A-Z MINI

Key to Map Pages	
Map Pages	
Index to Streets, etc	back cover

REFERENCE

Motorway	M1	**Church or Chapel**	†
A Road	A2	**Fire Station**	■
		Hospital	⊕
B Road	B519	**House Numbers** A & B Roads only	40 23
Dual Carriageway		**Information Centre**	🄸
One Way Street Traffic flow on A Roads is indicated by a heavy line on the drivers' left.	→	**National Grid Reference**	539
Junction Names	MARBLE ARCH	**Police Station**	▲
Pedestrianized Road		**Post Office**	★
Restricted Access		**Toilet with Facilities for the Disabled**	♿
Railway	Tunnel / Level Crossing	**Educational Establishment**	⌐
Stations:		**Hospital or Hospice**	⌐
National Rail Network	🚋	**Industrial Building**	⌐
Docklands Light Railway	DLR	**Leisure & Recreational Facility**	⌐
Underground Station	⊖ is the registered trade mark of Transport for London	**Place of Interest**	⌐
		Public Building	⌐
Map Continuation	84	**Shopping Centre or Market**	⌐
		Other Selected Building	⌐

SCALE
1:21,477
Approx. 3 inches (7.49 cm) to 1 mile
or 4.66 cm to 1 km

0	¼	½ Mile
0	250	500	750 Metres

Geographers' A-Z Map Company Ltd.

Head Office : Fairfield Road, Borough Green, Sevenoaks, Kent TN15 8PP   Tel: 01732 781000
Showrooms : 44 Gray's Inn Road, London WC1X 8HX   Tel: 020 7440 9500

Ordnance Survey® This product includes mapping data licensed from Ordnance Survey ® with the permission of the Controller of Her Majesty's Stationery Office.

© Crown Copyright 2001. Licence number 100017302

www.a-zmaps.co.uk   Copyright © Geographers' A-Z Map Co. Ltd. 2001   Edition 4 2001

KEY TO MAP PAGES

2

Kingsbury

HENDON

HORNSEY

Golders Green

Highgate

| 4 | 5 | 6 | 7 | 8 | 9 | 10 |

Neasden · Cricklewood

HAMPSTEAD

| 18 | 19 | 20 | 21 | 22 | 23 | 24 |

WILLESDEN

CAMDEN TOWN

ISLIN

Kensal Green · Kilburn

MARYLEBONE

FINS

| 32 | 33 | 34 | 35 | 36 | 37 | 38 |

ACTON

Holborn

Shepherd's Bush

PADDINGTON

WEST END

| 46 | 47 | 48 | 49 | 50 | 51 | 52 |

KENSINGTON

Westminster

LAM

CHISWICK

HAMMERSMITH

CHELSEA

| 60 | 61 | 62 | 63 | 64 | 65 | 66 |

BARNES

FULHAM

BATTERSEA

PUTNEY

CLAPHAM

BRIX

| 74 | 75 | 76 | 77 | 78 | 79 | 80 |

Roehampton

WANDSWORTH

Richmond Park

Balham

| 88 | 89 | 90 | 91 | 92 | 93 | 94 |

WIMBLEDON

Tooting

STREATHAM

SCALE

| 0 | 1 | 2 Miles |
| 0 | 1 | 2 | 3 Kilometres |

MITCHAM

TOTTENHAM WALTHAMSTOW

M11

A10
A104
A406
A12
A406
A13
A205
A207
A2
A20
A21

WANSTEAD

11 12 13 14 15 16 17
STOKE
NEWINGTON
LEYTON
Leytonstone

Highbury
Stratford
Manor-
Park
25 26 27 28 29 30 31
GTON HACKNEY
WEST HAM
EAST
HAM

BURY
BETHNAL
GREEN
BOW
Plaistow
39 40 41 42 43 44 45
CITY STEPNEY
London
City
Airport

Southwark
POPLAR Blackwall
Tunnel
53 54 55 56 57 58 59
Bermondsey
Woolwich
BETH

Peckham DEPTFORD GREENWICH Charlton
67 68 69 70 71 72 73
CAMBERWELL
Kidbrooke
Blackheath

TON
East
Dulwich
LEWISHAM
81 82 83 84 85 86 87
Lee ELTHAM

Dulwich
CATFORD
Mottingham
95 96 97 98 99 100 101
West
Norwood Sydenham
Grove
Park

PENGE

BECKENHAM

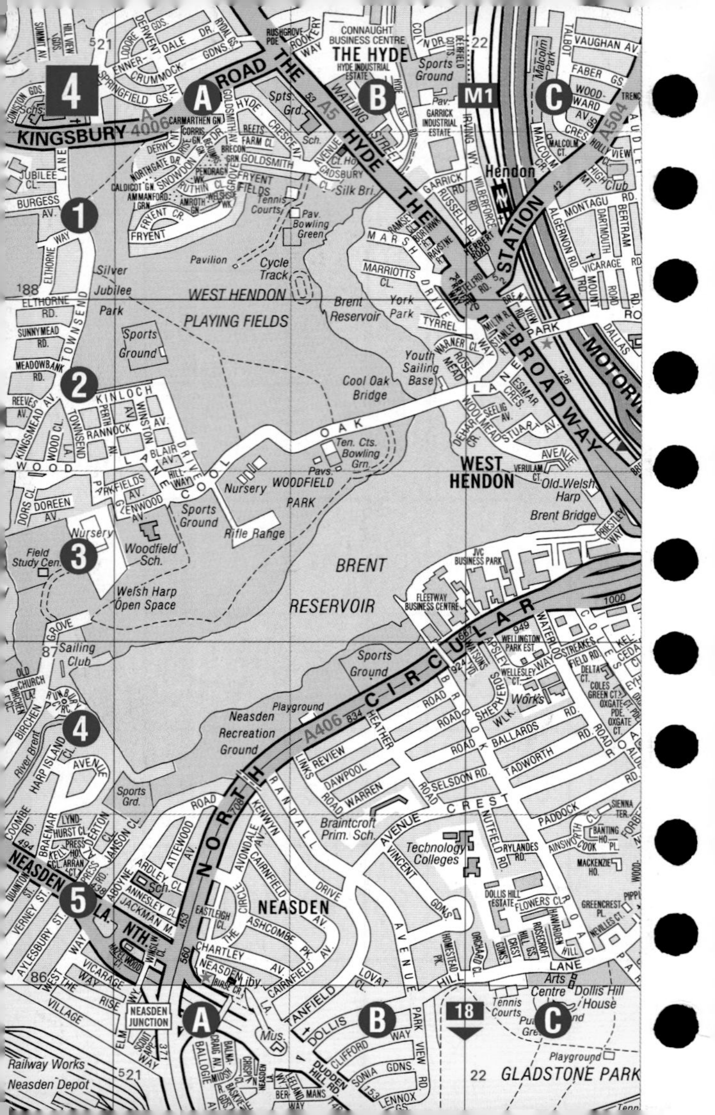

4
KINGSBURY ROAD
A4006
THE HYDE
CONNAUGHT BUSINESS CENTRE
HYDE INDUSTRIAL ESTATE
GARRICK INDUSTRIAL ESTATE
M1
A5
A504
Hendon
STATION ROAD
THE BROADWAY
M1 MOTORWAY
Silver Jubilee Park
WEST HENDON PLAYING FIELDS
Cycle Track
Pavilion
Brent Reservoir
York Park
Youth Sailing Base
Cool Oak Bridge
COOL OAK LANE
WOODFIELD PARK
Nursery
Rifle Range
Woodfield Sch.
Field Study Cen.
Welsh Harp Open Space
WEST HENDON
Old Welsh Harp
Brent Bridge
JVC BUSINESS PARK
FLEETWAY BUSINESS CENTRE
BRENT RESERVOIR
Sailing Club
Sports Ground
Neasden Recreation Ground
NORTH CIRCULAR
A406
Works
Braintcroft Prim. Sch.
Technology Colleges
DOLLIS HILL ESTATE
NEASDEN
NEASDEN JUNCTION
Neasden Liby.
Railway Works
Neasden Depot
Arts Centre
Dollis Hill House
Tennis Courts
GLADSTONE PARK
Playground
18
A B C
1 2 3 4 5
521
22
188
87
86

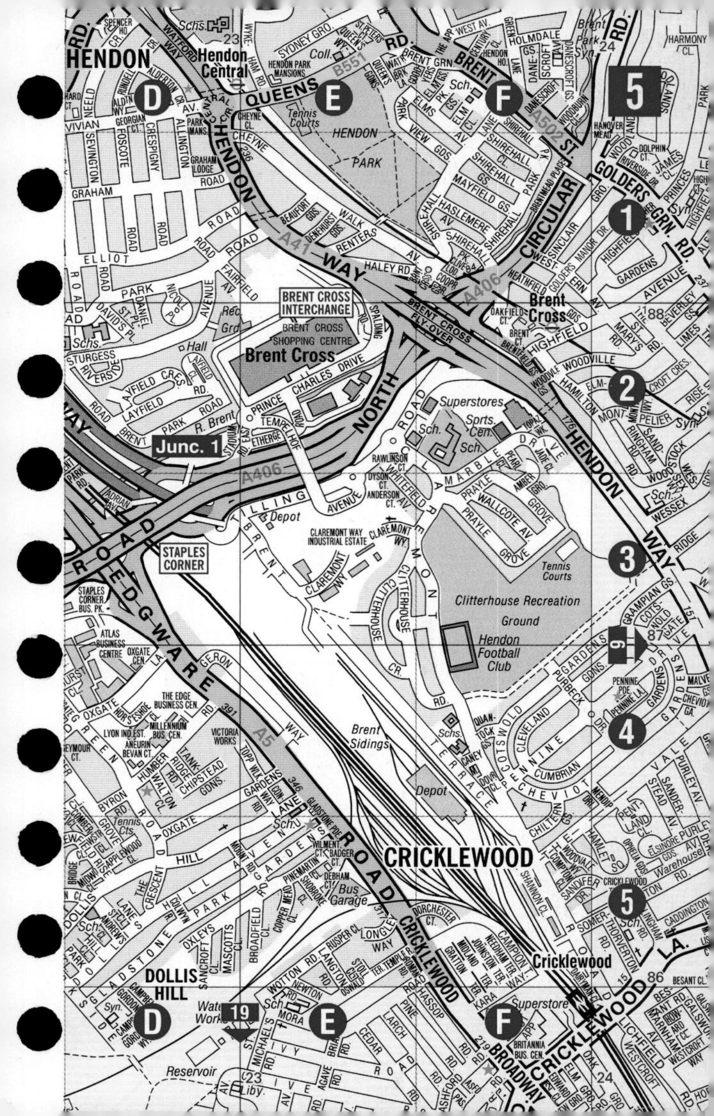
5
HENDON
Hendon Central
QUEENS RD.
HENDON PARK
BRENT ST.
A502
CIRCULAR
HENDON WAY
A41
Brent Cross
BRENT CROSS INTERCHANGE
BRENT CROSS SHOPPING CENTRE
BRENT CROSS FLY-OVER
NORTH CIRCULAR ROAD
A406
Junc. 1
STAPLES CORNER
EDGWARE ROAD
A5
Clitterhouse Recreation Ground
Hendon Football Club
Brent Sidings
Depot
Superstores
Tennis Courts
CRICKLEWOOD
Cricklewood
CRICKLEWOOD BROADWAY
CRICKLEWOOD LA.
DOLLIS HILL
GLADSTONE PARK
OXGATE LA.
Reservoir
Bus Garage
Superstore
D
E
F
1
2
3
4
5
6
19
23
24
86
87
88

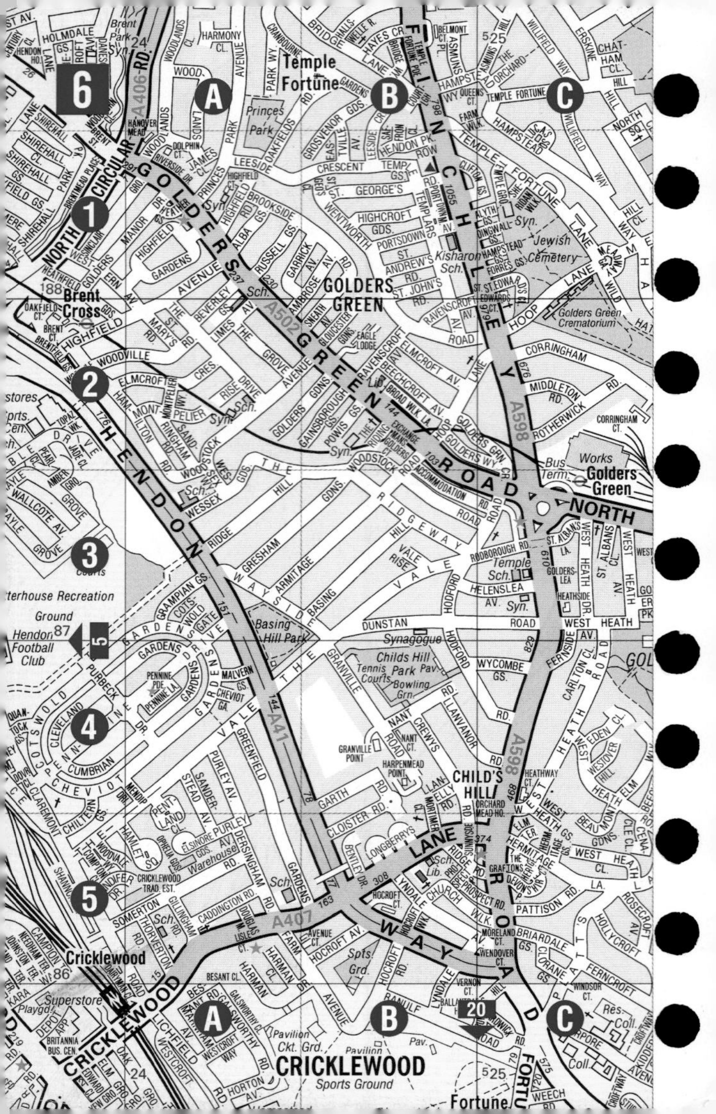

Temple Fortune
Princes Park
GOLDERS GREEN
Brent Cross
Golders Green
Jewish Cemetery
Golders Green Crematorium
Works
Bus Term.
NORTH CIRCULAR RD.
A406
GOLDERS GREEN ROAD
A502
FINCHLEY ROAD
A598
HENDON WAY
A41
CRICKLEWOOD LANE
A407
CRICKLEWOOD
Cricklewood
CHILD'S HILL
Basing Hill Park
Childs Hill Park
Tennis Courts
Bowling Grn.
Synagogue
Kisharon Sch.
Temple Sch.
Hendon Football Club
Ground
Sports Ground
Pavilion
Ckt. Grd.
Spts. Grd.
Superstore
CRICKLEWOOD TRAD. EST.
BRITANNIA BUS. CEN.
Warehouse
HOOP LANE
WEST HEATH RD.
TEMPLE FORTUNE LANE
HAMPSTEAD WAY
THE RIDGEWAY
WAYSIDE
DUNSTAN ROAD
GRANVILLE POINT
HARPENMEAD POINT
Fortune
5
20

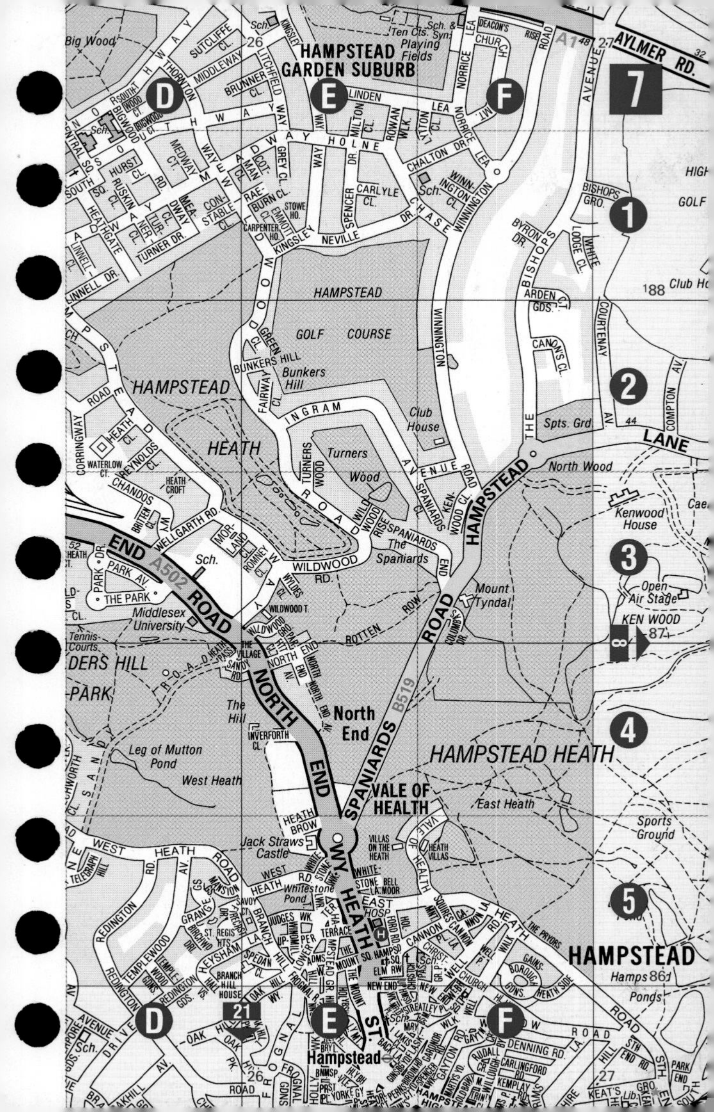
7
HAMPSTEAD GARDEN SUBURB
HAMPSTEAD GOLF COURSE
HAMPSTEAD HEATH
HEATH
Bunkers Hill
Club House
Turners Wood
Kenwood House
North Wood
The Spaniards
Mount Tyndal
Open Air Stage
KEN WOOD
Middlesex University
The Hill
Leg of Mutton Pond
West Heath
North End
VALE OF HEALTH
East Heath
Jack Straws Castle
Whitestone Pond
Sports Ground
HAMPSTEAD
Hampstead
NORTH END ROAD
SPANIARDS ROAD
HAMPSTEAD LANE
WINNINGTON ROAD
THE BISHOPS AVENUE
AYLMER RD.
WILDWOOD RD.
WEST HEATH ROAD
EAST HEATH RD.
A1
A502
B519
8
21

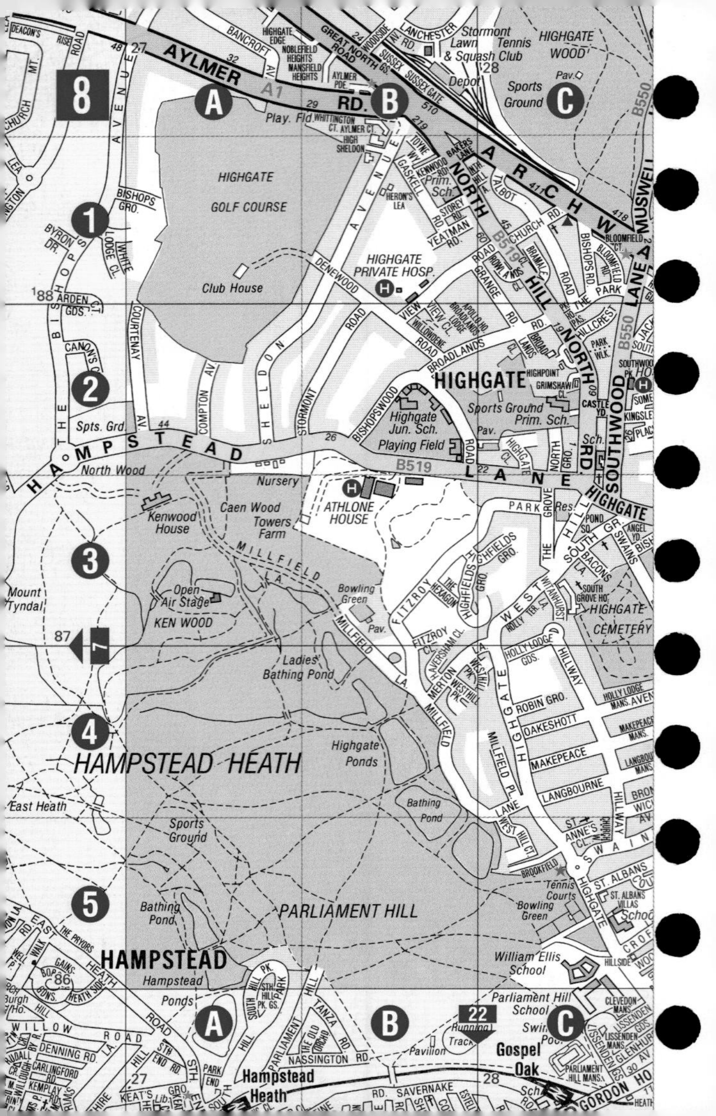
8
AYLMER RD.
HIGHGATE GOLF COURSE
Club House
HIGHGATE WOOD
Stormont Lawn Tennis & Squash Club
Sports Ground
ARCHWAY RD.
NORTH HILL
HIGHGATE PRIVATE HOSP.
HIGHGATE
Highgate Jun. Sch. Playing Field
HAMPSTEAD LANE
North Wood
Nursery
ATHLONE HOUSE
Kenwood House
Caen Wood Towers Farm
MILLFIELD LA.
Open Air Stage
KEN WOOD
Mount Tyndal
Bowling Green
Ladies' Bathing Pond
HAMPSTEAD HEATH
Highgate Ponds
Bathing Pond
East Heath
Sports Ground
PARLIAMENT HILL
Bathing Pond
HIGHGATE CEMETERY
HIGHGATE WEST HILL
SWAINS LANE
William Ellis School
Parliament Hill School
HAMPSTEAD
Hampstead Ponds
Hampstead Heath
Gospel Oak
87
7
22
A
B
C
1
2
3
4
5

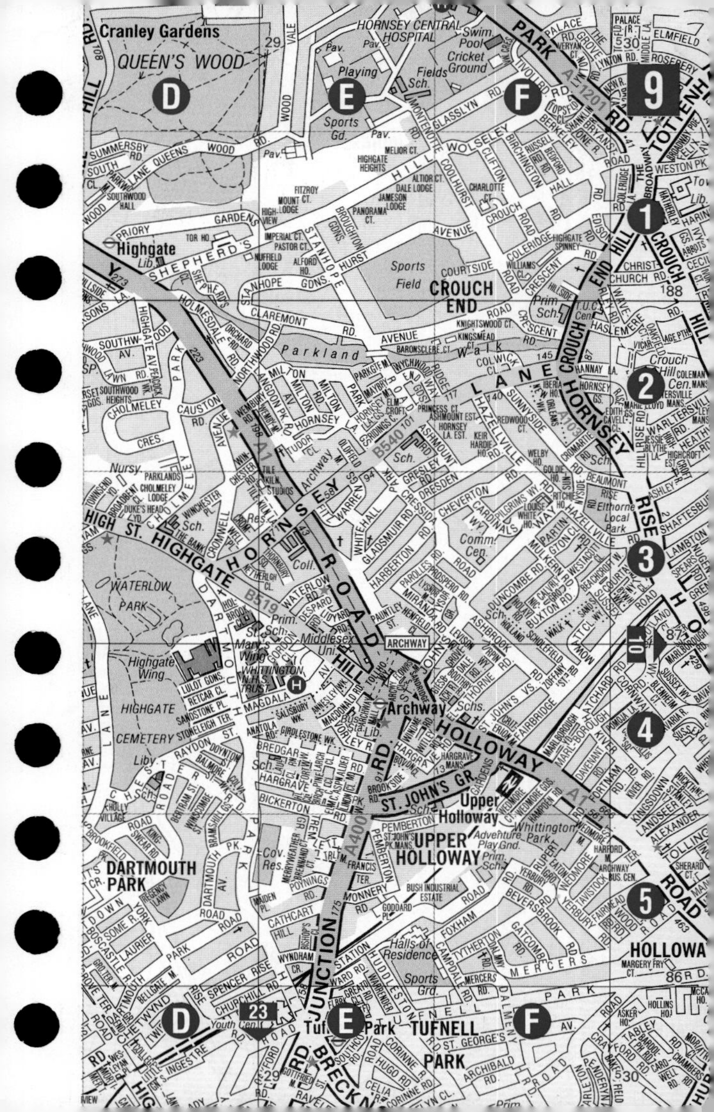
9
D
E
F
1
2
3
4
5
10
23
Cranley Gardens
QUEEN'S WOOD
HORNSEY CENTRAL HOSPITAL
Swim Pool
Cricket Ground
Playing Fields
Sports Gd.
PARK RD.
A1201
WOLSELEY RD.
GLASSLYN RD.
MONTENOTTE RD.
SHEPHERD'S HILL
Highgate
Lib.
PRIORY GARDENS
STANHOPE GDNS.
HURST AVENUE
Sports Field
CROUCH END
CROUCH END HILL
CHRIST CHURCH RD.
CROUCH HILL
CLAREMONT RD.
Parkland Walk
HORNSEY LANE
B540
A103
HORNSEY RISE
HORNSEY RD.
A1
ARCHWAY RD.
HIGHGATE HILL
HIGH ST. HIGHGATE
B519
WATERLOW PARK
Highgate Wing
WHITTINGTON N.H.S. TRUST
Middlesex Uni.
ARCHWAY
Archway
HOLLOWAY RD.
HIGHGATE CEMETERY
DARTMOUTH PARK HILL
DARTMOUTH PARK
Upper Holloway
UPPER HOLLOWAY
Whittington Park
Adventure Play Gnd.
A400
JUNCTION RD.
Halls of Residence
Sports Grd.
MERCERS RD.
DALMENY AV.
TUFNELL PARK RD.
Tufnell Park
TUFNELL PARK
HOLLOWAY
Elthorne Local Park
Comm. Cen.
Coll.
Sch.
Prim. Sch.

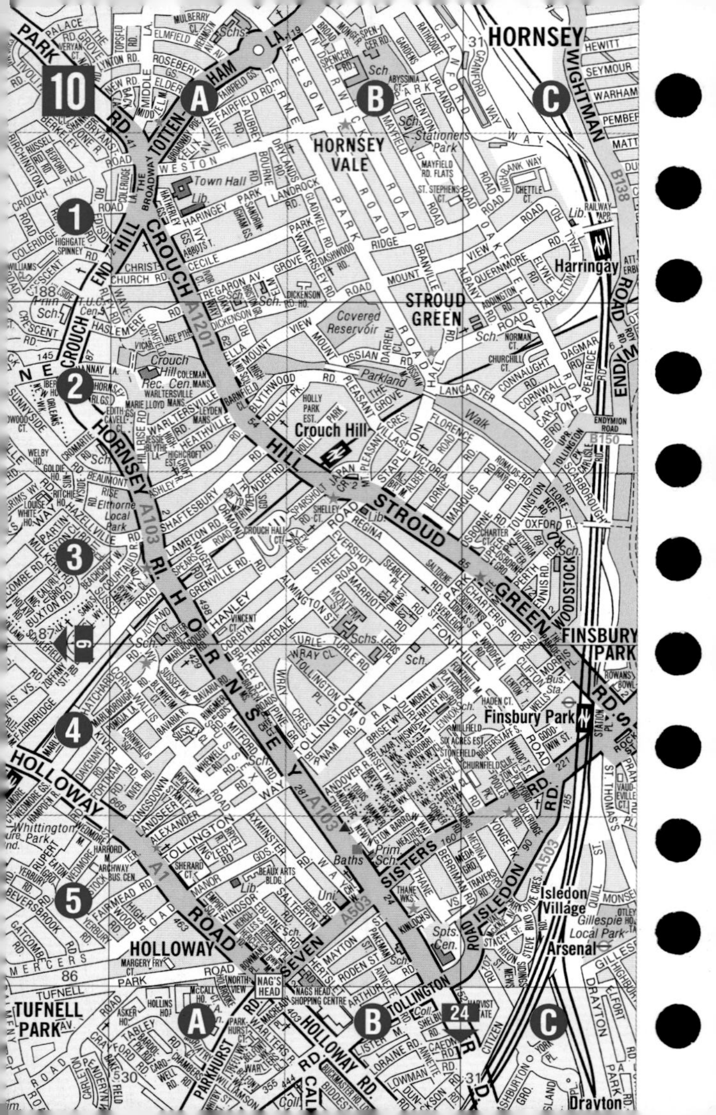
10
HORNSEY
HORNSEY VALE
Town Hall
Lib.
CROUCH END HILL
CROUCH HILL
A1201
STROUD GREEN
Covered Reservoir
Parkland Walk
Crouch Hill
Rec. Cen.
Crouch Hill
STROUD GREEN RD.
HORNSEY RI.
HORNSEY RD.
A103
Elthorne Local Park
FINSBURY PARK
Finsbury Park
Bus Sta.
Harringay
WIGHTMAN RD.
B138
B150
HOLLOWAY RD.
A1
HOLLOWAY
Whittington Park
TUFNELL PARK
PARK RD.
SEVEN SISTERS RD.
A503
Isledon Village
Gillespie Local Park
Arsenal
Drayton
NAG'S HEAD
NAGS HEAD SHOPPING CENTRE
Stationers Park
TOLLINGTON PARK
TOLLINGTON RD.
ISLEDON RD.
Spts. Cen.
Baths
Prim. Sch.
Uni.
A
B
C
1
2
3
4
5
9
24

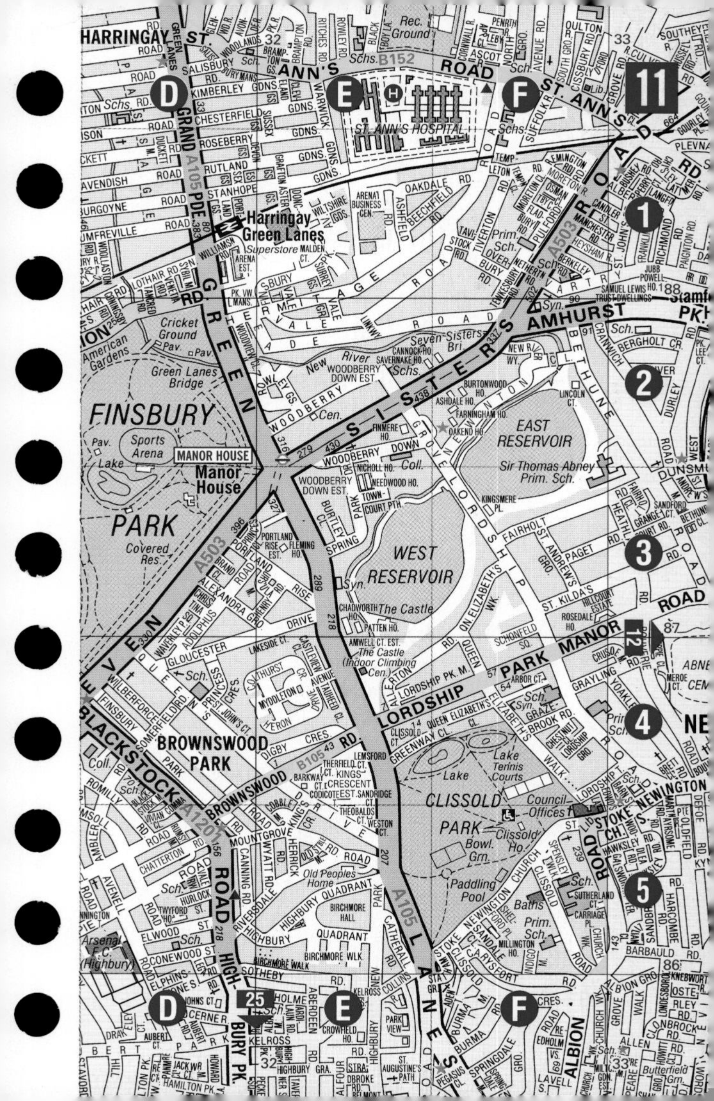
11
HARRINGAY
GREEN LANES
ST. ANN'S ROAD
B152
ST. ANN'S HOSPITAL
SALISBURY RD.
KIMBERLEY GDNS.
CHESTERFIELD GDNS.
ROSEBERRY GDNS.
RUTLAND GDNS.
STANHOPE GDNS.
GRAND PDE.
A105
Harringay Green Lanes
Superstore
ARENA BUSINESS CEN.
OAKDALE RD.
BEECHFIELD RD.
ASHFIELD RD.
ETHERIDGE RD.
HERMITAGE ROAD
VALE ROAD
SEVEN SISTERS ROAD
A503
AMHURST PK.
Seven Sisters Bri.
New River
WOODBERRY DOWN EST.
WOODBERRY DOWN
Cricket Ground
American Gardens
Green Lanes Bridge
FINSBURY PARK
Sports Arena
Lake
MANOR HOUSE
Manor House
Covered Res.
EAST RESERVOIR
Sir Thomas Abney Prim. Sch.
WEST RESERVOIR
The Castle
The Castle (Indoor Climbing Cen.)
LORDSHIP PARK
MANOR ROAD
ST. KILDA'S RD.
BLACKSTOCK RD.
A1201
BROWNSWOOD PARK
BROWNSWOOD RD.
B105
QUEEN'S DRIVE
CLISSOLD PARK
Lake
Tennis Courts
Council Offices
Clissold Ho.
Bowl. Grn.
Paddling Pool
Baths
STOKE NEWINGTON CHURCH ST.
STOKE NEWINGTON
HIGHBURY QUADRANT
BIRCHMORE HALL
HIGHBURY PK.
Arsenal F.C. (Highbury)
Old Peoples Home
ALBION RD.
Butterfield Grn.
12
25
86
87
88
32
33
D
E
F
1
2
3
4
5

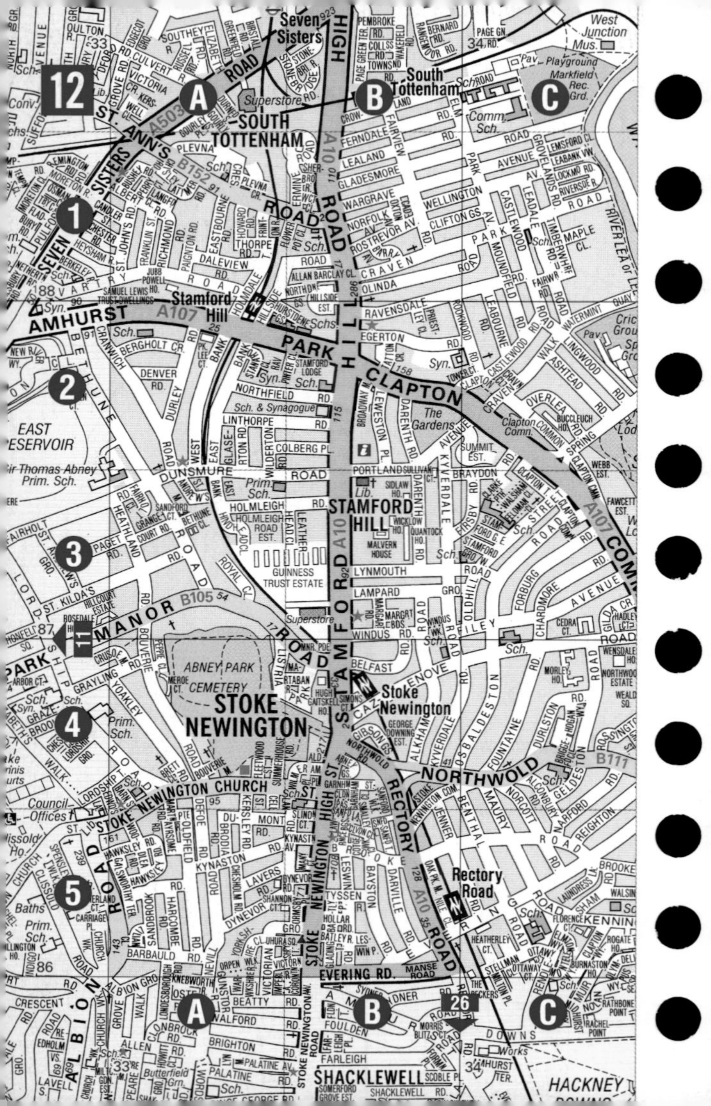
12
A
B
C
1
2
3
4
5
Seven Sisters
SEVEN SISTERS ROAD
A503
ST. ANN'S ROAD
B152
SOUTH TOTTENHAM
South Tottenham
Superstore
HIGH ROAD
A10
West Junction Mus.
Playground
Markfield Rec. Grd.
Comm. Sch.
PAGE GREEN TER.
FERNDALE RD.
LEALAND RD.
GLADESMORE RD.
WARGRAVE AV.
NORFOLK AV.
ROSTREVOR AV.
FAIRVIEW RD.
WELLINGTON AV.
CLIFTON GS.
CRAVEN PARK ROAD
OLINDA RD.
RAVENSDALE RD.
EGERTON RD.
CASTLEWOOD RD.
MOUNDFIELD RD.
LEADALE RD.
GROVELANDS RD.
TIMBERWHARF RD.
MAPLE CL.
RIVERSIDE RD.
LEABOURNE RD.
ROOKWOOD RD.
WATERMINT QUAY
LINGWOOD RD.
ASHTEAD RD.
OVERLEA RD.
SPRING HILL
CLAPTON COMMON
Clapton Comn.
VARTRY ROAD
DALEVIEW RD.
FRANKLIN ST.
RICHMOND RD.
PAIGNTON RD.
EASTBOURNE RD.
THORPE RD.
PLEVNA CR.
Stamford Hill
AMHURST PARK
A107
BERGHOLT CR.
DENVER RD.
NORTHFIELD RD.
LINTHORPE RD.
COLBERG PL.
PORTLAND AV.
STAMFORD HILL
A10
STAMFORD HILL
Lib.
The Gardens
EAST RESERVOIR
Sir Thomas Abney Prim. Sch.
DUNSMURE ROAD
BETHUNE RD.
HEATHLAND RD.
PAGET RD.
LORDSHIP RD.
ST. KILDA'S RD.
MANOR ROAD
B105
HOLMLEIGH RD.
GUINNESS TRUST ESTATE
LYNMOUTH RD.
LAMPARD GRO.
WINDUS RD.
BRAYDON RD.
FIRSBY RD.
FORBURG RD.
CHARDMORE RD.
FILEY AVENUE
ROYAL CL.
11
PARK
GRAYLING RD.
YOAKLEY RD.
ABNEY PARK CEMETERY
STOKE NEWINGTON
BELFAST RD.
Stoke Newington
GEORGE DOWNING EST.
NORTHWOLD ROAD
B111
OSBALDESTON RD.
FOUNTAYNE RD.
DURLSTON RD.
KYVERDALE RD.
ALKHAM RD.
STOKE NEWINGTON CHURCH ST.
STOKE NEWINGTON HIGH ST.
RECTORY ROAD
Rectory Road
Council Offices
LORDSHIP T.
CHURCH WALK
KYNASTON RD.
LAVERS RD.
DYNEVOR RD.
TYSSEN RD.
BAYSTON RD.
DARVILLE RD.
HARCOMBE RD.
SANDBROOK RD.
BARBAULD RD.
EVERING RD.
MANSE ROAD
NORTHWOLD RD.
NORCOTT RD.
MAURY RD.
BENTHAL RD.
JENNER RD.
NARFORD RD.
REIGHTON RD.
BROOKE RD.
KENNINGHALL
Baths
Prim. Sch.
ALBION ROAD
86
87
88
BEATTY RD.
WALFORD RD.
FOULDEN RD.
BRIGHTON RD.
FARLEIGH RD.
PALATINE RD.
SHACKLEWELL
SHACKLEWELL RD.
26
DOWNS
Works
HACKNEY
RATHBONE POINT
RACHEL POINT
ROGATE HO.
FLORENCE CT.
33
34

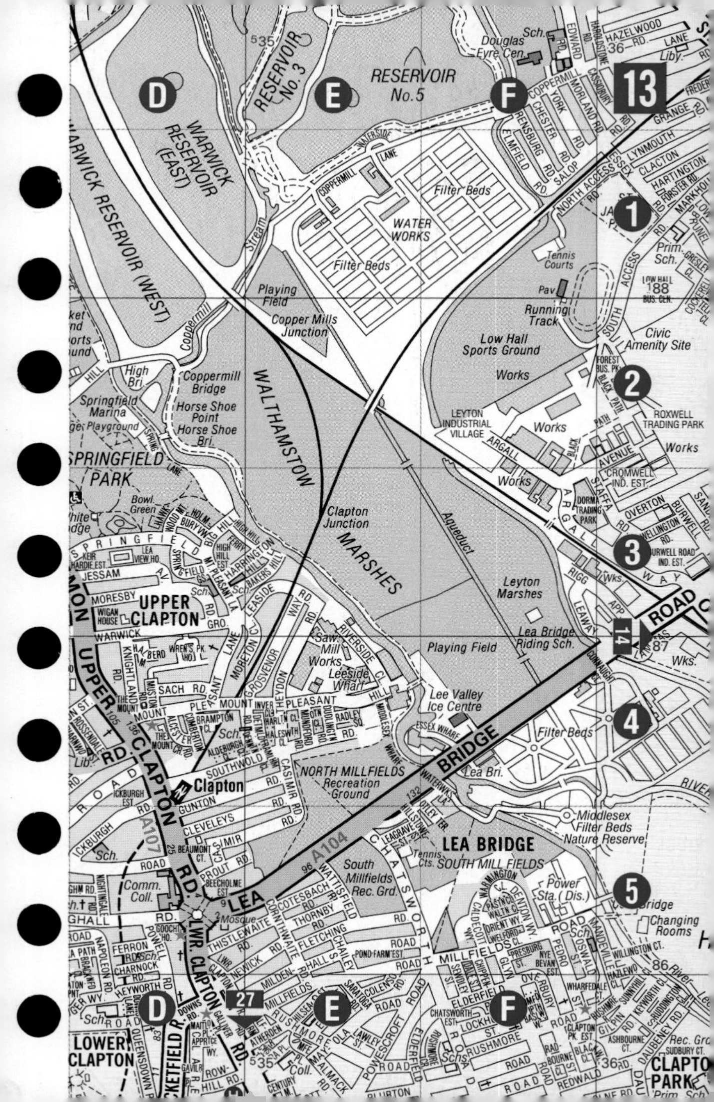

13
RESERVOIR No.5
RESERVOIR No.3
WARWICK RESERVOIR (EAST)
WARWICK RESERVOIR (WEST)
Douglas Eyre Cen.
Filter Beds
WATER WORKS
Playing Field
Copper Mills Junction
Tennis Courts
Running Track
Low Hall Sports Ground
Works
LOW HALL BUS. CEN.
Civic Amenity Site
LEYTON INDUSTRIAL VILLAGE
ROXWELL TRADING PARK
CROMWELL IND. EST.
DORMA TRADING PARK
BURWELL ROAD IND. EST.
High Bri.
Coppermill Bridge
Horse Shoe Point
Horse Shoe Bri.
Springfield Marina
Playground
SPRINGFIELD PARK
Bowl. Green
WALTHAMSTOW
MARSHES
Clapton Junction
Aqueduct
Leyton Marshes
Lea Bridge Riding Sch.
Playing Field
UPPER CLAPTON
Saw Mill Works
Leeside Wharf
Lee Valley Ice Centre
LEA BRIDGE ROAD
Filter Beds
Lea Bri.
NORTH MILLFIELDS Recreation Ground
Clapton
Middlesex Filter Beds Nature Reserve
LEA BRIDGE
A104
A107
South Millfields Rec. Grd.
SOUTH MILL FIELDS
Power Sta. (Dis.)
Changing Rooms
Comm. Coll.
Mosque
LOWER CLAPTON
CLAPTON PARK
14
27

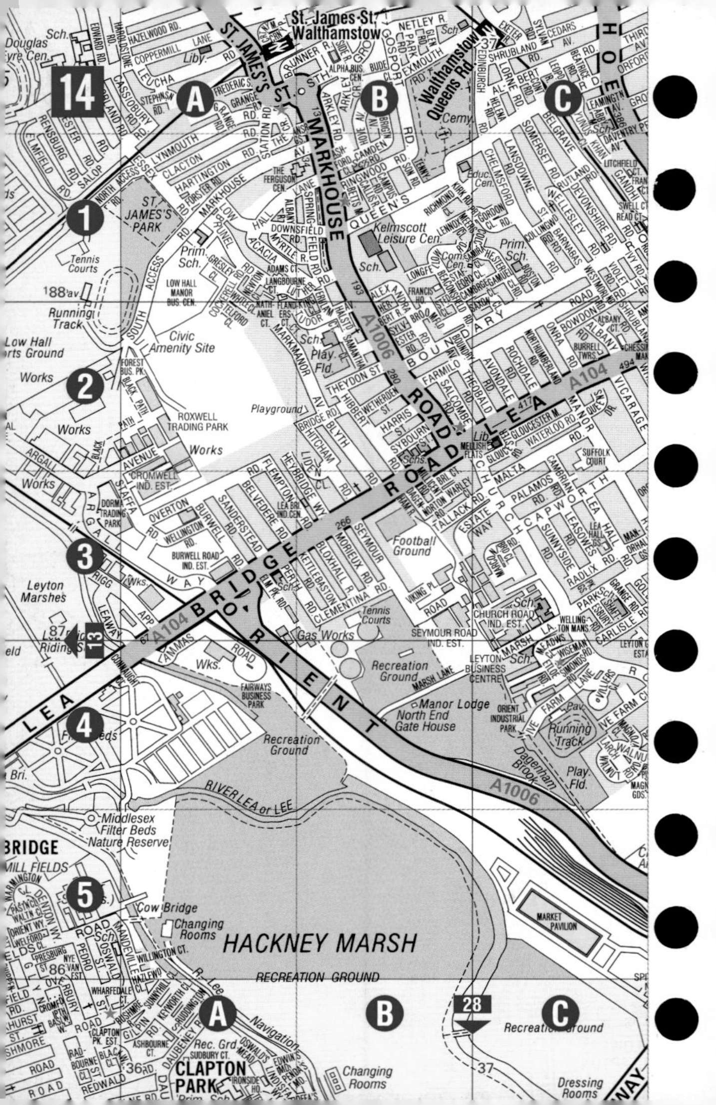

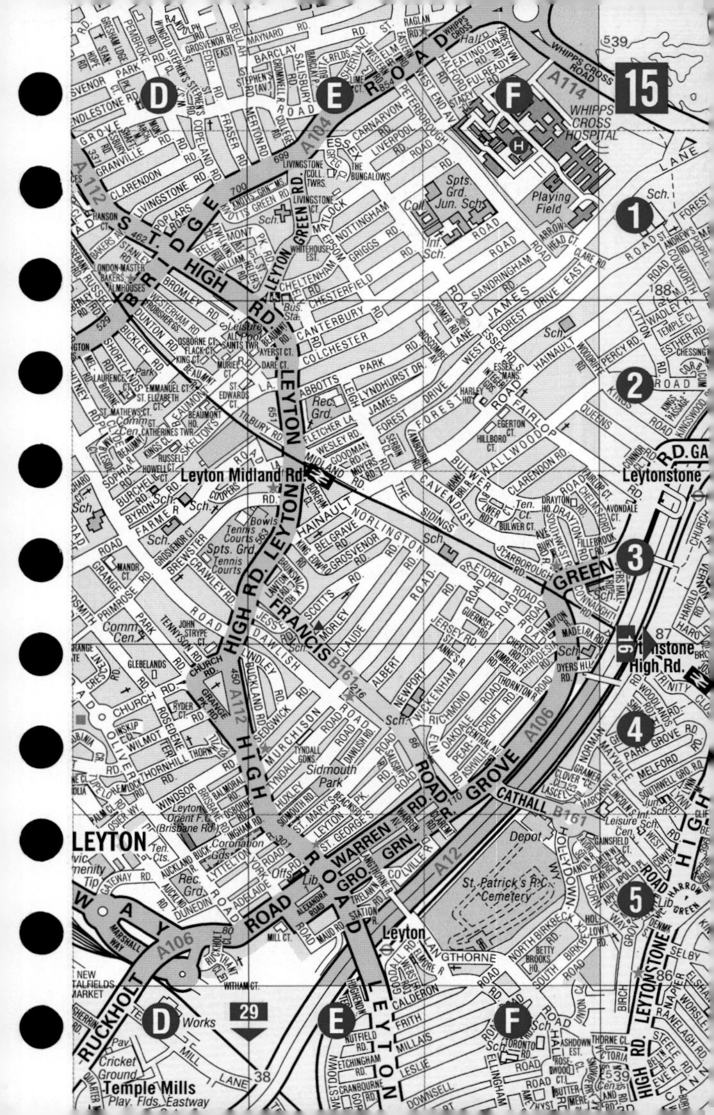
15
D
E
F
1
2
3
4
5
16
29
WHIPPS CROSS HOSPITAL
WHIPPS CROSS ROAD
A114
A104
A112
A106
A12
B161
LEA BRIDGE ROAD
HIGH RD. LEYTON
LEYTON GREEN RD.
ESSEX RD.
FOREST DRIVE EAST
FOREST DRIVE WEST
JAMES LANE
HAINAULT RD.
CAVENDISH
NORLINGTON
FRANCIS RD.
GROVE GREEN RD.
CATHALL RD.
GRANGE PARK RD.
CHURCH RD.
RUCKHOLT RD.
CALDERON
LEYTON
Leyton Midland Rd.
Leytonstone
Leytonstone High Rd.
LEYTON
Leyton Orient F.C. (Brisbane Rd.)
Sidmouth Park
St. Patrick's R.C. Cemetery
Depot
Playing Field
Temple Mills
Cricket Ground
NEW SPITALFIELDS MARKET
Works
Leisure Pool
Bus Sta.
Rec. Grd.
Spts. Grd.
Tennis Courts
Bowls
Comm. Cen.
Coronation Gdns.
Jun. Sch.
Inf. Sch.
Sch.
Coll.
Lib.
Offs.
Park
Leisure Cen.
539
88
87
86
38
LEYTONSTONE HIGH RD.

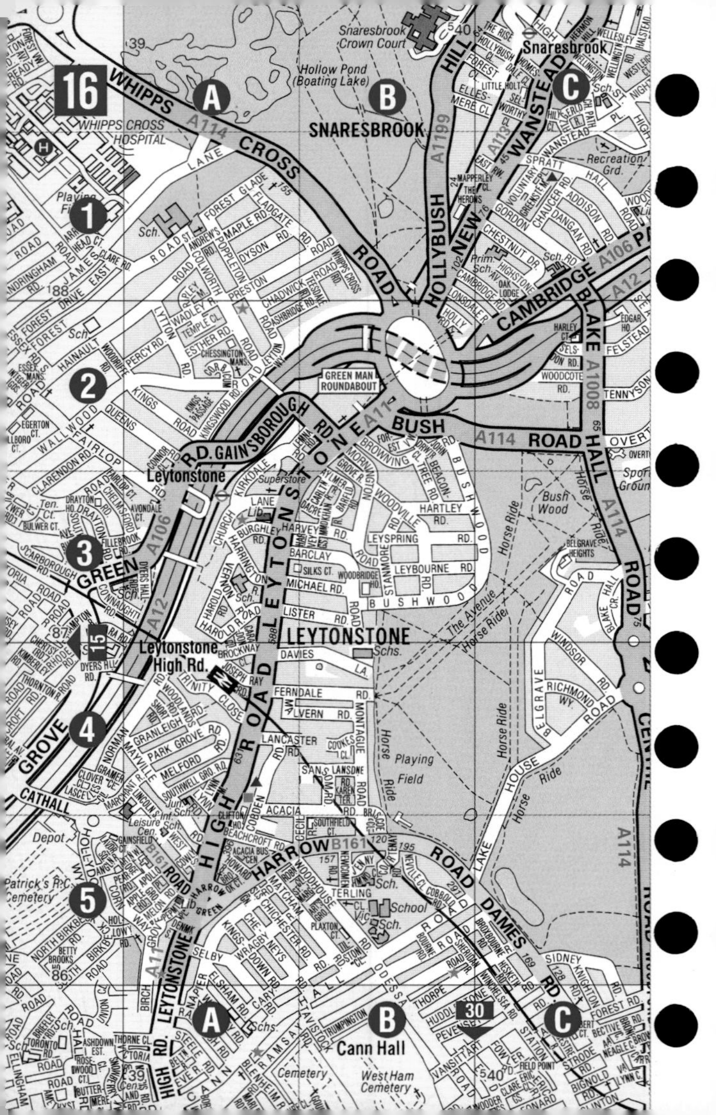

16
A
B
C
1
2
3
4
5
WHIPPS CROSS ROAD
A114
WHIPPS CROSS HOSPITAL
Snaresbrook Crown Court
Hollow Pond (Boating Lake)
SNARESBROOK
Snaresbrook
HOLLYBUSH HILL
A1199
NEW WANSTEAD
A113
Recreation Grd.
CAMBRIDGE PARK
A106
A12
BLAKE HALL ROAD
A1008
GREEN MAN ROUNDABOUT
BUSH ROAD
A114
Leytonstone
GAINSBOROUGH RD.
LEYTONSTONE HIGH ROAD
A11
GREEN
A12
LEYTONSTONE
Leytonstone High Rd.
15
Bush Wood
Horse Ride
The Avenue
Playing Field
HARROW ROAD
B161
DAMES RD.
LAKE HOUSE ROAD
CATHALL
GROVE
Depot
Patrick's R.C. Cemetery
Cann Hall
Cemetery
West Ham Cemetery
30
Sch.
Lib.
Superstore
Schs.
School

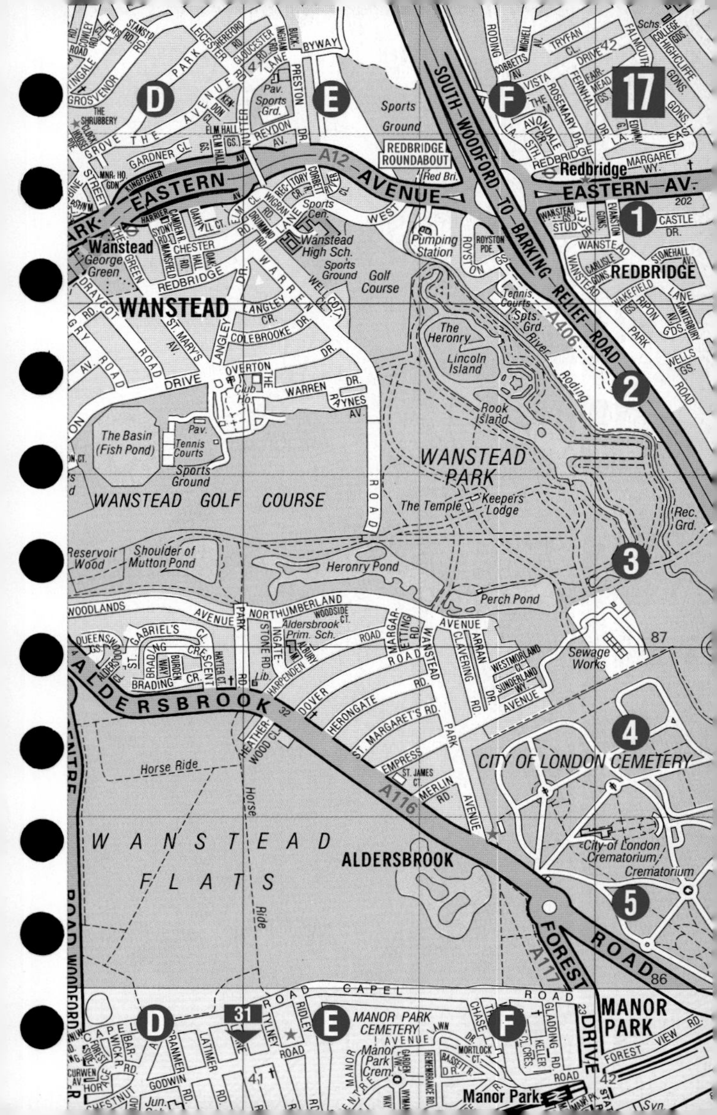
17
WANSTEAD
Wanstead
REDBRIDGE
Redbridge
REDBRIDGE ROUNDABOUT
EASTERN AVENUE
SOUTH WOODFORD TO BARKING RELIEF ROAD
WANSTEAD PARK
WANSTEAD GOLF COURSE
The Basin (Fish Pond)
Heronry Pond
Shoulder of Mutton Pond
Perch Pond
The Heronry
Lincoln Island
Rook Island
The Temple
Keepers Lodge
Sewage Works
CITY OF LONDON CEMETERY
City of London Crematorium
WANSTEAD FLATS
ALDERSBROOK
ALDERSBROOK ROAD
FOREST ROAD
MANOR PARK
MANOR PARK CEMETERY
Manor Park
CAPEL ROAD
NORTHUMBERLAND AVENUE
Wanstead High Sch.
Aldersbrook Prim. Sch.
Horse Ride
Reservoir Wood

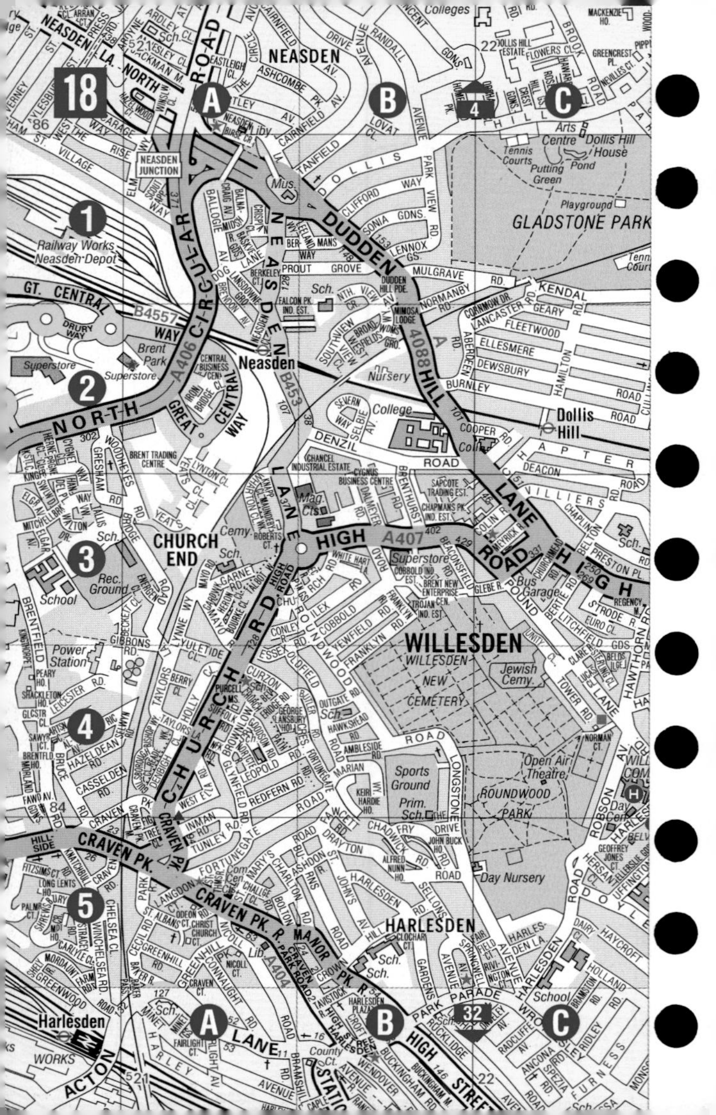
18
NEASDEN
A
B
C
1
2
3
4
5
NEASDEN LA. NORTH
NORTH CIRCULAR ROAD
A406
NEASDEN JUNCTION
Railway Works
Neasden Depot
GT. CENTRAL WAY
B4557
DRURY WAY
Superstore
Brent Park
CENTRAL BUSINESS CEN.
IRON BRIDGE CL.
GREAT CENTRAL WAY
BRENT TRADING CENTRE
Neasden
NEASDEN LANE
B453
DUDDEN HILL LANE
4088
DOLLIS HILL
Arts Centre
Dollis Hill House
Tennis Courts
Putting Green
Pond
Playground
GLADSTONE PARK
MULGRAVE RD.
KENDAL
GEARY
FLEETWOOD
ELLESMERE
DEWSBURY
BURNLEY
HAMILTON ROAD
Dollis Hill
CHAPTER ROAD
DEACON
VILLIERS
Nursery
College
DENZIL ROAD
CHANCEL INDUSTRIAL ESTATE
CYGNUS BUSINESS CENTRE
SAPCOTE TRADING EST.
CHAPMANS PK. IND. EST.
Mag. Cts.
HIGH ROAD
A407
CHURCH END
Cemy.
Sch.
Rec. Ground
School
Superstore
Bus Garage
POUND LANE
WILLESDEN
WILLESDEN NEW CEMETERY
Jewish Cemy.
Power Station
CHURCH RD.
ROUNDWOOD ROAD
Sports Ground
Prim. Sch.
Open Air Theatre
ROUNDWOOD PARK
Day Nursery
CRAVEN PK.
CRAVEN PK. RD.
HILLSIDE
MANOR PK. RD.
A404
HARLESDEN
HARLESDEN LA.
PARK PARADE
Harlesden
WORKS
ACTON LANE
HIGH STREET HARLESDEN
County Ct.
STATION
HIGH STREET
32
22
521

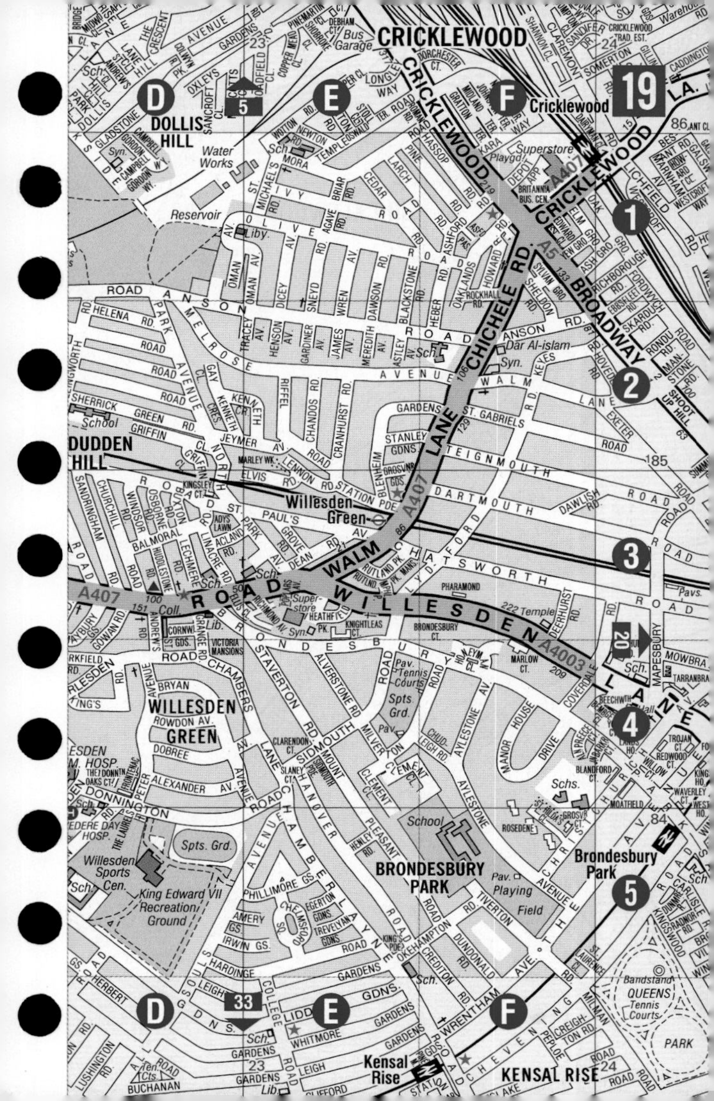
CRICKLEWOOD
19
D
E
F
5
Cricklewood
DOLLIS HILL
Water Works
Reservoir
Bus Garage
Superstore
BRITANNIA BUS. CEN.
CRICKLEWOOD LANE
CRICKLEWOOD BROADWAY
A5
A407
1
2
3
4
5
CHICHELE RD.
ANSON RD.
OLIVE RD.
MELROSE AVENUE
WALM LANE
Dar Al-islam
Syn.
DUDDEN HILL
TEIGNMOUTH ROAD
DARTMOUTH ROAD
Willesden Green
CHATSWORTH ROAD
WILLESDEN LANE
A4003
PHARAMOND
222 Temple
BRONDESBURY CT.
BRONDESBURY ROAD
Superstore
Coll.
Lib.
20
Pav.
Tennis Courts
Spts. Grd.
WILLESDEN GREEN
MANOR HOUSE DRIVE
Schs.
School
BRONDESBURY PARK
Pav. Playing Field
Brondesbury Park
Spts. Grd.
Willesden Sports Cen.
King Edward VII Recreation Ground
SIDMOUTH RD.
HANOVER RD.
CHAMBERLAYNE ROAD
33
Kensal Rise
KENSAL RISE
Bandstand
QUEENS PARK
Tennis Courts
Ten. Cts.
23
24
84
185
209

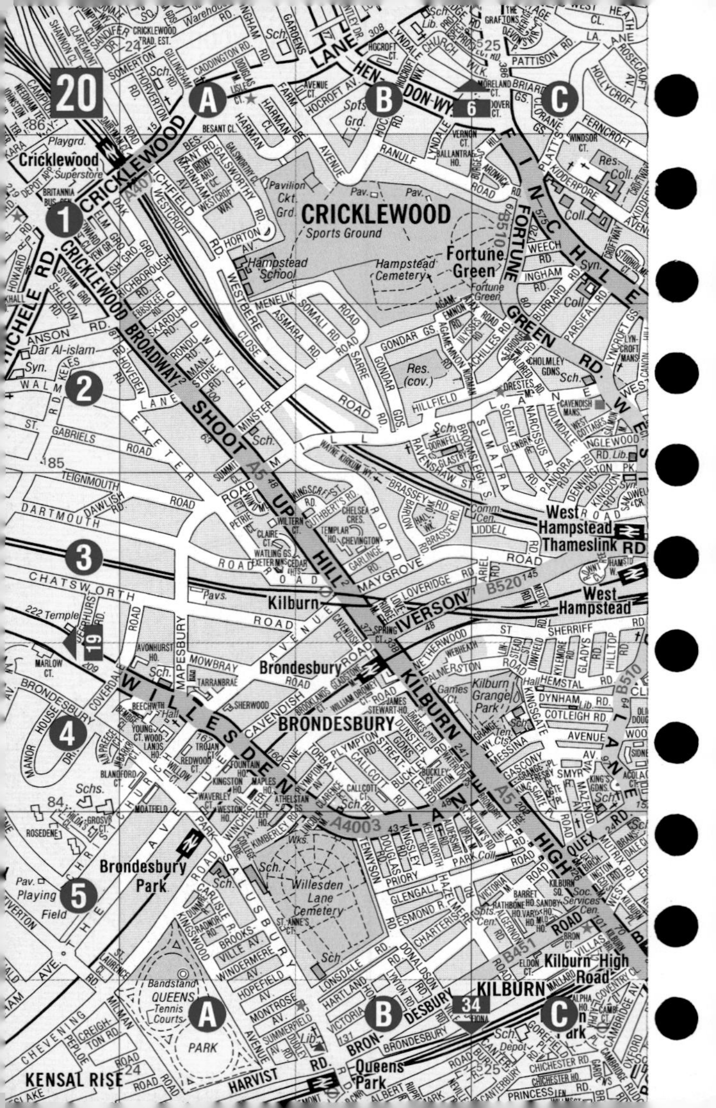

20
A
B
C
6
1
2
3
4
5
19
34
24
25
CRICKLEWOOD
Sports Ground
Cricklewood
Superstore
CRICKLEWOOD BROADWAY
SHOOT UP HILL
KILBURN HIGH ROAD
Fortune Green
FORTUNE GREEN RD.
FINCHLEY RD.
HENDON WY.
Hampstead School
Hampstead Cemetery
West Hampstead Thameslink
West Hampstead
Kilburn
Brondesbury
BRONDESBURY
Brondesbury Park
Kilburn Grange Park
WILLESDEN LANE
Willesden Lane Cemetery
Kilburn High Road
KILBURN
Queens Park
KENSAL RISE
QUEENS PARK
Playing Field
Dar Al-islam
Syn.
Sch.
Schs.
MAYGROVE
IVERSON RD.
MAPESBURY
CHATSWORTH ROAD
DARTMOUTH
TEIGNMOUTH
WALM LANE
ANSON RD.
GABRIELS ROAD
EXETER RD.
HILLFIELD
SUMATRA
GONDAR GS.
MENELIK
SOMALI RD.
ASMARA RD.
WESTBERE
RANULF
LYNDALE
PATTISON RD.
FERNCROFT
MOWBRAY
CAVENDISH
PLYMPTON
TORBAY
DYNE
BROOKSVILLE AV.
WINDERMERE
HOPEFIELD
MONTROSE AV.
SALUSBURY
HARVIST RD.
CHEVENING
MILMAN
PRIORY
GLENGALL
CHARTERIS
HEMSTAL
DYNHAM
COTLEIGH RD.
MESSINA
GASCONY
QUEX RD.
A5
A407
A4003
B510
B520
B451

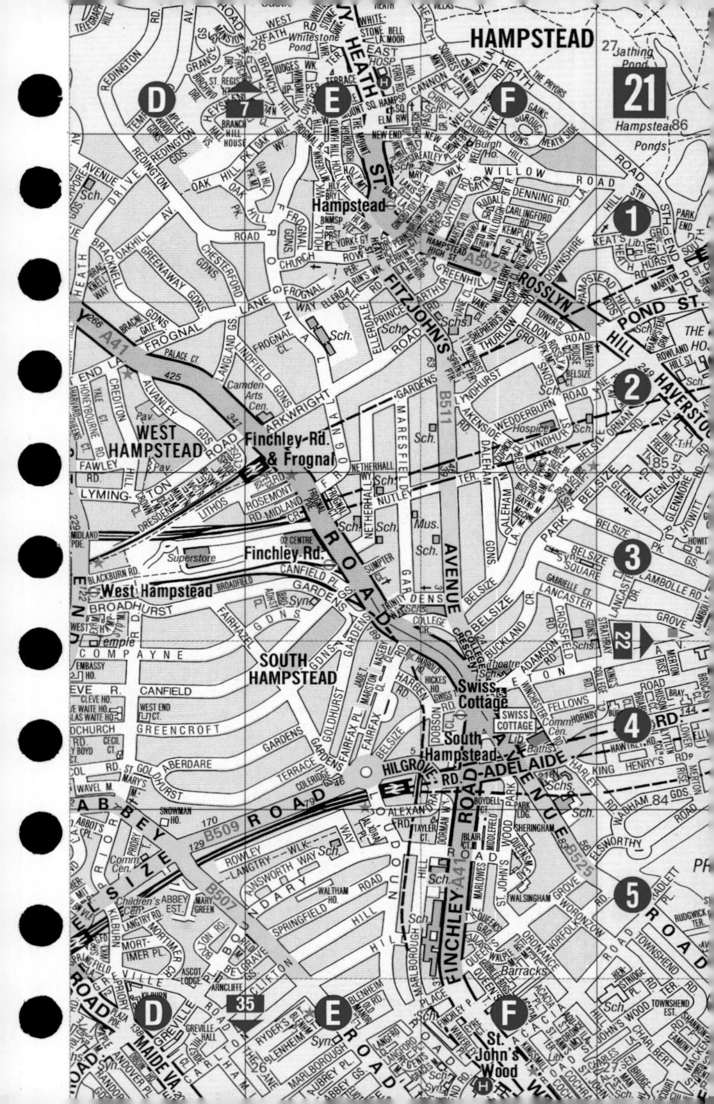
HAMPSTEAD
21
D
E
F
7
1
2
3
4
5
22
35
Hampstead
Hampstead Ponds
Whitestone Pond
Bathing Pond
FITZJOHN'S
AVENUE
B511
A41
A502
ROSSLYN
HILL
POND ST.
HAVERSTOCK
WEST HAMPSTEAD
Finchley Rd. & Frognal
Finchley Rd.
West Hampstead
SOUTH HAMPSTEAD
Swiss Cottage
South Hampstead
FINCHLEY ROAD
ADELAIDE RD.
ABBEY ROAD
B509
B507
B525
St. John's Wood
Barracks
Superstore
Camden Arts Cen.
COMPAYNE
GREENCROFT
CANFIELD
ABERDARE
BELSIZE
FROGNAL
REDINGTON
HEATH
WILLOW ROAD
LYNDHURST
WEDDERBURN
MARESFIELD
NETHERHALL
ARKWRIGHT
ELLERDALE
GOLDHURST TERRACE
BOUNDARY ROAD
SPRINGFIELD
ACACIA
WORONZOW

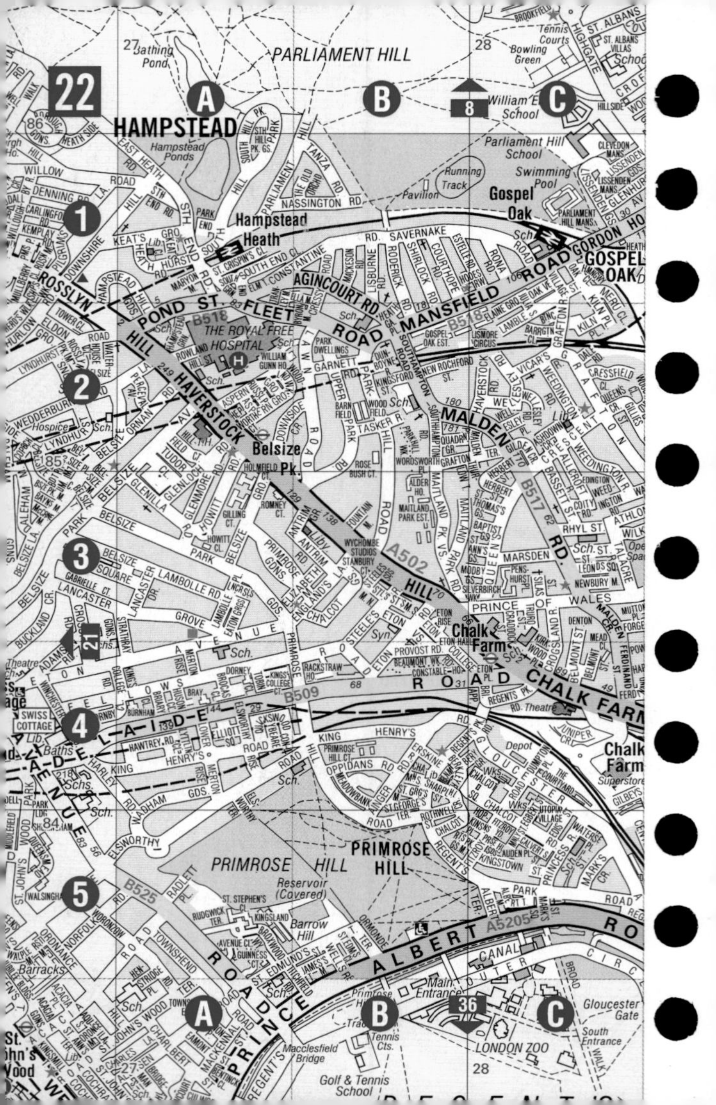

HAMPSTEAD
PARLIAMENT HILL
Hampstead Ponds
Hampstead Heath
Parliament Hill School
Gospel Oak
GOSPEL OAK
THE ROYAL FREE HOSPITAL
Belsize Pk.
HAVERSTOCK HILL
MALDEN RD.
AGINCOURT RD.
FLEET ROAD
MANSFIELD ROAD
GORDON HOUSE
POND ST.
ROSSLYN HILL
CHALK FARM ROAD
Chalk Farm
PRIMROSE HILL
ADELAIDE ROAD
ETON AVENUE
PRINCE ALBERT ROAD
PRINCE OF WALES RD.
SWISS COTTAGE
LONDON ZOO
Macclesfield Bridge
St. John's Wood

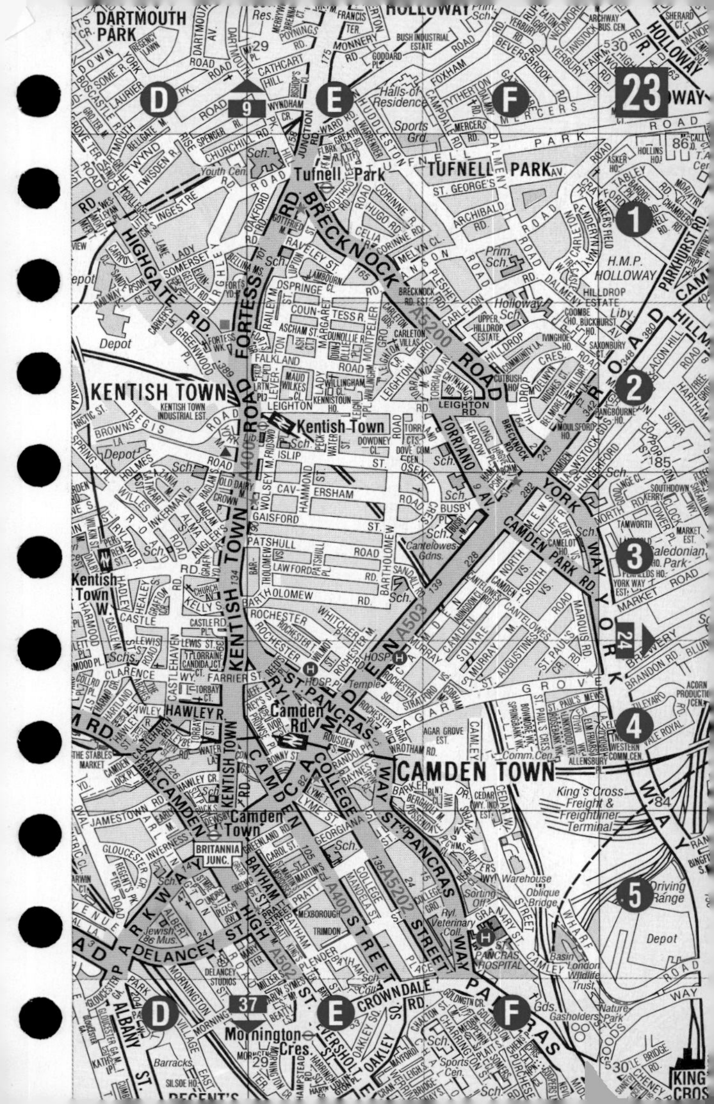
23
DARTMOUTH PARK
HOLLOWAY
TUFNELL PARK
Tufnell Park
KENTISH TOWN
Kentish Town
H.M.P. HOLLOWAY
CAMDEN TOWN
Camden Town
Camden Rd.
Kentish Town W.
King's Cross Freight & Freightliner Terminal
Mornington Cres.
ST. PANCRAS HOSPITAL
BRITANNIA JUNC.
Caledonian Park
KING'S CROSS

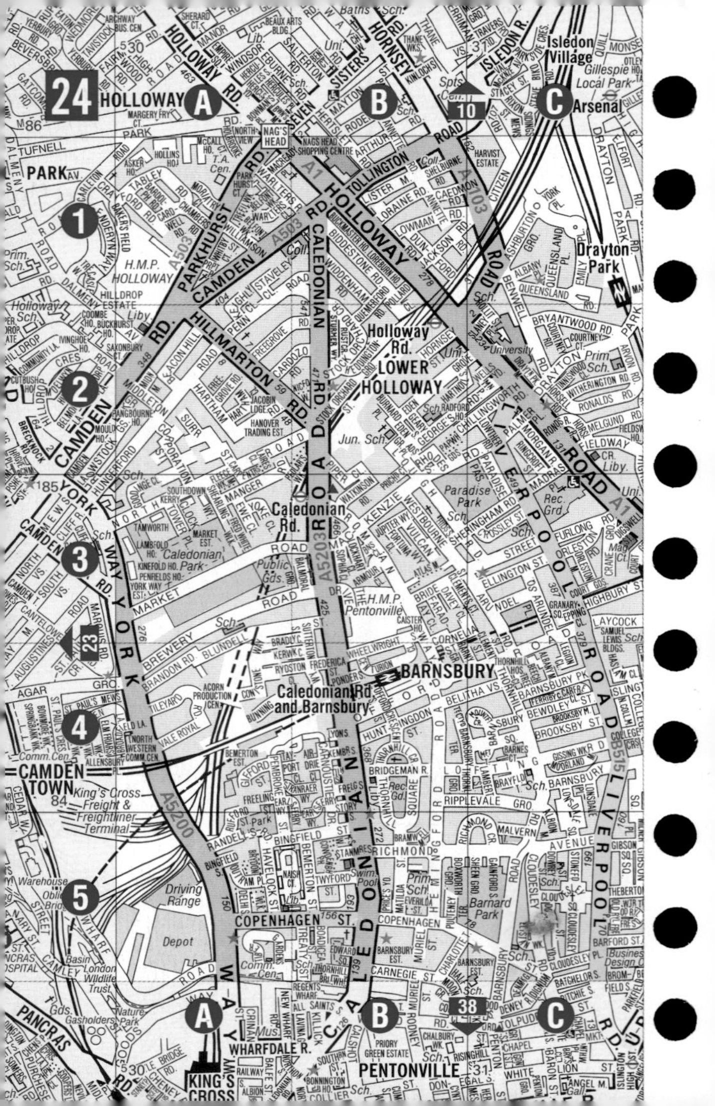
24
HOLLOWAY
A
B
C
10
Isledon Village
Gillespie Local Park
Arsenal
HOLLOWAY RD.
HORNSEY RD.
SEVEN SISTERS
NAG'S HEAD
NAGS HEAD SHOPPING CENTRE
TOLLINGTON
TUFNELL PARK AV.
DALMENY RD.
DRAYTON PARK
Drayton Park
1
2
3
4
5
H.M.P. HOLLOWAY
HILLDROP ESTATE
PARKHURST RD.
CAMDEN RD.
A503
A1
A103
CALEDONIAN RD.
HOLLOWAY RD.
HILLMARTON RD.
Holloway Rd.
LOWER HOLLOWAY
BENWELL RD.
CITIZEN RD.
University
ASHBURTON GRO.
QUEENSLAND RD.
BRYANTWOOD RD.
DRAYTON PARK
CAMDEN
YORK WAY
MIDDLETON GRO.
Caledonian Rd.
Caledonian Park
MARKET ROAD
Public Gds.
A5203
H.M.P. Pentonville
Paradise Park
LIVERPOOL ROAD
Rec. Grd.
HIGHBURY ST.
ELLINGTON ST.
BREWERY ROAD
BLUNDELL
BARNSBURY
Caledonian Rd. and Barnsbury
23
BARNSBURY PK.
BEWDLEY ST.
BROOKSBY ST.
B515
CAMDEN TOWN
King's Cross Freight & Freightliner Terminal
A5200
COPENHAGEN ST.
RICHMOND AV.
Barnard Park
Driving Range
Depot
Warehouse
ST. PANCRAS HOSPITAL
Camley Street Natural Park
London Wildlife Trust
Gasholders
PANCRAS RD.
KING'S CROSS
WHARFDALE R.
PENTONVILLE
CARNEGIE ST.
38
CLOUDESLEY SQ.
WHITE LION ST.
ANGEL M.

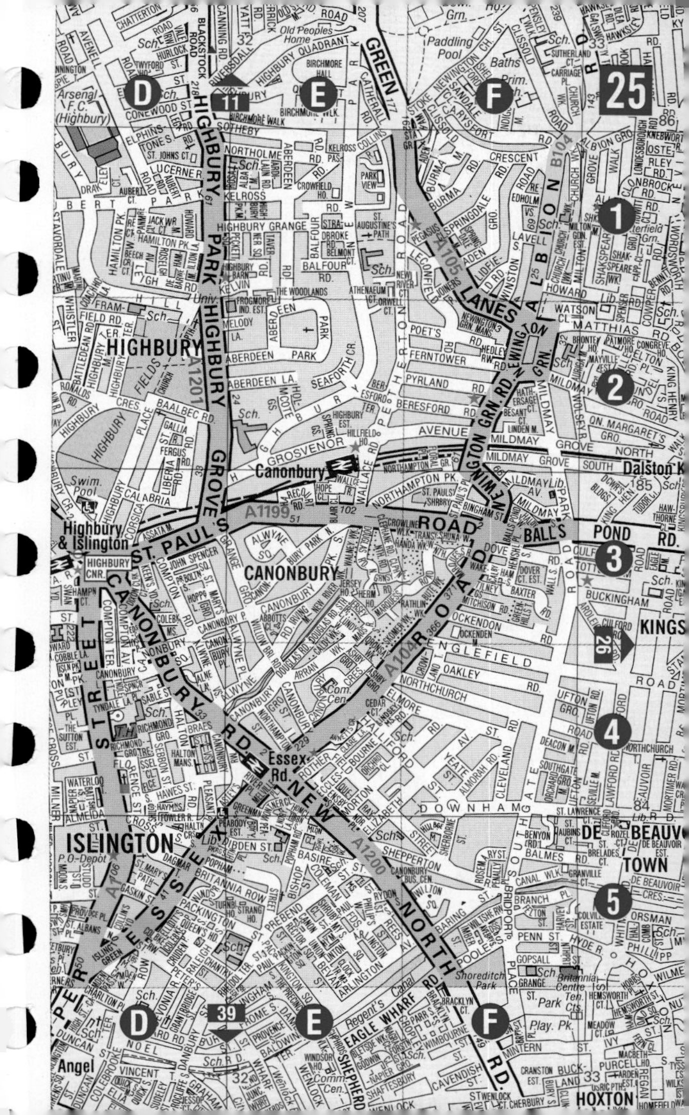
25
11
39
26
D
E
F
1
2
3
4
5
HIGHBURY
CANONBURY
ISLINGTON
DE BEAUVOIR TOWN
KINGSLAND
HOXTON
Angel
Highbury & Islington
Canonbury
Essex Rd.
Dalston Kingsland
Arsenal F.C. (Highbury)
HIGHBURY PARK
HIGHBURY GROVE
ST. PAUL'S ROAD
BALL'S POND RD.
ESSEX ROAD
NEW NORTH RD.
CANONBURY RD.
UPPER STREET
NEWINGTON GRN. RD.
ALBION ROAD
GREEN LANES
Regent's Canal
Shoreditch Park
Paddling Pool
Swim. Pool
A1199
A1201
A104
A105
A1200
B104

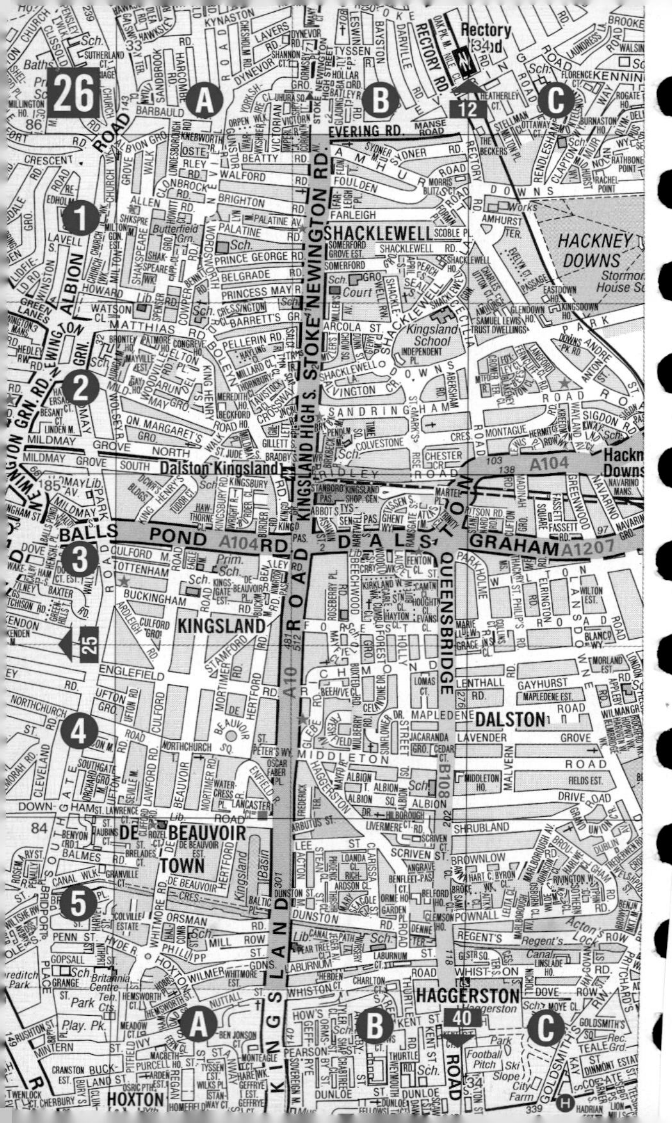

26
A
B
C
1
2
3
4
5
12
25
40
Rectory Rd.
SHACKLEWELL
HACKNEY DOWNS
Hackney Downs
Dalston Kingsland
KINGSLAND
DALSTON
DE BEAUVOIR TOWN
HAGGERSTON
HOXTON
BALLS POND RD.
A104
A1207
A10
B108
STOKE NEWINGTON RD.
KINGSLAND HIGH ST.
KINGSLAND ROAD
QUEENSBRIDGE ROAD
DALSTON LA.
GRAHAM RD.
EVERING RD.
AMHURST ROAD
DOWNS PARK ROAD
SANDRINGHAM ROAD
RIDLEY ROAD
FOREST ROAD
RICHMOND ROAD
MIDDLETON ROAD
ALBION ROAD
NEWINGTON GRN. RD.
MILDMAY GROVE NORTH
MILDMAY GROVE SOUTH
MILDMAY PARK
ESSEX ROAD
SOUTHGATE ROAD
DOWNHAM ROAD
BALMES RD.
ORSMAN RD.
PHILLIPP ST.
HOXTON ST.
NUTTALL ST.
WHISTON RD.
REGENT'S ROW
Regent's Canal
Kingsland Basin
Acton's Lock
Kingsland School
Butterfield Grn.
Britannia Centre
Play. Pk.
Football Pitch
Ski Slope
City Farm
Haggerston Park

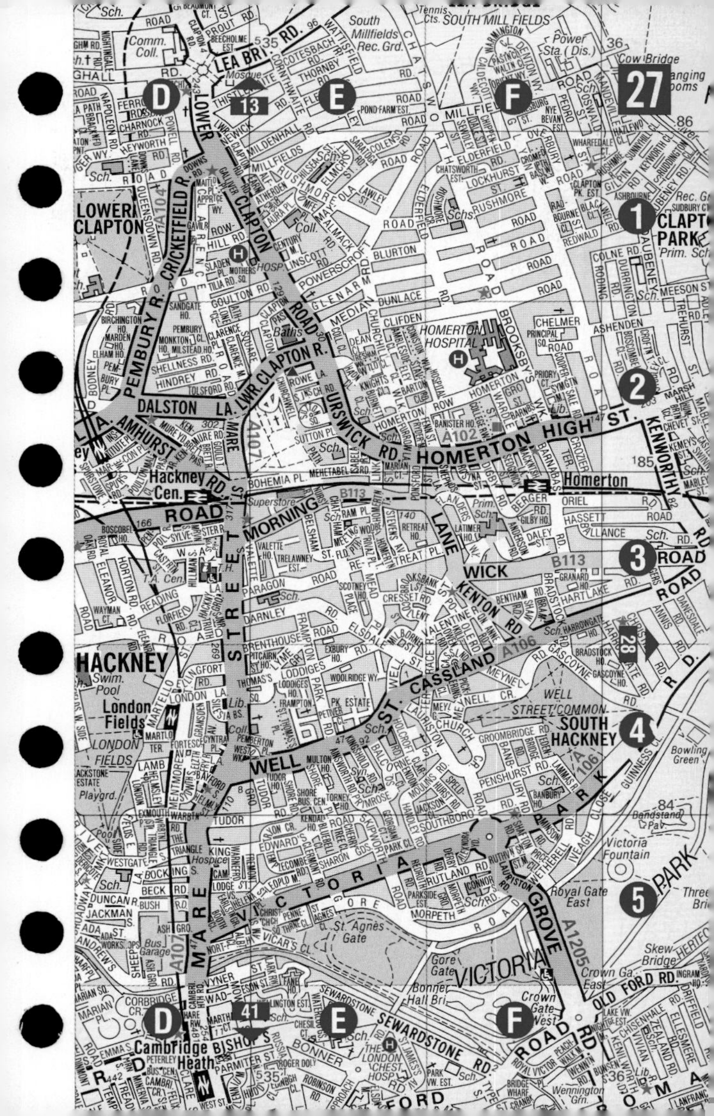

27
13
28
41
D
E
F
1
2
3
4
5
LOWER CLAPTON
CLAPTON PARK
HACKNEY
SOUTH HACKNEY
VICTORIA
Cambridge Heath
Hackney Cen.
Homerton
London Fields
SOUTH MILL FIELDS
South Millfields Rec. Grd.
Power Sta. (Dis.)
Cow Bridge
HOMERTON HOSPITAL
WELL STREET COMMON
LONDON FIELDS
Victoria Fountain
Royal Gate East
Crown Gate East
Crown Gate West
Gore Gate
St. Agnes Gate
Bonner Hall Bri.
Skew Bridge
Bowling Green
Bandstand Pav.
THE LONDON CHEST HOSP.
LEA BRI. RD.
LOWER CLAPTON RD.
LWR. CLAPTON R.
CLAPTON ROAD
PEMBURY R.
CRICKETFIELD R.
DALSTON LA.
AMHURST RD.
MARE STREET
MORNING LANE
URSWICK RD.
HOMERTON HIGH ST.
HOMERTON ROW
WICK ROAD
KENTON RD.
ST. CASSLAND RD.
WELL ST.
VICTORIA PARK ROAD
GROVE ROAD
OLD FORD RD.
SEWARDSTONE RD.
BISHOP'S
MILLFIELDS ROAD
CHATSWORTH ROAD
KENWORTHY RD.
BROOKSBY'S WK.
A102
A104
A106
A107
A1205
B113

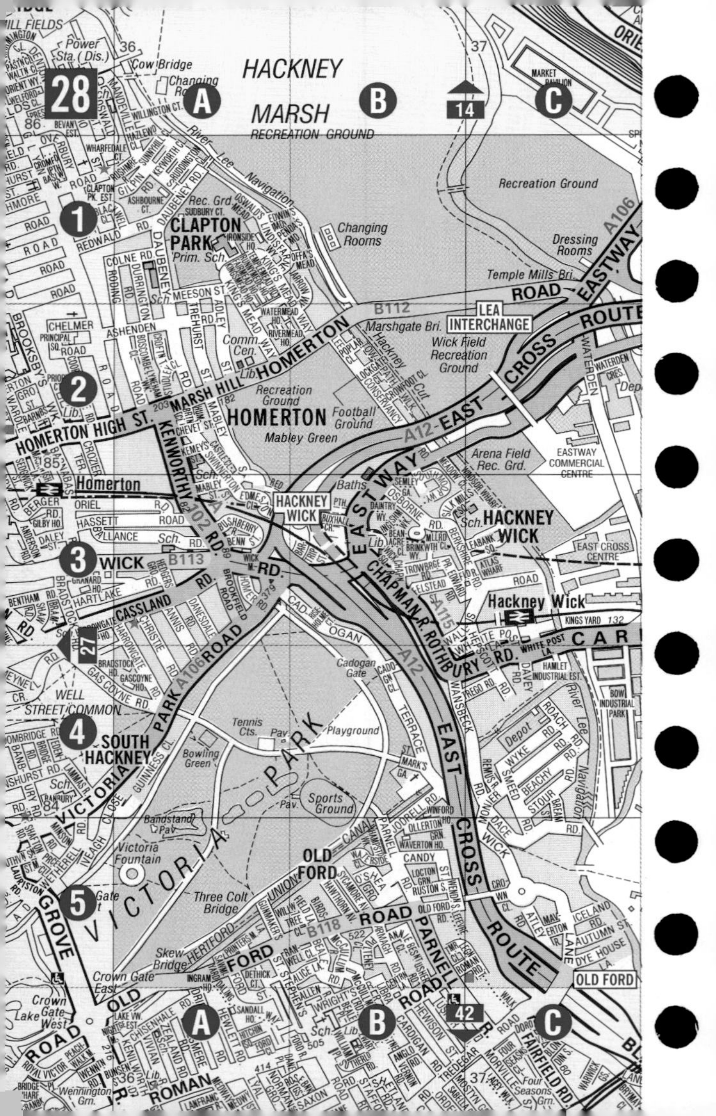28
HACKNEY
MARSH
RECREATION GROUND
Cow Bridge
Changing Rooms
Power Sta. (Dis.)
River Lee Navigation
Recreation Ground
Dressing Rooms
Temple Mills Bri.
EASTWAY
ROAD
A106
LEA INTERCHANGE
EAST CROSS ROUTE
B112
Marshgate Bri.
Wick Field Recreation Ground
Hackney Cut
CLAPTON PARK
Prim. Sch.
Rec. Grd.
Comm. Cen.
Lib.
HOMERTON
MARSH HILL
HOMERTON HIGH ST.
Recreation Ground
Football Ground
Mabley Green
A12
Arena Field Rec. Grd.
EASTWAY COMMERCIAL CENTRE
Homerton
HACKNEY WICK
Baths
HACKNEY WICK
EAST CROSS CENTRE
Hackney Wick
KINGS YARD
WICK RD.
B113
KENWORTHY RD.
CASSLAND ROAD
CHAPMAN RD.
ROTHBURY RD.
WHITE POST LA.
HAMLET INDUSTRIAL EST.
BOW INDUSTRIAL PARK
River Lee Navigation
Cadogan Gate
WELL STREET COMMON
SOUTH HACKNEY
VICTORIA PARK ROAD
Tennis Cts.
Pav.
Playground
Bowling Green
Sports Ground
Bandstand Pav.
Victoria Fountain
VICTORIA PARK
Three Colt Bridge
OLD FORD
UNION CANAL
OLD FORD ROAD
B118
PARNELL ROAD
Skew Bridge
Crown Gate East
Crown Gate West
Lake
OLD FORD ROAD
GROVE
ROMAN R.
Wennington Grn.
Four Seasons Grn.
FAIRFIELD RD.
OLD FORD
Depot
Sch.
A
B
C
1
2
3
4
5
14
27
42

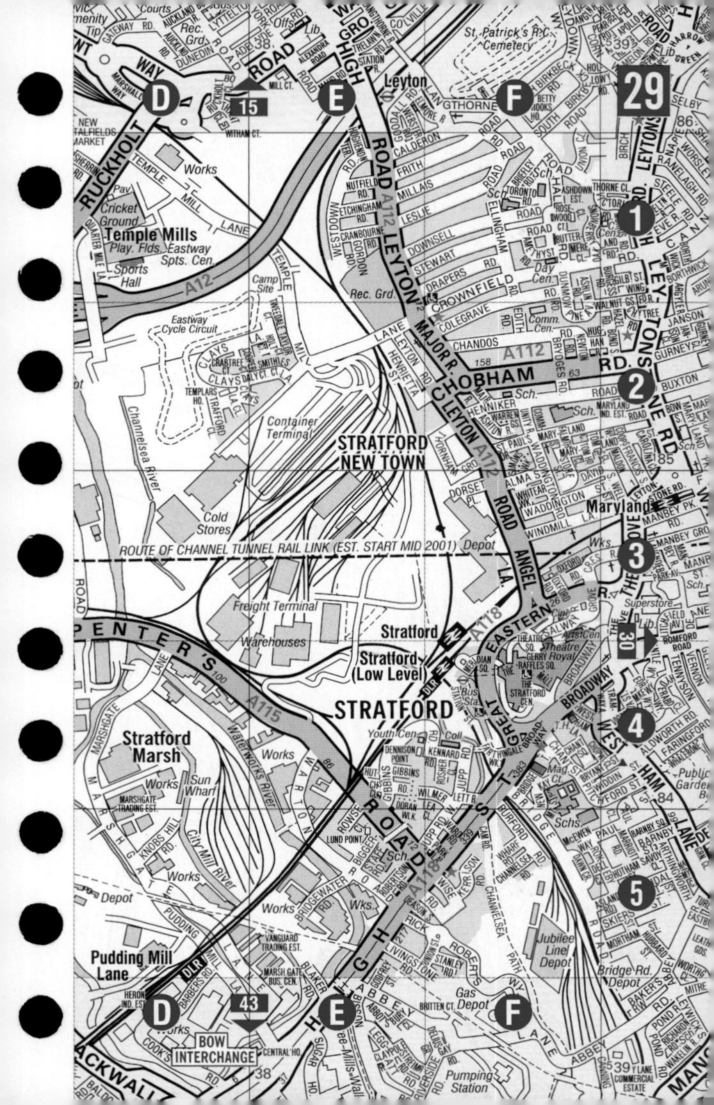

29
Leyton
St. Patrick's R.C. Cemetery
Temple Mills
Play. Flds.
Eastway Spts. Cen.
Sports Hall
Cricket Ground
Eastway Cycle Circuit
Camp Site
Channelsea River
Container Terminal
STRATFORD NEW TOWN
Cold Stores
ROUTE OF CHANNEL TUNNEL RAIL LINK (EST. START MID 2001)
Depot
Freight Terminal
Warehouses
Stratford
Stratford (Low Level)
STRATFORD
Stratford Marsh
Sun Wharf
City Mill River
Waterworks River
Maryland
Jubilee Line Depot
Pudding Mill Lane
BOW INTERCHANGE
Gas Depot
Pumping Station
Bridge Rd. Depot
Public Gardens
HIGH ROAD LEYTON
CHOBHAM RD.
ANGEL LA.
GREAT EASTERN RD.
BROADWAY
CARPENTER'S ROAD
HIGH ST.
ABBEY LANE
RUCKHOLT ROAD
MARSHGATE LANE
WEST HAM LANE
LEYTONSTONE RD.
A12
A112
A115
A118
15
30
43

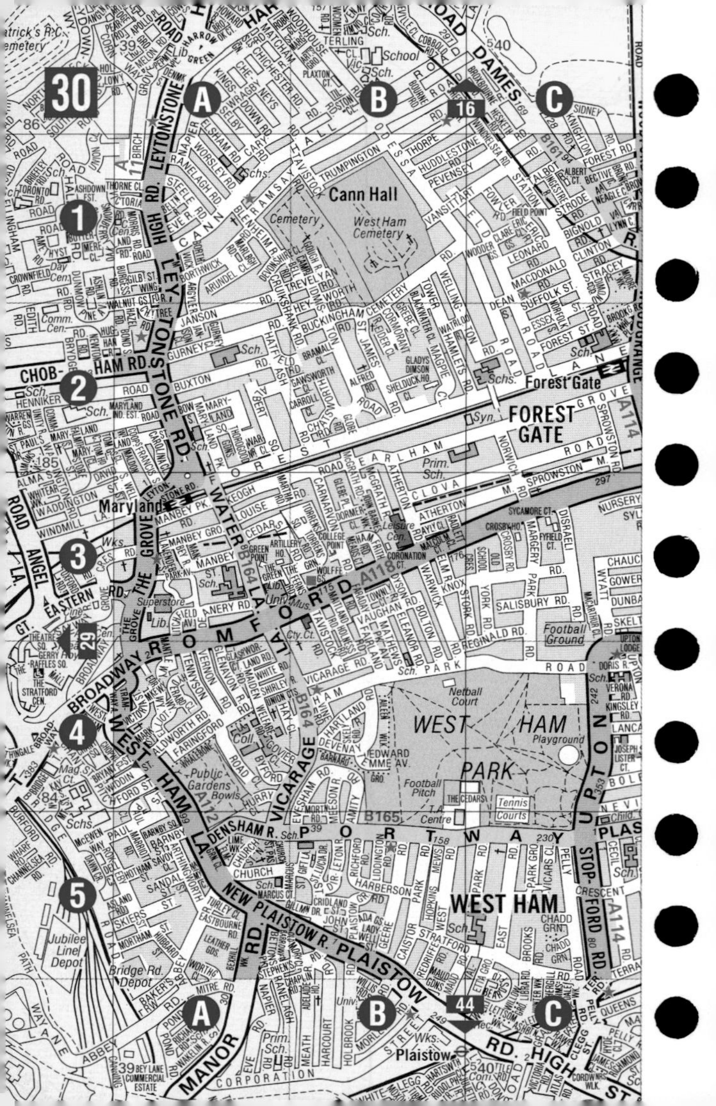
30
A
B
C
16
1
2
3
4
5
29
44
Cann Hall
Cemetery
West Ham Cemetery
Forest Gate
FOREST GATE
Maryland
Superstore
Lib.
Public Gardens
Bowls
Football Ground
Netball Court
WEST HAM PARK
Playground
Football Pitch
THE CEDARS
Tennis Courts
T.A. Centre
WEST HAM
Jubilee Line Depot
Bridge Rd. Depot
Plaistow
Leisure Cen.
Prim. Sch.
HIGH RD. LEYTONSTONE
LEYTONSTONE RD.
ROMFORD RD.
WATER LA.
VICARAGE LA.
PORTWAY
UPTON LA.
STOPFORD RD.
WEST HAM LA.
NEW PLAISTOW RD.
BROADWAY
THE GROVE
FOREST RD.
EARLHAM GROVE
CANN HALL RD.
DAMES RD.
CHOBHAM RD.
ANGEL LA.
EASTERN RD.
MANOR RD.
ABBEY RD.
ABBEY LANE
CORPORATION ST.
HIGH ST.
CLOVA RD.
SPROWSTON RD.
PLAISTOW RD.
A118
A112
A114
B164
B165
B161

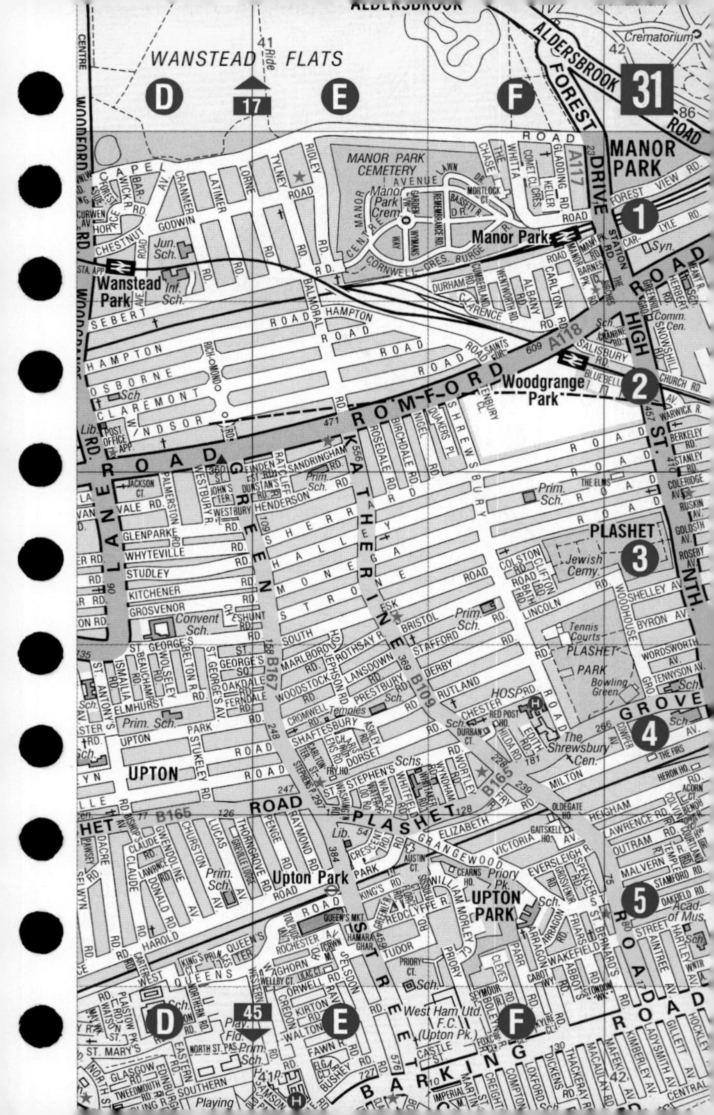

ALDERSBROOK
WANSTEAD FLATS
D
E
F
17
31
Crematorium
ALDERSBROOK
FOREST
DRIVE
ROAD
MANOR PARK
FOREST VIEW RD.
MANOR PARK CEMETERY
Manor Park Crem.
Manor Park
Wanstead Park
CAPEL
CHESTNUT
GODWIN
Jun. Sch.
Inf. Sch.
CRANMER
LATIMER
LORNE
TYLNEY
RIDLEY
BALMORAL
HAMPTON
SEBERT ROAD
OSBORNE
CLAREMONT
WINDSOR
RICHMOND
ROMFORD
A118
A117
HIGH ST. NTH.
SALISBURY
BLUEBELL
Woodgrange Park
DURHAM
CUMBERLAND
WENTWORTH
ALBANY
CARLTON
CLARENCE
SHREWSBURY
ROSEDALE
BIRCHDALE
NIGEL
QUAKERS PL.
GREEN
KATHERINE
B167
B109
B165
HENDERSON
SHERRARD
HALLEY
MONEGA
STRONE
SANDRINGHAM
Prim. Sch.
PLASHET
Jewish Cemy.
PLASHET PARK
Tennis Courts
Bowling Green
GROVE
The Shrewsbury Cen.
COLSTON
LINCOLN
WOODHOUSE
SHELLEY AV.
BYRON AV.
WORDSWORTH AV.
TENNYSON AV.
BRISTOL
STAFFORD
DERBY
RUTLAND
CHESTER
HOSP.
Temples
SHAFTESBURY
DORSET
Schs.
WYNDHAM
WORTLEY
MILTON
LANE
JACKSON CT.
VALE RD.
GLENPARKE
WHYTEVILLE
STUDLEY
KITCHENER
GROSVENOR
Convent Sch.
ST. GEORGE'S
UPTON PARK
UPTON
STUKELEY
PLASHET ROAD
ELIZABETH
GRANGEWOOD
VICTORIA
Upton Park
Lib.
Priory Pk.
UPTON PARK
WILLIAM MORLEY
QUEEN'S MKT.
WEST HAM Utd. F.C. (Upton Pk.)
GREEN STREET
BARKING ROAD
HAROLD
QUEENS
CLAUDE
DONALD RD.
LUCAS
CHURSTON
THORNGROVE RD.
PENGE
RAYMOND RD.
CASTLE ST.
STANDARD
HEIGHAM
LAWRENCE RD.
OUTRAM
MALVERN
STAMFORD RD.
OAKFIELD RD.
Acad. of Mus.
ST. BERNARD'S
AINTREE AV.
KIMBERLEY AV.
LADYSMITH AV.
CENTRAL
45
Play. Fld.
Playing
SOUTHERN
GLASGOW
TWEEDMOUTH
ST. MARY'S
NORTH ST. PAS.
WALTON
KIRTON
FAWN
BUSHEY
DICKENS
THACKERAY
MACAULAY
MAFEKING

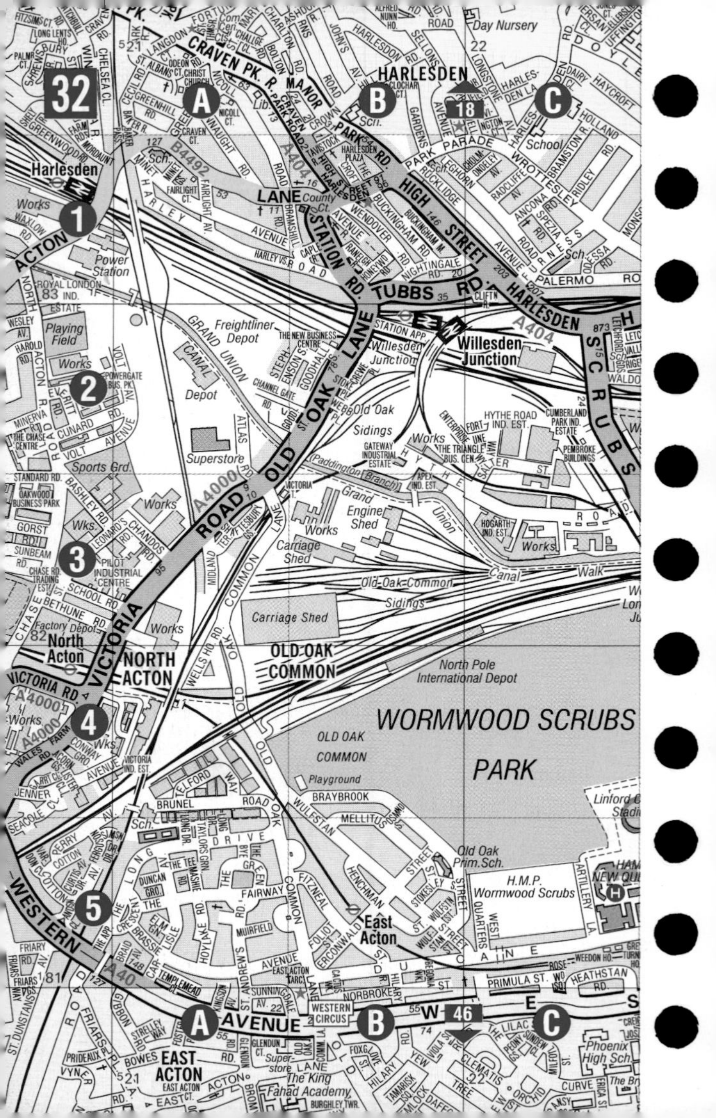

32
HARLESDEN
Harlesden
Day Nursery
CRAVEN PK. R.
MANOR
CRAVEN PARK ROAD
PARK RD.
HIGH STREET
HARLESDEN
Works
ACTON
Power Station
ROYAL LONDON IND. ESTATE
Playing Field
GRAND UNION
Canal Depot
Freightliner Depot
THE NEW BUSINESS CENTRE
TUBBS RD.
STATION RD.
OLD OAK LANE
Willesden Junction
Old Oak Sidings
HYTHE ROAD IND. EST.
CUMBERLAND PARK IND. ESTATE
PEMBROKE BUILDINGS
GATEWAY INDUSTRIAL ESTATE
THE TRIANGLE BUS. CEN.
APEX IND. EST.
Grand Union
Engine Shed
HOGARTH IND. EST.
Canal Walk
POWERGATE BUS. PK.
THE CHASE CENTRE
Sports Grd.
Superstore
STANDARD RD.
OAKWOOD BUSINESS PARK
PILOT INDUSTRIAL CENTRE
CHASE RD. TRADING EST.
Factory Depot
VICTORIA ROAD
A4000
Carriage Shed
Old Oak Common Sidings
OLD OAK COMMON
North Acton
NORTH ACTON
North Pole International Depot
WORMWOOD SCRUBS PARK
OLD OAK COMMON
Playground
VICTORIA IND. EST.
Old Oak Prim.Sch.
H.M.P. Wormwood Scrubs
East Acton
WESTERN AVENUE
A40
EAST ACTON
WESTERN CIRCUS
Phoenix High Sch.
The King Fahad Academy
46
18

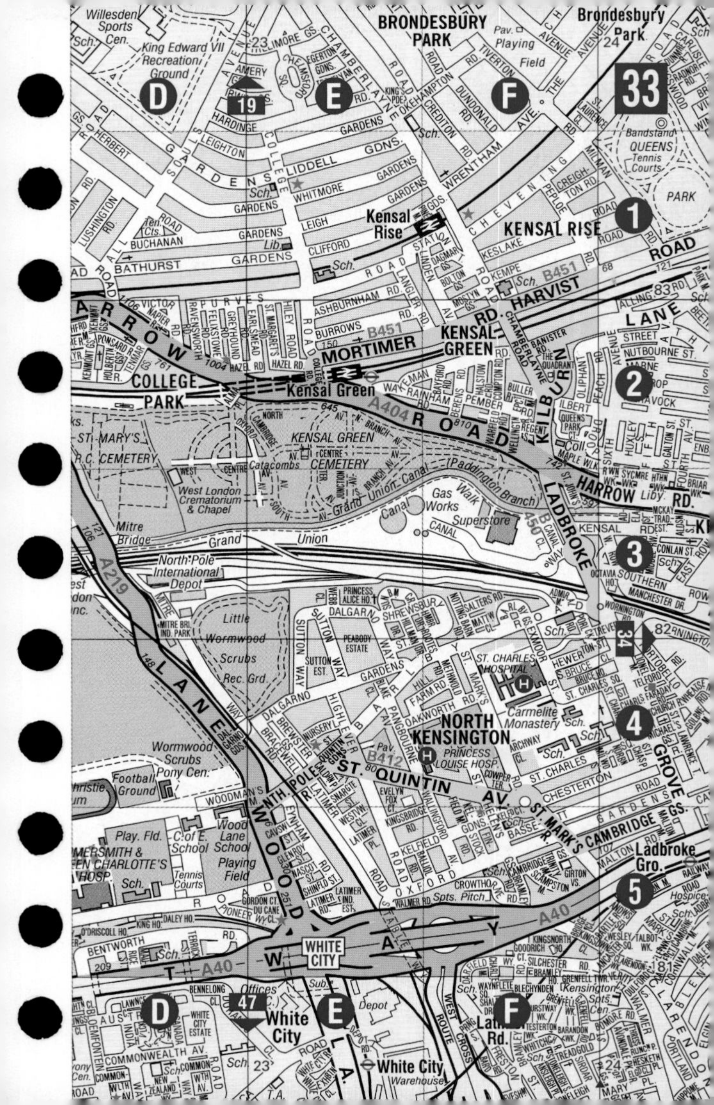
33
Willesden Sports Cen.
King Edward VII Recreation Ground
BRONDESBURY PARK
Brondesbury Park
Playing Field
D
E
F
19
1
2
3
4
5
Bandstand
QUEENS PARK
Tennis Courts
KENSAL RISE
Kensal Rise
CHAMBERLAYNE ROAD
COLLEGE ROAD
HARDINGE ROAD
LEIGHTON GARDENS
LIDDELL GDNS.
WHITMORE GARDENS
LEIGH GARDENS
CLIFFORD GARDENS
BATHURST GARDENS
BUCHANAN GARDENS
LUSHINGTON RD.
HERBERT GARDENS
WRENTHAM AVE.
CHEVENING ROAD
KESLAKE ROAD
HARVIST ROAD
B451
MORTIMER ROAD
KENSAL GREEN
Kensal Green
HARROW ROAD
A404
COLLEGE PARK
KILBURN LANE
LADBROKE GROVE
ST. MARY'S R.C. CEMETERY
KENSAL GREEN CEMETERY
Catacombs
West London Crematorium & Chapel
Grand Union Canal
Paddington Branch
Gas Works
Superstore
Mitre Bridge
North Pole International Depot
A219
Little Wormwood Scrubs Rec. Grd.
SCRUBS LANE
DALGARNO GARDENS
PEABODY ESTATE
ST. CHARLES HOSPITAL
Carmelite Monastery
NORTH KENSINGTON
PRINCESS LOUISE HOSP.
ST. QUINTIN AV.
B412
Wormwood Scrubs Pony Cen.
Football Ground
Play. Fld.
C. of E. School
Wood Lane School
Playing Field
Tennis Courts
WOOD LANE
OXFORD ROAD
ST. MARK'S RD.
CAMBRIDGE GARDENS
CHESTERTON ROAD
Ladbroke Gro.
A40
WESTWAY
WHITE CITY
White City
47
34
Offices
Depot
Latimer Rd.
WEST CROSS ROUTE
White City
Warehouse
COMMONWEALTH AV.
Kensington Spts. Cen.
WALMER RD.
CLARENDON RD.

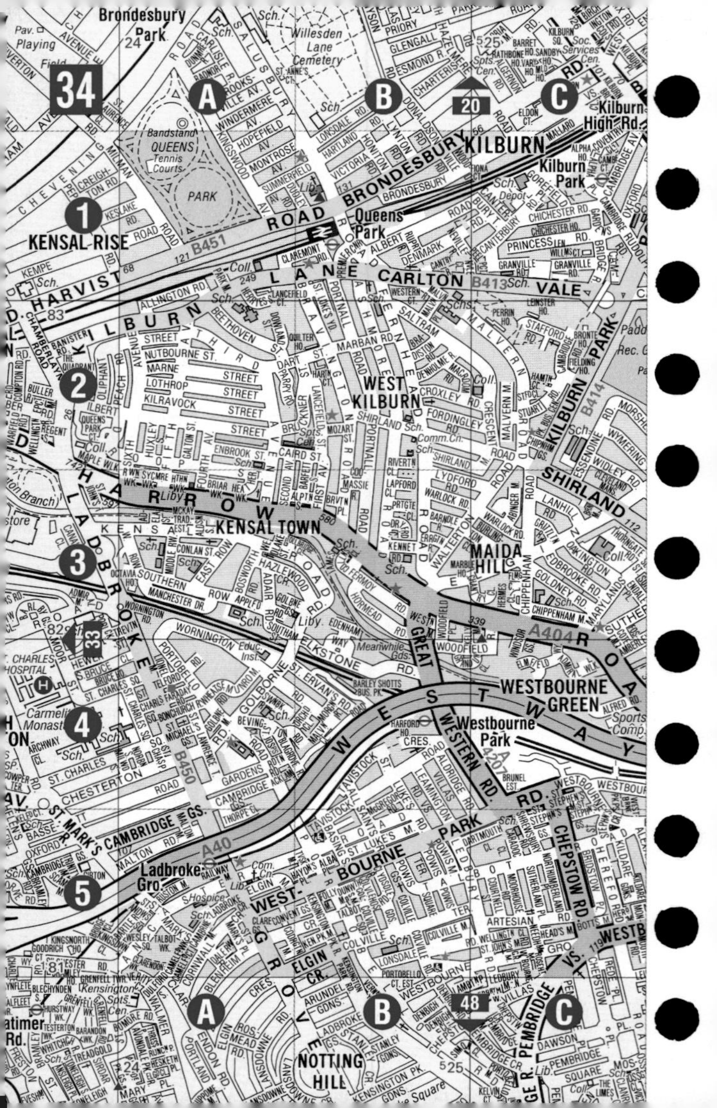
Brondesbury Park
Willesden Lane Cemetery
KILBURN
Kilburn High Rd.
Kilburn Park
QUEENS PARK
Bandstand
Tennis Courts
KENSAL RISE
Queens Park
BRONDESBURY ROAD
B451
HARVIST ROAD
CARLTON VALE
B413
KILBURN LANE
WEST KILBURN
SHIRLAND ROAD
KILBURN PARK ROAD
B414
HARROW ROAD
KENSAL TOWN
MAIDA HILL
LADBROKE GROVE
GREAT WESTERN RD.
A404
WESTBOURNE GREEN
WESTWAY
A40
Westbourne Park
ST. CHARLES HOSPITAL
Carmelite Monastery
CAMBRIDGE GS.
B450
Ladbroke Gro.
WESTBOURNE PARK RD.
CHEPSTOW RD.
WESTBOURNE GROVE
ELGIN CR.
NOTTING HILL
PEMBRIDGE
Latimer Rd.
A
B
C
1
2
3
4
5
20
33
48

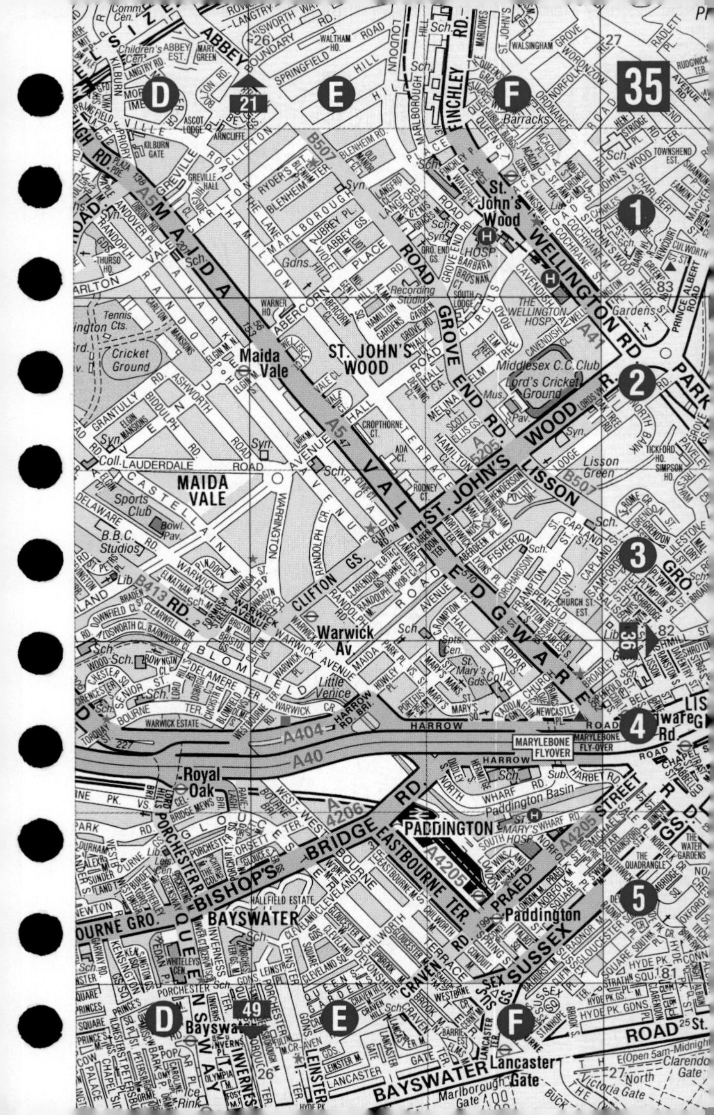
35
D
E
F
1
2
3
4
5
21
49
36
ST. JOHN'S WOOD
MAIDA VALE
Maida Vale
St. John's Wood
Warwick Av.
Royal Oak
PADDINGTON
Paddington
BAYSWATER
Bayswater
Lancaster Gate
Edgware Rd.
Little Venice
Paddington Basin
Lord's Cricket Ground
Middlesex C.C. Club
Lisson Green
Cricket Ground
Tennis Cts.
Sports Club
B.B.C. Studios
Recording Studio
THE WELLINGTON HOSP.
Barracks
MAIDA VALE
EDGWARE RD.
WELLINGTON RD.
GROVE END RD.
ST. JOHN'S WOOD RD.
LISSON GRO.
HARROW ROAD
MARYLEBONE FLYOVER
BISHOP'S BRIDGE RD.
EASTBOURNE TER.
PRAED ST.
SUSSEX GDNS.
BAYSWATER ROAD
QUEENSWAY
PORCHESTER TER.
WESTBOURNE GRO.
CLIFTON GDS.
WARWICK AVENUE
RANDOLPH AVENUE
ABERCORN PL.
HAMILTON TER.
ABBEY RD.
BOUNDARY RD.
FINCHLEY RD.
BLOMFIELD RD.
LAUDERDALE ROAD
ELGIN AV.
SUSSEX GDNS.
HYDE PK. GDNS.
A5
A41
A404
A40
A4206
A4205
A5205
B507
B413

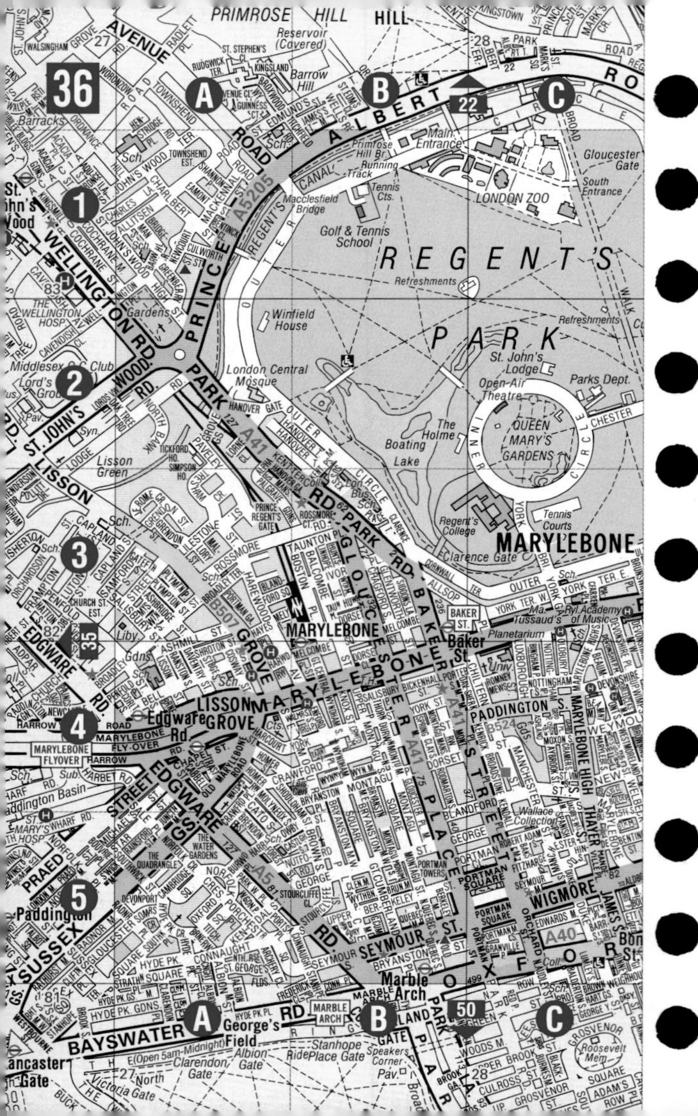
36
PRIMROSE HILL
Reservoir (Covered)
Barrow Hill
ALBERT ROAD
PRINCE ALBERT ROAD
22
REGENT'S PARK
LONDON ZOO
Main Entrance
Gloucester Gate
South Entrance
Golf & Tennis School
Macclesfield Bridge
REGENT'S CANAL
Winfield House
London Central Mosque
Refreshments
St. John's Lodge
Open-Air Theatre
QUEEN MARY'S GARDENS
Parks Dept.
Boating Lake
The Holme
Regent's College
Tennis Courts
MARYLEBONE
Clarence Gate
St. John's Wood
WELLINGTON RD.
THE WELLINGTON HOSP.
Middlesex C.C. Club
Lord's Ground
ST. JOHN'S WOOD RD.
LISSON GROVE
Lisson Green
PARK RD.
BAKER ST.
Baker St.
Madame Tussaud's
Planetarium
Ryl. Academy of Music
MARYLEBONE
GLOUCESTER PL.
MARYLEBONE RD.
35
EDGWARE RD.
Edgware Rd.
MARYLEBONE FLYOVER
Paddington Basin
ST. MARY'S HOSP.
PRAED ST.
Paddington
SUSSEX GDNS.
THE WATER GARDENS
THE QUADRANGLE
PORTMAN TOWERS
PORTMAN SQUARE
Wallace Collection
WIGMORE ST.
MARYLEBONE HIGH ST.
THAYER ST.
SEYMOUR ST.
Marble Arch
OXFORD ST.
BAYSWATER RD.
George's Field
(Open 5am-Midnight)
Stanhope Place Gate
Albion Gate
Clarendon Gate
Victoria Gate
Speakers Corner
Lancaster Gate
PARK LANE
50
GROSVENOR SQUARE
Roosevelt Mem.
1
2
3
4
5
A
B
C

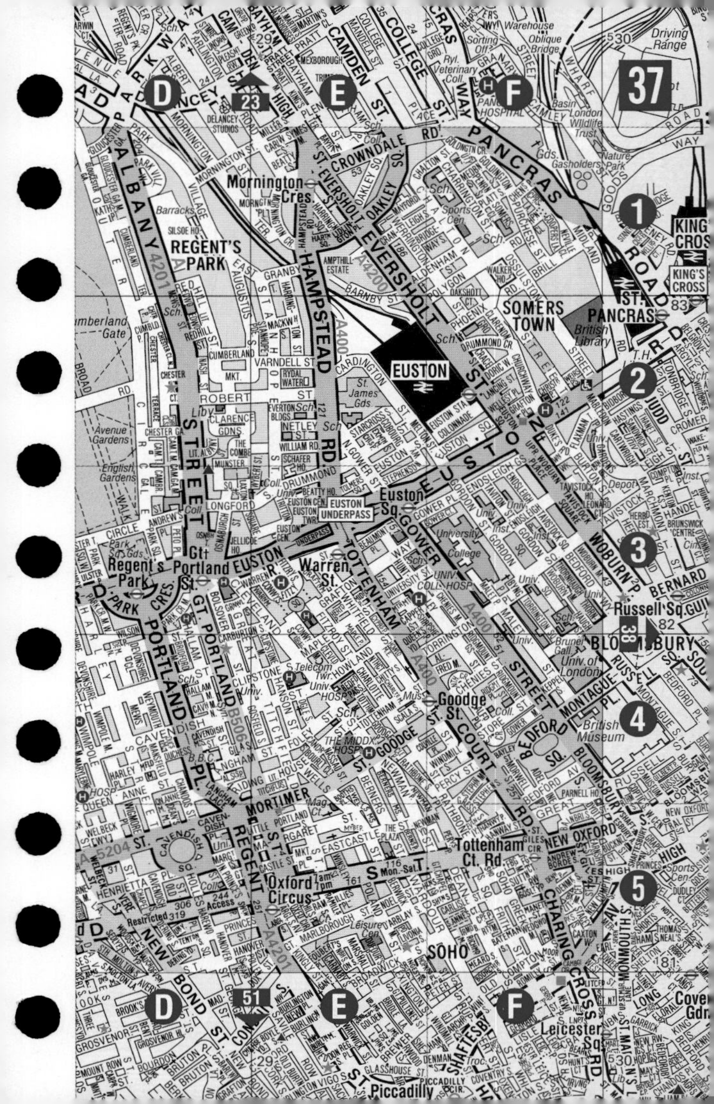
37
D
E
F
1
2
3
4
5
23
51
38
REGENT'S PARK
SOMERS TOWN
EUSTON
ST. PANCRAS
KING'S CROSS
British Library
Mornington Cres.
Euston Sq.
Warren St.
Regent's Park
Great Portland St.
Goodge St.
Tottenham Ct. Rd.
Oxford Circus
Russell Sq.
Leicester Sq.
Piccadilly
SOHO
BLOOMSBURY
British Museum
University College
Univ. of London
HAMPSTEAD RD.
EVERSHOLT ST.
EUSTON RD.
GOWER ST.
TOTTENHAM COURT RD.
PORTLAND PL.
ALBANY STREET
PARKWAY
CROWNDALE RD.
PANCRAS RD.
MORTIMER ST.
OXFORD ST.
REGENT ST.
NEW BOND ST.
CHARING CROSS RD.
NEW OXFORD ST.
WOBURN PL.
BEDFORD SQ.
CAVENDISH SQ.
Driving Range
London Wildlife Trust
Camley St. Nature Park
Gasholders
Ryl. Veterinary Coll.
Cumberland Gate
Avenue Gardens
English Gardens
Telecom Twr.
THE MIDDX. HOSP.
Brunei Gall.
EUSTON UNDERPASS

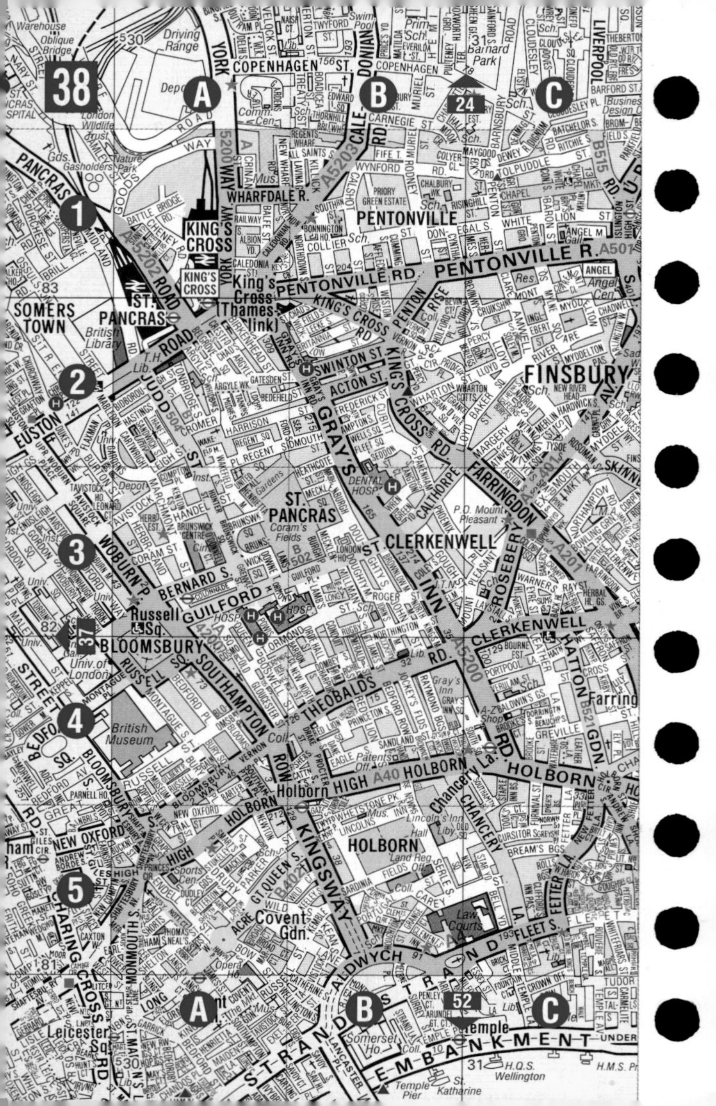

38
A
B
C
24
52
37
1
2
3
4
5
Warehouse
Oblique Bridge
Driving Range
Depot
London Wildlife Trust
Nature Park
Gasholders
Gds.
PANCRAS
MIDLAND
YORK
COPENHAGEN ST.
CALEDONIAN RD.
Barnard Park
CARNEGIE ST.
FIFE T.
WYNFORD
WHARFDALE R.
KILLICK
PRIORY GREEN ESTATE
PENTONVILLE
TOLPUDDLE
CHAPEL
WHITE LION
ANGEL M.
PENTONVILLE R.
A501
ANGEL
Angel Cen.
KING'S CROSS
KING'S CROSS
King's Cross (Thameslink)
ST. PANCRAS
SOMERS TOWN
British Library
BATTLE BRIDGE
RAILWAY
ALBION YD.
CALEDONIA ST.
COLLIER
PENTONVILLE RD.
KING'S CROSS RD
SWINTON ST.
ACTON ST.
FREDERICK ST.
CUBITT
GRAY'S INN RD.
PERCY CIR.
WHARTON COTTS.
LLOYD BAKER
FINSBURY
NEW RIVER HEAD
MYDDELTON
JUDD
CROMER
HARRISON
REGENT SQ.
SIDMOUTH
HEATHCOTE
DENTAL HOSP.
CALTHORPE
FARRINGDON
P.O. Mount Pleasant
ST. PANCRAS
Coram's Fields
ST. CLERKENWELL
ROSEBERY
A201
EUSTON
TAVISTOCK SQUARE
WOBURN
BERNARD S.
GUILFORD
CORAM ST.
BRUNSWICK CENTRE
Russell Sq.
BLOOMSBURY
Univ. of London
RUSSELL SQ.
SOUTHAMPTON
THEOBALDS RD.
CLERKENWELL
HATTON
Farring
Gray's Inn
A5200
British Museum
MONTAGUE S.
BEDFORD SQ.
BLOOMSBURY
HOLBORN
HIGH A40 HOLBORN
Holborn
Chancery La.
CHANCERY
Lincoln's Inn
NEW OXFORD
KINGSWAY
HOLBORN
Land Reg. Offs.
Law Courts
FLEET S.
FETTER LA.
Covent Gdn.
ACRE
ALDWYCH
STRAND
Opera Ho.
Leicester Sq.
CHARING CROSS RD.
SHAFTESBURY
MONMOUTH S.
Somerset Ho.
Temple
EMBANKMENT
H.Q.S. Wellington
Temple Pier
St. Katharine
H.M.S. Pr

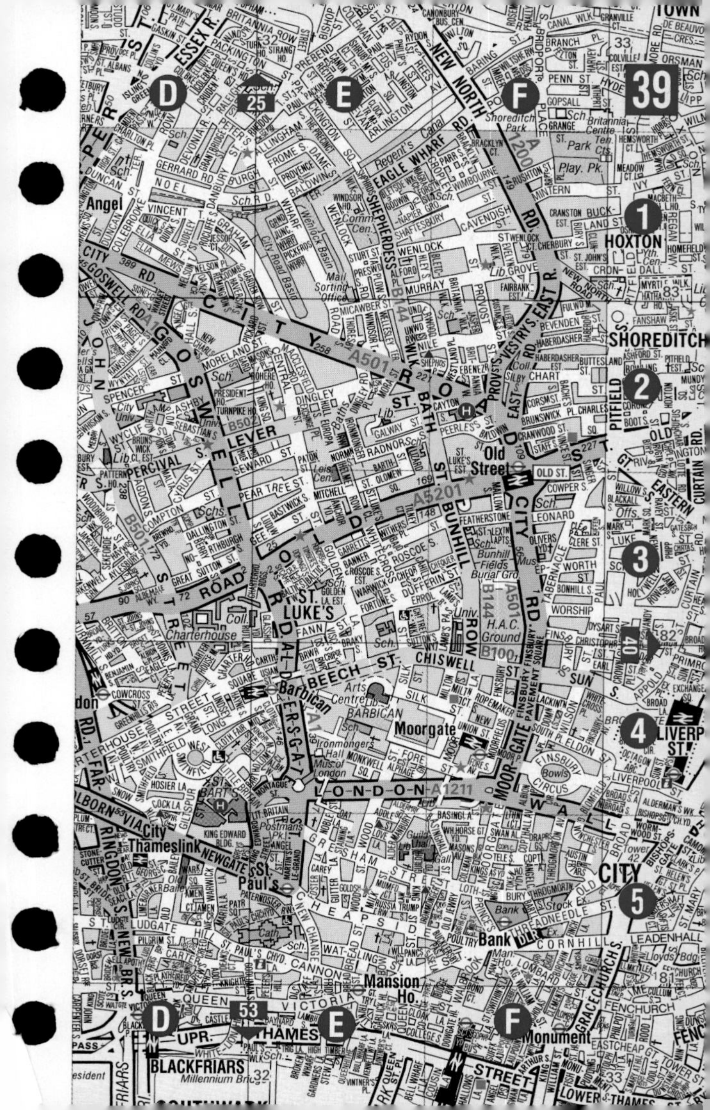

39
D
E
F
1
2
3
4
5
25
40
53
Angel
HOXTON
SHOREDITCH
CITY
Old Street
Barbican
Moorgate
Bank
Mansion Ho.
Monument
City Thameslink
St. Paul's
BLACKFRIARS
LIVERPOOL ST.
ST. LUKE'S
Charterhouse
City Road Basin
Wenlock Basin
Regent's Canal
Mail Sorting Office
Shoreditch Park
H.A.C. Ground
Bunhill Fields Burial Grd.
Finsbury Circus
Barbican Arts Centre
Mus. of London
Ironmongers Hall
Guildhall
Millennium Bridge
CITY RD.
GOSWELL RD.
ST. JOHN ST.
OLD ST.
LONDON WALL
CHEAPSIDE
NEWGATE ST.
QUEEN VICTORIA ST.
UPR. THAMES ST.
CANNON ST.
CORNHILL
LEADENHALL
FENCHURCH
GRACECHURCH S.
BISHOPSGATE
MOORGATE
NEW NORTH RD.
EAST RD.
ALDERSGATE ST.
BEECH ST.
CHISWELL
BUNHILL ROW
WHITECROSS
CLERKENWELL RD.
HOLBORN VIA.
FARRINGDON RD.
LUDGATE HILL
A1
A501
A5201
A1211
A1200
B144
B100
B501
B502

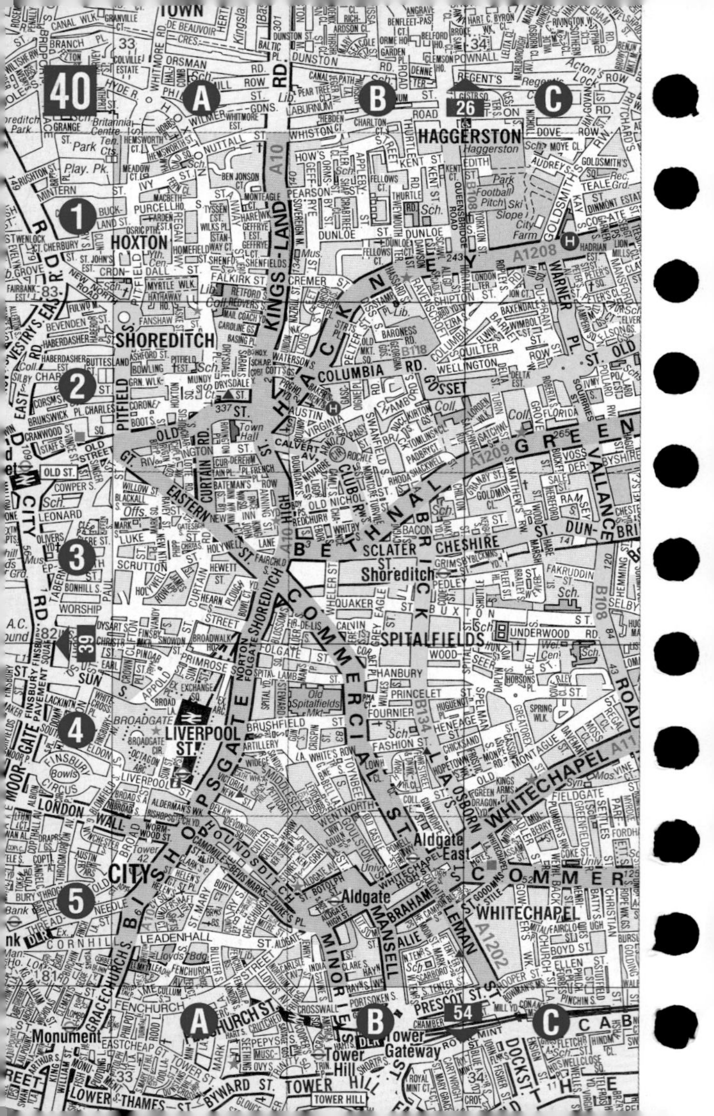
40
A
B
C
1
2
3
4
5
26
39
54
HAGGERSTON
Haggerston
HOXTON
SHOREDITCH
Shoreditch
SPITALFIELDS
LIVERPOOL ST.
Aldgate
Aldgate East
WHITECHAPEL
CITY
Monument
Tower Hill
Tower Gateway
Bank
KINGSLAND RD.
HACKNEY RD.
BETHNAL GREEN RD.
COMMERCIAL ST.
SHOREDITCH HIGH ST.
NORTON FOLGATE
BISHOPSGATE
HOUNDSDITCH
MINORIES
MANSELL
LEMAN
WHITECHAPEL
COMMERCIAL RD.
GREAT EASTERN ST.
OLD ST.
CITY RD.
COLUMBIA RD.
GOSSET
BRICK LANE
CHESHIRE
SCLATER
CURTAIN RD.
PITFIELD
LONDON WALL
LEADENHALL
FENCHURCH
GRACECHURCH
CORNHILL
EASTCHEAP
LOWER THAMES ST.
BYWARD ST.
TOWER HILL
PRESCOT ST.
REGENT'S ROW
Acton's Lock
DOVE ROW
WARNER PL.
GOLDSMITH'S
VALLANCE RD.
FINSBURY CIRCUS
BROADGATE
Old Spitalfields Mkt.
Town Hall
Park
Football Pitch
Ski Slope
City Farm
Play. Pk.
Britannia Centre
A10
A1208
A1209
A1202
A11
B108
B118
B134

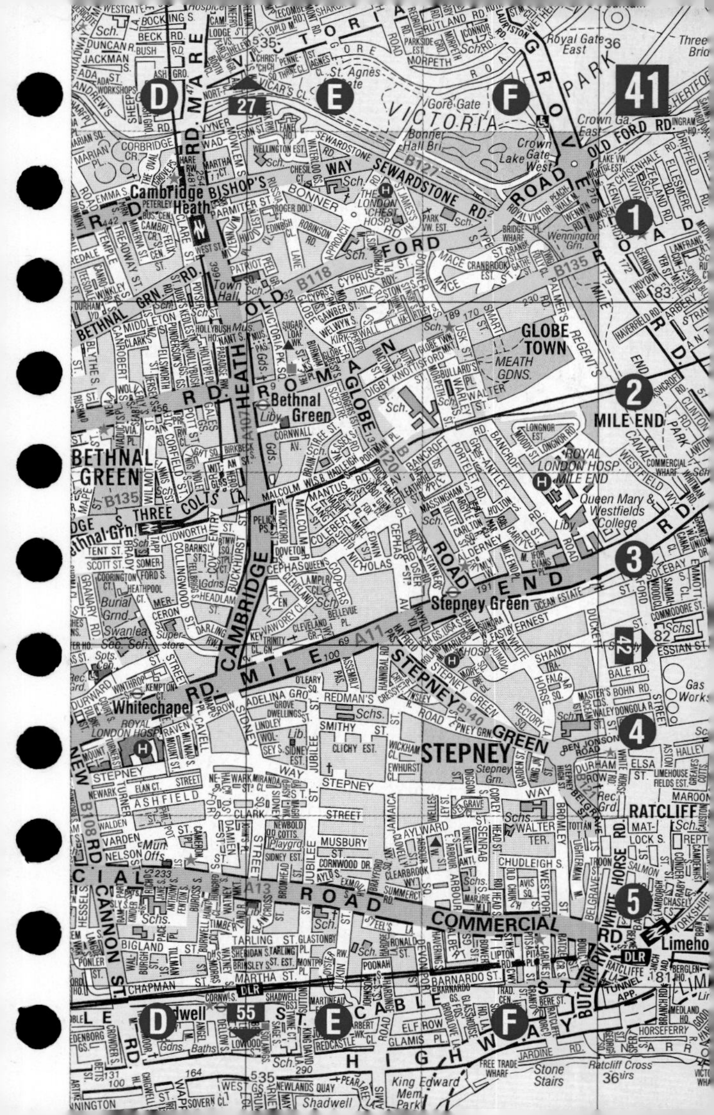
41
D
E
F
1
2
3
4
5
27
42
55
VICTORIA PARK
Royal Gate East
Gore Gate
Crown Gate East
Crown Gate West
Lake
Bonner Hall Bri.
OLD FORD RD.
GROVE ROAD
SEWARDSTONE RD.
B127
BISHOP'S WAY
Cambridge Heath
MARE ST.
HACKNEY RD.
THE LONDON CHEST HOSP.
ROMAN RD.
OLD FORD RD.
B118
B135
GLOBE TOWN
MEATH GDNS.
REGENT'S CANAL
MILE END
MILE END RD.
ROYAL LONDON HOSP. MILE END
Queen Mary & Westfields College
BETHNAL GREEN
Bethnal Green
Liby.
CAMBRIDGE HEATH RD.
A107
GLOBE RD.
BANCROFT RD.
THREE COLTS LA.
Bethnal Grn.
Stepney Green
STEPNEY GREEN
B140
OCEAN ESTATE
A11
MILE END RD.
Whitechapel
ROYAL LONDON HOSP.
STEPNEY
STEPNEY WAY
CLICHY EST.
RATCLIFF
Gas Works
WHITE HORSE RD.
COMMERCIAL ROAD
A13
NEW RD.
B108
CANNON ST. RD.
JUBILEE ST.
SIDNEY ST.
ARBOUR SQ.
Limehouse
DLR
Shadwell
CABLE ST.
THE HIGHWAY
GLAMIS PL.
Ratcliff Cross Stairs
King Edward Mem. Park
NARROW ST.
BUTCHER ROW
Stone Stairs
FREE TRADE WHARF
Shadwell

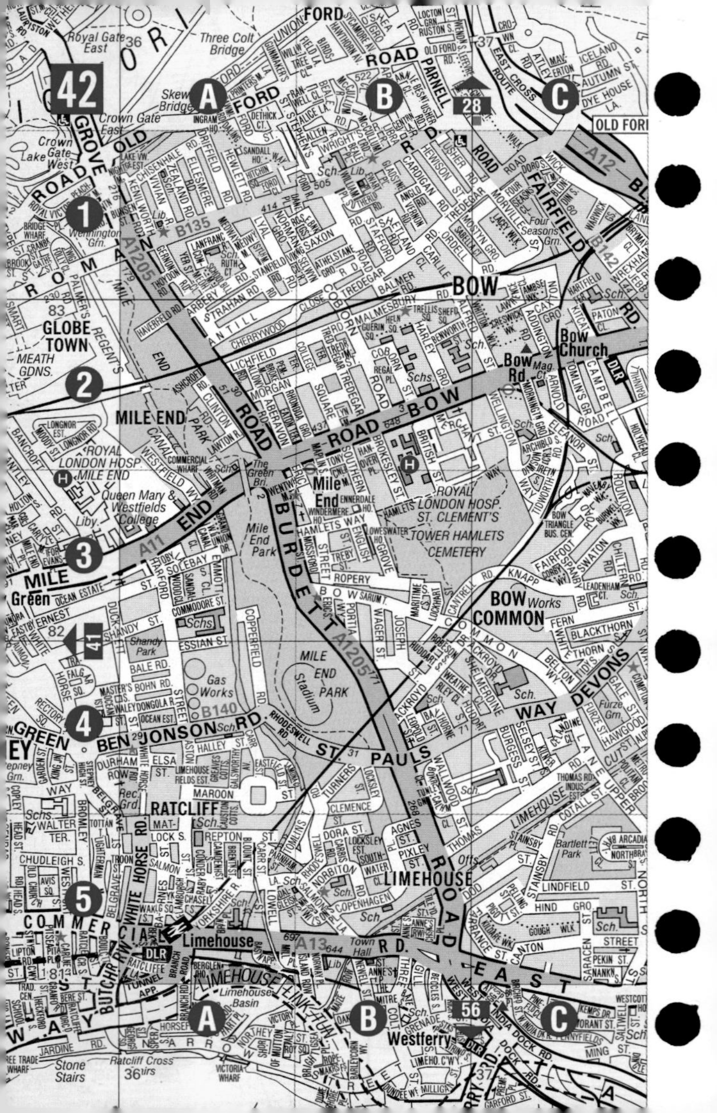

42
A
B
C
1
2
3
4
5
28
41
56
FORD
ROAD
PARNELL
OLD FORD RD.
EAST CROSS ROUTE
ICELAND RD.
AUTUMN ST.
DYE HOUSE LA.
OLD FORD
A12
Royal Gate East
Three Colt Bridge
Skew Bridge
Crown Gate East
Crown Gate West
Lake
GROVE ROAD
OLD FORD
ROMAN
B135
A1205
Lib.
Sch.
Wennington Grn.
BRIDGE WHARF
TREDEGAR RD.
SAXON RD.
FAIRFIELD
B142
Four Seasons Grn.
WRIGHT'S RD.
HEWISON ST.
CARDIGAN RD.
USHER RD.
CARLILE CL.
BOW
MALMESBURY RD.
ANTILL RD.
CHERRYWOOD CLOSE
COBORN RD.
HARLEY GRO.
ALFRED ST.
ADDINGTON RD.
Bow Church
DLR
Bow Rd.
Mag. Ct.
TOMLIN'S GRO.
CAMPBELL RD.
GLOBE TOWN
MEATH GDNS.
REGENT'S CANAL
MILE END
ROAD
BOW
MORGAN ST.
TREDEGAR SQUARE
CLINTON RD.
ASHCROFT
MERCHANT ST.
BRITISH ST.
WELLINGTON WAY
ELEANOR ST.
ROYAL LONDON HOSP. MILE END
Queen Mary & Westfields College
Liby.
LONGNOR EST.
BANCROFT RD.
The Green Bri.
Mile End
ROYAL LONDON HOSP. ST. CLEMENT'S
TOWER HAMLETS CEMETERY
HAMLETS WAY
BURDETT
BOW TRIANGLE BUS. CEN.
FAIRFOOT RD.
CHILTERN RD.
A11
END
MILE
Mile End Park
ROPERY ST.
BOW COMMON
Works
KNAPP RD.
FERN ST.
BLACKTHORN ST.
Green
OCEAN ESTATE
ERNEST ST.
SHANDY ST.
Shandy Park
ESSIAN ST.
COPPERFIELD RD.
COMMODORE ST.
Schs.
Gas Works
BALE RD.
B140
MILE END PARK
Stadium
A1205
DEVONS
WAY
COMMON
Furze Grn.
BELTON WY.
Sch.
BEN JONSON RD.
RHODESWELL RD.
ST. PAULS WAY
GREEN
Stepney Grn.
DURHAM ROW
ELSA ST.
HALLEY ST.
Rec. Grd.
MAROON ST.
RATCLIFF
CLEMENCE ST.
BURGESS ST.
SELSEY ST.
LIMEHOUSE CUT
UPPER NORTH
Bartlett Park
WALTER TER.
CHUDLEIGH S.
WHITE HORSE RD.
REPTON ST.
DORA ST.
AGNES ST.
PIXLEY ST.
LIMEHOUSE
ROAD
Offs.
STAINSBY RD.
LINDFIELD ST.
HIND GRO.
COMMERCIAL
Limehouse
A13
Town Hall
RD.
EAST
INDIA DOCK RD.
CANTON ST.
PEKIN ST.
SARACEN ST.
LIMEHOUSE LINK TUN.
Limehouse Basin
Westferry
NARROW ST.
JARDINE RD.
Stone Stairs
Ratcliff Cross Stairs
VICTORIA WHARF
36
37
81
82
83

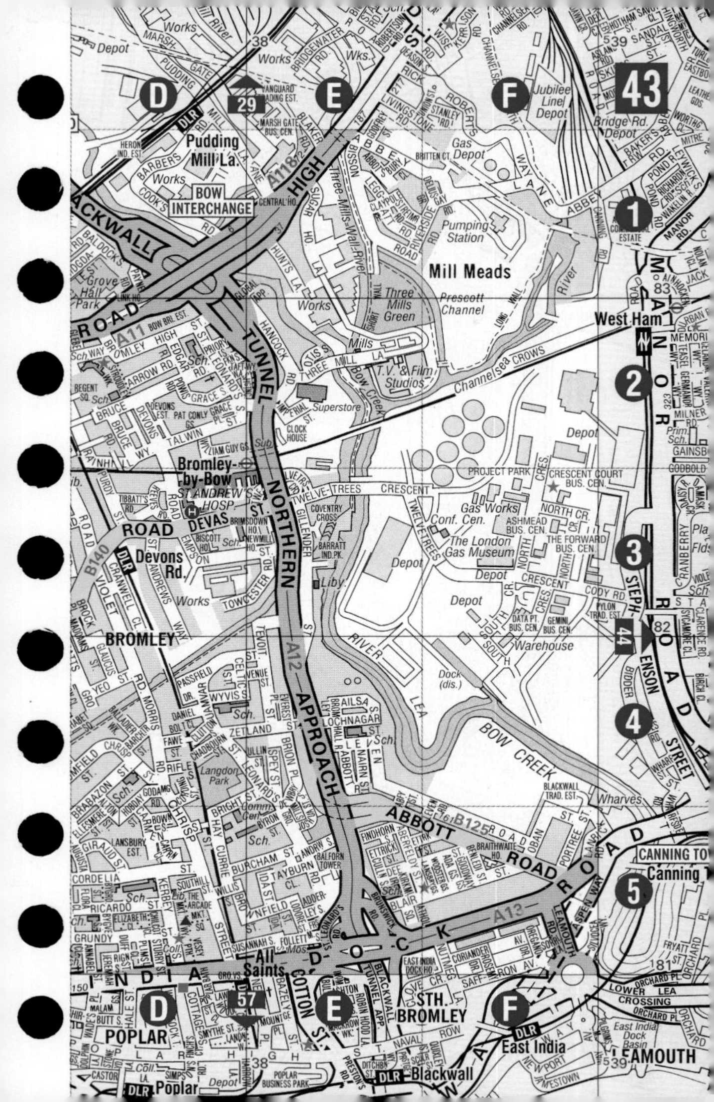

43
D
E
F
29
Works
Depot
Pudding Mill La.
BOW INTERCHANGE
Jubilee Line Depot
Bridge Rd. Depot
Gas Depot
Pumping Station
Mill Meads
Three Mills Green
Prescott Channel
West Ham
T.V. & Film Studios
Superstore
Bromley-by-Bow
ST. ANDREW'S HOSP.
Devons Rd.
BROMLEY
The London Gas Museum
Conf. Cen.
Gas Works
Warehouse
Dock (dis.)
BOW CREEK
Langdon Park
CANNING TOWN
Canning Town
All Saints
POPLAR
STH. BROMLEY
East India
Blackwall
LEAMOUTH
East India Dock Basin
LOWER LEA CROSSING
57
44
NORTHERN APPROACH
TUNNEL
ABBOTT ROAD
BLACKWALL TUNNEL APP.
HIGH ST.
STEPHENSON STREET
MANOR ROAD
A11
A12
A13
A118
B125
B140
1
2
3
4
5

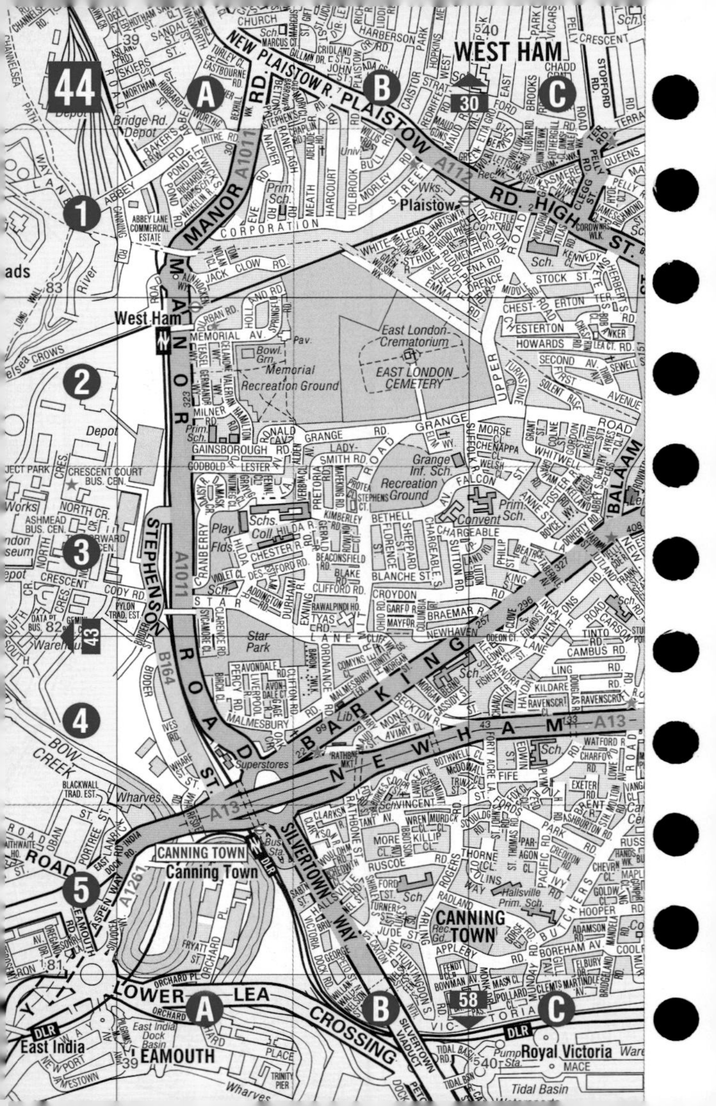

44
A
B
C
1
2
3
4
5
30
43
58
WEST HAM
West Ham
Plaistow
CANNING TOWN
Canning Town
East India
Royal Victoria
LEAMOUTH
NEW PLAISTOW R.
PLAISTOW RD.
HIGH ST.
MANOR RD.
MANOR ROAD
A1011
A112
A13
A1261
B164
CORPORATION
JACK CLOW RD.
MEMORIAL AV.
Bowl. Grn.
Memorial Recreation Ground
East London Crematorium
EAST LONDON CEMETERY
UPPER ROAD
GRANGE RD.
Grange Inf. Sch.
Recreation Ground
Convent
Prim. Sch.
STEPHENSON ST.
STAR LANE
Star Park
BARKING ROAD
NEWHAM WAY
BALAAM ST.
CHARGEABLE LA.
Superstores
Lib.
SILVERTOWN WAY
SILVERTOWN VIADUCT
LOWER LEA CROSSING
VICTORIA DOCK RD.
Hallsville Prim. Sch.
BUTCHERS RD.
BOW CREEK
BLACKWALL TRAD. EST.
Wharves
CRESCENT COURT BUS. CEN.
ASHMEAD BUS. CEN.
ABBEY LANE COMMERCIAL ESTATE
Bridge Rd. Depot
Depot
Works
East India Dock Basin
TRINITY PIER
Tidal Basin
Pump Sta.
Rec. Gd.
Bus Sta.
DLR

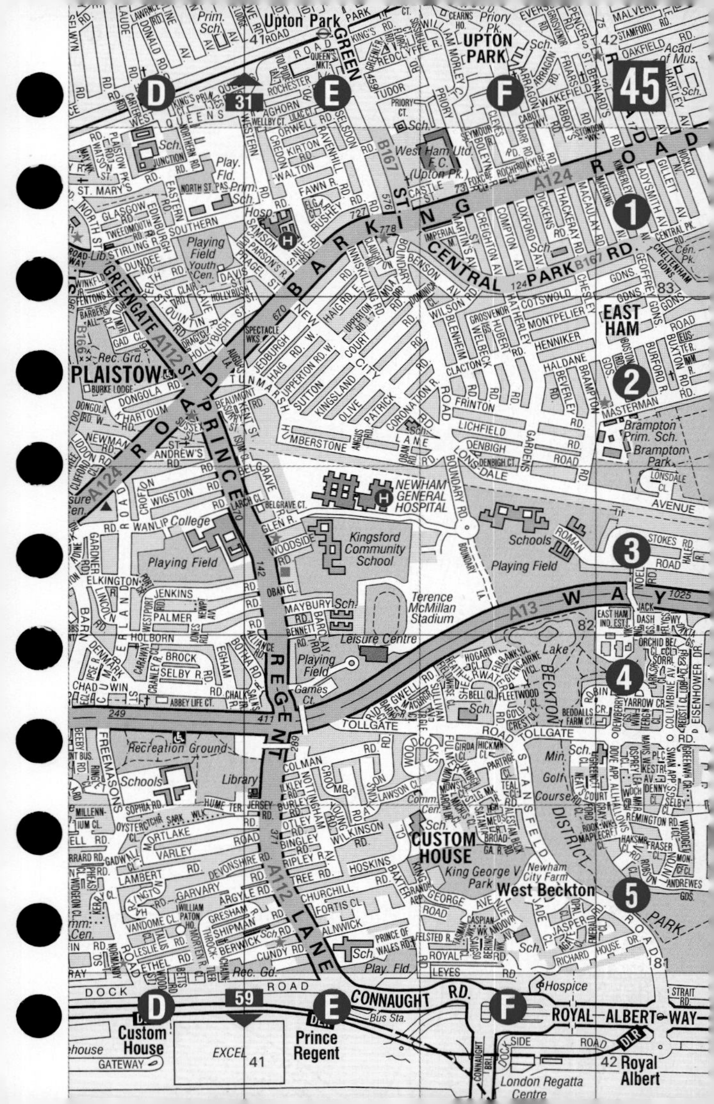

Upton Park
UPTON PARK
PLAISTOW
EAST HAM
CUSTOM HOUSE
West Beckton
BARKING ROAD
A124
CENTRAL PARK RD.
B167
West Ham Utd. F.C. (Upton Pk.)
PRINCE REGENT LANE
A112
A13
WAY
NEWHAM GENERAL HOSPITAL
Kingsford Community School
Terence McMillan Stadium
Leisure Centre
Playing Field
Schools
Recreation Ground
Library
King George V Park
Newham City Farm
Brampton Prim. Sch.
Brampton Park
Min. Golf Course
BECKTON DISTRICT PARK
TOLLGATE RD.
CONNAUGHT RD.
ROYAL ALBERT WAY
DOCK ROAD
Hospice
Custom House
Prince Regent
Royal Albert
EXCEL
London Regatta Centre
GREENGATE ST.
BOUNDARY RD.
AVENUE
STOKES RD.
31
59
D
E
F
1
2
3
4
5
41
42

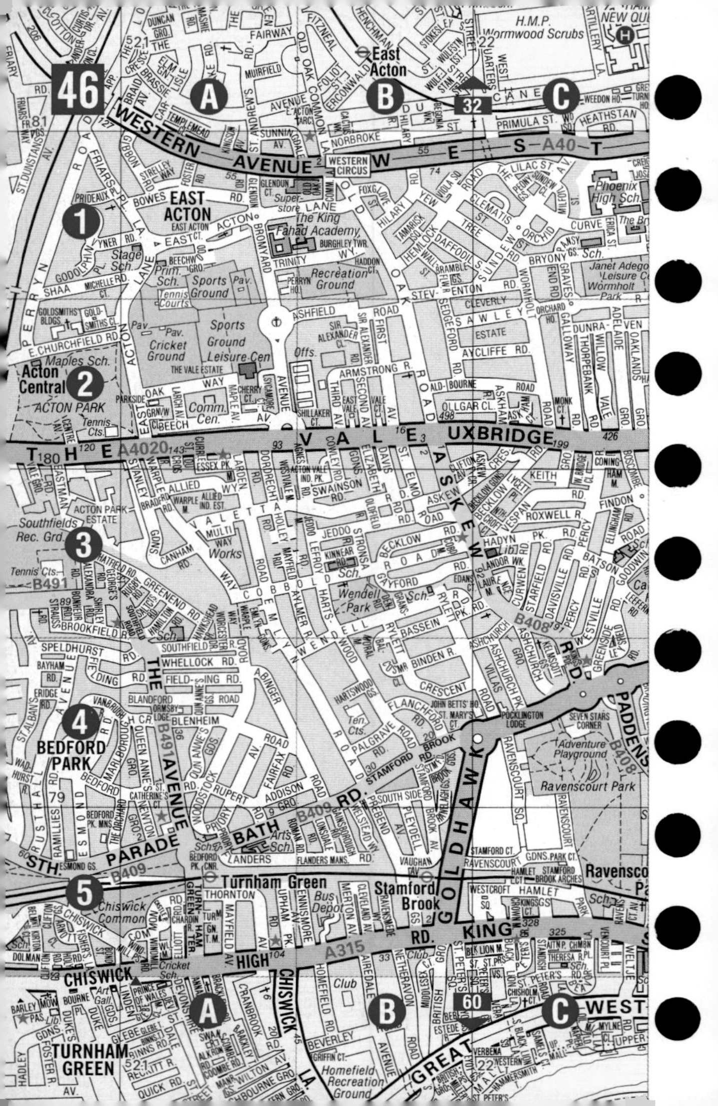
46
A
B
C
1
2
3
4
5
32
60
H.M.P. Wormwood Scrubs
East Acton
EAST ACTON
WESTERN AVENUE
WESTERN CIRCUS
WEST A40
DU CANE RD.
PRIMULA ST.
HEATHSTAN RD.
OLD OAK COMMON LA.
Phoenix High Sch.
The King Fahad Academy
Recreation Ground
Sports Ground
Cricket Ground
Leisure Cen
THE VALE ESTATE
Acton Central
ACTON PARK
Maples Sch.
SAWLEY ESTATE
Janet Adegoke Leisure Centre
Wormholt Park
UXBRIDGE
THE VALE A4020
ACTON PARK ESTATE
Southfields Rec. Grd.
ACTON VALE IND. PK.
Works
Wendell Park
COBBOLD RD.
ASKEW RD.
B491
B408
B409
BEDFORD PARK
THE AVENUE
BATH RD.
STH. PARADE
Turnham Green
Stamford Brook
GOLDHAWK RD.
Ravenscourt Park
Adventure Playground
SEVEN STARS CORNER
PADDENSWICK RD.
Bus Depot
Chiswick Common
CHISWICK
CHISWICK HIGH RD. A315
KING ST.
TURNHAM GREEN
Homefield Recreation Ground
GREAT WEST RD.
HAMMERSMITH

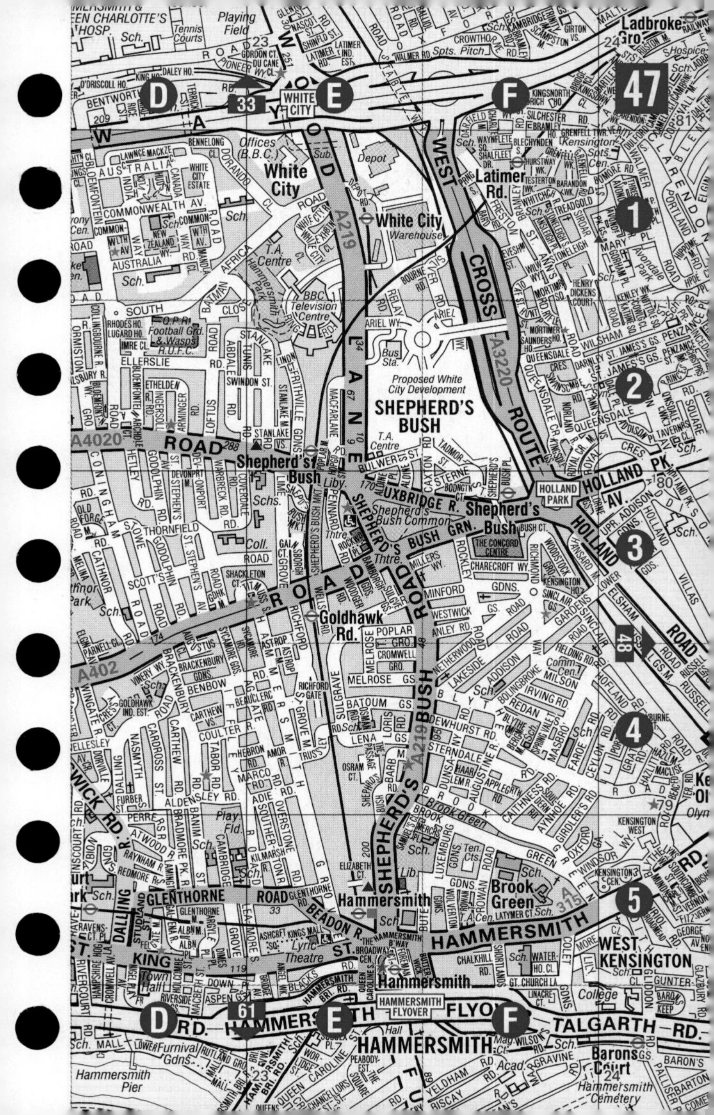
47
D
E
F
1
2
3
4
5
33
61
48
White City
Latimer Rd.
Shepherd's Bush
Goldhawk Rd.
Hammersmith
Ladbroke Gro.
SHEPHERD'S BUSH
Proposed White City Development
BBC Television Centre
Q.P.R. Football Grd. & Wasps R.U.F.C.
WEST CROSS ROUTE
A3220
A219
A4020
A402
WOOD LANE
UXBRIDGE R.
SHEPHERD'S BUSH GRN.
SHEPHERD'S BUSH ROAD
GOLDHAWK ROAD
GLENTHORNE ROAD
KING ST.
HAMMERSMITH ROAD
HAMMERSMITH FLYOVER
TALGARTH RD.
HOLLAND PARK
HOLLAND PK. AV.
HOLLAND ROAD
WEST KENSINGTON
Brook Green
Barons Court
HAMMERSMITH
Hammersmith Pier
Hammersmith Cemetery
THE CONCORD CENTRE
Lyric Theatre
Avondale Park
Ravenscourt Park

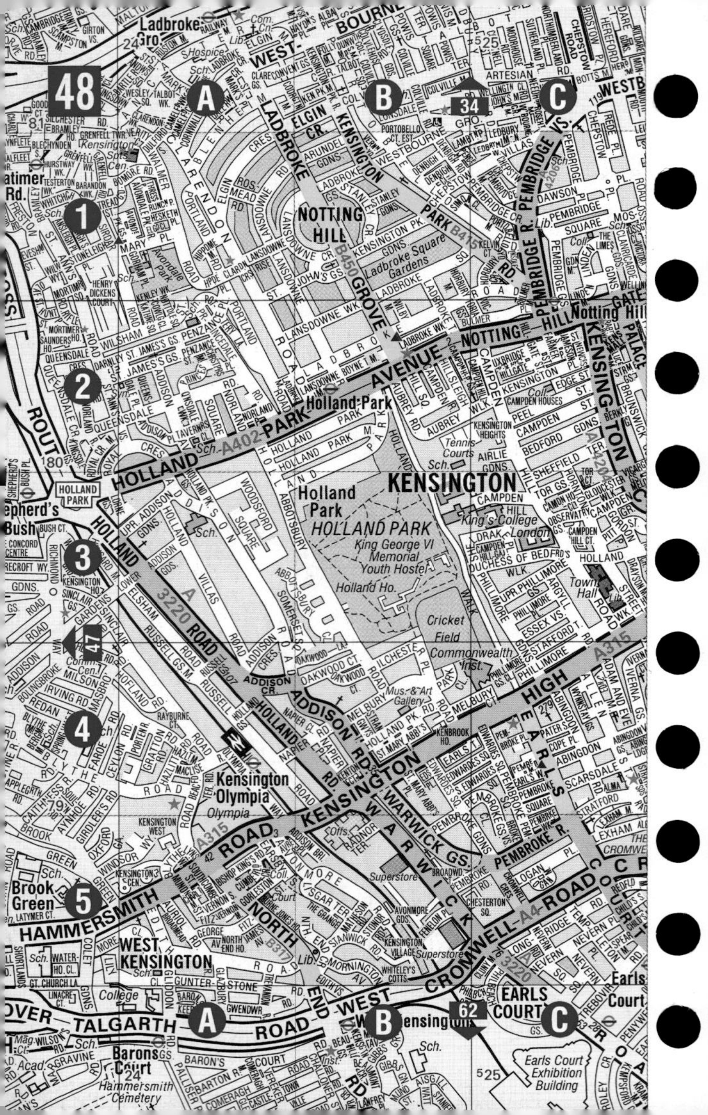

48
A
B
C
1
2
3
4
5
34
47
62
Ladbroke Gro.
NOTTING HILL
Notting Hill Gate
KENSINGTON
Holland Park
HOLLAND PARK
King George VI Memorial Youth Hostel
Holland Ho.
Cricket Field
Commonwealth Inst.
Mus. & Art Gallery
King's College London
Town Hall
Ladbroke Square Gardens
Avondale Park
Kensington Olympia
Olympia
Shepherd's Bush
Latimer Rd.
Brook Green
WEST KENSINGTON
West Kensington
Barons Court
Hammersmith Cemetery
EARLS COURT
Earls Court
Earls Court Exhibition Building
Superstore
HOLLAND PARK AVENUE
NOTTING HILL GATE
KENSINGTON HIGH STREET
KENSINGTON ROAD
HAMMERSMITH ROAD
CROMWELL ROAD
TALGARTH ROAD
WEST CROMWELL ROAD
NORTH END ROAD
WARWICK GS.
ADDISON RD.
HOLLAND ROAD
LADBROKE GROVE
KENSINGTON PARK ROAD
PEMBRIDGE VS.
CAMPDEN HILL
WESTBOURNE GRO.
A402
A315
A3220
A4
B450
B415
B317
A4206
A4204

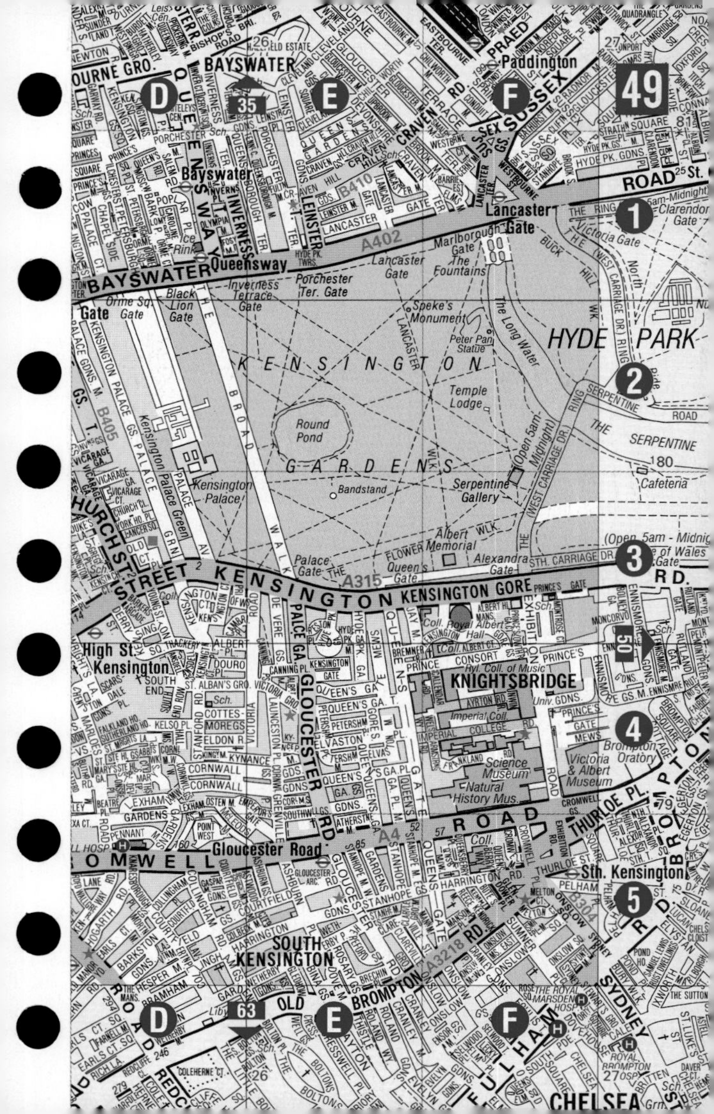
BAYSWATER
Paddington
Bayswater
Queensway
Lancaster Gate
HYDE PARK
KENSINGTON GARDENS
Round Pond
Bandstand
Kensington Palace
Speke's Monument
Peter Pan Statue
The Long Water
Temple Lodge
Serpentine Gallery
THE SERPENTINE
Cafeteria
Albert Memorial
Marlborough Gate
The Fountains
Victoria Gate
Lancaster Gate
Porchester Ter. Gate
Inverness Terrace Gate
Black Lion Gate
Orme Sq. Gate
Palace Gate
Queen's Gate
Alexandra Gate
KENSINGTON GORE
KENSINGTON
BAYSWATER
A402
A315
A4
B410
B405
B304
A3218
Royal Albert Hall
Ryl. Coll. of Music
KNIGHTSBRIDGE
Imperial Coll.
IMPERIAL COLLEGE
Science Museum
Natural History Mus.
Victoria & Albert Museum
Brompton Oratory
High St. Kensington
Gloucester Road
Sth. Kensington
SOUTH KENSINGTON
CROMWELL ROAD
BROMPTON
FULHAM
CHELSEA
THE ROYAL MARSDEN HOSP.
ROYAL BROMPTON HOSP.
(Open 5am-Midnight)
35
50
63
D
E
F
1
2
3
4
5

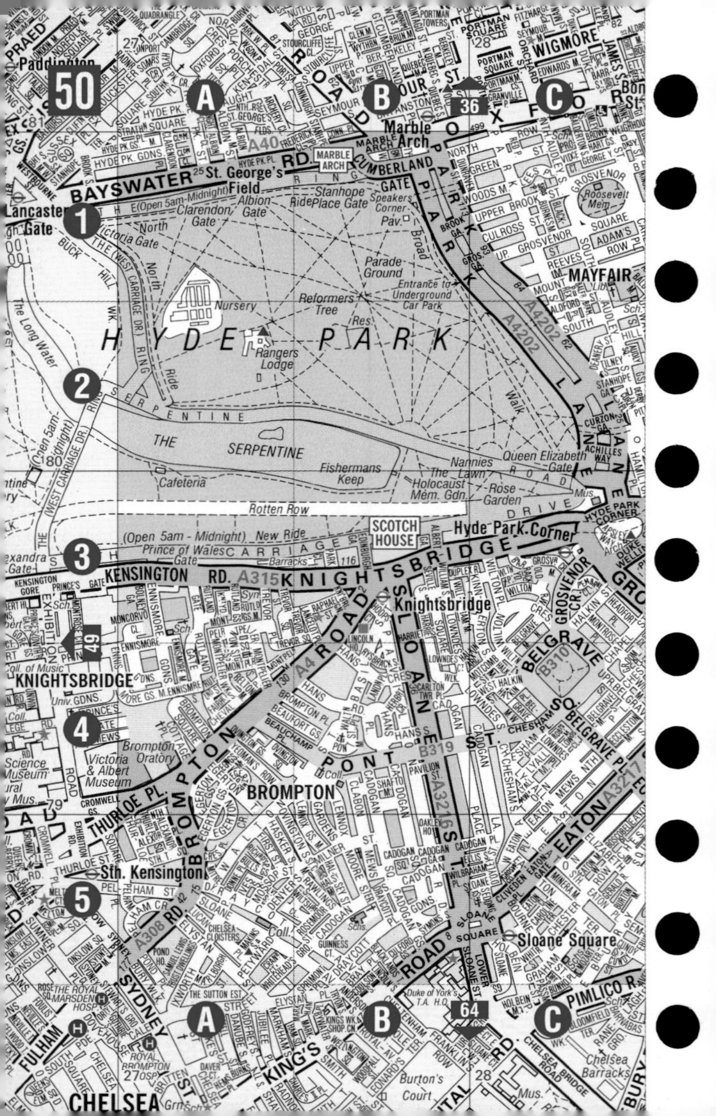

50
A
B
C
1
2
3
4
5
36
49
64
Paddington
Lancaster Gate
Marble Arch
MARBLE ARCH
BAYSWATER RD.
St. George's Field
(Open 5am-Midnight)
Clarendon Gate
Albion Gate
Stanhope Place Gate
Ride
Speakers Corner
CUMBERLAND GATE
Victoria Gate
North
Broad
Parade Ground
Entrance to Underground Car Park
Reformers Tree
Nursery
HYDE PARK
Rangers Lodge
Res.
The Long Water
SERPENTINE
THE SERPENTINE
Fishermans Keep
Cafeteria
Nannies Lawn
The Holocaust Mem. Gdn.
Rose Garden
Queen Elizabeth Gate
Rotten Row
(Open 5am - Midnight) New Ride
Prince of Wales Gate
SCOTCH HOUSE
Hyde Park Corner
HYDE PARK CORNER
PARK LANE
A4202
A40
A315
A4
B310
B319
A3216
A3217
A308
KENSINGTON RD.
KNIGHTSBRIDGE
Knightsbridge
BROMPTON ROAD
SLOANE ST.
BELGRAVE SQ.
MAYFAIR
WIGMORE ST.
OXFORD ST.
GROSVENOR SQUARE
Roosevelt Mem.
Coll. of Music
Science Museum
Victoria & Albert Museum
Brompton Oratory
BROMPTON
PONT ST.
CADOGAN
THURLOE PL.
Sth. Kensington
CROMWELL RD.
EATON SQ.
EATON PL.
Sloane Square
SLOANE SQUARE
KING'S RD.
Duke of York's T.A. H.Q.
PIMLICO R.
Chelsea Barracks
CHELSEA BRIDGE ROAD
Burton's Court
FULHAM RD.
SYDNEY ST.
THE ROYAL MARSDEN HOSP.
ROYAL BROMPTON HOSP.
CHELSEA

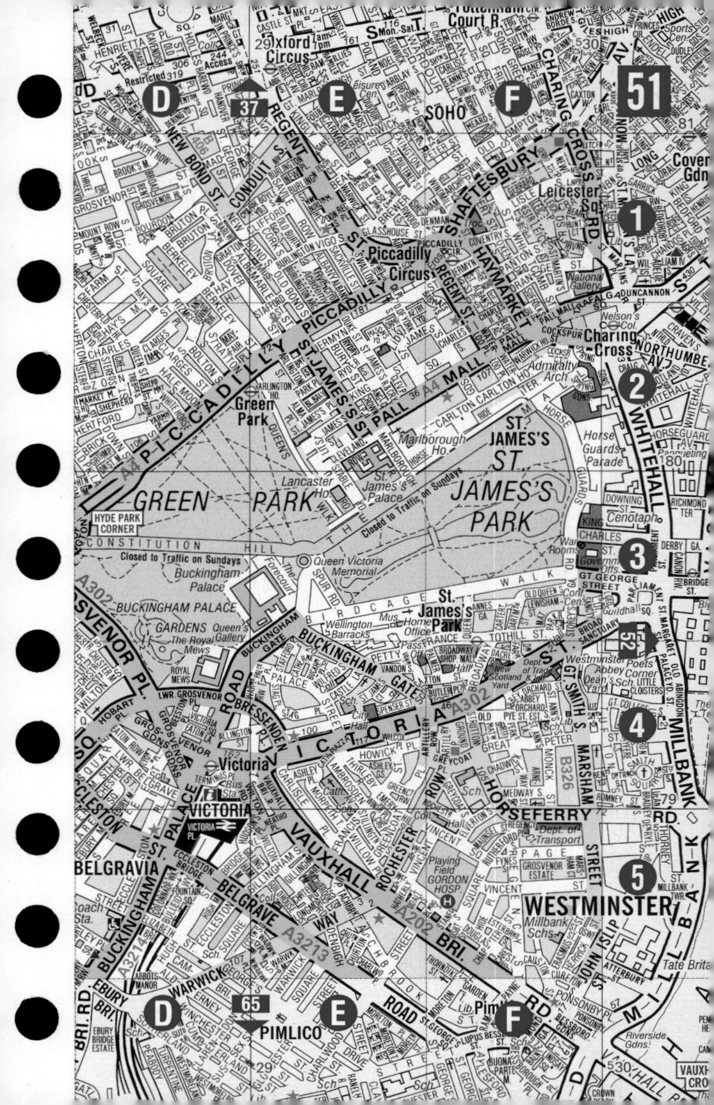
51
D
E
F
37
Oxford Circus
SOHO
Court R.
CHARING CROSS RD.
Leicester Sq.
SHAFTESBURY AV.
NEW BOND ST.
CONDUIT ST.
REGENT ST.
GROSVENOR ST.
BERKELEY SQUARE
Piccadilly Circus
PICCADILLY
HAYMARKET
National Gallery
Nelson's Col.
Charing Cross
NORTHUMBERLAND AV.
TRAFALGAR SQ.
DUNCANNON ST.
PALL MALL
ST. JAMES'S ST.
ST. JAMES'S SQ.
Admiralty Arch
Green Park
GREEN PARK
ST. JAMES'S PARK
Lancaster Ho.
St. James's Palace
Marlborough Ho.
Horse Guards Parade
WHITEHALL
Banqueting
Cenotaph
DOWNING ST.
KING CHARLES ST.
War Rooms
Govern. Offs.
HYDE PARK CORNER
CONSTITUTION HILL
Closed to Traffic on Sundays
Buckingham Palace
BUCKINGHAM PALACE GARDENS
Queen Victoria Memorial
The Royal Mews
Queen's Gallery
BIRDCAGE WALK
Wellington Barracks
St. James's Park
BUCKINGHAM GATE
Home Office
PETTY FRANCE
TOTHILL ST.
BROADWAY
New Scotland Yard
Westminster Abbey
Poets' Corner
Dean's Yard
BROAD SANCTUARY
GT. GEORGE STREET
PARLIAMENT SQ.
Guildhall
52
GT. SMITH ST.
MARSHAM
MILLBANK
VICTORIA ST.
A302
BRESSENDEN PL.
Victoria
VICTORIA
Bus Sta.
Westminster Cath.
HORSEFERRY RD.
Dept. of Transport
GROSVENOR ESTATE
VAUXHALL BRIDGE RD.
ROCHESTER ROW
Playing Field
GORDON HOSP.
WESTMINSTER
Millbank Schs.
JOHN ISLIP ST.
ATTERBURY
BELGRAVIA
BUCKINGHAM PALACE RD.
BELGRAVE RD.
ECCLESTON BRIDGE
ECCLESTON SQUARE
WARWICK WAY
A3213
A3214
A202
EBURY BRI.
EBURY BRIDGE ESTATE
Coach Sta.
PIMLICO
Pimlico
65
ST. GEORGE'S SQ.
BESSBOROUGH
PONSONBY PL.
Riverside Gdns.
Tate Brita
1
2
3
4
5

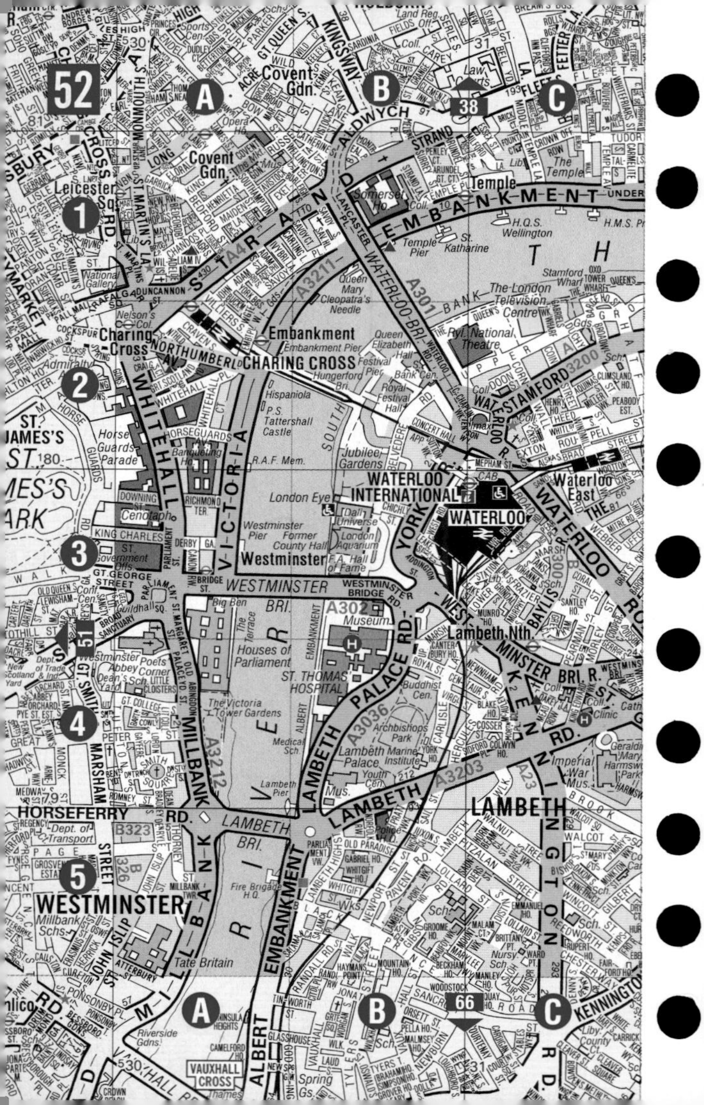

52
A
B
C
38
Covent Gdn.
Kingsway
Aldwych
Strand
Fleet St.
The Temple
Temple
Somerset Ho.
Embankment
Leicester Sq.
National Gallery
Trafalgar Sq.
Charing Cross
CHARING CROSS
Embankment Pier
Cleopatra's Needle
Waterloo Bri.
Queen Elizabeth Hall
Royal Festival Hall
Ryl. National Theatre
The London Television Centre
Stamford Wharf
OXO Tower Wharf
H.Q.S. Wellington
Temple Pier
St. Katharine
H.M.S. Pr
Upper Ground
Stamford St.
Waterloo
Waterloo East
WATERLOO INTERNATIONAL
WATERLOO
Whitehall
Horse Guards Parade
Banqueting Ho.
Downing St.
Cenotaph
King Charles St.
Government Offs.
St. James's Park
Victoria Embankment
R.A.F. Mem.
Jubilee Gardens
London Eye
Dali Universe
London Aquarium
Former County Hall
F.A. Hall of Fame
Westminster Pier
Westminster
Westminster Bridge
Big Ben
Houses of Parliament
Westminster Abbey
Poets Corner
Guildhall
Dept. of Trade & Ind.
New Scotland Yard
St. Thomas's Hospital
Museum
Lambeth Palace Rd.
Lambeth Nth.
Westminster Bri. Rd.
Baylis Rd.
Kennington Rd.
York Rd.
The Victoria Tower Gardens
Millbank
Archbishops Park
Lambeth Palace
Lambeth Pier
Imperial War Mus.
Geraldine Mary Harmsworth Park
Lambeth Rd.
Lambeth Bri.
LAMBETH
Horseferry Rd.
Dept. of Transport
Smith Square
Marsham St.
Page St.
Westminster
Millbank Schs.
Tate Britain
Fire Brigade H.Q.
Albert Embankment
Black Prince Rd.
Kennington
1
2
3
4
5
66
51
Riverside Gdns.
Vauxhall Cross
Spring Gs.
River Thames
A4
A3211
A301
A3200
A302
A3036
A3212
A3203
A23
A300
B323
B326

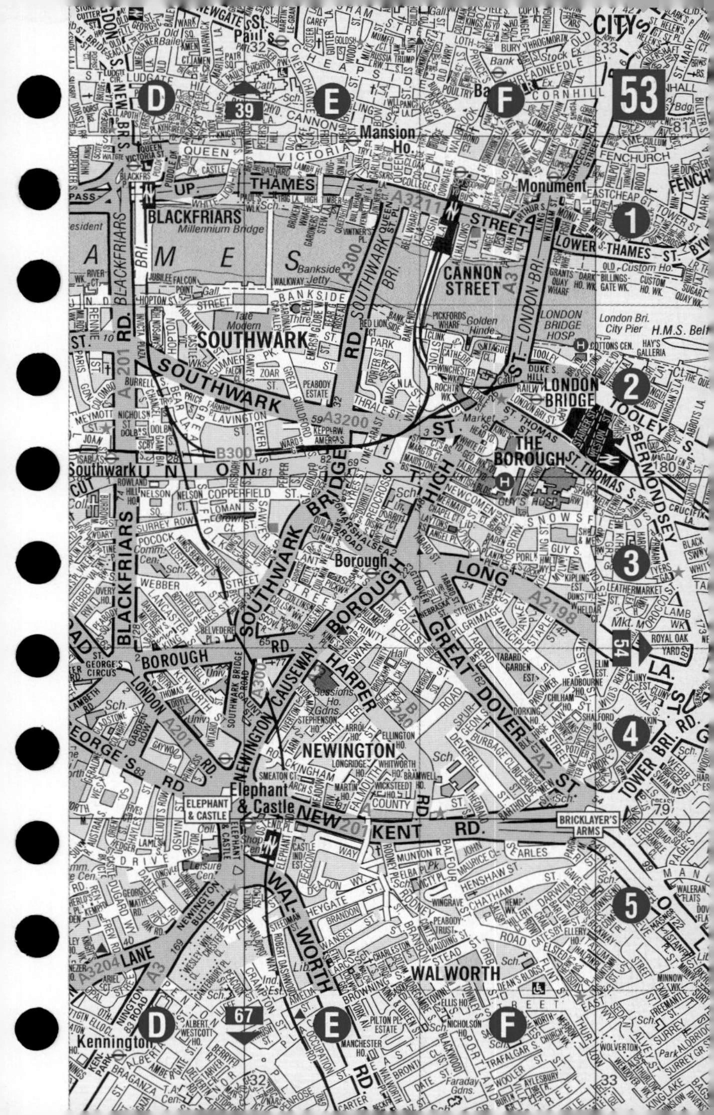

53
D
E
F
39
67
1
2
3
4
5
54
CITY
St. Paul's
CHEAPSIDE
CANNON
Mansion Ho.
VICTORIA
QUEEN
UP. THAMES
THAMES
BLACKFRIARS
Millennium Bridge
SOUTHWARK
Tate Modern
BANKSIDE
CANNON STREET
Monument
LOWER THAMES ST.
EASTCHEAP
FENCHURCH
CORNHILL
THREADNEEDLE
LONDON BRIDGE HOSP
London Bri. City Pier
H.M.S. Belfast
HAY'S GALLERIA
Golden Hinde
LONDON BRIDGE
TOOLEY
THE BOROUGH
GUY'S HOSP.
BERMONDSEY
SOUTHWARK ST.
A3200
B300
Southwark
UNION ST.
BLACKFRIARS RD.
SOUTHWARK BRIDGE RD.
BOROUGH HIGH ST.
Borough
LONG LA.
A2198
GREAT DOVER ST.
A2
BOROUGH RD.
ST. GEORGE'S CIRCUS
LONDON RD.
A201
A300
NEWINGTON CAUSEWAY
NEWINGTON
HARPER RD.
Elephant & Castle
ELEPHANT & CASTLE
NEW KENT RD.
BRICKLAYER'S ARMS
TOWER BRI. RD.
WALWORTH RD.
WALWORTH
A3204
Kennington
KENNINGTON LANE
A3
EAST ST.
OLD KENT RD.

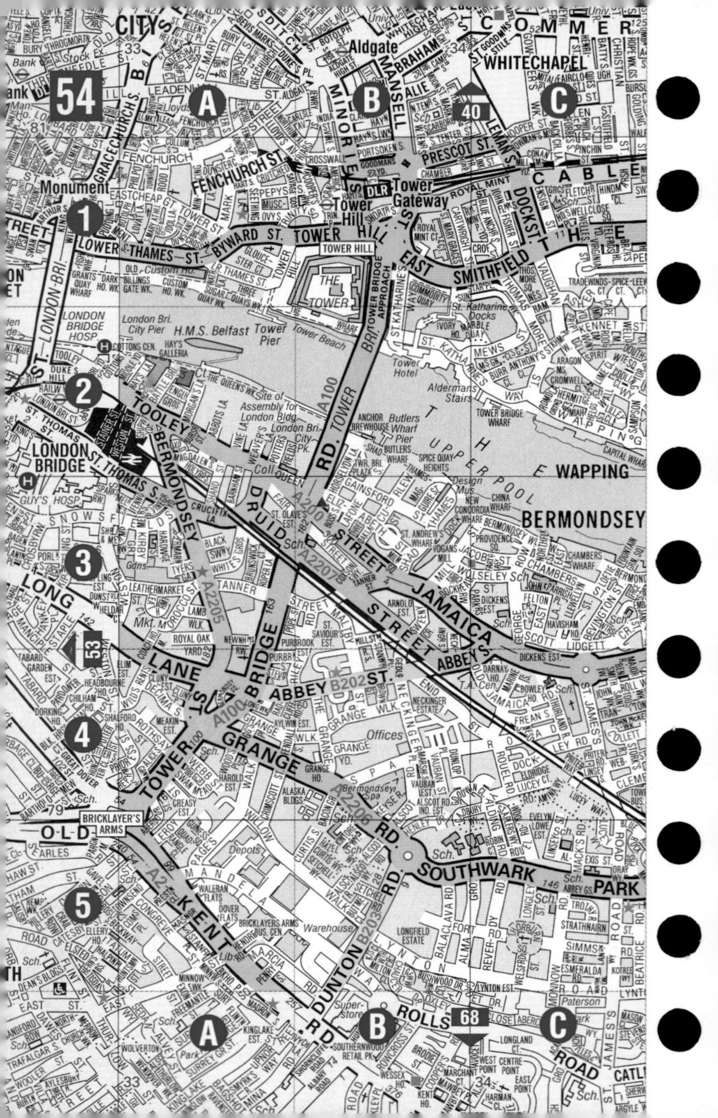

54
CITY
WHITECHAPEL
Aldgate
Monument
Tower Hill
Tower Gateway
DLR
FENCHURCH ST.
TOWER HILL
LOWER THAMES ST.
BYWARD ST.
EAST SMITHFIELD
PRESCOT ST.
CABLE
DOCK ST.
MINORIES
MANSELL
LEMAN S.
THE TOWER
TOWER BRIDGE APPROACH
St. Katharine Docks
H.M.S. Belfast
Tower Pier
Tower Beach
London Bri. City Pier
LONDON BRIDGE HOSP.
LONDON BRIDGE
GUY'S HOSP.
TOOLEY
BERMONDSEY
UPPER POOL
WAPPING
BERMONDSEY
TOWER BRIDGE WHARF
Butlers Wharf
Design Mus.
DRUID STREET
JAMAICA STREET
ABBEY ST.
LONG LANE
SNOWSFIELDS
BRIDGE
GRANGE
TOWER BRIDGE RD.
A100
A200
A2207
A2205
A2206
B202
B203
A2
Bermondsey Spa
Offices
SOUTHWARK PARK RD.
BRICKLAYER'S ARMS
OLD KENT RD.
MANDELA
Depots
Warehouse
DUNTON RD.
ROLLS RD.
LONGFIELD ESTATE
LYNTON RD.
Super-store
SOUTHERNWOOD RETAIL PK.
EAST ST.
TRAFALGAR S.
A
B
C
1
2
3
4
5
40
53
68

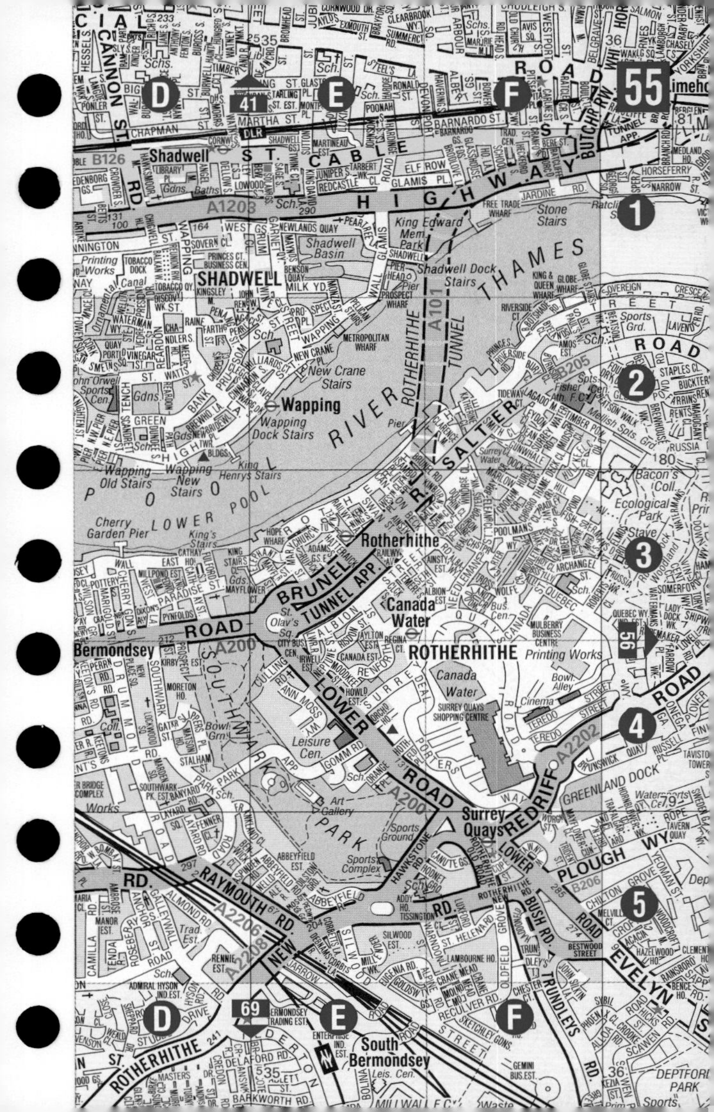

55
D
E
F
1
2
3
4
5
41
56
69
CANNON ST.
CABLE ST.
HIGHWAY
A1203
B126
Shadwell
SHADWELL
Shadwell Basin
King Edward Mem. Park
Shadwell Dock Stairs
RIVER THAMES
ROTHERHITHE TUNNEL
A101
Wapping
Wapping Dock Stairs
Wapping Old Stairs
Wapping New Stairs
King Henrys Stairs
New Crane Stairs
POOL
LOWER POOL
Cherry Garden Pier
King's Stairs
Rotherhithe
ROTHERHITHE
SALTER RD.
BRUNEL RD.
TUNNEL APP.
Canada Water
Surrey Quays
SURREY QUAYS SHOPPING CENTRE
REDRIFF RD.
A2202
LOWER ROAD
A200
SOUTHWARK PARK
Bermondsey
ROAD
RAYMOUTH RD.
A2206
A2208
NEW RD.
PLOUGH WY.
B206
B205
EVELYN STREET
GREENLAND DOCK
Ecological Park
Bacon's Coll.
Stave
Printing Works
Leisure Cen.
Art Gallery
Sports Ground
Sports Complex
South Bermondsey
ROTHERHITHE NEW RD.
TRUNDLEYS RD.
STUBBS DRIVE
RENNIE EST.
DEPTFORD PARK
JARDINE RD.
GLAMIS PL.
ELF ROW
BARNARDO ST.
MARTHA ST.
CHAPMAN
WAPPING HIGH

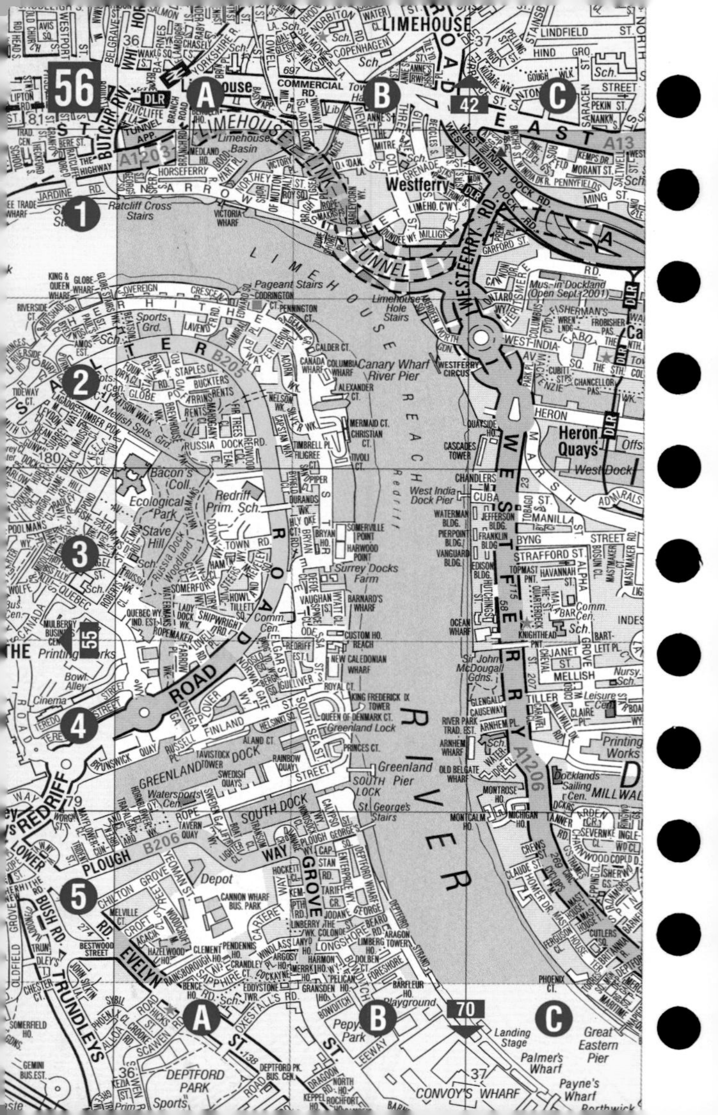

56
LIMEHOUSE
Limehouse
COMMERCIAL RD.
DLR
A
B
C
42
EAST
A13
LIMEHOUSE LINK
Limehouse Basin
A1203
NARROW ST.
THE HIGHWAY
JARDINE RD.
Ratcliff Cross Stairs
VICTORIA WHARF
Westferry
WEST INDIA DOCK RD.
PENNYFIELDS
MING ST.
GARFORD ST.
TUNNEL
LIMEHOUSE
Pageant Stairs
CODRINGTON CT.
PENNINGTON CT.
Limehouse Hole Stairs
WESTFERRY
Mus. in Dockland (Open Sept. 2001)
FISHERMAN'S WALK
WEST INDIA AV
CABOT SQ.
CHANCELLOR PAS.
HERON
Heron Quays
West Dock
1
2
3
4
5
ROTHERHITHE
B205
SALTER
Sports Grd.
Sch.
CALDER CT.
CANADA WHARF
COLUMBIA WHARF
Canary Wharf River Pier
WESTFERRY CIRCUS
ALEXANDER CT.
REACH
Redriff
MERMAID CT.
CHRISTIAN CT.
CASCADES TOWER
QUAYSIDE HO.
Mellish Sps. Grd.
RUSSIA DOCK RD.
TIMBRELL PL.
FILIGREE CT.
TIVOLI CT.
Bacon's Coll.
Ecological Park
Redriff Prim. Sch.
Stave Hill
Russia Dock Woodland
TOWN RD.
SOMERVILLE POINT
HARWOOD POINT
Surrey Docks Farm
West India Dock Pier
CHANDLERS M.
CUBA
MANILLA ST.
ADMIRALS
WATERMAN BLDG.
PIERPOINT BLDG.
VANGUARD BLDG.
JEFFERSON BLDG.
FRANKLIN BLDG.
EDISON BLDG.
BYNG ST.
STRAFFORD ST.
HAVANNAH ST.
ALPHA
TOPMAST PNT.
QUARTERDECK
MALTA ST.
BAR
Comm. Cen.
Sch.
INDES
QUEBEC
QUEBEC WY. IND. EST.
SOMERFORD
SHIPWRIGHT RD.
ROPEMAKER RD.
BARNARD'S WHARF
VAUGHAN
Comm. Cen.
CUSTOM HO. REACH
NEW CALEDONIAN WHARF
OCEAN WHARF
KNIGHTHEAD PNT.
JANET ST.
MELLISH
Nursy. Sch.
Sir John McDougall Gdns.
55
Printing Works
Bowl. Alley
Cinema
ROAD
ROYAL CT.
KING FREDERICK IX TOWER
QUEEN OF DENMARK CT.
Greenland Lock
RIVER
GLENGALL CAUSEWAY
RIVER PARK TRAD. EST.
ARNHEM PL.
ARNHEM WHARF
TILLER
Leisure Cen.
Printing Works
A1206
FINLAND ST.
BRUNSWICK QUAY
GREENLAND DOCK
TAVISTOCK TOWER
SWEDISH QUAYS
RAINBOW QUAY
PRINCES CT.
Greenland Pier
SOUTH LOCK
OLD BELGATE WHARF
Docklands Sailing Cen.
MILLWALL
REDRIFF
79
Watersports Cen.
SOUTH DOCK
St. George's Stairs
MONTROSE HO.
MONTCALM HO.
MICHIGAN HO.
TANNER
ARDEN CR.
SEVERNKE
CHARNWOOD
B206
PLOUGH WAY
GROVE
LOWER
TAVERN QUAY
CREWS ST.
CLAUDE ST.
HOMER DR.
Depot
CANNON WHARF BUS. PARK
CHILTON GROVE
YEOMAN ST.
MASTHOUSE TER.
BUSH RD.
MELVILLE CT.
LONGSHORE
ARAGON TOWER
CUTLERS SQ.
BESTWOOD STREET
EVELYN ST.
TRUNDLEYS
PENDENNIS HO.
HARMON HO.
PELICAN HO.
FORESHORE
STRAND
PHOENIX CT.
EDDYSTONE TWR.
OXESTALL'S RD.
GRANSDEN HO.
BARFLEUR HO.
Playground
70
Pepys Park
LEEWAY
Landing Stage
Great Eastern Pier
SOMERFIELD HO.
GEMINI BUS. EST.
36
DEPTFORD PARK
DEPTFORD PK. BUS. CEN.
37
CONVOY'S WHARF
Palmer's Wharf
Payne's Wharf
Sports

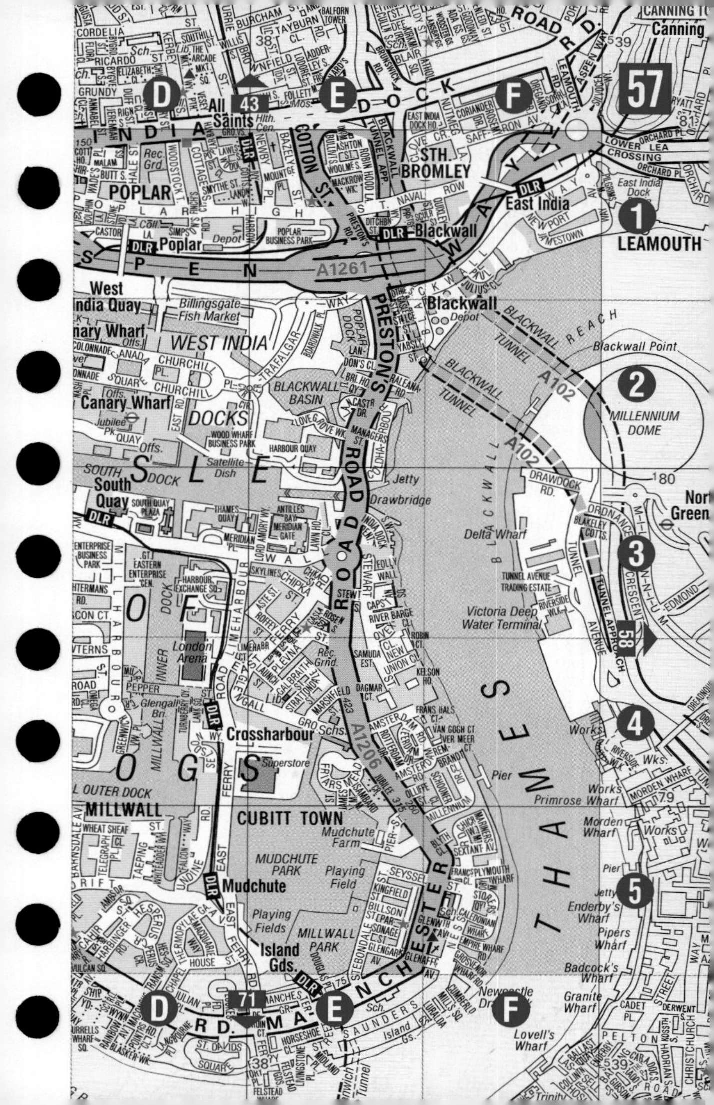
57
D
E
F
43
58
71
1
2
3
4
5
POPLAR
Poplar
All Saints
STH. BROMLEY
East India
Blackwall
LEAMOUTH
West India Quay
Billingsgate Fish Market
WEST INDIA
DOCKS
Canary Wharf
BLACKWALL BASIN
HARBOUR QUAY
South Quay
MILLENNIUM DOME
Blackwall Point
BLACKWALL REACH
BLACKWALL TUNNEL
A102
A1261
A1206
Delta Wharf
Victoria Deep Water Terminal
TUNNEL AVENUE TRADING ESTATE
London Arena
Crossharbour
CUBITT TOWN
Mudchute Farm
MUDCHUTE PARK
Mudchute
MILLWALL PARK
Island Gds.
THAMES
Primrose Wharf
Morden Wharf
Enderby's Wharf
Pipers Wharf
Badcock's Wharf
Granite Wharf
Lovell's Wharf
ISLE OF DOGS
MILLWALL
MANCHESTER RD.
PRESTON'S ROAD
EAST INDIA DOCK RD.
POPLAR HIGH ST.
ASPEN WAY
Canning

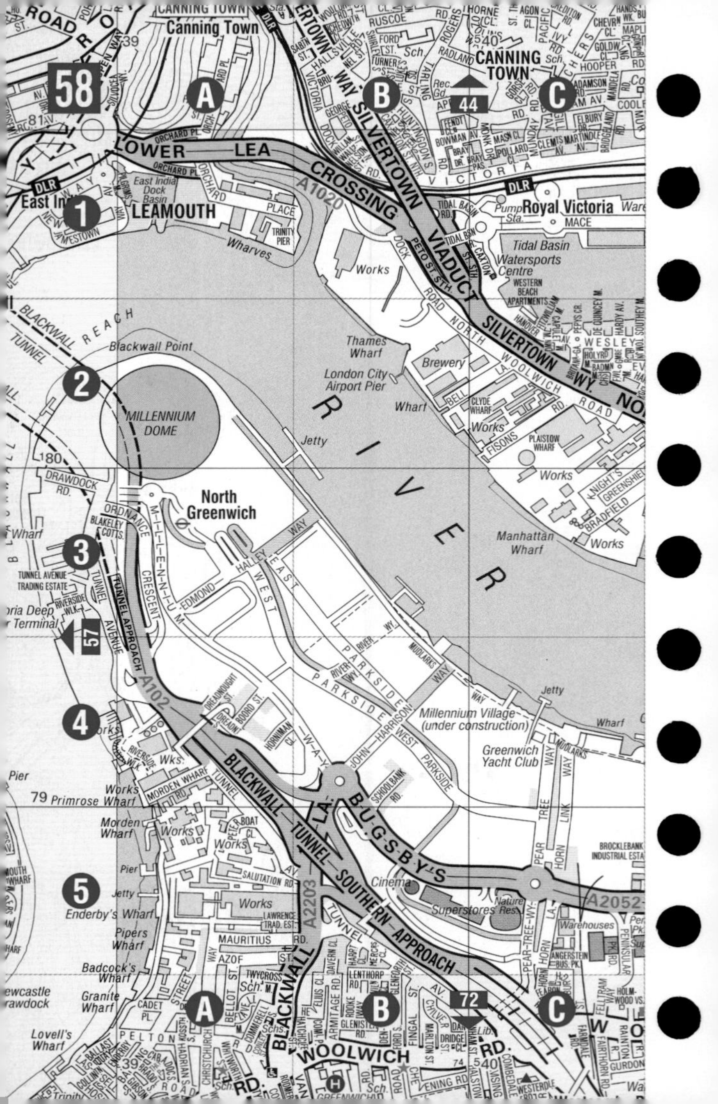
Canning Town
CANNING TOWN
LOWER LEA CROSSING
A1020
SILVERTOWN WAY
VICTORIA DOCK RD.
East India Dock Basin
LEAMOUTH
TRINITY PIER
Wharves
Royal Victoria
Tidal Basin Watersports Centre
WESTERN BEACH APARTMENTS
SILVERTOWN VIADUCT
NORTH WOOLWICH ROAD
Works
Thames Wharf
London City Airport Pier
Brewery
BLACKWALL REACH
Blackwall Point
BLACKWALL TUNNEL
MILLENNIUM DOME
RIVER
Jetty
Wharf
Works
CLYDE WHARF
PLAISTOW WHARF
North Greenwich
MILLENNIUM WAY
Manhattan Wharf
TUNNEL AVENUE TRADING ESTATE
TUNNEL APPROACH
A102
Millennium Village (under construction)
Greenwich Yacht Club
BLACKWALL TUNNEL SOUTHERN APPROACH
BUGSBY'S WAY
A2203
A2052
Cinema
Superstores
Nature Res.
Warehouses
BROCKLEBANK INDUSTRIAL ESTATE
Primrose Wharf
Morden Wharf
Enderby's Wharf
Pipers Wharf
Badcock's Wharf
Granite Wharf
Lovell's Wharf
WOOLWICH RD.
A B C
1 2 3 4 5
44
57
72

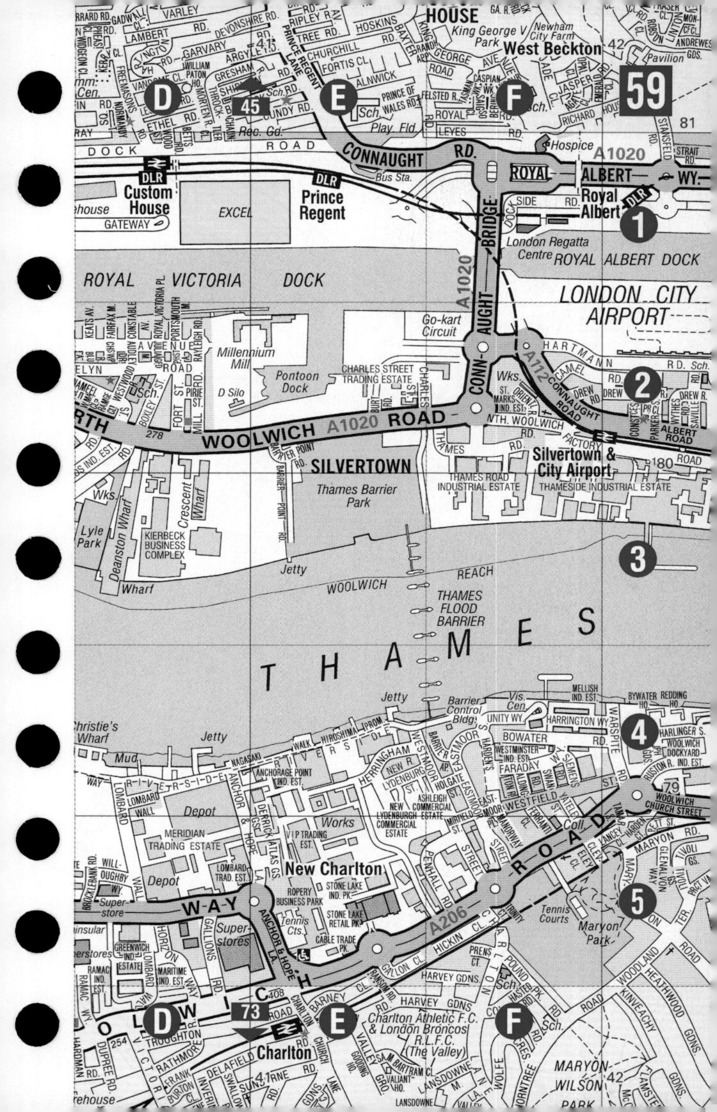
59
HOUSE
King George V Park
Newham City Farm
West Beckton
Pavilion
Hospice
A1020
DLR
Custom House
Prince Regent
Royal Albert
EXCEL
GATEWAY
DOCK ROAD
CONNAUGHT RD.
ROYAL ALBERT WY.
CONNAUGHT BRIDGE
DOCK SIDE RD.
London Regatta Centre
ROYAL ALBERT DOCK
ROYAL VICTORIA DOCK
LONDON CITY AIRPORT
Go-kart Circuit
HARTMANN RD.
A112
CONNAUGHT ROAD
ALBERT ROAD
Millennium Mill
Pontoon Dock
D Silo
CHARLES STREET TRADING ESTATE
WOOLWICH A1020 ROAD
NTH. WOOLWICH
FACTORY
Silvertown & City Airport
SILVERTOWN
Thames Barrier Park
THAMES ROAD INDUSTRIAL ESTATE
THAMESIDE INDUSTRIAL ESTATE
Crescent Wharf
Deanston Wharf
Lyle Park
KIERBECK BUSINESS COMPLEX
Jetty
WOOLWICH REACH
THAMES FLOOD BARRIER
THAMES
Barrier Control Bldg.
Vis. Cen.
MELLISH IND. EST.
BYWATER HO.
REDDING HO.
HARRINGTON WY.
UNITY WY.
BOWATER RD.
WESTMINSTER IND. EST.
FARADAY
HARLINGER S.
WOOLWICH DOCKYARD IND. EST.
WOOLWICH CHURCH STREET
Christie's Wharf
Mud
NAGASAKI WALK
HIROSHIMA PROM.
RIVERSIDE
ANCHORAGE POINT IND. EST.
HERRINGHAM
NEW LYDENBURGH COMMERCIAL ESTATE
ASHLEIGH COMMERCIAL ESTATE
WESTFIELD ST.
Coll.
Depot
Works
MERIDIAN TRADING ESTATE
V I P TRADING EST.
LOMBARD TRAD. EST.
New Charlton
ROPERY BUSINESS PARK
STONE LAKE IND. PK.
STONE LAKE RETAIL PK.
CABLE TRADE PK.
Tennis Cts.
Superstore
Superstores
GREENWICH IND. ESTATE
MARITIME IND. EST.
ANCHOR & HOPE LA.
A206
ROAD
Tennis Courts
Maryon Park
MARYON RD.
HARVEY GDNS.
Charlton Athletic F.C. & London Broncos R.L.F.C. (The Valley)
Charlton
CHARLTON CHURCH LA.
MARYON-WILSON PARK
WOODLAND TER.
45
73
D
E
F
1
2
3
4
5
41
42
79
81
180
278
254
408

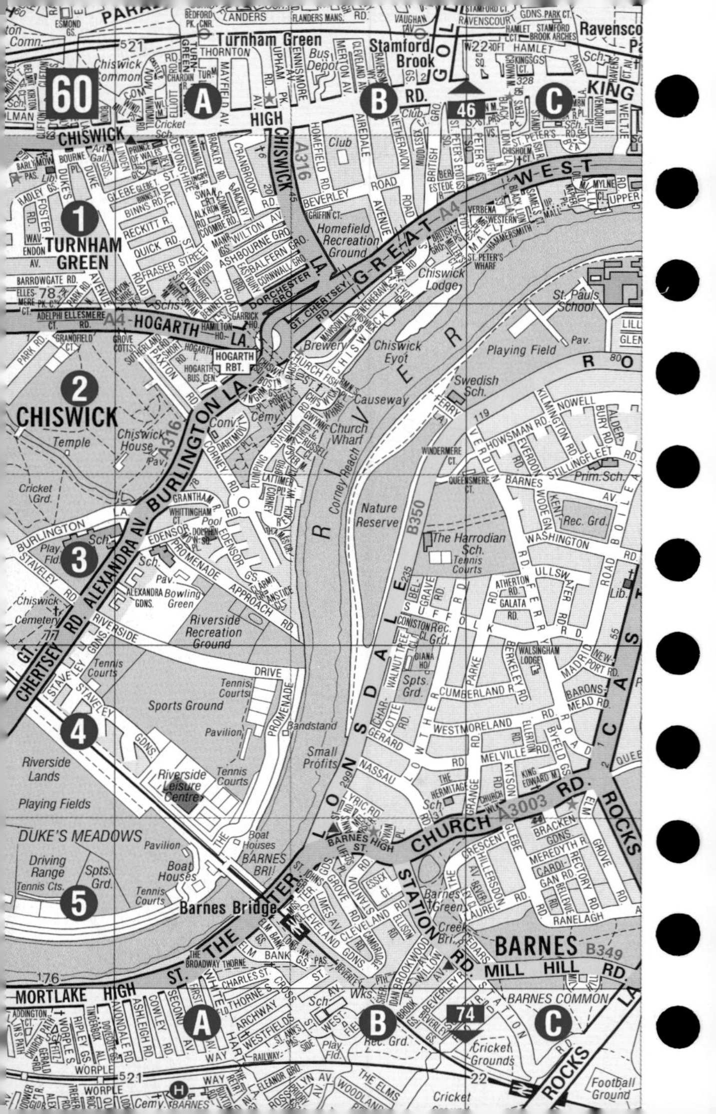
60
A
B
C
46
74
1
2
3
4
5
Turnham Green
Stamford Brook
Chiswick Common
HIGH
CHISWICK
A316
TURNHAM GREEN
CHISWICK
GREAT WEST RD.
A4
HOGARTH LA.
HOGARTH RBT.
BURLINGTON LA.
ALEXANDRA AV.
CHERTSEY RD.
Chiswick House
Temple
Cricket Grd.
Homefield Recreation Ground
Chiswick Lodge
Chiswick Eyot
Brewery
Causeway
Church Wharf
Corney Reach
RIVER
St. Pauls School
Playing Field
Swedish Sch.
Nature Reserve
The Harrodian Sch.
LONSDALE RD.
B350
Riverside Recreation Ground
Sports Ground
Riverside Lands
Playing Fields
Riverside Leisure Centre
DUKE'S MEADOWS
Driving Range
Barnes Bridge
BARNES BRI.
Bandstand
Small Profits
CHURCH RD.
A3003
CASTELNAU
ROCKS LA.
STATION RD.
BARNES
B349
MILL HILL RD.
BARNES COMMON
Cricket Grounds
Football Ground
MORTLAKE HIGH ST.
THE TERRACE
WORPLE WAY
Ravenscourt Park

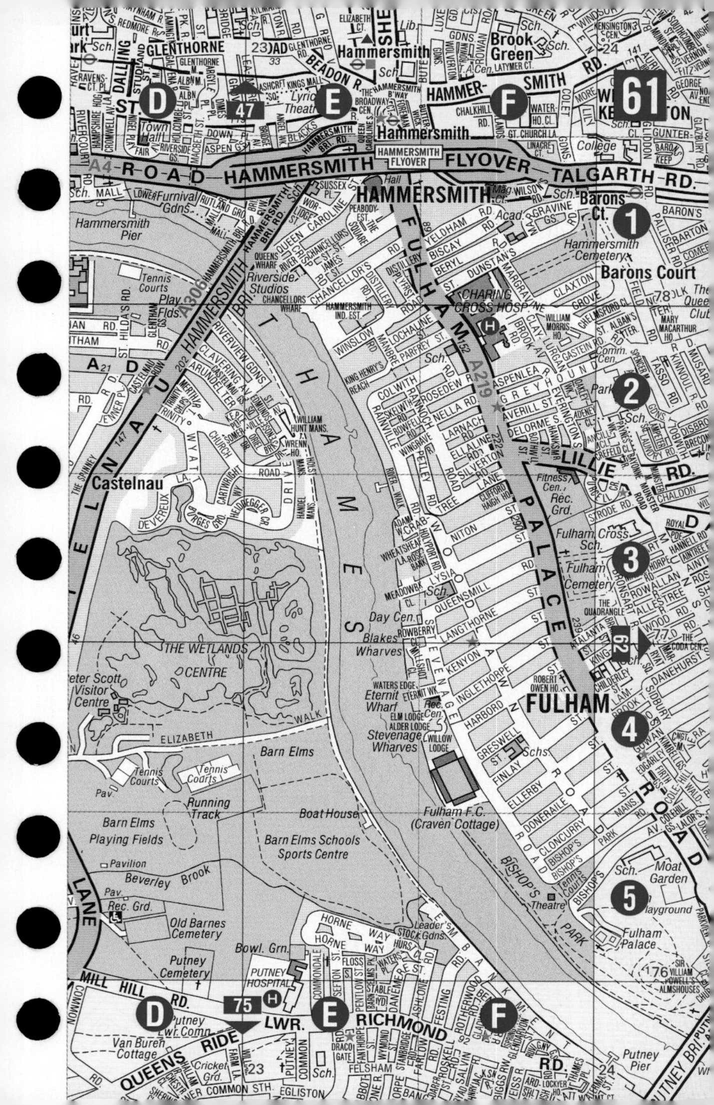

61
HAMMERSMITH
Hammersmith
Brook Green
HAMMERSMITH RD.
HAMMERSMITH FLYOVER
A4 ROAD
TALGARTH RD.
Barons Ct.
Barons Court
Hammersmith Cemetery
Hammersmith Pier
Lyric Theatre
Town Hall
Riverside Studios
CHARING CROSS HOSP.
FULHAM PALACE ROAD
A219
A306
HAMMERSMITH BRI.
LILLIE RD.
Castelnau
THAMES
THE WETLANDS CENTRE
Peter Scott Visitor Centre
Barn Elms
Barn Elms Playing Fields
Barn Elms Schools Sports Centre
Boat House
Running Track
Tennis Courts
Beverley Brook
Old Barnes Cemetery
Putney Cemetery
PUTNEY HOSPITAL
Fulham F.C. (Craven Cottage)
FULHAM
Fulham Cross Sch.
Fulham Cemetery
Blakes Wharves
Eternit Wharf
Stevenage Wharves
BISHOP'S PARK
Fulham Palace
Moat Garden
Putney Pier
PUTNEY BRI.
LWR. RICHMOND RD.
QUEENS RIDE
Putney Lwr. Comn.
Van Buren Cottage
MILL HILL RD.
47
62
75
1
2
3
4
5
D
E
F

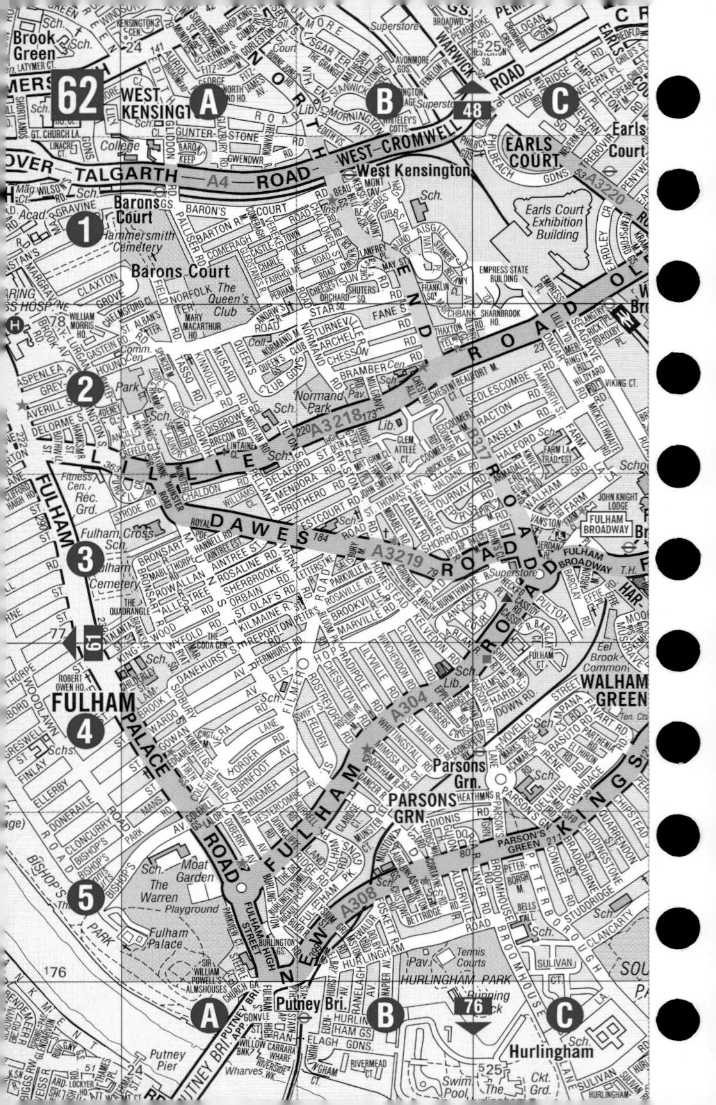

62
A
B
C
1
2
3
4
5
48
61
76
Brook Green
WEST KENSINGTON
West Kensington
Barons Court
Hammersmith Cemetery
TALGARTH ROAD
A4
WEST CROMWELL ROAD
NORTH END ROAD
EARLS COURT
Earls Court
A3220
Earls Court Exhibition Building
EMPRESS STATE BUILDING
The Queen's Club
LILLIE ROAD
A3218
Normand Park
DAWES ROAD
A3219
B317
FULHAM BROADWAY
Fulham Broadway
FULHAM
FULHAM PALACE ROAD
Fulham Cross
Fulham Cemetery
A304
FULHAM ROAD
NEW KINGS ROAD
A308
Parsons Grn.
PARSONS GRN.
WALHAM GREEN
Eel Brook Common
Moat Garden
The Warren
Playground
Fulham Palace
BISHOP'S PARK
FULHAM HIGH STREET
Putney Bri.
PUTNEY BRIDGE
Putney Pier
Wharves
HURLINGHAM PARK
Tennis Courts
Hurlingham
Swim Pool
Ckt. Grd.
Superstore

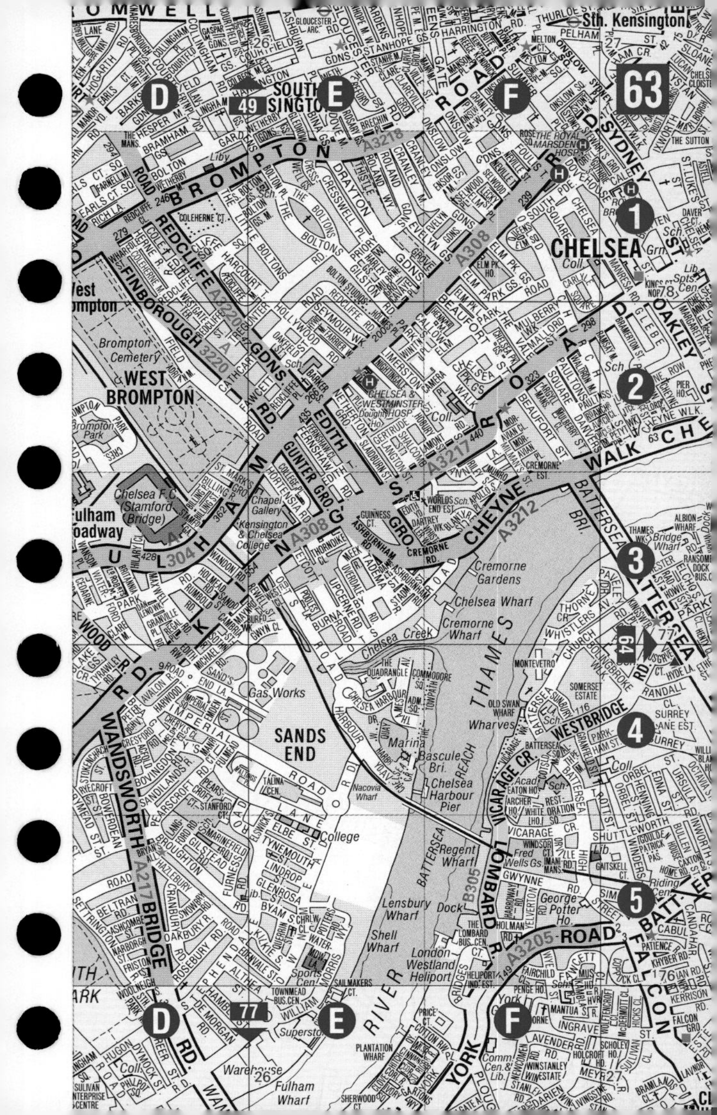

63
D
E
F
1
2
3
4
5
49
64
77
Sth. Kensington
SOUTH KENSINGTON
BROMPTON ROAD
A3218
CHELSEA
WEST BROMPTON
West Brompton
Brompton Cemetery
Chelsea F.C. (Stamford Bridge)
Fulham Broadway
FULHAM ROAD
A304
A308
A3217
A3212
A3220
A3205
A217
B305
KINGS ROAD
CHEYNE WALK
FINBOROUGH ROAD
REDCLIFFE GDNS.
EDITH GRO.
GUNTER GRO.
LOTS ROAD
CREMORNE RD.
BATTERSEA BRI.
BATTERSEA
WESTBRIDGE
VICARAGE CR.
LOMBARD R.
WANDSWORTH BRIDGE RD.
SANDS END
Gas Works
Chelsea Creek
Chelsea Harbour
Chelsea Harbour Pier
Cremorne Gardens
Chelsea Wharf
Cremorne Wharf
RIVER THAMES
Lensbury Wharf
Shell Wharf
London Westland Heliport
Regent Wharf
Nacovia Wharf
Marina
Bascule Bri.
THE ROYAL MARSDEN HOSP.
CHELSEA & WESTMINSTER Doughty HOSP.
Chapel Gallery
Kensington & Chelsea College
Brompton Park
Fulham Wharf
YORK ROAD
SYDNEY ST.
OAKLEY ST.
ELM PARK GS.
THE BOLTONS

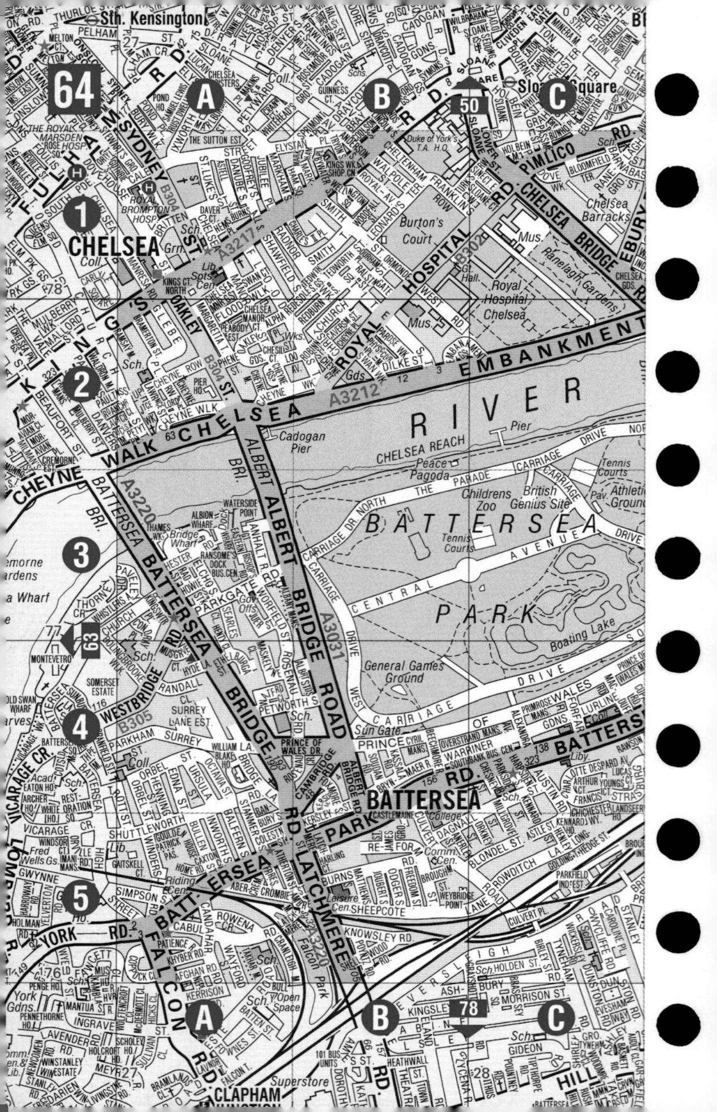

64
Sth. Kensington
Sloane Square
A
B
C
50
CHELSEA
SYDNEY
FULHAM
KING'S
OAKLEY
ST.
B304
A3217
Burton's Court
ROYAL HOSPITAL
B302
Royal Hospital Chelsea
Chelsea Barracks
Ranelagh Gardens
CHELSEA BRIDGE
EBURY
PIMLICO
RD.
Duke of York's T.A. H.Q.
CHELTENHAM
FRANKLIN'S ROW
EMBANKMENT
A3212
CHELSEA
WALK
CHEYNE
CHEYNE WLK
BEAUFORT
DANVERS
RIVER
Cadogan Pier
Pier
CHELSEA REACH
Peace Pagoda
THE PARADE
CARRIAGE DRIVE
CARRIAGE DR. NORTH
Childrens Zoo
British Genius Site
Tennis Courts
Athletic Ground
BATTERSEA
CENTRAL AVENUE
PARK
Boating Lake
General Games Ground
WEST CARRIAGE DRIVE
ALBERT BRIDGE ROAD
A3031
BATTERSEA BRIDGE
BATTERSEA BRI.
A3220
Bridge Wharf
WATERSIDE POINT
PARKGATE RD.
RANSOME'S DOCK BUS.CEN.
Gov. Offs.
1
2
3
4
5
77
63
Cremorne Gardens
WESTBRIDGE RD.
B305
SURREY LANE EST.
SOMERSET ESTATE
MONTEVETRO
VICARAGE CR.
PRINCE OF WALES DR.
Sun Gate
PRINCE OF WALES
BATTERSEA
PARK RD.
Liby.
LATCHMERE RD.
BATTERSEA
SHEEPCOTE
Leisure Cen.
KNOWSLEY RD.
CULVERT PL.
PARKFIELD IND. EST.
ROWENA CR.
YORK RD.
FALCON RD.
CANDAHAR
Falcon Park
Open Space
78
MORRISON ST.
HOLDEN ST.
TYNEHAM
DUNSTON
GIDEON
STANLEY
CLAPHAM
Superstore
101 BUS. UNITS
HEATHWALL
THEATRE
York Gdns.
INGRAVE
WINSTANLEY ESTATE
LAVENDER

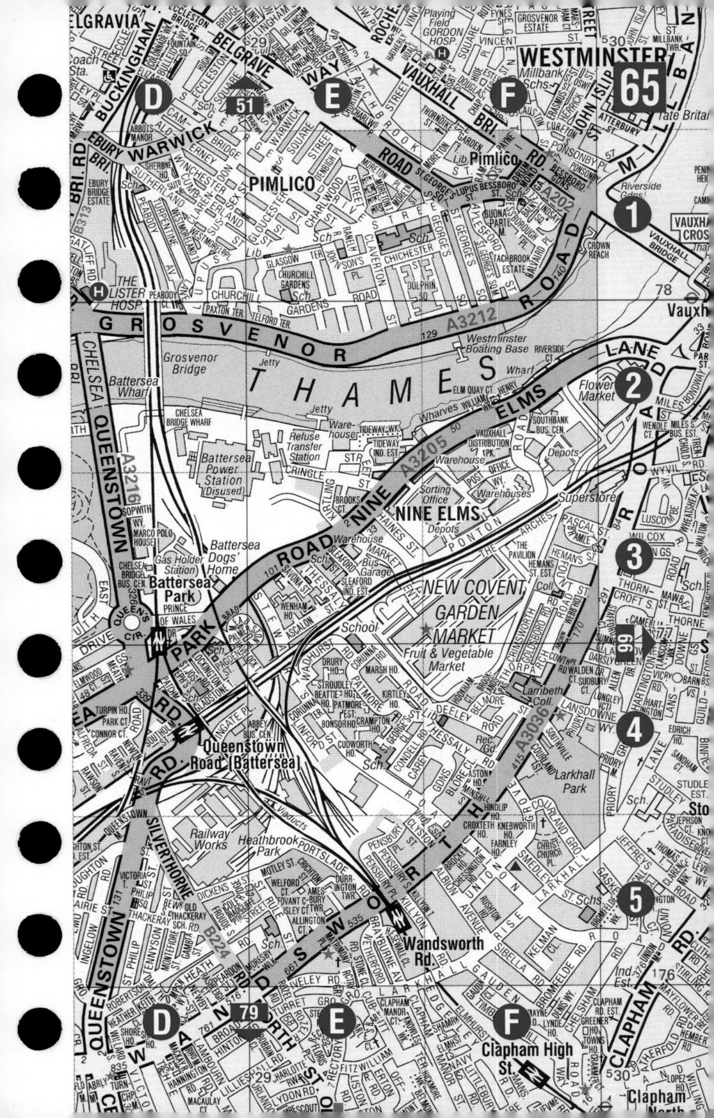

65
BELGRAVIA
WESTMINSTER
PIMLICO
Pimlico
NINE ELMS
THAMES
GROSVENOR ROAD
A3212
NINE ELMS LANE
A3205
QUEENSTOWN ROAD
A3216
WANDSWORTH ROAD
A3036
VAUXHALL BRIDGE ROAD
A202
BELGRAVE ROAD
WARWICK WAY
LUPUS ST.
CHURCHILL GARDENS
Grosvenor Bridge
Battersea Wharf
Battersea Power Station (Disused)
Refuse Transfer Station
Battersea Dogs' Home
Battersea Park
Queenstown Road (Battersea)
NEW COVENT GARDEN MARKET
Fruit & Vegetable Market
Sorting Office
Westminster Boating Base
Flower Market
Tate Britain
Millbank Schs.
THE LISTER HOSP.
Railway Works
Heathbrook Park
Larkhall Park
Lambeth Coll.
Wandsworth Rd.
Clapham High St.
CLAPHAM RD.
SILVERTHORNE RD.
B224
B313
LARKHALL LANE
PRIORY GROVE
PONTON RD.
Viaducts
51
79
66
D
E
F
1
2
3
4
5

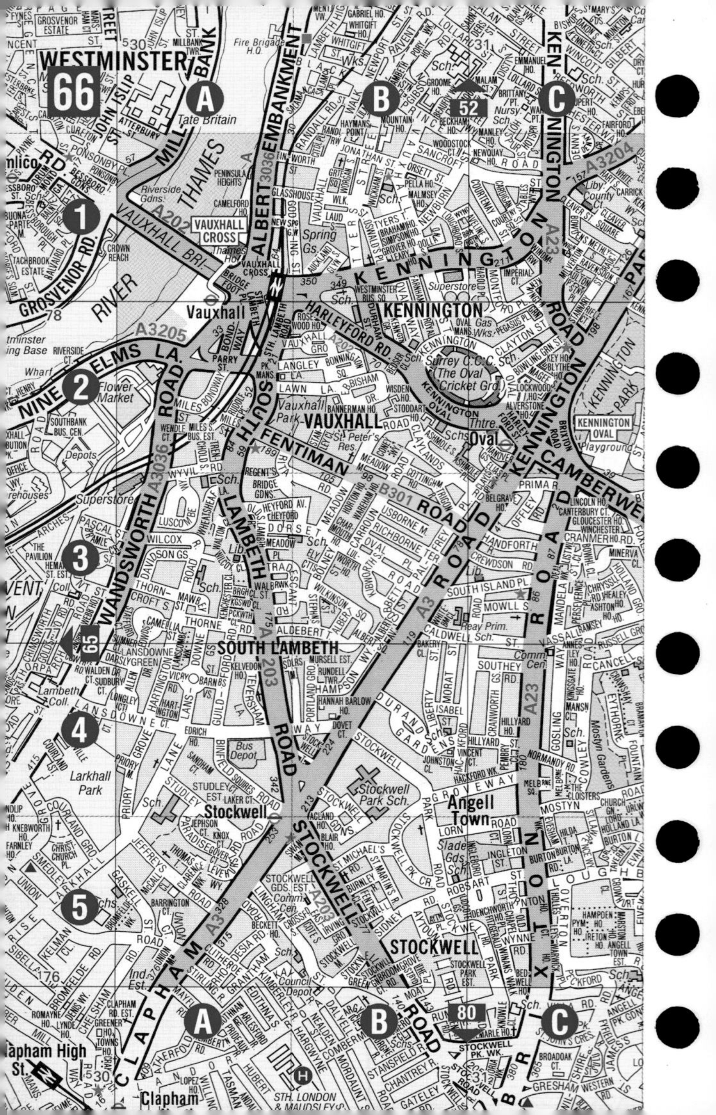

66
WESTMINSTER
A
B
C
52
Tate Britain
MILLBANK
THAMES
RIVER
Riverside Gdns.
VAUXHALL BRI.
VAUXHALL CROSS
ALBERT EMBANKMENT
Fire Brigade H.Q.
Spring Gs.
KENNINGTON
KENNINGTON ROAD
KENNINGTON PARK
KENNINGTON OVAL
Surrey C.C.C. (The Oval Cricket Grd.)
Oval
Vauxhall
VAUXHALL
Vauxhall Park
HARLEYFORD RD.
NINE ELMS LA.
Flower Market
WANDSWORTH ROAD
SOUTH LAMBETH ROAD
FENTIMAN ROAD
CAMBERWELL
BRIXTON ROAD
CLAPHAM ROAD
STOCKWELL
Stockwell
STOCKWELL ROAD
Stockwell Park Sch.
SOUTH LAMBETH
Angell Town
Larkhall Park
LANSDOWNE
Mostyn Gardens
Lambeth Coll.
Bus Depot
Superstore
GROSVENOR RD.
Pimlico
1
2
3
4
5
65
80
A3
A23
A202
A203
A3036
A3204
A3205
B301
Clapham High St.
Clapham
STH. LONDON & MAUDSLEY

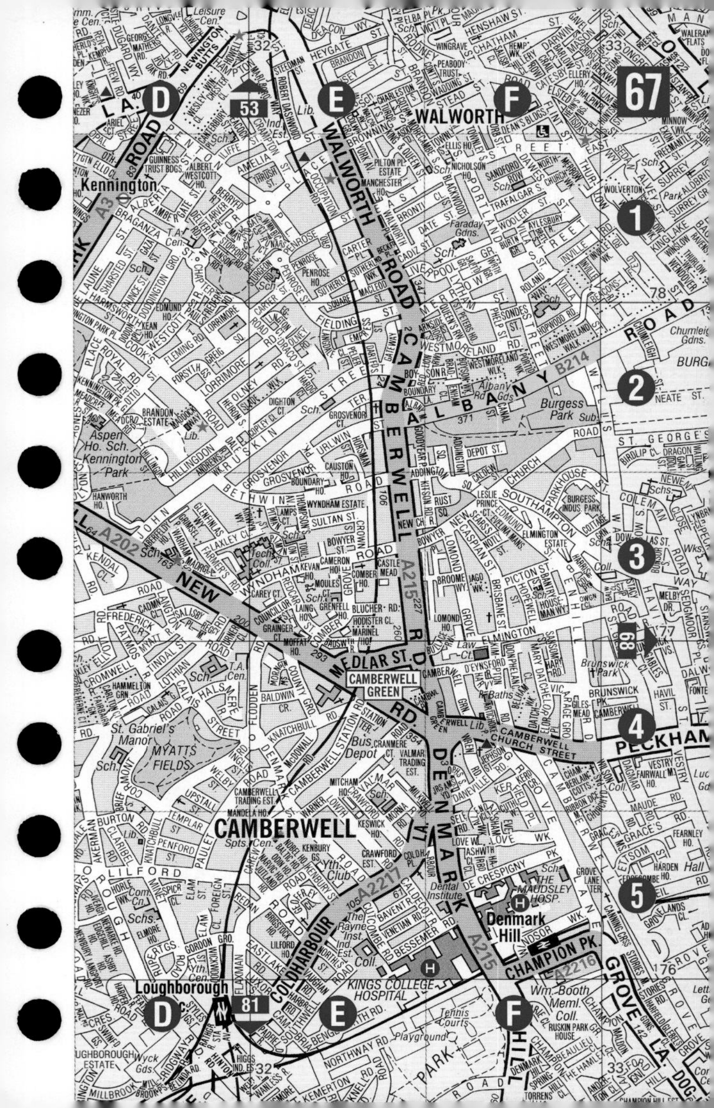

67
D
E
F
53
WALWORTH
Kennington
WALWORTH ROAD
CAMBERWELL RD.
ALBANY RD.
B214
Burgess Park
NEW RD.
A202
A215
A3
MEDLAR ST.
CAMBERWELL GREEN
CAMBERWELL
DENMARK HILL
CAMBERWELL CHURCH STREET
PECKHAM
Brunswick Park
St. Gabriel's Manor
MYATTS FIELDS
Aspen Ho. Sch.
Kennington Park
COLDHARBOUR LA.
A2217
KINGS COLLEGE HOSPITAL
Dental Institute
THE MAUDSLEY HOSP.
Denmark Hill
CHAMPION PK.
A2216
GROVE LA.
Loughborough Jc.
81
Wm. Booth Meml. Coll.
Faraday Gdns.
1
2
3
4
5
68

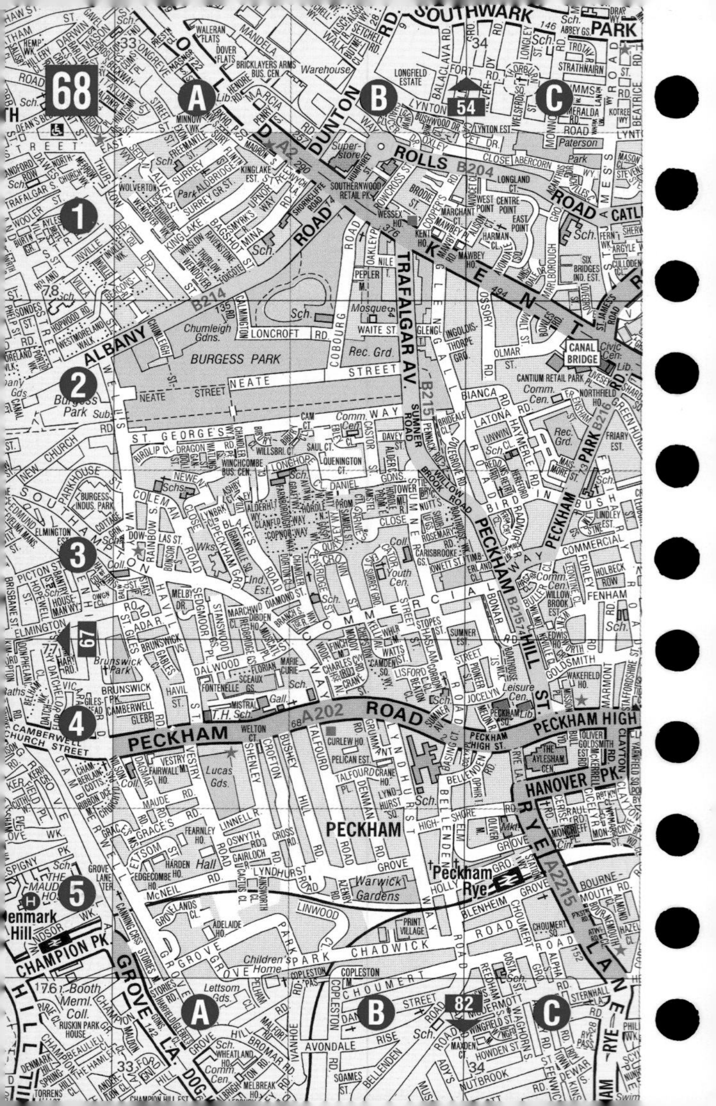
68
A
B
C
1
2
3
4
5
54
67
82
SOUTHWARK PARK
ROLLS ROAD
B204
OLD KENT ROAD
A2
DUNTON ROAD
ALBANY ROAD
B214
BURGESS PARK
Chumleigh Gdns.
LONCROFT RD.
NEATE STREET
ST. GEORGE'S WAY
COBOURG ROAD
TRAFALGAR AV.
B215
SUMNER ROAD
PECKHAM HILL ST.
PECKHAM PARK RD.
B216
COMMERCIAL WAY
WILLOWBROOK ROAD
BIRD IN BUSH RD.
PECKHAM ROAD
A202
PECKHAM HIGH ST.
HANOVER PK.
RYE LANE
A2215
PECKHAM
Peckham Rye
Warwick Gardens
Lucas Gds.
Burgess Park
CAMBERWELL CHURCH STREET
CAMBERWELL GROVE
GROVE PARK
CHADWICK ROAD
CHOUMERT ROAD
Lettsom Gds.
GROVE LA.
DOG KENNEL HILL
CHAMPION PK.
Denmark Hill
Booth Meml. Coll.
LINWOOD
PRINT VILLAGE
Children's Home
SOUTHAMPTON WAY
Super-store
SOUTHERNWOOD RETAIL PK.
CANTIUM RETAIL PARK
CANAL BRIDGE
Civic Cen.
Mosque
Rec. Grd.
Youth Cen.
Leisure Cen.
THE AYLESHAM CEN.
Paterson Park
BRICKLAYERS ARMS BUS. CEN.
LONGFIELD ESTATE
SIX BRIDGES IND. EST.
BURGESS INDUS. PARK
WINCHCOMBE BUS. CEN.
Brunswick Park
Ind. Est.
Gall.
T.H. Sch.

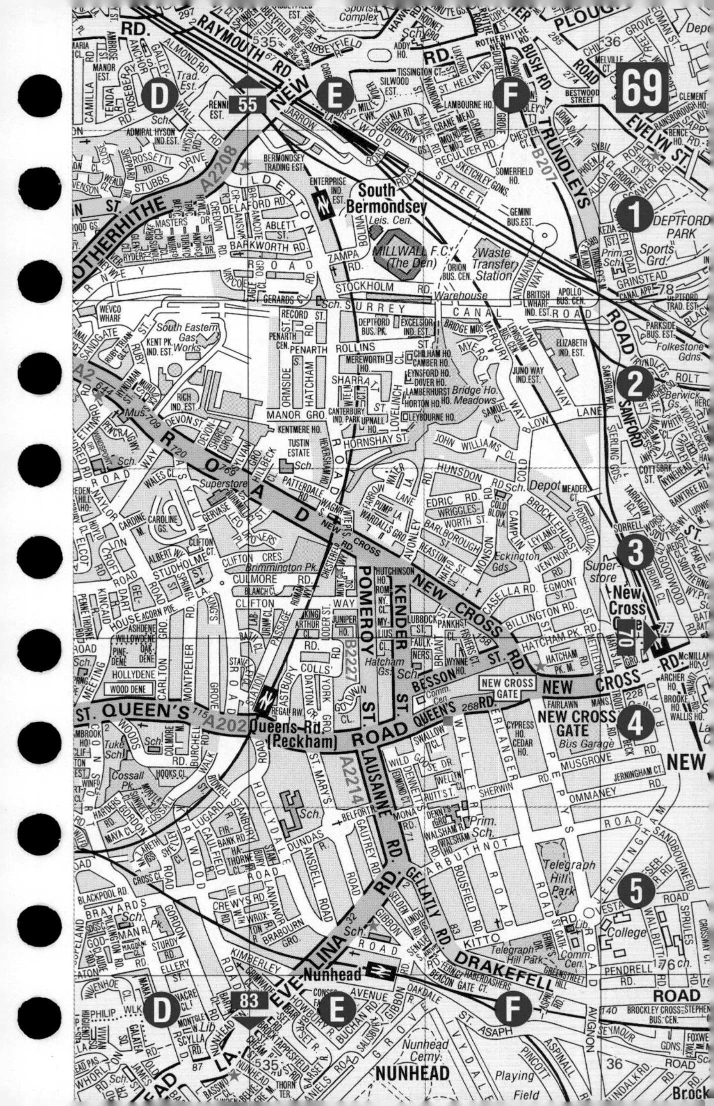
69
55
83
D
E
F
1
2
3
4
5
RAYMOUTH RD.
NEW RD.
ABBEYFIELD RD.
PLOUGH
ROAD
EVELYN ST.
BESTWOOD STREET
BUSH RD.
TRUNDLEYS ROAD
B207
ROTHERHITHE NEW RD.
A2208
SILWOOD ST.
SOUTH BERMONDSEY
South Bermondsey
ILDERTON ROAD
Leis. Cen.
MILLWALL F.C. (The Den)
Waste Transfer Station
Warehouse
SURREY CANAL ROAD
BERMONDSEY TRADING EST.
ENTERPRISE IND. EST.
ORION BUS. CEN.
BRITISH WHARF IND. EST.
APOLLO BUS. CEN.
SOMERFIELD HO.
GEMINI BUS. EST.
DEPTFORD PARK
Sports Grd.
Prim. Sch.
GRINSTEAD RD.
PARKSIDE BUS. EST.
Folkestone Gdns.
DEPTFORD TRAD. EST.
STOCKHOLM RD.
ZAMPA RD.
BOLINA RD.
BARKWORTH RD.
DELAFORD RD.
ABLETT ST.
WEVCO WHARF
South Eastern Gas Works
KENT PK. IND. EST.
RICH IND. EST.
A2
OLD KENT ROAD
A202
ASYLUM ROAD
PENARTH CEN.
PENARTH ST.
ROLLINS ST.
DEPTFORD BUS. PK.
EXCELSIOR IND. EST.
BRIDGE MDS.
Bridge Ho. Meadows
ELIZABETH IND. EST.
JUNO WAY IND. EST.
JUNO WAY
MERCURY WAY
LANDMANN WAY
LEWISHAM BUS. CEN.
SANFORD ST.
MANOR GRO.
ORMSIDE ST.
HATCHAM RD.
HORNSHAY ST.
TUSTIN ESTATE
Sch.
Superstore
JOHN WILLIAMS CL.
HUNSDON RD.
Depot
EDRIC RD.
WRIGGLESWORTH ST.
BARLBOROUGH ST.
NEW CROSS RD.
NEW CROSS
New Cross Gate
NEW CROSS GATE
Bus Garage
Eckington Gdns.
CASELLA RD.
BILLINGTON RD.
HATCHAM PK. RD.
ST. JAMES
Brimmington Pk.
CLIFTON CRES.
CULMORE RD.
CLIFTON WAY
POMEROY ST.
KENDER ST.
B2227
Hatcham Gs.
BESSON ST.
Comm. Cen.
QUEEN'S ROAD
Queens Rd. (Peckham)
ST. QUEEN'S RD.
A2214
LAUSANNE RD.
Tuke Sch.
Cossall Pk.
COSSALL WALK
STUDHOLME ST.
HOLLYDENE
WOOD DENE
CARLTON GRO.
MONTPELIER RD.
BURCHELL RD.
HOLLYDALE RD.
ST. MARY'S RD.
WALLER RD.
ERLANGER RD.
PEPYS RD.
MUSGROVE RD.
OMMANEY RD.
JERNINGHAM RD.
SANDBOURNE RD.
ARBUTHNOT RD.
BOUSFIELD RD.
SHERWIN RD.
Telegraph Hill Park
Telegraph Hill Park
Prim. Sch.
College
Lib.
GELLATLY RD.
EVELINA RD.
KITTO RD.
DRAKEFELL RD.
HABERDASHERS
PENDRELL RD.
BROCKLEY CROSS BUS. CEN.
ROAD
AVIGNON RD.
SEYMOUR
Nunhead
NUNHEAD
Nunhead Cemy.
NUNHEAD GROVE
KIMBERLEY AVENUE
OAKDALE RD.
ST. ASAPH RD.
LIVYDALE
Playing Field
ASPINALL RD.
PINCOTT RD.
BRAYARDS RD.
GORDON RD.
LUGARD RD.
CAULFIELD RD.
BRABOURN GRO.
CREWYS RD.
GIBBON RD.
BUCHAN RD.
HOWBURY RD.
NUNHEAD LA.
Lib
Brock

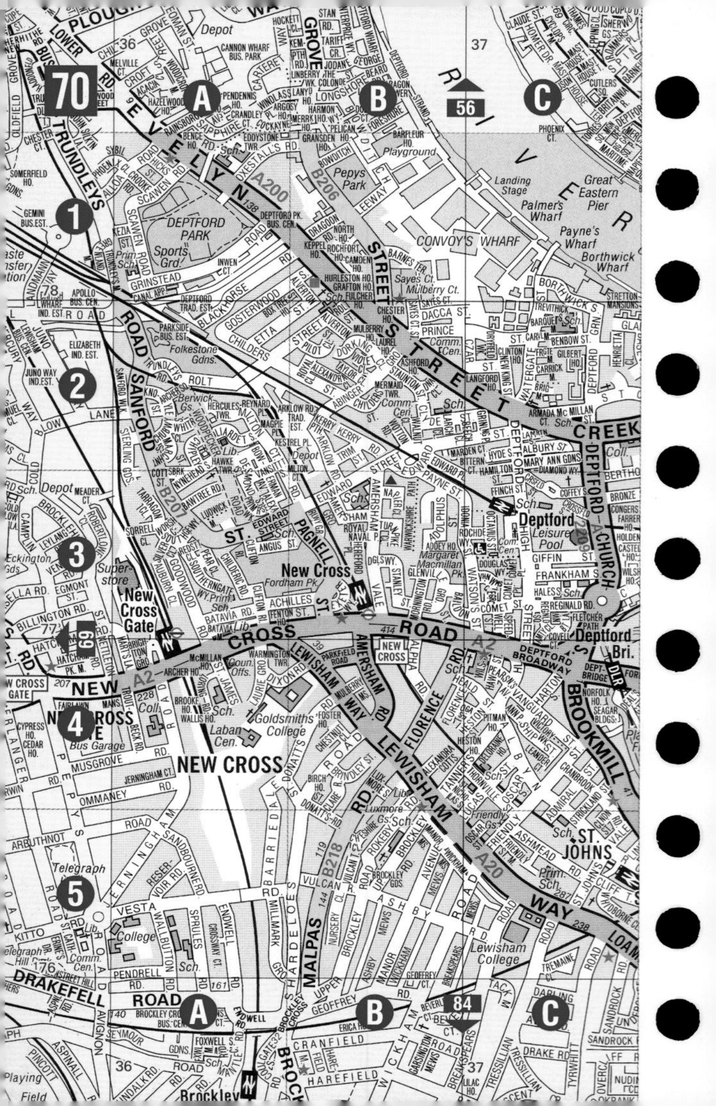

70
A
B
C
56
84
69
36
37
1
2
3
4
5
RIVER
EVELYN
A200
B206
STREET
DEPTFORD PARK
Sports Grd.
Pepys Park
Playground
Landing Stage
Palmer's Wharf
Great Eastern Pier
Payne's Wharf
Borthwick Wharf
CONVOY'S WHARF
Sayes Ct.
Mulberry Ct.
TRUNDLEYS
GEMINI BUS.EST.
GRINSTEAD
CANAL APP.
APOLLO BUS. CEN.
DEPTFORD TRAD. EST.
BLACKHORSE
GOSTERWOOD
CHILDERS
Folkestone Gdns.
PARKSIDE BUS. EST.
ELIZABETH IND. EST.
JUNO WAY IND.EST.
SANFORD
ROAD
B207
ROLT
Berwick Gs.
Lib.
Depot
Comm. Cen.
Sch.
CREEK
DEPTFORD
CHURCH
B209
Deptford Leisure Pool
Margaret Macmillan Pk.
Deptford
Deptford Bri.
DLR
ST. EDWARD STREET
PAGNELL
New Cross
Fordham Pk.
Super-store
New Cross Gate
NEW CROSS
CROSS ROAD
A2
DEPTFORD BROADWAY
BROOKMILL
LEWISHAM WAY
AMERSHAM RD.
FLORENCE
Goldsmiths College
Laban Cen.
Bus Garage
NEW CROSS
LEWISHAM
A20
WAY
B218
MALPAS
Luxmore Gs.
Friendly Gs.
ST. JOHNS
Prim. Sch.
Lewisham College
Telegraph Hill Park
College
DRAKEFELL ROAD
BROCKLEY CROSS BUS. CEN.
Brockley
Playing Field
HAREFIELD
CRANFIELD

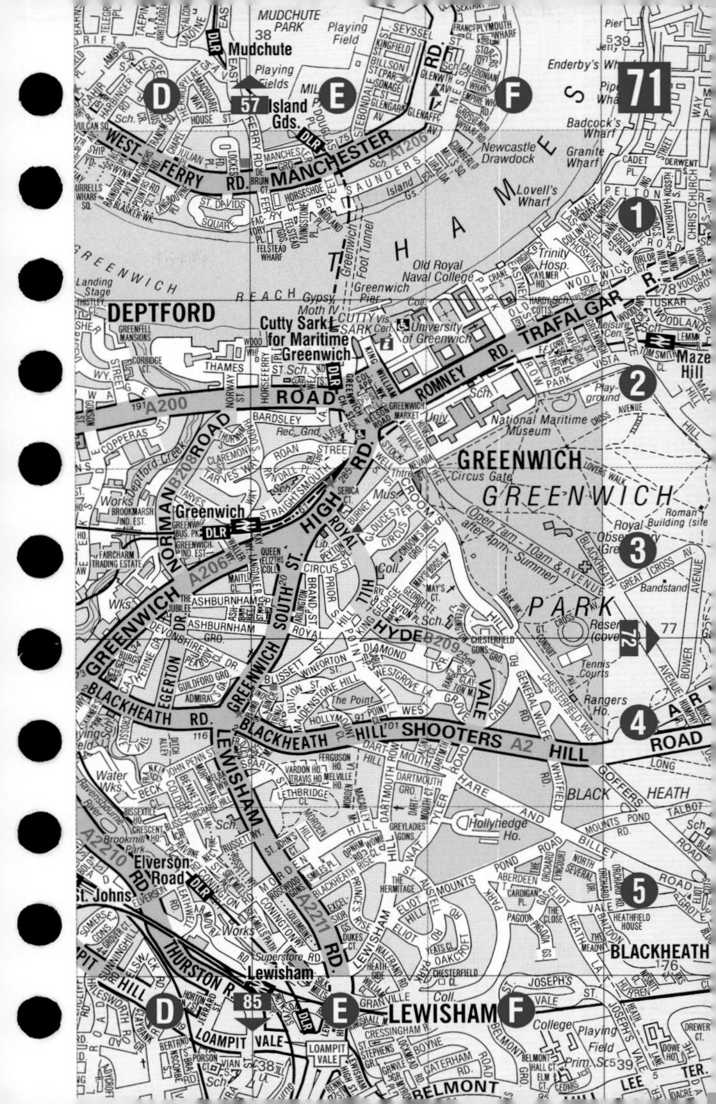
MUDCHUTE PARK
Mudchute
Playing Fields
Playing Field
Island Gds.
57
D
E
F
1
2
3
4
5
WEST FERRY RD.
MANCHESTER RD.
A1206
SAUNDERS NESS RD.
ST. DAVIDS SQUARE
Island Gs.
Newcastle Drawdock
Granite Wharf
Badcock's Wharf
Enderby's Wharf
Lovell's Wharf
THAMES
GREENWICH REACH
Greenwich Foot Tunnel
DEPTFORD
Landing Stage
Trinity Hosp.
Old Royal Naval College
Gypsy Moth IV
Greenwich Pier
Cutty Sark for Maritime Greenwich
University of Greenwich
TRAFALGAR RD.
ROMNEY RD.
Maze Hill
PARK VISTA
Playground
National Maritime Museum
A200
ROAD
CREEK ROAD
B208
NORMAN ROAD
GREENWICH HIGH RD.
Greenwich
DLR
A206
GREENWICH
GREENWICH PARK
Circus Gate
(Open 7am - 10am & after 4pm - Summer)
Royal Observatory Greenwich
Roman Building (site)
BLACKHEATH AVENUE
GREAT CROSS AV.
Bandstand
Reservoir (covered)
72
77
Tennis Courts
Rangers Ho.
CROOM'S HILL
ROYAL HILL
HYDE VALE
B209
GREENWICH SOUTH ST.
ASHBURNHAM GRO.
BLACKHEATH RD.
BLACKHEATH HILL
SHOOTERS HILL ROAD
A2
LEWISHAM RD.
A2210
Elverson Road
St. Johns
Brookmill Park
Ravensbourne River
Water Wks.
DARTMOUTH ROW
BLACKHEATH
GOFFERS RD.
Hollyhedge Ho.
MOUNTS POND RD.
A2211
Lewisham
Superstore
THURSTON R.
LOAMPIT VALE
LOAMPIT HILL
85
LEWISHAM
ST. JOSEPH'S VALE
College Playing Field
BELMONT
Coll.

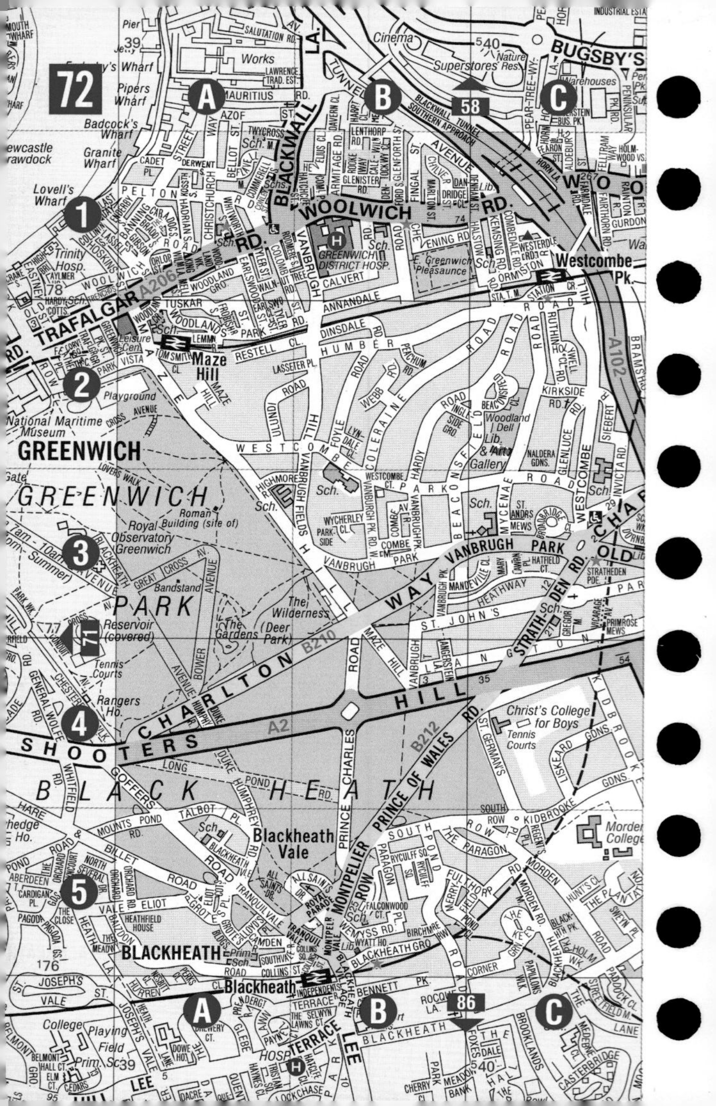

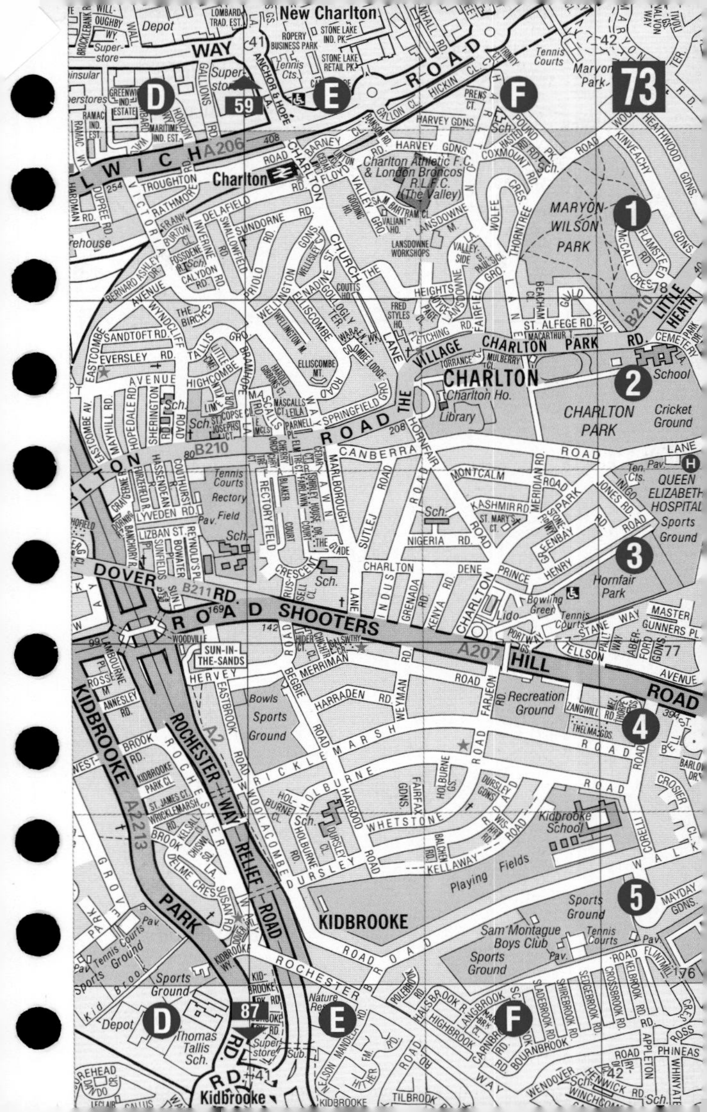
73
New Charlton
LOMBARD TRAD. EST.
ROPERY BUSINESS PARK
STONE LAKE IND. PK.
STONE LAKE RETAIL PK.
Tennis Cts.
Tennis Courts
Maryon Park
Depot
Super-store
WAY
ROAD
41
42
59
ANCHOR & HOPE LA.
D
E
F
GREENWICH IND. ESTATE
MARITIME IND. EST.
GALLIONS RD.
HORIZON WAY
HICKIN CL.
GALLON CL.
HARVEY GDNS.
PRENS CT.
POUND PK. RD.
HASTED RD.
TRINITY
HEATHWOOD GDNS.
KINVEACHY GDNS.
A206
408
WOOLWICH
Charlton
254
TROUGHTON
RATHMORE RD.
VICTORIA
BARNEY CL.
CHARLTON
FLOYD RD.
VALLEY GRO.
Charlton Athletic F.C. & London Broncos R.L.F.C. (The Valley)
SAM BARTRAM CL.
VALIANT HO.
LANSDOWNE M.
LANSDOWNE WORKSHOPS
COXMOUNT RD.
WOLFE CRES.
THORNTREE
MARYON-WILSON PARK
1
McCALL CRES.
FLAMSTEED RD.
78
B210
LITTLE HEATH
HARDMAN RD.
DUPREE RD.
DELAFIELD
FRANK BURTON CL.
SUNDORNE RD.
SWALLOWFIELD
INVERINE RD.
FOSSDENE RD.
CALYDON RD.
BERNARD ASHLEY DR.
AVENUE
PRIOLO RD.
WELLINGTON GDNS.
NADINE ST.
CHURCH
THE
COUTTS HO.
HEIGHTS
JOYCE PAGE CL.
VALLEY-SIDE
ST. PAUL'S CL.
FAIRFIELD GRO.
BEACHAM CL.
GUILD ROAD
LANE
WYNDCLIFF
THE BIRCHES
TALLIS GRO.
BRAMHOPE
WELLINGTON M.
ELLISCOMBE
GOLLOGLY TER.
FRED STYLES HO.
FETCHING
ST. ALFEGE RD.
MACARTHUR T.
CHARLTON PARK RD.
CEMETERY LA.
SANDTOFT RD.
EVERSLEY RD.
EASTCOMBE
HIGHCOMBE
ELLISCOMBE MT.
COOMBE LODGE
WARREN WK.
VILLAGE
TORRANCE CL.
MULBERRY
CHARLTON
Charlton Ho.
Library
2
School
CHARLTON PARK
Cricket Ground
AVENUE
SHERINGTON
Sch.
ROAD
ST. JOSEPHS CT.
COPSE CL.
MASCALLS
PARNELL
SPRINGFIELD GRO.
THE ROAD
208
HORNFAIR
EASTCOMBE AV.
MAYHILL RD.
HOPEDALE RD.
80
B210
CANBERRA ROAD
LANE
CHERRY
CEDAR
ELM
MARLBOROUGH
LAWN
TENNIS Courts
Rectory Field
Pav.
HASSENDEAN
COUTHURST
LYVEDEN RD.
SUTLEJ ROAD
MONTCALM
MERIDIAN RD.
KASHMIR RD.
ST. MARY'S CT.
JONES RD.
INIGO
Ten. Cts.
Pav.
QUEEN ELIZABETH HOSPITAL
Sports Ground
PARK
GREENBAY
ROAD
HENRY
PRINCE
DENE
NIGERIA RD.
CHARLTON
RECTORY FIELD
COURT
BLAKER
SHIRLEY HOUSE DR.
FAIRLAWN
THE GLADE
CRESCENT
LIZBAN ST.
SUNFIELDS
BOWATER
REYNOLD'S PL.
DOVER
B211 RD.
169
ROAD
SHOOTERS
142
LANE
INDUS
GRENADA RD.
KENYA RD.
Lido
Bowling Green
Tennis Courts
Hornfair Park
3
STANE WAY
MASTER GUNNERS PL.
PORTWAY GDNS.
TELLSON
A207
HILL
77
AVENUE
ROAD
WOODVILLE
99
SUN-IN-THE-SANDS
HERVEY
MERRIMAN
EASTBROOK
BEGBIE
HARRADEN RD.
WEYMAN
FARJEON RD.
Recreation Ground
ZANGWILL RD.
THELMA GDS.
4
394
Bowls Sports Ground
WRICKLEMARSH
ROAD
ROCHESTER
A2
KIDBROOKE
LAMBOURNE
ROSSE M.
ANNESLEY RD.
BROOK RD.
KIDBROOKE PARK CL.
ST. JAMES CT.
WRICKLEMARSH RD.
A2213
HOLBURNE
HARGOOD
FAIRFAX GDNS.
HOLBURNE GS.
DURSLEY GDNS.
HOLBURNE CL.
WHETSTONE
BALCHEN RD.
Kidbrooke School
CORELLI
CROSIER
BARLOW DR.
WAY
RELIEF
WOOLACOMBE
DURSLEY
KELLAWAY
Playing Fields
WALK
5
MAYDAY GDNS.
PARK
GROVE
BROOK
DELME CRES.
SUSAN RD.
PARK
ROAD
KIDBROOKE
Sports Ground
Tennis Courts
Sam Montague Boys Club
Pav.
Sports Ground
Kid Brook
Sports Ground
Pav.
Tennis Courts
KIDBROOKE WY.
ROAD
ROCHESTER
Nature Res.
POLEBROOK
HALSBROOK R.
HIGHBROOK
LANGBROOK
SLADEBROOK RD.
SHIREBROOK RD.
SEDGEBROOK RD.
CROSSBROOK RD.
KELBROOK RD.
FLINTMILL
176
87
D
E
F
Depot
Thomas Tallis Sch.
Super-store
Sub.
41
NELSON MANDELA RD.
HITHER FM. RD.
CARNBROOK RD.
BOURNBROOK
APPLETON
PHINEAS
WHINYATE
ROSS
WENDOVER
HENWICK RD.
WINCHCOMB
42
Sch.
WAY
RD.
Kidbrooke
KIDBROOKE
TILBROOK

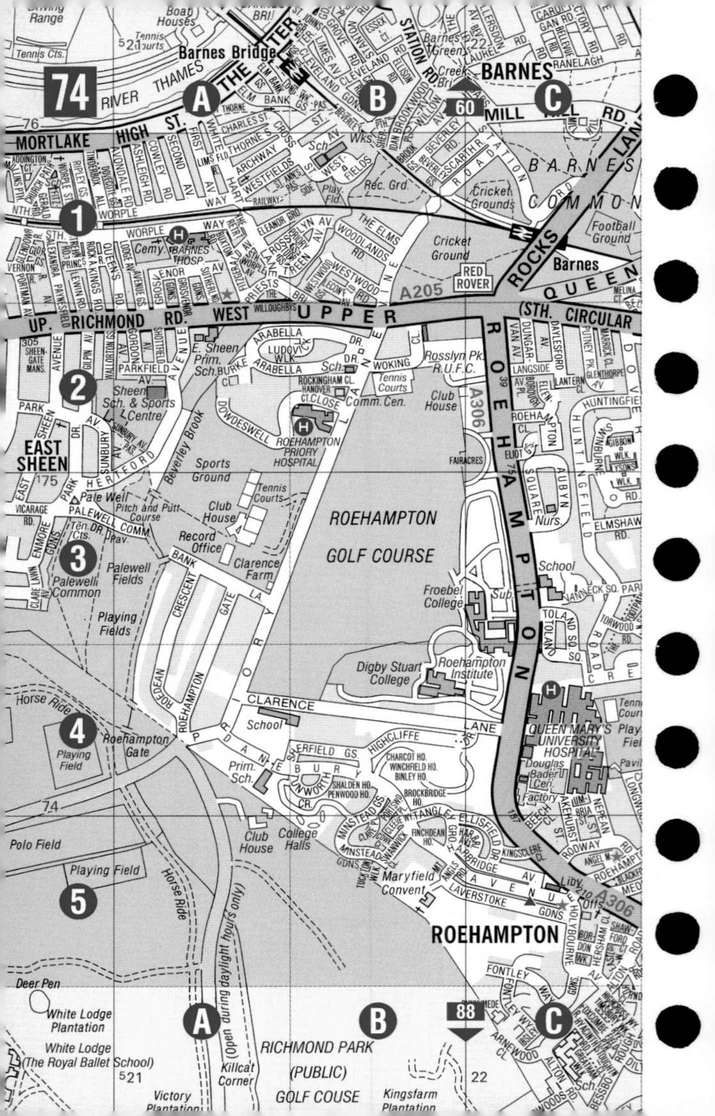
Driving Range
Boat Houses
Tennis Courts
Tennis Cts.
Barnes Bridge
RIVER THAMES
THE TER.
STATION RD.
Barnes Green
BARNES
60
MILL HILL RD.
MORTLAKE HIGH ST.
CHARLES ST.
THORNE ST.
ARCHWAY
WESTFIELDS
CLEVELAND GDNS.
CLEVELAND RD.
ELM BANK GS.
Rec. Grd.
BARNES COMMON
Cricket Grounds
Football Ground
ROCKS LANE
Barnes
QUEEN
WORPLE WAY
WORPLE
Cemy.
BARNES HOSP.
THE ELMS
WOODLANDS RD.
WESTWOOD RD.
Cricket Ground
RED ROVER
A205
UP. RICHMOND RD. WEST
UPPER RICHMOND RD.
(STH. CIRCULAR
SHEEN GATE MANS.
PARKFIELD AV.
E. Sheen Prim. Sch.
Sheen Sch. & Sports Centre
ARABELLA DR.
LUDOVICK WLK.
WOKING CL.
Tennis Courts
Rosslyn Pk. R.U.F.C.
Club House
A306
Comm. Cen.
DOWDESWELL CL.
ROEHAMPTON PRIORY HOSPITAL
ROEHAMPTON LANE
EAST SHEEN
HERTFORD AV.
Beverley Brook
Sports Ground
Tennis Courts
Club House
Pale Well
Pitch and Putt Course
PALEWELL COMM. DR.
Record Office
ROEHAMPTON GOLF COURSE
FAIRACRES
AUBYN SQUARE
HUNTINGFIELD
ELMSHAW RD.
Nurs.
School
Clarence Farm
BANK LA.
Palewell Fields
Palewell Common
Playing Fields
CRESCENT
GATE
PRIORY LANE
Froebel College
DANEBURY AV.
Digby Stuart College
Roehampton Institute
CLARENCE LANE
School
ROEDEAN CRES.
ROEHAMPTON GATE
Horse Ride
Playing Field
Roehampton Gate
QUEEN MARY'S UNIVERSITY HOSPITAL
Douglas Bader Cen.
Factory
Prim. Sch.
HIGHCLIFFE DR.
CHARCOT HO.
WINCHFIELD HO.
BINLEY HO.
SHALDEN HO.
PENWOOD HO.
BROCKBRIDGE HO.
FINCHDEAN HO.
ELLISFIELD DR.
MINSTEAD GDNS.
TANGLEY GRO.
HARBRIDGE AV.
KINGSCLERE CL.
Polo Field
Club House
College Halls
Playing Field
Horse Ride
Maryfield Convent
LAVERSTOKE GDNS.
ALTON RD.
Liby.
Offs.
ROEHAMPTON
HOLYBOURNE AV.
FONTLEY WAY
Deer Pen
White Lodge Plantation
White Lodge (The Royal Ballet School)
(Open during daylight hours only)
RICHMOND PARK (PUBLIC) GOLF COUSE
Killcat Corner
Victory Plantation
Kingsfarm Plantation
88
ARNEWOOD CL.

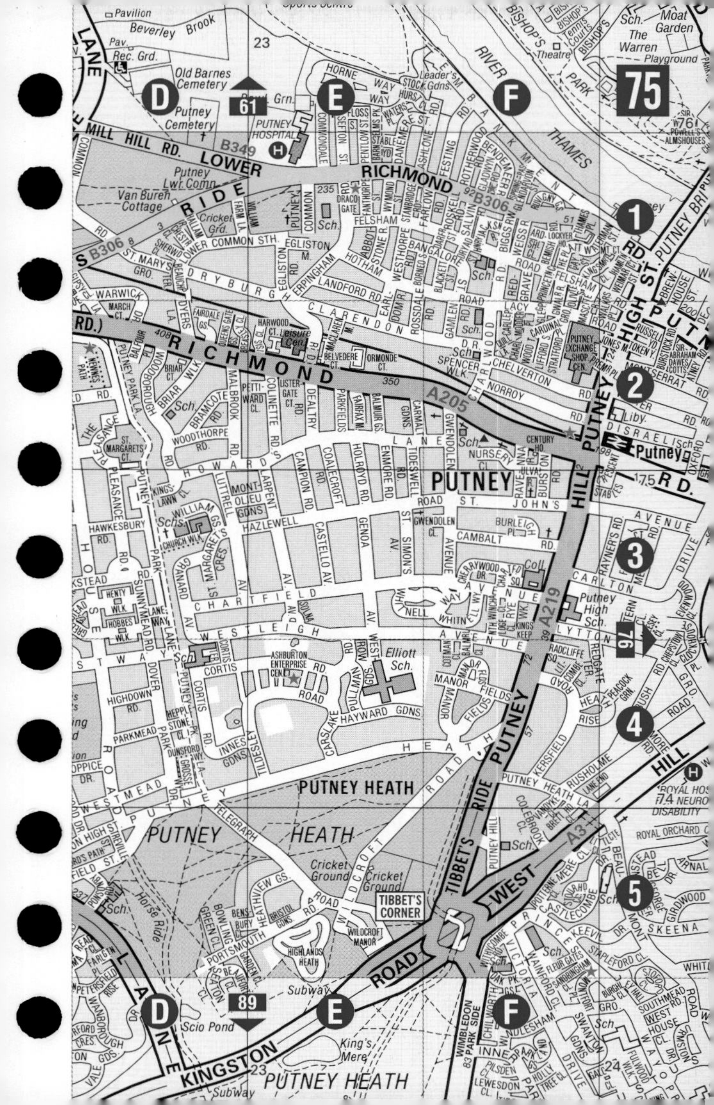

Pavilion
Beverley Brook
Rec. Grd.
Old Barnes Cemetery
Putney Cemetery
61
23
D
E
F
PUTNEY HOSPITAL
Leader's Gdns.
RIVER
THAMES
BISHOP'S PARK
Theatre
Tennis Courts
Moat Garden
The Warren
Playground
76
SIR W. POWELL'S ALMSHOUSES
MILL HILL RD.
LOWER
RICHMOND
B349
B306
Putney Lwr. Comn.
Van Buren Cottage
RIDE
Cricket Grd.
LOWER COMMON STH.
PUTNEY COMMON
FELSHAM
DRYBURGH
CLARENDON
LANDFORD RD.
HOTHAM
ERPINGHAM
EGLISTON
EMBANKMENT
1
PUTNEY BRIDGE
HIGH ST.
PUTNEY EXCHANGE SHOP CEN.
RICHMOND
A205
HARWOOD CT.
Leisure Cen.
BELVEDERE CT.
ORMONDE CT.
CHELVERTON
NORROY
MONTSERRAT
2
Liby.
DISRAELI
Putney
RD.
CENTURY HO.
NURSERY
LANE
PUTNEY
HOWARDS
ST. JOHN'S
HILL
GWENDOLEN
CAMBALT
HAZLEWELL
WILLIAM
Schs.
CHURCH WLK.
ST. MARGARET'S CRES.
3
AVENUE
CARLTON
CHARTFIELD
WHITNELL WAY
Putney High Sch.
Coll.
A219
WESTLEIGH
LYTTON
76
CORTIS
ASHBURTON ENTERPRISE CEN.
Elliott Sch.
MANOR FIELDS
PUTNEY
HAYWARD GDNS.
HEATH
4
HIGHDOWN RD.
PARKMEAD
WESTMEAD
PUTNEY HEATH
PUTNEY
HEATH
KERSFIELD
RUSHOLME
PUTNEY HEATH LA.
ROYAL HOSPITAL FOR NEURO-DISABILITY
TELEGRAPH
WILDCROFT
Cricket Ground
Cricket Ground
TIBBET'S RIDE
TIBBET'S CORNER
WILDCROFT MANOR
HIGHLANDS HEATH
A3
WEST
PRINCES
5
ROYAL ORCHARD
Horse Ride
Sch.
PORTSMOUTH
ROAD
D
E
F
89
Subway
Scio Pond
KINGSTON
ROAD
King's Mere
PUTNEY HEATH
WIMBLEDON PARK SIDE
VICTORIA
Subway
24

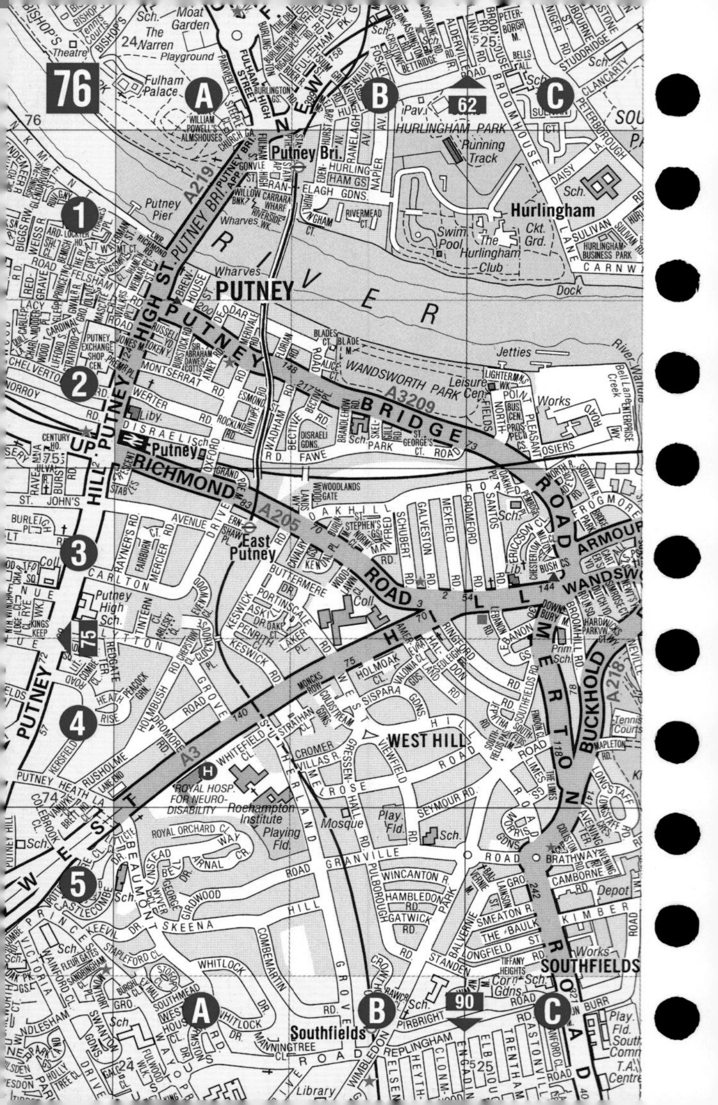
76
A
B
C
62
1
2
3
4
5
75
90
74
24
25
Theatre
Tennis Courts
Moat Garden
The Narren
Playground
Fulham Palace
WILLIAM POWELL'S ALMSHOUSES
FULHAM HIGH STREET
BURLINGTON GS.
HURLINGHAM PARK
Running Track
Putney Bri.
HAM GS.
ELAGH GDNS.
NAPIER
RANELAGH AV.
ALDERVILLE RD.
BROOMHOUSE LANE
PETERBOROUGH
CLANCARTY
STUDDRIDGE
NIGER RD.
SULIVAN
DAISY LA.
Sch.
Hurlingham
Swim Pool
The Hurlingham Club
Ckt. Grd.
HURLINGHAM BUSINESS PARK
CARNWATH
Dock
Putney Pier
CARRARA WHARF
Wharves WK.
RIVERMEAD CT.
Wharves
PUTNEY
RIVER
A219
PUTNEY BRIDGE APP.
ST. PUTNEY BRI.
HIGH ST.
PUTNEY BRIDGE
A3209
ROAD
WANDSWORTH PARK
Jetties
River Wandle
Leisure Cen.
Works
Bell Lane Creek
POINT PLEASANT
OSIERS
PUTNEY EXCHANGE SHOP CEN.
MONTSERRAT RD.
WERTER RD.
Liby.
DISRAELI
Putney
RICHMOND ROAD
A205
Sch.
DEODAR
MERIVALE
FLORIAN RD.
BLADES CT.
ALICE
ESMOND
ROCKLAND
WADHAM RD.
BECTIVE
DISRAELI GDNS.
BRANDLEHOW RD.
ST. GEORGE'S CT.
FAWE PARK ROAD
CENTURY HO.
UP. PUTNEY HILL
ST. JOHN'S
BURLEIGH PL.
Coll.
CARLTON
Putney High Sch.
LYTTON
PUTNEY HILL
HEATH RISE
KERSFIELD
PUTNEY HEATH LA.
RUSHOLME
AVENUE
RAYNER'S RD.
FAIRBURN CT.
MERCIER RD.
TINTERN
HOLMBUSH
GROVE
DROMORE
East Putney
OAKHILL
ST. STEPHEN'S GS.
MANFRED
SCHUBERT
GALVESTON
MEXFIELD
CROMFORD
SANTOS
Lib.
BUSH CS.
WANDSWORTH
ARMOURY
FROGMORE
BUCKHOLD
A218
ERICSSON CL.
CHESTERTON
BUTTERMERE DR.
PORTINSCALE
KESWICK
LAKER PL.
Coll.
WEST HILL
A3
HOLMOAK CL.
SISPARA GDNS.
RINGFORD
LEBANON
MERTON ROAD
Prim. Sch.
BROOMHILL RD.
Tennis Courts
MAPLETON RD.
LONGSTAFF
WHITEFIELD CL.
STRATHAN CL.
COLDSTREAM GDNS.
CROMER VILLAS R.
MELROSE
GRESSENHALL RD.
VIEWFIELD
WEST HILL
ROAD
SEYMOUR RD.
ROYAL HOSP. FOR NEURO-DISABILITY
Roehampton Institute
Playing Fld.
Mosque
Play. Fld.
Sch.
ROYAL ORCHARD CL.
GRANVILLE ROAD
WINCANTON R.
HAMBLEDON RD.
GATWICK RD.
PULBOROUGH
BRATHWAY
CAMBORNE RD.
Depot
KIMBER ROAD
SMEATON R.
THE BAULK
LONGFIELD ST.
Works
SOUTHFIELDS
TIFFANY HEIGHTS
Corn. Sch.
BEAUMONT
GIRDWOOD
SKEENA HILL
CASTLECOMBE
PRINCES WAY
VICTORIA
WAINFORD CL.
FLEUR GATES
SANDRINGHAM
WHITLOCK DR.
SOUTHMEAD
COMBEMARTIN
GROVE
STANDEN RD.
Sch.
PIRBRIGHT
BURR RD.
Play. Fld.
T.A. Centre
Southfields
MANNINGTREE
ROAD
WIMBLEDON
REPLINGHAM
Library
HOLLY TREE CL.
PUTNEY HILL
Sch.

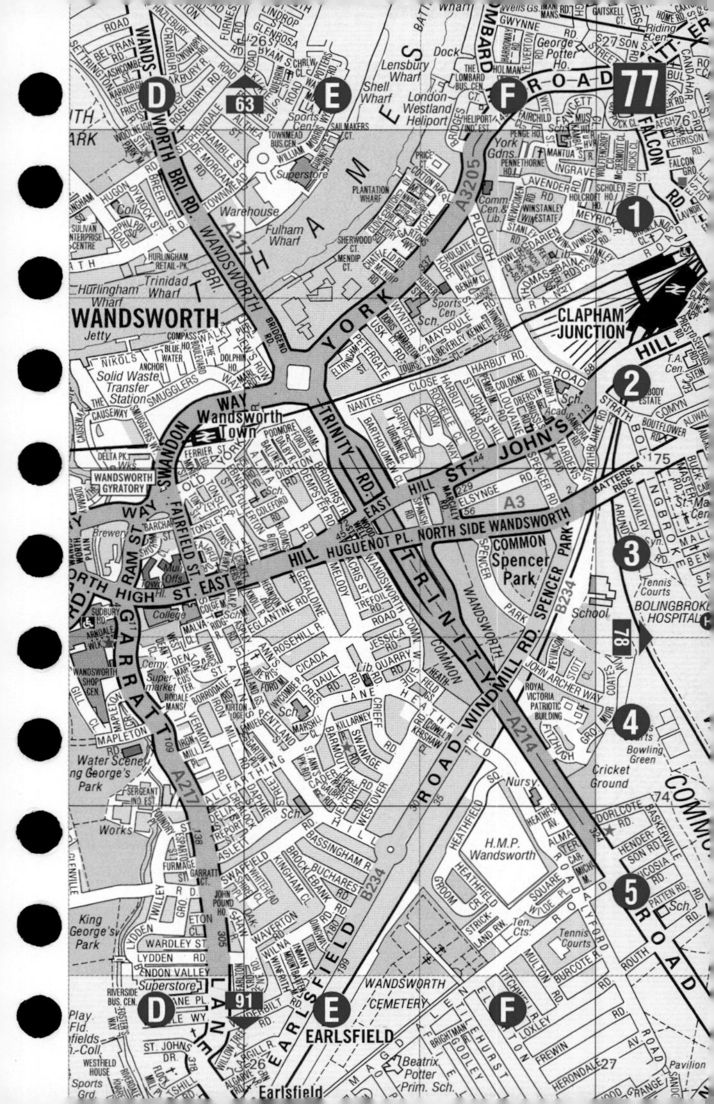

77
63
91
78
D
E
F
1
2
3
4
5
WANDSWORTH
CLAPHAM JUNCTION
EARLSFIELD
Earlsfield
Wandsworth Town
WANDSWORTH GYRATORY
WANDSWORTH BRI. RD.
WANDSWORTH BRI.
YORK ROAD
A3205
A217
A214
A3
B234
TRINITY RD.
ST. JOHN'S HILL
EAST HILL
NORTH SIDE WANDSWORTH
COMMON
HUGUENOT PL.
WANDSWORTH HIGH ST.
GARRATT LANE
SWANDON WAY
FAIRFIELD ST.
RAM ST.
OLD YORK RD.
WINDMILL RD.
SPENCER PARK
Spencer Park
WANDSWORTH COMMON W. SIDE
HEATHFIELD RD.
EARLSFIELD RD.
MAGDALEN RD.
ALLFARTHING LANE
BATTERSEA RISE
PLOUGH RD.
FALCON RD.
LOMBARD RD.
BOLINGBROKE HOSPITAL
H.M.P. Wandsworth
WANDSWORTH CEMETERY
King George's Park
Superstore
Warehouse
Fulham Wharf
Hurlingham Wharf
Trinidad Wharf
Shell Wharf
Lensbury Wharf
London Westland Heliport
Solid Waste Transfer Station
Brewery
College
Cemy.
Water Scene
Works
Tennis Courts
Bowling Green
Cricket Ground
ROYAL VICTORIA PATRIOTIC BUILDING
Beatrix Potter Prim. Sch.
Pavilion
Sch.
Lib.
Sports Cen.

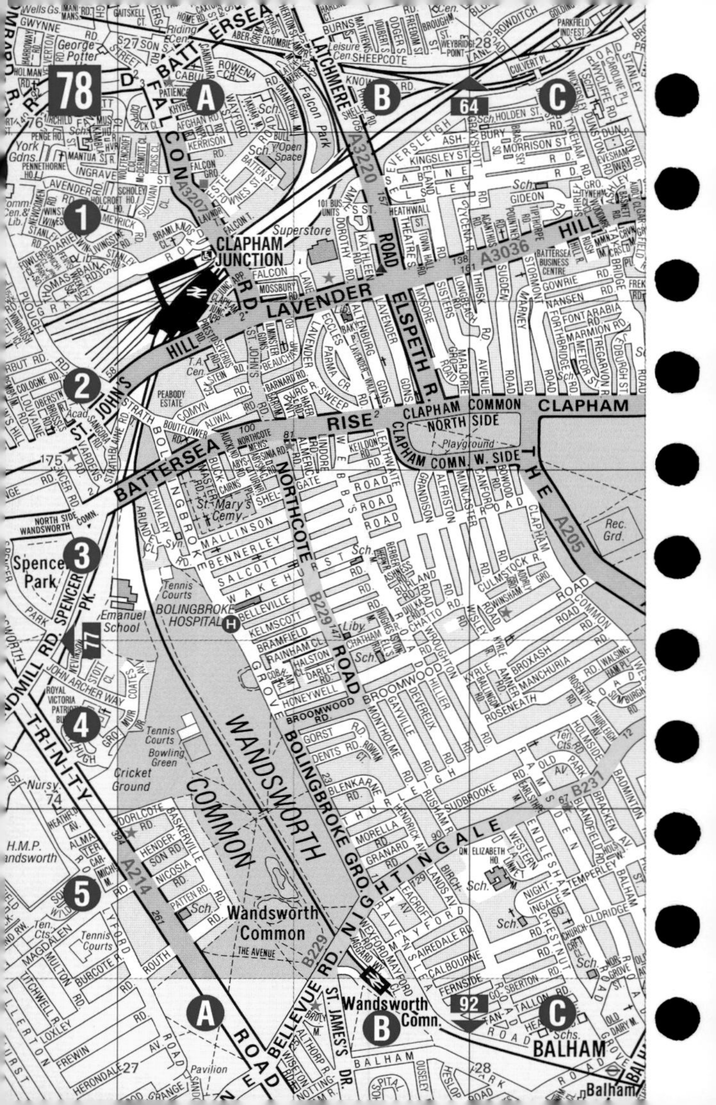
64
77
92
A
B
C
1
2
3
4
5
CLAPHAM JUNCTION
LAVENDER HILL
ST. JOHN'S HILL
BATTERSEA RISE
CLAPHAM COMMON NORTH SIDE
CLAPHAM COMMON WEST SIDE
NORTHCOTE ROAD
BOLINGBROKE GROVE
WANDSWORTH COMMON
NIGHTINGALE LANE
TRINITY ROAD
WINDMILL RD.
BELLEVUE RD.
ELSPETH R.
FALCON RD.
LATCHMERE RD.
Falcon Park
Superstore
St. Mary's Cemy.
Spencer Park
Emanuel School
BOLINGBROKE HOSPITAL
Tennis Courts
Bowling Green
Cricket Ground
H.M.P. Wandsworth
Wandsworth Common
Wandsworth Comn.
BALHAM
Rec. Grd.
Playground
A3207
A3220
A3036
A205
A214
B229
B237

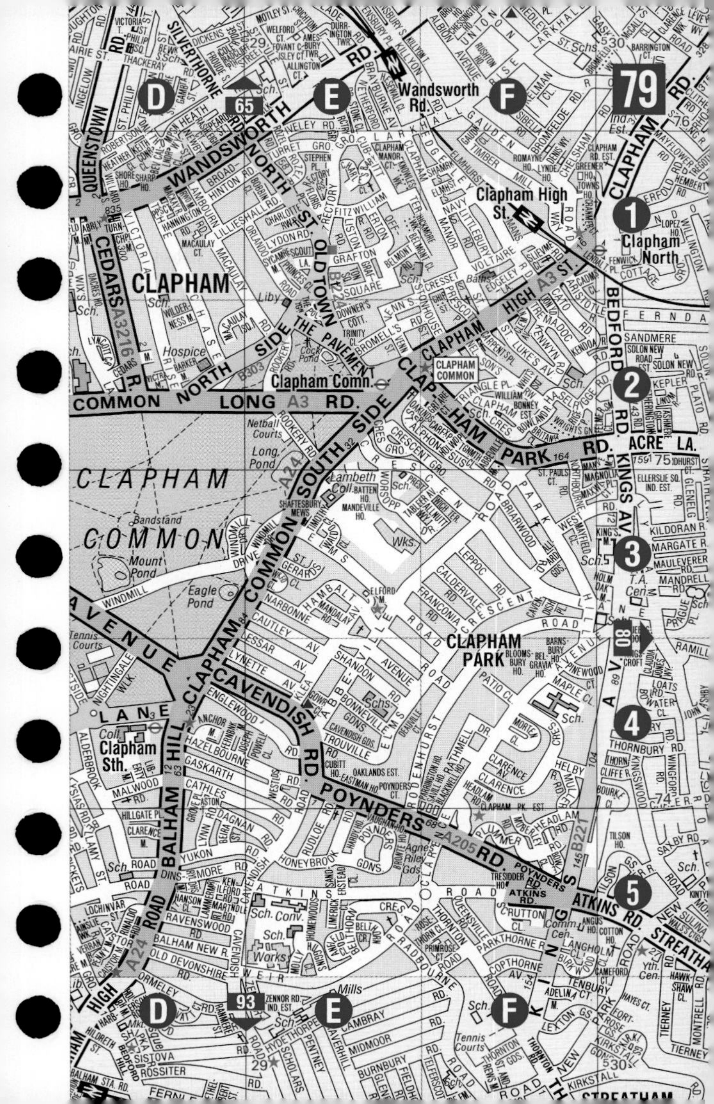
79
65
80
93
D
E
F
1
2
3
4
5
CLAPHAM
CLAPHAM COMMON
CLAPHAM PARK
Wandsworth Rd.
Clapham High St.
Clapham North
Clapham Comn.
Clapham Sth.
WANDSWORTH RD.
NORTH ST.
OLD TOWN
THE PAVEMENT
NORTH SIDE
COMMON NORTH SIDE
LONG RD.
CLAPHAM HIGH ST.
CLAPHAM PARK RD.
ACRE LA.
BEDFORD RD.
KINGS AV.
SOUTH SIDE
COMMON SIDE
CLAPHAM COMMON SOUTH SIDE
WINDMILL DRIVE
AVENUE
NIGHTINGALE LANE
CEDARS RD.
QUEENSTOWN RD.
SILVERTHORNE RD.
CAVENDISH RD.
POYNDERS RD.
CLARENCE AV.
ATKINS RD.
BALHAM HILL
BALHAM HIGH RD.
KINGS AV.
STREATHAM
NEW PARK RD.
A3
A24
A205
A3216
B221
B224
B303
Mount Pond
Eagle Pond
Long Pond
Cock Pond
Bandstand
Netball Courts
Tennis Courts
Hospice
Lambeth Coll.
Wks.
Works
Sch.
Liby
Baths

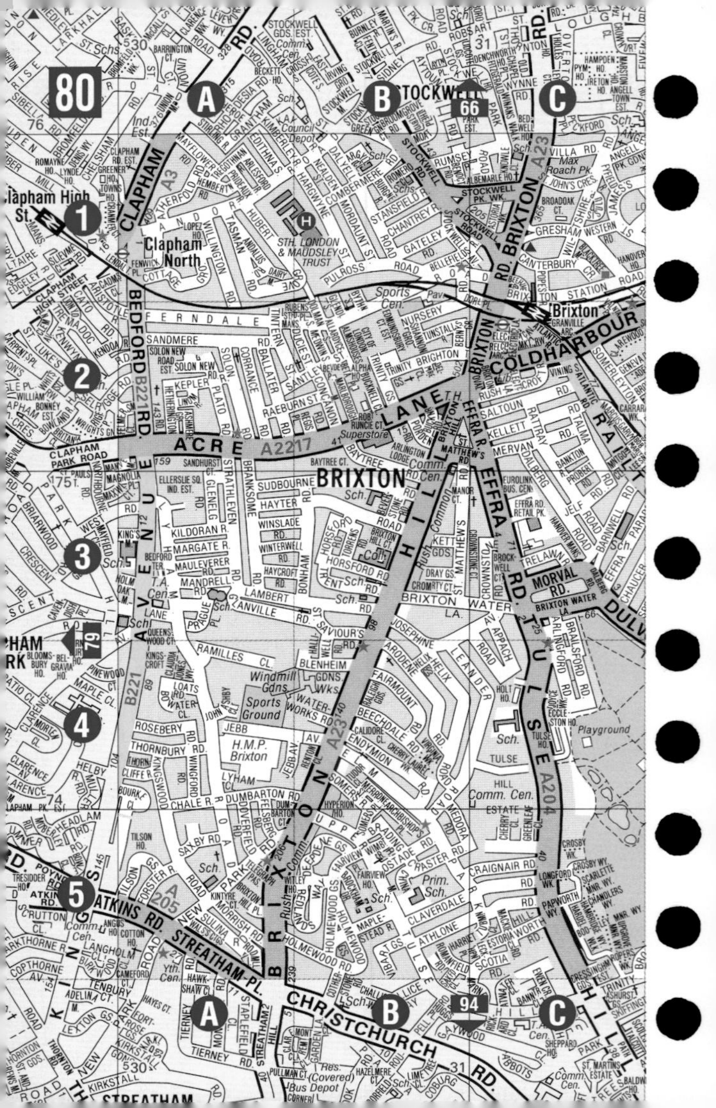

80
A
B
C
STOCKWELL
66
1
2
3
4
5
79
94
Clapham High St.
Clapham North
CLAPHAM
BEDFORD
B221 RD.
FERNDALE
ACRE LANE A2217
BRIXTON
COLDHARBOUR
BRIXTON RD.
A23
BRIXTON HILL
EFFRA RD.
TULSE HILL
A204
STH. LONDON & MAUDSLEY TRUST
Sports Cen.
Superstore
Windmill Gdns.
Sports Ground
H.M.P. Brixton
Max Roach Pk.
Playground
ATKINS RD.
STREATHAM PL.
CHRISTCHURCH RD.
KING'S AVENUE
STREATHAM

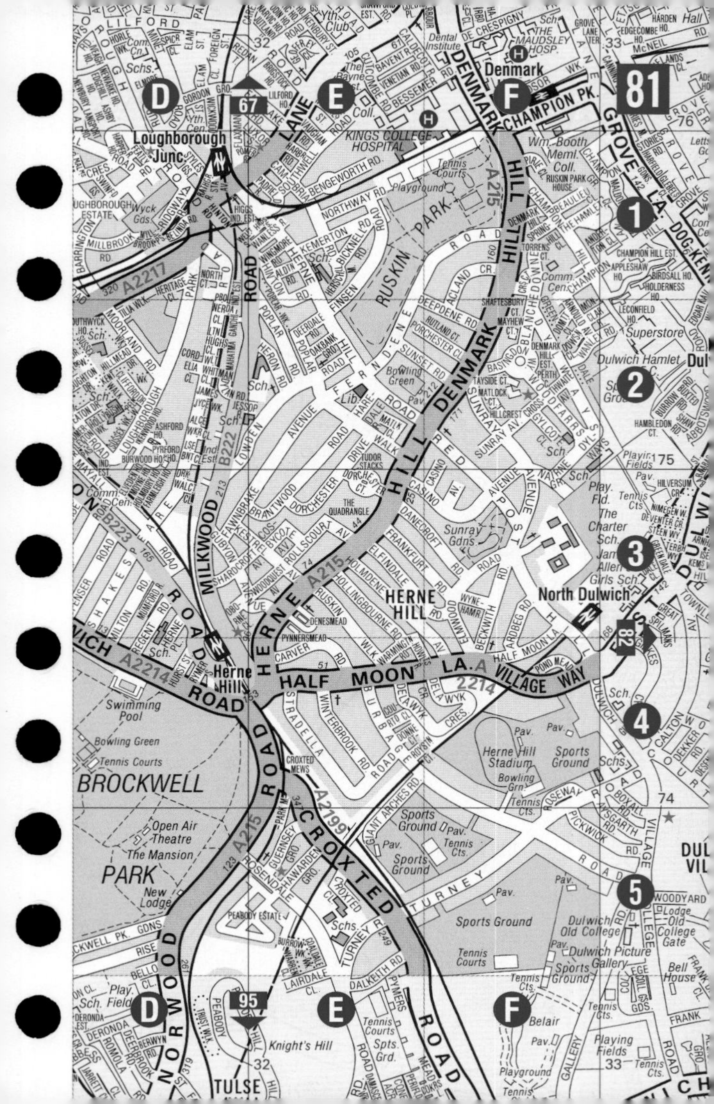

81
D
E
F
1
2
3
4
5
67
82
95
Loughborough Junc.
Denmark Hill
CHAMPION PK.
KINGS COLLEGE HOSPITAL
Dental Institute
DE CRESPIGNY
THE MAUDSLEY HOSP.
Wm. Booth Meml. Coll.
RUSKIN PARK HOUSE
RUSKIN PARK
Tennis Courts
Playground
CHAMPION HILL
CHAMPION HILL EST.
GROVE LA.
DOG KENNEL HILL
Superstore
Dulwich Hamlet F.C.
COLDHARBOUR LANE
HERNE HILL
DENMARK HILL
A215
A2217
A2214
A2199
B222
B223
MILKWOOD ROAD
LOUGHBOROUGH ESTATE
Wyck Gds.
MILLBROOK RD.
BENGEWORTH RD.
NORTHWAY RD.
FERNDENE ROAD
DEEPDENE RD.
SUNSET RD.
Bowling Green
Lib.
RED POST HILL
CASINO AV.
Sunray Gdns.
SUNRAY AV.
NORTH DULWICH
North Dulwich
The Charter Sch.
James Allen's Girls Sch.
Playing Fields
HALF MOON LA.
VILLAGE WAY
Herne Hill
HERNE HILL
DULWICH ROAD
Swimming Pool
Bowling Green
Tennis Courts
BROCKWELL PARK
Open Air Theatre
The Mansion
New Lodge
NORWOOD ROAD
CROXTED ROAD
STRADELLA RD.
WINTERBROOK RD.
BURBAGE ROAD
Herne Hill Stadium
Sports Ground
Bowling Grn.
ROSEWAY
GIANT ARCHES RD.
TURNEY ROAD
Sports Ground
Dulwich Old College
Dulwich Picture Gallery
Old College Gate
Bell House
PEABODY ESTATE
Knight's Hill
TULSE HILL
Belair
Playing Fields
Playground
GALLERY ROAD
DULWICH VILLAGE
COURT LANE
CALTON AV.

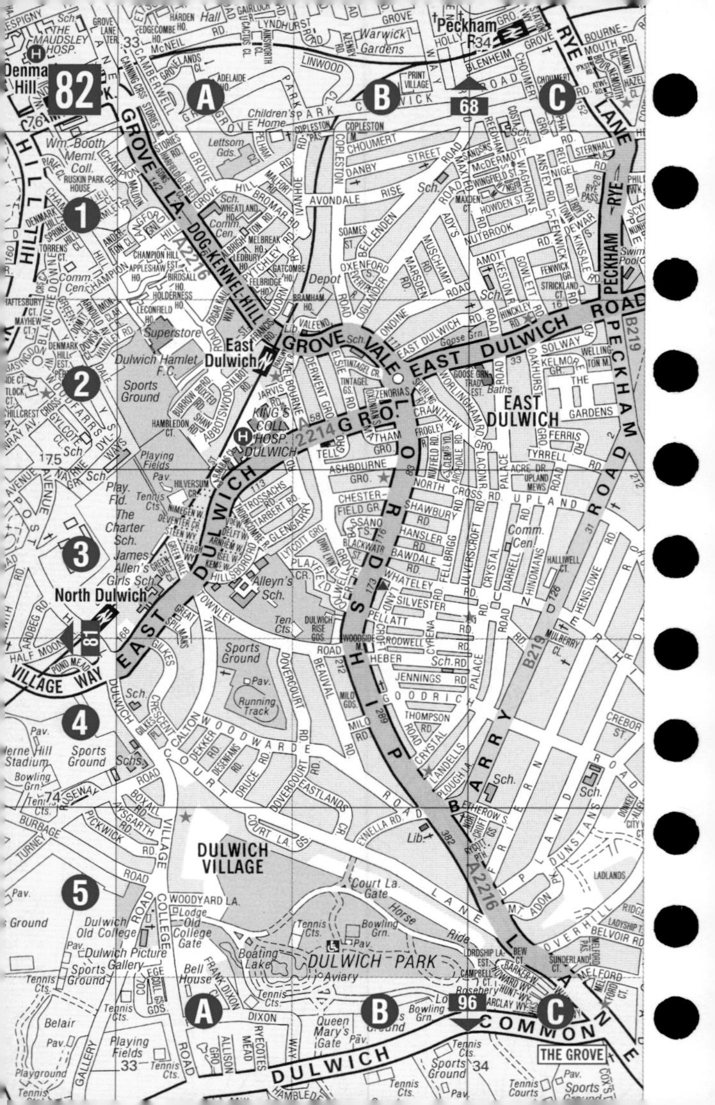
Peckham
East Dulwich
North Dulwich
EAST DULWICH
DULWICH VILLAGE
DULWICH PARK
GROVE LA.
DOG KENNEL HILL
A2216
GROVE VALE
EAST DULWICH ROAD
LORDSHIP LANE
BARRY ROAD
PECKHAM RYE
B219
DULWICH GRO.
A2214
EAST DULWICH GROVE
VILLAGE WAY
COURT LANE
DULWICH COMMON
CALTON AV.
WOODWARDE RD.
GOODRICH RD.
UPLAND ROAD
CRYSTAL PALACE ROAD
NORTH CROSS RD.
OVERHILL RD.
UPLAND RD.
ST. DUNSTANS RD.
AVONDALE RISE
DANBY STREET
CHOUMERT RD.
NUTBROOK ST.
MUSCHAMP ROAD
ONDINE RD.
SOLWAY RD.
THE GARDENS
TYRRELL RD.
CHAMPION HILL
DENMARK HILL
ASHBOURNE GRO.
SHAWBURY RD.
HANSLER RD.
BAWDALE RD.
WHATELEY RD.
SILVESTER RD.
PELLATT RD.
RODWELL RD.
HEBER RD.
JENNINGS RD.
THOMPSON RD.
TROSSACHS RD.
TARBERT RD.
GLENGARRY RD.
KING'S COLL. HOSP. DULWICH
Alleyn's Sch.
James Allen's Girls Sch.
The Charter Sch.
Wm. Booth Meml. Coll.
Dulwich Hamlet F.C.
Sports Ground
Playing Fields
Running Track
Lettsom Gds.
Children's Home
Superstore
Depot
Baths
Comm. Cen.
Lib.
Sch.
Court La. Gate
Horse Ride
Boating Lake
Aviary
Bowling Grn.
Tennis Cts.
Dulwich Old College
Old College Gate
Dulwich Picture Gallery
Bell House
Queen Mary's Gate
THE GROVE
Herne Hill Stadium
Belair
Playground
A
B
C
1
2
3
4
5
68
81
96
33
34

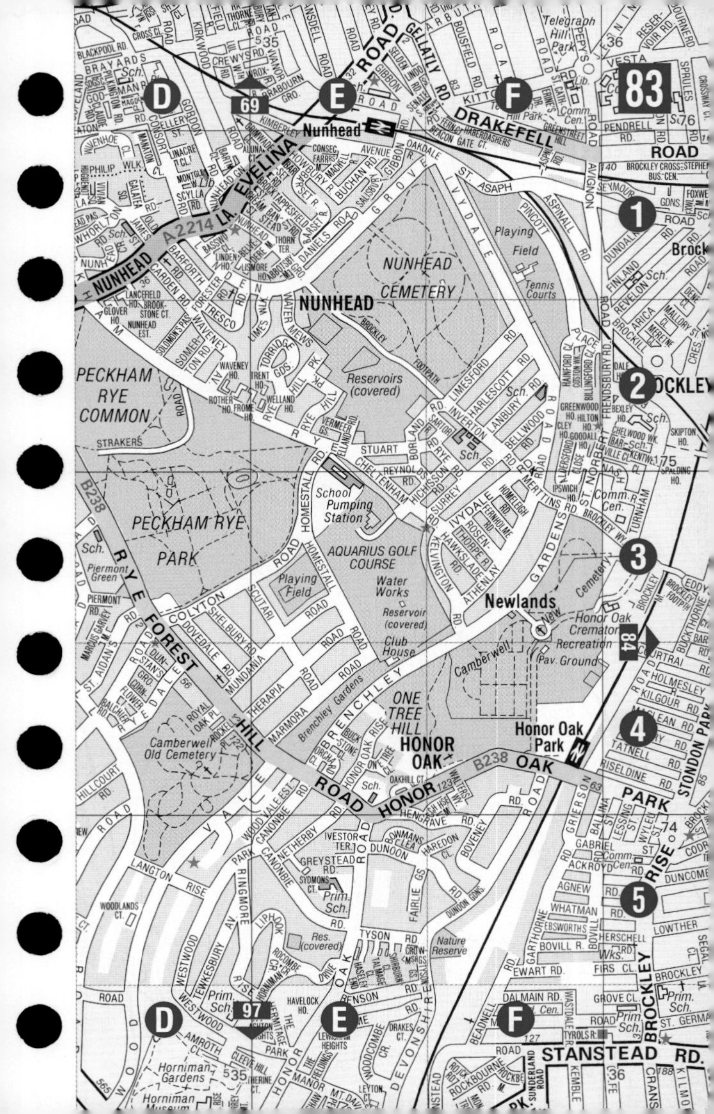

83
D
E
F
69
97
84
1
2
3
4
5
NUNHEAD
NUNHEAD CEMETERY
PECKHAM RYE COMMON
PECKHAM RYE PARK
AQUARIUS GOLF COURSE
ONE TREE HILL
HONOR OAK
Newlands
Honor Oak Park
Nunhead
Camberwell Old Cemetery
Horniman Gardens
Reservoirs (covered)
School Pumping Station
Playing Field
Water Works
Reservoir (covered)
Club House
Honor Oak Crematorium
Recreation Ground
Nature Reserve
Telegraph Hill Park
EVELINA RD.
NUNHEAD LA.
A2214
DRAKEFELL ROAD
FOREST HILL
HONOR OAK ROAD
B238
RYE
STANSTEAD RD.
BROCKLEY RISE
STONDON PARK
BROCKLEY RD.
LINDEN GROVE
ST. ASAPH RD.
IVYDALE RD.
CHELTENHAM RD.
COLYTON RD.
BRENCHLEY GARDENS
WOOD VALE
LANGTON RISE

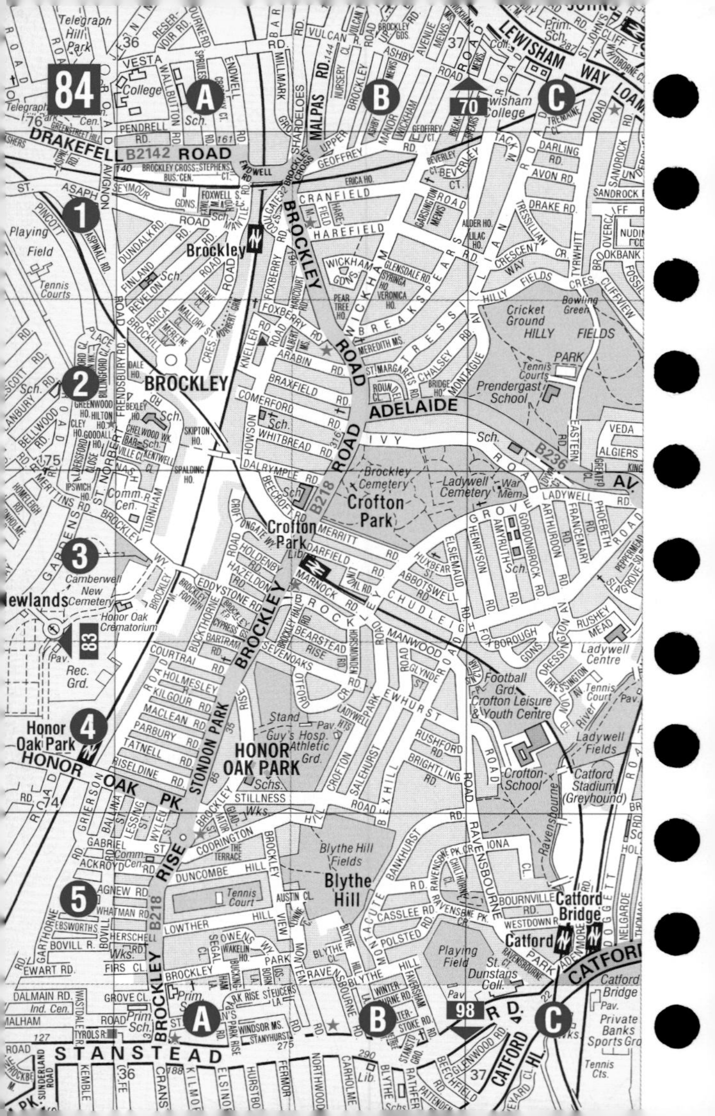

84
A
B
C
1
2
3
4
5
70
83
98
36
37
76
74
75
Telegraph Hill Park
Vesta Rd.
College
Sch.
Drakefell Road
B2142 Road
Brockley Cross Bus. Cen.
Stephens Ct.
Endwell Rd.
Vulcan Rd.
Millmark
Shardeloes
Malpas Rd.
Nursery Cl.
Brockley Mews
Ashby Road
Avenue
Lewisham Way
Lewisham College
Loampit
Prim. Sch.
Upper Geoffrey Rd.
Wickham
Beverley Ct.
Tack Mews
Darling Rd.
Avon Rd.
Drake Rd.
Sandrock
Asaph St.
Pincott
Seymour Gdns.
Foxwell St.
Mantle Rd.
Brockley
Cranfield Rd.
Harefield Rd.
Brockley Road
Playing Field
Tennis Courts
Dundalk Rd.
Finland Revelon Rd.
Arica
Mallory St.
Brockill Cres.
Foxberry Rd.
Wickham Gdns.
Glensdale Rd.
Breakspears Rd.
Tressillian
Crescent Way
Hilly Fields Cres.
Cliffview
Cricket Ground
Hilly Fields
Bowling Green
Park
Tennis Courts
Prendergast School
Brockley
Kneller Rd.
Arabin Rd.
Braxfield Rd.
Comerford Rd.
Whitbread Rd.
Howson
St. Margarets Rd.
Chalsey Rd.
Montague Av.
Adelaide
Ivy Road
B236
Veda
Algiers
Dalrymple Rd.
Beecroft Rd.
Brockley Cemetery
Ladywell Cemetery
War Mem.
Crofton Park
Ladywell Rd.
Grove
Arthurdon Rd.
Francemary Rd.
Phoebeth Road
Merritt
Darfield Rd.
Huxbear St.
Abbotswell
Chudleigh Rd.
Manwood
Foxborough Gdns.
Rushey Mead
Ladywell Centre
Elsiemaud Rd.
Henryson Rd.
Amyruth Sch.
Gordonbrock Rd.
Scott Rd.
Sch.
Bellwood Rd.
Greenwood Ho.
Hilton Ho.
Chelwood Wk.
Skipton Ho.
Spalding Ho.
Mertins Rd.
St. Norbert
Comm. Cen.
Turnham
Ipswich Ho.
Gardens
Camberwell New Cemetery
Honor Oak Crematorium
Newlands
Pav.
Rec. Grd.
Eddystone Rd.
Holdenby Rd.
Hazeldon Rd.
Brockley Footpath
Buckthorne Rd.
Cypress Gdns.
Bartram Rd.
Courtrai Rd.
Holmesley Rd.
Kilgour Rd.
Maclean Rd.
Parbury Rd.
Tatnell Rd.
Riseldine Rd.
Brockley
Standon Park
Bearstead Rise
Sevenoaks
Otford Cr.
Horsmonden Rd.
Marnock Rd.
Brockley Hall Rd.
Glynde St.
Ewhurst
Rushford Rd.
Brightling Rd.
Football Grd.
Crofton Leisure & Youth Centre
Crofton School
Ladywell Fields
Tennis Court
River
Catford Stadium (Greyhound)
Ravensbourne
Honor Oak Park
Honor Oak Pk.
Stand
Pav.
Guy's Hosp. Athletic Grd.
Honor Oak Park
Schs.
Stillness Road
Wks.
Crofton
Salehurst
Bexhill
Grierson
Ballina
Lessing St.
Wyleu St.
Codrington
The Terrace
Gabriel St.
Ackroyd Rd.
Comm. Cen.
Brockley Rise
B218
Duncombe Hill
Tennis Court
Blythe Hill Fields
Blythe Hill
Bankhurst Rd.
Iona Cl.
Ravensbourne Pk.
Montacute Rd.
Casslee Rd.
Polsted Rd.
Bournville Rd.
Westdown Rd.
Catford Bridge
Catford
Playing Field
St. Dunstans Coll.
Agnew Rd.
Whatman Rd.
Ebsworth St.
Herschell Rd.
Bovill Rd.
Garthorne Rd.
Wks.
Ewart Rd.
Firs Cl.
Lowther Hill
Owens Wy.
Austin Cl.
Blythe Hill
Brockley Park
Ravensbourne Rd.
Winter Bourne Rd.
Faversham
Stoke Rd.
Dalmain Rd.
Ind. Cen.
Grove Cl.
Prim. Sch.
Malham Road
Tyrols Rd.
Wastdale Rd.
Windsor Ms.
Stanyhurst
Stanstead Road
Kemble
Cranston
Kilmorie
Elsinore
Hurstbourne
Fermor
Northwood
Carholme
Blythe
Rathfern
Lib.
Schs.
Glenwood Rd.
Beechfield Rd.
Catford Hl.
Catford Rd.
Adenmore
Doggett
Nelgarde
Catford Bridge
Pav.
Private Banks Sports Grd.
Tennis Cts.

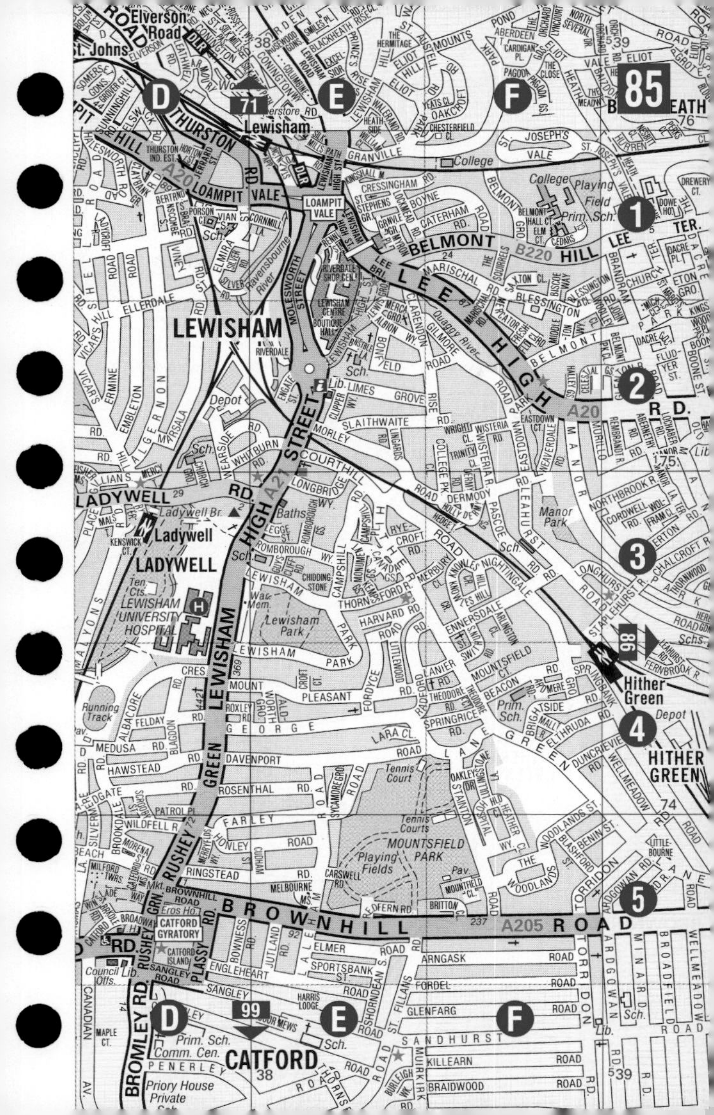
85
71
99
86
D
E
F
1
2
3
4
5
Elverson Road
St. Johns
Lewisham
LEWISHAM
LADYWELL
Ladywell
HITHER GREEN
Hither Green
CATFORD
CATFORD GYRATORY
LOAMPIT VALE
THURSTON RD.
LOAMPIT HILL
A20
A21
B220
A205
BELMONT HILL
LEE HIGH RD.
LEE TER.
LEWISHAM HIGH STREET
MOLESWORTH STREET
LADYWELL RD.
COURTHILL RD.
LEWISHAM PARK
MOUNT PLEASANT RD.
GEORGE LANE
HITHER GREEN LANE
RUSHEY GREEN
BROWNHILL ROAD
BROMLEY RD.
SANDHURST ROAD
TORRIDON ROAD
MANOR PARK
STAPLEHURST RD.
NIGHTINGALE GROVE
LEAHURST RD.
ELLERDALE ST.
VICAR'S HILL
ALGERNON RD.
LIMES GROVE
SLAITHWAITE RD.
GRANVILLE PK.
ST. JOSEPH'S VALE
MOUNTSFIELD PARK
Playing Fields
Lewisham Park
LEWISHAM UNIVERSITY HOSPITAL
LEWISHAM CENTRE
RIVERDALE SHOP. CEN.
Manor Park
Ravensbourne River
Quaggy River
Running Track
Council Offs.
Priory House Private
Prim. Sch.
Comm. Cen.
Depot
College
Baths
Lib.
539
38
76
74
175

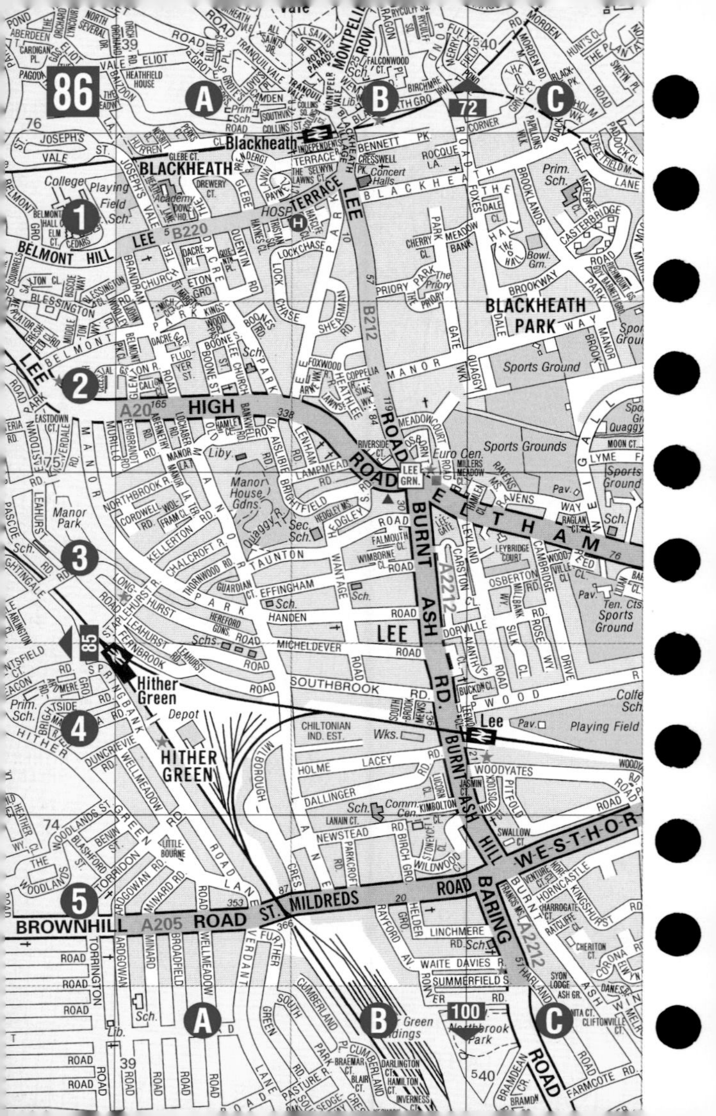

86
A
B
C
72
1
2
3
4
5
85
100
Blackheath
BLACKHEATH
BLACKHEATH PARK
LEE
Lee
Hither Green
HITHER GREEN
Northbrook Park
BELMONT HILL
LEE TERRACE
BLACKHEATH VILLAGE
MONTPELIER ROW
TRANQUIL VALE
ALL SAINTS DR.
ROYAL PARADE
ELIOT VALE
HEATHFIELD HOUSE
ST. JOSEPH'S VALE
GLEBE CT.
DREWERY CT.
BENNETT PK.
CRESSWELL PK.
Concert Halls
ROCQUE LA.
BLACKHEATH
BROOKLANDS
FOXES DALE
THE HALL
Bowl. Grn.
CASTERBRIDGE ROAD
BROOKWAY
PARK WAY
MANOR WAY
Sports Ground
Sports Grounds
Prim. Sch.
Playing Field
College
Sch.
HOSP.
LOCK CHASE
SHEARMAN RD.
B220
B212
A20
HIGH ROAD
LEE HIGH ROAD
A2212
BURNT ASH RD.
BURNT ASH HILL
ELTHAM RD.
LEE GRN.
Euro Cen.
MILLERS MEADOW CL.
RIVERSIDE CT.
LAMPMEAD RD.
Liby.
Manor House Gdns.
Quaggy R.
Sec. Sch.
TAUNTON RD.
EFFINGHAM
HANDEN ROAD
MICHELDEVER ROAD
SOUTHBROOK RD.
MANOR PARK
Manor Park
LEAHURST RD.
STAPLEHURST RD.
FERNBROOK RD.
SPRINGBANK RD.
Depot
CHILTONIAN IND. EST.
Wks.
HOLME LACEY RD.
DALLINGER RD.
NEWSTEAD RD.
Comm. Cen.
KIMBOLTON CL.
WILDWOOD CL.
WOODYATES RD.
SWALLOW CT.
WESTHORNE AV.
BARING ROAD
ST. MILDREDS ROAD
BROWNHILL ROAD
A205
LINCHMERE RD.
WAITE DAVIES RD.
SUMMERFIELD ST.
TORRIDON RD.
MINARD RD.
BROADFIELD RD.
WELLMEADOW RD.
VERDANT LANE
FURTHER GREEN RD.
CUMBERLAND
Lib.
Colfe Sch.
Pav.
Ten. Cts.
COLLINS ST.

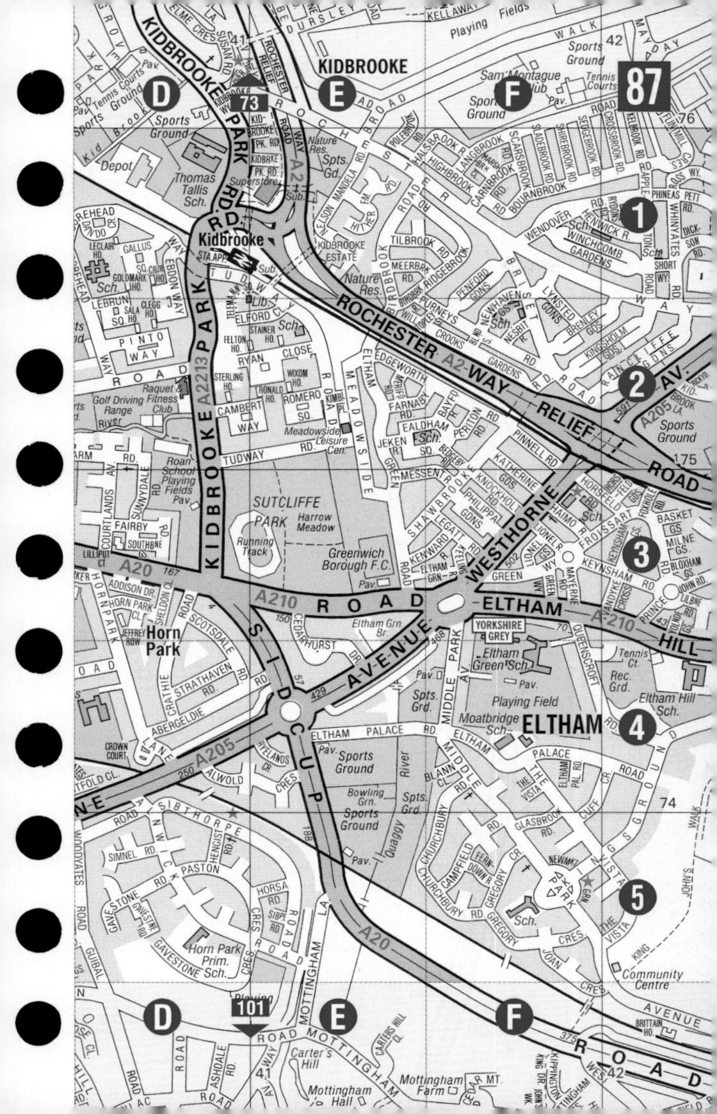
87
73
101
KIDBROOKE
Kidbrooke
ELTHAM
Horn Park
KIDBROOKE PARK RD.
KIDBROOKE PARK ROAD
ROCHESTER WAY
ROCHESTER WAY RELIEF ROAD
A2
A20
A205
A210
A2213
ELTHAM ROAD
WESTHORNE AVENUE
SIDCUP ROAD
ELTHAM HILL
ELTHAM PALACE ROAD
MIDDLE PARK AV.
TUDWAY RD.
SUTCLIFFE PARK
Harrow Meadow
Running Track
Greenwich Borough F.C.
Meadowside Leisure Cen.
Thomas Tallis Sch.
Sam Montague Club
Golf Driving Range
Raquet & Fitness Club
Roan School Playing Fields
YORKSHIRE GREY
Eltham Green Sch.
Moatbridge Sch.
Eltham Hill Sch.
Horn Park Prim. Sch.
Community Centre
Mottingham Farm
Mottingham Hall
Carter's Hill
Quaggy River
Playing Field
Sports Ground
Nature Res.
Superstore
MOTTINGHAM ROAD
COURT ROAD
BRISET WAY
SIBTHORPE ROAD
GAVESTONE RD.
HORN PARK LA.
CEDARHURST DR.
QUEENSCROFT
GLASBROOK RD.
CHURCHBURY RD.
GREGORY CR.
ALWOLD CRES.
LILLIPUT CT.
ADDISON DR.
SCOTSDALE RD.
STRATHAVEN RD.
ABERGELDIE
CROWN COURT
D
E
F
1
2
3
4
5

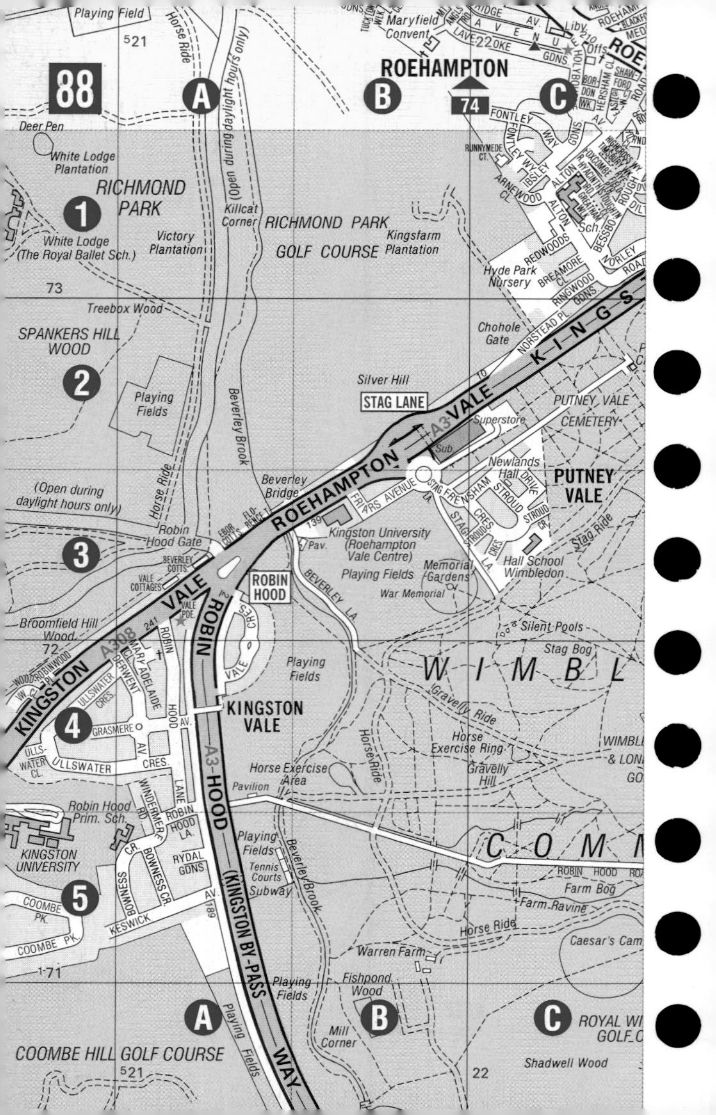
88
ROEHAMPTON
74
RICHMOND PARK
White Lodge Plantation
White Lodge (The Royal Ballet Sch.)
Victory Plantation
Killcat Corner
RICHMOND PARK GOLF COURSE
Kingsfarm Plantation
Treebox Wood
SPANKERS HILL WOOD
Playing Fields
Beverley Brook
Silver Hill
STAG LANE
ROEHAMPTON VALE
KINGSTON VALE
PUTNEY VALE
PUTNEY VALE CEMETERY
Superstore
Kingston University (Roehampton Vale Centre)
Robin Hood Gate
ROBIN HOOD
Memorial Gardens
War Memorial
Hall School Wimbledon
Silent Pools
Stag Bog
WIMBL
Gravelly Ride
Horse Exercise Ring
Gravelly Hill
Horse Exercise Area
Broomfield Hill Wood
A3 ROBIN HOOD (KINGSTON BY-PASS) WAY
Robin Hood Prim. Sch.
KINGSTON UNIVERSITY
COMM
Farm Bog
Farm Ravine
Horse Ride
Warren Farm
Fishpond Wood
Mill Corner
Caesar's Camp
ROYAL WI GOLF C
Shadwell Wood
COOMBE HILL GOLF COURSE
Hyde Park Nursery
Chohole Gate
Deer Pen

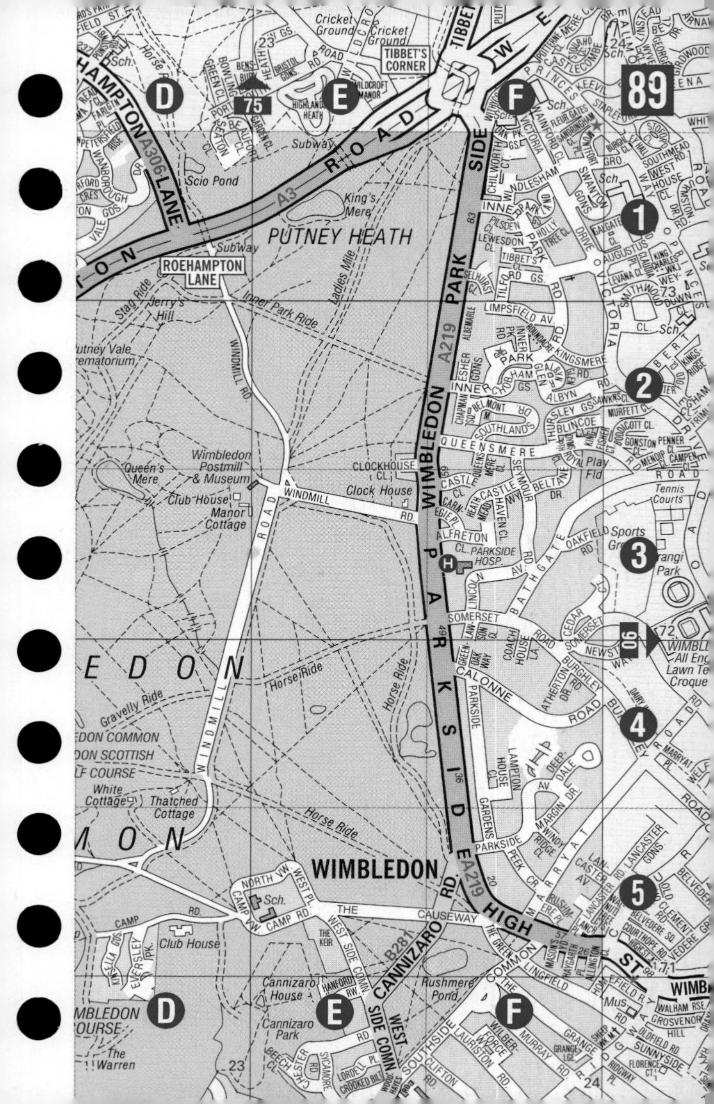
PUTNEY HEATH
WIMBLEDON
TIBBET'S CORNER
ROEHAMPTON LANE
Scio Pond
King's Mere
Queen's Mere
Wimbledon Postmill & Museum
Club House
Manor Cottage
Clock House
Putney Vale Crematorium
Jerry's Hill
Inner Park Ride
Ladies Mile
Horse Ride
Gravelly Ride
White Cottage
Thatched Cottage
PARKSIDE HOSP.
Rushmere Pond
Cannizaro House
Cannizaro Park
The Warren
WIMBLEDON PARK SIDE
WINDMILL RD.
CANNIZARO RD.
HIGH ST.
THE CAUSEWAY
Sports Gr
Tennis Courts
Play Fld
Mus.

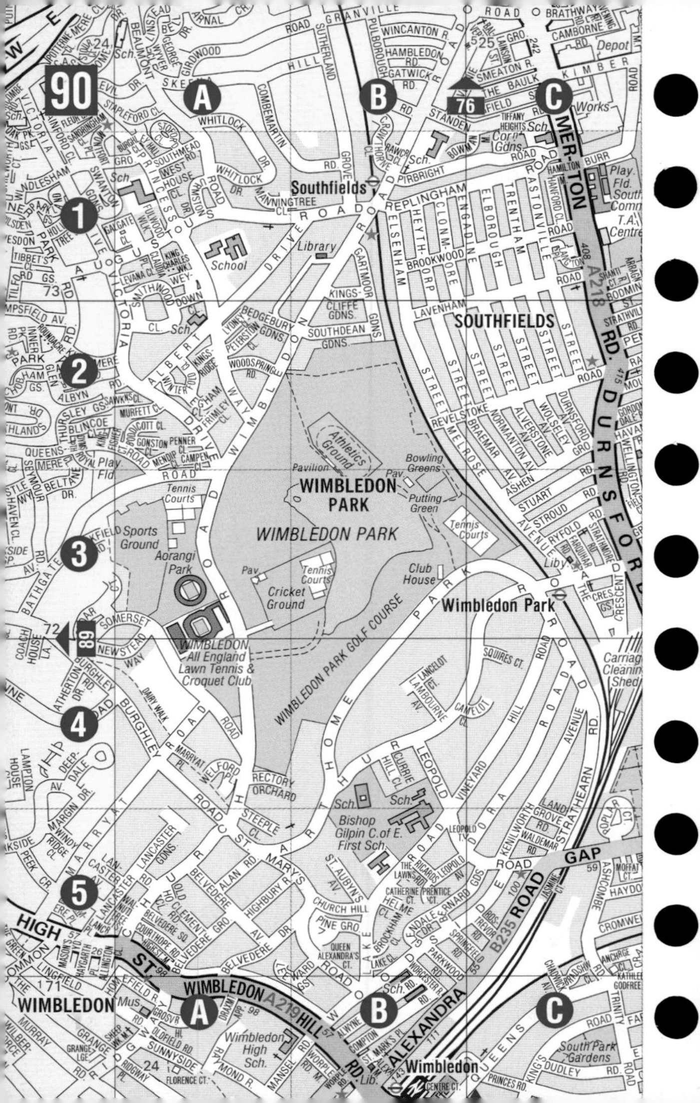
90
A
B
C
76
72
89
1
2
3
4
5
GRANVILLE
ROAD
BRATHWAY
CAMBORNE
Depot
KIMBER
ROAD
WINCANTON R.
HAMBLEDON RD.
GATWICK RD.
SUTHERLAND
PULBOROUGH
HILL
GIRDWOOD
SKEENA
BEAUMONT
Sch.
WHITLOCK DR.
COMBEMARTIN
STANDEN
SMEATON R.
THE BAULK
Works
TIFFANY HEIGHTS
Corn' Gdns.
BOWMAN
MERTON
BURR
Play. Fld.
T.A. Centre
Southfields
MANNINGTREE CL.
PIRBRIGHT
REPLINGHAM
ELSENHAM
CLONMORE
ENGADINE
ELBOROUGH
TRENTHAM
ASTONVILLE
BROOKWOOD
LAVENHAM
SOUTHFIELDS
A218
DURNSFORD RD.
Library
School
PRINCESS
AUGUSTUS
VICTORIA
WEST HOUSE CL.
SOUTHMEAD
KING CHARLES WK.
WEYDOWN CL.
SMITHWOOD
KINGSCLIFFE GDNS.
GARTMOOR GDNS.
BEDGEBURY GDNS.
SOUTHDEAN GDNS.
WOODSPRING RD.
WIMBLEDON PARK
WIMBLEDON PARK GOLF COURSE
Athletics Ground
Pavilion
Pav.
Bowling Greens
Putting Green
Tennis Courts
Club House
Cricket Ground
Sports Ground
Aorangi Park
WIMBLEDON All England Lawn Tennis & Croquet Club
Wimbledon Park
REVELSTOKE
MELROSE
BRAEMAR
NORMANTON AV.
ALVERSTONE AV.
WOLSELEY AV.
ASHEN
STUART
STROUD
RYFOLD RD.
ARTHUR RD.
HOME PARK RD.
Liby.
THE CRESCENT
Carriage Cleaning Shed
SQUIRES CT.
LANCELOT CT.
LAMBOURNE AV.
CAMELOT CL.
VINEYARD HILL ROAD
LEOPOLD
DORA ROAD
AVENUE
STRATHEARN RD.
KENILWORTH
GROVE RD.
WALDEMAR RD.
GAP ROAD
B235
ALBERT DRIVE
EGHAM CL.
FRIMLEY CL.
QUEENSMERE RD.
BELTANE DR.
BATHGATE RD.
SOMERSET RD.
NEWSTEAD WAY
BURGHLEY RD.
DAIRY WALK
MARRYAT RD.
WELFORD PL.
RECTORY ORCHARD
STEEPLE CL.
ST. MARY'S RD.
CHURCH RD.
Bishop Gilpin C.of E. First Sch.
CURRIE HILL CL.
LANCASTER GDNS.
ALAN RD.
BELVEDERE GRO.
HIGHBURY R.
ST. AUBYN'S AV.
CHURCH HILL
PINE GRO.
QUEEN ALEXANDRA'S CT.
HIGH ST.
WIMBLEDON HILL RD.
A219
WIMBLEDON
Mus.
ALEXANDRA RD.
QUEENS RD.
Wimbledon High Sch.
South Park Gardens
DUDLEY RD.
PRINCES RD.
Wimbledon
CENTRE CT.
MARGIN DR.
LAMPTON HOUSE
DEEPDALE
ATHERTON DR.
COACH HOUSE LA.

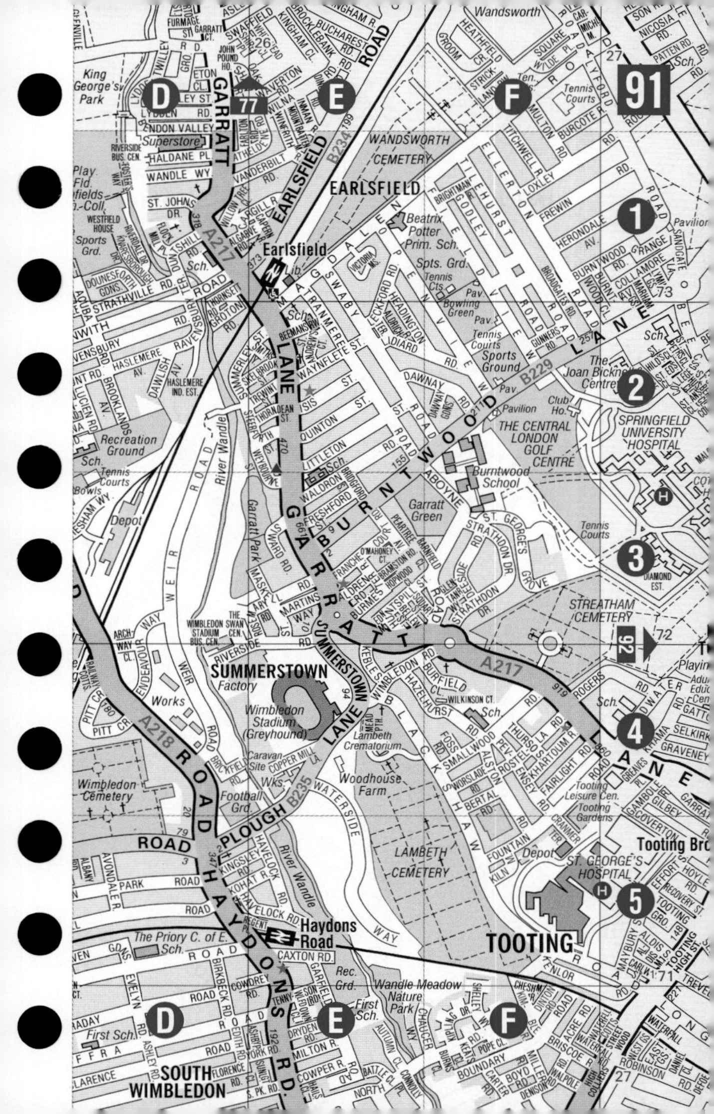

91
77
92
D
E
F
1
2
3
4
5
Wandsworth
King George's Park
Superstore
WANDSWORTH CEMETERY
EARLSFIELD
Earlsfield
GARRATT LANE
EARLSFIELD ROAD
BURNTWOOD LANE
Beatrix Potter Prim. Sch.
The Joan Bicknell Centre
SPRINGFIELD UNIVERSITY HOSPITAL
THE CENTRAL LONDON GOLF CENTRE
Burntwood School
Garratt Green
Garratt Park
Recreation Ground
River Wandle
WEIR ROAD
STREATHAM CEMETERY
SUMMERSTOWN
Wimbledon Stadium (Greyhound)
Lambeth Crematorium
Woodhouse Farm
LAMBETH CEMETERY
BLACKSHAW ROAD
Wimbledon Cemetery
PLOUGH LANE
HAYDONS ROAD
Haydons Road
Wandle Meadow Nature Park
ST. GEORGE'S HOSPITAL
TOOTING
Tooting Leisure Cen.
Tooting Gardens
SOUTH WIMBLEDON
The Priory C. of E. Sch.
A217
A218
B229
B234
B235

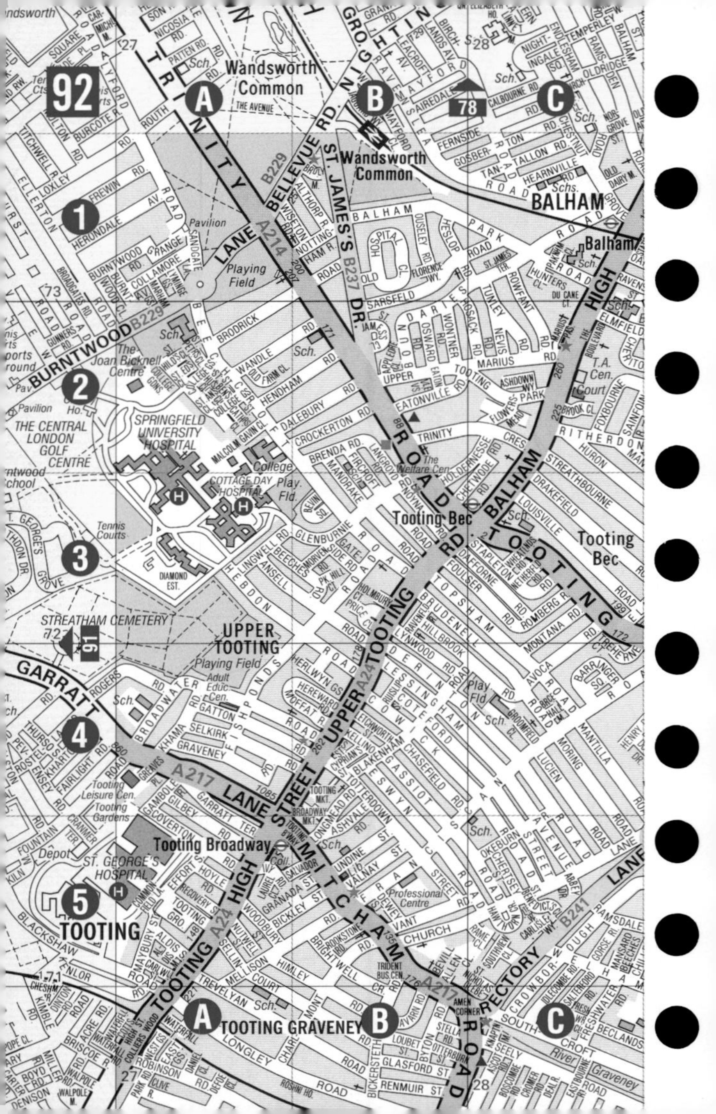
92
Wandsworth Common
Wandsworth Common
BALHAM
Balham
TRINITY ROAD
BELLEVUE RD.
ST. JAMES'S DR.
BALHAM PARK ROAD
BURNTWOOD LANE
SPRINGFIELD UNIVERSITY HOSPITAL
COTTAGE DAY HOSPITAL
THE CENTRAL LONDON GOLF CENTRE
STREATHAM CEMETERY
UPPER TOOTING
Tooting Bec
Tooting Bec
UPPER TOOTING ROAD
BALHAM HIGH ROAD
TOOTING BEC RD.
GARRATT LANE
Tooting Leisure Cen.
Tooting Gardens
Tooting Broadway
ST. GEORGE'S HOSPITAL
TOOTING
TOOTING HIGH STREET
MITCHAM ROAD
Professional Centre
TOOTING GRAVENEY
RECTORY LANE
AMEN CORNER
River Graveney
78
91
A
B
C
1
2
3
4
5
27
28
A214
A24
A217
B229
B237
B241

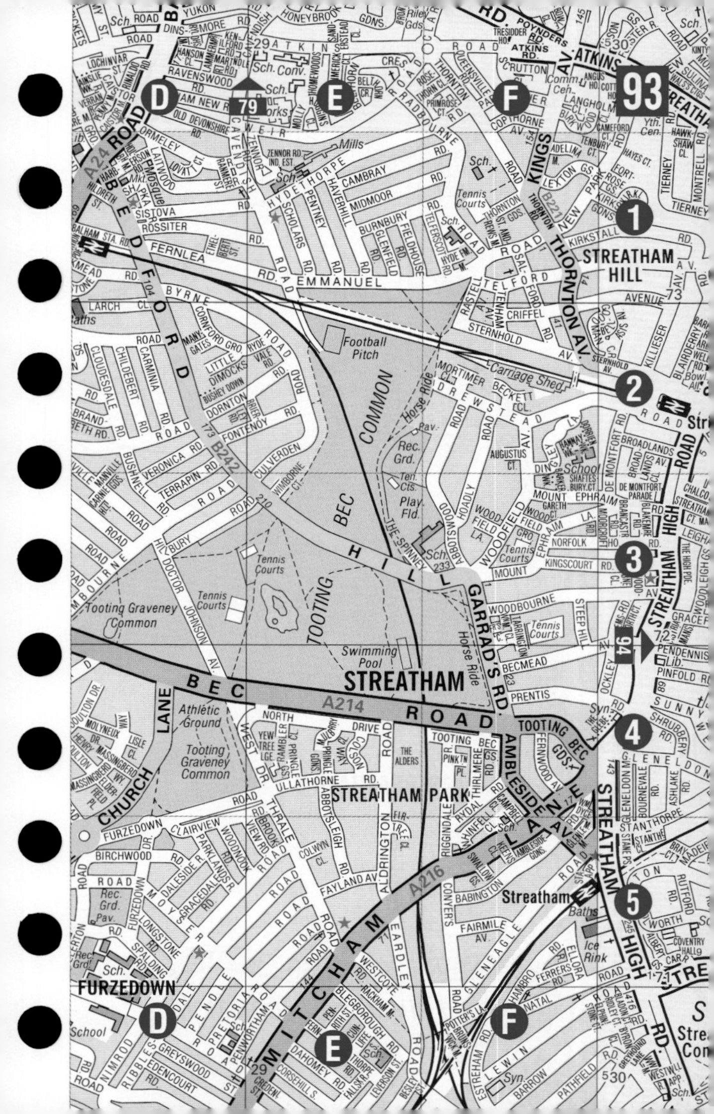

93
79
94
D
E
F
1
2
3
4
5
STREATHAM HILL
STREATHAM
STREATHAM PARK
FURZEDOWN
Streatham
TOOTING BEC COMMON
Tooting Graveney Common
Athletic Ground
Football Pitch
Swimming Pool
Tennis Courts
Rec. Grd.
Play Fld.
Horse Ride
Carriage Shed
Ice Rink
Baths
Mills
BEDFORD ROAD
A24
B242
A214
A216
BEC ROAD
BEC HILL
TOOTING BEC ROAD
CHURCH LANE
MITCHAM ROAD
MITCHAM LANE
GARRAD'S RD.
AMBLESIDE AV.
STREATHAM HIGH ROAD
KINGS AV.
THORNTON AV.
B221
EMMANUEL ROAD
TELFORD ROAD
STERNHOLD AV.
DREWSTEAD ROAD
MOUNT EPHRAIM RD.
WOODBOURNE AV.
BECMEAD AV.
PRENTIS RD.
FURZEDOWN DR.
MOYSER ROAD
ALDRINGTON RD.
EARDLEY ROAD
RAVENSWOOD RD.
HYDETHORPE RD.
CAMBRAY RD.
MIDMOOR RD.
BURNBURY RD.
FERNLEA RD.
ELMFIELD ROAD
CULVERDEN ROAD
VERONICA RD.
TERRAPIN RD.
FONTENOY RD.
ULLATHORNE RD.
THRALE ROAD
ABBOTSWOOD RD.
WOODFIELD AV.
NORFOLK HO. RD.
KINGSCOURT RD.
STEEP HILL
GLENELDON RD.
FAIRMILE AV.
GLENEAGLE RD.
BABINGTON RD.
RIGGINDALE RD.
PENDENNIS RD.
SUNNYHILL RD.
SHRUBBERY RD.
STANTHORPE RD.
BLEGBOROUGH RD.
DAHOMEY RD.
GREYSWOOD ST.
EDENCOURT RD.
NIMROD RD.
ESTREHAM RD.
LEWIN RD.
PATHFIELD RD.

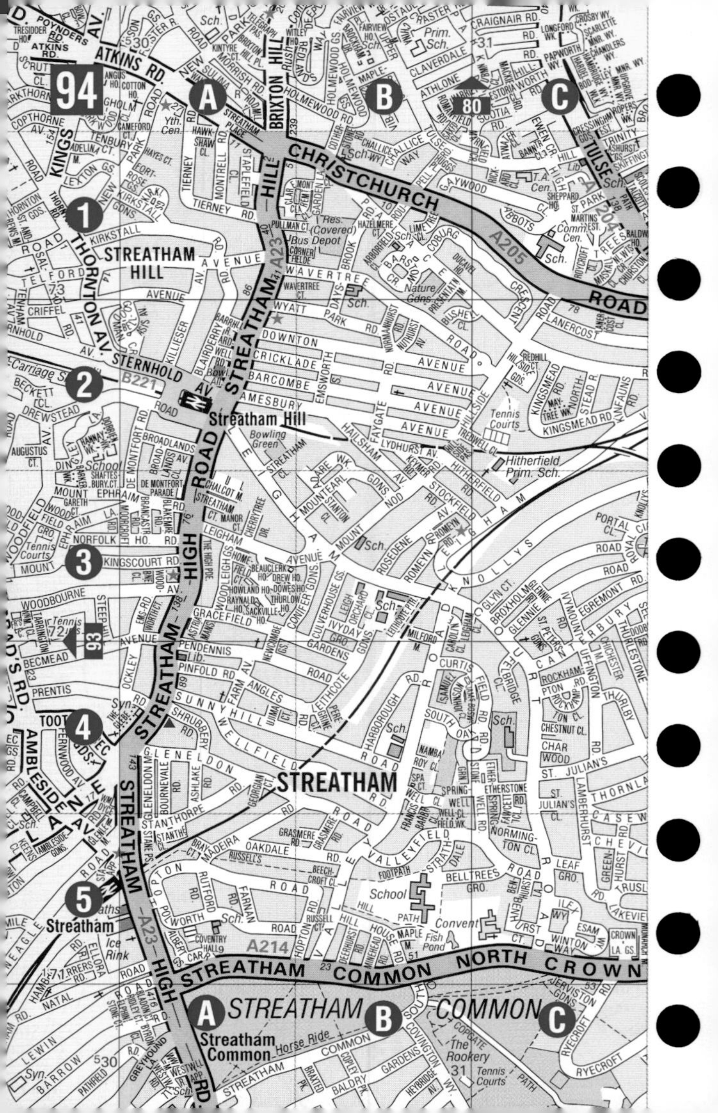
94
A
B
C
1
2
3
4
5
80
93
STREATHAM HILL
Streatham Hill
STREATHAM
Streatham
Streatham Common
STREATHAM COMMON
ATKINS RD.
POYNDERS RD.
KINGS AV.
THORNTON AV.
THORNTON RD.
KIRKSTALL RD.
KIRKSTALL GDNS.
TELFORD AV.
STERNHOLD AV.
B221
CHRISTCHURCH ROAD
A205
BRIXTON HILL
STREATHAM HILL
A23
STREATHAM HIGH ROAD
STREATHAM PLACE
HOLMEWOOD RD.
HOLMEWOOD GDNS.
TULSE HILL
A204
TIERNEY RD.
WAVERTREE RD.
WYATT PARK RD.
DOWNTON AVENUE
CRICKLADE AVENUE
BARCOMBE AVENUE
AMESBURY AVENUE
EMSWORTH ST.
FAYGATE RD.
HAILSHAM AV.
LYDHURST AV.
LEIGHAM AVENUE
LEIGHAM COURT RD.
MOUNT NOD RD.
MOUNT EARL GDNS.
ROMEYN RD.
ROSEDENE AV.
STOCKFIELD RD.
HITHERFIELD RD.
Hitherfield Prim. Sch.
KNOLLYS ROAD
KINGSMEAD RD.
LANERCOST RD.
PALACE ROAD
COBURG CRESCENT
HILLSIDE RD.
Tennis Courts
Bowling Green
BROADLANDS AV.
DE MONTFORT RD.
EPHRAIM RD.
NORFOLK HO. RD.
KINGSCOURT RD.
MOUNT EPHRAIM LA.
WOODBOURNE AV.
PENDENNIS RD.
PINFOLD RD.
ANGLES RD.
SUNNYHILL RD.
WELLFIELD ROAD
GLENELDON RD.
BOURNEVALE RD.
ASHLAKE RD.
STANTHORPE RD.
GRACEFIELD GDNS.
CONIFER GDNS.
CULVERHOUSE GDNS.
IVYDAY GROVE
GARDENS ROAD
LEITHCOTE GDNS.
HARBOROUGH RD.
VALLEY ROAD
VALLEYFIELD RD.
OAKDALE RD.
MADEIRA RD.
RUSSELL'S FOOTPATH
GRASMERE RD.
ETHERSTONE RD.
NORMINGTON CL.
BELLTREES GRO.
CURTIS FIELD RD.
ST. JULIAN'S FARM RD.
LAMBERHURST RD.
THORNLAW RD.
CASEWICK RD.
CHESTNUT CL.
CHARWOOD
CROWN LA. GDS.
School
Convent
Fish Pond
HOPTON RD.
POLWORTH RD.
RUTFORD RD.
FARNAN RD.
A214
STREATHAM COMMON NORTH
CROWN
ROOKERY
The Rookery
Tennis Courts
Horse Ride
COMMON GARDENS
COVINGTON WAY
COPLEY PK.
BRAXTED PK.
BALDRY GDNS.
HEYBRIDGE AV.
RYECROFT RD.
JERVISTON GDNS.
LEWIN RD.
BARROW RD.
NATAL RD.
ELLORA RD.
GREYHOUND LA.
STREATHAM HIGH RD.
Ice Rink
AMBLESIDE AV.
FERNWOOD AV.
PRENTIS RD.
BECMEAD AV.
OCKLEY RD.
Syn.
Lib.
Sch.
Bus Depot
Res. (Covered)
Nature Gdns.
Comm. Cen.
Yth. Cen.
T.A. Cen.
Baths
30
31
530
73
72

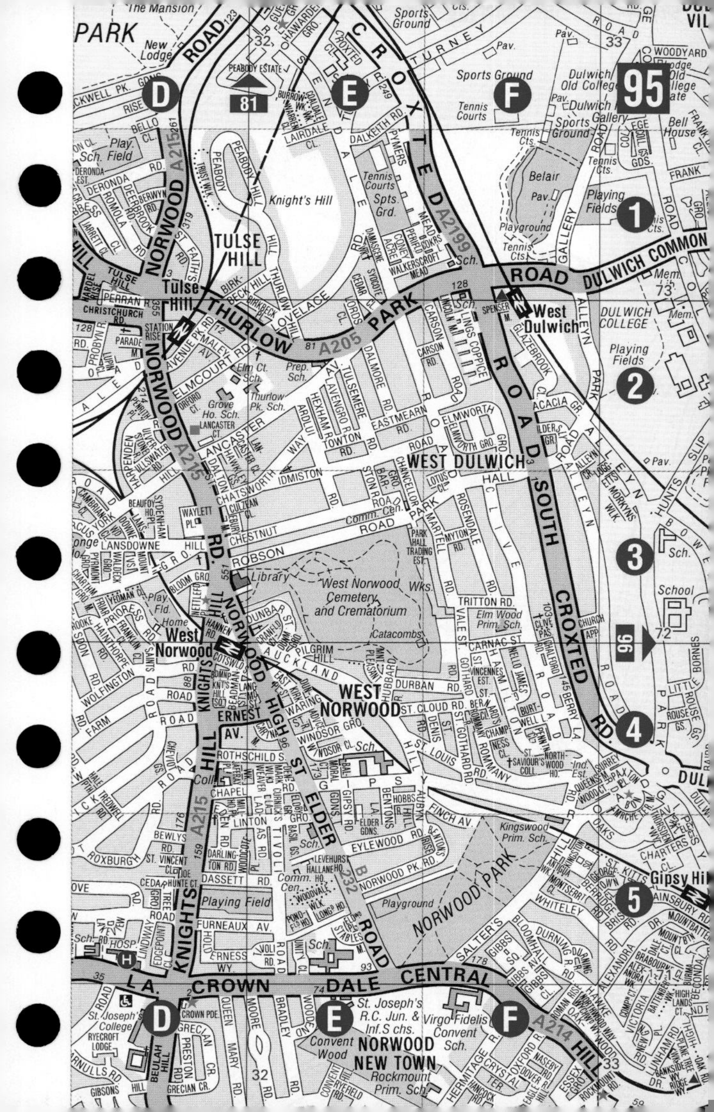
95
PARK
New Lodge
ROAD
PEABODY ESTATE
81
D
E
F
CROXTED
TURNEY
Sports Ground
Tennis Courts
Dulwich Old College
Dulwich Gallery
Bell House
WOODYARD
FRANK
Play. Sch. Field
DERONDA
NORWOOD
A215
Knight's Hill
TULSE HILL
Tulse Hill
Belair
Playing Fields
1
Playground
DULWICH COMMON
ROAD
CROXTED
DA2199
THURLOW PARK
A205
West Dulwich
DULWICH COLLEGE
Playing Fields
2
CHRISTCHURCH RD.
ELMCOURT RD.
Elm Ct. Sch.
Prep. Sch.
Thurlow Pk. Sch.
Grove Ho. Sch.
LANCASTER
TULSEMERE
DALMORE
CARSON RD.
EASTMEARN RD.
ELMWORTH
ACACIA GR.
WEST DULWICH
SOUTH CROXTED ROAD
ALLEYN PARK
IDMISTON
CHATSWORTH WAY
HALL
HUNTS SLIP
CHESTNUT ROAD
ROBSON
LANSDOWNE HILL
3
Library
West Norwood Cemetery and Crematorium
Catacombs
Elm Wood Prim. Sch.
School
West Norwood
96
72
AUCKLAND
PILGRIM HILL
WEST NORWOOD
DURBAN RD.
ST. CLOUD RD.
4
WOLFINGTON
KNIGHTS HILL
HIGH ST
ELDER
GIPSY RD.
ROTHSCHILD S.
ST. LOUIS
FINCH AV.
Kingswood Prim. Sch.
NORWOOD PARK
EYLEWOOD RD.
NORWOOD PK. RD.
ROXBURGH
Playing Field
Playground
Gipsy Hill
5
B232
ROAD
FURNEAUX AV.
CROWN DALE CENTRAL HILL
A214
35
74
St. Joseph's College
CROWN PDE.
St. Joseph's R.C. Jun. & Inf.S chs.
Virgo Fidelis Convent Sch.
Convent Wood
NORWOOD NEW TOWN
Rockmount Prim. Sch.
BEULAH HILL
GRECIAN CR.
33
32

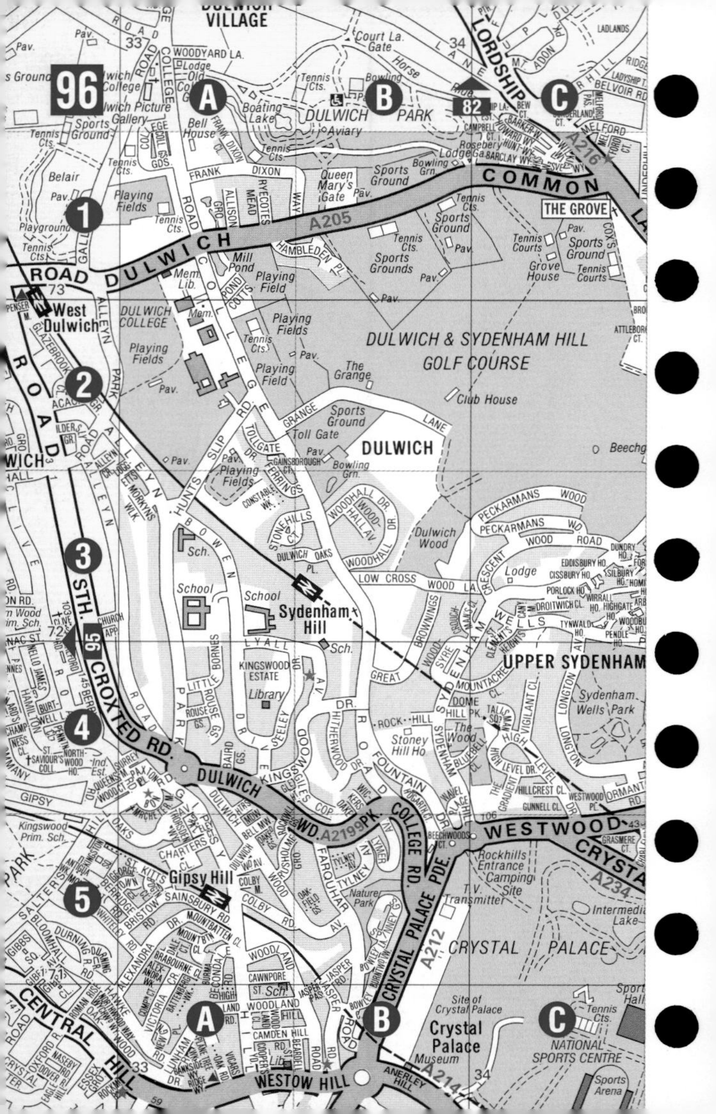
96
DULWICH VILLAGE
Court La. Gate
LORDSHIP LANE
Horse Ride
82
DULWICH PARK
Boating Lake
Aviary
Bell House
FRANK DIXON WAY
Queen Mary's Gate
Sports Ground
Bowling Grn.
COMMON
A216
THE GROVE
A205
DULWICH ROAD
Belair
Playing Fields
Tennis Cts.
Pav.
Playground
West Dulwich
DULWICH COLLEGE
Mem. Lib.
Mill Pond
Playing Field
HAMBLEDEN PL.
Sports Grounds
Grove House
Tennis Courts
DULWICH & SYDENHAM HILL
GOLF COURSE
The Grange
Club House
COLLEGE RD.
GRANGE LANE
Toll Gate
DULWICH
TOLLGATE DR.
Bowling Grn.
HUNTS SLIP RD.
ALLEYN PARK
ALLEYN RD.
Dulwich Wood
PECKARMANS WOOD
WOOD ROAD
LOW CROSS WOOD LA.
DULWICH OAKS PL.
WOODHALL DR.
BOWEN DR.
Sch.
School
Sydenham Hill
Lodge
UPPER SYDENHAM
SYDENHAM HILL
KINGSWOOD ESTATE
Library
KINGSWOOD DR.
SEELEY DR.
GREAT BROWNINGS
MOUNTACRE CL.
DOME HILL PK.
ROCK HILL
Stoney Hill Ho.
The Wood
Sydenham Wells Park
LONGTON AV.
HIGH LEVEL DR.
HILLCREST CL.
WESTWOOD PL.
FOUNTAIN DR.
CROXTED RD.
STH. CROXTED ROAD
95
DULWICH WD. A2199 PK.
COLLEGE RD.
WESTWOOD HILL
A234
CRYSTAL PALACE PDE.
Rockhills Entrance
Camping Site
T.V. Transmitter
Intermediate Lake
A212
CRYSTAL PALACE
Kingswood Prim. Sch.
GIPSY HILL
Gipsy Hill
SAINSBURY RD.
COLBY RD.
WOODLAND RD.
FARQUHAR RD.
Nature Park
Site of Crystal Palace
Crystal Palace Museum
NATIONAL SPORTS CENTRE
Sports Arena
CENTRAL HILL
WESTOW HILL
ANERLEY HILL
A214
ALEXANDRA DR.
A
B
C
1
2
3
4
5
33
34

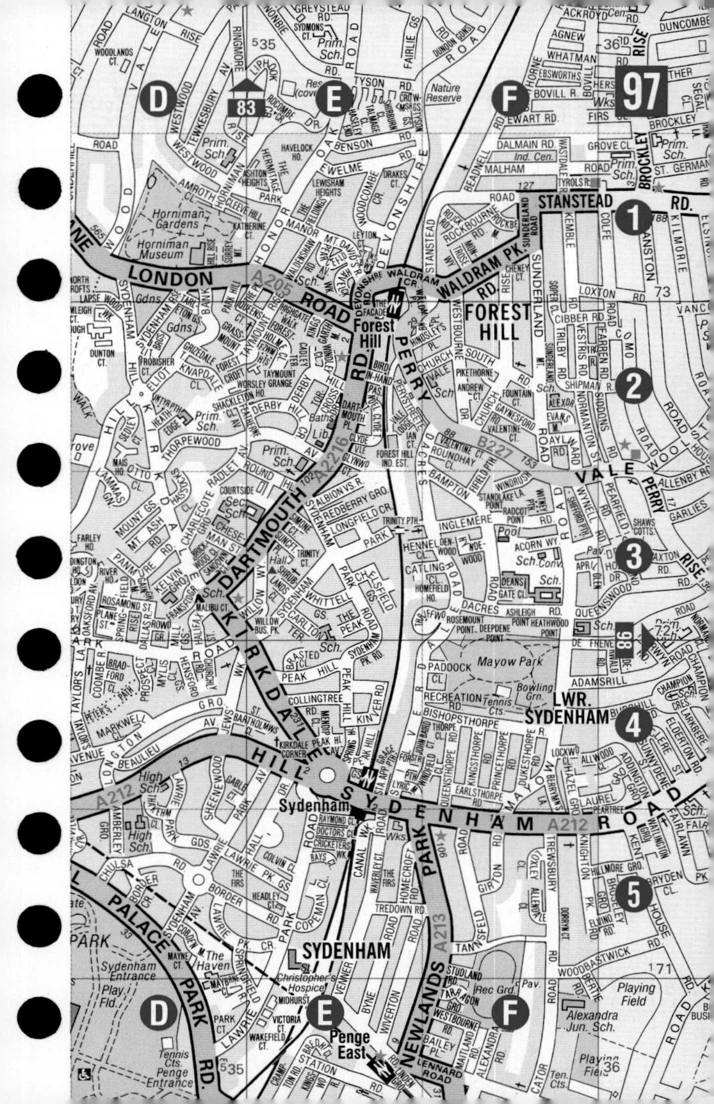

97
D
E
F
1
2
3
4
5
83
98
72
535
36
73
171
FOREST HILL
Forest Hill
LWR. SYDENHAM
SYDENHAM
Sydenham
Penge East
LONDON ROAD
A205
DARTMOUTH RD.
A2216
KIRKDALE
SYDENHAM HILL
SYDENHAM ROAD
A212
PERRY VALE
B227
PERRY RISE
WALDRAM PK. RD.
WALDRAM CR.
DEVONSHIRE RD.
STANSTEAD RD.
SUNDERLAND ROAD
BROCKLEY RISE
BROCKLEY RD.
DACRES ROAD
SILVERDALE
NEWLANDS PARK
A213
SYDENHAM PARK
PALACE RD.
CRYSTAL PALACE PARK
LAWRIE PARK RD.
WESTWOOD PARK
HONOR OAK RD.
Horniman Gardens
Horniman Museum
Nature Reserve
Mayow Park
Bowling Grn.
Tennis Cts.
Rec Grd.
Playing Field
Alexandra Jun. Sch.
St. Christopher's Hospice
Sydenham Entrance
Penge Entrance
Play. Fld.
The Haven
High Sch.
Prim. Sch.
Sec. Sch.
Baths
Lib.
Pool
Ind. Cen.
FOREST HILL IND. EST.
THE FACADE
TRINITY PTH.
KIRKDALE CORNER
STATION RD.
LENNARD ROAD

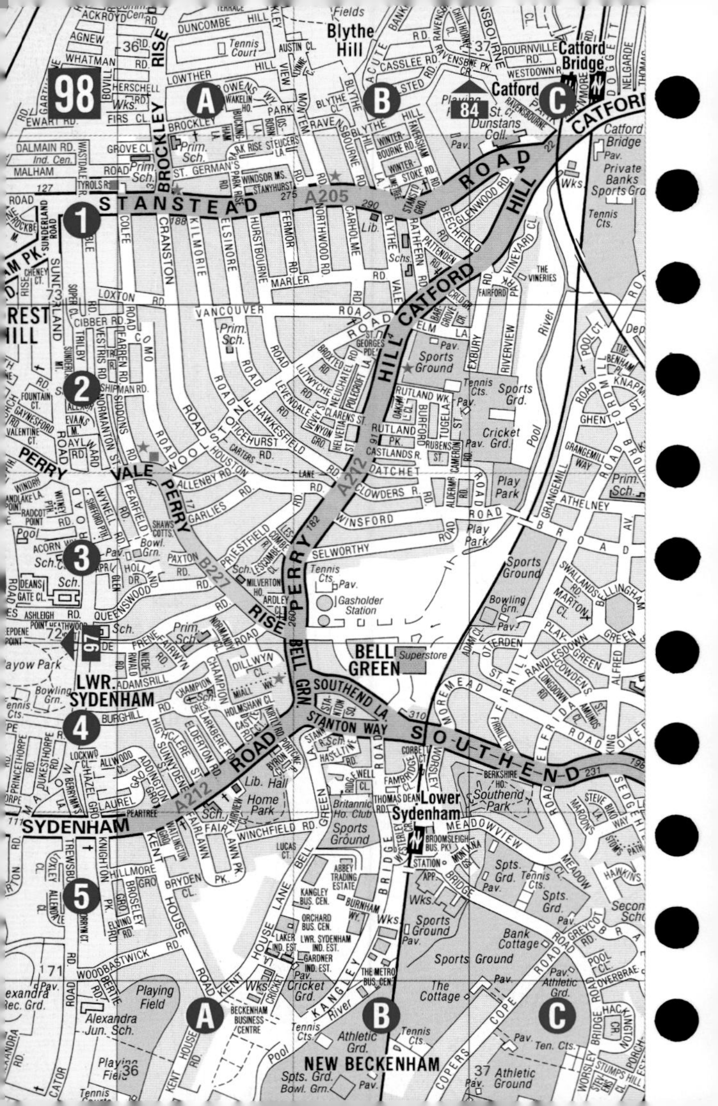
98
Blythe Hill
Catford Bridge
Catford
84
St. Dunstans Coll.
A
B
C
1
2
3
4
5
STANSTEAD ROAD
A205
CATFORD HILL
CATFORD
FOREST HILL
PERRY VALE
PERRY RISE
B227
PERRY HILL
A212
BELL GREEN
SOUTHEND LA.
STANTON WAY
SOUTHEND ROAD
LWR. SYDENHAM
SYDENHAM
SYDENHAM ROAD
Lower Sydenham
Southend Park
NEW BECKENHAM
Gasholder Station
Superstore
Sports Ground
Cricket Grd.
Play Park
Home Park
Mayow Park
Playing Field
Alexandra Rec. Grd.
Alexandra Jun. Sch.
Bank Cottage
The Cottage
Athletic Grd.
Athletic Ground
Private Banks Sports Grd.
River Pool
BROCKLEY RISE
BROCKLEY
BROADWAY
BELLINGHAM
KANGLEY BRIDGE RD.
BELL GREEN LANE
HOUSE
WOOLSTONE ROAD
HAWKESFIELD RD.
VANCOUVER ROAD
WINSFORD ROAD
SELWORTHY ROAD
MOREMEAD
FIRHILL
ELFRIDA
MEADOWVIEW
COPERS COPE ROAD
GREYCOT RD.
WOODBASTWICK RD.
BECKENHAM BUSINESS CENTRE
LWR. SYDENHAM IND. EST.
ABBEY TRADING ESTATE
36
37
72
97
171

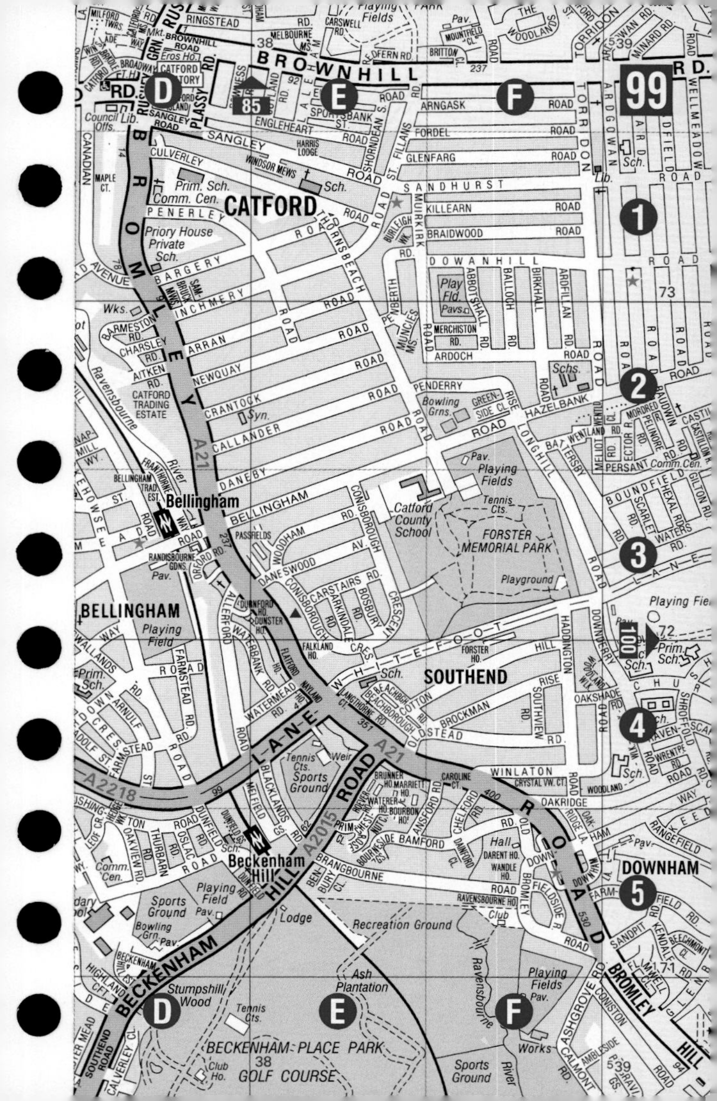

99
85
100
D
E
F
1
2
3
4
5
CATFORD
BELLINGHAM
SOUTHEND
DOWNHAM
BROWNHILL RD.
BROMLEY ROAD
A21
A2218
A2015
Bellingham
Beckenham Hill
Catford County School
FORSTER MEMORIAL PARK
Recreation Ground
BECKENHAM PLACE PARK
GOLF COURSE
Ash Plantation
Stumpshill Wood
Priory House Private Sch.
CATFORD TRADING ESTATE
Ravensbourne
River
WHITEFOOT LANE
BECKENHAM HILL
BROMLEY HILL
SANGLEY ROAD
SANDHURST ROAD
DOWANHILL ROAD
TORRIDON ROAD
LONGHILL ROAD
BELLINGHAM ROAD

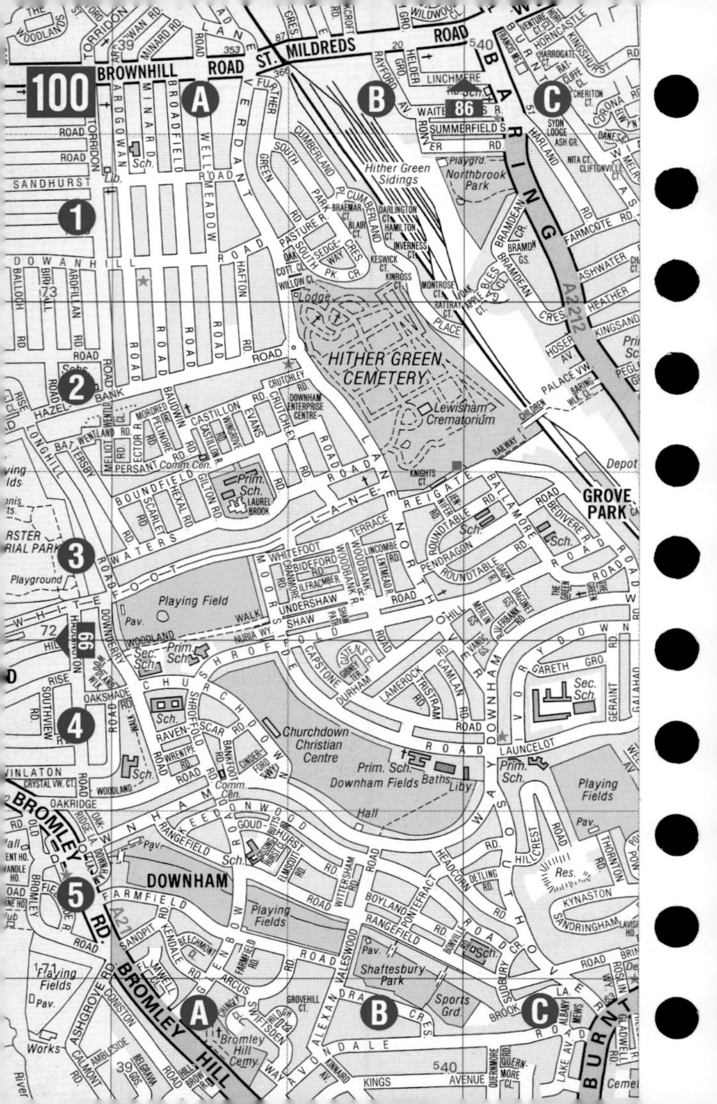

100
BROWNHILL ROAD
ST. MILDREDS ROAD
86
HITHER GREEN CEMETERY
Lewisham Crematorium
Hither Green Sidings
Northbrook Park
GROVE PARK
BARING ROAD
A2212
DOWNHAM
DOWNHAM WAY
WHITEFOOT LANE
VERDANT LANE
BROMLEY ROAD
A21
BROMLEY HILL
Bromley Hill Cemy.
Churchdown Christian Centre
Prim. Sch. Downham Fields
Playing Field
Playing Fields
Shaftesbury Park
Sports Grd.
AVONDALE ROAD
KINGS AVENUE
BURNT ASH HILL
99
540

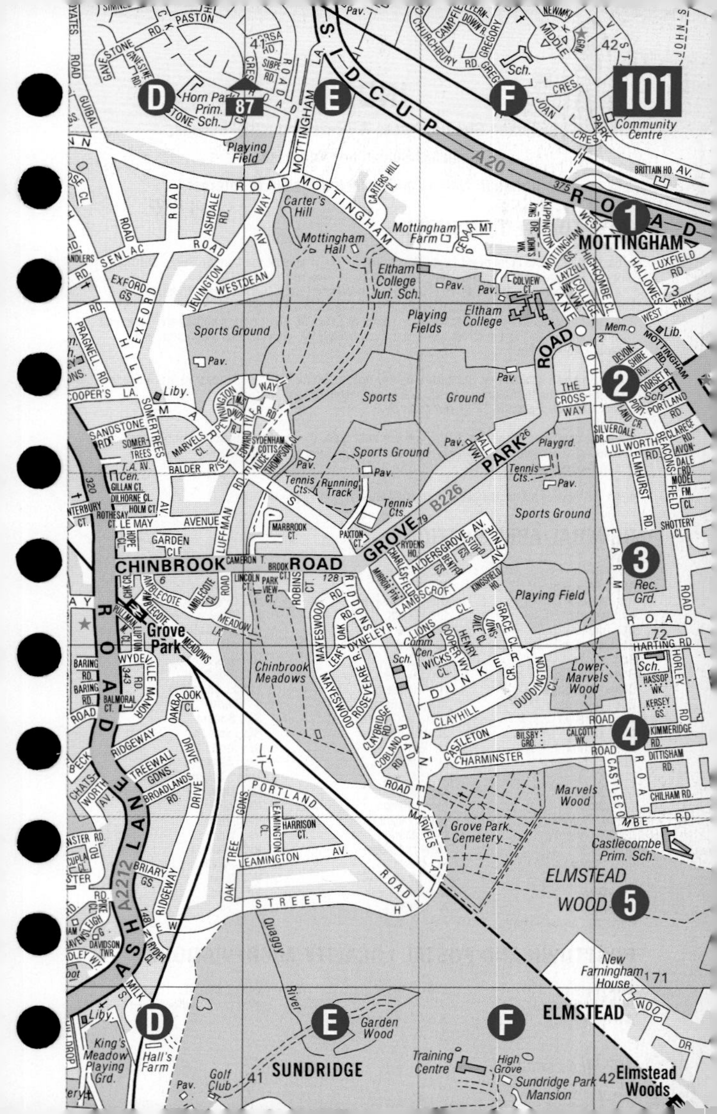
101
MOTTINGHAM
SIDCUP ROAD
A20
MOTTINGHAM ROAD
CHINBROOK ROAD
GROVE PARK ROAD
B226
Grove Park
Sports Ground
Playing Fields
Eltham College
Eltham College Jun. Sch.
Mottingham Hall
Carter's Hill
Mottingham Farm
Community Centre
Horn Park Prim. Sch.
Playing Field
Chinbrook Meadows
Lower Marvels Wood
Marvels Wood
Grove Park Cemetery
Castlecombe Prim. Sch.
ELMSTEAD WOOD
New Farningham House
ELMSTEAD
SUNDRIDGE
Garden Wood
Training Centre
High Grove
Sundridge Park Mansion
Golf Club
Elmstead Woods
King's Meadow Playing Grd.
Hall's Farm
Quaggy River
BAMBLE LANE
A2212
Rec. Grd.
Running Track
DUNKERY ROAD
MARVELS LANE
PORTLAND ROAD
LEAMINGTON AV.
OAK TREE GDNS.
STREET
87

INDEX

Including Streets, Places & Areas, Industrial Estates,

Selected Subsidiary Addresses,

Junction Names and Selected Places of Interest.

HOW TO USE THIS INDEX

1. Each street name is followed by its Postal District (or, if outside the London Postal Districts, by its Posttown or Postal Locality), and then by its map reference;
   e.g. Abbeville Rd. *SW4* —4E **79** is in the South West 4 Postal District and is found in square 4E on page **79**. The page number being shown in bold type.
   A strict alphabetical order is followed in which Av., Rd., St. etc. (though abbreviated) are read in full and as part of the street name; e.g. Abbotsleigh Rd. appears after Abbots La. but before Abbots Mnr.

2. Streets and a selection of Subsidiary names not shown on the Maps, appear in this index in *Italics* with the thoroughfare to which it is connected shown in brackets;
   e.g. *Abady Ho. SW1* —5F **51** *(off Page St.)*

3. Places and areas are shown in the index in **bold type**, the map reference referring to the actual map square in which the town or area is located and not to the place name;
   e.g. **Aldersbrook.** —4D **17**

4. An example of a selected place of interest is Admiralty Arch. —2F **51**

GENERAL ABBREVIATIONS

All : Alley	Est : Estate	Pde : Parade
App : Approach	Fld : Field	Pk : Park
Arc : Arcade	Gdns : Gardens	Pas : Passage
Av : Avenue	Gth : Garth	Pl : Place
Bk : Back	Ga : Gate	Quad : Quadrant
Boulevd : Boulevard	Gt : Great	Res : Residential
Bri : Bridge	Grn : Green	Ri : Rise
B'way : Broadway	Gro : Grove	Rd : Road
Bldgs : Buildings	Ho : House	Shop : Shopping
Bus : Business	Ind : Industrial	S : South
Cvn : Caravan	Info : Information	Sq : Square
Cen : Centre	Junct : Junction	Sta : Station
Chu : Church	La : Lane	St : Street
Chyd : Churchyard	Lit : Little	Ter : Terrace
Circ : Circle	Lwr : Lower	Trad : Trading
Cir : Circus	Mc : Mac	Up : Upper
Clo : Close	Mnr : Manor	Va : Vale
Comn : Common	Mans : Mansions	Vw : View
Cotts : Cottages	Mkt : Market	Vs : Villas
Ct : Court	Mdw : Meadow	Vis : Visitors
Cres : Crescent	M : Mews	Wlk : Walk
Cft : Croft	Mt : Mount	W : West
Dri : Drive	Mus : Museum	Yd : Yard
E : East	N : North	
Embkmt : Embankment	Pal : Palace	

POSTTOWN AND POSTAL LOCALITY ABBREVIATIONS

Bark : Barking	*Chst* : Chislehurst	*Slou* : Slough
Beck : Beckenham	*Ilf* : Ilford	*Wfd G* : Woodford Green
Brom : Bromley	*King T* : Kingston Upon Thames	

INDEX

101 Bus. Units. *SW11*
—1B **78**
198 Gallery. —4D **81**
(off Railton Rd.)
1 Owen St. *EC1* —1D **39**
(off Goswell St.)
3 Cranes Wlk. *EC4* —1E **53**
(off Bell Wharf La.)

Abady Ho. *SW1* —5F **51**
(off Page St.)
Abberley M. *SW4* —1D **79**
Abbess Clo. *SW2* —1D **95**
Abbeville M. *SW4* —2F **79**
Abbeville Rd. *SW4* —4E **79**
Abbey Bus. Cen. *SW8* —4E **65**
Abbey Ct. NW8 —1E **35**
(off Abbey Rd.)
Abbey Ct. SE17 —1E **67**
(off Macleod St.)
Abbey Dri. *SW17* —5C **92**
Abbey Est. *NW8* —5D **21**
Abbeyfield Est. *SE16* —5E **55**
Abbeyfield Rd. *SE16* —5E **55**
(in two parts)
Abbey Gdns. *NW8* —1E **35**
Abbey Gdns. *SE16* —5C **54**
Abbey Gdns. *W6* —2A **62**
Abbey Ho. E15 —1A **44**
(off Baker's Row)
Abbey Ho. NW8 —2E **35**
(off Garden Rd.)
Abbey La. *E15* —1E **43**
Abbey La. Commercial Est.
E15 —1A **44**
Abbey Life Ct. *E16* —4D **45**
Abbey Lodge. NW1 —2A **36**
(off Park Rd.)
Abbey M. *E17* —1C **14**
Abbey Orchard St. *SW1*
—4F **51**
Abbey Orchard St. Est. *SW1*
(in two parts) —4F **51**
Abbey Rd. *E15* —1F **43**
Abbey Rd. *NW6 & NW8*
—4D **21**
Abbey St. *E13* —3C **44**
Abbey St. *SE1* —4A **54**
Abbey Trad. Est. *SE26* —5B **98**
Abbot Clo. SW8 —3A **66**
(off Hartington Rd.)
Abbot Ho. *E14* —1D **57**
Abbotsbury Clo. *E15* —1E **43**
Abbotsbury M. *SE15* —1E **83**
Abbotsbury Rd. *W14* —3A **48**
Abbotshade Rd. *SE16* —2F **55**
Abbotshall Rd. *SE6* —1F **99**
Abbot's Ho. W14 —4B **48**
Abbots La. *SE1* —2A **54**
Abbotsleigh Rd. *SW16*
—4E **93**
Abbots Mnr. *SW1* —5D **51**

Abbots Pk. *SW2* —1C **94**
Abbot's Pl. *NW6* —5D **21**
Abbot's Rd. *E6* —5F **31**
Abbots Ter. *N8* —1A **10**
Abbotstone Rd. *SW15* —1E **75**
Abbot St. *E8* —3B **26**
Abbots Wlk. *W8* —4D **49**
Abbotswell Rd. *SE4* —3B **84**
Abbotswood Rd. *SE22*
—2A **82**
Abbotswood Rd. *SW16*
—3F **93**
Abbott Rd. *E14* —4E **43**
(in two parts)
Abbottsbury Clo. *W14* —3A **48**
Abbotts Clo. *N1* —3E **25**
Abbotts Ho. SW1 —1F **65**
(off Aylesford St.)
Abbotts Pk. Rd. *E10* —2E **15**
Abbotts Wharf. *E14* —5C **42**
Abchurch La. *EC4* —1F **53**
(in two parts)
Abchurch Yd. EC4 —1F **53**
(off Abchurch La.)
Abdale Rd. *W12* —2D **47**
Abel Ho. SE11 —2C **66**
(off Kennington Rd.)
Aberavon Rd. *E3* —2A **42**
Abercorn Clo. *NW8* —2E **35**
Abercorn Pl. *SE10* —3D **71**
(off Tarves Way)
Abercorn Mans. NW8 —1E **35**
(off Abercorn Pl.)
Abercorn Pl. *NW8* —2E **35**
Abercorn Way. *SE1* —1C **68**
Abercrombie St. *SW11*
—5A **64**
Aberdare Gdns. *NW6* —4D **21**
Aberdeen Ct. W9 —3E **35**
(off Lanark Rd.)
Aberdeen La. *N5* —2E **25**
Aberdeen Mans. WC1
(off Kenton St.) —3A **38**
Aberdeen Pk. *N5* —2E **25**
Aberdeen Pl. *NW8* —3F **35**
Aberdeen Rd. *N5* —1E **25**
Aberdeen Rd. *NW10* —2B **18**
Aberdeen Sq. *E14* —2B **56**
Aberdeen Ter. *SE3* —5F **71**
Aberdour St. *SE1* —5A **54**
Aberfeldy St. *SE5* —3D **67**
(in two parts)
Aberfeldy St. *E14* —5E **43**
(in two parts)
Aberford Gdns. *SE18* —4F **73**
Abergeldie Rd. *SE12* —4D **87**
Abernethy Rd. *SE13* —2A **86**
Abersham Rd. *E8* —2B **26**
Abingdon. W14 —5B **48**
(off Kensington Village)
Abingdon Clo. *NW1* —3F **23**
Abingdon Clo. *SE1* —5B **54**
(off Bushwood Dri.)

Abingdon Ct. *W8* —4C **48**
(off Abingdon Vs.)
Abingdon Gdns. *W8* —4C **48**
Abingdon Ho. *E2* —3B **40**
(off Boundary St.)
Abingdon Lodge. *W8* —4C **48**
Abingdon Rd. *W8* —4C **48**
Abingdon St. *SW1* —4A **52**
Abingdon Vs. *W8* —4C **48**
Abinger Gro. *SE8* —2B **70**
Abinger Ho. SE1 —3F **53**
(off Gt. Dover St.)
Abinger M. *W9* —3C **34**
Abinger Rd. *W4* —4A **46**
Ablett St. *SE16* —1E **69**
Abney Gdns. *N16* —4B **12**
Aboyne Rd. *NW10* —5A **4**
Aboyne Rd. *SW17* —3F **91**
Abyssinia Clo. *SW11* —2A **78**
Abyssinia Ct. *N8* —1B **10**
Abyssinia Rd. *SW11* —2A **78**
Acacia Bus. Cen. *E11* —5A **16**
Acacia Clo. *SE8* —5A **56**
Acacia Gdns. *NW8* —1F **35**
Acacia Gro. *SE21* —2F **95**
Acacia Pl. *NW8* —1F **35**
Acacia Rd. *E11* —4A **16**
Acacia Rd. *E17* —1A **14**
Acacia Rd. *NW8* —1F **35**
Academy Bldgs. N1 —2A **40**
(off Fanshaw St.)
Academy Ct. E2 —2E **41**
(off Kirkwall Pl.)
Academy Ho. *E3* —4D **43**
Acanthus Dri. *SE1* —1C **68**
Acanthus Rd. *SW11* —1C **78**
Accommodation Rd. *NW11*
—3B **6**
Acfold Rd. *SW6* —4D **63**
Achilles Clo. *SE1* —1C **68**
Achilles Ho. E2 —1D **41**
(off Old Bethnal Grn. Rd.)
Achilles Rd. *NW6* —2C **20**
Achilles St. *SE14* —3A **70**
Achilles Way. *W1* —2C **50**
Acklam Rd. *W10* —4A **34**
(in two parts)
Ackmar Rd. *SW6* —4C **62**
Ackroyd Dri. *E3* —4C **42**
Ackroyd Rd. *SE23* —5F **83**
Acland Cres. *SE5* —1F **81**
Acland Ho. *SW9* —4B **66**
Acland Rd. *NW2* —3D **19**
Acol Ct. *NW6* —4C **20**
Acol Rd. *NW6* —4C **20**
Acorn Ct. *E6* —4F **31**
Acorn Gdns. *W3* —4A **32**
Acorn Pde. *SE15* —3D **69**
Acorn Production Cen. N7
—4A **24**
Acorn Wlk. *SE16* —2A **56**
Acorn Way. *SE23* —3F **97**
Acre Dri. *SE22* —2C **82**

Acre Rd. *SW19* —5F **91**
Acris St. *SW18* —3E **77**
Acton Ho. *E8* —5B **26**
(off Lee St.)
Acton La. *NW10* —1A **32**
Acton M. *E8* —5B **26**
Acton Pk. Est. *W3* —3A **46**
Acton St. *WC1* —2B **38**
Acton Va. Ind. Pk. *W3*
—2B **46**
Acuba Rd. *SW18* —2D **91**
Ada Ct. N1 —5E **25**
(off Packington St.)
Ada Ct. *NW8* —2E **35**
Ada Gdns. *E14* —5F **43**
Ada Gdns. *E15* —5B **30**
Ada Ho. E2 —5C **26**
(off Ada Pl.)
Adair Rd. *W10* —3A **34**
Adair Tower. W10 —3A **34**
(off Appleford Rd.)
Ada Kennedy Ct. SE10
—3E **71**
(off Greenwich S. St.)
Adam & Eve Ct. W1 —5E **37**
(off Oxford St.)
Adam & Eve M. *W8* —4C **48**
Adam Clo. *SE6* —4B **98**
Adam Ct. SE11 —5D **53**
(off Opal St.)
Adam Ct. SW7 —5E **49**
(off Gloucester Rd.)
Adams Ct. *E17* —1A **14**
Adams Ct. *EC2* —5A **40**
Adams Gdns. Est. *SE16*
—3E **55**
Adams Ho. *E14* —5F **43**
Adamson Rd. *E16* —5C **44**
Adamson Rd. *NW3* —4F **21**
Adams Pl. E14 —2D **57**
(off N. Colonnade, The)
Adams Pl. *N7* —2B **24**
Adamsrill Rd. *SE26* —4F **97**
Adam's Row. *W1* —1C **50**
Adam St. *WC2* —1A **52**
Adam Wlk. SW6 —3E **61**
(off Crabtree La.)
Ada Pl. E2 —5C **26**
Adare Wlk. *SW16* —3B **94**
Ada Rd. *SE5* —3A **68**
Adastral Ho. WC1 —4B **38**
(off New North St.)
Ada St. *E8* —5D **27**
Ada Workshops. *E8* —5D **27**
Adderley Gro. *SW11* —3C **78**
Adderley St. *E14* —5E **43**
Addey Ho. *SE8* —3B **70**
Addington Ct. *SW14* —1A **74**
Addington Gro. *SE26* —4A **98**
Addington Ho. SW9 —5B **66**
(off Stockwell Rd.)
Addington Rd. *E3* —2C **42**
Addington Rd. *E16* —3A **44**
Addington Rd. *N4* —1C **10**
Addington Sq. *SE5* —2F **67**
(in two parts)
Addington St. *SE1* —3B **52**

Addis Ho. *E1* —4E **41**
(off Lindley St.)
Addisland Ct. W14 —3A **48**
(off Holland Vs. Rd.)
Addison Av. *W11* —2A **48**
Addison Bri. Pl. *W14* —5B **48**
Addison Cres. *W14* —4A **48**
Addison Dri. *SE12* —3D **87**
Addison Gdns. *W14* —4F **47**
Addison Gro. *W4* —4A **46**
Addison Ho. NW8 —2F **35**
(off Grove End Rd.)
Addison Pl. *W11* —2A **48**
Addison Rd. *E11* —1C **16**
Addison Rd. *W14* —3A **48**
Addle Hill. *EC4* —5D **39**
Addle St. *EC2* —5E **39**
Addy Ho. *SE16* —5E **55**
Adelaide Av. *SE4* —2B **84**
Adelaide Ct. *NW8* —1E **35**
(off Abercorn Pl.)
Adelaide Gro. *W12* —2C **46**
Adelaide Ho. *E15* —1B **44**
Adelaide Ho. *SE5* —5A **68**
Adelaide Ho. W11 —5B **34**
(off Portobello Rd.)
Adelaide Rd. *E10* —5D **15**
Adelaide Rd. *NW3* —4F **21**
Adelaide Rd. *SW18* —3C **76**
Adelaide St. *WC2* —1A **52**
Adela St. *W10* —3A **34**
Adelina Gro. *E1* —4E **41**
Adelina M. *SW12* —1F **93**
Adeline Pl. *WC1* —4F **37**
Adelphi Ct. *W4* —2A **60**
Adelphi Ter. WC2 —1A **52**
Adeney Clo. *W6* —2F **61**
Aden Gro. *N16* —1F **25**
Adenmore Rd. *SE6* —5C **84**
Aden Ter. *N16* —1F **25**
Adeyfield Ho. EC1 —2F **39**
(off Cranwood St.)
Adie Rd. *W6* —4E **47**
Adine Rd. *E13* —3D **45**
Adler St. *E1* —5C **40**
Adley St. *E5* —2A **28**
Admiral Ct. SW10 —4E **63**
(off Admiral Sq.)
Admiral Ct. W1 —4C **36**
(off Blandford St.)
Admiral Ho. SW1 —5E **51**
(off Willow Pl.)
Admiral Hyson Ind. Est. *SE1*
—1D **69**
Admiral M. *W10* —3F **33**
Admiral St. *SE16* —2A **56**
Admirals Ct. SE1 —2B **54**
(off Horselydown La.)
Admiral's Ga. *SE10* —4D **71**
Admiral Pl. *E14* —3C **56**
Admiral Sq. *SW10* —4E **63**
Admiral St. *SE8* —5C **70**
Admirals Wlk. *NW3* —5D **7**
Admiralty Arch. —2F **51**
Admiralty Clo. *SE8* —3C **70**
Admiral Wlk. *W9* —4C **34**

Adolf St. *SE6* —4D **99**
Adolphus Rd. *N4* —4D **11**
Adolphus St. *SE8* —3B **70**
Adpar St. *W2* —4F **35**
Adrian Av. *NW2* —3D **5**
Adrian Boult Ho. E2 —2D **41**
(off Mansford St.)
Adrian Ho. N1 —5B **24**
(off Barnsbury Est.)
Adrian Ho. SW8 —3A **66**
(off Wyvil Rd.)
Adrian M. *SW10* —2D **63**
Adriatic Building. *E14*
—1A **56**
Adron Ho. *SE16* —5E **55**
(off Millender Wlk.)
Adstock Ho. *N1* —4D **25**
(off Sutton Est., The)
Advance Rd. *SE27* —4E **95**
Adventurers Ct. *E14* —1F **57**
Adys Lawn. *NW2* —3D **19**
Ady's Rd. *SE15* —1B **82**
Aegon Ho. E14 —4D **57**
(off Lanark Sq.)
Affleck St. *N1* —1B **38**
Afghan Rd. *SW11* —5A **64**
Afsil Ho. EC1 —4C **38**
(off Viaduct Bldgs.)
Agamemnon Rd. *NW6*
—1B **20**
Agar Gro. *NW1* —4E **23**
Agar Gro. Est. *NW1* —4F **23**
Agar Pl. *NW1* —4E **23**
Agar St. *WC2* —1A **52**
Agate Clo. *E16* —5F **45**
Agate Rd. *W6* —4E **47**
Agatha Clo. *E1* —2D **55**
Agave Rd. *NW2* —1E **19**
Agdon St. *EC1* —3D **39**
Agincourt Rd. *NW3* —1B **22**
Agnes Ho. *W11* —1F **47**
(off St Ann's Rd.)
Agnes Rd. *W3* —2B **46**
Agnes St. *E14* —5B **42**
Agnew Rd. *SE23* —5F **83**
Aigburth Mans. *SW9* —3C **66**
(off Mowll St.)
Aileen Wlk. *E15* —4B **30**
Ailsa St. *E14* —4E **43**
Ainger M. NW3 —4B **22**
(off Ainger Rd., in two parts)
Ainger Rd. *NW3* —4B **22**
Ainsdale. *NW1* —1E **37**
(off Harrington St.)
Ainsdale Dri. *SE1* —1C **68**
Ainsley St. *E2* —2D **41**
Ainslie Wlk. *SW12* —5D **79**
Ainsty Est. *SE16* —3F **55**
Ainsty St. *SE16* —3E **55**
Ainsworth Clo. *NW2* —5C **4**
Ainsworth Clo. *SE15* —5A **68**
Ainsworth Ho. *NW8* —5D **21**
Ainsworth Rd. *E9* —4E **27**
Ainsworth Way. *NW8* —5E **21**
Aintree Av. *E6* —5F **31**
Aintree Est. SW6 —3A **62**
(off Aintree St.)

Aintree St. *SW6* —3A **62**
Aird Ho. *E1* —4E **53**
(off Rockingham St.)
Airdrie Clo. *N1* —4B **24**
Airedale Av. *W4* —5B **46**
Airedale Av. S. *W4* —1B **60**
Airedale Rd. *SW12* —5B **78**
Airlie Gdns. *W8* —2C **48**
Air St. *W1* —1E **51**
Aisgill Av. *W14* —1B **62**
(in two parts)
Aislibie Rd. *SE12* —2A **86**
Aiten Pl. *W6* —5C **46**
Aithan Ho. *E14* —5B **42**
Aitken Clo. *E8* —5C **26**
Aitken Rd. *SE6* —2D **99**
Ajax Ho. *E2* —1D **41**
(off Old Bethnal Grn. Rd.)
Ajax Rd. *NW6* —1B **20**
Akbar Ho. *E14* —5D **57**
Akehurst St. *SW15* —4C **74**
Akenside Rd. *NW3* —2F **21**
Akerman Rd. *SW9* —5D **67**
Akintaro Ho. *SE8* —2B **70**
(off Alverton St.)
Aland Ct. *SE16* —4A **56**
Alan Hocken Way. *E15*
—1A **44**
Alan Preece Ct. *NW6* —4F **19**
Alan Rd. *SW19* —5A **90**
Alanthus Clo. *SE12* —4C **86**
Alaska Bldgs. *SE1* —4B **54**
Alaska St. *SE1* —2C **52**
Albacore Cres. *SE13* —4D **85**
Alba Gdns. *NW11* —1A **6**
Alban Highwalk. *EC2* —2E **39**
(off Addle St., in two parts)
Albany. *W1* —1E **51**
Albany Ct. *E10* —2C **14**
Albany Ct. *NW8* —1F **35**
(off Abbey Rd.)
Albany Courtyard. *W1*
(off Piccadilly) —1E **51**
Albany Mans. *SW11* —3A **64**
Albany M. *N1* —4C **24**
Albany M. *SE5* —2E **67**
Albany M. *Brom* —5C **100**
Albany Pl. *N7* —1C **24**
Albany Rd. *E10* —2C **14**
Albany Rd. *E12* —1F **31**
Albany Rd. *E17* —1A **14**
Albany Rd. *N4* —1C **10**
Albany Rd. *SE5* —2F **67**
Albany Rd. *SW19* —5D **91**
Albany Rd. *NW1* —1D **37**
Albany Ter. *NW1* —3D **37**
(off Marylebone Rd.)
Alba Pl. *W11* —5B **34**
Albatross Ct. *SE8* —2B **70**
(off Childers St.)
Albatross Way. *SE16* —3F **55**
Albemarle. *SW19* —2F **89**
Albemarle Ho. *SE8* —5B **56**
(off Foreshore)
Albemarle Ho. *SW9* —1C **80**
Albemarle St. *W1* —1D **51**
Albemarle Way. *EC1* —3D **39**

Alberta Est. *SE17* —1D **67**
(off Alberta St.)
Alberta Ho. *E14* —2E **57**
Alberta St. *SE17* —1D **67**
Albert Av. *SW8* —3B **66**
Albert Barnes Ho. *SE1*
(off New Kent Rd.) —4E **53**
Albert Bigg Point. *E15*
(off Godfrey St.) —1E **43**
Albert Bri. *SW3 & SW11*
—2A **64**
Albert Bri. Rd. *SW11* —3A **64**
Albert Carr Gdns. *SW16*
—5A **94**
Albert Clo. *E9* —5D **27**
Albert Cotts. *E1* —4C **40**
(off Deal St.)
Albert Ct. *E7* —1C **30**
Albert Ct. *SW7* —4F **49**
Albert Ct. Ga. *SW7* —3B **50**
(off Knightsbridge)
Albert Dri. *SW19* —2A **90**
Albert Embkmt. *SE1* —4B **52**
(Lambeth Pal. Rd.)
Albert Embkmt. *SE1* —1A **66**
(Vauxhall Cross)
Albert Gdns. *E1* —5F **41**
Alberta Ga. *SW1* —3B **50**
Albert Gray Ho. *SW10*
—3F **63**
(off Worlds End Est.)
Albert Hall Mans. *SW7*
(in two parts) —3F **49**
Albert Memorial. —3F **49**
Albert M. *E14* —1A **56**
Albert M. *N4* —3B **10**
Albert M. *SE4* —2B **84**
Albert M. *W8* —4E **49**
Albert Pal. Mans. SW11
(off Lurline Gdns.) —4D **65**
Albert Pl. *W8* —4D **49**
Albert Rd. *E10* —4E **15**
Albert Rd. *E16* —2F **59**
Albert Rd. *E17* —1C **14**
Albert Rd. *N4* —3B **10**
Albert Rd. *N15* —1A **12**
Albert Rd. *NW6* —1B **34**
Albert Sq. *SW8* —3B **66**
Albert Starr Ho. SE8 —5F **55**
(off Bush Rd.)
Albert St. *NW1* —5D **23**
Albert Studios. *SW11* —4B **64**
Albert Ter. *NW1* —5C **22**
Albert Ter. M. *NW1* —5C **22**
Albert Way. *SE15* —3C **67**
Albert Westcott Ho. *SE17*
—1D **67**
Albion Av. *SW8* —5F **65**
Albion Clo. *W2* —1A **50**
Albion Dri. *E8* —4B **26**
(in two parts)
Albion Est. *SE16* —3F **55**
Albion Gdns. *W6* —5D **47**
Albion Ga. *W2* —1A **50**
(off Albion St., in two parts)
Albion Gro. *N16* —1A **26**

Albion Ho. *SE8* —3C **70**
(off Watsons St.)
Albion M. *N1* —5C **24**
Albion M. *W2* —1A **50**
Albion M. *W6* —5D **47**
Albion Pl. *EC1* —4D **39**
Albion Pl. *EC2* —4F **39**
Albion Pl. *W6* —5D **47**
Albion Rd. *N16* —1F **25**
Albion Sq. *E8* —4B **26**
Albion St. *SE16* —3E **55**
Albion St. *W2* —5A **36**
Albion Ter. *E8* —4B **26**
Albion Vs. Rd. *SE26* —3E **97**
Albion Way. *EC1* —4E **39**
Albion Way. *SE13* —2E **85**
Albion Wharf. *SW11* —3A **64**
Albion Yd. *N1* —1A **38**
Albrighton Rd. *SE22* —1A **82**
Albury Ho. *SE1* —3D **53**
(off Boyfield St.)
Albury M. *E12* —4E **17**
Albury St. *SE8* —2C **70**
Albyn Rd. *SE8* —4C **70**
Alcester Cres. *E5* —4D **13**
Alconbury Rd. *E5* —4C **12**
Aldam Pl. *N16* —4B **12**
Aldbourne Rd. *W3* —2B **46**
(in two parts)
Aldbridge St. *SE17* —1A **68**
Aldburgh M. *W1* —5C **36**
(in two parts)
Aldbury Ho. *SW3* —5A **50**
(off Ixworth Pl.)
Aldebert Ter. *SW8* —3A **66**
Aldeburgh Clo. *E5* —4D **13**
Aldeburgh St. *SE10* —1C **72**
Alden Av. *E15* —2B **44**
Aldenham Ho. *NW1* —1E **37**
(off Aldenham St.)
Aldenham St. *NW1* —1E **37**
Alden Ho. *E8* —5D **27**
(off Duncan Rd.)
Aldensley Rd. *W6* —4D **47**
Alderbrook Rd. *SW12*
—4D **79**
Alderbury Rd. *SW13* —2C **60**
Alder Clo. *SE15* —2B **68**
Alder Gro. *NW2* —4C **4**
Alderholt Way. *SE15* —3A **68**
Alder Ho. *NW3* —3B **22**
Alder Ho. *SE4* —1C **84**
Alder Ho. SE15 —2B **68**
(off Alder Clo.)
Alder Lodge. *SW6* —4E **61**
Aldermanbury. *EC2* —5B **39**
Aldermanbury Sq. *EC2*
—4E **39**
Aldermans Wlk. *EC2* —4A **40**
Alder M. *N19* —4E **9**
Aldermoor Rd. *SE6* —3B **98**
Alderney Rd. *E1* —3F **41**
Alderney St. *SW1* —5D **51**
Aldersbrook. —4D **17**
Aldersbrook Rd. *E11 & E12*
—4D **17**
Alders Clo. *E11* —4D **17**

Aldersford Clo. SE4 —3F **83**
Aldersgate St. EC1 —4E **39**
Aldersgrove Av. SE9
　　　　　　　　—3F **101**
Aldershot Rd. NW6 —5B **20**
Alderson St. W10 —3A **34**
Alders, The. SW16 —4E **93**
Alderton Rd. NW10 —5A **4**
Alderton Cres. NW4 —1D **5**
Alderton Rd. SE24 —1E **81**
Alderton Way. NW4 —1D **5**
Alderville Rd. SW6 —5B **62**
Aldford Rd. W1 —2C **50**
　　(off Park St.)
Aldford St. W1 —2C **50**
Aldgate. (Junct.) —5B **40**
Aldgate. E1 —5B **40**
　　(off Whitechapel High St.)
Aldgate. EC3 —5A **40**
Aldgate Av. E1 —5B **40**
Aldgate Barrs. E1 —5B **40**
　　(off Whitechapel High St.)
Aldgate High St. EC3 —5B **40**
Aldgate Triangle. E1 —5C **40**
　　(off Coke St.)
Aldham Ho. SE4 —5B **70**
Aldine Ct. W12 —3E **47**
　　(off Aldine St.)
Aldine Pl. W12 —3E **47**
Aldine St. W12 —3E **47**
Aldington Ct. E8 —4C **26**
　　(off Lansdowne Dri.)
Aldington Rd. SE18 —4F **59**
Aldis M. SW17 —5A **92**
Aldis St. SW17 —5A **92**
Aldred Rd. NW6 —2C **20**
Aldren Rd. SW17 —3E **91**
Aldrich Ter. SW18 —2E **91**
Aldrick Ho. N1 —5B **24**
　　(off Barnsbury Est.)
Aldridge Rd. Vs. W11 —4B **34**
Aldrington Rd. SW16 —5E **93**
Aldsworth Clo. W9 —3D **35**
Aldworth Gro. SE13 —4E **85**
Aldworth Rd. E15 —4A **30**
Aldwych. WC2 —5B **38**
Aldwyn Ho. SW8 —3A **66**
　　(off Davidson Gdns.)
Alestan Beck Rd. E16 —5F **45**
Alexa Ct. W8 —5C **48**
Alexander Av. NW10 —4D **19**
Alexander Ct. SE16 —2B **56**
Alexander Evans M. SE23
　　　　　　　　—2F **97**
Alexander Fleming Mus.
　　(off Praed St.) —5F **35**
Alexander Ho. E14 —4C **56**
Alexander M. W2 —5D **35**
Alexander Pl. SW7 —5A **50**
Alexander Rd. N19 —5A **10**
Alexander Sq. SW3 —5A **50**
Alexander St. W2 —5C **34**
Alexander Studios. SW11
　　(off Haydon Way) —2F **77**
Alexandra Av. SW11 —4C **64**
Alexandra Av. W4 —3A **60**
Alexandra Clo. SE8 —2B **70**

Alexandra Cotts. SE14
　　　　　　　　—4B **70**
*Alexandra Ct. SW7 —4E **49***
　　(off Queen's Ga.)
*Alexandra Ct. W2 —1D **49***
　　(off Moscow Rd.)
*Alexandra Ct. W9 —3E **35***
　　(off Maida Va.)
Alexandra Cres. Brom
　　　　　　　　—5B **100**
Alexandra Dri. SE19 —5A **96**
Alexandra Gdns. W4 —3A **60**
Alexandra Gro. N4 —3D **11**
Alexandra Mans. SW3
　　(off Moravian Clo.) —2F **63**
Alexandra M. SW19 —5B **90**
Alexandra Pl. NW8 —5E **21**
Alexandra Rd. E10 —5E **15**
Alexandra Rd. E17 —1B **14**
Alexandra Rd. NW8 —5E **21**
Alexandra Rd. SE26 —5F **97**
Alexandra Rd. SW14 —1A **74**
Alexandra Rd. SW19 —5B **90**
Alexandra Rd. W4 —3A **46**
Alexandra St. E16 —4C **46**
Alexandra St. SE14 —3A **70**
Alexandra Ter. E14 —1D **71**
Alexandra Wlk. SE19 —5A **96**
Alexandra Yd. E9 —5F **27**
Alexis St. SE16 —5C **54**
Alfearn Rd. E5 —1E **27**
Alford Ct. N1 —1E **39**
　　(in two parts)
Alford Ho. N6 —1E **9**
Alford Pl. N1 —1E **39**
Alfreda St. SW11 —4D **65**
Alfred Clo. W4 —5A **46**
*Alfred Ho. E9 —2A **28***
　　(off Homerton Rd.)
*Alfred Ho. E12 —4F **31***
　　(off Tennyson Av.)
Alfred M. W1 —4F **37**
Alfred Nunn Ho. NW10
　　　　　　　　—5B **18**
Alfred Pl. WC1 —4F **37**
Alfred Rd. E15 —2B **30**
Alfred Rd. W2 —4C **34**
Alfred St. E3 —2B **42**
Alfreton Clo. SW19 —3F **89**
Alfriston Rd. SW11 —3B **78**
*Algar Ho. SE1 —3D **53***
　　(off Webber Row)
Algarve Rd. SW18 —1D **91**
Algernon Rd. NW4 —1C **4**
Algernon Rd. NW6 —5C **20**
Algernon Rd. SE13 —2D **85**
Algiers Rd. SE13 —2C **84**
Alice Ct. SW15 —2B **76**
*Alice Gilliatt Ct. W14 —2B **62***
　　(off Star Rd.)
Alice La. E3 —5B **28**
Alice Owen Technology Cen.
　　　　　　EC1 —2D **39**
Alice Shepherd Ho. E14
　　　　　　　　—3E **57**
Alice St. SE1 —4A **54**
　　(in two parts)

Alice Thompson Clo. SE12
　　　　　　　　—2E **101**
Alice Walker Clo. SE24
　　　　　　　　—2D **81**
Alie St. E1 —5B **40**
Alison Ct. SE1 —1C **68**
Aliwal Rd. SW11 —2A **78**
Alkerden Rd. W4 —1A **60**
Alkham Rd. N16 —4B **12**
Allan Barclay Clo. N15 —1B **12**
*Allanson Ct. E10 —4C **14***
　　(off Leyton Grange Est.)
Allard Gdns. SW4 —3F **79**
Allardyce St. SW4 —2B **80**
Allcroft Rd. NW5 —2C **22**
Allenby Rd. SE23 —3A **98**
*Allen Ct. E17 —1C **14***
　　(off Yunus Khan Clo.)
Allendale Clo. SE5 —5F **67**
Allendale Clo. SE26 —5F **97**
Allen Edwards Dri. SW8
　　　　　　　　—4A **66**
*Allenford Ho. SW15 —4B **74***
　　(off Tunworth Cres.)
Allen Rd. E3 —1B **42**
Allen Rd. N16 —1A **26**
Allensbury Pl. NW1 —4F **23**
Allen St. W8 —4C **48**
Allerford Rd. SE6 —3D **99**
*Allerton Ho. N1 —2F **39***
　　(off Provost Est.)
Allerton Rd. N16 —4E **11**
Allerton St. N1 —2F **39**
Allerton Wlk. N7 —4B **10**
Allestree Rd. SW6 —3A **62**
Alleyn Cres. SE21 —2F **95**
*Alleyn Ho. SE1 —4F **53***
　　(off Burbage Clo.)
Alleyn Pk. SE21 —2F **95**
Alleyn Rd. SE21 —3F **95**
Allfarthing La. SW18 —4D **77**
Allgood St. E2 —1B **40**
Allhallows La. EC4 —1F **53**
Allhallows Rd. E6 —4F **45**
Alliance Rd. E13 —4E **45**
Allied Ind. Est. W3 —3A **46**
Allied Way. W3 —3A **46**
Allingham St. N1 —1E **39**
Allington Clo. SW19 —5F **89**
*Allington Ct. SW1 —4D **51***
　　(off Allington St.)
Allington Ct. SW8 —5E **65**
Allington Rd. NW4 —1D **5**
Allington Rd. W10 —2A **34**
Allington St. SW1 —4D **51**
Allison Clo. SE10 —4E **71**
Allison Gro. SE21 —1A **96**
Allison Rd. N8 —1C **10**
*Alliston Ho. E2 —2B **40***
　　(off Gibraltar Wlk.)
Allitsen Rd. NW8 —1A **36**
　　(in two parts)
Allnutt Way. SW4 —3F **79**
Alloa Rd. SE8 —1F **69**
*Allom Ho. W11 —1A **48***
　　(off Clarendon Rd.)
Alloway Rd. E3 —2A **42**

Allport Ho. SE5 —1F **81**
 (off Denmark Hill)
All Saints Ct. SW11 —3D **65**
 (off Prince of Wales Dri.)
All Saints Dri. SE3 —5A **72**
All Saints Ho. W11 —4B **34**
All Saints Pas. SW18 —3C **76**
All Saints Rd. W11 —4B **34**
All Saints St. N1 —1B **38**
All Saints Tower. E10 —2D **15**
All Seasons Ct. E1 —2C **54**
 (off Aragon M.)
Allsop Pl. NW1 —3E **36**
All Souls Av. NW10 —1D **33**
All Souls' Pl. W1 —4D **37**
Allwood Clo. SE26 —4F **97**
Almack Rd. E5 —1E **27**
Alma Gro. SE1 —5B **54**
Alma Pl. NW10 —2D **33**
Alma Sq. NW8 —1E **35**
Alma St. E15 —3F **29**
Alma St. NW5 —3D **23**
Alma Ter. SW18 —5F **77**
Alma Ter. W8 —4C **48**
Almeida St. N1 —5D **25**
Almeric Rd. SW11 —2B **78**
Almington St. N4 —3B **10**
Almond Clo. SE15 —5C **68**
Almond Rd. SE16 —5D **55**
Almondsbury Ct. SE15
 (off Newent Clo.) —3A **68**
Almorah Rd. N1 —4F **25**
Alnwick Rd. E16 —5E **45**
Alnwick Rd. SE12 —4D **87**
Alperton St. W10 —3B **34**
Alphabet Sq. E3 —4C **42**
Alpha Bus. Cen. E17 —1B **14**
Alpha Clo. NW1 —3A **36**
Alpha Gro. E14 —3C **56**
Alpha Ho. NW1 —3A **36**
 (off Ashbridge St.)
Alpha Ho. NW6 —1C **34**
Alpha Ho. SW9 —2B **80**
Alpha Pl. NW6 —1C **34**
Alpha Pl. SW3 —2A **64**
Alpha Rd. SE14 —4B **70**
Alpha St. SE15 —5C **68**
Alpine Rd. SE16 —5E **55**
 (in two parts)
Alric Av. NW10 —4A **18**
Alroy Rd. N4 —2C **10**
Alsace Rd. SE17 —1A **68**
Alscot Rd. SE1 —5B **54**
 (in two parts)
Alscot Rd. Ind. Est. SE1
 —4B **54**
Alscot Way. SE1 —5B **54**
Alston Rd. SW17 —4F **91**
Altenburg Gdns. SW11
 —2B **78**
Althea St. SW6 —5D **63**
Althorpe M. SW11 —1F **63**
Althorp Rd. SW17 —1B **92**
Altior Ct. N6 —1E **9**
Alton Rd. SW15 —1C **88**
Alton St. E14 —4D **43**

Aluna Ct. SE15 —1E **83**
Alvanley Gdns. NW6 —2D **21**
Alverstone Av. SW19 —2C **90**
Alverstone Ho. SE11 —2C **66**
Alverstone Rd. NW2 —4E **19**
Alverton St. SE8 —1B **70**
 (in two parts)
Alvey St. SE17 —1A **68**
Alvington Cres. E8 —2B **26**
Alwold Cres. SE12 —4D **87**
Alwyne La. N1 —4D **25**
Alwyne Pl. N1 —3E **25**
Alwyne Rd. N1 —4E **25**
Alwyne Rd. SW19 —5B **90**
Alwyne Sq. N1 —3E **25**
Alwyne Vs. N1 —4D **25**
Alyth Gdns. NW11 —1C **6**
Amazon St. E1 —5C **40**
Ambassadors' Ct. SW1
 (off St James' Pal.) —2E **51**
Ambassador Sq. E14 —5D **57**
Ambergate St. SE17 —1D **67**
Amber Gro. NW2 —3F **5**
Amberley Gro. SE26 —5D **97**
Amberley Rd. E10 —2C **14**
Amberley Rd. W9 —4C **34**
Amblecote Clo. SE12
 —3D **101**
Amblecote Meadows. SE12
 —3D **101**
Amblecote Rd. SE12
 —3D **101**
Ambler Rd. N4 —5D **11**
Ambleside. NW1 —1D **37**
 (off Augustus St.)
Ambleside. Brom —5F **99**
Ambleside Av. SW16 —4F **93**
Ambleside Clo. E9 —2E **27**
Ambleside Clo. E10 —2D **15**
Ambleside Gdns. SW16
 —5F **93**
Ambleside Point. SE15
 (off Tustin Est.) —3E **69**
Ambleside Rd. NW10 —4B **18**
Ambrosden Av. SW1 —4E **51**
Ambrose Av. NW11 —2A **6**
Ambrose Ho. E14 —4C **42**
Ambrose M. SW11 —5B **64**
Ambrose St. SE16 —5D **55**
Ambrose Wlk. E3 —1C **42**
Amelia St. SE17 —1E **67**
Amen Corner. EC4 —5D **39**
Amen Corner. SW17 —5B **92**
Amen Ct. EC4 —5D **39**
America Sq. EC3 —1B **54**
America St. SE1 —2E **53**
Amerland Rd. SW18 —3B **76**
Amersham Gro. SE14 —3B **70**
Amersham Rd. SE14 —4B **70**
Amersham Va. SE14 —3B **70**
Amery Gdns. NW10 —5E **19**
Amery Ho. SE17 —1A **68**
 (off Kinglake St.)
Amesbury Av. SW2 —2A **94**
Amesbury Tower. SW8
 —5E **65**
Ames Cotts. E14 —4A **42**

Amethyst Rd. E15 —1F **29**
Amhurst Pk. N16 —2F **11**
Amhurst Pas. E8 —2C **26**
Amhurst Rd. E8 —2D **27**
Amhurst Rd. N16 & E8
 —1B **26**
Amhurst Ter. E8 —1C **26**
Amias Ho. EC1 —3E **39**
 (off Central St.)
Amiel St. E1 —3E **41**
Amies St. SW11 —1B **78**
Amigo Ho. SE1 —4C **52**
 (off Morley St.)
Amina Way. SE16 —4C **54**
Amity Rd. E15 —4B **30**
Ammanford Grn. NW9 —1A **4**
Amner Rd. SW11 —4C **78**
Amor Rd. W6 —4E **47**
Amory Ho. N1 —5B **24**
 (off Barnsbury Est.)
Amos Est. SE16 —2F **55**
Amott Rd. SE15 —1C **82**
Amoy Pl. E14 —5B **42**
 (in two parts)
Ampthill Est. NW1 —1E **38**
Ampton Pl. WC1 —2B **38**
Ampton St. WC1 —2B **38**
Amroth Clo. SE23 —1D **97**
Amroth Grn. NW9 —1A **4**
Amstel Ct. SE15 —3B **68**
 (off Garnies Clo.)
Amsterdam Rd. E14 —4E **57**
Amundsen Ct. E14 —1C **70**
Amunsden Ho. NW10 —4A **18**
 (off Stonebridge Pk.)
Amwell Ct. Est. N16 —4E **11**
Amwell St. N1 —2C **38**
Amyruth Rd. SE4 —3C **84**
Anatola Rd. N19 —4D **9**
Anchor. SW18 —2D **77**
Anchorage Clo. SW19 —5C **90**
Anchorage Ho. E14 —1F **57**
 (off Clove Cres.)
Anchorage Ho. E14 —3B **56**
 (off Cuba St.)
Anchorage Point Ind. Est. SE7
 —4E **59**
Anchor & Hope La. SE7
 —4D **59**
Anchor Brewhouse. SE1
 —2B **54**
Anchor Ct. SW1 —5F **51**
 (off Vauxhall Bri. Rd.)
Anchor Ho. E16 —4B **44**
 (off Barking Rd.)
Anchor Ho. E16 —5E **45**
 (off Prince Regent La.)
Anchor Ho. EC1 —3E **39**
 (off Old St.)
Anchor M. SW12 —4D **79**
Anchor St. SE16 —5D **55**
Anchor Wharf. E3 —4D **43**
Anchor Yd. EC1 —3E **39**
Ancill Clo. W6 —2A **62**
Ancona Rd. NW10 —1C **32**
Andalus Rd. SW9 —1A **80**
Anderson Clo. W3 —5A **32**

Anderson Ct. NW2 —3E **5**
Anderson Rd. E9 —3F **27**
Anderson Sq. N1 —5D **25** (off Gaskin St.)
Anderson St. SW3 —1B **64**
Anderton Clo. SE5 —1F **81**
Andover Av. E16 —5F **45**
Andover Pl. NW6 —1D **35**
Andover Rd. N7 —4B **10**
Andoversford Ct. SE15 (off Bibury Clo.) —2A **68**
Andre St. E8 —2C **26**
Andrew Borde St. WC2 —5F **37**
Andrew Ct. SE23 —2F **97**
Andrewes Gdns. E6 —5F **45**
Andrewes Highwalk. EC2 (off Fore St.) —4E **39**
Andrewes Ho. EC2 —4E **39** (off Fore St.)
Andrew Pl. SW8 —3F **65**
Andrews Crosse. WC2 (off Chancery La.) —5C **38**
Andrew's Rd. E8 —5D **27**
Andrew St. E14 —5E **43**
Andrews Wlk. SE17 —2D **67**
Anerley Hill. SE19 —5B **96**
Anerley St. SW11 —5B **64**
Aneurin Bevan Ct. NW2 —4D **5**
Anfield Clo. SW12 —5E **79**
Angel. (Junct.) —1C **38**
Angela Davies Ind. Est. SE24 —2D **81**
Angel All. E1 —5B **40** (off Whitechapel High St.)
Angel Cen., The. N1 —1C **38** (off St John St.)
Angel Ct. EC2 —5F **39**
Angel Ct. SW1 —2E **51**
Angel Ga. EC1 —2D **39** (in three parts)
Angelina Ho. SE15 —4C **68** (off Goldsmith Rd.)
Angel La. E15 —3F **29**
Angell Pk. Gdns. SW9 —1C **80**
Angell Rd. SW9 —1C **80**
Angell Town. —4C 66
Angell Town Est. SW9 —5C **66**
Angel M. E1 —1D **55**
Angel M. N1 —1C **38**
Angel M. SW15 —5C **74**
Angel Pas. EC4 —1F **53**
Angel Pl. SE1 —3F **53**
Angel Sq. N1 —1C **38**
Angel St. EC1 —5E **39**
Angel Wlk. W6 —5E **47**
Angel Yd. N6 —3C **8**
Angerstein Bus. Pk. SE10 —5C **58**
Angerstein La. SE3 —4B **72**
Anglebury. W2 —5C **34** (off Talbot Rd.)
Angler's La. NW5 —3D **23**
Anglesey Ho. E14 —5C **42**
Angles Rd. SW16 —4A **94**
Anglia Ho. E14 —5A **42**
Anglian Rd. E11 —5F **15**
Anglo Rd. E3 —1B **42**
Angrave Ct. E8 —5B **26** (off Scriven St.)
Angrave Pas. E8 —5B **26**
Angus Ho. SW2 —5F **79**
Angus Rd. E13 —2E **45**
Angus St. SE14 —3A **70**
Anhalt Rd. SW11 —3A **64**
Anley Rd. W6 —3F **47**
Annabel Clo. E14 —5D **43**
Anna Clo. E8 —5B **26**
Annandale Rd. SE10 —2B **72**
Annandale Rd. W4 —1A **60**
Anna Neagle Clo. E7 —1C **30**
Annesley Clo. NW10 —5A **4**
Annesley Ho. SW9 —4C **66**
Annesley Rd. SE3 —4D **73**
Annesley Wlk. N19 —4E **9**
Anne St. E13 —3C **44**
Annette Rd. N7 —5B **10** (in two parts)
Annetts Cres. N1 —4E **25**
Annie Besant Clo. E3 —5B **28**
Anning St. EC2 —3A **40**
Annis Rd. E9 —3A **28**
Ann La. SW10 —2F **63**
Ann Moss Way. SE16 —4E **55**
Ann's Clo. SW1 —3B **50** (off Kinnerton St.)
Ann's Pl. E1 —4B **40** (off Wentworth St.)
Ansar Gdns. E17 —1B **14**
Ansdell Rd. SE15 —5E **69**
Ansdell St. W8 —4D **49**
Ansdell Ter. W8 —4D **49**
Ansell Ho. E1 —4E **41** (off Mile End Rd.)
Ansell Rd. SW17 —3A **92**
Anselm Rd. SW6 —2C **62**
Ansford Rd. Brom —5E **99**
Ansleigh Pl. W11 —1F **47**
Anson Ho. SW1 —2E **65** (off Churchill Gdns.)
Anson Rd. N19 —1E **23**
Anson Rd. NW2 —1D **19**
Anstey Rd. SE15 —1C **82**
Anstice Clo. W4 —3A **60**
Antenor Ho. E2 —1D **41** (off Old Bethnal Grn. Rd.)
Anthony Cope Ct. N1 —2F **39** (off Chart St.)
Anthony Ho. NW1 —3A **36** (off Ashbridge St.)
Anthony St. E1 —5D **41**
Antigua Wlk. SE19 —5F **95**
Antilles Bay. E14 —3E **57**
Antill Rd. E3 —2A **42**
Antill Ter. E1 —5F **41**
Anton St. E8 —2C **26**
Antony Ho. SE14 —3F **69** (off Barlborough St.)
Antony Ho. SE16 —5E **55** (off Raymouth Rd.)
Antrim Gro. NW3 —3B **22**
Antrim Rd. NW3 —3B **22**
Apex Ind. Est. NW10 —3B **32**
Aphrodite Ct. E14 —5C **56**
Apollo Bus. Cen. SE8 —1F **69**
Apollo Ct. E1 —1C **54** (off Thomas More St.)
Apollo Ct. SW9 —4C **66** (off Southey Rd.)
Apollo Ho. E2 —1D **41** (off St Jude's Rd.)
Apollo Ho. N6 —2C **8**
Apollo Ho. SW10 —3F **63** (off Riley St.)
Apollo Pl. E11 —5A **16**
Apollo Pl. SW10 —3F **63**
Apothecary St. EC4 —5D **39**
Appach Rd. SW2 —3C **80**
Apple Blossom Ct. SW8 (off Pascal St.) —3F **65**
Appleby Clo. N15 —1F **11**
Appleby Rd. E8 —4C **26**
Appleby Rd. E16 —5B **44**
Appleby St. E2 —1B **40**
Appledore Clo. SW17 —2B **92**
Appleford Ho. W10 —3A **34** (off Bosworth Rd.)
Appleford Rd. W10 —3A **34**
Applegarth Ho. SE1 —3D **53** (off Nelson Sq.)
Applegarth Ho. SE15 —3C **68** (off Bird in Bush Rd.)
Applegarth Rd. W14 —4F **47**
Apple Rd. E11 —5A **16**
Appleshaw Ho. SE5 —1A **82**
Appleton Rd. SE3 —1F **87**
Apple Tree Yd. SW1 —2E **51**
Applewood Clo. NW2 —5D **5**
Appold St. EC2 —4A **40**
Apprentice Way. E5 —1D **27**
Approach Clo. N16 —1A **26**
Approach Rd. E2 —1E **41**
Approach, The. NW4 —1F **5**
Approach, The. W3 —5A **32**
April Ct. E2 —1C **40** (off Teale St.)
April Glen. SE23 —3F **97**
April St. E8 —1B **26**
Apsley Ho. NW8 —1F **35** (off Finchley Rd.)
Apsley Way. NW2 —4C **4**
Apsley Way. W1 —3C **50** (in two parts)
Aquila St. NW8 —1F **35**
Aquinas St. SE1 —2C **52**
Arabella Dri. SW15 —2A **74**
Arabin Rd. SE4 —2A **84**
Aragon M. E1 —2C **54**
Aragon Tower. SE8 —5B **56**
Arapiles Ho. E14 —5F **43**
Arbery Rd. E3 —2A **42**
Arbon Ct. N1 —5E **25** (off Linton St.)
Arbor Ct. N16 —4F **11**
Arborfield Clo. SW2 —1B **94**
Arborfield Ho. E14 —1C **56**
Arbour Sq. E1 —5F **41**

Arbroath Rd. SE9 —1F **87**
Arbury Ter. SE26 —3C **96**
Arbuthnot Rd. SE14 —5F **69**
Arbutus St. E8 —5B **26**
Arcade, The. E14 —5D **43**
Arcade, The. EC2 —4A ***40***
(off Liverpool St.)
Arcadia Ct. E1 —4B ***40***
(off Old Castle St.)
Arcadia St. E14 —5C **42**
Archangel St. SE16 —3F **55**
Archbishop's Pl. SW2 —5B **80**
Archdale Ct. W12 —2D **47**
Archdale Ho. SE1 —4A ***54***
(off Long La.)
Archdale Rd. SE22 —3B **82**
Archel Rd. W14 —2B **62**
Archer Ho. SE14 —4A **70**
Archer Ho. SW11 —4F **63**
Archer Ho. W11 —1B ***48***
(off Westbourne Gro.)
Archers Lodge. SE16 —1C ***68***
(off Culloden Clo.)
Archer Sq. SE14 —2A **70**
Archer St. W1 —1F **51**
Archery Clo. W2 —5A **36**
Archery Steps. W2 —1A ***50***
(off St George's Fields)
Arches, The. NW1 —4D **23**
Arches, The. SW8 —3F **65**
Arches, The. WC2 —2A ***52***
(off Villiers St.)
Archibald M. W1 —1C **50**
Archibald Rd. N7 —1F **23**
Archibald St. E3 —2C **42**
Arch St. SE1 —4E **53**
Archway. (Junct.) —4E **9**
Archway Bus. Cen. N19 —5F **9**
Archway Clo. N19 —4E **9**
Archway Clo. SW19 —3D **91**
Archway Clo. W10 —4F **33**
Archway Mall. N19 —4E **9**
Archway Rd. N6 & N19 —1C **8**
Archway St. SW13 —1A **74**
Arcola St. E8 —2B **26**
Arctic St. NW5 —2D **23**
Arcus Rd. Brom —5A **100**
Ardbeg Rd. SE24 —3F **81**
Arden Ct. Gdns. N2 —1F **7**
Arden Cres. E14 —5C **56**
Arden Est. N1 —1A **40**
Arden Ho. N1 —1A ***40***
(off Arden Est.)
Arden Ho. SE11 —5B ***52***
(off Black Prince Rd.)
Arden Ho. SW9 —5A ***66***
(off Grantham Rd.)
Ardfillan Rd. SE6 —1F **99**
Ardgowan Rd. SE6 —5A **86**
(in two parts)
Ardilaun Rd. N5 —1E **25**
Ardleigh Rd. N1 —3A **26**
Ardley Clo. NW10 —5A **4**
Ardley Clo. SE6 —3A **98**
Ardlui Rd. SE27 —2E **95**
Ardmere Rd. SE13 —4F **85**
Ardoch Rd. SE6 —2F **99**
Ardshiel Clo. SW15 —1F **75**
Ardwell Rd. SW2 —2A **94**
Ardwick Rd. NW2 —1C **20**
Arena Bus. Cen. N4 —1E **11**
Arena Est. N4 —1D **11**
Ares Ct. E14 —5C **56**
Arethusa Ho. E14 —5C **56**
Argall Av. E10 —2F **13**
Argall Way. E10 —3F **13**
Argon M. SW6 —3C **62**
Argos Ct. SW9 —4C ***66***
(off Caldwell St.)
Argos Ho. E2 —1D ***41***
(off Old Bethnal Grn. Rd.)
Argosy Ho. SE8 —5A **56**
Argyle Ho. E14 —4E **57**
Argyle Pl. W6 —5D **47**
Argyle Rd. E1 —3F **41**
Argyle Rd. E15 —1A **30**
Argyle Rd. E16 —5D **45**
Argyle Sq. WC1 —2A **38**
Argyle St. NW1 —2A **38**
Argyle Wlk. WC1 —2A **38**
Argyle Way. SE16 —1C ***68***
(off St James Rd.)
Argyll Clo. SW9 —1B **80**
Argyll Mans. SW3 —2F **63**
Argyll Mans. W14 —5A ***48***
(off Hammersmith Rd.)
Argyll Rd. W8 —3C **48**
Argyll St. W1 —5E **37**
Arica Ho. SE16 —4D ***55***
(off Slippers Pl.)
Arica Rd. SE4 —2A **84**
Ariel Ct. SE11 —5D **53**
Ariel Rd. NW6 —3C **20**
Ariel Way. W12 —2E **47**
Aristotle Rd. SW4 —1F **79**
Arkindale Rd. SE6 —3E **99**
Arkley Cres. E17 —1B **14**
Arkley Rd. E17 —1B **14**
Arklow Ho. SE5 —2F ***67***
(off Albany Rd.)
Arklow Rd. SE14 —2B **70**
Arklow Rd. Trad. Est. SE14 —2A **70**
Arkwright Ho. SW2 —5A ***80***
(off Streatham Pl.)
Arkwright Rd. NW3 —2E **21**
Arlesey Clo. SW15 —3A **76**
Arlesford Rd. SW9 —1A **80**
Arlingford Rd. SW2 —3C **80**
Arlington Av. N1 —5E **25**
(in two parts)
Arlington Clo. SE13 —3F **85**
Arlington Ho. EC1 —2C ***38***
(off Arlington Way)
Arlington Ho. SE8 —2B ***70***
(off Evelyn St.)
Arlington Ho. SW1 —2E **51**
Arlington Lodge. SW2 —2B **80**
Arlington Pl. SE10 —3E **71**
Arlington Rd. NW1 —5D **23**
Arlington Sq. N1 —5E **25**
Arlington St. W1 —2E **51**
Arlington Way. EC1 —2C **38**
Armada Ct. SE8 —2C **70**
Armadale Rd. SW6 —3C **62**
Armada St. SE8 —2C ***70***
(off McMillan St.)
Armagh Rd. E3 —5B **28**
Arminger Rd. W12 —2D **47**
Armitage Rd. NW11 —3A **6**
Armitage Rd. SE10 —1B **72**
Armour Clo. N7 —3B **24**
Armoury Rd. SE8 —5D **71**
Armoury Way. SW18 —3C **76**
Armsby Ho. E1 —4E ***41***
(off Stepney Way)
Armstrong Rd. SW7 —4F **49**
Armstrong Rd. W3 —2B **46**
Arnal Cres. SW18 —5A **76**
Arncliffe. NW6 —1D **35**
Arndale Wlk. SW18 —3D **77**
Arne Ho. SE11 —1B ***66***
(off Worgan St.)
Arne St. WC2 —5A **38**
Arne Wlk. SE3 —2B **86**
Arneway St. SW1 —4F **51**
Arnewood Clo. SW15 —1C **88**
Arngask Rd. SE6 —5F **85**
Arnhem Pl. E14 —4C **56**
Arnhem Way. SE22 —3A **82**
Arnhem Wharf. E14 —4B **56**
Arnold Cir. E2 —2B **40**
Arnold Est. SE1 —3B **54**
(in two parts)
Arnold Ho. SE3 —3E ***73***
(off Shooters Hill Rd.)
Arnold Ho. SE17 —1D ***67***
(off Doddington Gro.)
Arnold Mans. W14 —2B ***62***
(off Queen's Club Gdns.)
Arnold Rd. E3 —2C **42**
Arnot Ho. SE5 —3E ***67***
(off Comber Gro.)
Arnott Clo. W4 —5A **46**
Arnould Av. SE5 —2F **81**
Arnside St. SE17 —2F **67**
Arnulf St. SE6 —4D **99**
Arnulls Rd. SW16 —5D **95**
Arodene Rd. SW2 —4B **80**
Arragon Rd. E6 —5F **31**
Arragon Rd. SW18 —1C **90**
Arran Ct. NW10 —5A **4**
Arran Dri. E12 —3F **17**
Arran Ho. E14 —2E **57**
Arran Rd. SE6 —2D **99**
Arran Wlk. N1 —4E **25**
Arrol Ho. SE1 —4E **53**
Arrow Ct. SW5 —5C ***48***
(off W. Cromwell Rd.)
Arrowhead Ct. E11 —1F **15**
Arrow Rd. E3 —2D **43**
Arrowsmith Ho. SE11
(off Wickham St.) —1B ***66***
Arsenal F.C. —5D 11
Artemis Ct. E14 —5C **56**
Artesian Clo. NW10 —4A **18**
Artesian Rd. W2 —5C **34**
Artesian Wlk. E11 —5A **16**
Arthingworth St. E15 —5A **30**
Arthur Ct. SW11 —4C **64**

Arthur Ct. W2 —5D **35**
(off Queensway)
Arthur Ct. W10 —5F **33**
(off Silchester Rd.)
Arthur Deakin Ho. E1 —4C **40**
(off Hunton St.)
Arthurdon Rd. SE4 —3C **84**
Arthur Henderson Ho. SW6
(off Fulham Rd.) —5B **62**
Arthur Horsley Wlk. E7
—2B **30**
(off Tower Hamlets Rd.)
Arthur Rd. N7 —1B **24**
Arthur Rd. SW19 —5B **90**
Arthur St. EC4 —1F **53**
Artichoke Hill. E1 —1D **55**
Artichoke M. SE5 —4F **67**
(off Artichoke Pl.)
Artichoke Pl. SE5 —4F **67**
Artillery Ho. E15 —3A **30**
Artillery La. E1 —4A **40**
Artillery La. W12 —5C **32**
Artillery Pas. E1 —4B **40**
(off Artillery La.)
Artillery Pl. SW1 —4F **51**
Artillery Row. SW1 —4E **51**
Artizan St. E1 —5B **40**
(off Harrow Pl.)
Arundel Bldgs. SE1 —4A **54**
(off Swan Mead)
Arundel Clo. E15 —1A **30**
Arundel Clo. SW11 —3A **78**
Arundel Ct. SW3 —1A **64**
(off Jubilee Pl.)
Arundel Gdns. W11 —1B **48**
Arundel Gt. Ct. WC2 —1B **52**
Arundel Gro. N16 —2A **26**
Arundel Mans. SW6 —4B **62**
(off Kelvedon Rd.)
Arundel Pl. N1 —3C **24**
Arundel Sq. N7 —3C **24**
Arundel St. WC2 —1B **52**
Arundel Ter. SW13 —2D **61**
Arvon Rd. N5 —2C **24**
(in two parts)
Ascalon Ho. SW8 —3E **65**
(off Thessaly Rd.)
Ascalon St. SW8 —3E **65**
Ascham St. NW5 —2E **23**
Ascot Cl. NW8 —2F **35**
(off Grove End Rd.)
Ascot Ho. NW1 —2D **37**
(off Redhill St.)
Ascot Ho. W9 —3C **34**
(off Harrow Rd.)
Ascot Lodge. NW6 —5D **21**
Ascot Rd. N15 —1F **11**
Ascot Rd. SW17 —5C **92**
Ashbee Ho. E2 —2E **41**
(off Portman Pl.)
Ashbourne Av. NW11 —1B **6**
Ashbourne Ct. E5 —1A **28**
Ashbourne Gro. SE22 —2B **82**
Ashbourne Gro. W4 —1A **60**
Ashbridge Rd. E11 —2A **16**
Ashbridge St. NW8 —3A **36**
Ashbrook Rd. N19 —3F **9**

Ashburn Gdns. SW7 —5E **49**
Ashburnham Gro. SE10
—3D **71**
Ashburnham Mans. SW10
—3E **63**
(off Ashburnham Rd.)
Ashburnham Pl. SE10
—3D **71**
Ashburnham Retreat. SE10
—3D **71**
Ashburnham Rd. NW10
—2E **33**
Ashburnham Rd. SW10
—3E **63**
Ashburnham Tower. SW10
—3F **63**
(off Worlds End Est.)
Ashburn Pl. SW7 —5E **49**
Ashburton Enterprise Cen.
SW15 —4E **75**
Ashburton Gro. N7 —1C **24**
Ashburton Rd. W9 —3B **34**
(off Fernhead Rd.)
Ashburton Rd. E16 —5C **44**
Ashburton Ter. E13 —1C **44**
Ashbury Pl. SW19 —5E **91**
Ashbury Rd. SW11 —1B **78**
Ashby Ct. NW8 —3F **35**
(off Pollitt Dri.)
Ashby Gro. N1 —4E **25**
Ashby Ho. N1 —4E **25**
(off Essex Rd.)
Ashby Ho. SW9 —5D **67**
Ashby M. SE4 —5B **70**
Ashby Rd. SE4 —5B **70**
Ashby St. EC1 —2D **39**
Ashchurch Gro. W12 —4C **46**
Ashchurch Pk. Vs. W12
—4C **46**
Ashchurch Ter. W12 —4C **46**
Ashcombe Pk. NW2 —5A **4**
Ashcombe Rd. SW19 —5C **90**
Ashcombe St. SW6 —5D **63**
Ash Ct. NW5 —2C **23**
Ash Ct. W1 —5B **36**
(off Harrowby St.)
Ashcroft Ho. SW8 —4E **65**
(off Wadhurst Rd.)
Ashcroft Rd. E3 —2A **42**
Ashcroft Sq. W6 —5E **47**
Ashdale Ho. N4 —2F **11**
Ashdale Rd. SE12 —1D **101**
Ashdene. SE15 —3D **69**
Ashdon Rd. NW10 —5B **18**
Ashdown Cres. NW5 —2C **22**
Ashdown Est. E11 —1F **29**
Ashdown Ho. SW1 —4E **51**
(off Victoria St.)
Ashdown Wlk. E14 —5C **56**
(off Copeland Dri.)
Ashdown Way. SW17 —2C **92**
Ashenden. SE1 —5E **53**
(off Deacon Way)
Ashenden Rd. E5 —2A **28**
Ashen Gro. SW19 —3C **90**
Ashentree Ct. EC4 —5C **38**
(off Whitefriars St.)

Asher Way. E1 —1C **54**
Ashfield Ho. W14 —1B **62**
Ashfield Rd. N4 —1E **11**
Ashfield Rd. W3 —2B **46**
Ashfield St. E1 —4D **41**
Ashfield Yd. E1 —4E **41**
Ashford Clo. E17 —1B **14**
Ashford Ho. SE8 —2B **70**
Ashford Ho. SW9 —2D **81**
Ashford Pas. NW2 —1F **19**
Ashford Rd. NW2 —1F **19**
Ashford St. N1 —2A **40**
Ash Gro. E8 —5D **27**
(in two parts)
Ash Gro. NW2 —1F **19**
Ash Gro. SE12 —1C **100**
Ashgrove Ct. W9 —4C **34**
(off Elmfield Way)
Ashgrove Ho. SW1 —1F **65**
(off Lindsay Sq.)
Ashgrove Rd. Brom —5F **99**
Ash Ho. E14 —3E **57**
(off Longfield Est.)
Ash Ho. SE1 —5B **54**
Ash Ho. W10 —3A **34**
(off Heather Wlk.)
Ashington Ho. E1 —3D **41**
(off Barnsley St.)
Ashington Rd. SW6 —5B **62**
Ashlake Rd. SW16 —4A **94**
Ashland Pl. W1 —4C **36**
Ashleigh Commercial Est. SE7
—4E **59**
Ashleigh Point. SE23 —3F **97**
Ashleigh Rd. SW14 —1A **74**
Ashley Ct. SW1 —4E **51**
(off Morpeth Ter.)
Ashley Cres. SW11 —1C **78**
Ashley Gdns. SW1 —4E **51**
(in three parts)
Ashley Pl. SW1 —4E **51**
(in two parts)
Ashley Rd. E7 —4E **31**
Ashley Rd. N19 —3A **10**
Ashley Rd. SW19 —5D **91**
Ashlin Rd. E15 —1F **29**
Ashlone Rd. SW15 —1E **75**
Ashmead Bus. Cen. E3
—3F **43**
Ashmead Ho. E9 —2A **28**
(off Homerton Rd.)
Ashmead Rd. SE8 —5C **70**
Ashmere Gro. SW2 —2A **80**
Ashmill St. NW1 —4A **36**
Ashmole Pl. SW8 —2B **66**
(in two parts)
Ashmole St. SW8 —2B **66**
Ashmore. NW1 —4F **23**
(off Agar Gro.)
Ashmore Ho. W14 —4A **48**
(off Russell Rd.)
Ashmore Rd. W9 —1B **34**
Ashmount Est. N19 —2F **9**
Ashmount Rd. N6 —2E **9**
Ashness Rd. SW11 —3B **78**
Ashpark Ho. E14 —5B **42**
Ash Rd. E15 —2A **30**

Ashtead Rd. *E5*—2C **12**
Ashton Heights. *SE23* —1E **97**
Ashton Ho. *SW9*—3C **66**
Ashton Rd. *E15*—2F **29**
Ashton St. *E14*—1E **57**
Ashurst Gdns. *SW2*—1C **94**
Ashvale Rd. *SW17*—5B **92**
Ashville Rd. *E11*—4F **15**
Ashwater Rd. *SE12*—1C **100**
Ashwin St. *E8*—3B **26**
Ashworth Clo. *SE5*—5F **67**
Ashworth Mans. W9 —2D ***35*** *(off Elgin Av.)*
Ashworth Rd. *W9*—2D **35**
Aske Ho. N1 —2A ***40*** *(off Fanshaw St., in two parts)*
Asker Ho. *N7*—1A **24**
Aske St. *N1*—2A **40**
Askew Cres. *W12*—3B **46**
Askew Est. W12 —2B ***46*** *(off Uxbridge Rd.)*
Askew Rd. *W12*—2B **46**
Askham Ct. *W12*—2C **46**
Askham Rd. *W12*—2C **46**
Askill Dri. *SW15*—3A **76**
Asland Rd. *E15*—5A **30**
Aslett St. *SW18*—5D **77**
Asmara Rd. *NW2*—2A **20**
Asmuns Hill. *NW11*—1C **6**
Asmuns Pl. *NW11*—1B **6**
Asolando Dri. SE17 —5E ***53*** *(off King & Queen St.)*
Aspen Clo. *N19*—4E **9**
Aspen Gdns. *W6*—1D **61**
Aspen Ho. SE15 —2E ***69*** *(off Sharratt St.)*
Aspenlea Rd. *W6*—2F **61**
Aspen Lodge. *W8*—4D **49**
Aspen Way. *E14*—1D **57**
Aspern Gro. *NW3*—2A **22**
Aspinall Rd. *SE4*—1F **83**
Aspinden Rd. *SE16*—5D **55**
Aspley Rd. *SW18*—3D **77**
Assam St. *E1*—5C **40**
Assata M. *N1*—3D **25**
Assembly Pas. *E1*—4E **41**
Astbury Ho. SE11 —4C ***52*** *(off Lambeth Wlk.)*
Astbury Rd. *SE15*—4E **69**
Astell St. *SW3*—1A **64**
Aste St. *E14*—3E **57**
Astey's Row. *N1*—4E **25**
Astle St. *SW11*—5C **64**
Astley Av. *NW2*—2E **19**
Astley Ho. SE1 —1B ***68*** *(off Rowcross St.)*
Aston Ho. *SW8*—4F **65**
Aston Ho. W11 —1B ***48*** *(off Westbourne Gro.)*
Aston St. *E14*—4A **42**
Aston Ter. *SW12*—4D **79**
Astonville St. *SW18*—1C **90**
Astor Ct. E16 —5E ***45*** *(off Ripley Rd.)*
Astoria Mans. *SW16*—3A **94**
Astoria Wlk. *SW9*—1C **80**
Astra Ho. SE14 —2B ***70*** *(off Arklow Rd.)*
Astrop M. *W6*—4E **47**
Astrop Ter. *W6*—3E **47**
Astwood M. *SW7*—5E **49**
Asylum Rd. *SE15*—3D **69**
Atalanta St. *SW6*—3F **61**
Atheldene Rd. *SW18*—1D **91**
Athelney St. *SE6*—3C **98**
Athelstane Gro. *E3*—1B **42**
Athelstane M. *N4*—3C **10**
Athelstan Gdns. *NW6*—4A **20**
Athenaeum Ct. *N5*—1E **25**
Athenia Ho. *E14*—5F **43**
Athenlay Rd. *SE15*—3F **83**
Athens Gdns. W9 —3C ***34*** *(off Harrow Rd.)*
Atherden Rd. *E5*—1E **27**
Atherfold Rd. *SW9*—1A **80**
Atherstone Ct. W2 —4D ***35*** *(off Delamere Ter.)*
Atherstone M. *SW7*—5E **49**
Atherton Dri. *SW19*—4F **89**
Atherton M. *E7*—3B **30**
Atherton Rd. *E7*—3B **30**
Atherton Rd. *SW13*—3C **60**
Atherton St. *SW11*—5A **64**
Athlone Clo. *E5*—2D **27**
Athlone Rd. *SW2*—5B **80**
Athlone St. *NW5*—3C **22**
Atholl Ho. W9 —2E ***35*** *(off Maida Va.)*
Athol Sq. *E14*—5E **43**
Atkin Building. WC1 —4B ***38*** *(off Raymond Bldgs.)*
Atkinson Ct. E10 —2D ***15*** *(off Kings Clo.)*
Atkinson Ho. E2 —1C ***40*** *(off Pritchards Rd.)*
Atkinson Ho. E13 —3B ***44*** *(off Sutton Rd.)*
Atkinson Ho. SE17 —5F ***53*** *(off Catesby St.)*
Atkinson Rd. *E16*—4E **45**
Atkins Rd. *E10*—1D **15**
Atkins Rd. *SW12*—5E **79**
Atlantic Ct. *E14*—1F **57**
Atlantic Rd. *SW9*—2C **80**
Atlas Bus. Cen. *NW2*—3D **5**
Atlas Gdns. *SE7*—5E **59**
Atlas M. *E8*—3B **26**
Atlas M. *N7*—3B **24**
Atlas Rd. *E13*—1C **44**
Atlas Rd. *NW10*—2A **32**
Atlas Wharf. *E9*—3C **28**
Atley Rd. *E3*—5C **28**
Atney Rd. *SW15*—2A **76**
Atterbury Rd. *N4*—1C **10**
Atterbury St. *SW1*—5A **52**
Attewood Av. *NW10*—5A **4**
Attilburgh Ho. SE1 —4B ***54*** *(off Abbey St.)*
Attleborough Ct. *SE26* —2C **96**
Attneave St. *WC1*—2C **38**
Atwater Clo. *SW2*—1C **94**
Atwell Clo. *E10*—1D **15**
Atwell Rd. *SE15*—5C **68**
Atwood Rd. *W6*—5D **47**
Aubert Ct. *N5*—1D **25**
Aubert Pk. *N5*—1D **25**
Aubert Rd. *N5*—1D **25**
Aubrey Beardsley Ho. SW1 —5E ***51*** *(off Vauxhall Bri. Rd.)*
Aubrey Mans. NW1 —4A ***36*** *(off Lisson St.)*
Aubrey Moore Point. E15 (off Abbey La.) —1E ***43***
Aubrey Pl. *NW8*—1E **35**
Aubrey Rd. *N8*—1A **10**
Aubrey Rd. *W8*—2B **48**
Aubrey Wlk. *W8*—2B **48**
Auburn Clo. *SE14*—3A **70**
Aubyn Hill. *SE27*—4E **95**
Aubyn Sq. *SW15*—3C **74**
Auckland Hill. *SE27*—4E **95**
Auckland Ho. W12 —1D ***47*** *(off White City Est.)*
Auckland Rd. *E10*—5D **15**
Auckland Rd. *SW11*—2A **78**
Auckland St. *SE11*—1B **66**
Auden Pl. *NW1*—5C **22** (in two parts)
Audley Clo. *SW11*—1C **78**
Audley Dri. *E16*—2D **59**
Audley Rd. *NW4*—1C **4**
Audley Sq. *W1*—2C **50**
Audrey St. *E2*—1C **40**
Augurs La. *E13*—2D **45**
Augusta St. *E14*—5D **43**
Augustine Rd. *W14*—4F **47**
Augustus Clo. *W12*—3D **47**
Augustus Ct. *SW16*—2F **93**
Augustus Ho. NW1 —1E ***37*** *(off Augustus St.)*
Augustus Rd. *SW19*—1F **89**
Augustus St. *NW1*—1D **37**
Aulton Pl. *SE11*—1C **66**
Auriga M. *N1*—2F **25**
Auriol Rd. *W14*—5A **48**
Aurora Ho. *E14*—5D **43**
Austen Ho. NW6 —2C ***34*** *(off Cambridge Rd.)*
Austen Ho. NW6 —2C ***34*** *(off Cambridge Rd.)*
Austin Clo. *SE23*—5A **84**
Austin Ct. *E6*—5E **31**
Austin Ct. SE15 —1C ***82*** *(off Philip Wlk.)*
Austin Friars. *EC2*—5F **39** (in two parts)
Austin Friars Pas. EC2 (off Austin Friars) —5F ***39***
Austin Friars Sq. EC2 —5F ***39*** *(off Austin Friars)*
Austin Ho. SE14 —3B ***70*** *(off Achilles St.)*
Austin Rd. *SW11*—4C **64**
Austin St. *E2*—2B **40**
Austin Ter. *SE1*—4C **52**
Australia Rd. *W12*—1D **47**
Austral St. *SE11*—5D **53**

Autumn Clo. *SW19* —5E **91**
Autumn St. *E3* —5C **28**
Avalon Rd. *SW6* —4D **63**
Avarn Rd. *SW17* —5B **92**
*Avebury Ct. N1 —5F **25***
(off Imber St.)
Avebury Rd. *E11* —3F **15**
Avebury St. *N1* —5F **25**
Aveline St. *SE11* —1C **66**
Ave Maria La. *EC4* —5D **39**
Avenell Rd. *N5* —5D **11**
*Avenfield Ho. W1 —1B **50***
(off Park La.)
Avening Rd. *SW18* —5C **76**
Avening Ter. *SW18* —5C **76**
Avenons Rd. *E13* —3C **44**
Avenue Clo. *NW8* —5A **22**
(in two parts)
Avenue Ct. *NW2* —5B **6**
*Avenue Ct. SW3 —5B **50***
(off Draycott Av.)
Avenue Gdns. *SW14* —1A **74**
*Avenue Ho. NW8 —1A **36***
(off Allitsen Rd.)
*Avenue Lodge. NW8 —4F **21***
(off Avenue Rd.)
*Avenue Mans. NW3 —2D **21***
(off Finchley Rd.)
Avenue Pk. Rd. *SE27* —2D **95**
Avenue Rd. *E7* —1D **31**
Avenue Rd. *N6* —2E **9**
Avenue Rd. *N15* —1F **11**
Avenue Rd. *NW3 & NW8* —4F **21**
Avenue Rd. *NW10* —1B **32**
Avenue, The. *E11* —1D **17**
Avenue, The. *NW6* —5F **19**
Avenue, The. *SE10* —3F **71**
Avenue, The. *SW4* —3C **78**
Avenue, The. *SW18* —5A **78**
Avenue, The. *W4* —4A **46**
Averill St. *W6* —2F **61**
Avery Farm Row. *SW1* —5C **50**
Avery Row. *W1* —1D **51**
Aviary Clo. *E16* —4B **44**
Avignon Rd. *SE4* —1F **83**
*Avington Ct. SE1 —5A **54***
(off Old Kent Rd.)
Avington Way. *SE15* —3B **68**
Avis Sq. *E1* —5F **41**
Avoca Rd. *SW17* —4C **92**
Avocet Clo. *SE1* —1C **68**
Avondale Av. *NW2* —5A **4**
Avondale Ct. *E11* —3A **16**
Avondale Ct. *E16* —4A **44**
Avondale Cres. *Ilf* —1F **17**
*Avondale Ho. SE1 —1C **68***
(off Avondale Sq.)
Avondale Pk. Gdns. *W11* —1A **48**
Avondale Pk. Rd. *W11* —1A **48**
Avondale Ri. *SE15* —1B **82**
Avondale Rd. *E16* —4A **44**
Avondale Rd. *E17* —2C **14**
Avondale Rd. *N15* —1D **11**
Avondale Rd. *SE9* —2F **101**
Avondale Rd. *SW14* —1A **74**
Avondale Rd. *SW19* —5D **91**
Avondale Rd. *Brom* —5A **100**
Avondale Sq. *SE1* —1C **68**
*Avon Ho. W8 —4C **48***
(off Allen St.)
*Avon Ho. W14 —5B **48***
(off Avonmore Rd.)
Avonhurst Ho. *NW2* —4A **20**
Avonley Rd. *SE14* —3E **69**
Avonmore Gdns. *W14* —5B **48**
*Avonmore Pl. W14 —5A **48***
(off Avonmore Rd.)
Avonmore Rd. *W14* —5A **48**
Avonmouth St. *SE1* —4E **53**
Avon Pl. *SE1* —3E **53**
Avon Rd. *SE4* —1C **84**
*Avro Ho. SW8 —3D **65***
(off Havelock Ter.)
Axminster Rd. *N7* —5A **10**
Aybrook St. *W1* —4C **36**
Aycliffe Rd. *W12* —2C **46**
Ayerst Ct. *E10* —2E **15**
Aylesbury Clo. *E7* —3B **30**
*Aylesbury Ho. SE15 —2C **68***
(off Friary Est.)
Aylesbury Rd. *SE17* —1F **67**
Aylesbury St. *EC1* —3D **39**
Aylesbury St. *NW10* —5A **4**
*Aylesford Ho. SE1 —3F **53***
(off Long La.)
Aylesford St. *SW1* —1F **65**
Aylesham Cen., The. *SE15* —4C **68**
Aylestone Av. *NW6* —4F **19**
Aylmer Ct. *N2* —1B **8**
Aylmer Ho. *SE10* —1F **71**
Aylmer Pde. *N2* —1B **8**
Aylmer Rd. *E11* —3B **16**
Aylmer Rd. *N2* —1A **8**
Aylmer Rd. *W12* —3B **46**
Aylton Est. *SE16* —3E **55**
Aylward Rd. *SE23* —2F **97**
Aylward St. *E1* —5E **41**
(in two parts)
Aylwin Est. *SE1* —4A **54**
*Aynhoe Mans. W14 —5F **47***
(off Aynhoe Rd.)
Aynhoe Rd. *W14* —5F **47**
Ayres Clo. *E13* —2C **44**
Ayres St. *SE1* —3E **53**
Ayrsome Rd. *N16* —5A **12**
Ayrton Rd. *SW7* —4F **49**
Aysgarth Rd. *SE21* —5A **82**
*Ayshford Ho. E2 —2D **41***
(off Viaduct St.)
*Ayston Ho. SE16 —5F **55***
(off Plough Way)
*Ayton Ho. SE5 —3F **67***
(off Edmund St.)
Aytoun Pl. *SW9* —5B **66**
Aytoun Rd. *SW9* —5B **66**
*Azalea Ho. SE14 —3B **70***
(off Achilles St.)
Azania M. *NW5* —3D **23**
Azenby Rd. *SE15* —5B **68**
Azof St. *SE10* —5A **58**

Baalbec Rd. *N5* —2D **25**
*Babington Ct. WC1 —4A **38***
(off Orde Hall St.)
*Babington Ho. SE1 —3E **53***
(off Disney St.)
Babington Rd. *SW16* —5F **93**
Babmaes St. *SW1* —1F **51**
*Bacchus Wlk. N1 —1A **40***
(off Regan Way)
Bache's St. *N1* —2F **39**
*Back All. EC3 —5A **40***
(off Northumberland All.)
Bk. Church La. *E1* —5C **40**
Back Hill. *EC1* —3C **38**
*Backhouse Pl. SE17 —5A **54***
(off Surrey Sq.)
Back La. *N8* —1A **10**
Back La. *NW3* —1E **21**
Bacon Gro. *SE1* —4B **54**
Bacons La. *N6* —3C **8**
Bacon St. *E1 & E2* —3B **40**
Bacton St. *E2* —2E **41**
*Baddesley Ho. SE11 —1B **66***
(off Jonathan St.)
*Baddow Wlk. N1 —5E **25***
(off New N. Rd.)
Baden Pl. *SE1* —3F **53**
Baden Powell Ho. SW7
*(off Queens Ga.) —5E **49***
Badger Ct. *NW2* —5E **5**
Badminton M. *E16* —2C **58**
Badminton Rd. *SW12* —4C **78**
Badsworth Rd. *SE5* —4E **67**
*Baffin Way. E14 —2E **57***
(off Blackwall Way)
Bagley's La. *SW6* —4D **63**
*Bagnigge Ho. WC1 —2C **38***
(off Margery St.)
*Bagshot Ho. NW1 —2D **37***
(off Redhill St.)
Bagshot St. *SE17* —1A **68**
*Baildon. E2 —1E **41***
(off Cyprus St.)
Baildon St. *SE8* —3B **70**
Bailey Pl. *SE26* —5F **97**
Bainbridge St. *WC1* —5F **37**
Baird Clo. *E10* —3C **14**
Baird Gdns. *SE19* —4A **96**
*Baird Ho. W12 —1D **47***
(off White City Est.)
Baird St. *EC1* —3E **39**
Baizdon Rd. *SE3* —5A **72**
Baker Pass. *NW10* —5A **18**
Baker Rd. *NW10* —5A **18**
Bakers Av. *E17* —1D **15**
Baker's Fld. *N7* —1A **24**
*Bakers Hall Ct. EC3 —1A **54***
(off Cross La.)
Bakers Hill. *E5* —3E **13**
Bakers La. *N6* —1B **8**
Baker's M. *W1* —5C **36**
*Bakers Pas. NW3 —1E **21***
(off Heath St.)

Baker's Rents. *E2* —2B **40**
Baker's Row. *E15* —1A **44**
Baker's Row. *EC1* —3C **38**
Baker Street. (Junct.) —4B **36**
Baker St. *NW1 & W1* —3B **36**
*Baker's Yd. EC1 —3C **38***
(off Bakers Rd.)
Bakery Clo. *SW9* —3B **66**
Bakery Pl. *SW11* —2B **78**
Balaam St. *E13* —3C **44**
Balaclava Rd. *SE1* —5B **54**
Balchen Rd. *SE3* —5F **73**
Balchier Rd. *SE22* —4D **83**
*Balcombe Ho. NW1 —3A **36***
(off Taunton Pl.)
Balcombe St. *NW1* —3B **36**
Balcorne St. *E9* —4E **27**
Balder Ri. *SE12* —2D **101**
*Balderton Flats. W1 —5C **36***
(off Balderton St.)
Balderton St. *W1* —5C **36**
Baldock St. *E3* —1D **43**
*Baldrey Ho. SE10 —1B **72***
(off Blackwall La.)
Baldwin Cres. *SE5* —4E **67**
Baldwin Ho. *SW2* —1C **94**
Baldwins Gdns. *WC1* —4C **38**
Baldwin St. *EC1* —2F **39**
Baldwin Ter. *N1* —1E **39**
Bale Rd. *E1* —4A **42**
Balfern Gro. *W4* —1A **60**
Balfern St. *SW11* —5A **64**
Balfe St. *N1* —1A **38**
Balforn Tower. *E14* —5E **43**
*Balfour Ho. W10 —4F **33***
(off St Charles Sq.)
Balfour M. *W1* —2C **50**
Balfour Pl. *SW15* —2D **75**
Balfour Pl. *W1* —1C **50**
Balfour Rd. *N5* —1E **25**
Balfour St. *SE17* —5F **53**
Balfron Tower. *E14* —5E **43**
Balham. —1D 93
*Balham Continental Mkt. SW12 —1D **93***
(off Shipka Rd.)
Balham Gro. *SW12* —5C **78**
Balham High Rd. *SW17 & SW12* —3C **92**
Balham Hill. *SW12* —5D **79**
Balham New Rd. *SW12* —5D **79**
Balham Pk. Rd. *SW12* —1B **92**
Balham Sta. Rd. *SW12* —1D **93**
*Balin Ho. SE1 —3F **53***
(off Long La.)
Balkan Wlk. *E1* —1D **55**
Balladier Wlk. *E14* —4D **43**
Ballamore Rd. *Brom* —3C **100**
Ballance Rd. *E9* —3F **27**
Ballantine St. *SW18* —2E **77**
Ballantrae Ho. *NW2* —1B **20**
*Ballard Ho. SE10 —2D **71***
(off Thames St.)
Ballards Rd. *NW2* —4C **4**
Ballast Quay. *SE10* —1F **71**
Ballater Rd. *SW2* —2A **80**
*Ball Ct. EC3 —5F **39***
(off Cornhill)
Ballina St. *SE23* —5F **83**
Ballin Ct. *E14* —3E **57**
Ballingdon Rd. *SW11* —4C **78**
Balliol Rd. *W10* —5E **33**
Balloch Rd. *SE6* —1F **99**
Ballogie Av. *NW10* —1A **18**
Ballow Clo. *SE5* —3A **68**
Ball's Pond Pl. *N1* —3F **25**
Balls Pond Rd. *N1* —3F **25**
*Balman Ho. SE16 —5F **55***
(off Rotherhithe New Rd.)
Balmer Rd. *E3* —1B **42**
Balmes Rd. *N1* —5F **25**
Balmoral Clo. *SW15* —4F **75**
Balmoral Ct. *SE12* —4D **101**
*Balmoral Ct. SE16 —2F **55***
(off King & Queen Wharf)
Balmoral Ct. *SE27* —4E **95**
Balmoral Gro. *N7* —3B **24**
Balmoral Ho. *E14* —4D **57**
*Balmoral Ho. W14 —5A **48***
(off Windsor Way)
Balmoral M. *W12* —4B **46**
Balmoral Rd. *E7* —1E **31**
Balmoral Rd. *E10* —4D **15**
Balmoral Rd. *NW2* —3D **19**
Balmore St. *N19* —4D **9**
Balmuir Gdns. *SW15* —2E **75**
Balnacraig Av. *NW10* —1A **18**
Balniel Ga. *SW1* —1F **65**
Balsam Ho. *E14* —1D **57**
Baltic Ct. *SE16* —3F **55**
Baltic Ho. *SE5* —5E **67**
Baltic Pl. *N1* —5A **26**
Baltic St. E. *EC1* —3E **39**
Baltic St. W. *EC1* —3E **39**
*Baltimore Ho. SE11 —1C **66***
(off Hotspur St.)
Balvaird Pl. *SW1* —1F **65**
Balvernie Gro. *SW18* —5B **76**
Balvernie M. *SW18* —5C **76**
Bamborough Gdns. *W12* —3E **47**
Bamford Ct. *E15* —2D **29**
Bamford Rd. *Brom* —5E **99**
Bampton Rd. *SE23* —3F **97**
*Banbury Ct. WC2 —1A **52***
(off Long Acre)
Banbury Ho. *E9* —4F **27**
Banbury Rd. *E9* —4F **27**
Banbury St. *SW11* —5A **64**
Banchory Rd. *SE3* —3D **73**
Bancroft Av. *N2* —1A **8**
*Bancroft Ct. SW8 —3A **66***
(off Allen Edwards Dri.)
*Bancroft Ho. E1 —3E **41***
(off Cephas St.)
Bancroft Rd. *E1* —2E **41**
Bangalore St. *SW15* —1E **75**
Banim St. *W6* —5D **47**
Banister Ho. *E9* —2F **27**
*Banister Ho. SW8 —4E **65***
(off Wadhurst Rd.)
*Banister Ho. W10 —2A **34***
(off Bruckner St.)
Banister Rd. *W10* —2F **33**
Bank End. *SE1* —2E **53**
Bankfoot Rd. *Brom* —4A **100**
Bankhurst Rd. *SE6* —5B **84**
Bank La. *SW15* —3A **74**
Bank of England. —5F 39
Bank of England Mus. —5F 39
(off Bartholomew La.)
Bank of England Offices. EC4
*(off New Change) —5E **39***
*Banks Ho. SE1 —4E **53***
(off Rockingham St.)
Bankside. *SE1* —1E **53**
(in two parts)
Bankside Art Gallery. —1D 53
Bankside Way. *SE19* —5A **96**
Bank, The. *N6* —3D **9**
Bankton Rd. *SW2* —2C **80**
Bankwell Rd. *SE13* —2A **86**
Bannerman Ho. *SW8* —2B **66**
Banner St. *EC1* —3E **39**
Banning St. *SE10* —1A **72**
Bannister Clo. *SW2* —1C **94**
*Bannister Ho. SE14 —2F **69***
(off John Williams Clo.)
Banqueting House. —2A 52
Banstead St. *SE15* —1E **83**
Banting Ho. *NW2* —5C **4**
*Bantock Ho. W10 —2A **34***
(off Third Av.)
Bantry St. *SE5* —3F **67**
Banyard Rd. *SE16* —4D **55**
Baptist Gdns. *NW5* —3C **22**
Barandon Wlk. *W11* —1F **47**
*Barbanel Ho. E1 —3E **41***
(off Cephas St.)
Barbara Brosnan Ct. *NW8* —1F **35**
Barbauld Rd. *N16* —5A **12**
Barbers All. *E13* —2D **45**
Barbers Rd. *E15* —1D **43**
*Barbican. EC2 —4E **39***
(off Beech St.)
Barbican Arts Cen. —4E 39
Barb M. *W6* —4E **47**
Barbon Clo. *WC1* —4B **38**
Barchard St. *SW18* —3D **77**
Barchester St. *E14* —4D **43**
Barclay Clo. *SW6* —3C **62**
Barclay Path. *E17* —1E **15**
Barclay Rd. *E11* —3B **16**
Barclay Rd. *E13* —3E **45**
Barclay Rd. *E17* —1E **15**
Barclay Rd. *SW6* —3C **62**
Barclay Way. *SE22* —1C **96**
Barcombe Av. *SW2* —2A **94**
*Bardell Ho. SE16 —3C **54***
(off Dickens Est.)
Bardolph Rd. *N7* —1A **24**
Bard Rd. *W10* —1F **47**
*Bardsey Pl. E1 —3E **41***
(off Mile End Rd.)
*Bardsey Wlk. N1 —3E **25***
(off Douglas Rd. N.)

Bardsley Ho. *SE10* —2E *71*
　(off Bardsley La.)
Bardsley La. *SE10* —2E *71*
Barfett St. *W10* —3B *34*
Barfield Rd. *E11* —3B *16*
Barfleur Ho. *SE8* —1B *70*
Barford St. *N1* —5C *24*
Barforth Rd. *SE15* —1D *83*
Barge Ho. St. *SE1* —2C *52*
Bargery Rd. *SE6* —1D *99*
Bargrove Cres. *SE6* —2B *98*
Barham Ho. *SE17* —1A *68*
　(off Kinglake St.)
Baring Ho. *E14* —5C *42*
Baring Rd. *SE12* —5C *86*
Baring St. *N1* —5F *25*
Barker Dri. *NW1* —4E *23*
Barker M. *SW4* —2D *79*
Barkers Arc. *W8* —3D *49*
Barker St. *SW10* —2E *63*
Barker Wlk. *SW16* —3F *93*
Barker Way. *SE22* —5C *82*
Barkham Ter. *SE1* —4C *52*
　(off Lambeth Rd.)
Barking Rd. *E13 & E6*
　—1E *45*
Barking Rd. *E16 & E13*
　—4B *44*
Bark Pl. *W2* —1D *49*
Barkston Gdns. *SW5*
　—5D *49*
Barkway Ct. *N4* —4E *11*
Barkwith Ho. *SE14* —2F *69*
　(off Cold Blow La.)
Barkworth Rd. *SE16*
　—1D *69*
Barlborough St. *SE14*
　—3F *69*
Barlby Gdns. *W10* —3F *33*
Barlby Rd. *W10* —4E *33*
Barleycorn Way. *E14*
　(in two parts) —1B *56*
Barley Mow Pas. *EC1*
　(off Long La.) —4D *39*
Barley Mow Pas. *W4*
　—1A *60*
Barley Shotts Bus. Pk.
　W10 —4B *34*
Barlings Ho. *SE4* —2F *83*
　(off Frendsbury Rd.)
Barlow Dri. *SE18* —4F *73*
Barlow Ho. *N1* —2F *39*
　(off Provost St.)
Barlow Ho. *SE16* —5D *55*
　(off Rennie Est.)
Barlow Ho. *W11* —1A *48*
　(off Walmer Rd.)
Barlow Pl. *W1* —1D *51*
Barlow Rd. *NW6* —3B *20*
Barlow St. *SE17* —5F *53*
Barmeston Rd. *SE6* —2D *99*
Barmouth Rd. *SW18*
　—4E *77*
Barnabas Rd. *E9* —2F *27*
Barnaby Cl. *E16* —3C *54*
　(off Scott Lidgett Cres.)

Barnaby Pl. *SW7* —5F *49*
　(off Brompton Rd.)
Barnard Gro. *E15* —4B *30*
Barnard Ho. *E2* —2D *41*
　(off Ellsworth St.)
Barnard Lodge. *W9* —4C *34*
　(off Admiral Wlk.)
Barnard M. *SW11* —2A *78*
Barnardo Gdns. *E1* —1F *55*
Barnardo St. *E1* —5F *41*
Barnard Rd. *SW11* —2A *78*
Barnard's Inn. *EC4* —5C *38*
　(off Fetter La.)
Barnard's Wharf. *SE16*
　—3B *56*
Barnbrough. *NW1* —5E *23*
　(off Camden St.)
Barnby Sq. *E15* —5A *30*
Barnby St. *E15* —5A *30*
Barnby St. *NW1* —1E *37*
Barn Clo. *NW5* —2F *23*
　(off Torriano Av.)
Barn Elms Pk. *SW15* —1E *75*
Barnes. —5B 60
Barnes Av. *SW13* —3C *60*
Barnes Clo. *E12* —1F *31*
Barnes Ct. *E16* —4E *45*
Barnes Ct. *N1* —4C *24*
Barnes High St. *SW13*
　—5B *60*
Barnes Ho. *SE14* —2F *69*
　(off John Williams Clo.)
Barnes St. *E14* —5A *42*
Barnes Ter. *SE8* —1B *70*
Barnet Gro. *E2* —2C *40*
Barnett St. *E1* —5D *41*
Barney Clo. *SE7* —1E *73*
Barn Fld. *NW3* —2B *22*
Barnfield Clo. *N4* —2A *10*
Barnfield Clo. *SW17* —3F *91*
Barnfield Pl. *E14* —5C *56*
Barnham St. *SE1* —3A *54*
Barnsbury. —4B 24
Barnsbury Est. *N1* —5B *24*
　(in two parts)
Barnsbury Gro. *N7* —4B *24*
Barnsbury Rd. *SW4* —4F *79*
Barnsbury Pk. *N1* —4C *24*
Barnsbury Rd. *N1* —1C *38*
Barnsbury Sq. *N1* —4C *24*
Barnsbury St. *N1* —4C *24*
Barnsbury Ter. *N1* —4B *24*
Barnsdale Av. *E14* —5C *56*
Barnsdale Rd. *W9* —3B *34*
Barnsley St. *E1* —3D *41*
Barnstable La. *SE13* —2E *85*
Barnstaple Ho. *SE10* —3D *71*
　(off Devonshire Dri.)
Barnstaple Ho. *SE12* —3B *86*
　(off Taunton Rd.)
Barnston Wlk. *N1* —5E *25*
　(off Popham St.)
Barn St. *N16* —4A *12*
Barnwell Ho. *SE5* —4A *68*
　(off St Giles Rd.)
Barnwell Rd. *SW2* —3C *80*
Barnwood Clo. *W9* —3D *35*

Baroness Rd. *E2* —2B *40*
Baronsclere Ct. *N6* —2E *9*
Barons Court. —1A 62
Baron's Ct. Rd. *W14* —1A *62*
Barons Court Theatre.
　—1A *62*
Barons Keep. *W14* —1A *62*
Baronsmead Rd. *SW13*
　—4C *60*
Baron's Pl. *SE1* —3C *52*
Baron St. *N1* —1C *38*
Baron Wlk. *E16* —4B *44*
Barque M. *SE8* —2C *70*
Barratt Ho. *N1* —4D *25*
　(off Sable St.)
Barratt Ind. Pk. *E3* —3E *43*
Barret Ho. *NW6* —5C *20*
Barret Ho. *SW9* —18 *80*
　(off Benedict Rd.)
Barrett Ho. *SE17* —1E *67*
　(off Browning St.)
Barrett's Gro. *N16* —2A *26*
Barrett St. *W1* —5C *36*
Barrhill Rd. *SW2* —2A *94*
Barriedale. *SE14* —5A *70*
Barrie Est. *W2* —1F *49*
Barrie Ho. *W2* —1E *49*
　(off Lancaster Ga.)
Barrier App. *SE7* —4F *59*
Barrier Point Rd. *E16* —2E *59*
Barringer Sq. *SW17* —4C *92*
Barrington Clo. *NW5* —2C *22*
Barrington Ct. *NW5* —2C *22*
Barrington Ct. *SW4* —5A *66*
Barrington Rd. *SW9* —1D *81*
Barrow Clo. *SE6* —1B *100*
　(off Cumberland Pk.)
Barrowgate Rd. *W4* —1A *60*
Barrow Hill Est. *NW8* —1A *36*
　(off Barrow Hill Rd.)
Barrow Hill Rd. *NW8* —1A *36*
Barrow Ho. *SW16* —5F *93*
Barry Av. *N15* —1B *12*
Barry Ho. *SE16* —5D *55*
　(off Rennie Est.)
Barry Rd. *E6* —5F *45*
Barry Rd. *SE22* —4C *82*
Barset Rd. *SE15* —1E *83*
　(in three parts)
Barston Rd. *SE27* —3E *95*
Barstow Cres. *SW2* —1B *94*
Barter St. *WC1* —4A *38*
Bartholomew Clo. *EC1*
　(in two parts) —4E *39*
Bartholomew Clo. *SW18*
　—2E *77*
Bartholomew Ct. *E14* —1F *57*
Bartholomew Ct. *EC1* —3E *39*
　(off Old St.)
Bartholomew La. *EC2* —5F *39*
Bartholomew Pl. *EC1* —4E *39*
　(off Kinghorn St.)
Bartholomew Rd. *NW5*
　—3E *23*
Bartholomew Sq. *E1* —3D *41*
Bartholomew Sq. *EC1* —3E *39*
Bartholomew St. *SE1* —4F *53*

Bartholomew Vs. *NW5*
— —3E **23**
Bartle Rd. *W11* —5A **34**
Bartlett Clo. *E14* —5C **42**
Bartlett Ct. *EC4* —5C **38**
Bartletts Pas. *EC4* —5C **38**
(off Fetter La.)
Barton Clo. *E9* —2E **27**
Barton Clo. *SE15* —1D **83**
Barton Ct. *W14* —1A **62**
(off Baron's Ct. Rd.)
Barton Ho. *N1* —4D **25**
(off Sable St.)
Barton Ho. *SW6* —1D **77**
(off Wandsworth Bri. Rd.)
Barton Rd. *W14* —1A **62**
Barton St. *SW1* —4A **52**
Bartonway. *NW8* —5F **21**
(off Queen's Ter.)
Bartram Rd. *SE4* —3A **84**
Bartrip St. *E9* —3B **28**
Barville Clo. *SE4* —3A **84**
Barwell Ho. *E2* —3C **40**
(off Menotti St.)
Barwick Rd. *E7* —1D **31**
Basevi Way. *SE8* —2C **70**
Bashley Rd. *NW10* —3A **32**
Basildon Ct. *W1* —4C **36**
(off Devonshire Rd.)
Basil Gdns. *SE27* —5E **95**
Basil Ho. *SW8* —3A **66**
(off Wyvil Rd.)
Basil St. *SW3* —4B **50**
Basin App. *E14* —5A **42**
Basing Ct. *SE15* —4B **68**
Basingdon Way. *SE5* —2F **81**
Basinghall Av. *EC2* —5F **39**
Basinghall St. *EC2* —5F **39**
Basing Hill. *NW11* —3B **6**
Basing Ho. Yd. *E2* —2A **40**
Basing Pl. *E2* —2A **40**
Basing St. *W11* —5B **34**
Basire St. *N1* —5E **25**
Baskerville Gdns. *NW10*
— —1A **18**
Baskerville Rd. *SW18* —5A **78**
Basket Gdns. *SE9* —3F **87**
Baslow Wlk. *E5* —1F **27**
Basnett Rd. *SW11* —1C **78**
Basque Ct. *SE16* —3F **55**
(off Garter Way)
Bassano St. *SE22* —3B **82**
Bassein Pk. Rd. *W12* —3B **46**
Bassett Rd. *E7* —1F **31**
Bassett Rd. *W10* —5F **33**
Bassett St. *NW5* —3C **22**
Bassingbourn Ho. *N1* —4C **24**
(off Sutton Est., The)
Bassingham Rd. *SW18*
— —5E **77**
Bassishaw Highwalk. *EC2*
(off London Wall) —4F **39**
Basswood Clo. *SE15* —1D **83**
Basterfield Ho. *EC1* —3E **39**
(off Golden La. Est.)
Bastion Highwalk. *EC2*
(off London Wall) —4E **39**

Bastion Ho. *EC2* —4E **39**
(off London Wall)
Bastwick St. *EC1* —3E **39**
Basuto Rd. *SW6* —4C **62**
Batavia Ho. *SE14* —3A **70**
(off Batavia Rd.)
Batavia M. *SE14* —3A **70**
Batavia Rd. *SE14* —3A **70**
Batchelor St. *N1* —5C **24**
Bateman Ho. *SE11* —2D **67**
(off Brandon Est.)
Bateman's Bldgs. *W1* —5F **37**
(off Bateman St.)
Bateman's Row. *EC2* —3A **40**
Bateman St. *W1* —5F **37**
Bates Point. *E13* —5C **30**
(off Pelly Rd.)
Bate St. *E14* —1B **56**
Bath Clo. *SE15* —3D **69**
Bath Ct. *EC1* —3C **38**
(off St Lukes Est.)
Bath Ct. *SE26* —3C **96**
(off Droitwich Clo.)
Bathgate Rd. *SW19* —3F **89**
Bath Gro. *E2* —1C **40**
(off Horatio St.)
Bath Ho. *E2* —3C **40**
(off Ramsey St.)
Bath Ho. *SE1* —4E **53**
(off Bath Ter.)
Bath Pl. *EC2* —2A **40**
Bath Pl. *W6* —1E **61**
(off Fulham Pal. Rd.)
Bath Rd. *E7* —3F **31**
Bath Rd. *W4* —5A **46**
Baths App. *SW6* —3B **62**
Bath St. *EC1* —2E **39**
Bath Ter. *SE1* —4E **53**
Bathurst Gdns. *NW10*
— —1D **33**
Bathurst M. *W2* —5F **35**
Bathurst St. *W2* —1F **49**
Batley Pl. *N16* —5B **12**
Batley Rd. *N16* —5B **12**
Batman Clo. *W12* —2D **47**
Batoum Gdns. *W6* —4E **47**
Batson Ho. *E1* —5C **40**
(off Fairclough St.)
Batson St. *W12* —3C **46**
Battenberg Wlk. *SE19*
— —5A **96**
Batten Ho. *SW4* —3E **79**
Batten Ho. *W10* —2A **34**
(off Third Av.)
Batten St. *SW11* —1A **78**
Battersby Rd. *SE9* —1A **102**
Battersea. —4C **64**
Battersea Bri. *SW3 & SW11*
— —3F **63**
Battersea Bri. Rd. *SW11*
— —3A **64**
Battersea Bus. Cen. *SW11*
— —1C **78**
Battersea Chu. Rd. *SW11*
— —4F **63**
Battersea Dogs' Home.
— —3D **65**

Battersea High St. *SW11*
(in two parts) —4F **63**
Battersea Pk. —3C **64**
Battersea Pk. Children's
Zoo. —3C **64**
Battersea Pk. Rd. *SW11 &*
SW8 —5A **64**
Battersea Ri. *SW11* —3A **78**
Battersea Sq. *SW11* —4F **63**
Battishill St. *N1* —4D **25**
Battlebridge Ct. *N1* —1A **38**
(off Wharfdale Rd.)
Battle Bri. La. *SE1* —2A **54**
Battle Bri. Rd. *NW1* —1A **38**
Battle Clo. *SW19* —5E **91**
Battledean Rd. *N5* —2D **25**
Battle Ho. *SE15* —2C **68**
(off Haymerle Rd.)
Batty St. *E1* —5C **40**
Baudwin Rd. *SE6* —2A **100**
Baulk, The. *SW18* —5C **76**
Bavaria Rd. *N19* —4A **10**
(in two parts)
Bavent Rd. *SE5* —5E **67**
Bawdale Rd. *SE22* —3B **82**
Bawtree Rd. *SE14* —3A **70**
Baxendale St. *E2* —2C **40**
Baxter Rd. *E16* —5E **45**
Baxter Rd. *N1* —3F **25**
Bayer Ho. *EC1* —3E **39**
(off Golden La. Est.)
Bayfield Ho. *SE4* —2F **83**
(off Coston Wlk.)
Bayfield Rd. *SE9* —2F **87**
Bayford M. *E8* —4D **27**
(off Bayford St.)
Bayford Rd. *NW10* —2F **33**
Bayford St. *E8* —4D **27**
Bayford St. Ind. Est. *E9*
— —4A **28**
Bayham Pl. *NW1* —5E **23**
Bayham Rd. *W4* —4A **46**
Bayham St. *NW1* —5E **23**
Bayley St. *W1* —4F **37**
Baylis Rd. *SE1* —3C **52**
Baynard St. *EC4* —1E **53**
Baynes M. *NW3* —3F **21**
Baynes St. *NW1* —4E **23**
Bayonne Rd. *W6* —2A **62**
Bays Clo. *SE26* —5E **97**
Bayston Rd. *N16* —5B **12**
Bayswater. —1E **49**
Bayswater Rd. *W2* —1D **49**
Baythorne St. *E3* —4B **42**
Bayton Ct. *E8* —4C **26**
(off Lansdowne Dri.)
Baytree Ct. *SW2* —2B **80**
Baytree Rd. *SW2* —2B **80**
Bazalgette Ho. *NW8* —3F **35**
(off Orchardson St.)
Bazeley Ho. *SE1* —3D **53**
(off Library St.)
Bazely St. *E14* —1E **57**
Beacham Clo. *SE7* —1F **73**
Beachborough Rd. *Brom*
— —4E **99**
Beachcroft Rd. *E11* —5A **16**

Beachcroft Way. *N19* —3F **9**
Beach Ho. *SW5* —1C *62*
(off Philbeach Gdns.)
Beachy Rd. *E3* —4C **28**
Beacon Ga. *SE14* —1F **83**
Beacon Hill. *N7* —2A **24**
Beacon Ho. *E14* —1D **71**
Beacon Ho. SE5 —3A 68
(off Southampton Way)
Beacon Rd. *E13* —4F **85**
Beacons Clo. *E6* —4F **45**
Beaconsfield Clo. *SE3* —2C **72**
Beaconsfield Pde. *SE9*
—4F **101**
Beaconsfield Rd. *E10* —4E **15**
Beaconsfield Rd. *E16* —3B **44**
Beaconsfield Rd. *E17* —1B **14**
Beaconsfield Rd. *NW10*
—3B **18**
Beaconsfield Rd. *SE3* —3B **72**
Beaconsfield Rd. *SE9*
—2F **101**
Beaconsfield Rd. *SE17*
—1F **67**
Beaconsfield Ter. Rd. *W14*
—4A **48**
Beaconsfield Wlk. *SW6*
—4B **62**
Beacontree Rd. *E11* —3B **16**
Beadman St. *SE27* —4D **95**
Beadnell Rd. *SE23* —1F **97**
Beadon Rd. *W6* —5E **47**
Beak St. *W1* —1E **51**
Beale Pl. *E3* —1B **42**
Beale Rd. *E3* —5B **28**
Beaminster Ho. SW8 —3B 66
(off Dorset Rd.)
Beamish Ho. SE16 —5D 55
(off Rennie Est.)
Beanacre Clo. *E9* —3B **28**
Bear All. *EC4* —5D **39**
Beardell St. *SE19* —5B **96**
Beardsfield. *E13* —1C **44**
Bear Gdns. *SE1* —2E **53**
Bear La. *SE1* —2D **53**
Bearsted Ri. *SE4* —3B **84**
Bear St. *WC2* —1F **51**
Beaton Clo. *SE15* —4B **68**
Beatrice Clo. *E13* —3C **44**
Beatrice Pl. *W8* —4D **49**
Beatrice Rd. *E17* —1C **14**
Beatrice Rd. *N4* —2C **10**
Beatrice Rd. *SE1* —5C **54**
Beatrix Ho. SW5 —1D 63
(off Old Brompton Rd.)
Beatson Wlk. *SE16* —2A **56**
(in two parts)
Beattie Ho. *SW8* —4E **65**
Beatty Ho. E14 —3C 56
(off Admirals Way)
Beatty Ho. *NW1* —3E **37**
Beatty Ho. SW1 —1E 65
(off Dolphin Sq.)
Beatty Rd. *N16* —1A **26**
Beatty St. *NW1* —1E **37**
Beauchamp Pl. *SW3* —4A **50**
Beauchamp Rd. *E7* —4D **31**

Beauchamp Rd. *SW11*
—2A **78**
Beauchamp St. *EC1* —4C **38**
Beauchamp Ter. *SW15*
—1D **75**
Beauclerc Rd. *W6* —4D **47**
Beauclerk Ho. *SW16* —3A **94**
Beaufort Clo. *SW15* —5D **75**
Beaufort Gdns. *NW4* —1E **5**
Beaufort Gdns. *SW3* —4A **50**
Beaufort Ho. E14 —3C 56
Beaufort Ho. SW1 —1F 65
(off Aylesford St.)
Beaufort M. *SW6* —2B **62**
Beaufort St. *SW3* —2F **63**
Beaufort Ter. *E14* —1E **71**
Beaufoy Ho. *SE27* —3D **95**
Beaufoy Ho. SW8 —3B 66
(off Rita Rd.)
Beaufoy Wlk. *SE11* —5B **52**
Beaulieu Av. *E16* —2D **59**
Beaulieu Av. *SE26* —4D **97**
Beaulieu Clo. *SE5* —1F **81**
Beaumaris Grn. *NW9* —1A **4**
Beaumont. W14 —5B 48
(off Avonmore Rd.)
Beaumont Av. W14 —1B 62
Beaumont Bldgs. WC2
(off Martlett Ct.) —5A **38**
Beaumont Ct. *E5* —5D **13**
Beaumont Ct. W1 —4C 36
(off Beaumont St.)
Beaumont Cres. *W14* —1B **62**
Beaumont Gdns. *NW3* —5C **6**
Beaumont Gro. *E1* —3F **41**
Beaumont Ho. *E10* —2D **15**
Beaumont Ho. E15 —5B 30
(off John St.)
Beaumont Lodge. E8 —3C 26
(off Greenwood Rd.)
Beaumont M. *W1* —4C **36**
Beaumont Pl. *W1* —3E **37**
Beaumont Ri. *N19* —3F **9**
Beaumont Rd. *E10* —2D **15**
(in three parts)
Beaumont Rd. *E13* —2D **45**
Beaumont Rd. *SE19* —5E **95**
Beaumont Rd. *SW19* —3A **76**
Beaumont Sq. *E1* —4F **41**
Beaumont St. *W1* —4C **36**
Beaumont Ter. SE13 —5A 86
(off Wellmeadow Rd.)
Beaumont Wlk. *NW3* —4B **22**
Beauval Rd. *SE22* —4B **82**
Beaux Arts Building. *N7*
—3A **10**
Beavor Gro. *W6* —1C *60*
(off Beavor La.)
Beavor La. *W6* —1C **60**
Beccles St. *E14* —5B **42**
Bechervaise Ct. E10 —3D 15
(off Leyton Grange Est.)
Beck Clo. *SE13* —4D **71**
Beckenham Bus. Cen. *Beck*
—5A **98**
Beckenham Hill Est. *Beck*
—5D **99**

Beckenham Hill Rd. *Beck &*
SE6 —5D **99**
Beckers, The. *N16* —1C **26**
Becket Ho. SE1 —3F 53
(off Tabard St.)
Becket St. *SE1* —4F **53**
Beckett Clo. *NW10* —3A **18**
Beckett Clo. *SW16* —2F **93**
Beckett Ho. E1 —4E 41
(off Jubilee St.)
Beckett Ho. *SW9* —5A **66**
Beckfoot. *NW1* —1E **37**
(off Ampthill Est.)
Beckford Ho. *N16* —2A **26**
Beckford Pl. *SE17* —1E **67**
Beckham Gdns. *SE11* —5B **52**
Becklow Gdns. W12 —3C 46
(off Becklow Rd.)
Becklow M. W12 —3C 46
(off Becklow Rd.)
Becklow Rd. *W12* —3B **46**
(in two parts)
Beck Rd. *E8* —5D **27**
Beckton Rd. *E16* —4B **44**
Beckway St. *SE17* —5A **54**
(in two parts)
Beckwith Rd. *SE24* —3F **81**
Beclands Rd. *SW17* —5C **92**
Becmead Av. *SW16* —4F **93**
Becondale Rd. *SE19* —5A **96**
Bective Pl. *SW15* —2B **76**
Bective Rd. *E7* —1C **30**
Bective Rd. *SW15* —2B **76**
Bedale St. *SE1* —2F **53**
Beddalls Farm Ct. *E6* —4F **45**
Bedefield. *WC1* —2A **38**
Bede Ho. *SE4* —4B **70**
Bedford Av. *WC1* —4F **37**
Bedfordbury. *WC2* —1A **52**
Bedford Clo. *W4* —2A **60**
Bedford Corner. W4 —5A 46
(off South Pde.)
Bedford Ct. *WC2* —1A **52**
(in two parts)
Bedford Ct. Mans. WC1
(off Bedford Av.) —4F **37**
Bedford Gdns. *W8* —2C **48**
Bedford Hill. *SW12 &*
SW16 —1D **93**
Bedford Ho. SW4 —2A 80
(off Solon New Rd. Est.)
Bedford Park. —4A 46
Bedford Pk. Corner. *W4*
—5A **46**
Bedford Pk. Mans. *W4*
—5A **46**
Bedford Pas. *SW6* —3A *62*
(off Dawes Rd.)
Bedford Pas. *W1* —4E **37**
Bedford Pl. *WC1* —4A **38**
Bedford Rd. *N8* —1F **9**
Bedford Rd. *SW4* —2A **80**
Bedford Rd. *W4* —4A **46**
Bedford Row. *WC1* —4B **38**
Bedford Sq. *WC1* —4F **37**
Bedford St. *WC2* —1A **52**
Bedford Ter. *SW4* —3A **80**

Bedford Way. *WC1* —3F **37**
Bedgebury Gdns. *SW19*
—2A **90**
Bedgebury Rd. *SE9* —2F **87**
Bedivere Rd. *Brom* —3C **100**
Bedmond Ho. SW3 —1A *64*
(off Ixworth Pl.)
Bedser Clo. *SE11* —2B **66**
Bedwell Ho. *SW9* —5C **66**
Beeby Rd. *E16* —4D **45**
Beech Av. *W3* —2A **46**
Beech Clo. *SE8* —2C **70**
Beech Clo. *SW15* —5C **74**
Beech Clo. *SW19* —5E **89**
Beech Ct. W1 —5B *36*
(off Harrowby St.)
Beech Cres. Ct. *N5* —1D **25**
Beechcroft Av. *NW11* —2B **6**
Beechcroft Clo. *SW16*
—5B **94**
Beechcroft Ct. NW11 —2B *6*
(off Beechcroft Av.)
Beechcroft Rd. *SW17* —2A **92**
Beechdale Rd. *SW2* —4B **80**
Beechdene. SE15 —4D *69*
(off Carlton Gro.)
Beechen Pl. *SE23* —2F **97**
Beeches Rd. *SW17* —3A **92**
Beechey Ho. E1 —2D *55*
(off Wats St.)
Beechfield Rd. *N4* —1E **11**
Beechfield Rd. *SE6* —1B **98**
Beech Gdns. EC2 —4E *39*
(off Beech St.)
Beech Ho. SE16 —3E *55*
(off Ainsty Est.)
Beechmont Clo. *Brom*
—5A **100**
Beechmore Rd. *SW11* —4B **64**
Beecholme Est. *E5* —5D **13**
Beech St. *EC2* —4E **39**
Beech Tree Clo. *N1* —4C **24**
Beechwood Gro. *W3* —1A **46**
Beechwood Ho. E2 —1C *40*
(off Teale St.)
Beechwood Rd. *E8* —3B **26**
Beechwoods Ct. *SE19* —5B **96**
Beechworth. *NW6* —4A **20**
Beechworth Clo. *NW3* —4C **6**
Beecroft Rd. *SE4* —3A **84**
Beehive Clo. *E8* —4B **26**
Beehive Pl. *SW9* —1C **80**
Beemans Row. *SW18* —2E **91**
Bee Pas. EC3 —5A *40*
(off Lime St.)
Beeston Clo. *E8* —2C **26**
Beeston Ho. SE1 —4F *53*
(off Burbage Clo.)
Beeston Pl. *SW1* —4D **51**
Beethoven St. *W10* —2A **34**
Begbie Rd. *SE3* —4E **73**
Begonia Wlk. *W12* —5B **32**
Beira St. *SW12* —5D **79**
Bekesbourne St. *E14* —5A **42**
Beldanes Lodge. *NW10*
—4C **18**
Belfast Rd. *N16* —4B **12**

Belfont Wlk. *N7* —1A **24**
(in two parts)
Belford Ho. *E8* —5B **26**
Belfort Rd. *SE15* —5E **69**
Belfry Clo. *SE16* —1D **69**
Belgrade Rd. *N16* —1A **26**
Belgrave Ct. *E13* —3E **45**
Belgrave Ct. SW8 —3E *65*
(off Ascalon St.)
Belgrave Gdns. *NW8* —5D **21**
Belgrave Heights. *E11* —3C **16**
Belgrave Ho. *SW9* —3C **66**
Belgrave M. N. *SW1* —3C **50**
Belgrave M. S. *SW1* —4C **50**
Belgrave M. W. *SW1* —4C **50**
Belgrave Pl. *SW1* —4C **50**
Belgrave Rd. *E10* —3E **15**
Belgrave Rd. *E11* —4C **16**
Belgrave Rd. *E13* —3E **45**
Belgrave Rd. *E17* —1C **14**
Belgrave Rd. *SW1* —5D **51**
Belgrave Rd. *SW13* —3B **60**
Belgrave Sq. *SW1* —4C **50**
Belgrave St. *E1* —4F **41**
Belgrave Yd. SW1 —4D *51*
(off Lwr. Belgrave St.)
Belgravia. —4C 50
Belgravia Ct. SW1 —4D *51*
(off Ebury St.)
Belgravia Gdns. *Brom*
—5A **100**
Belgravia Ho. SW1 —4C *50*
(off Halkin Pl.)
Belgravia Ho. *SW4* —4F **79**
Belgravia Workshops. N19
—4A *10*
(off Marlborough Rd.)
Belgrove St. *NW1* —2A **38**
Belham Wlk. *SE5* —4F **67**
Belinda Rd. *SW9* —1D **81**
Belitha Vs. *N1* —4B **24**
Bellamy Clo. *E14* —3C **56**
Bellamy St. *SW14* —1B **62**
Bellamy's Ct. SE16 —2F *55*
(off Abbotshade Rd.)
Bellamy St. *SW12* —5D **79**
Bellasis Av. *SW2* —2A **94**
Bell Dri. *SW18* —5A **76**
Bellefields Rd. *SW9* —1B **80**
Bellenden Rd. *SE15* —4B **68**
Belleville Rd. *SW11* —3A **78**
Bellevue Pl. E1 —3E *41*
Bellevue Rd. *SW13* —5C **60**
Bellevue Rd. *SW17* —1A **92**
Bellew St. *SW17* —3E **91**
Bellflower Clo. *E6* —4F **45**
Bell Gdns. *E10* —3C **14**
(off Church Rd.)
Bellgate M. *NW5* —1D **23**
Bell Green. —4A 98
Bell Grn. *SE26* —4B **98**
Bell Grn. La. *SE26* —5B **98**
Bell Ho. SE10 —2E *71*
(off Haddo St.)
Bellina M. *NW5* —1D **23**
Bellingham. —3D 99
Bellingham Grn. *SE6* —3C **98**

Bellingham Rd. *SE6* —3D **99**
Bellingham Trad. Est. *SE6*
—3D **99**
Bell Inn Yd. *EC3* —5F **39**
Bell La. *E1* —4B **40**
Bell La. *E16* —2B **58**
Bell Mdw. *SE19* —5A **96**
Bell Moor. NW3 —5E *7*
(off E. Heath Rd.)
Bello Clo. *SE24* —5D **81**
Bellot Gdns. SE10 —1A *72*
(off Bellot St.)
Bellot St. *SE10* —1A **72**
Bells All. *SW6* —5C **62**
Bell St. *NW1* —4A **36**
Bell St. *SE18* —4F **73**
Belltrees Gro. *SW16* —5B **94**
Bell Wharf La. *EC4* —1E **53**
Bellwood Rd. *SE15* —2F **83**
Bell Yd. *WC2* —5C **38**
Belmont Clo. *SW4* —1E **79**
Belmont Ct. *N5* —1E **25**
Belmont Ct. *NW11* —1B **6**
Belmont Gro. *SE13* —1F **85**
Belmont Gro. *W4* —5A **46**
Belmont Hall Ct. *SE13* —1F **85**
Belmont Hill. *SE13* —1E **85**
Belmont M. *SW19* —2F **89**
Belmont Pk. *SE13* —2F **85**
Belmont Pk. Clo. *SE13*
—2A **86**
Belmont Pk. Rd. *E10* —1D **15**
Belmont Rd. *SW4* —1E **79**
Belmont Rd. *NW1* —4C **22**
Belmont Ter. *W4* —5A **46**
Belmore La. *N7* —2F **23**
Belmore St. *SW8* —4F **65**
Beloe Clo. *SW15* —2C **74**
Belsham St. *E9* —3E **27**
Belsize Av. *NW3* —3F **21**
Belsize Ct. *NW3* —2F **21**
Belsize Ct. Garages. NW3
(off Belsize La.) —2F *21*
Belsize Cres. *NW3* —3F **21**
Belsize Gro. *NW3* —3A **22**
Belsize La. *NW3* —3F **21**
Belsize M. *NW3* —3F **21**
Belsize Pk. *NW3* —3F **21**
Belsize Pk. Gdns. *NW3*
—3F **21**
Belsize Pk. M. *NW3* —3F **21**
Belsize Pl. *NW3* —2F **21**
Belsize Rd. *NW6* —5C **20**
Belsize Sq. *NW3* —3F **21**
Belsize Ter. *NW3* —3F **21**
Beltane Dri. *SW19* —3F **89**
Belthorn Cres. *SW12* —5E **79**
Belton Rd. *E7* —4D **31**
Belton Rd. *E11* —1A **30**
Belton Rd. *NW2* —3C **18**
Belton Way. *E3* —4C **42**
Beltran Rd. *SW6* —5D **63**
Belvedere Av. *SW19* —5A **90**
Belvedere Bldgs. *SE1* —3D **53**
Belvedere Ct. *SW15* —2E **75**
Belvedere Dri. *SW19* —5A **90**
Belvedere Gro. *SW19* —5A **90**

Belvedere M. SE15 —1E 83
Belvedere Pl. SE1 —3D 53
Belvedere Pl. SW2 —2B 80
Belvedere Rd. E10 —3A 14
Belvedere Rd. SE1 —2B 52
Belvedere Sq. SW19 —5A 90
Belvedere, The. SW10 —4E 63 (off Chelsea Harbour)
Belvoir Rd. SE22 —5C 82
Bembridge Clo. NW6 —4A 20
Bembridge Ho. SE8 —5B 56 (off Longshore)
Bemersyde Point. E13 —2D 45 (off Dongola Rd. W.)
Bemerton Est. N1 —4A 24
Bemerton St. N1 —5B 24
Bemish Rd. SW15 —1F 75
Benbow Ho. SE8 —2C 70 (off Benbow St.)
Benbow Rd. W6 —4D 47
Benbow St. SE8 —2C 70
Benbury Clo. Brom —5E 99
Bence Ho. SE8 —1A 70
Bendall M. NW1 —4A 36 (off Bell St.)
Bendemeer Rd. SW15 —1F 75
Benden Ho. SE13 —3E 85 (off Monument Gdns.)
Bendish Rd. E6 —4F 31
Bendon Valley. SW18 —5D 77
Benedict Rd. SW9 —1B 80
Ben Ezra Ct. SE17 —5E 53 (off Asolando Dri.)
Benfleet Ct. E8 —5B 26
Bengal Ct. EC3 —5F 39 (off Birchin La.)
Bengeworth Rd. SE5 —1E 81
Benham Clo. SW11 —1F 77
Benham's Pl. NW3 —1E 21
Benhill Rd. SE5 —3F 67
Benhurst Ct. SW16 —5C 94
Benhurst La. SW16 —5C 94
Benin St. SE13 —5F 85
Benjamin Clo. E8 —5C 26
Benjamin St. EC1 —4D 39
Ben Jonson Ct. N1 —1A 40
Ben Jonson Ho. EC2 —4E 39 (off Beech St.)
Ben Jonson Pl. EC2 —4E 39 (off Beech St.)
Ben Jonson Rd. E1 —4F 41
Benledi St. E14 —5F 43
Bennelong Clo. W12 —1D 47
Bennerley Rd. SW11 —3A 78
Bennet's Hill. EC4 —1E 53
Bennet St. SW1 —2E 51
Bennett Ct. N7 —5B 10
Bennett Gro. SE13 —4D 71
Bennett Ho. SW1 —5F 51 (off Page St.)
Bennett Pk. SE3 —1B 86
Bennett Rd. E13 —3E 45
Bennett Rd. N16 —1A 26
Bennetts Copse. Chst —5F 101
Bennett St. W4 —2A 60
Bennett's Yd. SW1 —4F 51
Benn St. E9 —3A 28
Bensbury Clo. SW15 —5D 75
Ben Smith Way. SE16 —4C 54
Benson Av. E6 —1E 45
Benson Ho. E2 —3B 40 (off Ligonier St.)
Benson Ho. SE1 —2D 53 (off Hatfields)
Benson Quay. E1 —1E 55
Benson Rd. SE23 —1E 97
Bentfield Gdns. SE9 —3F 101
Benthal Rd. N16 —5C 12
Bentham Ct. N1 —4E 25 (off Ecclesbourne Rd.)
Bentham Ct. SE1 —4F 53 (off Falmouth Rd.)
Bentham Rd. E9 —3F 27
Bentinck Clo. NW8 —1A 36
Bentinck M. W1 —5C 36
Bentinck St. W1 —5C 36
Bentley Dri. NW2 —5B 6
Bentley Ho. SE5 —4A 68 (off Peckham Rd.)
Bentley Rd. N1 —3A 26
Bentons La. SE27 —4E 95
Benton's Ri. SE27 —5F 95
Bentworth Ct. E2 —3C 40 (off Granby St.)
Bentworth Rd. W12 —5D 33
Benville Ho. SW8 —3B 66 (off Oval Pl.)
Benwell Rd. N7 —1C 24
Benwick Clo. SE16 —5D 55
Benworth St. E3 —2B 42
Benyon Ct. N1 —5A 26 (off De Beauvoir Est.)
Benyon Ho. EC1 —2C 38 (off Myddelton Pas.)
Benyon Rd. N1 —5F 25
Berberis Ho. E3 —4C 42
Berber Pl. E14 —1C 56
Berber Rd. SW11 —3B 78
Berenger Tower. SW10 —3F 63 (off Worlds End Est.)
Berenger Wlk. SW10 —3F 63 (off Worlds End Est.)
Berens Rd. NW10 —2F 33
Beresford Rd. N5 —2F 25
Beresford Ter. N5 —2E 25
Berestede Rd. W4 —1B 60
Bere St. E1 —1F 55
Bergen Ho. SE5 —5E 67 (off Carew St.)
Bergen Sq. SE16 —4A 56
Berger Rd. E9 —3F 27
Berghem M. W14 —4F 47
Bergholt Cres. N16 —2A 12
Bergholt M. NW1 —4E 23
Berglen Ct. E14 —5A 42
Berglen Ho. E14 —5A 42
Bering Sq. E14 —1C 70
Bering Wlk. E16 —5F 45
Berisford M. SW18 —4E 77
Berkeley Ct. NW1 —3B 36 (off Marylebone Rd.)
Berkeley Ct. NW10 —1A 18
Berkeley Ct. NW11 —2B 6 (off Ravenscroft Av.)
Berkeley Gdns. W8 —2C 48
Berkeley Ho. SE8 —1B 70 (off Grove St.)
Berkeley M. W1 —5B 36
Berkeley Rd. E12 —2F 31
Berkeley Rd. N8 —1F 9
Berkeley Rd. N15 —1F 11
Berkeley Rd. SW13 —4C 60
Berkeley Sq. W1 —1D 51
Berkeley St. W1 —1D 51
Berkeley Wlk. N4 —4B 10 (off Durham Rd.)
Berkley Gro. NW1 —4C 22
Berkley Rd. NW1 —4B 22
Berkshire Ho. SE6 —4C 98
Berkshire Rd. E9 —3B 28
Bermans Way. NW10 —1A 18
Bermondsey. —3C 54
Bermondsey Sq. SE1 —4A 54
Bermondsey St. SE1 —2A 54
Bermondsey Trad. Est. SE16 —1E 69
Bermondsey Wall E. SE16 —3C 54
Bermondsey Wall W. SE16 —3C 54
Bernard Angell Ho. SE10 (off Trafalgar Rd.) —2F 71
Bernard Ashley Dri. SE7 —1D 73
Bernard Cassidy St. E16 —4B 44
Bernard Gdns. SW19 —5B 90
Bernard Mans. WC1 —3A 38
Bernard Rd. N15 —1B 12
Bernard Shaw Ct. NW1 —4E 23 (off St Pancras Way)
Bernard St. WC1 —3A 38
Bernard Sunley Ho. SW9 (off S. Island Pl.) —3C 66
Bernays Gro. SW9 —2B 80
Berners Ho. N1 —1C 38 (off Barnsbury Est.)
Berners M. W1 —4E 37
Berners Pl. W1 —5E 37
Berners Rd. N1 —5D 25
Berners St. W1 —4E 37
Berner Ter. E1 —5C 40 (off Fairclough St.)
Berridge M. NW6 —2C 20
Berridge Rd. SE19 —5F 95
Berriman Rd. N7 —5B 10
Berry Clo. NW10 —4A 18
Berryfield Rd. SE17 —1D 67
Berry Ho. E1 —3D 41 (off Headlam St.)
Berry La. SE21 —4F 95
Berryman's La. SE26 —4F 97
Berry Pl. EC1 —2D 39
Berry St. EC1 —3D 39
Bertal Rd. SW17 —4F 91
Berthon St. SE8 —3C 70
Bertie Rd. NW10 —3C 18

Bertie Rd. *SE26* —5F **97**
Bertram Rd. *NW4* —1C **4**
Bertram St. *N19* —4D **9**
*Bertrand Ho. SW16 —3A **94***
(off Leigham Av.)
Bertrand St. *SE13* —1D **85**
Berwick Rd. *E16* —5D **45**
Berwick St. *W1* —5E **37**
Berwyn Rd. *SE24* —1D **95**
Beryl Rd. *W6* —1F **61**
Besant Clo. *NW2* —5A **6**
Besant Ct. *N1* —2F **25**
*Besant Ho. NW8 —5E **21***
(off Boundary Rd.)
Besant Rd. *NW2* —1A **20**
Besant Wlk. *N7* —4B **10**
*Besford Ho. E2 —1C **40***
(off Pritchard's Rd.)
Besley St. *SW16* —5E **93**
Bessborough Gdns. *SW1* —1F **65**
Bessborough Pl. *SW1* —1F **65**
Bessborough Rd. *SW15* —1C **88**
Bessborough St. *SW1* —1F **65**
*Bessemer Ct. NW1 —4E **23***
(off Rochester Sq.)
Bessemer Rd. *SE5* —5E **67**
*Bessingham Wlk. SE4 —2F **83***
(off Aldersford Clo.)
Besson St. *SE14* —4E **69**
Bessy St. *E2* —2E **41**
Bestwood St. *SE8* —5F **55**
Beswick M. *NW6* —3D **21**
Beta Pl. *SW9* —2B **80**
*Bethal Est. SE1 —2A **54***
(off Tooley St.)
Bethell Av. *E16* —3B **44**
*Bethersden Ho. SE17 —1A **68***
(off Kinglake St.)
Bethlehem Ho. *E14* —1B **56**
Bethnal Green. —2D 41
Bethnal Green Mus. of Childhood. —2E 41
Bethnal Grn. Rd. *E1 & E2* —3B **40**
Bethune Clo. *N16* —3A **12**
Bethune Rd. *N16* —2F **11**
Bethune Rd. *NW10* —3A **32**
Bethwin Rd. *SE5* —3D **67**
*Betsham Ho. SE1 —3F **53***
(off Newcomen St.)
*Betterton Ho. WC2 —5A **38***
(off Betterton St.)
Betterton St. *WC2* —5A **38**
Bettons Pk. *E15* —5A **30**
Bettridge Rd. *SW6* —5B **62**
*Betts Ho. E1 —1D **55***
(off Betts St.)
Betts M. *E17* —1B **14**
Betts Rd. *E16* —1D **59**
Betts St. *E1* —1D **55**
Betty Brooks Ho. *E11* —5F **15**
Betty May Gray Ho. *E14* —5E **57**
Beulah Hill. *SE19* —5D **95**
Beulah Path. *E17* —1E **15**
Beulah Rd. *E17* —1D **15**
*Bevan Ho. WC1 —4A **38***
(off Boswell St.)
Bevan St. *N1* —5E **25**
Bev Callender Clo. *SW8* —1D **79**
Bevenden St. *N1* —2F **39**
Beverley Clo. *SW11* —2F **77**
Beverley Clo. *SW13* —5C **60**
Beverley Cotts. *SW15* —3A **88**
Beverley Ct. *SE4* —1B **84**
Beverley Gdns. *NW11* —2A **6**
Beverley Gdns. *SW13* —1B **74**
*Beverley Ho. Brom —5F **99***
(off Brangbourne Rd.)
Beverley La. *SW15* —3B **88**
Beverley Path. *SW13* —5B **60**
Beverley Rd. *E6* —2F **45**
Beverley Rd. *SW13* —1B **74**
Beverley Rd. *W4* —1B **60**
Beversbrook Rd. *N19* —5F **9**
Beverstone Rd. *SW2* —3B **80**
*Beverston M. W1 —4B **36***
(off Up. Montagu St.)
Bevill Allen Clo. *SW17* —5B **92**
Bevin Clo. *SE16* —2A **56**
Bevin Ct. *WC1* —2B **38**
Bevington Rd. *W10* —4A **34**
Bevington St. *SE16* —3C **54**
*Bevin Ho. E2 —2E **41***
(off Butler St.)
Bevin Sq. *SW17* —3B **92**
Bevin Way. *WC1* —1C **38**
Bevis Marks. *EC3* —5A **40**
Bew Ct. *SE22* —5C **82**
Bewdley St. *N1* —4C **24**
Bewick St. *SW8* —5D **65**
*Bewley Ho. E1 —1D **55***
(off Bewley St.)
Bewley St. *E1* —1E **55**
Bewlys Rd. *SE27* —5D **95**
Bexhill Rd. *SE4* —4B **84**
Bexhill Wlk. *E15* —5A **30**
Bexley Ho. *SE4* —2A **84**
Bianca Rd. *SE15* —2C **68**
Bibury Clo. *SE15* —2A **68**
(in two parts)
*Bickenhall Mans. NW1 —4B **36***
(off Bickenhall St., in two parts)
Bickenhall St. *W1* —4B **36**
Bickersteth Rd. *SW17* —5B **92**
Bickerton Rd. *N19* —4E **9**
Bickley Rd. *E10* —2D **15**
Bickley St. *SW17* —5A **92**
*Bicknell Ho. E1 —5C **40***
(off Ellen St.)
Bicknell Rd. *SE5* —1E **81**
Bidborough St. *WC1* —2A **38**
*Biddenham Ho. SE16 —5F **55***
(off Plough Way)
Bidder St. *E16* —4A **44**
(in two parts)
*Biddesden Ho. SW3 —5B **50***
(off Cadogan St.)
Biddestone Rd. *N7* —1B **24**
*Biddulph Mans. W9 —2D **35***
(off Elgin Av.)
Biddulph Rd. *W9* —2D **35**
Bideford Rd. *Brom* —3B **100**
Bidwell St. *SE15* —4D **69**
Big Ben. —3A 52
Biggerstaff Rd. *E15* —5E **29**
Biggerstaff St. *N4* —4C **10**
Biggs Row. *SW15* —1F **75**
Big Hill. *E5* —3D **13**
Bigland St. *E1* —5D **41**
Bignold Rd. *E7* —1C **30**
Bigwood Ct. *NW11* —1D **7**
Bigwood Rd. *NW11* —1D **7**
Bilberry Ho. *E3* —4C **42**
Billingford Clo. *SE4* —2F **83**
*Billingley. NW1 —5E **23***
(off Pratt St.)
Billing Pl. *SW10* —3D **63**
Billing Rd. *SW10* —3D **63**
Billingsgate Fish Market. —2D 57
Billingsgate Rd. *E14* —1C **56**
Billing St. *SW6* —3D **63**
Billington Rd. *SE14* —3F **69**
*Billiter Sq. EC3 —5A **40***
(off Fenchurch Av.)
Billiter St. *EC3* —5A **40**
Billson St. *E14* —5E **57**
Bilsby Gro. *SE9* —4F **101**
*Bilton Towers. W1 —5B **36***
(off Gt. Cumberland Pl.)
Bina Gdns. *SW5* —5E **49**
*Binbrook Ho. W10 —4E **33***
(off Sutton Way)
Binden Rd. *W12* —4B **46**
Binfield Rd. *SW8* —4A **66**
Bingfield St. *N1* —5A **24**
(in two parts)
*Bingham Ct. N1 —4D **25***
(off Halton Rd.)
Bingham Pl. *W1* —4C **36**
Bingham St. *N1* —3F **25**
Bingley Rd. *E16* —5E **45**
Binley Ho. *SW15* —4B **74**
Binney St. *W1* —5C **36**
*Binnie Ct. SE10 —3D **71***
(off Greenwich High Rd.)
*Binnie Ho. SE1 —4E **53***
(off Bath Ter.)
Binns Rd. *W4* —1A **60**
Binns Ter. *W4* —1A **60**
*Bircham Path. SE4 —2F **83***
(off Aldersford Clo.)
Birch Clo. *E16* —4A **44**
Birch Clo. *N19* —4E **9**
*Birch Clo. SE15 —5C **68***
(off Bournemouth Clo.)
Birchdale Rd. *E7* —2E **31**
Birchen Clo. *NW9* —4A **4**
Birchen Gro. *NW9* —4A **4**
Birches, The. *E12* —1F **31**
Birches, The. *SE7* —2D **73**
Birchfield Ho. *E14* —1C **56**
Birchfield St. *E14* —1C **56**
Birch Gro. *E11* —1A **30**

Birch Gro. *SE12* —5B **86**
Birch Ho. *SE14* —4B **70**
Birch Ho. SW2 —4C *80*
(off Tulse Hill)
Birch Ho. *W10* —3A *34*
(off Droop St.)
Birchington Av. *NW6* —5D *21*
(off W. End La.)
Birchington Ho. *E5* —2D **27**
Birchington Rd. *N8* —1F **9**
Birchington Rd. *NW6* —5C **20**
Birchin La. *EC3* —5F **39**
Birchlands Av. *SW12* —5B **78**
Birchmere Lodge. SE16
—1D *69*
(off Sherwood Gdns.)
Birchmere Row. *SE3* —5B **72**
Birchmore Hall. *N5* —5E **11**
Birchmore Wlk. *N5* —5E **11**
Birch Va. Ct. NW8 —3F *35*
(off Pollitt Dri.)
Birchwood Dri. *NW3* —5D **7**
Birchwood Rd. *SW17* —5D **93**
Birdbrook Ho. N1 —4E *25*
(off Popham Rd.)
Birdbrook Rd. *SE3* —2E **87**
Birdcage Wlk. *SW1* —3E **51**
Birdhurst Rd. *SW18* —3E **77**
Bird in Bush Rd. SE15
—3C **68**
Bird-in-Hand Pas. *SE23*
—2E **97**
Bird in Hand Yd. NW3 —1E **21**
Birdlip Clo. *SE15* —2A **68**
Birdsall Ho. *SE5* —1A **82**
Birdsfield La. *E3* —5B **28**
Bird St. *W1* —5C **36**
Birkbeck Hill. *SE21* —1D **95**
Birkbeck M. *E8* —2B **26**
Birkbeck Pl. *SE21* —2E **95**
Birkbeck Rd. *E8* —2B **26**
Birkbeck Rd. *SW19* —5D **91**
Birkbeck St. *E2* —2D **41**
Birkdale Clo. *SE16* —1D **69**
Birkenhead St. *WC1* —2A **38**
Birkhall Rd. *SE6* —1F **99**
Birkwood Clo. *SW12* —5F **79**
Birley Lodge. NW8 —1F *35*
(off Acacia Rd.)
Birley St. *SW11* —5C **64**
Birnam Rd. *N4* —4B **10**
Birnbeck Ct. *NW11* —1B **6**
Birrell Ho. SW9 —5B **66**
(off Stockwell Rd.)
Birse Cres. *NW10* —5A **4**
Birstall Rd. *N15* —1A **12**
Biscay Rd. *W6* —1F **61**
Biscoe Way. *SE13* —1F **85**
Biscott Ho. *E3* —3D **43**
Bisham Gdns. *N6* —3C **8**
Bishop King's Rd. W14
—5A **48**
Bishop's Av. *E13* —5D **31**
Bishop's Av. *SW6* —5F **61**
Bishops Av., The. *N2* —1F **7**
Bishop's Bri. Rd. *W2* —5D **35**
Bishop's Clo. *N19* —5E **9**

Bishop's Ct. *EC4* —5D *39*
(off Old Bailey)
Bishops Ct. *W2* —5D *35*
(off Bishop's Bri. Rd.)
Bishop's Ct. *WC2* —5C *38*
(off Star Yd.)
Bishopsdale Ho. *NW6* —5C *20*
(off Kilburn Va.)
Bishopsgate. *EC2* —5A **40**
Bishopsgate Arc. EC2 —4A *40*
(off Bishopsgate)
Bishopsgate Chu. Yd. *EC2*
—4A **40**
*Bishopsgate Institute &
Libraries.* —4A *40*
(off Bishopsgate)
Bishops Gro. *N2* —1A **8**
Bishops Ho. *SW8* —3A **66**
Bishop's Mans. *SW6* —5F **61**
(in two parts)
Bishops Mead. SE5 —3E *67*
(off Camberwell Rd.)
Bishop's Pk. Rd. *SW6* —5F **61**
Bishops Rd. *N6* —1C **8**
Bishops Rd. *SW6* —4A **62**
Bishop's Rd. *SW11* —3A **64**
Bishop's Ter. *SE11* —5C **52**
Bishopsthorpe Rd. SE26
—4F **97**
Bishop St. *N1* —5E **25**
Bishop's Way. *E2* —1D **41**
Bishopswood Rd. *N6* —2B **8**
Bishop Way. *NW10* —4A **19**
Bishop Wilfred Wood Clo.
SE15 —5C **68**
Bishop Wilfred Wood Ct. E13
(off Pragel St.) —1F **45**
Bissextile Ho. *SE8* —5D **71**
Bisson Rd. *E15* —1E **43**
Bittern Ct. *SE8* —2C **70**
Bittern Ho. SE1 —3E *53*
(off Gt. Suffolk St.)
Bittern St. *SE1* —3E **53**
Blackall St. *EC2* —3A **40**
Blackbird Yd. *E2* —2B **40**
Black Boy La. *N15* —1E **11**
Blackburne's M. *W1* —1C **50**
Blackburn Rd. *NW6* —3D **21**
Blackett St. *SW15* —1F **75**
Blackford's Path. SW15
—5C **74**
Blackfriars Bri. *SE1 & EC4*
—1D **53**
Blackfriars Ct. EC4 —1D *53*
(off New Bri. St.)
Black Friars La. *EC4* —5D **39**
(in two parts)
Blackfriars Pas. *EC4* —1D **53**
Blackfriars Rd. *SE1* —3D **53**
Blackfriars Underpass. EC4
—1C **52**
Blackheath. —5B **72**
Blackheath Av. *SE10* —3F **71**
Blackheath Bus. Est. SE10
(off Blackheath Hill) —4E *71*
Blackheath Gro. *SE3* —5B **72**
Blackheath Hill. *SE10* —4E **71**

Blackheath Park. —2C **86**
Blackheath Pk. *SE3* —1B **86**
Blackheath Ri. *SE13* —5E **71**
Blackheath Rd. *SE10* —4D **71**
Blackheath Vale. —5B **72**
Blackheath Va. *SE3* —5A **72**
Blackheath Village. *SE3*
—5B **72**
Black Horse Ct. SE1 —4F *53*
(off Gt. Dover St.)
Blackhorse Rd. *SE8* —2A **70**
Blacklands Rd. *SE6* —4E **99**
Blacklands Ter. *SW3* —5B **50**
Black Lion La. *W6* —5C **46**
Black Lion M. *W6* —5C **46**
Blackmans Yd. E2 —3C *40*
(off Grimsby St.)
Blackmore Ho. N1 —5B *24*
(off Barnsbury Est.)
Black Path. *E10* —2A **14**
Blackpool Rd. *SE15* —5D **69**
Black Prince Rd. SE1 & SE11
—5B **52**
Blackshaw Rd. *SW17* —4E **91**
Blacks Rd. *W6* —1E **61**
Blackstock M. *N4* —4D **11**
Blackstock Rd. *N4 & N5*
—4D **11**
Blackstone Est. *E8* —4D **27**
Blackstone Ho. SW1 —1E *65*
(off Churchill Gdns.)
Blackstone Rd. *NW2* —2E **19**
Black Swan Yd. *SE1* —3A **54**
Blackthorne Ct. SE15 —3B *68*
(off Cator St.)
Blackthorn St. *E3* —3C **42**
Blacktree M. *SW9* —1C **80**
Blackwall. —1E **57**
Blackwall La. *SE10* —1A **72**
(in two parts)
Blackwall Trad. Est. *E14*
—4F **43**
Blackwall Tunnel. *E14 &*
(in two parts) *SE10* —2F **57**
Blackwall Tunnel App. *E14*
—1E **57**
Blackwall Tunnel Northern
App. E3 & E14—1D **43**
Blackwall Tunnel Southern
App. SE10 —4A **58**
Blackwall Way. *E14* —1E **57**
Blackwater Clo. E7 —1B **30**
Blackwater Ho. NW8 —4F *35*
(off Church St.)
Blackwater St. *SE22* —3B **82**
Blackwell Clo. *E5* —1F **27**
Blackwell Ho. *SW4* —4F **79**
Blackwood Ho. E1 —3D *41*
(off Collingwood St.)
Blackwood St. *SE17* —1F **67**
Blade M. *SW15* —2B **76**
Blades Ct. *SW15* —2B **76**
Blades Ho. SE11 —2C *66*
(off Kennington Oval)
Bladon Ct. *SW16* —5A **94**
Blagdon Rd. *SE13* —4D **85**
Blagrove Rd. *W10* —4A **34**

Blair Av. *NW9* —2A **4**
Blair Clo. *N1* —3E **25**
Blair Ct. *NW8* —5F **21**
Blair Ct. *SE6* —1B **100**
Blairderry Rd. *SW2* —2A **94**
Blair Ho. *SW9* —5B **66**
Blair St. *E14* —5E **43**
Blake Clo. *W10* —4E **33**
*Blake Ct. NW6 —2C **34***
(off Stafford Clo.)
*Blake Ct. SE16 —1D **69***
(off Stubbs Dri.)
Blake Gdns. *SW6* —4D **63**
Blake Hall Cres. *E11* —3C **16**
Blake Hall Rd. *E11* —2C **16**
*Blake Ho. E14 —3C **56***
(off Admirals Way)
Blake Ho. *SE1* —4C **52**
*Blake Ho. SE8 —2C **70***
(off New King St.)
Blakeley Cotts. *SE10* —3F **57**
Blakemore Rd. *SW16* —3A **94**
Blakeney Clo. *E8* —2C **26**
Blakeney Clo. *NW1* —4F **23**
Blakenham Rd. *SW17* —4B **92**
Blaker Ct. *SE7* —3E **73**
(in two parts)
Blake Rd. *E16* —3B **44**
Blaker Rd. *E15* —5E **29**
Blake's Rd. *SE15* —3A **68**
Blanchard Clo. *SE9* —3F **101**
Blanchard Way. *E8* —3C **26**
Blanch Clo. *SE15* —3E **69**
Blanchedowne. *SE5* —2F **81**
Blanche St. *E16* —3B **44**
Blandfield Rd. *SW12* —5C **78**
*Blandford Ct. E8 —4A **26***
(off St Peter's Way)
Blandford Ct. *NW6* —4F **19**
*Blandford Ho. SW8 —3B **66***
(off Richborne Ter.)
Blandford Rd. *W4* —4A **46**
Blandford Sq. *NW1* —3A **36**
Blandford St. *W1* —5B **36**
*Bland Ho. SE11 —1B **66***
(off Vauxhall St.)
Bland St. *SE9* —2F **87**
Blann Clo. *SE9* —4F **87**
Blantyre St. *SW10* —3F **63**
Blantyre Tower. SW10
*(off Blantyre St.) —3F **63***
*Blantyre Wlk. SW10 —3F **63***
(off Worlds End Est.)
*Blashford. NW3 —4B **22***
(off Adelaide Rd.)
Blashford St. *SE13* —5F **85**
Blasker Wlk. *E14* —1D **71**
*Blaxland Ho. W12 —1D **47***
(off White City Est.)
*Blazer Ct. NW8 —2F **35***
(off St John's Wood Rd.)
Blechynden St. *W10* —1F **47**
*Bledlow Ho. NW8 —3F **35***
(off Capland St.)
Bleeding Heart Yd. EC1
*(off Greville St.) —4C **38***
Blegborough Rd. *SW16* —5E **93**
*Blendon Row. SE17 —5F **53***
(off Townley St.)
Blendworth Way. SE15
*(off Clanfield Way) —3A **68***
Blenheim Ct. *N19* —4A **10**
*Blenheim Ct. SE16 —2F **55***
(off King & Queen Wharf)
Blenheim Cres. *W11* —1A **48**
Blenheim Gdns. *NW2* —3E **19**
Blenheim Gdns. *SW2* —4B **80**
Blenheim Gro. *SE15* —5C **68**
Blenheim Pas. *NW8* —1E **35**
(in two parts)
Blenheim Rd. *E6* —2F **45**
Blenheim Rd. *E15* —1A **30**
Blenheim Rd. *NW8* —1E **35**
Blenheim Rd. *W4* —4A **46**
Blenheim St. *W1* —5D **37**
Blenheim Ter. *NW8* —1E **35**
Blenkarne Rd. *SW11* —4B **78**
Blessington Clo. *SE13* —1F **85**
Blessington Rd. *SE13* —1F **85**
*Bletchley Ct. N1 —1F **39***
(off Bletchley St.,
in two parts)
Bletchley St. *N1* —1F **39**
Bletsoe Wlk. *N1* —1E **39**
*Blick Ho. SE16 —4E **55***
(off Neptune St.)
Blincoe Clo. *SW19* —2F **89**
Bliss Cres. *SE13* —5D **71**
Blissett St. *SE10* —4E **71**
*Blisworth Ho. E2 —5C **26***
(off Whiston Rd.)
Blithfield St. *W8* —4D **49**
Bloemfontein Av. *W12* —2D **47**
Bloemfontein Rd. *W12* —1D **47**
Bloemfontein Way. *W12* —2D **47**
*Blomfield Ct. W9 —3E **35***
(off Lanark Pl.)
Blomfield Rd. *W9* —4D **35**
Blomfield St. *EC2* —4F **39**
Blomfield Vs. *W2* —4D **35**
Blondel St. *SW11* —5C **64**
Blondin St. *E3* —1C **42**
Bloomburg St. *SW1* —5F **51**
Bloomfield Ct. *N6* —1C **8**
*Bloomfield Ho. E1 —4C **40***
(off Old Montague St.)
*Bloomfield Pl. W1 —1D **51***
(off Grosvenor Hill)
Bloomfield Rd. *N6* —1C **8**
Bloomfield Ter. *SW1* —1C **64**
Bloom Gro. *SE27* —3D **95**
Bloomhall Rd. *SE19* —5F **95**
Bloom Pk. Rd. *SW6* —3B **62**
Bloomsbury. —4A 38
*Bloomsbury Ct. WC1 —4A **38***
(off Barter St.)
Bloomsbury Ho. *SW4* —4F **79**
Bloomsbury Pl. *SW18* —3E **77**
Bloomsbury Pl. *WC1* —4A **38**
Bloomsbury Sq. *WC1* —4A **38**
Bloomsbury St. *WC1* —4F **37**
Bloomsbury Way. *WC1* —4A **38**
Blore Clo. *SW8* —4F **65**
*Blore Ct. W1 —5F **37***
(off Berwick St.)
Blossom St. *E1* —3A **40**
Blount Ho. *E14* —4A **42**
Blount St. *E14* —4A **42**
Bloxam Gdns. *SE9* —3F **87**
Bloxhall Rd. *E10* —3B **14**
Blucher Rd. *SE5* —3E **67**
Blue Anchor La. *SE16* —5C **54**
Blue Anchor Yd. *E1* —1C **54**
Blue Ball Yd. *SW1* —2E **51**
Bluebell Av. *E12* —2F **31**
Bluebell Clo. *E9* —5E **27**
Bluebell Clo. *SE26* —4B **96**
Blue Water. *SW18* —2D **77**
*Blundell Ho. SE14 —3A **70***
(off Goodwood Rd.)
Blundell St. *N7* —4A **24**
Blurton Rd. *E5* —1E **27**
Blyth Clo. *E14* —5F **57**
Blythe Clo. *SE6* —5B **84**
Blythe Hill. —5B 84
Blythe Hill. *SE6* —5B **84**
Blythe Hill La. *SE6* —5B **84**
Blythe Ho. *SE11* —2C **66**
Blythe M. *W14* —4F **47**
*Blythendale Ho. E2 —1C **40***
(off Mansford St.)
Blythe Rd. *W14* —4F **47**
Blythe St. *E2* —2D **41**
Blythe Va. *SE6* —1B **98**
Blyth Hill Pl. *SE6* —5D **85**
Blyth Rd. *E17* —2B **14**
Blythwood Rd. *N4* —2A **10**
Boades M. *NW3* —1F **21**
Boadicea St. *N1* —5B **24**
Boardwalk Pl. *E14* —2E **57**
*Boarley Ho. SE17 —5A **54***
(off Massinger St.)
Boathouse Wlk. *SE15* —3B **68**
(in two parts)
Boat Lifter Way. *SE16* —5A **56**
Bob Anker Clo. *E13* —2C **44**
Bobbin Clo. *SW4* —1E **79**
Bob Marley Way. *SE24* —2C **80**
Bocking St. *E8* —5D **27**
Boddicott Clo. *SW19* —2A **90**
*Boddington Ho. SE14 —4E **69***
(off Pomeroy St.)
*Bodeney Ho. SE5 —4A **68***
(off Peckham Rd.)
*Boden Ho. E1 —4C **40***
(off Woodseer St.)
Bodington Ct. *W12* —3F **47**
Bodley Mnr. Way. *SW2* —5C **80**
Bodmin Pl. *SE27* —4D **95**
Bodmin St. *SW18* —1C **90**

Bodney Rd.—Bovingdon Clo.

Bodney Rd. *E8* —2D **27**
Bohemia Pl. *E8* —3E **27**
Bohn Rd. *E1* —4A **42**
Boileau Rd. *SW13* —3C **60**
Bolden St. *SE8* —5D **71**
Boldero Pl. NW8 —3A **36**
(off Gateforth St.)
Boleyn Rd. *E6* —1F **45**
Boleyn Rd. *E7* —4C **30**
Boleyn Rd. *N16* —2A **26**
Bolina Rd. *SE16* —1E **69**
Bolingbroke Gro. *SW11*
—2A **78**
Bolingbroke Rd. *W14* —4F **47**
Bolingbroke Wlk. *SW11*
—4F **63**
Bolney Ga. *SW7* —3A **50**
Bolney St. *SW8* —3B **66**
Bolsover St. *W1* —3D **37**
Bolt Ct. *EC4* —5C **38**
Bolton Cres. *SE5* —3D **67**
Bolton Gdns. *NW10* —1F **33**
Bolton Gdns. *SW5* —1D **63**
Bolton Gdns. M. *SW10*
—1E **63**
Bolton Ho. SE10 —1A 72
(off Trafalgar Rd.)
Bolton Pl. NW8 —5D 21
(off Bolton Rd.)
Bolton Rd. *E15* —3B **30**
Bolton Rd. *NW8* —5D **21**
Bolton Rd. *NW10* —5A **18**
Boltons Ct. SW5 —1D 63
(off Old Brompton Rd.)
Boltons Pl. *SW5* —1E **63**
Boltons, The. *SW10* —1E **63**
Bolton St. *W1* —2D **51**
Bolton Studios. *SW10* —1E **63**
Bolton Wlk. N4 —4B 10
(off Durham Rd.)
Bombay St. *SE16* —5D **55**
Bomore Rd. *W11* —1A **48**
Bonar Rd. *SE15* —3C **68**
Bonchurch Rd. *W10* —4A **34**
Bond Ct. *EC4* —1F **53**
Bond Ho. NW6 —1B 34
(off Rupert Rd.)
Bond Ho. SE14 —3A 70
(off Goodwood Rd.)
Bonding Yd. Wlk. *SE16*
—4A **56**
Bond St. *E15* —2A **30**
Bond St. *W4* —5A **46**
Bondway. *SW8* —2A **66**
Bonfield Rd. *SE13* —2E **85**
Bonham Rd. *SW2* —3B **80**
Bonheur Rd. *W4* —3A **46**
Bonhill St. *EC2* —3F **39**
Bonington Ho. N1 —1B 38
Bon Marche Ter. M. SE27
—4A **96**
Bonner Rd. *E2* —1E **41**
Bonner St. *E2* —1E **41**
Bonneville Gdns. *SW4* —4E **79**
Bonnington Sq. *SW8* —2B **66**
Bonny St. *NW1* —4E **23**
Bonsor Ho. *SW8* —4E **65**

Bonsor St. *SE5* —3A **68**
Bonville Rd. *Brom* —5B **100**
Booker Clo. *E14* —4B **42**
Boones Rd. *SW13* —2A **86**
Boone St. *SE13* —2A **86**
Boord St. *SE10* —4A **56**
Boothby Rd. *N19* —4F **9**
Booth Clo. *E9* —5D **27**
Booth La. EC4 —1E 53
(off Baynard St.)
Booth's Pl. *W1* —4E **37**
Boot St. *N1* —2A **40**
Border Cres. *SE26* —5D **97**
Border Rd. *SE26* —5D **97**
Bordon Wlk. *SW15* —5C **74**
Boreas Wlk. N1 —1D 39
(off Nelson Pl.)
Boreham Av. *E16* —5C **44**
Boreham Clo. *E10* —3E **15**
Boreman Ho. SE10 —2E 71
(off Thames St.)
Borland Rd. *SE15* —2E **83**
Borneo St. *SW15* —1E **75**
Borough High St. *SE1* —3E **53**
Borough Rd. *SE1* —4D **53**
Borough Sq. SE1 —3E 53
(off McCoid Way)
Borough, The. —3F 53
Borrett Clo. *SE17* —1E **67**
Borrodaile Rd. *SW18* —4D **77**
Borrowdale. NW1 —2E 37
(off Robert St.)
Borthwick M. *E15* —1A **30**
Borthwick Rd. *E15* —1A **30**
Borthwick Rd. *NW9* —1B **4**
Borthwick St. *SE8* —1C **70**
Bosbury Rd. *SE6* —3E **99**
Boscastle Rd. *NW5* —5D **9**
Boscobel Ho. *E8* —3D **27**
Boscobel Pl. *SW1* —5C **50**
Boscobel St. *W2* —3F **35**
Boscombe Av. *E10* —2F **15**
Boscombe Clo. *E5* —2A **28**
Boscombe Rd. *SW17* —5C **92**
Boscombe Rd. *W12* —2C **46**
Boss Ho. SE1 —3B 54
(off Boss St.)
Boss St. *SE1* —3B **54**
Boston Gdns. *W4* —2A **60**
Boston Pl. *NW1* —3B **36**
Boston Rd. *E6* —2F **45**
Boston Rd. *E17* —1C **14**
Bosun Clo. *E14* —3C **56**
Boswell Ct. W14 —4F 47
(off Blythe Rd.)
Boswell Ct. *WC1* —4A **38**
Boswell Ho. WC1 —4A 38
(off Boswell St.)
Boswell St. *WC1* —4A **38**
Bosworth Ho. *W10* —3A **34**
(off Bosworth Rd.)
Bosworth Rd. *W10* —3A **34**
Botha Rd. *E13* —4D **45**
Bothwell Clo. *E16* —4B **44**
Bothwell St. *SW6* —2F **61**
Botolph All. *EC3* —1A **54**
(off Botolph La.)

Botolph La. *EC3* —1A **54**
Botts M. *W2* —5C **34**
Boughton Ho. SE1 —3F 53
(off Tennis St.)
Boulcott St. *E1* —5F **41**
Boulevard, The. *SW17*
—2C **92**
Boulevard, The. *SW18*
—2D **77**
Boulogne Ho. SE1 —4B 54
(off Abbey St.)
Boulter Ho. SE14 —4E 69
(off Kender St.)
Boundaries Rd. *SW12*
—2B **92**
Boundary Av. *E17* —2B **14**
Boundary Ho. *SE5* —3E **67**
Boundary La. *E13* —2F **45**
Boundary La. *SE5* —2E **67**
Boundary M. NW8 —5E 21
(off Boundary Rd.)
Boundary Pas. *E1* —3B **40**
Boundary Rd. *E13* —1E **45**
Boundary Rd. *E17* —2B **14**
Boundary Rd. *NW8* —5D **21**
Boundary Rd. *SW19* —5F **91**
Boundary Row. *SE1* —3D **53**
Boundary St. E2 —2B 40
(in two parts)
Boundfield Rd. *SE6* —3A **100**
Bourbon Ho. *SE6* —5E **99**
Bourchier St. *W1* —1F **51**
(in two parts)
Bourdon Pl. W1 —1D 51
(off Bourdon St.)
Bourdon St. *W1* —1D **51**
Bourke Clo. *NW10* —3A **18**
Bourke Clo. *SW4* —4A **80**
Bourlet Clo. *W1* —4E **37**
Bournbrook Rd. *SE3* —1F **87**
Bourne Est. *EC1* —4C **38**
Bourne M. *W1* —5C **20**
Bournemouth Clo. *SE15*
—5C **68**
Bournemouth Rd. *SE15*
—5C **68**
Bourne Pl. *W4* —1A **60**
Bourne Rd. *E7* —5B **16**
Bourne Rd. *N8* —1A **10**
Bournes Ho. N15 —1A 12
(off Chisley Rd.)
Bourneside Gdns. *SE6*
—5E **99**
Bourne St. *SW1* —5C **50**
Bourne Ter. *W2* —4D **35**
Bournevale Rd. *NW6* —4A **94**
Bournville Rd. *SE6* —5C **84**
Bousfield Rd. *SE14* —5F **69**
Boutflower Rd. *SW11* —2A **78**
Boutique Hall. SE13 —2E 85
Bouverie M. *N16* —4A **12**
Bouverie Pl. *W2* —5F **35**
Bouverie Rd. *N16* —4A **12**
Bouverie St. *EC4* —5C **38**
Boveney Rd. *SE23* —5F **83**
Bovill Rd. *SE23* —5F **83**
Bovingdon Clo. *N19* —4E **9**

Bovingdon Rd. *SW6* —4D **63**
Bow. —2C 42
Bowater Clo. *SW2* —4A **50**
Bowater Ho. *EC1* —3E **39**
 (off Golden La. Est.)
Bowater Pl. *SE3* —3D **73**
Bowater Rd. *SE18* —4F **59**
Bow Bri. Est. *E3* —2D **43**
Bow Chyd. *EC4* —5E **39**
 (off Cheapside)
Bow Common. —4C 42
Bow Comn. La. *E3* —3B **42**
Bowden St. *SE11* —1C **66**
Bowditch. *SE8* —5B **56**
 (in two parts)
Bowdon Rd. *E17* —2C **14**
Bowen Dri. *SE21* —3A **96**
Bowen St. *E14* —5D **43**
Bower Av. *SE10* —4A **72**
Bowerdean St. *SW6* —4D **63**
Bower Ho. *SE14* —4F **69**
 (off Besson St.)
Bowerman Av. *SE14* —2A **70**
Bowerman Ct. *N19* —4F **9**
 (off St John's Way)
Bower St. *E1* —5F **41**
Bowes-Lyon Hall. *E16* —2C **58**
 (off Wesley Av., in two parts)
Bowes Rd. *W3* —1A **46**
Bowfell Rd. *W6* —2E **61**
Bowhill Clo. *SW9* —3C **66**
Bowie Clo. *SW4* —5F **79**
Bow Ind. Pk. *E15* —4C **28**
Bow Interchange. (Junct.)
 —1D **43**
Bowland Rd. *SW4* —2F **79**
Bowland Yd. *SW1* —3B **50**
 (off Kinnerton St.)
Bow La. *EC4* —5E **39**
Bowl Ct. *EC2* —3A **40**
Bowles Rd. *SE1* —2C **68**
Bowley Clo. *SE19* —5B **96**
Bowley Ho. *SE16* —4C **54**
Bowley La. *SE19* —5B **96**
Bowling Grn. Clo. *SW15*
 —5D **75**
Bowling Grn. La. *EC1* —3C **38**
Bowling Grn. Pl. *SE1* —3F **53**
Bowling Grn. St. *SE11*
 —2C **66**
Bowling Grn. Wlk. *N1* —2A **40**
Bowman Av. *E16* —1B **58**
Bowman M. *SW18* —1B **90**
Bowman's Bldgs. NW1
 (off Penfold Pl.) —4A **36**
Bowmans Lea. *SE23* —5E **83**
Bowman's M. *E1* —1C **54**
Bowman's M. *N7* —5A **10**
Bowman's Pl. *N7* —5A **10**
Bowmore Wlk. *NW1* —4F **23**
Bowness Clo. E8 —3B **26**
 (off Beechwood Rd.)
Bowness Cres. *SW15* —5A **88**
Bowness Ho. SE15 —3E **69**
 (off Hillbeck Clo.)
Bowness Rd. *SE6* —5D **85**
Bowood Rd. *SW11* —3C **78**

Bow Rd. *E3* —2B **42**
Bowry Ho. *E14* —4B **42**
Bowsprit Point. *E14* —4C **56**
Bow St. *E15* —2A **30**
Bow St. *WC2* —5A **38**
Bow Triangle Bus. Cen. *E3*
 —3C **42**
Bowyer Ho. *N1* —5A **26**
 (off Whitmore Est.)
Bowyer Pl. *SE5* —3E **67**
Bowyer St. *SE5* —3E **67**
Boxall Rd. *SE21* —4A **82**
Boxley St. *E16* —2D **59**
Boxmoor Ho. W11 —2F **47**
 (off Queensdale Cres.)
Box Tree Ho. *SE8* —2A **70**
Boxworth Gro. *N1* —5B **24**
Boyce Ho. W10 —2B **34**
 (off Bruckner St.)
Boyce Way. *E13* —3C **44**
Boydell Ct. *NW8* —4F **21**
 (in two parts)
Boyd Rd. *SW19* —5F **91**
Boyd St. *E1* —5C **40**
Boyfield St. *SE1* —3D **53**
Boyland Rd. *Brom* —5B **100**
Boyle St. *W1* —1E **51**
Boyne Rd. *SE13* —1E **85**
Boyne Ter. M. *W11* —2B **48**
Boyson Rd. *SE5* —2E **67**
 (in two parts)
Boyson Wlk. *SE17* —2F **67**
Boyton Clo. *E1* —3E **41**
Boyton Ho. NW8 —1F **35**
 (off Wellington Rd.)
Brabant Ct. EC3 —1A **54**
 (off Philpot La.)
Brabazon St. *E14* —5D **43**
Brabner Ho. E2 —2C **40**
 (off Wellington Row)
Brabourne Clo. *SE19* —5A **96**
Brabourn Gro. *SE15* —5E **69**
Bracer Ho. N1 —1A **40**
 (off Whitmore Est.)
Bracewell Rd. *W10* —4E **33**
Bracey M. *N19* —4A **10**
Bracey St. *N4* —4A **10**
Bracken Av. *SW12* —4C **78**
Brackenbury. *N4* —3C **10**
 (off Osborne Rd.)
Brackenbury Gdns. *W6*
 —4D **47**
Brackenbury Rd. *W6* —4D **47**
Brackenfield Clo. *E5* —5D **13**
Bracken Gdns. *SW13* —5C **60**
Bracken Ho. *E3* —4C **42**
Brackley Ct. NW8 —3F **35**
 (off Henderson St.)
Brackley Rd. *W4* —1A **60**
Brackley St. *EC1* —3E **39**
Brackley Ter. *W4* —1A **60**
Bracklyn Ct. *N1* —1F **39**
 (in three parts)
Bracklyn St. *N1* —1F **39**
Bracknell Gdns. *NW3* —1D **21**
Bracknell Ga. *NW3* —2D **21**
Bracknell Way. *NW3* —1D **21**

Bradbeer Ho. *E2* —2E **41**
 (off Cornwall Av.)
Bradbourne St. *SW6* —5C **62**
Bradbury M. N16 —2A **26**
 (off Bradbury St.)
Bradbury St. *N16* —2A **26**
Braddyll St. *SE10* —1A **72**
Bradenham. SE17 —2F **67**
 (off Bradenham Clo.)
Bradenham Clo. *SE17* —2F **67**
Braden St. *W9* —3D **35**
Bradfield Ct. NW1 —4D **23**
 (off Hawley Rd.)
Bradfield Rd. *E16* —3C **58**
Bradford Clo. *SE26* —4D **97**
Bradford Rd. *W3* —3A **46**
Bradgate Rd. *SE6* —4D **85**
Brading Cres. *E11* —4D **17**
Brading Rd. *SW2* —5B **80**
Brading Ter. *W12* —4C **46**
Bradiston Rd. *W9* —2B **34**
Bradley Clo. *N7* —3A **24**
Bradley Ho. E2 —1C **40**
 (off Claredale St.)
Bradley Ho. SE16 —5E **55**
 (off Raymouth Rd.)
Bradley M. *SW17* —1B **92**
Bradley Rd. *SE19* —5E **95**
Bradley's Clo. *N1* —1C **38**
Bradmead. *SW8* —3D **65**
Bradmore Ho. E1 —4E **41**
 (off Jamaica St.)
Bradmore Pk. Rd. *W6* —5D **47**
Bradshaw Clo. *SW19* —5C **90**
Bradstock Ho. *E9* —4F **27**
Bradstock Rd. *E9* —3F **27**
Brad St. *SE1* —2C **52**
Bradwell Ho. NW6 —5D **21**
 (off Mortimer Cres.)
Brady Ho. SW8 —4E **65**
 (off Corunna Rd.)
Brady St. *E1* —3D **41**
Braemar Av. *NW10* —5A **4**
Braemar Av. *SW19* —2C **90**
Braemar Ct. *SE6* —1B **100**
Braemar Ho. W9 —2E **35**
 (off Maida Va.)
Braemar Rd. *E13* —3B **44**
Braemar Rd. *N15* —1A **12**
Braemer Clo. SE16 —1D **69**
 (off Masters Dri.)
Braeside. *Beck* —5C **98**
Braes St. *N1* —4D **25**
Braganza St. *SE17* —1D **67**
Braham St. *E1* —5B **40**
Braham St. *E1* —5B **40**
Braid Av. *W3* —5A **32**
Braid Ho. SE10 —4E **71**
 (off Blackheath Hill)
Braidwood Pas. EC1 —4E **39**
 (off Aldersgate St.)
Braidwood Rd. *SE6* —1F **99**
Brailsford Rd. *SW2* —3C **80**
Braintree Ho. E1 —3E **41**
 (off Malcolm St.)
Braintree St. *E2* —2E **41**
Braithwaite Ho. *E14* —5F **43**

Braithwaite Ho. EC1 —3F 39 (off Bunhill Row)
Braithwaite Tower. W2 (off Hall Pl.) —4F 35
Bramah Grn. SW9 —4C 66
Bramah Tea & Coffee Mus. (off Maguire St.) —3B 54
Bramalea Clo. N6 —1C 8
Bramall Clo. E15 —2B 30
Bramall Ct. N7 —2B 24 (off George's Rd.)
Bramber. WC1 —2A 38 (off Cromer St.)
Bramber Rd. W14 —2B 62
Bramble Gdns. W12 —1B 46
Bramble Ho. E3 —4C 42
Brambles, The. SW19 —5B 90 (off Woodside)
Brambling Ct. SE8 —2B 70 (off Abinger Gro.)
Bramcote Gro. SE16 —1E 69
Bramcote Rd. SW15 —2D 75
Bramdean Cres. SE12 —1C 100
Bramdean Gdns. SE12 —1C 100
Bramerton St. SW3 —2A 64
Bramfield Ct. N4 —5E 11 (off Queens Dri.)
Bramfield Rd. SW11 —4A 78
Bramford Rd. SW18 —2E 77
Bramham Gdns. SW5 —1D 63
Bramham Ho. SE15 —1B 82
Bramhope La. SE7 —2D 73
Bramlands Clo. SW11 —1A 78
Bramley Cres. SW8 —3F 65
Bramley Ho. SW15 —4B 74 (off Tunworth Cres.)
Bramley Ho. W10 —5F 33
Bramley Rd. W10 —5F 33
Brampton. WC1 —4B 38 (off Red Lion Sq.)
Brampton Clo. E5 —4D 13
Brampton Gdns. N15 —1E 11
Brampton Rd. E6 —2F 45
Brampton Rd. N15 —1E 11
Bramshaw Rd. E9 —3F 27
Bramshill Gdns. NW5 —5D 9
Bramshill Rd. NW10 —1B 32
Bramshot Av. SE7 —2C 72
Bramshurst. NW8 —5D 21 (off Abbey Rd.)
Bramston Rd. NW10 —1C 32
Bramston Rd. SW17 —3E 91
Bramwell Ho. SE1 —4E 53
Bramwell Ho. SW1 —1E 65 (off Churchill Gdns.)
Bramwell M. N1 —5B 24
Brancaster Rd. SW16 —3A 94
Branch Hill. NW3 —5E 7
Branch Hill Ho. NW3 —5D 7
Branch Pl. N1 —5F 25
Branch Rd. E14 —1A 56
Branch St. SE5 —3A 68
Brand Clo. N4 —3D 11
Brandlehow Rd. SW15 —2B 76
Brandon Est. SE17 —2D 67
Brandon Ho. Beck —5D 99 (off Beckenham Hill Rd.)
Brandon Mans. W14 —2A 62 (off Queen's Club Gdns.)
Brandon M. EC2 —4F 39 (off Silk St.)
Brandon Rd. N7 —4A 24
Brandon St. SE17 —5E 53 (in three parts)
Brandram M. SE13 —2A 86 (off Brandram Rd.)
Brandram Rd. SE13 —1A 86
Brandreth Rd. SW17 —2D 93
Brand St. SE10 —3E 71
Brangbourne Rd. Brom —5E 99
Brangton Rd. SE11 —1B 66
Brangwyn Ct. W14 —4A 48 (off Blythe Rd.)
Branksea St. SW6 —3A 62
Branksome Ho. SW8 —3B 66 (off Meadow Rd.)
Branksome Rd. SW2 —3A 80
Branscombe. NW1 —5E 23 (off Plender St.)
Branscombe St. SE13 —1D 85
Bransdale Clo. NW6 —5C 20
Brantwood Ho. SE5 —3E 67 (off Wyndam Est.)
Brantwood Rd. SE24 —3E 81
Brasenose Dri. SW13 —2E 61
Brassett Point. E15 —5A 30 (off Abbey Rd.)
Brassey Ho. E14 —5D 57
Brassey Rd. NW6 —3B 20
Brassey Sq. SW11 —1C 78
Brassie Av. W3 —5A 32
Brass Tally All. SE16 —3F 55
Brasted Clo. SE26 —4E 97
Brathay. NW1 —1E 37 (off Ampthill Est.)
Brathway Rd. SW18 —5C 76
Bratley St. E1 —3C 40
Bravington Pl. W9 —3B 34
Bravington Rd. W9 —1B 34
Brawne Ho. SE17 —2D 67 (off Brandon Est.)
Braxfield Rd. SE4 —2A 84
Braxted Pk. SW16 —5B 94
Bray. NW3 —4A 22
Brayards Rd. SE15 —5D 69
Brayards Rd. Est. SE15 (off Brayards Rd.) —5E 69
Braybrook St. W12 —4B 32
Brayburne Av. SW4 —5E 65
Bray Ct. SW16 —5A 94
Bray Cres. SE16 —3F 55
Braydon Rd. N16 —3C 12
Bray Dri. E16 —1B 58
Brayfield Ter. N1 —4C 24
Brayford Sq. E1 —5E 41
Bray Pas. E16 —1C 58
Bray Pl. SW3 —5B 50
Bread St. EC4 —5E 39 (in two parts)
Breakspears M. SE4 —5B 70
Breakspears Rd. SE4 —2B 84
Breamore Clo. SW15 —1C 88
Breamore Ho. SE15 —3C 68 (off Friary Est.)
Bream's Bldgs. EC4 —5C 38
Bream St. E3 —4C 28
Breasley Clo. SW15 —2D 75
Brechin Pl. SW7 —5E 49
Brecknock Rd. N19 & N7 —1E 23
Brecknock Rd. Est. N19 —1E 23
Brecon Grn. NW9 —1A 4
Brecon Ho. W2 —5E 35 (off Hallfield Est.)
Brecon M. NW5 —2F 23
Brecon Rd. W6 —2A 62
Bredel Ho. E14 —4C 42
Bredgar Rd. N19 —4E 9
Bredhurst Clo. SE20 —5E 97
Breer St. SW6 —1D 77
Breezers Ct. E1 —1C 54 (off Highway, The)
Breezer's Hill. E1 —1C 54
Bremner Rd. SW7 —4E 49
Brenchley Gdns. SE23 —4E 83
Brenda Rd. SW17 —2B 92
Brendon Av. NW10 —1A 18
Brendon St. W1 —5A 36
Brenley Gdns. SE9 —2F 87
Brenley Ho. SE1 —3F 53 (off Tennis St.)
Brennand Ct. N19 —5E 9
Brent Ct. NW11 —2F 5
Brent Cross. —2E 5
Brent Cross Fly-Over. NW2 —2F 5
Brent Cross Gdns. NW4 —1F 5
Brent Cross Interchange. (Junct.) —2F 5
Brent Cross Shop. Cen. NW4 —2E 5
Brentfield Gdns. NW2 —2F 5
Brentfield Ho. NW10 —4A 18
Brentfield Rd. NW10 —3A 18
Brent Grn. NW4 —1E 5
Brenthouse Rd. E9 —4E 27
Brenthurst Rd. NW10 —3B 18
Brentmead Pl. NW11 —1F 5
Brent New Enterprise Cen. NW10 —3B 18
Brenton St. E14 —5A 42
Brent Pk. Rd. NW9 & NW4 (in two parts) —2D 5
Brent Rd. E16 —5C 44
Brent Ter. NW2 —3E 5 (in two parts)
Brent Trad. Cen. NW10 —2A 18
Brent Vw. Rd. NW9 —1C 4
Brentwood Ho. SE18 —3F 73 (off Portway Gdns.)
Brentwood Lodge. NW4 (off Holmdale Gdns.) —1F 5
Bressenden Pl. SW1 —4D 51

Breton Highwalk. EC2 —4E ***39***
(off Golden La.)
Breton Ho. EC1 —4E ***39***
(off Beech St.)
Breton Ho. SE1 —4B ***54***
(off Abbey St.)
Brett Clo. *N16* —4A **12**
Brettell St. *SE17* —1F **67**
Brett Ho. Clo. *SW15* —5F **75**
Brettinghurst. SE1 —1C ***68***
(off Avondale Sq.)
Brett Pas. *E8* —2D **27**
Brett Rd. *E8* —2D **27**
Brewer's Grn. SW1 —4F ***51***
(off Buckingham Ga.)
Brewer's Hall Garden. EC2
(off London Wall) —4E ***39***
Brewer St. *W1* —1E **51**
Brewery Ind. Est., The. *N1* —1E **39**
Brewery Rd. *N7* —4A **24**
Brewery Sq. SE1 —3B ***54***
(off Horselydown La.)
Brewhouse La. *E1* —2D **55**
Brewhouse St. *SW15* —1A **76**
Brewhouse Wlk. *SE16* —2A **56**
Brewhouse Yd. *EC1* —3D **39**
Brewster Gdns. *W10* —4E **33**
Brewster Ho. *E14* —1B **56**
Brewster Ho. SE1 —5B ***54***
(off Dunton Rd.)
Brewster Rd. *E10* —3D **15**
Briant Ho. SE1 —4B ***52***
(off Hercules Rd.)
Briant St. *SE14* —4F **69**
Briar Ct. *SW15* —2D **75**
Briardale Gdns. *NW3* —5C **6**
Briar Rd. *NW2* —1E **19**
Briar Wlk. *SW15* —2D **75**
Briar Wlk. *W10* —3A **34**
Briarwood Rd. *SW4* —3F **79**
Briary Clo. *NW3* —4A **22**
Briary Gdns. *Brom* —5D **101**
Brickbarn Clo. SW10 —3E ***63***
(off King's Barn)
Brick Ct. *EC4* —5C **38**
Brickfield Rd. *SW19* —4D **91**
Brick La. *E2 & E1* —2B **40**
Bricklayers Arms. (Junct.) —4F **53**
Bricklayers Arms Bus. Cen. *SE1* —5A **54**
Brick St. *W1* —2D **51**
Brickwood Clo. *SE26* —3D **97**
Brideale Clo. *SE15* —2B **68**
Bride Ct. EC4 —5D ***39***
(off Bride La.)
Bride La. *EC4* —5D **39**
Bridel M. N1 —5D ***25***
(off Colebrook Row)
Bride St. *N7* —3B **24**
Bridewain St. *SE1* —4B **54**
(in two parts)
Bridewell Pl. *E1* —2D **55**
Bridewell Pl. *EC4* —5D **39**
Bridford M. *W1* —4D **37**
Bridge App. *NW1* —4C **22**
Bridge Av. *W6* —5E **47**
Bridge Clo. *W10* —5F **33**
Bridge Ct. *E10* —3B **14**
Bridgefoot. *SE1* —1A **66**
Bridge Ho. E9 —3F ***27***
(off Shepherds La.)
Bridge Ho. NW3 —4C ***22***
(off Adelaide Rd.)
Bridge Ho. *SE4* —2B **84**
Bridge Ho. *SW1* —1D **65**
Bridgehouse Ct. *SE1* —3D **53**
Bridge Ho. Quay. *E14* —2E **57**
Bridgeland Rd. *E16* —1C **58**
Bridge La. *NW11* —1B **6**
Bridge La. *SW11* —4A **64**
Bridgeman Rd. *N1* —4B **24**
Bridgeman St. *NW8* —1A **36**
Bridge Meadows. *SE14* —2F **69**
Bridgend Rd. *SW18* —2E **77**
Bridgen Ho. E1 —5D ***41***
(off Nelson St.)
Bridgepark. *SW18* —3C **76**
Bridge Pl. *SW1* —5D **51**
Bridgeport Pl. *E1* —2C **54**
Bridge Rd. *E15* —4F **29**
Bridge Rd. *E17* —2B **14**
Bridge Rd. *NW10* —3A **18**
Bridges Ct. *SW11* —1F **77**
(in two parts)
Bridges Ho. SE5 —3F ***67***
(off Elmington Est.)
Bridgeside Ho. N1 —1E ***39***
(off Wharf Rd.)
Bridges Pl. *SW6* —4B **62**
Bridge St. *SW1* —3A **52**
Bridge Ter. *E15* —4F **29**
(in two parts)
Bridgetown Clo. *SE19* —5A **96**
Bridge Vw. *W6* —1E **61**
Bridgewalk Heights. SE1
(off Weston St.) —3F ***53***
Bridgewater Highwalk. EC2
(off Beech St.) —4E ***39***
Bridgewater Rd. *E15* —5E **29**
Bridgewater Sq. *EC2* —4E **39**
Bridgewater St. *EC2* —4E **39**
Bridge Way. *NW11* —1B **6**
Bridgeway St. *NW1* —1E **37**
Bridge Wharf. *E2* —1F **41**
Bridge Yd. *SE1* —2F **53**
Bridgford St. *SW18* —3E **91**
Bridgnorth Ho. SE15 —2C ***68***
(off Friary Est.)
Bridgwater Ho. W2 —5E ***35***
(off Hallfield Est.)
Bridle La. *W1* —1E **51**
Bridport. SE17 —1F ***67***
(off Date St.)
Bridport Ho. N1 —5F ***25***
(off Bridport Pl.)
Bridport Pl. *N1* —5F **25**
(in two parts)
Bridstow Pl. *W2* —5C **34**
Brief St. *SE5* —4D **67**
Brierfield. NW1 —5E ***23***
(off Arlington Rd.)
Brierley Rd. *E11* —1F **29**
Brierley Rd. *SW12* —2E **93**
Brierly Gdns. *E2* —1E **41**
Brigade St. *SE3* —5B **72**
Briggeford Clo. *E5* —4C **12**
Briggs Ho. E2 —2B ***40***
(off Chambord St.)
Brightfield Rd. *SE12* —3A **86**
Brightling Rd. *SE4* —4B **84**
Brightlingsea Pl. *E14* —1B **56**
Brightman Rd. *SW18* —1F **91**
Brighton Av. *E17* —1B **14**
Brighton Bldgs. SE1 —4A ***54***
(off Tower Bri. Rd.)
Brighton Gro. *SE14* —4A **70**
Brighton Rd. *N16* —1A **26**
Brighton Ter. *SW9* —2B **80**
Brightside Rd. *SE13* —4F **85**
Bright St. *E14* —5D **43**
Brightwell Cres. *SW17* —5B **92**
Brig M. *SE8* —2C **70**
Brigstock Ho. *SE5* —5E **67**
Brill Pl. *NW1* —1F **37**
Brimsdown Ho. *E3* —3D **43**
Brimstone Ho. E15 —4A ***30***
(off Victoria St.)
Brindley St. *SE14* —4B **70**
Brindley Way. *Brom* —5C **100**
Brinklow Ho. W2 —4D ***35***
(off Torquay St.)
Brinkworth Way. *E9* —3B **28**
Brinsley St. *E1* —5D **41**
Brinton Wlk. SE1 —2D ***53***
(off Chancel St.)
Brion Pl. *E14* —4E **43**
Brisbane Rd. *E10* —4D **15**
Brisbane St. *SE5* —3F **67**
Briscoe Clo. *E11* —4B **16**
Briscoe Rd. *SW19* —5F **91**
Briset Rd. *SE9* —1F **87**
Briset St. *EC1* —4D **39**
Briset Way. *N7* —4B **10**
Bristol Gdns. *SW15* —5E **75**
Bristol Gdns. *W9* —3D **35**
Bristol Ho. SE11 —4C ***52***
(off Lambeth Wlk.)
Bristol M. *W9* —3D **35**
Bristol Rd. *E7* —3E **31**
Briston Gro. *N8* —1A **10**
Bristow Rd. *SE19* —5A **96**
Britain Vis. Cen. —2F 51
(off Regent St.)
Britania Bus. Cen. *NW2* —1F **19**
Britannia Bri. *E14* —5B **42**
Britannia Clo. *SW4* —2F **79**
Britannia Ga. *E16* —2C **58**
Britannia Junction. (Junct.) —5D **23**
Britannia Rd. *E14* —5C **56**
Britannia Rd. *SW6* —3D **63**
(in two parts)
Britannia Row. *N1* —5D **25**
Britannia St. *WC1* —2B **38**
Britannia Wlk. *N1* —1F **39**
(in two parts)

*Britannia Way. SW6 —3D **63***
(off Britannia Rd.)
Britannic Highwalk. EC2
*(off Moor La.) —4F **39***
*Britannic Tower. EC2 —4F **39***
(off Ropemaker St.)
British Gro. *W4* —1B **60**
British Gro. Pas. *W4* —1B **60**
British Gro. S. *W4* —1B **60**
British Library. —2F 37
British Mus. —4A 38
British St. *E3* —2B **42**
British Telecom Cen. EC1
*(off Newgate St.) —5E **39***
British Wharf Ind. Est. *SE14*
—1F **69**
Britley Ho. *E14* —5B **42**
Brittain Ho. *SE9* —1F **101**
Brittany Point. *SE11* —5C **52**
Britten Clo. *NW11* —3D **7**
Britten Ct. *E15* —1F **43**
Britten St. *SW3* —1A **64**
Britton Clo. *SE6* —5F **85**
Britton St. *EC1* —3D **39**
Brixton. —2B 80
Brixton Hill. *SW2* —5A **80**
Brixton Hill Ct. *SW2* —3B **80**
Brixton Hill Pl. *SW2* —5A **80**
Brixton Oval. *SW9* —2C **80**
Brixton Sta. Rd. *SW9* —1C **80**
Brixton Water La. *SW2*
—3B **80**
Broadbent Clo. *N6* —3D **9**
Broadbent St. *W1* —1D **51**
Broadbridge Clo. *SE3* —3C **72**
Broad Comn. Est. N16
*—3C **12***
(off Osbaldeston Rd.)
Broad Ct. *WC2* —5A **38**
Broadfield. *NW6* —3D **21**
Broadfield Clo. *NW2* —5E **5**
Broadfield La. *NW1* —4A **24**
Broadfield Rd. *SE6* —5A **86**
Broadfields Way. *NW10*
—2B **18**
*Broadgate. EC2 —4A **40***
(off Broadgate Cir.)
*Broadgate Circ. EC2 —4A **40***
(off Broadgate)
Broadgate Rd. *E16* —5F **45**
*Broadgates Ct. SE11 —1C **66***
(off Cleaver St.)
Broadgates Rd. *SW18* —1F **91**
Broadhinton Rd. *SW4* —1D **79**
Broadhurst Clo. *NW6* —3E **21**
Broadhurst Gdns. *NW6*
—3D **21**
Broadlands Av. *SW16* —2A **94**
Broadlands Clo. *N6* —2C **8**
Broadlands Clo. *SW16*
—2A **94**
Broadlands Lodge. *N6* —2B **8**
Broadlands Rd. *N6* —2B **8**
Broadlands Rd. *Brom*
—4D **101**
Broad La. *EC2* —4A **40**
(in two parts)
Broad La. *N8* —1B **10**
Broadley St. *NW8* —4F **35**
Broadley Ter. *NW1* —3A **36**
*Broadmayne. SE17 —1F **67***
(off Portland St.)
Broadmead. *SE6* —3C **98**
Broadmead. *W14* —5A **48**
Broadoak Ct. *SW9* —1C **80**
*Broadoak Ho. NW6 —5D **21***
(off Mortimer Cres.)
Broad Sanctuary. *SW1*
—3F **51**
*Broadstone Ho. SW8 —3B **66***
(off Dorset Rd.)
Broadstone Pl. *W1* —4C **36**
Broad St. Av. *EC2* —4A **40**
*Broad St. Pl. EC2 —4F **39***
(off Blomfield St.)
Broad Wlk. *NW1* —5C **22**
Broad Wlk. *SE3* —5E **73**
Broad Wlk. *W1* —1B **50**
*Broadwalk Ct. W8 —2C **48***
(off Palace Gdns. Ter.)
Broadwalk Ho. *EC2* —3A **40**
*Broadwalk Ho. SW7 —3E **49***
(off Broadwalk Ho.)
Broad Wlk. La. *NW11* —2B **6**
Broad Wlk., The. *W8* —2D **49**
Broadwall. *SE1* —2C **52**
Broadwater Rd. *SW17*
—4A **92**
Broadway. *E13* —1D **45**
Broadway. *E15* —4F **29**
(in two parts)
Broadway. *SW1* —4F **51**
*Broadway Arc. W6 —5E **47***
(off Hammersmith B'way.)
Broadway Cen., The. *W6*
—5E **47**
Broadway Ho. *E8* —5D **27**
*Broadway Ho. Brom —5F **99***
(off Bromley Rd.)
Broadway Mkt. *E8* —5D **27**
Broadway Mkt. *SW17* —4B **92**
Broadway Mkt. M. *E8* —5C **26**
Broadway M. *N16* —2B **12**
Broadway Pde. *N8* —1A **10**
Broadway Shop. Mall. *SW1*
—4F **51**
Broadway, The. *N8* —1A **10**
Broadway, The. *NW9* —1B **4**
Broadway, The. *SW14*
—5A **60**
Broadwick St. *W1* —1E **51**
*Broadwood Ter. W14 —5B **48***
(off Warwick Rd.)
Broad Yd. *EC1* —3D **39**
Brocas Clo. *NW3* —4A **22**
Brockbridge Ho. *SW15*
—4B **74**
Brocket Ho. *SW8* —5F **65**
Brockham Clo. *SW19* —5B **90**
Brockham Dri. *SW2* —5B **80**
*Brockham Ho. NW1 —5E **23***
(off Bayham Pl.)
*Brockham Ho. SW2 —5B **80***
(off Brockham Dri.)
Brockham St. *SE1* —4E **53**
Brockill Cres. *SE4* —2A **84**
Brocklebank Ind. Est. *SE7*
—5C **58**
Brocklebank Rd. *SE7* —5D **59**
Brocklebank Rd. *SW18*
—5E **77**
Brocklehurst St. *SE14* —3F **69**
Brockley. —2B 84
Brockley Cross. *SE4* —1A **84**
Brockley Cross Bus. Cen.
SE4 —1A **84**
Brockley Footpath. *SE4*
(in two parts) —3A **84**
Brockley Footpath. *SE15*
—2E **83**
Brockley Gdns. *SE4* —5B **70**
Brockley Gro. *SE4* —3B **84**
Brockley Hall Rd. *SE4*
—3A **84**
Brockley M. *SE4* —3A **84**
Brockley Pk. *SE23* —5A **84**
Brockley Ri. *SE23* —1A **98**
Brockley Rd. *SE4* —1B **84**
Brockley Vw. *SE23* —5A **84**
Brockley Way. *SE4* —3F **83**
Brockman Ri. *Brom* —4F **99**
*Brockmer Ho. E1 —1D **55***
(off Crowder St.)
Brock Pl. *E3* —3D **43**
Brock Rd. *E13* —4D **45**
Brock St. *SE15* —1E **83**
Brockway Clo. *E11* —4A **16**
*Brockweir. E2 —1E **41***
(off Cyprus St.)
Brockwell Ct. *SW2* —3C **80**
*Brockwell Ho. SE11 —2B **66***
(off Vauxhall St.)
Brockwell Pk. Gdns. *SE24*
—5C **80**
Brodia Rd. *N16* —5A **12**
*Brodie Ho. SE1 —1B **68***
(off Cooper's Rd.)
Brodie St. *SE1* —1B **68**
Brodlove La. *E1* —1F **55**
Brodrick Rd. *SW17* —2A **92**
Broken Wharf. *EC4* —1E **53**
Brokesley St. *E3* —2B **42**
Broke Wlk. *E8* —5B **26**
Bromar Rd. *SE5* —1A **82**
Bromell's Rd. *SW4* —2E **79**
Bromfelde Rd. *SW4* —1F **79**
Bromfelde Wlk. *SW4* —5F **65**
Bromfield St. *N1* —5C **24**
Bromhead St. *E1* —5E **41**
Bromleigh Ct. *SE23* —2C **96**
*Bromleigh Ho. SE1 —4B **54***
(off Abbey St.)
Bromley. —2D 43
Bromley Hall Rd. *E14* —4E **43**
Bromley High St. *E3* —2D **43**
Bromley Hill. *Brom* —5A **100**
Bromley Pl. *W1* —4E **37**
Bromley Rd. *E10* —1D **15**
Bromley Rd. *SE6 & Brom*
—1D **99**
Bromley St. *E1* —4F **41**

Brompton. —4A 50
Brompton Arc. SW1 —3B 50 (off Brompton Rd.)
Brompton Pk. Cres. *SW6* —2D **63**
Brompton Pl. *SW3* —4A **50**
Brompton Rd. *SW3 & SW1* —5A **50**
Brompton Sq. *SW3* —4A **50**
Bromwich Av. *N6* —4C **8**
Bromyard Av. *W3* —1A **46**
Bromyard Ho. SE15 —3D 69 (off Commercial Way)
Bron Ct. *NW6* —5C **20**
Brondesbury. —4B 20
Brondesbury Ct. *NW2* —3F **19**
Brondesbury M. *NW6* —4C **20**
Brondesbury Park. —5A 20
Brondesbury Pk. *NW2 & NW6* —3D **19**
Brondesbury Rd. *NW6* —1B **34**
Brondesbury Vs. *NW6* —1B **34**
Bronsart Rd. *SW6* —3A **62**
Bronte Clo. *E7* —1C **30**
Bronte Ho. *N16* —2A **26**
Bronte Ho. NW6 —2C 34 (off Cambridge Rd.)
Bronte Ho. *SW4* —5E **79**
Bronti Clo. *SE17* —1E **67**
Bronwen Ct. NW8 —2F 35 (off Grove End Rd.)
Bronze St. *SE8* —3C **70**
Brookbank Rd. *SE13* —1C **84**
Brook Clo. *SW17* —2C **92**
Brook Ct. *E11* —5A **16**
Brook Ct. E15 —2D 29 (off Clays La.)
Brook Ct. *SE12* —3E **101**
Brookdale Rd. *SE6* —5D **85** (in two parts)
Brook Dri. *SE11* —4C **52**
Brooke Ho. *SE14* —4A **70**
Brookehowse Rd. *SE6* —2C **98**
Brooke Rd. *E5* —5C **12**
Brooke Rd. *N16* —5B **12**
Brooke's Ct. *WC1* —4C **38**
Brooke's Mkt. EC1 —4C 38 (off Dorrington St.)
Brooke St. *EC1* —4C **38**
Brookfield. *N6* —5C **8**
Brookfield Pk. *NW5* —5D **9**
Brookfield Rd. *E9* —3A **28**
Brookfield Rd. *W4* —3A **46**
Brook Gdns. *SW13* —1B **74**
Brook Ga. *W1* —1B **50**
Brook Green. —5F 47
Brook Grn. *W6* —4F **47**
Brook Houses. NW1 —1E 37 (off Cranleigh St.)
Brooking Rd. *E7* —2C **30**
Brooklands Av. *SW19* —2D **91**
Brooklands Ct. *NW6* —4B **20**
Brooklands Pk. *SE3* —1C **86**
Brooklands Pas. *SW8* —4F **65**
Brook La. *SE3* —5D **73**
Brook La. *Brom* —5C **100**
Brookmarsh Ind. Est. *SE8* —3D **71**
Brook M. *WC2* —5F **37**
Brook M. N. *W2* —1E **49**
Brookmill Rd. *SE8* —4C **70**
Brook Pas. *SW6* —3C **62**
Brook Rd. *NW2* —4B **4**
Brooksbank St. *E9* —3E **27**
Brooksby M. *N1* —4C **24**
Brooksby St. *N1* —4C **24**
Brooksby's Wlk. *E9* —2F **27**
Brooks Ct. *SW8* —3E **65**
Brookside Rd. *N19* —4E **9**
Brookside Rd. *NW11* —1A **6**
Brooks M. *W1* —1D **51**
Brooks Rd. *E13* —5C **30**
Brookstone Ct. *SE15* —2D **83**
Brook St. *W1* —1D **51**
Brook St. *W2* —1F **49**
Brooksville Av. *NW6* —5A **20**
Brookview Rd. *SW16* —5E **93**
Brookville Rd. *SW6* —3B **62**
Brookway. *SE3* —1C **86**
Brookwood Av. *SW13* —5B **60**
Brookwood Ho. SE1 —3D 53 (off Webber St.)
Brookwood Rd. *SW18* —1B **90**
Broome Way. *SE5* —3F **67**
Broomfield. *E17* —2B **14**
Broomfield. NW1 —4C 22 (off Ferdinand St.)
Broomfield Ct. SE16 —4C 54 (off Ben Smith Way)
Broomfield Ho. SE17 —5A 54 (off Massinger St.)
Broomfield St. *E14* —4C **42**
Broomgrove Rd. *SW9* —5B **66**
Broomhill Rd. *SW18* —3C **76**
Broomhouse La. *SW6* —5C **62**
Broomhouse Rd. *SW6* —5C **62**
Broomsleigh Bus. Pk. *SE26* —5B **98**
Broomsleigh St. *NW6* —2B **20**
Broomwood Rd. *SW11* —4B **78**
Broseley Gro. *SE26* —5A **98**
Brougham Rd. *E8* —5C **26**
Brougham St. *SW11* —5B **64**
Brough Clo. *SW8* —3A **66**
Broughton Dri. *SW9* —2C **80**
Broughton Gdns. *N6* —1E **9**
Broughton Rd. *SW6* —5D **63**
Broughton St. *SW8* —5C **64**
Broughton St. Ind. Est. *SW11* —5C **64**
Browne Ho. SE8 —3C 70 (off Deptford Chu. St.)
Brownfield Area. *E14* —5E **43**
Brownfield St. *E14* —5D **43**
Brown Hart Gdns. *W1* —1C **50**
Brownhill Rd. *SE6* —5D **85**
Browning Clo. *W9* —3E **35**
Browning M. *W1* —4D **37**
Browning Rd. *E11* —2B **16**
Browning St. *SE17* —1E **67**
Brownlow Ho. SE16 —3C 54 (off George Row)
Brownlow M. *WC1* —3B **38**
Brownlow Rd. *E7* —1C **30**
Brownlow Rd. *E8* —5B **26**
Brownlow Rd. *NW10* —4A **18**
Brownlow St. *WC1* —4B **38**
Browns Arc. W1 —1E 51 (off Regent St.)
Brown's Bldgs. *EC3* —5A **40**
Browns La. *NW5* —2D **23**
Brown St. *W1* —5B **36**
Brownswood Park. —4D 11
Brownswood Rd. *N4* —5D **11**
Broxash Rd. *SW11* —4C **78**
Broxbourne Rd. *E7* —5C **16**
Broxholme Ho. SW6 —4D 63 (off Harwood Rd.)
Broxholm Rd. *SW16* —3C **94**
Broxted Rd. *SE23* —2B **98**
Broxwood Way. *NW8* —5A **22**
Bruce Clo. *W10* —4F **33**
Bruce Hall M. *SW17* —4C **92**
Bruce Ho. *W10* —4F **33**
Bruce Rd. *E3* —2D **43**
Bruce Rd. *NW10* —4A **18**
Bruckner St. *W10* —2A **34**
Brudenell Rd. *SW17* —3B **92**
Bruges Pl. NW1 —4E 23 (off Randolph St.)
Brune Ho. E1 —4B 40 (off Bell La.)
Brunei Gallery. —4F 37
Brunel Est. *W2* —4C **34**
Brunel Ho. *E14* —1D **71**
Brunel Rd. *E17* —1A **14**
Brunel Rd. *SE16* —3E **55**
Brunel Rd. *W3* —4A **32**
Brunel St. *E16* —5B **44**
Brune St. *E1* —4B **40**
Brunlees Ho. SE1 —4E 53 (off Bath Ter.)
Brunner Clo. *NW11* —1D **7**
Brunner Ho. *SE6* —4E **99**
Brunner Rd. *E17* —1A **14**
Brunswick Cen. *WC1* —3A **38**
Brunswick Clo. Est. *EC1* —2D **39**
Brunswick Ct. EC1 —2D 39 (off Tompion St.)
Brunswick Ct. *SE1* —3A **54**
Brunswick Ct. SW1 —5F 51 (off Regency St.)
Brunswick Gdns. *W8* —2C **48**
Brunswick Ho. E2 —1B 40 (off Thurtle Rd.)
Brunswick Mans. WC1 (off Handel St.) —3A 38
Brunswick M. *SW16* —5F **93**
Brunswick M. *W1* —5B **36**
Brunswick Pk. *SE5* —4A **68**

Brunswick Pl. *N1* —2F **39**
Brunswick Pl. *NW1* —3C **36**
Brunswick Quay. *SE16* —4F **55**
Brunswick Rd. *E10* —3E **15**
Brunswick Rd. *E14* —5E **43**
Brunswick Sq. *WC1* —3A **38**
Brunswick St. *E17* —1E **15**
Brunswick Vs. *SE5* —4A **68**
Brunton Pl. *E14* —5A **42**
Brushfield St. *EC2* —4A **40** (in two parts)
Brussels Rd. *SW11* —2F **77**
Bruton La. *W1* —1D **51**
Bruton Pl. *W1* —1D **51**
Bruton St. *W1* —1D **51**
Brutus Ct. SE11 —5D ***53*** *(off Kennington La.)*
Bryan Av. *NW10* —4D **19**
Bryan Ho. *SE16* —3B **56**
Bryan Rd. *SE16* —3B **56**
Bryan's All. *SW6* —5D **63**
Bryanston Ct. W1 —5B ***36*** *(off Seymour Pl., in two parts)*
Bryanstone Rd. *N8* —1F **9**
Bryanston Mans. W1 —4B ***36*** *(off York St.)*
Bryanston M. E. *W1* —4B **36**
Bryanston M. W. *W1* —4B **36**
Bryanston Pl. *W1* —4B **36**
Bryanston Sq. *W1* —5B **36**
Bryanston St. *W1* —5B **36**
Bryant Ct. E2 —1B ***40*** *(off Whiston Rd., in two parts)*
Bryant St. *E15* —4F **29**
Bryantwood Rd. *N7* —2C **24**
Bryce Ho. SE14 —2F ***69*** *(off John Williams Clo.)*
Brydale Ho. SE16 —5F ***55*** *(off Rotherhithe New Rd.)*
Bryden Clo. *SE26* —5A **98**
Brydges Pl. *WC2* —1A **52**
Brydges Rd. *E15* —2F **29**
Brydon Wlk. *N1* —5A **24**
Bryer Ct. EC2 —4E ***39*** *(off Beech St.)*
Bryet Rd. *N7* —5A **10**
Bryher Ct. SE11 —1C ***66*** *(off Sancroft St.)*
Brymay Clo. *E3* —1C **42**
Brynmaer Rd. *SW11* —4B **64**
Bryony Rd. *W12* —1C **46**
Buccleugh Ho. *E5* —2C **12**
Buchanan Ct. SE16 —5F ***55*** *(off Worgan St.)*
Buchanan Gdns. *NW10* —1D **33**
Buchan Rd. *SE15* —1E **83**
Bucharest Rd. *SW18* —5E **77**
Buckden Clo. *SE12* —4C **86**
Buckfast St. *E2* —2C **40**
Buck Hill Wlk. *W2* —1F **49**
Buckhold Rd. *SW18* —4C **76**
Buckhurst Ho. *N7* —2F **23**
Buckhurst St. *E1* —3D **41**
Buckingham Arc. WC2 (off Strand) —1A ***52***
Buckingham Chambers. SW1 (off Greencoat Pl.) —5E ***51***
Buckingham Ga. *SW1* —4E **51**
Buckingham La. *SE23* —5A **84**
Buckingham Mans. NW6 (off W. End La.) —2D ***21***
Buckingham M. *N1* —3A **26**
Buckingham M. *NW10* —1B **32**
Buckingham M. SW1 —4E ***51*** *(off Stafford Pl.)*
Buckingham Palace. —3D 51
Buckingham Pal. Rd. *SW1* —5D **51**
Buckingham Pl. *SW1* —4E **51**
Buckingham Rd. *E10* —5D **15**
Buckingham Rd. *E11* —1E **17**
Buckingham Rd. *E15* —2B **30**
Buckingham Rd. *N1* —3A **26**
Buckingham Rd. *NW10* —1B **32**
Buckingham St. *WC2* —1A **52**
Buckland Ct. N1 —1A ***40*** *(off St Johns Est.)*
Buckland Cres. *NW3* —4F **21**
Buckland Rd. *E10* —4E **15**
Buckland St. *N1* —1F **39**
Bucklebury. NW1 —3E ***37*** *(off Stanhope St.)*
Bucklers All. *SW6* —2B **62** (in two parts)
Bucklersbury. EC2 —5F ***39*** *(off Queen Victoria St., in two parts)*
Bucklersbury Pas. *EC2* —5F **39**
Buckle St. *E1* —5B **40**
Buckley Ct. *NW6* —4B **20**
Buckley Rd. *NW6* —4B **20**
Buckmaster Clo. SW9 —1C ***80*** *(off Stockwell Pk. Rd.)*
Buckmaster Ho. *N7* —1B **24**
Buckmaster Rd. *SW11* —2A **78**
Bucknall St. *WC1* —5A **38**
Bucknell Clo. *SW9* —2B **80**
Buckner Rd. *SW2* —2B **80**
Bucknill Ho. SW1 —1D ***65*** *(off Ebury Bri. Rd.)*
Buckridge Ho. EC1 —4C ***38*** *(off Portpool La.)*
Buckstone Clo. *SE23* —4E **83**
Buck St. *NW1* —4D **23**
Buckters Rents. *SE16* —2A **56**
Buckthorne Rd. *SE4* —3A **84**
Bude Clo. *E17* —1B **14**
Budge Row. *EC4* —1F **53**
Budge's Wlk. W2 —2E ***49*** *(off Broad Wlk., The)*
Budleigh Ho. SE15 —3C ***68*** *(off Bird in Bush Rd.)*
Buer Rd. *SW6* —5A **62**
Bugsby's Way. *SE10 & SE7* —5B **58**
Bulbarrow. NW8 —5D ***21*** *(off Abbey Rd.)*
Bullace Row. *SE5* —4F **67**
Bullard's Pl. *E2* —2F **41**
Bulleid Way. *SW1* —5D **51**
Bullen Ho. E1 —3D ***41*** *(off Collingwood St.)*
Bullen St. *SW11* —5A **64**
Buller Clo. *SE15* —3C **68**
Buller Rd. *NW10* —2F **33**
Bullingham Mans. W8 (off Pitt St. La.) —3C ***48***
Bull Inn Ct. WC2 —1A ***52*** *(off Strand)*
Bullivant St. *E14* —1E **57**
Bull Rd. *E15* —1B **44**
Bull's All. *SW14* —5A **60**
Bulls Gdns. *SW3* —5A **50** (in two parts)
Bulls Head Pas. EC3 —5A ***40*** *(off Gracechurch St.)*
Bull Wharf La. *EC4* —1E **53**
Bull Yd. *SE15* —4C **68**
Bulmer M. *W11* —1C **48**
Bulmer Pl. *W11* —2C **48**
Bulow Est. SW6 —4D ***63*** *(off Pearscroft Rd.)*
Bulstrode Pl. *W1* —4C **36**
Bulstrode St. *W1* —5C **36**
Bulwer Ct. *E11* —3F **15**
Bulwer Ct. Rd. *E11* —3F **15**
Bulwer Rd. *E11* —2F **15**
Bulwer St. *W12* —2E **47**
Bunbury Ho. SE15 —3C ***68*** *(off Fenham Rd.)*
Bungalows, The. *E10* —1E **15**
Bunhill Row. *EC1* —3F **39**
Bunhouse Pl. *SW1* —1C **64**
Bunkers Hill. *NW11* —2E **7**
Bunning Way. *N7* —4A **24**
Bunsen St. *E3* —1A **42**
Bunyan Ct. EC2 —4E ***39*** *(off Beech St.)*
Buonaparte M. *SW1* —1F **65**
Burbage Clo. *SE1* —4F **53**
Burbage Ho. N1 —5F ***25*** *(off Poole St.)*
Burbage Ho. SE14 —2F ***69*** *(off Samuel Clo.)*
Burbage Rd. *SE24 & SE21* —4E **81**
Burcham St. *E14* —5D **43**
Burchell Ho. SE11 —1B ***66*** *(off Jonathan St.)*
Burchell Rd. *E10* —3D **15**
Burchell Rd. *SE15* —4D **69**
Burcote Rd. *SW18* —5F **77**
Burden Ho. SW8 —3A ***66*** *(off Thorncroft St.)*
Burden Way. *E11* —4D **17**
Burder Clo. *N1* —3A **26**
Burder Rd. *N1* —3A **26**
Burdett M. *NW3* —3F **21**
Burdett M. *W2* —5D **35**

Burdett Rd. *E3 & E14* —3A **42**
Burfield Clo. *SW17* —4F **91**
Burford Rd. *E6* —2F **45**
Burford Rd. *E15* —5F **29**
Burford Rd. *SE6* —2B **98**
Burford Wlk. *SW6* —3E **63**
Burge Rd. *E7* —1F **31**
Burges Gro. *SW13* —3D **61**
Burgess Av. *NW9* —1A **4**
Burgess Hill. *NW2* —1C **20**
Burgess Ind. Pk. *SE5* —3F **67**
Burgess Pk. —2A **68**
Burgess Rd. *E15* —1A **30**
Burgess St. *E14* —4C **42**
Burge St. *SE1* —4F **53**
Burghill Rd. *SE26* —4A **98**
Burghley Hall Clo. *SW19* —1A **90**
Burghley Rd. *E11* —3A **16**
Burghley Rd. *NW5* —1D **23**
Burghley Rd. *SW19* —4F **89**
Burghley Tower. *W3* —1B **46**
Burgh St. *N1* —1D **39**
Burgon St. *EC4* —5D **39**
Burgos Gro. *SE10* —4D **71**
Burgoyne Rd. *N4* —1D **11**
Burgoyne Rd. *SW9* —1B **80**
Burke Clo. *SW15* —2A **74**
Burke Lodge. *E13* —2D **45**
Burke St. *E16* —4B **44**
Burland Rd. *SW11* —3B **78**
*Burleigh Ho. SW3 —2F **63***
(off Beaufort St.)
*Burleigh Ho. W10 —4A **34***
(off St Charles Sq.)
Burleigh Pl. *SW15* —3F **75**
Burleigh St. *WC2* —1B **52**
Burleigh Wlk. *SE6* —1E **99**
Burley Rd. *E16* —5E **45**
Burlington Arc. *W1* —1E **51**
Burlington Clo. *W9* —3C **34**
Burlington Gdns. *SW6* —5A **62**
Burlington Gdns. *W1* —1E **51**
Burlington La. *W4* —3A **60**
Burlington M. *SW15* —3B **76**
Burlington Pl. *SW6* —5A **62**
Burlington Rd. *SW6* —5A **62**
Burma M. *N16* —1F **25**
Burma Rd. *N16* —1F **25**
Burma Ter. *SE19* —5A **96**
Burmester Rd. *SW17* —3E **91**
Burnaby St. *SW10* —3E **63**
Burnard Pl. *N7* —2B **24**
Burnaston Ho. *E5* —5C **12**
Burnbury Rd. *SW12* —1E **93**
Burne Jones Ho. W14
*(off N. End Rd.) —5A **48***
*Burnell Wlk. SE1 —1B **68***
(off Abingdon Clo.)
Burness Clo. *N7* —3B **24**
Burne St. *NW1* —4A **36**
Burnett Clo. *E9* —2E **27**
*Burnett Ho. SE13 —5E **71***
(off Lewisham Hill)
Burney St. *SE10* —3E **71**
Burnfoot Av. *SW6* —4A **62**
Burnham. *NW3* —4A **22**
Burnham Clo. *SE1* —5B **54**
*Burnham Ct. W2 —1D **49***
(off Moscow Rd.)
*Burnham Est. E2 —2E **41***
(off Burnham St.)
Burnham St. *E2* —2E **41**
Burnham Way. *SE26* —5B **98**
Burnley Rd. *NW10* —2B **18**
Burnley Rd. *SW9* —5B **66**
Burnmill Clo. *SE15* —3D **69**
Burnsall St. *SW3* —1A **64**
Burns Clo. *SW19* —5F **91**
*Burns Ho. E2 —2E **41***
(off Cornwall Av.)
*Burns Ho. SE17 —1D **67***
(off Doddington Gro.)
Burnside Clo. *SE16* —2F **55**
Burns Rd. *NW10* —5B **18**
Burns Rd. *SW11* —5B **64**
Burnt Ash Hill. *SE12* —4B **86**
(in two parts)
Burnt Ash La. *Brom* —5C **100**
Burnt Ash Rd. *SE12* —3B **86**
Burnthwaite Rd. *SW6* —3B **62**
Burntwood Clo. *SW18* —1A **92**
Burntwood Grange Rd. *SW18* —1F **91**
Burntwood La. *SW17* —3E **91**
Burntwood Vw. *SE19* —5B **96**
Buross St. *E1* —5D **41**
*Burrage Ct. SE16 —5F **55***
(off Worgan St.)
Burrard Rd. *E16* —5D **45**
Burrard Rd. *NW6* —2C **20**
Burr Clo. *E1* —2C **54**
Burrell St. *SE1* —2D **53**
Burrell Towers. *E10* —2C **14**
*Burrmill Ct. SE16 —4F **55***
(off Worgan St.)
*Burrow Ho. SW9 —5C **66***
(off Stockwell Pk. Rd.)
Burrow Rd. *SE22* —2A **82**
Burrows M. *SE1* —3D **53**
Burrows Rd. *NW10* —2E **33**
Burrow Wlk. *SE21* —5E **81**
Burr Rd. *SW18* —1C **90**
*Bursar St. SE1 —2A **54***
(off Tooley St.)
Burslem St. *E1* —5C **40**
Burstock Rd. *SW15* —2A **76**
Burston Rd. *SW15* —3F **75**
Burtley Clo. *N4* —3E **11**
*Burton Bank. N1 —4F **25***
(off Yeate St.)
*Burton Ct. SW3 —1B **64***
(off Turks Row, in two parts)
Burton Gro. *SE17* —1F **67**
*Burton Ho. SE16 —3D **55***
(off Cherry Garden St.)
Burton La. *SW9* —5C **66**
(in two parts)
Burton M. *SW1* —5C **50**
Burton Pl. *WC1* —3F **37**
Burton Rd. *NW6* —4B **20**
Burton Rd. *SW9* —5D **67**
(Akerman Rd.)
Burton Rd. *SW9* —5C **66**
(Brixton Rd.)
Burton St. *WC1* —2F **37**
Burtonwood Ho. *N4* —2F **11**
Burt Rd. *E16* —2E **59**
*Burtt Ho. N1 —2A **40***
(off Aske St.)
Burtwell La. *SE27* —4F **95**
*Burwash Ho. SE1 —3F **53***
(off Kipling Est.)
Burwell Clo. *E1* —5D **41**
Burwell Rd. *E10* —3A **14**
Burwell Rd. Ind. Est. *E10* —3A **14**
Burwell Wlk. *E3* —3C **42**
Burwood Ho. *SW9* —2D **81**
Burwood Pl. *W2* —5A **36**
Bury Clo. *SE16* —2F **55**
Bury Ct. *EC3* —5A **40**
Bury Pl. *WC1* —4A **38**
Bury St. *EC3* —5A **40**
Bury St. *SW1* —2E **51**
Bury Wlk. *SW3* —5A **50**
Busbridge Ho. *E14* —4C **42**
Busby M. *NW5* —3F **23**
Busby Pl. *NW5* —3F **23**
Bushbaby Clo. *SE1* —4A **54**
Bushberry Rd. *E9* —3A **28**
Bush Cotts. *SW18* —3C **76**
Bush Ct. *W12* —3F **47**
Bushell Clo. *SW2* —2B **94**
Bushell St. *E1* —2C **54**
Bushey Down. *SW12* —2D **93**
Bushey Hill Rd. *SE5* —4A **68**
Bushey Rd. *E13* —1E **45**
Bushey Rd. *N15* —1A **12**
Bush Ind. Est. *N19* —5E **9**
Bush La. *EC4* —1F **53**
Bushnell Rd. *SW17* —2D **93**
Bush Rd. *E8* —5D **27**
Bush Rd. *E11* —2B **16**
Bush Rd. *SE8* —5F **55**
Bushwood. *E11* —3B **16**
Bushwood Dri. *SE1* —5B **54**
Butcher Row. *E14 & E1* —1F **55**
Butchers Rd. *E16* —5C **44**
Bute Gdns. *W6* —5F **47**
Bute St. *SW7* —5F **49**
Bute Wlk. *N1* —3F **25**
*Butfield Ho. E9 —3E **27***
(off Stevens Av.)
*Butler Ho. E2 —2E **41***
(off Bacton St.)
Butler Ho. *E14* —5B **42**
*Butler Ho. SW9 —4D **67***
(off Lothian Rd.)
*Butler Pl. SW1 —4F **51***
(off Palmer St.)
Butler Rd. *NW10* —4B **18**
Butlers & Colonial Wharf. SE1
*(off Shad Thames) —3B **54***
Butler St. *E2* —2E **41**
*Butlers Wharf. SE1 —2B **54***
(off Shad Thames)

Butley Ct. E3 —1A 42
(off Ford St.)
Butterfield Clo. SE16 —3D 55
Butterfields. E17 —1E 15
Butterfly Wlk. SE5 —5F 67
(off Denmark Hill)
Buttermere. NW1 —2D 37
(off Augustus St.)
Buttermere Clo. E15 —1F 29
Buttermere Clo. SE1 —5B 54
Buttermere Ct. NW8 —5F 21
(off Boundary Rd.)
Buttermere Dri. SW15 —3A 76
Buttermere Wlk. E8 —3B 26
Butterwick. W6 —5F 47
Buttesland St. N1 —2F 39
Butts Rd. Brom —5A 100
Buxhall Cres. E9 —3B 28
Buxted Rd. E8 —4B 26
Buxted Rd. SE22 —2A 82
Buxton Ct. N1 —2E 39
(off Thoresby St., in two parts)
Buxton Rd. E6 —2F 45
Buxton Rd. E15 —2A 30
Buxton Rd. N19 —3F 9
Buxton Rd. NW2 —3D 19
Buxton Rd. SW14 —1A 74
Buxton St. E1 —3B 40
Byam St. SW6 —5E 63
Byards Ct. SE16 —5F 55
(off Worgan St.)
Byelands Clo. SE16 —2F 55
Bye, The. W3 —5A 32
Byfeld Gdns. SW13 —4C 60
Byfield Clo. SE16 —3B 56
Byford Clo. E15 —4A 30
Bygrove St. E14 —5D 43
(in two parts)
Byne Rd. SE26 —5E 97
Byng Pl. WC1 —3F 37
Byng St. E14 —3C 56
Byrne Rd. SW12 —1D 93
Byron Av. E12 —3F 31
Byron Clo. E8 —5C 26
Byron Clo. SE26 —4A 98
Byron Clo. SW16 —5A 94
Byron Ct. NW6 —4E 21
(off Fairfax Rd.)
Byron Ct. W9 —3C 34
(off Lanhill Rd.)
Byron Ct. WC1 —3B 38
(off Mecklenburgh Sq.)
Byron Dri. N2 —1F 7
Byron M. NW3 —2B 22
Byron M. W9 —3C 34
Byron Rd. E10 —3D 15
Byron Rd. NW2 —4D 5
Byron St. E14 —5E 43
Bythorn St. SW9 —1B 80
Byton Rd. SW17 —5B 92
Byward St. EC3 —1A 54
Bywater Ho. SE18 —4F 59
Bywater Pl. SE16 —2A 56
Bywater St. SW3 —1B 64
Byway. E11 —1E 17
Bywell Pl. W1 —4E 37
(off Wells St.)
Byworth Wlk. N19 —3A 10

Cabbell St. NW1 —4A 36
Cabinet War Rooms. —3F 51
Cable Ho. WC1 —2C 38
(off Gt. Percy St.)
Cable Pl. SE10 —4E 71
Cable St. E1 —1C 54
Cable Trade Pk. SE7 —5E 59
Cabot Ct. SE16 —5F 55
(off Worgan St.)
Cabot Sq. E14 —2C 56
Cabot Way. E6 —5F 31
Cab Rd. SE1 —3C 52
(off West Rd.)
Cabul Rd. SW11 —5A 64
Caci Ho. W14 —5B 48
(off Avonmore Rd.)
Cactus Clo. SE15 —5A 68
Cactus Wlk. W12 —5B 32
Cadbury Way. SE16 —4B 54
(in two parts)
Caddington Rd. NW2 —5A 6
Cadell Clo. E2 —1B 40
Cade Rd. SE10 —4F 71
Cader Rd. SW18 —4E 77
Cadet Dri. SE1 —5B 54
Cadet Pl. SE10 —1A 72
Cadiz St. SE17 —1E 67
Cadley Ter. SE23 —2E 97
Cadman Clo. SW9 —3D 67
Cadmore Ho. N1 —4D 25
(off Sutton Est., The)
Cadmus Clo. SW4 —1F 79
Cadmus Ct. SW9 —4C 66
(off Southey Rd.)
Cadnam Lodge. E14 —4E 57
Cadogan Clo. E9 —4B 28
Cadogan Ct. SW3 —5B 50
(off Draycott Av.)
Cadogan Gdns. SW3 —5B 50
Cadogan Ga. SW1 —5B 50
Cadogan Ho. SW3 —2F 63
(off Beaufort St.)
Cadogan La. SW1 —4C 50
Cadogan Pl. SW1 —4B 50
Cadogan Sq. SW1 —4B 50
Cadogan St. SW3 —5B 50
Cadogan Ter. E9 —3B 28
Cadoxton Av. N15 —1B 12
Caedmon Rd. N7 —1B 24
Caernarvon Ho. W2 —5E 35
(off Hallfield Est.)
Cahill St. EC1 —3E 39
Cahir St. E14 —5D 57
Caird St. W10 —2A 34
Cairnfield Av. NW2 —5A 4
Cairns Rd. SW11 —3A 78
Caister Ho. N7 —3B 24
Caistor Ho. E15 —5B 30
(off Caistor Pk. Rd.)
Caistor M. SW12 —5D 79
Caistor Pk. Rd. E15 —5B 30
Caistor Rd. SW12 —5D 79
Caithness Ho. N1 —5B 24
(off Twyford St.)
Caithness Rd. W14 —4F 47
Calabria Rd. N5 —3D 25
Calais Ga. SE5 —4D 67
Calais St. SE5 —4D 67
Calbourne Rd. SW12 —5B 78
Calcott Ct. W14 —4A 48
(off Blythe Rd.)
Calcott Wlk. SE9 —4F 101
Calcraft Ho. E2 —1E 41
(off Bonner Rd.)
Caldecot Rd. SE5 —5E 67
Caldecott Way. E5 —5F 13
Calder Ct. SE16 —2B 56
Calderon Ho. NW8 —1A 36
(off Townshend Est.)
Calderon Pl. W10 —4E 33
Calderon Rd. E11 —1E 29
Caldervale Rd. SW4 —3F 79
Caldew St. SE5 —3F 67
Caldicot Grn. NW9 —1A 4
Caldwell St. SW9 —3B 66
Caldy Wlk. N1 —4E 25
Caleb St. SE1 —3E 53
Caledonia Ho. E14 —5A 42
Caledonian Rd. N7 & N1 —1B 24
Caledonian Wharf. E14 —5F 57
Caledonia St. N1 —1A 38
Cale St. SW3 —1A 64
Caletock Way. SE10 —1B 72
Calgarth. NW1 —1E 37
(off Ampthill Est.)
Calgary Ct. SE16 —3E 55
(off Canada Est.)
Caliban Tower. N1 —1A 40
(off Arden Est.)
Calico Row. SW11 —1E 77
Calidore Clo. SW2 —4B 80
Callaby Ter. N1 —3F 25
Callaghan Clo. SE13 —2A 86
Callaghan Cotts. E1 —4E 41
(off Lindley St.)
Callander Rd. SE6 —2D 99
Callcott Ct. NW6 —4B 20
Callcott Rd. NW6 —4B 20
Callcott St. W8 —2C 48
Callendar Rd. SW7 —4F 49
Callingham Clo. E14 —4B 42
Callis Rd. E17 —1B 14
Callow St. SW3 —2F 63
Callum Welch Ho. EC1
(off Goswell Rd.) —3E 39
Calmington Rd. SE5 —2A 68
Calmont Rd. Brom —5F 99
Calonne Rd. SW19 —4F 89
Calshot Ho. N1 —1B 38
(off Priory Grn. Est.)
Calshot St. N1 —1B 38
Calstock. NW1 —5F 23
(off Royal College St.)
Calstock Ho. SE11 —1C 66
(off Kennings Way)
Calthorpe St. WC1 —3B 38

Calton Av. *SE21* —4A **82**
Calverley Clo. *Beck* —5D **99**
Calverley Gro. *N19* —3F **9**
Calvert Av. *E1* —2A **40**
*Calverton. SE17 —2A **68***
(off Albany Rd.)
Calvert Rd. *SE10* —1B **72**
Calvert's Bldgs. *SE1* —2F **53**
Calvert St. *NW1* —5C **22**
Calvin St. *E1* —3B **40**
Calydon Rd. *SE7* —1D **73**
Calypso Way. *SE16* —4B **56**
Cambalt Rd. *SW15* —3F **75**
Camber Ho. *SE15* —2E **69**
*Camberley Ho. NW1 —1D **37***
(off Redhill St.)
Cambert Way. *SE3* —2D **87**
Camberwell. —4F 67
Camberwell Chu. St. *SE5* —4F **67**
Camberwell Glebe. *SE5* —4A **68**
Camberwell Green. (Junct.) —4F **67**
Camberwell Grn. *SE5* —4F **67**
Camberwell Gro. *SE5* —4F **67**
Camberwell New Rd. *SE5* —2C **66**
Camberwell Pl. *SE5* —4E **67**
Camberwell Rd. *SE17 & SE5* —2E **67**
Camberwell Sta. Rd. *SE5* —4E **67**
Camberwell Trad. Est. *SE5* —4D **67**
Camborne Rd. *SW18* —5C **76**
*Cambourne M. W11 —5A **34***
(off St Mark's Rd.)
Cambray Rd. *SW12* —1E **93**
Cambria Ho. *E14* —5A **42**
*Cambria Ho. SE26 —4C **96***
(off High Level Dri.)
Cambrian Clo. *SE27* —3D **95**
*Cambrian Grn. NW9 —1A **4***
(off Snowden Dri.)
Cambrian Rd. *E10* —2C **14**
Cambria Rd. *SE5* —1E **81**
Cambria St. *SW6* —3D **63**
Cambridge Av. *NW6* —1C **34**
Cambridge Av. *NW10* —2E **33**
Cambridge Cir. *WC2* —5F **37**
Cambridge Clo. *E17* —1B **14**
*Cambridge Ct. E2 —1D **41***
(off Cambridge Heath Rd.)
*Cambridge Ct. N15 —2A **12***
(off Amhurst Pk.)
Cambridge Ct. *NW6* —1C **34**
(in three parts)
*Cambridge Ct. W2 —4A **36***
(off Edgware Rd.)
Cambridge Cres. *E2* —1D **41**
Cambridge Dri. *SE12* —3C **86**
Cambridge Gdns. *NW6* —1C **34**
Cambridge Gdns. *W10* —5F **33**
Cambridge Ga. *NW1* —3D **37**
Cambridge Ga. M. *NW1* —3D **37**
Cambridge Gro. *W6* —5D **47**
Cambridge Heath Rd. *E1 & E2* —4D **41**
Cambridge Lodge Vs. *E8* —5D **27**
Cambridge Pk. *E11* —2C **16**
Cambridge Pk. Rd. *E11* —2B **16**
Cambridge Pl. *W8* —3D **49**
Cambridge Rd. *E11* —1B **16**
Cambridge Rd. *NW6* —1C **34**
(in two parts)
Cambridge Rd. *SW11* —4B **64**
Cambridge Rd. *SW13* —5B **60**
Cambridge Sq. *W2* —5A **36**
Cambridge St. *SW1* —5D **51**
Cambridge Ter. *NW1* —2D **37**
Cambridge Ter. M. *NW1* —2D **37**
Cambus Rd. *E16* —4C **44**
Cam Ct. *SE15* —2B **68**
Camden Arts Cen. —2E 21
*Camden Ct. NW1 —4E **23***
(off Rousden St.)
Camden Gdns. *NW1* —4D **23**
Camden High St. *NW1* —4D **23**
Camden Hill Rd. *SE19* —5A **96**
Camden Ho. *SE8* —1B **70**
Camdenhurst St. *E14* —5A **42**
Camden La. *N7* —2F **23**
Camden Lock Market. —4D 23
Camden Lock Pl. *NW1* —4D **23**
Camden M. *NW1* —4E **23**
Camden Pk. Rd. *NW1* —3F **23**
Camden Passage. —1D 39
Camden Pas. *N1* —5D **25**
(in two parts)
Camden Rd. *E11* —1D **17**
Camden Rd. *E17* —1B **14**
Camden Rd. *NW1 & N7* —4E **23**
Camden Row. *SE3* —5A **72**
Camden Sq. *NW1* —4F **23**
Camden Sq. *SE15* —4B **68**
Camden St. *NW1* —4E **23**
*Camden Studios. NW1 —5E **23***
(off Camden St.)
Camden Ter. *NW1* —3F **23**
Camden Town. —5D 23
Camden Wlk. *N1* —5D **25**
(in two parts)
Cameford Ct. *SW2* —5A **80**
*Camelford. NW1 —5E **23***
(off Royal College St.)
Camelford Ct. *W11* —5A **34**
Camelford Ho. *SE1* —1A **66**
Camelford Wlk. *W11* —5A **34**
*Camellia Ho. SE8 —3B **70***
(off Idonia St.)
Camellia St. *SW8* —3A **66**
Camelot Clo. *SW19* —4B **90**
Camelot Ho. *NW1* —3F **23**
Camel Rd. *E16* —2F **59**
Camera Pl. *SW10* —2F **63**
*Cameret Ct. W11 —3F **47***
(off Lorne Gdns.)
*Cameron Ho. NW8 —1A **36***
(off St John's Wood Ter.)
Cameron Ho. *SE5* —3E **67**
Cameron Pl. *E1* —5D **41**
Cameron Rd. *SE6* —2B **98**
Cameron Ter. *SE12* —3D **101**
Camerton Clo. *E8* —3B **26**
Camilla Rd. *SE16* —5D **55**
Camlan Rd. *Brom* —4B **100**
Camlet St. *E2* —3B **40**
Camley St. *NW1* —4F **23**
Camomile St. *EC2* —5A **40**
Campana Rd. *SW6* —4C **62**
*Campania Building. E1 —1F **55***
(off Jardine Rd.)
Campbell Clo. *SW16* —4F **93**
Campbell Ct. *SE21* —5C **82**
*Campbell Ct. SW7 —4E **49***
(off Gloucester Rd.)
Campbell Gordon Way. *NW2* —1D **19**
*Campbell Ho. SW1 —1E **65***
(off Churchill Gdns.)
*Campbell Ho. W12 —1D **47***
(off White City Est.)
Campbell Rd. *E3* —2C **42**
Campbell Rd. *E15* —1B **30**
*Campbell Wlk. N1 —5A **24***
(off Outram Pl.)
Campdale Rd. *N7* —5F **9**
Campden Gro. *W8* —3C **48**
Campden Hill. *W8* —3C **48**
Campden Hill Ct. *W8* —3C **48**
Campden Hill Gdns. *W8* —2C **48**
Campden Hill Ga. *W8* —3C **48**
*Campden Hill Mans. W8 —2C **48***
(off Kensington Church St.)
Campden Hill Pl. *W11* —2B **48**
Campden Hill Rd. *W11* —2C **48**
Campden Hill Sq. *W11* —2B **48**
Campden Ho. *NW6* —4F **21**
Campden Ho. *W8* —2C **48**
Campden Ho. Clo. *W8* —3C **48**
*Campden Houses. W8 —2C **48***
(off Peel St.)
Campden St. *W8* —2C **48**
Campen Clo. *SW19* —2A **90**
Camperdown St. *E1* —5B **40**
Campfield Rd. *SE9* —5F **87**
Campion Rd. *SW15* —2E **75**
Campion Ter. *NW2* —5F **5**
Camplin St. *SE14* —3F **69**
Camp Rd. *SW19* —5D **89**
(in two parts)
Campshill Pl. *SE13* —3E **85**
Campshill Rd. *SE13* —3E **85**
Campus Rd. *E17* —1B **14**
Camp Vw. *SW19* —5D **89**

Cam Rd. *E15* —5F **29**
Canada Est. *SE16* —4E **55**
Canada Gdns. *SE13* —3E **85**
Canada Sq. *E14* —2D **57**
Canada St. *SE16* —3F **55**
Canada Way. *W12* —1D **47**
Canada Wharf. *SE16* —2B **56**
Canadian Av. *SE6* —1D **99**
Canal App. *SE8* —1A **70**
Canal Bridge. (Junct.) —2C **68**
*Canal Building. N1 —1E **39***
(off Shepherdess Wlk.)
Canal Clo. *E1* —3A **42**
Canal Clo. *W10* —3F **33**
Canal Gro. *SE15* —2D **69**
Canal Path. *E2* —5B **26**
Canal Rd. *E3* —3A **42**
Canal St. *SE5* —2F **67**
Canal Wlk. *N1* —5F **25**
Canal Wlk. *SE26* —5E **97**
Canal Way. *W10* —3F **33**
Canary Wharf. —2D 57
Canberra Rd. *SE7* —2E **73**
Canbury M. *SE26* —3C **96**
Cancell Rd. *SW9* —4C **66**
Candahar Rd. *SW11* —5A **64**
Candida Ct. *NW1* —4D **23**
Candler St. *N15* —1F **11**
Candover St. *W1* —4E **37**
Candy St. *E3* —5B **28**
Caney M. *NW2* —4F **5**
Canfield Gdns. *NW6* —4D **21**
*Canfield Ho. N15 —1A **12***
(off Albert Rd.)
Canfield Pl. *NW6* —3E **21**
Canford Rd. *SW11* —3C **78**
Canham Rd. *W3* —3A **46**
Cann Hall. —1A 30
Cann Hall Rd. *E11* —1A **30**
*Cann Ho. W14 —4A **48***
(off Russell Rd.)
Canning Cross. *SE5* —5A **68**
*Canning Ho. W12 —1D **47***
(off White City Est.)
Canning Pas. *W8* —4E **49**
(in two parts)
Canning Pl. *W8* —4E **49**
*Canning Pl. M. W8 —4E **49***
(off Canning Pl.)
Canning Rd. *E15* —1F **43**
Canning Rd. *N5* —5D **11**
Canning Town. —5B 44
Canning Town. (Junct.) —4A **44**
Cannizaro Rd. *SW19* —5E **89**
Cannock Ho. *N4* —2E **11**
Cannon Dri. *E14* —1C **56**
Cannon Hill. *NW6* —2C **20**
*Cannon Ho. SE11 —5B **52***
(off Beaufoy Wlk.)
Cannon La. *NW3* —5F **7**
Cannon Pl. *NW3* —5F **7**
Cannon St. *EC4* —5E **39**
Cannon St. Rd. *E1* —5D **41**
Cannon Wharf Bus. Pk. *SE8* —5A **56**
Cannon Workshops. *E14* —1C **56**
Canonbie Rd. *SE23* —5E **83**
Canonbury. —3E 25
Canonbury Bus. Cen. *N1* —5F **25**
*Canonbury Ct. N1 —4D **25***
(off Hawes St.)
Canonbury Cres. *N1* —4E **25**
Canonbury Gro. *N1* —4E **25**
Canonbury La. *N1* —4D **25**
Canonbury Pk. N. *N1* —3E **25**
Canonbury Pk. S. *N1* —3E **25**
Canonbury Pl. *N1* —3D **25**
(in two parts)
Canonbury Rd. *N1* —3D **25**
Canonbury Sq. *N1* —4D **25**
Canonbury St. *N1* —4E **25**
Canonbury Vs. *N1* —4D **25**
Canon Row. *SW1* —3A **52**
(in two parts)
Canon's Clo. *N2* —2F **7**
Canon St. *N1* —5E **25**
Canrobert St. *E2* —1D **41**
Cantelowes Rd. *NW1* —3F **23**
Canterbury Av. *Ilf* —2F **17**
*Canterbury Clo. SE5 —5E **67***
(off Lilford Rd.)
Canterbury Ct. *NW6* —1C **34**
Canterbury Ct. *SE12* —3D **101**
Canterbury Cres. *SW9* —1C **80**
Canterbury Gro. *SE27* —4C **94**
Canterbury Ho. *SE1* —4B **52**
Canterbury Ho. *SW9* —3C **66**
Canterbury Ind. Pk. *SE15* —2E **69**
Canterbury Pl. *SE17* —1D **67**
Canterbury Rd. *E10* —2E **15**
Canterbury Rd. *NW6* —1B **34**
(in two parts)
Canterbury Ter. *NW6* —1C **34**
Cantium Retail Pk. *SE1* —2C **68**
Canton St. *E14* —5C **42**
Cantrell Rd. *E3* —3B **42**
Canute Gdns. *SE16* —5F **55**
Canvey St. *SE1* —2E **53**
Cape Henry Ct. *E14* —1F **57**
*Cape Ho. E8 —3B **26***
(off Dalston La.)
*Capel Ct. EC2 —5F **39***
(off Bartholomew La.)
Capel Rd. *E7 & E12* —1D **31**
*Capener's Clo. SW1 —3C **50***
(off Kinnerton St.)
Capern Rd. *SW18* —1E **91**
*Cape Yd. E1 —1C **54***
(off Kennet St.)
Capital Wharf. *E1* —2C **54**
*Capland Ho. NW8 —3F **35***
(off Capland St.)
Capland St. *NW8* —3F **35**
*Caple Ho. SW10 —3E **63***
(off King's Rd.)
Caple Rd. *NW10* —1B **32**
Capper St. *W1* —3E **37**
*Capstan Ho. E14 —1F **57***
(off Clove Cres.)
*Capstan Ho. E14 —5E **57***
(off Stebondale St.)
Capstan Rd. *SE8* —5B **56**
Capstan Sq. *E14* —3E **57**
Capstan Way. *SE16* —2A **56**
Capstone Rd. *Brom* —4B **100**
Capulet M. *E16* —2C **58**
Capworth St. *E10* —3C **14**
Caradoc Clo. *W2* —5C **34**
Caradoc St. *SE10* —1A **72**
Caradon Clo. *E11* —3A **16**
Caravel Clo. *E14* —4C **56**
Caravel M. *SE8* —2C **70**
Caraway Clo. *E13* —4D **45**
*Caraway Heights. E14 —1E **57***
(off Poplar High St.)
Carbis Rd. *E14* —5B **42**
Carburton St. *W1* —4D **37**
Cardale St. *E14* —4E **57**
Carden Rd. *SE15* —1D **83**
*Cardiff Ho. SE15 —2C **68***
(off Friary Est.)
Cardigan Pl. *SE3* —5F **71**
Cardigan Rd. *E3* —1B **42**
Cardigan Rd. *SW13* —5C **60**
Cardigan St. *SE11* —1C **66**
*Cardigan Wlk. N1 —4E **25***
(off Ashby Gro.)
Cardinal Bourne St. *SE1* —4F **53**
Cardinal Cap All. *SE1* —2E **53**
*Cardinal Ct. E1 —1C **54***
(off Thomas More St.)
Cardinal Pl. *SW15* —2F **75**
Cardinals Way. *N19* —3F **9**
Cardine M. *SE15* —3D **69**
Cardington St. *NW1* —2E **37**
Cardozo Rd. *N7* —2A **24**
Cardross St. *W6* —4D **47**
Cardwell Rd. *N7* —1A **24**
*Career Ct. SE16 —3F **55***
(off Christopher Clo.)
Carew Clo. *N7* —4B **10**
*Carew Ct. SE14 —2F **69***
(off Samuel Clo.)
Carew St. *SE5* —5E **67**
Carey Ct. *SE5* —3E **67**
Carey Gdns. *SW8* —4E **65**
Carey La. *EC2* —5E **39**
*Carey Mans. SW1 —5F **51***
(off Rutherford St.)
*Carey Pl. SW1 —5F **51***
(off Vauxhall Bri. Rd.)
Carey St. *WC2* —5B **38**
Carfax Pl. *SW4* —2F **79**
Carfree Clo. *N1* —4C **24**
Cargill Rd. *SW18* —1D **91**
Carholme Rd. *SE23* —1B **98**
Carina M. *SE27* —4E **95**
Carisbrooke Gdns. *SE15* —3B **68**
Carker's La. *NW5* —2D **23**
Carleton Gdns. *N19* —2E **23**
Carleton Rd. *N19* —2F **23**

Carleton Vs. *NW5* —2E **23**
Carlile Clo. *E3* —1B **42**
Carlingford Rd. *NW3* —1F **21**
Carlisle Av. *EC3* —5B **40**
Carlisle Av. *W3* —5A **32**
Carlisle Gdns. *IIf* —1F **17**
Carlisle La. *SE1* —4B **52**
Carlisle Mans. SW1 —5E **51**
(off Carlisle Pl.)
Carlisle Pl. *SW1* —4E **51**
Carlisle Rd. *E10* —3C **14**
Carlisle Rd. *N4* —2C **10**
Carlisle Rd. *NW6* —5A **20**
Carlisle St. *W1* —5F **37**
Carlisle Wlk. *E8* —3B **26**
Carlisle Way. *SW17* —5C **92**
Carlos Pl. *W1* —1C **50**
Carlow St. *NW1* —1E **37**
Carlton Clo. *NW3* —4C **6**
Carlton Ct. *SW9* —4D **67**
Carlton Ct. W9 —1D **35**
(off Maida Va.)
Carlton Dri. *SW15* —3F **75**
Carlton Gdns. *SW1* —2F **51**
Carlton Gro. *SE15* —4D **69**
Carlton Hill. *NW8* —1D **35**
Carlton Ho. NW6 —1C **34**
(off Canterbury Ter.,
in five parts)
Carlton Ho. Ter. *SW1* —2F **51**
Carlton Lodge. N4 —2C **10**
(off Carlton Rd.)
Carlton Mans. NW6 —4C **20**
(off W. End La.)
Carlton Mans. *W9* —2D **35**
Carlton Rd. *E11* —3B **16**
Carlton Rd. *E12* —1F **31**
Carlton Rd. *N4* —2C **10**
Carlton Sq. *E1* —3F **41**
(in two parts)
Carlton St. *SW1* —1F **51**
Carlton Ter. *E7* —4E **31**
Carlton Ter. *SE26* —3E **97**
Carlton Tower Pl. SW1
—4B **50**
Carlton Vs. *NW6* —1B **34**
Carlwell St. *SW17* —5A **92**
Carlyle Clo. *N2* —1E **7**
Carlyle Clo. *NW10* —5A **18**
Carlyle Ct. SW6 —4D **63**
(off Maltings Pl.)
Carlyle Ct. SW10 —4E **63**
(off Chelsea Harbour)
Carlyle Pl. *E1* —3F **41**
Carlyle Pl. *SW15* —2F **75**
Carlyle Rd. *E12* —1F **31**
Carlyle's House. —2A **64**
Carlyle Sq. *SW3* —1F **63**
Carmalt Gdns. *SW15* —2E **75**
Carmarthen Grn. *NW9* —1A **4**
Carmarthen Pl. *SE1* —3A **54**
Carmel Ct. W8 —3D **49**
(off Holland St.)
Carmelite St. *EC4* —1C **52**
Carmen St. *E14* —5D **43**
Carmichael Clo. *SW11*
—1F **77**

Carmichael Ct. *SW13* —5B **60**
(off Grove Rd.)
Carmichael Ho. *E14* —1E **57**
Carmichael M. *SW18* —5F **77**
Carminia Rd. *SW17* —2D **93**
Carnaby St. *W1* —5E **37**
Carnac St. *SE27* —4F **95**
Carnarvon Rd. *E10* —1E **15**
Carnarvon Rd. *E15* —3B **30**
Carnbrook Rd. *SE3* —1F **87**
Carnegie Pl. *SW19* —3F **89**
Carnegie St. *N1* —5B **24**
Carnie Hall. *SW17* —3D **93**
Carnoustie Dri. *N1* —4B **24**
(in two parts)
Carnwath Rd. *SW6* —1C **76**
Carolina Clo. *E15* —2A **30**
Caroline Clo. *SW16* —3B **94**
Caroline Clo. W2 —1D **49**
(off Bayswater Rd.)
Caroline Ct. *SE6* —4E **99**
Caroline Gdns. *E2* —2A **40**
Caroline Gdns. *SE15* —3D **69**
Caroline Pl. *SW11* —5C **64**
Caroline Pl. *W2* —1D **49**
Caroline Pl. M. *W2* —1D **49**
Caroline St. *E1* —5F **41**
Caroline Ter. *SW1* —5C **50**
Caroline Wlk. W6 —2A **62**
(off Lillie Rd.)
Carol St. *NW1* —5E **23**
Caronia Ct. SE16 —5A **56**
(off Plough Way)
Carpenter Ho. *E14* —4C **42**
Carpenter Ho. NW11 —1E **7**
Carpenters Ct. NW1 —5E **23**
(off Pratt St.)
Carpenters M. *N7* —2A **24**
Carpenters Pl. *SW4* —2F **79**
Carpenter's Rd. *E15* —3C **28**
Carpenter St. *W1* —1D **51**
Carradale Ho. *E14* —5E **43**
Carrara Wlk. *SE24* —2C **80**
Carrara Wharf. *SW6* —1A **76**
Carriage Dri. E. *SW11*
—3C **64**
Carriage Dri. N. *SW11*
(in two parts) —3B **64**
Carriage Dri. S. *SW11*
—4B **64**
Carriage Dri. W. *SW11*
—3B **64**
Carriage Pl. *N16* —5F **11**
Carrick Ho. *N7* —3B **24**
(off Caledonian Rd.)
Carrick Ho. *SE11* —1C **66**
(off Kennington Pk. Rd.)
Carrick M. *SE8* —2C **70**
Carrington Gdns. *E7* —1C **30**
Carrington Ho. W1 —2D **51**
(off Carrington St.)
Carrington St. *W1* —2D **51**
Carrol Clo. *NW5* —1D **23**
Carroll Clo. *E15* —2B **30**
Carroll Ho. W2 —1F **49**
(off Craven Ter.)
Carron Clo. *E14* —5D **43**

Carroun Rd. *SW8* —3B **66**
Carr St. *E14* —5A **42**
(in two parts)
Carslake Rd. *SW15* —4E **75**
Carson Rd. *E16* —3C **44**
Carson Rd. *SE21* —2F **95**
Carstairs Rd. *SE6* —3E **99**
Carston Clo. *SE12* —3B **86**
Carswell Rd. *SE6* —5E **85**
Carter Ct. EC4 —5D **39**
(off Carter La.)
Carteret St. *SW1* —3F **51**
Carteret Way. *SE8* —5A **56**
Carter Ho. E1 —4B **40**
(off Brune St.)
Carter La. *EC4* —5D **39**
Carter Pl. *SE17* —1E **67**
Carter Rd. *E13* —5D **31**
Carter Rd. *SW19* —5F **91**
Carters Clo. *NW5* —2F **23**
(off Torriano Av.)
Carters Hill Clo. *SE9* —1E **101**
Carters La. *SE23* —2A **98**
Carter St. *SE17* —2E **67**
Carter's Yd. *SW18* —3C **76**
Carthew Rd. *W6* —4D **47**
Carthew Vs. *W6* —4D **47**
Carthusian St. *EC1* —4E **39**
Cartier Circ. *E14* —2D **57**
Carting La. *WC2* —1A **52**
Cartmel. NW1 —2E **37**
(off Hampstead Rd.)
Carton Ho. *SE16* —4C **54**
(off Marine St.)
Carton Ho. W11 —2F **47**
(off St Ann's Rd.)
Cartwright Gdns. *WC1*
—2A **38**
Cartwright Ho. SE1 —4E **53**
(off County St.)
Cartwright St. *E1* —1B **54**
Cartwright Way. SW13
—3D **61**
Carvel Ho. *E14* —1E **71**
Carver Rd. *SE24* —4E **81**
Cary Rd. *E11* —1A **30**
Carysfort Rd. *N16* —5F **11**
Casby Rd. SE16 —4C **54**
(off Marine St.)
Cascades Tower. *E14* —2C **56**
Casella Rd. *SE14* —3F **69**
Casewick Rd. *SE27* —5C **94**
Casimir Rd. *E5* —4E **13**
Casino Av. *SE24* —3E **81**
Caspian St. *SE5* —3F **67**
Caspian Wlk. *E16* —5F **45**
Casselden Rd. *NW10* —4A **18**
Cassell Ho. SW9 —5A **66**
(off Stockwell Gdns. Est.)
Cassidy Rd. *SW6* —3C **62**
(in two parts)
Cassiobury Rd. *E17* —1A **14**
Cassland Rd. *E9* —4F **27**
Casslee Rd. *SE6* —5B **84**
Casson Ho. E1 —4C **40**
(off Spelman St.)
Casson St. *E1* —4C **40**

Castalia Sq. *E14* —3E **57**
Castellain Mans. *W9* —3D **35**
(off Castellain Rd.)
Castellain Rd. *W9* —3D **35**
Castell Ho. *SE8* —3C **70**
Castello Av. *SW15* —3E **75**
Castelnau. —2D **61**
Castelnau. *SW13* —4C **60**
Castelnau Gdns. *SW13*
—2D **61**
Castelnau Row. *SW13*
—2D **61**
Casterbridge. *NW6* —5D **21**
(off Abbey Rd.)
Casterbridge. *W11* —5B **34**
(off Dartmouth Clo.)
Casterbridge Rd. *SE3* —1C **86**
Casterton St. *E8* —3D **27**
Castillon Rd. *SE6* —2A **100**
Castlands Rd. *SE6* —2B **98**
Castleacre. *W2* —5A **36**
(off Hyde Pk. Cres.)
Castle Baynard St. *EC4*
—1D **53**
Castlebrook Clo. *SE11*
(off Brook Dri.) —5D **53**
Castle Clo. *E9* —2A **28**
Castle Clo. *SW19* —3F **89**
Castlecombe Dri. *SW19*
—5F **75**
Castlecombe Rd. *SE9*
—4F **101**
Castle Ct. *EC3* —5F **39**
(off Birchin La.)
Castle Ct. *SE26* —4A **98**
Castle Dri. *Ilf* —1F **17**
Castleford Ct. *NW8* —3F **35**
(off Henderson Dri.)
Castlehaven Rd. *NW1* —4D **23**
Castle Ho. *SE1* —5E **53**
(off Walworth Rd.)
Castle Ho. *SW8* —3A **66**
(off S. Lambeth Rd.)
Castle Ind. Est. *SE17* —5E **53**
Castlemaine. *SW11* —5B **64**
Castle Mead. *SE5* —3E **67**
Castle M. *NW1* —3D **23**
Castle Pl. *NW1* —3D **23**
Castle Pl. *W4* —5A **46**
Castle Point. *E13* —1E **45**
(off Boundary Rd.)
Castlereagh St. *W1* —5A **36**
Castle Rd. *NW1* —3D **23**
Castle Rd. *E6* —1E **45**
Castleton Ho. *E14* —5E **57**
Castleton Rd. *SE9* —4F **101**
Castletown Rd. *W14* —1A **62**
Castleview Clo. *N4* —4E **11**
Castle Way. *SW19* —3F **89**
Castle Wharf. *E14* —1A **58**
Castlewood Rd. *N15 & N16*
—1C **12**
Castle Yd. *N6* —2C **8**
Castle Yd. *SE1* —2D **53**
Castor La. *E14* —1D **57**
Caterham Rd. *SE13* —1F **85**

Catesby St. *SE17* —5F **53**
Catford. —5D **85**
Catford B'way. *SE6* —5D **85**
Catford Greyhound Stadium.
—4C **84**
Catford Gyratory. (Junct.)
—5D **85**
Catford Hill. *SE6* —1B **98**
Catford Island. *SE6* —5D **85**
Catford M. *SE6* —5D **85**
Catford Rd. *SE6* —5C **84**
Catford Trad. Est. *SE6*
—2D **99**
Cathall Rd. *E11* —4F **15**
Cathay Ho. *SE16* —3D **55**
Cathay St. *SE16* —3D **55**
Cathcart Hill. *N19* —5E **9**
Cathcart Rd. *SW10* —2D **63**
Cathcart St. *NW5* —3D **23**
Cathedral Lodge. *EC1* —4E **39**
(off Aldersgate St.)
Cathedral Mans. *SW1* —5E **51**
(off Vauxhall Bri. Rd.)
Cathedral Piazza. *SW1*
—4E **51**
Cathedral Pl. *EC4* —5E **39**
(off Paternoster Row)
Cathedral St. *SE1* —2F **53**
Catherall Rd. *N5* —5E **11**
Catherine Ct. *SW19* —5B **90**
Catherine Griffiths Ct. *EC1*
(off Pine St.) —3C **38**
Catherine Gro. *SE10* —4D **71**
Catherine Ho. *N1* —5A **26**
(off Whitmore Est.)
Catherine Pl. *SW1* —4E **51**
Catherine Pl. *WC2* —1B **52**
Catherine Wheel All. *EC2*
—4A **40**
Catherine Wheel Yd. *SW1*
—2E **51**
(off Lit. St James's St.)
Catherwood Ct. *N1* —1F **39**
(off Murray Gro.)
Cathles Rd. *SW12* —4D **79**
Cathnor Rd. *W12* —3D **47**
Catinthia Ct. *SE16* —5A **56**
(off Plough Way)
Catling Clo. *SE23* —3E **97**
Catlin St. *SE16* —1C **68**
Cato Rd. *SW4* —1F **79**
Cator Rd. *SE26* —5F **97**
Cator St. *SE15* —3B **68**
(Commercial Way)
Cator St. *SE15* —2B **68**
(St George's Way)
Cato St. *W1* —4A **36**
Catton St. *WC1* —4B **38**
Caudwell Ter. *SW18* —4F **77**
Caughley Ho. *SE11* —4C **52**
(off Lambeth Wlk.)
Caulfield Rd. *SE15* —5D **69**
Causeway, The. *SW18*
(in two parts) —3D **77**
Causeway, The. *SW19*
—5E **89**
Causton Cotts. *E14* —4A **42**

Causton Ho. *SE5* —3E **67**
Causton Rd. *N6* —2D **9**
Causton St. *SW1* —5F **51**
Cautley Av. *SW4* —3E **79**
Cavalry Gdns. *SW15* —3B **76**
Cavaye Pl. *SW10* —1E **63**
Cavell Ho. *N1* —5A **26**
(off Colville Est.)
Cavell St. *E1* —4D **41**
Cavendish Av. *NW8* —1F **35**
Cavendish Clo. *NW6* —3B **20**
Cavendish Clo. *NW8* —2F **35**
Cavendish Ct. *EC3* —5A **40**
(off Devonshire Row)
Cavendish Dri. *E11* —3F **15**
Cavendish Gdns. *SW4*
—4E **79**
Cavendish Ho. *NW8* —1F **35**
(off Cavendish Av.)
Cavendish Mans. *EC1* —3C **38**
(off Rosebery Av.)
Cavendish Mans. *NW6*
—2C **20**
Cavendish M. N. *W1* —4D **37**
Cavendish M. S. *W1* —4D **37**
Cavendish Pde. *SW12* —4D **79**
(off Clapham Comn. S. Side)
Cavendish Pl. *SW4* —3F **79**
Cavendish Pl. *W1* —5D **37**
Cavendish Rd. *N4* —1D **11**
Cavendish Rd. *NW6* —4A **20**
Cavendish Rd. *SW12* —4D **79**
Cavendish Sq. *W1* —5D **37**
Cavendish St. *N1* —1F **39**
Cave Rd. *E13* —2D **45**
Caversham Ho. *SE15* —2C **68**
(off Haymerle Rd.)
Caversham Rd. *NW5* —3E **23**
Caversham St. *SW3* —2B **64**
Caverswall St. *W12* —5E **33**
Cavour Ho. *SE17* —1D **67**
(off Alberta Est.)
Cawnpore St. *SE19* —5A **96**
Caxton Ct. *SW11* —5A **64**
Caxton Gro. *E3* —2C **42**
Caxton Rd. *SW19* —5E **91**
Caxton Rd. *W12* —3F **47**
Caxton St. *SW1* —4E **51**
Caxton St. N. *E16* —5B **44**
Caxton St. S. *E16* —1C **58**
Caxton Wlk. *WC2* —5F **37**
Cayton Pl. *EC1* —2F **39**
(off Cayton St.)
Cayton St. *EC1* —2F **39**
Cazenove Rd. *N16* —4B **12**
Cearns Ho. *E6* —5F **31**
Cecil Ct. *NW6* —4D **21**
Cecil Ct. *SW10* —2E **63**
(off Hollywood Rd.)
Cecil Ct. *WC2* —1A **52**
Cecile Pk. *N8* —1A **10**
Cecilia Rd. *E8* —2B **26**
Cecil Rhodes Ho. *NW1*
(off Goldington St.) —1F **37**
Cecil Rd. *E11* —5B **16**
Cecil Rd. *E13* —5C **30**
Cecil Rd. *NW10* —5A **18**

Cedar Clo. SE21 —1E 95
Cedar Ct. N1 —4E 25
Cedar Ct. SE7 —2E 73
Cedar Ct. SW19 —3F 89
Cedar Ct. W1 —5A 36
(off Harrowby St.)
Cedar Heights. NW2 —3B 20
Cedar Ho. E14 —3E 57
Cedar Ho. SE14 —4F 69
Cedar Ho. SE16 —3F 55
(off Woodland Cres.)
Cedar Ho. W8 —4D 49
(off Marloes Rd.)
Cedarhurst Dri. SE9 —3E 87
Cedar Mt. SE9 —1F 101
Cedarne Rd. SW6 —3D 63
Cedar Pl. SE7 —1E 73
Cedar Rd. NW2 —1E 19
Cedars Av. E17 —1C 14
Cedars Clo. SE13 —1F 85
Cedars M. SW4 —2D 79
(in two parts)
Cedars Rd. E15 —3A 30
Cedars Rd. SW4 —1D 79
Cedars Rd. SW13 —5C 60
Cedars, The. E15 —4B 30
Cedar Tree Gro. SE27
—5D 95
Cedar Way. NW1 —4F 23
Cedar Way Ind. Est. NW1
—4F 23
Cedra Ct. N16 —3C 12
Celandine Clo. E3 —4C 42
Celandine Dri. E8 —4B 26
Celandine Way. E15 —2A 44
Celbridge M. W2 —5D 35
Celestial Gdns. SE13 —2F 85
Celia Ho. N1 —1A 40
(off Arden Est.)
Celia Rd. N19 —1E 23
Celtic St. E14 —4D 43
Cemetery La. SE7 —2F 73
Cemetery Rd. E7 —2B 30
Cenacle Clo. NW3 —5C 6
Cenotaph. —3A 52
Centaur St. SE1 —4B 52
Central Av. E11 —4F 15
Central Av. SW11 —3B 64
Central Bus. Cen. NW10
—2A 18
Central Cir. NW4 —1D 5
Central Criminal Court.
(Old Bailey) —5D 39
Central Hill. SE19 —5E 95
Central Ho. E15 —1E 43
Central Mans. NW4 —1D 5
(off Watford Way)
Central Markets. EC1 —4D 39
(off Charterhouse St.)
Central Markets (Smithfield).
—4D 39
(off Charterhouse St.)
Central Pk. Rd. E6 —1F 45
Central Sq. NW11 —1D 7
Central St. EC1 —2E 39
Centre Av. NW10 —2E 33
Centre Av. W3 —2A 46

Centre Dri. E7 —1E 31
Centre Heights. NW3 —4F 21
Centre Point. SE1 —1C 68
Centrepoint. WC1 —5F 37
(off St Giles High St.)
Centre Point Ho. WC2 —5F 37
Centre St. E2 —1D 41
Centric Clo. NW1 —5C 22
Centurion Clo. N7 —4B 24
Centurion La. E3 —5B 28
Century Clo. NW4 —1F 5
Century Ho. SW15 —2F 75
Century M. E5 —1E 27
Cephas Av. E1 —3E 41
Cephas Ho. E1 —3E 41
(off Doveton St.)
Cephas St. E1 —3E 41
Cerise Rd. SE15 —4C 68
Cerney M. W2 —1F 49
Cervantes Ct. W2 —5D 35
Cester St. E2 —5C 26
Ceylon Rd. W14 —4F 47
Chadacre Ct. E15 —5C 30
(off Vicars Clo.)
Chadacre Ho. SW9 —2D 81
(off Loughborough Pk.)
Chadbourn St. E14 —4D 43
Chadd Grn. E13 —5C 30
(in two parts)
Chadston Ho. N1 —4D 25
(off Halton Rd.)
Chadswell. WC1 —2A 38
(off Cromer St.)
Chadwell St. EC1 —2C 38
Chadwick Clo. SW19 —5C 90
Chadwick Gdns. SW15 —5B 74
Chadwick Rd. E11 —1A 16
Chadwick Rd. NW10 —5B 18
Chadwick Rd. SE15 —5B 68
Chadwick St. SW1 —4F 51
Chadwin Rd. E13 —4D 45
Chadworth Ho. EC1 —2E 39
(off Lever St.)
Chadworth Ho. N4 —3E 11
Chagford St. NW1 —3B 36
Chailey St. E5 —5E 13
Chalbury Wlk. N1 —1B 38
Chalcot Cres. NW1 —5B 22
Chalcot Gdns. NW3 —3B 22
Chalcot M. SW16 —3A 94
Chalcot Rd. NW1 —4C 22
Chalcot Sq. NW1 —4C 22
(in two parts)
Chalcroft Rd. SE13 —3A 86
Chaldon Rd. SW6 —3A 62
Chale Rd. SW2 —4A 80
Chalfont Ct. NW1 —3B 36
(off Baker St.)
Chalfont Ho. SE16 —4D 55
(off Keetons Rd.)
Chalford Rd. SE21 —4F 95
Chalk Farm. —4C 22
Chalk Farm Rd. NW1 —4C 22
Chalkhill Rd. W6 —5F 47
Chalk Rd. E13 —4D 45
Challenge Clo. NW10 —5A 18

Challice Way. SW2 —1B 94
Challoner Cres. W14 —1B 62
Challoner St. W14 —1B 62
Chalmers Wlk. SE17 —2D 67
(off Hillingdon St.)
Chalsey Rd. SE4 —2B 84
Chalton Dri. N2 —1F 7
Chalton Ho. NW1 —2F 37
(off Chalton St.)
Chalton St. NW1 —1E 37
(in three parts)
Chamberlain Cotts. SE5
—4F 67
Chamberlain Ho. NW1
(off Ossulston St.) —1F 37
Chamberlain Ho. SE1 —3C 52
(off Westminster Bri. Rd.)
Chamberlain St. NW1 —4B 22
Chamberlayne Rd. NW10
—5E 19
Chambers La. NW10 —4D 19
Chambers Rd. N7 —1A 24
Chambers St. SE16 —3C 54
Chambers, The. SW10
—4E 63
(off Chelsea Harbour)
Chamber St. E1 —1B 54
Chambers Wharf. SE16
—3C 54
Chambon Pl. W6 —5C 46
Chambord St. E2 —2B 40
Chamomile Ct. E17 —1C 14
(off Yunus Khan Clo.)
Champion Cres. SE26 —4A 98
Champion Gro. SE5 —1F 81
Champion Hill. SE5 —1F 81
Champion Hill Est. SE5
—1A 82
Champion Pk. SE5 —5F 67
Champion Rd. SE26 —4A 98
Champlain Ho. W12 —1D 47
(off White City Est.)
Champness Clo. SE27 —4F 95
Chancel Ind. Est. NW10
—2B 18
Chancellor Gro. SE21 —2E 95
Chancellor Ho. E1 —2D 55
(off Green Bank)
Chancellor Pas. E14 —2C 56
Chancellors Ct. WC1 —4B 38
(off Olde Hall St.)
Chancellor's Rd. W6 —1E 61
Chancellor's St. W6 —1E 61
Chancellors Wharf. W6
—1E 61
Chancel St. SE1 —2D 53
Chancery Bldgs. E1 —1D 55
(off Lowood St.)
Chancery La. WC2 —5C 38
Chance St. E2 & E1 —3B 40
Chandler Av. E16 —4C 44
Chandlers Ct. SE12 —1D 101
Chandlers M. E14 —3C 56
Chandler St. E1 —2D 55
Chandlers Way. SW2 —5C 80
Chandler Way. SE15 —3B 68
(Diamond Way)

Chandler Way. *SE15* —2A **68**
(St George's Way)
Chandlery Ho. *E1* —5C **40**
(off Bk. Church La.)
Chandlery, The. *SE1* —4C **52**
(off Gerridge St.)
Chandos Pl. *WC2* —1A **52**
Chandos Rd. *E15* —2F **29**
Chandos Rd. *NW2* —2E **19**
Chandos Rd. *NW10* —3A **32**
Chandos St. *W1* —4D **37**
Chandos Way. *NW11* —3D **7**
Change All. *EC3* —5F **39**
Channel Ga. Rd. *NW10*
—2A **32**
Channel Islands Est. *N1*
(off Guernsey Rd.) —3E **25**
Channelsea Path. *E15*
—5F **29**
Channelsea Rd. *E15* —5F **29**
Chantrey Rd. *SW9* —1B **80**
Chantry Clo. *W9* —3B **34**
Chantry Sq. *W8* —4D **49**
Chantry St. *N1* —5D **25**
Chant Sq. *E15* —4F **29**
Chant St. *E15* —4F **29**
Chapel Ct. *SE1* —3F **53**
Chapel Ho. St. *E14* —1D **71**
Chapel Mkt. *N1* —1C **38**
Chapel Path. *E11* —1D **17**
(off Woodbine Pl.)
Chapel Pl. *EC2* —2A **40**
Chapel Pl. *N1* —1C **38**
Chapel Pl. *W1* —5D **37**
Chapel Rd. *SE27* —4D **95**
Chapel Side. *W2* —1D **49**
Chapel St. *SW1* —4C **50**
Chapel St. *W2* —4A **36**
Chapel Way. *N7* —5B **10**
Chapel Yd. *SW18* —3C **76**
(off Wandsworth High St.)
Chaplin Clo. *SE1* —3C **52**
Chaplin Rd. *E15* —1B **44**
Chaplin Rd. *NW2* —3C **18**
Chapman Ho. *E1* —5D **41**
(off Bigland St.)
Chapman Rd. *E9* —3B **28**
Chapmans Pk. Ind. Est.
NW10 —3B **18**
Chapman Sq. *SW19* —2F **89**
Chapman St. *E1* —1D **55**
Chapone Pl. *W1* —5F **37**
(off Dean St.)
Chapter Chambers. *SW1*
(off Chapter St.) —5F **51**
Chapter Ho. Ct. *EC4* —5E **39**
(off St Paul's Chyd.)
Chapter Rd. *NW2* —2C **18**
Chapter Rd. *SE17* —1D **67**
Chapter St. *SW1* —5F **51**
Charcot Ho. *SW15* —4B **74**
Charcroft Ct. *W14* —3F **47**
(off Minford Gdns.)
Chardin Ho. *SW9* —4C **66**
(off Gosling Way)
Chardin Rd. *W4* —5A **46**
Chardmore Rd. *N16* —3C **12**

Charecroft Way. *W12* —3F **47**
Charfield Ct. *W9* —3D **35**
(off Shirland Rd.)
Charford Rd. *E16* —4C **44**
Chargeable La. *E13* —3B **44**
Chargeable St. *E16* —3B **44**
Chargrove Clo. *SE16* —3F **55**
Charing Cross. *SW1* —2A **52**
(off Whitehall)
Charing Cross Rd. *WC2*
—5F **37**
Charing Ho. *SE1* —3C **52**
(off Windmill Wlk.)
Charlbert Ct. *NW8* —1A **36**
(off Charlbert St.)
Charlbert St. *NW8* —1A **36**
Charlecote Gro. *SE26* —3D **97**
Charles Auffray Ho. *E1*
(off Smithy St.) —4E **41**
Charles Barry Clo. *SW4*
—1E **79**
Charles Coveney Rd. *SE5*
—4B **68**
Charles Dickens Ho. *E2*
(off Mansford St.) —2C **40**
Charlesfield. *SE9* —3E **101**
Charles Flemwell M. *E16*
—2C **58**
Charles Gardner Ct. *N1*
—2F **39**
(off Haberdasher Est.)
Charles Harrod Ct. *SW13*
(off Somerville Av.) —2E **61**
Charles La. *NW8* —1A **36**
Charles MacKenzie Ho. *SE16*
(off Linsey St.) —5C **54**
Charles Pl. *NW1* —2E **37**
Charles Rd. *E7* —4E **31**
Charles Rowan Ho. *WC1*
(off Margery St.) —2C **38**
Charles II Pl. *SW3* —1B **64**
Charles II St. *SW1* —2F **51**
Charles Simmons Ho. *WC1*
(off Margery St.) —2B **38**
Charles Sq. *N1* —2F **39**
Charles Sq. Est. *N1* —2F **39**
(off Charles Sq.)
Charles St. *E16* —2E **59**
Charles St. *SW13* —5A **60**
Charles St. *W1* —2D **51**
Charles St. Trad. Est. *E16*
—2E **59**
Charleston St. *SE17* —5E **53**
Charles Townsend Ho. *EC1*
(off Finsbury Est.) —2D **39**
Charles Uton Ct. *E8* —1C **26**
Charles Whincup Rd. *E16*
—1D **72**
Charlesworth Ho. *E14* —5C **42**
Charleville Ct. *SE26* —5C **96**
Charleville Mans. *W14*
(off Charleville Rd.) —1A **62**
Charleville Rd. *W14* —1A **62**
Charlie Chaplin Wlk. *SE1*
—2B **52**
Charlmont Rd. *SW17* —5A **92**
Charlotte Ct. *N8* —1F **9**

Charlotte Ct. *SE17* —5A **54**
(off Old Kent Rd.)
Charlotte Despard Av. *SW11*
—4C **64**
Charlotte M. *W1* —4E **37**
Charlotte M. *W10* —5F **33**
Charlotte M. *W14* —5A **48**
Charlotte Pl. *SW1* —5E **51**
Charlotte Pl. *W1* —4E **37**
Charlotte Rd. *EC1* —2A **40**
Charlotte Rd. *SW13* —4B **60**
Charlotte Row. *SW4* —1E **79**
Charlotte St. *W1* —4E **37**
Charlotte Ter. *N1* —5B **24**
Charlow Clo. *SW6* —5E **63**
Charlton. —2F 73
Charlton Athletic F.C. —1E **73**
Charlton Chu. La. *SE7* —1E **73**
Charlton Ct. *E2* —5B **26**
Charlton Dene. *SE7* —3E **73**
Charlton King's Rd. *NW5*
—2F **23**
Charlton La. *SE7* —5F **59**
Charlton Pk. La. *SE7* —3F **73**
Charlton Pk. Rd. *SE7* —2F **73**
Charlton Pl. *N1* —1D **39**
Charlton Rd. *NW10* —5A **18**
Charlton Rd. *SE3 & SE7*
—3C **72**
Charlton Way. *SE3* —4A **72**
Charlwood Ho. *SW1* —5F **51**
(off Vauxhall Bri. Rd.)
Charlwood Houses. *WC1*
(off Midhope St.) —2A **38**
Charlwood Pl. *SW1* —5E **51**
Charlwood St. *SW15* —2F **75**
Charlwood St. *SW1* —1E **65**
(in two parts)
Charlwood Ter. *SW15* —2F **75**
Charmans Ho. *SW8* —3A **66**
(off Wandsworth Rd.)
Charminster Rd. *SE9* —4F **101**
Charmouth Ho. *SW8* —3B **66**
Charnock Rd. *E5* —5D **13**
Charnwood Gdns. *E14*
—5C **56**
Charnwood St. *E5* —4D **13**
Charrington St. *NW1* —1F **37**
Charsley Rd. *SE6* —2D **99**
Charter Ct. *N4* —3C **10**
Charter Ho. *WC2* —5A **38**
(off Crown Ct.)
Charterhouse Bldgs. *EC1*
—3E **39**
Charterhouse M. *EC1* —4D **39**
Charterhouse Sq. *EC1* —4D **39**
Charterhouse St. *EC1* —4C **38**
Charteris Rd. *N4* —3C **10**
Charteris Rd. *NW6* —5B **20**
Charters Clo. *SE19* —5A **96**
Chartes Ho. *SE1* —1A **54**
(off Abbey St.)
Chartfield Av. *SW15* —3D **75**
Chartfield Sq. *SW15* —3F **75**
Chartham Ct. *SW9* —1C **80**
(off Canterbury Cres.)
Chartham Gro. *SE27* —3D **95**

*Chartham Ho. SE1 —4F **53***
(off Weston St.)
Chart Ho. *E14* —1D **71**
Chartley Av. *NW2* —5A **4**
*Chartridge. SE17 —2F **67***
(off Westmoreland Rd.)
Chart St. *N1* —2F **39**
Charwood. *SW16* —4C **94**
Chase Cen., The. *NW10* —2A **32**
Chasefield Rd. *SW17* —4B **92**
Chaseley St. *E14* —5A **42**
Chasemore Ho. *SW6* —3A **62**
Chase Rd. *NW10* —3A **32**
Chase Rd. Trad. Est. *NW10* —3A **32**
Chase, The. *E12* —1F **31**
Chase, The. *SW4* —1D **79**
*Chaston St. NW5 —2C **22***
(off Grafton Ter.)
Chatfield Rd. *SW11* —1E **77**
Chatham Clo. *NW11* —1C **6**
Chatham Pl. *E9* —3E **27**
Chatham Rd. *SW11* —4B **78**
Chatham St. *SE17* —5F **53**
Chatsworth Av. *Brom* —4D **101**
*Chatsworth Ct. W8 —5C **48***
(off Pembroke Rd.)
Chatsworth Est. *E5* —1F **27**
Chatsworth Lodge. W4
*(off Bourne Pl.) —1A **60***
Chatsworth Rd. *E5* —5E **13**
Chatsworth Rd. *E15* —2B **30**
Chatsworth Rd. *NW2* —3E **19**
(in two parts)
Chatsworth Way. *SE27* —3D **95**
*Chatterton M. N4 —5D **11***
(off Chatterton Rd.)
Chatterton Rd. *N4* —5D **11**
Chatto Rd. *SW11* —3B **78**
Chaucer Dri. *SE1* —5B **54**
*Chaucer Ho. SW1 —1E **65***
(off Churchill Gdns.)
*Chaucer Mans. W14 —2A **62***
(off Queen's Club Gdns.)
Chaucer Rd. *E7* —3C **30**
Chaucer Rd. *E11* —1C **16**
Chaucer Rd. *SE24* —3C **80**
Chaucer Way. *SW19* —5E **91**
*Chaulden Ho. EC1 —2F **39***
(off Cranwood St.)
Chauntler Clo. *E16* —5D **45**
Cheadle Ct. *NW8* —3F **35**
Cheadle Ho. *E14* —5B **42**
Cheam St. *SE15* —1E **83**
Cheapside. *EC2* —5E **39**
*Chearsley. SE17 —5E **53***
(off Deacon Way)
*Cheddington Ho. E2 —5C **26***
(off Whiston Rd.)
Chedworth Clo. *E16* —5B **44**
Cheesemans Ter. *W14*
(in two parts) —1B **62**
Chelford Rd. *Brom* —5F **99**
Chelmer Rd. *E9* —2F **27**
Chelmsford Clo. *W6* —2F **61**
*Chelmsford Ho. N7 —1B **24***
(off Holloway Rd.)
Chelmsford Rd. *E11* —3F **15**
Chelmsford Rd. *E17* —1C **14**
Chelmsford Sq. *NW10* —5E **19**
Chelsea. —1A 64
Chelsea Bri. *SW1 & SW8* —2D **65**
Chelsea Bri. Bus. Cen. *SW8* —3D **65**
Chelsea Bri. Rd. *SW1* —1C **64**
Chelsea Bri. Wharf. *SW8* —2D **65**
Chelsea Cloisters. *SW3* —5A **50**
Chelsea Clo. *NW10* —5A **18**
Chelsea Cres. *NW2* —3B **20**
Chelsea Cres. *SW10* —4E **63**
Chelsea Embkmt. *SW3* —2A **64**
*Chelsea Farm Ho. Studios. SW10 —2F **63***
(off Milman's St.)
Chelsea F.C. —3D 63
Chelsea Gdns. *SW1* —1C **64**
*Chelsea Ga. SW1 —1C **64***
(off Ebury Bri. Rd.)
Chelsea Harbour Design Cen. *SW10* —4E **63**
Chelsea Harbour Dri. *SW10* —4E **63**
*Chelsea Lodge. SW3 —2B **64***
(off Tite St.)
Chelsea Mnr. Ct. *SW3* —2A **64**
Chelsea Mnr. Gdns. *SW3* —1A **64**
Chelsea Mnr. St. *SW3* —1A **64**
Chelsea Pk. Gdns. *SW3* —2F **63**
Chelsea Physic Garden. —2B 64
*Chelsea Reach Tower. SW10 —3F **63***
(off Worlds End Est.)
Chelsea Sq. *SW3* —1F **63**
Chelsea Studios. SW6
*(off Fulham Rd.) —3D **63***
*Chelsea Towers. SW3 —2A **64***
(off Chelsea Mnr. Gdns.)
*Chelsea Village. SW6 —3D **63***
(off Fulham Rd.)
*Chelsea Wharf. SW10 —3F **63***
(off Lots Rd.)
Chelsfield Gdns. *SE26* —3E **97**
*Chelsfield Ho. SE17 —5A **54***
(off Massinger St.)
Chelsham Rd. *SW4* —1F **79**
Cheltenham Gdns. *E6* —1F **45**
Cheltenham Rd. *E10* —1E **15**
Cheltenham Rd. *SE15* —2E **83**
Cheltenham Ter. *SW3* —1B **64**
Chelverton Rd. *SW15* —2F **75**
*Chelwood Ho. W2 —5F **35***
(off Gloucester Sq.)
Chelwood Wlk. *SE4* —2A **84**
Chenappa Clo. *E13* —2C **44**
Cheney Ct. *SE23* —1F **97**
Cheney Rd. *NW1* —1A **38**
Cheneys Rd. *E11* —5A **16**
*Chenies Ho. W4 —3B **60***
(off Corney Reach Way)
Chenies M. *WC1* —3F **37**
Chenies Pl. *NW1* —1F **37**
Chenies St. *WC1* —4F **37**
*Chenies, The. NW1 —1F **37***
(off Pancras Rd.)
Cheniston Gdns. *W8* —4D **49**
Chepstow Clo. *SW15* —4A **76**
*Chepstow Corner. W2 —5C **34***
(off Pembridge Vs.)
*Chepstow Ct. W2 —1C **48***
(off Chepstow Vs.)
Chepstow Cres. *W11* —1C **48**
Chepstow Pl. *W2* —5C **34**
Chepstow Rd. *W2* —5C **34**
Chepstow Vs. *W11* —1B **48**
Chepstow Way. *SE15* —3B **68**
*Chequers Ct. EC1 —3F **39***
(off Chequer St.)
*Chequers Ho. NW8 —3A **36***
(off Jerome Cres.)
Chequer St. *EC1* —3E **39**
(in two parts)
*Cherbury Ct. N1 —1F **39***
(off St John's Est.)
Cherbury St. *N1* —1F **39**
Cheriton Ct. *SE12* —5C **86**
Cheriton Sq. *SW17* —2C **92**
Cherry Clo. *SW2* —5C **80**
Cherry Ct. *W3* —2A **46**
*Cherry Garden Ho. SE16 —3D **55***
(off Cherry Garden St.)
Cherry Garden St. *SE16* —3D **55**
Cherry Laurel Wlk. *SW2* —4B **80**
Cherry Orchard. *SE7* —2E **73**
Cherry Tree Clo. *E9* —5E **27**
Cherry Tree Ct. *SE7* —2E **73**
Cherrytree Dri. *SW16* —3A **94**
Cherry Tree Rd. *E15* —2A **30**
Cherry Tree Wlk. *EC1* —3E **39**
Cherrywood Clo. *E3* —2A **42**
Cherrywood Dri. *SW15* —3F **75**
Chertsey Rd. *E11* —4F **15**
Chertsey St. *SW17* —5C **92**
*Cherwell Ho. NW8 —3F **35***
(off Church St. Est.)
Cheryls Clo. *SW6* —4D **63**
Cheseman St. *SE26* —3D **97**
*Chesham Clo. SW1 —4C **50***
(off Lyall St.)
*Chesham Flats. W1 —1C **50***
(off Brown Hart Gdns.)
*Chesham M. SW1 —4C **50***
(off Belgrave M. W.)
Chesham Pl. *SW1* —4C **50**
(in two parts)
Chesham Rd. *SW19* —5F **91**
Chesham St. *SW1* —4C **50**

Cheshire Clo. *SE4* —5B **70**
Cheshire Ct. *EC4* —5C **38**
(off Fleet St.)
Cheshire St. *E2* —3B **40**
Chesholm Rd. *N16* —5A **12**
Cheshunt Ho. *NW6* —5D **21**
(off Mortimer Cres.)
Cheshunt Rd. *E7* —3D **31**
Chesil Ct. *E2* —1E **41**
Chesil Ct. *SW3* —2A **64**
Chesilton Rd. *SW6* —4B **62**
Chesley Gdns. *E6* —1F **45**
Chesney Ct. *W9* —3C **34**
(off Shirland Rd.)
Chesney Ho. *SE13* —2F **85**
(off Mercator Rd.)
Chesney St. *SW11* —4C **64**
Chessington Ho. *SW8*
—5F **65**
Chessington Mans. *E10*
—2C **14**
Chessington Mans. *E11*
—2A **16**
Chesson Rd. *W14* —2B **62**
Chester Clo. *SW1* —3D **51**
Chester Clo. *SW13* —1D **75**
Chester Clo. N. *NW1* —2D **37**
Chester Clo. S. *NW1* —2D **37**
Chester Cotts. *SW1* —5C **50**
(off Bourne St.)
Chester Ct. *NW1* —2D **37**
Chester Ct. *SE5* —3F **67**
(off Lomond Gro.)
Chester Ct. *SE8* —1F **69**
Chester Cres. *E8* —2B **26**
Chesterfield Clo. *SE13* —5F **71**
Chesterfield Gdns. *N4*
—1D **11**
Chesterfield Gdns. *SE10*
—4F **71**
Chesterfield Gdns. *W1*
—2D **51**
Chesterfield Gro. *SE22*
—3B **82**
Chesterfield Hill. *W1* —2D **51**
Chesterfield Ho. *W1* —2C **50**
(off Chesterfield Gdns.)
Chesterfield Rd. *E10* —1E **15**
Chesterfield St. *W1* —2D **51**
Chesterfield Wlk. *SE10*
—4F **71**
Chesterfield Way. *SE15*
—3E **69**
Chesterford Gdns. *NW3*
—1D **21**
Chesterford Ho. *SE18* —4F **73**
(off Portway Gdns.)
Chester Ga. *NW1* —2D **37**
Chester Ho. *SW1* —5D **51**
(off Eccleston Pl.)
Chester Ho. *SW9* —3C **66**
(off Brixton Rd.)
Chesterman Ct. *W4* —3A **60**
(off Corney Reach Way)
Chester M. *SW1* —4D **51**
Chester Pl. *NW1* —2D **37**

Chester Rd. *E7* —4F **31**
Chester Rd. *E11* —1D **17**
Chester Rd. *E16* —3A **44**
Chester Rd. *E17* —1F **13**
Chester Rd. *N19* —4D **9**
Chester Rd. *NW1* —2C **36**
Chester Rd. *SW19* —5E **89**
Chester Row. *SW1* —5C **50**
Chester Sq. *SW1* —5C **50**
Chester Sq. M. *SW1* —4D **51**
(off Chester Sq.)
Chester St. *E2* —3C **40**
Chester St. *SW1* —4C **50**
Chester Ter. *NW1* —2D **37**
(in three parts)
Chesterton Clo. *SW18*
—3C **76**
Chesterton Rd. *E13* —2C **44**
Chesterton Rd. *W10* —4F **33**
Chesterton Sq. *W8* —5C **48**
Chesterton Ter. *E13* —2C **44**
Chester Way. *SE11* —5C **52**
Chestnut All. *SW6* —2B **62**
Chestnut Av. *E7* —1D **31**
Chestnut Av. *SW14* —1A **74**
Chestnut Clo. *N16* —4F **11**
Chestnut Clo. *SE6* —5E **99**
Chestnut Clo. *SE14* —4B **70**
Chestnut Clo. *SW16* —4C **94**
Chestnut Ct. *SW6* —2B **62**
Chestnut Ct. *W8* —4D **49**
Chestnut Dri. *E11* —1C **16**
Chestnut Gro. *SW12* —5C **78**
Chestnut Ho. *W4* —5A **46**
(off Orchard, The)
Chestnut Rd. *SE27* —3D **95**
Chestnuts, The. *N5* —1E **25**
(off Highbury Grange)
Chettle Clo. *SE1* —4F **53**
(off Spurgeon St.)
Chettle Ct. *N8* —1C **10**
Chetwode Ho. *NW8* —3A **36**
(off Grendon St.)
Chetwode Rd. *SW17* —3B **92**
Chetwood Wlk. *E6* —4F **45**
(off Greenwich Cres.)
Chetwynd Rd. *NW5* —1D **23**
Cheval Pl. *SW7* —4A **50**
Cheval St. *E14* —4C **56**
Chevening Rd. *NW6* —1F **33**
Chevening Rd. *SE10* —1B **72**
Cheverell Ho. *E2* —1C **40**
(off Pritchard's Rd.)
Cheverton Rd. *N19* —3F **9**
Chevet St. *E9* —2A **28**
Chevington. *NW2* —3B **20**
Cheviot Ct. *SE14* —2E **69**
(off Avonley Rd.)
Cheviot Gdns. *NW2* —4F **5**
Cheviot Gdns. *SE27* —4D **95**
Cheviot Ga. *NW2* —4A **6**
Cheviot Rd. *SE27* —5C **94**
Chevron Clo. *E16* —5C **44**
Cheylesmore Ho. *SW1*
(off Ebury Bri. Rd.) —1D **63**
Cheyne Clo. *NW4* —1E **5**
Cheyne Ct. *SW3* —2B **64**

Cheyne Gdns. *SW3* —2A **64**
Cheyne M. *SW3* —2A **64**
Cheyne Pl. *SW3* —2B **64**
Cheyne Row. *SW3* —2A **64**
Cheyne Wlk. *NW4* —1E **5**
Cheyne Wlk. *SW10 & SW3*
(in three parts) —3F **63**
Chichele Rd. *NW2* —2F **19**
Chicheley St. *SE1* —3B **52**
Chichester Clo. *SE3* —3E **73**
Chichester Ho. *NW6* —1C **34**
Chichester Ho. *SW9* —3C **66**
(off Brixton Rd.)
Chichester M. *SE27* —4C **94**
Chichester Rents. *WC2*
(off Chancery La.) —5C **38**
Chichester Rd. *E11* —5A **16**
Chichester Rd. *NW6* —1C **34**
Chichester Rd. *W2* —4D **35**
Chichester St. *SW1* —1E **65**
Chichester Way. *E14* —5F **57**
Chicksand Ho. *E1* —4C **40**
(off Chicksand St.)
Chicksand St. *E1* —4B **40**
(in two parts)
Chiddingstone. *SE13* —3E **85**
Chiddingstone St. *SW6*
—5C **62**
Chigwell Hill. *E1* —1D **55**
Chilcot Clo. *E14* —5D **43**
Childebert Rd. *SW17*
—2D **93**
Childeric Rd. *SE14* —3A **70**
Childerley St. *SW6* —4A **62**
Childers St. *SE8* —2A **70**
Child's Hill. —5C **6**
Childs Hill Wlk. *NW2* —5B **6**
(off Cricklewood La.)
Child's Pl. *SW5* —5C **48**
Child's St. *SW5* —5C **48**
Child's Wlk. *SW5* —5C **48**
Chilham Ho. *SE1* —4F **53**
Chilham Ho. *SE15* —2E **69**
Chilham Rd. *SE9* —4F **101**
Chilianwalla Memorial.
—2C **64**
(off Chelsea Embkmt.)
Chillerton Rd. *SW17* —5C **92**
Chillingworth Rd. *N7* —2C **24**
Chiltern Ct. *NW1* —3B **36**
(off Baker St.)
Chiltern Ct. *SE14* —3E **69**
(off Avonley Rd.)
Chiltern Gdns. *NW2* —5F **5**
Chiltern Ho. *SE17* —2F **67**
(off Portland St.)
Chiltern Rd. *E3* —3C **42**
Chiltern St. *W1* —4C **36**
Chilthorne Clo. *SE6* —5B **84**
Chilton Gro. *SE8* —5F **55**
Chiltonian Ind. Est. *SE12*
—4B **86**
Chilton St. *E2* —3B **40**
Chilver St. *SE10* —1B **72**
Chilworth M. *W2* —5F **35**
Chilworth St. *W2* —5E **35**

Chimney Ct. *E1* —2D **55**
(off Brewhouse La.)
China Ct. E1 —2D **55**
(off Asher Way)
China M. *SW2* —5B **80**
China Wharf. *SE16* —3C **54**
Chinbrook Cres. *SE12*
—3D **101**
Chinbrook Rd. *SE12* —3D **101**
Ching Ct. WC2 —5A **38**
(off Monmouth St.)
Chingley Clo. *Brom* —5A **100**
Chinnock's Wharf. E14
—1A **56**
Chipka St. *E14* —3E **57**
(in two parts)
Chipley St. *SE14* —2A **70**
Chippendale Ho. SW1 —1D **65**
(off Churchill Gdns.)
Chippendale St. *E5* —5F **13**
Chippenham Gdns. *NW6*
—2C **34**
Chippenham M. *W9* —3C **34**
Chippenham Rd. *W9* —3C **34**
Chipperfield Ho. SW3 —1A **64**
(off Ixworth Pl.)
Chipstead Gdns. *NW2* —4D **5**
Chipstead St. *SW6* —4C **62**
Chip St. *SW4* —1F **79**
Chisenhale Rd. *E3* —1A **42**
Chisholm Ct. *W6* —1C **60**
Chisledon Wlk. E9 —3B **28**
(off Osborne Rd.)
Chisley Rd. *N15* —1A **12**
Chiswell Sq. *SE3* —5D **73**
Chiswell St. *EC1* —4F **39**
Chiswick. —2A **60**
Chiswick Comn. Rd. *W4*
—5A **46**
Chiswick House. —2A **60**
Chiswick La. *W4* —1A **60**
Chiswick La. S. *W4* —2B **60**
Chiswick Mall. *W4 & W6*
—2B **60**
Chiswick Sq. *W4* —2A **60**
Chiswick Wharf. *W4* —2B **60**
Chitty St. *W1* —4E **37**
Chivalry Rd. *SW11* —3A **78**
Chobham Gdns. *SW19*
—2F **89**
Chobham Rd. *E15* —2F **29**
Cholmeley Cres. *N6* —2D **9**
Cholmeley Lodge. *N6* —3D **9**
Cholmeley Pk. *N6* —3D **9**
Cholmley Gdns. *NW6* —2C **20**
Cholmondeley Av. *NW10*
—1C **32**
Choppin's Ct. *E1* —2D **55**
Chopwell Clo. *E15* —4F **29**
Choumert Gro. *SE15* —5C **68**
Choumert Rd. *SE15* —1B **82**
Choumert Sq. *SE15* —5C **68**
Chow Sq. *E8* —2B **26**
Chrisp Ho. SE10 —2A **72**
(off Maze Hill)
Chrisp St. *E14* —4D **43**
(in two parts)

Christchurch Av. *NW6*
—5F **19**
Christchurch Ct. *NW10*
—5A **18**
Christchurch Hill. *NW3* —5F **7**
Christchurch Ho. SW2
—1B **94**
(off Christchurch Rd.)
Christchurch Pas. *NW3* —5E **7**
Christchurch Pl. *SW8* —5F **65**
Christchurch Rd. *N8* —1A **18**
Christchurch Rd. SW2
—1B **94**
Christchurch Sq. *E9* —5E **27**
Christchurch St. *SW3* —2B **64**
Christchurch Ter. SW3
—2B **64**
(off Christchurch St.)
Christchurch Way. *SE10*
—1A **72**
Christian Ct. *SE16* —2B **56**
Christian Pl. E1 —5C **40**
(off Burslem St.)
Christian St. *E1* —5C **40**
Christie Ct. *N19* —4A **10**
Christie Ho. SE10 —1B **72**
(off Blackwall La.)
Christie Rd. *E9* —3A **28**
Christina Sq. *N4* —3D **11**
Christina St. *EC2* —3A **40**
Christopher Clo. *SE16*
—3F **55**
Christopher Pl. *NW1* —2F **37**
Christophers M. *W11* —2A **48**
Christopher St. *EC2* —3F **39**
Chryssell Rd. *SW9* —3C **66**
Chubworthy St. *SE14* —2A **70**
Chudleigh Rd. *NW6* —4F **19**
Chudleigh Rd. *SE4* —3B **84**
Chudleigh St. *E1* —5F **41**
Chulsa Rd. *SE26* —5D **97**
Chumleigh St. *SE5* —2A **68**
Church App. *SE21* —3F **95**
Church Av. *NW1* —3D **23**
Churchbury Rd. *SE9* —5E **87**
Church Cloisters. EC3
(off Lovat La.) —1A **54**
Church Clo. *W8* —3D **49**
Church Ct. SE16 —3B **56**
(off Rotherhithe St.)
Church Cres. *E9* —4F **27**
Churchcroft Clo. *SW12*
—5C **78**
Churchdown. *Brom* —4A **100**
Church Entry. EC4 —5D **39**
(off Carter La.)
Churchfield Mans. *SW6*
—5B **62**
(off New King's Rd.)
Churchfields. *SE10* —2E **71**
Church Gth. N19 —4F **9**
(off Sth John's Gro.)
Church Ga. *SW6* —1A **76**
Church Grn. *SW9* —4C **66**
Church Gro. *SE13* —3D **85**
Church Hill. *SW19* —5B **90**

Church Ho. *SW1* —4F **51**
(off Gt. Smith St.)
Churchill Ct. *N4* —2C **10**
Churchill Gdns. *SW1* —1E **65**
Churchill Gdns. Rd. *SW1*
—1D **65**
Churchill Pl. *E14* —2D **57**
Churchill Rd. E16 —5E **45**
Churchill Rd. *NW2* —3D **19**
Churchill Rd. *NW5* —1D **23**
Churchill Wlk. *E9* —2E **27**
Church La. *E11* —3A **16**
Church La. *SW17* —5B **92**
Churchley Rd. *SE26* —4D **97**
Church Mead. SE5 —3E **67**
(off Camberwell Rd.)
Churchmead Rd. *NW10*
—3C **18**
Church Mt. *N2* —1F **7**
Church Pas. EC2 —5E **39**
(off Guildhall Yd.)
Church Path. *E11* —1C **16**
Church Path. *N5* —2D **25**
Church Path. *NW10* —4A **18**
Church Pl. *W1* —1E **51**
Church Ri. *SE23* —2F **97**
Church Rd. *E10* —3C **14**
Church Rd. *E12* —2F **31**
Church Rd. *N6* —1C **8**
Church Rd. *NW10* —4A **18**
Church Rd. *SW13* —5B **60**
Church Rd. *SW19* —5A **90**
Church Rd. Almshouses. E10
(off Church Rd.) —4D **15**
Church Rd. Ind. Est. *E10*
—3C **14**
Church Row. *NW3* —1E **21**
Church St. *E15* —5A **30**
Church St. *W2 & NW8*
—4F **35**
Church St. *W4* —2B **60**
Church St. Est. *NW8* —3F **35**
(in two parts)
Church St. N. *E15* —5A **30**
Church St. Pas. *E15* —5A **30**
Church Ter. *SE13* —1A **86**
Church Va. *SE23* —2F **97**
Church Wlk. *N6* —5C **8**
Church Wlk. *N16* —5F **11**
(in three parts)
Church Wlk. *NW2* —5B **6**
Church Wlk. *SW13* —4C **60**
Church Wlk. *SW15* —3D **75**
Churchward Ho. W14 —1B **62**
(off Ivatt Pl.)
Churchway. *NW1* —2F **37**
(in two parts)
Churchwell Path. *E9* —2E **27**
Churchyard Pas. *SE5* —5F **67**
Churchyard Row. *SE11*
—5D **53**
Churnfield. *N4* —4C **10**
Churston Av. *E13* —5D **31**
Churston Clo. *SW2* —1C **94**
Churton Pl. *SW1* —5E **51**
Churton St. *SW1* —5E **51**
Chusan Pl. *E14* —5B **42**

Chute Ho. SW9 —5C **66**
  (off Stockwell Pk. Rd.)
Cibber Rd. SE23 —2F **97**
Cicada Rd. SW18 —4E **77**
Cicely Ho. N1 —1F **35**
  (off Cochrane St.)
Cicely Rd. SE15 —4C **68**
Cinderford Way. Brom
  —4A **100**
Cinnamon Row. SW11
  —1E **77**
Cinnamon St. E1 —2D **55**
Cinnamon Wharf. SE1
  (off Shad Thames) —3B **54**
Circle, The. NW2 —5A **4**
Circle, The. SE1 —3B **54**
  (off Queen Elizabeth St.)
Circus Lodge. NW8 —2F **35**
  (off Circus Rd.)
Circus M. W1 —4B **36**
  (off Enford St.)
Circus Pl. EC2 —4F **39**
Circus Rd. NW8 —2F **35**
Circus St. SE10 —3E **71**
Cirencester St. W2 —4D **35**
Cissbury Ho. SE26 —3C **96**
Cissbury Rd. N15 —1F **11**
Citadel Pl. SE11 —1B **66**
Citizen Rd. N7 —1C **24**
Citrus Ho. SE8 —1B **70**
  (off Alverton St.)
City Bus. Cen. SE16 —4E **55**
City Central Est. EC1 —2E **39**
  (off Seward St.)
City Garden Row. N1 —1D **39**
City Harbour. E14 —4D **57**
City Heights. SE1 —2A **54**
  (off Weavers La.)
City of London. —5F **39**
City of London Almshouses.
  SW9 —2B **80**
City of London Crematorium.
  E12 —5F **17**
City Pavilion. EC1 —4D **39**
  (off Britton St.)
City Rd. EC1 —1D **39**
City Tower. EC2 —4F **39**
  (off Basinghall St.)
City Vw. Ct. SE22 —5C **82**
Clabon M. SW1 —4B **50**
Clack St. SE16 —3E **55**
Clacton Rd. E13 —2F **45**
Clacton Rd. E17 —1A **14**
Claire Ct. NW2 —3A **20**
Claire Pl. E14 —4C **56**
Clairview Rd. SW16 —5D **93**
Clairville Point. SE23 —3F **97**
  (off Dacres Rd.)
Clancarty Rd. SW6 —5C **62**
Clandeboye Ho. E15 —5B **30**
  (off John St.)
Clandon Ho. SE1 —3D **53**
  (off Webber St.)
Clandon St. SE8 —5C **70**
Clanfield Way. SE15 —3A **68**
Clanricarde Gdns. W2
  —1C **48**

Clapham. —2E **79**
Clapham Common. (Junct.)
  —2F **79**
Clapham Comn. N. Side.
  SW4 —2B **78**
Clapham Comn. S. Side.
  SW4 —4D **79**
Clapham Comn. W. Side.
  (in two parts) SW4 —2B **78**
Clapham Cres. SW4 —2F **79**
Clapham High St. SW4
  —2F **79**
Clapham Junction. —1A **78**
Clapham Junct. App. SW11
  —1A **78**
Clapham Mnr. Ct. SW4
  —1E **79**
Clapham Mnr. St. SW4
  —1E **79**
Clapham Park. —4F **79**
Clapham Pk. Est. SW4
  —4F **79**
Clapham Pk. Rd. SW4
  —2E **79**
Clapham Pk. Ter. SW4
  (off Kings Av.) —3A **80**
Clapham Rd. SW4 —1A **80**
Clapham Rd. Est. SW4
  —1A **80**
Clapton Comn. E5 —2B **12**
Clapton Park. —1F **27**
Clapton Pk. Est. E5 —1F **27**
Clapton Pas. E5 —2E **27**
Clapton Sq. E5 —2E **27**
Clapton Ter. N16 —3C **12**
Clapton Way. E5 —1C **26**
Clara Grant Ho. E14 —4C **56**
Clara Nehab Ho. NW11
  (off Leeside Cres.) —1B **6**
Clare Ct. WC1 —2A **38**
  (off Judd St.)
Claredale Ho. E2 —1D **41**
  (off Claredale St.)
Claredale St. E2 —1C **40**
Clare Gdns. E7 —1C **30**
Clare Gdns. W11 —5A **34**
Clare La. N1 —4E **25**
Clare Lawn Av. SW14 —3A **74**
Clare Mkt. WC2 —5B **38**
Clare M. SW6 —3D **63**
Claremont Clo. N1 —1C **38**
Claremont Clo. SW2 —1A **94**
Claremont Gro. W4 —3A **60**
Claremont Rd. E7 —2D **31**
Claremont Rd. E11 —5F **15**
Claremont Rd. N6 —2E **9**
Claremont Rd. NW2 —2F **5**
Claremont Rd. W9 —1A **34**
Claremont Sq. N1 —1C **38**
Claremont St. SE10 —2D **71**
Claremont Way. NW2 —3E **5**
  (in two parts)
Claremont Way Ind. Est.
  NW2 —3E **5**
Clarence Av. SW4 —4F **79**
Clarence Cres. SW4 —4F **79**
Clarence Gdns. NW1 —2D **37**

Clarence Ga. Gdns. NW1
  (off Glentworth St.) —3B **36**
Clarence House. —3E **51**
  (off St James's Pal.)
Clarence La. SW15 —4A **74**
Clarence M. E5 —2D **27**
Clarence M. SE16 —2F **55**
Clarence M. SW12 —5D **79**
Clarence Pas. NW1 —1A **38**
Clarence Pl. E5 —2D **27**
Clarence Rd. E5 —1D **27**
Clarence Rd. E12 —1F **31**
Clarence Rd. E16 —3A **44**
Clarence Rd. NW6 —4B **20**
Clarence Rd. SE9 —2F **101**
Clarence Rd. SW19 —5D **91**
Clarence Ter. NW1 —3B **36**
Clarence Wlk. SW4 —5A **66**
Clarence Way. NW1 —4D **23**
Clarendon Clo. E9 —4E **27**
Clarendon Clo. W2 —1A **50**
Clarendon Clo. NW2 —4E **19**
Clarendon Cross. W11
  —1A **48**
Clarendon Dri. SW15 —2E **75**
Clarendon Flats. W1 —5C **36**
  (off Balderton St.)
Clarendon Gdns. W9 —3E **35**
Clarendon Gro. NW1 —2F **37**
Clarendon Ho. NW1 —1E **37**
  (off Werrington St.)
Clarendon M. W2 —1A **50**
Clarendon Pl. W2 —1A **50**
Clarendon Ri. SE13 —2E **85**
Clarendon Rd. E11 —3F **15**
Clarendon Rd. E17 —1D **15**
Clarendon Rd. W11 —1A **48**
Clarendon St. SW1 —1D **65**
Clarendon Ter. W9 —3E **35**
Clarendon Wlk. W11 —5A **34**
Clarens St. SE6 —2B **98**
Clare Pl. SW15 —5B **74**
Clare Rd. E11 —1F **15**
Clare Rd. NW10 —4C **18**
Clare Rd. SE14 —4B **70**
Clare St. E2 —1D **41**
Clareville Gro. SW7 —5E **49**
Clareville Gro. M. SW7
  (off Clareville St.) —5E **49**
Clareville St. SW7 —5E **49**
Clarewood Ct. W1 —4B **36**
  (off Seymour Pl.)
Clarewood Wlk. SW9
  —2C **80**
Clarges M. W1 —2D **51**
Clarges St. W1 —2D **51**
Claribel Rd. SW9 —5D **67**
Claridge Ct. SW6 —5B **62**
Clarion Ho. SW1 —1E **65**
  (off Moreton Pl.)
Clarion Ho. W1 —5F **37**
  (off St Anne's Ct.)
Clarissa Ho. E14 —5D **43**
Clarissa St. E8 —5B **26**
Clarke Path. N16 —3C **12**
Clarke's M. W1 —4C **36**
Clarkson Rd. E16 —5B **44**

Clarkson Row. NW1 —1E 37
(off Mornington Ter.)
Clarkson St. E2 —2D 41
Clark's Pl. EC2 —5A 40
Clark St. E1 —4D 41
Claude Rd. E10 —4E 15
Claude Rd. E13 —5D 31
Claude Rd. SE15 —5D 69
Claude St. E14 —5C 56
Claudia Jones Way. SW2
—4A 80
Claudia Pl. SW19 —1A 90
Claughton Rd. E13 —1E 45
Clavell St. SE10 —2E 71
Claverdale Rd. SW2 —5B 80
Clavering Av. SW13 —2D 61
Clavering Ho. SE13 —2F 85
(off Blessington Rd.)
Clavering Rd. E12 —3F 17
Claverton St. SW1 —1E 65
Clave St. E1 —2E 55
Claxton Gro. W6 —1F 61
Claxton Path. SE4 —2F 85
(off Coston Wlk.)
Claybank Gro. SE13 —1D 85
Claybridge Rd. SE12
—4E 101
Claybrook Rd. W6 —2F 61
Claydon. SE17 —5E 53
(off Deacon Way)
Clayhill Cres. SE9 —4F 101
Claylands Pl. SW8 —3C 66
Claylands Rd. SW8 —2B 66
Claypole Ct. E17 —1C 14
(off Yunus Khan Clo.)
Claypole Rd. E15 —1E 43
Clays La. E15 —2D 29
Clays La. Clo. E15 —2D 29
Clay St. W1 —4B 36
Clayton M. SE10 —4F 71
Clayton Rd. SE15 —4C 68
Clayton St. SE11 —2C 66
Clearbrook Way. E1 —5E 41
Clearwater Ter. W11 —3A 48
(off Lorne Gdns.)
Clearwell Dri. W9 —3D 35
Cleaver Ho. NW3 —4B 22
Cleaver Sq. SE11 —1C 66
Cleaver St. SE11 —1C 66
Cleeve Hill. SE23 —1D 97
Cleeve Way. SW15 —5B 74
Cleeve Workshops. E1
(off Boundary Rd.) —2A 40
Clegg Ho. SE3 —2D 87
Clegg St. E1 —2D 55
Clegg St. E13 —1C 44
Clematis St. W12 —1C 46
Clem Attlee Ct. SW6 —2B 62
Clem Attlee Pde. SW6
(off N. End Rd.) —2B 62
Clemence St. E14 —4B 42
Clement Av. SW4 —2F 79
Clement Clo. NW6 —4E 19
Clement Ho. SE8 —5A 56
Clement Ho. W10 —4E 33
(off Dalgarno Gdns.)
Clementina Rd. E10 —3B 14

Clement Rd. SW19 —5A 90
Clement's Av. E16 —1C 58
Clement's Inn. WC2 —5B 38
Clement's Inn Pas. WC2
(off Grange Ct.) —5B 38
Clements La. EC4 —1F 53
Clement's Rd. SE16 —4C 54
Clemson Ho. E8 —5B 26
(off Queensbridge Rd.)
Clennam St. SE1 —3E 53
Clenston M. W1 —5B 36
Cleopatra's Needle. —1B 52
Clephane Rd. N1 —3E 25
Clephane Rd. N. N1 —3E 25
Clere Pl. EC2 —3F 39
Clere St. EC2 —3F 39
Clerkenwell. —3C 38
Clerkenwell Clo. EC1 —3C 38
(in two parts)
Clerkenwell Grn. EC1 —3C 38
Clerkenwell Rd. EC1 —3C 38
Clermont Rd. E9 —5E 27
Clevedon Clo. N16 —5B 12
Clevedon Mans. NW5 —1C 22
Clevedon Pas. N16 —4B 12
Cleve Ho. NW6 —4D 21
Cleveland Av. W4 —5B 46
Cleveland Gdns. N4 —1E 11
Cleveland Gdns. NW2 —4F 5
Cleveland Gdns. SW13
—5B 60
Cleveland Gdns. W2 —5E 35
Cleveland Gro. E1 —3E 41
Cleveland Mans. SW9
(off Mowll St.) —3C 66
Cleveland Mans. W9 —3C 34
Cleveland M. W1 —4E 37
Cleveland Pl. SW1 —2E 51
Cleveland Rd. N1 —4F 25
Cleveland Rd. SW13 —5B 60
Cleveland Row. SW1 —2E 51
Cleveland Sq. W2 —5E 35
Cleveland St. W1 —3D 37
Cleveland Ter. W2 —5E 35
Cleveland Way. E1 —3E 41
Cleveley Clo. SE7 —5E 59
Cleveleys Rd. E5 —5D 13
Cleverly Est. W12 —2C 46
Cleve Rd. NW6 —4D 21
Cleves Rd. E6 —5F 31
Clewer Ct. E10 —3C 14
(off Leyton Grange Est.)
Cley Ho. SE4 —2F 83
Clichy Est. E1 —4E 41
Clifden Rd. E5 —2E 27
Cliffe Ho. SE10 —1B 72
(off Blackwall La.)
Clifford Clo. W2 —4D 35
(off Westbourne Pk. Vs.)
Clifford Dri. SW9 —2D 81
Clifford Gdns. NW10 —1E 33
Clifford Haigh Ho. SW6
—3F 61
Clifford Ho. W14 —5B 48
(off Edith Vs.)
Clifford Rd. E16 —3B 44
Clifford Rd. N1 —5A 26

Clifford's Inn Pas. WC2
—5C 38
Clifford St. W1 —1E 51
Clifford Way. NW10 —1B 18
Cliff Rd. NW1 —3F 23
Cliffsend Ho. SW9 —4C 66
(off Cowley Rd.)
Cliff Ter. SE8 —5C 70
Cliffview Rd. SE13 —1C 84
Cliff Vs. NW1 —3F 23
Cliff Wlk. E16 —4B 44
(in two parts)
Clifton Av. W12 —2B 46
Clifton Ct. N4 —4C 10
Clifton Ct. NW8 —3F 35
(off Maida Va.)
Clifton Ct. SE15 —3D 69
Clifton Cres. SE15 —3D 69
Clifton Est. SE15 —4D 69
Clifton Gdns. N15 —1B 12
Clifton Gdns. NW11 —1B 6
Clifton Gdns. W4 —5A 46
(in two parts)
Clifton Gdns. W9 —3E 35
Clifton Gro. E8 —3C 26
Clifton Hill. NW6 —1D 35
Clifton Ho. E2 —2B 40
(off Club Row)
Clifton Ho. E11 —4A 16
Clifton Pl. SE16 —3E 55
Clifton Pl. W2 —5F 35
Clifton Ri. SE14 —3A 70
(in two parts)
Clifton Rd. E7 —3E 31
Clifton Rd. E16 —4A 44
Clifton Rd. N8 —1F 9
Clifton Rd. NW10 —1C 32
Clifton Rd. SW19 —5F 89
Clifton Rd. W9 —3E 35
Clifton St. EC2 —4A 40
Clifton Ter. N4 —4C 10
Clifton Vs. W9 —4E 35
Cliftonville Ct. SE12 —1C 100
Clifton Wlk. W6 —5D 47
(off King St.)
Clifton Way. SE15 —3D 69
Climsland Ho. SE1 —2C 52
Clinch Ct. E16 —4C 44
(off Plymouth Rd.)
Clinger Ct. N1 —5A 26
Clink Exhibition, The.
(off Clink St.) —2F 53
Clink St. SE1 —2F 53
Clink Wharf. SE1 —2F 53
(off Clink St.)
Clinton Ho. SE8 —2C 70
Clinton Rd. E3 —2A 42
Clinton Rd. E7 —1C 30
Clipper Clo. SE16 —3F 55
Clipper Ho. E14 —1E 71
Clipper Way. SE13 —2E 85
Clipstone M. W1 —4E 37
Clipstone St. W1 —4D 37
Clissold Ct. N4 —4E 11
Clissold Cres. N16 —5F 11
Clissold Rd. N16 —5F 11
Clitheroe Rd. SW9 —5A 66

Clitterhouse Cres. *NW2*
—3E **5**
Clitterhouse Rd. *NW2* —3E **5**
Clive Ct. W9 —3E **35**
(off Maida Va.)
Cliveden Pl. *SW1* —5C **50**
Clive Ho. SE10 —2E **71**
(off Haddo St.)
Clive Lloyd Ho. N15 —1E **11**
(off Woodlands Pk. Rd.)
Clive Lodge. *NW4* —1F **5**
Clive Pas. *SE21* —3F **95**
Clive Rd. *SE21* —3F **95**
Clive Rd. *SW19* —5A **92**
Cloak La. *EC4* —1E **53**
Clochar Ct. *NW10* —5B **18**
Clock Ho. *E3* —2E **43**
Clockhouse Clo. *SW19*
—2E **89**
Clock House Pde. *E11* .
—1D **17**
Clockhouse Pl. *SW15*
—4A **76**
Clock Pl. SE11 —5D **53**
(off Newington Butts)
Clock Tower M. *N1* —5E **25**
Clock Tower Pl. *N7* —3A **24**
Cloister Rd. *NW2* —5B **6**
Cloisters Bus. Cen. SW8
—3D **65**
(off Battersea Pk. Rd.)
Cloisters, The. E1 —4B **40**
(off Commercial St.)
Cloisters, The. *SW9* —4C **66**
Clonbrock Rd. N16 —1A **26**
Cloncurry St. *SW6* —5F **61**
Clonmel Rd. *SW6* —3B **62**
Clonmore St. *SW18* —1B **90**
Clorane Gdns. *NW3* —5C **6**
Close, The. *SE3* —5F **71**
Cloth Ct. EC1 —4D **39**
(off Cloth Fair)
Cloth Fair. *EC1* —4D **39**
Clothier St. *E1* —5A **40**
Cloth St. *EC1* —4E **39**
Cloudesdale Rd. SW17
—2D **93**
Cloudesley Pl. *N1* —5C **24**
Cloudesley Rd. *N1* —5C **24**
(in two parts)
Cloudesley Sq. *N1* —5C **24**
Cloudesley St. *N1* —5C **24**
Clova Rd. E7 —3B **30**
Clove Cres. E14 —1F **57**
Clove Hitch Quay. SW11
—1E **77**
Clovelly Ho. W2 —5E **35**
(off Hallfield Est.)
Clovelly Way. E1 —5E **41**
Clover Clo. E11 —4F **15**
Clover M. SW3 —2B **64**
Clove St. E13 —3C **44**
Clowders Rd. SE6 —3B **98**
Cloysters Grn. E1 —2C **54**
Club Row. E2 & E1 —3B **40**
Clunbury St. N1 —1F **39**
Cluny Est. *SE1* —4A **54**

Cluny M. *SW5* —5C **48**
Cluny Pl. *SE1* —4A **54**
Cluse Ct. N1 —1E **39**
(off St Peters St.,
in two parts)
Clutton St. E14 —4D **43**
Clyde Ct. NW1 —1F **37**
(off Hampden Clo.)
Clyde Flats. SW6 —3B **62**
(off Rhylston Rd.)
Clyde Pl. E10 —2D **15**
Clydesdale Ho. W11 —5B **34**
(off Clydesdale Rd.)
Clydesdale Rd. W11 —5B **34**
Clyde St. SE8 —2B **70**
Clyde Ter. SE23 —2E **97**
Clyde Va. SE23 —2E **97**
Clyde Wharf. E16 —2C **58**
Clyston St. SW8 —5E **65**
Coach & Horses Yd. W1
—1E **51**
Coach Ho. La. N5 —1D **25**
Coach Ho. La. SW19 —4F **89**
Coach Ho. M. SE1 —3A **54**
Coach Ho. M. SE23 —4F **83**
Coach Ho. Yd. NW3 —1E **21**
(off Hampstead High St.)
Coach Ho. Yd. SW18 —2D **77**
Coach Yd. M. N19 —3A **10**
Coaldale Wlk. SE21 —5E **81**
Coalecroft Rd. SW15 —2E **75**
Coalport Ho. SE11 —5C **52**
(off Walnut Tree Wlk.)
Coates Av. SW18 —4A **78**
Coate St. E2 —1C **40**
Cobalt Sq. SW8 —2B **66**
(off S. Lambeth Rd.)
Cobbetts Av. Ilf —1F **17**
Cobbett St. SW8 —3B **66**
Cobble La. N1 —4D **25**
Cobble M. N4 —5E **11**
Cobbold Ct. SW1 —5F **51**
(off Elverton St.)
Cobbold Ind. Est. NW10
—3B **18**
Cobbold M. W12 —3B **46**
Cobbold Rd. E11 —5B **16**
Cobbold Rd. NW10 —3B **18**
Cobbold Rd. W12 —3A **46**
Cobb's Ct. EC4 —5D **39**
(off Carter La.)
Cobb St. E1 —4B **40**
Cobden Ho. E2 —2C **40**
(off Nelson Gdns.)
Cobden Ho. NW1 —1E **37**
(off Arlington Rd.)
Cobden M. SE26 —5D **97**
Cobden Rd. E11 —5A **16**
Cobham Clo. SW11 —4A **78**
Cobham M. NW1 —4F **23**
Cobland Rd. SE12 —4E **101**
Coborn Rd. E3 —1B **42**
Coborn St. E3 —2B **42**
Cobourg Rd. SE5 —2B **68**
Cobourg St. NW1 —2E **37**
Coburg Clo. SW1 —5E **51**
(off Windsor Pl.)

Coburg Cres. SW2 —1B **94**
Cochrane Clo. NW8 —1F **35**
(off Cochrane St.)
Cochrane Ct. E10 —3C **14**
(off Leyton Grange Est.)
Cochrane Ho. E14 —3C **56**
(off Admirals Way)
Cochrane M. NW8 —1F **35**
Cochrane St. NW8 —1F **35**
Cockayne Way. SE8 —5A **56**
Cockburn Ho. SW1 —1F **65**
(off Aylesford St.)
Cockerell Rd. E17 —2A **14**
Cock Hill. E1 —4A **40**
Cock La. EC1 —4D **39**
Cockpit Steps. SW1 —3F **51**
(off Birdcage Wlk.)
Cockpit Yd. WC1 —4B **38**
Cockspur Ct. SW1 —2F **51**
Cockspur St. SW1 —2F **51**
Coda Cen., The. SW6 —3A **62**
Code St. E1 —3B **40**
Codicote Ho. SE8 —5F **55**
(off Chilton Gro.)
Codicote Ter. N4 —4D **11**
Codling Ho. E1 —2C **54**
Codling Clo. E1 —2C **54**
Codrington Ct. E1 —3D **41**
Codrington Ct. SE16 —1A **56**
Codrington Hill. SE23 —5A **84**
Codrington M. W11 —5A **34**
Cody Rd. E16 —3F **43**
Coffey St. SE8 —3C **70**
Coin St. SE1 —2C **52**
(in two parts)
Coity Rd. NW5 —3C **22**
Cokers La. SE21 —1F **95**
Coke St. E1 —5C **40**
Colas M. NW6 —5C **20**
Colbeck M. SW5 —5D **49**
Colberg Pl. N16 —2B **12**
Colborne Ho. E14 —1C **56**
Colby M. SE19 —5A **96**
Colby Rd. SE19 —5A **96**
Colchester Rd. E10 —2E **15**
Colchester Rd. E17 —1C **14**
Colchester St. E1 —5B **40**
Coldbath Sq. EC1 —3C **38**
Coldbath St. SE13 —4D **71**
(in two parts)
Cold Blow La. SE14 —3F **69**
(in two parts)
Coldharbour. E14 —3E **57**
Coldharbour La. SW9 & SE5
—2C **80**
Coldharbour Pl. SE5 —5E **67**
Coldstream Gdns. SW18
—4B **76**
Colebeck M. N1 —3D **25**
Colebert Av. E1 —3E **41**
Colebert Ho. E1 —3E **41**
(off Colebert Av.)
Colebrook Clo. SW15 —5F **75**
Colebrook Ct. SW3 —5A **50**
(off Makins St.)
Colebrooke Dri. E11 —2E **17**
Colebrooke Pl. N1 —5D **25**
Colebrooke Row. EC1 —1D **39**

Colebrook Ho. E14 —5D 43
Coleby Path. SE5 —3F 67
Colechurch Ho. SE1 —1C 68 (off Avondale Sq.)
Coleford Rd. SW18 —3E 77
Colegrave Rd. E15 —2F 29
Colegrove Rd. SE15 —2B 68
Coleherne Ct. SW5 —1D 63
Coleherne Mans. SW5 —1D 63 (off Old Brompton Rd.)
Coleherne M. SW10 —1D 63
Coleherne Rd. SW10 —1D 63
Colehill Gdns. SW6 —5A 62
Colehill La. SW6 —4A 62
Cole Ho. SE1 —3C 52 (off Baylis Rd.)
Coleman Fields. N1 —5E 25
Coleman Mans. N8 —2A 10
Coleman Rd. SE5 —3A 68
Coleman St. EC2 —5F 39
Coleman St. Bldgs. EC2 (off Coleman St.) —5F 39
Colenso Rd. E5 —1E 27
Coleraine Rd. SE3 —2B 72
Coleridge Av. E12 —3F 31
Coleridge Clo. SW8 —5D 65
Coleridge Ct. W14 —4F 47 (off Blythe Rd.)
Coleridge Gdns. NW6 —4E 21
Coleridge Ho. SE17 —1E 67 (off Browning St.)
Coleridge Ho. SW1 —1E 65 (off Churchill Gdns.)
Coleridge La. N8 —1A 10
Coleridge Rd. N4 —4C 10
Coleridge Rd. N8 —1F 9
Coles Grn. Ct. NW2 —4C 4
Coles Grn. Rd. NW2 —3C 4
Coleshill Flats. SW1 —5C 50 (off Pimlico Rd.)
Colestown St. SW11 —5A 64
Cole St. SE1 —3E 53
Colet Gdns. W14 —5F 47
Colet Ho. SE17 —1D 67 (off Doddington Gro.)
Colette Ct. SE16 —3F 55 (off Eleanor Clo.)
Coley St. WC1 —3B 38
Colfe & Hatcliffe Glebe. SE13 —3E 85 (off Lewisham High St.)
Colfe Rd. SE23 —1A 98
Colin Dri. NW9 —1B 4
Colinette Rd. SW15 —2E 75
Colin Rd. NW10 —3C 18
Colin Winter Ho. E1 —3E 41 (off Nicholas Rd.)
Coliston Pas. SW18 —5C 76
Coliston Rd. SW18 —5C 76
Collamore Av. SW18 —1A 92
Collard Pl. NW1 —4D 23
Collards Almshouses. E17 (off Maynard Rd.) —1E 15
College App. SE10 —2E 71
College Clo. E5 —2E 27
College Ct. SW3 —1B 64 (off West Rd.)
College Ct. W6 —1E 61 (off Queen Caroline St.)
College Cres. NW3 —3E 21 (in two parts)
College Cross. N1 —4C 24
College E. E1 —4B 40
College Gdns. SE21 —1A 96
College Gdns. SW17 —2A 92 (in three parts)
College Gdns. Ilf —1F 17
College Gro. NW1 —5E 23
College Hill. EC4 —1E 53
College La. NW5 —1D 23
College Mans. NW6 —5A 20 (off Winchester Av.)
College M. N1 —4C 24 (in two parts)
College M. SW1 —4A 52 (off Gt. College St.)
College M. SW18 —3D 77
College of Arms. —1D 53 (off Queen Victoria St.)
College Pde. NW6 —5A 20
College Park. —2D 33
College Pk. Clo. SE13 —2F 85
College Pl. NW1 —5E 23
College Pl. SW10 —3E 63
College Point. E15 —3B 30
College Rd. E17 —1E 15
College Rd. NW10 —1E 33
College Rd. SE21 & SE19 —5A 82
College Row. E9 —2F 27
College St. EC4 —1E 53
College Ter. E3 —2B 42
College Vw. SE9 —1F 101
College Yd. NW5 —1D 23
Collent St. E9 —3E 27
Collerston Ho. SE10 —1B 72 (off Armitage Rd.)
Colless Rd. N15 —1B 12
Collett Rd. SE16 —4C 54
Collier St. N1 —1B 38
Collingbourne Rd. W12 —2D 47
Collingham Gdns. SW5 —5D 49
Collingham Pl. SW5 —5D 49
Collingham Rd. SW5 —5D 49
Collington St. SE10 —1F 71
Collingtree Rd. SE26 —4E 97
Collingwood Ho. E1 —3D 41 (off Darling Row)
Collingwood Ho. SW1 (off Dolphin Sq.) —1F 65
Collingwood Ho. W1 —4E 37 (off Clipstone St.)
Collingwood Rd. E17 —1C 14
Collingwood St. E1 —3D 41
Collins Ct. E8 —3C 26
Collins Ho. E15 —5B 30 (off John St.)
Collins Ho. SE10 —1B 72 (off Armitage Rd.)
Collinson Ct. SE1 —3E 53 (off Gt. Suffolk St.)
Collinson Ho. SE15 —3C 68 (off Peckham Pk. Rd.)
Collinson St. SE1 —3E 53
Collinson Wlk. SE1 —3E 53
Collins Rd. N5 —1E 25
Collins Sq. SE3 —5B 72
Collins St. SE3 —5A 72 (in two parts)
Collin's Yd. N1 —5D 25
Colls Rd. SE15 —4E 69
Collyer Pl. SE15 —4C 68
Colman Rd. E16 —4E 45
Colmans Wharf. E14 —4D 43
Colmar Clo. E1 —3F 41
Colmore M. SE15 —4D 69
Colnbrook St. SE1 —4D 53
Colne Rd. E5 —1A 28
Colne St. E13 —2C 44
Cologne Rd. SW11 —2F 77
Colombo St. SE1 —2D 53
Colomb St. SE10 —1A 72
Colonnade. WC1 —3A 38
Colonnades, The. W2 —5D 35
Colonnade, The. SE8 —5B 56
Colonnade Wlk. SW1 —5D 51
Colosseum Ter. NW1 —2D 37 (off Albany St.)
Colour Ct. SW1 —2E 51 (off St James' Pal.)
Colson Way. SW16 —4E 93
Colstead Ho. E1 —5D 41 (off Watney Mkt.)
Colston Rd. E7 —3F 31
Colthurst Cres. N4 —4D 11
Coltman Ho. E14 —5A 42
Coltman Ho. SE10 —2E 71 (off Welland St.)
Colt St. E14 —1B 56
Columbas. E14 —2C 56
Columbas Dri. NW3 —3F 7
Columbia Ct. SE16 —4E 55 (off Surrey Quays Rd.)
Columbia Rd. E2 —2B 40
Columbia Rd. E16 —3B 44
Columbia Wharf. SE16 —2B 56
Columbine Av. E6 —4F 45
Columbine Way. SE13 —5E 71
Columbus Ct. SE16 —2E 55 (off Rotherhithe St.)
Columbus Courtyard. E14 —2C 56
Colva Wlk. N19 —4D 9
Colverson Ho. E1 —4E 41 (off Lindley St.)
Colvestone Cres. E8 —2B 26
Colview Ct. SE9 —1F 101
Colville Est. N1 —5A 26
Colville Est. W. E2 —2B 40 (off Turin St.)
Colville Gdns. W11 —5B 34 (in two parts)
Colville Houses. W11 —5B 34
Colville M. W11 —5B 34
Colville Pl. W1 —4E 37

Colville Rd. *E11* —5E **15**
Colville Rd. *W11* —5B **34**
Colville Sq. *W11* —5B **34**
Colville Sq. M. *W11* —5B **34**
Colville Ter. *W11* —5B **34**
Colvin Clo. *SE26* —5E **97**
Colvin Rd. *E6* —4F **31**
Colwell Rd. *SE22* —3B **82**
Colwick Clo. *N6* —2F **9**
Colwith Rd. *W6* —2E **61**
Colworth Gro. *SE17* —5E **53**
Colworth Rd. *E11* —1A **16**
Colwyn Clo. *SW16* —5E **93**
Colwyn Grn. *NW9* —1A **4**
 (off Snowden Dri.)
Colwyn Ho. *SE1* —4C **52**
Colwyn Rd. *NW2* —5D **5**
Colyer Clo. *N1* —1B **38**
Colyton Rd. *SE22* —3D **83**
Combe Av. *SE3* —3B **72**
Combedale Rd. *SE10*
 —1C **72**
Combemartin Rd. *SW18*
 —5A **76**
Combe M. *SE3* —3B **72**
Comber Clo. *NW2* —5D **5**
Comber Gro. *SE5* —3E **67**
Comber Ho. *SE5* —3E **67**
Combermere Rd. *SW9*
 —1B **80**
Comberton Rd. *E5* —4D **13**
Combe, The. *NW1* —2D **37**
 (in two parts)
Comeragh M. *W14* —1A **62**
Comeragh Rd. *W14* —1A **62**
Comerell Pl. *SE10* —1B **72**
Comerford Rd. *SE4* —2A **84**
Comet Clo. *E12* —1F **31**
Comet Pl. *SE8* —3C **70**
 (in two parts)
Comet St. *SE8* —3C **70**
Commercial Rd. *E1* —5C **40**
Commercial St. *E1* —3B **40**
Commercial Way. *SE15*
 —3B **68**
Commercial Wharf. *E1*
 —2A **42**
Commerell St. *SE10* —1A **72**
Commodity Quay. *E1* —1B **54**
Commodore St. *SE8* —4C **70**
 (off Albyn Rd.)
Commodore Ho. *E14* —1E **57**
Commodore Sq. *SW10*
 —4E **63**
Commodore St. *E1* —3A **42**
Commondale. *SW15* —1E **75**
Commonfield La. *SW17*
 —5A **92**
Common Rd. *SW13* —1D **75**
Commonwealth Av. *W12*
 (in three parts) —1D **47**
Community La. *N7* —2F **23**
Community Rd. *E15* —2F **29**
Como Rd. *SE23* —2A **98**
Compass Ct. *SE1* —2B **54**
 (off Shad Thames.)
Compass Ho. *SW18* —2D **77**

Compass Point. *E14* —1B **56**
 (off Grenade St.)
Compayne Gdns. *NW6*
 —4D **21**
Compton Av. *E6* —1F **45**
Compton Av. *N1* —3D **25**
Compton Av. *N6* —2A **8**
Compton Clo. *E3* —4C **42**
Compton Clo. *NW1* —2D **37**
 (off Robert St.)
Compton Clo. *NW11* —5F **5**
Compton Ct. *SE19* —5A **96**
Compton Pas. *EC1* —3D **39**
Compton Pl. *WC1* —3A **38**
Compton Rd. *N1* —3D **25**
Compton Rd. *NW10* —2F **33**
Compton Rd. *SW19* —5B **90**
Compton St. *EC1* —3D **39**
Compton Ter. *N1* —3D **25**
Comus Ho. *SE17* —5A **54**
 (off Comus Pl.)
Comus Pl. *SE17* —5A **54**
Comyn Rd. *SW11* —2A **78**
Comyns Clo. *E16* —4B **44**
Conant Ho. *SE11* —2D **67**
 (off St Agnes Pl.)
Conant M. *E1* —1C **54**
Concanon Rd. *SW2* —2B **80**
Concert Hall App. *SE1* —2B **52**
Concord Cen., The. *W12*
 —3F **47**
Concordia Wharf. *E14*
 —2E **57**
Condell Rd. *SW8* —4E **65**
Conder St. *E14* —5A **42**
Condray Pl. *SW11* —3A **64**
Conduit Av. *SE10* —4F **71**
Conduit Ct. *WC2* —1A **52**
 (off Floral St.)
Conduit M. *W2* —5F **35**
Conduit Pas. *W2* —5F **35**
 (off Conduit Pl.)
Conduit Pl. *W2* —5F **35**
Conduit Pl. *W2* —1D **51**
Conduit St. *W1* —1D **51**
Conduit St. *WC1* —3B **38**
Conewood St. *N5* —5D **11**
Coney Acre. *SE21* —1E **95**
Coney Way. *SW8* —2B **66**
Congers Ho. *SE8* —3C **70**
Congreve Ho. *N16* —2A **26**
Congreve St. *SE17* —5A **54**
Congreve Wlk. *E16* —4F **45**
 (off Stansfield Rd.)
Conifer Gdns. *SW16* —3A **94**
Conifer Ho. *SE4* —2B **84**
 (off Brockley Rd.)
Coniger Rd. *SW6* —5C **62**
Coningham Ct. *SW10*
 (off King's Rd.) —3E **63**
Coningham M. *W12* —2C **46**
Coningham Rd. *W12* —3D **47**
Coningsby Rd. *N4* —2D **11**
Conington Rd. *SE13* —5D **71**
Conisborough Cres. *SE6*
 —3E **99**
Conisbrough. *NW1* —5E **23**
 (off Bayham St.)

Coniston. *NW1* —2E **37**
 (off Harrington St.)
Coniston Clo. *SW13* —3B **60**
Coniston Ct. *SE16* —3F **55**
 (off Eleanor Clo.)
Coniston Ct. *W2* —5A **36**
 (off Kendal St.)
Conistone Way. *N7* —4A **24**
Coniston Ho. *E3* —3B **42**
 (off Southern Gro.)
Coniston Ho. *SE5* —3E **67**
 (off Wyndham Rd.)
Coniston Rd. *Brom* —5A **100**
Coniston Wlk. *E9* —2E **27**
Conlan St. *W10* —3A **34**
Conley Rd. *NW10* —3A **18**
Conley St. *SE10* —1A **72**
Connaught Bri. *E16* —2F **59**
Connaught Bus. Cen. *NW9*
 —1B **4**
Connaught Ct. *E11* —3F **15**
Connaught Ct. *E16* —1E **59**
 (in two parts)
Connaught Rd. *E17* —1C **14**
Connaught Clo. *W2* —5A **36**
 (off Connaught St.)
Connaught Ho. *W1* —1D **51**
 (off Davies St.)
Connaught Lodge. *N4* —2C **10**
 (off Connaught Rd.)
Connaught M. *SW6* —4A **62**
Connaught Pl. *W2* —1B **50**
Connaught Rd. *E11* —3F **15**
Connaught Rd. *E16* —1E **59**
 (in two parts)
Connaught Rd. *N4* —2C **10**
Connaught Rd. *NW10* —5A **18**
Connaught Sq. *W2* —5B **36**
Connaught St. *W2* —5A **36**
Connell Ct. *SE14* —2F **69**
 (off Myers La.)
Connett Ho. *E2* —1C **40**
 (off Mansford St.)
Connolly Pl. *SW19* —5E **91**
Connor Clo. *E11* —2A **16**
Connor St. *SW11* —4D **65**
Connor St. *E9* —5F **27**
Conrad Ho. *N16* —2A **26**
 (off Matthias Rd.)
Conrad Ho. *SW8* —3A **66**
 (off Wyvil Rd.)
Consec Farriers M. *SE15*
 —1E **83**
Consort Ho. *E14* —1D **71**
Consort Ho. *W2* —1D **49**
 (off Queensway)
Consort Lodge. *NW8* —5B **22**
 (off Prince Albert Rd.)
Consort Rd. *SE15* —4D **69**
Cons St. *SE1* —3C **52**
Constable Av. *E16* —2D **59**
Constable Clo. *NW11* —1D **7**
Constable Ct. *SE16* —1D **69**
 (off Stubbs Dri.)
Constable Cres. *N15* —1C **12**
Constable Ho. *NW3* —4B **22**
Constable Wlk. *SE21* —3A **96**
Constance St. *E16* —2F **59**
Constant Ho. *E14* —1D **57**

Constantine Rd. NW3 —1A 22
Constitution Hill. SW1 —3D 51
Content St. SE17 —5F 53
Convent Gdns. W11 —5A 34
Convent Hill. SE19 —5E 95
Conway Gro. W3 —4A 32
Conway Ho. E14 —5C 56
Conway Ho. E17 —1A 14
(off Mission Gro.)
Conway M. W1 —3E 37
(off Conway St.)
Conway Rd. NW2 —4E 5
Conway St. W1 —3E 37
(in two parts)
Conybeare. NW3 —4A 22
Conyer's Rd. SW16 —5F 93
Conyer St. E3 —1A 42
Cook Ct. SE16 —2E 55
(off Rotherhithe St.)
Cookes Clo. E11 —4B 16
Cookham Cres. SE16 —3F 55
Cookham Ho. E2 —3B 40
(off Montclare St.)
Cook's Rd. E15 —1D 43
Cook's Rd. SE17 —2D 67
Coolfin Rd. E16 —5C 44
Coolhurst Rd. N8 —1F 9
Cool Oak La. NW9 —3A 4
Coomassie Rd. W9 —3B 34
Coombe Ho. N7 —2F 23
Coombe Lodge. SE7 —2E 73
Coombe Pk. King T —5A 88
Coomber Ho. SW6 —1D 77
(off Wandsworth Bri. Rd.)
Coombe Rd. NW10 —5A 4
Coombe Rd. SE26 —4D 97
Coombe Rd. W4 —1A 60
Coombs St. N1 —1D 39
Coomer M. SW6 —2B 62
Coomer Pl. SW6 —2B 62
Coomer Rd. SW6 —2B 62
Cooper Clo. SE1 —3C 52
Cooper Ct. E15 —2D 29
Cooper Ho. NW8 —3F 35
(off Lyons Pl.)
Cooper Rd. NW4 —1F 5
Cooper Rd. NW10 —2B 18
Coopersale Rd. E9 —2F 27
Coopers Clo. E1 —3E 41
Coopers La. E10 —3D 15
Coopers La. NW1 —1F 37
Cooper's La. SE12 —2D 101
Cooper's Rd. SE1 —1B 68
Coopers Row. EC3 —1B 54
Cooper St. E16 —4B 44
Coopers Wlk. E15 —2A 30
Cooper's Yd. SE19 —5A 96
Cope Ho. EC1 —2E 39
(off Bath St.)
Copeland Dri. E14 —5C 56
Copeland Ho. SE11 —4C 52
(off Lambeth Wlk.)
Copeland Rd. E17 —1D 15
Copeland Rd. SE15 —5C 68
Copeman Clo. SE26 —5E 97
Copenhagen Ho. N1 —5B 24
(off Barnsbury Est.)
Copenhagen Pl. E14 —5B 42
(in two parts)
Copenhagen St. N1 —5A 24
Cope Pl. W8 —4C 48
Copers Cope Rd. Beck —5B 98
Cope St. SE16 —5F 55
Copford Wlk. N1 —5E 25
(off Popham St.)
Copgate Path. SW16 —5B 94
Copleston M. SE15 —5B 68
Copleston Pas. SE5 —5B 68
Copleston Rd. SE15 —1B 82
Copley Clo. SE17 —2E 67
Copley Pk. SW16 —5B 94
Copley St. E1 —4F 41
Copnor Way. SE15 —3A 68
Coppelia Rd. SE3 —2B 86
Copperas St. SE8 —2D 71
Copperbeech Clo. NW3 —2F 21
Copperfield Ho. SE1 —3C 54
(off Wolseley St.)
Copperfield Ho. W1 —4C 36
(off Marylebone High St.)
Copperfield Ho. W11 —2F 47
(off St Ann's Rd.)
Copperfield Rd. E3 —3A 42
Copperfield St. SE1 —3D 53
Copper Mead Clo. NW2 —5E 5
Coppermill La. E17 —1E 13
Copper Mill La. SW17 —4E 91
Copper Row. SE1 —2B 54
(off Horselydown La.)
Coppice Dri. SW15 —4D 75
Coppock Clo. SW11 —5A 64
Copse Clo. SE7 —2D 73
Copthall Av. EC2 —5F 39
(in three parts)
Copthall Bldgs. EC2 —5F 39
(off Copthall Av.)
Copthall Clo. EC2 —5F 39
Copthorne Av. SW12 —5F 79
Coptic St. WC1 —4A 38
Coral Row. SW11 —1E 77
Coral St. SE1 —3C 52
Coram Ho. W4 —1A 60
(off Wood St.)
Coram Ho. WC1 —3A 38
(off Herbrand St.)
Coram St. WC1 —3A 38
Corbden Clo. SE15 —4B 68
Corbet Ct. EC3 —5F 39
Corbet Ho. N1 —1C 38
(off Barnsbury Est.)
Corbet Pl. E1 —4B 40
Corbett Ct. SE26 —4B 98
Corbett Ho. SW10 —2E 63
(off Cathcart Rd.)
Corbett Rd. E11 —1E 17
Corbetts La. SE16 —5E 55
(in two parts)
Corbetts Pas. SE16 —5E 55
(off Corbetts La.)
Corbetts Wharf. SE16 —3D 55
(off Bermondsey Wall E.)
Corbicum. E11 —2A 16
Corbidge Ct. SE8 —2D 71
Corbiere Ho. N1 —5A 26
(off De Beauvoir Est.)
Corbridge Cres. E2 —1D 41
Corbyn St. N4 —3A 10
Corby Way. E3 —3C 42
Cordelia Clo. SE24 —2D 81
Cordelia Ho. N1 —1A 40
(off Arden Est.)
Cordelia St. E14 —5D 43
Cording St. E14 —4D 43
Cordwainers Wlk. E13 —1C 44
Cord Way. E14 —4C 56
Cordwell Rd. SE13 —3A 86
Corelli Ct. SW5 —5C 48
(off W. Cromwell Rd.)
Corelli Rd. SE3 —5F 73
Corfe Ho. SW8 —3B 66
(off Dorset Rd.)
Corfield St. E2 —2D 41
Coriander Av. E14 —5F 43
Corinne Rd. N19 —1E 23
Corker Wlk. N7 —4B 10
Cork Sq. E1 —2D 55
Cork St. W1 —1E 51
Cork St. M. W1 —1E 51
(off Cork St.)
Cork Tree Ho. SE27 —5D 95
(off Lakeview Rd.)
Corlett St. NW1 —4A 36
Cormont Rd. SE5 —4D 67
Cormorant Ct. SE8 —2B 70
(off Pilot Clo.)
Cormorant Rd. E7 —2B 30
Cornbury Ho. SE8 —2B 70
(off Evelyn St.)
Cornelia St. N7 —3B 24
Cornell Building. E1 —5C 40
(off Coke St.)
Corner Fielde. SW2 —1B 94
Corner Grn. SE3 —5C 72
Corner Ho. St. WC2 —2A 52
(off Northumberland St.)
Corney Reach Way. W4 —3A 60
Corney Rd. W4 —2A 60
Cornflower Ter. SE22 —4D 83
Cornford Gro. SW12 —2D 93
Cornhill. EC3 —5F 39
Cornick Ho. SE16 —4D 55
(off Slippers Pl.)
Cornish Ho. SE17 —2D 67
(off Brandon Est.)
Cornmill La. SE13 —1E 85
Cornmow Dri. NW10 —2B 18
Cornthwaite Rd. E5 —5E 13
Cornwall Av. E2 —2E 41
Cornwall Cres. W11 —5A 34
Cornwall Gdns. NW10 —3D 19
Cornwall Gdns. SW7 —4D 49
Cornwall Gdns. Wlk. SW7 —4D 49
Cornwall Gro. W4 —1A 60
Cornwallis Ct. SW8 —4A 66
(off Lansdowne Grn.)
Cornwallis Ho. W12 —1D 47
(off India Way)

Cornwallis Rd. N19—4A 10
Cornwallis Sq. N19—4A 10
Cornwall Mans. SW10
(off Cremorne Rd.) —3E 63
Cornwall M. S. SW7—4E 49
Cornwall M. W. SW7—4D 49
Cornwall Rd. N4—2C 10
Cornwall Rd. N15—1F 11
Cornwall Rd. SE1—2C 52
Cornwall Sq. SE11 —1D 67
(off Seaton Clo.)
Cornwall St. E1—1D 55
Cornwall Ter. NW1—3B 36
Cornwall Ter. M. NW1 —3B 36
(off Allsop Pl.)
Corn Way. E11—5F 15
Cornwell Cres. E7—1E 31
Cornwood Dri. E1—5E 41
Corona Rd. SE12—5C 86
Coronation Av. N16—1B 26
Coronation Ct. E15—3B 30
Coronation Ct. W10 —4E 33
(off Brewster Gdns.)
Coronation Rd. E13—2E 45
Coronet St. N1—2A 40
Corporation Row. EC1—3C 38
Corporation St. E15—1A 44
Corporation St. N7—2A 24
Corrance Rd. SW2—2A 80
Corringham Ct. NW11—2C 6
Corringham Rd. NW11—2C 6
Corringway. NW11—2D 7
Corris Grn. NW9—1A 4
Corry Ho. E14—1D 57
Corsehill St. SW16—5E 93
Corsham St. N1—2F 39
Corsica St. N1—3D 25
Corsley Way. E9 —3B 28
(off Osborne Rd.)
Cortayne Rd. SW6—5B 62
Cortis Rd. SW15—4D 75
Cortis Ter. SW15—4D 75
Corunna Rd. SW8—4E 65
Corunna Ter. SW8—4E 65
Corvette Sq. SE10—2F 71
Coryton Path. W9 —3B 34
(off Ashmore Rd.)
Cosbycote Av. SE24—3E 81
Cosgrove Ho. E2 —5C 26
(off Whiston Rd.)
Cosmo Pl. WC1—4A 38
Cosmur Clo. W12—4B 46
Cossall Wlk. SE15—5D 69
Cosser St. SE1—4C 52
Costa St. SE15—5C 68
Coston Wlk. SE4—2F 83
Cosway Mans. NW1 —4A 36
(off Shroton St.)
Cosway St. NW1—4A 36
Cotail St. E14—4C 42
Coteford St. SW17—4B 92
Cotesbach Rd. E5—5E 13
Cotes Ho. NW8 —3A 36
(off Broadley St.)
Cotham St. SE17—5E 53
Cotherstone Rd. SW2—1B 94
Cotleigh Rd. NW6—4C 20
Cotman Clo. NW11—1E 7
Cotman Clo. SW15—4F 75
Cotman Ho. NW8 —1A 36
(off Townshend Est.)
Cotswold Ct. EC1 —3E 39
(off Gee St.)
Cotswold Gdns. E6—2F 45
Cotswold Gdns. NW2—4F 5
Cotswold Ga. NW2—3A 6
Cotswold M. SW11—4F 63
Cotswold St. SE27—4D 95
Cottage Clo. E1 —3E 41
(off Mile End Rd.)
Cottage Grn. SE5—3F 67
Cottage Gro. SW9—1A 80
Cottage Pl. SW3—4A 50
Cottage St. E14—1D 57
Cottage Wlk. N16—5B 12
Cottesbrook St. SE14—3A 70
Cottesloe Ho. NW8 —3A 36
(off Jerome Cres.)
Cottesloe M. SE1 —4C 52
(off Emery St.)
Cottesmore Ct. W8 —4D 49
(off Stanford Rd.)
Cottesmore Gdns. W8—4D 49
Cottingham Rd. SW8—3B 66
Cottington St. SE11—1C 66
Cottle Way. SE16 —3D 55
(off Paradise St.)
Cotton Av. W3—5A 32
Cotton Hill. Brom—4E 99
Cotton Ho. SW2—5A 80
Cotton Row. SW11—1E 77
Cottons Cen. SE1—2A 54
Cotton's Gdns. E2—2A 40
Cottons La. SE1—2F 53
Cotton St. E14—1E 57
Coulgate St. SE4—1A 84
Coulson St. SW3—1B 64
Coulter Rd. W6—4D 47
Councillor St. SE5—3E 67
Counter Ct. SE1 —2F 53
(off Borough High St.)
Counter St. SE1 —2A 54
(off Hays La.)
Countess Rd. NW5—2E 23
County Gro. SE5—4E 67
County Hall Apartments. SE1
—3B 52
(off Westminster Bri. Rd.)
County St. SE1—4E 53
Courland Gro. SW8—4F 65
Courland St. SW8—4F 65
(in two parts)
Courtauld Ho. E2 —5C 26
(off Goldsmiths Row)
Courtauld Institute Galleries.
(off Strand) —1B 52
Courtauld Rd. N19—3A 10
Courtenay Av. N6—2A 8
Courtenay M. E17—1A 14
Courtenay Pl. E17—1A 14
Courtenay Rd. E11—5B 16
Courtenay Sq. SE11—1C 66
Courtenay St. SE11—1C 66
Court Farm Rd. SE9—2F 101
Courtfield Gdns. SW5—5D 49
Courtfield Ho. WC1 —4C 38
(off Baldwins Gdns.)
Courtfield M. SW5—5E 49
Courtfield Rd. SW7—5E 49
Court Gdns. N7—3C 24
(in two parts)
Courthill Rd. SE13—2E 85
Courthope Ho. SE16 —4E 55
(off Lower Rd.)
Courthope Ho. SW8 —3A 66
(off Hartington Rd.)
Courthope Rd. NW3—1B 22
Courthope Rd. SW19—5A 90
Courtland Rd. E6—5F 31
Courtlands Av. SE12—3D 87
Court La. SE21—4A 82
Court La. Gdns. SE21—5A 82
Courtleigh. NW11—1B 6
Courtmead Clo. SE24—4E 81
Courtnell St. W2—5C 34
Courtney Ct. N7—2C 24
Courtney Ho. W14 —4A 48
(off Russell Rd.)
Courtney Rd. N7—2C 24
Courtrai Rd. SE23—4A 84
Courtside. N8—1F 9
Courtside. SE26—3D 97
Court St. E1—4D 41
Courtville Ho. W10 —2A 34
(off Third Av.)
Courtyard, The. N1—4B 24
Courtyard, The. NW1—4C 22
Cousin La. EC4—1F 53
Couthurst Rd. SE3—2D 73
Coutt's Cres. NW5—5C 8
Coutts Ho. SE7—1E 73
Couzens Ho. E3—4B 42
Covell Ct. SE8—3C 70
Covent Garden. —1A 52
Covent Garden. —1A 52
Covent Garden. WC2—1A 52
Coventry Clo. NW6—1C 34
Coventry Cross. E3—3E 43
Coventry Hall. SW16—5A 94
Coventry Rd. E1 & E2—3D 41
Coventry St. W1—1F 51
Coverdale Rd. NW2—4F 19
Coverdale Rd. W12—3D 47
Coverley Clo. E1—4C 40
Coverley Point. SE11 —5B 52
(off Tyers St.)
Coverton Rd. SW17—5A 92
Covington Way. SW16
(in two parts) —5B 94
Cowan Clo. E6—4F 45
Cowcross St. EC1—4D 39
Cowdenbeath Path. N1
—5B 24
Cowden St. SE6—4C 98
Cowdrey Rd. SW19—5D 91
Cowdry Rd. E9—3A 28
Cowick Rd. SW17—4B 92
Cowley La. E11—5A 16
Cowley Rd. E11—1D 17
Cowley Rd. SW9—4C 66
Cowley Rd. SW14—1A 74

Cowley Rd. *W3* —2B **46**
Cowley St. *SW1* —4A **52**
Cowling Clo. *W11* —2A **48**
Cowper Av. *E6* —4F **31**
Cowper St. *SE17* —1E **67**
(off Browning St.)
Cowper Rd. *SW1* —1F **65**
(off Aylesford St.)
Cowper Rd. *N16* —2A **26**
Cowper Rd. *SW19* —5E **91**
Cowper's Ct. *EC3* —5F **39**
(off Birchin La.)
Cowper St. *EC2* —3F **39**
Cowper Ter. *W10* —4F **33**
Cowthorpe Rd. *SW8* —4F **65**
Cox Ho. *W6* —2A **62**
(off Field Rd.)
Coxmount Rd. *SE7* —1F **73**
Cox's Ct. *E1* —4B **40**
(off Bell La.)
Coxson Way. *SE1* —3B **54**
Cox's Wlk. *SE21* & *SE26*
—1C **96**
Crabtree Clo. *E2* —1B **40**
Crabtree Ct. *E15* —2D **29**
Crabtree La. *SW6* —3E **61**
(in two parts)
Crabtree Wlk. *SE15* —4B **68**
(off Peckham Rd.)
Craddock St. *NW5* —3C **22**
Crafts Council & Gallery.
—1C **38**
Cragie Ho. *SE1* —5B **54**
(off Balaclava Rd.)
Craigerne Rd. *SE3* —3D **73**
Craignair Rd. *SW2* —5C **80**
Craig's Ct. *SW1* —2A **52**
Craik Ct. *NW6* —1B **34**
(off Carlton Va.)
Crail Row. *SE17* —5F **53**
Cramer St. *W1* —4C **36**
Crammond Clo. *W6* —2A **62**
Crampton Ho. *SW8* —4E **65**
Crampton Rd. *SE20* —5D **97**
Crampton St. *SE17* —5E **53**
Cranberry La. *E16* —3A **44**
Cranbourn All. *WC2* —1F **51**
(off Cranbourn St.)
Cranbourne Gdns. *NW11*
—1A **6**
Cranbourne Rd. *E12* —2F **31**
Cranbourne Rd. *E15* —1E **29**
Cranbourn Ho. *SE16* —3D **55**
(off Marigold St.)
Cranbourn Pas. *SE16* —3D **55**
(off Wilson Gro.)
Cranbourn Pl. *SE16* —3D **55**
Cranbourn St. *WC2* —1F **51**
Cranbrook. *NW1* —5E **23**
(off Camden St.)
Cranbrook Est. *E2* —1F **41**
Cranbrook M. *E17* —1B **14**
Cranbrook Rd. *SE8* —4C **70**
Cranbrook Rd. *W4* —1A **60**
Cranbrook St. *E2* —1F **41**
Cranbury Rd. *SW6* —5D **63**
Crandley Ct. *SE8* —5A **56**

Crane Ct. *EC4* —5C **38**
Crane Gro. *N7* —3C **24**
Crane Ho. *SE15* —4B **68**
Crane Mead. *SE16* —5F **55**
Crane St. *SE10* —1F **71**
Crane St. *SE15* —4B **68**
Cranfield Clo. *SE27* —3E **95**
Cranfield Ct. *W1* —4A **36**
(off Homer St.)
Cranfield Ho. *WC1* —4A **38**
(off Southampton Row)
Cranfield Rd. *SE4* —1B **84**
Cranfield Row. *SE1* —4C **52**
(off Gerridge St.)
Cranford St. *E1* —1F **55**
(off Cranford St.)
Cranford Cotts. *E1* —1F **55**
(off Cranford St.)
Cranford Way. *N8* —1C **10**
Cranhurst Rd. *NW2* —2E **19**
Cranleigh Houses. *NW1*
(off Cranleigh St.) —1E **37**
Cranleigh St. *NW1* —1E **37**
Cranleigh M. *SW11* —5A **64**
Cranley Gdns. *SW7* —1E **63**
Cranley M. *SW7* —1E **63**
Cranley Pl. *SW7* —5E **49**
Cranley Rd. *E13* —4D **45**
Cranmer Ct. *SW3* —5A **50**
Cranmer Ct. *SW4* —1F **79**
Cranmere St. *SE5* —4E **67**
Cranmer Ho. *SW9* —3C **66**
(off Brixton Rd.)
Cranmer Rd. *E7* —1D **31**
Cranmer Rd. *SW9* —3C **66**
Cranmer Ter. *SW17* —5F **91**
Cranmore Rd. *Brom* —3B **100**
Cranston Est. *N1* —1F **39**
Cranston Rd. *SE23* —1A **98**
Cranswick Rd. *SE16* —1D **69**
Crantock Rd. *SE6* —2D **99**
Cranwell Clo. *E3* —3D **43**
Cranwich Rd. *N16* —2F **11**
Cranwood Ct. *EC1* —2F **39**
(off Vince St.)
Cranwood St. *EC1* —2F **39**
Cranworth Gdns. *SW9*
—4C **66**
Craster Rd. *SW2* —5B **80**
Crathie Rd. *SE12* —4D **87**
Craven Clo. *N16* —2C **12**
Craven Ct. *NW10* —5A **18**
Craven Gdns. *SW19* —5C **90**
Craven Hill. *W2* —1E **49**
Craven Hill Gdns. *W2* —1E **49**
(in two parts)
Craven Hill M. *W2* —1E **49**
Craven Lodge. *W2* —1E **49**
(off Craven Hill)
Craven M. *SW11* —1C **78**
Craven Pk. *NW10* —5A **18**
Craven Pk. M. *NW10* —5A **18**
Craven Pk. Rd. *N15* —1B **12**
Craven Pk. Rd. *NW10* —5A **18**
Craven Pas. *WC2* —2A **52**
(off Craven St.)
Craven Rd. *NW10* —5A **18**
Craven Rd. *W2* —1E **49**

Craven St. *WC2* —2A **52**
Craven Ter. *W2* —1E **49**
Craven Wlk. *N16* —2C **12**
Crawford Bldgs. *W1* —4A **36**
(off Homer St.)
Crawford Est. *SE5* —5E **67**
Crawford Mans. *W1* —4A **36**
(off Crawford St.)
Crawford M. *W1* —4B **36**
Crawford Pas. *EC1* —3C **38**
Crawford Pl. *W2* —5A **36**
Crawford Point. *E16* —5B **44**
(off Wouldham Rd.)
Crawford Rd. *SE5* —4E **67**
Crawford St. *W1* —4A **36**
Crawley Rd. *E10* —3D **15**
Crawshay Ct. *SW9* —4C **66**
Crawthew Gro. *SE22* —2B **82**
Crayford Clo. *E6* —5F **45**
Crayford Ho. *SE1* —3F **53**
(off Long La.)
Crayford Rd. *N7* —1F **23**
Crayle Ho. *EC1* —3D **39**
(off Malta St.)
Crealock St. *SW18* —4D **77**
Creasy Est. *SE1* —4A **54**
Crebor St. *SE22* —4C **82**
Credenhill Ho. *SE15* —3D **69**
Credenhill St. *SW16* —5E **93**
Crediton Hill. *NW6* —2D **21**
Crediton Rd. *E16* —5C **44**
Crediton Rd. *NW10* —5F **19**
Credon Rd. *E13* —1E **45**
Credon Rd. *SE16* —1D **69**
Creechurch La. *EC3* —5A **40**
(in two parts)
Creechurch Pl. *EC3* —5A **40**
(off Creechurch La.)
Creed St. *EC4* —5D **39**
(off Ludgate Hill)
Creed La. *EC4* —5D **39**
Creek Ho. *W14* —4A **48**
(off Russell Rd.)
Creek Rd. *SE8* & *SE10*
—2C **70**
Creekside. *SE8* —3D **71**
Creeland Gro. *SE6* —1B **98**
Crefeld Clo. *SW6* —2A **62**
Creighton Av. *E6* —1F **45**
Creighton Clo. *W12* —1C **46**
Creighton Rd. *NW6* —1F **33**
Cremer Bus. Cen. *E2* —1B **40**
(off Cremer St.)
Cremer Ho. *SE8* —3C **70**
(off Deptford Chu. St.)
Cremer St. *E2* —1B **40**
Cremorne Est. *SW10* —2F **63**
Cremorne Rd. *SW10* —3E **63**
Creon Ct. *SW9* —3C **66**
(off Caldwell St.)
Crescent. *EC3* —1B **54**
Crescent Ct. Bus. Cen. *E16*
—3F **43**
Crescent Gdns. *SW19* —3C **90**
Crescent Gro. *SW4* —2E **79**
Crescent Ho. *EC1* —3E **39**
(off Golden La. Est.)

Crescent Ho. SE8 —5D 71
Crescent La. SW4 —2E 79
Crescent Pl. SW3 —5A 50
Crescent Rd. E6 —5E 31
Crescent Rd. E10 —4D 15
Crescent Rd. E13 —5C 30
Crescent Rd. N8 —1F 9
Crescent Row. EC1 —3E 39
Crescent Stables. SW15 —3A 76
Crescent St. N1 —4B 24
Crescent, The. E17 —1A 14
Crescent, The. NW2 —5D 5
Crescent, The. SE7 —3E 73
Crescent, The. SW13 —5B 60
Crescent, The. SW19 —3C 90
Crescent, The. W3 —5A 32
Crescent Way. SE4 —1C 84
Crescent Wharf. E16 —2D 59
(off N. Woolwich Rd.)
Crescent Wood Rd. SE26 —3C 96
Cresford Rd. SW6 —4D 63
Crespigny Rd. NW4 —1D 5
Cressal Ho. E14 —4C 56
Cresset Rd. E9 —3E 27
Cresset St. SW4 —1F 79
Cressfield Clo. NW5 —2C 22
Cressida Rd. N19 —3E 9
Cressingham Gdns. Est. SW2 —5C 80
Cressingham Rd. SE13 —1E 85
Cressington Clo. N16 —2A 26
Cresswell Gdns. SW5 —1E 63
Cresswell Pk. SE3 —1B 86
Cresswell Pl. SW10 —1E 63
Cressy Ct. E1 —4E 41
Cressy Ct. W6 —4D 47
Cressy Houses. E1 —4E 41
(off Hannibal Rd.)
Cressy Pl. E1 —4E 41
Cressy Rd. NW3 —2B 22
Cresta Ho. NW3 —4F 21
Crestfield St. NW1 —2A 38
Crest Rd. NW2 —4C 4
Crestway. SW15 —4C 74
Creswick Wlk. E3 —2C 42
Crewdson Rd. SW9 —3C 66
Crewe Pl. NW10 —2B 32
Crewkerne Ct. SW11 —4F 63
(off Bolingbroke Wlk.)
Crews St. E14 —5C 56
Crewys Rd. NW2 —4B 6
Crewys Rd. SE15 —5D 69
Crichton St. SW8 —5E 65
Cricketers Ct. SE11 —5D 53
(off Kennington La.)
Cricketers M. SW18 —3D 77
Cricketers Wlk. SE26 —5E 97
Cricketfield Rd. E5 —1D 27
Cricket La. Beck —5A 98
Cricklade Av. SW2 —2A 94
Cricklewood. —5A 6
Cricklewood B'way. NW2 —5E 5
Cricklewood La. NW2 —1F 19
Cricklewood Trad. Est. NW2 —5A 6
Cridland St. E15 —5B 30
Crieff Rd. SW18 —4E 77
Criffel Av. SW2 —2F 93
Crimscott St. SE1 —4A 54
Crimsworth Rd. SW8 —4F 65
Crinan St. N1 —1A 38
Cringle St. SW8 —3E 65
Cripplegate St. EC2 —4E 39
Crispe Ho. N1 —5B 24
(off Barnsbury Est.)
Crispian Clo. NW10 —1A 18
Crispin St. E1 —4B 40
Crisp Rd. W6 —1E 61
Cristowe Rd. SW6 —5B 62
Criterion M. N19 —4F 9
Crockerton Rd. SW17 —2B 92
Croft Ct. SE13 —4E 85
Croftdown Rd. NW5 —5C 8
Crofters Ct. SE8 —5A 56
(off Croft St.)
Crofters Way. NW1 —5F 23
Croft Ho. W10 —2A 34
(off Third Av.)
Croftongate Way. SE4 —3A 84
Crofton Park. —3B 84
Crofton Pk. Rd. SE4 —4B 84
Crofton Rd. E13 —3D 45
Crofton Rd. SE5 —4A 68
Crofton Ter. E5 —2A 28
Crofts Ho. E2 —1C 40
(off Teale St.)
Crofts St. E1 —1C 54
Croft St. SE8 —5A 56
Croft, The. NW10 —1B 32
Croftway. NW3 —1C 20
Crogsland Rd. NW1 —4C 22
Cromartie Rd. N19 —2F 9
Cromarty Ct. SW2 —3B 80
Crombie M. SW11 —5A 64
Cromer Rd. E10 —2F 15
Cromer Rd. SW17 —5C 92
Cromer St. WC1 —2A 38
Cromer Ter. E8 —2C 26
Cromer Vs. Rd. SW18 —4B 76
Cromford Path. E5 —1F 27
Cromford Rd. SW18 —3C 76
Crompton Ho. SE1 —4E 53
(off County St.)
Crompton Ho. W2 —3F 35
(off Hall Pl.)
Crompton St. W2 —3F 35
Cromwell Av. N6 —3D 9
Cromwell Av. W6 —1D 61
Cromwell Clo. E1 —2C 54
Cromwell Cres. W8 —5C 48
Cromwell Gdns. SW7 —4F 49
Cromwell Gro. W6 —4E 47
Cromwell Highwalk. EC2
(off Beech St.) —4E 39
Cromwell Ind. Est. E10 —3A 14
Cromwell Lodge. E1 —3E 41
(off Cleveland Gro.)
Cromwell M. SW7 —5F 49
Cromwell Pl. EC2 —4E 39
(off Beech St.)
Cromwell Pl. N6 —3D 9
Cromwell Pl. SW7 —5F 49
Cromwell Rd. E7 —4E 31
Cromwell Rd. E17 —1E 15
Cromwell Rd. SW5 & SW7 —5C 48
Cromwell Rd. SW9 —4D 67
Cromwell Rd. SW19 —5C 90
Cromwell Tower. EC2 —4E 39
(off Beech St.)
Crondace Rd. SW6 —4C 62
Crondall Ct. N1 —1A 40
(off St John's Est.)
Crondall St. N1 —1F 39
Crone Ct. NW6 —1B 34
(off Denmark Rd.)
Cronin St. SE15 —3B 68
Crooked Billet. SW19 —5E 89
Crooked Billet Yd. E2 —2A 40
Crooke Rd. SE8 —1A 70
Crookham Rd. SW6 —4B 62
Croombs Rd. E16 —4E 45
Croom's Hill. SE10 —3E 71
Croom's Hill Gro. SE10 —3E 71
Cropley Ct. N1 —1F 39
(off Cropley St., in two parts)
Cropley St. N1 —1F 39
Cropthorne Ct. W9 —2E 35
Crosby Ct. SE1 —3F 53
(off Crosby Row)
Crosby Ho. E7 —3C 30
Crosby Ho. E14 —4E 57
Crosby Rd. E7 —3C 30
Crosby Row. SE1 —3F 53
Crosby Sq. EC3 —5A 40
Crosby Wlk. E8 —3B 26
Crosby Wlk. SW2 —5C 80
Crosby Way. SW2 —5C 80
Crosier Clo. SE3 —4F 73
Crosland Pl. SW11 —1C 78
Cross Av. SE10 —2F 71
Crossbrook Rd. SE3 —5F 73
Cross Clo. SE15 —5D 69
Crossfield Ho. W11 —1A 48
(off Mary Pl.)
Crossfield Rd. NW3 —3F 21
Crossfield St. SE8 —3C 70
Crossford St. SW9 —5B 66
Cross Keys Clo. W1 —4C 36
Cross Keys Sq. EC1 —4E 39
(off Little Britain)
Cross La. EC3 —1A 54
Crossleigh Ct. SE14 —3B 70
(off New Cross Rd.)
Crosslet St. SE17 —5F 53
Crosslet Va. SE10 —4D 71
Crossley St. N7 —3C 24
Crossmount Ho. SE5 —3E 67
(off Bowyer St.)
Cross St. N1 —5D 25
Cross St. SE5 —1F 81

Cross St. *SW13* —5A **60**
Crossthwaite Av. *SE5* —2F **81**
Crosswall. *EC3* —1B **54**
Crossway. *N16* —2A **26**
Crossway Ct. *SE4* —5A **70**
Crossways Ter. *E5* —1E **27**
Crossway, The. *SE9* —2F **101**
Croston St. *E8* —5C **26**
Crouch End. —2F 9
Crouch End Hill. *N8* —2F **9**
Crouch Hall Ct. *N19* —3A **10**
Crouch Hall Rd. *N8* —1F **9**
Crouch Hill. *N8 & N4* —1A **10**
Crouchman's Clo. *SE26*
　　　　　　　　—3B **96**
Crowborough Rd. *SW17*
　　　　　　　　—5C **92**
Crowder St. *E1* —1D **55**
Crowfield Ho. *N5* —1E **25**
Crowfoot Clo. *E9* —2B **28**
Crowhurst Clo. *SW9* —5C **66**
Crowhurst Ho. SW9 —5B 66
　(off Aytoun Rd.)
Crowland Ho. *NW8* —5E **21**
　(off Springfield Rd.)
Crowland Rd. *N15* —1B **12**
Crowland Ter. *N1* —4F **25**
Crowline Wlk. *N1* —3E **25**
Crowmarsh Gdns. *SE23*
　　　　　　　　—5E **83**
Crown Clo. *E3* —5C **28**
Crown Clo. *NW6* —3D **21**
Crown Clo. Bus. Cen. E3
　(off Crown Clo.) —5C **28**
Crown Ct. EC4 —5E 39
　(off Cheapside)
Crown Ct. *SE12* —4D **87**
Crown Dale. *SE19* —5D **95**
Crowndale Ct. NW1 —1F 37
　(off Crowndale Ct.)
Crowndale Rd. *NW1* —1E **37**
Crownfield Rd. *E15* —1F **29**
Crown Hill Rd. *NW10* —5B **18**
Crown La. *SW16* —5C **94**
Crown La. Gdns. *SW16*
　　　　　　　　—5C **94**
Crown Lodge. *SW3* —5A **50**
Crown M. *E13* —5E **31**
Crown M. *W6* —5C **46**
Crown Office Row. *EC4*
　　　　　　　　—1C **52**
Crown Pde. *SE19* —5D **95**
Crown Pl. *EC2* —4A **40**
Crown Pl. *NW5* —3D **23**
Crown Reach. *SW1* —1F **65**
Crownstone Ct. *SW2* —3C **80**
Crownstone Rd. *SW2* —3C **80**
Crown St. *SE5* —3E **67**
Crown Wharf. *E14* —2E **57**
Crown Wharf. SE8 —1B 70
　(off Grove St.)
Crows Rd. *E15* —2F **43**
Crowthorne Clo. *SW18*
　　　　　　　　—5B **76**
Crowthorne Rd. *W10* —5F **33**
Croxley Rd. *W9* —2B **34**

Croxted Clo. *SE21* —5E **81**
Croxted M. *SE24* —4E **81**
Croxted Rd. *SE24 & SE21*
　　　　　　　　—4E **81**
Croxteth Ho. *SW8* —5F **65**
Croydon Ho. SE1 —2C 52
　(off Wootton St.)
Croydon Rd. *E13* —3B **44**
Crozier Ho. *SE3* —1D **87**
Crozier Ho. SW8 —3B 66
　(off Wilkinson St.)
Crozier Ter. *E9* —2F **27**
Crucifix La. *SE1* —3A **54**
Cruden Ho. *SE5* —2D **67**
　(off Brandon Est.)
Cruden St. *N1* —5D **25**
Cruikshank Ho. NW8 —1A 36
　(off Townshend Rd.)
Cruikshank Rd. *E15* —1A **30**
Cruikshank St. *WC1* —2C **38**
Crummock Gdns. *NW9* —1A **4**
Crusoe M. *N16* —4F **11**
Crutched Friars. *EC3* —1A **54**
Crutchley Rd. *SE6* —2A **100**
Crystal Palace. —5B 96
Crystal Palace Mus. —5B 96
**Crystal Palace National
　　　Sports Centre. —5C 96**
Crystal Pal. Pde. *SE19*
　　　　　　　　—5B **96**
Crystal Pal. Pk. Rd. *SE26*
　　　　　　　　—5C **96**
Crystal Pal. Rd. *SE22* —4B **82**
Crystal Ter. *SE19* —5F **95**
Crystal Vw. Ct. *Brom* —4F **99**
Cuba St. *E14* —3C **56**
Cubitt Ho. *SW4* —4E **79**
Cubitt Steps. *E14* —2C **56**
Cubitt St. *WC1* —2B **38**
Cubitt's Yd. WC2 —1A 52
　(off James St.)
Cubitt Ter. *SW4* —1E **79**
Cubitt Town. —5E 57
Cuddington. SE17 —5E 53
　(off Deacon Way)
Cudham St. *SE6* —5E **85**
Cudworth Ho. *SW8* —4E **65**
Cudworth St. *E1* —3D **41**
Cuff Cres. *SE9* —4F **87**
Cuff Point. E2 —2B 40
　(off Columbia Rd.)
Culford Gdns. *SW3* —5B **50**
Culford Gro. *N1* —3A **26**
Culford Mans. *SW3* —5B **50**
Culford M. *N1* —3A **26**
Culford Rd. *N1* —4A **26**
　(in two parts)
Culham Ho. E2 —2B 40
　(off Palissy St.)
Culling Rd. *SE16* —4E **55**
Cullingworth Rd. *NW10*
　　　　　　　　—2C **18**
Culloden Clo. *SE1* —1C **68**
Culloden St. *E14* —5E **43**
Cullum St. *EC3* —1A **54**
Cullum Welch Ct. N1 —2F 39
　(off Haberdasher St.)

Culmore Rd. *SE15* —3D **69**
Culmstock Rd. *SW11* —3C **78**
Culpeper Ho. *E14* —5A **42**
Culpepper Ct. SE11 —5C 52
　(off Kennington Rd.)
Culross Bldgs. N1 —1A 38
　(off Battle Bri. Rd.)
Culross St. *W1* —1C **50**
Culverden Rd. *SW12* —2E **93**
Culverhouse. WC1 —4B 38
　(off Red Lion Sq.)
Culverhouse Gdns. *SW16*
　　　　　　　　—3B **94**
Culverley Rd. *SE6* —1D **99**
Culvert Pl. *SW11* —5C **64**
Culvert Rd. *N15* —1A **12**
Culvert Rd. *SW11* —5B **64**
Culworth Ho. *NW8* —1A **36**
　(off Allitsen Rd.)
Culworth St. *NW8* —1A **36**
Culzean Clo. *SE27* —3D **95**
Cumberland Clo. *E8* —3B **26**
Cumberland Ct. SW1 —1D 65
　(off Cumberland St.)
Cumberland Cres. *W14*
　　(in two parts)　—5A **48**
Cumberland Gdns. *WC1*
　　　　　　　　—2C **38**
Cumberland Ga. *W1* —1B **50**
Cumberland Mans. W1
　(off George St.) —5B **36**
Cumberland Mkt. *NW1*
　　　　　　　　—2D **37**
Cumberland Mills Sq. *E14*
　　　　　　　　—1F **71**
Cumberland Pk. Ind. Est.
　　　　　NW10 —2C **32**
Cumberland Pl. *NW1* —2D **37**
Cumberland Pl. *SE6* —1B **100**
Cumberland Rd. *E12* —1F **31**
Cumberland Rd. *E13* —4D **45**
Cumberland Rd. *SW13*
　　　　　　　　—4B **60**
Cumberland St. *SW1* —1D **65**
Cumberland Ter. *NW1* —1D **37**
Cumberland Ter. M. NW1
　　　　　　　　—1D **37**
　(off Cumberland Ter.)
Cumbrian Gdns. *NW2* —4F **5**
Cumming St. *N1* —1B **38**
Cumnor Clo. SW9 —5B 66
　(off Robsart St.)
Cunard Pl. *EC3* —5A **40**
Cunard Rd. *NW10* —2A **32**
Cunard Wlk. *SE16* —5F **55**
Cundy Rd. *E16* —5E **45**
Cundy St. *SW1* —5C **50**
Cunliffe St. *SW16* —5D **93**
Cunningham Ho. SE5 —3F 67
　(off Elmington Est.)
Cunningham Pl. *NW8* —3F **35**
Cupar Rd. *SW11* —4C **64**
Cupola Clo. *Brom* —5D **101**
Cureton St. *SW1* —5F **51**
Curlew Ho. *SE4* —2A **84**
　(off St Norbert Rd.)
Curlew Ho. *SE15* —4B **68**

Curlew St. SE1 —3B 54
Curnick's La. SE27 —4E 95
Curran Ho. SW3 —5A 50 (off Lucan Pl.)
Curricle St. W3 —2A 46
Currie Hill Clo. SW19 —4B 90
Currie Ho. E14 —5F 43
Cursitor St. WC2 —5C 38
Curtain Pl. EC2 —2A 40 (off Curtain Rd.)
Curtain Rd. EC2 —3A 40 (in two parts)
Curtis Dri. W3 —5A 32
Curtis Fld. Rd. SW16 —4B 94
Curtis Ho. SE17 —1F 67 (off Morecambe St.)
Curtis St. SE1 —5B 54
Curtis Way. SE1 —5B 54
Curve, The. W12 —1C 46
Curwen Av. E7 —1D 31
Curwen Rd. W12 —3C 46
Curzon Ct. SW6 —4D 63 (off Maltings Pl.)
Curzon Cres. NW10 —4A 18
Curzon Ga. W1 —2C 50
Curzon Pl. W1 —2C 50
Curzon St. W1 —2C 50
Custance Ho. N1 —1F 39 (off Provost Est.)
Custance St. N1 —2F 39
Custom House. —5E 45
Custom House. —1A 54
Custom Ho. Reach. SE16 —3B 56
Custom Ho. Wlk. EC3 —1A 54
Cutbush Ho. N7 —2F 23
Cutcombe Rd. SE5 —5E 67
Cuthbert Harrowing Ho. EC1 (off Golden La. Est.) —3E 39
Cuthbert Ho. W2 —4F 35 (off Hall Pl.)
Cuthbert St. W2 —4F 35
Cuthill Wlk. SE5 —4F 67
Cutlers Gdns. E1 —5A 40 (off Cutlers St.)
Cutlers Sq. E14 —5C 56
Cutler St. E1 —5A 40
Cut, The. SE1 —3C 52
Cutty Sark Clipper Ship. —2E 71
Cutty Sark Gdns. SE10 —2E 71 (off King William Wlk.)
Cyclops M. E14 —5C 56
Cygnet Clo. NW10 —2A 18
Cygnet St. E1 —3B 40
Cygnus Bus. Cen. NW10 —2B 18
Cynthia St. N1 —1B 38
Cyntra Pl. E8 —4D 27
Cypress Gdns. SE4 —3A 84
Cypress Ho. SE14 —4F 69
Cypress Pl. W1 —3E 37
Cyprus Clo. N4 —1D 11
Cyprus Pl. E2 —1E 41
Cyprus St. E2 —1E 41 (in two parts)
Cyrena Rd. SE22 —4B 82
Cyril Mans. SW11 —4B 64
Cyrus Ho. EC1 —3D 39
Cyrus St. EC1 —3D 39 (off Cyrus St.)
Czar St. SE8 —2C 70

Dabbs La. EC1 —3C 38 (off Farringdon Rd.)
Dabin Cres. SE10 —4E 71
Dacca St. SE8 —2B 70
Dace Rd. E3 —5C 28
Dacre Gdns. SE13 —2A 86
Dacre Ho. SW3 —2F 63 (off Beaufort St.)
Dacre Pk. SE13 —1A 86
Dacre Pl. SE13 —1A 86
Dacre Rd. E11 —3B 16
Dacre Rd. E13 —5D 31
Dacres Ho. SW4 —1D 79
Dacres Rd. SE23 —2F 97
Dacre St. SW1 —4F 51
Daffodil St. W12 —1B 46
Dafforne Rd. SW17 —3C 92
Dagenham Rd. E10 —3B 14
Dagleish St. E14 —5A 42
Dagmar Ct. E14 —4E 57
Dagmar Gdns. NW10 —1F 33
Dagmar Pas. N1 —5D 25 (off Cross St.)
Dagmar Rd. N4 —2C 10
Dagmar Rd. SE5 —4A 68
Dagmar Ter. N1 —5D 25
Dagnall St. SW11 —5B 64
Dagnan Rd. SW12 —5D 79
Dagobert Ho. E1 —4E 41 (off Smithy St.)
Dagonet Gdns. Brom —3C 100
Dagonet Rd. Brom —3C 100
Dahomey Rd. SW16 —5E 93
Dain Ct. W8 —5C 48 (off Lexham Gdns.)
Dainford Clo. Brom —5F 99
Daintry Way. E9 —3B 28
Dairy Clo. NW10 —5C 18
Dairyman Clo. NW2 —5F 5
Dairy M. SW9 —1A 80
Dairy Wlk. SW19 —4A 90
Daisy Dobbings Wlk. N19 —2A 10 (off Jessie Blythe La.)
Daisy La. SW6 —1C 76
Daisy Rd. E16 —3A 44
Dakota Gdns. E6 —3F 45
Dalberg Rd. SW2 —2C 80 (in two parts)
Dalby Rd. SW18 —2E 77
Dalby St. NW5 —3D 23
Dalebury Rd. SW17 —2B 92
Dale Clo. SE3 —1C 86
Daleham Gdns. NW3 —2F 21
Daleham M. NW3 —3F 21
Dalehead. NW1 —1E 37 (off Harrington Sq.)
Dale Ho. NW8 —5E 21 (off Boundary Rd.)
Dale Ho. SE4 —2A 84
Dale Lodge. N6 —1E 9
Dalemain M. E16 —2C 58
Dale Rd. NW5 —2C 22
Dale Rd. SE17 —2D 67
Dale Row. W11 —5A 34
Daleside Rd. SW16 —5D 93
Dale St. W4 —1A 60
Daleview Rd. N15 —1A 12
Daley Ho. W12 —5D 33
Daley St. E9 —3F 27
Daley Thompson Way. SW8 —5D 65
Dalgarno Gdns. W10 —4D 33
Dalgarno Way. W10 —3E 33
Dalgleish St. E14 —5A 42
Daling Way. E3 —5A 28
Dali Universe. —3B 52
Dalkeith Ct. SW1 —5F 51 (off Vincent St.)
Dalkeith Ho. SW9 —4D 67 (off Lothian Rd.)
Dalkeith Rd. SE21 —1E 95
Dallas Rd. NW4 —2C 4
Dallas Rd. SE26 —3D 97
Dallinger Rd. SE12 —4B 86
Dalling Rd. W6 —5D 47
Dallington St. EC1 —3D 39
Dalmain Rd. SE23 —1F 97
Dalmeny Av. N7 —1F 23
Dalmeny Rd. N7 —5F 9 (in three parts)
Dalmeyer Rd. NW10 —3B 18
Dalmore Rd. SE21 —2E 95
Dalo Lodge. E3 —4C 42
Dalrymple Rd. SE4 —2A 84
Dalston. —3B 26
Dalston La. E8 —3B 26
Dalton Ho. SE14 —2F 69 (off John Williams Clo.)
Dalton Ho. SW1 —1D 65 (off Ebury Bri. Rd.)
Dalton St. SE27 —2D 95
Dalwood St. SE5 —4A 68
Daly Ct. E15 —2D 29
Dalyell Rd. SW9 —1B 80
Damascene Wlk. SE21 —1E 95
Damask Cres. E16 —3A 44
Damer Ter. SW10 —3E 63
Dames Rd. E7 —5C 16
Dame St. N1 —1E 39
Damien Ct. E1 —5D 41 (off Damien St.)
Damien St. E1 —5D 41
Damory Ho. SE16 —5D 55 (off Abbeyfield Est.)
Danbury St. N1 —1D 39
Danby St. SE15 —1B 82
Dancer Rd. SW6 —4B 62
Dando Cres. SE3 —1D 87
Dandridge Clo. SE10 —1B 72
Dandridge Ho. E1 —4B 40 (off Lamb St.)
Danebury Av. SW15 —4A 74 (in two parts)
Daneby Rd. SE6 —3D 99

Danecroft Rd. *SE24* —3E **81**
Danehurst St. *SW6* —4A **62**
Danemere St. *SW15* —1E **75**
Dane Pl. *E3* —1B **42**
Danescombe. *SE12* —1C **100**
Danes Ct. *NW8* —5B **22**
(off St Edmund's Ter.)
Danescroft. *NW4* —1F **5**
Danescroft Av. *NW4* —1F **5**
Danescroft Gdns. *NW4* —1F **5**
Danesdale Rd. *E9* —3A **28**
Danesfield. *SE17* —2A **68**
(off Albany Rd.)
Danes Ho. *W10* —4E **33**
(off Sutton Way)
Dane St. *WC1* —4B **38**
Daneswood Av. *SE6* —3E **99**
Daneville Rd. *SE5* —4F **67**
Dangan Rd. *E11* —1C **16**
Daniel Bolt Clo. *E14* —4D **43**
Daniel Clo. *SW17* —5A **92**
Daniel Gdns. *SE15* —3B **68**
Daniel Ho. N1 —1F **39**
(off Cranston Est.)
Daniel Pl. *NW4* —2D **5**
Daniels Rd. *SE15* —1E **83**
Dan Leno Wlk. *SW6* —3D **63**
Dansey Pl. W1 —1F **51**
(off Wardour St.)
Danson Rd. *SE17* —1D **67**
Dante Pl. SE11 —5D **53**
(off Dante Rd.)
Dante Rd. *SE11* —5D **53**
Danube Ct. *SE15* —3B **68**
(off Daniel Gdns.)
Danube St. *SW3* —1A **64**
Danvers Ho. *E1* —5C **40**
(off Christian St.)
Danvers St. *SW3* —2F **63**
Da Palma Ct. SW6 —2C **62**
(off Anselm Rd.)
Daphne St. *SW18* —4E **77**
Daplyn St. *E1* —4C **40**
D'Arblay St. W1 —5E **37**
Darcy Ho. E8 —5D **27**
(off London Fields E. Side)
Dare Ct. *E10* —2E **15**
Darent Ho. NW8 —4F **35**
(off Church St. Est.)
Darent Ho. *Brom* —5F **99**
Darenth Rd. *E5* —2B **12**
Darfield. NW1 —5E **23**
(off Bayham St.)
Darfield Rd. *SE4* —3B **84**
Darfield Way. *W10* —5F **33**
Darfur St. *SW15* —1F **75**
Darien Rd. *SW11* —1F **77**
Dark Ho. Wlk. *EC3* —1F **53**
Darlan Rd. *SW6* —3B **62**
Darley Ho. SE11 —1B **66**
(off Laud St.)
Darley Rd. *SW11* —4B **78**
Darling Rd. *SE4* —1C **84**
Darling Row. *E1* —3D **41**
Darlington Ho. *SE12* —1B **100**
Darlington Ho. SW8 —3F **65**
(off Hemans St.)

Darlington Rd. *SE27* —5D **95**
Darnall Ho. SE10 —4E **71**
(off Royal Hill)
Darnay Ho. *SE1* —4C **54**
Darnley Ho. *E14* —5A **42**
Darnley Rd. *E9* —3E **27**
Darnley Ter. *W11* —2F **47**
Darrell Rd. *SE22* —3C **82**
Darren Clo. *N4* —2B **10**
Darsley Dri. *SW8* —4F **65**
Dartford Ho. *SE1* —5B **54**
(off Longfield Est.)
Dartford St. *SE17* —2E **67**
Dartington Ho. W1 —5E **23**
(off Plender St.)
Dartington Ho. SW8 —5F **65**
(off Union St.)
Dartington Ho. W2 —4D **35**
(off Senior St.)
Dartle Ct. *SE16* —3C **54**
(off Scott Lidgett Cres.)
Dartmoor Wlk. *E14* —5C **56**
(off Charnwood Gdns.)
Dartmouth Clo. *W11* —5B **34**
Dartmouth Ct. *SE10* —4E **71**
Dartmouth Gro. *SE10* —4E **71**
Dartmouth Hill. *SE10* —4E **71**
Dartmouth Park. —5D 9
Dartmouth Pk. Av. *NW5*
—5D **9**
Dartmouth Pk. Hill. *N19 &*
NW5 —3D **9**
Dartmouth Pk. Rd. *NW5*
—1D **23**
Dartmouth Pl. *SE23* —2E **97**
Dartmouth Pl. *W4* —2A **60**
Dartmouth Rd. *NW2* —3F **19**
Dartmouth Rd. *NW4* —1C **4**
Dartmouth Rd. *SE26 & SE23*
—3D **97**
Dartmouth Row. *SE10* —5E **71**
Dartmouth St. *SW1* —3F **51**
Dartmouth Ter. *SE10* —4F **71**
Dartrey Tower. SW10 —3E **63**
(off Worlds End Est.)
Dartrey Wlk. *SW10* —3E **63**
Dart St. *W10* —2A **34**
Darville Rd. *N16* —5B **12**
Darwin Ct. *NW1* —5C **22**
(in three parts)
Darwin Ho. SW1 —2E **65**
(off Grosvenor Rd.)
Darwin St. *SE17* —5F **53**
(in two parts)
Daryngton Ho. SW8 —3A **66**
(off Hartington Rd.)
Dashwood Ho. *N8* —1B **10**
Dassett Rd. *SE27* —5D **95**
Data Point Bus. Cen. E16
—3F **43**
Datchelor Pl. *SE5* —4F **67**
Datchet Ho. NW1 —2D **37**
(off Augustus St.)
Datchet Rd. *SE6* —2B **98**
Datchworth Ho. N1 —4D **25**
(off Sutton Est., The)
Date St. *SE17* —1F **67**

Daubeney Rd. *E5* —1A **28**
Daubeney Tower. SE8 —1B **70**
(off Bowditch)
Dault Rd. *SW18* —4E **77**
Dauncey Ho. SE1 —3D **53**
(off Webber Row)
Davenant Rd. *N19* —4F **9**
Davenant St. *E1* —4C **40**
Davenport Ho. *SE11* —5C **52**
(off Walnut Tree Wlk.)
Davenport Rd. *SE6* —4D **85**
Daventry Av. *E17* —1C **14**
Daventry St. *NW1* —4A **36**
Daver Ct. *SW3* —1A **64**
Davern Clo. *SE10* —5B **58**
Davey Clo. *N7* —3B **24**
Davey Rd. *E9* —4C **28**
Davey's Ct. WC2 —1A **52**
(off Bedfordbury)
Davey St. *SE15* —2B **68**
Davidge Ho. SE1 —3C **52**
(off Coral St.)
Davidge St. *SE1* —3D **53**
David Ho. *E14* —4D **43**
David Ho. SW8 —3A **66**
(off Wyvil Rd.)
David Lee Point. *E15* —5A **30**
(off Leather Gdns.)
David M. *W1* —4B **36**
Davidson Gdns. *SW8* —3A **66**
Davidson Terraces. E7
—2D **31**
(off Claremont Rd.,
in two parts)
Davidson Tower. Brom
—5D **101**
David's Rd. *SE23* —1E **97**
David St. *E15* —3F **29**
Davies La. *E11* —4A **16**
Davies M. *W1* —1D **51**
Davies St. *W1* —5D **37**
Da Vinci Ct. SE16 —1D **69**
(off Rossetti Rd.)
Davis Rd. *W3* —2B **46**
Davis St. *E13* —1D **45**
Davisville Rd. *W12* —3C **46**
Dawes Ho. SE17 —5F **53**
(off Orb St.)
Dawes Rd. *SW6* —3A **62**
Dawes St. *SE17* —1F **67**
Dawlish Av. *SW18* —2D **91**
Dawlish Rd. *E10* —3E **15**
Dawlish Rd. *NW2* —3F **19**
Dawnay Gdns. *SW18* —2F **91**
Dawnay Rd. *SW18* —2E **91**
Dawn Cres. *E15* —5F **29**
Dawpool Rd. *NW2* —4B **4**
Dawson Ho. E2 —2E **41**
(off Sceptre Rd.)
Dawson Pl. *W2* —1C **48**
Dawson Rd. *NW2* —2E **19**
Dawson St. *E2* —1B **40**
Day Ho. *SE5* —3E **67**
(off Bethwin Rd.)
Daylesford Av. *SW15* —2C **74**
Daysbrook Rd. *SW2* —1B **94**
Dayton Gro. *SE15* —4B **69**

Deacon Ho. SE11 —5B 52
(off Black Prince Rd.)
Deacon M. N1 —4F 25
Deacon Rd. NW2 —2C 18
Deacon's Ri. N2 —1F 7
Deacon Way. SE15 —1E 53
Deal Ho. SE15 —2F 69
(off Lovelinch La.)
Deal Porters Wlk. SE16
—3F 55
Deal Porters Way. SE16
—4E 55
Deal Rd. SW17 —5C 92
Deal's Gateway. SE10 —4C 70
Deal St. E1 —4C 40
Dealtry Rd. SW15 —2E 75
Deal Wlk. SW9 —3C 66
Dean Abbott Ho. SW1 —5F 51
(off Vincent St.)
Dean Bradley St. SW1 —4A 52
Dean Clo. E9 —2E 27
Dean Clo. SE16 —2F 55
Dean Ct. SW8 —3A 66
(off Thorncroft St.)
Deancross St. E1 —5E 41
Deanery M. W1 —2C 50
(off Deanery St.)
Deanery Rd. E15 —3A 30
Deanery St. W1 —2C 50
Dean Farrar St. SW1 —4F 51
Dean Ho. SE14 —3A 70
(off New Cross Rd.)
Dean Rd. NW2 —3E 19
Dean Ryle St. SW1 —5A 52
Dean's Bldgs. SE17 —5F 53
Dean's Ct. EC4 —5D 39
Deans Ga. Clo. SE23 —3F 97
Deanshanger Ho. SE8 —5F 55
(off Chilton Gro.)
Dean's M. W1 —5D 37
Dean Stanley St. SW1 —4A 52
Deanston Wharf. E16 —3D 59
(off N. Woolwich Rd.)
Dean St. E7 —2C 30
Dean St. W1 —5F 37
Dean's Yd. SW1 —4F 51
(off Sanctuary, The)
Dean Trench St. SW1 —4A 52
Deason St. E15 —5E 29
Deauville Ct. SE16 —3F 55
(off Eleanor Clo.)
Deauville Ct. SW4 —4E 79
De Barowe M. N5 —1D 25
Debdale Rd. E2 —5C 26
(off Whiston Rd.)
De Beauvoir Ct. N1 —4F 25
(off Northchurch Rd.)
De Beauvoir Cres. N1 —5A 26
De Beauvoir Est. N1 —5A 26
De Beauvoir Pl. N1 —3A 26
De Beauvoir Rd. N1 —5A 26
De Beauvoir Sq. N1 —4A 26
De Beauvoir Town. —5A 26
Debenham Ct. E8 —5C 26
(off Pownall Rd.)
Debham Ct. NW2 —5E 5
Debnams Rd. SE16 —5E 55

De Bruin Ct. E14 —1E 71
Decima St. SE1 —4A 54
Deck Clo. SE16 —2F 55
De Crespigny Pk. SE5 —5F 67
Deeley Rd. SW8 —4F 65
Deepdale. SW19 —4F 89
Deepdene Gdns. SW2 —5B 80
Deepdene Point. SE23 —3F 97
Deepdene Rd. SE5 —2F 81
Deepway. SE8 —1A 70
(off Evelyn St.)
Deerbrook Rd. SE24 —1D 95
Deerdale Rd. SE24 —2E 81
Deerfield Cotts. NW9 —1B 4
Deerhurst Ho. SE15 —2C 68
(off Haymerle Rd.)
Deerhurst Rd. NW6 —3F 19
Deerhurst Rd. SW16 —5B 94
Deeside Rd. SW17 —3F 91
Dee St. E14 —5E 43
Defoe Clo. SE16 —3B 56
Defoe Clo. SW17 —5A 92
Defoe Ho. EC2 —4F 39
(off Beech St.)
Defoe Pl. EC2 —4E 39
(off Beech St.)
Defoe Rd. N16 —5A 12
De Frene Rd. SE26 —4F 97
De Gama Pl. E14 —1C 70
Dehar Cres. NW9 —2B 4
Dekker Ho. SE5 —3F 67
(off Elmington Est.)
Dekker Rd. SE21 —4A 82
Delacourt Rd. SE3 —3D 73
Delafield Ho. E1 —5C 40
(off Christian St.)
Delafield Rd. SE7 —1D 73
Delaford Rd. SE16 —1D 69
Delaford St. SW6 —3A 62
Delamere Rd. W2 —5D 35
Delamere Ter. W2 —4D 35
Delancey Pas. NW1 —5D 23
(off Delancey St.)
Delancey St. NW1 —5D 23
Delancey Studios. NW1
—5D 23
Delany Ho. SE10 —2E 71
(off Thames St.)
Delarch Ho. SE1 —3D 53
(off Webber Row)
De Laune St. SE17 —1D 67
Delaware Mans. W9 —3D 35
(off Delaware Rd.)
Delaware Rd. W9 —3D 35
Delawyk Cres. SE24 —4E 81
Delft Way. SE22 —3A 82
Delhi St. N1 —5A 24
(in two parts)
Delia St. SW18 —5D 77
Delius Gro. E15 —1F 43
Della Path. E5 —5C 12
Dell Clo. E15 —5F 29
Dellow Ho. E1 —1D 55
(off Dellow St.)
Dellow St. E1 —1D 55
Dell's M. SW1 —5E 51
(off Churton Pl.)

Delmaine Ho. E14 —5A 42
Delmare Clo. SW9 —2B 80
Delme Cres. SE3 —5D 73
Delmerend Ho. SW3 —1A 64
(off Ixworth Pl.)
Deloraine Ho. SE8 —4C 70
Delorme St. W6 —2F 61
Delta Building. E14 —5E 43
Delta Clo. E2 —2C 40
Delta Ct. NW2 —4C 4
Delta Est. E2 —2C 40
Delta Pk. SW18 —2D 77
Delta St. E2 —2C 40
Delverton Ho. SE17 —1D 67
(off Delverton Rd.)
Delverton Rd. SE17 —1D 67
Delvino Rd. SW6 —4C 62
De Montfort Pde. SW16
—3A 94
De Montfort Rd. SW16
—3A 94
De Morgan Rd. SW6 —1D 77
Dempster Rd. SW18 —3E 77
Denbigh Clo. NW10 —4A 18
Denbigh Clo. W11 —1B 48
Denbigh Ct. E6 —2F 45
Denbigh Ho. SW1 —4B 50
Denbigh Ho. W11 —1B 48
(off Westbourne Gro.)
Denbigh M. SW1 —5E 51
(off Denbigh St.)
Denbigh Pl. SW1 —1E 65
Denbigh Rd. E6 —2F 45
Denbigh Rd. W11 —1B 48
Denbigh St. SW1 —5E 51
(in two parts)
Denbigh Ter. W11 —1B 48
Denby Ct. SE11 —5B 52
(off Lambeth Wlk.)
Dence Ho. E2 —2C 40
(off Turin St.)
Denchworth Ho. SW9 —5C 66
Dene Clo. SE4 —1A 84
Denehurst Gdns. NW4 —1E 5
Denesmead. SE24 —3E 81
Denewood Rd. N6 —1B 8
Denford St. SE10 —1B 72
Dengie Wlk. N1 —5E 25
(off Basire St.)
Denham Ct. SE26 —3D 97
(off Kirkdale)
Denham Ho. W12 —1D 47
(off White City Est.)
Denham St. SE10 —1C 72
Denholme Rd. W9 —2B 34
Denison Ho. E14 —5C 42
Denison Rd. SW19 —5F 91
Denis Way. SW4 —1F 79
Denland Ho. SW8 —3B 66
(off Dorset Rd.)
Denman Dri. NW11 —1C 6
Denman Dri. S. NW11 —1C 6
Denman Pl. W1 —1F 51
(off Denman St.)
Denman Rd. SE15 —4B 68
Denman St. W1 —1F 51
Denmark Gro. N1 —1C 38
Denmark Hill. SE5 —4F 67

Denmark Hill Est. *SE5* —2F **81**
Denmark Mans. *SE5* —5E **67**
　(off Coldharbour La.)
Denmark Pl. *WC2* —5F **37**
Denmark Rd. *NW6* —1B **34**
　(in two parts)
Denmark Rd. *SE5* —4E **67**
Denmark St. *E11* —3A **16**
Denmark St. *E13* —4D **45**
Denmark St. *WC2* —5F **37**
Denmark Wlk. *SE27* —4E **95**
Denmead Ho. *SW15* —4B **74**
　(off Highcliffe Dri.)
Denmead Way. *SE15* —3B **68**
　(off Pentridge St.)
Denne Ter. *E8* —5B **26**
Dennetts Gro. *SE14* —4E **69**
Denning Clo. *NW8* —2E **35**
Denning Point. *E1* —5B **40**
　(off Commercial St.)
Denning Rd. *NW3* —1F **21**
Dennington Clo. *E5* —4E **13**
Dennington Pk. Rd. *NW6*
　—3C **20**
Dennison Gro. *SW14* —1A **74**
Dennison Point. *E15* —4E **29**
Denny Clo. *E6* —4F **45**
Denny Cres. *SE11* —1C **66**
Denny St. *SE11* —1C **66**
Densham Ho. *NW8* —1F **35**
　(off Cochrane St.)
Densham Rd. *E15* —5A **30**
Denstone Ho. *SE15* —2C **68**
　(off Haymerle Rd.)
Dent Ho. *SE17* —5A **54**
　(off Tatum St.)
Denton. *NW1* —3C **22**
Denton Ho. *N1* —4D **25**
　(off Halton Rd.)
Denton St. *N8* —1B **10**
Denton St. *SW18* —4D **77**
Denton Way. *E5* —5F **13**
Dents Rd. *SW11* —4B **78**
Denver Rd. *N16* —2A **12**
Denwood. *SE23* —3F **97**
Denyer St. *SW3* —5A **50**
Denys Ho. *EC1* —4C **38**
Denzil Rd. *NW10* —2B **18**
Deodar Rd. *SW15* —2A **76**
Depot App. *NW2* —1F **19**
Depot Rd. *W12* —1E **47**
Depot St. *SE5* —2F **67**
Deptford. —3C **70**
Deptford Bri. *SE8* —4C **70**
Deptford B'way. *SE8* —4C **70**
Deptford Bus. Pk. SE15
　(off Rollins St.) —2E **69**
Deptford Chu. St. *SE8* —2C **70**
Deptford Creek Bri. SE8
　(off Creek Rd.) —2D **71**
Deptford Ferry Rd. *E14*
　—5C **56**
Deptford Grn. *SE8* —2C **70**
Deptford High St. *SE8* —2C **70**
Deptford Pk. Bus. Cen. *SE8*
　—1A **70**
Deptford Strand. *SE8* —5B **56**

Deptford Trad. Est. *SE8*
　—1A **70**
Deptford Wharf. *SE8* —5B **56**
　(in two parts)
De Quincey Ho. *SW1* —1E **65**
　(off Lupus St.)
De Quincey M. *E16* —2C **58**
Derby Ga. *SW1* —3A **52**
　(in two parts)
Derby Hill. *SE23* —2E **97**
Derby Hill Cres. *SE23* —2E **97**
Derby Ho. SE11 —5C **52**
　(off Walnut Tree Wlk.)
Derby Lodge. *WC1* —2B **38**
　(off Britannia St.)
Derby Rd. *E7* —4F **31**
Derby Rd. *E9* —5F **27**
Derbyshire St. *E2* —2C **40**
　(in two parts)
Derby St. *W1* —2C **50**
Dereham Ho. *SE4* —2F **83**
　(off Frendsbury Rd.)
Dereham Pl. *EC2* —2A **40**
　(in two parts)
Derek Walcott Clo. *SE24*
　—3D **81**
Dericote St. *E8* —5D **27**
Dering St. *W1* —5D **37**
Dering Yd. *W1* —5D **37**
Derinton Rd. *SW17* —4B **92**
Dermody Gdns. *SE13* —3F **85**
Dermody Rd. *SE13* —3F **85**
Deronda Est. *SW2* —1D **95**
Deronda Rd. *SE24* —1D **95**
Derrick Gdns. *SE7* —4E **59**
Derry St. *W8* —3D **49**
Dersingham Rd. *NW2* —5A **6**
Derwent. NW1 —2E **37**
　(off Robert St.)
Derwent Av. *NW9* —1A **4**
Derwent Av. *SW15* —5A **88**
Derwent Ct. *SE16* —3F **55**
　(off Eleanor Clo.)
Derwent Gro. *SE22* —2B **82**
Derwent Ho. E3 —3B **42**
　(off Southern Gro.)
Derwent Ho. SW7 —5E **49**
　(off Cromwell Rd.)
Derwent Ri. *NW9* —1A **4**
Derwent St. *SE10* —1A **72**
Desborough Clo. W2 —4D **35**
　(off Bourne Ter.)
Desborough Ho. W14
　(off N. End Rd.) —2B **62**
Desenfans Rd. *SE21* —4A **82**
Desford Rd. *E16* —3A **44**
Design Mus. —3B **54**
Desmond St. *SE14* —3A **70**
Despard Rd. *N19* —3E **9**
Dethick Ct. *E3* —5A **28**
Detling Ho. *SE17* —5A **54**
　(off Congreve St.)
Detling Rd. *Brom* —5C **100**
Detmold Rd. *E5* —4E **13**
Devas St. *E3* —3D **43**
Devenay Rd. *E15* —4B **30**
Deventer Cres. *SE22* —3A **82**

De Vere Gdns. *W8* —3E **49**
Deverell St. *SE1* —4F **53**
De Vere M. *W8* —4E **49**
　(off De Vere Gdns.)
Devereux Ct. *WC2* —5C **38**
　(off Essex St.)
Devereux La. *SW13* —3D **61**
Devereux Rd. *SW11* —4B **78**
Devitt Ho. *E14* —1D **57**
Devizes St. *N1* —5F **25**
　(off Avebury St.)
Devon Gdns. *N4* —1D **11**
Devonhurst Pl. *W4* —1A **60**
Devonia Rd. *N1* —1D **39**
Devon Mans. SE1 —3B **54**
　(off Tooley St.)
Devonport. *W2* —5A **36**
Devonport M. *W12* —3D **47**
Devonport Rd. *W12* —2D **47**
Devonport St. *E1* —5F **41**
Devons Est. *E3* —2D **43**
Devonshire Clo. *E15* —1A **30**
Devonshire Clo. *W1* —4D **37**
Devonshire Ct. E1 —2E **41**
　(off Bancroft Rd.)
Devonshire Ct. WC1 —4A **38**
　(off Boswell St.)
Devonshire Dri. *SE10* —3D **71**
Devonshire Gro. *SE15*
　—2D **69**
Devonshire Ho. NW6 —3B **20**
　(off Kilburn High Rd.)
Devonshire Ho. SE1 —4E **53**
　(off Bath Ter.)
Devonshire Ho. SW1 —1F **65**
　(off Lindsay Sq.)
Devonshire M. *W4* —1A **60**
Devonshire M. N. *W1* —4D **37**
Devonshire M. S. *W1* —4D **37**
Devonshire M. W. *W1* —3C **36**
Devonshire Pas. *W4* —1A **60**
Devonshire Pl. *NW1* —3C **36**
Devonshire Pl. *NW2* —5C **6**
Devonshire Pl. *W8* —4D **49**
Devonshire Pl. M. *W1* —4C **36**
Devonshire Rd. *E16* —5D **45**
Devonshire Rd. *E17* —1C **14**
Devonshire Rd. *SE9* —2F **101**
Devonshire Rd. *SE23* —1E **97**
Devonshire Rd. *W4* —1A **60**
Devonshire Row. *EC2* —4A **40**
Devonshire Row M. W1
　(off Devonshire St.) —3D **37**
Devonshire Sq. *EC2* —5A **40**
Devonshire St. *W1* —4C **36**
Devonshire St. *W4* —1A **60**
Devonshire Ter. *W2* —5E **35**
Devons Rd. *E3* —4C **42**
　(in two parts)
Devon St. *SE15* —2D **69**
Devon Wharf. *E14* —4E **43**
De Walden Ho. NW8 —1A **36**
　(off Allitsen Rd.)
De Walden St. *W1* —4C **36**
Dewar St. *SE15* —1C **82**
Dewberry Gdns. *E6* —4F **45**
Dewberry St. *E14* —4E **43**

Dewey Rd. N1 —1C 38
Dewey St. SW17 —5B 92
Dewhurst Rd. W6 —4F 47
Dewsbury Rd. NW10 —2C 18
Dewsbury Ter. NW1 —5D 23
D'Eynsford Rd. SE5 —4F 67
Dhonau Ho. SE1 —5B 54 (off Longfield Est.)
Diadem Ct. W1 —5F 37 (off Dean St.)
Dial Wlk., The. W8 —3D 49 (off Broad Wlk., The)
Diamond Est. SW17 —3A 92
Diamond St. SE5 —3A 68
Diamond Ter. SE10 —4E 71
Diamond Way. SE8 —2C 70
Diana Clo. SE8 —2B 70
Diana Ho. SW13 —4B 60
Dibden Ho. SE5 —3A 68
Dibden St. N1 —5E 25
Dibdin Ho. NW6 —1D 35 (in two parts)
Dicey Av. NW2 —1E 19
Dickens Est. SE1 —3C 54
Dickens Est. SE16 —4C 54
Dickens' House. —3B 38 (off Doughty St.)
Dickens Ho. NW6 —2C 34 (off Malvern Rd.)
Dickens Ho. NW8 —3F 35 (off Fisherton St.)
Dickens Ho. SE17 —1D 67 (off Doddington Gro.)
Dickens Ho. W9 —3C 34 (off Malvern Rd.)
Dickens Ho. WC1 —3A 38 (off Herbrand St.)
Dickens M. EC1 —4D 39 (off Turnmill St.)
Dickenson Ho. N8 —1B 10
Dickenson Rd. N8 —2A 10
Dickens Rd. E6 —1F 45
Dickens Sq. SE1 —4E 53
Dickens St. SW8 —5D 65
Dicksee Ho. NW8 —3F 35 (off Lyons Pl.)
Dickson Ho. E1 —5D 41 (off Philpot St.)
Dickson Rd. SE9 —1F 87
Digby Bus. Cen. E9 —3F 27 (off Digby Rd.)
Digby Cres. N4 —4E 11
Digby Mans. W6 —1D 61 (off Hammersmith Bri. Rd.)
Digby Rd. E9 —3F 27
Digby St. E2 —2E 41
Diggon St. E1 —4F 41
Dighton Ct. SE17 —2E 67 (off John Ruskin St.)
Dighton Rd. SW18 —3E 77
Dignum St. N1 —1C 38
Digswell St. N7 —3C 24
Dilhorne Clo. SE12 —3D 101
Dilke St. SW3 —2B 64
Dillwyn Clo. SE26 —4A 98
Dilston Gro. SE16 —5E 55
Dilton Gdns. SW15 —1C 88
Dimes Pl. W6 —5D 47
Dimond Clo. E7 —1C 30
Dimsdale Wlk. E13 —1C 44
Dimson Cres. E3 —2C 42
Dingle Gdns. E14 —1C 56
Dingley La. SW16 —2F 93
Dingley Pl. EC1 —2E 39
Dingley Rd. EC1 —2E 39
Dingwall Gdns. NW11 —1C 6
Dingwall Rd. SW18 —5E 77
Dinmont Est. E2 —1C 40
Dinmont Ho. E2 —1C 40 (off Pritchard's Rd.)
Dinmont St. E2 —1D 41
Dinnington Ho. E1 —3D 41 (off Coventry Rd.)
Dinsdale Rd. SE3 —2B 72
Dinsmore Rd. SW12 —5D 79
Dinton Ho. NW8 —3A 36 (off Lilestone St.)
Dinton Rd. SW19 —5F 91
Dirleton Rd. E15 —5B 30
Disbrowe Rd. W6 —2A 62
Discovery Bus. Pk. SE16 (off St James's Rd.) —4C 54
Discovery Ho. E14 —1E 57
Discovery Wlk. E1 —2D 55
Disney Pl. SE1 —3E 53
Disney St. SE1 —3E 53
Disraeli Gdns. SW15 —2B 76
Disraeli Rd. E7 —3C 30
Disraeli Rd. SW15 —2A 76
Diss St. E2 —2B 40
Distaff La. EC4 —1E 53
Distillery La. W6 —1E 61
Distillery Rd. W6 —1E 61
Distin St. SE11 —5C 52
Ditch All. SE10 —4D 71
Ditchburn St. E14 —1E 57
Dittisham Rd. SE9 —4F 101
Divis Way. SW15 —4D 75 (off Dover Pk. Dri.)
Dixon Clark Ct. N1 —3D 25
Dixon Ho. W10 —5F 33 (off Darfield Way)
Dixon Rd. SE14 —4A 70
Dixon's All. SE16 —3D 55
Dobree Av. NW10 —4D 19
Dobson Clo. NW6 —4F 21
Dobson Ho. SE5 —3F 67 (off Edmund St.)
Dobson Ho. SE14 —2F 69 (off John Williams Clo.)
Doby Ct. EC4 —1E 53 (off Skinners La.)
Dockers Tanner Rd. E14 —5C 56
Dockhead. SE1 —3B 54
Dockhead Wharf. SE1 —3B 54 (off Shad Thames)
Dock Hill Av. SE16 —2F 55
Dockley Rd. SE16 —4C 54
Dockley Rd. Ind. Est. SE16 (off Dockley Rd.) —4C 54
Dock Offices. SE16 —4E 55 (off Surrey Quays Rd.)
Dock Rd. E16 —1B 58
Dockside Rd. E16 —1F 59
Dock St. E1 —1C 54
Doctor Johnson Av. SW17 —3D 93
Doctors Clo. SE26 —5E 97
Docwra's Bldgs. N1 —3A 26
Dodbrooke Rd. SE27 —3C 94
Dodd Ho. SE16 —5D 55 (off Rennie Est.)
Doddington Gro. SE17 —2D 67
Doddington Pl. SE17 —2D 67
Dodson St. SE1 —3C 52
Dod St. E14 —5B 42
Dog and Duck Yd. WC1 (off Princeton St.) —4B 38
Doggett Rd. SE6 —5C 84
Dog Kennel Hill. SE5 —1A 82
Dog Kennel Hill Est. SE22 (off Albrighton Rd.) —1A 82
Dog La. NW10 —1A 18
Doherty Rd. E13 —3C 44
Dolben Ct. SE8 —5B 56
Dolben St. SE1 —2D 53 (in two parts)
Dolby Rd. SW6 —5B 62
Dolland Ho. SE11 —1B 66 (off Newburn St.)
Dolland St. SE11 —1B 66
Dollar Bay. E14 —3E 57
Dollis Hill. —4D 5
Dollis Hill Av. NW2 —5D 5
Dollis Hill Est. NW2 —5C 4
Dollis Hill La. NW2 —1B 18
Dolman Rd. W4 —5A 46
Dolman St. SW4 —2B 80
Dolphin Clo. SE16 —3F 55
Dolphin Ct. NW11 —1A 6
Dolphin Ct. SE8 —2B 70 (off Wotton Rd.)
Dolphin Ho. SW18 —2D 77
Dolphin La. E14 —1D 57
Dolphin Sq. SW1 —1E 65
Dolphin Sq. W4 —3A 60
Dolphin Tower. SE8 —2B 70 (off Abinger Gro.)
Dombey Ho. SE1 —3C 54 (off Wolseley St.)
Dombey Ho. W11 —2F 47 (off St Ann's Rd.)
Dombey St. WC1 —4B 38 (in two parts)
Dome Hill Pk. SE26 —4B 96
Domett Clo. SE5 —2F 81
Domfe Pl. E5 —1E 27
Domingo St. EC1 —3E 39
Dominica Clo. E13 —2E 45
Dominion Ho. E14 —1D 71
Dominion St. EC2 —4F 39
Donald Hunter Ho. E7 —2D 31 (off Post Office App., in two parts)
Donald Rd. E13 —5D 31
Donaldson Rd. NW6 —5B 20
Doncaster Gdns. N4 —1E 11
Donegal Ho. E1 —3D 41 (off Cambridge Heath Rd.)

Donegal St. *N1* —1B **38**
Doneraile Ho. *SW1* —1D **65**
(off Ebury Bri. Rd.)
Doneraile St. *SW6* —5F **61**
Dongola Rd. *E1* —4A **42**
Dongola Rd. *E13* —2D **45**
Dongola Rd. W. *E13* —2D **45**
Donkey All. *SE22* —5C **82**
Donkin Ho. *SE16* —5D **55**
(off Rennie Est.)
Donnatt's Rd. *SE14* —4B **70**
Donne Ct. *SE24* —4E **81**
Donne Ho. *E14* —5C **42**
Donne Ho. *SE14* —2F **69**
(off Samuel Clo.)
Donnelly Ct. *SW6* —3A **62**
(off Dawes Rd.)
Donne Pl. *SW3* —5A **50**
Donnington Ct. *NW1* —4D **23**
(off Castlehaven Rd.)
Donnington Ct. *NW10*
—4D **19**
Donnington Rd. *NW10*
—4D **19**
Donoghue Cotts. *E14* —4A **42**
(off Maroon St.)
Donovan Ct. *SW10* —1F **63**
(off Drayton Gdns.)
Don Phelan Clo. *SE5* —4F **67**
Doon St. *SE1* —2C **52**
Dora Ho. *E14* —5B **42**
Dora Ho. *W11* —1F **47**
(off St Ann's Rd.)
Dorando Clo. *W12* —1D **47**
Doran Mnr. *N2* —1B **8**
(off Gt. North Rd.)
Doran Wlk. *E15* —4E **29**
Dora Rd. *SW19* —5C **90**
Dora St. *E14* —5B **42**
Dorchester Ct. *N1* —4A **26**
(off Englefield Rd.)
Dorchester Ct. *NW2* —5F **5**
Dorchester Ct. *SE24* —3E **81**
Dorchester Dri. *SE24* —3E **81**
Dorchester Gro. *W4* —1A **60**
Dorchester Ter. *NW2* —5F **5**
(off Gratton Ter.)
Dordrecht Rd. *W3* —2A **46**
Doreen Av. *NW9* —3A **4**
Doreen Capstan Ho. *E11*
(off Apollo Pl.) —5A **16**
Doria Rd. *SW6* —5B **62**
Doric Way. *NW1* —2F **37**
Dorinda St. *N7* —3C **24**
Doris Emmerton Ct. *SW11*
—2E **77**
Doris Rd. *E7* —4C **30**
Dorking Clo. *SE8* —2B **70**
Dorking Ho. *SE1* —4F **53**
Dorlcote Rd. *SW18* —5A **78**
Dorman Way. *NW8* —5F **21**
Dorma Trad. Pk. *E10* —3F **13**
Dormay St. *SW18* —3D **77**
Dormer Clo. *E15* —3B **30**
Dormstone Ho. *SE17* —5A **54**
(off Beckway St.)
Dornberg Clo. *SE3* —3C **72**

Dornberg Rd. *SE3* —3D **73**
Dorncliffe Rd. *SW6* —5A **62**
Dorney. *NW3* —4A **22**
Dornfell St. *NW6* —2B **20**
Dornton Rd. *SW12* —2D **93**
Dorothy Rd. *SW11* —1B **78**
Dorrell Pl. *SW9* —1C **80**
Dorrien Wlk. *SW16* —2F **93**
Dorrington St. *EC1* —1C **38**
Dorrit Ho. *W11* —2F **47**
(off St Ann's Rd.)
Dorrit St. *SE1* —3E **53**
(off Quilp St.)
Dorryn Ct. *SE26* —5F **97**
Dors Clo. *NW9* —3A **4**
Dorset Bldgs. *EC4* —5D **39**
Dorset Clo. *NW1* —4B **36**
Dorset Ct. *N1* —4A **26**
(off Hertford Rd.)
Dorset Ho. *NW1* —3B **36**
(off Gloucester Pl.)
Dorset Pl. *E15* —3F **29**
Dorset Ri. *EC4* —5D **39**
Dorset Rd. *E7* —4E **31**
Dorset Rd. *SW8* —3A **66**
Dorset Sq. *NW1* —3A **36**
Dorset Sq. *NW1* —4B **36**
Dorton Clo. *SE5* —3A **68**
Dorville Cres. *W6* —4D **47**
Dorville Rd. *SE12* —3B **86**
Doughty Ct. *E1* —2D **55**
(off Prusom St.)
Doughty Ho. *SW10* —2E **63**
(off Netherton Gro.)
Doughty M. *WC1* —3B **38**
Doughty St. *WC1* —3B **38**
Douglas Ho. *NW6* —4C **20**
(off Quex Rd.)
Douglas Est. *N1* —3E **25**
Douglas Johnstone Ho. *SW6*
(off Clem Attlee Ct.) —2B **62**
Douglas M. *NW2* —5A **6**
Douglas Pl. *E14* —5E **57**
Douglas Pl. *SW1* —5F **51**
(off Douglas St.)
Douglas Rd. *E16* —4C **44**
Douglas Rd. *N1* —4E **25**
Douglas Rd. S. *N1* —3E **25**
Douglas Rd. S. *N1* —3E **25**
Douglas St. *SW1* —5F **51**
Douglas Waite Ho. *NW6*
—4C **20**
Douglas Way. *SE8* —3C **70**
Douglas Way. *SE14* —3B **70**
(in two parts)
Doulton Ho. *SE11* —4B **52**
(off Lambeth Wlk.)
Doulton M. *NW6* —3D **21**
Dounesforth Gdns. *SW18*
—1D **91**
Douro Pl. *W8* —4D **49**
Douro St. *E3* —1C **42**
Douthwaite Sq. *E1* —2C **54**
Dove App. *E6* —4F **45**

Dove Commercial Cen. *NW5*
—2E **23**
Dovecote Gdns. *SW14*
—1A **74**
Dove Ct. *EC2* —5F **39**
(off Old Jewry)
Dovedale Rd. *SE22* —3D **83**
Dovehouse St. *SW3* —1F **63**
Dove M. *SW5* —5E **49**
Dover Clo. *NW2* —4F **5**
Dovercourt Est. *N1* —3F **25**
Dovercourt Rd. *SE22* —4A **82**
Doverfield Rd. *SW2* —5A **80**
Dover Flats. *SE1* —5A **54**
Dover Ho. *SE15* —2E **69**
Dover Ho. Rd. *SW15* —2C **74**
Dove Rd. *N1* —3F **25**
Dove Row. *E2* —5C **26**
Dover Pk. Dri. *SW15* —4D **75**
Dover Patrol. *SE3* —5D **73**
Dover Rd. *E12* —4E **17**
Dover Rd. *SE19* —5F **95**
Dover St. *W1* —1D **51**
Dover Yd. *W1* —2E **51**
(off Berkeley St.)
Doves Yd. *N1* —5C **24**
Doveton Ho. *E1* —3E **41**
(off Doveton St.)
Doveton St. *E1* —3E **41**
Dove Wlk. *SW1* —1C **64**
Dovey Lodge. *N1* —4C **24**
(off Bewdley St.)
Dowanhill Rd. *SE6* —1F **99**
Dowdeswell Clo. *SW15*
—2A **74**
Dowding Ho. *N6* —2C **8**
(off Hillcrest)
Dowdney Clo. *NW5* —2E **23**
Dowe Ho. *SE3* —1A **86**
Dowes Ho. *SW16* —3A **94**
Dowgate Hill. *EC4* —1F **53**
Dowland St. *W10* —2A **34**
Dowlas St. *SE5* —3A **68**
Dowler Ho. *E1* —5C **40**
(off Burslem St.)
Downbury M. *SW18* —3C **76**
Downderry Rd. *Brom* —3F **99**
Downend Ct. *SE15* —2A **68**
(off Longhope Clo.)
Downer's Cottage. *SW4*
—2E **79**
Downfield Clo. *W9* —3D **35**
Downham. —5F **99**
Downham Enterprise Cen.
SE6 —2B **100**
Downham La. *Brom* —5F **99**
Downham Rd. *N1* —4F **25**
Downham Way. *Brom* —5F **99**
Downing St. *SW1* —3A **52**
Down Pl. *W6* —5D **47**
Downsell Rd. *E15* —1E **29**
Downshield Rd. *E17* —1A **14**
Downshire Hill. *NW3* —1F **21**
Downside Cres. *NW3* —2A **22**
Downs La. *E5* —1D **27**
Downs Pk. Rd. *E8 & E5*
—2B **26**

Downs Rd. *E5* —1C **26**
Down St. *W1* —2D **51**
Down St. M. *W1* —2D **51**
Downton Av. *SW2* —2A **94**
Downtown Rd. *SE16* —3A **56**
Dowrey St. *N1* —5C **24**
Dowson Clo. *SE5* —2F **81**
Doyce St. *SE1* —3E **53**
Doyle Gdns. *NW10* —5C **18**
D'Oyley St. *SW1* —5C **50**
Doynton St. *N19* —4D **9**
Draco Ga. *SW15* —1E **75**
Draco St. *SE17* —2E **67**
Dragonfly Clo. *E13* —2D **45**
Dragon Rd. *SE15* —2A **68**
Dragon Yd. WC2 —*5A 38*
   (off High Holborn)
Dragoon Rd. *SE8* —1B **70**
Drake Clo. *SE16* —3F **55**
Drakefell Rd. *SE14 & SE4*
   —5F **69**
Drakefield Rd. *SW17* —3C **92**
Drake Hall. E16 —*2D 59*
   (off Wesley Av., in two parts)
Drake Ho. E1 —*4E 41*
   (off Stepney Way)
Drake Ho. SW1 —*2F 65*
   (off Dolphin Sq.)
Drakeland Ho. W9 —*3B 34*
   (off Fernhead Rd.)
Drakeley Ct. *N5* —1D **25**
Drake Rd. *SE4* —1C **84**
Drakes Ct. *SE23* —1E **97**
Drakes Courtyard. NW6
   —*4B 20*
Drake St. *WC1* —4B **38**
Draper Ho. SE1 —*5D 53*
   (off Elephant & Castle)
Draper Pl. N1 —*5D 25*
   (off Dagmar Ter.)
Drapers Gdns. *EC2* —5F **39**
Drapers Rd. *E15* —1F **29**
Drappers Way. *SE16* —5C **54**
Drawdock Rd. *SE10* —3F **57**
Draycot Rd. *E11* —1D **17**
Draycott Av. *SW3* —5A **50**
Draycott Pl. *SW3* —5B **50**
Draycott Ter. *SW3* —5B **50**
Drayford Clo. *W9* —3B **34**
Dray Gdns. *SW2* —3B **80**
Drayson M. *W8* —3C **48**
Drayton Gdns. *SW10* —1E **63**
Drayton Ho. E11 —*1F 15*
Drayton Ho. SE5 —*3F 67*
   (off Elmington Rd.)
Drayton Pk. *N5* —1C **24**
Drayton Pk. M. *N5* —2C **24**
Drayton Rd. *E11* —1F **15**
Drayton Rd. *NW10* —5B **18**
Dreadnought St. *SE10*
   —4A **58**
Dreadnought Wharf. SE10
   (off Thames St.) —*2D 71*
Dresden Clo. *NW6* —3D **21**
Dresden Ho. SE11 —*5B 52*
   (off Lambeth Wlk.)
Dresden Rd. *N19* —3E **9**

Dressington Av. *SE4* —4C **84**
Drewery Ct. *SE3* —1A **86**
Drewett Ho. E1 —*5C 40*
   (off Christian St.)
Drew Ho. *SW16* —3A **94**
Drew Rd. *E16* —2F **59**
   (in three parts)
Drewstead Rd. *SW16* —2F **93**
Driffield Rd. *E3* —1A **42**
Drinkwater Ho. SE5 —*3F 67*
   (off Picton St.)
Drive Mans. SW6 —*5A 62*
   (off Fulham Rd.)
Drive, The. *N7* —3B **24**
Drive, The. *NW10* —5B **18**
Drive, The. *NW11* —2A **6**
Drive, The. *SW6* —5A **62**
Drive, The. *Ilf* —1F **17**
Driveway, The. E17 —*1D 15*
   (off Hoe St.)
Droitwich Clo. *SE26* —3C **96**
Dromore Rd. *SW15* —4A **76**
Dron Ho. E1 —*4E 41*
   (off Adelina Gro.)
Droop St. *W10* —2F **33**
Drovers Pl. *SE15* —3E **69**
Druce Rd. *SE21* —4A **82**
Druid St. *SE1* —3A **54**
Drummond Cres. *NW1*
   —2F **37**
Drummond Ga. *SW1* —1F **65**
Drummond Ho. E2 —*1C 40*
   (off Goldsmiths Row)
Drummond Rd. *E11* —1E **17**
Drummond Rd. *SE16*
   —4D **55**
Drummond St. *NW1* —3E **37**
Drum St. *E1* —5B **40**
Drury Ho. *SW8* —4E **65**
Drury La. *WC2* —5A **38**
Drury Way. *NW10* —2A **18**
Dryad St. *SW15* —1F **75**
Dryburgh Ho. *SW1* —1D **65**
   (off Abbots Mnr.)
Dryburgh Rd. *SW15* —1D **75**
Dryden Ct. *SE11* —5D **53**
Dryden Mans. W14 —*2A 62*
   (off Queen's Club Gdns.)
Dryden Rd. *SW19* —5E **91**
Dryden St. *WC2* —5A **38**
Dryfield Wlk. *SE8* —2C **70**
Drylands Rd. *N8* —1A **10**
Drysdale Ho. N1 —*2A 40*
   (off Drysdale St.)
Drysdale Pl. *N1* —2A **40**
Drysdale St. *N1* —2A **40**
Dublin Av. *E8* —5C **26**
Ducal St. *E2* —2B **40**
Du Cane Clo. *W12* —5E **33**
Du Cane Ct. *SW17* —1C **92**
Du Cane Rd. *W12* —5B **32**
Ducavel Ho. *SW2* —1B **94**
Duchess M. *W1* —4D **37**
Duchess of Bedford Ho. W8
   —*3C 48*
   *(off Duchess of
        Bedford's Wlk.)*

Duchess of Bedford's Wlk.
   W8 —*3C 48*
Duchess St. *W1* —4D **37**
Duchy St. *SE1* —2C **52**
   (in two parts)
Ducie St. *SW4* —2B **80**
Duckett M. *N4* —1D **11**
Duckett Rd. *N4* —1D **11**
Duckett St. *E1* —3F **41**
Duck La. W1 —*5F 37*
   (off Broadwick St.)
Du Cros Rd. *W3* —2A **46**
Dudden Hill. —2D **19**
Dudden Hill La. *NW10*
   —1B **18**
Dudden Hill Pde. *NW10*
   —1B **18**
Duddington Clo. *SE9* —4F **101**
Dudley Ct. W1 —*5B 36*
   (off Up. Berkeley St.)
Dudley Ct. *SW4* —2A **38**
Dudley Ho. W2 —*4F 35*
   (off N. Wharf Rd.)
Dudley Rd. *NW6* —1A **34**
Dudley Rd. *SW19* —5C **90**
Dudley St. *W2* —4F **35**
Dudlington Rd. *E5* —4E **13**
Dudmaston M. SW3 —*1F 63*
   (off Fulham Rd.)
Duffell Ho. SE11 —*1B 66*
   (off Loughborough St.)
Dufferin Av. *EC1* —3F **39**
   (off Loughborough St.)
Dufferin Ct. EC1 —*3F 39*
   (off Dufferin St.)
Dufferin St. *EC1* —3E **39**
Duff St. *E14* —5D **43**
Dufour's Pl. *W1* —5E **37**
Dugard Way. *SE11* —5D **53**
Duke Humphrey Rd. *SE3*
   —4A **72**
Duke of Wellington Pl. *SW1*
   —3C **50**
Duke of York Memorial.
   —*2F 51*
   (off Carlton Ho. Ter.)
Duke of York St. *SW1*
   —2E **51**
Duke Rd. *W4* —1A **60**
Duke's Av. *W4* —1A **60**
Dukes Ct. *SE13* —5E **71**
Duke's Head Yd. *N6* —3D **9**
Duke Shore Pl. *E14* —1B **56**
Duke Shore Wharf. *E14*
   —1B **56**
Duke's Ho. SW1 —*5F 51*
   (off Vincent St.)
Dukes La. *W8* —3D **49**
Duke's M. W1 —*5C 36*
   (off Duke St.)
Duke's Pl. *EC3* —5A **40**
Duke's Rd. *NW1* —2F **37**
Dukesthorpe Rd. *SE26*
   —4F **97**
Duke St. *SW1* —2E **51**
Duke St. *W1* —5C **36**
Duke St. Hill. *SE1* —2F **53**

Duke St. Mans. W1 —5C 36 (off Duke St.)
Duke's Yd. W1 —1C 50
Dulas St. N4 —3B 10
Dulford St. W11 —1A 48
Dulka Rd. SW11 —3B 78
Dulverton. NW1 —5E 23 (off Royal College St.)
Dulverton Mans. WC1 —3B 38 (off Gray's Inn Rd.)
Dulwich. —2A 96
Dulwich Comn. SE21 & SE22 —1A 96
Dulwich Hamlet F.C. —2A 82
Dulwich Lawn Clo. SE22 —3B 82
Dulwich Oaks Pl. SE21 —3A 96
Dulwich Picture Gallery. —5A 82
Dulwich Ri. Gdns. SE22 —3B 82
Dulwich Rd. SE24 —3C 80
Dulwich Village. —5A 82
Dulwich Village. SE21 —4F 81
Dulwich Wood Av. SE19 —4A 96
Dulwich Wood Pk. SE19 —4A 96
Dumain Ct. SE11 —5D 53 (off Opal St.)
Dumbarton Ct. SW2 —4A 80
Dumbarton Rd. SW2 —4A 80
Dumont Rd. N16 —5A 12
Dumpton Pl. NW1 —4C 22
Dunbar Rd. E7 —3C 30
Dunbar St. SE27 —3E 95
Dunbar Wharf. E14 —1B 56
Dunboyne Rd. NW3 —2B 22
Dunbridge Ho. SW15 —4B 74 (off Highcliffe Dri.)
Dunbridge St. E2 —3C 40
Duncan Gro. W3 —5A 32
Duncan Ho. SW1 —1E 65 (off Dolphin Sq.)
Duncannon Ho. SW1 —1F 65 (off Lindsay Sq.)
Duncannon St. WC2 —1A 52
Duncan Rd. E8 —5D 27
Duncan St. N1 —1D 39
Duncan Ter. N1 —1D 39 (in two parts)
Duncombe Hill. SE23 —5A 84
Duncombe Rd. N19 —3F 9
Duncrievie Rd. SE13 —4F 85
Dundalk Rd. SE4 —1A 84
Dundas Rd. SE15 —5E 69
Dundee Ct. E1 —2D 55 (off Wapping High St.)
Dundee Ho. W9 —2E 35 (off Maida Va.)
Dundee Rd. E13 —1D 45
Dundee St. E1 —2D 55
Dundee Wharf. E14 —1B 56
Dundonald Ho. E14 —3D 57
Dundonald Rd. NW10 —5F 19
Dundry Ho. SE26 —3C 96
Dunedin Rd. E10 —5D 15
Dunelm Gro. SE27 —3E 95
Dunelm St. E1 —5F 41
Dunfield Gdns. SE6 —5D 99
Dunfield Rd. SE6 —5D 99 (in two parts)
Dunford Rd. N7 —1B 24
Dungarvan Av. SW15 —2C 74
Dunkeld Ho. E14 —5F 43
Dunkery Rd. SE9 —4F 101
Dunkirk St. SE27 —4E 95
Dunlace Rd. E5 —1E 27
Dunlin Ho. SE16 —5F 55 (off Tawny Way)
Dunloe Ct. E2 —1B 40 (off Dawson St.)
Dunloe St. E2 —1B 40
Dunlop Pl. SE16 —4B 54
Dunmore Point. E2 —2B 40 (off Gascoigne Pl.)
Dunmore Rd. NW6 —5A 20
Dunmow Ho. SE11 —1B 66 (off Newburn St.)
Dunmow Rd. E15 —1F 29
Dunmow Wlk. N1 —5E 25 (off Popham St.)
Dunnage Cres. SE16 —5A 56
Dunnico Ho. SE17 —1A 68 (off East St.)
Dunn's Pas. WC1 —5A 38 (off High Holborn)
Dunn St. E8 —2B 26
Dunollie Pl. NW5 —2E 23
Dunollie Rd. NW5 —2E 23
Dunoon Gdns. SE23 —5F 83
Dunoon Ho. N1 —5B 24 (off Bemerton Est.)
Dunoon Rd. SE23 —5E 83
Dunraven Rd. W12 —2C 46
Dunraven St. W1 —1B 50
Dunsany Rd. W14 —4F 47
Dunsford Way. SW15 —4D 75
Dunsmure Rd. N16 —3A 12
Dunstable M. W1 —4C 36
Dunstan Houses. E1 —4E 41 (off Stepney Grn.)
Dunstan Rd. NW11 —3B 6
Dunstan's Gro. SE22 —4D 83
Dunstan's Rd. SE22 —5C 82
Dunster Ct. EC3 —1A 54
Dunster Gdns. NW6 —4B 20
Dunster Ho. SE6 —3E 99
Dunsterville Way. SE1 —3F 53
Dunston Rd. E8 —5B 26
Dunston Rd. SW11 —5C 64
Dunston St. E8 —5A 26
Dunton Ct. SE23 —2D 97
Dunton Rd. E10 —2D 15
Dunton Rd. SE1 —1B 68
Duntshill Rd. SW18 —1D 91
Dunworth M. W11 —5B 34
Duplex Ride. SW1 —3B 50
Dupree Rd. SE7 —1D 73
Durand Gdns. SW9 —4B 66
Durands Wlk. SE16 —3B 56
Durant St. E2 —1C 40
Durban Ct. E7 —4F 31
Durban Rd. E15 —2A 44
Durban Rd. SE27 —4E 95
Durfey Ho. SE5 —3F 67 (off Edmund St.)
Durford Cres. SW15 —1D 89
Durham Ct. NW6 —1C 34 (off Kilburn Pk. Rd., in two parts)
Durham Hill. Brom —4B 100
Durham Ho. St. WC2 —1A 52 (off John Adam St.)
Durham Pl. SW3 —1B 64
Durham Rd. E12 —1F 31
Durham Rd. E16 —3A 44
Durham Rd. N7 —4B 10
Durham Row. E1 —4F 41
Durham St. SE11 —2B 66
Durham Ter. W2 —5D 35
Durham Yd. E2 —2D 41
Durley Rd. N16 —2A 12
Durlston Rd. E5 —4C 12
Durnford Ho. SE6 —3E 99
Durnford St. N15 —1A 12
Durnford St. SE10 —2E 71
Durning Rd. SE19 —5F 95
Durnsford Av. SW19 —2C 90
Durnsford Rd. SW19 —2C 90
Durrell Rd. SW6 —4B 62
Durrels Ho. W14 —5B 48 (off Warwick Rd.)
Durrington Rd. E5 —1A 28
Durrington Tower. SW8 —5E 65
Durrisdeer Ho. NW2 —1B 20 (off Lyndale)
Dursley Clo. SE3 —5E 73
Dursley Ct. SE15 —3A 68 (off Lydney Clo.)
Dursley Gdns. SE3 —4F 73
Dursley Rd. SE3 —5E 73
Durward St. E1 —4D 41
Durweston M. W1 —4B 36 (off Crawford St.)
Durweston St. W1 —4B 36
Dutch Yd. SW18 —3C 76
Duthie St. E14 —1E 57
Dutton St. SE10 —4E 71
Dye Ho. La. E3 —5C 28
Dyer's Bldgs. EC1 —4C 38
Dyers Hall Rd. E11 —3A 16
Dyers Hill Rd. E11 —4F 15
Dyers La. SW15 —2D 75
Dylan Rd. SE24 —2D 81
Dylways. SE5 —2F 81
Dymes Path. SW19 —2F 89
Dymock Ct. SE15 —3A 68 (off Lydney Clo.)
Dymock St. SW6 —1D 77
Dyneley Rd. SE12 —3E 101
Dyne Rd. NW6 —4A 20
Dynevor Rd. N16 —5A 12
Dynham Rd. NW6 —4C 20
Dyott St. WC1 —5F 37
Dysart St. EC2 —3F 39
Dyson Ct. NW2 —3E 5
Dyson Ho. SE10 —1B 72 (off Blackwall La.)

Dyson Rd. *E11* —1A **16**
Dyson Rd. *E15* —3B **30**

Eade Rd. *N4* —2E **11**
Eagle Clo. *SE16* —1E **69**
Eagle Ct. *EC1* —4D **39**
Eagle Hill. *SE19* —5F **95**
*Eagle Ho. E1 —3D **41***
(off Headlam St.)
Eagle Lodge. *NW11* —2B **6**
Eagle M. *N1* —3A **26**
*Eagle Pl. SW10 —1E **63***
(off Rolandway)
*Eagle Pl. W1 —1E **51***
(off Piccadilly)
Eagle St. *WC1* —4B **38**
*Eagle Wharf Ct. SE1 —2B **54***
(off Lafone St.)
*Eagle Wharf E. E14 —1A **56***
(off Narrow St.)
Eagle Wharf Rd. *N1* —1E **39**
*Eagle Wharf W. E14 —1A **56***
(off Narrow St.)
Ealdham Sq. *SE9* —2E **87**
*Eamont Ct. NW8 —1A **36***
(off Eamont St.)
Eamont St. *NW8* —1A **36**
Eardley Cres. *SW5* —1C **62**
Eardley Rd. *SW16* —5E **93**
Earldom Rd. *SW15* —2E **75**
Earlham Gro. *E7* —2B **30**
Earlham St. *WC2* —5A **38**
*Earl Ho. NW8 —3A **36***
(off Lisson Gro.)
*Earlom Ho. WC1 —2C **38***
(off Margery St.)
Earls Court. —1C 62
Earl's Court Exhibition Building. —1C 62
Earls Ct. Gdns. *SW5* —5D **49**
Earls Ct. Rd. *W8 & SW5* —4C **48**
Earl's Ct. Sq. *SW5* —1D **63**
Earlsferry Way. *N1* —4A **24**
(in two parts)
Earlsfield. —1E 91
Earlsfield Rd. *SW18* —1E **91**
Earlsmead Rd. *NW10* —2E **33**
Earls Ter. *W8* —4B **48**
Earlsthorpe M. *SW12* —4C **78**
Earlsthorpe Rd. *SE26* —4F **97**
Earlstoke St. *EC1* —2D **39**
Earlston Gro. *E9* —5D **27**
Earl St. *EC2* —4F **39**
Earls Wlk. *W8* —4C **48**
Earlswood Clo. *SE10* —2A **72**
Earlswood St. *SE10* —1A **72**
Early M. *NW1* —5D **23**
Earnshaw St. *WC2* —5F **37**
Earsby St. *W14* —5A **48**
(in three parts)
*Easley's M. W1 —5C **36***
(off Wigmore St.)
East Acton. —1A 46
E. Acton Arc. *W3* —5A **32**
E. Acton Ct. *W3* —1A **46**
E. Acton La. *W3* —2A **46**
E. Arbour St. *E1* —5F **41**
East Bank. *N16* —2A **12**
*East Block. SE1 —3B **52***
(off York Rd.)
Eastbourne M. *W2* —5E **35**
Eastbourne Rd. *E15* —5A **30**
Eastbourne Rd. *N15* —1A **12**
Eastbourne Rd. *SW17* —5C **92**
Eastbourne Ter. *W2* —5E **35**
Eastbrook Rd. *SE3* —4D **73**
Eastbury Gro. *W4* —1A **60**
Eastbury Ter. *E1* —3F **41**
Eastcastle St. *W1* —5E **37**
Eastcheap. *EC3* —1A **54**
E. Churchfield Rd. *W3* —2A **46**
Eastcombe Av. *SE7* —2D **73**
Eastcote St. *SW9* —5B **66**
E. Cross Cen. *E15* —3C **28**
E. Cross Route. *E9 & E3* —4B **28**
Eastdown Ct. *SE13* —2F **85**
Eastdown Ho. *E8* —1C **26**
Eastdown Pk. *SE13* —2F **85**
East Dulwich. —2B 82
E. Dulwich Gro. *SE22* —3A **82**
E. Dulwich Rd. *SE22 & SE15* —2B **82**
Eastern Av. *E11 & Ilf* —1D **17**
Eastern Rd. *E13* —1D **45**
Eastern Rd. *E17* —1E **15**
Eastern Rd. *SE4* —2C **84**
E. Ferry Rd. *E14* —5D **57**
Eastfield St. *E14* —4A **42**
East Gdns. *SW17* —5A **92**
E. Ham Ind. Est. *E6* —3F **45**
E. Harding St. *EC4* —5C **38**
E. Heath Rd. *NW3* —5E **7**
East Hill. *SW18* —3D **77**
E. India Bldgs. *E14* —1C **56**
E. India Dock Ho. *E14* —5E **43**
E. India Dock Rd. *E14* —5C **42**
E. India Dock Wall Rd. *E14* —1F **57**
*Eastlake Ho. NW8 —3F **35***
(off Frampton St.)
Eastlake Rd. *SE5* —5E **67**
Eastlands Cres. *SE21* —4B **82**
East La. *SE16* —3C **54**
(Chambers St.)
East La. *SE16* —3C **54**
(Scott Lidgett Cres., in two parts)
Eastlea M. *E16* —3A **44**
Eastleigh Clo. *NW2* —5A **4**
Eastleigh Wlk. *SW15* —5C **74**
East London Crematorium. *E13* —2B **44**
Eastman Ho. *SW4* —4E **79**
Eastman Rd. *W3* —3A **46**
East Mascalls. *SE7* —2E **73**
Eastmearn Rd. *SE27* —2E **95**
Eastmoor Pl. *SE7* —4F **59**
Eastmoor St. *SE7* —4F **59**
E. Mount St. *E1* —4D **41**
Eastney St. *SE10* —1F **71**
Easton St. *WC1* —3C **38**
East Parkside. *SE10* —3A **58**
*East Pas. EC1 —4E **39***
(off Cloth St.)
East Pier. *E1* —2D **55**
East Pl. *SE27* —4E **95**
East Point. *SE1* —1C **68**
E. Poultry Av. *EC1* —4D **39**
East Rd. *E15* —5C **30**
East Rd. *EC1* —2F **39**
East Row. *E11* —1C **16**
East Row. *W10* —3A **34**
*Eastry Ho. SW8 —3A **66***
(off Hartington Rd.)
E. Sheen Av. *SW14* —3A **74**
East Smithfield. *E1* —1B **54**
East St. *SE17* —1E **67**
E. Surrey Gro. *SE15* —3B **68**
E. Tenter St. *E1* —5B **40**
East Va. *W3* —2B **46**
Eastville Av. *NW11* —1B **6**
Eastway. *E9* —3B **28**
(in two parts)
East Way. *E11* —1D **17**
Eastway Commercial Cen. *E15* —2C **28**
*Eastwell Ho. SE1 —4F **53***
(off Weston St.)
Eatington Rd. *E10* —1F **15**
Eaton Clo. *SW1* —5C **50**
Eaton Dri. *SW9* —2D **81**
Eaton Garages. *NW3* —3A **22**
Eaton Ga. *SW1* —5C **50**
Eaton Gro. *N19* —5F **9**
Eaton Ho. *SW11* —4F **63**
Eaton La. *SW1* —4D **51**
*Eaton Mans. SW1 —5C **50***
(off Bourne St.)
Eaton M. N. *SW1* —5C **50**
Eaton M. S. *SW1* —5C **50**
Eaton M. W. *SW1* —5C **50**
Eaton Pl. *SW1* —5C **50**
Eaton Row. *SW1* —4D **51**
Eaton Sq. *SW1* —5C **50**
Eaton Ter. *E3* —2A **42**
Eaton Ter. *SW1* —5C **50**
*Eaton Ter. M. SW1 —5C **50***
(off Eaton Ter.)
Eatonville Rd. *SW17* —2B **92**
Eatonville Vs. *SW17* —2B **92**
Ebbisham Dri. *SW8* —2B **66**
Ebbsfleet Rd. *NW2* —2A **20**
Ebdon Way. *SE3* —1D **87**
Ebenezer Ho. *SE11* —5D **53**
Ebenezer Mussel Ho. E2
*(off Patriot Sq.) —1E **41***
Ebenezer St. *N1* —2F **39**
Ebley Clo. *SE15* —2B **68**
Ebner St. *SW18* —3D **77**
Ebor Cotts. *SW15* —3A **88**
Ebor St. *E2* —3B **40**
Ebsworth St. *SE23* —5F **83**
Eburne Rd. *N7* —5A **10**
Ebury Bri. *SW1* —1D **65**
Ebury Bri. Est. *SW1* —1D **65**
Ebury Bri. Rd. *SW1* —1C **64**
Ebury M. *SE27* —3D **95**
Ebury M. *SW1* —5D **51**

Ebury M. E. *SW1* —4D **51**
Ebury Sq. *SW1* —5C **50**
Ebury St. *SW1* —5C **50**
Ecclesbourne Rd. *N1* —4E **25**
Eccles Rd. *SW11* —2B **78**
Eccleston Bri. *SW1* —5D **51**
Eccleston Ho. *SW2* —4C **80**
Eccleston M. *SW1* —4C **50**
Eccleston Pl. *SW1* —5D **51**
Eccleston Sq. *SW1* —5D **51**
Eccleston Sq. M. *SW1* —5D **51**
Eccleston St. *SW1* —4D **51**
Eckford St. *N1* —1C **38**
*Eckington Ho. N15 —1F **11***
(off Fladbury Rd.)
Eckstein Rd. *SW11* —2A **78**
Eclipse Rd. *E13* —4D **45**
Ector Rd. *SE6* —2A **100**
Edans Ct. *W12* —3B **46**
Edbrooke Rd. *W9* —3C **34**
Eddington St. *N4* —3C **10**
Eddisbury Ho. *SE26* —3C **96**
Eddiscombe Rd. *SW6* —5B **62**
Eddystone Rd. *SE4* —3A **84**
Eddystone Tower. *SE8* —1A **70**
Edenbridge Clo. SE16
*(off Masters Dri.) —1D **69***
Edenbridge Rd. *E9* —4F **27**
Eden Clo. *NW3* —4C **6**
Eden Clo. *W8* —4C **48**
Edencourt Rd. *SW16* —5D **93**
Eden Gro. *E17* —1D **15**
Eden Gro. *N7* —2B **24**
Edenham Way. *W10* —3B **34**
*Eden Ho. NW8 —3A **36***
(off Church St.)
Edenhurst Av. *SW6* —1B **76**
Eden M. *SW17* —3E **91**
Eden Rd. *E17* —1D **15**
Eden Rd. *SE27* —4D **95**
Edensor Gdns. *W4* —3A **60**
Edensor Rd. *W4* —3A **60**
Edenvale St. *SW6* —5D **63**
*Edgar Ho. E9 —2A **28***
(off Homerton Rd.)
Edgar Ho. *E11* —2C **16**
*Edgar Ho. SW8 —3A **66***
(off Wyvil Rd.)
Edgar Kail Way. *SE22* —2A **82**
Edgarley Ter. *SW6* —4A **62**
Edgar Rd. *E3* —2D **43**
Edge Bus. Cen., The. *NW2* —4D **5**
Edgecombe Ho. *SE5* —5A **68**
Edgecot Gro. *N15* —1A **12**
Edgefoot Gro. *N15* —1A **12**
Edgehill Ho. *SW9* —5D **67**
Edgeley La. *SW4* —1F **79**
Edgeley Rd. *SW4* —1F **79**
Edgel St. *SW18* —2D **77**
Edgepoint Clo. *SE27* —5D **95**
Edge St. *W8* —2C **48**
Edgeworth Av. *NW4* —1C **4**
Edgeworth Clo. *NW4* —1C **4**
*Edgeworth Ho. NW8 —5E **21***
(off Boundary Rd.)
Edgeworth Rd. *SE9* —2E **87**
Edgington Rd. *SW16* —5F **93**
*Edgson Ho. SW1 —1D **65***
(off Ebury Bri. Rd.)
Edgware Rd. *NW2* —3D **5**
Edgware Rd. *W2* —3F **35**
Edinburgh Clo. *E2* —1E **41**
*Edinburgh Ct. SE16 —2F **55***
(off Rotherhithe St.)
Edinburgh Ga. *SW1* —3B **50**
*Edinburgh Ho. W9 —2D **35***
(off Maida Va.)
Edinburgh Rd. *E13* —1D **45**
Edinburgh Rd. *E17* —1C **14**
Edington. *NW5* —3C **22**
Edison Building. *E14* —3C **56**
Edison Clo. *E17* —1C **14**
Edison Rd. *N8* —1F **9**
Edis St. *NW1* —5C **22**
Edith Brinson Ho. *E14* —5F **43**
Edith Cavell Clo. *N19* —2A **10**
Edith Gro. *SW10* —2E **63**
*Edith Ho. W6 —1E **61***
(off Queen Caroline St.)
Edithna St. *SW9* —1A **80**
Edith Neville Cotts. *NW1* —2F **37**
Edith Rd. *E6* —4F **31**
Edith Rd. *E15* —2F **29**
Edith Rd. *SW19* —5D **91**
Edith Rd. *W14* —5A **48**
Edith Row. *SW6* —4D **63**
Edith St. *E2* —1C **40**
*Edith Summerskill Ho. SW6 —3B **62***
(off Clem Attlee Est.)
Edith Ter. *SW10* —3E **63**
Edith Vs. *W14* —5B **48**
Edith Yd. *SW10* —3E **63**
Edmeston Clo. *E9* —3A **28**
Edmond Ct. *SE14* —4E **69**
Edmond Halley Way. *SE10* —3A **58**
*Edmonton Ct. SE16 —4E **55***
(off Canada Est.)
Edmund Ho. *SE17* —2D **67**
Edmundsbury Ct. Est. *SW9* —2B **80**
Edmund St. *SE5* —3F **67**
*Ednam Ho. SE15 —2C **68***
(off Haymerle Rd.)
Edna St. *SW11* —4A **64**
*Edred Ho. E9 —1A **28***
(off Lindisfarne Way)
Edrich Ho. *SW4* —4A **66**
*Edric Ho. SW1 —5F **51***
(off Page St.)
Edric Rd. *SE14* —3F **69**
Edward Bond Ho. WC1
*(off Cromer St.) —2A **38***
Edward Clo. *NW2* —1F **19**
Edward Ct. *E16* —4C **44**
*Edward Dodd Ct. N1 —2F **39***
(off Haberdasher St.)
Edward Edward's Ho. SE1
*(off Nicholson St.) —2D **53***
Edwardes Pl. *W8* —4B **48**
Edwardes Sq. *W8* —4B **48**
*Edward Ho. SE11 —1B **66***
(off Newburn St.)
*Edward Mann Clo. E1 —5F **41***
(off Caroline St.)
Edward M. *NW1* —2D **37**
Edward Pl. *SE8* —2B **70**
Edward Robinson Ho. SE14
*(off Reaston St.) —3F **69***
Edwards Cotts. *N1* —3D **25**
Edward's La. *N16* —4F **11**
Edwards M. *N1* —4D **25**
Edwards M. *W1* —5C **36**
Edward Sq. *N1* —5B **24**
Edward Sq. *SE16* —2A **56**
Edward St. *E16* —3C **44**
Edward St. *SE14* —3A **70**
Edward Temme Av. *E15* —4B **30**
Edward Tyler Rd. *SE12* —2E **101**
Edwina Gdns. *Ilf* —1F **17**
Edwin's Mead. *E9* —1A **28**
Edwin St. *E1* —3E **41**
Edwin St. *E16* —4C **44**
Edwis Ho. *SE15* —3C **68**
Effie Pl. *SW6* —3C **62**
Effie Rd. *SW6* —3C **62**
Effingham Rd. *SE12* —3A **86**
Effort St. *SW17* —5A **92**
*Effra Ct. SW2 —3B **80***
(off Brixton Hill)
Effra Pde. *SW2* —3C **80**
Effra Rd. *SW2* —2C **80**
Effra Rd. *SW19* —5D **91**
Effra Rd. Retail Pk. *SW2* —3C **80**
Egbert St. *NW1* —5C **22**
*Egbury Ho. SW15 —4B **74***
(off Tangley Gro.)
Egerton Ct. *E11* —2F **15**
Egerton Cres. *SW3* —5A **50**
Egerton Dri. *SE10* —4D **71**
Egerton Gdns. *NW10* —5E **19**
Egerton Gdns. *SW3* —5A **50**
Egerton Gdns. M. *SW3* —4A **50**
Egerton Pl. *SW3* —4A **50**
Egerton Rd. *N16* —2B **12**
Egerton Ter. *SW3* —4A **50**
Egham Clo. *SW19* —2A **90**
Egham Rd. *E13* —4D **45**
Eglantine Rd. *SW18* —3E **77**
Eglington Ct. *SE17* —2E **67**
Egliston M. *SW15* —1E **75**
Egliston Rd. *SW15* —1E **75**
Eglon M. *NW1* —4B **22**
Egmont St. *SE14* —3F **69**
*Egremont Ho. SE13 —5D **71***
(off Russett Way)
Egremont Rd. *SE27* —3C **94**
*Egret Ho. SE16 —5F **55***
(off Tawny Way)
Eider Clo. *E7* —2B **30**
*Eider Ct. SE8 —2B **70***
(off Pilot Clo.)

Eileen Wilkinson Ho. SW6 (off Clem Attlee Ct.) —2B ***62***
Eisenhower Dri. *E6* —4F **45**
Elaine Gro. *NW5* —2C **22**
Elam Clo. *SE5* —5D **67**
Elam St. *SE5* —5D **67**
Elan Ct. *E1* —4D **41**
Eland Rd. *SW11* —1B **78**
Elba Pl. *SE17* —5E **53**
Elbe St. *SW6* —5E **63**
Elborough St. *SW18* —1C **90**
Elbourne Ct. SE16 —4F ***55*** *(off Worgan St.)*
Elbourn Ho. SW3 —1A ***64*** *(off Cale St.)*
Elbury Dri. *E16* —5C **44**
Elcho St. *SW11* —3A **64**
Elcot Av. *SE15* —3D **69**
Elder Av. *N8* —1A **10**
Elderberry Gro. *SE27* —4E **95**
Elderfield Ho. *E14* —1C **56**
Elderfield Pl. *SW17* —4D **93**
Elderfield Rd. *E5* —1F **27**
Elderflower Way. *E15* —4A **30**
Elder Gdns. *SE27* —5E **95**
Elder Rd. *SE27* —4E **95**
Elder St. *E1* —3B **40** (in two parts)
Elderton Rd. *SE26* —4A **98**
Elder Wlk. N1 —5D ***25*** *(off Popham St.)*
Elderwood Pl. *SE27* —5E **95**
Eldon Ct. *NW6* —5C **20**
Eldon Gro. *NW3* —2F **21**
Eldon Rd. *W8* —4D **49**
Eldon St. *EC2* —4F **39**
Eldridge Ct. *SE16* —4C **54**
Eleanor Clo. *SE16* —3F **55**
Eleanor Gro. *SW13* —1A **74**
Eleanor Rd. *E8* —3D **27**
Eleanor Rd. *E15* —3B **30**
Eleanor St. *E3* —2C **42**
Electric Av. *SW9* —2C **80**
Electric La. *SW9 & SW2* (in two parts) —2C **80**
Elephant & Castle. (Junct.) —4D **53**
Elephant & Castle. *SE1* —5D **53**
Elephant La. *SE16* —3E **55**
Elephant Rd. *SE17* —5E **53**
Elfindale Rd. *SE24* —3E **81**
Elford Clo. *SE3* —2D **87**
Elford M. *SW4* —3E **79**
Elfort Rd. *N5* —1C **24**
Elfrida Cres. *SE6* —4C **98**
Elf Row. *E1* —1E **55**
Elgar Av. *NW10* —3A **18** (in two parts)
Elgar Clo. *E13* —1E **45**
Elgar Clo. *SE8* —3C **70**
Elgar Ct. W14 —4A ***48*** *(off Blythe Rd.)*
Elgar Ho. *NW6* —4E **21**
Elgar Ho. SW1 —1D ***65*** *(off Churchill Gdns.)*
Elgar St. *SE16* —4A **56**
Elgin Av. *W9* —3B **34**
Elgin Av. *W12* —3D **47**
Elgin Ct. *W9* —3D **35**
Elgin Cres. *W11* —1A **48**
Elgin Est. W9 —3C ***34*** *(off Elgin Av.)*
Elgin Ho. *E14* —5D **43**
Elgin Mans. *W9* —2D **35**
Elgin M. *W11* —5A **34**
Elgin M. N. *W9* —2D **35**
Elgin M. S. *W9* —2D **35**
Elgood Clo. *W11* —1A **48**
Elgood Ho. NW8 —1F ***35*** *(off Wellington Rd.)*
Elham Ho. *E5* —2D **27**
Elia M. *N1* —1D **39**
Elias Pl. *SW8* —2C **66**
Elia St. *N1* —1D **39**
Elim Est. *SE1* —4A **54**
Elim St. *SE1* —4F **53** (in two parts)
Elim Way. *E13* —2B **44**
Eliot Bank. *SE23* —2D **97**
Eliot Cotts. *SE3* —5A **72**
Eliot Gdns. *SW15* —2C **74**
Eliot Hill. *SE13* —5E **71**
Eliot M. *NW8* —1E **35**
Eliot Pk. *SE13* —5E **71**
Eliot Pl. *SE3* —5A **72**
Eliot Va. *SE3* —5F **71**
Elizabeth Av. *N1* —5E **25**
Elizabeth Barnes Ct. *SW6* —5D **63**
Elizabeth Bri. *SW1* —5D **51**
Elizabeth Clo. *E14* —5D **43**
Elizabeth Clo. *W9* —3E **35**
Elizabeth Ct. SW1 —4F ***51*** *(off Milmans Ct.)*
Elizabeth Ct. *SW10* —2F **63**
Elizabeth Ct. *W6* —5E **47**
Elizabeth Fry Rd. *E8* —4D **27**
Elizabeth Gdns. *W3* —2B **46**
Elizabeth Ho. SE11 —5C ***52*** *(off Reedworth St.)*
Elizabeth Ind. Est. *SE14* —2F **69**
Elizabeth M. *NW3* —3A **22**
Elizabeth Newcomen Ho. SE1 (off Newcomen St.) —3F ***53***
Elizabeth Rd. *E6* —5F **31**
Elizabeth Rd. *N15* —1A **12**
Elizabeth Sq. SE16 —1A ***56*** *(off Sovereign Cres.)*
Elizabeth St. *SW1* —5C **50**
Elkington Point. SE11 (off Lollard St.) —5C ***52***
Elkington Rd. *E13* —3D **45**
Elkstone Ct. SE15 —2A ***68*** *(off Birdlip Clo.)*
Elkstone Rd. *W10* —4B **34**
Ellaline Rd. *W6* —2F **61**
Ella M. *NW3* —1B **22**
Elland Ho. *E14* —5B **42**
Elland Rd. *SE15* —2E **83**
Ella Rd. *N8* —2A **10**
Ellenborough Ho. W12 (off White City Est.) —1D ***47***
Ellenborough Pl. *SW15* —2C **74**
Ellen St. *E1* —5C **40**
Ellerby St. *SW6* —4F **61**
Ellerdale Clo. *NW3* —1E **21**
Ellerdale Rd. *NW3* —2E **21**
Ellerdale St. *SE13* —2D **85**
Ellerslie Gdns. *NW10* —5C **18**
Ellerslie Rd. *W12* —2D **47**
Ellerslie Sq. Ind. Est. *SW2* —3A **80**
Ellerton Rd. *SW13* —4C **60**
Ellerton Rd. *SW18* —1F **91**
Ellery Ho. *SE17* —5F **53**
Ellery St. *SE15* —5D **69**
Ellesmere Clo. *E11* —1B **16**
Ellesmere Ct. *W4* —1A **60**
Ellesmere Gdns. *Ilf* —1F **17**
Ellesmere Rd. *E3* —1A **42**
Ellesmere Rd. *NW10* —2C **18**
Ellesmere Rd. *W4* —2A **60**
Ellesmere St. *E14* —5D **43**
Ellingfort Rd. *E8* —4D **27**
Ellingham Rd. *E15* —1F **29**
Ellingham Rd. *W12* —3C **46**
Ellington Ho. *SE1* —4E **53**
Ellington St. *N7* —3C **24**
Elliot Clo. *E15* —4A **30**
Elliot Ho. W1 —4A ***36*** *(off Molyneux St.)*
Elliot Rd. *NW4* —1D **5**
Elliott Rd. *SW9* —4D **67**
Elliott Rd. *W4* —5A **46**
Elliott's Pl. *N1* —5D **25**
Elliott Sq. *NW3* —4A **22**
Elliotts Row. *SE11* —5D **53**
Ellis Clo. *NW10* —3D **19**
Elliscombe Mt. *SE7* —2E **73**
Elliscombe Rd. *SE7* —1E **73**
Ellisfield Dri. *SW15* —5C **74**
Ellis Franklin Ct. NW8 —1E ***35*** *(off Abbey Rd.)*
Ellis Ho. SE17 —1F ***67*** *(off Brandon St.)*
Ellison Ho. SE13 —5D ***71*** *(off Lewisham Rd.)*
Ellison Rd. *SW13* —5B **60**
Ellis St. *SW1* —5C **50**
Ellora Rd. *SW16* —5F **93**
Ellsworth St. *E2* —2D **41**
Ellwood Ct. W9 —3D ***35*** *(off Clearwell Dri.)*
Elm Bank Gdns. *SW13* —5A **60**
Elmbourne Rd. *SW17* —3C **92**
Elmbridge Wlk. *E8* —4C **26**
Elm Clo. *E11* —1D **17**
Elm Clo. *N19* —4E **9**
Elm Clo. *NW4* —1F **5**
Elm Ct. EC4 —5C ***38*** *(off Terrace, The)*
Elm Ct. *SE13* —1F **85**
Elmcourt Rd. *SE27* —2D **95**
Elmcroft. *N6* —2E **9**
Elmcroft Av. *NW11* —2B **6**
Elmcroft Cres. *NW11* —2A **6**
Elmcroft St. *E5* —1E **27**

Elmer Ho.—Empress State Building

Elmer Ho. *NW1* —4A **36**
(off Broadley St.)
Elmer Rd. *SE6* —5E **85**
Elmfield Av. *N8* —1A **10**
Elmfield Rd. *E17* —1F **13**
Elmfield Rd. *SW17* —2C **92**
Elmfield Way. *W9* —4C **34**
Elm Friars Wlk. *NW1* —4F **23**
Elm Grn. *W3* —5A **32**
Elm Gro. *N8* —1A **10**
Elm Gro. *NW2* —1F **19**
Elm Gro. *SE15* —5B **68**
Elm Gro. Rd. *SW13* —4C **60**
Elm Hall Gdns. *E11* —1D **17**
(in two parts)
Elm Ho. *E14* —3E **57**
Elm Ho. W10 —3A **34**
(off Briar Wlk.)
Elmhurst Mans. *SW4* —1F **79**
Elmhurst Rd. *E7* —4D **31**
Elmhurst Rd. *SE9* —2F **101**
Elmhurst St. *SW4* —1F **79**
Elmington Est. *SE5* —3F **67**
Elmington Rd. *SE5* —3F **67**
Elmira St. *SE13* —1D **85**
Elm La. *SE6* —2B **98**
Elm Lodge. *SW6* —4E **61**
Elmore Ho. *SW9* —5D **67**
Elmore Rd. *E11* —5E **15**
Elmore Row. *N1* —4E **25**
Elm Pk. *SW2* —4B **80**
Elm Pk. Av. *N15* —1B **12**
Elm Pk. Chambers. *SW10*
—1F **63**
Elm Pk. Gdns. *NW4* —1F **5**
Elm Pk. Gdns. *SW10* —1F **63**
Elm Pk. Ho. *SW10* —1F **63**
Elm Pk. La. *SW3* —1F **63**
Elm Pk. Mans. SW10 —2E **63**
(off Park Wlk.)
Elm Pk. Rd. *E10* —3A **14**
Elm Pk. Rd. *SW3* —2F **63**
Elm Pl. *SW7* —1F **63**
Elm Quay Ct. *SW8* —2F **65**
Elm Rd. *E7* —3B **30**
Elm Rd. *E11* —4F **15**
Elm Rd. *E17* —1E **15**
Elm Row. *NW3* —5E **7**
Elms Av. *NW4* —1F **5**
Elmscott Rd. *Brom* —5A **100**
Elms Cres. *SW4* —4E **79**
Elmshaw Rd. *SW15* —3C **74**
Elmslie Point. *E3* —4B **42**
Elms M. *W2* —1F **49**
Elms Rd. *SW4* —3E **79**
Elms, The. *E12* —3F **31**
Elms, The. *SW13* —1B **74**
Elmstone Rd. *SW6* —4C **62**
Elm St. *WC1* —3B **38**
Elm Ter. *NW2* —5C **6**
Elm Ter. *NW3* —1A **22**
Elmton Ct. NW8 —3F **35**
(off Cunningham Pl.)
Elmton Way. *E5* —5C **12**
Elm Tree Clo. *NW8* —2F **35**
Elm Tree Ct. NW8 —2F **35**
(off Elm Tree Rd.)

Elm Tree Ct. *SE7* —2E **73**
Elm Tree Rd. *NW8* —2F **35**
Elm Wlk. *NW3* —4C **6**
Elm Way. *NW10* —1A **18**
Elmwood Ct. E10 —3C **14**
(off Goldsmith Rd.)
Elmwood Ct. *SW11* —4D **65**
Elmwood Rd. *SE24* —3F **81**
Elmworth Gro. *SE21* —2F **95**
Elnathan M. *W9* —3D **35**
Elphinstone Ct. *SW16* —5A **94**
Elphinstone St. *N5* —1D **25**
Elrington Rd. *E8* —3C **26**
Elsa St. *E1* —4A **42**
Elsdale St. *E9* —3E **27**
Elsden M. *E2* —1E **41**
Elsenham St. *SW18* —1B **90**
Elsham Rd. *E11* —5A **16**
Elsham Rd. *W14* —3A **48**
Elsham Ter. W14 —4A **48**
(off Elsham Rd.)
Elsie La. Ct. W2 —4C **34**
(off Westbourne Pk. Vs.)
Elsiemaud Rd. *SE4* —3B **84**
Elsie Rd. *SE22* —2B **82**
Elsinore Gdns. *NW2* —5A **6**
Elsinore Ho. N1 —5C **24**
(off Denmark Gro.)
Elsinore Rd. *SE23* —1A **98**
Elsley Rd. *SW11* —1B **78**
Elsmore Ho. SE5 —5E **67**
(off Denmark Rd.)
Elspeth Rd. *SW11* —2B **78**
Elstead Ho. SW2 —5B **80**
(off Redlands Way)
Elsted St. *SE17* —5F **53**
Elswick Rd. *SE13* —5D **71**
Elswick St. *SW6* —5E **63**
Elsworthy Ri. *NW3* —4A **22**
Elsworthy Rd. *NW3* —5A **22**
Elsworthy Ter. *NW3* —4A **22**
Elsynge Rd. *SW18* —3F **77**
Eltham Grn. *SE9* —3F **87**
Eltham Grn. Rd. *SE9* —2E **87**
Eltham Hill. *SE9* —3F **87**
Eltham Pal. Rd. *SE9* —4E **87**
Eltham Rd. *SE12 & SE9*
—3B **87**
Elthiron Rd. *SW6* —4C **62**
Elthorne Rd. *N19* —4F **9**
Elthorne Way. *NW9* —1A **4**
Elthruda Rd. *SE13* —4F **85**
Elton Ho. E3 —5B **28**
(off Candy St.)
Elton Pl. *N16* —2A **26**
Eltringham St. *SW18* —2E **77**
Elvaston M. *SW7* —4E **49**
Elvaston Pl. *SW7* —4E **49**
Elveden Rd. *SE24* —3D **81**
Elver Gdns. E2 —2C **40**
(off St Peter's Clo.)
Elverson Rd. *SE8* —5D **71**
Elverton St. *SW1* —5F **51**
Elvino Rd. *SE26* —5A **98**
Elvis Rd. *NW2* —3E **19**
Elwin St. *E2* —2C **40**
Elwood St. *N5* —5D **11**

Elworth Ho. *SW8* —3B **66**
(off Oval Pl.)
Elwyn Gdns. *SE12* —5C **86**
Ely Cotts. *SW8* —3B **66**
Ely Ct. EC1 —4C **38**
(off Ely Pl.)
Ely Ct. NW6 —1C **34**
(off Chichester Rd.,
in two parts)
Ely Gdns. *Ilf* —2F **17**
Ely Ho. SE15 —3C **68**
(off Friary Est.)
Elyne Rd. *N4* —1C **10**
Ely Pl. *EC1* —4C **38**
Ely Rd. *E10* —1E **15**
Elysium Pl. SW6 —5B **62**
(off Elysium St.)
Elysium St. *SW6* —5B **62**
Elystan Pl. *SW3* —1A **64**
Elystan St. *SW3* —5A **50**
Elystan Wlk. *N1* —5C **24**
Embankment. *SW15* —5F **61**
Embankment Gdns. *SW3*
—2B **64**
Embankment Pl. WC2 —2A **52**
Embassy Ct. *NW8* —1F **35**
(off Wellington Rd.)
Embassy Ho. *NW6* —4D **21**
Emba St. *SE16* —3C **54**
Emberton. *SE17* —2A **68**
(off Albany Rd.)
Emberton Ct. EC1 —2D **39**
(off Tompion St.)
Embleton Rd. *SE13* —2D **85**
Embley Point. E5 —1D **27**
(off Tiger Way)
Emden St. *SW6* —4D **63**
Emerald Clo. *E16* —5F **45**
Emerald St. *WC1* —4B **38**
Emerson St. *SE1* —2E **53**
Emery Hill St. *SW1* —4E **51**
Emery St. *SE1* —4C **52**
Emily Pl. *N7* —1C **24**
Emily St. E16 —5B **44**
(off Jude St.)
Emlyn Gdns. *W12* —3A **46**
Emlyn Rd. *W12* —3A **46**
Emmanuel Ct. *E10* —2D **15**
Emmanuel Ho. *SE11* —5C **52**
Emmanuel Rd. *SW12* —1E **93**
Emma Rd. *E13* —1B **44**
Emma St. *E2* —1D **41**
Emminster. *NW6* —5D **21**
(off Abbey Rd.)
Emmott Clo. *E1* —3A **42**
Emmott Clo. *NW11* —1E **7**
Emperor's Ga. *SW7* —4E **49**
Empingham Ho. SE8 —5F **55**
(off Chilton St.)
Empire Sq. *N7* —5A **10**
Empire Wharf. E3 —5A **28**
(off Old Ford Rd.)
Empire Wharf Rd. *E14* —5F **57**
Empress Av. *E12* —4E **17**
Empress Pl. *SW6* —1C **62**
Empress State Building. *W14*
—1C **62**

Empress St. *SE17*—2E **67**
Empson St. *E3*—3D **43**
Emsworth Ct. *SW16*—3A **94**
Emsworth St. *SW2*—2B **94**
Emu Rd. *SW8*—5D **65**
Enbrook St. *W10*—2A **34**
Endeavour Way. *SW19* —4D **91**
Endell St. *WC2*—5A **38**
Enderby St. *SE10*—1F **71**
Endlesham Rd. *SW12*—5C **78**
Endsleigh Gdns. *WC1*—3F **37**
Endsleigh Pl. *WC1*—3F **37**
Endsleigh St. *WC1*—3F **37**
Endwell Rd. *SE4*—5A **70**
Endymion Rd. *N4*—2C **10**
Endymion Rd. *SW2*—4B **80**
Energen Clo. *NW10*—3A **18**
*Enfield Cloisters. N1 —2A **40***
(off Fanshaw St.)
*Enfield Ho. SW9 —5A **66***
(off Stockwell Rd.)
Enfield Rd. *N1*—4A **26**
Enford St. *W1*—4B **36**
Engadine St. *SW18*—1B **90**
Engate St. *SE13*—2E **85**
*Engine Ct. SW1 —2E **51***
(off St James's Pal.)
England's La. *NW3*—3B **22**
*Englefield. NW1 —2E **37***
(off Clarence Gdns.)
Englefield Rd. *N1*—4F **25**
Engleheart Rd. *SE6*—5D **85**
Englewood Rd. *SW12*—4D **79**
English Grounds. *SE1*—2A **54**
English St. *E3*—3B **42**
Enid St. *SE16*—4B **54**
Enmore Gdns. *SW14*—3A **74**
Enmore Rd. *SW15*—2E **75**
*Ennerdale. NW1 —2E **37***
(off Varndell St.)
Ennerdale Dri. *NW9*—1A **4**
Ennerdale Ho. *E3*—3B **42**
Ennersdale Rd. *SE13*—3F **85**
Ennis Ho. *E14*—5D **43**
Ennismore Av. *W4*—5B **46**
Ennismore Gdns. *SW7* —3A **50**
Ennismore Gdns. M. *SW7* —4A **50**
Ennismore M. *SW7*—4A **50**
Ennismore St. *SW7*—4A **50**
Ennis Rd. *N4*—3C **10**
*Ensbury Ho. SW8 —3B **66***
(off Carroun Rd.)
Ensign Ho. *E14*—3C **56**
*Ensign Ind. Cen. E1 —1C **54***
(off Ensign St.)
Ensign St. *E1*—1C **54**
Ensor M. *SW7*—1F **63**
Enterprise Bus. Pk. *E14* —3D **57**
Enterprise Cen., The. Beck
*(off Cricket La.) —5A **98***
Enterprise Ho. *E14*—1D **71**
Enterprise Ind. Est. *SE16* —1E **69**
Enterprise Way. *NW10* —2B **32**
Enterprise Way. *SW18* —2C **76**
Enterprize Way. *SE8*—5B **56**
Epcot M. *NW10*—2F **33**
Epirus M. *SW6*—3C **62**
Epirus Rd. *SW6*—3B **62**
Epping Clo. *E14*—5C **56**
Epping Pl. *N1*—3C **24**
Epple Rd. *SW6*—4B **62**
Epsom Rd. *E10*—1E **15**
Epworth St. *EC1*—3F **39**
*Equity Sq. E2 —2B **40***
(off Shacklewell St.)
Erasmus St. *SW1*—5F **51**
Erconwald St. *W12*—5B **32**
*Eresby Ho. SW7 —3A **50***
(off Rutland Ga.)
Eresby Pl. *NW6*—4C **20**
Erica Ho. *SE4*—1B **84**
Erica St. *W12*—1C **46**
Eric Clo. *E7*—1C **30**
Ericcson Clo. *SW18*—3C **76**
*Eric Fletcher Ct. N1 —4E **25***
(off Essex Rd.)
Eric Rd. *E7*—1C **30**
Eric Rd. *NW10*—3B **18**
*Ericson Ho. SE13 —2F **85***
(off Blessington Rd.)
Eric St. *E3*—3B **42**
(in two parts)
*Eric Wilkins Ho. SE1 —1C **68***
(off Old Kent Rd.)
Eridge Rd. *NW10*—4A **18**
Eridge Rd. *W4*—4A **46**
Erlanger Rd. *SE14*—4F **69**
*Erlich Cotts. E1 —4E **41***
(off Sidney St.)
Ermine Rd. *N15*—1B **12**
Ermine Rd. *SE13*—2D **85**
Ernest Av. *SE27*—4D **95**
Ernest Harriss Ho. W9
*(off Elgin Av.) —3C **34***
Ernest St. *E1*—3F **41**
Ernshaw Pl. *SW15*—3A **76**
Eros. —1F 51
Eros Ho. Shops. SE23
*(off Brockley Pk.) —5A **84***
Erpingham Rd. *SW15* —1E **75**
Errington Rd. *W9*—3B **34**
Errol St. *EC1*—3E **39**
Erskine Hill. *NW11*—1C **6**
*Erskine Ho. SW1 —1E **65***
(off Churchill Gdns.)
*Erskine M. NW3 —4B **22***
(off Erskine Rd.)
Erskine Rd. *NW3*—4B **22**
Esam Way. *SW16*—5C **94**
Escott Gdns. *SE9*—4F **101**
Esher Gdns. *SW19*—2F **89**
*Eskdale. NW1 —1E **37***
(off Stanhope St.)
Esk Rd. *E13*—3C **44**
Esmar Cres. *NW9*—2C **4**
Esmeralda Rd. *SE1*—5C **54**
*Esmond Ct. W8 —4D **49***
(off Ansdell St.)
Esmond Gdns. *W4*—5A **46**
Esmond Rd. *NW6*—5B **20**
Esmond Rd. *W4*—5A **46**
Esmond St. *SW15*—2A **76**
Esparto St. *SW18*—5D **77**
Essendine Rd. *W9*—2C **34**
Essex Ct. *SW13*—5B **60**
*Essex Ct. WC2 —5C **38***
(off Brick Ct.)
Essex Gdns. *N4*—1D **11**
Essex Gro. *SE19*—5F **95**
Essex Ho. *E14*—5D **43**
Essex Mans. *E11*—2F **15**
Essex Pk. M. *W3*—2A **46**
Essex Rd. *E10*—1E **15**
Essex Rd. *E17*—1A **14**
Essex Rd. *N1*—5D **25**
Essex Rd. *NW10*—4A **18**
Essex Rd. S. *E11*—2F **15**
Essex St. *E7*—2C **30**
Essex St. *WC2*—5C **38**
Essex Vs. *W8*—3C **48**
Essex Wharf. *E5*—4F **13**
Essian St. *E1*—4A **42**
Estate Way. *E10*—3B **14**
Estcourt Rd. *SW6*—3B **62**
*Estella Ho. W11 —1F **47***
(off St Ann's Rd.)
Estelle Rd. *NW3*—1B **22**
Esterbrooke St. *SW1*—5F **51**
Este Rd. *SW11*—1A **78**
Esther Rd. *E11*—2A **16**
Estoria Clo. *SW2*—5C **80**
Estorick Collection of Modern Italian Art. —3D 25
(off Canonbury Sq.)
Estreham Rd. *SW16*—5F **93**
Eswyn Rd. *SW17*—4B **92**
*Etal Ho. N1 —4D **25***
(off Sutton Est., The)
Etcetera Theatre. —4D 23
Etchingham Rd. *E15*—1E **29**
Eternit Wlk. *SW6*—4E **61**
Ethelbert St. *SW12*—1D **93**
Ethelburga St. *SW11*—4A **64**
Ethelden Rd. *W12*—2D **47**
Ethel Rd. *E16*—5D **45**
Ethel St. *SE17*—5E **53**
Etheridge Rd. *NW4*—2E **5**
Etherley Rd. *N15*—1E **11**
Etherow St. *SE22*—5C **82**
Etherstone Grn. *SW16* —4C **94**
Etherstone Rd. *SW16*—4C **94**
Ethnard Rd. *SE15*—2D **69**
Etloe Rd. *E10*—4C **14**
Eton Av. *NW3*—4F **21**
Eton Clo. *SW18*—5D **77**
Eton College Rd. *NW3*—3B **22**
Eton Gro. *SE13*—1A **86**
Eton Hall. *NW3*—3B **22**
*Eton Ho. N5 —1D **25***
(off Leigh Rd.)
*Eton Mnr. Ct. E10 —4C **14***
(off Leyton Grange Est.)

Eton Pl. *NW3* —4C **22**
Eton Ri. *NW3* —3B **22**
Eton Rd. *NW3* —4B **22**
Eton Vs. *NW3* —3B **22**
Etta St. *SE8* —2A **70**
Ettrick St. *E14* —5E **43**
(in two parts)
Eugene Cotter Ho. SE17 (off Tatum St.) —5F ***53***
Eugenia Rd. *SE16* —5E **55**
Euro Clo. *NW10* —3C **18**
Eurolink Bus. Cen. *SW2* —3C **80**
Europa Pl. *EC1* —2E **39**
Eustace Ho. SE1 —5B ***52*** *(off Old Paradise St.)*
Eustace Rd. *E6* —2F **45**
Eustace Rd. *SW6* —3C **62**
Euston Cen. *NW1* —3E **37**
(in two parts)
Euston Gro. NW1 —2F ***37*** *(off Euston Sq.)*
Euston Rd. *NW1 & N1* —3D **37**
Euston Sq. *NW1* —2F **37**
(in two parts)
Euston Sta. Colonnade. *NW1* —2F **37**
Euston St. *NW1* —2E **37**
Euston Tower. *NW1* —3E **37**
Euston Underpass. (Junct.) —3E **37**
Evandale Rd. *SW9* —5C **66**
Evangelist Rd. *NW5* —1D **23**
Evans Clo. *E8* —3B **26**
Evans Ho. SW8 —3F ***65*** *(off Wandsworth Rd.)*
Evans Ho. W12 —1D ***47*** *(off White City Est.)*
Evans Rd. *SE6* —2A **100**
Evanston Gdns. *Ilf* —1F **17**
Evelina Mans. *SE5* —3F **67**
Evelina Rd. *SE15* —1E **83**
Evelyn Ct. *E8* —1C **26**
Evelyn Ct. N1 —1F ***39*** *(off Evelyn Wlk., in two parts)*
Evelyn Denington Ct. N1 (off Upper St.) —4D ***25***
Evelyn Fox Ct. *W10* —4E **33**
Evelyn Gdns. *SW7* —1E **63**
Evelyn Ho. W12 —3B ***46*** *(off Cobbold Rd.)*
Evelyn Lowe Est. *SE16* —4C **54**
Evelyn Mans. SW1 —4E ***51*** *(off Carlisle Pl.)*
Evelyn Mans. W14 —2A ***62*** *(off Queen's Club Gdns.)*
Evelyn Rd. *E16* —2C **58**
Evelyn Rd. *SW19* —5D **91**
Evelyn St. *SE8* —5A **56**
Evelyn Wlk. *N1* —1F **39**
Evelyn Yd. *W1* —5F **37**
Evenwood Clo. *SW15* —3A **76**
Everard Ho. E1 —5C ***40*** *(off Boyd St.)*
Everatt Clo. *SW18* —4B **76**
Everdon Rd. *SW13* —2C **60**
Everest Pl. *E14* —4E **43**
Everett Ho. *SE17* —1F **67**
Everilda St. *N1* —5B **24**
Evering Rd. *N16 & E5* —5B **12**
Everington St. *W6* —2F **61**
(in two parts)
Everitt Rd. *NW10* —2A **32**
Everleigh St. *N4* —3B **10**
Eve Rd. *E11* —1A **30**
Eve Rd. *E15* —1A **44**
Eversholt St. *NW1* —1E **37**
Evershot Rd. *N4* —3B **10**
Eversleigh Rd. *E6* —5F **31**
Eversleigh Rd. *SW11* —1B **78**
Eversley Ho. E2 —2C ***40*** *(off Gossett St.)*
Eversley Pk. *SW19* —5D **89**
Eversley Rd. *SE7* —2D **73**
Everthorpe Rd. *SE15* —1B **82**
Everton Bldgs. *NW1* —2E **37**
Evesham Ho. E2 —1E ***41*** *(off Old Ford Rd.)*
Evesham Ho. NW8 —5E ***21*** *(off Abbey Rd.)*
Evesham Rd. *E15* —4B **30**
Evesham St. *W11* —1F **47**
Evesham Wlk. *SE5* —5F **67**
Evesham Wlk. *SW9* —5C **66**
Evesham Way. *SW11* —1C **78**
Ewald Rd. *SW6* —5B **62**
Ewart Pl. *E3* —1B **42**
Ewart Rd. *SE23* —5F **83**
Ewe Clo. *N7* —3A **24**
Ewelme Rd. *SE23* —1E **97**
Ewen Cres. *SW2* —5C **80**
Ewen Ho. N1 —5B ***24*** *(off Barnsbury Est.)*
Ewer St. *SE1* —2E **53**
Ewhurst Clo. *E1* —4E **41**
Ewhurst Rd. *SE4* —4B **84**
Exbury Ho. *E9* —4E **27**
Exbury Ho. SW1 —1F ***65*** *(off Rampayne St.)*
Exbury Rd. *SE6* —2C **98**
Excel. —1D 59
Excel Ct. WC2 —1F ***51*** *(off Whitcomb St.)*
Excelsior Gdns. *SE13* —5E **71**
Excelsior Ind. Est. SE15 —2E ***69*** *(off Surrey Canal Rd.)*
Exchange Arc. *EC2* —4A **40**
Exchange Building. E1 —3B ***40*** *(off Commercial St.)*
Exchange Ct. *WC2* —1A **52**
Exchange Ho. EC2 —4A ***40*** *(off Exchange Sq.)*
Exchange Mans. *NW11* —2B **6**
Exchange Pl. *EC2* —4A **40**
Exchange Sq. *EC2* —4A **40**
Exchange St. *EC1* —2E **39**
Exeter Ct. NW6 —1C ***34*** *(off Cambridge Rd.)*
Exeter Ho. SE15 —2C ***68*** *(off Friary Est.)*
Exeter Ho. W2 —5E ***35*** *(off Hallfield Est.)*
Exeter Mans. *NW2* —3A **20**
Exeter M. *NW6* —3D **21**
Exeter M. *SW6* —3C **62**
Exeter Rd. *E16* —4C **44**
Exeter Rd. *E17* —1C **14**
Exeter Rd. *NW2* —2A **20**
Exeter St. *WC2* —1A **52**
Exeter Way. *SE14* —3B **70**
Exford Gdns. *SE12* —1D **101**
Exford Rd. *SE12* —2D **101**
Exhibition Clo. *W12* —1E **47**
Exhibition Rd. *SW7* —3F **49**
Exmoor St. *W10* —3F **33**
Exmouth Ho. *E14* —5D **57**
Exmouth Ho. EC1 —3C ***38*** *(off Pine St.)*
Exmouth Mkt. *EC1* —3C **38**
Exmouth M. *NW1* —2E **37**
Exmouth Pl. *E8* —4D **27**
Exmouth Rd. *E17* —1B **14**
Exmouth St. *E1* —5E **41**
Exning Rd. *E16* —3B **44**
Exonbury. NW8 —5D ***21*** *(off Abbey Rd.)*
Exon St. *SE17* —1A **68**
Express Newspapers. SE1 (off Blackfriars Rd.) —2D ***53***
Express Wharf. *E14* —3C **56**
Exton St. *SE1* —2C **52**
Eyhurst Clo. *NW2* —4C **4**
Eylewood Rd. *SE27* —5E **95**
Eynella Rd. *SE22* —5B **82**
Eynham Rd. *W12* —5E **33**
Eynsford Ho. SE1 —3F ***53*** *(off Crosby Row)*
Eynsford Ho. *SE15* —2E **69**
Eynsford Ho. SE17 —5A ***54*** *(off Beckway St.)*
Eyot Gdns. *W6* —1B **60**
Eyot Grn. *W4* —1B **60**
Eyre Ct. *NW8* —1F **35**
Eyre St. Hill. *EC1* —3C **38**
Eythorne Rd. *SW9* —4C **66**
Ezra St. *E2* —2B **40**

Faber Gdns. *NW4* —1C **4**
Fabian Rd. *SW6* —3B **62**
Facade, The. *SE23* —2E **97**
Factory Pl. *E14* —1E **71**
Factory Rd. *E16* —2F **59**
Fairacres. *SW15* —2B **74**
Fairbairn Grn. *SW9* —4D **67**
Fairbank Est. *N1* —1F **39**
Fairbridge Rd. *N19* —4F **9**
Fairburn Ct. *SW15* —3A **76**
Fairburn Ho. W14 —1B ***62*** *(off Ivatt Pl.)*
Fairby Ho. SE1 —5B ***54*** *(off Longfield Est.)*
Fairby Rd. *SE12* —3D **87**
Faircharm Trad. Est. *SE8* —3D **71**

Fairchild Clo. *SW11* —5F **63**
Fairchild Ho. *N1* —2A **40**
(off Fanshaw St.)
Fairchild Pl. *EC2* —3A **40**
(off Gt. Eastern St.)
Fairchild St. *EC2* —3A **40**
Fairclough St. *E1* —5C **40**
Fairdale Gdns. *SW15* —2D **75**
Fairfax Gdns. *SE3* —4E **73**
Fairfax M. *E16* —2D **59**
Fairfax M. *SW15* —2E **75**
Fairfax Pl. *NW6* —4E **21**
Fairfax Rd. *NW6* —4E **21**
Fairfax Rd. *W4* —4A **46**
Fairfield. E1 —4E **41**
(off Redman's Rd.)
Fairfield. NW1 —1E **23**
(off Arlington Rd.)
Fairfield Av. *NW4* —1D **5**
Fairfield Ct. *NW10* —5C **18**
Fairfield Dri. *SW18* —3D **77**
Fairfield Gdns. *N8* —1A **10**
Fairfield Gro. *SE7* —2F **73**
Fairfield Rd. *E3* —1C **42**
Fairfield Rd. *N8* —1A **10**
Fairfield St. *SW18* —3D **77**
Fairfoot Rd. *E3* —3C **42**
Fairford. *SE6* —1C **98**
Fairford Ho. *SE11* —5C **52**
Fairhazel Gdns. *NW6* —3D **21**
Fairholme Rd. *W14* —1A **62**
Fairholt Clo. *N16* —3A **12**
Fairholt Rd. *N16* —3F **11**
Fairholt St. *SW7* —4A **50**
Fairland Rd. *E15* —3B **30**
Fairlawn. *SE7* —3E **73**
Fairlawn Ct. *SE7* —3E **73**
(in two parts)
Fairlawn Mans. *SE14* —4F **69**
Fairlawn Pk. *SE26* —5A **98**
Fairlie Gdns. *SE23* —5E **83**
Fairlight Av. *NW10* —1A **32**
Fairlight Ct. *NW10* —1A **32**
Fairlight Rd. *SW17* —4F **91**
Fairlop Ct. *E11* —3F **15**
Fairlop Rd. *E11* —2F **15**
Fairmead Gdns. *Ilf* —1F **17**
Fairmead Ho. *E9* —1A **28**
Fairmead Rd. *N19* —5F **9**
Fairmile Av. *SW16* —5F **93**
Fairmount Rd. *SW2* —4B **80**
Fairstead Wlk. N1 —5E **25**
(off Popham St.)
Fair St. *SE1* —3A **54**
Fairthorn Rd. *SE7* —1C **72**
Fairview Clo. *SE26* —5A **98**
Fairview Ho. *SW2* —5B **80**
Fairview Pl. *SW2* —5B **80**
Fairview Rd. *N15* —1B **12**
Fairwall Ho. *SE5* —4A **68**
Fairway Clo. *NW11* —2E **7**
Fairway Ct. SE16 —3F **55**
(off Christopher Clo.)
Fairways Bus. Pk. *E10* —4A **14**
Fairway, The. *W3* —5A **32**
Fairweather Rd. *N16* —1C **12**
Fairwyn Rd. *SE26* —4A **98**

Fakruddin St. *E1* —3C **40**
Falcon. *WC1* —4A **38**
(off Old Gloucester St.)
Falconberg Ct. *W1* —5F **37**
Falconberg M. *W1* —5F **37**
Falcon Clo. *SE1* —2D **53**
Falcon Ct. *EC4* —5C **38**
Falcon Ct. N1 —1D **39**
(off City Garden Row)
Falconer Wlk. *N7* —4B **10**
Falconet, The. E1 —2D **55**
(off Wapping High St.)
Falcon Gro. *SW11* —1A **78**
Falcon Ho. *E14* —1D **71**
Falcon La. *SW11* —1A **78**
Falcon Lodge. W9 —4C **34**
(off Admiral Wlk.)
Falcon Pk. Ind. Est. *NW10*
—1A **18**
Falcon Point. *SE1* —1D **53**
Falcon Rd. *SW11* —5A **64**
Falcon St. *E13* —3B **44**
Falcon Ter. *SW11* —1A **78**
Falcon Way. *E14* —5D **57**
Falconwood Ct. *SE3* —5B **72**
Falkirk Ct. SE16 —2F **55**
(off Rotherhithe St.)
Falkirk Ho. W9 —1D **35**
(off Maida Va.)
Falkirk St. *N1* —1A **40**
Falkland Ho. *SE6* —4E **99**
Falkland Ho. *W8* —4D **49**
Falkland Ho. W14 —1B **62**
(off Edith Vs.)
Falkland Pl. *NW5* —2E **23**
Falkland Rd. *NW5* —2E **23**
Fallodon Ho. W11 —4B **34**
(off St Luke's Rd.)
Fallow Ct. SE16 —1C **68**
(off Argyle Way)
Fallsbrook Rd. *SW16* —5E **93**
Falmouth Clo. *SE12* —3B **86**
Falmouth Ho. *SE11* —1C **66**
(off Seaton Clo.)
Falmouth Ho. W2 —1A **50**
(off Clarendon Pl.)
Falmouth Rd. *SE1* —4E **53**
Falmouth St. *E15* —2F **29**
Falstaff Ct. SE11 —5D **53**
(off Opal St.)
Falstaff Ho. N1 —1A **40**
(off Arden Est.)
Fambridge Clo. *SE26* —4B **98**
Fane Ho. *E2* —5E **27**
Fane St. *W14* —2B **62**
Fan Mus. —3E **71**
Fann St. *EC1 & EC2* —3E **39**
(in two parts)
Fanshaw St. *N1* —2A **40**
Fanthorpe St. *SW15* —1E **75**
Faraday Clo. *N7* —3B **24**
Faraday Ho. *E14* —1B **56**
Faraday Mans. W14 —2A **62**
(off Queen's Club Gdns.)
Faraday Mus. —1E **51**
Faraday Rd. *E15* —3B **30**
Faraday Rd. *SW19* —5C **90**

Faraday Rd. *W10* —4A **34**
Faraday Way. *SE18* —4F **59**
Fareham St. *W1* —5F **37**
Faringford Rd. *E15* —4A **30**
Farjeon Ho. NW3 —4F **21**
(off Hilgrove Rd.)
Farjeon Rd. *SE3* —4F **73**
Farleigh Pl. *N16* —1B **26**
Farleigh Rd. *N16* —1B **26**
Farley Ct. NW1 —3B **36**
(off Allsop Pl.)
Farley Ho. *SE26* —3D **97**
Farley Rd. *SE6* —5D **85**
Farlington Pl. *SW15* —5D **75**
Farlow Rd. *SW15* —1F **75**
Farlton Rd. *SW18* —1D **91**
Farm Av. *NW2* —5A **6**
Farm Av. *SW16* —4A **94**
Farm Clo. *SW6* —3C **62**
Farmcote Rd. *SE12* —1C **100**
Farmdale Rd. *SE10* —1C **72**
Farmer Rd. *E10* —3D **15**
Farmer's Rd. *SE5* —3D **67**
Farmer St. *W11* —2C **48**
Farmfield Rd. *Brom* —5A **100**
Farmilo Rd. *E17* —2B **14**
Farm La. *SW6* —2C **62**
Farm La. Trad. Est. *SW6*
—2C **62**
Farmleigh Ho. *SW9* —3D **81**
Farm Pl. *W8* —2C **48**
Farm Rd. *NW10* —5A **18**
Farmstead Rd. *SE6* —4D **99**
Farm St. *W1* —1D **51**
Farm Wlk. *NW11* —1B **6**
Farnaby Ho. W10 —2B **34**
(off Bruckner St.)
Farnaby Rd. *SE9* —2E **87**
Farnan Rd. *SW16* —5A **94**
Farnborough Way. *SE15*
—3A **68**
Farncombe St. *SE16* —3C **54**
Farndale Ho. NW6 —5D **21**
(off Kilburn Va.)
Farnell M. *SW5* —1D **63**
Farnham Ho. NW1 —3A **36**
(off Harewood Av.)
Farnham Pl. *SE1* —2D **53**
Farnham Royal. *SE11* —1B **66**
Farningham Ho. *N4* —2F **11**
Farnley Ho. *SW8* —5F **65**
Farnworth Ho. *E14* —5F **57**
Faroe Rd. *W14* —4F **47**
Farquhar Rd. *SE19* —5B **96**
Farquhar Rd. *SW19* —3C **90**
Farrance St. *E14* —5B **42**
Farren Rd. *SE23* —2A **98**
Farrer Ho. *SE8* —3C **70**
Farriers Ho. EC1 —3E **39**
(off Errol St.)
Farrier St. *NW1* —4D **23**
Farrier Wlk. *SW10* —2E **63**
Farringdon La. *EC1* —3C **38**
Farringdon Rd. *EC1* —3C **38**
Farringdon St. *EC4* —4D **39**
Farrins Rents. *SE16* —2A **56**
Farrow La. *SE14* —3E **69**

Farrow Pl. SE16 —4A 56
Farthingale Wlk. E15 —4F 29
Farthing All. SE1 —3C 54
Farthing Fields. E1 —2D 55
Fashion St. E1 —4B 40
Fassett Rd. E8 —3C 26
Fassett Sq. E8 —3C 26
Faulkners All. EC1 —4D 39
Faulkner St. SE14 —4E 69
Faunce Ho. SE17 —2D 67 (off Doddington Gro.)
Faunce St. SE17 —1D 67
Favart Rd. SW6 —4C 62
Faversham Ho. NW1 —5E 23 (off Bayham Pl.)
Faversham Ho. SE17 —1A 68 (off Kinglake St.)
Faversham Rd. SE6 —5B 84
Fawcett Clo. SW11 —5F 63
Fawcett Clo. SW16 —5C 94
Fawcett Est. E5 —3C 12
Fawcett Rd. NW10 —4B 18
Fawcett St. SW10 —2E 63
Fawe Pk. Rd. SW15 —2B 76
Fawe St. E14 —4D 43
Fawkham Ho. SE1 —5B 54 (off Longfield Est.)
Fawley Lodge. E14 —5F 57
Fawley Rd. NW6 —2D 21
Fawnbrake Av. SE24 —3D 81
Fawn Rd. E13 —1E 45
Fawood Av. NW10 —14 18
Faygate Rd. SW2 —2B 94
Fayland Av. SW16 —5E 93
Fearnley Ho. SE5 —5A 68
Fearon St. SE10 —1C 72
Feathers Pl. SE10 —2F 71
Featherstone Av. SE23 —2D 97
Featherstone St. EC1 —3F 39
Featley Rd. SW9 —1D 81
Felbridge Clo. SW16 —4C 94
Felbridge Ho. SE22 —1A 82
Felday Rd. SE13 —4D 85
Felden St. SW6 —4B 62
Feldman Clo. N16 —3C 12
Felgate M. W6 —5D 47
Felix Av. N8 —1A 10
Felixstowe Rd. NW10 —2D 33
Felix St. E2 —1D 41
Fellbrigg Rd. SE22 —3B 82
Fellbrigg St. E1 —3D 41
Fellows Ct. E2 —1B 40 (in four parts)
Fellows Rd. NW3 —4F 21
Felltram Way. SE7 —1C 72
Felmersham Clo. SW4 —2A 80
Felnex Trad. Est. NW10 —1A 32
Felsberg Rd. SW2 —4A 80
Felsham Rd. SW15 —1E 75
Felstead Gdns. E14 —1E 71
Felstead Rd. E9 —3B 28
Felstead Rd. E11 —2C 16
Felstead St. E9 —3B 28
Felstead Wharf. E14 —1E 71
Felsted Rd. E16 —5F 45
Felton Ho. N1 —5F 25 (off Colville Est.)
Felton Ho. SE3 —2D 87
Felton St. N1 —5F 25
Fenchurch Av. EC3 —5A 40
Fenchurch Bldgs. EC3 —5A 40
Fenchurch Pl. EC3 —5A 40
Fenchurch St. EC3 —1A 54
Fen Ct. EC3 —5A 40
Fendall St. SE1 —4A 54 (in two parts)
Fendt Clo. E16 —5B 44
Fenelon Pl. W14 —5B 48
Fenham Rd. SE15 —3C 68
Fenn Clo. Brom —5C 100
Fennel Clo. E16 —3A 44
Fenner Clo. SE16 —5D 55
Fenner Ho. E1 —2D 55 (off Watts St.)
Fenner Sq. SW11 —1F 77
Fenning St. SE1 —3A 54
Fenn St. E9 —2E 27
Fenstanton. N4 —3B 10 (off Marquis Rd.)
Fen St. E16 —1B 58
Fentiman Rd. SW8 —2A 66
Fenton Clo. E8 —3B 26
Fenton Clo. SW9 —5B 66
Fenton House. —1E 21 (off Windmill Hill)
Fenton Ho. SE14 —3A 70
Fentons Av. E13 —2D 45
Fenton St. E1 —5D 41
Fenwick Gro. SE15 —1C 82
Fenwick Pl. SW9 —1A 80
Fenwick Rd. SE15 —1C 82
Ferdinand Pl. NW1 —4C 22
Ferdinand St. NW1 —4C 22
Ferguson Cen., The. E17 —1A 14
Ferguson Clo. E14 —5C 56
Ferguson Dri. W3 —5A 32
Ferguson Ho. SE10 —4E 71
Fergus Rd. N5 —2D 25
Fermain Ct. E. N1 —5A 26 (off De Beauvoir Est.)
Fermain Ct. N. N1 —5A 26 (off De Beauvoir Est.)
Fermain Ct. W. N1 —5A 26 (off De Beauvoir Est.)
Ferme Pk. Rd. N8 & N4 —1A 10
Fermor Rd. SE23 —1A 98
Fermoy Rd. W9 —3B 34
Fernbank M. SW12 —4D 79
Fernbrook Cres. SE13 (off Fernbrook Rd.) —4A 86
Fernbrook Rd. SE13 —4A 86
Ferncliff Rd. E8 —2C 26
Fern Clo. N1 —1A 40
Fern Ct. SE14 —5F 69
Ferncroft Av. NW3 —5C 6
Ferndale Rd. E7 —4D 31
Ferndale Rd. E11 —4A 16
Ferndale Rd. N15 —1B 12
Ferndale Rd. SW4 & SW9 —2A 80
Ferndene Rd. SE24 —2E 81
Ferndown Lodge. E14 —4E 57
Ferndown Rd. SE9 —5F 87
Fernhall Dri. Ilf —1F 17
Fernhead Rd. W9 —1B 34
Fernholme Rd. SE15 —3F 83
Fernhurst Rd. SW6 —4A 62
Fernlea Rd. SW12 —1D 93
Fernsbury St. WC1 —2C 38
Fernshaw Clo. SW10 —2E 63
Fernshaw Rd. SW10 —2E 63
Fernside. NW11 —4C 6
Fernside Rd. SW12 —1B 92
Ferns Rd. E15 —3B 30
Fern St. E3 —3C 42
Fernthorpe Rd. SW16 —5E 93
Ferntower Rd. N5 —2F 25
Fern Wlk. SE1 —1C 68 (off Argyle Way)
Fernwood Av. SW16 —4F 93
Ferranti Clo. SE18 —4F 59
Ferrers Rd. SW16 —5F 93
Ferriby Clo. N1 —4C 24
Ferrier Ind. Est. SW18 (off Ferrier St.) —2D 77
Ferrier Point. E16 —4C 44 (off Forty Acre La.)
Ferrier St. SW18 —2D 77
Ferrings. SE21 —3A 96
Ferris Rd. SE22 —2C 82
Ferron Rd. E5 —5D 13
Ferrybridge Ho. SE11 —4C 52 (off Lambeth Wlk.)
Ferry Ho. E5 —3D 13 (off High Hill Ferry)
Ferry La. SW13 —2B 60
Ferry Rd. SW13 —3C 60
Ferry St. E14 —1E 71
Festing Rd. SW15 —1F 75
Fetter La. EC4 —5C 38 (in two parts)
Fettes Ho. NW8 —1F 35 (off Cochrane St.)
Ffinch St. SE8 —3C 70
Field Ct. SW19 —3C 90
Field Ct. WC1 —4B 38
Fieldgate Mans. E1 —4C 40 (off Fieldgate St., in two parts)
Fieldgate St. E1 —4C 40
Fieldhouse Rd. SW12 —1E 93
Fielding Ho. NW6 —2C 34 (off Cambridge Rd.)
Fielding Ho. W4 —2A 60 (off Devonshire Rd.)
Fielding M. SW13 —2D 61 (off Jenner Pl.)
Fielding Rd. W4 —4A 46
Fielding Rd. W14 —4F 47
Fieldings, The. SE23 —1E 97
Fielding St. SE17 —2E 67
Field Point. E7 —1C 30
Field Rd. E7 —1B 30
Field Rd. W6 —1A 62

Fields Est.—Flaxman Ter.

Fields Est. E8 —4C 26
Fieldside Rd. Brom —5F 99
Field St. WC1 —2B 38
Fieldsway Ho. N5 —2C 24
Fieldview. SW18 —1F 91
Fieldway Cres. N5 —2C 24
Fife Rd. E16 —4C 44
Fife Ter. N1 —1B 38
Fifield Path. SE23 —3F 97
Fifth Av. W10 —2A 34
Fig Tree Clo. NW10 —5A 18
Figure Ct. SW3 —1B 64 (off Royal Hospital Rd.)
Filey Av. N16 —3C 12
Filigree Ct. SE16 —2B 56
Fillebrook Rd. E11 —3F 15
Filmer Rd. SW6 —4A 62
Filton Ct. SE14 —3E 69 (off Farrow La.)
Finborough Ho. SW10 (off Fawcett St.) —2E 63
Finborough Rd. SW10 —1D 63
Finborough Theatre, The. —2D 63
Finch Av. SE27 —4F 95
Finchdean Ho. SW15 —5B 74
Finch Ho. SE8 —3D 71 (off Bronze St.)
Finch La. EC3 —5F 39
Finchley Pl. NW8 —1F 35
Finchley Rd. NW3 —1C 20
Finchley Rd. NW8 —5F 21
Finchley Rd. NW11 & NW2 —1B 6
Finch Lodge. W2 —4C 34 (off Admiral Wlk.)
Finch M. SE15 —4B 68
Finch's Ct. E14 —1D 57
Finden Rd. E7 —2E 31
Findhorn St. E14 —5E 43
Findon Clo. SW18 —4C 76
Findon Rd. W12 —3C 46
Fingal St. SE10 —1B 72
Fingest Ho. NW8 —3A 36 (off Lilestone St.)
Finland Rd. SE4 —1A 84
Finland St. SE16 —4A 56
Finlay St. SW6 —4F 61
Finmere Ho. N4 —2E 11
Finnemore Ho. N1 —5E 25 (off Britannia Row)
Finn Ho. N1 —2F 39 (off Bevenden St.)
Finnis St. E2 —2D 41
Finsbury. —2C 38
Finsbury Av. EC2 —4F 39 (in two parts)
Finsbury Av. Sq. EC2 —4A 40 (off Finsbury Av.)
Finsbury Cir. EC2 —4F 39
Finsbury Est. EC1 —2C 38
Finsbury Mkt. EC2 —3A 40 (in two parts)
Finsbury Park. —3C 10
Finsbury Pk. Av. N4 —1E 11
Finsbury Pk. Rd. N4 —4D 11
Finsbury Pavement. EC2 —4F 39
Finsbury Sq. EC2 —4F 39
Finsbury St. EC2 —4F 39
Finsen Rd. SE5 —2E 81
Finstock Rd. W10 —5F 33
Finwhale Ho. E14 —4D 57
Fiona Ct. NW6 —1C 34
Firbank Clo. E16 —4F 45
Firbank Rd. SE15 —5D 69
Fircroft Rd. SW17 —2B 92
Firecrest Dri. NW3 —5D 7
Firefly Gdns. E6 —3F 45
Firhill Rd. SE6 —4C 98
Fir Ho. W10 —3A 34 (off Droop St.)
Firle Ho. W10 —4E 33 (off Sutton Way)
Firsby Rd. N16 —3C 12
Firs Clo. SE23 —5A 84
First Av. E12 —1F 31
First Av. E13 —2C 44
First Av. SW14 —1A 74
First Av. W3 —2B 46
First Av. W10 —3B 34
Firs, The. E6 —4F 31
Firs, The. SE26 —5D 97 (Lawrie Pk. Gdns.)
Firs, The. SE26 —5E 97 (Venner Rd.)
First St. SW3 —5A 50
Firth Gdns. SW6 —4A 62
Firth Ho. E2 —2C 40 (off Barnet Gro.)
Firtree Clo. SW16 —5E 93
Fir Tree Ho. SE14 —3E 69 (off Avonley Rd.)
Fir Trees Clo. SE16 —2A 56
Fishemans Wlk. E14 —2C 56
Fisher Athletic F.C. —2F 55
Fisher Ho. N1 —5C 24 (off Barnsbury Est.)
Fishermans Dri. SE16 —3F 55
Fisherman's Pl. W4 —2B 60
Fisherman's Wlk. E14 —2C 56
Fisher's Clo. SW16 —3F 93
Fishers Ct. SE14 —4F 69
Fisher's La. W4 —5A 46
Fisher St. E16 —4C 44
Fisher St. WC1 —4B 38
Fisherton St. NW8 —3F 35
Fishmongers Hall Wharf. EC4 (off Swan La.) —1F 53
Fishponds Rd. SW17 —4A 92
Fish St. Hill. EC3 —1F 53
Fish Wharf. EC3 —1F 53 (off Lwr. Thames St.)
Fisons Rd. E16 —2C 58
Fitzalan St. SE11 —5C 52
Fitzgeorge Av. W14 —5A 48
Fitzgerald Av. SW14 —1A 74
Fitzgerald Ct. E10 —3D 15 (off Leyton Grange Est.)
Fitzgerald Ho. E14 —5D 43
Fitzgerald Ho. SW9 —5C 66
Fitzgerald Rd. E11 —1C 16
Fitzgerald Rd. SW14 —1A 74
Fitzhardinge Ho. W1 —5C 36 (off Portman Sq.)
Fitzhardinge St. W1 —5C 36
Fitzhugh Gro. SW18 —4F 77
Fitzjames Av. W14 —5A 48
Fitzjohn's Av. NW3 —1E 21
Fitzmaurice Ho. SE16 —5D 55 (off Rennie Est.)
Fitzmaurice Pl. W1 —2D 51
Fitzneal St. W3 —5B 32
Fitzroy Clo. N6 —3B 8
Fitzroy Ct. N6 —1E 9
Fitzroy Ct. W1 —3E 37 (off Tottenham Ct. Rd.)
Fitzroy Ho. E14 —4B 42
Fitzroy Ho. SE1 —1B 68 (off Coopers La.)
Fitzroy M. W1 —3E 37 (off Cleveland St.)
Fitzroy Pk. N6 —3B 8
Fitzroy Rd. NW1 —5C 22
Fitzroy Sq. W1 —3E 37
Fitzroy St. W1 —3E 37 (in two parts)
Fitzroy Yd. NW1 —5C 22
Fitzsimmons Ct. NW10 —5A 18
Fitzwarren Gdns. N19 —3E 9
Fitzwilliam Heights. SE23 —2E 97
Fitzwilliam M. E16 —2C 58
Fitzwilliam Rd. SW4 —1E 79
Five Bell All. E14 —5B 42
Fives Ct. SE11 —4D 53
Fiveways Rd. SW9 —5C 66
Flack Ct. E10 —2D 15
Fladbury Rd. N15 —1F 11
Fladgate Rd. E11 —1A 16
Flamborough Ho. SE15 (off Clayton Rd.) —4C 68
Flamborough St. E14 —5A 42
Flamborough Wlk. E14 —5A 42
Flamingo Ct. SE8 —3C 70 (off Hamilton St.)
Flamstead Ho. SW3 —1A 64 (off Cale St.)
Flamsteed Rd. SE7 —1F 73
Flanchford Rd. W12 —4B 46
Flanders Ct. E17 —2A 14
Flanders Mans. W4 —5B 46
Flanders Rd. W4 —5A 46
Flanders Way. E9 —3F 27
Flank St. E1 —1C 54
Flansham Ho. E14 —5B 42
Flask Wlk. NW3 —1E 21
Flatford Ho. SE6 —4E 99
Flatiron Yd. SE1 —2E 53 (off Ayres St.)
Flavell M. SE10 —1A 72
Flaxman Ct. W1 —5F 37 (off Wardour St.)
Flaxman Ct. WC1 —2F 37
Flaxman Ho. W4 —1A 60 (off Devonshire St.)
Flaxman Rd. SE5 —1D 81
Flaxman Ter. WC1 —2F 37

*Flecker Ho. SE5 —3F **67*** *(off Lomond Gro.)*
Fleece Wlk. *N7* —3A **24**
*Fleetbank Ho. EC4 —5C **38*** *(off Salisbury Sq.)*
*Fleet Building. EC4 —5D **39*** *(off Shoe La.)*
*Fleetfield. WC1 —2A **38*** *(off Birkenhead St.)*
*Fleet Pl. EC4 —5D **39*** *(off Limeburner La., in two parts)*
Fleet Rd. *NW3* —2A **22**
Fleet Sq. *WC1* —2B **38**
Fleet St. *EC4* —5C **38**
Fleet St. Hill. *E1* —3C **40**
*Fleetway. WC1 —2A **38*** *(off Birkenhead St.)*
Fleetway Bus. Cen. *NW2* —3B **4**
Fleetwood Clo. *E16* —4F **45**
Fleetwood Rd. *NW10* —2C **18**
Fleetwood St. *N16* —4A **12**
Fleming Clo. *W9* —3C **34**
*Fleming Ct. W2 —4F **35*** *(off St Marys Sq.)*
Fleming Ho. *N4* —3E **11**
*Fleming Ho. SE16 —3C **54*** *(off George Row)*
*Fleming Lodge. W2 —4C **34*** *(off Admiral Wlk.)*
Fleming Rd. *SE17* —2D **67**
Flempton Rd. *E10* —3A **14**
*Fletcher Bldgs. WC2 —5A **38*** *(off Martlett Ct.)*
Fletcher La. *E10* —2E **15**
Fletcher Path. *SE8* —3C **70**
Fletcher St. *E1* —1C **54**
Fletching Rd. *E5* —5E **13**
Fletching Rd. *SE7* —2E **73**
Fleur-de-Lis St. *E1* —3B **40** (in two parts)
Fleur Gates. *SW19* —5F **75**
Flimwell Clo. *Brom* —5A **100**
*Flinders Ho. E1 —2D **55*** *(off Green Bank)*
Flintmill Cres. *SE3* —5F **73** (in three parts)
Flinton St. *SE17* —1A **68**
Flint St. *SE17* —5F **53**
Flitcroft St. *WC2* —5F **37**
*Flitton Ho. N1 —4D **25*** *(off Sutton Est., The)*
Flock Mill Pl. *SW18* —1D **91**
Flockton St. *SE16* —3C **54**
Flodden Rd. *SE5* —4E **67**
Flood St. *SW3* —1A **64**
Flood Wlk. *SW3* —2A **64**
Flora Clo. *E14* —5D **43**
*Flora Gdns. W6 —5D **47*** *(off Albion Gdns.)*
Floral Pl. *N1* —2F **25**
Floral St. *WC2* —1A **52**
Florence Ct. *E5* —5C **12**
*Florence Ct. N1 —4D **25*** *(off Florence St.)*
Florence Ct. *SW19* —5A **90**
*Florence Ct. W9 —2E **35*** *(off Maida Va.)*
*Florence Ho. SE16 —1D **69*** *(off Rotherhithe New Rd.)*
Florence Ho. *W11* —1F **47**
*Florence Mans. NW4 —1D **5*** *(off Vivian Av.)*
Florence Nightingale Mus. —3B 52
Florence Rd. *E6* —5E **31**
Florence Rd. *E13* —1B **44**
Florence Rd. *N4* —2B **10** (in two parts)
Florence Rd. *SE14* —4B **70**
Florence Rd. *SW19* —5D **91**
Florence St. *E16* —3B **44**
Florence St. *N1* —4D **25**
Florence Ter. *SE14* —4B **70**
Florence Ter. *SW15* —3A **88**
Florence Way. *SW12* —1B **92**
*Florey Lodge. W9 —4C **34*** *(off Admiral Wlk.)*
*Florfield Pas. E8 —3D **27*** *(off Florfield Rd.)*
Florfield Rd. *E8* —3D **27**
Florian. *SE5* —4A **68**
Florian Rd. *SW15* —2A **76**
Florida St. *E2* —2C **40**
*Florin Ct. SE1 —3B **54*** *(off Tanner St.)*
Floris Pl. *SW4* —1E **79**
Floss St. *SW15* —5E **61**
Flower & Dean Wlk. *E1* (in two parts) —4B **40**
Flowerpot Clo. *N15* —1B **12**
Flowers Clo. *NW2* —5C **4**
Flowersmead. *SW17* —2C **92**
Flowers M. *N19* —4E **9**
Flower Wlk., The. *SW7* —3E **49**
Floyd Rd. *SE7* —1E **73**
Fludyer St. *SE13* —2A **86**
Foley St. *W1* —4E **37**
Folgate St. *E1* —4A **40** (in two parts)
*Foliot Ho. N1 —1B **38*** *(off Priory Grn. Est.)*
Foliot St. *W3* —5B **32**
*Follett Ho. SW10 —3F **63*** *(off Worlds End Est.)*
Follett St. *E14* —5E **43**
*Follingham Ct. N1 —2A **40*** *(off Drysdale Pl.)*
Folly M. *W11* —5B **34**
Folly Wall. *E14* —3E **57**
Fontarabia Rd. *SW11* —2C **78**
Fontenelle Gdns. *SE5* —4A **68**
*Fontenoy Ho. SE11 —5D **53*** *(off Kennington La.)*
Fontenoy Rd. *SW12* —2D **93**
Fonthill M. *N4* —4B **10**
Fonthill Rd. *N4* —3B **10**
Fontley Way. *SW15* —5C **74**
Football Association Hall of Fame. —3B 52
Footpath, The. *SW15* —4C **74**
*Forber Ho. E2 —2E **41*** *(off Cornwall Av.)*
Forbes Clo. *NW2* —5C **4**
Forbes St. *E1* —5C **40**
Forburg Rd. *N16* —3C **12**
Ford Clo. *E3* —1A **42**
Fordel Rd. *SE6* —1F **99**
Fordham St. *E1* —5C **40**
Fordingley Rd. *W9* —2B **34**
Fordington Ho. *SE26* —3C **96**
Fordmill Rd. *SE6* —2C **98**
Ford Rd. *E3* —1B **42**
Fords Pk. Rd. *E16* —4C **44**
Ford Sq. *E1* —4D **41**
Ford St. *E3* —5A **28**
Ford St. *E16* —5B **44**
Fordwych Rd. *NW2* —1A **20**
Fordyce Rd. *SE13* —4E **85**
Foreign St. *SE5* —5D **67**
*Foreland Ho. W11 —1A **48*** *(off Walmer Rd.)*
Foreman Ct. *W6* —5E **47**
Foreshore. *SE8* —5B **56**
Forest Bus. Pk. *E17* —2A **14**
Forest Clo. *E11* —1C **16**
Forest Cft. *SE23* —2D **97**
Forest Dri. *E12* —5F **17**
Forest Dri. E. *E11* —2F **15**
Forest Dri. W. *E11* —2E **15**
Forester Rd. *SE15* —1D **83**
Forest Gate. —2D 31
Forest Glade. *E11* —1A **16**
Forest Gro. *E8* —3B **26**
Forest Hill. —2E 97
*Forest Hill Bus. Cen. SE23 (off Clyde Va.) —2E **97***
Forest Hill Ind. Est. *SE23* —2E **97**
Forest Hill Rd. *SE22 & SE23* —3D **83**
Forestholme Clo. *SE23* —2E **97**
Forest La. *E15 & E7* —2A **30**
*Forest Lodge. SE26 —3E **97*** *(off Dartmouth Rd.)*
*Forest Point. E7 —2D **31*** *(off Windsor Rd.)*
Fore St. *EC2* —4E **39**
Fore St. Av. *EC2* —4F **39**
Forest Rd. *E7* —1C **30**
Forest Rd. *E8* —3B **26**
Forest Rd. *E11* —2F **15**
Forest Side. *E7* —1D **31**
Forest St. *E7* —2C **30**
Forest Vw. *E11* —2B **16**
Forest Vw. Av. *E10* —1F **15**
Forest Vw. Rd. *E12* —1F **31**
Forest Way. *N19* —4E **9**
Forfar Rd. *SW11* —4C **64**
Forge Pl. *NW1* —3C **22**
Forman Pl. *N16* —1B **26**
*Formby Ct. N7 —2C **24*** *(off Morgan Rd.)*
Former County Hall. —3B 52
Formosa St. *W9* —3D **35**
Formunt Clo. *E16* —4B **44**
Forres Gdns. *NW11* —1C **6**

Forrester Path. SE26 —4E **97**
Forset Ct. W2 —5A ***36*** *(off Harrowby St.)*
Forset St. W1 —5A **36**
Forster Ho. Brom —4F **99**
Forster Rd. E17 —1A **14**
Forster Rd. SW12 —5A **80**
Forston St. N1 —1E **39**
Forsyth Gdns. SE17 —2D **67**
Forsyth Ho. SW1 —1E ***65*** *(off Tachbrook St.)*
Fortescue Av. E8 —4D **27**
Fortess Gro. NW5 —2E **23**
Fortess Rd. NW5 —2D **23**
Fortess Wlk. NW5 —2D **23**
Fortess Yd. NW5 —1D **23**
Forthbridge Rd. SW11 —2C **78**
Fortis Clo. E16 —5E **45**
Fortnam Rd. N19 —4F **9**
Fort Rd. SE1 —5B **54**
Fortrose Gdns. SW2 —1A **94**
Fort St. E1 —4A **40**
Fort St. E16 —2D **59**
Fortuna Clo. N7 —3B **24**
Fortunegate Rd. NW10 —5A **18**
Fortune Green. —1C 20
Fortune Grn. Rd. NW6 —1C **20**
Fortune Ho. EC1 —3E ***39*** *(off Fortune St.)*
Fortune Ho. SE11 —5C ***52*** *(off Marylee Way)*
Fortune St. EC1 —3E **39**
Fortune Way. NW10 —2C **32**
Forty Acre La. E16 —4C **44**
Forum Magnus Sq. SE1 (off York Rd.) —3B ***52***
Forward Bus. Cen. E16 —3F **43**
Fosbrooke Ho. SW8 —3A ***66*** *(off Davidson Gdns.)*
Fosbury M. W2 —1D **49**
Foscote M. W9 —3C **34**
Foscote Rd. NW4 —1D **5**
Foskett Rd. SW6 —5B **62**
Fossdene Rd. SE7 —1D **73**
Fossil Rd. SE13 —1C **84**
Foss Rd. SW17 —4F **91**
Foster Ct. NW1 —4E ***23*** *(off Royal College St.)*
Foster Ho. SE14 —4B **70**
Foster La. EC2 —5E **39**
Foster Rd. E13 —3C **44**
Foster Rd. W3 —1A **46**
Foster Rd. W4 —1A **60**
Foster's Way. SW18 —1D **91**
Fothergill Clo. E13 —1C **44**
Foubert's Pl. W1 —5E **37**
Foulden Rd. N16 —1B **26**
Foulden Ter. N16 —1B **26**
Foulis Ter. SW7 —1F **63**
Foulser Rd. SW17 —3B **92**
Founders Ct. EC2 —5F ***39*** *(off Lothbury)*
Founders Ho. SW1 —1F ***65*** *(off Aylesford St.)*
Foundling Ct. WC1 —3A ***38*** *(off Brunswick Cen.)*
Foundry Clo. SE16 —2A **56**
Foundry Ho. E14 —4D **43**
Foundry M. NW1 —3E ***37*** *(off Drummond St.)*
Foundry Pl. SW18 —5D **77**
Fountain Ct. EC4 —1C **52**
Fountain Ct. SE23 —2F **97**
Fountain Ct. SW1 —5D ***51*** *(off Buckingham Pal. Rd.)*
Fountain Dri. SE19 —4B **96**
Fountain Grn. Sq. SE16 —3C **54**
Fountain Ho. NW6 —4A **20**
Fountain Ho. W1 —2C ***50*** *(off Park St.)*
Fountain M. N5 —1E ***25*** *(off Highbury Grange)*
Fountain M. NW3 —3B **22**
Fountain Pl. SW9 —4C **66**
Fountain Rd. SW17 —5F **91**
Fountain Sq. SW1 —5D **51**
Fountayne Rd. N16 —4C **12**
Fount St. SW8 —3F **65**
Fournier St. E1 —4B **40**
Four Seasons Clo. E3 —1C **42**
Fourth Av. W10 —3A **34**
Fovant Ct. SW8 —5E **65**
Fowey Av. Ilf —1F **17**
Fowey Clo. E1 —2D **55**
Fowey Ho. SE11 —1C ***66*** *(off Kennings Way)*
Fowler Clo. SW11 —1F **77**
Fowler Ho. N15 —1F ***11*** *(off South Gro)*
Fowler Rd. E7 —1C **30**
Fowler Rd. N1 —5D **25**
Fownes St. SW11 —1A **78**
Fox & Knot St. EC1 —4D ***39*** *(off Charterhouse Sq.)*
Foxberry Rd. SE4 —1A **84**
Foxborough Gdns. SE4 —3C **84**
Foxbourne Rd. SW17 —2C **92**
Fox Clo. E1 —3E **41**
Fox Clo. E16 —4C **44**
Foxcombe Clo. E6 —1F **45**
Foxcombe Rd. SW15 —1C **88**
Foxcote. SE5 —1A **68**
Foxcroft. WC1 —1B ***38*** *(off Penton Ri.)*
Foxes Dale. SE3 —1C **86**
Foxfield. NW1 —5D ***23*** *(off Arlington Rd.)*
Foxglove St. W12 —1B **46**
Foxham Rd. N19 —5F **9**
Foxhole Rd. SE9 —3F **87**
Foxley Clo. E8 —2C **26**
Foxley Rd. SW9 —3C **66**
Foxley Sq. SW9 —4D **67**
Foxmore St. SW11 —4B **64**
Fox Rd. E16 —4B **44**
Foxwell M. SE4 —1A **84**
Foxwell St. SE4 —1A **84**
Foxwood Rd. SE3 —2B **86**
Foyle Rd. SE3 —2B **72**
Framfield Rd. N5 —2D **25**
Framlingham Clo. E5 —4E **13**
Frampton. NW1 —4F ***23*** *(off Wrotham Rd.)*
Frampton Ho. NW8 —3F ***35*** *(off Frampton St.)*
Frampton Pk. Est. E9 —4E **27**
Frampton Pk. Rd. E9 —3E **27**
Frampton St. W2 —3F **35**
Francemary Rd. SE4 —3C **84**
Frances Ct. E17 —1C **14**
Franche Ct. Rd. SW17 —3E **91**
Francis Barber Clo. SW16 —5B **94**
Franciscan Rd. SW17 —5B **92**
Francis Chichester Way. SW11 —4C **64**
Francis Clo. E14 —5F **57**
Francis Ct. EC1 —4D ***39*** *(off Briset St.)*
Francis Ct. SE14 —2F ***69*** *(off Myers La.)*
Francis Ho. E17 —1B **14**
Francis Ho. N1 —5A ***26*** *(off Colville Est.)*
Francis M. SE12 —5C **86**
Francis Rd. E10 —3E **15**
Francis St. E15 —2A **30**
Francis St. SW1 —5E **51**
Francis Ter. N19 —5E **9**
Francis Wlk. N1 —5B **24**
Franconia Rd. SW4 —3F **79**
Frank Beswick Ho. SW6 (off Clem Attlee Ct.) —2B ***62***
Frank Burton Clo. SE7 —1D **73**
Frank Dixon Clo. SE21 —5A **82**
Frank Dixon Way. SE21 —1A **96**
Frankfurt Rd. SE24 —3E **81**
Frankham Ho. SE8 —3C ***70*** *(off Frankham St.)*
Frankham St. SE8 —3C **70**
Frank Ho. SW8 —3A ***66*** *(off Wyvil Rd.)*
Frankland Clo. SE16 —4D **55**
Frankland Rd. SW7 —4F **49**
Franklin Building. E14 —3C **56**
Franklin Clo. SE13 —4D **71**
Franklin Clo. SE27 —3D **95**
Franklin Ho. E1 —2D ***55*** *(off Watts St.)*
Franklin Pas. SE9 —1F **87**
Franklin Sq. W14 —1B **62**
Franklin's Row. SW3 —1B **64**
Franklin St. E3 —2D **43**
Franklin St. N15 —1A **12**
Franklyn Rd. NW10 —3B **18**
Frank Soskice Ho. SW6 (off Clem Attlee Ct.) —2B ***62***
Frank St. E13 —3C **44**
Frank Whymark Ho. SE16 (off Rupack St.) —3E ***55***
Fransfield Gro. SE26 —3D **97**

Frans Hals Ct. *E14* —4E **57**
Franthorne Way. *SE6* —2D **99**
Fraser Clo. *E6* —5F **45**
Fraser Ct. *E14* —1E **71**
Fraser Rd. *E17* —1D **15**
Fraser St. *W4* —1A **60**
Frazier St. *SE1* —3C **52**
Frean St. *SE16* —4C **54**
Frearson Ho. *WC1* —2B **38**
(off Penton Ri.)
Freda Corbett Clo. *SE15*
—3C **68**
Frederica St. *N7* —4B **24**
Frederick Charrington Ho. E1
(off Wickford St.) —3E **41**
Frederick Clo. *W2* —1B **50**
Frederick Cres. *SW9* —3D **67**
Frederick Rd. *SE17* —2D **67**
Frederick's Pl. *EC2* —5F **39**
Frederick Sq. SE16 —1A 56
(off Sovereign Cres.)
Frederick's Row. *EC1* —2D **39**
Frederick St. *WC1* —2B **38**
Frederick Ter. *E8* —4B **26**
Frederic M. SW1 —3B 50
(off Kinnerton St.)
Frederic St. *E17* —1A **14**
Fred Styles Ho. *SE7* —2E **73**
Fred White Wlk. *N7* —3A **24**
Freedom St. *SW11* —5B **64**
Freegrove Rd. *N7* —2A **24**
(in two parts)
Freeling Ho. NW8 —5F 21
(off Dorman Way)
Freeling St. *N1* —4A **24**
(in two parts)
Freemantle Ho. E1 —3D 41
(off Somerford St.)
Freemantle St. *SE17* —1A **68**
Freemasons Rd. *E16* —4D **45**
Free Trade Wharf. *E1* —1F **55**
Freke Rd. *SW11* —1C **78**
Fremont St. *E9* —5D **27**
French Ordinary Ct. EC3
(off Crutched Friars) —1A **54**
French Pl. *E1* —2A **40**
Frendsbury Rd. *SE4* —2A **84**
Frensham Dri. *SW15* —3B **88**
Frensham St. *SE15* —2C **68**
Frere St. *SW11* —5A **64**
Freshfield Av. *E8* —4B **26**
Freshfield Clo. *SE13* —2E **85**
Freshford St. *SW17* —3E **91**
Freshwater Clo. *SW17* —5C **92**
Freshwater Ct. W1 —4A 36
(off Crawford St.)
Freshwater Rd. *SW17* —5C **92**
Freston Rd. *W10 & W11*
—1F **47**
Freswick Ho. SE8 —5F 55
(off Chilton Gro.)
Freud Mus., The. —3E 21
(off Maresfield Gdns.)
Frewell Ho. EC1 —4C 38
(off Bourne Est.)
Frewin Rd. *SW18* —1F **91**
Friar M. *SE27* —3D **95**

Friars Av. *SW15* —3B **88**
Friars Clo. SE1 —2D 53
(off Bear La.)
Friars Gdns. *W3* —5A **32**
Friars Mead. *E14* —4E **57**
Friars Pl. La. *W3* —1A **46**
Friars Rd. *E6* —5F **31**
Friar St. *EC4* —5D **39**
Friars Way. *W3* —5A **32**
Friary Ct. SW1 —2E 51
(off St James' Pal.)
Friary Est. SE15 —2C 68
(in two parts)
Friary Rd. *SE15* —3C **68**
Friday St. *EC4* —1E **53**
Frideswide Pl. NW5 —2E 23
Friendly Pl. *SE13* —4D **71**
Friendly St. *SE8* —5C **70**
Friendly St. M. *SE8* —5C **70**
Friend St. *EC1* —2D **39**
Friern Rd. *SE22* —5C **82**
Frigate Ho. *E14* —5E **57**
Frigate M. *SE8* —2C **70**
Frimley Clo. *SW19* —2A **90**
Frimley Way. *E1* —3F **41**
Frinstead Ho. W10 —1F 47
(off Freston Rd.)
Frinton Rd. *E6* —2F **45**
Frinton Rd. *N15* —1A **12**
Friston St. *SW6* —5D **63**
Frith Ho. NW8 —3F 35
(off Frampton St.)
Frith Rd. *E11* —1E **29**
Frith St. *W1* —5F **37**
Frithville Gdns. *W12* —2E **47**
Frobisher Ct. SE10 —2F 71
(off Old Woolwich Rd.)
Frobisher Ct. *SE23* —2D **97**
Frobisher Ct. W12 —3E 47
(off Lime Gro.)
Frobisher Cres. EC2 —4E 39
(off Beech St.)
Frobisher Gdns. *E10* —2D **15**
Frobisher Ho. E1 —2D 55
(off Watts St.)
Frobisher Ho. SW1 —2E 65
(off Dolphin Sq.)
Frobisher Pas. *E14* —2C **56**
Frobisher St. *SE10* —2A **72**
Frogley Rd. *SE22* —2B **82**
Frogmore. *SW18* —3C **76**
Frogmore Ind. Est. *N5*
—2E **25**
Frognal. *NW3* —1E **21**
Frognal Clo. *NW3* —2E **21**
Frognal Ct. *NW3* —3E **21**
Frognal Gdns. *NW3* —1E **21**
Frognal La. *NW3* —2D **21**
Frognal Pde. *NW3* —3E **21**
Frognal Ri. *NW3* —1E **21**
Frognal Way. *NW3* —1E **21**
Froissart Rd. *SE9* —3F **87**
Frome Ho. *SE15* —2D **83**
Frome St. *N1* —1E **39**
Frontenac. *NW10* —4D **19**
Frostic Wlk. E1 —4C 40
(off Hopetown St.)

Froude St. *SW8* —5D **65**
Fruiterers Pas. EC4 —1E 53
(off Queen St Pl.)
Fryatt St. *E14* —5A **44**
Fryent Cres. *NW9* —1A **4**
Fryent Fields. *NW9* —1A **4**
Fryent Gro. *NW9* —1A **4**
Fry Ho. *E7* —4E **31**
Frying Pan All. E1 —4B 40
(off Bell La.)
Fry Rd. *E6* —4F **31**
Fry Rd. *NW10* —5B **18**
Fulbeck Rd. *N19* —1E **23**
Fulbourne St. *E1* —4D **41**
Fulbrook M. *N19* —1E **23**
Fulcher Ho. N1 —5A 26
(off Colville Ho.)
Fulcher Ho. *SE8* —1B **70**
Fulford St. *SE16* —3D **55**
Fulham. —5A 62
Fulham Broadway. (Junct.)
—3C **62**
Fulham B'way. *SW6* —3C **62**
Fulham Ct. *SW6* —4C **62**
Fulham F.C. —4F 61
Fulham High St. *SW6* —5A **62**
Fulham Pal. Rd. *W6 & SW6*
—1E **61**
Fulham Pk. Gdns. *SW6*
—5B **62**
Fulham Pk. Rd. *SW6* —5B **62**
Fulham Rd. *SW6* —5A **62**
Fulham Rd. *SW10 & SW3*
—2E **63**
Fuller Clo. E2 —3C 40
(off Cheshire St.)
Fuller's Griffin Brewery &
Vis. Cen. —2B 60
Fullerton Rd. *SW18* —3D **77**
Fullwood's M. *N1* —2E **39**
Fulmar Ho. SE16 —5F 55
(off Tawny Way)
Fulmead St. *SW6* —4D **63**
Fulmer Ho. NW1 —3A 36
(off Rossmore Rd.)
Fulmer Rd. *E16* —4F **45**
Fulneck. *E1* —4E **41**
(off Mile End Rd.)
Fulready Rd. *E10* —1F **15**
Fulthorp Rd. *SE3* —5B **72**
Fulton M. *W2* —1E **49**
(off Porchester Ter.)
Fulwood Pl. *WC1* —4B **38**
Fulwood Wlk. *SW19* —1A **90**
Furber St. *W6* —4D **47**
Furley Ho. SE15 —3C 68
(off Peckham Pk. Rd.)
Furley Rd. *SE15* —3C **68**
Furlong Rd. *N7* —3C **24**
Furmage St. *SW18* —5D **77**
Furneaux Av. *SE27* —5D **95**
Furness Ho. *SW1* —1D **65**
(off Abbots Mnr.)
Furness Rd. *NW10* —1C **32**
Furness Rd. *SW6* —5D **63**
Furnival Mans. *W1* —4E **37**
(off Wells St.)

Furnival St. EC4 —5C 38
Furrow La. E9 —2E 27
Fursecroft. W1 —5B 36 (off George St.)
Further Grn. Rd. SE6 —5A 86
Furzedown. —5D 93
Furzedown Dri. SW17 —5D 93
Furzedown Rd. SW17 —5D 93
Furzefield Rd. SE3 —2D 73
Furze St. E3 —4C 42
Fye Foot La. EC4 —1E 53 (off Queen Victoria St., in two parts)
Fyfield. N4 —4C 10 (off Six Acres Est.)
Fyfield Ct. E7 —3C 30
Fyfield Rd. SW9 —1C 80
Fynes St. SW1 —5F 51

Gable Ct. SE26 —4D 97
Gables Clo. SE5 —4A 68
Gables Clo. SE12 —1C 100
Gabriel Ho. SE11 —5B 52
Gabrielle Ct. NW3 —3F 21
Gabriel St. SE23 —5F 83
Gabriels Wharf. SE1 —2C 52
Gad Clo. E13 —2D 45
Gaddesden Ho. EC1 —2F 39 (off Cranwood St.)
Gadebridge Ho. SW3 —1A 64 (off Cale St.)
Gadsbury Clo. NW9 —1B 4
Gadsden Ho. W10 —3A 34 (off Hazlewood Cres.)
Gadwall Clo. E16 —5D 45
Gage Rd. E16 —4A 44
Gage St. WC1 —4A 38
Gainford Ho. E2 —2D 41 (off Ellsworth St.)
Gainford St. N1 —5C 24
Gainsborough Ct. SE16 (off Stubbs Dri.) —1D 69
Gainsborough Ct. SE21 —2A 96
Gainsborough Ct. W12 —3E 47
Gainsborough Gdns. NW3 —5F 7
Gainsborough Gdns. NW11 —2B 6
Gainsborough Ho. SW1 (off Erasmus St.) —5F 51
Gainsborough Mans. W14 —2A 62 (off Queen's Club Gdns.)
Gainsborough M. SE26 —3D 97
Gainsborough Rd. E11 —2A 16
Gainsborough Rd. E15 —2A 44
Gainsborough Rd. W4 —5B 46
Gainsfield Ct. E11 —5A 16
Gainsford St. SE1 —3B 54
Gairloch Ho. NW1 —4F 23 (off Stratford Vs.)
Gairloch Rd. SE5 —5A 68
Gaisford St. NW5 —3E 23
Gaitskell Ct. SW11 —5A 64
Gaitskell Ho. E6 —5F 31
Gaitskell Ho. SE17 —2A 68 (off Villa St.)
Galahad Rd. Brom —4C 100
Galata Rd. SW13 —3C 60
Galatea Sq. SE15 —1D 83
Galbraith St. E14 —4E 57
Galena Rd. W6 —5D 47
Galen Pl. WC1 —4A 38
Galesbury Rd. SW18 —4E 77
Gales Gdns. E2 —2D 41
Gale St. E3 —4C 42
Galgate Clo. SW19 —1F 89
Galleon Clo. SE16 —3F 55
Galleon Ho. E14 —5E 57
Gallery Ct. SE1 —3F 53 (off Pilgrimage St.)
Gallery Ct. SW10 —2E 63
Gallery Rd. SE21 —1F 95
Galleywall Rd. SE16 —5D 55
Galleywall Rd. Trad. Est. SE16 —5D 55 (off Galleywall Rd.)
Gallia Rd. N5 —2D 25
Gallions Rd. SE7 —5D 59 (in two parts)
Galliver Pl. E5 —1D 27
Gallon Clo. SE7 —5E 59
Galloway Rd. W12 —2C 46
Gallus Sq. SE3 —1D 87
Galsworth Clo. NW2 —1A 20
Galsworthy Av. E14 —4A 42
Galsworthy Cres. SE3 —4E 73
Galsworthy Ho. W11 —5A 34
Galsworthy Rd. NW2 —1A 20
Galsworthy Ter. N16 —5A 12
Galton St. W10 —2A 34
Galveston Rd. SW15 —3B 76
Galway Clo. SE16 —1D 69 (off Masters Dri.)
Galway Ho. EC1 —2E 39 (off Radnor St.)
Galway St. EC1 —2E 39
Gambetta St. SW8 —5D 65
Gambia St. SE1 —2D 53
Gambier Ho. EC1 —2E 39 (off Mora St.)
Gambole Rd. SW17 —4A 92
Gamlen Rd. SW15 —2F 75
Gamuel Clo. E17 —1C 14
Gandhi Clo. E17 —1C 14
Gandolfi St. SE15 —2A 68
Ganton St. W1 —1E 51
Gap Rd. SW19 —5C 90
Garbett Ho. SE17 —2D 67 (off Doddington Gro.)
Garbutt Pl. W1 —4C 36
Garden Clo. SE12 —3D 101
Garden Clo. SW15 —5E 75
Garden Ct. WC2 —1C 52 (off Temple)
Garden La. SW2 —1B 94
Garden M. W2 —1C 48
Garden Pl. E8 —5B 26
Garden Rd. NW8 —2E 35
Garden Row. SE1 —4D 53
Gardens, The. SE22 —2C 82
Garden St. E1 —4F 41
Garden Ter. SW1 —1F 65
Garden Ter. SW7 —3A 50 (off Trevor Pl.)
Garden Vw. E7 —1E 31
Garden Wlk. EC2 —2A 40
Gardiner Av. NW2 —2E 19
Gardner Clo. E11 —1D 17
Gardner Ind. Est. SE26 —5B 98
Gardner Rd. E13 —3D 45
Gardners La. EC4 —1E 53
Gardnor Rd. NW3 —1F 21
Gard St. EC1 —2D 39
Gareth Ct. SW16 —3F 93
Gareth Gro. Brom —4C 100
Garfield M. SW11 —1C 78
Garfield Rd. E13 —3B 44
Garfield Rd. SW11 —1C 78
Garfield Rd. SW19 —5E 91
Garford St. E14 —1C 56
Garganey Ct. NW10 —3A 18 (off Elgar Av.)
Garlick Hill. EC4 —1E 53
Garlies Rd. SE23 —3A 98
Garlinge Rd. NW2 —3B 20
Garnault M. EC1 —2C 38 (off Rosebery Av.)
Garnault Pl. EC1 —2C 38
Garner St. E2 —1C 40
Garnet Rd. NW10 —3A 18
Garnet St. E1 —1E 55
Garnett Rd. NW3 —2B 22
Garnham Clo. N16 —4B 12
Garnham St. N16 —4B 12
Garnies Clo. SE15 —3B 68
Garrad's Rd. SW16 —3F 93
Garrard Wlk. NW10 —3A 18
Garratt Ct. SW18 —5D 77
Garratt La. SW18 & SW17 —4D 77
Garratt Ter. SW17 —4A 92
Garrett Clo. W3 —4A 32
Garrett St. EC1 —3E 39
Garrick Av. NW11 —1A 6
Garrick Clo. SW18 —2E 77
Garrick Ho. W1 —2D 51
Garrick Ho. W4 —2A 60
Garrick Ind. Est. NW9 —1B 4
Garrick Rd. NW9 —1B 4
Garrick St. WC2 —1A 52
Garrick Yd. WC2 —1A 52 (off St Martin's La.)
Garsdale Ter. W14 —1B 62
Garsington M. SE4 —1B 84
Garson Ho. W2 —1F 49 (off Gloucester Ter.)
Garston Ho. N1 —4D 25 (off Sutton Est., The)
Garter Way. SE16 —3F 55
Garthorne Rd. SE23 —5F 83

Garth Rd. *NW2* —4B **6**
Gartmoor Gdns. *SW19*
—1B **90**
Garton Pl. *SW18* —4E **77**
Gartons Way. *SW11* —1E **77**
Garvary Rd. *E16* —5D **45**
Garway Rd. *W2* —5D **35**
Gascoigne Pl. *E2* —2B **40**
(in two parts)
Gascony Av. *NW6* —4C **20**
Gascoyne Ho. *E9* —4A **28**
Gascoyne Rd. *E9* —4F **27**
Gaselee St. *E14* —1E **57**
Gaskarth Rd. *SW12* —4D **79**
Gaskell Rd. *N6* —1B **8**
Gaskell St. *SW4* —5A **66**
Gaskin St. *N1* —5D **25**
Gaspar Clo. *SW5* —5D **49**
(off Courtfield Gdns.)
Gaspar M. *SW5* —5D **49**
Gassiot Rd. *SW17* —4B **92**
Gasson Rd. *SE14* —2F **69**
(off John Williams Clo.)
Gastein Rd. *W6* —2F **61**
Gastigny Ho. *EC1* —2E **39**
(off Lever St.)
Gataker Ho. *SE16* —4D **55**
(off Slippers Pl.)
Gataker St. *SE16* —4D **55**
Gatcombe Ho. *SE22* —1A **82**
Gatcombe Rd. *E16* —2C **58**
Gatcombe Rd. *N19* —5F **9**
Gateforth St. *NW8* —3A **36**
Gate Hill Ct. *W11* —2B **48**
(off Ladbroke Ter.)
Gatehouse Sq. *SE1* —2E **53**
(off Porter St.)
Gateley Ho. *SE4* —2F **83**
(off Coston Wlk.)
Gateley Rd. *SW9* —1B **80**
Gate Lodge. *W9* —4C **34**
Gate M. *SW7* —3A **50**
(off Rutland Ga.)
Gatesborough St. *EC2* —3A **40**
Gates Ct. *SE17* —1E **67**
Gatesden. *WC1* —2A **38**
Gateside Rd. *SW17* —3B **92**
Gate St. *WC2* —5B **38**
Gate Theatre, The. —2C **48**
Gateway. *SE17* —2E **67**
Gateway Arc. *N1* —1D **39**
Gateway Ind. Est. *NW10*
—2B **32**
Gateway M. *E8* —2B **26**
Gateway Rd. *E10* —5D **15**
Gateways, The. *SW3* —5A **50**
(off Sprimont Pl.)
Gathorne St. *E2* —1F **41**
Gatliff Clo. *SW1* —1D **65**
(off Ebury Bri. Rd.)
Gatliff Rd. *SW1* —1D **65**
(in two parts)
Gattis Wharf. *N1* —1A **38**
(off New Wharf Rd.)
Gatton Rd. *SW17* —4A **92**
Gatwick Ho. *E14* —5B **42**
Gatwick Rd. *SW18* —5B **76**

Gauden Clo. *SW4* —1F **79**
Gauden Rd. *SW4* —5F **65**
Gaugin Ct. *SE16* —1D **69**
(off Stubbs Dri.)
Gaumont Ter. *W12* —3E **47**
(off Lime Gro.)
Gaunt St. *SE1* —4E **53**
Gautrey Rd. *SE15* —5E **69**
Gavel St. *SE17* —5F **53**
Gavestone Cres. *SE12*
—5D **87**
Gavestone Rd. *SE12* —5D **87**
Gaviller Pl. *E5* —1D **27**
Gawber St. *E2* —2E **41**
Gawsworth Clo. *E15* —2B **30**
Gay Clo. *NW2* —2D **19**
Gaydon Ho. *W2* —4D **35**
(off Bourne Ter.)
Gayfere St. *SW1* —4A **52**
Gayford Rd. *W12* —3B **46**
Gay Ho. *N1* —2A **26**
Gayhurst. *SE17* —2F **67**
(off Hopwood Rd.)
Gayhurst Ho. *NW8* —3A **36**
(off Mallory St.)
Gayhurst Rd. *E8* —4C **26**
Gaymead. *NW8* —5D **21**
(off Abbey Rd.)
Gaynesford Rd. *SE23* —2F **97**
Gay Rd. *E15* —1F **43**
Gaysley Ho. *SE11* —5C **52**
(off Hotspur St.)
Gay St. *SW15* —1F **75**
Gaythorne St. *E3* —3B **42**
Gayton Cres. *NW3* —1F **21**
Gayton Rd. *NW3* —1F **21**
Gayville Rd. *SW11* —4B **78**
Gaywood Clo. *SW2* —1B **94**
Gaywood St. *SE1* —4D **53**
Gaza St. *SE17* —1D **67**
Gaze Ho. *E14* —5F **43**
Geary Rd. *NW10* —2C **18**
Geary St. *N7* —2B **24**
Gedling Pl. *SE1* —4B **54**
Geere Rd. *E15* —5B **30**
Gees Ct. *W1* —5C **36**
Gee St. *EC1* —3E **39**
Geffrye Ct. *N1* —1A **40**
Geffrye Est. *N1* —1A **40**
Geffrye Mus. —1B **40**
Geffrye St. *E2* —1B **40**
Geldart Rd. *SE15* —3D **69**
Geldeston Rd. *E5* —4C **12**
Gellatly Rd. *SE14* —5E **69**
Gemini Bus. Cen. *E16* —3F **43**
Gemini Bus. Est. *SE14*
—1F **69**
Gemini Ct. *E1* —1C **54**
(off Vaughan Way)
General Wolfe Rd. *SE10*
—4F **71**
Geneva Dri. *SW9* —2C **80**
Genoa Av. *SW15* —3E **75**
Gentry Gdns. *E13* —3C **44**
Geoffrey Clo. *SE5* —5E **67**
Geoffrey Ct. *SE4* —5B **70**
Geoffrey Gdns. *E6* —1F **45**

Geoffrey Ho. *SE1* —4F **53**
(off Pardoner St.)
Geoffrey Jones Ct. *NW10*
—5C **18**
Geoffrey Rd. *SE4* —1B **84**
Geographers A-Z Shop.
—4C **38**
George Beard Rd. *SE8*
—5B **56**
George Ct. *WC2* —1A **52**
(off John Adam St.)
George Downing Est. *N16*
—4B **12**
George Eliot Ho. *SW1* —5E **51**
(off Vauxhall Bri. Rd.)
George Elliston Ho. *SE1*
(off Old Kent Rd.) —1C **68**
George Eyre Ho. *NW8* —1F **35**
(off Cochrane St.)
George Gillett Ct. *EC1* —3E **39**
(off Banner St.)
George Inn Yd. *SE1* —2F **53**
George La. *SE13* —4D **85**
George Lansbury Ho. *NW10*
—4A **18**
George Lindgren Ho. *SW6*
(off Clem Attlee Ct.) —3B **62**
George Loveless Ho. *E2*
(off Diss St.) —2B **40**
George Lowe Ct. *W2* —4D **35**
(off Bourne Ter.)
George Mathers Rd. *SE11*
—5D **53**
George M. *NW1* —2E **37**
(off N. Gower St.)
George Peabody Ct. *NW1*
(off Bell St.) —4A **36**
George Row. *SE16* —3C **54**
George's Rd. *N7* —2B **24**
George's Sq. *SW6* —2B **62**
(off N. End Rd.)
George St. *E16* —5B **44**
George St. *W1* —5B **36**
George Tingle Ho. *SE1*
(off Grange Wlk.) —4B **54**
Georgetown Clo. *SE19*
—5A **96**
Georgette Pl. *SE10* —3E **71**
George Walter Ho. *SE16*
(off Millender Wlk.) —5E **55**
George Wyver Clo. *SW19*
—5A **76**
George Yd. *EC3* —5F **39**
George Yd. *W1* —1C **50**
Georgiana St. *NW1* —5E **23**
Georgian Ct. *E9* —5E **27**
Georgian Ct. *NW4* —1D **5**
Georgian Ct. *SW16* —4A **94**
Georgina Gdns. *E2* —2B **40**
Geraint Rd. *Brom* —4C **100**
Geraldine Rd. *SW18* —3E **77**
Geraldine St. *SE11* —4D **53**
Gerald M. *SW1* —5C **50**
(off Gerald Rd.)
Gerald Rd. *E16* —3B **44**
Gerald Rd. *SW1* —5C **50**
Gerard Rd. *SW13* —4B **60**

Gerards Clo. *SE16* —1E **69**
Germander Way. *E15* —2A **44**
Gernon Rd. *E3* —1A **42**
Geron Way. *NW2* —4D **5**
Gerrard Rd. SE14 —3E **69**
(off Briant St.)
Gerrard Pl. *W1* —1F **51**
Gerrard Rd. *N1* —1D **39**
Gerrard St. *W1* —1F **51**
Gerridge Ct. SE1 —4C **52**
(off Gerridge St.)
Gerridge St. *SE1* —4C **52**
Gerry Raffles Sq. *E15* —4F **29**
Gertrude St. *SW10* —2E **63**
Gervase St. *SE15* —3D **69**
Ghent St. *SE6* —2C **98**
Ghent Way. *E8* —3B **26**
Giant Arches Rd. *SE24*
—5E **81**
Gibbings Ho. SE1 —3D **53**
(off King James St.)
Gibbins Rd. *E15* —4E **29**
(in three parts)
Gibbon Ho. NW8 —3F **35**
(off Fisherton St.)
Gibbon Rd. *SE15* —5E **69**
Gibbon Rd. *W3* —1A **46**
Gibbon's Rents. SE1 —2A **54**
(off Magdalen St.)
Gibbons Rd. *NW10* —3A **18**
Gibbon Wlk. *SW15* —2C **74**
Gibbs Av. *SE19* —5F **95**
Gibbs Clo. *SE19* —5F **95**
Gibbs Grn. *W14* —1B **62**
(in three parts)
Gibbs Sq. *SE19* —5F **95**
Gibney Ter. *Brom* —4B **100**
Gibraltar Wlk. E2 —2B **40**
(off Tomlinson Clo.)
Gibson Clo. *E1* —3E **41**
Gibson Gdns. *N16* —4B **12**
Gibson Rd. *SE11* —5B **52**
Gibsons Hill. *SW16* —5D **95**
Gibson Sq. *N1* —5C **24**
Gibson St. *SE10* —1A **72**
Gideon Rd. *SW11* —1C **78**
Giesbach Rd. *N19* —4F **9**
Giffen Sq. Mkt. SE8 —3C **70**
(off Giffen St.)
Giffin St. *SE8* —3C **70**
Gifford Ho. *SE10* —1F **71**
(off Eastney St.)
Gifford Ho. *SW1* —1E **65**
(off Churchill Gdns.)
Gifford St. *N1* —4A **24**
Gift La. *E15* —5B **30**
Gilbert Bri. EC2 —4E **39**
(off Barbican)
Gilbert Ho. EC2 —4E **39**
(off Beech St.)
Gilbert Ho. *SE8* —2C **70**
Gilbert Ho. SW1 —1D **65**
(off Churchill Gdns.)
Gilbert Ho. SW8 —3A **66**
(off Wyvil Rd.)
Gilbert Rd. *SE11* —5C **52**

Gilbert Sheldon Ho. W2
(off Edgware Rd.) —4F **35**
Gilbertson Ho. *E14* —4C **56**
Gilbert St. *E15* —1A **30**
Gilbert St. *W1* —5C **36**
Gilbey Rd. *SW17* —4A **92**
Gilbeys Yd. *NW1* —4C **22**
Gilda Cres. *N16* —3C **12**
Gildea St. *W1* —4D **37**
Gilden Cres. *NW5* —2C **22**
Giles Coppice. *SE19* —4B **96**
Giles Ho. SE16 —4C **54**
(off Old Jamaica Rd.)
Gilesmead. *SE5* —4F **67**
Gilkes Cres. *SE21* —4A **82**
Gilkes Pl. *SE21* —4A **82**
Gillam Ho. SE16 —5E **55**
(off Silwood St.)
Gillan Ct. *SE12* —3D **101**
Gillender St. *E3 & E14* —3E **43**
Gillender St. *E14* —3E **43**
Gillespie Rd. *N5* —5C **10**
Gillett Av. *E6* —1F **45**
Gillett Pl. *N16* —2A **26**
Gillett St. *N16* —2A **26**
Gillfoot. NW1 —1E **37**
(off Hampstead Rd.)
Gillian St. *SE13* —3D **85**
Gillies St. *NW5* —2C **22**
Gilling Ct. *NW3* —3A **22**
Gillingham M. *SW1* —5E **51**
Gillingham Rd. *NW2* —5A **6**
Gillingham Row. *SW1* —5E **51**
Gillingham St. *SW1* —5E **51**
Gillison Wlk. *SE16* —4D **55**
Gillman Dri. *E15* —5B **30**
Gillman Ho. E2 —1C **40**
(off Pritchard's Rd.)
Gill St. *E14* —5B **42**
Gilmore Rd. *SE13* —2F **85**
Gilpin Av. *SW14* —2A **74**
Gilpin Rd. *E5* —1A **28**
Gilray Ho. W2 —1F **49**
(off Gloucester Ter.)
Gilstead Rd. *SW6* —5D **63**
Gilston Rd. *SW10* —1E **63**
Gilton Rd. *SE6* —3A **100**
Giltspur St. *EC1* —5D **39**
Ginsburg Yd. *NW3* —1E **21**
Gipsy Hill. *SE19* —4A **96**
Gipsy La. *SW15* —1D **75**
Gipsy Rd. *SE27* —4E **95**
Gipsy Rd. Gdns. *SE27*
—4E **95**
Giralda Clo. *E16* —4F **45**
Giraud St. *E14* —5D **43**
Girdler's Rd. *W14* —5F **47**
Girdlestone Wlk. *N19* —4E **9**
Girdwood Rd. *SW18* —5A **76**
Girling Ho. N1 —5A 26
(off Colville Est.)
Gironde Rd. *SW6* —3B **62**
Girton Rd. *SE26* —5F **97**
Girton Vs. *W10* —5F **33**
Gisburn Ho. SE15 —2C **68**
(off Friary Est.)

Gissing Wlk. *N1* —4C **24**
Gittens Clo. *Brom* —4B **100**
Given Wilson Wlk. *E13*
—1B **44**
Gladding Rd. *E12* —1F **31**
Gladesmore Rd. *N15* —1B **12**
Glade, The. *SE7* —3E **73**
Gladiator St. *SE23* —5A **84**
Glading Ter. *N16* —5B **12**
Gladsmuir Rd. *N19* —3E **9**
Gladstone Ct. SW1 —5F 51
(off Regency St.)
Gladstone Ho. *E14* —5C **42**
Gladstone M. *NW6* —4B **20**
Gladstone Pde. *NW2* —4E **5**
Gladstone Pk. Gdns. *NW2*
—5D **5**
Gladstone Pl. *E3* —1B **42**
Gladstone St. *SE1* —4D **53**
Gladstone Ter. SE27 —5E 95
(off Bentons La.)
Gladstone Ter. *SW8* —4D **65**
Gladwell Rd. *N8* —1B **10**
Gladwell Rd. *Brom* —5C **100**
Gladwin Ho. NW1 —1E 37
(off Cranleigh St.)
Gladwyn Rd. *SW15* —1F **75**
Gladys Dimson Ho. E7
—2B **30**
Gladys Rd. *NW6* —4C **20**
Glaisher St. *SE8* —2C **70**
Glamis Pl. *E1* —1E **55**
Glamis Rd. *E1* —1E **55**
Glanville Rd. *SW2* —3A **80**
Glasbrook Rd. *SE9* —5F **87**
Glaserton Rd. *N16* —2A **12**
Glasford St. *SW17* —5B **92**
Glasgow Ho. W9 —1D 35
(off Maida Va.)
Glasgow Rd. *E13* —1D **45**
Glasgow Ter. *SW1* —1E **65**
Glasier Ct. *E15* —4A **30**
Glasshill St. *SE1* —3D **53**
Glasshouse Fields. *E1* —1F **55**
Glasshouse St. *W1* —1E **51**
Glasshouse Wlk. *SE1* —1A **66**
Glasshouse Yd. *EC1* —3E **39**
Glasslyn Rd. *N8* —1F **9**
Glass St. *E2* —3D **41**
Glastonbury Ct. SE14 —3E 69
(off Farrow La.)
Glastonbury Ho. SE12
(off Wantage Rd.) —3B **86**
Glastonbury Ho. SW1
(off Abbots Mnr.) —1D **65**
Glastonbury Pl. *E1* —5E **41**
Glastonbury St. *NW6* —2B **20**
Glaucus St. *E3* —4D **43**
Glazbury Rd. *W14* —5A **48**
Glazebrook Clo. *SE21* —2F **95**
Glebe Clo. *W4* —1A **60**
Glebe Ct. SE3 —1A 86
(off Glebe, The)
Glebe Ho. SE16 —4D 55
(off Slippers Pl.)
Glebe Hyrst. *SE19* —4A **96**
Glebelands. *E10* —4D **15**

Glebelands Clo. *SE5* —1A **82**
Glebe Pl. *SW3* —2A **64**
Glebe Rd. *E8* —4B **26**
Glebe Rd. *NW10* —3C **18**
Glebe Rd. *SW13* —5C **60**
Glebe St. *W4* —1A **60**
Glebe Ter. *E3* —2D **43**
Glebe Ter. *W4* —1A **60**
Glebe, The. *SE3* —1A **86**
Glebe, The. *SW16* —4F **93**
Gledhow Gdns. *SW5* —5E **49**
Gledstanes Rd. *W14* —1A **62**
Glegg Pl. *SW15* —2F **75**
Glenaffric Av. *E14* —5F **57**
Glen Albyn Rd. *SW19* —2F **89**
Glenallan Ho. W14 —5B **48**
   (off N. End Cres.)
Glenalvon Way. *SE18* —5F **59**
Glenarm Rd. *E5* —1E **27**
Glenavon Rd. *E15* —4A **30**
Glenbow Rd. *Brom* —5A **100**
Glenbrook Rd. *NW6* —2C **20**
Glenburnie Rd. *SW17* —3B **92**
Glencairne Clo. *E16* —4F **45**
Glencoe Mans. SW9 —3C **66**
   (off Mowll St.)
Glendale Dri. *SW19* —5B **90**
Glendall St. *SW9* —2B **80**
Glendarvon St. *SW15* —1F **75**
Glendower Gdns. *SW14*
   —1A **74**
Glendower Pl. *SW7* —5F **49**
Glendower Rd. *SW14* —1A **74**
Glendown Rd. *E8* —2C **26**
Glendun Ct. *W3* —1A **46**
Glendun Rd. *W3* —1A **46**
Gleneagle M. *SW16* —5F **93**
Gleneagle Rd. *SW16* —5F **93**
Gleneagles Clo. SE16 —1D **69**
   (off Ryder Dri.)
Gleneldon M. *SW16* —4A **94**
Gleneldon Rd. *SW16* —4A **94**
Glenelg Rd. *SW2* —3A **80**
Glenfarg Rd. *SE6* —1E **99**
Glenfield Rd. *SW12* —1E **93**
Glenfinlas Way. *SE5* —3D **67**
Glenforth St. *SE10* —1B **72**
Glengall Gro. *E14* —4D **57**
Glengall Pas. NW6 —5C **20**
   *(off Priory Pk. Rd.,
      in two parts)*
Glengall Rd. *NW6* —5B **20**
Glengall Rd. *SE15* —1B **68**
Glengall Ter. *SE15* —2B **68**
Glengariff Mans. SW9
   (off S. Island Pl.) —3C **66**
Glengarnock Av. *E14* —5E **57**
Glengarry Rd. *SE22* —3A **82**
Glenhurst Av. *NW5* —1C **22**
Glenilla Rd. *NW3* —3A **22**
Glenister Rd. *SE10* —1B **72**
Glenkerry Ho. *E14* —5E **43**
Glenloch Rd. *NW3* —3A **22**
Glenluce Rd. *SE3* —2C **72**
Glenmore Rd. *NW3* —3A **22**
Glennie Ho. SE10 —4E **71**
   (off Blackheath Hill)

Glennie Rd. *SE27* —3C **94**
Glenparke Rd. *E7* —3D **31**
Glenridding. NW1 —1E **37**
   (off Ampthill Est.)
Glen Rd. *E13* —3E **45**
Glen Rd. *E17* —1B **14**
Glenrosa St. *SW6* —5E **63**
Glenroy St. *W12* —5E **33**
Glensdale Rd. *SE4* —1B **84**
Glenshaw Mans. SW9
   (off Brixton Rd.) —3C **66**
Glentanner Way. SW17
   —3F **91**
Glentham Gdns. *SW13*
   —2D **61**
Glentham Rd. *SW13* —2C **60**
Glenthorne M. *W6* —5D **47**
Glenthorne Rd. *E17* —1A **14**
Glenthorne Rd. *W6* —5D **47**
Glenthorpe Av. *SW15* —2C **74**
Glenton Rd. *SE13* —2A **86**
Glentworth St. *NW1* —3B **36**
Glenville Gro. *SE8* —3B **70**
Glenville M. *SW18* —5D **77**
Glenwood Av. *NW9* —3A **4**
Glenwood Rd. *N15* —1D **11**
Glenwood Rd. *SE6* —1B **98**
Glenworth Av. *E14* —5F **57**
Gliddon Rd. *W14* —5A **48**
Global App. *E3* —1D **43**
Globe Pond Rd. *SE16* —2A **56**
Globe Rd. *E2 & E1* —2E **41**
   (in two parts)
Globe Rd. *E15* —2B **30**
Globe Rope Wlk. *E14* —5D **57**
Globe Stairs. *SE16* —1F **55**
Globe St. *SE1* —4F **53**
Globe Ter. *E2* —2E **41**
Globe Town. —2F **41**
Globe Town Mkt. *E2* —2F **41**
Globe Wharf. *SE16* —1F **55**
Globe Yd. W1 —5D **37**
   (off S. Molton St.)
Gloucester Arc. *SW7* —5E **49**
Gloucester Av. *NW1* —4C **22**
Gloucester Cir. *SE10* —3E **71**
Gloucester Ct. *EC3* —1A **54**
Gloucester Ct. NW11 —2B **6**
   (off Golders Grn. Rd.)
Gloucester Cres. *NW1* —5D **23**
Gloucester Dri. *N4* —4D **11**
Gloucester Gdns. *NW11*
   —2B **6**
Gloucester Gdns. *W2* —5E **35**
Gloucester Ga. *NW1* —1D **37**
   (in two parts)
Gloucester Ga. M. *NW1*
   —1D **37**
Gloucester Ho. NW6 —1C **34**
   (off Cambridge Rd.)
Gloucester Ho. *SE5* —3C **66**
Gloucester M. *E10* —2C **14**
Gloucester M. *W2* —5E **35**
Gloucester M. W. *W2* —5E **35**
Gloucester Pl. *NW1 & W1*
   —3B **36**

Gloucester Pl. M. *W1*
   —4B **36**
Gloucester Rd. *E10* —2C **14**
Gloucester Rd. *E11* —1D **17**
Gloucester Rd. *SW7* —4E **49**
Gloucester Sq. *E2* —5C **26**
Gloucester Sq. *W2* —5F **35**
Gloucester Sq. *SW1* —1E **65**
Gloucester Ter. *W2* —5D **35**
Gloucester Wlk. *W8* —3C **48**
Gloucester Way. *EC1* —2C **38**
Glover Ho. *NW6* —4E **21**
Glover Ho. *SE15* —2D **83**
Glycena Rd. *SW11* —1B **78**
Glyn Ct. *SW16* —3C **94**
Glynde M. SW3 —4A **50**
   (off Walton St.)
Glynde Reach. WC1 —2A **38**
   (off Harrison St.)
Glynde St. *SE4* —4B **84**
Glynfield Rd. *NW10* —4A **18**
Glyn Rd. *E5* —5F **13**
Glyn St. *SE11* —1B **66**
Glynwood Ct. *SE23* —2E **97**
Goater's All. SW6 —3B **62**
   (off Dawes Rd.)
Godalming Rd. *E14* —4D **43**
Godbold Rd. *E15* —3A **44**
Goddard Pl. *N19* —5E **9**
Godfrey Ho. EC1 —2F **39**
   (off St Luke's Est.)
Godfrey St. *E15* —1E **43**
Godfrey St. *SW3* —1A **64**
Goding St. *SE11* —1A **66**
Godley Rd. *SW18* —1F **91**
Godliman St. *EC4* —5D **39**
Godman Rd. *SE15* —5D **69**
Godolphin Pl. *W3* —1A **46**
Godolphin Rd. *W12* —2D **47**
   (in two parts)
Godstone Ho. SE1 —4F **53**
   (off Pardoner St.)
Godwin Clo. *N1* —1E **39**
Godwin Ct. NW1 —1E **37**
   (off Chalton St.)
Godwin Ho. NW6 —1D **35**
   *(off Tollgate Gdns.,
      in three parts)*
Godwin Rd. *E7* —1D **31**
Goffers Rd. *SE3* —4A **72**
Golborne Gdns. *W10* —3A **34**
Golborne Ho. W10 —3A **34**
   (off Adair Rd.)
Golborne M. *W10* —4A **34**
Golborne Rd. *W10* —4A **34**
Goldcrest Clo. *E16* —4F **45**
Golden Cross M. W11
   (off Portobello Rd.) —5B **34**
Golden Hinde Educational
   Mus. —2F **53**
Golden Hind Pl. SE8 —5B **56**
   (off Grove St.)
Golden La. *EC1* —3E **39**
Golden La. Est. *EC1* —3E **39**
Golden Plover Clo. *E16*
   —5C **44**
Golden Sq. *W1* —1E **51**

Golden Yd. NW3 —1E **21**
(off Holly Mt.)
Golders Ct. NW11 —2B **6**
Golders Gdns. NW11 —2A **6**
Golders Green. —1A 6
Golders Green Crematorium.
NW11 —2C **6**
Golders Grn. Cres. NW11
—2B **6**
Golders Grn. Rd. NW11
—1A **6**
Golders Mnr. Dri. NW11
—1F **5**
Golders Pk. Clo. NW11 —3C **6**
Golders Way. NW11 —2B **6**
Goldeslea. NW11 —3C **6**
Goldhawk Ind. Est. W12
—4D **47**
Goldhawk M. W12 —3D **47**
Goldhawk Rd. W6 & W12
—5B **46**
Goldhurst Gdns. NW6
—4E **21**
Goldhurst Ter. NW6 —4D **21**
Goldie Ho. N19 —2F **9**
Golding St. E1 —5C **40**
Golding Ter. E1 —5C **40**
Golding Ter. SW11 —5C **64**
Goldington Ct. NW1 —5F **23**
(off Royal College St.)
Goldington Cres. NW1
—1F **37**
Goldington St. NW1 —1F **37**
Goldman Clo. E2 —3C **40**
Goldmark Ho. SE3 —1D **87**
Goldney Rd. W9 —3C **34**
Goldsborough Ho. E14
—1D **71**
Goldsborough Rd. SW8
—4F **65**
Goldsmith Av. E12 —3F **31**
Goldsmith Av. NW9 —1A **4**
Goldsmith Ct. WC2 —5A **38**
(off Stukeley St.)
Goldsmith Rd. E10 —3C **14**
Goldsmith Rd. SE15 —4C **68**
Goldsmith's Bldgs. W3
—2A **46**
Goldsmiths Clo. W3 —2A **46**
Goldsmith's Pl. NW6 —5D **21**
(off Springfield La.)
Goldsmith's Row. E2 —1C **40**
Goldsmith's Sq. E2 —1C **40**
Goldsmith St. EC2 —5E **39**
Goldsworthy Gdns. SE16
—1E **69**
Goldthorpe. NW1 —5E **23**
(off Camden St.)
Goldwell Ho. SE22 —1A **82**
Goldwin Clo. SE14 —4E **69**
Goldwing Clo. E16 —5C **44**
Gollogly Ter. SE7 —1E **73**
Gomm Rd. SE16 —4E **55**
Gondar Gdns. NW6 —2B **20**
Gonson St. SE8 —2D **71**
Gonston Clo. SW19 —2A **90**
Gonville St. SW6 —1A **76**

Gooch Ho. E5 —5D **13**
Gooch Ho. WC1 —4C **38**
(off Portpool La.)
Goodall Ho. SE4 —2F **83**
Goodall Rd. E11 —5E **15**
Goodge Pl. W1 —4E **37**
Goodge St. W1 —4E **37**
Goodhall St. NW10 —2B **32**
(in two parts)
Goodhart Pl. E14 —1A **56**
Good Hart Pl. E14 —1A **56**
Goodinge Clo. N7 —3A **24**
Gooding Ho. SE7 —1E **73**
Goodman Cres. SW2 —2A **94**
Goodman Rd. E10 —2E **15**
Goodman's Ct. E1 —1B **54**
(off Goodman's Yd.)
Goodman's Stile. E1 —5C **40**
Goodmans Yd. EC3 —1B **54**
Goodrich Ct. W10 —5F **33**
Goodrich Rd. SE22 —4B **82**
Goodson Rd. NW10 —4A **18**
Goodson St. N1 —1C **38**
Goods Way. NW1 —1A **38**
Goodway Gdns. E14 —5F **43**
Goodwill Ho. E14 —1D **57**
Goodwin Clo. SE16 —4B **54**
Goodwin Rd. W12 —3C **46**
Goodwins Ct. WC2 —1A **52**
Goodwin St. N4 —4C **10**
Goodwood Ct. W1 —4D **37**
(off Devonshire St.)
Goodwood Ho. SE14 —4A **70**
(off Goodwood St.)
Goodwood Rd. SE14 —3A **70**
Goodyear Pl. SE5 —2E **67**
Goodyer Ho. SW1 —1F **65**
(off Tachbrook St.)
Goodyers Gdns. NW4 —1F **5**
Goosander Ct. SE8 —2A **70**
(off Childers St.)
Goose Grn. Trad. Est. SE22
—2B **82**
Gophir La. EC4 —1F **53**
Gopsall St. N1 —5F **25**
Gordon Av. SW14 —2A **74**
Gordonbrock Rd. SE4 —3C **84**
Gordon Clo. E17 —1C **14**
Gordon Clo. N19 —3E **9**
Gordon Ct. W12 —5E **33**
Gordondale Rd. SW19
—2C **90**
Gordon Gro. SE5 —5D **67**
Gordon Ho. E1 —1E **55**
(off Glamis Rd.)
Gordon Ho. SE10 —3D **71**
(off Tarves Way)
Gordon Ho. Rd. NW5 —1C **22**
Gordon Mans. WC1 —3F **37**
(off Torrington Pl.)
Gordon Pl. W8 —3C **48**
Gordon Rd. E11 —1C **16**
Gordon Rd. E15 —1E **29**
Gordon Rd. SE15 —5D **69**
Gordon Sq. WC1 —3F **37**
Gordon St. E13 —2C **44**
Gordon St. WC1 —3F **37**

Gorefield Ho. NW6 —1C **34**
(off Canterbury Rd.)
Gorefield Pl. NW6 —1C **34**
Gore Rd. E9 —5E **27**
Gore St. SW7 —4E **49**
Gorham Pl. W11 —1A **48**
Goring St. EC3 —5A **40**
(off Houndsditch)
Gorleston St. W14 —5A **48**
(in two parts)
Gorse Clo. E16 —5C **44**
Gorsefield Ho. E14 —1C **56**
Gorse Ri. SW17 —5C **92**
Gorst Rd. NW10 —3A **32**
Gorst Rd. SW11 —4B **78**
Gorsuch Pl. E2 —2B **40**
Gorsuch St. E2 —1B **40**
Gosberton Rd. SW12 —1B **92**
Gosfield St. W1 —4E **37**
Goslett Yd. WC2 —5F **37**
Gosling Ct. SE8 —2B **70**
(off Wotton Rd.)
Gosling Way. SW9 —4C **66**
Gospel Oak. —1C 22
Gospel Oak Est. NW5 —2B **22**
Gosport Rd. E17 —1B **14**
Gosport Way. SE15 —3B **68**
Gosset St. E2 —2B **40**
Gosterwood St. SE8 —2A **70**
Goswell Pl. EC1 —2D **39**
(off Goswell Rd.)
Goswell Rd. EC1 —1D **39**
Gothic Ct. SE5 —3E **67**
(off Wyndham Rd.)
Gottfried M. NW5 —1E **23**
Goudhurst Rd. Brom —5A **100**
Gough Ho. N1 —5D **25**
(off Windsor St.)
Gough Rd. E15 —1B **30**
Gough Sq. EC4 —5C **38**
Gough St. WC1 —3B **38**
Gough Wlk. E14 —5C **42**
Goulden Ho. SW11 —5A **64**
Gouldman Ho. E1 —3E **41**
(off Wyllen Clo.)
Gould Ter. E8 —2D **27**
Goulston St. E1 —5B **40**
Goulton Rd. E5 —1D **27**
Gourley Pl. N15 —1A **12**
Gourley St. N15 —1A **12**
Govan St. E2 —5C **26**
Gover Ct. SW4 —5A **66**
Govier Clo. E15 —4A **30**
Gowan Av. SW6 —4A **62**
Gowan Ho. E2 —2B **40**
(off Chambord St.)
Gowan Rd. NW10 —3D **19**
Gower Clo. SW4 —4E **79**
Gower Ct. WC1 —3F **37**
Gower Ho. SE17 —1E **67**
Gower M. WC1 —4F **37**
Gower M. Mans. WC1
(off Gower M.) —4F **37**
Gower Pl. WC1 —3F **37**
Gower Rd. E7 —3C **30**
Gower St. WC1 —3E **37**
Gower's Wlk. E1 —5C **40**

Gowlett Rd. SE15—1C 82
Gowrie Rd. SW11—1C 78
Gracechurch St. EC3—1F 53
Grace Clo. SE9—3F 101
Gracedale Rd. SW16—5D 93
Gracefield Gdns. SW16 —3A 94
Gracehill. E1—4E 41 (off Hannibal Rd.)
Grace Ho. SE11—2B 66 (off Vauxhall St.)
Grace Jones Clo. E8—3C 26
Grace Path. SE26—4E 97
Grace Pl. E3—2D 43
Graces All. E1—1C 54
Graces M. NW8—1E 35
Grace's M. SE5—5F 67
Grace's Rd. SE5—5A 68
Grace St. E3—2D 43
Gradient, The. SE26—4C 96
Grafely Way. SE15—3B 68
Grafton Cres. NW1—3D 23
Grafton Gdns. N4—1E 11
Grafton Ho. SE8—1B 70
Grafton M. N1—1E 39 (off Frome St.)
Grafton M. W1—3E 37
Grafton Pl. NW1—2F 37
Grafton Rd. NW5—2C 22
Grafton Sq. SW4—1E 79
Graftons, The. NW2—5C 6
Grafton St. W1—1D 51
Grafton Ter. NW5—2B 22
Grafton Way. W1 & WC1 —3E 37
Grafton Yd. NW5—3D 23
Graham Ct. SE14—2F 69 (off Myers La.)
Graham Lodge. NW4—1D 5
Graham Rd. E8—3C 26
Graham Rd. E13—2C 44
Graham Rd. NW4—1D 5
Graham St. N1—1D 39
Graham Ter. SW1—5C 50
Grainger Ct. SE5—3E 67
Gramer Clo. E11—4F 15
Grampian Gdns. NW2—3A 6
Grampians, The. W12—3F 47 (off Shepherd's Bush Rd.)
Granada St. SW17—5A 92
Granard Av. SW15—3D 75
Granard Ho. E9—3F 27
Granard Rd. SW12—5B 78
Granary Rd. E1—3D 41
Granary Sq. N1—3C 24
Granary St. NW1—5F 23
Granby Pl. SE1—3C 52 (off Station App. Rd.)
Granby St. E2—3C 40 (in two parts)
Granby Ter. NW1—1E 37
Grand Av. EC1—4D 39 (in two parts)
Grandfield Ct. W4—2A 60
Grandison Rd. SW11—3B 78
Grand Junct. Wharf. N1 —1E 39
Grand Pde. N4—1D 11
Grand Pde. M. SW15—3A 76
Grand Union Cen. W10 (off West Row) —3F 33
Grand Union Clo. W9—4B 34
Grand Union Cres. E8 —5C 26
Grand Union Wlk. NW1 —4D 23 (off Kentish Town Rd.)
Grand Vitesse Ind. Cen. SE1 (off Dolben St.) —2D 53
Grand Wlk. E1—3A 42
Granfield St. SW11—4F 63
Grange Ct. NW10—5A 4 (off Neasden La.)
Grange Ct. WC2—5B 38
Grangecourt Rd. N16—3A 12
Grangefield. NW1—4F 23 (off Marquis Rd.)
Grange Gdns. NW3—5D 7
Grange Gro. N1—3E 25
Grange Ho. SE1—4B 54
Grange La. SE21—2B 96
Grange Lodge. SW19—5F 89
Grangemill Rd. SE6—3C 98
Grangemill Way. SE6—2C 98
Grange Mus. of Community History.—1A 18
Grange Pk. Rd. E10—3D 15
Grange Pl. NW6—4C 20
Grange Rd. E10—3C 14
Grange Rd. E13—2B 44
Grange Rd. E17—1A 14 (in two parts)
Grange Rd. N6—1C 8
Grange Rd. NW10—3D 19
Grange Rd. SE1—4A 54
Grange Rd. SW13—4C 60
Grange St. N1—5F 25
Grange, The. E17—1A 14 (off Grange Rd.)
Grange, The. SE1—4B 54
Grange, The. SW19—5F 89
Grange, The. W14—5B 48
Grange Wlk. SE1—4A 54
Grange Wlk. M. SE1—4A 54 (off Grange Wlk.)
Grange Way. NW6—4C 20
Grangewood St. E6—5F 31
Grange Yd. SE1—4B 54
Granleigh Rd. E11—4A 16
Gransden Av. E8—4D 27
Gransden Ho. SE8—1B 70
Gransden Rd. W12—3B 46
Grantbridge St. N1—1D 39
Grantham Ct. SE16—3F 55 (off Eleanor Clo.)
Grantham Ho. SE15—2C 68 (off Friary Est.)
Grantham Pl. W1—2D 51
Grantham Rd. SW9—5A 66
Grantham Rd. W4—3A 60
Grantley Ho. SE14—2F 69 (off Myers La.)
Grantley St. E1—2F 41
Grant Rd. SW11—2F 77
Grants Quay Wharf. EC3 —1F 53
Grant St. E13—2C 44
Grant St. N1—1C 38
Grantully Rd. W9—2D 35
Granville Arc. SW9—2C 80
Granville Ct. N1—5A 26 (off Colville Est.)
Granville Ct. SE14—3A 70 (off Nynehead St.)
Granville Gro. SE13—1E 85
Granville Ho. E14—5C 42
Granville Pk. SE13—1E 85
Granville Pl. SW6—3D 63
Granville Pl. W1—5C 36
Granville Point. NW2—4B 6
Granville Rd. E17—1D 15
Granville Rd. N4—1B 10
Granville Rd. NW2—4B 6
Granville Rd. NW6—1C 34 (in two parts)
Granville Rd. SW18—5B 76
Granville Sq. SE15—3A 68
Granville Sq. WC1—2B 38
Granville St. WC1—2B 38
Grape St. WC2—5A 38
Graphite Sq. SE11—1B 66
Grasmere. NW1—2D 37 (off Osnaburgh St.)
Grasmere Av. SW15—4A 88
Grasmere Ct. SE26—5C 96
Grasmere Point. SE15 (off Old Kent Rd.) —3E 69
Grasmere Rd. E13—1C 44
Grasmere Rd. SW16—5B 94
Grassmount. SE23—2D 97
Gratton Rd. W14—4A 48
Gratton Ter. NW2—5F 5
Gravel La. E1—5B 40
Gravely Ho. SE8—5A 56 (off Chilton Gro.)
Gravenel Gdns. SW17 (off Nutwell St.) —5A 92
Graveney Rd. SW17—4A 92
Gravesend Rd. W12—1C 46
Gray Ho. SE17—1E 67
Grayling Clo. E16—3A 44
Grayling Rd. N16—4F 11
Grayling Sq. E2—2C 40 (off Nelson Gdns.)
Grayshott Rd. SW11—5C 64
Gray's Inn.—4B 38
Gray's Inn Bldgs. EC1—3C 38 (off Rosebery Av.)
Gray's Inn Pl. WC1—4B 38
Gray's Inn Rd. WC1—2A 38
Gray's Inn Sq. WC1—4B 38
Grayson Ho. EC1—2E 39 (off Pleydell Est.)
Gray St. SE1—3C 52
Gray's Yd. W1—5C 36 (off James St.)
Grazebrook Rd. N16—4F 11
Grazeley Ct. SE19—5A 96
Gt. Acre Ct. SW4—2F 79
Gt. Arthur Ho. EC1—3E 39 (off Golden La. Est.)

Gt. Bell All. *EC2* —5F **39**
Great Brownings. *SE21*
    —4B **96**
Gt. Castle St. *W1* —5D **37**
Gt. Central St. *NW1* —4B **36**
Gt. Central Way. *NW10*
    —2A **18**
Gt. Chapel St. *W1* —5F **37**
Gt. Chertsey Rd. *W4* —4A **60**
Gt. Church La. *W6* —5F **47**
Gt. College St. *SW1* —4A **52**
Great Cft. WC1 —2A **38**
  (off Cromer St.)
Gt. Cross Av. *SE10* —3F **71**
  (in three parts)
Gt. Cumberland M. *W1*
    —5B **36**
Gt. Cumberland Pl. *W1*
    —5B **36**
Gt. Dover St. *SE1* —3E **53**
Gt. Eastern Bldgs. E1 —4C **40**
  (off Fieldgate St.)
Gt. Eastern Enterprise Cen.
    E14 —3D **57**
Gt. Eastern Rd. *E15* —4F **29**
Gt. Eastern St. *EC2* —2A **40**
Gt. Eastern Wlk. EC2 —4A **40**
  (off Bishopsgate)
Gt. Eastern Wharf. *SW11*
    —3A **64**
Greatfield Clo. *N19* —1E **23**
Greatfield Clo. *SE4* —2C **84**
Gt. George St. *SW1* —3F **51**
Gt. Guildford Bus. Sq. SE1
    —2E **53**
  (off Gt. Guildford St.)
Gt. Guildford St. *SE1* —2E **53**
Greatham Wlk. *SW15* —1C **88**
Gt. James St. *WC1* —4B **38**
Gt. Marlborough St. *W1*
    —5E **37**
Gt. Maze Pond. *SE1* —3F **53**
  (in two parts)
Gt. Newport St. *WC2* —1A **52**
Gt. New St. *EC4* —5C **39**
Gt. North Rd. *N2 & N6* —1B **8**
Greatorex Ho. E1 —4C **40**
  (off Greatorex St.)
Greatorex St. *E1* —4C **40**
Gt. Ormond St. *WC1* —4A **38**
Gt. Percy St. *WC1* —2B **38**
Gt. Peter St. *SW1* —4F **51**
Gt. Portland St. *W1* —3D **37**
Gt. Pulteney St. *W1* —1E **51**
Gt. Queen St. *WC2* —5A **38**
Gt. Russell St. *WC1* —5F **37**
St Helen's. *EC2* —5A **40**
Gt. St Thomas Apostle. *EC4*
    —1E **53**
Gt. Scotland Yd. *SW1* —2A **52**
Gt. Smith St. *SW1* —4F **51**
Great Spilmans. *SE22* —3A **82**
Gt. Suffolk St. *SE1* —2D **53**
Gt. Sutton St. *EC1* —3D **39**
Gt. Swan All. *EC2* —5F **39**
  (in two parts)
Gt. Titchfield St. *W1* —3D **37**

Gt. Tower St. *EC3* —1A **54**
Gt. Trinity La. *EC4* —1E **53**
Great Turnstile. *WC1* —4B **38**
Gt. Western Rd. *W9 & W11*
    —4B **34**
Gt. West Rd. *W4 & W6*
    —1B **60**
Gt. Winchester St. *EC2*
    —5F **39**
Gt. Windmill St. *W1* —1F **51**
Great Yd. SE1 —3A **54**
  (off Crucifix La.)
Greaves Cotts. *E14* —4A **42**
Greaves Pl. *SW17* —4A **92**
Greaves Tower. SW10 —3E **63**
  (off Worlds End Est.)
Grebe Clo. *E7* —2B **30**
Grebe Ct. *E14* —3E **57**
Grebe Ct. SE8 —2B **70**
  (off Dorking Clo.)
Grecian Cres. *SE19* —5D **95**
Greek St. *W1* —5F **37**
Greek St. *W1* —5F **37**
Greenacre Sq. *SE16* —3F **55**
Grn. Arbour Ct. EC4 —5D **39**
  (off Old Bailey)
Greenaway Gdns. *NW3*
    —1D **21**
Greenaway Ho. NW8 —5E **21**
  (off Boundary Rd.)
Greenaway Ho. WC1 —2C **38**
  (off Fernsbury St.)
Green Bank. *E1* —2D **55**
Greenbay Rd. *SE7* —3F **73**
Greenberry St. *NW8* —1A **36**
Green Clo. *E15* —5A **30**
Green Clo. *NW11* —2E **7**
Greencoat Mans. SW1
  (off Greencoat Row) —4E **51**
Greencoat Pl. *SW1* —5E **51**
Greencoat Row. *SW1* —4E **51**
Greencrest Pl. *NW2* —5C **4**
Greencroft Clo. *E6* —4F **45**
Greencroft Gdns. *NW6*
    —4D **21**
Green Dale. *SE5* —2F **81**
Green Dale. *SE22* —3A **82**
Grn. Dale Clo. *SE22* —3A **82**
Grn. Dragon Ct. SE1 —2F **53**
  (off Bedale St.)
Grn. Dragon Yd. *E1* —4C **40**
Greene Ct. *SE14* —2F **69**
  (off Samuel Clo.)
Greene Ho. SE1 —4F **53**
  (off Burbage Rd.)
Greenend Rd. *W4* —3A **46**
Greener Ho. *SW4* —1F **79**
Greenfell Mans. *SE8* —2D **71**
Greenfield Gdns. *NW2* —4A **6**
Greenfield Rd. *E1* —4C **40**
Greenfield Rd. *N15* —1A **12**
Greengate Lodge. E13
  (off Hollybush St.) —1D **45**
Greengate St. *E13* —1D **45**
Greenham Clo. *SE1* —3C **52**
Greenheath Bus. Cen. E2
  (off Three Colts La.) —3D **41**

Greenhill. *NW3* —1F **21**
Greenhill Gro. *E12* —1F **31**
Greenhill Pk. *NW10* —5A **18**
Greenhill Rd. *NW10* —5A **18**
Greenhill's Rents. *EC1* —4D **39**
Greenhills Ter. *N1* —3F **25**
Grn. Hundred Rd. *SE15*
    —2C **68**
Greenhurst Rd. *SE27* —5C **94**
Greenland M. *SE8* —1F **69**
Greenland Pl. *NW1* —5D **23**
Greenland Quay. *SE16* —5F **55**
Greenland Rd. *NW1* —5E **23**
Greenland St. *NW1* —5D **23**
Green Lanes. *N8 & N4*
    —1D **11**
Greenleaf Clo. *SW2* —5C **80**
Greenleaf Rd. *E6* —5E **31**
Green Man Roundabout.
  (Junct.) —2B **16**
Greenman St. *N1* —4E **25**
Greenoak Way. *SW19* —4F **89**
Green Pk. —3D **51**
Green Point. *E15* —3A **30**
Green's Ct. W1 —1F **51**
  (off Brewer St.)
Greenshields Ind. Est. *E16*
    —3C **58**
Greenside Clo. *SE6* —2F **99**
Greenside Rd. *W12* —4C **46**
Greenstead Gdns. *SW15*
    —3D **75**
Greenstone M. *E11* —1C **16**
Green St. *E7 & E13* —3D **31**
Green St. *W1* —1C **50**
Greenstreet Hill. *SE14* —5F **69**
Green Ter. *EC1* —2C **38**
Green, The. *E11* —1D **17**
Green, The. *E15* —3A **30**
Green, The. *SW19* —5F **89**
Green, The. *W3* —5A **32**
Green, The. *Brom* —3C **100**
  (in two parts)
Greenview Clo. *W3* —2A **46**
Green Wlk. *SE1* —4A **54**
Green Way. *SE9* —3F **87**
Greenway Clo. *N4* —4E **11**
Greenwell St. *W1* —3D **37**
Greenwich. —3E **71**
Greenwich Bus. Cen. SE10
    —3D **71**
  (off Greenwich High Rd.)
Greenwich Bus. Pk. *SE10*
    —3D **71**
Greenwich Chu. St. *SE10*
    —2E **71**
Greenwich Ct. E1 —5D **41**
  (off Cavell St.)
Greenwich Cres. *E6* —4F **45**
Greenwich Gateway Vis. Cen.
    —2E **71**
Greenwich High Rd. *SE10*
    —4D **71**
Greenwich Ind. Est. *SE7*
    —5D **59**
Greenwich Ind. Est. *SE10*
    —3D **71**

Greenwich Mkt. *SE10* —2E **71**
Greenwich Pk. —3A **72**
Greenwich Pk. St. *SE10* —2F **71**
Greenwich S. St. *SE10* —4D **71**
Greenwich Vw. Pl. *E14* —4D **57**
Greenwood Ho. *SE4* —2F **83**
Greenwood Pl. *NW5* —2D **23**
Greenwood Rd. *E8* —3C **26**
Greenwood Rd. *E13* —1B **44**
Greenwood Ter. *NW10* —5A **18**
*Green Yd. WC1 —3B **38***
(off Gough St.)
*Green Yd., The. EC3 —5A **40***
(off Leadenhall St.)
*Greet Ho. SE1 —3C **52***
(off Frazier St.)
Greet St. *SE1* —2C **52**
Greg Clo. *E10* —1E **15**
Gregory Cres. *SE9* —5F **87**
Gregory Pl. *W8* —3D **49**
Greig Clo. *N8* —1A **10**
Greig Ter. *SE17* —2D **67**
Grenada Ho. *E14* —1B **56**
Grenada Rd. *SE7* —3E **73**
Grenade St. *E14* —1B **56**
*Grendon Ho. E9 —4E **27***
(off Shore Pl.)
*Grendon Ho. N1 —1B **38***
(off Priory Grn. Est.)
Grendon St. *NW8* —3A **36**
Grenfell Ho. *SE5* —3E **67**
Grenfell Rd. *W11* —1F **47**
Grenfell Tower. *W11* —1F **47**
Grenfell Wlk. *W11* —1F **47**
*Grenville Ho. SE8 —2C **70***
(off New King St.)
*Grenville Ho. SW1 —2F **65***
(off Dolphin Sq.)
*Grenville M. SW7 —5E **49***
(off Harrington Gdns.)
Grenville Pl. *SW7* —4E **49**
Grenville Rd. *N19* —3A **10**
Grenville St. *WC1* —3A **38**
Gresham Gdns. *NW11* —3A **6**
Gresham Lodge. *E17* —1D **15**
Gresham Rd. *E16* —5D **45**
Gresham Rd. *NW10* —2A **18**
Gresham Rd. *SW9* —1C **80**
Gresham St. *EC2* —5E **39**
Gresham Way. *SW19* —3D **91**
Gresley Clo. *E17* —1A **14**
Gresley Rd. *N19* —3E **9**
Gressenhall Rd. *SW18* —4B **76**
Gresse St. *W1* —5F **37**
Greswell St. *SW6* —4F **61**
*Gretton Ho. E2 —2E **41***
(off Globe Rd.)
Greville Hall. *NW6* —1D **35**
Greville Lodge. *E13* —5D **31**
*Greville M. NW6 —5D **21***
(off Greville Rd.)
Greville Pl. *NW6* —1D **35**
Greville Rd. *NW6* —1D **35**
Greville St. *EC1* —4C **38**
(in two parts)
Grey Clo. *NW11* —1E **7**
*Greycoat Gdns. SW1 —4F **51***
(off Greycoat St.)
Greycoat Pl. *SW1* —4F **51**
Greycoat St. *SW1* —4F **51**
Greycot Rd. *Beck* —5C **98**
Grey Eagle St. *E1* —3B **40**
*Greyfriars. SE26 —3C **96***
(off Wells Pk. Rd.)
Greyfriars Pas. *EC1* —5D **39**
Greyhound Ct. *WC2* —1B **52**
Greyhound La. *SW16* —5A **94**
*Greyhound Mans. W6 —2A **62***
(off Greyhound Rd.)
Greyhound Rd. *NW10* —2D **33**
Greyhound Rd. *W6 & W14* —2F **61**
*Grey Ho. W12 —1D **47***
(off White City Est.)
Greyladies Gdns. *SE10* —5E **71**
Greystead Rd. *SE23* —5E **83**
*Greystoke Ho. SE15 —2C **68***
(off Peckham Pk. Rd.)
Greystoke Pl. *EC4* —5C **38**
*Greystone Path. E11 —2B **16***
(off Mornington Rd.)
Greyswood St. *SW16* —5D **93**
Grey Turner Ho. *W12* —5C **32**
Grierson Rd. *SE23* —5F **83**
Griffin Clo. *NW10* —2D **19**
Griffin Ct. *W4* —1B **60**
Griffin Ho. *E14* —5D **43**
*Grigg's Pl. SE1 —4A **54***
(off Grange Rd.)
Griggs Rd. *E10* —1E **15**
*Grimaldi Ho. N1 —1B **38***
(off Priory Grn. Est.)
Grimsby St. *E2* —3B **40**
Grimsel Path. *SE5* —3D **67**
Grimshaw Clo. *N6* —2C **8**
Grimston Rd. *SW6* —5B **62**
*Grimthorpe Ho. EC1 —3D **39***
(off Agdon St.)
Grimwade Clo. *SE15* —1E **83**
*Grindall Ho. E1 —3D **41***
(off Darling Row)
Grindal St. *SE1* —3C **52**
Grindley Ho. *E3* —4B **42**
Grinling Pl. *SE8* —2C **70**
Grinstead Rd. *SE8* —1A **70**
*Grisedale. NW1 —2E **37***
(off Cumberland Mkt.)
Grittleton Rd. *W9* —3C **34**
Grizedale Ter. *SE23* —2D **97**
Grocer's Hall Ct. *EC2* —5F **39**
Grocer's Hall Gdns. EC2
*(off Prince's St.) —5F **39***
Groombridge Rd. *E9* —4F **27**
Groom Cres. *SW18* —5F **77**
Groome Ho. *SE11* —5B **52**
Groomfield Clo. *SW17* —4C **92**
Groom Pl. *SW1* —4C **50**
Grosse Way. *SW15* —4D **75**
Grosvenor Av. *N5* —2E **25**
Grosvenor Av. *SW14* —1A **74**
Grosvenor Cotts. *SW1* —5C **50**
Grosvenor Ct. *E10* —3D **15**
Grosvenor Ct. *NW6* —5F **19**
Grosvenor Ct. *SE5* —2E **67**
Grosvenor Ct. Mans. W2
*(off Edgware Rd.) —5B **36***
Grosvenor Cres. *SW1* —3C **50**
Grosvenor Cres. M. *SW1* —3C **50**
Grosvenor Est. *SW1* —5F **51**
Grosvenor Gdns. *E6* —2F **45**
Grosvenor Gdns. *NW2* —3E **19**
Grosvenor Gdns. *NW11* —1B **6**
Grosvenor Gdns. *SW1* —4D **51**
Grosvenor Gdns. *SW14* —1A **74**
Grosvenor Gdns. M. E. SW1
*(off Beeston Pl.) —4D **51***
Grosvenor Gdns. M. N. SW1
*(off Ebury St.) —4D **51***
Grosvenor Gdns. M. S. SW1
*(off Ebury St.) —4D **51***
Grosvenor Ga. *W1* —1C **50**
Grosvenor Hill. *SW19* —5A **90**
Grosvenor Hill. *W1* —1D **51**
Grosvenor Hill Ct. W1
*(off Bourdon St.) —1D **51***
Grosvenor Pk. *SE5* —3E **67**
Grosvenor Pk. Rd. *E17* —1C **14**
Grosvenor Pl. *SW1* —3C **50**
Grosvenor Ri. E. *E17* —1D **15**
Grosvenor Rd. *E6* —5F **31**
Grosvenor Rd. *E7* —3D **31**
Grosvenor Rd. *E10* —3E **15**
Grosvenor Rd. *E11* —1D **17**
Grosvenor Rd. *SW1* —2D **65**
Grosvenor Sq. *W1* —1C **50**
Grosvenor St. *W1* —1D **51**
Grosvenor Ter. *SE5* —3E **67**
Grosvenor Way. *E5* —4E **13**
Grosvenor Wharf Rd. *E14* —5F **57**
Grotes Bldgs. *SE3* —5A **72**
Grote's Pl. *SE3* —5A **72**
Groton Rd. *SW18* —2D **91**
Grotto Ct. *SE1* —3D **53**
Grotto Pas. *W1* —4C **36**
Grove Clo. *SE23* —1A **98**
Grove Cotts. *W4* —2A **60**
*Grove Ct. NW8 —2F **35***
(off Grove End Rd.)
*Grove Ct. SW10 —1E **63***
(off Drayton Gdns.)
Grove Cres. Rd. *E15* —3F **29**
Grovedale Rd. *N19* —4F **9**
Grove Dwellings. *E1* —4E **41**
Grove End. *NW5* —1D **23**
Grove End Gdns. *NW8* —1F **35**

Grove End Ho. NW8 —2F 35 (off Grove End Ho.)
Grove End Rd. NW8 —1F 35
Grove Gdns. NW8 —2A 36
Grove Grn. Rd. E10 —5E 15
Grove Hall Ct. NW8 —2E 35
Grovehill Ct. Brom —5B 100
Grove Hill Rd. SE5 —1A 82
Grove Ho. SW3 —2A 64
Groveland Ct. EC4 —5E 39 (off Bow La.)
Grovelands Clo. SE5 —5A 68
Grovelands Rd. N15 —1C 12
Grove La. SE5 —4F 67
Grove La. Ter. SE5 —5F 67
Grove M. W6 —4E 47
Grove Park. —3D 101
Grove Pk. E11 —1D 17
Grove Pk. SE5 —5A 68
Gro. Park Rd. SE9 —3E 101
Grove Pas. E2 —1D 41
Grove Pl. NW3 —5F 7
Grove Pl. SW12 —5D 79
Grover Ct. SE13 —5D 71
Grover Ho. SE11 —1B 66
Grove Rd. E3 —5F 27
Grove Rd. E11 —2B 16
Grove Rd. E17 —1D 15
Grove Rd. N15 —1A 12
Grove Rd. NW2 —3E 19
Grove Rd. SW13 —5B 60
Grove St. SE8 —5B 56
Grove Ter. NW5 —5D 9
Grove Ter. M. NW5 —5D 9
Grove, The. (Junct.) —1C 96
Grove, The. E15 —3A 30
Grove, The. N4 —2B 10
Grove, The. N6 —3C 8
Grove, The. N8 —1F 9
Grove, The. NW9 —1A 4
Grove, The. NW11 —2A 6
Grove Va. SE22 —2B 82
Grove Vs. E14 —1D 57
Groveway. SW9 —4B 66
Grummant Rd. SE15 —4B 68
Grundy St. E14 —5D 43
Guardian Ct. SE12 —3A 86
Guard's Mus. —3E 51
Gubyon Av. SE24 —3D 81
Guerin Sq. E3 —2B 42
Guernsey Gro. SE24 —5E 81
Guernsey Ho. N1 —3E 25 (off Douglas Rd. N.)
Guernsey Rd. E10 —3F 15
Guernsey Rd. N1 —3E 25
Guibal Rd. SE12 —5D 87
Guildford Gro. SE10 —4D 71
Guildford Rd. SW8 —4A 66
Guildhall. —5F 39
Guildhall Bldgs. EC2 —5F 39 (off Basinghall St.)
Guildhall Library. —5E 39
Guildhall Offices. EC2 —5E 39 (off Basinghall St.)
Guildhall Yd. EC2 —5E 39
Guildhouse St. SW1 —5E 51
Guild Rd. SE7 —2F 73
Guilford Pl. WC1 —3B 38
Guilford St. WC1 —3A 38
Guillemot Ct. SE8 —2B 70 (off Alexandra Clo.)
Guilsborough Clo. NW10 —4A 18
Guinness Clo. E9 —4A 28
Guinness Ct. E1 —5B 40 (off Mansell St.)
Guinness Ct. EC1 —2E 39 (off Lever St.)
Guinness Ct. NW8 —5A 22
Guinness Ct. SE1 —3A 54 (off Snowsfields)
Guinness Ct. SW3 —5B 50
Guinness Sq. SE1 —5A 54
Guinness Trust Bldgs. SE17 —1D 67
Guinness Trust Bldgs. W6 (off Fulham Pal. Rd.) —1F 61
Guinness Trust Est. E15 —5B 30
Guinness Trust Est. N16 —3A 12
Guion Rd. SW6 —5B 62
Gulland Wlk. N1 —3E 25 (off Oronsay Wlk.)
Gulliver's Ho. EC1 —3E 39 (off Goswell Rd.)
Gulliver St. SE16 —4A 56
Gulston Wlk. SW3 —5B 50 (off Blackland Ter.)
Gunmaker's La. E3 —5A 28
Gunnell Clo. SE26 —4C 96
Gunners Rd. SW18 —2F 91
Gunpowder Sq. EC4 —5C 38 (off Gough Sq., in two parts)
Gunstor Rd. N16 —1A 26
Gun St. E1 —4B 40
Gunter Gro. SW10 —2E 63
Gunterstone Rd. W14 —5A 48
Gunthorpe St. E1 —4B 40
Gunton Rd. E5 —5D 13
Gunwhale Clo. SE16 —2F 55
Gun Wharf Bus. Cen. E3 (off Old Ford Rd.) —5A 28
Gurdon Ho. E14 —5C 42
Gurdon Rd. SE7 —1C 72
Gurney Clo. E15 —2A 30
Gurney Ho. E2 —1C 40 (off Goldsmith Row)
Gurney Rd. E15 —2A 30
Gurney Rd. SW6 —1E 77
Guthrie Ct. SE1 —4C 52 (off Morley St.)
Guthrie St. SW3 —1F 63
Gutter La. EC2 —5E 39
Guy Barnett Gro. SE3 —1C 86
Guyscliff Rd. SE13 —3E 85
Guy St. SE1 —3F 53
Gwalior Rd. SW15 —2F 75
Gwendolen Av. SW15 —2F 75
Gwendolen Clo. SW15 —3F 75
Gwendoline Av. E13 —5D 31
Gwendwr Rd. W14 —1A 62
Gwent Ct. SE16 —2F 55 (off Rotherhithe St.)
Gwilym Maries Ho. E2 (off Blythe St.) —2D 41
Gwyn Clo. SW6 —3E 63
Gwynne Clo. W4 —2B 60
Gwynne Ho. E1 —4D 41 (off Turner St.)
Gwynne Ho. WC1 —2C 38 (off Lloyd Baker St.)
Gwynne Pl. WC1 —2B 38
Gwynne Rd. SW11 —5F 63
Gylcote Clo. SE5 —2F 81

Haarlem Rd. W14 —4F 47
Haberdasher Est. N1 —2F 39
Haberdasher Pl. N1 —2F 39
Haberdashers Ct. SE14 —1F 83
Haberdasher St. N1 —2F 39
Habington Ho. SE5 —3F 67 (off Notley St.)
Hackford Rd. SW9 —4B 66
Hackford Wlk. SW9 —4B 66
Hackington Cres. Beck —5C 98
Hackney. —3D 27
Hackney Gro. E8 —3D 27
Hackney Rd. E2 —2A 40
Hackney Wick. —3C 28
Hackney Wick. (Junct.) —3B 28
Haddington Ct. SE10 —3D 71 (off Tarves Way)
Haddington Rd. Brom —3F 99
Haddo Ho. SE10 —2D 71 (off Haddo St.)
Haddon Ct. W3 —1B 46
Haddonfield. SE8 —5F 55
Haddo St. SE10 —2D 71
Haden Ct. N4 —4C 10
Hadfield Ho. E1 —5C 40 (off Ellen St.)
Hadleigh Clo. E1 —3E 41
Hadleigh Ho. E1 —3E 41 (off Hadleigh Clo.)
Hadleigh St. E2 —2E 41
Hadley Ct. N16 —3C 12
Hadley Gdns. W4 —1A 60
Hadley St. NW1 —3D 23 (in two parts)
Hadlow Ho. SE17 —1A 68 (off Kinglake Est.)
Hadrian Est. E2 —1C 40 (off Hackney Rd.)
Hadrian St. SE10 —1A 72
Hadstock Ho. NW1 —2F 37 (off Ossulston St.)
Hadyn Pk. Ct. W12 —3C 46 (off Curwen Rd.)
Hadyn Pk. Rd. W12 —3C 46
Hafer Rd. SW11 —2B 78
Hafton Rd. SE6 —1A 100
Haggerston. —1B 40
Haggerston Rd. E8 & E2 —4B 26
Hague St. E2 —2C 40

*Haig Ho. E2 —1C **40***
(off Shipton St.)
Haig Rd. E. *E13* —2E **45**
Haig Rd. W. *E13* —2E **45**
Hailes Clo. *SW19* —5E **91**
Hailsham Av. *SW2* —2B **94**
Haimo Rd. *SE9* —3F **87**
Hainault Rd. *E11* —3E **15**
Haines St. *SW8* —3E **65**
Hainford Clo. *SE4* —2F **83**
Hainthorpe Rd. *SE27* —3D **95**
Hainton Clo. *E1* —5D **41**
Halberd M. *E5* —4D **13**
Halcomb St. *N1* —5A **26**
Halcrow St. *E1* —4D **41**
*Halcyon Wharf. E1 —2C **54***
(off Hermitage Wall)
Haldane Pl. *SW18* —1D **91**
Haldane Rd. *E6* —2F **45**
Haldane Rd. *SW6* —3B **62**
Haldon Rd. *SW18* —4B **76**
*Hale Ho. SW1 —1F **65***
(off Lindsay Sq.)
Hale Path. *SE27* —4D **95**
Hale Rd. *E6* —3F **45**
*Hales Prior. N1 —1B **38***
(off Calshot St.)
Hales St. *SE8* —3C **70**
Hale St. *E14* —1D **57**
Halesworth Clo. *E5* —4E **13**
Halesworth Rd. *SE13* —1D **85**
Haley Rd. *NW4* —1E **5**
*Half Moon Ct. EC1 —4E **39***
(off Bartholomew Clo.)
Half Moon Cres. *N1* —1B **38**
(in two parts)
Half Moon La. *SE24* —4E **81**
Half Moon Pas. *E1* —5B **40**
(in two parts)
Half Moon St. *W1* —2D **51**
Halford Rd. *E10* —1F **15**
Halford Rd. *SW6* —2C **62**
*Haliday Ho. N1 —3F **25***
(off Mildmay St.)
Haliday Wlk. *N1* —3F **25**
Halidon Clo. *E9* —2E **27**
Halifax St. *SE26* —3D **97**
*Haliwell Ho. NW6 —5D **21***
(off Mortimer Cres.)
Halkin Arc. *SW1* —4B **50**
(in two parts)
Halkin M. *SW1* —4C **50**
Halkin Pl. *SW1* —4C **50**
Halkin St. *SW1* —3C **50**
*Hallam Ct. W1 —4D **37***
(off Hallam St.)
*Hallam Ho. SW1 —1E **65***
(off Churchill Gdns.)
Hallam M. *W1* —4D **37**
Hallam Rd. *SW13* —1D **75**
Hallam St. *W1* —3D **37**
Hallane Ho. *SE27* —5E **95**
Hall Dri. *SE26* —5E **97**
Halley Gdns. *SE13* —2F **85**
*Halley Ho. E2 —1C **40***
(off Pritchards Rd.)
*Halley Ho. SE10 —1B **72***
(off Armitage Rd.)
Halley Rd. *E7 & E12* —3E **31**
Halley St. *E14* —4A **42**
Hallfield Est. *W2* —5E **35**
(in two parts)
Hall Ga. *NW8* —2F **35**
Halliford St. *N1* —4E **25**
Halliwell Ct. *SE22* —3C **82**
Halliwell Rd. *SW2* —4B **80**
Hall Oak Wlk. *NW6* —3B **20**
Hall Pl. *W2* —3F **35**
(in two parts)
Hall Rd. *E15* —1F **29**
Hall Rd. *NW8* —2E **35**
Hall St. *EC1* —2D **39**
Hallsville Rd. *E16* —5B **44**
Hallswelle Rd. *NW11* —1B **6**
Hall, The. *SE3* —1C **86**
*Hall Tower. W2 —4F **35***
(off Hall Pl.)
Hall Vw. *SE9* —2F **101**
Halpin Pl. *SE17* —5F **53**
Halsbrook Rd. *SE3* —1E **87**
Halsbury Rd. *W12* —2D **47**
Halsey M. *SW3* —5B **50**
Halsey St. *SW3* —5B **50**
Halsmere Rd. *SE5* —4D **67**
Halstead Ct. *E17* —2B **14**
*Halstead Ct. N1 —1F **39***
(off Fairbank Est.)
Halstead Rd. *E11* —1C **16**
Halston Clo. *SW11* —4B **78**
Halstow Rd. *NW10* —2F **33**
Halstow Rd. *SE10* —1C **72**
Halton Cross St. *N1* —5D **25**
Halton Mans. *N1* —4D **25**
Halton Pl. *N1* —5E **25**
Halton Rd. *N1* —4D **25**
Halyard Ho. *E14* —4E **57**
Hamara Ghar. *E13* —5E **31**
Hambalt Rd. *SW4* —3E **79**
Hambleden Pl. *SE21* —1A **96**
*Hambledon. SE17 —2F **67***
(off Villa St.)
Hambledon Ct. *SE22* —2A **82**
Hambledon Rd. *SW18* —5B **76**
Hamble St. *SW6* —1D **77**
*Hambley Ho. SE16 —5D **55***
(off Camilla Rd.)
Hambridge Way. *SW2* —5C **80**
Hambro Rd. *SW16* —5F **93**
Hamfrith Rd. *E15* —3B **30**
*Hamilton Bldgs. EC2 —3A **40***
(off Gt. Eastern St.)
Hamilton Clo. *NW8* —2F **35**
Hamilton Clo. *SE16* —3A **56**
Hamilton Ct. *SE6* —1B **100**
Hamilton Ct. *SW15* —1A **76**
*Hamilton Ct. W9 —2E **35***
(off Maida Va.)
Hamilton Gdns. *NW8* —2E **35**
Hamilton Ho. *E14* —1D **71**
*Hamilton Ho. NW8 —2F **35***
(off Hall Rd.)
Hamilton Ho. *W4* —2A **60**
Hamilton La. *N5* —1D **25**
*Hamilton Lodge. E1 —3E **41***
(off Cleveland Gro.)
Hamilton M. *SW18* —1C **90**
Hamilton M. *W1* —3D **51**
Hamilton Pk. *N5* —1D **25**
Hamilton Pk. W. *N5* —1D **25**
Hamilton Pl. *W1* —2C **50**
Hamilton Rd. *E15* —2A **44**
Hamilton Rd. *NW10* —2C **18**
Hamilton Rd. *NW11* —2F **5**
Hamilton Rd. *SE27* —4F **95**
Hamilton Rd. *W4* —3A **46**
Hamilton Rd. Ind. Est. SE27
*(off Hamilton Rd.) —4F **95***
*Hamilton Sq. SE1 —3F **53***
(off Kipling St.)
Hamilton St. *SE8* —2C **70**
Hamilton Ter. *NW8* —1D **35**
Hamlea Clo. *SE12* —3C **86**
Hamlet Clo. *SE13* —2A **86**
*Hamlet Ct. SE11 —1D **67***
(off Opal St.)
Hamlet Ct. *W6* —5C **46**
Hamlet Gdns. *W6* —5C **46**
Hamlet Ind. Est. *E9* —4C **28**
Hamlet Sq. *NW2* —5A **6**
Hamlets Way. *E3* —3B **42**
(in two parts)
Hamlet, The. *SE5* —1F **81**
Hamlet Way. *SE1* —3F **53**
Hammelton Grn. *SW9* —4D **67**
*Hammerfield Ho. SW3 —1A **64***
(off Marlborough St.)
Hammersley Ho. SE14
*(off Pomeroy St.) —3E **69***
Hammersmith. —5E 47
Hammersmith Bri. *SW13 & W6* —2D **61**
Hammersmith Bri. Rd. *W6*
(in two parts) —1E **61**
Hammersmith Broadway.
(Junct.) —5E **47**
Hammersmith B'way. *W6* —5E **47**
Hammersmith Flyover.
(Junct.) —1E **61**
Hammersmith Flyover. *W6* —1E **61**
Hammersmith Gro. *W6* —3E **47**
Hammersmith Ind. Est. *W6* —2E **61**
Hammersmith Rd. *W6 & W14* —5F **47**
Hammersmith Ter. *W6* —1C **60**
Hammett St. *EC3* —1B **54**
Hammond Ct. *E10* —4D **15**
Hammond Ho. *E14* —4C **56**
*Hammond Ho. SE14 —3E **69***
(off Lubbock St.)
Hammond Lodge. W9
*(off Admiral Wlk.) —4C **34***
Hammond St. *NW5* —3E **23**
*Hamond Sq. N1 —1A **40***
(off Hoxton St.)

Ham Pk. Rd. *E15 & E7*
    —4B 30
Hampden Clo. *NW1* —1F 37
Hampden Gurney St. *W1*
    —5B 36
Hampden Ho. *SW9* —5C 66
Hampden Rd. *N19* —4F 9
Hampshire Hog La. *W6*
    —1D 61
Hampshire St. *NW5* —3F 23
Hampson Way. *SW8* —4B 66
Hampstead. —1F 21
Hampstead Gdns. *NW11*
    —1C 6
Hampstead Grn. *NW3* —2A 22
Hampstead Gro. *NW3* —5E 7
Hampstead Heath. —4A 8
Hampstead High St. *NW3*
    —1F 21
Hampstead Hill Gdns. *NW3*
    —1F 21
Hampstead La. *NW3 & N6*
    —3F 7
Hampstead Mus. —1F 21
(off New End Sq.)
Hampstead Rd. *NW1* —1E 37
Hampstead Sq. *NW3* —5E 7
Hampstead Theatre Club.
    —4F 21
Hampstead Wlk. *E3* —5B 28
Hampstead Way. *NW11*
    —1B 6
Hampstead W. *NW6* —3C 20
Hampton Clo. *NW6* —2C 34
Hampton Ct. *N1* —3D 25
Hampton Ct. *SE16* —1F 55
(off King & Queen Wharf)
Hampton M. *NW10* —2A 32
Hampton Rd. *E7* —2D 31
Hampton Rd. *E11* —3F 15
Hampton St. *SE17 & SE1*
    —5D 53
Ham Yd. *W1* —1F 51
Hanameel St. *E16* —2D 59
Hanbury Ho. *E1* —4C 40
(off Hanbury St.)
Hanbury Ho. *SW8* —3A 66
(off Regent's Bri. Gdns.)
Hanbury M. *N1* —5E 25
Hanbury St. *E1* —4B 40
Hancock Rd. *E3* —2E 43
Hancock Rd. *SE19* —5F 95
Handa Wlk. *N1* —3F 25
Hand Ct. *WC1* —4B 38
Handel Mans. *SW13* —3E 61
Handel Mans. *WC1* —3A 38
(off Handel St.)
Handel Pl. *NW10* —3A 18
Handel St. *WC1* —3A 38
Handen Rd. *SE12* —3A 86
Handforth Rd. *SW9* —3C 66
Handley Rd. *E9* —4E 27
Hands Wlk. *E16* —5C 44
Hanford Clo. *SW18* —1C 90
Hanford Row. *SW19* —5E 89
Hanging Sword All. *EC4*
(off Whitefriars St.) —5C 38

Hankey Pl. *SE1* —3F 53
Hanley Gdns. *N4* —3B 10
Hanley Rd. *N4* —3A 10
Hanmer Wlk. *N7* —4B 10
Hannah Barlow Ho. *SW8*
    —4B 66
Hannah Mary Way. *SE1*
    —5C 54
Hannay La. *N8* —2F 9
Hannay Wlk. *SW16* —2F 93
Hannell Rd. *SW6* —3A 62
Hannen Rd. *SE27* —3D 95
Hannibal Rd. *E1* —4E 41
Hannington Point. *E9* —3B 28
(off Eastway)
Hannington Rd. *SW4* —1D 79
Hanover Av. *E16* —2C 58
Hanover Ct. *W12* —2C 46
(off Uxbridge Rd.)
Hanover Flats. *W1* —1C 50
(off Binney St.)
Hanover Gdns. *SE11* —2C 66
Hanover Ga. *NW8* —2A 36
Hanover Ga. Mans. *NW1*
    —3A 36
Hanover Ho. *NW8* —1A 36
(off St John's Wood
    High St.)*
Hanover Ho. *SW9* —1C 80
Hanover Mans. *SW2* —3C 80
Hanover Mead. *NW11* —1A 6
Hanover Pk. *SE15* —4C 68
Hanover Pl. *E3* —2B 42
Hanover Pl. *WC2* —5A 38
Hanover Rd. *NW10* —4E 19
Hanover Sq. *W1* —5D 37
Hanover Steps. *W2* —5A 36
(off St George's Fields)
Hanover St. *W1* —5D 37
Hanover Ter. *NW1* —2A 36
Hanover Ter. M. *NW1* —2A 36
Hanover Trad. Est. *N7* —2A 24
Hanover Yd. *N1* —1E 39
(off Noel Rd.)
Hansard M. *W14* —3F 47
(in two parts)
Hans Cres. *SW1* —4B 50
Hansler Rd. *SE22* —3B 82
Hanson Clo. *SW12* —5D 79
Hanson Ct. *E17* —1D 15
Hanson St. *W1* —4E 37
Hans Pl. *SW1* —4B 50
Hans Rd. *SW3* —4B 50
Hans St. *SW1* —4B 50
Hanway Pl. *W1* —5F 37
Hanway St. *W1* —5F 37
Hanworth Ho. *SE5* —3D 67
(in two parts)
Harad's Pl. *E1* —1C 54
Harben Pde. *NW3* —4E 21
Harben Rd. *NW6* —4E 21
Harberson Rd. *E15* —5B 30
Harberson Rd. *SW12* —1D 93
Harberton Rd. *N19* —3E 9
Harbet Rd. *W2* —4F 35
Harbinger Rd. *E14* —5D 57

Harbledown Ho. *SE1* —3F 53
(off Manciple St.)
Harbledown Rd. *SW6* —4C 62
Harbord Clo. *SE5* —5F 67
Harbord St. *SW6* —4F 61
Harborough Rd. *SW16*
    —4B 94
Harbour Av. *SW10* —4E 63
Harbour Exchange Sq. *E14*
    —3D 57
Harbour Quay. *E14* —2E 57
Harbour Rd. *SE5* —1E 81
Harbour Yd. *SW10* —4E 63
Harbridge Av. *SW15* —5B 74
Harbut Rd. *SW11* —2F 77
Harcombe Rd. *N16* —5A 12
Harcourt Bldgs. *EC4* —1C 52
(off Middle Temple La.)
Harcourt Rd. *E15* —1B 44
Harcourt Rd. *SE4* —1B 84
Harcourt Ter. *NW1* —4A 36
Harcourt Ter. *SW10* —1D 63
Hardel Ri. *SW2* —1D 95
Hardel Wlk. *SW2* —5C 80
Harden Ct. *SE7* —5F 59
Harden Ho. *SE5* —5A 68
Harden's Manorway. *SE7*
(in three parts) —4F 59
Harders Rd. *SE15* —5D 69
Hardess St. *SE24* —1E 81
Harding Clo. *SE17* —2E 67
Harding La. *E1* —5E 41
Hardinge Rd. *NW10* —5D 19
Hardinge St. *E1* —5E 41
Hardman Rd. *SE7* —1D 73
Hardwicke M. *WC1* —2C 38
(off Lloyd Baker St.)
Hardwick Ho. *NW8* —3A 36
(off Lilestone St.)
Hardwick St. *EC1* —2C 38
Hardwicks Way. *SW18*
    —3C 76
Hardwidge St. *SE1* —3A 54
Hardy Av. *E16* —2C 58
Hardy Clo. *SE16* —3F 55
Hardy Cotts. *SE10* —2F 71
Hardy Ho. *SW4* —5E 79
Hardy Rd. *SE3* —3B 72
Hare & Billet Rd. *SE3* —4F 71
Hare Ct. *EC4* —5C 38
Harecourt Rd. *N1* —3E 25
Haredale Rd. *SE24* —2E 81
Haredon Clo. *SE23* —5F 83
Harefield M. *SE4* —1B 84
Harefield Rd. *SE4* —1B 84
Hare Marsh. *E2* —3C 40
Hare Pl. *EC4* —5C 38
(off Pleydell St.)
Hare Row. *E2* —1D 41
Hare Wlk. *N1* —1A 40
Harewood Av. *NW1* —3A 36
Harewood Ho. *NW1* —5D 37
Harewood Row. *NW1*
    —4A 36
Harfield Gdns. *SE5* —1A 82
Harfleur Ct. *SE11* —5D 53
(off Opal St.)

Harford Ho. *SE5* —2E **67**
(off Bethwin Rd.)
Harford Ho. *W11* —4B **34**
Harford M. *N19* —5F **9**
Harford St. *E1* —3A **42**
Hargood Ho. *SE3* —4E **73**
Hargrave Mans. *N19* —4F **9**
Hargrave Pk. *N19* —4E **9**
Hargrave Pl. *NW5* —2F **23**
Hargrave Rd. *N19* —4E **9**
Hargraves Ho. *W12* —1D **47**
(off White City Est.)
Hargwyne St. *SW9* —1B **80**
Haringey Pk. *N8* —1A **10**
Harkness Ho. *E1* —5C **40**
(off Christian St.)
Harland St. *SE12* —1C **100**
Harlequin Ct. *NW10* —3A **18**
(off Mitchellbrook Way)
Harlescott Rd. *SE15* —2F **83**
Harlesden. —1B 32
Harlesden Gdns. *NW10*
—5B **18**
Harlesden La. *NW10* —5C **18**
Harlesden Plaza. *NW10*
—1B **32**
Harlesden Rd. *NW10* —5C **18**
Harleston Clo. *E5* —4E **13**
Harley Ct. *E11* —2C **16**
Harleyford Ct. *SE11* —2B **66**
(off Harleyford Rd.)
Harleyford Rd. *SE11* —2B **66**
Harleyford St. *SE11* —2C **66**
Harley Gdns. *SW10* —1E **63**
Harley Gro. *E3* —2B **42**
Harley Ho. *E11* —2F **15**
Harley Ho. *NW1* —3C **36**
(off Marylebone Rd.)
Harley Pl. *W1* —1D **37**
Harley Rd. *NW3* —4F **21**
Harley Rd. *NW10* —1A **32**
Harley St. *W1* —3D **37**
Harley Vs. *NW10* —1A **32**
Harling Ct. *SW11* —5B **64**
Harlinger St. *SE18* —4F **59**
Harlowe Clo. *E8* —5C **26**
Harlowe Ho. *E8* —5B **26**
(off Clarissa St.)
Harlynwood. *SE5* —3E **67**
(off Wyndham Rd.)
Harman Clo. *NW2* —5A **6**
Harman Clo. *SE1* —1C **68**
Harman Dri. *NW2* —5A **6**
Harmon Ho. *SE8* —5B **56**
Harmont Ho. *W1* —4D **37**
(off Harley St.)
Harmony Clo. *NW11* —1A **6**
Harmood Gro. *NW1* —4D **23**
Harmood Ho. *NW1* —4D **23**
Harmood St. *NW1* —3D **23**
Harmsworth M. *SE1* —4C **52**
Harmsworth St. *SE17* —1D **67**
Harold Ct. *SE16* —3F **55**
(off Christopher Clo.)
Harold Est. *SE1* —4A **54**
Harold Gibbons Ct. *SE7*
—2E **73**

Harold Laski Ho. *EC1* —2D **39**
(off Percival St.)
Harold Maddison Ho. *SE17*
(off Penton Pl.) —1D **67**
Harold Pl. *SE11* —1C **66**
Harold Rd. *E11* —3A **16**
Harold Rd. *E13* —5D **31**
Harold Rd. *NW10* —2A **32**
Haroldstone Rd. *E17* —1F **13**
Harold Wilson Ho. *SW6*
(off Clem Attlee Ct.) —2B **62**
Harp All. *EC4* —5D **39**
Harp Bus. Cen. *NW2* —3C **4**
(off Apsley Way)
Harpenden Rd. *E12* —4E **17**
Harpenden Rd. *SE27* —3D **95**
Harpenmead Point. *NW2*
—4B **6**
Harper Ho. *SW9* —1D **81**
Harper Rd. *SE1* —4E **53**
Harp Island Clo. *NW10* —4A **4**
Harp La. *EC3* —1A **54**
Harpley Sq. *E1* —3E **41**
Harpsden St. *SW11* —4C **64**
Harpur M. *WC1* —4B **38**
Harpur St. *WC1* —4B **38**
Harraden Rd. *SE3* —4E **73**
Harrier Av. *E11* —1D **17**
Harriet Clo. *E8* —5C **26**
Harriet Ho. *SW6* —3D **63**
(off Wandon Rd.)
Harriet St. *SW1* —3B **50**
Harriet Tubman Clo. *SW2*
—5B **80**
Harriet Wlk. *SW1* —3B **50**
Harringay. —1D 11
Harringay Rd. *N15* —1D **11**
(in two parts)
Harrington Ct. *W10* —2B **34**
Harrington Gdns. *SW7*
—5D **49**
Harrington Hill. *E5* —3D **13**
Harrington Ho. *NW1* —2E **37**
(off Harrington St.)
Harrington Rd. *E11* —3A **16**
Harrington Rd. *SW7* —5F **49**
Harrington Sq. *NW1* —1E **37**
Harrington St. *NW1* —1E **37**
(in two parts)
Harrington Way. *SE18* —4F **59**
Harriott Clo. *SE10* —5B **58**
Harris Bldgs. *E1* —5C **40**
(off Burslem St.)
Harris Ho. *SW9* —1C **80**
(off St James's Cres.)
Harris Lodge. *SE6* —1E **99**
Harrison Ho. *SE17* —1F **67**
(off Brandon St.)
Harrisons Ct. *SE14* —2F **69**
(off Myers La.)
Harrison St. *WC1* —2A **38**
Harris St. *E17* —2B **14**
Harris St. *SE5* —3F **67**
Harrogate Ct. *SE12* —5C **86**
Harrogate Rd. *SE26* —3C **96**
(off Droitwich Clo.)
Harrold Ho. *NW3* —4E **21**

Harrold Ho. *NW6* —4E **21**
Harroway Rd. *SW11* —5F **63**
Harrowby St. *W2* —5A **36**
Harrowgate Ho. *E9* —3F **27**
Harrowgate Rd. *E9* —3A **28**
Harrow Grn. *E11* —5A **16**
Harrow La. *E14* —1E **57**
Harrow Lodge. *NW8* —3F **35**
(off Northwick Ter.)
Harrow Pl. *E1* —5A **40**
Harrow Rd. *E6* —5F **31**
Harrow Rd. *E11* —5A **16**
Harrow Rd. *NW10* —2D **33**
Harrow Rd. *W2 & NW1*
(in two parts) —4E **35**
Harrow Rd. *W10 & W9*
—3A **34**
Harrow Rd. Bri. *W2* —4E **35**
Harrow St. *NW1* —4A **36**
(off Daventry St.)
Harry Hinkins Ho. *SE17*
(off Bronti Clo.) —1E **67**
Harry Lambourn Ho. *SE15*
(off Gervase St.) —3D **69**
Hartfield Ter. *E3* —1C **42**
Hartham Clo. *N7* —2A **24**
Hartham Rd. *N7* —2A **24**
Harting Rd. *SE9* —3F **101**
Hartington Ct. *SW8* —4A **66**
Hartington Rd. *SW1* —1F **65**
(off Drummond Ga.)
Hartington Rd. *E16* —5D **45**
Hartington Rd. *E17* —1A **14**
Hartington Rd. *SW8* —4A **66**
Hartismere Rd. *SW6* —3B **62**
Hartlake Rd. *E9* —3F **27**
Hartland. *NW1* —5E **23**
(off Royal College St.)
Hartland Rd. *E15* —4B **30**
Hartland Rd. *NW1* —4D **23**
Hartland Rd. *NW6* —1B **34**
Hartley Av. *E6* —5F **31**
Hartley Ho. *SE1* —5B **54**
(off Longfield Est.)
Hartley Rd. *E11* —3B **16**
Hartley St. *E2* —2E **41**
(in two parts)
Hartmann Rd. *E16* —2F **59**
Hartnoll St. *N7* —2B **24**
Harton St. *SE8* —4C **70**
Hartop Point. *SW6* —3A **62**
(off Pellant Rd.)
Hartshorn All. *EC3* —5A **40**
(off Leadenhall St.)
Hart's La. *SE14* —4A **70**
Hart St. *EC3* —1A **54**
Hartswood Gdns. *W12*
—4B **46**
Hartswood Rd. *W12* —3B **46**
Hartsworth Clo. *E13* —1B **44**
Hartwell Ho. *SE7* —1D **73**
(off Troughton Rd.)
Hartwell St. *E8* —3B **26**
Harvard Clo. *NW6* —2D **21**
Harvard Ho. *SE17* —2D **67**
(off Doddington Gro.)
Harvard Rd. *SE13* —3E **85**

Harvey Ct. *E17* —1C **14**
Harvey Gdns. *E11* —3B **16**
Harvey Gdns. *SE7* —1E **73**
Harvey Ho. *E1* —3D **41**
(off Brady St.)
Harvey Ho. *N1* —5F **25**
(off Colville Est.)
Harvey Ho. *SW1* —1F **65**
(off Aylesford St.)
Harvey Lodge. *W9* —4C **34**
(off Admiral Wlk.)
Harvey Point. *E16* —4C **44**
(off Fife Rd.)
Harvey Rd. *E11* —3A **16**
Harvey Rd. *SE5* —4F **67**
(in two parts)
Harvey's Bldgs. *WC2* —1A **52**
Harvey St. *N1* —5F **25**
Harvington Wlk. *E8* —4C **26**
Harvist Est. *N7* —1C **24**
Harvist Rd. *NW6* —1F **33**
Harwood Ct. *N1* —5F **25**
(off Colville Est.)
Harwood Ct. *SW15* —2E **75**
Harwood Ho. *E2* —2D **41**
(off Pott St.)
Harwood Point. *SE16* —3B **56**
Harwood Rd. *SW6* —3C **62**
Harwood Ter. *SW6* —4D **63**
Haseley End. *SE23* —5E **83**
Haselrigge Rd. *SW4* —2F **79**
Haseltine Rd. *SE26* —4B **98**
Hasker St. *SW3* —5A **50**
Haslam Clo. *N1* —4C **24**
Haslam St. *SE15* —3B **68**
Haslemere Av. *NW4* —1F **5**
Haslemere Av. *SW18* —2D **91**
Haslemere Ind. Est. *SW18*
—2D **91**
Haslemere Rd. *N8* —2F **9**
Haslers Wharf. *E3* —5A **28**
(off Old Ford Rd.)
Hassard St. *E2* —1B **40**
Hassendean Rd. *SE3* —2D **73**
Hassett Rd. *E9* —3F **27**
Hassocks Clo. *SE26* —3D **97**
Hassop Rd. *NW2* —1F **19**
Hassop Wlk. *SE9* —4F **101**
Hasted Rd. *SE7* —1F **73**
Hastings Clo. *SE15* —3C **68**
Hastings Ho. *W12* —1D **47**
(off White City Est.)
Hastings Ho. *WC1* —2A **38**
(off Hastings St.)
Hastings St. *WC1* —2A **38**
Hastingwood Ct. *E17* —1D **15**
Hat & Mitre Ct. *EC1* —3D **39**
(off St John St.)
Hatcham M. Bus. Cen.
SE14 —4F **69**
Hatcham Pk. M. *SE14*
—4F **69**
Hatcham Pk. Rd. *SE14*
—4F **69**
Hatcham Rd. *SE15* —2E **69**
Hatchard Rd. *N19* —4F **9**
Hatchcliffe St. *SE10* —1B **72**

Hatchfield Ho. *N15* —1A **12**
(off Albert Rd.)
Hatcliffe Almshouses. *SE10*
(off Tuskar St.) —1A **72**
Hatcliffe Clo. *SE3* —1B **86**
Hatfield Clo. *SE14* —3F **69**
Hatfield Ct. *SE3* —3C **72**
Hatfield Ho. *EC1* —3E **39**
(off Golden La. Est.)
Hatfield Rd. *E15* —2A **30**
Hatfield Rd. *W4* —3A **46**
Hatfields. *SE1* —2C **52**
Hathaway Ho. *N1* —1A **40**
Hatherley Ct. *W2* —5D **35**
(off Hatherley Gro.)
Hatherley Gdns. *E6* —2F **45**
Hatherley Gdns. *N8* —1A **10**
Hatherley Gro. *W2* —5D **35**
Hatherley St. *SW1* —5E **51**
Hathersage Ct. *N1* —2F **25**
Hathorne Clo. *SE15* —5D **69**
Hathway St. *SE15* —5F **69**
Hathway Ter. *SE15* —5F **69**
(off Hathway St.)
Hatley Rd. *N7* —4B **10**
Hatteraick St. *SE16* —3E **55**
Hatton Garden. *EC1* —4C **38**
Hatton Pl. *EC1* —4C **38**
Hatton Row. *NW8* —3F **35**
(off Hatton St.)
Hatton St. *NW8* —3F **35**
Hatton Wall. *EC1* —4C **38**
Haunch of Venison Yd. *W1*
—5D **37**
Hauteville Ct. Gdns. *W6*
(off South Side) —4B **46**
Havana Rd. *SW19* —2C **89**
Havannah St. *E14* —3C **56**
Havelock Clo. *W12* —1D **47**
Havelock Ho. *SE23* —1E **97**
Havelock Rd. *SW19* —5E **91**
Havelock St. *N1* —5A **24**
Havelock Ter. *SW8* —4D **65**
Havelock Wlk. *SE23* —1E **97**
Haven Clo. *SW19* —3F **89**
Haven M. *E3* —4B **42**
Havenpool. *NW8* —5D **21**
(off Abbey Rd.)
Haven St. *NW1* —4D **23**
Haverfield Rd. *E3* —2A **42**
Haverhill Rd. *SW12* —1E **93**
Havering St. *E1* —5F **41**
Haversham Pl. *N6* —4B **8**
Haverstock Hill. *NW3* —2A **22**
Haverstock Pl. *EC1* —2D **39**
(off Haverstock St.)
Haverstock Rd. *NW5* —2C **22**
Haverstock St. *N1* —1D **39**
Havil St. *SE5* —3A **68**
Havisham Ho. *SE16* —3C **54**
Hawarden Gro. *SE24* —5E **81**
Hawarden Hill. *NW2* —5C **4**
Hawbridge Rd. *E11* —3F **15**
Hawes St. *N1* —4D **25**
Hawgood St. *E3* —4C **42**
Hawke Pl. *SE16* —3F **55**
Hawke Rd. *SE19* —5F **95**

Hawkesbury Rd. *SW15*
—3D **75**
Hawkesfield Rd. *SE23* —2A **98**
Hawke Tower. *SE14* —2A **70**
Hawkins Ct. *SE18* —5F **59**
Hawkins Ho. *SE8* —2C **70**
(off New King St.)
Hawkins Ho. *SW1* —2E **65**
(off Dolphin Sq.)
Hawkins Way. *SE6* —5C **98**
Hawkley Gdns. *SE27* —2D **95**
Hawkshaw Clo. *SW2* —5A **80**
Hawkshead. *NW1* —2E **37**
(off Stanhope St.)
Hawkshead Rd. *NW10*
—4B **18**
Hawkshead Rd. *W4* —3A **46**
Hawkslade Rd. *SE15* —3F **83**
Hawksley Rd. *N16* —5A **12**
Hawks M. *SE10* —3E **71**
Hawksmoor Clo. *E6* —5F **45**
Hawksmoor M. *E1* —1D **55**
Hawksmoor Pl. *E2* —3C **40**
(off Cheshire St.)
Hawksmoor St. *W6* —2F **61**
Hawkstone Rd. *SE16* —5E **55**
Hawkwell Wlk. *N1* —5E **25**
(off Maldon Rd.)
Hawkwood Mt. *E5* —3D **13**
Hawley Cres. *NW1* —4D **23**
Hawley M. *NW1* —4D **23**
Hawley Rd. *NW1* —4D **23**
(in three parts)
Hawley St. *NW1* —4D **23**
Hawstead Rd. *SE6* —4D **85**
Hawthorn Av. *E3* —5B **28**
Hawthorn Cres. *SW17* —5C **92**
Hawthorne Clo. *N1* —3A **26**
Hawthorne Ho. *SW1* —1E **65**
(off Churchill Gdns.)
Hawthorn Rd. *NW10* —4C **18**
Hawthorn Wlk. *W10* —3A **34**
Hawtrey Rd. *NW3* —4A **22**
Hay Clo. *E15* —4A **30**
Haycroft Gdns. *NW10* —5C **18**
Haycroft Rd. *SW2* —3A **80**
Hay Currie St. *E14* —5D **43**
Hayday Rd. *E16* —4C **44**
Hayden's Pl. *W11* —5B **34**
Haydon Pk. Rd. *SW19*
—5C **90**
Haydons Rd. *SW19* —5D **91**
Haydon St. *EC3* —1B **54**
Haydon Wlk. *E1* —5B **40**
Haydon Way. *SW11* —2F **77**
Hayes Ct. *SE5* —3E **67**
(off Camberwell New Rd.)
Hayes Cres. *NW11* —1B **6**
Hayes Pl. *NW1* —3A **36**
Hayfield Pas. *E1* —3E **41**
Hayfield Yd. *E1* —3E **41**
Haygarth Pl. *SW19* —5F **89**
Hay Hill. *W1* —1D **51**
Hayles Bldgs. *SE11* —5D **53**
(off Elliotts Row)
Hayles St. *SE11* —5D **53**

Hayling Clo. N16 —2A 26
Haymans Point. SE11 —5B 52
Hayman St. N1 —4D 25
Haymarket. SW1 —1F 51
Haymarket Arc. SW1 —1F 51
(off Haymarket)
Haymerle Ho. SE15 —2C 68
(off Haymerle Rd.)
Haymerle Rd. SE15 —2C 68
Hayne Ho. N11 —2A 48
(off Penzance Pl.)
Haynes Clo. SE3 —1A 86
Hayne St. EC1 —4D 39
Hay's Galleria. SE1 —2A 54
Hays La. SE1 —2A 54
Hay's M. W1 —2D 51
Hay St. E2 —5C 26
Hayter Ct. E11 —4D 17
Hayter Rd. SW2 —3A 80
Hayton Clo. E8 —3B 26
Hayward Clo. SW9 —5A 66
(off Clapham Rd.)
Hayward Gallery. —2B 52
(off Belvedere Rd.)
Hayward Gdns. SW15 —4E 75
Hayward's Pl. EC1 —3D 39
Haywards Yd. SE4 —3B 84
(off Lindal Rd.)
Hazelbank Rd. SE6 —2F 99
Hazelbourne Rd. SW12
 —4D 79
Hazel Clo. N19 —4E 9
Hazel Clo. SE15 —5C 68
Hazeldean Rd. NW10 —4A 18
Hazeldon Rd. SE4 —3A 84
Hazel Gro. SE26 —4F 97
Hazelhurst Ct. SE6 —5E 99
(off Beckenham Hill Rd.)
Hazelhurst Rd. SW17 —4E 91
Hazellville Rd. N19 —2F 9
Hazelmere Ct. SW2 —1B 94
Hazelmere Rd. NW6 —5B 20
Hazel Rd. E15 —2A 30
Hazel Rd. NW10 —2D 33
(in two parts)
Hazel Way. SE1 —5B 54
Hazelwood Ct. NW10 —5A 4
Hazelwood Ho. SE8 —5A 56
Hazelwood Rd. E17 —1A 14
Hazlebury Rd. SW6 —5D 63
Hazlewell Rd. SW15 —3E 75
Hazlewood Clo. E5 —5A 14
Hazlewood Cres. W10 —3A 34
Hazlewood Tower. W10
 —3A 34
(off Golborne Gdns.)
Hazlitt M. W14 —4A 48
Hazlitt Rd. W14 —4A 48
Headbourne Ho. SE1 —4F 53
(off Law St.)
Headcorn Rd. Brom —5B 100
Headfort Pl. SW1 —3C 50
Headington Rd. SW18
 —2E 91
Headlam Rd. SW4 —4F 79
(in two parts)
Headlam St. E1 —3D 41

Headley Ct. SE26 —5E 97
Head's M. W11 —5C 34
Head St. E1 —5F 41
(in two parts)
Heald St. SE14 —4C 70
Healey Ho. SW9 —3C 66
Healey St. NW1 —3D 23
Hearn's Bldgs. SE17 —5F 53
Hearn St. EC2 —3A 40
Hearnville Rd. SW12 —1C 92
Heath Brow. NW3 —5E 7
Heath Clo. NW11 —2D 7
Heathcock Ct. WC2 —1A 52
(off Exchange Ct.)
Heathcote St. WC1 —3B 38
Heathcroft. NW11 —3D 7
Heath Dri. NW3 —1D 21
Heathedge. SE26 —2D 97
Heather Clo. N7 —5B 10
Heather Clo. SE13 —5F 85
Heather Clo. SW8 —1D 79
Heather Gdns. NW11 —1A 6
Heather Ho. E14 —5E 43
Heatherley St. E5 —5C 12
Heather Rd. NW2 —4B 4
Heather Rd. SE12 —2C 100
Heather Wlk. W10 —3A 34
Heatherwood Clo. E12
 —4E 17
Heathfield Av. SW18 —5F 77
Heathfield Clo. E16 —4F 45
Heathfield Gdns. NW11 —1F 5
Heathfield Gdns. SE3 —5A 72
(off Baizdon Rd.)
Heathfield Gdns. SW18
 —4F 77
Heathfield Ho. SE3 —5A 72
Heathfield Pk. NW2 —3E 19
Heathfield Rd. SW18 —4E 77
Heathfield Sq. SW18 —5F 77
Heathfield St. W11 —1A 48
(off Portland Rd.)
Heathgate. NW11 —1D 7
Heathgate Pl. NW3 —2B 22
Heath Hurst Rd. NW3
 —1A 22
Heathland Rd. N16 —3A 12
Heath La. SE3 —5F 71
(in two parts)
Heathlee Rd. SE3 —2B 86
Heathmans Rd. SW6 —4B 62
Heath Mead. SW19 —3F 89
Heath Pas. NW3 —3E 7
Heathpool Ct. E1 —3D 41
(off Brady St.)
Heath Ri. SW15 —4F 75
Heath Rd. SW8 —5D 65
Heath Side. NW3 —1F 21
Heathside. NW11 —3C 6
Heathside. SE13 —5E 71
Heathstan Rd. W12 —5C 32
Heath St. NW3 —5E 7
Heathview. NW5 —1C 22
Heathview Gdns. SW15
 —5E 75
Heath Vs. NW3 —5F 7
Heathville Rd. N19 —2A 10

Heathwall St. SW11 —1B 78
Heathway. SE3 —3C 72
Heathway Ct. NW11 —4C 6
Heathwood Gdns. SE7 —5F 59
Heathwood Point. SE23
 —3F 97
Heaton Rd. SE15 —5D 69
Heaver Rd. SW11 —1F 77
Hebden Ct. E2 —5B 26
Hebdon Rd. SW17 —3A 92
Heber Mans. W14 —2A 62
(off Queen's Club Gdns.)
Heber Rd. NW2 —2F 19
Heber Rd. SE22 —4B 82
Hebron Rd. W6 —4E 47
Heckfield Pl. SW6 —3C 62
Heckford Ho. E14 —5D 43
Heckford St. E1 —1F 55
Heckford St. Bus. Cen. E1
(off Heckford St.) —1F 55
Hector Clo. SW9 —3C 66
(off Caldwell St.)
Hector Ho. E2 —1D 41
(off Old Bethnal Grn. Rd.)
Heddington Gro. N7 —2B 24
Heddon St. W1 —1E 51
(in two parts)
Hedgers Gro. E9 —3A 28
Hedger St. SE11 —5D 53
Hedge Wlk. SE6 —5D 99
Hedgley M. SE12 —3B 86
Hedgley St. SE12 —3B 86
Hedingham Clo. N1 —4E 25
Hedley Ho. E14 —4E 57
Hedley Row. N5 —2F 25
Hedsor Ho. E2 —3B 40
(off Ligonier St.)
Hega Ho. E14 —4E 43
Heidegger Cres. SW13
 —3D 61
Heigham Rd. E6 —5F 31
Heights, The. SE7 —1E 73
Heiron St. SE17 —2D 67
Helby Rd. SW4 —4F 79
Heldar Ct. SE1 —3F 53
Helder Gro. SE12 —5B 86
Helena Pl. E9 —5D 27
Helena Rd. E13 —1B 44
Helena Rd. E17 —1C 14
Helena Rd. NW10 —2D 19
Helena Sq. SE16 —1A 56
(off Sovereign Cres.)
Helen Gladstone Ho. SE1
(off Surrey Row) —3D 53
Helen Ho. E2 —1D 41
(off Old Bethnal Grn. Rd.)
Helen Mackay Ho. E14
 —5F 43
Helen Peele Cotts. SE16
(off Lower Rd.) —4E 55
Helenslea Av. NW11 —3C 6
Helen's Pl. E2 —2E 41
Helen Taylor Ho. SE16
 —4C 54
(off Evelyn Lowe Est.)

Heliport Ind. Est. SW11 —5F 63
Helix Gdns. SW2 —4B 80
Helix Rd. SW2 —4B 80
Hellings St. E1 —2C 54
Helme Clo. SW19 —5B 90
Helmet Row. EC1 —3E 39
(in two parts)
Helmsdale Ho. NW6 —1D 35
(off Carlton Va.)
Helmsley Pl. E8 —4D 27
Helmsley St. E8 —4D 27
Helsby Ct. NW8 —3F 35
(off Pollitt Dri.)
Helsinki Sq. SE16 —4A 56
Helston. NW1 —1E 37
(off Camden St.)
Helston Ct. N15 —1A 12
(off Culvert Rd.)
Helston Ho. SE11 —1C 66
(off Kennings Way)
Helvetia St. SE6 —2B 98
Hemans St. SW8 —3F 65
Hemans St. Est. SW8 —3F 65
Hemberton Rd. SW9 —1A 80
Hemingford Rd. N1 —5B 24
Hemingway Clo. NW5 —1C 22
Hemlock Rd. E10 —4D 15
Hemlock Rd. W12 —1B 46
(in two parts)
Hemming St. E1 —3C 40
Hemp Wlk. SE17 —5F 53
Hemstal Rd. NW6 —4C 20
Hemsworth Ct. N1 —1A 40
Hemsworth St. N1 —1A 40
Hemus Pl. SW3 —1A 64
Henchman St. W12 —5B 32
Henderson Ct. SE14 —2F 69
(off Myers La.)
Henderson Dri. NW8 —3F 35
Henderson Rd. E7 —3E 31
Henderson Rd. SW18 —5A 78
Hendham Rd. SW17 —2A 92
Hendon. —1D 5
Hendon F.C. —4F 5
Hendon Ho. NW4 —1F 5
Hendon Pk. Mans. NW4 —1E 5
Hendon Pk. Row. NW11 —1B 6
Hendon Way. NW4 & NW2 —1D 5
Hendre Rd. SE1 —5A 54
Hendrick Av. SW12 —5B 78
Heneage La. EC3 —5A 40
Heneage Pl. EC3 —5A 40
Heneage St. E1 —4B 40
Henfield Clo. N19 —3E 9
Hengist Rd. SE12 —5D 87
Hengrave Rd. SE23 —4E 83
Henley Clo. SE16 —3E 55
(off St Marychurch St.)
Henley Dri. SE1 —5B 54
Henley Ho. E2 —3B 40
(off Swanfield St.)
Henley Prior. N1 —1B 38
(off Collier St.)
Henley Rd. NW10 —5E 19
Henley St. SW11 —5C 64
Hennel Clo. SE23 —3E 97
Henniker Gdns. E6 —2F 45
Henniker M. SW3 —2F 63
Henniker Point. E15 —2A 30
(off Leytonstone Rd.)
Henniker Rd. E15 —2F 29
Henning St. SW11 —4A 64
Henrietta Clo. SE8 —2C 70
Henrietta Ho. N15 —1A 12
(off St Ann's Rd.)
Henrietta Ho. W6 —1E 61
(off Queen Caroline St.)
Henrietta M. WC1 —3A 38
Henrietta Pl. W1 —5D 37
Henrietta St. E15 —2E 29
Henrietta St. WC2 —1A 52
Henriques St. E1 —5C 40
Henry Cooper Way. SE9 —3F 101
Henry Dickens Ct. W11 —1F 47
Henry Doulton Dri. SW17 —4C 92
Henry Ho. SE1 —2C 52
Henry Ho. SW8 —3A 66
(off Wyvil Rd.)
Henry Jackson Rd. SW15 —1F 75
Henry Rd. N4 —3E 11
Henryson Rd. SE4 —3C 84
Henry Wise Ho. SW1 —5E 51
(off Vauxhall Bri. Rd.)
Hensford Gdns. SE26 —4D 97
Henshall St. N1 —3F 25
Henshaw St. SE17 —5F 53
Henslowe Rd. SE22 —3C 82
Henslow Ho. SE15 —3C 68
(off Peckham Pk. Rd.)
Henson Av. NW2 —2E 19
Henstridge Pl. NW8 —5A 22
Henty Clo. SW11 —3A 64
Henty Wlk. SW15 —3D 75
Henwick Rd. SE9 —1F 87
Hepburn M. SW11 —3B 78
Hepplestone Clo. SW15 —4D 75
Hepscott Rd. E9 —3C 28
Hepworth Ct. N1 —5D 25
(off Gaskin St.)
Hepworth Ct. NW3 —2A 22
Hera Ct. E14 —5C 56
Herald's Pl. SE11 —5D 53
Herald St. E2 —3D 41
Herbal Hill. EC1 —3C 38
Herbal Hill Gdns. EC1 —3C 38
Herbal Pl. EC1 —3C 38
(off Herbal Hill)
Herbert Cres. SW1 —4B 50
Herbert Gdns. NW10 —1D 33
Herbert Ho. E1 —5B 40
(off Old Castle St.)
Herbert Morrison Ho. SW6
(off Clem Attlee Ct.) —2B 62
Herbert Rd. E12 —1F 31
Herbert Rd. E17 —2B 14
Herbert Rd. NW9 —1C 4
Herbert St. E13 —1C 44
Herbert St. NW5 —3C 22
Herbrand Est. WC1 —3A 38
Herbrand St. WC1 —3A 38
Hercules Pl. N7 —5A 10
(in two parts)
Hercules Rd. SE1 —4B 52
Hercules St. N7 —5A 10
Hercules Tower. SE14 —2A 70
Hercules Wharf. E14 —1A 58
Hercules Yd. N7 —5A 10
Hereford Bldgs. SW3 —2F 63
Hereford Gdns. SE13 —3A 86
Hereford Ho. NW6 —1C 34
(off Carlton Va.)
Hereford Ho. SW3 —4A 50
(off Old Brompton Rd.)
Hereford Ho. SW10 —3D 63
(off Fulham Rd.)
Hereford M. W2 —5C 34
Hereford Pl. SE14 —3B 70
Hereford Retreat. SE15 —3C 68
Hereford Rd. E11 —1D 17
Hereford Rd. W2 —5C 34
Hereford Sq. SW7 —5E 49
Hereford St. E2 —3C 40
Hereward Rd. SW17 —4B 92
Heriot Rd. NW4 —1E 5
Heritage Clo. SW9 —1D 81
Heritage Ct. SE8 —1F 69
(off Trundley's Rd.)
Herlwyn Gdns. SW17 —4B 92
Hermes Clo. W9 —3C 34
Hermes Ct. SW9 —4C 66
(off Southey Rd.)
Hermes St. N1 —1C 38
Herm Ho. N1 —3E 25
Hermiston Av. N8 —1A 10
Hermitage Ct. E1 —2C 54
(off Knighten St.)
Hermitage Ct. NW2 —5C 6
Hermitage Gdns. NW2 —5C 6
Hermitage La. NW2 —5C 6
Hermitage Rd. N4 & N15 —2D 11
Hermitage Rd. SE19 —5F 95
Hermitage Row. E8 —2C 26
Hermitage St. W2 —4F 35
Hermitage, The. SE13 —5E 71
Hermitage, The. SE23 —1E 97
Hermitage, The. SW13 —4B 60
Hermitage Wall. E1 —2C 54
Hermit Pl. NW6 —5D 21
Hermit Rd. E16 —4B 44
Hermit St. EC1 —2D 39
Hermon Hill. E11 & E18 —1C 16
Herndon Rd. SW18 —3E 77
Herne Clo. NW10 —2A 18
Herne Hill. —3E 81
Herne Hill. SE24 —4E 81
Herne Hill Ho. SE24 —4D 81
(off Railton Rd.)

Herne Hill Rd. *SE24* —1E **81**
Herne Hill Stadium. —2F **81**
Herne Pl. *SE24* —3D **81**
Heron Clo. *NW10* —3A **18**
Heron Ct. *E14* —4E **57**
Herondale Av. *SW18* —1F **91**
Herongate Rd. *E12* —4E **17**
Heron Ho. *E6* —4F **31**
Heron Ho. *NW8* —1A **36**
  (off Barrow Hill Est.)
Heron Ho. *SW11* —3A **64**
  (off Searles Clo.)
Heron Ind. Est. *E15* —1D **43**
Heron Pl. *SE16* —2A **56**
Heron Pl. *W1* —5C **36**
  (off Thayer St.)
Heron Quay. *E14* —2C **56**
Heron Rd. *SE24* —2E **81**
Heron's Lea. *N6* —1B **8**
Herons, The. *E11* —1B **16**
Herrick Ho. *SE5* —3F **67**
  (off Elmington Est.)
Herrick Rd. *N5* —5E **11**
Herrick St. *SW1* —5F **51**
Herries St. *W10* —1A **34**
Herringham Rd. *SE7* —4E **59**
Hersant Clo. *NW10* —5C **18**
Herschell M. *SE5* —1E **81**
Herschell Rd. *SE23* —5A **84**
Hersham Clo. *SW15* —5C **74**
Hertford Av. *SW14* —3A **74**
Hertford Pl. *W1* —3E **37**
Hertford Rd. *N1* —5A **26**
  (in two parts)
Hertford St. *W1* —2D **51**
Hertslet Rd. *N7* —5B **10**
Hertsmere Rd. *E14* —1C **56**
Hertsmere Rd. *E14* —2C **56**
Hervey Rd. *SE3* —4D **73**
Hesewall Clo. *SW4* —5E **65**
Hesketh Pl. *W11* —1A **48**
Hesketh Rd. *E7* —5C **16**
Heslop Rd. *SW12* —1B **92**
Hesper M. *SW5* —5D **49**
Hesperus Clo. *E14* —5D **57**
Hesperus Cres. *E14* —5D **57**
Hessel St. *E1* —5D **41**
Hestercombe Av. *SW6*
  —5A **62**
Hester Rd. *SW11* —3A **64**
Heston Ho. *SE8* —4C **70**
Heston St. *SE14* —4C **70**
Hetherington Rd. *SW4*
  —2A **80**
Hethpool Ho. *W2* —3F **35**
  (off Hall Pl.)
Hetley Ho. *W12* —3D **47**
  (off Hetley Rd.)
Hetley Rd. *W12* —2D **47**
Hevelius Clo. *SE10* —1B **72**
Hever Ho. *SE15* —2F **69**
  (off Lovelinch Clo.)
Heversham Ho. *SE15* —2E **69**
Hewer St. *W10* —4F **33**
Hewett St. *EC2* —3A **40**
Hewison St. *E3* —1B **42**

Hewitt Rd. *N8* —1C **10**
Hewlett Ho. *SW8* —3D **65**
  (off Havelock Ter.)
Hewlett Rd. *E3* —1A **42**
Hexagon, The. *N6* —3B **8**
Hexal Rd. *SE6* —3A **100**
Hexham Rd. *SE27* —2E **95**
Heybridge Av. *SW16* —5B **94**
Heybridge Way. *E10* —2A **14**
Heydon Ho. *SE14* —4E **69**
  (off Kender St.)
Heyford Av. *SW8* —3A **66**
Heyford Ter. *SW8* —3A **66**
Heygate St. *SE17* —5E **53**
Heylyn Sq. *E3* —2B **42**
Heysham La. *NW3* —5D **7**
Heysham Rd. *N15* —1F **11**
Heythorp St. *SW18* —1B **90**
Heywood Ho. *SE14* —2F **69**
  (off Myers La.)
Heyworth Rd. *E5* —1D **27**
Heyworth Rd. *E15* —2B **30**
Hibbert Rd. *E17* —2B **14**
Hibbert St. *SW11* —1F **77**
Hichisson Rd. *SE15* —3E **83**
Hickes Ho. *NW6* —4F **21**
Hickin Clo. *SE7* —5E **59**
Hickin St. *E14* —4E **57**
Hickleton. *NW1* —5E **23**
  (off Camden St.)
Hickling Ho. *SE16* —4D **55**
  (off Slippers Pl.)
Hickman Clo. *E16* —4F **45**
Hickmore Wlk. *SW4* —1F **79**
Hicks Clo. *SW11* —1A **78**
Hicks St. *SE8* —1A **70**
Hide Pl. *SW1* —5F **51**
Hider Ct. *SE3* —3E **73**
Hides St. *N7* —2B **24**
Hide Tower. *SW1* —5F **51**
  (off Regency St.)
Higgins Ho. *N1* —5A **26**
  (off Colville Est.)
Higginson Ho. *NW3* —4B **22**
Higgs Ind. Est. *SE24* —1D **81**
Highbank Way. *N8* —1C **10**
High Bri. *SE10* —1F **71**
Highbridge Ct. *SE14* —3E **69**
  (off Farrow La.)
High Bri. Wharf. *SE10*
  (off High Bri.)   —1F **71**
Highbrook Rd. *SE3* —1F **87**
Highbury. —1D 25
Highbury Barn. *N5* —1E **25**
Highbury Corner. (Junct.)
  —3D **25**
Highbury Cres. *N5* —2D **25**
Highbury Est. *N5* —2E **25**
Highbury Grange. *N5* —1E **25**
Highbury Gro. *N5* —2D **25**
Highbury Hill. *N5* —5C **10**
Highbury M. *N7* —3C **24**
Highbury New Pk. *N5* —2E **25**
Highbury Pk. *N5* —5C **10**
Highbury Pk. M. *N5* —1E **25**
Highbury Pl. *N5* —3D **25**
Highbury Quad. *N5* —5E **11**

Highbury Rd. *SW19* —5A **90**
Highbury Sta. Rd. *N1* —3C **24**
Highbury Ter. *N5* —2D **25**
Highbury Ter. M. *N5* —2D **25**
Highclere St. *SE26* —4A **98**
Highcliffe Dri. *SW15* —4B **74**
Highcliffe Gdns. *Ilf* —1F **17**
Highcombe. *SE7* —2D **73**
Highcombe Clo. *SE9* —1F **101**
Highcroft Est. *N19* —2A **10**
Highcroft Gdns. *NW11* —1B **6**
Highcroft Rd. *N19* —2A **10**
Highcross Way. *SW15*
  —1C **88**
Highdown Rd. *SW15* —4D **75**
Highfield Av. *NW11* —2F **5**
Highfield Clo. *SE13* —4F **85**
Highfield Ct. *NW11* —1A **6**
Highfield Gdns. *NW11* —1A **6**
Highfield Rd. *NW11* —1A **6**
Highfields Gro. *N6* —3B **8**
Highgate. —3D 9
Highgate Av. *N6* —2D **9**
Highgate Cemetery. —4D **9**
Highgate Clo. *N6* —2C **8**
Highgate Edge. *N2* —1A **8**
Highgate Heights. *N6* —1E **8**
Highgate High St. *N6* —3C **8**
Highgate Hill. *N6 & N19*
  —3D **9**
Highgate Ho. *SE26* —3C **96**
Highgate Rd. *N6* —5C **8**
Highgate Spinney. *N8* —1A **10**
Highgate Wlk. *SE23* —2E **97**
Highgate W. Hill. *N6* —4C **8**
High Hill Est. *E5* —3D **13**
High Hill Ferry. *E5* —3D **13**
High Holborn. *WC1* —5A **38**
Highland Cft. *Beck* —5D **99**
Highland Rd. *SE19* —5A **96**
Highlands Clo. *N4* —2A **10**
Highlands Ct. *SW19* —5A **96**
Highlands Heath. *SW15*
  —5E **75**
Highland Ter. *SE13* —1D **85**
  (off Claybank Gro.)
High Level Dri. *SE26* —4C **96**
Highlever Rd. *W10* —4E **33**
High Meads Rd. *E16* —5F **45**
Highmore Rd. *SE3* —3A **72**
Highmt. *NW4* —1C **4**
High Pde., The. *SW16* —3A **94**
Highpoint. *N6* —2C **8**
High Pk. *N15 & N17* —1B **12**
High Rd. *NW10* —3A **18**
High Rd. Leyton. *E10 & E15*
  —1D **15**
High Rd. Leytonstone. *E11 &*
  E15 —1A **30**
High Sheldon. *N6* —1B **8**
Highshore Rd. *SE15* —5B **68**
  (in two parts)
Highstone Av. *E11* —1C **16**
Highstone Ct. *E11* —1B **16**
  (off New Wanstead)
Highstone Mans. *NW1*
  (off Camden Rd.)   —4E **23**

High St.—Hogarth Ho.

High St. *E13* —1C **44**
High St. *E15* —1E **43**
High St. *E17* —1A **14**
High St. *SW19* —5F **91**
(Colliers Wood)
High St. *SW19* —5F **89**
(Wimbledon)
High St. Harlesden. *NW10*
—1B **32**
High St. M. *SW19* —5A **90**
High St. N. *E12 & E6* —2F **31**
High Timber St. *EC4* —1E **53**
High Trees. *SW2* —1C **94**
Highview. *N6* —1E **9**
Highway, The. *E1 & E14*
—1C **54**
Highway Trad. Cen., The. E1
(off Heckford St.) —1F **55**
Highwood Rd. *N19* —5A **10**
Highworth St. NW1 —4A 36
(off Daventry St.)
Hilary Clo. *E11* —1C **16**
Hilary Clo. *SW6* —3D **63**
Hilary Rd. *W12* —5B **32**
(in two parts)
Hilborough Ct. *E8* —4B **26**
Hilda Rd. *E6* —4F **31**
Hilda Rd. *E16* —3A **44**
Hilda Ter. *SW9* —5C **66**
Hildenborough Gdns. Brom
—5A **100**
Hildreth St. *SW12* —1D **93**
Hildyard Rd. *SW6* —2C **62**
Hiley Rd. *NW10* —2E **33**
Hilgrove Rd. *NW6* —4E **21**
Hillbeck Clo. *SE15* —3E **69**
Hillboro Ct. *E11* —2F **15**
Hillbrook Rd. *SW17* —3B **92**
Hillbrow Rd. Brom —5A **100**
Hillbury Rd. *SW17* —3D **93**
Hill Clo. *NW2* —5D **5**
Hill Clo. *NW11* —1C **6**
Hillcourt Est. *N16* —3F **11**
Hillcourt Rd. *SE22* —4D **83**
Hillcrest. *N6* —2C **8**
Hillcrest. *SE5* —2F **81**
Hillcrest Clo. *SE26* —4C **96**
Hillcrest Gdns. *NW2* —5C **4**
Hillcrest Rd. Brom —5C **100**
Hilldrop Cres. *N7* —2F **23**
Hilldrop Est. *N7* —1F **23**
Hilldrop La. *N7* —2F **23**
Hilldrop Rd. *N7* —2F **23**
Hilldrop Rd. Brom —5D **101**
Hillersden Ho. SW1 —1D 65
(off Ebury Bri. Rd.)
Hillersdon Av. *SW13*
—5C **60**
Hillery Clo. *SE17* —5F **53**
Hill Farm Rd. *W10* —4E **33**
Hillfield Av. *N8* —1A **10**
Hillfield Ct. *NW3* —2A **22**
Hillfield Ho. *N5* —2E **25**
Hillfield Rd. *NW6* —2B **20**
Hillgate Pl. *SW12* —5D **79**
Hillgate Pl. *W8* —2C **48**
Hillgate St. *W11* —2C **48**

Hill Ho. *E5* —3D **13**
(off Harrington Hill)
Hill Ho. Rd. *SW16* —5B **94**
Hilliard Ho. *E1* —2D **55**
(off Prusom St.)
Hilliards Ct. *E1* —2E **55**
Hillier Rd. *SW11* —4B **78**
Hillingdon St. *SE5 & SE17*
(in two parts) —2D **67**
Hillman Dri. *W10* —3E **33**
Hillman St. *E8* —3D **27**
Hillmarton Rd. *N7* —2A **24**
Hillmead Dri. *SW9* —2D **81**
Hillmore Ct. SE13 —1F 85
(off Belmont Hill)
Hillmore Gro. *SE26* —5A **98**
Hill Path. *SW16* —5B **94**
Hill Ri. *SE23* —1D **97**
Hillrise Mans. N19 —2A 10
(off Warltersville Rd.)
Hillrise Rd. *N19* —2A **10**
Hill Rd. *NW8* —2E **35**
Hillsboro' Rd. *SE22* —3A **82**
Hillsborough Ct. NW6 —5D 21
(off Mortimer Cres.)
Hillside. *N8* —1F **9**
Hillside. *NW5* —5C **8**
Hillside. *NW10* —5A **18**
Hillside Clo. *NW8* —1D **35**
Hillside Est. *N15* —1B **12**
Hillside Gdns. *N6* —1D **9**
Hillside Gdns. *SW2* —2C **94**
Hillside Pas. *SW16* —2B **94**
Hillside Rd. *N16* —2A **12**
Hillside Rd. *SW2* —2B **94**
Hillsleigh Rd. *W8* —2B **48**
Hills Pl. *W1* —5E **37**
Hillstowe St. *E5* —5E **13**
Hill St. *W1* —2C **50**
Hilltop Ct. NW8 —4E 21
(off Alexandra Rd.)
Hilltop Rd. *NW6* —4C **20**
Hillway. *N6* —4C **8**
Hillway. *NW9* —3A **4**
Hillwood Ho. NW1 —1E 37
(off Polygon Rd.)
Hillworth Rd. *SW2* —5C **80**
Hillyard Ho. *SW9* —4C **66**
Hillyard St. *SW9* —4C **66**
Hilly Fields Cres. *SE4* —1C **84**
Hilsea St. *E5* —1E **27**
Hilton Ho. *SE4* —2F **83**
Hilton's Wharf. SE10 —2D 71
(off Norman Rd.)
Hilversum Cres. *SE22* —3A **82**
Himley Rd. *SW17* —5A **92**
Hinchinbrook Ho. NW6
(off Mortimer Cres.) —5D **21**
Hinckley Rd. *SE15* —2C **82**
Hind Ct. *EC4* —5C **38**
Hinde Ho. W1 —5C 36
(off Hinde St.)
Hinde M. W1 —5C 36
(off Marlebone La.)
Hinde St. *W1* —5C **36**
Hind Gro. *E14* —5C **42**
Hindhead Clo. *N16* —3A **12**

Hind Ho. *SE14* —2F **69**
(off Myers La.)
Hindlip Ho. *SW8* —4F **65**
Hindmans Rd. *SE22* —3C **82**
Hindmarsh Clo. *E1* —1C **54**
Hindrey Rd. *E5* —2D **27**
Hindsley's Pl. *SE23* —2E **97**
Hinstock. NW6 —5D 21
(off Belsize Rd.)
Hinton Ct. E10 —4D 15
(off Leyton Grange Est.)
Hinton Rd. *SW9* —1D **81**
Hippodrome M. *W11* —1A **48**
Hippodrome Pl. *W11* —1A **48**
Hiroshima Promenade. SE7
—4E **59**
Hitcham Rd. *E17* —2B **14**
Hitchin Sq. *E3* —1A **42**
Hither Farm Rd. *SE3* —1E **87**
Hitherfield Rd. *SW16* —2B **94**
Hither Green. —4A 86
Hither Grn. La. *SE13* —3E **85**
Hitherwood Dri. *SE19*
—4B **96**
HMS Belfast. —2A **54**
Hoadly Rd. *SW16* —3F **93**
Hobart Pl. *SW1* —4D **51**
Hobbes Wlk. *SW15* —3D **75**
Hobbs Ct. SE1 —3B 54
(off Mill St.)
Hobbs Pl. *N1* —5A **26**
Hobbs Pl. Est. N1 —5A 26
(off Hobbs Pl.)
Hobbs Rd. *SE27* —4E **95**
Hobday St. *E14* —5D **43**
Hobson's Pl. *E1* —4C **40**
Hobury St. *SW10* —2E **63**
Hocker St. *E2* —2B **40**
Hockett Clo. *SE8* —5A **56**
Hockley Av. *E6* —1F **45**
Hockliffe Ho. W10 —4E 33
(off Sutton Way)
Hockney Ct. SE16 —1D 69
(off Rossetti Rd.)
Hocroft Av. *NW2* —5B **6**
Hocroft Ct. *NW2* —5B **6**
Hocroft Rd. *NW2* —5B **6**
Hocroft Wlk. *NW2* —5B **6**
Hodes Row. *NW3* —1C **22**
Hodford Rd. *NW11* —3B **6**
Hodister Clo. *SE5* —3E **67**
Hodnet Gro. *SE16* —5F **55**
Hoever Ho. *SE6* —4E **99**
Hofland Rd. *W14* —4A **48**
Hogan M. *W2* —4E **35**
Hogan Way. *E5* —4C **12**
Hogarth Bus. Cen. W4
—2A **60**
Hogarth Clo. *E16* —4F **45**
Hogarth Ct. E1 —5C 40
(off Batty St.)
Hogarth Ct. *EC3* —5A **40**
Hogarth Ct. NW1 —4E 23
(off St Pancras Way)
Hogarth Ct. *SE19* —4B **96**
Hogarth Ho. SW1 —5F 51
(off Erasmus St.)

Hogarth Ind. Est. NW10 —3C 32
Hogarth La. W4 —2A 60
Hogarth Pl. SW5 —5D 49
(off Hogarth Rd.)
Hogarth Rd. SW5 —5D 49
Hogarth Roundabout. (Junct.) —2A 60
Hogarth's House. —2A 60
Hogarth Ter. W4 —2A 60
Hogshead Pas. E1 —1D 55
(off Pennington St.)
Holbeach M. SW12 —1D 93
Holbeach Rd. SE6 —5C 84
Holbeck Row. SE15 —3C 68
Holbein Ho. SW1 —1C 64
(off Holbein M.)
Holbein M. SW1 —1C 64
Holbein Pl. SW1 —5C 50
Holberton Gdns. NW10 —2D 33
Holborn. —4C 38
Holborn. WC1 —4C 38
Holborn Cir. EC1 —4C 38
Holborn Pl. WC2 —4B 38
(off High Holborn)
Holborn Rd. E13 —4D 45
Holborn Viaduct. EC4 —4C 38
Holbrook Clo. N19 —3D 9
Holbrooke Ct. N7 —5A 10
Holbrook Rd. E15 —1B 44
Holburne Clo. SE3 —4E 73
Holburne Gdns. SE3 —4F 73
Holburne Rd. SE3 —4E 73
Holcombe Ho. SW9 —1A 80
(off Landor Rd.)
Holcombe Pl. SE4 —1A 84
(off St Asaph Rd.)
Holcombe St. W6 —5D 47
Holcroft Ct. W1 —4E 37
(off Clipstone St.)
Holcroft Ho. SW11 —1F 77
Holcroft Rd. E9 —4E 27
Holdenby Rd. SE4 —3A 84
Holden Ho. N1 —5E 25
(off Prebend St.)
Holden Ho. SE8 —3C 70
Holden St. SW11 —5C 64
Holdernesse Rd. SW17 —3B 92
Holderness Ho. SE5 —1A 82
Holderness Way. SE27 —5D 95
Holford Ho. SE16 —5D 55
(off Camilla Rd.)
Holford M. WC1 —2C 38
(off Cruikshank St.)
Holford Pl. WC1 —2B 38
Holford Rd. NW3 —5E 7
Holford St. WC1 —2B 38
Holford Yd. WC1 —1C 38
Holgate Av. SW11 —1F 77
Holgate St. SE7 —4F 59
Holland Dri. SE23 —3A 98
Holland Gdns. W14 —4A 48
Holland Gro. SW9 —3C 66
Holland Park. —2B 48
Holland Park. (Junct.) —3F 47
Holland Pk. —3B 48
Holland Pk. W11 —2A 48
Holland Pk. Av. W11 —3A 48
Holland Pk. Gdns. W14 —3A 48
Holland Pk. M. W11 —2A 48
Holland Pk. Rd. W14 —4B 48
Holland Pk. Theatre. —3B 48
Holland Pas. N1 —5E 25
(off Basire St.)
Holland Pl. W8 —3D 49
(off Kensington Chu. St.)
Holland Pl. Chambers. W8
(off Pitt St. La.) —3D 49
Holland Ri. Ho. SW9 —3B 66
(off Clapham Rd.)
Holland Rd. E15 —2A 44
Holland Rd. NW10 —5C 18
Holland Rd. W14 —3F 47
Holland St. SE1 —2D 53
Holland St. W8 —3C 48
Holland Vs. Rd. W14 —3A 48
Holland Wlk. N19 —3F 9
Holland Wlk. W8 —2B 48
(off Holland Pk. Av.)
Hollar Rd. N16 —5B 12
Hollen St. W1 —5F 37
Holles Ho. SW9 —5C 66
Holles St. W1 —5D 37
Holley Rd. W3 —3A 46
Holliday Sq. SW11 —1F 77
(off Fowler Clo.)
Hollies, The. E11 —1C 16
(off New Wanstead)
Hollies Way. SW12 —5C 78
Hollingbourne Rd. SE24 —3E 81
Hollins Ho. N7 —1A 24
Hollisfield. WC1 —2A 38
(off Cromer St.)
Holloway. —5A 10
Holloway Ho. NW2 —5E 5
Holloway Rd. E11 —5F 15
Holloway Rd. N19 & N7 —4F 9
Hollyberry La. NW3 —1E 21
Hollybush Clo. E11 —1C 16
Hollybush Gdns. E2 —2D 41
Hollybush Hill. E11 —1B 16
Hollybush Hill. NW3 —1E 21
Hollybush Ho. E2 —2D 41
Hollybush Pl. E2 —2D 41
Hollybush Steps. NW3
(off Holly Mt.) —1E 21
Hollybush St. E13 —2D 45
Holly Bush Va. NW3 —1E 21
Hollybush Wlk. SW9 —2D 81
Holly Clo. NW10 —4A 18
Hollycroft Av. NW3 —5C 6
Hollydale Rd. SE15 —4E 69
Holly Dene. SE15 —4D 69
Hollydown Way. E11 —5F 15
Holly Gro. SE15 —5B 68
Holly Hedge Ter. SE13 —3F 85
Holly Hill. NW3 —1E 21
Holly Ho. W10 —3A 34
(off Hawthorn Wlk.)
Holly Lodge Gdns. N6 —4C 8
Holly Lodge Mans. N6 —4C 8
Holly M. SW10 —1E 63
(off Drayton Gdns.)
Holly Mt. NW3 —1E 21
Hollymount Clo. SE10 —4E 71
Holly Pk. N4 —2A 10
(in two parts)
Holly Pk. Est. N4 —2B 10
Holly Pl. NW3 —1E 21
(off Holly Berry La.)
Holly Rd. E11 —2B 16
Holly Rd. W4 —5A 46
Holly St. E8 —4B 26
Holly Ter. N6 —3C 8
Holly Tree Clo. SW19 —1F 89
Holly Tree Ho. SE4 —1B 84
(off Brockley Rd.)
Holly Vw. Clo. NW4 —1C 4
Holly Village. N6 —4D 9
Holly Wlk. NW3 —1E 21
Hollywood M. SW10 —2E 63
Hollywood Rd. SW10 —2E 63
Holman Hunt Ho. W6 —1A 62
(off Field Rd.)
Holman Rd. SW11 —5F 63
Holmbrook. NW1 —1E 37
(off Eversholt St.)
Holmbrook Dri. NW4 —1F 5
Holmbury Ct. SW17 —3B 92
Holmbury Ho. SE24 —3D 81
Holmbury Vw. E5 —3D 13
Holmbush Rd. SW15 —4A 76
Holmcote Gdns. N5 —2E 25
Holm Ct. SE12 —3D 101
Holmdale Gdns. NW4 —1F 5
Holmdale Rd. NW6 —2C 20
Holmdale Ter. N15 —2A 12
Holmdene Av. SE24 —3E 81
Holmead Rd. SW6 —3D 63
Holme Lacey Rd. SE12 —4B 86
Holme Rd. E6 —5F 31
Holmesdale Ho. NW6 —5C 20
(off Kilburn Va.)
Holmesdale Rd. N6 —2D 9
Holmesley Rd. SE23 —4A 84
Holmes Pl. SW10 —2E 63
Holmes Rd. NW5 —2D 23
Holmes Ter. SE1 —3C 52
(off Waterloo Rd.)
Holmewood Gdns. SW2 —5B 80
Holmewood Rd. SW2 —5A 80
Holmfield Av. NW4 —1F 5
Holmfield Ct. NW3 —2A 22
Holmleigh Rd. N16 —3A 12
Holmleigh Rd. Est. N16 —3A 12
Holmoak Clo. SW15 —4B 76
Holm Oak M. SW4 —3A 80
Holmsdale Ho. E14 —1D 57
Holmshaw Clo. SE26 -
Holmside Rd. SW12 -

Holmsley Ho. SW15 —5B 74 (off Tangley Gro.)
Holm Wlk. SE3 —5C 72
Holmwood Vs. SE7 —1C 72
Holne Chase. N2 —1E 7
Holness Rd. E15 —3B 30
Holroyd Rd. SW15 —2E 75
Holst Ct. SE1 —4C 52 (off Westminster Bri. Rd.)
Holst Mans. SW13 —2E 61
Holsworthy Sq. WC1 —3B 38 (off Elm St.)
Holt Ct. E15 —2E 29
Holt Ho. SW2 —4C 80
Holton St. E1 —3F 41
Holwood Pl. SW4 —2F 79
Holybourne Av. SW15 —5C 74
Holyhead Clo. E3 —2C 42
Holy Oake Ct. SE16 —3B 56
Holyoak Rd. SE11 —5D 53
Holyport Rd. SW6 —3F 61
Holyrood M. E16 —2C 58 (off Badminton M.)
Holyrood St. SE1 —2A 54
Holywell Clo. SE3 —2C 72
Holywell Clo. SE16 —1D 69
Holywell La. EC2 —3A 40
Holywell Row. EC2 —3A 40
Homecroft Rd. SE26 —5E 97
Homefield Ct. SW16 —3A 94
Homefield Ho. SE23 —3F 97
Homefield Rd. SW19 —5F 89
Homefield Rd. W4 —5B 46
Homefield St. N1 —1A 40
Homeleigh Rd. SE15 —3F 83
Home Pk. Rd. SW19 —4B 90
Homer Dri. E14 —5C 56
Home Rd. SW11 —5A 64
Homer Rd. E9 —3A 28
Homer Row. W1 —4A 36
Homer St. NW1 —4A 36
Homerton. —2F 27
Homerton Gro. E9 —2F 27
Homerton High St. E9 —2F 27
Homerton Rd. E9 —2A 28
Homerton Row. E9 —2E 27
Homerton Ter. E9 —3E 27 (in two parts)
Homesdale Clo. E11 —1C 16
Homestall Rd. SE22 —3E 83
Homestead Pk. NW2 —5B 4
Homestead Rd. SW6 —3B 62
Homewoods. SW12 —5E 79
Homildon Ho. SE26 —3C 96
Honduras St. EC1 —3E 39
Honeybourne Rd. NW6 —2D 21
Honeybrook Rd. SW12 —5E 79
Honey La. EC2 —5E 39 (off Trump St.)
Honeyman Clo. NW6 —4F 19 (in two parts)
Honeywell Rd. SW11 —4B 78
Honeywood Rd. NW10 —1B 32
Honiton Gdns. SE15 —5E 69 (off Gibbon Rd.)
Honiton Rd. NW6 —1B 34
Honley Rd. SE6 —5D 85
Honor Oak. —4E 83
Honor Oak Crematorium. SE23 —3A 84
Honor Oak Park. —5A 84
Honor Oak Pk. SE23 —4E 83
Honor Oak Ri. SE23 —4E 83
Honor Oak Rd. SE23 —1E 97
Hood Ct. EC4 —5C 38 (off Fleet St.)
Hood Ho. SE5 —3F 67 (off Elmington Est.)
Hood Ho. SW1 —1F 65 (off Dolphin Sq.)
Hookham Ct. SW8 —4F 65
Hooks Clo. SE15 —4D 69
Hooks Way. SE22 —1C 96
Hooper Rd. E16 —5C 44
Hooper's Ct. SW3 —3B 50
Hooper Sq. E1 —5C 40 (off Hooper St.)
Hooper St. E1 —5C 40
Hoop La. NW11 —2B 6 (in two parts)
Hope Clo. N1 —3E 25
Hope Clo. SE12 —3D 101
Hopedale Rd. SE7 —2D 73
Hopefield Av. NW6 —1A 34
Hope St. SW11 —1F 77
Hopetown St. E1 —4B 40
Hopewell St. SE5 —3F 67
Hope Wharf. SE16 —3E 55
Hop Gdns. WC2 —1A 52
Hopgood St. W12 —2E 47
Hopkins Ho. E14 —5C 42
Hopkins M. E15 —5B 30
Hopkinsons Pl. NW1 —5C 22
Hopkins St. W1 —5E 37
Hopping La. N1 —3D 25
Hopton Rd. SW16 —5A 94
Hopton's Gdns. SE1 —2D 53 (off Hopton St.)
Hopton St. SE1 —2D 53
Hopwood Clo. SW17 —3E 91
Hopwood Rd. SE17 —2F 67
Hopwood Wlk. E8 —4C 26
Horace Rd. E7 —1D 31
Horatio Ct. SE16 —2E 55 (off Rotherhithe St.)
Horatio Ho. E2 —1B 40 (off Horatio St.)
Horatio Pl. E14 —3E 57 (off Preston's Rd.)
Horatio St. E2 —1B 40 (in two parts)
Horbury Cres. W11 —1C 48
Horbury M. W11 —1B 48
Horder Rd. SW6 —4A 62
Hordle Promenade E. SE15 —3B 68
Hordle Promenade N. SE15 —3B 68
Hordle Promenade S. SE15 (off Quarley Way) —3B 68
Hordle Promenade W. SE15 (off Clanfield Way) —3A 68
Horizon Building. E14 (off Hertsmere Rd.) —1C 56
Horizon Way. SE7 —5D 59
Horle Wlk. SW9 —5D 67
Horley Rd. SE9 —4F 101
Hormead Rd. W9 —3B 34
Hornbeam Clo. SE11 —5C 52
Hornblower Clo. SE16 —4A 56
Hornby Clo. NW3 —4F 21
Hornby Ho. SE11 —2C 66 (off Clayton St.)
Horncastle Clo. SE12 —5C 86
Horncastle Rd. SE12 —5C 86
Horndean Clo. SW15 —1C 88
Horner Ho. N1 —5A 26 (off Whitmore Est.)
Horne Way. SW15 —5E 61
Hornfair Rd. SE7 —2E 73
Horniman Clo. SE10 —4A 58
Horniman Dri. SE23 —1D 97
Horniman Mus. —1D 97
Horn La. SE10 —1C 72 (in three parts)
Horn Park. —3D 87
Horn Pk. Clo. SE12 —3D 87
Hornpark La. SE12 —3D 87
Hornsey La. N6 —3D 9
Hornsey La. Est. N19 —2F 9
Hornsey La. Gdns. N6 —2E 9
Hornsey Ri. N19 —2F 9
Hornsey Ri. Gdns. N19 —2F 9
Hornsey Rd. N19 & N7 —3A 10
Hornsey St. N7 —2B 24
Hornsey Vale. —1B 10
Hornshay St. SE15 —2E 69
Hornton Ct. W8 —3C 48 (off Kensington High St.)
Hornton Pl. W8 —3D 49
Hornton St. W8 —3C 48
Horsa Rd. SE12 —5E 87
Horse & Dolphin Yd. W1 (off Macclesfield St.) —1F 51
Horseferry Pl. SE10 —2E 71
Horseferry Rd. E14 —1A 56
Horseferry Rd. SW1 —4F 51
Horseferry Rd. Est. SW1 (off Horseferry Rd.) —4F 51
Horseguards Av. SW1 —2A 52
Horse Guards Rd. SW1 —2F 51
Horsell Rd. N5 —2C 24 (in two parts)
Horselydown La. SE1 —3B 54
Horselydown Mans. SE1 (off Lafone St.) —3B 54
Horsemongers M. SE1 (off Cole St.) —3E 53
Horse Ride. SW1 —2E 51 (off Mall, The)
Horseshoe Clo. E14 —1E 71
Horseshoe Clo. NW2 —4D 5
Horseshoe Wharf. SE1 (off Clink St.) —2F 53

Horse Yd. N1 —5D 25
(off Essex Rd.)
Horsfeld Gdns. SE9 —3F 87
Horsfeld Rd. SE9 —3F 87
Horsfield Ho. N1 —4E 25
(off Northampton St.)
Horsford Rd. SW2 —3B 80
Horsley St. SE17 —2F 67
Horsman Ho. SE5 —2E 67
(off Bethwin Rd.)
Horsman St. SE5 —2E 67
Horsmonden Rd. SE4 —3B 84
Hortensia Ho. SW10 —3E 63
(off Hortensia Rd.)
Hortensia Rd. SW10 —3E 63
Horton Av. NW2 —1A 20
Horton Ho. SE15 —2E 69
Horton Ho. SW8 —3B 66
Horton Ho. W6 —1A 62
(off Field Rd.)
Horton Rd. E8 —3D 27
Horton St. SE13 —1D 85
Horwood Ho. NW8 —3A 36
(off Paveley St.)
Hosack Rd. SW17 —2C 92
Hoser Av. SE12 —2C 100
Hosier La. EC1 —4D 39
Hoskins Clo. E16 —5E 45
Hoskins St. SE10 —1F 71
Hospital Rd. E9 —2F 27
Hospital Way. SE13 —5F 85
Hotham Rd. SW15 —1E 75
Hotham St. E15 —5A 30
Hothfield Pl. SE16 —4E 55
Hotspur St. SE11 —5C 52
Houghton Clo. E8 —3B 26
Houghton St. WC2 —5B 38
(in two parts)
Houndsditch. EC3 —5A 40
Houseman Way. SE5 —3F 67
Houses of Parliament. —4A 52
Houston Rd. SE23 —2A 98
Hove Av. E17 —1B 14
Hoveden Rd. NW2 —2A 20
Howard Clo. NW2 —1A 20
Howard Ho. SE8 —2B 70
(off Evelyn St.)
Howard Ho. SW1 —1E 65
(off Dolphin Sq.)
Howard Ho. SW9 —1D 81
(off Barrington Rd.)
Howard Ho. W1 —3D 37
(off Cleveland St.)
Howard M. N5 —1D 25
Howard Rd. E11 —5A 16
Howard Rd. N15 —1A 12
Howard Rd. N16 —1F 25
Howard Rd. NW2 —1F 19
Howard's La. SW15 —2D 75
Howards Rd. E13 —2C 44
Howard Way. SE22 —5C 82
Howarth Ct. E15 —2D 29
Howbury Rd. SE15 —1E 83
Howden St. SE15 —1C 82
Howell Ct. E10 —2D 15
Howell Wlk. SE17 —5D 53
Howick Pl. SW1 —4E 51
Howie St. SW11 —3A 64
Howitt Clo. N16 —1A 26
Howitt Clo. NW3 —3A 22
Howitt Rd. NW3 —3A 22
Howland Est. SE16 —4E 55
Howland Ho. SW16 —3A 94
Howland M. E. W1 —4E 37
Howland St. W1 —4E 37
Howland Way. SE16 —3A 56
Howlett's Rd. SE24 —4E 81
Howley Pl. W2 —4E 35
Howsman Rd. SW13 —2C 60
Howson Rd. SE4 —2A 84
How's St. E2 —1B 40
Hoxton. —1A 40
Hoxton Mkt. N1 —2A 40
(off Coronet St.)
Hoxton Sq. N1 —2A 40
Hoxton St. N1 —5A 26
Hoylake Rd. W3 —5A 32
Hoyland Clo. SE15 —3D 69
Hoyle Rd. SW17 —5A 92
Hoy St. E16 —5B 44
Hubbard Rd. SE27 —4E 95
Hubbard St. E15 —5A 30
Huberd Ho. SE1 —4F 53
(off Manciple St.)
Hubert Gro. SW9 —1A 80
Hubert Ho. NW8 —3A 36
Hubert Rd. E6 —2F 45
Hucknall Ct. NW8 —3F 35
(off Cunningham Pl.)
Huddart St. E3 —4B 42
(in two parts)
Huddleston Clo. E2 —1E 41
Huddlestone Rd. E7 —1B 30
Huddlestone Rd. NW2 —3D 19
Huddleston Rd. N7 —5E 9
Hudson Clo. W12 —1D 47
Hudson Ct. E14 —1C 70
Hudson's Pl. SW1 —5D 51
(off Bridge Pl.)
Huggin Ct. EC4 —1E 53
(off Huggin Hill)
Huggin Hill. EC4 —1E 53
Huggins Pl. SW2 —1B 94
Hughan Rd. E15 —2F 29
Hugh Astor Ct. SE1 —4D 53
(off Keyworth St.)
Hugh Dalton Av. SW6 —2B 62
Hughenden Ho. NW8 —3A 36
(off Jerome Cres.)
Hughendon Ter. E15 —1E 29
Hughes Ct. N7 —2F 23
Hughes Ho. E2 —2E 41
(off Sceptre Ho.)
Hughes Ho. SE8 —2C 70
(off Benbow St.)
Hughes Ho. SE17 —5D 53
(off Peacock St.)
Hughes Mans. E1 —3C 40
Hughes M. SW11 —3B 78
Hughes Ter. E16 —4B 44
(off Clarkson Rd.)
Hugh Gaitskell Clo. SW6 —2B 62
Hugh Gaitskell Ho. N16 —4B 12
Hugh M. SW1 —5D 51
Hugh Platt Ho. E2 —1D 41
(off Patriot Sq.)
Hugh St. SW1 —5D 51
Hugon Rd. SW6 —1D 77
Hugo Rd. N19 —1E 23
Huguenot Pl. E1 —4B 40
Huguenot Pl. SW18 —3E 77
Huguenot Sq. SE15 —1D 83
Hullbridge M. N1 —5F 25
Hull Clo. SE16 —3F 55
Hull St. EC1 —2E 39
Hulme Ho. W11 —2F 47
Hulme Pl. SE1 —3E 53
Humber Dri. W10 —3F 33
Humber Rd. NW2 —4D 5
Humber Rd. SE3 —2B 72
Humberstone Rd. E13 —2E 45
Humberton Clo. E9 —2A 28
Humbolt Rd. W6 —2A 62
Hume Ct. N1 —4D 25
(off Hawes St.)
Hume Ho. W11 —2F 47
(off Queensdale Cres.)
Hume Ter. E16 —4D 45
Humphrey St. SE1 —1B 68
Hungerford Ho. SW1 —2E 65
(off Churchill Gdns.)
Hungerford La. WC2 —2A 52
(off Craven St., in two parts)
Hungerford Rd. N7 —3F 23
Hungerford St. E1 —5D 41
Hunsdon Rd. SE14 —3F 69
Hunslett St. E2 —2E 41
Hunstanton Ho. NW1 —4A 36
(off Cosway St.)
Hunter Clo. SE1 —4F 53
Hunter Ho. SE1 —3D 53
(off Lancaster St.)
Hunter Ho. SW5 —1C 62
(off Old Brompton Rd.)
Hunter Ho. SW8 —3F 65
Hunter Ho. WC1 —3A 38
(off Hunter St.)
Hunter Lodge. W9 —4C 34
(off Admiral Wlk.)
Hunters Clo. SW12 —1C 92
Hunters Mdw. SE19 —4A 96
Hunter St. WC1 —3A 38
Hunter Wlk. E13 —1C 44
Huntingdon St. E16 —5B 44
Huntingdon St. N1 —4B 24
Huntingfield Rd. SW15 —2C 74
Huntley St. WC1 —3E 37
Hunton St. E1 —4C 40
Hunt's Clo. SE3 —5C 72
Hunt's Ct. WC2 —1F 51
Hunts La. E15 —1E 43
Huntsman St. SE17 —5A 54
Huntspill St. SW17 —3E 91
Hunts Slip Rd. SE21 —3A 96
Hunt St. W11 —2F 47

Huntsworth M. *NW1* —3B **36**
Hunt Way. *SE22* —1C **96**
Hurdwick Pl. *NW1* —1E **37**
(off Hampstead Rd.)
Hurleston Ho. *SE8* —1B **70**
Hurley Cres. *SE16* —3F **55**
Hurley Ho. *SE11* —5D **53**
Hurlingham. —1D **77**
Hurlingham Bus. Pk. *SW6*
—1C **76**
Hurlingham Ct. *SW6* —1B **76**
Hurlingham Gdns. *SW6*
—1B **76**
Hurlingham Retail Pk. *SW6*
—1D **77**
Hurlingham Rd. *SW6* —5B **62**
Hurlingham Sq. *SW6* —1C **76**
Hurlock St. *N5* —5D **11**
Huron Rd. *SW17* —2C **92**
Hurren Clo. *SE3* —1A **86**
Hurry Clo. *E15* —4A **30**
Hurst Av. *N6* —1E **9**
Hurstbourne Ho. *SW15*
(off Tangley Gro.) —4B **74**
Hurstbourne Rd. *SE23*
—1A **98**
Hurst Clo. *NW11* —1D **7**
Hurst Ct. *E6* —4F **45**
(off Tollgate Rd.)
Hurstdene Gdns. *N15* —2A **12**
Hurst Ho. *WC1* —1B **38**
(off Penton Ri.)
Hurst St. *SE24* —4D **81**
Hurstway Wlk. *W11* —1F **47**
Husborne Ho. *SE8* —5A **56**
(off Chilton Gro.)
Huson Clo. *NW3* —4A **22**
Hutchings St. *E14* —3C **56**
Hutchins Clo. *E15* —4E **29**
Hutchinson Ho. *SE14*
—3E **69**
Hutton Ct. *N4* —3B **10**
(off Victoria Rd.)
Hutton St. *EC4* —5D **39**
Huxbear St. *SE4* —3B **84**
Huxley Ho. *NW8* —3F **35**
(off Fisherton St.)
Huxley Rd. *E10* —4E **15**
Huxley St. *W10* —2A **34**
Hyacinth Rd. *SW15* —1C **88**
Hyde Clo. *E13* —1C **44**
Hyde Cres. *NW9* —1A **4**
Hyde Est. Rd. *NW9* —1B **4**
Hyde Farm M. *SW12* —1F **93**
Hyde Ind. Est., The. *NW9*
—1B **4**
Hyde La. *SW11* —4A **64**
Hyde Pk. —2F **49**
Hyde Park Corner. (Junct.)
—3C **50**
Hyde Pk. Corner. *W1* —3C **50**
Hyde Pk. Cres. *W2* —5A **36**
Hyde Pk. Gdns. *W2* —1F **49**
Hyde Pk. Gdns. M. *W2*
(in two parts) —1F **49**
Hyde Pk. Ga. *SW7* —3E **49**
(in two parts)

Hyde Pk. Ga. M. *SW7* —3E **49**
Hyde Pk. Mans. *NW1* —4A **36**
(off Cabbell St.)
Hyde Pk. Pl. *W2* —1A **50**
Hyde Pk. Sq. *W2* —5A **36**
Hyde Pk. Sq. M. *W2* —5A **36**
(off Southwick Pl.)
Hyde Pk. St. *W2* —5A **36**
Hyde Pk. Towers. *W2* —1E **49**
Hyderbad Way. *E15* —4A **30**
Hyde Rd. *N1* —5A **26**
Hydes Pl. *N1* —4D **25**
Hyde St. *SE8* —2C **70**
Hyde, The. —1B **4**
Hyde, The. *NW9* —1B **4**
Hydethorpe Rd. *SW12*
—1E **93**
Hyde Va. *SE10* —3E **71**
Hydra Building, The. *EC1*
(off Amwell St.) —2C **38**
Hyndewood. *SE23* —3F **97**
Hyndman St. *SE15* —2D **69**
Hyperion Ho. *SW2* —4B **80**
Hyson Rd. *SE16* —1D **69**
Hythe Ho. *SE16* —3E **55**
(off Swan Rd.)
Hythe Rd. *NW10* —2B **32**
Hythe Rd. Ind. Est. *NW10*
—2C **32**

Ian Bowater Ct. *N1* —2F **39**
(off East Rd.)
Ian Ct. *SE23* —2E **97**
Ibberton Ho. *SW8* —3B **66**
(off Meadow Rd.)
Ibberton Ho. *W14* —4A **48**
(off Russell Rd.)
Ibbotson Av. *E16* —5B **44**
Ibbott St. *E1* —3E **41**
Iberia Ho. *N19* —2F **9**
Ibis Ct. *SE8* —2B **70**
(off Edward Pl.)
Ibsley Gdns. *SW15* —1C **88**
Iceland Rd. *E3* —5C **28**
Ice Wharf Marina. *N1* —1A **38**
(off New Wharf Rd.)
Ickburgh Est. *E5* —5D **13**
Ickburgh Rd. *E5* —5D **13**
Icknield Ho. *SW3* —1A **64**
(off Marlborough St.)
Ida St. *E14* —5E **43**
(in three parts)
Idlecombe Rd. *SW17* —5C **92**
Idmiston Rd. *E15* —1B **30**
Idmiston Rd. *SE27* —3E **95**
Idol La. *EC3* —1A **54**
Idonia St. *SE8* —3C **70**
Iffley Rd. *W6* —4D **47**
Ifield Rd. *SW10* —2D **63**
Ifor Evans Pl. *E1* —3F **41**
Ightham Ho. *SE17* —5A **54**
(off Comus Pl.)
Ilbert St. *W10* —2F **33**
Ilchester Gdns. *W2* —1D **45**
Ilchester Pl. *W14* —4B **48**
Ildersly Gro. *SE21* —2F **95**

Ilderton Rd. *SE16 & SE15*
—1E **69**
Ilderton Wharf. *SE15* —2E **69**
(off Rollins St.)
Ilex Rd. *NW10* —3B **18**
Ilex Way. *SW16* —5C **94**
Ilford Ho. *N1* —3F **25**
(off Dove Rd.)
Ilfracombe Flats. *SE1* —3E **53**
(off Marshalsea Rd.)
Ilfracombe Rd. *Brom* —3B **100**
Iliffe St. *SE17* —1D **67**
Iliffe Yd. *SE17* —1D **67**
(off Crampton St.)
Ilkeston Ct. *E5* —1F **27**
(off Clapton Pk. Est.)
Ilkley Rd. *E16* —4E **45**
Ilminster Gdns. *SW11* —2A **78**
Imani Mans. *SW11* —5F **63**
IMAX Cinema. —2C **52**
Imber St. *N1* —5F **25**
Imperial Av. *N16* —1A **26**
Imperial College Rd. *SW7*
—4F **49**
Imperial Ct. *N6* —1E **9**
Imperial Ct. *NW8* —1A **36**
(off Prince Albert Rd.)
Imperial Ct. *SE11* —1C **66**
Imperial M. *E6* —1F **45**
Imperial Pde. *EC4* —5D **39**
(off New Bri. St.)
Imperial Rd. *SW6* —4D **63**
Imperial Sq. *SW6* —4D **63**
Imperial St. *E3* —2E **43**
Imperial War Mus. —4C **52**
Imre Clo. *W12* —2D **47**
Inchmery Rd. *SE6* —2D **99**
Independent Pl. *E8* —2B **26**
Independents Rd. *SE3* —1B **86**
Inderwick Rd. *N8* —1B **10**
Indescon Ct. *E14* —3C **56**
India Pl. *WC2* —1B **52**
(off Montreal Pl.)
India St. *EC3* —5B **40**
India Way. *W12* —1D **47**
Indigo M. *E14* —5E **43**
Indigo M. *N16* —5F **11**
Indus Rd. *SE7* —3E **73**
Infirmary Ct. *SW3* —2B **64**
(off West Rd.)
Ingal Rd. *E13* —3C **44**
Ingate Pl. *SW8* —4D **65**
Ingatestone Rd. *E12* —3E **17**
Ingelow Ho. *W8* —3D **49**
(off Holland St.)
Ingelow Rd. *SW8* —5D **65**
Ingersoll Rd. *W12* —2D **47**
Ingestre Pl. *W1* —5E **37**
Ingestre Rd. *E7* —1C **30**
Ingestre Rd. *NW5* —1D **23**
Ingham Rd. *NW6* —1C **20**
Inglebert St. *EC1* —2C **38**
Ingleborough St. *SW9* —5C **66**
Ingleby Rd. *N7* —5A **10**
Inglefield Sq. *E1* —2D **55**
(off Prusom St.)
Inglemere Rd. *SE23* —3F **97**

Inglesham Wlk. *E9* —3B **28**
Ingleside Gro. *SE3* —2B **72**
Inglethorpe St. *SW6* —4F **61**
Ingleton St. *SW9* —5C **66**
Inglewood Clo. *E14* —5C **56**
Inglewood Rd. *NW6* —2C **20**
Inglis St. *SE5* —4D **67**
Ingoldisthorpe Gro. *SE15*
—2B **68**
Ingram Av. *NW11* —2E **7**
Ingram Clo. *SE11* —5B **52**
Ingram Ho. *E3* —3A **28**
Ingrave St. *SW11* —1F **77**
Ingrebourne Ho. *NW8* —4F **35**
(off Broadley St.)
Ingrebourne Ho. Brom —5F **99**
(off Brangbourne Rd.)
Ingress St. *W4* —1A **60**
Inigo Jones Rd. *SE7* —3F **73**
Inigo Pl. *WC2* —1A **52**
(off Bedford St.)
Inkerman Rd. *NW5* —3D **23**
Inkerman Ter. *W8* —4C **48**
(off Allen St.)
Inman Rd. *NW10* —5A **18**
Inman Rd. *SW18* —5E **77**
Inner Circ. *NW1* —2C **36**
Inner Pk. Rd. *SW19* —1F **89**
Inner Temple Hall. —5C **38**
(off Middle Temple La.)
Inner Temple La. *EC4* —5C **38**
Innes Gdns. *SW15* —4D **75**
Innis Ho. *SE17* —1A **68**
(off East St.)
Inniskilling Rd. *E13* —1E **45**
Innovation Cen., The. *E14*
—3E **57**
Inskip Clo. *E10* —4D **15**
Institute Pl. *E8* —2D **27**
Integer Gdns. *E11* —2F **15**
International Ho. *E1* —1B **54**
(off St Katharine's Way)
Inver Clo. *E5* —4E **13**
Inver Ct. *W2* —5D **35**
Inverforth Clo. *NW3* —4E **7**
Invergarry Ho. *W9* —1D **35**
(off Carlton Va.)
Inverine Rd. *SE7* —1D **73**
Inverness Ct. *SE6* —1B **100**
Inverness Gdns. *W8* —2D **49**
Inverness M. *W2* —1D **49**
Inverness Pl. *W2* —1D **49**
Inverness St. *NW1* —5D **23**
Inverness Ter. *W2* —5D **35**
Inverton Rd. *SE15* —2F **83**
Invicta Plaza. *SE1* —2D **53**
Invicta Rd. *SE3* —3C **72**
Inville Rd. *SE17* —1F **67**
Inville Wlk. *SE17* —1F **67**
Inwen Ct. *SE8* —1A **70**
Inwood Ct. *NW1* —4E **23**
(off Rochester Sq.)
Inworth St. *SW11* —5A **64**
Inworth Wlk. *N1* —5E **25**
(off Popham St.)
Iona Clo. *SE6* —5C **84**
Ion Ct. *E2* —1C **40**

Ionian Building. *E14* —1A **56**
Ion Sq. *E2* —1C **40**
Ipsden Bldgs. *SE1* —3C **52**
(off Great St.)
Ipswich Ho. *SE4* —3F **83**
Ireland Yd. *EC4* —5D **39**
Irene Rd. *SW6* —4C **62**
Ireton Ho. *SW9* —5C **66**
Ireton St. *E3* —2C **42**
Iris Ct. *SE14* —4E **69**
(off Briant St.)
Iron Bri. Clo. *NW10* —2A **18**
Iron Mill Pl. *SW18* —4D **77**
Iron Mill Rd. *SW18* —4D **77**
Ironmonger La. *EC2* —5E **39**
Ironmonger Pas. *EC1* —2E **39**
(off Ironmonger Row)
Ironmonger Row. *EC1*
—2E **39**
Ironmongers Pl. *E14* —5C **56**
Ironside Clo. *SE16* —3F **55**
Ironside Ho. *E9* —1A **28**
Irvine Ho. *E14* —4D **43**
Irvine Ho. *N7* —3B **24**
(off Caledonian Rd.)
Irving Gro. *SW9* —5B **66**
Irving Ho. *SE17* —1D **67**
(off Doddington Gro.)
Irving Mans. *W14* —2A **62**
(off Queen's Club Gdns.)
Irving M. *N1* —3E **25**
Irving Rd. *W14* —4F **47**
Irving St. *WC2* —1C **52**
Irving Way. *NW9* —1C **4**
Irwell Est. *SE16* —4E **55**
Irwin Gdns. *NW10* —5D **19**
Isabella Ho. *SE11* —1D **67**
(off Othello Clo.)
Isabella Rd. *E9* —2E **27**
Isabella St. *SE1* —2D **53**
Isabel St. *SW9* —4B **66**
Isambard M. *E14* —4E **57**
Isambard Pl. *SE16* —2E **55**
Isel Way. *SE22* —3A **82**
Isis Clo. *SW15* —2E **75**
Isis Ho. *NW8* —3F **35**
(off Church St. Est.)
Isis St. *SW18* —2E **91**
Island Row. *E14* —5B **42**
Islay Wlk. *N1* —3E **25**
Isleden Ho. *N1* —5E **25**
(off Prebend St.)
Isledon Rd. *N7* —5C **10**
Isleton Village. —5C **10**
Isley Ct. *SW8* —5C **65**
Islington. —4D **25**
Islington Grn. *N1* —5D **25**
Islington High St. *N1* —1C **38**
(in two parts)
Islington Pk. M. *N1* —4D **25**
Islington Pk. St. *N1* —4C **24**
Islip St. *NW5* —2E **23**
Ismailia Rd. *E7* —4D **31**
Isom Clo. *E13* —2D **45**
Ivanhoe Rd. *SE5* —1B **82**
Ivatt Pl. *W14* —1B **62**
Iveagh Clo. *E9* —5F **27**

Iveagh Ct. *EC3* —5B **40**
(off Haydon Wlk.)
Iveagh Ho. *SW9* —5D **67**
Iveagh Ho. *SW10* —3E **63**
(off King's Rd.)
Ive Farm Clo. *E10* —4C **14**
Ive Farm La. *E10* —4C **14**
Iveley Rd. *SW4* —5E **65**
Iverna Ct. *W8* —4C **48**
Iverna Gdns. *W8* —4C **48**
Iverson Rd. *NW6* —3B **20**
Ives Rd. *E16* —4A **44**
Ives St. *SW3* —5A **50**
Ivestor Ter. *SE23* —5E **83**
Ivimey St. *E2* —2C **40**
Ivinghoe Ho. *N7* —2F **23**
Ivor Ct. *N8* —1A **10**
Ivor Ct. *NW1* —3B **36**
(off Gloucester Pl.)
Ivories, The. *N1* —4E **25**
(off Northampton St.)
Ivor Pl. *NW1* —3B **36**
Ivor St. *NW1* —4E **23**
Ivorydown. Brom —4C **100**
Ivory Ho. *E1* —2B **54**
Ivory Sq. *SW11* —1E **77**
Ivybridge La. *WC2* —1A **52**
Ivychurch La. *SE17* —1B **68**
Ivy Cotts. *E14* —1D **57**
Ivy Ct. *SE16* —1C **68**
(off Argyle Way)
Ivydale Rd. *SE15* —1F **83**
Ivyday Gro. *SW16* —3B **94**
Ivy Gdns. *N8* —1A **10**
Ivymount Rd. *SE27* —3C **94**
Ivy Rd. *E16* —5C **44**
Ivy Rd. *E17* —1C **14**
Ivy Rd. *NW2* —1E **19**
Ivy Rd. *SE4* —2B **84**
Ivy Rd. *SW17* —5A **92**
Ivy St. *N1* —1A **40**
Ixworth Pl. *SW3* —1A **64**

Jacaranda Gro. *E8* —4B **26**
Jack Clow Rd. *E15* —1A **44**
Jack Dash Ho. *E14* —3E **57**
Jack Dash Way. *E6* —3F **45**
Jackman Ho. *E1* —2D **55**
(off Watts St.)
Jackman M. *NW10* —5A **4**
Jackman St. *E8* —5D **27**
Jackson Clo. *E9* —4E **27**
Jackson Ct. *E7* —3D **31**
Jackson Rd. *N7* —1B **24**
Jacksons La. *N6* —2C **8**
Jack Walker Ct. *N5* —1D **25**
Jacobin Lodge. *N7* —2A **24**
Jacobs Ho. *E13* —2E **45**
(off New City Rd.)
Jacob St. *SE1* —3C **54**
Jacob's Well M. *W1* —4C **36**
Jacqueline Creft Ter. *N6*
(off Grange Rd.)   —1C **8**
Jade Clo. *E16* —5F **45**
Jade Clo. *NW2* —2F **5**
Jade Ter. *NW6* —4E **21**

Jaffray Pl. *SE27* —4D **95**
Jaggard Way. *SW12* —5B **78**
Jagger Ho. *SW11* —4B **64**
(off Worfield St.)
Jago Wlk. *SE5* —3F **67**
Jamaica Rd. *SE1 & SE16*
—3B **54**
Jamaica St. *E1* —5E **41**
James Anderson Ct. *N1*
(off Kingsland Rd.) —1A **40**
James Av. *NW2* —2E **19**
James Boswell Clo. *SW16*
—4B **94**
James Brine Ho. *E2* —2B **40**
(off Ravenscroft St.)
James Campbell Ho. *E2*
(off Old Ford Rd.) —1E **41**
James Clo. *E13* —1C **44**
James Clo. *NW11* —1A **6**
James Collins Clo. *W9*
—3B **34**
James Ct. *N1* —5E **25**
(off Raynor Pl.)
James Docherty Ho. *E2*
(off Patriot Sq.) —1D **41**
James Hammett Ho. *E2*
(off Ravenscroft St.) —2B **40**
James Joyce Wlk. *SE24*
—2D **81**
James La. *E10 & E11* —2E **15**
James Lind Ho. *SE8* —5B **56**
(off Grove St.)
James Middleton Ho. *E2*
(off Middleton St.) —2D **41**
Jameson Ct. *E2* —1E **41**
(off Russia La.)
Jameson Ho. *SE11* —1B **66**
(off Glasshouse Wlk.)
Jameson Lodge. *N6* —1E **9**
Jameson St. *W8* —2C **48**
James Stewart Ho. *NW6*
—4B **20**
James St. *W1* —5C **36**
James St. *WC2* —1A **52**
James Stroud Ho. *SE17*
(off Bronti Clo.) —1E **67**
James Ter. *SW14* —1A **74**
(off Church Path)
Jamestown Rd. *NW1* —5D **23**
Jamestown Way. *E14* —1F **57**
Jamuna Clo. *E14* —4A **42**
Jane Austen Hall. *E16* —2D **59**
(off Wesley Av., in two parts)
Jane Austen Ho. *SW1* —1E **65**
(off Churchill Gdns.)
Jane St. *E1* —5D **41**
Janet St. *E14* —4C **56**
Janeway Pl. *SE16* —3D **55**
Janeway St. *SE16* —3C **54**
Jansen Wlk. *SW11* —1F **77**
Janson Clo. *E15* —2A **30**
Janson Clo. *NW10* —5A **4**
Janson Rd. *E15* —2A **30**
Japan Cres. *N4* —3B **10**
Jardine Rd. *E1* —1F **55**
Jarman Ho. *E1* —4E **41**
(off Jubilee St.)

Jarman Ho. *SE16* —5F **55**
(off Hawkstone Rd.)
Jarrett Clo. *SW2* —1D **95**
Jarrow Rd. *SE16* —5E **55**
Jarrow Way. *E9* —1B **28**
Jarvis Rd. *SE22* —2A **82**
Jasmin Ct. *SE12* —4B **86**
Jasmine St. *SW19* —5C **90**
Jasmin Lodge. *SE16* —1D **69**
(off Sherwood Gdns.)
Jason Ct. *SW9* —4C **66**
(off Southey Rd.)
Jason Ct. *W1* —5C **36**
(off Wigmore St.)
Jasper Pas. *SE19* —5B **96**
Jasper Rd. *E16* —5F **45**
Jasper Rd. *SE19* —5B **96**
Jasper Wlk. *N1* —2F **39**
Java Wharf. *SE1* —3B **54**
(off Shad Thames)
Jay M. *SW7* —3E **49**
Jean Darling Ho. *SW10*
(off Milman's St.) —2F **63**
Jean Pardies Ho. *E1* —4E **41**
(off Jubilee St.)
Jebb Av. *SW2* —4A **80**
(in two parts)
Jebb St. *E3* —1C **42**
Jedburgh Rd. *E13* —2E **45**
Jedburgh St. *SW11* —2C **78**
Jeddo M. *W3* —3B **46**
Jeddo Rd. *W12* —3B **46**
Jefferson Building. *E14*
—3C **56**
Jeffrey Row. *SE12* —3D **87**
Jeffrey's Pl. *NW1* —4E **23**
Jeffreys Rd. *SW4* —5A **66**
Jeffrey's St. *NW1* —4E **23**
Jeger Av. *E2* —5B **26**
Jeken Rd. *SE9* —2E **87**
Jelf Rd. *SW2* —3C **80**
Jellicoe Ho. *E2* —1C **40**
(off Ropley St.)
Jellicoe Ho. *NW1* —3D **37**
Jellicoe Rd. *E13* —3C **44**
Jemotts Ho. *SE14* —2F **69**
(off Myers La.)
Jenkins Rd. *E13* —3D **45**
Jenner Av. *W3* —4A **32**
Jenner Ho. *SE3* —2A **72**
(off Restell Clo.)
Jenner Ho. *WC1* —3A **38**
(off Hunter St.)
Jenner Pl. *SW13* —2D **61**
Jenner Rd. *N16* —5B **12**
Jennifer Ho. *SE11* —5C **52**
(off Reedworth St.)
Jennifer Rd. Brom —3B **100**
Jenningsbury Ho. *SW3*
—1A **64**
(off Marlborough St.)
Jennings Ho. *SE10* —1F **71**
(off Old Woolwich Rd.)
Jennings Rd. *SE22* —4B **82**
Jenny Hammond Clo. *E11*
—5B **16**
Jephson Ct. *SW4* —5A **66**

Jephson Ho. *SE17* —2D **67**
(off Doddington Gro.)
Jephson Rd. *E7* —4E **31**
Jephson St. *SE5* —4F **67**
Jephtha Rd. *SW18* —4C **76**
Jepson Ho. *SW6* —4D **63**
(off Pearscroft Rd.)
Jerdan Pl. *SW6* —3C **62**
Jeremiah St. *E14* —5D **43**
Jeremy Bentham Ho. *E2*
(off Mansford St.) —2C **40**
Jermyn St. *SW1* —2E **51**
(in two parts)
Jerningham Ct. *SE14* —4A **70**
Jerningham Rd. *SE14* —5A **70**
Jerome Cres. *NW8* —3A **36**
Jerome Ho. *NW1* —4A **36**
(off Lisson Gro.)
Jerome Ho. *SW7* —5F **49**
(off Glendower Pl.)
Jerome St. *E1* —3B **40**
(off Commercial St.)
Jerrard St. *SE13* —1D **85**
Jerrold St. *N1* —1A **40**
Jersey Ho. *N1* —3E **25**
Jersey Rd. *E11* —3F **15**
Jersey Rd. *E16* —5E **45**
Jersey Rd. *N1* —3E **25**
Jersey St. *E2* —2D **41**
Jerusalem Pas. *EC1* —3D **39**
Jervis Bay Ho. *E14* —5F **43**
Jervis Ct. *SE10* —4E **71**
(off Blissett St.)
Jervis Ct. *W1* —5D **37**
(off Princes St.)
Jerviston Gdns. *SW16*
—5C **94**

Jerwood Space Art Gallery.
(off Union St.) —3D **53**
Jessam Av. *E5* —3D **13**
Jesse Ho. *SW1* —5F **51**
(off Page St.)
Jessel Ho. *WC1* —2A **38**
(off Judd St.)
Jessel Mans. *W14* —2A **62**
(off Queen's Club Gdns.)
Jesse Rd. *E10* —3E **15**
Jessica Rd. *SW18* —4E **77**
Jessie Blythe La. *N19* —2A **10**
Jessie Wood Ct. *SW9*
(off Caldwell St.) —3C **66**
Jesson Ho. *SE17* —5F **53**
(off Orb St.)
Jessop Ct. *N1* —1D **39**
Jessop Rd. *SE24* —2D **81**
Jessop Sq. *E14* —2C **56**
Jevington Way. *SE12*
—1D **101**

Jewish Mus. —5D **23**
Jewry St. *EC3* —5B **40**
Jew's Row. *SW18* —2D **77**
Jews Wlk. *SE26* —4D **97**
Jeymer Av. *NW2* —2D **19**
Jeypore Pas. *SW18* —4E **77**
Jeypore Rd. *SW18* —5E **77**
Jim Griffiths Ho. *SW6*
(off Clem Attlee Ct.) —2B **62**

Joan Cres. SE9 —5F 87
Joan St. SE1 —2D 53
Jocelin Ho. N1 —5B 24 (off Barnsbury Est.)
Jocelyn St. SE15 —4C 68
Jockey's Fields. WC1 —4B 38
Jodane St. SE8 —5B 56
Jodrell Rd. E3 —5B 28
Joe Hunte Ct. SE27 —5D 95
Johanna St. SE1 —3C 52
John Adam St. WC2 —1A 52
John Aird Ct. W2 —4E 35 (off Howley Pl., in two parts)
John Archer Way. SW18 —4F 77
John Ashby Clo. SW2 —4A 80
John Baird Ct. SE26 —4F 97
John Barker Ct. NW6 —4A 20
John Barnes Wlk. E15 —3B 30
John Betts' Ho. W12 —4B 46
John Brent Ho. SE8 —5F 55 (off Bush Rd.)
John Buck Ho. NW10 —5B 18
John Campbell Rd. N16 —2A 26
John Carpenter St. EC4 —1D 53
John Cartwright Ho. E2 —2D 41 (off Old Bethnal Grn. Rd.)
John Drinkwater Clo. E11 —2B 16
John Felton Rd. SE16 —3C 54
John Fielden Ho. E2 —2D 41 (off Canrobert St.)
John Fisher St. E1 —1C 54
John Harrison Way. SE10 —4B 58
John Islip St. SW1 —5F 51
John Kennedy Ct. N1 —3F 25 (off Newington Grn. Rd.)
John Kennedy Ho. SE16 —5F 55 (off Rotherhithe Old Rd.)
John Knight Lodge. SW6 (off Vanston Pl.) —3C 62
John Masefield Ho. N15 (off Fladbury Rd.) —1F 11
John Maurice Clo. SE17 —5F 53
John McDonald Ho. E14 —4E 57
John McKenna Wlk. SE16 —4C 54
John Parker Sq. SW11 —1F 77
John Parry Ct. N1 —1A 40 (off Hare Wlk.)
John Penn St. SE13 —4D 71
John Pound Ho. SW18 —5D 77
John Prince's St. W1 —5D 37
John Pritchard Ho. E1 (off Buxton St.) —3C 40
John Ratcliffe Ho. NW6 —2C 34 (off Chippenham Gdns.)
John Rennie Wlk. E1 —2D 55
John Roll Way. SE16 —4C 54
John Ruskin St. SE5 —3D 67
John Scurr Ho. E14 —5A 42
John Silkin La. SE8 —5F 55
John's M. WC1 —3B 38
John Smith Av. SW6 —3B 62
Johnson Clo. E8 —5C 26
Johnson Ho. E2 —2C 40 (off Roberta St.)
Johnson Ho. NW1 —1E 37 (off Cranleigh St.)
Johnson Ho. SW1 —5C 50 (off Cundy St.)
Johnson Ho. SW8 —3F 65 (off Wandsworth Rd.)
Johnson Lodge. W2 —4C 34 (off Admiral Wlk.)
Johnson Mans. W14 —2A 62 (off Queen's Club Gdns.)
Johnson's Ct. EC4 —5C 38
Johnson's Pl. SW1 —1E 65
Johnson St. E1 —1E 55
John Spencer Sq. N1 —3D 25
John's Pl. E1 —5D 41
Johnston Clo. SW9 —4B 66
Johnstone Ho. SE13 —1F 85 (off Belmont Hill)
John Strachey Ho. SW6 (off Clem Attlee Ct.) —2B 62
John St. E15 —5B 30
John St. WC1 —3B 38
John Strype Ct. E10 —3D 15
John Trundle Ct. EC2 —4E 39 (off Beech St.)
John Trundle Highwalk. EC2 (off Beech St.) —4E 39
John Tucker Ho. E14 —4C 56
John Wesley Highwalk. EC1 (off Barbican) —4E 39
John Wheatley Ho. SW6 (off Clem Attlee Ct.) —2B 62
John Williams Clo. SE14 —2F 69
John Woolley Clo. SE13 —2A 86
Joiners Arms Yd. SE5 —4F 67
Joiners Pl. N5 —1F 25
Jonathan St. SE11 —1B 66
Jones Ho. E14 —5F 43
Jones M. SW15 —2A 76
Jones Rd. E13 —4D 45
Jones St. W1 —1D 51
Jonson Ho. SE1 —4F 53 (off Burbage Clo.)
Jordan Ho. N1 —5F 25 (off Colville Est.)
Jordan Ho. SE4 —2F 83 (off St Norbert Rd.)
Jordans Ho. NW8 —3F 35 (off Capland St.)
Joscoyne Ho. E1 —5D 41 (off Philpot St.)
Joseph Conrad Ho. SW1 (off Tachbrook St.) —5E 51
Joseph Ct. N15 —1A 12 (off Amhurst Pk.)
Josephine Av. SW2 —3B 80
Joseph Irwin Ho. E14 —1B 56
Joseph Lister Ct. E7 —4C 30
Joseph Powell Clo. SW12 —4D 79
Joseph Ray Rd. E11 —4A 16
Joseph St. E3 —3B 42
Joseph Trotter Clo. EC1 (off Finsbury Est.) —2C 38
Joshua St. E14 —4E 43
Joslings Clo. W12 —1C 46
Josseline Ct. E3 —1A 42 (off Ford St.)
Joubert St. SW11 —5B 64
Jowett St. SE15 —3B 68
Joyce Page Clo. SE7 —2F 73
Joyce Wlk. SW2 —4C 80
Jubb Powell Ho. N15 —1A 12
Jubilee Bldgs. NW8 —5F 21 (off Queen's Ter.)
Jubilee Clo. NW9 —1A 4
Jubilee Cres. E14 —4E 57
Jubilee Ho. SE11 —5C 52 (off Reedworth St.)
Jubilee Ho. WC1 —3B 38 (off Gray's Inn Rd.)
Jubilee Pl. SW3 —1A 64
Jubilee St. E1 —5E 41
Jubilee, The. SE10 —3D 71
Jubilee Walkway. SE1 —1D 53
Jubilee Yd. SE1 —3B 54 (off Lafone St.)
Judd St. WC1 —2A 38
Jude St. E16 —5B 44
Judges Wlk. NW3 —5E 7
Juer St. SW11 —3A 64
Julia Ct. E17 —1D 15
Julia Garfield M. E16 —2D 59
Julian Pl. E14 —1D 71
Julian Taylor Path. SE23 —2D 97
Julia St. NW5 —1C 22
Juliet Ho. N1 —1A 40 (off Arden Est.)
Juliette Rd. E13 —1C 44
Julius Nyerere Clo. N1 —5B 24 (off Copenhagen St.)
Junction App. SE13 —1E 85
Junction App. SW11 —1A 78
Junction Av. NW10 —3E 33
Junction M. W2 —5A 36
Junction Pl. W2 —5F 35 (off Praed St.)
Junction Rd. E13 —1D 45
Junction Rd. N19 —1E 23
Juniper Ct. W8 —4D 49 (off St Marys Pl.)
Juniper Cres. NW1 —4C 22
Juniper Ho. SE15 —3E 69
Juniper Ho. W10 —3A 34 (off Fourth Av.)
Juniper St. E1 —1E 55
Juno Ct. SW9 —3C 66 (off Caldwell St.)
Juno Way. SE14 —2F 69

Juno Way Ind. Est. *SE14* —2F **69**
*Jupiter Ct. SW9 —3C **66***
(off Caldwell St.)
Jupiter Ho. *E14* —1D **71**
Jupiter Way. *N7* —3B **24**
Jupp Rd. *E15* —4F **29**
Jupp Rd. W. *E15* —5F **29**
*Jura Ho. SE16 —5F **55***
(off Plough Way)
*Jurston Ct. SE1 —3C **52***
(off Gerridge St.)
*Justice Wlk. SW3 —2A **64***
(off Lawrence St.)
Jutland Clo. *N19* —3A **10**
Jutland Ho. *SE5* —5E **67**
Jutland Rd. *E13* —3C **44**
Jutland Rd. *SE6* —5E **85**
Juxon St. *SE11* —5B **52**
JVC Bus. Pk. *NW2* —3C **4**

Kambala Rd. *SW11* —1F **77**
Kangley Bri. Rd. *SE26* —5B **98**
Kangley Bus. Cen. *SE26* —5B **98**
Kara Way. *NW2* —1F **19**
Karen Ter. *E11* —4B **16**
Kashmir Rd. *SE7* —3F **73**
Kassala Rd. *SW11* —4B **64**
Katherine Clo. *SE16* —2F **55**
Katherine Ct. *SE23* —1D **97**
Katherine Gdns. *SE9* —2F **87**
Katherine Rd. *E7 & E6* —2E **31**
Katherine Sq. *W11* —2A **48**
Kathleen Godfree Ct. *SW19* —5C **90**
Kathleen Rd. *SW11* —1B **78**
Kay Rd. *SW9* —5A **66**
Kay St. *E2* —1C **40**
Kay St. *E15* —4F **29**
Kay Way. *SE10* —3E **71**
Kean Ho. *SE17* —2D **67**
Kean St. *WC2* —5B **38**
Keats Av. *E16* —2D **59**
Keats Clo. *E11* —1D **17**
Keat's Clo. *NW3* —1A **22**
Keats Clo. *SE1* —5B **54**
Keats Clo. *SW19* —5F **91**
Keat's Gro. *NW3* —1A **22**
Keats House. —1A 22
(off Keat's Gro.)
*Keats Ho. E2 —2E **41***
(off Roman Rd.)
*Keats Ho. SE5 —3E **67***
(off Elmington Est.)
*Keats Ho. SW1 —2E **65***
(off Churchill Gdns.)
*Keats Pl. EC2 —4F **39***
(off Moorfields)
*Kebbell Ter. E7 —2D **31***
(off Claremont Rd.)
Keble St. *SW17* —4E **91**
Kedge Ho. *E14* —4C **56**
Kedleston Wlk. *E2* —2D **41**
Keedonwood Rd. *Brom* —5A **100**
Keel Clo. *SE16* —2F **55**
Keeley St. *WC2* —5B **38**
*Keeling Ho. E2 —1D **41***
(off Claredale St.)
Keeling Rd. *SE9* —3F **87**
Keens Clo. *SW16* —5F **93**
Keen's Yd. *N1* —3D **25**
Keepier Wharf. *E14* —1F **55**
Keep, The. *SE3* —5C **72**
Keeton's Rd. *SE16* —4D **55**
(in two parts)
Keevil Dri. *SW19* —5F **75**
Keighley Clo. *N7* —2A **24**
Keildon Rd. *SW11* —2B **78**
Keir Hardie Est. *E5* —3D **13**
Keir Hardie Ho. *N19* —2F **9**
Keir, The. *SW19* —5E **89**
Keith Connor Clo. *SW8* —1D **79**
Keith Gro. *W12* —3C **46**
*Keith Ho. W9 —2D **35***
(off Carlton Va.)
Kelbrook Rd. *SE3* —5F **73**
Kelceda Clo. *NW2* —4C **4**
Kelfield Ct. *W10* —5F **33**
Kelfield Gdns. *W10* —5E **33**
Kelfield M. *W10* —5F **33**
Kelland Clo. *N8* —1F **9**
Kelland Rd. *E13* —3C **44**
Kellaway Rd. *SE3* —5F **73**
Keller Cres. *E12* —1F **31**
Kellerton Rd. *SE13* —3A **86**
*Kellet Houses. WC1 —2A **38***
(off Tankerton St.)
*Kellett Ho. N1 —5A **26***
(off Colville Est.)
Kellett Rd. *SW2* —2C **80**
Kellino St. *SW17* —4B **92**
*Kellow Ho. SE1 —3F **53***
(off Tennis St.)
Kell St. *SE1* —4D **53**
Kelly Av. *SE15* —3B **68**
Kelly Clo. *NW10* —5A **4**
Kelly M. *W9* —3B **34**
Kelly St. *NW1* —3D **23**
Kelman Clo. *SW4* —5F **65**
Kelmore Gro. *SE22* —2C **82**
Kelmscott Gdns. *W12* —4C **46**
Kelmscott Rd. *SW11* —3A **78**
Kelross Pas. *N5* —1E **25**
Kelross Rd. *N5* —1E **25**
Kelsall Clo. *SE3* —5D **73**
Kelsey St. *E2* —3C **40**
Kelson Ho. *E14* —4E **57**
Kelso Pl. *W8* —4D **49**
Kelvedon Ho. *SW8* —4A **66**
Kelvedon Rd. *SW6* —3B **62**
Kelvin Ct. *W11* —1C **48**
Kelvin Gro. *SE26* —3D **97**
Kelvington Rd. *SE15* —3F **83**
Kelvin Rd. *N5* —1E **25**
Kember St. *N1* —4B **24**
*Kemble Ct. SE15 —3A **68***
(off Lydney Clo.)
*Kemble Ho. SW9 —1D **81***
(off Barrington Rd.)
Kemble Rd. *SE23* —1F **97**
Kemble St. *WC2* —5B **38**
Kemerton Rd. *SE5* —1E **81**
Kemeys St. *E9* —2A **28**
*Kemp Ct. SW8 —3A **66***
(off Hartington Rd.)
*Kempe Ho. SE1 —4F **53***
(off Burge St.)
Kempe Rd. *NW6* —1F **33**
*Kemp Ho. W1 —1F **51***
(off Berwick St.)
Kempis Way. *SE22* —3A **82**
Kemplay Rd. *NW3* —1F **21**
*Kemps Ct. W1 —5F **37***
(off Hopkins St.)
Kemps Dri. *E14* —1C **56**
Kemp's Dri. *E14* —1C **56**
Kempsford Gdns. *SW5* —1C **62**
Kempsford Rd. *SE11* —5C **52**
(in two parts)
Kemps Gdns. *SE13* —3E **85**
Kempson Rd. *SW6* —4C **62**
Kempthorne Rd. *SE8* —5B **56**
Kempton Ct. *E1* —4D **41**
*Kemsing Ho. SE1 —3F **53***
(off Long La.)
Kemsing Rd. *SE10* —1C **72**
Kenbrook Ho. *W14* —4B **48**
Kenbury Gdns. *SE5* —5E **67**
*Kenbury Mans. SE5 —5E **67***
(off Kenbury St.)
Kenbury St. *SE5* —5E **67**
Kenchester Clo. *SW8* —3A **66**
*Kendal. NW1 —2D **37***
(off Augustus St.)
Kendal Clo. *SW9* —3D **67**
Kendale Rd. *Brom* —5A **100**
Kendal Ho. *E9* —5E **27**
*Kendal Ho. N1 —1B **38***
(off Priory Grn. Est.)
Kendall Pl. *W1* —4C **36**
Kendal Pl. *SW15* —3B **76**
Kendal Rd. *NW10* —1C **18**
*Kendal Steps. W2 —5A **36***
(off St George's Fields)
Kendal St. *W2* —5A **36**
Kender St. *SE14* —3E **69**
Kendoa Rd. *SW4* —2F **79**
Kendon Clo. *E11* —1D **17**
*Kendrick Ct. SE15 —4D **69***
(off Woods Rd.)
Kendrick M. *SW7* —5F **49**
Kendrick Pl. *SW7* —5F **49**
Kenilford Rd. *SW12* —5D **79**
Kenilworth Av. *SW19* —5C **90**
Kenilworth Rd. *E3* —1A **42**
Kenilworth Rd. *NW6* —5B **20**
Kenley Wlk. *W11* —1A **48**
Kenlor Rd. *SW17* —5F **91**
Kenmont Gdns. *NW10* —2D **33**
Kenmure Rd. *E8* —2D **27**
Kenmure Yd. *E8* —2D **27**
Kennacraig Clo. *E16* —2C **58**
Kennard Ho. *SW11* —5C **64**
Kennard Rd. *E15* —4F **29**
Kennard St. *SW11* —4C **64**

Kennedy Clo. *E13* —1C **44**
Kennedy Cox Ho. E16 (off Burke St.) —4B ***44***
Kennedy Ho. SE11 —1B ***66*** *(off Vauxhall Wlk.)*
Kennedy Wlk. SE17 —5F ***53*** *(off Elsted St.)*
Kennet Clo. *SW11* —2F **77**
Kenneth Campbell Ho. NW8 (off Orchardson St.) —3F ***35***
Kenneth Ct. *SE11* —5C **52**
Kenneth Cres. *NW2* —2D **19**
Kennet Ho. NW8 —3F ***35*** *(off Church St. Est.)*
Kenneth Younger Ho. SW6 —2B ***62*** *(off Clem Attlee Ct.)*
Kennet Rd. *W9* —3B **34**
Kennet St. *E1* —2C **54**
Kennett Wharf La. *EC4* —1E **53**
Kenninghall Rd. *E5* —5C **12**
Kenning Ho. N1 —5A ***26*** *(off Colville Est.)*
Kenning St. *SE16* —3E **55**
Kennings Way. *SE11* —1C **66**
Kennington. —2C 66
Kennington Grn. *SE11* —1C **66**
Kennington Gro. *SE11* —2B **66**
Kennington La. *SE11* —1B **66**
Kennington Oval. (Junct.) —2C **66**
Kennington Oval. *SE11* —2B **66**
Kennington Pal. Ct. SE11 (off Sancroft St.) —1C ***66***
Kennington Pk. Gdns. *SE11* —2D **67**
Kennington Pk. Ho. SE11 —1C ***66*** *(off Kennington Pk. Pl.)*
Kennington Pk. Pl. *SE11* —2C **66**
Kennington Pk. Rd. *SE11* —2C **66**
Kennington Rd. *SE1 & SE11* —4C **52**
Kennistoun Ho. *NW5* —2E **23**
Kennyland Ct. NW4 —1D ***5*** *(off Hendon Way)*
Kenrick Pl. *W1* —4C **36**
Kensal Green. —2E 33
Kensal Ho. W10 —3F ***33*** *(off Ladbroke Gro.)*
Kensal Rise. —1F 33
Kensal Rd. *W10* —3A **34**
Kensal Town. —3A 34
Kensington. —3D 49
Kensington Arc. W8 —3D ***49*** *(off Kensington High St.)*
Kensington Av. *E12* —3F **31**
Kensington Cen. *W14* (in two parts) —5A **48**
Kensington Chu. Ct. *W8* —3D **49**
Kensington Chu. St. *W8* —2C **48**
Kensington Chu. Wlk. *W8* (in two parts) —3D **49**
Kensington Ct. SE16 —2F ***55*** *(off King & Queen Wharf)*
Kensington Ct. *W8* —3D **49**
Kensington Ct. Gdns. W8 —4D ***49*** *(off Kensington Ct. Pl.)*
Kensington Ct. M. W8 —4D ***49*** *(off Kensington Ct. Pl.)*
Kensington Ct. Pl. *W8* —4D **49**
Kensington Gardens. —2E 49
Kensington Gdns. Sq. *W2* —5D **35**
Kensington Ga. *W8* —4E **49**
Kensington Gore. *SW7* —3E **49**
Kensington Hall Gdns. *W14* —1B **62**
Kensington Heights. *W8* —2C **48**
Kensington High St. *W14 & W8* —4B **48**
Kensington Ho. *W14* —3F **47**
Kensington Mall. *W8* —2C **48**
Kensington Mans. SW5 —1C ***62*** *(off Trebovir Rd., in two parts)*
Kensington Palace. —2D 49
Kensington Pal. Gdns. *W8* —2D **49**
Kensington Pk. Gdns. *W11* —1B **48**
Kensington Pk. M. *W11* —5B **34**
Kensington Pk. Rd. *W11* —5B **34**
Kensington Pl. *W8* —2C **48**
Kensington Rd. *W8 & SW7* —3E **49**
Kensington Sq. *W8* —4D **49**
Kensington Village. *W14* —5B **48**
Kensington W. *W14* —5A **48**
Kenswick Ct. *SE13* —3D **85**
Kensworth Ho. EC1 —2F ***39*** *(off Cranwood St.)*
Kent Ct. *E2* —1B **40**
Kent Ho. *SE1* —1B **68**
Kent Ho. SW1 —1F ***65*** *(off Aylesford St.)*
Kent Ho. W4 —1A ***60*** *(off Devonshire St.)*
Kent Ho. La. *Beck* —5A **98**
Kent Ho. Rd. *SE26 & Beck* —5A **98**
Kentish Bldgs. SE1 —3F ***53*** *(off Borough High St.)*
Kentish Town. —2D 23
Kentish Town Ind. Est. *NW5* —2D **23**
Kentish Town Rd. *NW1 & NW5* —4D **23**
Kentmere Ho. *SE15* —2E **69**
Kenton Ct. SE26 —4A ***98*** *(off Adamsrill Rd.)*
Kenton Ct. *W14* —4B **48**
Kenton Ho. E1 —3E ***41*** *(off Mantus Clo.)*
Kenton Rd. *E9* —3F **27**
Kenton St. *WC1* —3A **38**
Kent Pk. Ind. Est. *SE15* —2D **69**
Kent Pas. *NW1* —3B **36**
Kent St. *E2* —1B **40**
Kent St. *E13* —2D **45**
Kent Ter. *NW1* —2A **36**
Kent Wlk. *SW9* —2D **81**
Kentwell Clo. *SE4* —2A **84**
Kent Wharf. SE8 —3D ***71*** *(off Creekside)*
Kentwode Grn. *SW13* —3C **60**
Kent Yd. *SW7* —3A **50**
Kenward Rd. *SE9* —3E **87**
Kenway Rd. *SW5* —5D **49**
Ken Wilson Ho. E2 —1C ***40*** *(off Pritchards Rd.)*
Kenwood Clo. *NW3* —3F **7**
Kenwood House. —3A 8
Kenwood Ho. *SW9* —2D **81**
Kenwood Rd. *N6* —1B **8**
Kenworthy Rd. *E9* —2A **28**
Kenwrick Ho. N1 —5B ***24*** *(off Barnsbury Est.)*
Kenwyn Dri. *NW2* —4A **4**
Kenwyn Rd. *SW4* —2F **79**
Kenya Rd. *SE7* —3F **73**
Kenyon Mans. W14 —2A ***62*** *(off Queen's Club Gdns.)*
Kenyon St. *SW6* —4F **61**
Keogh Rd. *E15* —3A **30**
Keple Pl. *SW13* —2D **61**
Kepler Ho. SE10 —1B ***72*** *(off Armitagge Rd.)*
Kepler Rd. *SW4* —2A **80**
Keppel Ho. *SE8* —1B **70**
Keppel Row. *SE1* —2E **53**
Keppel St. *WC1* —4F **37**
Kerbela St. *E2* —3C **40**
Kerbey St. *E14* —5D **43**
Kerfield Cres. *SE5* —4F **67**
Kerfield Pl. *SE5* —4F **67**
Kerridge Ct. N1 —3A ***26*** *(off Balls Pond Rd.)*
Kerrison Rd. *E15* —5F **29**
Kerrison Rd. *SW11* —1A **78**
Kerry. *N7* —3A **24**
Kerry Clo. *E16* —5D **45**
Kerry Path. *SE14* —2B **70**
Kerry Rd. *SE14* —2B **70**
Kersey Gdns. *SE9* —4F **101**
Kersfield Rd. *SW15* —4F **75**
Kershaw Clo. *SW18* —4F **77**
Kersley M. *SW11* —4B **64**
Kersley Rd. *N16* —4A **12**
Kersley St. *SW11* —5B **64**
Kerswell Clo. *N15* —1A **12**
Kerwick Clo. *N7* —4A **24**
Keslake Mans. NW10 —1F ***33*** *(off Station Ter.)*
Keslake Rd. *NW6* —1F **33**

Kessock Clo. *N17* —1D **13**
Keston Ho. *SE17* —1A **68**
(off Kinglake St.)
Keston Rd. *SE15* —1C **82**
Kestrel Av. *E6* —4F **45**
Kestrel Av. *SE24* —3D **81**
Kestrel Clo. *NW10* —2A **18**
Kestrel Ct. SE8 —2B **70**
(off Abinger Gro.)
Kestrel Ho. *EC1* —2E **39**
(off Pickard St.)
Kestrel Pl. *SE14* —2A **70**
Keswick Av. *SW15* —5A **88**
Keswick Ct. *SE6* —1B **100**
Keswick Ho. *SE5* —5E **67**
Keswick Rd. *SW15* —3A **76**
Kett Gdns. *SW2* —3B **80**
Kettlebaston Rd. *E10* —3B **14**
Kettleby Ho. *SW9* —1D **81**
(off Barrington Rd.)
Ketton Ho. *W10* —3E **33**
(off Sutton Way)
Kevan Ho. *SE5* —3E **67**
Keybridge Ho. SW8 —2A **66**
(off Miles St.)
Key Clo. *E1* —3E **41**
Keyes Ho. *SW1* —1F **65**
(off Dolphin Sq.)
Keyes Rd. *NW2* —2F **19**
Key Ho. *SE11* —2C **66**
Keymer Rd. *SW2* —2B **94**
Keynsham Gdns. *SE9* —3F **87**
Keynsham Rd. *SE9* —3F **87**
Keyse Rd. *SE1* —4B **54**
Keystone Cres. *N1* —1A **38**
Keyworth Clo. *E5* —1A **28**
Keyworth Pl. SE1 —4D **53**
(off Keyworth St.)
Keyworth St. *SE1* —4D **53**
Kezia St. *SE8* —1A **70**
Khama Rd. *SW17* —4A **92**
Khartoum Rd. *E13* —2D **45**
Khartoum Rd. *SW17* —4F **91**
Khyber Rd. *SW11* —5A **64**
Kibworth St. *SW8* —3B **66**
Kidbrooke. —5D **73**
Kidbrooke Est. *SE3* —1E **87**
Kidbrooke Gdns. *SE3* —5C **72**
Kidbrooke Gro. *SE3* —4C **72**
Kidbrooke La. *SE9* —2F **87**
Kidbrooke Pk. Clo. *SE3*
—4D **73**
Kidbrooke Pk. Rd. *SE3*
—4D **73**
Kidbrooke Way. *SE3* —5D **73**
Kidderpore Av. *NW3* —1C **20**
Kidderpore Gdns. *NW3*
—1C **20**
Kidd Pl. *SE7* —1F **73**
Kierbeck Bus. Complex. *E16*
—3D **59**
Kier Hardie Ct. *NW10* —4B **18**
Kiffen St. *EC2* —3F **39**
Kilbrennan Ho. *E14* —5E **43**
Kilburn. —5C **20**
Kilburn Bri. *NW6* —5C **20**
Kilburn Ga. *NW6* —1D **35**

Kilburn High Rd. *NW6*
—4B **20**
Kilburn La. *W10* & *W9*
—2F **33**
Kilburn Pk. Rd. *NW6* —2C **34**
Kilburn Pl. *NW6* —5C **20**
Kilburn Priory. *NW6* —5D **21**
Kilburn Sq. *NW6* —5C **20**
Kilburn Va. *NW6* —5D **21**
Kilburn Va. Est. *NW6* —5D **21**
(off Kilburn Va.)
Kildare Gdns. *W2* —5C **34**
Kildare Rd. *E16* —4C **44**
Kildare Ter. *W2* —5C **34**
Kildare Wlk. *E14* —5C **42**
Kildoran Rd. *SW2* —3A **80**
Kilgour Rd. *SE23* —4A **84**
Kilkie St. *SW6* —5E **63**
Killarney Rd. *SW18* —4E **77**
Killearn Rd. *SE6* —1F **99**
Killick St. *N1* —1B **38**
Killieser Av. *SW2* —2A **94**
Killip Clo. *E16* —5B **44**
Killowen Rd. *E9* —3F **27**
Killyon Rd. *SW8* —5E **65**
Killyon Ter. *SW8* —5E **65**
Kilmaine Rd. *SW6* —3A **62**
Kilmarsh Rd. *W6* —5E **47**
Kilmington Rd. *SW13* —2C **60**
Kilmore Ho. *E14* —5D **43**
Kilmorie Rd. *SE23* —1A **98**
Kilmuir Ho. SW1 —5C **50**
(off Bury St.)
Kiln Ct. *E14* —1B **56**
Kilner Ho. *SE11* —2C **66**
(off Clayton St.)
Kilner St. *E14* —4C **42**
Kiln M. *SW17* —5F **91**
Kiln Pl. *NW5* —2C **22**
Kilravock St. *W10* —2A **34**
Kimbell Gdns. *SW6* —4A **62**
Kimbell Pl. *SE3* —2E **87**
Kimberley Av. *E6* —1F **45**
Kimberley Av. *SE15* —5D **69**
Kimberley Gdns. *N4* —1D **11**
Kimberley Ho. *E14* —4E **57**
Kimberley Rd. *E11* —4F **15**
Kimberley Rd. *E16* —3B **44**
Kimberley Rd. *NW6* —5A **20**
Kimberley Rd. *SW9* —5A **66**
Kimber Rd. *SW18* —5C **76**
Kimble Ho. *NW8* —3A **36**
(off Lilestone St.)
Kimble Rd. *SW19* —5F **91**
Kimbolton Clo. *SE12* —4B **86**
Kimbolton Ct. SW3 —5A **50**
(off Fulham Rd.)
Kimbolton Row. SW3 —5A **50**
(off Fulham Rd.)
Kimmeridge Gdns. *SE9*
—4F **101**
Kimmeridge Rd. *SE9* —4F **101**
Kimpton Rd. *SE5* —4F **67**
Kinburn St. *SE16* —3F **55**
Kincaid Rd. *SE15* —3D **69**
Kincardine Gdns. W9 —3C **34**
(off Harrow Rd.)

Kinder Ho. *N1* —1F **39**
(off Cranston Est.)
Kindersley Ho. *E1* —5C **40**
(off Pinchin St.)
Kinder St. *E1* —5D **41**
Kinefold Ho. *N7* —3A **24**
Kinfauns Rd. *SW2* —2C **94**
King Alfred Av. *SE6* —4C **98**
(in two parts)
King & Queen St. *SE17*
—1E **67**
King & Queen Wharf. *SE16*
—1F **55**
King Arthur Clo. *SE15*
—3E **69**
King Charles Ct. *SE17*
—2D **67**
(off Royal Rd.)
King Charles Ho. SW6
(off Wandon Rd.) —3D **63**
King Charles's Ct. SE10
(off Park Row) —2E **71**
King Charles St. *SW1* —3F **51**
King Charles Ter. E1 —1D **55**
(off Sovereign Clo.)
King Charles Wlk. *SW19*
—1A **90**
King Ct. *E10* —2D **15**
King David La. *E1* —1E **55**
Kingdon Ho. *E14* —4E **57**
Kingdon Rd. *NW6* —3C **20**
King Edward Building. *EC1*
—5D **39**
King Edward Mans. E8
(off Mare St.) —5D **27**
King Edward Mans. SW6
(off Fulham Rd.) —3C **62**
King Edward M. *SW13*
—4C **60**
King Edward's Rd. *E10* —3E **15**
King Edward's Rd. *E8* —5D **27**
King Edward St. *EC1* —5E **39**
King Edward III M. *SE16*
—3D **55**
King Edward Wlk. *SE1*
—4C **52**
Kingfield St. *E14* —5E **57**
Kingfisher Av. *E11* —1D **17**
Kingfisher Ct. *E14* —3E **57**
Kingfisher Ct. *SW19* —2F **89**
Kingfisher M. *SE13* —2C **84**
Kingfisher Sq. SE8 —2B **70**
(off Clyde St.)
Kingfisher Way. *NW10*
—3A **18**
King Frederick IX Tower. *SE16*
—4B **56**
King George Av. *E16* —5E **45**
King George St. *SE10* —3E **71**
Kingham Clo. *SW18* —5E **77**
Kingham Clo. W11 —3A **48**
(off Holland Pk. Av.)
King Henry's Reach. *W6*
—2E **61**
King Henry's Rd. *NW3*
—4A **22**
King Henry St. *N16* —2A **26**
King Henry's Wlk. *N1* —3A **26**

*King Henry Ter. E1 —1D **55***
(off Sovereign Clo.)
Kinghorn St. *EC1* —4E **39**
King Ho. *W12* —5D **33**
*King James Ct. SE1 —3D **53***
(off King James St.)
King James St. *SE1* —3D **53**
King John Ct. *EC2* —3A **40**
King John St. *E1* —4F **41**
King John's Wlk. *SE9* —5F **87**
(Middle Pk. Av.)
King John's Wlk. *SE9*
(Mottingham La.) —1F **101**
Kinglake Est. *SE17* —1A **68**
Kinglake St. *SE17* —1A **68**
(in two parts)
*Kingly Ct. W1 —1E **51***
(off Beak St.)
Kingly St. *W1* —5E **37**
Kingsand Rd. *SE12* —2C **100**
*Kings Arms Ct. E1 —4C **40***
(off Whitechapel Rd.)
Kings Arms Yd. *EC2* —5F **39**
Kings Av. *SW12 & SW4*
—1F **93**
Kings Av. *Brom* —5B **100**
King's Bench St. *SE1* —3D **53**
King's Bench Wlk. *EC4*
—5C **38**
*Kingsbridge Ct. E14 —4C **56***
(off Dockers Tanner Rd.)
Kingsbridge Rd. *W10* —5E **33**
Kingsbury Rd. *N1* —3A **26**
Kingsbury Ter. *N1* —3A **26**
Kingsclere Clo. *SW15* —5C **74**
Kingscliffe Gdns. *SW19*
—1B **90**
Kings Clo. *E10* —2D **15**
Kings College Ct. *NW3*
—4A **22**
King's College Rd. *NW3*
—4A **22**
Kingscote St. *EC4* —1D **53**
King's Ct. *E13* —5D **31**
*Kings Ct. NW8 —5B **22***
(off Prince Albert Rd.)
King's Ct. *SE1* —3D **53**
Kings Ct. *W6* —5C **46**
*Kings Ct. N. SW3 —1A **64***
(off King's Rd.)
Kingscourt Rd. *SW16* —3F **93**
*Kings Ct. S. SW3 —1A **64***
(off King's Rd.)
King's Cres. *N4* —5E **11**
Kings Cres. Est. *N4* —4E **11**
Kingscroft. *SW4* —4A **80**
Kingscroft Rd. *NW2* —3B **20**
King's Cross. —1A 38
Kings Cross. (Junct.) —2A **38**
*King's Cross Bri. WC1 —2A **38***
(off Gray's Inn Rd.)
King's Cross Rd. *WC1* —2B **38**
Kingsdale Gdns. *W11* —2F **47**
Kingsdown Av. *W3* —1A **46**
Kingsdown Clo. SE16
*(off Masters Dri.) —1D **69***
Kingsdown Clo. *W10* —5F **33**
Kingsdown Ho. *E8* —2C **26**
Kingsdown Rd. *E11* —5A **16**
Kingsdown Rd. *N19* —4A **10**
Kingsfield Ho. *SE9* —3F **101**
Kingsford St. *NW5* —2B **22**
King's Gdns. *NW6* —4C **20**
Kings Gth. M. *SE23* —2E **97**
Kingsgate Est. *N1* —3A **26**
Kingsgate Ho. *SW9* —4C **66**
Kingsgate Mans. WC1
*(off Red Lion Sq.) —4B **38***
*Kingsgate Pde. SW1 —4E **51***
(off Victoria St.)
Kingsgate Pl. *NW6* —4C **20**
Kingsgate Rd. *NW6* —4C **20**
Kingsground. *SE9* —5F **87**
King's Gro. *SE15* —3D **69**
(in two parts)
Kingshall M. *SE13* —1E **85**
*Kings Head Pas. SW4 —2F **79***
(off Clapham Pk. Rd.)
Kings Head Theatre. —5D 25
King's Head Yd. *SE1* —2F **53**
Kingshill. *SE17* —5E **53**
Kingshold Rd. *E9* —4E **27**
Kingsholm Gdns. *SE9* —2F **87**
*Kings Ho. SW8 —3A **66***
(off S. Lambeth Rd.)
Kingshurst Rd. *SE12* —5C **86**
Kings Keep. *SW15* —3F **75**
Kingsland. —3A 26
Kingsland. *NW8* —5A **22**
Kingsland Grn. *E8* —3A **26**
Kingsland High St. *E8* —3B **26**
Kingsland Pas. *E8* —3A **26**
Kingsland Rd. *E2 & E8*
—2A **40**
Kingsland Rd. *E13* —2E **45**
Kingsland Shop. Cen. *E8*
—3B **26**
Kingslawn Clo. *SW15* —3D **75**
Kingsley Clo. *N2* —1E **7**
Kingsley Ct. *NW10* —3D **19**
*Kingsley Flats. SE1 —5A **54***
(off Old Kent Rd.)
*Kingsley Ho. SW3 —2F **63***
(off Beaufort St.)
*Kingsley Mans. W14 —2A **62***
(off Greyhound Rd.)
Kingsley M. *E1* —1D **55**
Kingsley M. *W8* —4D **49**
Kingsley Pl. *N6* —2C **8**
Kingsley Rd. *E7* —4C **30**
Kingsley Rd. *NW6* —5B **20**
Kingsley Rd. *SW19* —5D **91**
Kingsley St. *SW11* —1B **78**
Kingsley Way. *NW11* —1E **7**
Kings Mall. *W6* —5E **47**
Kingsmead Av. *NW9* —2A **4**
Kingsmead Ct. *N6* —2F **9**
Kingsmead Ho. *E9* —1A **28**
Kingsmead Rd. *SW2* —2C **94**
King's Mead Way. *E9* —1A **28**
Kingsmere Clo. *SW15* —1F **75**
Kingsmere Pl. *N16* —3F **11**
Kingsmere Rd. *SW19* —2F **89**
King's M. *SW4* —3A **80**
King's M. *WC1* —3B **38**
*Kingsmill. NW8 —1F **35***
(off Kingsmill Ter.)
*Kingsmill Ho. SW3 —1A **64***
(off Marlborough St.)
Kingsmill Ter. *NW8* —1F **35**
Kingsnorth Ho. *W10* —5F **33**
King's Pde. *NW10* —5E **19**
Kings Pde. *W12* —4C **46**
Kings Pas. *E11* —2A **16**
King's Pl. *SE1* —3E **53**
King Sq. *EC1* —2E **39**
*King's Quay. SW10 —4E **63***
(off Chelsea Harbour)
Kings Reach Tower. SE1
*(off Hatfields) —2C **52***
Kingsridge. *SW19* —2A **90**
King's Rd. *E6* —5E **31**
Kings Rd. *E11* —2A **16**
King's Rd. *NW10* —4D **19**
King's Rd. *SW6* —3D **63**
Kings Rd. *SW14* —1A **74**
Kings Rd. *SW19* —5C **90**
King's Scholars' Pas. SW1
*(off Carlisle Pl.) —4E **51***
King Stairs Clo. *SE16* —3D **55**
King's Ter. *NW1* —5E **23**
Kingsthorpe Rd. *SE26* —4F **97**
Kingston By-Pass.
SW15 & SW20 —4A **88**
Kingston Ho. *NW6* —4A **20**
*Kingston Ho. E. SW7 —3A **50***
(off Prince's Ga.)
*Kingston Ho. N. SW7 —3A **50***
(off Prince's Ga.)
*Kingston Ho. S. SW7 —3A **50***
(off Ennismore Gdns.)
Kingston Rd. *SW15 & SW19*
—2C **88**
Kingston Sq. *SE19* —5F **95**
Kingston Vale. —4A 88
Kingston Va. *SW15* —4A **88**
Kingstown St. *NW1* —5C **22**
(in two parts)
King St. *E13* —3C **44**
King St. *EC2* —5E **39**
King St. *SW1* —2E **51**
King St. *W6* —5C **46**
King St. *WC2* —1A **52**
Kings Wlk. Shop. Cen. *SW3*
—1B **64**
Kingswater Pl. *SW11* —3A **64**
Kingsway. *WC2* —5B **38**
Kingsway Mans. WC1
*(off Red Lion Sq.) —4B **38***
*Kingsway Pl. EC1 —3C **38***
(off Corporation Row)
Kingswear Rd. *NW5* —5D **9**
*Kingswood. E2 —1E **41***
(off Cyprus St.)
Kingswood Av. *NW6* —5A **20**
Kingswood Clo. *SW8* —3A **66**
*Kingswood Ct. NW6 —4C **20***
(off W. End La.)
Kingswood Dri. *SE19* —4A **96**
Kingswood Est. *SE21* —4A **96**
Kingswood Pl. *SE13* —2A **86**

Kingswood Rd. *E11* —2A **16**
Kingswood Rd. *SE20* —5E **97**
Kingswood Rd. *SW2* —4A **80**
Kings Yd. *E9* —3C **28**
Kings Yd. SW15 —1E **75**
  (off Lwr. Richmond Rd.)
Kingthorpe Rd. *NW10* —4A **18**
Kingthorpe Ter. *NW10* —3A **18**
Kington Ho. NW6 —5D **21**
  (off Mortimer Cres.)
Kingward Ho. E1 —4C **40**
  (off Hanbury St.)
King William La. *SE10* —1A **72**
King William's Ct. SE10
  (off Park Row) —2F **71**
King William St. *EC4* —5F **39**
King William Wlk. *SE10*
  (in two parts) —2E **71**
Kingwood Rd. *SW6* —4A **62**
Kinloch Dri. *NW9* —2A **4**
Kinloch St. *N7* —5B **10**
Kinnaird Av. *Brom* —5B **100**
Kinnear Rd. *W12* —3B **46**
Kinnerton Pl. N. SW1 —3B **50**
  (off Kinnerton St.)
Kinnerton Pl. S. SW1 —3B **50**
  (off Kinnerton St.)
Kinnerton St. *SW1* —3C **50**
Kinnerton Yd. SW1 —3C **50**
  (off Kinnerton St.)
Kinnoul Rd. *W6* —2A **62**
Kinross Ct. *SE6* —1B **100**
Kinsale Rd. *SE15* —1C **82**
Kinsella Gdns. *SW19* —5D **89**
Kinsham Ho. E2 —3C **40**
  (off Ramsey St.)
Kintore Way. *SE1* —5B **54**
Kintyre Ct. *SW2* —5A **80**
Kintyre Ho. *E14* —2E **57**
Kinveachy Gdns. *SE7* —1F **73**
Kinver Rd. *SE26* —4E **97**
Kipling Dri. *SW19* —5F **91**
Kipling Est. *SE1* —3F **53**
Kipling Ho. SE5 —3F **67**
  (off Elmington Est.)
Kipling St. *SE1* —3F **53**
Kippington Dri. *SE9* —1F **101**
Kirby Est. *SE16* —4D **55**
Kirby Gro. *SE1* —3A **54**
Kirby St. *EC1* —4C **38**
Kirkdale *SE26* —2D **97**
Kirkdale Corner. *SE26* —4E **97**
Kirkdale Rd. *E11* —3A **16**
Kirkeby Ho. EC1 —4C **38**
  (off Leather La.)
Kirkham Rd. *E6* —5F **45**
Kirkland Ho. E14 —1D **71**
  (off St Davids Sq.)
Kirkland Ho. E14 —1D **71**
  (off Westferry Rd.)
Kirkland Wlk. *E8* —3B **26**
Kirkman Pl. W1 —4F **37**
  (off Tottenham Ct. Rd.)
Kirkmichael Rd. *E14* —5E **43**
Kirk Rd. *E17* —1B **14**
Kirkside Rd. *SE3* —2C **72**
Kirk's Pl. *E14* —4B **42**

Kirkstall Gdns. *SW2* —1A **94**
Kirkstall Rd. *SW2* —1F **93**
Kirkstone. NW1 —2E **37**
  (off Harrington St.)
Kirk St. WC1 —3D **38**
  (off Northington St.)
Kirkwall Pl. *E2* —2E **41**
Kirkwood La. *NW1* —4C **22**
Kirkwood Rd. *SE15* —5D **69**
Kirtley Ho. *SW8* —4E **65**
Kirtley Rd. *SE26* —4A **98**
Kirtling St. *SW8* —3E **65**
Kirton Clo. *W4* —5A **46**
Kirton Gdns. *E2* —2B **40**
  (in two parts)
Kirton Lodge. *SW18* —4D **77**
Kirton Rd. *E13* —1E **45**
Kirwyn Way. *SE5* —3D **67**
Kitcat Ter. *E3* —2C **42**
Kitchener Rd. *E7* —3D **31**
Kite Pl. E2 —2C **40**
  (off Lampern St.)
Kite Yd. SW11 —4B **64**
  (off Cambridge Rd.)
Kitson Rd. *SE5* —3F **67**
Kitson Rd. *SW13* —4C **60**
Kittiwake Ct. SE8 —2B **70**
  (off Abinger Gro.)
Kitto Rd. *SE14* —5F **69**
Kiver Rd. *N19* —4F **9**
Klea Av. *SW4* —4E **79**
Klein's Wharf. *E14* —4C **56**
Knapdale Clo. *SE23* —2D **97**
Knapmill Rd. *SE6* —2C **98**
Knapmill Way. *SE6* —2D **99**
Knapp Clo. *NW10* —3A **18**
Knapp Rd. *E3* —3C **42**
Knapton M. *SW17* —5C **92**
Knaresborough Dri. *SW18*
  —1D **91**
Knaresborough Pl. *SW5*
  —5D **49**
Knatchbull Rd. *NW10* —5A **18**
Knatchbull Rd. *SE5* —5D **67**
Knebworth Ho. *SW8* —5F **65**
Knebworth Rd. *N16* —1A **26**
Kneller Rd. *SE4* —2A **84**
Knighten St. *E1* —2D **55**
Knighthead Point. *E14*
  —3C **56**
Knight Ho. SE17 —5A **54**
  (off Tatum St.)
Knightland Rd. *E5* —4D **13**
Knightleas Ct. *NW2* —3E **19**
Knighton Pk. Rd. *SE26*
  —5F **97**
Knighton Rd. *E7* —5C **16**
Knightrider Ct. EC4 —1E **53**
  (off Knightrider St.)
Knightrider St. *EC4* —5D **39**
Knights Arc. SW1 —3B **50**
  (off Knightsbridge)
Knightsbridge. —3A 50
Knightsbridge. *SW7 & SW1*
  —3B **50**
Knightsbridge. SW1
  (off Sloane St.) —3B **50**

Knightsbridge Grn. *SW1*
  (in two parts) —3B **50**
Knights Clo. *E9* —2E **27**
Knights Ct. *Brom* —3B **100**
Knights Hill. *SE27* —5D **95**
Knight's Hill Sq. *SE27*
  —4D **95**
Knights Ho. SW8 —3A **66**
  (off S. Lambeth Rd.)
Knight's Rd. *E16* —3C **58**
Knight's Wlk. *SE11* —5D **53**
  (in two parts)
Knightswood Ct. *N6* —2F **9**
Knivet Rd. *SW6* —2C **62**
Knobs Hill Rd. *E15* —5D **29**
Knockholt Rd. *SE9* —3F **87**
Knoll Ho. NW8 —1E **35**
  (off Carlton Hill)
Knoll Rd. *SW18* —3E **77**
Knollys Clo. *SW16* —3C **94**
Knolly's Ho. WC1 —3A **38**
  (off Tavistock Pl.)
Knollys Rd. *SW16* —3B **94**
Knottisford St. *E2* —2E **41**
Knotts Grn. M. *E10* —1D **15**
Knotts Grn. Rd. *E10* —1D **15**
Knowle Clo. *SW9* —1C **80**
Knowles Hill Cres. *SE13*
  —3F **85**
Knowles Wlk. *SW4* —1E **79**
Knowlton Ho. SW9 —4C **66**
  (off Cowley Rd.)
Knowsley Rd. *SW11* —5B **64**
Knox Ct. *SW4* —5A **66**
Knox Rd. *E7* —3B **30**
Knox St. *W1* —4B **36**
Knoyle St. *SE14* —2A **70**
Kohat Rd. *SW19* —5D **91**
Kossuth St. *SE10* —1A **72**
Kotree Way. *SE1* —5C **54**
Kramer M. *SW5* —1C **62**
Kreedman Wlk. *E8* —2C **26**
Krupnik Pl. EC2 —3A **40**
  (off Bateman's Row)
Kubrick Bus. Est. E7 —1D **31**
  (off Station App.)
Kuhn Way. *E7* —2C **30**
Kylemore Clo. *E6* —1F **45**
Kylemore Rd. *NW6* —4C **20**
Kylestrome Ho. SW1 —5C **50**
  (off Cundy St.)
Kynance M. *SW7* —4D **49**
Kynance Pl. *W8* —4E **49**
Kynaston Av. *N16* —5B **12**
Kynaston Rd. *N16* —5A **12**
Kynaston Rd. *Brom* —5C **100**
Kyrle Rd. *SW11* —4C **78**
Kyverdale Rd. *N16* —3B **12**

Laburnum Clo. *SE15* —3E **69**
Laburnum Ct. *E2* —5B **26**
  (in two parts)
Laburnum Ct. SE16 —3E **55**
  (off Albion St.)
Laburnum St. *E2* —5B **26**
Lacey Wlk. *E3* —1C **42**

Lacine Ct. *SE16* —3F **55**
(off Christopher Clo.)
Lackington St. *EC2* —4F **39**
Lackland Ho. *SE1* —1B **68**
(off Rowcross St.)
Lacland Ho. *SW10* —3F **63**
(off Worlds End Est.)
Lacon Ho. *WC1* —4B **38**
(off Theobalds Rd.)
Lacon Rd. *SE22* —2C **82**
Lacy Rd. *SW15* —2F **75**
Ladas Rd. *SE27* —4E **95**
Ladbroke Cres. *W11* —5A **34**
Ladbroke Gdns. *W11* —1B **48**
Ladbroke Gro. *W10 & W11*
—3F **33**
Ladbroke Gro. Ho. *W11*
—1B **48**
Ladbroke M. *W11* —2A **48**
Ladbroke Rd. *W11* —2B **48**
Ladbroke Sq. *W11* —1B **48**
Ladbroke Ter. *W11* —1B **48**
Ladbroke Wlk. *W11* —2B **48**
Ladlands. *SE22* —5C **82**
Ladycroft Rd. *SE13* —1D **85**
Lady Dock Wlk. *SE16* —3A **56**
Lady Margaret Rd. *NW5 &
N19* —2E **23**
Lady Micos Almshouses. *E1*
(off Aylward St.) —5E **41**
Ladyship Ter. *SE22* —5C **82**
Ladysmith Av. *E6* —1F **45**
Ladysmith Rd. *E16* —2B **44**
Lady Somerset Rd. *NW5*
—1D **23**
Ladywell. —3D 85
Ladywell Clo. *SE4* —3C **84**
Ladywell Heights. *SE4* —4B **84**
Ladywell Rd. *SE13* —3C **84**
Ladywell St. *E15* —5B **30**
Lafone St. *SE1* —3B **54**
Lagado M. *SE16* —2F **55**
Laing Ho. *SE5* —3E **67**
Lainson St. *SW18* —5C **76**
Lairdale Clo. *SE21* —1E **95**
Laird Ho. *SE5* —3E **67**
(off Redcar St.)
Lairs Clo. *N7* —2A **24**
Laitwood Rd. *SW12* —1D **93**
Lakanal. *SE5* —4A **68**
(off Dalwood St.)
Lake Av. *Brom* —5C **100**
Lake Clo. *SW19* —5B **90**
Lake Ho. *SE1* —3E **53**
(off Southwark Bri. Rd.)
Lake Ho. Rd. *E11* —5C **16**
Laker Ct. *SW4* —4A **66**
Laker Ind. Est. *SE26* —5A **98**
(off Kent Ho. La.)
Lake Rd. *SW19* —5B **90**
Laker Pl. *SW15* —4A **76**
Lakeside Ct. *N4* —4E **11**
Lakeside Rd. *W14* —4F **47**
Lakeside Ter. *EC2* —4E **39**
(off Beech St.)
Lake Vw. Ct. *SW1* —4D **51**
(off Bressenden Pl.)

Lake Vw. Est. *E3* —1A **42**
Lakeview Rd. *SE27* —5C **94**
Lakis Clo. *NW3* —1E **21**
Laleham Ho. *E2* —2B **40**
(off Camlet St.)
Laleham Rd. *SE6* —5E **85**
Lalor St. *SW6* —5A **62**
Lambard Ho. *SE10* —3E **71**
(off Langdale Rd.)
Lamb Ct. *E14* —1A **56**
(off Narrow St.)
Lamberhurst Ho. *SE15*
—2E **69**
Lamberhurst Rd. *SE27*
—4C **94**
Lambert Jones M. *EC2*
(off Beech St.) —4E **39**
Lambert Rd. *E16* —5D **45**
Lambert Rd. *SW2* —3A **80**
Lambert St. *N1* —4C **24**
Lambeth. —4B 52
Lambeth Bri. *SW1 & SE1*
—5A **52**
Lambeth Crematorium. *SW17*
—4E **91**
Lambeth High St. *SE1* —5B **52**
Lambeth Hill. *EC4* —1E **53**
Lambeth Pal. Rd. *SE1* —4B **52**
Lambeth Rd. *SE1 & SE11*
—5B **52**
Lambeth Towers. *SE11* —4C **52**
(off Kennington Rd.)
Lambeth Wlk. *SE11* —5B **52**
(in two parts)
Lambfold Ho. *N7* —3A **24**
Lamb Ho. *SE5* —3E **67**
(off Elmington Est.)
Lamb Ho. *SE10* —2E **71**
(off Haddo St.)
Lamb La. *E8* —4D **27**
Lamble St. *NW5* —2C **22**
Lambolle Pl. *NW3* —3A **22**
Lambolle Rd. *NW3* —3A **22**
Lambourn Clo. *NW5* —1E **23**
Lambourne Av. *SW19* —4B **90**
Lambourne Ho. *NW8* —4F **35**
(off Broadley St.)
Lambourne Rd. *SE16* —5F **55**
Lambourne Pl. *SE3* —4D **73**
Lambourne Rd. *E11* —2E **15**
Lambourn Rd. *SW8* —1D **79**
Lambrook Ho. *SE15* —4C **68**
Lambrook Ter. *SW6* —4A **62**
Lamb's Bldgs. *EC1* —3F **39**
Lamb's Conduit Pas. *WC1*
(off Red Lion St.) —4B **38**
Lamb's Conduit St. *WC1*
(in three parts) —3B **38**
Lambscroft Av. *SE9* —3E **101**
Lamb's M. *N1* —5D **25**
Lamb's Pas. *EC1* —3F **39**
Lamb St. *E1* —4A **40**
Lambton Pl. *W11* —1B **48**
Lambton Rd. *N19* —3A **10**
Lamb Wlk. *SE1* —3A **54**
LAMDA Theatre. —5C 48
Lamerock Rd. *Brom* —4B **100**

Lamerton St. *SE8* —2C **70**
Lamington St. *W6* —5D **47**
Lamlash St. *SE11* —5D **53**
Lamley Ho. *SE10* —3D **71**
(off Ashburnham Pl.)
Lammas Grn. *SE26* —3D **97**
Lammas Rd. *E9* —4F **27**
Lammas Rd. *E10* —4A **14**
Lammermoor Rd. *SW12*
—5D **79**
Lamont Rd. *SW10* —2F **63**
Lamont Rd. Pas. *SW10*
(off Lamont Rd.) —2F **63**
Lampard Gro. *N16* —3B **12**
Lampern Sq. *E2* —2C **40**
Lampeter Sq. *W6* —2A **62**
Lamplighter Clo. *E1* —3E **41**
Lampmead Rd. *SE12* —3B **86**
Lamp Office Ct. *WC1* —3B **38**
(off Conduit St.)
Lamps Ct. *SE5* —3E **67**
Lampton Ho. Clo. *SW19*
—4F **89**
Lanain Ct. *SE12* —5B **86**
Lanark Ho. *SE1* —1C **68**
(off Old Kent Rd.)
Lanark Mans. *W9* —3E **35**
(off Lanark Rd.)
Lanark M. *W9* —2E **35**
Lanark Pl. *W9* —3E **35**
Lanark Rd. *W9* —1D **35**
Lanark Sq. *E14* —4D **57**
Lanbury Rd. *SE15* —2F **83**
Lancashire Ct. *W1* —1D **51**
(off New Bond St.)
Lancaster Av. *SE27* —2D **95**
Lancaster Av. *SW19* —5F **89**
Lancaster Clo. *N1* —4A **26**
Lancaster Clo. *SE27* —2D **95**
Lancaster Clo. *W2* —1D **49**
(off St Petersburgh Pl.)
Lancaster Ct. *SE27* —2D **95**
Lancaster Ct. *SW6* —3B **62**
Lancaster Ct. *W2* —1E **49**
(off Lancaster Ga.)
Lancaster Dri. *E14* —2E **57**
Lancaster Dri. *NW3* —3A **22**
Lancaster Gdns. *SW19*
—5A **90**
Lancaster Ga. *W2* —1E **49**
Lancaster Gro. *NW3* —3F **21**
Lancaster Hall. E16 —2C 58
(off Wesley Av., in two parts)
Lancaster Lodge. *W11*
(off Lancaster Rd.) —5A **34**
Lancaster M. *SW18* —3D **77**
Lancaster M. *W2* —1E **49**
Lancaster Pl. *SW19* —5F **89**
Lancaster Rd. *WC2* —1B **52**
Lancaster Rd. *E7* —4C **30**
Lancaster Rd. *E11* —4A **16**
Lancaster Rd. *N4* —2B **10**
Lancaster Rd. *NW10* —2C **18**
Lancaster Rd. *SW19* —5F **89**
Lancaster Rd. *W11* —5A **34**
Lancaster Stables. *NW3*
—3A **22**

Lancaster St.—Larch Ho.

Lancaster St. *SE1* —3D **53**
Lancaster Ter. *W2* —1F **49**
Lancaster Wlk. *W2* —2E **49**
Lancefield Ct. *W10* —1A **34**
Lancefield Ho. *SE15* —1D **83**
Lancefield St. *W10* —2B **34**
Lancell St. *N16* —4A **12**
Lancelot Pl. *SW7* —3D **50**
Lancer Sq. *W8* —3D **49**
Lancey Clo. *SE7* —5F **59**
Lanchester Ct. *W2* —5B **36**
  (off Seymour St.)
Lanchester Rd. *N6* —1B **8**
Lancing St. *NW1* —2F **37**
Lancresse Ct. *N1* —5A **26**
  (off De Beauvoir Est.)
Landale Ho. *SE16* —4E **55**
  (off Lower Rd.)
Landcroft Rd. *SE22* —3B **82**
Landells Rd. *SE22* —4B **82**
Landford Rd. *SW15* —1E **75**
Landgrove Rd. *SW19* —5C **90**
Landin Ho. *E14* —5C **42**
Landleys Fld. *NW5* —2F **23**
  (off Long Mdw.)
Landmann Ho. *SE16* —5D **55**
  (off Rennie Est.)
Landmann Way. *SE14*
  —1F **69**
Landon Pl. *SW1* —4B **50**
Landon's Clo. *E14* —2E **57**
Landon Wlk. *E14* —1D **57**
Landor Ho. *SE5* —3F **67**
  (off Elmington Est.)
Landor Rd. *SW4* —1A **80**
Landor Wlk. *W12* —3C **46**
Landrake. *NW1* —5E **23**
  (off Plender St.)
Landridge Rd. *SW6* —5B **62**
Landrock Rd. *N8* —1A **10**
Landseer Ho. *NW8* —3F **35**
  (off Frampton St.)
Landseer Ho. *SW1* —5F **51**
  (off Herrick St.)
Landseer Ho. *SW11* —4C **64**
Landseer Rd. *N19* —5A **10**
  (in two parts)
Landulph Ho. *SE11* —1C **66**
  (off Kennings Way)
Landward Ct. *W1* —5A **36**
  (off Harrowby St.)
Lane Clo. *NW2* —5D **5**
Lane End. *SW15* —4F **75**
Lanercost Clo. *SW2* —2C **94**
Lanercost Rd. *SW2* —2C **94**
Lanesborough Pl. *SW1*
  (off Grosvenor Pl.) —3C **50**
Lane, The. *NW8* —1E **35**
Lane, The. *SE3* —1C **86**
Laneway. *SW15* —3D **75**
Laney Ho. *EC1* —4C **38**
  (off Leather La.)
Lanfranc Rd. *E3* —1A **42**
Lanfrey Pl. *W14* —1B **62**
Langbourne Av. *N6* —4C **8**
Langbourne Ct. *E17* —1A **14**
Langbourne Mans. *N6* —4C **8**

Langbourne Pl. *E14* —1D **71**
Langbrook Rd. *SE3* —1F **87**
Langdale. *NW1* —2E **37**
  (off Stanhope St.)
Langdale Clo. *SE17* —2E **67**
Langdale Ho. *SW1* —1F **65**
  (off Churchill Gdns.)
Langdale Rd. *SE10* —3E **71**
Langdale St. *E1* —5D **41**
Langdon Ct. *EC1* —1D **39**
  (off City Rd.)
Langdon Ct. *NW10* —5A **18**
Langdon Ho. *E14* —5E **43**
Langdon Pk. Rd. *N6* —2E **9**
Langdon Way. *SE1* —5C **54**
Langford Clo. *E8* —2C **26**
Langford Clo. *N15* —1A **12**
Langford Clo. *NW8* —1E **35**
Langford Ct. *NW8* —1E **35**
  (off Abbey Rd.)
Langford Grn. *SE5* —1A **82**
Langford Ho. *SE8* —2C **70**
Langford Pl. *NW8* —1E **35**
Langford Rd. *SW6* —5D **63**
Langham Mans. *SW5* —1D **63**
  (off Earl's Ct. Sq.)
Langham Pl. *W1* —4D **37**
Langham Pl. *W4* —2A **60**
Langham St. *W1* —4D **37**
Langholm Clo. *SW12* —5F **79**
Langhorne Ct. *NW8* —4F **21**
  (off Dorman Way)
Lang Ho. *SW8* —3A **66**
  (off Hartington Rd.)
Langland Gdns. *NW3* —2D **21**
Langland Ho. *SE5* —3F **67**
  (off Edmund St.)
Langler Rd. *NW10* —1E **33**
Langley Ct. *SW2* —1A **52**
Langley Cres. *E11* —2E **17**
Langley Dri. *E11* —2D **17**
Langley La. *SW8* —2A **66**
Langley Mans. *SW8* —2B **66**
  (off Langley La.)
Langley St. *WC2* —5A **38**
Langmead St. *SE27* —4D **95**
Langmore Ho. *E1* —5C **40**
  (off Stutfield St.)
Langport Ho. *SW9* —5D **67**
Langroyd Rd. *SW17* —2B **92**
Langside Av. *SW15* —2C **74**
Langston Hughes Clo. *SE24*
  —2D **81**
Lang St. *E1* —3E **41**
Langthorn Ct. *EC2* —2F **39**
Langthorne Ct. *SE6* —4E **99**
Langthorne Rd. *E11* —5E **15**
Langthorne St. *SW6* —3F **61**
Langton Clo. *WC1* —3B **38**
Langton Ho. *SE11* —5B **52**
  (off Lambeth Wlk.)
Langton Pl. *SW18* —1C **90**
Langton Ri. *SE23* —5D **83**
Langton Rd. *NW2* —5E **5**
Langton Rd. *SW9* —3D **67**
Langton St. *SW10* —2E **63**
Langton Way. *SE3* —4B **72**

Langtry Pl. *SW6* —2C **62**
Langtry Rd. *NW8* —5D **21**
Langtry Wlk. *NW8* —5D **21**
Lanhill Rd. *W9* —3C **34**
Lanier Rd. *SE13* —4F **85**
Lannoy Point. *SW6* —3A **62**
  (off Pellant Rd.)
Lanrick Ho. *E14* —5F **43**
Lanrick Rd. *E14* —5F **43**
Lansbury Est. *E14* —5D **43**
Lansbury Gdns. *E14* —5F **43**
Lanscombe Wlk. *SW8* —4A **66**
Lansdell Ho. *SW2* —4C **80**
  (off Tulse Hill)
Lansdowne Ct. *W11* —1A **48**
  (off Lansdowne Ri.)
Lansdowne Cres. *W11*
  —1A **48**
Lansdowne Dri. *E8* —3C **26**
Lansdowne Gdns. *SW8*
  —4A **66**
Lansdowne Grn. *SW8* —4A **66**
Lansdowne Ho. *NW10*
  —1A **18**
Lansdowne Hill. *SE27* —3D **95**
Lansdowne La. *SE7* —2F **73**
Lansdowne M. *SE7* —1F **73**
Lansdowne M. *W11* —2B **48**
Lansdowne Pl. *SE1* —4F **53**
Lansdowne Ri. *W11* —1A **48**
Lansdowne Rd. *E11* —4B **16**
Lansdowne Rd. *E17* —1C **14**
Lansdowne Rd. *W11* —1A **48**
Lansdowne Row. *W1* —2D **51**
Lansdowne Ter. *WC1* —3A **38**
Lansdowne Wlk. *W11* —2A **48**
Lansdowne Way. *SW8* —4F **65**
Lansdowne Wood Clo. *SE27*
  —3D **95**
Lansdowne Workshops. *SE7*
  —1E **73**
Lansdown Rd. *E7* —4E **31**
Lantern Clo. *SW15* —2C **74**
Lanterns Ct. *E14* —3D **57**
Lant Ho. *SE1* —3E **53**
  (off Toulmin St.)
Lant St. *SE1* —3E **53**
Lanvanor Rd. *SE15* —5E **69**
Lanyard Ho. *SE8* —5B **56**
Lapford Clo. *W9* —3B **34**
Lapse Wood Wlk. *SE23*
  —1D **97**
Lapwing Tower. *SE8* —2B **70**
  (off Abinger Gro.,
    in two parts)
Lapworth Ct. *W2* —4D **35**
  (off Chichester Rd.)
Lara Clo. *SE13* —4B **85**
Larch Av. *W3* —2A **46**
Larch Clo. *E13* —3D **45**
Larch Clo. *N19* —4E **9**
Larch Clo. *SE8* —2B **70**
Larch Clo. *SW12* —2D **93**
Larch Ho. *SE16* —3E **55**
  (off Ainsty Est.)
Larch Ho. *W10* —3A **34**
  (off Rowan Wlk.)

Larch Rd. *E10* —4C **14**
Larch Rd. *NW2* —2E **19**
Larcom St. *SE17* —5E **53**
Larden Rd. *W3* —2A **46**
Larissa St. *SE17* —1F **67**
Larkbere Rd. *SE26* —4A **98**
Larkhall La. *SW4* —5F **65**
Larkhall Ri. *SW4* —1E **79**
Lark Row. *E2* —5E **27**
Larkspur Clo. *E6* —4F **45**
Larnach Rd. *W6* —2F **61**
Larpent Av. *SW15* —3E **75**
Lascelles Clo. *E11* —4F **15**
Lascelles Ho. NW1 —3A **36**
 (off Harewood Av.)
Lassell St. *SE10* —1F **71**
Lasseter Pl. *SE3* —2A **72**
Latchmere Pas. *SW11* —5A **64**
Latchmere Rd. *SW11* —5B **64**
Latchmere St. *SW11* —5B **64**
Latham Clo. W14 —5C **48**
 (off W. Cromwell Rd.)
Latimer Ho. *E9* —3F **27**
Latimer Ho. W11 —1B **48**
 (off Kensington Pk. Rd.)
Latimer Ind. Est. *W10* —5E **33**
Latimer Pl. *W10* —5E **33**
Latimer Rd. *E7* —1D **31**
Latimer Rd. *N15* —1A **12**
Latimer Rd. *W10* —4E **33**
 (in two parts)
Latona Ct. SW9 —3C **66**
 (off Caldwell St.)
Latona Rd. *SE15* —2C **68**
Lattimer Pl. *W4* —3A **60**
Latymer Ct. *W6* —5F **47**
Lauderdale Ho. SW9 —4C **66**
 (off Gosling Way)
Lauderdale Mans. W9 —2D **35**
 (off Lauderdale Rd.,
 in two parts)
Lauderdale Pl. EC2 —4E **39**
 (off Beech St.)
Lauderdale Rd. *W9* —2D **35**
Lauderdale Tower. EC2
 (off Beech St.) —4E **39**
Laud St. *SE11* —1B **66**
Launcelot Rd. *Brom* —4C **100**
Launcelot St. *SE1* —3C **52**
Launceston Pl. *W8* —4E **49**
Launch St. *E14* —4E **57**
Laundress La. *N16* —5C **12**
Laundry La. *N1* —5E **25**
Laundry Rd. *W6* —2A **62**
Laura Pl. *E5* —1E **27**
Laurel Bank Gdns. *SW6*
 —5B **62**
Laurelbrook. *SE6* —3A **100**
Laurel Clo. *N19* —4E **9**
Laurel Clo. *SW17* —5A **92**
Laurel Gro. *SE26* —4F **97**
Laurel Ho. *SE8* —2B **70**
Laurel Rd. *SW13* —5C **60**
Laurels, The. *NW10* —5D **19**
Laurel St. *E8* —3B **26**
Laurence Ct. *E10* —2D **15**
Laurence M. *W12* —3C **46**

Laurence Pountney Hill. *EC4*
 —1F **53**
Laurence Pountney La. *EC4*
 —1F **53**
Laurie Gro. *SE14* —4A **70**
Laurie Ho. SE1 —4D **53**
 (off St George's Rd.)
Laurier Rd. *NW5* —5D **9**
Lauriston Rd. *E9* —4E **27**
Lauriston Rd. *SW19* —5F **89**
Lausanne Rd. *SE15* —4E **69**
Lavell St. *N16* —1F **25**
Lavender Clo. *SW3* —2F **63**
Lavender Gdns. *SW11*
 —2B **78**
Lavender Gro. *E8* —4C **26**
Lavender Hill. *SW11* —2A **78**
Lavender Ho. SE16 —2F **55**
 (off Rotherhithe St.)
Lavender Rd. *SE16* —2A **56**
Lavender Rd. *SW11* —1F **77**
Lavender Sq. *E11* —5F **15**
Lavender St. *E15* —3A **30**
Lavender Sweep. *SW11*
 —2B **78**
Lavender Ter. *SW11* —1A **78**
Lavender Wlk. *SW11* —2B **78**
Lavendon Ho. NW8 —3A **36**
 (off Paveley St.)
Lavengro Rd. *SE27* —2E **95**
Lavenham Rd. *SW18* —2B **90**
Lavers Rd. *N16* —5A **12**
Laverstoke Gdns. *SW15*
 —5B **74**
Laverton M. *SW5* —5D **49**
Laverton Pl. *SW5* —5D **49**
Lavina Gro. *N1* —1B **38**
Lavington St. *SE1* —2D **53**
Lavisham Ho. Brom —5C **100**
Lawford Rd. *N1* —4A **26**
Lawford Rd. *NW5* —3E **23**
Lawless Ho. *E14* —1E **57**
Lawless St. *E14* —1D **57**
Lawley St. *E5* —1E **27**
Lawn Dri. *E7* —1F **31**
Lawn La. *SW8* —2A **66**
Lawn Rd. *NW3* —2B **22**
Lawnside. *SE3* —2B **86**
Lawns, The. *SE3* —1B **86**
Lawns, The. *SW19* —5B **90**
Lawn Ter. *SE3* —1A **86**
Lawrence Bldgs. *N16* —5B **12**
Lawrence Clo. *E3* —2C **42**
Lawrence Clo. *W12* —1D **47**
 (off Cureton St.)
Lawrence La. *EC2* —5A **39**
Lawrence Pl. N1 —5A **24**
 (off Brydon Wlk.)
Lawrence Rd. *E6* —5F **31**
Lawrence Rd. *E13* —5D **31**
Lawrence Rd. *E16* —4B **44**
Lawrence St. *SW3* —2A **64**
Lawrence Trad. Est. *SE10*
 —5A **58**
Lawrie Pk. Av. *SE26* —5D **97**

Lawrie Pk. Cres. *SE26*
 —5D **97**
Lawrie Pk. Gdns. *SE26*
 —4D **97**
Lawrie Pk. Rd. *SE26* —5D **97**
Lawson Clo. *E16* —4E **45**
Lawson Clo. *SW19* —3F **89**
Lawson Ct. N4 —3B **10**
 (off Lorne Rd.)
Lawson Ho. W12 —1D **47**
 (off White City Est.)
Law St. *SE1* —4F **53**
Lawton Rd. *E3* —2A **42**
Lawton Rd. *E10* —3E **15**
Laxfield Ct. E8 —5C **26**
 (off Pownall Rd.)
Laxford Ho. SW1 —5C **50**
 (off Cundy St.)
Laxley Clo. *SE5* —3D **67**
Laxton Pl. *NW1* —3D **37**
Layard Rd. *SE16* —5D **55**
Layard Sq. *SE16* —5D **55**
Laybourne Ho. E14 —3C **56**
 (off Admirals Way)
Laycock St. *N1* —3C **24**
Layfield Clo. *NW4* —2D **5**
Layfield Cres. *NW4* —2D **5**
Layfield Ho. SE10 —1C **72**
 (off Kemsing Rd.)
Layfield Rd. *NW4* —2D **5**
Laystall Ct. EC1 —3C **38**
 (off Mt. Pleasant)
Laystall St. *EC1* —3C **38**
Layton's Bldgs. *SE1* —3F **53**
Layzell Wlk. *SE9* —1F **101**
Lazar Wlk. *N7* —4B **10**
Lazenby Ct. WC2 —1A **52**
 (off Floral St.)
Leabank Sq. *E9* —3C **28**
Leabank Vw. *N15* —1C **12**
Lea Bon Ct. E15 —5B **30**
 (off Plaistow Gro.)
Leabourne Rd. *N16* —2C **12**
Lea Bridge. —5F 13
Lea Bri. Ind. Cen. *E10* —3A **14**
Lea Bri. Rd. *E5 & E10*
 —5E **13**
Lea Bri. Rd. *E10* —2C **14**
Lea Ct. *E13* —2C **44**
Leacroft Av. *SW12* —5B **78**
Leadale Rd. *N15 & N16*
 —1C **12**
Leadbetter Ct. NW10
 (off Melville Rd.) —4A **18**
Leadenhall Market. —5A **40**
Leadenhall Mkt. *EC3* —5A **40**
Leadenhall Pl. *EC3* —5A **40**
Leadenhall St. *EC3* —5A **40**
Leadenham Ct. *E3* —3C **42**
Leaf Gro. *SE27* —5C **94**
Leafield Clo. *SW16* —5D **95**
Leafy Oak Rd. *SE12* —4E **101**
Leagrave St. *E5* —5E **13**
Lea Hall Gdns. *E10* —3C **14**
Lea Hall Rd. *E10* —3C **14**
Lea Ho. NW8 —3A **36**
 (off Salisbury St.)

Leahurst Rd. *SE13* —3F **85**
Lea Interchange. (Junct.)
    —2C **28**
Leake Ct. *SE1* —3B **52**
Leake St. *SE1* —3B **52**
  (in two parts)
Lealand Rd. *N15* —1B **12**
Leamington Av. *E17* —1C **14**
Leamington Av. *Brom*
    —5E **101**
Leamington Clo. *Brom*
    —4E **101**
Leamington Rd. Vs. *W11*
    —4B **34**
Leamore St. *W6* —5E **47**
Leamouth. —1A **58**
Leamouth Rd. *E14* —5F **43**
Leander Ct. *SE8* —4C **70**
Leander Rd. *SW2* —4B **80**
Lea Pk. Trad. Est. *E10*
  (off Warley Clo.) —3B **14**
Leapold M. *E9* —5E **27**
Leary Ho. *SE11* —1B **66**
Leaside Rd. *E5* —3E **13**
Leasowes Rd. *E10* —3C **14**
Leatherdale St. *E1* —3E **41**
  (in two parts)
Leather Gdns. *E15* —5A **30**
Leatherhead Clo. *N16* —3B **12**
Leather La. *EC1* —4C **38**
  (in two parts)
Leathermarket Ct. *SE1*
    —3A **54**
Leathermarket St. *SE1*
    —3A **54**
Leathwaite Rd. *SW11* —2B **78**
Leathwell Rd. *SE8* —5D **71**
Lea Vw. Ho. *E5* —3D **13**
Leaway. *E10* —3F **13**
Lebanon Gdns. *SW18* —4C **76**
Lebanon Rd. *SW18* —3C **76**
Lebrun Sq. *SE3* —2D **87**
Lebus Ho. *NW8* —1A **36**
  (off Cochrane St.)
Le Caye Apartments. *E14*
    —5F **57**
Lechmere Rd. *NW2* —3D **19**
Leckford Rd. *SW18* —2E **91**
Leckhampton Pl. *SW2* —5C **80**
Lecky St. *SW7* —1F **63**
Leclair Ho. *SE3* —1D **87**
Leconfield Av. *SW13* —1B **74**
Leconfield Ho. *SE5* —2A **82**
Leconfield Rd. *N5* —1F **25**
Leda Ct. *SW9* —3C **66**
  (off Caldwell St.)
Ledam Ho. *EC1* —4C **38**
  (off Bourne Est.)
Ledbury Ho. *SE22* —1A **82**
Ledbury Ho. *W11* —5B **34**
  (off Colville Rd.)
Ledbury M. N. *W11* —1C **48**
Ledbury M. W. *W11* —1C **48**
Ledbury Rd. *W11* —5B **34**
Ledbury St. *SE15* —3C **68**
Lee. —3B **86**
Lee Bri. *SE13* —1E **85**

Lee Chu. St. *SE13* —2A **86**
Lee Conservancy Rd. *E9*
    —2B **28**
Lee Ct. *SE13* —2F **85**
Leeds Pl. *N4* —3B **10**
Leefern Rd. *W12* —3C **46**
Leegate. *SE12* —3B **86**
Lee Green. (Junct.) —3B **86**
Lee High Rd. *SE13 & SE12*
    —1E **85**
Lee Ho. *EC2* —4E **39**
  (off Monkwell Sq.)
Leeke St. *WC1* —2B **38**
Leeland Way. *NW10* —1B **18**
Lee Pk. *SE3* —2B **86**
Leerdam Dri. *E14* —4E **57**
Lee Rd. *SE3* —1B **86**
Lees Ct. *W1* —1C **50**
  (off Lees Pl.)
Leeside Cres. *NW11* —1A **6**
Leeson Rd. *SE24* —2C **80**
Lees Pl. *W1* —1C **50**
Lee St. *E8* —5B **26**
Lee Ter. *SE3* —1A **86**
Lee Valley Ice Centre.
    —4F **13**
Leeward Ct. *E1* —1C **54**
Leeward Gdns. *SW19* —5A **90**
Leeway. *SE8* —1B **70**
Leewood Clo. *SE12* —4C **86**
Lefevre Wlk. *E3* —5B **28**
Leff Ho. *NW6* —4A **20**
Lefroy Ho. *SE1* —4E **53**
  (off Southwark Bri. Rd.)
Lefroy Rd. *W12* —3B **46**
Legard Rd. *N5* —5D **11**
Legatt Rd. *SE9* —3F **87**
Leggatt Rd. *E15* —1E **43**
Legge St. *SE13* —3E **85**
Leghorn Rd. *NW10* —1B **32**
Legion Clo. *N1* —4C **24**
Legion Ter. *E3* —5B **28**
Leicester Ct. *WC2* —1F **51**
  (off Lisle St.)
Leicester Ho. *SW9* —1D **81**
  (off Loughborough Rd.)
Leicester Pl. *WC2* —1F **51**
Leicester Rd. *E11* —1D **17**
Leicester Rd. *NW10* —4A **18**
Leicester Sq. *WC2* —1F **51**
Leicester St. *WC2* —1F **51**
Leigham Av. *SW16* —3A **94**
Leigham Clo. *SW16* —3B **94**
Leigham Ct. Rd. *SW16*
    —2A **94**
Leigham Hall Pde. *SW16*
    —3A **94**
  (off Streatham High Rd.)
Leigham Va. *SW16 & SW2*
    —3B **94**
Leigh Gdns. *NW10* —1E **33**
Leigh Orchard Clo. *SW16*
    —3B **94**
Leigh Pl. *EC1* —4C **38**
Leigh Rd. *E10* —2E **15**
Leigh Rd. *N5* —1D **25**
Leigh St. *WC1* —2A **38**

Leighton Cres. *NW5* —2E **23**
Leighton Gdns. *NW10* —1D **33**
Leighton Gro. *NW5* —2E **23**
Leighton Ho. *SW1* —5F **51**
  (off Herrick St.)
Leighton House Art Gallery.
    —4B **48**
Leighton House Mus. —4B **48**
Leighton Mans. *W14* —2A **62**
  (off Greyhound Rd.)
Leighton Pl. *NW5* —2E **23**
Leighton Rd. *NW5* —2E **23**
Leila Parnell Pl. *SE7* —2E **73**
Leinster Ct. *NW6* —2C **34**
Leinster Gdns. *W2* —5E **35**
Leinster Ho. *NW6* —2C **34**
Leinster M. *W2* —1E **49**
Leinster Pl. *W2* —5E **35**
Leinster Sq. *W2* —5C **34**
Leinster Ter. *W2* —1E **49**
Leith Clo. *NW9* —3A **4**
Leithcote Gdns. *SW16*
    —4B **94**
Leithcote Path. *SW16* —3B **94**
Leith Mans. *W9* —2D **35**
  (off Grantully Rd.)
Lelita Clo. *E8* —5C **26**
Leman Pas. *E1* —5C **40**
  (off Leman St.)
Leman St. *E1* —5B **40**
Le May Av. *SE12* —3D **101**
Lemmon Rd. *SE10* —2A **72**
Lemna Rd. *E11* —2B **16**
Lemsford Clo. *N15* —1C **12**
Lemsford Ct. *N4* —4E **11**
Lemuel St. *SW18* —4E **77**
Lena Gdns. *W6* —4E **47**
Lenanton Steps. *E14* —3C **56**
Lendal Ter. *SW4* —1F **79**
Len Freeman Pl. *SW6*
    —2B **62**
Lenham Ho. *SE1* —4F **53**
  (off Long La.)
Lenham Rd. *SE12* —2B **86**
Lennard Rd. *SE20 & Beck*
    —5F **97**
Lennon Rd. *NW2* —2E **19**
Lennox Gdns. *NW10* —1B **18**
Lennox Gdns. *SW1* —4B **50**
Lennox Gdns. M. *SW1*
    —4B **50**
Lennox Rd. *E17* —1B **14**
Lennox Rd. *N4* —4B **10**
Lens Rd. *E7* —4E **31**
Lenthall Ho. *SW1* —1E **65**
  (off Churchill Gdns.)
Lenthall Rd. *E8* —4C **26**
Lenthorp Rd. *SE10* —5B **58**
Lentmead Rd. *Brom* —3B **100**
Len Williams Ct. *NW6* —1C **34**
Leof Cres. *SE6* —5D **99**
Leonard Ct. *WC1* —3F **37**
Leonard Rd. *E7* —1C **30**
Leonard's Rd. *E14* —4E **43**
Leonard St. *EC1* —3F **39**
Leonora Ho. *W9* —3E **35**
  (off Lanark Rd.)

Leontine Clo. SE15 —3C 68
Leopards Ct. EC1 —4C 38
(off Baldwins Gdns.)
Leopold Av. SW19 —5B 90
Leopold Bldgs. E2 —2B 40
(off Columbia Rd.)
Leopold M. E9 —5E 27
Leopold Rd. E17 —1C 14
Leopold Rd. NW10 —4A 18
Leopold Rd. SW19 —4B 90
Leopold St. E3 —4B 42
Leopold Ter. SW19 —5B 90
Leo St. SE15 —3D 69
Leo Yd. EC1 —3D 39
(off St John St.)
Leppoc Rd. SW4 —3F 79
Leroy St. SE1 —5A 54
Lerry Clo. W14 —2B 62
Lescombe Clo. SE23 —3A 98
Lescombe Rd. SE23 —3A 98
Leslie Prince Ct. SE5 —3F 67
Leslie Rd. E11 —1E 29
Leslie Rd. E16 —5D 45
Lessar Av. SW4 —4E 79
Lessingham Av. SW17 —4B 92
Lessing St. SE23 —5A 84
Lester Av. E15 —3A 44
Leswin Pl. N16 —5B 12
Leswin Rd. N16 —5B 12
Letchford Gdns. NW10 —2C 32
Letchford M. NW10 —2C 32
Letchworth St. SW17 —4B 92
Lethbridge Clo. SE13 —4E 71
Letterstone Rd. SW6 —3B 62
Lettice St. SW6 —4B 62
Lett Rd. E15 —4F 29
Lettsom St. SE5 —5A 68
Lettsom Wlk. E13 —1C 44
Leucha Rd. E17 —1A 14
Levana Clo. SW19 —1A 90
Levehurst Ho. SE27 —5E 95
Levendale Rd. SE23 —2A 98
Levenhurst Way. SW4 —5A 66
Leven Rd. E14 —4E 43
Leverett St. SW3 —5A 50
Leverington Pl. N1 —2F 39
(off Charles Sq.)
Leverson St. SW16 —5E 93
Leverstock Ho. SW3 —1A 64
(off Cale St.)
Lever St. EC1 —2D 39
Leverton Pl. NW5 —2E 23
Leverton St. NW5 —2E 23
Levison Way. N19 —3F 9
Levita Ho. NW1 —2F 37
(off Ossulston St., in two parts)
Lewesdon Clo. SW19 —1F 89
Lewes Ho. SE1 —3A 54
Lewes Ho. SE15 —2C 68
(off Friary Est.)
Leweston Pl. N16 —2B 12
Lewey Ho. E3 —3B 42
Lewin Rd. SW14 —1A 74
Lewin Rd. SW16 —5F 93
Lewis Ct. SE16 —1D 69
(off Stubbs Dri.)
Lewis Gro. SE13 —2E 85
Lewisham. —1E 85
Lewisham Bus. Cen. SE14 —2F 69
Lewisham Cen. SE13 —2E 85
Lewisham Crematorium. SE6 —2B 100
Lewisham Heights. SE23 —1E 97
Lewisham High St. SE13 —4D 85
Lewisham Hill. SE13 —5E 71
Lewisham Model Mkt. SE13 —2E 85
(off Lewisham High St.)
Lewisham Pk. SE13 —3E 85
Lewisham Rd. SE13 —4D 71
Lewisham St. SW1 —3F 51
(in two parts)
Lewisham Way. SE14 & SE4 —4B 70
Lewis Ho. E14 —2E 57
Lewis Silkin Ho. SE15
(off Lovelinch Clo.) —2E 69
Lewis St. NW1 —3D 23
(in two parts)
Lexham Gdns. W8 —5C 48
Lexham Gdns. M. W8 —4D 49
Lexham M. W8 —5C 48
Lexham Wlk. W8 —4D 49
Lexington Apartments. EC1 —3F 39
Lexington St. W1 —1E 51
Lexton Gdns. SW12 —1F 93
Leybourne Ho. E14 —5B 42
Leybourne Ho. SE15 —2E 69
Leybourne Rd. E11 —3B 16
Leybourne Rd. NW1 —4D 23
Leybourne St. NW1 —4D 23
Leybridge Ct. SE12 —3C 86
Leyden Mans. N19 —2A 10
Leyden St. E1 —4B 40
Leydon Clo. SE16 —2F 55
Leyes Rd. E16 —5F 45
Leyland Ho. E14 —1D 57
Leyland Rd. SE12 —3C 86
Leylang Rd. SE14 —3F 69
Leys Ct. SW9 —5C 66
Leysdown Ho. SE17 —1A 68
(off Madron St.)
Leysfield Rd. W12 —4C 46
Leyspring Rd. E11 —3B 16
Leyton. —5E 15
Leyton Bus. Cen. E10 —4C 14
Leyton Ct. SE23 —1E 97
Leyton Grange Est. E10 —4C 14
Leyton Grn. Rd. E10 —1E 15
Leyton Ind. Village. E17 —2F 13
Leyton Orient F.C. —5D 15
Leyton Pk. Rd. E10 —5E 15
Leyton Rd. E15 —2E 29
Leytonstone. —3A 16
Leytonstone Rd. E15 —1A 30
Leyton Way. E11 —2A 16
Leywick St. E15 —1A 44
Liardet St. SE14 —2A 70
Liberia Rd. N5 —3D 25
Liberty M. SW12 —4D 79
Liberty St. SW9 —4B 66
Libra Rd. E13 —1C 44
Library Pde. NW10 —5A 18
(off Craven Pk. Rd.)
Library Pl. E1 —1D 55
Library St. SE1 —3D 53
Lichfield Rd. E3 —2A 42
Lichfield Rd. E6 —2F 45
Lichfield Rd. NW2 —1A 20
Lickey Ho. W14 —2B 62
(off N. End Rd.)
Lidcote Gdns. SW9 —5B 66
Liddell Gdns. NW10 —1E 33
Liddell Rd. NW6 —3C 20
Liddington Rd. E15 —5B 30
Liddon Rd. E13 —2D 45
Liden Clo. E17 —2B 14
Lidfield Rd. N16 —1F 25
Lidgate Rd. SE15 —3B 68
Lidiard Rd. SW18 —2E 91
Lidlington Pl. NW1 —1E 37
Lidyard Rd. N19 —3E 9
Liffords Pl. SW13 —5B 60
Lifford St. SW15 —2F 75
Lighter Clo. SE16 —5A 56
Lighterman Ho. E14 —1E 57
Lighterman M. E1 —5F 41
Lightermans Rd. E14 —3C 56
Lightermans Wlk. SW18 —2C 76
Light Horse Ct. SW3 —1C 64
(off Royal Hospital Rd.)
Ligonier St. E2 —3B 40
Lilac Ct. E13 —5E 31
Lilac Ho. SE4 —1C 84
Lilac Pl. SE11 —5B 52
Lilac St. W12 —1C 46
Lilburne Gdns. SE9 —3F 87
Lilburne Rd. SE9 —3F 87
Lilestone Ho. NW8 —3F 35
(off Frampton St.)
Lilestone St. NW8 —3A 36
Lilford Ho. SE5 —5E 67
Lilford Rd. SE5 —5D 67
Lilian Barker Clo. SE12 —3C 86
Lilian Clo. N16 —5A 12
Lilley Clo. E1 —2C 54
Lillian Rd. SW13 —2C 60
Lillie Mans. W14 —2A 62
(off Lillie Rd.)
Lillie Rd. SW6 —2F 61
Lillieshall Rd. SW4 —1D 79
Lillie Yd. SW6 —2C 62
Lillington Gdns. Est. SW1 —5E 51
(off Vauxhall Bri. Rd.)
Lilliput Ct. SE12 —3D 87
Lily Clo. W14 —5F 47
(in two parts)
Lily Pl. EC1 —4C 38

Lily Rd. *E17* —1C **14**
Lilyville Rd. *SW6* —4B **62**
Limberg Ho. *SE8* —5B **56**
Limborough Ho. *E14* —4C **42**
Limburg Rd. *SW11* —2A **78**
Limeburner La. *EC4* —5D **39**
Lime Clo. *E1* —2C **54**
*Lime Ct. E11 —4A **16***
(off Trinity Clo.)
Lime Ct. *E17* —1E **15**
Lime Gro. *W12* —3E **47**
Limeharbour. *E14* —4D **57**
Limeharbour Ct. *E14* —4D **57**
Limehouse. —5B 42
Limehouse Causeway. *E14* —1B **56**
Limehouse Cut. *E14* —4D **43**
Limehouse Fields Est. *E1* —4A **42**
Limehouse Link. *E14* —5A **42**
Lime Kiln Dri. *SE7* —2D **73**
Limerick Clo. *SW12* —5E **79**
Limerston St. *SW10* —2E **63**
Limes Av. *E12* —5F **17**
Limes Av. *NW11* —2A **6**
Limes Av. *SW13* —5B **60**
Limes Fld. Rd. *SW14* —1A **74**
Limesford Rd. *SE15* —2F **83**
Limes Gdns. *SW18* —4C **76**
Limes Gro. *SE13* —2E **85**
Limes, The. *SW18* —4C **76**
*Limes, The. W2 —1C **48***
(off Linden Gdns.)
Lime St. *EC3* —1A **54**
Lime St. Pas. *EC3* —5A **40**
Limes Wlk. *SE15* —2E **83**
Limetree Clo. *SW2* —1B **94**
Limetree Ter. *SE6* —1B **98**
Limetree Wlk. *SW17* —5C **92**
Lime Wlk. *E15* —5A **30**
Limpsfield Av. *SW19* —2F **89**
Linacre Clo. *SE15* —1D **83**
*Linacre Ct. W6 —1F **61***
(off Talgarth Rd.)
Linacre Rd. *NW2* —3D **19**
*Linale Ho. N1 —1F **39***
(off Murray Gro.)
Linberry Wlk. *SE8* —5B **56**
Linchmere Rd. *SE12* —5B **86**
Lincoln Av. *SW19* —3F **89**
Lincoln Ct. *N16* —2F **11**
Lincoln Ct. *SE12* —3E **101**
Lincoln Ho. *SW3* —3B **50**
Lincoln Ho. *SW9 & SE5* —3C **66**
Lincoln M. *NW6* —5B **20**
Lincoln M. *SE21* —2F **95**
Lincoln Rd. *E7* —3F **31**
Lincoln Rd. *E13* —3D **45**
Lincoln's Inn. —5B 38
Lincolns Inn Fields. *WC2* —5B **38**
Lincoln St. *E11* —4A **16**
Lincoln St. *SW3* —5B **50**
Lincombe Rd. *Brom* —3B **100**
Lindal Rd. *SE4* —3B **84**
Linden Av. *NW10* —1F **33**
Linden Ct. *W12* —2E **47**
Linden Gdns. *W2* —1C **48**
Linden Gdns. *W4* —1A **60**
Linden Gro. *SE15* —1D **83**
Linden Gro. *SE26* —5E **97**
Linden Ho. *SE15* —1D **83**
Linden Lea. *N2* —1E **7**
Linden M. *N1* —2F **25**
Linden M. *W2* —1C **48**
Linden Wlk. *N19* —4E **9**
Lindfield Gdns. *NW3* —2D **21**
Lindfield St. *E14* —5C **42**
Lindisfarne Way. *E9* —1A **28**
Lindley Est. *SE15* —3C **68**
*Lindley Ho. E1 —4E **41***
(off Lindley St.)
*Lindley Ho. SE15 —3C **68***
(off Peckham Pk. Rd.)
Lindley Rd. *E10* —4E **15**
Lindley St. *E1* —4E **41**
Lindore Rd. *SW11* —2B **78**
Lindo St. *SE15* —5E **69**
Lindrop St. *SW6* —5E **63**
Lindsay Sq. *SW1* —1F **65**
Lindsell St. *SE10* —4E **71**
Lindsey M. *N1* —4E **25**
Lindsey St. *EC1* —4D **39**
Lind St. *SE8* —5C **70**
Lindway. *SE27* —5D **95**
*Linfield. WC1 —2B **38***
(off Sidmouth St.)
Linford Christie Stadium. —5C 32
Linford St. *SW8* —4E **65**
Lingard Ho. *E14* —4E **57**
Lingards Rd. *SE13* —2E **85**
*Lingfield Ho. SE1 —3D **53***
(off Lancaster St.)
Lingfield Rd. *SW19* —5F **89**
Lingham St. *SW9* —5A **66**
Ling Rd. *E16* —4C **44**
Lings Coppice. *SE21* —2F **95**
Lingwell Rd. *SW17* —3A **92**
Lingwood Rd. *E5* —2C **12**
Linhope St. *NW1* —3B **36**
*Linkenholt Mans. W6 —5B **46***
(off Stamford Brook Av.)
Link Ho. *E3* —1D **43**
Link Rd. *E1* —1C **54**
Links Rd. *NW2* —4B **4**
Link St. *E9* —3E **27**
*Linksview. N2 —1B **8***
(off Gt. North Rd.)
*Links Yd. E1 —4C **40***
(off Spelman St.)
Linkway. *N4* —2E **11**
Linkwood Wlk. *NW1* —4F **23**
Linley Sambourne House.
(off Stafford Ter.) —4C 48
Linnell Clo. *NW11* —1D **7**
Linnell Dri. *NW11* —1D **7**
*Linnell Ho. E1 —4B **40***
(off Folgate St.)
Linnell Rd. *SE5* —5A **68**
Linnet M. *SW12* —5C **78**
Linom Rd. *SW4* —2A **80**
Linscott Rd. *E5* —1E **27**
*Linsey Ct. E10 —3C **14***
(off Grange Rd.)
Linsey St. *SE16* —5C **54**
(in two parts)
Linslade Ho. *E2* —5C **26**
*Linslade Ho. NW8 —3A **36***
(off Paveley St.)
Linstead St. *NW6* —4C **20**
Linstead Way. *SW18* —5A **76**
Lintaine Clo. *SW6* —2A **62**
Linthorpe Rd. *N16* —2A **12**
Linton Clo. *SE7* —1E **73**
Linton Gdns. *E6* —5F **45**
Linton Gro. *SE27* —5D **95**
Linton Ho. *E14* —4C **42**
Linton St. *N1* —5E **25**
(in two parts)
Linver Rd. *SW6* —5C **62**
Linwood Clo. *SE5* —5B **68**
Lion Clo. *SE4* —4C **84**
*Lion Ct. N1 —5B **24***
(off Copenhagen St.)
*Lion Ct. SE1 —2A **54***
(off Magdalen St.)
Lionel Gdns. *SE9* —3F **87**
Lionel M. *W10* —4A **34**
Lionel Rd. *SE9* —3F **87**
Lion Mills. *E2* —1C **40**
Lions Clo. *SE9* —3F **101**
Lion Yd. *SW4* —2F **79**
Liphook Cres. *SE23* —5E **83**
Lipton Rd. *E1* —5F **41**
Lisburne Rd. *NW3* —1B **22**
Lisford St. *SE15* —4B **68**
Lisgar Ter. *W14* —5B **48**
Liskeard Gdns. *SE3* —4C **72**
*Liskeard Ho. SE11 —1C **66***
(off Kennings Way)
Lisle Clo. *SW17* —4D **93**
Lisle Ct. *NW2* —5A **6**
Lisle St. *WC2* —1F **51**
*Lismore. SW19 —5B **90***
(off Woodside)
Lismore Cir. *NW5* —2C **22**
Lismore Ho. *SE15* —1D **83**
*Lismore Wlk. N1 —3E **25***
(off Clephane Rd.)
Lissenden Gdns. *NW5* —1C **22**
(in two parts)
Lissenden Mans. *NW5* —1C **22**
Lisson Grn. Est. *NW8* —3A **36**
Lisson Grove. —4A 36
Lisson Gro. *NW8 & NW1* —3F **35**
*Lisson Ho. NW1 —4A **36***
(off Lisson St.)
Lisson St. *NW1* —4A **36**
Lister Clo. *W3* —4A **32**
Listergate Ct. *SW15* —2E **75**
Lister Ho. *E1* —4C **40**
*Lister Ho. SE3 —2A **72***
(off Restell Clo.)
*Lister Lodge. W2 —4C **34***
(off Admiral Wlk.)
Lister M. *N7* —1B **24**
Lister Rd. *E11* —3A **16**

Liston Rd. *SW4* —1E **79**
Listowel Clo. *SW9* —3C **66**
Listria Pk. *N16* —4A **12**
Litchfield Av. *E15* —3A **30**
Litchfield Ct. *E17* —1C **14**
Litchfield Gdns. *NW10*
—3C **18**
Litchfield St. *WC2* —1F **51**
Litchfield Way. *NW11* —1E **7**
Lithos Rd. *NW3* —3D **21**
Lit. Albany St. NW1 —2D **37**
(off Longford St.,
in two parts)
Little Angel Theatre. —5D 25
Lit. Argyll St. *W1* —5E **37**
Lit. Boltons, The.
SW5 & SW10 —1D **63**
Little Bornes. *SE21* —4A **96**
Littlebourne. *SE13* —5A **86**
Little Britain. *EC1* —4D **39**
Little Brownings. *SE23*
—2D **97**
Littlebury Rd. *SW4* —1F **79**
Lit. Chester St. *SW1* —4D **51**
Little Cloisters. *SW1* —4A **52**
Lit. College La. EC4 —1F **53**
(off College St.)
Lit. College St. *SW1* —4A **52**
Littlecombe. *SE7* —2D **73**
Littlecombe Clo. *SW15*
—4F **75**
Littlecote Clo. *SW19* —5A **76**
Lit. Dean's Yd. SW1 —4A **52**
(off Dean's Yd.)
Little Dimocks. *SW12*
—2D **93**
Lit. Dorrit Ct. *SE1* —3E **53**
Lit. Edward St. *NW1* —2D **37**
Lit. Essex St. WC2 —1C **52**
(off Essex St.)
Littlefield Clo. *N19* —1E **23**
Lit. George St. *SW1* —3A **52**
Lit. Green St. *NW5* —1D **23**
Little Heath. *SE7* —2F **73**
Little Holt. *E11* —1C **16**
Lit. London Ct. SE1 —3B **54**
(off Wolseley St.)
Lit. Marlborough St. W1
(off Kingly St.) —5E **37**
Lit. Newport St. *WC2* —1F **51**
Lit. New St. *EC4* —5C **38**
Lit. Portland St. *W1* —5E **37**
Lit. Russell St. *WC1* —4A **38**
Lit. St James's St. *SW1*
—2E **51**
Little Sanctuary. *SW1* —3F **51**
Lit. Smith St. *SW1* —4F **51**
Lit. Somerset St. *E1* —5B **40**
Lit. Titchfield St. *W1* —4E **37**
Littleton Ho. SW1 —1E **65**
(off Lupus St.)
Littleton St. *SW18* —2E **91**
Lit. Trinity La. *EC4* —1E **53**
Little Turnstile. *WC1* —4B **38**
Littlewood. *SE13* —4E **85**
Livermere Ct. E8 —5B **26**
(off Queensbridge Rd.)

Livermere Rd. *E8* —5B **26**
Liverpool Gro. *SE17* —1E **67**
Liverpool Rd. *E10* —1E **15**
Liverpool Rd. *E16* —4A **44**
Liverpool Rd. *N7 & N1*
—2C **24**
Liverpool St. *EC2* —4A **40**
Livesey Mus. —2D 69
Livesey Pl. *SE15* —2C **68**
Livingstone College Towers.
E10 —1E **15**
Livingstone Ct. *E10* —1E **15**
Livingstone Ho. SE5 —3E **67**
(off Wyndam Rd.)
Livingstone Lodge. W2
(off Admiral Wlk.) —4C **34**
Livingstone Mans. *W14*
—2A **62**
(off Queen's Club Gdns.)
Livingstone Pl. *E14* —1E **71**
Livingstone Rd. *E15* —5E **29**
Livingstone Rd. *E17* —1D **15**
Livingstone Rd. *SW11* —1F **77**
Livonia St. *W1* —5E **37**
Lizard St. *EC1* —2E **39**
Lizban St. *SE3* —3D **73**
Llandovery Ho. *E14* —3E **57**
Llanelly Rd. *NW2* —4B **6**
Llanvanor Rd. *NW2* —4B **6**
Llewellyn St. *SE16* —3C **54**
Lloyd Baker Ho. WC1 —2B **38**
(off Lloyd Baker St.)
Lloyd Baker St. *WC1* —2B **38**
(in two parts)
Lloyd's Av. *EC3* —5A **40**
Lloyds Building. —5A 40
Lloyd's Pl. *SE3* —5A **72**
Lloyd Sq. *WC1* —2C **38**
Lloyd's Row. *EC1* —2C **38**
Lloyd St. *WC1* —2C **38**
Lloyds Wharf. SE1 —3B **54**
(off Mill St.)
Loampit Hill. *SE13* —5C **70**
Loampit Vale. (Junct.) —1E **85**
Loampit Va. *SE13* —1D **85**
Loanda Clo. *E8* —5B **26**
Loats Rd. *SW2* —4A **80**
Lobelia Clo. *E6* —4F **45**
Lochaber Rd. *SE13* —2A **86**
Lochaline St. *W6* —2E **61**
Lochinvar St. *SW12* —5D **79**
Lochmore Ho. SW1 —5C **50**
(off Cundy St.)
Lochnagar St. *E14* —4E **43**
Lockbridge Rd. W9 —4C **34**
(off Elmfield Way)
Lock Chase. *SE3* —1A **86**
Locke Ho. SW8 —4E **65**
(off Wadhurst Rd.)
Lockesfield Pl. *E14* —1D **71**
Lockgate Clo. *E9* —2B **28**
Lockhart Clo. *N7* —3B **24**
Lockhart Ho. *SE10* —3D **71**
(off Tarves Way)
Lockhart St. *E3* —3B **42**
Lockhurst St. *E5* —1F **27**
Lockington Rd. *SW8* —4D **65**

Lock Keepers Quay. *SE16*
—4F **55**
(off Brunswick Quay)
Lockmead Rd. *N15* —1C **12**
Lockmead Rd. *SE13* —1E **85**
Locksfield Pl. *E14* —1D **71**
Locksfields. SE17 —5F **53**
(off Catesby St.)
Lockside. *E14* —1A **56**
(off Narrow St.)
Locksley Est. *E14* —5B **42**
Locksley St. *E3* —4B **42**
Lock Vw. Ct. *E14* —1A **56**
Lockwood Clo. *SE26* —4F **97**
Lockwood Ho. *SE11* —2C **66**
Lockwood Sq. *SE16* —4D **55**
Lockyer Est. SE1 —3F **53**
(off Kipling St., in two parts)
Lockyer Ho. *SE10* —1B **72**
(off Blackwall La.)
Lockyer Ho. SW8 —3F **65**
(off Wandsworth Rd.)
Lockyer St. *SE1* —3F **53**
Locton Grn. *E3* —5B **28**
Loddiges Ho. *E9* —4E **27**
Loddiges Rd. *E9* —4E **27**
Loder St. *SE15* —3E **69**
Lodge Av. *SW14* —1A **74**
Lodge Rd. *NW8* —2F **35**
Lodore Gdns. *NW9* —1A **4**
Lodore St. *E14* —5E **43**
Loftie St. *SE16* —3C **54**
Lofting Rd. *N1* —4B **24**
Loftus Rd. *W12* —2D **47**
Logan M. *W8* —5C **48**
Logan Pl. *SW5* —5C **48**
Loggetts. *SE21* —2A **96**
Lohmann Ho. SE11 —2C **66**
(off Kennington Oval)
Lolesworth Clo. *E1* —4B **40**
Lollard St. *SE11* —5B **52**
(in two parts)
Loman St. *SE1* —3D **53**
Lomas Ct. *E8* —4C **40**
Lombard Bus. Cen., The.
SW11 —5F **63**
Lombard Ct. *EC3* —1F **53**
Lombard La. *EC4* —5C **38**
Lombard Rd. *SW11* —5F **63**
Lombard St. *EC3* —5F **39**
Lombard Trad. Est. *SE7*
—5D **59**
Lombard Wall. *SE7* —4D **59**
(in two parts)
Lombardy Pl. *W2* —1D **49**
Lomond Gro. *SE5* —3F **67**
Lomond Ho. *SE5* —3F **67**
Loncroft Rd. *SE5* —2A **68**
Londesborough Rd. *N16*
—1A **26**
Londinium Tower. E1 —1B **54**
(off W. Tenter St.)
London Aquarium. —3B 52
London Arena. —4D 57
London Bri. *SE1 & EC4*
—2F **53**

London Bri. St. *SE1* —2F **53**
London Bri. Wlk. *SE1* —2F *53*
(off Duke St. Hill)
London Broncos R.L.F.C.
—1E 73
(Charlton Athletic
Football Ground)
London Canal Mus. —1A 38
London City Airport. —2F 59
London City Airport. *E16*
—1F 59
London Commonwealth
Institute. —4C 48
London Dungeon. —2F 53
(off Tooley St.)
London Eye. —3B 52
London Fields E. Side. *E8*
(in two parts) —4D 27
London Fields W. Side. *E8*
—4C 26
London Ho. NW8 —1A **36**
(off Avenue Rd.)
London Ho. *WC1* —3B 38
London Knights Ice Hockey.
(London Arena) —4D 57
London La. *E8* —4D 27
London Leopards Basketball.
(London Arena) —4D 57
London Master Bakers
Almshouses. *E10* —1D **15**
London M. *W2* —5F 35
London Planetarium.
—3C 36
London Rd. *E13* —1C 44
London Rd. *SE1* —4D 53
London Rd. *SE23* —1D 97
London St. *EC3* —1A 54
London St. *W2* —5F 35
London Ter. *E2* —1C 40
London Towers Basketball.
—5C 96
(Crystal Palace National
Sports Centre)
London Transport Mus.
—1A 52
London Underwriting Cen.
EC3 —1A 54
London Wall. *EC2* —4E 39
London Wall Bldgs. EC2
(off London Wall) —4F **39**
London Westland Heliport.
—5D 63
London Wharf. E2 —5D 27
(off Wharf Pl.)
London Zoo. —1C 36
Long Acre. *WC2* —1A 52
Longbeach Rd. *SW11*
—1B 78
Longberrys. *NW2* —5B 6
Longbridge Way. *SE13*
—3E 85
Longdown Rd. *SE6* —4C 98
Long Dri. *W3* —5A 32
Longfellow Rd. *E17* —1B 14
Longfellow Way. *SE1* —5B 54
Longfield Cres. *SE26* —3E 97
Longfield Est. *SE1* —5B 54

Longfield St. *SW18* —5C 76
Longford Ho. Brom —5F **99**
(off Brangbourne Rd.)
Longford St. *NW1* —3D 37
Longford Wlk. *SW2* —5C 88
Longhedge Ho. SE26 —4C **96**
(off High Level Dri.)
Longhedge St. *SW11* —5C 64
Longhill Rd. *SE6* —2F 99
Longhope Clo. *SE15* —2A 68
Longhurst Rd. *SE13* —3F 85
Longland Ct. *SE1* —1C 68
Longlands Ct. W11 —1B **48**
(off Westbourne Gro.)
Long La. *EC1* —4D 39
Long La. *SE1* —3F 53
Longleat Ho. SW1 —1F **65**
(off Rampayne St.)
Longleigh Ho. SE5 —4A **68**
(off Peckham Rd.)
Long Lents Ho. *NW10*
—5A 18
Longley Ct. *SW8* —4A 66
Longley Ho. *SW17* —5A 92
Longley St. *SE1* —5C 54
Longley Way. *NW2* —5E 5
Longman Ho. E8 —5B **26**
(off Haggerston Rd.)
Long Mark Rd. *E16* —4F 45
Longmead Ho. *SE27* —5E **95**
Long Mdw. *NW5* —2F 23
Longmead Rd. *SW17* —5B 92
Longmoore St. *SW1* —5E 51
Longnor Est. *E1* —2F 41
Longnor Rd. *E1* —2F 41
Long Pond Rd. *SE3* —4A 72
Longridge Ho. *SE1* —4E 53
Longridge Rd. *SW5* —5C 48
Long Rd. *SW4* —2D 79
Long's Ct. WC2 —1F **51**
(off Orange St.)
Longshore. *SE8* —5B 56
Longshott Ct. SW5 —5C **48**
(off W. Cromwell Rd.)
Longstaff Cres. *SW18* —4C 76
Longstaff Rd. *SW18* —4C 76
Longstone Av. *NW10* —4B 18
Longstone Rd. *SW17* —5D 93
Long St. *E2* —2B 40
Longton Av. *SE26* —4D 97
Longton Gro. *SE26* —4D 97
Longville Rd. *SE11* —5D 53
Long Wlk. *SE1* —4A 54
Long Wlk. *SW13* —5A 60
Long Wall. *E15* —2F 43
Longwood Dri. *SW15* —4C 74
Long Yd. *WC1* —3B 38
Lonsdale Av. *E6* —2F 45
Lonsdale Clo. *E6* —3F 45
Lonsdale Clo. *SE9* —3F 101
Lonsdale Ho. *W11* —5B 34
Lonsdale M. W11 —5B **34**
(off Lonsdale Rd.)
Lonsdale Pl. *N1* —4C 24
Lonsdale Rd. *E11* —1B 16
Lonsdale Rd. *NW6* —5B 20
Lonsdale Rd. *SW13* —4B 60

Lonsdale Rd. *W4* —5B 46
Lonsdale Rd. *W11* —5B 34
Lonsdale Sq. *N1* —4C 24
Lonsdale Rd. *W11* —1C 48
Lopez Ho. *SW9* —1B 80
Loraine Rd. *N7* —1B 24
Lord Amory Way. *E14* —3E 57
Lordell Pl. *SW19* —5E 89
Lorden Wlk. *E2* —2C 40
Lord Hills Bri. *W2* —4D 35
Lord Hills Rd. *W2* —4D 35
Lord Holland La. *SW9* —5C 66
Lord Napier Pl. *W6* —1C 60
Lord N. St. *SW1* —4A 52
Lord Roberts M. *SW6* —3D 63
Lords Clo. *SE21* —2E 95
Lord's Cricket Ground.
—2F 35
Lordship Gro. *N16* —4F 11
Lordship La. *SE22* —2B 82
Lordship La. Est. *SE21*
—5C 82
Lordship Pk. *N16* —4E 11
Lordship Pk. M. *N16* —4E 11
Lordship Pl. *SW3* —2A 64
Lordship Rd. *N16* —3F 11
Lordship Ter. *N16* —4F 11
Lords Vw. *NW8* —2F 35
(in two parts)
Loreburn Ho. *N7* —1B 24
Lorenzo St. *WC1* —2B 38
Loring Rd. *SE14* —4A 70
Loris Rd. *W6* —4E 47
Lorn Ct. *SW9* —5C 66
Lorne Clo. *NW8* —2A 36
Lorne Gdns. *W11* —3F 47
Lorne Rd. *E7* —1D 31
Lorne Rd. *E17* —1C 14
Lorne Rd. *N4* —3B 10
Lorn Rd. *SW9* —5B 66
Lorraine Ct. *NW1* —4D 23
Lorrimore Rd. *SE17* —2D 67
Lorrimore Sq. *SE17* —2D 67
Lorton Ho. NW6 —5C **20**
(off Kilburn Va.)
Lothair Rd. N. *N4* —1D 11
Lothair Rd. S. *N4* —2C 10
Lothbury. *EC2* —5B 39
Lothian Rd. *SW9* —4D 67
Lothrop St. *W10* —2A 34
Lots Rd. *SW10* —3E 63
Lotus Clo. *SE21* —3F 95
Loubet St. *SW17* —5B 92
Loudoun Rd. *NW8* —5E 21
Loughborough Est. *SW9*
—1D 81
Loughborough Pk. *SW9*
—2D 81
Loughborough Rd. *SW9*
—5C 66
Loughborough St. *SE11*
—1B 81
Lough Rd. *N7* —2B 24
Louisa Gdns. *E1* —3F 41
Louisa St. *E1* —3F 41
Louise Bennett Clo. *SE24*
—2D 81

Louise De Marillac Ho.—Lyal Rd.

Louise De Marillac Ho. *E1*
(off Smithy St.)
—4E *41*
Louise Rd. *E15* —3A **30**
Louise White Ho. *N19* —3F **9**
Louisville Rd. *SW17* —3C **92**
Louvaine Rd. *SW11* —2F **77**
Lovat Ct. *EC3* —1A **54**
(in two parts)
Lovatt Ct. *SW12* —1D **93**
Lovegrove St. *SE1* —1C **68**
Lovegrove Wlk. *E14* —2E **57**
Lovelace Ho. *E8* —5B **26**
(off Haggerston Rd.)
Lovelace Rd. *SE21* —2E **95**
Love La. *EC2* —5E **39**
Lovelinch Clo. *SE15* —2E **69**
Lovell Ho. *E8* —5C **26**
(off Shrubland Rd.)
Lovell Pl. *SE16* —4A **56**
Loveridge M. *NW6* —3B **20**
Loveridge Rd. *NW6* —3B **20**
Lovers Wlk. *SE10* —2F **71**
Lovers' Wlk. *W1* —2C **50**
Love Wlk. *SE5* —5F **67**
Low Cross Wood La. *SE21*
—3B **96**
Lowden Rd. *SE24* —2D **81**
Lowder Ho. *E1* —2D **55**
(off Wapping La.)
Lowe Av. *E16* —4C **44**
Lowell Ho. *SE5* —3E **67**
(off Wyndham Est.)
Lowell St. *E14* —5A **42**
Lwr. Addison Gdns. *W14*
—3A **48**
Lwr. Belgrave St. *SW1*
—4D **51**
Lower Clapton. —1D 27
Lwr. Clapton Rd. *E5* —5D **13**
Lwr. Clarendon Wlk. W11
(off Clarendon Rd.) —5A *34*
Lwr. Common S. *SW15*
—1D **75**
Lwr. Grosvenor Pl. *SW1*
—4D **51**
Lower Holloway. —2B 24
Lwr. James St. *W1* —1E **51**
Lwr. John St. *W1* —1E **51**
Lwr. Lea Crossing. *E14*
—1A **58**
Lower Mall. *W6* —1D **61**
Lwr. Marsh. *SE1* —3C **52**
Lwr. Merton Ri. *NW3* —4A **22**
Lwr. Richmond Rd. *SW15*
—1D **75**
Lower Rd. *SE1* —3C **52**
Lower Rd. *SE16 & SE8*
(in two parts) —3E **55**
Lwr. Sloane St. *SW1* —5C **50**
Lower Sydenham. —4F 97
Lwr. Sydenham Ind. Est. *SE26*
—5B **98**
Lower Ter. *NW3* —5E **7**
Lwr. Thames St. *EC3* —1F **53**
Lowerwood Ct. W11 —5A 34
(off Westbourne Pk. Rd.)

Lowestoft Clo. *E5* —4E **13**
(off Mt. Pleasant Hill)
Loweswater Ho. *E3* —3B **42**
Lowfield Rd. *NW6* —4C **20**
Low Hall La. *E17* —1A **14**
Low Hall Mnr. Bus. Cen. *E17*
—1A **14**
Lowman Rd. *N7* —1B **24**
Lowndes Clo. *SW1* —4C **50**
Lowndes Ct. *SW1* —4B **50**
Lowndes Ct. W1 —5E 37
(off Kingly St.)
Lowndes Pl. *SW1* —4C **50**
Lowndes Sq. *SW1* —3B **50**
Lowndes St. *SW1* —4C **50**
Lowood Ho. *E1* —1E **55**
(off Bewley St.)
Lowood St. *E1* —1D **55**
Lowry Ct. SE16 —1D 69
(off Stubbs Dri.)
Lowther Gdns. *SW7* —3F **49**
Lowther Hill. *SE23* —5A **84**
Lowther Ho. *E8* —5B **26**
Lowther Ho. SW1 —1E 65
(off Churchill Gdns.)
Lowther Rd. *N7* —2C **24**
Lowther Rd. *SW13* —4B **60**
Lowth Rd. *SE5* —4E **67**
Loxford Av. *E6* —1F **45**
Loxham St. *WC1* —2A **38**
Loxley Clo. *SE26* —5F **97**
Loxley Rd. *SW18* —1F **91**
Loxton Rd. *SE23* —1F **97**
Lubbock Ho. *E14* —1D **57**
(off Colville Est.)
Lubbock St. *SE14* —3E **69**
Lucan Ho. *N1* —5F **25**
(off Colville Est.)
Lucan Pl. *SW3* —5A **50**
Lucas Av. *E13* —5D **31**
Lucas Ct. *SE26* —5A **98**
Lucas Ct. *SW11* —4C **64**
Lucas Ho. *NW10* —4C **18**
Lucas Sq. *NW11* —1C **6**
Lucas St. *SE8* —4C **70**
Lucerne M. *W8* —2C **48**
Lucerne Rd. *N5* —1D **25**
Lucey Rd. *SE16* —4C **56**
Lucey Way. *SE16* —4C **54**
(in two parts)
Lucien Rd. *SW17* —4C **92**
Lucien Rd. *SW19* —2D **91**
Lucorn Clo. *SE12* —4B **86**
Lucy Brown Ho. SE1 —2E 53
(off Park St.)
Ludgate B'way. *EC4* —5D **39**
Ludgate Cir. *EC4* —5D **39**
Ludgate Hill. *EC4* —5D **39**
Ludgate Sq. *EC4* —5D **39**
Ludlow St. *EC1* —3E **39**
Ludovick Wlk. *SW15* —2A **74**
Ludwick M. *SE14* —3A **70**
Luffman Rd. *SE12* —3D **101**
Lugard Ho. *W12* —2D **47**
Lugard Rd. *SE15* —5D **69**
Luke Ho. *E1* —5D **41**
(off Tillman St.)
Luke St. *EC2* —3A **40**

Lukin St. *E1* —5E **41**
Lullingstone Ho. SE15
(off Lovelinch Clo.) —2E *69*
Lullingstone La. *SE13* —4F **85**
Lulot Gdns. *N19* —4D **9**
Lulworth. *NW1* —4F **23**
(off Wrotham Rd.)
Lulworth. *SE17* —1F **67**
(off Portland St.)
Lulworth Ho. *SW8* —3B **66**
Lulworth Rd. *SE9* —2F **101**
Lulworth Rd. *SE15* —5D **69**
Lumiere Building, The. E7
(off Romford Rd.) —2F *31*
Lumley Ct. *WC2* —1A **52**
Lumley Flats. SW1 —1C 64
(off Holbein Pl.)
Lumley St. *W1* —5C **36**
Lumsdon. *NW8* —5D **21**
(off Abbey Rd.)
Lund Point. *E15* —5E **29**
Lundy Wlk. *N1* —3E **25**
Lunham Rd. *SE19* —5A **96**
Luntley Pl. *E1* —4C **40**
Lupin Clo. *SW2* —2D **95**
Lupin Point. *SE1* —3B **54**
(off Abbey St.)
Lupton Clo. *SE12* —3D **101**
Lupton St. *NW5* —1E **23**
(in two parts)
Lupus St. *SW1* —1D **65**
Luralda Gdns. *E14* —1E **71**
Lurgan Av. *W6* —2F **61**
Lurline Gdns. *SW11* —4C **64**
Luscombe Way. *SW8* —3A **66**
Lushington Rd. *NW10*
—1D **33**
Lushington Rd. *SE6* —4D **99**
Lushington Ter. E8 —2C 26
(off Wayland Av.)
Luther King Clo. *E17* —1B **14**
Luton Ho. *E13* —3C **44**
(off Luton Rd.)
Luton Pl. *SE10* —3E **71**
Luton Rd. *E13* —3C **44**
Luton St. *NW8* —3F **35**
Lutton Ter. NW3 —1E 21
(off Heath St.)
Luttrell Av. *SW15* —3D **75**
Lutwyche Rd. *SE6* —2B **98**
Lutyens Ho. SW1 —1E 65
(off Churchill Gdns.)
Luxborough Ho. *W1* —4C **36**
(off Luxborough St.)
Luxborough St. *W1* —4C **36**
Luxborough Tower. W1
(off Luxborough St.) —4C *36*
Luxemburg Gdns. *W6* —5F **47**
Luxfield Rd. *SE9* —1F **101**
Luxford St. *SE16* —5F **55**
Luxmore St. *SE4* —4B **70**
Luxor St. *SE5* —1E **81**
Lyall Av. *SE21* —4A **96**
Lyall M. *SW1* —4C **50**
Lyall M. W. *SW1* —4C **50**
Lyall St. *SW1* —4C **50**
Lyal Rd. *E3* —1A **42**

Lycett Pl. *W12* —3C **46**
Lydden Gro. *SW18* —5D **77**
Lydden Rd. *SW18* —5D **77**
*Lydford. NW1 —5E **23***
(off Royal College St.)
*Lydford Clo. N16 —2A **26***
(off Pellerin Rd.)
Lydford Rd. *N15* —1F **11**
Lydford Rd. *NW2* —3E **19**
Lydford Rd. *W9* —3B **34**
Lydhurst Av. *SW2* —2B **94**
Lydney Clo. *SE15* —3A **68**
Lydney Clo. *SW19* —2A **90**
Lydon Rd. *SW4* —1E **79**
Lyford Rd. *SW18* —5F **77**
Lyford St. *SE7* —5F **59**
*Lygon Ho. E2 —2B **40***
(off Gosset St.)
*Lygon Ho. SW6 —4A **62***
(off Fulham Pal. Rd.)
Lygon Pl. *SW1* —4D **51**
Lyham Clo. *SW2* —4A **80**
Lyham Rd. *SW2* —3A **80**
*Lyly Ho. SE1 —4F **53***
(off Burbage Clo.)
Lyme Farm Rd. *SE12* —2C **86**
Lyme Gro. *E9* —4E **27**
Lymer Av. *SE19* —5B **96**
Lyme St. *NW1* —4E **23**
Lyme Ter. *NW1* —4E **23**
Lyminge Gdns. *SW18* —1A **92**
Lymington Rd. *NW6* —3D **21**
Lympstone Gdns. *SE15* —3C **68**
Lynbrook Clo. *SE15* —3A **68**
Lynch Wlk. *SE8* —2B **70**
Lyncott Cres. *SW4* —2D **79**
Lyncourt. *SE3* —5F **71**
Lyncroft Gdns. *NW6* —2C **20**
Lyncroft Mans. *NW6* —2C **20**
Lyndale. *NW2* —1B **20**
Lyndale Av. *NW2* —5B **6**
Lyndale Clo. *SE3* —2B **72**
Lynde Ho. *SW4* —1F **79**
Lyndhurst Clo. *NW10* —5A **4**
*Lyndhurst Ct. NW8 —5F **21***
(off Finchley Rd.)
Lyndhurst Dri. *E10* —2E **15**
Lyndhurst Gdns. *NW3* —2F **21**
Lyndhurst Gro. *SE15* —5A **68**
Lyndhurst Lodge. *E14* —5F **57**
Lyndhurst Rd. *NW3* —2F **21**
Lyndhurst Sq. *SE15* —4B **68**
Lyndhurst Ter. *NW3* —2F **21**
Lyndhurst Way. *SE15* —4B **68**
Lyneham Wlk. *E5* —2A **28**
Lynette Av. *SW4* —4D **79**
Lyn M. *E3* —2B **42**
Lyn M. *N16* —1A **26**
Lynmouth Rd. *E17* —1A **14**
Lynmouth Rd. *N16* —3B **12**
Lynne Clo. *SE23* —5B **84**
Lynne Way. *NW10* —3A **18**
*Lynn Ho. SE15 —2D **69***
(off Friary Est.)
Lynn M. *E11* —4A **16**
Lynn Rd. *E11* —4A **16**
Lynn Rd. *SW12* —5D **79**
Lynsted Gdns. *SE9* —1F **87**
Lynton Clo. *NW10* —2A **18**
Lynton Est. *SE1* —5C **54**
*Lynton Ho. W2 —5E **35***
(off Hallfield Est.)
*Lynton Mans. SE1 —4C **52***
(off Kennington Rd.)
Lynton Rd. *N8* —1F **9**
(in two parts)
Lynton Rd. *NW6* —1B **34**
Lynton Rd. *SE1* —5B **54**
Lynwood Rd. *SW17* —3B **92**
Lyon Ho. *NW8* —3A **36**
Lyon Ind. Est. *NW2* —4D **5**
Lyons Pl. *NW8* —3F **35**
Lyon St. *N1* —4B **24**
Lyons Wlk. *W14* —5A **48**
Lyric M. *SE26* —4E **97**
Lyric Rd. *SW13* —4B **60**
Lyric Theatre. —5E 47
Lysander Gro. *N19* —3F **9**
*Lysander Ho. E2 —1D **41***
(off Temple St.)
Lysander M. *N19* —3E **9**
Lysias Rd. *SW12* —4D **79**
Lysia St. *SW6* —3F **61**
Lysons Wlk. *SW15* —2C **74**
Lytcott Gro. *SE22* —3A **82**
Lytham St. *SE17* —1F **67**
Lyttelton Clo. *NW3* —4A **22**
Lyttelton Rd. *E10* —5D **15**
Lytton Clo. *N2* —1F **7**
Lytton Gro. *SW15* —3F **75**
Lytton Rd. *E11* —2A **16**
Lyveden Rd. *SE3* —3D **73**

*Mabledon Ct. WC1 —2F **37***
(off Mabledon Pl.)
Mabledon Pl. *NW1* —2F **37**
Mablethorpe Rd. *SW6* —3A **62**
Mabley St. *E9* —2A **28**
Macarthur Clo. *E7* —3C **30**
Macarthur Ter. *SE7* —2F **73**
*Macartney Ho. SW9 —4C **66***
(off Gosling Way)
Macaulay Ct. *SW4* —1D **79**
Macaulay Rd. *E6* —1F **45**
Macaulay Rd. *SW4* —1D **79**
Macaulay Sq. *SW4* —2D **79**
McAuley Clo. *SE1* —4C **52**
Macauley M. *SE13* —4E **71**
Macbeth Ho. *N1* —1A **40**
Macbeth St. *W6* —1D **61**
McCall Clo. *SW4* —5A **66**
McCall Cres. *SE7* —1F **73**
McCall Ho. *N7* —1A **24**
*Macclesfield Ho. EC1 —2E **39***
(off Central St.)
Macclesfield Rd. *EC1* —2E **39**
Macclesfield St. *W1* —1F **51**
McCoid Way. *SE1* —3E **53**
McCrone M. *NW3* —3F **21**
McCullum Rd. *E3* —5B **28**
McDermott Clo. *SW11* —1A **78**
McDermott Rd. *SE15* —1C **82**
Macdonald Rd. *E7* —1C **30**
Macdonald Rd. *N19* —4E **9**
McDowall Clo. *E16* —4B **44**
McDowall Rd. *SE5* —4E **67**
Macduff Rd. *SW11* —4C **64**
Mace Clo. *E1* —2D **55**
Mace Gateway. *E16* —1C **58**
Mace St. *E2* —1F **41**
McEwen Way. *E15* —5F **29**
*Macey St. SE10 —2E **71***
(off Thames St.)
Macfarlane Rd. *W12* —2E **47**
Macfarren Pl. *NW1* —3C **36**
*McGlashon Ho. E1 —3C **40***
(off Hunton St.)
McGrath Rd. *E15* —2B **30**
*McGregor Ct. N1 —2A **40***
(off Hoxton St.)
MacGregor Rd. *E16* —4E **45**
McGregor Rd. *W11* —5B **34**
Machell Rd. *SE15* —1E **83**
*McIndoe Ct. N1 —5F **25***
(off Sherborne St.)
*McIntosh Ho. SE16 —5E **55***
(off Millender Wlk.)
*Macintosh Ho. W1 —4C **36***
(off Beaumont St.)
*Mackay Ho. W12 —1D **47***
(off White City Est.)
Mackay Rd. *SW8* —1D **79**
McKay Trad. Est. *W10* —3A **34**
Mackennal St. *NW8* —1A **36**
Mackenzie Clo. *W12* —1D **47**
Mackenzie Ho. *NW2* —5C **4**
Mackenzie Rd. *N7* —3B **24**
Mackenzie Wlk. *E14* —2C **56**
McKerrell Rd. *SE15* —4C **68**
Mackeson Rd. *NW3* —1B **22**
Mackie Rd. *SW2* —5C **80**
Mackintosh La. *E9* —2F **27**
Macklin St. *WC2* —5A **38**
*Mackonochie Ho. EC1 —4C **38***
(off Baldwins Gdns.)
Mackrow Wlk. *E14* —1E **57**
Mack's Rd. *SE16* —5C **54**
*Mackworth Ho. NW1 —2E **37***
(off Augustus St.)
Mackworth St. *NW1* —2E **37**
Maclaren M. *SW15* —2E **75**
Maclean Rd. *SE23* —4A **84**
McLeod's M. *SW7* —5D **49**
Macleod St. *SE17* —1E **67**
*Maclise Ho. SW1 —5A **52***
(off Marsham St.)
Maclise Rd. *W14* —4A **48**
*McMillan Ho. SE4 —1A **84***
(off Arica Rd.)
McMillan St. *SE8* —2C **70**
*Macnamara Ho. SW10 —3F **63***
(off Worlds End Est.)
McNeil Rd. *SE5* —5A **68**
Maconochies Rd. *E14* —1D **71**
Macquarie Way. *E14* —5D **57**
*Macready Ho. W1 —4A **36***
(off Crawford St.)

Macready Pl. *N7* —1A **24**
Macroom Rd. *W9* —2B **34**
Mac's Pl. *EC4* —5C **38**
Madame Tussaud's. —3C **36**
Maddams St. *E3* —3D **43**
Maddocks Ho. *E1* —1D **55**
  (off Cornwall St.)
Maddock Way. *SE17* —2D **67**
Maddox St. *W1* —1D **51**
Madeira Rd. *E11* —3F **15**
Madeira Rd. *SW16* —5A **94**
Madinah Rd. *E8* —3C **26**
Madras Pl. *N7* —3C **24**
Madrid Rd. *SW13* —4C **60**
Madrigal La. *SE5* —3D **67**
Madron St. *SE17* —1A **68**
Mafeking Av. *E6* —1F **45**
Mafeking Rd. *E16* —3B **44**
Magdala Av. *N19* —4E **9**
Magdalene Clo. *SE15* —5D **69**
Magdalen Pas. *E1* —1B **54**
Magdalen Rd. *SW18* —1E **91**
Magdalen St. *SE1* —2A **54**
Magee St. *SE11* —2C **66**
Magellan Ct. *NW10* —4A **18**
  (off Stonebridge Pk.)
Magellan Pl. *E14* —5C **56**
Magnin Clo. *E8* —5C **26**
Magnolia Clo. *E10* —4C **14**
Magnolia Gdns. *E10* —4C **14**
Magnolia Ho. *SE8* —2B **70**
Magnolia Lodge. *W8* —4D **49**
Magnolia Pl. *SW4* —3A **80**
Magpie All. *EC4* —5C **38**
Magpie Clo. *E7* —2B **30**
Magpie Pl. *SE14* —2A **70**
Magri Wlk. *E1* —4E **41**
Maguire St. *SE1* —3B **54**
Mahatma Gandhi Ind. Est.
  SE24 —2D **81**
Mahogany Clo. *SE16* —2A **56**
Maida Av. *W2* —4E **35**
Maida Hill. —3B 34
Maida Vale. —2D 35
Maida Va. *W9* —1D **35**
Maiden La. *NW1* —4F **23**
Maiden La. *SE1* —2E **53**
Maiden La. *WC2* —1A **52**
Maiden Pl. *N19* —5E **9**
Maiden Rd. *E15* —4A **30**
Maidenstone Hill. *SE10*
  —4E **71**
Maidstone Bldgs. *SE1* —2E **53**
Maidstone Ho. *E14* —5D **43**
Mail Coach Yd. *E2* —2A **40**
Mais Ho. *SE26* —2C **97**
Maismore St. *SE15* —2C **68**
Maitland Clo. *SE10* —3D **71**
Maitland Ct. *W2* —1F **49**
  (off Lancaster Ter.)
Maitland Ho. *SW1* —2E **65**
  (off Churchill Gdns.)
Maitland Pk. Est. *NW3*
  —3B **22**
Maitland Pk. Rd. *NW3* —3B **22**
Maitland Pk. Vs. *NW3* —3B **22**
Maitland Pl. *E5* —1D **27**

Maitland Rd. *E15* —3B **30**
Maitland Rd. *SE26* —5F **97**
Maize Row. *E14* —1B **56**
Major Rd. *E15* —2F **29**
Major Rd. *SE16* —4C **54**
Makepeace Av. *N6* —4C **8**
Makepeace Mans. *N6* —4C **8**
Makins St. *SW3* —5A **50**
Malabar Ct. *W12* —1D **47**
  (off India Way)
Malabar St. *E14* —3C **56**
Malam Ct. *SE11* —5C **52**
Malam Gdns. *E14* —1D **57**
Malbrook Rd. *SW15* —2D **75**
Malcolm Ct. *E7* —3B **30**
Malcolm Ct. *NW4* —1C **4**
Malcolm Cres. *NW4* —1C **4**
Malcolm Gavin Clo. *SW17*
  —2A **92**
Malcolm Ho. *N1* —1A **40**
  (off Arden Est.)
Malcolm Pl. *E2* —3E **41**
Malcolm Rd. *E1* —3E **41**
Malcolmson Ho. *SW1* —1F **65**
  (off Aylesford St.)
Malden Ct. *N4* —1E **11**
Malden Cres. *NW5* —3C **22**
Malden Pl. *NW5* —2C **22**
Malden Rd. *NW5* —2B **22**
Maldon Clo. *E15* —2A **30**
Maldon Ho. *N1* —5E **25**
Maldon Rd. *SE5* —1A **82**
Malet Pl. *WC1* —3F **37**
Malet St. *WC1* —3F **37**
Maley Av. *SE27* —2D **95**
Malfort Rd. *SE5* —1A **82**
Malham Rd. *SE23* —1F **97**
Malibu Ct. *SE26* —3D **97**
Mallams M. *SW9* —1D **81**
Mallard Clo. *E9* —3B **28**
Mallard Clo. *NW6* —1C **34**
Mallard Ho. *NW8* —1A **36**
  (off Barrow Hill Est.)
Mallards. *E11* —2C **16**
  (off Blake Hall Rd.)
Mall Chambers. *W8* —2C **48**
  (off Kensington Mall)
Mallet Rd. *SE13* —4F **85**
Mall Galleries. —2F **51**
  (off Carlton Ho. Ter.)
Mall Gallery. *WC2* —5A **38**
  (off Thomas Neals
    Shop. Mall)
Mallinson Rd. *SW11* —3A **78**
Mallon Gdns. *E1* —5B **40**
  (off Commercial St.)
Mallord St. *SW3* —2F **63**
Mallory Clo. *SE4* —2A **84**
Mallory St. *NW8* —3A **36**
Mallow St. *EC1* —3F **39**
Mall Rd. *W6* —1D **61**
Mall, The. *E15* —4F **29**
Mall, The. *SW1* —3E **51**
Malmesbury. *E2* —1E **41**
  (off Cyprus St.)
Malmesbury Rd. *E3* —2B **42**
Malmesbury Rd. *E16* —4A **44**

Malmesbury Ter. *E16* —4B **44**
Malmsey Ho. *SE11* —1B **66**
Malpas Rd. *E8* —2D **27**
Malpas Rd. *SE4* —5B **70**
Malsmead Ho. *E9* —2B **28**
  (off Homerton Rd.)
Malta Rd. *E10* —3C **14**
Malta St. *EC1* —3D **39**
Maltby St. *SE1* —3B **54**
Malthouse Dri. *W4* —2B **60**
Malthouse Pas. *SW13*
  —5B **60**
Malting Ho. *E14* —1B **56**
Maltings Clo. *SW13* —5B **60**
Maltings Lodge. *W4* —2A **60**
  (off Corney Reach Way)
Maltings Pl. *SE1* —3A **54**
  (off Tower Bri. Rd.)
Maltings Pl. *SW6* —4D **63**
Malton M. *W10* —5A **34**
Malton Rd. *W10* —5A **34**
Maltravers St. *WC2* —1B **52**
Malt St. *SE1* —2C **68**
Malva Clo. *SW18* —3D **77**
Malvern Clo. *W10* —4B **34**
Malvern Ct. *SW7* —5F **49**
  (off Onslow Sq.)
Malvern Ct. *W12* —3C **46**
  (off Hadyn Pk. Rd.)
Malvern Gdns. *NW2* —4A **6**
Malvern Ho. *N16* —3B **12**
Malvern M. *NW6* —2C **34**
Malvern Pl. *NW6* —2B **34**
Malvern Rd. *E6* —5F **31**
Malvern Rd. *E8* —4C **26**
Malvern Rd. *E11* —4A **16**
Malvern Rd. *NW6* —2C **34**
  (in two parts)
Malvern Ter. *N1* —5C **24**
Malwood Rd. *SW12* —4D **79**
Malyons Rd. *SE13* —4B **85**
Malyons Ter. *SE13* —3D **85**
Managers St. *E14* —2E **57**
Manaton Clo. *SE15* —1D **83**
Manbey Gro. *E15* —3A **30**
Manbey Pk. Rd. *E15* —3A **30**
Manbey Rd. *E15* —3A **30**
Manbey St. *E15* —3A **30**
Manbre Rd. *W6* —2E **61**
Manchester Dri. *W10* —3A **34**
Manchester Gro. *E14* —1E **71**
Manchester Ho. *SE17* —1E **67**
Manchester M. *W1* —4C **36**
  (off Manchester St.)
Manchester Rd. *E14* —3E **57**
Manchester Rd. *N15* —1F **11**
Manchester Sq. *W1* —5C **36**
Manchester St. *W1* —4C **36**
Manchuria Rd. *SW11* —4C **78**
Manciple St. *SE1* —3F **53**
Mandalay Rd. *SW4* —3E **79**
Mandarin Ct. *NW8* —1A **18**
  (off Mitchellbrook Way)
Mandarin Ct. *SE8* —2C **70**
  (off Edward St.)
Mandela Clo. *W12* —1D **47**

*Mandela Ho. E2 —2B **40***
(off Virginia Rd.)
Mandela Ho. *SE5* —5D **67**
Mandela Rd. *E16* —5C **44**
Mandela St. *NW1* —5E **23**
Mandela St. *SW9* —3C **66**
(in two parts)
Mandela Way. *SE1* —5A **54**
Mandeville Clo. *SE3* —3B **72**
*Mandeville Ho. SE1 —1B **68***
(off Rolls Rd.)
Mandeville Ho. *SW4* —3E **79**
Mandeville M. *SW4* —2F **79**
Mandeville Pl. *W1* —5C **36**
Mandeville St. *E5* —5A **14**
Mandrake Rd. *SW17* —3B **92**
Mandrake Way. *E15* —4A **30**
Mandrell Rd. *SW2* —3A **80**
Manette St. *W1* —5F **37**
Manfred Rd. *SW15* —3B **76**
Manger Rd. *N7* —3A **24**
Manilla St. *E14* —3C **56**
*Manitoba Ct. SE16 —3E **55***
(off Canada Est.)
Manley Ct. *N16* —5B **12**
Manley Ho. *SE11* —5C **52**
Manley St. *NW1* —5C **22**
*Manneby Prior. N1 —1B **38***
(off Cumming St.)
Manningford Clo. *EC1* —2D **39**
Manningtree Clo. *SW19* —1A **90**
Manningtree St. *E1* —5C **40**
Manny Shinwell Ho. SW6
*(off Clem Attlee Ct.) —2B **62***
Manor Av. *E7* —1E **31**
Manor Av. *SE4* —5B **70**
Manor Brook. *SE3* —2C **86**
Manor Ct. *E10* —3D **15**
*Manor Ct. N2 —1B **8***
(off Aylmer Rd.)
Manor Ct. *SW2* —3B **80**
Manor Ct. *SW6* —4D **63**
Manor Ct. *SW16* —3A **94**
Mnr. Deerfield Cotts. *NW9* —1B **4**
Manor Est. *SE16* —5D **55**
*Manorfield Clo. N19 —1E **23***
(off Fulbrook M.)
Manor Fields. *SW15* —4F **75**
Manor Gdns. *N7* —5A **10**
*Manor Gdns. SW4 —5E **65***
(off Larkhall Ri.)
Manor Gdns. *W4* —1A **60**
Manor Gro. *SE15* —2E **69**
Manorhall Gdns. *E10* —3C **14**
Manor House. (Junct.) —3E **11**
*Manor Ho. NW1 —4A **36***
(off Marylebone Rd.)
*Manor Ho. Ct. W9 —3E **35***
(off Warrington Gdns.)
Manor Ho. Dri. *NW6* —4F **19**
Mnr. Ho. Garden. *E11* —1D **17**
Manor La. *SE13 & SE12* —3A **86**
Manor La. Ter. *SE13* —2A **86**
*Manor M. NW6 —1C **34***
(off Cambridge Rd., in two parts)
Manor M. *SE4* —5B **70**
Manor Mt. *SE23* —1E **97**
Manor Pde. *N16* —4B **12**
*Manor Pde. NW10 —1B **32***
(off High St.)
Manor Pk. *SE13* —2F **85**
Manor Park Crematorium. *E7* —1E **31**
*Mnr. Park Pde. SE13 —2F **85***
(off Lee High Rd.)
Mnr. Park Rd. *E12* —1F **31**
Mnr. Park Rd. *NW10* —5B **18**
Manor Pl. *SE17* —1D **67**
Manor Rd. *E10* —2C **14**
Manor Rd. *E15 & E16* —1A **44**
Manor Rd. *N16* —4F **11**
Manor Way. *SE3* —2B **86**
Manresa Rd. *SW3* —1A **64**
Mansard Beeches. *SW17* —5C **92**
Mansell St. *E1* —5B **40**
Mansel Rd. *SW19* —5A **90**
Manse Rd. *N16* —5B **12**
*Mansfield Ct. E2 —5B **26***
(off Whiston Rd.)
Mansfield Heights. *N2* —1B **8**
Mansfield M. *W1* —4D **37**
Mansfield Pl. *NW3* —1E **21**
Mansfield Rd. *E11* —1D **17**
Mansfield Rd. *NW3* —2B **22**
Mansfield St. *W1* —4D **37**
Mansford St. *E2* —1C **40**
Mansion Clo. *SW9* —4C **66**
(in two parts)
Mansion Gdns. *NW3* —5D **7**
Mansion House. —5F 39
Mansion Ho. Pl. *EC4* —5F **39**
*Mansion Ho. St. EC2 —5F **39***
(off Victoria St.)
Mansions, The. *SW5* —1D **63**
Manson M. *SW7* —5F **49**
Manson Pl. *SW7* —5F **49**
*Manston. NW1 —4E **23***
(off Agar Gro.)
Manstone Rd. *NW2* —2A **20**
*Manston Ho. W14 —4A **48***
(off Russell Rd.)
Mantilla Rd. *SW17* —4C **92**
Mantle Rd. *SE4* —1A **84**
Mantle Way. *E15* —4A **30**
Mantua St. *SW11* —1F **77**
Mantus Clo. *E1* —3E **41**
Mantus Rd. *E1* —3E **41**
Manville Gdns. *SW17* —3D **93**
Manville Rd. *SW17* —2C **92**
Manwood Rd. *SE4* —3B **84**
Manygates. *SW12* —2D **93**
Mapesbury Rd. *NW2* —4A **20**
Mapeshill Pl. *NW2* —3E **19**
Mapes Ho. *NW6* —4A **20**
Mape St. *E2* —2D **41**
(in two parts)
Maple Av. *W3* —2A **46**
Maple Clo. *N16* —1C **12**
Maple Clo. *SW4* —4F **79**
Maple Ct. *SE6* —1D **99**
Maplecroft Clo. *E6* —5F **45**
Mapledene Est. *E8* —4C **26**
Mapledene Rd. *E8* —4B **26**
*Maple Ho. SE8 —3B **70***
(off Idonia St.)
Maple Leaf Sq. *SE16* —3F **55**
Maple Lodge. *W8* —4D **49**
Maple M. *NW6* —1D **35**
Maple M. *SW16* —5B **94**
Maple Pl. *W1* —3E **37**
Maple Rd. *E11* —1A **16**
Maples Pl. *E1* —4D **41**
Maplestead Rd. *SW2* —5B **80**
Maple St. *W1* —4E **37**
Mapleton Cres. *SW18* —4D **77**
Mapleton Rd. *SW18* —4C **76**
(in two parts)
Maple Wlk. *W10* —2F **33**
Maplin Rd. *E16* —5C **44**
Maplin St. *E3* —2B **42**
Mapperley Clo. *E11* —1B **16**
*Marathon Ho. NW1 —4B **36***
(off Marylebone Rd.)
Marban Rd. *W9* —2B **34**
Marble Arch. (Junct.) —1B **50**
Marble Arch. —1B 50
(off Marble Arch)
Marble Arch. *W1* —1B **50**
Marble Dri. *NW2* —3F **5**
Marble Ho. *W9* —3B **34**
Marble Quay. *E1* —2C **54**
Marbrook Ct. *SE12* —3E **101**
Marchant Ct. *SE1* —1B **68**
Marchant Rd. *E11* —4F **15**
Marchant St. *SE14* —2A **70**
Marchbank Rd. *W14* —2B **62**
March Ct. *SW15* —2D **75**
Marchmont St. *WC1* —3A **38**
Marchwood Clo. *SE5* —3A **68**
Marcia Rd. *SE1* —5A **54**
Marcilly Rd. *SW18* —3F **77**
*Marcon Ct. E8 —2D **27***
(off Amhurst Rd.)
Marconi Rd. *E10* —3C **14**
Marcon Pl. *E8* —2D **27**
Marco Polo Ho. *SW8* —3D **65**
Marco Rd. *W6* —4E **47**
Marcus Ct. *E15* —5A **30**
Marcus Garvey M. *SE22* —4D **83**
Marcus Garvey Way. *SE24* —2C **80**
Marcus St. *E15* —5A **30**
Marcus St. *SW18* —4D **77**
Marcus Ter. *SW18* —4D **77**
Mardale Dri. *NW9* —1A **4**
Marden Ct. *SE8* —2B **70**
Marden Ho. *E5* —2D **27**
Marden Sq. *SE16* —4D **55**

Mardyke Ho. SE17 —5F ***53***
(off Mason St.)
Maresfield Gdns. *NW3* —2E **21**
Mare St. *E8* —2D **27**
Margaret Bldgs. *N16* —3B **12**
Margaret Ct. W1 —5E ***37***
(off Margaret St.)
Margaret Herbison Ho. SW6
(off Clem Attlee Ct.) —2B ***62***
Margaret Ingram Clo. SW6
(off Rylston Rd.) —2B ***62***
Margaret Rd. *N16* —3B **12**
Margaret St. *W1* —5D **37**
Margaretta Ter. *SW3* —2A **64**
Margaretting Rd. *E12* —3E **17**
Margaret Way. *Ilf* —1F **17**
Margaret White Ho. NW1
(off Chalton St.) —2F ***37***
Margate Rd. *SW2* —3A **80**
Margery Fry Ct. *N7* —5A **10**
Margery Pk. Rd. *E7* —3C **30**
Margery St. *WC1* —2C **38**
Margin Dri. *SW19* —5F **89**
Margravine Gdns. *W6* —1F **61**
Margravine Rd. *W6* —1F **61**
Marham Gdns. *SW18* —1A **92**
Maria Clo. *SE1* —5D **55**
Marian Ct. *E9* —2E **27**
Marian Pl. *E2* —1D **41**
Marian Sq. *E2* —1D **41**
Marian St. *E2* —1D **41**
Marian Way. *NW10* —4B **18**
Maria Ter. *E1* —4F **41**
Maribor. SE10 —3E ***71***
(off Burney St.)
Marie Lloyd Gdns. *N19* —2A **10**
Marie Lloyd Ho. N1 —1F ***39***
(off Murray Gro.)
Marie Lloyd Wlk. *E8* —3B **26**
Marigold All. SE1 —1D ***53***
(off Up. Ground)
Marigold St. *SE16* —3D **55**
Marinefield Rd. *SW6* —5D **63**
Marinel Ho. *SE5* —3E **67**
Mariners M. *E14* —5F **57**
Marine St. *SE16* —4C **54**
Marine Tower. SE8 —2B ***70***
(off Abinger Gro.)
Marischal Rd. *SE13* —1F **85**
Maritime Ind. Est. *SE7* —5D **59**
Maritime Quay. *E14* —1C **70**
Maritime St. *E3* —3B **42**
Marius Pas. *SW17* —2C **92**
Marius Rd. *SW17* —2C **92**
Marjorie Gro. *SW11* —2B **78**
Marjorie M. *E1* —5F **41**
Market Ct. W1 —5E ***37***
(off Market Pl.)
Market Entrance. *SW8* —3E **65**
Market Est. *N7* —3A **24**
Market M. *W1* —2D **51**
Market Pde. E10 —1E ***15***
(off High Rd. Leyton)
Market Pavilion. *E10* —5C **14**
Market Pl. *SE16* —5C **54**
(in two parts)
Market Pl. *W1* —5E **37**
Market Rd. *N7* —3A **24**
Market Row. *SW9* —2C **80**
Market Sq. *E14* —5D **43**
Market Way. *E14* —5D **43**
Markham Pl. *SW3* —1B **64**
Markham Sq. *SW3* —1B **64**
Markham St. *SW3* —1A **64**
Markhouse Av. *E17* —1A **14**
Markhouse Pas. E17 —1B ***14***
(off Markhouse Rd.)
Markhouse Rd. *E17* —1B **14**
Markland Ho. W10 —1F ***47***
(off Darfield Way)
Mark La. *EC3* —1A **54**
Markmanor Av. *E17* —2A **14**
Mark Sq. *EC2* —3A **40**
Markstone Ho. SE1 —3D ***53***
(off Lancaster St.)
Mark St. *E15* —4A **30**
Mark St. *EC2* —3A **40**
Markwell Clo. *SE26* —4D **97**
Marlborough Av. *E8* —5C **26**
(in three parts)
Marlborough Clo. *SE17* —5E **53**
Marlborough Ct. W1 —1E ***51***
(off Kingly St.)
Marlborough Ct. W8 —5C ***48***
(off Pembroke Rd.)
Marlborough Cres. *W4* —4A **46**
Marlborough Flats. SW3
(off Walton St.) —5A ***50***
Marlborough Gro. *SE1* —1C **68**
Marlborough Hill. *NW8* —1E **35**
Marlborough House. —2E 51
Marlborough Ho. NW1
(off Osnaburgh St.) —3D ***37***
Marlborough La. *SE7* —2E **73**
Marlborough Mans. NW6
(off Canon Hill) —2D ***21***
Marlborough M. *SW2* —2B **80**
Marlborough Pl. *NW8* —1E **35**
Marlborough Rd. *E7* —4E **31**
Marlborough Rd. *E15* —1A **30**
Marlborough Rd. *N19* —4F **9**
(in two parts)
Marlborough Rd. *SW1* —2E **51**
Marlborough St. *SW3* —5A **50**
Marlborough Yd. *N19* —4F **9**
Marlbury. NW8 —5D ***21***
(off Abbey Rd.)
Marler Rd. *SE23* —1A **98**
Marley Ho. W11 —1F ***47***
(off St Ann's Rd.)
Marley Wlk. *NW2* —2E **19**
Marloes Rd. *W8* —4D **49**
Marlow Ct. *NW6* —4F **19**
Marlow Ct. *W2* —5D **35**
Marlowe Bus. Cen. SE14
(off Batavia Rd.) —3A ***70***
Marlowe Ct. *SW3* —5A **50**
Marlowe Ho. SE8 —1B ***70***
(off Bowditch)
Marlowes, The. *NW8* —5F **21**
Marlow Ho. E2 —2B ***40***
(off Calvert Av.)
Marlow Ho. SE1 —4B ***54***
(off Maltby St.)
Marlow Way. *SE16* —3F **55**
Marl Rd. *SW18* —2E **77**
Marlton St. *SE10* —1B **72**
Marmion M. *SW11* —1C **78**
Marmion Rd. *SW11* —2C **78**
Marmont Rd. *SE15* —4C **68**
Marmora Rd. *SE22* —4E **83**
Marne St. *W10* —2A **34**
Marney Rd. *SW11* —2C **78**
Marnfield Cres. *SW2* —1C **94**
Marnham Av. *NW2* —1A **20**
Marnock Ho. SE17 —1F ***67***
(off Brandon St.)
Marnock Rd. *SE4* —3B **84**
Maroon Ho. *E14* —4A **42**
Maroon St. *E14* —4A **42**
Maroons Way. *SE6* —4C **98**
Marquess Rd. *N1* —3F **25**
Marquess Rd. N. *N1* —3E **25**
Marquess Rd. S. *N1* —3E **25**
Marquis Ct. N4 —3B ***10***
(off Marquis Rd.)
Marquis Rd. *N4* —3B **10**
Marquis Rd. *NW1* —3F **23**
Marrick Clo. *SW15* —2C **74**
Marrick Ho. NW6 —5D ***21***
(off Mortimer Cres.)
Marriett Ho. *SE6* —4E **99**
Marriott Rd. *E15* —5A **30**
Marriott Rd. *N4* —3B **10**
Marriotts Clo. *NW9* —1B **4**
Marryat Ho. SW1 —1E ***65***
(off Churchill Gdns.)
Marryat Pl. *SW19* —4A **90**
Marryat Rd. *SW19* —5F **89**
Marryat Sq. *SW6* —4A **62**
Marsala Rd. *SE13* —2D **85**
Marsden Rd. *SE15* —1B **82**
Marsden St. *NW5* —3C **22**
(in two parts)
Marshall Clo. *SW18* —4E **77**
Marshall Ho. N1 —1F ***39***
(off Cranston Est.)
Marshall Ho. NW6 —1B ***34***
(off Albert Rd.)
Marshall Ho. SE1 —4A ***54***
(off Page's Wlk.)
Marshall Ho. *SE17* —1F **67**
Marshall's Pl. *SE16* —4B **54**
Marshall St. *W1* —5E **37**
Marshall Way. *E10* —5D **15**
Marshalsea Rd. *SE1* —3E **53**
Marsham Ct. SW1 —5F ***51***
(off Marsham St.)
Marsham St. *SW1* —4F **51**

Marshbrook Clo. SE3 —1F 87
Marsh Cen., The. E1 —5B 40 (off Whitechapel High St.)
Marsh Ct. E8 —4B 26 (off St Philip's Rd.)
Marsh Dri. NW9 —1B 4
Marshfield St. E14 —4E 57
Marsh Ga. Bus. Cen. E15 —5E 29
Marshgate La. E15 —4D 29
Marshgate Trad. Est. E15 —4D 29
Marsh Hill. E9 —2A 28
Marsh Ho. SW1 —1F 65 (off Aylesford St.)
Marsh Ho. SW8 —4E 65
Marsh La. E10 —4B 14
Marsh St. E14 —5D 57
Marsh Wall. E14 —2C 56
Marshwood Ho. NW6 —5C 20 (off Kilburn Va.)
Marsland Clo. SE17 —1D 67
Marsom Ho. N1 —1F 39 (off Provost Est.)
Marston Clo. NW6 —4E 21
Marston Ho. SW9 —5C 66
Marsworth Ho. E2 —5C 26 (off Whiston Rd.)
Martaban Rd. N16 —4B 12
Martello St. E8 —4D 27
Martello Ter. E8 —4D 27
Martell Rd. SE21 —3F 95
Martel Pl. E8 —3B 26
Martha Ct. E2 —1D 41
Martha Rd. E15 —3A 30
Martha St. E1 —5E 41
Martin Ct. E14 —3E 57
Martindale Av. E16 —1C 58
Martindale Ho. E14 —1D 57
Martindale Rd. SW12 —5D 79
Martineau Est. E1 —1E 55
Martineau Ho. SW1 —1E 65 (off Churchill Gdns.)
Martineau M. N5 —1D 25
Martineau Rd. N5 —1D 25
Martin Ho. SE1 —4E 53
Martin Ho. SW8 —3A 66 (off Wyvil Rd.)
Martin La. EC4 —1F 53 (in two parts)
Martlett Ct. WC2 —5A 38
Marton Clo. SE6 —3C 98
Marton Rd. N16 —4A 12
Martys Yd. NW3 —1F 21
Marvell Ho. SE5 —3F 67 (off Camberwell Rd.)
Marvels Clo. SE12 —2D 101
Marvels La. SE12 —2D 101
Marville Rd. SW6 —3B 62
Marvin St. E8 —3D 27
Mary Adelaide Clo. SW15 —4A 88
Mary Ann Gdns. SE8 —2C 70
Mary Datchelor Clo. SE5 —4F 67
Mary Flux Ct. SW5 —1D 63 (off Bramham Gdns.)
Mary Grn. NW8 —5D 21
Mary Jones Ho. E14 —1C 56
Maryland Ho. E15 —3A 30 (off Manbey Pk. Rd.)
Maryland Ind. Est. E15 (off Maryland Rd.) —2A 30
Maryland Pk. E15 —2A 30
Maryland Point. E15 —3A 30 (off Grove, The)
Maryland Rd. E15 —2F 29
Maryland Sq. E15 —2A 30
Marylands Rd. W9 —3C 34
Maryland St. E15 —2F 29
Maryland Wlk. N1 —5E 25 (off Popham St.)
Mary Lawrenson Pl. SE3 —3C 72
Marylebone. —4C 36
Marylebone Flyover. (Junct.) —4A 36
Marylebone Fly-Over. W2 —4F 35
Marylebone High St. W1 —4C 36
Marylebone La. W1 —4C 36
Marylebone M. W1 —4D 37
Marylebone Pas. W1 —5E 37
Marylebone Rd. NW1 —4A 36
Marylebone St. W1 —4C 36
Marylee Way. SE11 —5B 52
Mary Macarthur Ho. W6 —2A 62
Maryon Gro. SE7 —5F 59
Maryon M. NW3 —1A 22
Maryon Rd. SE7 & SE18 —5F 59
Mary Pl. W11 —1A 48
Mary Seacole Clo. E8 —5B 26
Mary Smith Ct. SW5 —5C 48 (off Trebovir Rd.)
Marysmith Ho. SW1 —1F 65 (off Cureton St.)
Mary St. E16 —4B 44
Mary St. N1 —5E 25
Mary Ter. NW1 —5D 23
Mary Wharrie Ho. NW3 —4B 22
Masbro' Rd. W14 —4F 47
Mascalls Ct. SE7 —2E 73
Mascalls Rd. SE7 —2E 73
Mascotte Rd. SW15 —2F 75
Mascotts Clo. NW2 —5D 5
Masefield Ho. NW6 —2C 34 (off Stafford Rd.)
Mashie Rd. W3 —5A 32
Maskall Clo. SW2 —1C 94
Maskell Rd. SW17 —3E 91
Maskelyne Clo. SW11 —4A 64
Mason Clo. E16 —1C 58
Mason Clo. SE16 —1C 68
Mason's Arms M. W1 —5D 37
Mason's Av. EC2 —5F 39
Mason's Pl. EC1 —2E 39
Mason St. SE17 —5F 53
Mason's Yd. SW1 —2E 51
Mason's Yd. SW19 —5F 89
Massey Ct. E6 —5E 31 (off Florence Rd.)
Massie Rd. E8 —3C 26
Massingberd Way. SW17 —4D 93
Massinger St. SE17 —5A 54
Massingham St. E1 —3F 41
Mast Ct. SE16 —5A 56 (off Boat Lifter Way)
Master Gunners Pl. SE18 —3F 73
Masterman Ho. SE5 —3F 67 (off Elmington Est.)
Masterman Rd. E6 —2F 45
Masters Dri. SE16 —1D 69
Master's St. E1 —4F 41
Masthouse Ter. E14 —5C 56
Mast Ho. Ter. E14 —5C 56 (in two parts)
Mastmaker Ct. E14 —3C 56
Mastmaker Rd. E14 —3C 56
Matcham Rd. E11 —5A 16
Matham Gro. SE22 —2B 82
Matheson Lang Ho. SE1 (off Baylis Rd.) —3C 52
Matheson Rd. W14 —5B 48
Mathews Pk. Av. E15 —3B 30
Mathews Yd. WC2 —5A 38
Mathieson Ct. SE1 —3D 53 (off King James St.)
Matilda Ho. E1 —2C 54 (off St Katherine's Way)
Matilda St. N1 —5B 24
Matlock Clo. SE24 —2E 81
Matlock Ct. SE5 —2F 81
Matlock Rd. E10 —1E 15
Matlock St. E1 —5A 42
Matlock St. E14 —5A 42
Maton Ho. SW6 —3B 62 (off Estcourt Rd.)
Matrimony Pl. SW8 —5E 65
Matson Ho. SE16 —4D 55
Matthew Clo. W10 —3F 33
Matthew Parker St. SW1 —3F 51
Matthews Ho. E14 —4C 42
Matthews St. SW11 —5B 64
Matthias Rd. N16 —2A 26
Mattingley Way. SE15 —3B 68
Mattison Rd. N4 —1C 10
Maude Ho. E2 —1C 40 (off Ropley St.)
Maude Rd. SE5 —4A 68
Maud Gdns. E13 —5B 30
Maudlins Grn. E1 —2C 54
Maud Rd. E10 —5E 15
Maud Rd. E13 —1B 44
Maud St. E16 —4B 44
Maud Wilkes Clo. NW5 —2E 23
Mauleverer Rd. SW2 —3A 80
Maundeby Wlk. NW10 —3A 18
Maunsel St. SW1 —5F 51

Mauretania Building. E1
 (off Jardine Rd.) —1F 55
Maurice Bishop Ter. N6
 (off View Rd.) —1C 8
Maurice Drummond Ho. SE10
 (off Catherine Gro.) —4D 71
Maurice St. W12 —5D 33
Mauritius Rd. SE10 —5A 58
Maury Rd. N16 —4C 12
Maverton Rd. E3 —5C 28
Mavis Wlk. E6 —4F 45
 (off Greenwich Cres.)
Mavor Ho. N1 —5B 24
 (off Barnsbury Est.)
Mawbey Ho. SE1 —1B 68
Mawbey Pl. SE1 —1B 68
Mawbey Rd. SE1 —1B 68
Mawbey St. SW8 —3A 66
Mawdley Ho. SE1 —3C 52
 (off Webber Row)
Mawson Ho. EC1 —4C 38
 (off Baldwins Gdns.)
Mawson La. W4 —2B 60
Maxden Ct. SE15 —1C 82
Maxted Rd. SE15 —1B 82
Maxwell St. SW4 —3F 79
Maxwell Rd. SW6 —3D 63
Maya Clo. SE15 —5D 69
Mayall Rd. SE24 —3D 81
Maybourne Clo. SE26 —5D 97
Maybury Ct. W1 —4C 36
 (off Marylebone St.)
Maybury Gdns. NW10
 —3D 19
Maybury M. N6 —2E 9
Maybury Rd. E13 —3E 45
Maybury St. SW17 —5A 92
Mayday Gdns. SE3 —5F 73
Maydew Ho. SE16 —5E 55
 (off Abbeyfield Est.)
Maydwell Ho. E14 —4C 42
Mayerne Rd. SE9 —3F 87
Mayeswood Rd. SE12
 —4E 101
Mayfair. —1D 51
Mayfair M. NW1 —4B 22
 (off Regents Pk. Rd.)
Mayfair Pl. W1 —2D 51
Mayfield Av. W4 —5A 46
Mayfield Clo. E8 —3B 26
Mayfield Clo. SW4 —3F 79
Mayfield Gdns. NW4 —1F 5
Mayfield Ho. E2 —1D 41
 (off Cambridge Heath Rd.)
Mayfield Rd. E8 —4B 26
Mayfield Rd. E13 —3B 44
Mayfield Rd. N8 —1B 10
Mayfield Rd. W12 —3A 46
Mayfield Rd. Flats. N8 —1B 10
Mayflower Clo. SE16 —5F 55
Mayflower Clo. SE16 —3D 55
Mayflower Rd. SW9 —1A 80
Mayflower St. SE16 —3E 55
Mayford. NW1 —1E 37
 (in three parts)
Mayford Clo. SW12 —5B 78

Mayford Rd. SW12 —5B 78
Maygood St. N1 —1C 38
Maygrove Rd. NW6 —3B 20
Mayhew Ct. SE5 —2F 81
Mayhill Rd. SE7 —2D 73
Maylands Ho. SW3 —5A 50
 (off Elystan St.)
Maynard Clo. SW6 —3D 63
Maynard Rd. E17 —1E 15
Maynards Quay. E1 —1E 55
Mayne Ct. SE26 —5D 97
Mayo Ho. E1 —4E 41
 (off Lindley St.)
Mayola Rd. E5 —1E 27
Mayo Rd. NW10 —3A 18
Mayow Rd. SE26 & SE23
 —4F 97
May Rd. E13 —1C 44
May's Bldgs. M. SE10 —3E 71
May's Ct. SE10 —3F 71
Mays Ct. WC2 —1A 52
Maysoule Rd. SW11 —2F 77
May St. W14 —1B 62
Mayton St. N7 —5B 10
May Tree Ho. SE4 —1B 84
 (off Wickham Rd.) ·
Maytree Wlk. SW2 —2C 94
Mayville Est. N16 —2A 26
Mayville Rd. E11 —4A 16
May Wlk. E13 —1D 45
Mayward Ho. SE5 —4A 68
 (off Peckham Rd.)
May Wynne Ho. E16 —1D 59
 (off Murray Sq.)
Maze Hill. SE10 & SE3
 —2A 72
Maze Hill Lodge. SE10
 (off Park Vista) —2F 71
Mazenod Av. NW6 —4C 20
M.C.C. Cricket Mus. —2F 35
Mead Clo. NW1 —4C 22
Meadcroft Rd. SE11 —2D 67
 (in two parts)
Meader Ct. SE14 —3F 69
Mead Ho. W11 —2B 48
 (off Ladbroke Rd.)
Mead Lodge. W4 —3A 46
Meadowbank. NW3 —4B 22
Meadow Bank. SE3 —1B 86
Meadowbank Clo. SW6
 —3E 61
Meadowbank Rd. NW9
 —2A 4
Meadow Clo. E9 —2B 28
Meadow Clo. SE6 —5C 98
Meadow Ct. N1 —1A 40
Meadowcourt Rd. SE3
 —2B 86
Meadow La. SE12 —3D 101
Meadow M. SW8 —2B 66
Meadow Pl. SW8 —3A 66
Meadow Pl. W4 —3A 60
Meadow Rd. SW8 —3B 66
Meadow Row. SE1 —4E 53
Meadows Clo. E10 —4C 14
Meadowside. SE9 —2E 87

Meadowsweet Clo. E16
 —4F 45
Meadowview Rd. SE6 —5B 98
Mead Path. SW17 —4E 91
Mead Pl. E9 —3E 27
Mead Row. SE1 —4C 52
Meads Ct. E15 —3B 30
Meadway. NW11 —1C 6
Meadway Clo. NW11 —1D 7
Meadway Ct. NW11 —1D 7
Meadway Ga. NW11 —1C 6
Meadway, The. SE3 —5F 71
Meakin Est. SE1 —4A 54
Meanley Rd. E12 —1F 31
Meard St. W1 —5F 37
 (in two parts)
Meath Rd. E15 —1B 44
Meath St. SW11 —4D 65
Mechanics Path. SE8 —3C 70
Mecklenburgh Pl. WC1
 —3B 38
Mecklenburgh Sq. WC1
 —3B 38
Mecklenburgh St. WC1
 —3B 38
Medburn St. NW1 —1F 37
Medebourne Clo. SE3 —1C 86
Mede Ho. Brom. —5D 101
 (off Pike Clo.)
Medfield St. SW15 —5C 74
Medhurst Clo. E3 —1A 42
Median Rd. E5 —2E 27
Medina Gro. N7 —5C 10
Medina Rd. N7 —5C 10
Medland Ho. E14 —1A 56
Medlar St. SE5 —4E 67
Medley Rd. NW6 —3C 20
Medora Rd. SW2 —5B 80
Medusa Rd. SE6 —4D 85
Medway Ct. WC1 —2A 38
 (off Judd St.)
Medway Ho. NW8 —3A 36
 (off Penfold St.)
Medway Ho. SE1 —3F 53
 (off Hankey Pl.)
Medway M. E3 —1A 42
Medway Rd. E3 —1A 42
Medway St. SW1 —4F 51
Medwin St. SW4 —2B 80
Meek Rd. SW10 —3E 63
Meerbrook Rd. SE3 —1E 87
Meeson Rd. E15 —4B 30
Meeson St. E5 —5A 28
Meeting Fld. Path. E9 —3E 27
Meetinghouse All. E1 —2D 55
Meeting Ho. La. SE15 —4D 69
Mehetabel Rd. E9 —2E 27
Melba Way. SE13 —4D 71
Melbourne Ct. W9 —3E 35
 (off Clifton Rd.)
Melbourne Gro. SE22 —2A 82
Melbourne Ho. W8 —2C 48
 (off Kensington Pl.)
Melbourne Mans. W6 —2A 62
 (off Musard Rd.)
Melbourne M. SE6 —5E 85

Melbourne M.—Metro Central Heights

Melbourne M. *SW9* —4C **66**
Melbourne Pl. *WC2* —5B **38**
Melbourne Rd. *E10* —2D **15**
Melbourne Sq. *SW9* —4C **66**
Melbray M. *SW6* —5B **62**
Melbreak Ho. *SE22* —1A **82**
Melbury Ct. *W8* —4B **48**
Melbury Dri. *SE5* —3A **68**
Melbury Ho. SW8 —3B **66**
  (off Richborne Ter.)
Melbury Rd. *W14* —4B **48**
Melbury Ter. *NW1* —3A **36**
Melchester. W11 —5B **34**
  (off Ledbury Rd.)
Melchester Ho. N19 —5F **9**
  (off Wedmore St.)
Melcombe Ct. *NW1* —4B **36**
  (off Melcombe Pl.)
Melcombe Ho. *SW8* —3B **66**
  (off Dorset Rd.)
Melcombe Pl. *NW1* —4B **36**
Melcombe Regis Ct. W1
  (off Weymouth St.) —4C **36**
Melcombe St. *NW1* —3B **36**
Meldon Clo. *SW6* —4D **63**
Melfield Gdns. *SE6* —4E **99**
Melford Ct. SE1 —4A **54**
  (off Fendall St.)
Melford Ct. *SE22* —1C **96**
Melford Pas. *SE22* —5C **82**
Melford Rd. *E11* —4A **16**
Melford Rd. *SE22* —5C **82**
Melgund Rd. *N5* —2C **24**
Melina Ct. *SW15* —1C **74**
Melina Pl. *NW8* —2F **35**
Melina Rd. *W12* —3D **47**
Melior Ho. *N6* —1E **9**
Melior Pl. *SE1* —3A **54**
Melior St. *SE1* —3A **54**
Meliot Rd. *SE6* —2F **99**
Mellish Flats. *E10* —2C **14**
Mellish Ho. E1 —5D **41**
  (off Varden St.)
Mellish Ind. Est. *SE18* —4F **59**
Mellish St. *E14* —4C **56**
Mellison Rd. *SW17* —5A **92**
Mellitus St. *W12* —4B **32**
Mell St. *SE10* —1A **72**
Melody La. *N5* —2E **25**
Melody Rd. *SW18* —3E **77**
Melon Pl. *W8* —3C **48**
Melon Rd. *E11* —5A **16**
Melon Rd. *SE15* —4C **68**
Melrose Av. *NW2* —2D **19**
Melrose Av. *SW19* —2B **90**
Melrose Clo. *SE12* —1C **100**
Melrose Gdns. *W6* —4E **47**
Melrose Ho. *E14* —4D **57**
Melrose Ho. NW6 —2C **34**
  (off Carlton Va.)
Melrose Rd. *SW13* —5B **60**
Melrose Rd. *SW18* —4B **76**
Melrose Ter. *W6* —4E **47**
Melthorpe Gdns. *SE3* —4F **73**
Melton Ct. *SW7* —5F **49**
Melton St. *NW1* —2E **37**

Melville Ct. *SE8* —5A **56**
Melville Ct. W12 —4D **47**
  (off Goldhawk Rd.)
Melville Ho. *SE10* —4E **71**
Melville Pl. *N1* —4E **25**
Melville Rd. *SW13* —4C **60**
Melwood Ho. E1 —5D **41**
  (off Watney Mkt.)
Melyn Clo. *N7* —1E **23**
Memel Ct. EC1 —3E **39**
  (off Memel St.)
Memel St. *EC1* —3E **39**
Memorial Av. *E15* —2A **44**
Mendham Ho. SE1 —4A **54**
  (off Cluny Pl.)
Mendip Clo. *SE26* —4E **97**
Mendip Clo. *SW19* —2A **90**
Mendip Ct. SE14 —2E **69**
  (off Avonley Rd.)
Mendip Dri. *NW2* —4A **6**
Mendip Houses. E2 —2E **41**
  (off Welwyn St.)
Mendip Rd. *SW11* —1E **77**
Mendora Rd. *SW6* —3A **62**
Menelik Rd. *NW2* —1A **20**
Menotti St. *E2* —3C **40**
Menteath Ho. *E14* —5C **42**
Mentmore Ter. *E8* —4D **27**
Mepham St. *SE1* —2C **52**
Merbury Clo. *SE13* —3F **85**
Mercator Pl. *E14* —1C **70**
Mercator Rd. *SE13* —2F **85**
Mercer Ho. SW1 —1D **65**
  (off Ebury Bri. Rd.)
Merceron Houses. E2 —2E **41**
  (off Globe Rd.)
Merceron St. *E1* —3D **41**
Mercers Clo. *SE10* —5B **58**
Mercers Pl. W6 —5F **47**
Mercers Rd. *N19* —5F **9**
  (in two parts)
Merchant St. *WC2* —5A **38**
Merchant St. *E3* —2B **42**
Merchiston Rd. *SE6* —2F **99**
Marcia Gro. *SE13* —2E **85**
Mercia Ho. SE5 —5E **67**
  (off Denmark Rd.)
Mercier Rd. *SW15* —3A **76**
Mercury Ct. *E14* —5C **56**
Mercury Way. *SE14* —2F **69**
Mercy Ter. *SE13* —3D **85**
Mere Clo. *SW15* —5F **75**
Meredith Av. *NW2* —2E **19**
Meredith Ho. *N16* —2A **26**
Meredith M. *SE4* —2B **84**
Meredith St. *E13* —2C **44**
Meredith St. *EC1* —2D **39**
Meredyth Rd. *SW13* —5C **60**
Meretone Clo. *SE4* —2A **84**
Mereworth Ho. *SE15* —2E **69**
Merganser Ct. SE8 —2B **70**
  (off Edward St.)
Meriden Ct. SW3 —1A **64**
  (off Chelsea Mnr. St.)
Meridian Ga. *E14* —3E **57**

Meridian Ho. *SE10* —5A **58**
  (off Azof St.)
Meridian Ho. *SE10* —3E **71**
  (off Royal Hill)
Meridian Pl. *E14* —3E **57**
Meridian Rd. *SE7* —3F **73**
Meridian Sq. *E15* —4F **29**
Meridian Trad. Est. *SE7*
  —5D **59**
Merifield Rd. *SE9* —2E **87**
Merivale Rd. *SW15* —2A **76**
Merlin Gdns. *Brom* —3C **100**
Merlin Ho. *E12* —4F **17**
Merlins Ct. WC1 —2C **38**
  (off Margery St.)
Merlin St. *WC1* —2C **38**
Mermaid Ct. *SE1* —3F **53**
Mermaid Ct. *SE16* —2B **56**
Mermaid Ho. *E14* —1E **57**
Mermaid Tower. SE8 —2B **70**
  (off Abinger Gro.)
Meroe Ct. *N16* —4A **12**
Merredene St. SW2 —4B **80**
Merrick Ho. *SE8* —5B **56**
Merrick Sq. *SE1* —4F **53**
Merriman Rd. *SE3* —4E **73**
Merrington Rd. *SW6* —2C **62**
Merritt Rd. *SE4* —3B **84**
Merritt's Bldgs. EC2 —3A **40**
  (off Worship St.)
Merrivale. NW1 —5E **23**
  (off Camden St.)
Merrow St. *SE17* —1F **67**
Merrow Wlk. *SE17* —1F **67**
Merryfield. *SE3* —5B **72**
Merryfield Ho. SE9 —3E **101**
  (off Grove Pk. Rd.)
Merryfields Way. *SE6* —5D **85**
Merryweather Ct. *N19* —5E **9**
Merthyr Ter. *SW13* —2D **61**
Merton Av. *W4* —5B **46**
Merton La. *N6* —4B **8**
Merton Mans. SE8 —4C **70**
  (off Brookmill Rd.)
Merton Ri. *NW3* —4A **22**
  (in two parts)
Merton Rd. *E17* —1E **15**
Merton Rd. *SW18* —4C **76**
Mertoun Ter. W1 —4B **36**
  (off Seymour Pl.)
Merttins Rd. *SE15 & SE4*
  —3F **83**
Meru Clo. *NW5* —1C **22**
Mervan Rd. *SW2* —2C **80**
Messent Rd. *SE9* —3E **87**
Messina Av. *NW6* —4C **20**
Messiter Ho. N1 —5B **24**
  (off Barnsbury Est.)
Meteor St. *SW11* —2C **78**
Methley St. *SE11* —1C **66**
Methwold Rd. *W10* —4F **33**
Metro Bus. Cen., The. *SE26*
  —5B **98**

Metro Central Heights. SE1
  —4E **53**
  (off Newington Causeway)

Metropolis. SE11 —4D ***53***
(off Oswin St.)
Metropolitan Bus. Cen. N1
(off Enfield Rd.) —4A ***26***
Metropolitan Clo. *E14* —4C **42**
Metropolitan Wharf. *E1* —2E **55**
Mews St. *E1* —2C **54**
Mews, The. *N1* —5E **25**
Mews, The. *Ilf* —1F **17**
Mexborough. *NW1* —5E **23**
Mexfield Rd. *SW15* —3B **76**
Meymott St. *SE1* —2D **53**
Meynell Cres. *E9* —4F **27**
Meynell Gdns. *E9* —4F **27**
Meynell Rd. *E9* —4F **27**
Meyrick Ho. *E14* —4C **42**
Meyrick Rd. *NW10* —3C **18**
Meyrick Rd. *SW11* —1F **77**
Miah Ter. *E1* —2C **54**
Miall Wlk. *SE26* —4A **98**
Micawber Ct. N1 —2E ***39***
(off Windsor Ter.)
Micawber Ho. SE16 —3C ***54***
(off Llewellyn St.)
Micawber St. *N1* —2E **39**
Michael Cliffe Ho. EC1
(off Finsbury Est.) —2D ***39***
Michael Faraday Ho. SE17
—1A ***68***
(off Beaconsfield Rd.)
Michael Manley Ind. Est. SW8
(off Clyston St.) —5E ***65***
Michael Rd. *E11* —3B **16**
Michael Rd. *SW6* —4D **63**
Michael's Clo. *SE13* —2A **86**
Michael Stewart Ho. SW6
(off Clem Attlee Ct.) —2B ***62***
Michelangelo Ct. SE16
(off Stubbs Dri.) —1D ***69***
Micheldever Rd. *SE12* —4A **86**
Michelle Ct. *W3* —1A **46**
Michelson Ho. SE11 —5B ***52***
(off Black Prince Rd.)
Michigan Ho. *E14* —4C **56**
Mickledore. NW1 —1E ***37***
(off Ampthill Est.)
Micklethwaite Rd. *SW6* —2C **62**
Middlefield. *NW8* —5F **21**
Middle La. *N8* —1A **10**
Middle La. M. *N8* —1A **10**
Middle Pk. Av. *SE9* —4F **87**
Middle Rd. *E13* —1C **44**
Middle Row. *W10* —3A **34**
Middlesex County Cricket Club. —2F 35
Middlesex Ct. *W4* —1B **60**
Middlesex Pas. EC1 —4D ***39***
(off Bartholomew Clo.)
Middlesex Pl. E9 —3E ***27***
(off Elsdale St.)
Middlesex St. *E1* —4A **40**
Middlesex Wharf. *E5* —4E **13**
Middle St. *EC1* —4E **39**
Middle Temple Hall. —1C 52
(off Middle Temple La.)
Middle Temple La. *EC4* —5C **38**
Middleton Bldgs. W1 —4E ***37***
(off Langham St.)
Middleton Dri. *SE16* —3F **55**
Middleton Gro. *N7* —2A **24**
Middleton Ho. *E8* —4B **26**
Middleton Ho. SE1 —4F ***53***
(off Burbage Clo.)
Middleton Ho. SW1 —5F ***51***
(off Causton St.)
Middleton M. *N7* —2A **24**
Middleton Rd. *E8* —4B **26**
Middleton Rd. *NW11* —2C **6**
Middleton St. *E2* —2D **41**
Middleton Way. *SE13* —2F **85**
Middleway. *NW11* —1D **7**
Middle Yd. *SE1* —2A **54**
Midford Pl. *W1* —3E **37**
Midhope Ho. WC1 —2A ***38***
(off Midhope St.)
Midhope St. *WC1* —2A **38**
Midhurst. *SE26* —5E **97**
Midhurst Ho. *E14* —5B **42**
Midhurst Way. *E5* —1C **26**
Midland Cres. *NW3* —3E **21**
Midland Pde. *NW6* —3D **21**
Midland Pl. *E14* —1E **71**
Midland Rd. *E10* —2E **15**
Midland Rd. *NW1* —1F **37**
Midland Ter. *NW2* —5F **5**
Midland Ter. *NW10* —3A **32**
(in two parts)
Midmoor Rd. *SW12* —1E **93**
Midship Clo. *SE16* —2F **55**
Midship Point. E14 —3C ***56***
(off Quarterdeck, The)
Midstrath Rd. *NW10* —1A **18**
Midway Ho. EC1 —2D ***39***
(off Manningford Clo.)
Midwood Clo. *NW2* —5D **5**
Mighell Av. *Ilf* —1F **17**
Milborne Gro. *SW10* —1E **63**
Milborne St. *E9* —3E **27**
Milborough Cres. *SE12* —4A **86**
Milcote St. *SE1* —3D **53**
Mildenhall Rd. *E5* —1E **27**
Mildmay Av. *N1* —3F **25**
Mildmay Gro. N. *N1* —2F **25**
Mildmay Gro. S. *N1* —2F **25**
Mildmay Pk. *N1* —2F **25**
Mildmay Pl. *N16* —2A **26**
Mildmay Rd. *N1* —2F **25**
Mildmay St. *N1* —3F **25**
Mile End. —3B 42
Mile End Pk. —2A 42
Mile End Pl. *E1* —3F **41**
Mile End Rd. *E1 & E3* —4E **41**
Miles Bldgs. NW1 —4A ***36***
(off Penfold Pl.)
Miles Ct. E1 —5D ***41***
(off Tillman St.)
Miles Ho. SE10 —1A ***72***
(off Tuskar St.)
Miles Pl. NW8 —4F ***35***
(off Broadley St.)
Miles St. *SW8* —2A **66**
Miles St. Bus. Est. *SW8* —2A **66**
Milfoil St. *W12* —1C **46**
Milford La. *WC2* —1C **52**
Milford M. *SW16* —3B **94**
Milford Towers. *SE6* —5D **85**
Milk St. *EC2* —5E **39**
Milk St. *Brom* —5D **101**
Milkwell Yd. *SE5* —4E **67**
Milkwood Rd. *SE24* —3D **81**
Milk Yd. *E1* —1E **55**
Millais Ho. SW1 —5A ***52***
(off Marsham St.)
Millais Rd. *E11* —1E **29**
Millard Clo. *N16* —2A **26**
Millard Ho. SE8 —1B ***70***
(off Leeway)
Millbank. *SW1* —4A **52**
Millbank Ct. SW1 —5A ***52***
(off John Islip St.)
Millbank Tower. SW1 —5A ***52***
(off Millbank)
Millbank Way. *SE12* —3C **86**
Millbrook Ho. SE15 —2C ***68***
(off Peckham Pk. Rd.)
Millbrook Pas. *SW9* —1D **81**
Millbrook Pl. NW1 —1E ***37***
(off Hampstead Rd.)
Millbrook Rd. *SW9* —1D **81**
Mill Ct. *E10* —5E **15**
Millcroft Ho. SE6 —4E ***99***
(off Melfield Gdns.)
Millender Wlk. *SE16* —5E **55**
Millennium Bridge. —1D 53
Millennium Bus. Cen. *NW2* —4D **5**
Millennium Clo. *E16* —5D **45**
Millennium Dri. *E14* —5F **57**
Millennium Pl. *E2* —1D **41**
Millennium Sq. *SE1* —3B **54**
Millennium Way. *SE10* —3A **58**
Miller Rd. *SW19* —5F **91**
Miller's Av. *E8* —2B **26**
Miller's Ct. *W4* —1B **60**
Millers Mdw. Clo. *SE3* —3B **86**
Miller's Ter. *E8* —2B **26**
Miller St. *NW1* —1E **37**
(in two parts)
Millers Way. *W6* —3E **47**
Millers Wharf Ho. E1 —2C ***54***
(off St Katherine's Way)
Miller Wlk. *SE1* —2C **52**
Millfield. *N4* —4C **10**
Millfield La. *N6* —3A **8**
(in two parts)
Millfield Pl. *N6* —4C **8**
Millfields Rd. *E5* —1E **27**
Mill Gdns. *SE26* —3D **97**
Millgrove St. *SW11* —4C **64**
Millharbour. *E14* —3D **57**

Mill Harbour—Monarch Dri.

Mill Harbour. *E14* —4D **57**
Mill Hill. *SW13* —5C **60**
Mill Hill Rd. *SW13* —5C **60**
Millhouse Pl. *SE27* —4D **95**
Millicent Rd. *E10* —3B **14**
Milligan St. *E14* —1B **56**
Millington Ho. *N16* —5F **11**
Mill La. *NW6* —2B **20**
Millman M. *WC1* —3B **38**
Millman Pl. *WC1* —3B *38*
  (off Millman St.)
Millman St. *WC1* —3B **38**
Millmark Gro. *SE14* —5A **70**
Mill Meads. —1F 43
Mill Pl. *E14* —5A **42**
Millpond Est. *SE16* —3D **55**
Mill Rd. *E16* —2D **59**
Mill Row. *N1* —5A **26**
Mills Ct. *EC2* —2A *40*
  (off Curtain Rd.)
Mills Gro. *E14* —4E **43**
Millshot Clo. *SW6* —4E **61**
Mills Ho. *SW8* —4E *65*
  (off Thessaly Rd.)
Millstream Ho. *SE16* —3D *55*
  (off Jamaica St.)
Millstream Rd. *SE1* —3B **54**
Mill St. *SE1* —3B **54**
Mill St. *W1* —1D **51**
Millwall. —5C 56
Millwall Dock Rd. *E14* —4C **56**
Millwall F.C. —1E **69**
Millwood St. *W10* —4A **34**
Mill Yd. *E1* —1C **54**
Milman Rd. *NW6* —1F **33**
Milman's St. *SW10* —2F **63**
Milne Gdns. *SE9* —3F **87**
Milner Pl. *N1* —5C **24**
Milner Rd. *E15* —2A **44**
Milner Sq. *N1* —4D **25**
Milner St. *SW3* —5B **50**
Milo Gdns. *SE22* —4B **82**
Milo Rd. *SE22* —4B **82**
Milroy Wlk. *SE1* —2D **53**
Milson Rd. *W14* —4F **47**
Milstead Ho. *E5* —2D **27**
Milton Av. *E6* —4F **31**
Milton Av. *N6* —2E **9**
Milton Clo. *N2* —1E **7**
Milton Clo. *SE1* —5B **54**
Milton Ct. *EC2* —4F **39**
Milton Ct. *SE14* —2B **70**
Milton Ct. *SW18* —3C **76**
Milton Ct. Highwalk. *EC2*
  (off Silk St.) —4F *39*
Milton Ct. Rd. *SE14* —2A **70**
Milton Garden Est. *N16*
  —1F **25**
Milton Gro. *N16* —1F **25**
Milton Ho. *E2* —2E *41*
  (off Roman Rd.)
Milton Ho. *SE5* —3F *67*
  (off Elmington Est.)
Milton Mans. *W14* —2A *62*
  (off Queen's Club Gdns.)
Milton Pk. *N6* —2E **9**

Milton Pl. *N7* —2C **24**
Milton Rd. *N6* —2E **9**
Milton Rd. *NW9* —2C **4**
Milton Rd. *SE24* —3D **81**
Milton Rd. *SW19* —5E **91**
Milton St. *EC2* —4F **39**
Milverton Ho. *SE23* —3A **98**
Milverton Rd. *NW6* —4E **19**
Milverton St. *SE11* —1C **66**
Milward Wlk. *E1* —4D **41**
Mimosa Lodge. *NW10*
  —2B **18**
Mimosa St. *SW6* —4B **62**
Minard Rd. *SE6* —5A **86**
  (in two parts)
Mina Rd. *SE17* —1A **68**
Minchin Ho. *E14* —5C **42**
Mincing La. *EC3* —1A **54**
Minehead Rd. *SW16* —5B **94**
Minera M. *SW1* —5C **50**
Minerva Clo. *SW9* —3C **66**
  (in two parts)
Minerva Rd. *NW10* —2A **32**
Minerva St. *E2* —1D **41**
Minet Av. *NW10* —1A **32**
Minet Gdns. *NW10* —1A **32**
Minet Rd. *SW9* —5D **67**
Minford Gdns. *W6* —3F **47**
Mingard Wlk. *N7* —4B **10**
Ming St. *E14* —1C **56**
Miniver Pl. *EC4* —1E *53*
  (off Garlick Hill)
Minnow St. *SE17* —5A **54**
Minnow Wlk. *SE17* —5A **54**
Minories. *EC3* —5B **40**
Minshill St. *SW8* —4F **65**
Minson Rd. *E9* —5F **27**
Minstead Gdns. *SW15*
  —5B **74**
Minster Ct. *EC3* —1A *54*
  (off Mincing La.)
Minster Pavement. *EC3*
  (off Mincing La.) —1A **54**
Minster Rd. *NW2* —2A **20**
Mint Bus. Pk. *E16* —4D **45**
Mintern St. *N1* —1F **39**
Minton Ho. *SE11* —5C *52*
  (off Walnut Tree Wlk.)
Minton M. *NW6* —3D **21**
Mint St. *SE1* —3E **53**
Mirabel Rd. *SW6* —3B **62**
Miranda Clo. *E1* —4E **41**
Miranda Rd. *N19* —3E **9**
Mirfield St. *SE7* —5F **59**
Mirror Path. *SE9* —3E **101**
Missenden. *SE17* —1F *67*
  (off Roland Way)
Missenden Ho. *NW8* —3A *36*
  (off Jerome Cres.)
Mission Gro. *E17* —1A **14**
Mission Pl. *SE15* —4C **68**
Mission, The. *E14* —5B **42**
Mistral. *SE5* —4A **68**
Mitali Pas. *E1* —5C **40**
  (in two parts)
Mitcham Ho. *SE5* —4E **67**

Mitcham La. *SW16* —5E **93**
Mitcham Rd. *E6* —2F **45**
Mitcham Rd. *SW17* —5B **92**
Mitcheldean Ct. *SE15* —3A *68*
  (off Newent Clo.)
Mitchellbrook Way. *NW10*
  —3A **18**
Mitchell Ho. *W12* —1D *47*
  (off White City Est.)
Mitchell's Pl. *SE21* —4A *82*
  (off Aysgarth Rd.)
Mitchell St. *EC1* —3E **39**
  (in two parts)
Mitchell Wlk. *E6* —4F *45*
  (off Neats Ct. Rd.)
Mitchison Rd. *N1* —3F **25**
Mitford Rd. *N19* —4A **10**
Mitre Bri. Ind. Pk. *W10*
  —3D **33**
Mitre Ct. *EC2* —5E *39*
  (off Wood St.)
Mitre Rd. *E15* —1A **44**
Mitre Rd. *SE1* —3C **52**
Mitre Sq. *EC3* —5A **40**
Mitre St. *EC3* —5A **40**
Mitre, The. *E14* —1B **56**
Mitre Way. *NW10* —3D **33**
Mitre Yd. *SW3* —5A **50**
Moat Dri. *E13* —1E **45**
Moatfield. *NW6* —4A **20**
Moatlands Ho. *WC1* —2A *38*
  (off Cromer St.)
Moat Pl. *SW9* —1B **80**
Moberley Rd. *SW4* —5F **79**
Mobil Ct. *WC2* —5B *38*
  (off Clement's Inn)
Modbury Gdns. *NW5* —3C **22**
Modder Pl. *SW15* —2F **75**
Model Bldgs. *WC1* —2B *38*
  (off Cubitt St.)
Model Farm Clo. *SE9*
  —3F **101**
Modern Ct. *EC4* —5D *39*
  (off Farringdon St.)
Moelwyn. *N7* —2F **23**
Moffat Ct. *SW19* —5C **90**
Moffat Ho. *SE5* —3E **67**
Moffat Rd. *SW17* —4B **92**
Mohmmad Khan Rd. *E11*
  —3B **16**
Moland Mead. *SE16* —1F **69**
Molasses Ho. *SW11* —1E *77*
  (off Clove Hitch Quay)
Molasses Row. *SW11* —1E **77**
Molesford Rd. *SW6* —4C **62**
Molesworth Ho. *SE17* —2D **67**
Molesworth St. *SE13* —2E **85**
Mollis Ho. *E3* —4C **42**
Molly Huggins Clo. *SW12*
  —5E **79**
Molton Ho. *N1* —5B *24*
  (off Barnsbury Est.)
Molyneux Dri. *SW17* —4D **93**
Molyneux St. *W1* —4A **36**
Monarch Ct. *N2* —1F **7**
Monarch Dri. *E16* —4F **45**

Monarch M. E17—1D 15
Monarch M. SW16—5C 94
Mona Rd. SE15—5E 69
Mona St. E16—4B 44
Moncks Row. SW15—4B 76 (off West Hill Rd.)
Monck St. SW1—4F 51
Monclar Rd. SE5—2F 81
Moncorvo Clo. SW7—3A 50 (off Ennismore Gdns.)
Moncreiff Pl. SE15—5C 68
Moncrieff Clo. E6—5F 45
Moncrieff St. SE15—5C 68
Monega Rd. E7 & E12—3E 31
Monet Ct. SE16—1D 69 (off Stubbs Dri.)
Moneyer Ho. N1—1F 39 (off Provost Est.)
Monica Shaw Ct. NW1—1F 37 (off Purchese St., in two parts)
Monier Rd. E3—4C 28
Monk Ct. W12—2C 46
Monk Dri. E16—1C 58
Monk Pas. E16—1C 58 (off Monk Dri.)
Monkton Ho. E5—2D 27
Monkton St. SE11—5C 52
Monkwell Sq. EC2—4E 39
Monmouth Pl. W2—5D 35 (off Monmouth Rd.)
Monmouth Rd. W2—5C 34
Monmouth St. WC2—5A 38
Monnery Rd. N19—5E 9
Monnow Rd. SE1—1C 68
Monsell Rd. N4—5C 10
Monson Rd. NW10—1C 32
Monson Rd. SE14—3F 69
Montacute Rd. SE6—5B 84
Montague Av. SE4—2B 84
Montague Clo. SE1—2F 53
Montague Pl. E14—1E 57
Montague Pl. WC1—4F 37
Montague Rd. E8—2C 26
Montague Rd. E11—4B 16
Montague Rd. N8—1B 10
Montague Sq. SE15—3E 69
Montague St. EC1—4E 39
Montague St. WC1—4A 38
Montagu Mans. W1—4B 36
Montagu M. N. W1—4B 36
Montagu M. S. W1—5B 36
Montagu M. W. W1—5B 36
Montagu Pl. W1—4B 36
Montagu Rd. NW4—1C 4
Montagu Row. W1—4B 36
Montagu Sq. W1—4B 36
Montagu St. W1—5B 36
Montana Gdns. SE26—5B 98
Montana Rd. SW17—3C 92
Montcalm Ho. E14—5C 56
Montcalm Rd. SE7—3F 73
Montclare St. E2—3B 40
Monteagle Ct. N1—1A 40
Monteagle Way. E5—5C 12
Monteagle Way. SE15—1D 83
Montefiore St. SW8—5D 65
Montego Clo. SE24—2C 80
Montem Rd. SE23—5B 84
Montem St. N4—3B 10
Montenotte Rd. N8—1E 9
Montesquieu Ter. E16—5B 44 (off Clarkson Rd.)
Montevetro. SW11—4F 63
Montford Pl. SE11—1C 66
Montfort Ho. E2—2E 41 (off Victoria Pk. Sq.)
Montfort Ho. E14—4E 57
Montfort Pl. SW19—1F 89
Montgomery Lodge. E1 (off Cleveland Gro.)—3E 41
Montholme Rd. SW11—4B 78
Monthope Rd. E1—4C 40 (off Hopetown St., in two parts)
Montolieu Gdns. SW15—3D 75
Montpelier Gdns. E6—2F 45
Montpelier Gro. NW5—2E 23
Montpelier M. SW7—4A 50
Montpelier Pl. E1—5E 41
Montpelier Pl. SW7—4A 50
Montpelier Ri. NW11—2A 6
Montpelier Rd. SE15—4D 69
Montpelier Row. SE3—5B 72
Montpelier Sq. SW7—3A 50
Montpelier St. SW7—4A 50
Montpelier Ter. SW7—3A 50
Montpelier Va. SE3—5B 72
Montpelier Wlk. SW7—4A 50
Montpelier Way. NW11—2A 6
Montreal Pl. WC2—1B 52
Montrell Rd. SW2—1A 94
Montrose Av. NW6—1A 34
Montrose Ct. SE6—1B 100
Montrose Ct. SW7—3F 49
Montrose Ho. E14—4C 56
Montrose Pl. SW1—3C 50
Montrose Way. SE23—1F 97
Montserrat Clo. SE19—5F 95
Montserrat Rd. SW15—2A 76
Monument Gdns. SE13—3E 85
Monument St. EC3—1F 53
Monument, The.—1F 53 (off Monument St.)
Monza St. E1—1E 55
Moodkee St. SE16—4E 55
Moody Rd. SE15—4B 68
Moody St. E1—2F 41
Moon Ct. SE12—2C 86
Moon St. N1—5D 25
Moorcroft Rd. SW16—3A 94
Moore Ct. N1—5D 25 (off Gaskin St.)
Moorehead Way. SE3—1C 86
Moore Ho. E2—2E 41 (off Roman Rd.)
Moore Ho. SE10—1B 72 (off Armitage Rd.)
Moore Pk. Ct. SW6—3D 63 (off Fulham Rd.)
Moore Pk. Rd. SW6—3C 62
Moore Rd. SE19—5E 95
Moore St. SW3—5B 50
Moore Wlk. E7—1C 30
Moorey Clo. E15—5B 30
Moorfields. EC2—4F 39
Moorfields Highwalk. EC2—4F 39 (off Moor La., in two parts)
Moorgate. EC2—5F 39
Moorgate Pl. EC2—5F 39 (off Swan All.)
Moorgreen Ho. EC1—2D 39 (off Spencer St.)
Moorhen Ct. SE8—2B 70 (off Rolt St.)
Moorhouse Rd. W2—5C 34
Moorings, The. E16—4E 45 (off Prince Regent La.)
Moorland M. N1—4C 24
Moorland Rd. SW9—2D 81
Moor La. EC2—4F 39 (in two parts)
Moor Pl. EC2—4F 39
Moorside Rd. Brom—3A 100
Moor St. W1—5F 37
Moran Ho. E1—2D 55 (off Wapping La.)
Morant St. E14—1C 56
Mora Rd. NW2—1E 19
Mora St. EC1—2E 39
Morat St. SW9—4B 66
Moravian Clo. SW10—2F 63
Moravian Pl. SW10—2F 63
Moravian St. E2—1E 41
Moray M. N7—4B 10
Moray Rd. N4—4B 10
Mordaunt Ho. NW10—5A 18
Mordaunt Rd. NW10—5A 18
Mordaunt St. SW9—1B 80
Morden Hill. SE13—5E 71
Morden La. SE13—4E 71
Morden Rd. SE3—5C 72
Morden Rd. M. SE3—5C 72
Morden St. SE13—4D 71
Morden Wharf. SE10—4A 58 (off Morden Wharf Rd.)
Morden Wharf Rd. SE10—4A 58
Mordern Ho. NW1—3A 36 (off Harewood Av.)
Mordred Rd. SE6—2A 100
Morecambe Clo. E1—4F 41
Morecambe St. SE17—5E 53
More Clo. E16—5B 44
More Clo. W14—5F 47
Moreland Ct. NW2—5C 6
Moreland St. EC1—2D 39
Morella Rd. SW12—5B 78
Moremead Rd. SE6—4B 98
Morena St. SE6—5D 85
Moresby Rd. E5—3D 13
Moresby Wlk. SW8—5E 65
More's Garden. SW3—2F 63 (off Cheyne Wlk.)
Moreton Clo. E5—4D 13

Moreton Clo. *N15* —1F **11**
Moreton Ho. *SW1* —1E **65**
(off Moreton Ter.)
Moreton Ho. *SE16* —4D **55**
Moreton Pl. *SW1* —1E **65**
Moreton Rd. *N15* —1F **11**
Moreton St. *SW1* —1E **65**
Moreton Ter. *SW1* —1E **65**
Moreton Ter. M. N. *SW1*
　　　　　—1E **65**
Moreton Ter. M. S. *SW1*
　　　　　—1E **65**
Morgan Ho. *SW1* —5E **51**
(off Vauxhall Bri. Rd.)
Morgan Ho. *SW8* —4E **65**
(off Wadhurst Rd.)
Morgan Mans. *N7* —2C **24**
(off Morgan Rd.)
Morgan Rd. *N7* —2C **24**
Morgan Rd. *W10* —4B **34**
Morgan's La. *SE1* —2A **54**
Morgan St. *E3* —2A **42**
Morgan St. *E16* —4B **44**
Moriarty Clo. *N7* —1A **24**
Morie St. *SW18* —3D **77**
Morieux Rd. *E10* —3B **14**
Moring Rd. *SW17* —4C **92**
Morkyns Wlk. *SE21* —3A **96**
Morland Clo. *NW11* —3D **7**
Morland Est. *E8* —4C **26**
Morland Gdns. *NW10* —4A **18**
Morland Ho. *NW1* —1E **37**
(off Cranleigh St.)
Morland Ho. *NW6* —5C **20**
(off Brondesbury Rd.)
Morland Ho. *SW1* —5A **52**
(off Marsham St.)
Morland Ho. *W11* —5A **34**
(off Lancaster Rd.)
Morland Rd. *E17* —1F **13**
Morley Ho. *N16* —4C **12**
Morley Rd. *E10* —3E **15**
Morley Rd. *E15* —1B **44**
Morley Rd. *SE13* —2E **85**
Morley St. *SE1* —4C **52**
Morna Rd. *SE5* —5E **67**
Morning La. *E9* —3E **27**
Mornington Av. *W14* —5B **48**
Mornington Ct. *NW1* —1E **37**
(off Mornington Cres.)
Mornington Cres. *NW1*
　　　　　—1E **37**
Mornington Gro. *E3* —2C **42**
Mornington M. *SE5* —4E **67**
Mornington Pl. *NW1* —1E **37**
Mornington Pl. *SE8* —3B **70**
(off Mornington Rd.)
Mornington Rd. *E11* —2B **16**
Mornington Rd. *SE14* —3B **70**
Mornington St. *NW1* —1D **37**
Mornington Ter. *NW1* —5D **23**
Morocco St. *SE1* —3A **54**
Morpeth Gro. *E9* —5F **27**
Morpeth Mans. *SW1* —5E **51**
(off Morpeth Ter.)
Morpeth Rd. *E9* —5F **27**

Morpeth St. *E2* —2F **41**
Morpeth Ter. *SW1* —4E **51**
Morrel Ct. *E2* —1C **40**
(off Goldsmiths Row)
Morris Blitz Ct. *N16* —1B **26**
Morris Gdns. *SW18* —5C **76**
Morris Ho. *E2* —2E **41**
(off Roman Rd.)
Morris Ho. *NW8* —3A **36**
(off Salisbury St.)
Morrish Rd. *SW2* —5A **80**
Morrison Bldgs. N. *E1* —5C **40**
(off Commercial St.)
Morrison Bldgs. S. *E1* —5C **40**
(off Commercial Rd.)
Morrison St. *SW11* —1C **78**
Morris Pl. *N4* —4C **10**
Morris Rd. *E14* —4D **43**
Morriss Ho. *SE16* —3D **55**
(off Cherry Garden St.)
Morris St. *E1* —5D **41**
Morse Clo. *E13* —2C **44**
Morshead Mans. *W9* —2C **34**
(off Morshead Rd.)
Morshead Rd. *W9* —2C **34**
Mortain Ho. *SE16* —5D **55**
(off Roseberry St.)
Morten Clo. *SW4* —4F **79**
Mortham St. *E15* —5A **30**
Mortimer Clo. *NW2* —4B **6**
Mortimer Clo. *SW16* —2F **93**
Mortimer Ct. *NW8* —1E **35**
(off Abercorn Pl.)
Mortimer Cres. *NW6* —5D **21**
Mortimer Est. *NW6* —5D **21**
(off Mortimer Pl.)
Mortimer Ho. *W11* —2F **47**
(off Queensdale Cres.)
Mortimer Ho. *W14* —5A **48**
(off N. End Rd.)
Mortimer Mkt. *WC1* —3E **37**
Mortimer Mkt. Cen. *W1*
　　　　　—3E **37**
Mortimer Pl. *NW6* —5D **21**
Mortimer Rd. *N1* —4A **26**
(in two parts)
Mortimer Rd. *NW10* —2E **33**
Mortimer Sq. *W11* —1F **47**
Mortimer St. *W1* —5E **37**
Mortimer Ter. *NW5* —1D **23**
Mortlake High St. *SW14*
　　　　　—1A **74**
Mortlake Rd. *E16* —5D **45**
Mortlock Clo. *SE15* —4D **69**
Mortlock Ct. *E7* —1F **31**
Morton Ho. *SE17* —2D **67**
Morton M. *SW5* —5D **49**
Morton Pl. *SE1* —4C **52**
Morton Rd. *E15* —4B **30**
Morton Rd. *N1* —4E **25**
Morval Rd. *SW2* —3C **80**
Morven Rd. *SW17* —3B **92**
Morville St. *E3* —1C **42**
Morwell St. *WC1* —4F **37**
Moscow Pl. *W2* —1D **49**
Moscow Rd. *W2* —1C **48**

Mosedale. *NW1* —2E **37**
(off Cumberland Mkt.)
Mossbury Rd. *SW11* —1A **78**
Moss Clo. *E1* —4C **40**
Mossford St. *E3* —3B **42**
Mossington Gdns. *SE16*
　　　　　—5E **55**
Mossop St. *SW3* —5A **50**
Mostyn Gdns. *NW10* —2F **33**
Mostyn Gro. *E3* —1C **42**
Mostyn Rd. *SW9* —4C **66**
Motcomb St. *SW1* —4C **50**
Mothers Sq. *E5* —1D **27**
Motley Av. *EC2* —3A **40**
(off Christina St.)
Motley St. *SW8* —5E **65**
Mottingham. —2F 101
Mottingham Gdns. *SE9*
　　　　　—1F **101**
Mottingham La. *SE12 & SE9*
　　　　　—1E **101**
Mottingham Rd. *SE9* —2F **101**
Moules Ct. *SE5* —3E **67**
Moulins Rd. *E9* —4E **27**
Moulsford Ho. *N7* —2F **23**
Moundfield Rd. *N16* —1C **12**
Mounsey Ho. *W10* —2A **34**
(off Third Av.)
Mountacre Clo. *SE26* —4B **96**
Mt. Adon Pk. *SE22* —5C **82**
Mountague Pl. *E14* —1E **57**
Mountain Ho. *SE11* —5B **52**
Mt. Angelus Rd. *SW15*
　　　　　—5B **74**
Mt. Ash Rd. *SE26* —3D **97**
Mountbatten Clo. *SE19*
　　　　　—5A **96**
Mountbatten Ct. *SE16* —2E **55**
(off Rotherhithe St.)
Mountbatten Ho. *N6* —2C **8**
(off Hillcrest)
Mountbatten M. *SW18*
　　　　　—5E **77**
Mt. Carmel Chambers. W8
(off Pitt St. La.) —3C **48**
Mount Ct. *SW15* —1A **76**
Mountearl Gdns. *SW16*
　　　　　—3B **94**
Mt. Ephraim La. *SW16*
　　　　　—3F **93**
Mt. Ephraim Rd. *SW16*
　　　　　—3F **93**
Mountfield Clo. *SE6* —5F **85**
Mountford Rd. *E8* —2C **26**
Mountford St. *E1* —5C **40**
Mountfort Cres. *N1* —4C **24**
Mountfort Ter. *N1* —4C **24**
Mount Gdns. *SE26* —3D **97**
Mountgrove Rd. *N5* —5D **11**
Mountjoy Clo. EC2 —4E **39**
(off Beech St.)
Mountjoy Ho. EC2 —4E **39**
(off Beech St.)
Mount Lodge. *N6* —1E **9**
Mount Mills. *EC1* —2D **39**
Mt. Nod Rd. *SW16* —3B **94**

Mount Pleasant. SE27 —4E **95**
Mount Pleasant. WC1 —3C **38**
Mt. Pleasant Cres. N4 —3B **10**
Mt. Pleasant Hill. E5 —4D **13**
Mt. Pleasant La. E5 —3D **13**
Mt. Pleasant Rd. NW10 —4E **19**
Mt. Pleasant Rd. SE13 —4D **85**
Mt. Pleasant Vs. N4 —2B **10**
Mount Rd. NW2 —5D **5**
Mount Rd. NW4 —1C **4**
Mount Rd. SW19 —2C **90**
Mount Row. W1 —1D **51**
Mountsfield Ct. SE13 —4F **85**
Mounts Pond Rd. SE3 (in two parts) —5F **71**
Mount Sq., The. NW3 —5E **7**
Mount St. W1 —1C **50**
Mount St. M. W1 —1D **51**
Mount Ter. E1 —4D **41**
Mount, The. E5 —4D **13** (in two parts)
Mount, The. NW3 —5E **7**
Mount Vernon. NW3 —1E **21**
Mount Vw. Rd. N4 —2A **10**
Mount Vs. SE27 —3D **95**
Mowatt Clo. N19 —4F **9**
Mowbray Rd. NW6 —4A **20**
Mowlem St. E2 —1D **41**
Mowll St. SW9 —3C **66**
Moxon Clo. E13 —1B **44**
Moxon St. W1 —4C **36**
Moye Clo. E2 —1C **40**
Moyers Rd. E10 —2E **15**
Moylan Rd. W6 —2A **62**
*Moyle Ho. SW1 —1E **65** (off Churchill Gdns.)*
Moyne Ho. SW9 —3D **81**
Moyser Rd. SW16 —5D **93**
Mozart St. W10 —2B **34**
Mozart Ter. SW1 —5C **50**
Mudlarks Way. SE10 & SE7 (in two parts) —4B **58**
Muir Dri. SW18 —4A **78**
Muirfield. W3 —5A **32**
Muirfield Clo. SE16 —1D **69**
Muirfield Cres. E14 —4D **57**
Muirkirk Rd. SE6 —1E **99**
Muir Rd. E5 —1C **26**
Mulberry Bus. Cen. SE16 —3F **55**
Mulberry Clo. N8 —1A **10**
Mulberry Clo. NW3 —1F **21**
Mulberry Clo. SE7 —2F **73**
Mulberry Clo. SE22 —3C **82**
Mulberry Clo. SW3 —2F **63**
Mulberry Clo. SW16 —4E **93**
*Mulberry Ct. EC1 —2D **39** (off Tompion St.)*
*Mulberry Ho. E2 —2E **41** (off Victoria Pk. Sq.)*
Mulberry Ho. SE8 —2B **70**
*Mulberry Housing Co-operative. SE1—2C **52** (off Upper Rd.)*
Mulberry M. SE14 —4B **70**
Mulberry Pl. E14 —1E **57**
Mulberry Pl. W6 —1C **60**
Mulberry Rd. E8 —4B **26**
Mulberry St. E1 —5C **40**
Mulberry Wlk. SW3 —2F **63**
Mulgrave Rd. NW10 —1B **18**
Mulgrave Rd. SW6 —2B **62**
Mulkern Rd. N19 —3F **9**
*Mullberry Pl. E14 —1E **57** (off Clove Cres.)*
*Mullen Tower. EC1 —3C **38** (off Mt. Pleasant)*
Muller Rd. SW4 —4F **79**
Mullet Gdns. E2 —2C **40**
*Mulletsfield. WC1 —2A **38** (off Cromer St.)*
Mullins Path. SW14 —1A **74**
*Mull Wlk. N1 —3E **25** (off Clephane Rd.)*
*Mulready Ho. SW1 —5A **52** (off Marsham St.)*
Mulready St. NW8 —3A **36**
Multi Way. W3 —3A **46**
Multon Rd. SW18 —5F **77**
Mulvaney Way. SE1 —3F **53** (in two parts)
Mumford Ct. EC2 —5E **39**
Mumford Rd. SE24 —3D **81**
Muncaster Rd. SW11 —3B **78**
Muncies M. SE6 —2E **99**
Mundania Rd. SE22 —4D **83**
*Munday Ho. SE1 —4F **53** (off Deverell St.)*
Munday Rd. E16 —1C **58**
Munden St. W14 —5A **48**
Mundford Rd. E5 —4E **13**
Mund St. W14 —1B **62**
Mundy St. N1 —2A **40**
Munro Ho. SE1 —3C **52**
Munro M. W10 —4A **34** (in two parts)
Munro Ter. SW10 —3F **63**
Munster Ct. SW6 —5B **62**
Munster M. SW6 —3A **62**
Munster Rd. SW6 —3A **62**
Munster Sq. NW1 —2D **37**
Munton Rd. SE17 —5E **53**
Murchison Rd. E10 —4E **15**
*Murdoch Ho. SE16 —4E **55** (off Moodkee St.)*
Murdock Clo. E16 —5B **44**
Murdock St. SE15 —2D **69**
Murfett Clo. SW19 —2A **90**
Muriel Ct. E10 —2D **15**
Muriel St. N1 —1B **38** (in two parts)
Murillo Rd. SE13 —2F **85**
*Murphy Ho. SE1 —4D **53** (off Borough Rd.)*
Murphy St. SE1 —3C **52**
Murray Gro. N1 —1E **39**
Murray M. NW1 —4F **23**
Murray Rd. SW19 —5F **89**
Murray Sq. E16 —5C **44**
Murray St. NW1 —4E **23**
Murray Ter. NW3 —1E **21**
Mursell Est. SW8 —4B **66**
Musard Rd. W6 —2A **62**
Musbury St. E1 —5E **41**
*Muscal. W6 —2A **62** (off Field Rd.)*
Muscatel Pl. SE5 —4A **68**
Muschamp Rd. SE15 —1B **82**
Muscovy St. EC3 —1A **54**
*Museum Chambers. WC1 (off Bury Pl.) —4A **38***
Mus. in Docklands. —1C 56
*Museum La. SW7 —4F **49** (off Exhibition Rd.)*
Mus. of Fulham Palace. —5A 62
Mus. of Gardening History. —4B 52
Mus. of London. —4E 39
Mus. of Methodism. —3F 39
Museum Pas. E2 —2E **41**
Museum St. WC1 —4A **38**
Musgrave Ct. SW11 —4A **64**
Musgrave Cres. SW6 —3C **62**
Musgrove Rd. SE14 —4F **69**
Musjid Rd. SW11 —5F **63**
Muston Rd. E5 —4D **13**
Mustow Pl. SW6 —5B **62**
Muswell Hill Rd. N6 & N10 —1C **8**
Mutrix Rd. NW6 —5C **20**
Mutton Pl. NW1 —3C **22**
Myatt Rd. SW9 —4D **67**
*Myatts Fields S. SW9 —5C **66** (off St Lawrence Way)*
Mycenae Rd. SE3 —3C **72**
Myddelton Pas. EC1 —2C **38**
Myddelton Sq. EC1 —2C **38**
Myddelton St. EC1 —2C **38**
Myddleton Av. N4 —4E **11**
*Myddleton Ho. WC1 —1C **38** (off Pentonville Rd.)*
Myers La. SE14 —2F **69**
Mylis Clo. SE26 —4D **97**
Mylius Clo. SE14 —3E **69**
Mylne Clo. W6 —1C **60**
Mylne St. EC1 —2C **38**
Myron Pl. SE13 —1E **85**
*Myrtleberry Clo. E8 —3B **26** (off Beechwood Rd.)*
Myrtle Rd. E17 —1A **14**
Myrtle Wlk. N1 —1A **40**
Mysore Rd. SW11 —1B **78**
Myton Rd. SE21 —3F **95**
*Mytton Ho. SW8 —3B **66** (off St Stephens Ter.)*

Nadine St. SE7 —1E **73**
Nagasaki Wlk. SE7 —4D **59**
Nag's Head. (Junct.) —5A **10**
*Nags Head Ct. EC1 —3E **39** (off Golden La.)*
Nags Head Shop. Cen. N7 —1B **24**

*Nailsworth Ct. SE15 —2A **68***
(off Birdlip Clo.)
*Nainby Ho. SE11 —5C **52***
(off Hotspur St.)
Nairne Gro. *SE24* —3F **81**
Nairn St. *E14* —4E **43**
Naish Ct. *N1* —5A **24**
(in three parts)
Naldera Gdns. *SE3* —2C **72**
Namba Roy Clo. *SW16* —4B **94**
Nankin St. *E14* —5C **42**
*Nansen Ho. NW10 —4A **18***
(off Stonebridge Pk.)
Nansen Rd. *SW11* —1C **78**
Nant Ct. *NW2* —4B **6**
Nantes Clo. *SW18* —2E **77**
*Nantes Pas. E1 —4B **40***
(off Lamb St.)
Nant Rd. *NW2* —4B **6**
Nant St. *E2* —2D **41**
Naoroji St. *WC1* —2C **38**
Napier Av. *E14* —1C **70**
Napier Av. *SW6* —1B **76**
Napier Clo. *SE8* —3B **70**
Napier Clo. *W14* —4A **48**
*Napier Ct. N1 —1F **39***
(off Cropley St.)
*Napier Ct. SW6 —1B **76***
(off Ranelagh Gdns.)
Napier Gro. *N1* —1E **39**
Napier Pl. *W14* —4B **48**
Napier Rd. *E11* —1A **30**
Napier Rd. *E15* —1A **44**
(in two parts)
Napier Rd. *NW10* —2D **33**
Napier Rd. *W14* —4A **48**
*Napier St. SE8 —3B **70***
(off Napier Clo.)
Napier Ter. *N1* —4D **25**
Napoleon Rd. *E5* —5D **13**
Narbonne Av. *SW4* —3E **79**
Narborough St. *SW6* —5D **63**
Narcissus Rd. *NW6* —2C **20**
Narford Rd. *E5* —5C **12**
Narrow St. *E14* —1F **55**
Narvic Ho. *SE5* —5E **67**
Nascot St. *W12* —5E **33**
Naseby Clo. *NW6* —4E **21**
Naseby Rd. *SE19* —5F **95**
*Naseby Tower. SE14 —3A **70***
(off Desmond St.)
*Nash Ct. E14 —2D **57***
(off S. Colonnade, The)
*Nashe Ho. SE1 —4F **53***
(off Burbage Clo.)
*Nash Ho. SW1 —1D **65***
(off Lupus St.)
Nash Pl. *E14* —2D **57**
Nash Rd. *SE4* —2A **84**
Nash St. *NW1* —2D **37**
Nasmyth St. *W6* —4D **47**
Nassau Rd. *SW13* —4B **60**
Nassau St. *W1* —4E **37**
Nassington Rd. *NW3* —1B **22**
Natal Rd. *SW16* —5F **93**
*Nathan Ho. SE11 —5C **52***
(off Reedworth St.)
Nathaniel Clo. *E1* —4B **40**
Nathaniel Ct. *E17* —2A **14**
National Army Mus. —2B 64
National Film Theatre.
(off Waterloo Rd.) —2B 52
National Gallery. —1F 51
National Maritime Mus. —2F 71
National Portrait Gallery.
(off St Martin's Pl.) —1F 51
Natural History Mus. —4F 49
Nautilus Building, The. EC1
*(off Myddelton Pas.) —2C **38***
Naval Ho. *E14* —1F **57**
Naval Row. *E14* —1E **57**
Navarino Gro. *E8* —3C **26**
Navarino Mans. *E8* —3C **26**
Navarino Rd. *E8* —3C **26**
Navarre St. *E2* —3B **40**
Navenby Wlk. *E3* —3C **42**
Navy St. *SW4* —1F **79**
Nayland Ho. *SE6* —4E **99**
Naylor Rd. *SE15* —3D **69**
Nazareth Gdns. *SE15* —5D **69**
Nazrul St. *E2* —2B **40**
*Neagle Ho. NW2 —5E **5***
(off Stoll Clo.)
Nealden St. *SW9* —1B **80**
Neal St. *WC2* —5A **38**
Neal's Yd. *WC2* —5A **38**
Neasden. —5A 4
Neasden Clo. *NW10* —2A **18**
Neasden Junction. (Junct.) —1A **18**
Neasden La. *NW10* —5A **4**
Neasden La. N. *NW10* —5A **4**
Neate St. *SE5* —2A **68**
(in two parts)
*Neath Ho. SE24 —4D **81***
(off Dulwich Rd.)
Neathouse Pl. *SW1* —5E **51**
Neatscourt Rd. *E6* —4F **45**
Nebraska St. *SE1* —3F **53**
Neckinger. *SE1* —4B **54**
Neckinger Est. *SE16* —4B **54**
Neckinger St. *SE1* —3B **54**
Nectarine Way. *SE13* —5D **71**
*Needham Ho. SE11 —1C **66***
(off Hotspur St.)
Needham Rd. *W11* —5C **34**
Needham Ter. *NW2* —5F **5**
Needleman St. *SE16* —3F **55**
Needwood Ho. *N4* —3E **11**
Neeld Cres. *NW4* —1D **5**
Neil Wates Cres. *SW2* —1C **94**
Nelgarde Rd. *SE6* —5C **84**
Nella Rd. *W6* —2F **61**
Nelldale Rd. *SE16* —5E **55**
Nello James Gdns. *SE27* —4F **95**
Nelson Ct. *SE1* —3D **53**
Nelson Gdns. *E2* —2C **40**
*Nelson Ho. SW1 —2E **65***
(off Dolphin Sq.)
Nelson Mandela Rd. *SE3* —1E **87**
Nelson Pas. *EC1* —2E **39**
Nelson Pl. *N1* —1D **39**
Nelson Rd. *N8* —1B **10**
Nelson Rd. *SE10* —2E **71**
Nelson's Column. —2A 52
Nelson Sq. *SE1* —3D **53**
Nelson's Row. *SW4* —2F **79**
Nelson St. *E1* —5D **41**
Nelson St. *E16* —1B **58**
(in two parts)
*Nelsons Yd. NW1 —1E **37***
(off Mornington Cres.)
Nelson Ter. *EC1* —1D **39**
Nelson Wlk. *SE16* —2A **56**
Nepaul Rd. *SW11* —5A **64**
Nepean St. *SW15* —4C **74**
Neptune Ct. *E14* —5C **56**
*Neptune Ho. SE16 —4E **55***
(off Moodkee St.)
Neptune St. *SE16* —4E **55**
Nesbit Rd. *SE9* —2F **87**
Nesbitt Clo. *SE3* —1A **86**
Nesham St. *E1* —2C **54**
Ness St. *SE16* —4C **54**
*Nestor Ho. E2 —1D **41***
(off Old Bethnal Grn. Rd.)
Netheravon Rd. *W4* —5B **46**
Netheravon Rd. S. *W4* —1B **60**
Netherby Rd. *SE23* —5E **83**
Netherfield Rd. *SW17* —3C **92**
Netherford Rd. *SW4* —5E **65**
Netherhall Gdns. *NW3* —3E **21**
Netherhall Way. *NW3* —2E **21**
Netherleigh Clo. *N6* —3D **9**
Netherton Gro. *SW10* —2E **63**
Netherton Rd. *N15* —1F **11**
Netherwood Rd. *W6* —4F **47**
Netherwood St. *NW6* —4B **20**
*Netley. SE5 —4A **68***
(off Redbridge Gdns.)
Netley Rd. *E17* —1B **14**
Netley St. *NW1* —2E **37**
*Nettlecombe. NW1 —4F **23***
(off Agar Gro.)
*Nettleden Ho. SW3 —5A **50***
(off Marlborough St.)
Nettlefold Pl. *SE27* —3D **95**
*Nettleton Ct. EC2 —4E **39***
(off London Wall)
Nettleton Rd. *SE14* —4F **69**
Neuchatel Rd. *SE6* —2B **98**
Nevada St. *SE10* —2E **71**
*Nevern Mans. SW5 —1C **62***
(off Warwick Rd.)
Nevern Pl. *SW5* —5C **48**
Nevern Rd. *SW5* —5C **48**
Nevern Sq. *SW5* —5C **48**
*Nevil Ho. SW9 —5D **67***
(off Loughborough Est.)
*Nevill Ct. EC4 —5C **38***
(off E. Harding St.)
Neville Clo. *E11* —5B **16**

Neville Clo. NW1 —1F 37
Neville Clo. NW6 —1B 34
Neville Clo. SE15 —4C 68
Neville Ct. NW8 —1F 35 (off Abbey Rd.)
Neville Dri. N2 —1E 7
Neville Gill Clo. SW18 —4C 76
Neville Rd. E7 —4C 30
Neville Rd. NW6 —1B 34
Nevilles Ct. NW2 —5C 4
Neville St. SW7 —1F 63
Neville Ter. SW7 —1F 63
Nevill Rd. N16 —1A 26
Nevinson Clo. SW18 —4F 77
Nevis Rd. SW17 —2C 92
Nevitt Ho. N1 —1F 39 (off Cranston Est.)
Newall Ho. SE1 —4E 53 (off Bath Ter.)
Newarke Ho. SW9 —5D 67
Newark St. E1 —4D 41 (in two parts)
New Atlas Wharf. E14 —4C 56 (off Glengall Causeway)
New Baltic Wharf. SE8 (off Evelyn St.) —1A 70
New Barn St. E13 —3C 44
New Beckenham. —5B 98
New Bentham Ct. N1 —4E 25 (off Ecclesbourne Rd.)
Newbery Ho. N1 —4E 25 (off Northampton St.)
Newbold Cotts. E1 —5E 41
Newbolt Ho. SE17 —1F 67 (off Brandon St.)
New Bond St. W1 —5D 37
Newbridge Point. SE23 (off Windrush La.) —3F 97
New Bri. St. EC4 —5D 39
New Broad St. EC2 —4A 40
Newburgh St. W1 —5E 37
New Burlington M. W1 —1E 51
New Burlington Pl. W1 —1E 51
New Burlington St. W1 —1E 51
Newburn Ho. SE11 —1B 66 (off Newburn St.)
Newburn St. SE11 —1B 66
Newbury Ho. SW9 —5D 67
Newbury Ho. W2 —5D 35 (off Hallfield Est.)
Newbury M. NW5 —3C 22
Newbury St. EC1 —4E 39
New Bus. Cen., The. NW10 —2B 32
New Butt La. SE8 —3C 70 (in two parts)
New Butt La. N. SE8 —3C 70 (off Reginald Rd.)
Newby. NW1 —2E 37 (off Robert St.)
Newby Pl. E14 —1E 57
Newby St. SW8 —1D 79
New Caledonian Wharf. SE16 —4B 56
Newcastle Clo. EC4 —5D 39
Newcastle Ct. EC4 —1E 53 (off College Hill)
Newcastle Ho. W1 —4C 36 (off Luxborough St.)
Newcastle Pl. W2 —4F 35
Newcastle Row. EC1 —3C 38
New Cavendish St. W1 —4C 36
New Change. EC4 —5E 39
New Charles St. EC1 —2D 39
New Charlton. —5E 59
New Chu. Rd. SE5 —3E 67 (in two parts)
New City Rd. E13 —2E 45
New College Ct. NW3 —3E 21 (off College Cres.)
New College M. N1 —4C 24
New College Pde. NW3 (off College Cres.) —3F 21
Newcombe Gdns. SW16 —4A 94
Newcombe St. W8 —2C 48
Newcomen Rd. E11 —5B 16
Newcomen Rd. SW11 —1F 77
Newcomen St. SE1 —3F 53
New Compton St. WC2 —5F 37
New Concordia Wharf. SE1 —3C 54
New Ct. EC4 —1C 52 (off Fountain Ct.)
Newcourt Ho. E2 —2D 41 (off Pott St.)
Newcourt St. NW8 —1A 36
New Covent Garden Market. —3F 65
New Coventry St. W1 —1F 51
New Crane Pl. E1 —2E 55
New Cross. —3B 70
New Cross. (Junct.) —4B 70
New Cross Gate. —4F 69
New Cross Gate. (Junct.) —4F 69
New Cross Rd. SE15 & SE14 —3E 69
Newdigate Ho. E14 —5B 42
Newell St. E14 —5B 42
New End. NW3 —1E 21
New End Sq. NW3 —1F 21
Newent Clo. SE15 —3A 68
New Era Est. N1 —5A 26 (off Phillipp St.)
New Fetter La. EC4 —5C 38
Newfield Ri. NW2 —5D 5
Newgate St. EC1 —5D 39
New Globe Wlk. SE1 —2E 53
New Goulston St. E1 —5B 40
New Grn. Pl. SE19 —5A 96
Newham's Row. SE1 —3A 54
Newham Way. E16 & E6 —4B 44
Newhaven Gdns. SE9 —2F 87
Newhaven La. E16 —3B 44
Newick Rd. E5 —1D 27
Newington. —4E 53
Newington Barrow Way. N7 —5B 10
Newington Butts. SE11 & SE1 —5D 53
Newington Causeway. SE1 —4D 53
Newington Ct. Bus. Cen. SE1 —4E 53 (off Newington Causeway)
Newington Grn. N1 & N16 —2F 25
Newington Grn. Mans. N16 —2F 25
Newington Grn. Rd. N1 —3F 25
Newington Ind. Est. SE17 (off Crampton St.) —5E 53
New Inn B'way. EC2 —3A 40
New Inn Pas. WC2 —5B 38 (off Houghton St.)
New Inn Sq. EC2 —3A 40 (off Bateman's Row)
New Inn St. EC2 —3A 40
New Inn Yd. EC2 —3A 40
New Kent Rd. SE1 —4E 53
New Kings Rd. SW6 —5B 62
New King St. SE8 —2C 70
Newland Ct. EC1 —3F 39 (off St Luke's Est.)
Newland Ho. SE14 —2F 69 (off John Williams Clo.)
Newlands. —3F 83
Newlands. NW1 —2E 37 (off Harrington St.)
Newlands Pk. SE26 —5E 97
Newlands Quay. E1 —1E 55
New London St. EC3 —1A 54 (off Hart St.)
New Lydenburg Commercial Est. SE7 —4E 59
New Lydenburg St. SE7 —4E 59
Newlyn. NW1 —5E 23 (off Plender St.)
Newman Pas. W1 —4E 37
Newman Rd. E13 —2D 45
Newman's Ct. EC3 —5F 39 (off Cornhill)
Newman's Row. WC2 —4B 38
Newman St. W1 —4E 37
Newman Yd. W1 —5E 37
Newmarket Grn. SE9 —5F 87
Newmill Ho. E3 —3E 43
New Mt. St. E15 —4F 29
Newnes Path. SW15 —2D 75
Newnham Ter. SE1 —4C 52
New N. Pl. EC2 —3A 40
New N. Rd. N1 —4E 25
New N. St. WC1 —4B 38
Newnton Clo. N4 —2F 11 (in two parts)
New Orleans Wlk. N19 —2F 9
New Oxford St. WC1 —5F 37

*New Pk. Pde. SW2 —5A **80***
(off New Pk. Rd.)
New Pk. Rd. *SW2* —1F **93**
New Pl. Sq. *SE16* —4D **55**
New Plaistow Rd. *E15* —5A **30**
Newport Av. *E13* —3D **45**
Newport Av. *E14* —1F **57**
Newport Ct. *WC2* —1F **51**
Newport Pl. *WC2* —1F **51**
Newport Rd. *E10* —4E **15**
Newport Rd. *SW13* —4C **60**
Newport St. *SE11* —5B **52**
*New Priory Ct. NW6 —4C **20***
(off Mazenod Av.)
Newquay Ho. *SE11* —1C **66**
Newquay Rd. *SE6* —2D **99**
New Quebec St. *W1* —5B **36**
New Ride. *SW7 & SW1* —3F **49**
New River Ct. *N5* —1E **25**
New River Head. *EC1* —2C **38**
*New River Wlk. N1 —4E **25***
(off Canonbury Rd.)
New River Way. *N4* —2F **11**
New Rd. *E1* —4D **41**
New Rd. *N8* —1A **10**
New Rochford St. *NW5* —2B **22**
New Row. *WC2* —1A **52**
New Spitalfields Market. —5C 14
New Spitalfields Mkt. *E10* —5D **15**
New Spring Gdns. Wlk. *SE1* —1A **66**
New Sq. *WC2* —5C **38**
*New Sq. Pas. WC2 —5C **38***
(off Star Yd.)
Newstead Rd. *SE12* —5B **86**
Newstead Way. *SW19* —4F **89**
New St. *EC2* —4A **40**
New St. Hill. *Brom* —5D **101**
New St. Sq. *EC4* —5C **38**
Newton Clo. *E17* —1A **14**
Newton Gro. *W4* —5A **46**
*Newton Ho. E1 —1D **55***
(off Corwall St.)
*Newton Ho. NW8 —5D **21***
(off Abbey Rd.)
*Newton Mans. W14 —2A **62***
(off Queen's Club Gdns.)
*Newton Point. E16 —5B **44***
(off Clarkson Rd.)
Newton Rd. *E15* —2F **29**
Newton Rd. *NW2* —1E **19**
Newton Rd. *W2* —5D **35**
Newton St. *WC1* —5A **38**
Newton's Yd. *SW18* —3C **76**
New Tower Bldgs. *E1* —2D **55**
Newtown St. *SW11* —4D **65**
New Turnstile. *WC1* —4B **38**
New Union Clo. *E14* —4E **57**
New Union St. *EC2* —4F **39**
New Wanstead. *E11* —1B **16**
New Wharf Rd. *N1* —1A **38**
New Zealand Way. *W12* —1D **47**
Niagra Clo. *N1* —1E **39**
*Niagra Ct. SE16 —4E **55***
(off Canada Est.)
*Nicholas Ct. W4 —2A **60***
(off Corney Reach Way)
Nicholas La. *EC4* —1F **53**
(in two parts)
*Nicholas Pas. EC4 —1F **53***
(off Nicholas La.)
Nicholas Rd. *E1* —3E **41**
Nicholay Rd. *N19* —3F **9**
Nicholl Ho. *N4* —3E **11**
Nichollsfield Wlk. *N7* —2B **24**
*Nicholls Point. E13 —5C **30***
(off Park Gro.)
Nicholl St. *E2* —5C **26**
*Nichols Clo. N4 —3C **10***
(off Osborne Rd.)
Nicholson Ho. *SE17* —1F **67**
Nicholson St. *SE1* —2D **53**
*Nickleby Ho. SE16 —3C **54***
(off George Row)
Nicoll Ct. *NW10* —5A **18**
Nicoll Pl. *NW4* —1D **5**
Nicoll Rd. *NW10* —5A **18**
Nicosia Rd. *SW18* —5A **78**
Niederwald Rd. *SE26* —4A **98**
*Nigel Ho. EC1 —4C **38***
(off Portpool La.)
Nigel Playfair Av. *W6* —5D **47**
Nigel Rd. *E7* —2E **31**
Nigel Rd. *SE15* —1C **82**
Nigeria Rd. *SE7* —3E **73**
Nightingale Ct. *E14* —3E **57**
*Nightingale Ct. N4 —4B **10***
(off Tollington Pk.)
*Nightingale Ct. SW6 —4D **63***
(off Maltings Pl.)
Nightingale Gro. *SE13* —3F **85**
*Nightingale Ho. E1 —2C **54***
(off Thomas More St.)
*Nightingale Ho. N1 —5A **26***
(off Wilmer Gdns.)
Nightingale La. *E11* —1C **16**
Nightingale La. *SW12 & SW4* —5B **78**
Nightingale Lodge. W9
*(off Admiral Wlk.) —4C **34***
Nightingale M. *E3* —1F **41**
Nightingale Pl. *SW10* —2E **63**
Nightingale Rd. *E5* —5D **13**
Nightingale Rd. *NW10* —1B **32**
Nightingale Sq. *SW12* —5C **78**
Nightingale Wlk. *SW4* —4D **79**
Nikols Wlk. *SW18* —2D **77**
Nile Clo. *N16* —5B **12**
Nile Rd. *E13* —1E **45**
Nile St. *N1* —2E **39**
Nile Ter. *SE15* —1B **68**
Nimegen Way. *SE22* —3A **82**
*Nimrod Ho. E16 —4D **45***
(off Vanguard Clo.)
Nimrod Pas. *N1* —3A **26**
Nimrod Rd. *SW16* —5D **93**
Nina Mackay Clo. *E15* —5A **30**
Nine Acres Clo. *E12* —2F **31**
Nine Elms. —3E 65
Nine Elms La. *SW8* —3E **65**
Nita Ct. *SE12* —1C **100**
Niton St. *SW6* —3F **61**
Nobel Ho. *SE5* —5E **67**
*Noble Ct. E1 —1D **55***
(off Cable St., in two parts)
Noblefield Heights. *N2* —1A **8**
Noble St. *EC2* —5E **39**
*Noel Coward Ho. SW1 —5E **51***
(off Vauxhall Bri. Rd.)
Noel Ho. *NW3* —4F **21**
Noel Rd. *E6* —3F **45**
Noel Rd. *N1* —1D **39**
Noel St. *W1* —5E **37**
Noel Ter. *SE23* —2E **97**
Nolan Way. *E5* —1C **26**
Norbiton Rd. *E14* —5B **42**
Norbroke St. *W12* —1B **46**
Norburn St. *W10* —4A **34**
*Norcombe Ho. N19 —5F **9***
(off Wedmore St.)
Norcott Rd. *N16* —4C **12**
Norcroft Gdns. *SE22* —5C **82**
*Norden Ho. E2 —2D **41***
(off Pott St.)
Norfolk Av. *N15* —1B **12**
Norfolk Cres. *W2* —5A **36**
Norfolk Ho. *SE8* —4C **70**
*Norfolk Ho. SW1 —5F **51***
(off Page St.)
Norfolk Ho. Rd. *SW16* —3F **93**
*Norfolk Mans. SW11 —4B **64***
(off Prince of Wales Dri.)
*Norfolk M. W10 —4B **34***
(off Blagrove Rd.)
Norfolk Pl. *W2* —5F **35**
(in two parts)
Norfolk Rd. *NW8* —5F **21**
Norfolk Rd. *NW10* —4A **18**
Norfolk Row. *SE1* —5B **52**
(in two parts)
Norfolk Sq. *W2* —5F **35**
*Norfolk Sq. M. W2 —5F **35***
(off London St.)
Norfolk St. *E7* —2C **30**
Norfolk Ter. *W6* —1A **62**
Norgrove St. *SW12* —5C **78**
*Norland Ho. W11 —2F **47***
(off Queensdale Cres.)
Norland Pl. *W11* —2A **48**
*Norland Rd. W11 —2F **47***
(off Queensdale Cres.)
Norland Sq. *W11* —2A **48**
Norland Sq. Mans. W11
*(off Norland Sq.) —2A **48***
Norley Va. *SW15* —1C **88**
Norlington Rd. *E10 & E11* —3E **15**
Normanby Clo. *SW15* —3B **76**
Normanby Rd. *NW10* —1B **18**
Norman Ct. *N4* —2C **10**
Norman Ct. *NW10* —4C **18**

*Normand Gdns. W14 —2A **62***
(off Greyhound Rd.)
Normand M. *W14* —2A **62**
Normand Rd. *W14* —2B **62**
Normandy Clo. *SE26* —3A **98**
Normandy Rd. *SW9* —4C **66**
Normandy Ter. *E16* —5D **45**
Norman Gro. *E3* —1A **42**
*Norman Ho. SW8 —3A **66***
(off Wyvil Rd.)
Normanhurst Rd. *SW2* —2B **94**
Norman Rd. *E11* —4F **15**
Norman Rd. *N15* —1B **12**
Norman Rd. *SE10* —3D **71**
Norman St. *EC1* —2E **39**
Normanton Av. *SW19* —2C **90**
Normanton St. *SE23* —2F **97**
Normington Clo. *SW16* —5C **94**
Norrice Lea. *N2* —1F **7**
*Norris Ho. N1 —5A **26***
(off Colville Est.)
*Norris Ho. SE8 —1B **70***
(off Grove St.)
Norris St. *SW1* —1F **51**
Norroy Rd. *SW15* —2F **75**
Norstead Pl. *SW15* —2C **88**
N. Access Rd. *E17* —1F **13**
N. Acton Rd. *NW10* —1A **32**
Northampton Gro. *N1* —2E **25**
Northampton Pk. *N1* —3E **25**
Northampton Rd. *EC1* —3C **38**
Northampton Row. EC1
*(off Rosoman Pl.) —3C **38***
Northampton Sq. *EC1* —2D **39**
Northampton St. *N1* —4E **25**
N. Audley St. *W1* —5C **36**
North Av. *NW10* —2E **33**
North Bank. *NW8* —2A **36**
North Beckton. —4F 45
N. Birkbeck Rd. *E11* —5F **15**
*North Block. SE1 —3B **52***
(off York Rd.)
Northbourne Rd. *SW4* —3F **79**
N. Branch Av. *NW10* —2E **33**
Northbrook Rd. *SE13* —3A **86**
Northburgh St. *EC1* —3D **39**
N. Carriage Dri. *W2* —1A **50**
Northchurch. *SE17* —1F **67**
(in three parts)
Northchurch Rd. *N1* —4F **25**
(in two parts)
Northchurch Ter. *N1* —4A **26**
(in two parts)
N. Circular Rd. *NW2* —5A **4**
N. Circular Rd. *NW4* —2E **5**
N. Circular Rd. *NW10* —2A **18**
N. Colonnade, The. *E14* —2C **56**
Northcote M. *SW11* —2A **78**
Northcote Rd. *NW10* —4A **18**
Northcote Rd. *SW11* —3A **78**
North Ct. *SE24* —1D **81**
*North Ct. SW1 —4A **52***
(off Gt. Peter St.)
North Ct. *W1* —4E **37**
North Cres. *E16* —3F **43**
North Cres. *WC1* —4F **37**
Northcroft Ct. *W12* —3C **46**
North Crofts. *SE23* —1D **97**
N. Cross Rd. *SE22* —3B **82**
Northdene Gdns. *N15* —1B **12**
Northdown St. *N1* —1A **38**
North Dri. *SW16* —4E **93**
N. East Pier. *E1* —2D **55**
North End. —4E 7
North End. *NW3* —4E **7**
N. End Av. *NW3* —4E **7**
N. End Cres. *W14* —5B **48**
N. End Ho. *W14* —5A **48**
*N. End Pde. W14 —5A **48***
(off N. End Rd.)
N. End Rd. *NW11* —3C **6**
N. End Rd. *W14 & SW6* —5A **48**
N. End Way. *NW3* —4E **7**
Northern Rd. *E13* —1D **45**
*Northesk Ho. E1 —3D **41***
(off Tent St.)
N. Eyot Gdns. *W6* —1B **60**
Northey St. *E14* —1A **56**
Northfield Ho. *SE15* —2C **68**
Northfield Rd. *N16* —2A **12**
Northfields. *SW18* —2C **76**
Northfields Prospect Bus. Cen. *SW18* —2C **76**
*Northfleet Ho. SE1 —3F **53***
(off Tennis St.)
N. Flock St. *SE16* —3C **54**
*N. Flower Wlk. W2 —1E **49***
(off Lancaster Wlk.)
North Garden. *E14* —2B **56**
*North Ga. NW8 —1A **36***
(off Prince Albert Rd.)
Northgate Dri. *NW9* —1A **4**
Northgate Ho. *E14* —1C **56**
N. Gower St. *NW1* —2E **37**
North Gro. *N6* —2C **8**
North Gro. *N15* —1F **11**
North Hill. *N6* —1B **8**
N. Hill Av. *N6* —1C **8**
North Ho. *SE8* —1B **70**
*Northiam. WC1 —2A **38***
(off Cromer St.)
Northiam St. *E8 & E9* —5D **27**
Northington St. *WC1* —3B **38**
North Kensington. —4F 33
Northlands St. *SE5* —5E **67**
*Northleach Ct. SE15 —2A **68***
(off Birdlip Clo.)
N. Lodge Clo. *SW15* —3F **75**
North M. *WC1* —3B **38**
Northolme Rd. *N5* —1E **25**
Northover. *Brom* —3B **100**
North Pl. *SW18* —3C **76**
N. Pole Rd. *W10* —4E **33**
Northport St. *N1* —5F **25**
North Ride. *W2* —1A **50**
North Ri. *W2* —5A **36**
North Rd. *N6* —2C **8**
North Rd. *N7* —3A **24**
North Rd. *SW19* —5E **91**
North Row. *W1* —1B **50**
*N. Row Bldgs. W1 —1C **50***
(off North Row)
North Several. *SE3* —5F **71**
N. Side Wandsworth Comn. *SW18* —3F **77**
North Sq. *NW11* —1C **6**
Northstead Rd. *SW2* —2C **94**
North St. *E13* —1D **45**
North St. *SW4* —1E **79**
N. Street Pas. *E13* —1D **45**
N. Tenter St. *E1* —5B **40**
North Ter. *SW3* —4A **50**
Northumberland All. *EC3*
(in two parts) —5A **40**
Northumberland Av. *E12* —3E **17**
Northumberland Av. *WC2* —2A **52**
*Northumberland Ho. SW1 —2A **52***
(off Northumberland Av.)
Northumberland Pl. *W2* —5C **34**
Northumberland Rd. *E17* —2C **14**
Northumberland St. *WC2* —2A **52**
Northumbria St. *E14* —5C **42**
N. Verbena Gdns. *W6* —1C **60**
Northview. *N7* —5A **10**
North Vw. *SW19* —5E **89**
N. View Cres. *NW10* —1B **18**
North Vs. *NW1* —3F **23**
*North Wlk. W8 —1D **49***
(off Bayswater Rd.)
Northway. *NW11* —1D **7**
Northway Rd. *SE5* —1E **81**
*Northways Pde. NW3 —4F **21***
(off College Cres.)
N. Western Commercial Cen. *NW1* —4A **24**
N. West Pier. *E1* —2D **55**
Northwest Pl. *N1* —1C **38**
North Wharf. *E14* —2E **57**
N. Wharf Rd. *W2* —4F **35**
Northwick Clo. *NW8* —3F **35**
*Northwick Ho. W9 —3E **35***
(off St John's Wood Rd.)
Northwick Ter. *NW8* —3F **35**
Northwold Est. *E5* —4C **12**
Northwold Rd. *N16 & E5* —4B **12**
Northwood Ho. *SE27* —4F **95**
Northwood Rd. *N6* —2D **9**
Northwood Rd. *SE23* —1B **98**
Northwood Way. *SE19* —5F **95**
N. Woolwich Rd. *E16* —2B **58**
N. Worple Way. *SW14* —1A **74**
Norton Folgate. *EC2* —4A **40**
Norton Folgate Almshouses.
*(off Puma Ct.) E1 —4B **40***
*Norton Ho. E1 —5D **41***
(off Bigland St.)

*Norton Ho. SW1 —4F **51***
(off Arneway St.)
*Norton Ho. SW9 —5B **66***
(off Aytoun Rd.)
Norton Rd. *E10* —3B **14**
Norway Ga. *SE16* —4A **56**
Norway Pl. *E14* —5B **42**
Norway St. *SE10* —2D **71**
Norway Wharf. *E14* —5B **42**
Norwich Ho. *E14* —5D **43**
Norwich Rd. *E7* —2C **30**
Norwich St. *EC4* —5C **38**
Norwood High St. *SE27* —3D **95**
Norwood Ho. *E14* —1D **57**
Norwood New Town. —5E 95
Norwood Pk. Rd. *SE27* —5E **95**
Norwood Rd. *SE24* —1D **95**
Norwood Rd. *SE27* —2D **95**
Notley St. *SE5* —3F **67**
Notting Barn Rd. *W10* —3F **33**
Nottingdale Sq. *W11* —2A **48**
Nottingham Av. *E16* —4E **45**
Nottingham Ct. *WC2* —5A **38**
Nottingham Ho. *WC2* —5A **38**
Nottingham Pl. *W1* —4C **36**
Nottingham Rd. *E10* —1E **15**
Nottingham Rd. *SW17* —1B **92**
Nottingham St. *W1* —4C **36**
*Nottingham Ter. NW1 —3C **36***
(off York Ter. W.)
Notting Hill. —1B 48
Notting Hill Ga. *W11* —2C **48**
Nottingwood Ho. W11
*(off Clarendon Rd.) —1A **48***
Novello St. *SW6* —4C **62**
Nowell Rd. *SW13* —2C **60**
Noyna Rd. *SW17* —3B **92**
Nubia Way. *Brom* —3A **100**
Nuding Clo. *SE13* —1C **84**
Nuffield Lodge. *N6* —1E **9**
*Nuffield Lodge. W2 —4C **34***
(off Admiral Wlk.)
Nugent Rd. *N19* —3A **10**
Nugent Ter. *NW8* —1E **35**
*Nun Ct. EC2 —5F **39***
(off Coleman St.)
Nunhead. —1D 83
Nunhead Cres. *SE15* —1D **83**
Nunhead Est. *SE15* —2D **83**
Nunhead Grn. *SE15* —1D **83**
Nunhead Gro. *SE15* —1D **83**
Nunhead La. *SE15* —1D **83**
Nunhead Pas. *SE15* —1C **82**
Nunnington Clo. *SE9* —3F **101**
Nursery Clo. *SE4* —5B **70**
Nursery Clo. *SW15* —2F **75**
Nursery La. *E2* —5B **26**
Nursery La. *E7* —3C **30**
Nursery La. *W10* —4E **33**
Nursery Rd. *E9* —3E **27**
Nursery Rd. *SW9* —2B **80**
Nutbourne St. *W10* —2A **34**
Nutbrook St. *SE15* —1C **82**
Nutcroft Rd. *SE15* —3D **69**
Nutfield Rd. *E15* —1E **29**
Nutfield Rd. *NW2* —5C **4**
Nutfield Rd. *SE22* —2B **82**
Nutford Pl. *W1* —5B **36**
Nuthurst Av. *SW2* —2B **94**
Nutley Ter. *NW3* —3E **21**
Nutmeg Clo. *E16* —3A **44**
Nutmeg La. *E14* —5F **43**
Nuttall St. *N1* —1A **40**
Nutter La. *E11* —1E **17**
Nutt St. *SE15* —3B **68**
Nutwell St. *SW17* —5A **92**
Nye Bevan Est. *E5* —5F **13**
*Nye Bevan Ho. SW6 —3B **62***
(off St Thomas's Way)
Nynehead St. *SE14* —3A **70**
Nyon Gro. *SE6* —2B **98**
*Nyssa Ct. E15 —2A **44***
(off Teasel Way)
Nyton Clo. *N19* —3A **10**

Oak Apple Ct. *SE12* —1C **100**
Oakbank Gro. *SE24* —2E **81**
Oakbrook Clo. *Brom* —4D **101**
Oakbury Rd. *SW6* —5D **63**
Oak Cottage Clo. *SE6* —1B **100**
*Oak Ct. SE15 —3B **68***
(off Sumner Rd.)
Oak Cres. *E16* —4A **44**
Oakcroft Rd. *SE13* —5F **71**
Oakdale Rd. *E7* —4D **31**
Oakdale Rd. *E11* —4F **15**
Oakdale Rd. *N4* —1E **11**
Oakdale Rd. *SE15 & SE4* —1E **83**
Oakdale Rd. *SW16* —5A **94**
Oakdene. *SE15* —4D **69**
Oakden St. *SE11* —5C **52**
Oake Ct. *SW15* —3A **76**
*Oakeford Ho. W14 —4A **48***
(off Russell Rd.)
Oakend Ho. *N4* —2F **11**
Oakeshott Av. *N6* —4C **8**
Oakey La. *SE1* —4C **52**
Oakfield Ct. *N8* —2A **10**
Oakfield Ct. *NW11* —2F **5**
Oakfield Gdns. *SE19* —5A **96**
(in two parts)
Oakfield Ho. *E3* —4C **42**
Oakfield Rd. *E6* —5F **31**
Oakfield Rd. *N8* —1C **10**
Oakfield Rd. *SW19* —3F **89**
Oakfields Rd. *NW11* —1A **6**
Oakfield St. *SW10* —2E **63**
Oakford Rd. *NW5* —1E **23**
Oak Gro. *NW2* —1A **20**
Oakhall Ct. *E11* —1D **17**
Oak Hall Rd. *E11* —1D **17**
Oakham Clo. *SE6* —2B **98**
Oakhill Av. *NW3* —1D **21**
Oakhill Ct. *SE23* —4E **83**
Oak Hill Pk. *NW3* —1D **21**
Oak Hill Pk. M. *NW3* —1E **21**
Oakhill Pl. *SW15* —3C **76**
Oakhill Rd. *SW15* —3B **76**
Oak Hill Way. *NW3* —1E **21**
*Oak Ho. W10 —3A **34***
(off Sycamore Wlk.)
Oakhurst Gro. *SE22* —2C **82**
Oakington Rd. *W9* —3C **34**
Oakington Way. *N8* —2A **10**
Oakland Rd. *E15* —1F **29**
*Oaklands Ct. NW10 —5A **18***
(off Nicoll Rd.)
Oaklands Est. *SW4* —4E **79**
Oaklands Gro. *W12* —2C **46**
*Oaklands M. NW2 —1F **19***
(off Oaklands Rd.)
*Oaklands Pas. NW2 —1F **19***
(off Oaklands Rd.)
Oaklands Pl. *SW4* —2E **79**
Oaklands Rd. *NW2* —1F **19**
Oak La. *E14* —1B **56**
Oakley Cres. *EC1* —1D **39**
Oakley Dri. *SE13* —4F **85**
Oakley Gdns. *SW3* —2A **64**
Oakley Ho. *SW1* —5B **50**
Oakley Pl. *SE1* —1B **68**
Oakley Rd. *N1* —4F **25**
Oakley Sq. *NW1* —1E **37**
Oakley St. *SW3* —2A **64**
Oakley Wlk. *W6* —2F **61**
*Oakley Yd. E2 —3B **40***
(off Bacon St.)
Oak Lodge. *E11* —1C **16**
*Oak Lodge. W8 —4D **49***
(off Chantry Sq.)
Oakmead Rd. *SW12* —1C **92**
Oak Pk. Gdns. *SW19* —1F **89**
Oak Pk. M. *N16* —5B **12**
Oak Pl. *SW18* —3D **77**
Oakridge La. *Brom* —5F **99**
Oakridge Rd. *Brom* —4F **99**
Oaks Av. *SE19* —5A **96**
Oaksford Av. *SE26* —3D **97**
Oakshade Rd. *Brom* —4F **99**
Oakshaw Rd. *SW18* —5D **77**
Oakshott Ct. *NW1* —1F **37**
(in two parts)
Oaks, The. *NW10* —4D **19**
Oak Tree Gdns. *Brom* —5D **101**
*Oak Tree Ho. W9 —3C **34***
(off Shirland Rd.)
Oak Tree Rd. *NW8* —2A **36**
*Oakview Lodge. NW11 —2B **6***
(off Beechcroft Av.)
Oakview Rd. *SE6* —5D **99**
Oak Village. *NW5* —1C **22**
*Oak Vs. NW11 —1B **6***
(off Hendon Pk. Row)
Oak Way. *W3* —2A **46**
Oakwood Bus. Pk. *NW10* —3A **32**
Oakwood Ct. *E6* —4F **31**
Oakwood Ct. *W14* —4B **48**
Oakwood Dri. *SE19* —5F **95**
Oakwood La. *W14* —4B **48**
Oakworth Rd. *W10* —4E **33**

Oast Ct. E14 —1B 56
Oast Lodge. W4 —3A 60
(off Corney Reach Way)
Oatfield Ho. N15 —1A 12
(off Perry Ct.)
Oat La. EC2 —2E 39
Oatwell Ho. SW3 —1A 64
Oban Clo. E13 —3E 45
Oban Ho. E14 —5F 43
Oban Rd. E13 —2E 45
Oban St. E14 —5F 43
Oberon Ho. N1 —1A 40
(off Arden Est.)
Oberstein Rd. SW11 —2F 77
Oborne Clo. SE24 —3D 81
Observatory Gdns. W8
—3C 48
Observatory M. E14 —5F 57
Occupation Rd. SE17 —1E 67
Ocean Est. E1 —3F 41
(in two parts)
Ocean St. E1 —4F 41
Ocean Wharf. E14 —3C 56
Ockbrook. E1 —4E 41
(off Hannibal Rd.)
Ockenden M. N1 —3F 25
Ockendon Rd. N1 —3F 25
Ockley Rd. SW16 —4A 94
Octagon Arc. EC2 —4A 40
Octagon Ct. SE16 —2F 55
(off Rotherhithe St.)
Octavia St. SW1 —4F 51
Octavia Ho. W10 —3A 94
Octavia St. SW11 —4A 64
Octavius St. SE8 —3C 70
Odeon Ct. E16 —4C 44
Odeon Ct. NW10 —5A 18
Odessa Rd. E7 —5B 16
Odessa Rd. NW10 —1C 32
Odessa St. SE16 —3B 56
Odger St. SW11 —5B 64
Odhams Wlk. WC2 —5A 38
Odin Ho. SE5 —5E 67
O'Donnell Ct. WC1 —3A 38
O'Driscoll Ho. W12 —5D 33
Offa's Mead. E9 —1B 28
Offerton Rd. SW4 —1E 79
Offham Ho. SE17 —5A 54
(off Beckway St.)
Offley Rd. SW9 —3C 66
Offord Rd. N1 —4B 24
Offord St. N1 —4B 24
Oglander Rd. SE15 —2B 82
Ogle St. W1 —4E 37
O'Gorman Ho. SW10 —3E 63
(off King's Rd.)
Ohio Rd. E13 —3B 44
Oil Mill La. W6 —1C 60
Okeburn Rd. SW17 —5C 92
Okehampton Rd. NW10
—5E 19
Olaf St. W11 —1F 47
Oldacre M. SW12 —5C 78
Old Bailey. EC4 —5D 39
Old Barge Ho. All. SE1
(off Barge Ho. St.) —1C 52

Old Barrack Yd. SW1 —3C 50
(in two parts)
Old Barrowfield. E15 —5A 30
Old Belgate Wharf. E14
—4C 56
Old Bellgate Wharf. E14
—4C 56
Old Bethnal Grn. Rd. E2
—2C 40
Old Billingsgate Mkt. EC3
—1A 54
(off Lwr. Thames St.)
Old Billingsgate Wlk. EC3
—1A 54
Old Bond St. W1 —1E 51
Old Brewer's Yd. WC2 —5A 38
Old Brewery M. NW3 —1F 21
Old Broad St. EC2 —2F 39
Old Bromley Rd. Brom
—5F 99
Old Brompton Rd. SW5 &
SW7 —1C 62
Old Bldgs. WC2 —5C 38
(off Chancery La.)
Old Burlington St. W1 —1E 51
Oldbury Pl. W1 —4C 36
Old Castle St. E1 —5B 40
Old Cavendish St. W1 —5D 37
Old Change Ct. EC4 —5E 39
(off Carter La.)
Old Chapel Pl. SW9 —5C 66
Old Chelsea M. SW3 —2A 64
Old Chiswick Yd. W4 —2A 60
(off Pumping Sta. Rd.)
Old Church La. NW9 —4A 4
Old Church Rd. E1 —5F 41
Old Church St. SW3 —1F 63
Old Compton St. W1 —1F 51
Old Ct. Ho. W8 —3D 49
(off Old Ct. Pl.)
Old Ct. Pl. W8 —3D 49
Old Dairy M. NW5 —3D 23
Old Dairy M. SW12 —1C 92
Old Devonshire Rd. SW12
—5D 79
Old Dover Rd. SE3 —3C 72
Oldegate Ho. E6 —4F 31
Old Farm Clo. SW17 —2A 92
Oldfield Gro. SE16 —5F 55
Oldfield Ho. W4 —1A 60
(off Devonshire Rd.)
Oldfield M. N6 —2E 9
Oldfield Rd. N16 —5A 12
Oldfield Rd. NW10 —4A 18
Oldfield Rd. SW19 —5A 90
Oldfield Rd. W3 —3B 46
Old Fish St. Hill. EC4 —1E 53
(off Victoria St.)
Old Fleet La. EC4 —5D 39
Old Ford. —5B 28
Old Ford. (Junct.) —1C 42
Old Ford Rd. E2 & E3 —2E 41
Old Forge M. W12 —3D 47
Old Gloucester St. WC1
—4A 38
Oldhill St. N16 —3C 12

Old Hospital Clo. SW17
—1B 92
Old Ho. Clo. SW19 —5A 90
Old Jamaica Rd. SE16
—4C 54
Old James St. SE15 —1D 83
Old Jewry. EC2 —5F 39
Old Kent Rd. SE1 & SE15
—5A 54
Old Mnr. Ct. NW8 —1E 35
Old Mnr. Yd. SW5 —5D 49
Old Mkt. Sq. E2 —2B 40
Old Marylebone Rd. NW1
—4A 36
Old Mitre Ct. EC4 —5C 38
Old Montague St. E1 —4C 40
Old Nichol St. E2 —3B 40
Old N. St. WC1 —4B 38
(off Theobald's Rd.)
Old Oak Common. —3A 32
Old Oak Comn. La. W3 &
NW10 —4A 32
Old Oak La. NW10 —2A 32
Old Oak Rd. W3 —1B 46
Old Orchard, The. NW3
—1B 22
Old Pal. Yd. SW1 —4A 52
Old Paradise St. SE1 —5B 52
Old Pk. Av. SW12 —4C 78
Old Pk. La. W1 —2D 51
Old Pye St. SW1 —4F 51
Old Pye St. Est. SW1 —4F 51
(off Old Pye St.)
Old Quebec St. W1 —5B 36
Old Queen St. SW1 —3F 51
Oldridge Rd. SW12 —5C 78
Old Rd. SE13 —2A 86
Old Royal Free Pl. N1 —5C 24
(off Liverpool Rd.)
Old Royal Free Sq. N1 —5C 24
(off Old Royal Free Pl.)
Old Royal Naval College.
—2F 71
Old School Cres. E7 —3C 30
Old School Sq. E14 —5C 42
(off Pelling St.)
Old Seacoal La. EC4 —5D 39
(in two parts)
Old S. Lambeth Rd. SW8
—3A 66
Old Spitalfields Market.
—4B 40
Old Sq. WC2 —5B 38
Old Stable M. N5 —5E 11
Oldstead Rd. Brom —4E 99
Old Street. (Junct.) —2F 39
Old St. E13 —1D 45
Old St. EC1 —3E 39
Old Sun Wharf. E14 —1A 56
(off Narrow St.)
Old Swan Wharf. SW11
—4F 63
Old Thackeray School.
—5D 65
Old Theatre Ct. SE1 —2E 53
(off Porter St.)

Old Town. SW4 —1E **79**
Old Woolwich Rd. SE10 —2F **71**
Old York Rd. SW18 —3D **77**
O'Leary Sq. E1 —4E **41**
Olinda Rd. N16 —1B **12**
Oliphant St. W10 —2F **33**
Oliver Goldsmith Est. SE15 —4C **68**
*Oliver Ho. SE16 —3C **54***
(off George Row)
*Oliver Ho. SW8 —3A **66***
(off Wyvil Rd.)
Oliver M. SE15 —5C **68**
Olive Rd. E13 —2E **45**
Olive Rd. NW2 —1E **19**
Oliver Rd. E10 —4D **15**
*Olivers Wharf. E1 —2D **55***
(off Wapping High St.)
Olivers Yd. EC1 —3F **39**
*Olive Tree Ho. SE15 —2E **69***
(off Sharratt St.)
Olivette St. SW15 —1F **75**
Olive Waite Ho. NW6 —4C **20**
Ollerton Grn. E3 —5B **28**
Ollgar Clo. W12 —2B **46**
Olliffe St. E14 —4E **57**
Olmar St. SE1 —2C **68**
*Olney Ho. NW8 —3A **36***
(off Tresham Cres.)
Olney Rd. SE17 —2D **67**
(in two parts)
Olympia. —4A 48
Olympia M. W2 —1D **49**
Olympia Way. W14 —4A **48**
Olympus Sq. E5 —5C **12**
O'Mahoney Ct. SW17 —3E **91**
Oman Av. NW2 —1E **19**
O'Meara St. SE1 —2E **53**
Omega Clo. E14 —4D **57**
*Omega Pl. N1 —1A **38***
(off Caledonian Rd.)
Omega St. SE14 —4C **70**
Ommaney Rd. SE14 —4F **69**
Ondine Rd. SE15 —2B **82**
Onega Ga. SE16 —4A **56**
*O'Neill Ho. NW8 —1A **36***
(off Cochrane St.)
One Tree Clo. SE23 —4E **83**
Ongar Rd. SW6 —2C **62**
Onra Rd. E17 —2C **14**
Onslow Gdns. SW7 —5F **49**
Onslow M. E. SW7 —5F **49**
Onslow M. W. SW7 —5F **49**
Onslow Sq. SW7 —5F **49**
Onslow St. EC1 —3C **38**
Ontario St. SE1 —4D **53**
Ontario Way. E14 —1C **56**
(in two parts)
Opal Clo. E16 —5F **45**
Opal M. NW6 —5B **20**
Opal St. SE11 —1D **67**
Openview. SW18 —1E **91**
Operating Theatre Mus.
(off St Thomas St.) —2F 53
Ophelia Gdns. NW2 —5A **6**
Ophir Ter. SE15 —4C **68**
*Opie Ho. NW8 —1A **36***
(off Townshend Est.)
Oppenheim Rd. SE13 —5E **71**
Oppidans Rd. NW3 —4B **22**
Orange Gro. E11 —5A **16**
(in two parts)
Orange Pl. SE16 —4E **55**
Orange St. SW1 —1F **51**
*Orange Yd. W1 —5F **37***
(off Manette St.)
*Oratory La. SW3 —1F **63***
(off Stewart's Gro.)
Oratory, The. —4A 50
Orbain Rd. SW6 —3A **62**
Orbel St. SW11 —4A **64**
Orb St. SE17 —5F **53**
Orchard Bus. Cen. SE26 —5B **98**
Orchard Clo. N1 —4E **25**
Orchard Clo. NW2 —5C **4**
Orchard Clo. SE23 —4E **83**
Orchard Clo. W10 —4B **34**
Orchard Ct. E10 —3D **15**
Orchard Dri. SE3 —5F **71**
Orchard Hill. SE13 —5D **71**
*Orchard Ho. SE5 —4E **67***
(off County Gro.)
Orchard Ho. SE16 —4E **55**
*Orchard Ho. SW6 —3A **62***
(off Varna Rd.)
*Orchard Ho. W1 —5C **36***
(off Fitzhardinge St.)
Orchard Ho. W12 —2C **46**
Orchard Mead Ho. NW2 —4C **6**
Orchard M. N1 —4F **25**
Orchard Pl. E14 —1A **58**
(in two parts)
Orchard Rd. N6 —2D **9**
Orchard Rd. SE3 —5A **72**
*Orchardson Ho. NW8 —3F **35***
(off Orchardson St.)
Orchardson St. NW8 —3F **35**
Orchard Sq. W14 —1B **62**
Orchard St. W1 —5C **36**
Orchard, The. NW11 —1C **6**
Orchard, The. SE3 —5F **71**
Orchard, The. W4 —5A **46**
Orchard Wharf. E14 —1A **58**
Orchid Clo. E6 —4F **45**
Orchid St. W12 —1C **46**
Orde Hall St. WC1 —3B **38**
Ordell Rd. E3 —1B **42**
Ordnance Cres. SE10 —3F **57**
Ordnance Hill. NW8 —5F **21**
Ordnance M. NW8 —1F **35**
Ordnance Rd. E16 —4B **44**
Oregano Dri. E14 —5F **43**
Orestes M. NW6 —2C **20**
Orford Ct. SE27 —2D **95**
Orford Rd. E17 —1C **14**
Orford Rd. SE6 —3D **99**
Oriel Ct. NW3 —1E **21**
Oriel Dri. SW13 —2E **61**
*Oriel Pl. NW3 —1E **21***
(off Heath St.)
Oriel Rd. E9 —3F **27**
Oriental Rd. E16 —2F **59**
Oriental St. E14 —1C **56**
Orient Ind. Pk. E10 —4C **14**
Orient St. SE11 —5D **53**
Orient Way. E5 —5F **13**
Orient Way. E10 —3A **14**
Orion Bus. Cen. SE14 —1F **69**
*Orion Ho. E1 —3D **41***
(off Coventry Rd.)
*Orkney Ho. N1 —5B **24***
(off Bemerton Est.)
Orkney St. SW11 —5C **64**
Orlando Rd. SW4 —1E **79**
Orleston M. N7 —3C **24**
Orleston Rd. N7 —3C **24**
Orlop St. SE10 —1A **72**
Ormanton Rd. SE26 —4C **96**
Orme Ct. W2 —1D **49**
*Orme Ct. M. W2 —1D **49***
(off Orme La.)
Orme Ho. E8 —5B **26**
Orme La. W2 —1D **49**
Ormeley Rd. SW12 —1D **93**
Orme Sq. W2 —1D **49**
Ormiston Gro. W12 —2D **47**
Ormiston Rd. SE10 —1C **72**
Ormond Clo. WC1 —4A **38**
Ormonde Ct. SW15 —2E **75**
Ormonde Ga. SW3 —1B **64**
Ormonde Pl. SW1 —5C **50**
Ormonde Ter. NW8 —5B **22**
Ormond M. WC1 —3A **38**
Ormond Rd. N19 —3A **10**
Ormond Yd. SW1 —2E **51**
Ormsby Lodge. W4 —4A **46**
Ormsby Pl. N16 —5B **12**
Ormsby St. E2 —1B **40**
Ormside St. SE15 —2E **69**
Ornan Rd. NW3 —2A **22**
Oronsay Wlk. N1 —4E **25**
Orpen Wlk. N16 —5A **12**
Orpheus St. SE5 —4F **67**
*Orpheus Tower. SE14 —3A **70***
(off Desmond St.)
Orsett M. W2 —5D **35**
(in two parts)
Orsett St. SE11 —1B **66**
Orsett Ter. W2 —5D **35**
Orsman Rd. N1 —5A **26**
Orton St. E1 —2C **54**
Orville Rd. SW11 —5F **63**
*Orwell Ct. E8 —5C **26***
(off Pownall Rd.)
Orwell Ct. N5 —1E **25**
Orwell Rd. E13 —1E **45**
Osbaldeston Rd. N16 —4C **12**
Osberton Rd. SE12 —3C **86**
Osbert St. SW1 —5F **51**
Osborn Clo. E8 —5C **26**
Osborne Ct. E10 —2D **15**
Osborne Gro. N4 —3C **10**
Osborne Rd. E7 —2D **31**

Osborne Rd. E9—3B 28
Osborne Rd. E10—4D 15
Osborne Rd. N4—3C 10
Osborne Rd. NW2—3D 19
Osborne Ter. SW17—5B 92
(off Church La.)
Osborn La. SE23—5A 84
Osborn St. E1—4B 40
Osborn Ter. SE3—2B 86
Oscar Faber Pl. N1—4A 26
Oscar St. SE4—5C 70
(in two parts)
Oseney Cres. NW5—2E 23
O'Shea Gro. E3—5B 28
Osier Ct. E1—3F 41
(off Osier St.)
Osier M. W4—2A 60
Osiers Rd. SW18—2C 76
Osier St. E1—3E 41
Osier Way. E10—5D 15
Oslac Rd. SE6—5D 99
Oslo Ct. NW8—1A 36
(off Prince Albert Rd.)
Oslo Ho. SE5—5E 67
(off Carew St.)
Oslo Sq. SE16—4A 56
Osman Clo. N15—1F 11
Osman Rd. W6—4E 47
Osmington Ho. SW8—3B 66
(off Dorset Rd.)
Osmund St. W12—4B 32
Osnaburgh St. NW1—2D 37
(off Robert St.)
Osnaburgh St. NW1—3D 37
(Longford St.)
Osnaburgh Ter. NW1—3D 37
Osprey Clo. E6—4F 45
Osprey Est. SE16—5A 56
(off Plough Way)
Osprey Est. SE16—5A 56
(off Greenland Quay)
Ospringe Ho. SE1—3C 52
(off Wootton St.)
Ospringe Rd. NW5—1E 23
Osram Ct. W6—4E 47
Osric Path. N1—1A 40
Ossian M. N4—2B 10
Ossian Rd. N4—2B 10
Ossington Bldgs. W1—4C 36
Ossington Clo. W2—1C 48
Ossington St. W2—1C 48
Ossory Rd. SE1—2C 68
Ossulston St. NW1—1F 37
Ostade Rd. SW2—5B 80
Ostend Pl. SE1—5E 53
Osten M. SW7—4D 49
Osterley Ho. E14—5D 43
Osterley Rd. N16—1A 26
Oswald's Mead. E9—1A 28
Oswald St. E5—5F 13
Oswald Ter. NW2—5E 5
Osward Rd. SW17—2B 92
Oswell Ho. E1—2D 55
(off Farthing Fields)
Oswin St. SE11—5D 53
Oswyth Rd. SE5—5A 68
Otford Cres. SE4—4B 84
Otford Ho. SE1—3F 53
(off Staple St.)
Otford Ho. SE15—2E 69
(off Lovelinch Clo.)
Othello Clo. SE11—1D 67
Otis St. E3—2E 43
Otley Ho. N4—5C 10
Otley Rd. E16—5E 45
Otley Ter. E5—5F 13
Ottaway Ct. E5—5C 12
Ottaway St. E5—5C 12
Otterburn Ho. SE5—3E 67
(off Sultan St.)
Otterburn St. SW17—5B 92
Otterden St. SE6—4C 98
Otto Clo. SE26—3D 97
Otto St. SE17—2D 67
Oulton Clo. E5—4E 13
Oulton Rd. N15—1F 11
Ouseley Rd. SW12—1B 92
Outer Circ. NW1—2A 36
Outgate Rd. NW10—4B 18
Outram Pl. N1—5A 24
Outram Rd. E6—5F 31
Outwich St. EC3—5A 40
(off Houndsditch)
Outwood Ho. SW2—5B 80
(off Deepdene Gdns.)
Oval Cricket Ground. —2B 66
Oval House Theatre. —2C 66
Oval Mans. SE11—2B 66
Oval Pl. SW8—3B 66
Oval Rd. NW1—5D 23
Oval, The. E2—1D 41
Oval Way. SE11—1B 66
Overbrae. Beck—5C 98
Overbury Rd. N15—1F 11
Overbury St. E5—1F 27
Overcliff Rd. SE13—1C 84
Overdown Rd. SE6—4C 98
Overhill Rd. SE22—5C 82
Overlea Rd. E5—2C 12
Oversley Ho. W2—4C 34
(off Alfred Rd.)
Overstone Ho. E14—5C 42
Overstone Rd. W6—4E 47
Overstrand Mans. SW11—4B 64
Overton Ct. E11—2C 16
Overton Dri. E11—2C 16
Overton Ho. SW15—5B 74
(off Tangley Gro.)
Overton Rd. E10—3A 14
Overton Rd. SW9—5C 66
Overy Ho. SE1—3D 53
Ovex Clo. E14—3E 57
Ovington Gdns. SW3—4A 50
Ovington M. SW3—4A 50
(off Ovington M.)
Ovington Sq. SW3—4A 50
Ovington St. SW3—5A 50
Owen Mans. W14—2A 62
(off Queen's Club Gdns.)
Owen's Ct. EC1—2D 39
Owen's Row. EC1—2D 39
Owen St. EC1—1D 39
(in two parts)
Owens Way. SE23—5A 84
Owgan Clo. SE5—3F 67
Oxberry Av. SW6—5A 62
Oxendon St. W1—1F 51
Oxenford St. SE15—1B 82
Oxenham Ho. SE8—2C 70
(off Benbow St.)
Oxenholme. NW1—1E 37
(off Harrington Sq.)
Oxestall's Rd. SE8—1A 70
Oxford & Cambridge Mans. NW1—4A 36
(off Old Marylebone Rd.)
Oxford Av. NW10—2D 33
Oxford Cir. W1—5E 37
(off Oxford St.)
Oxford Cir. Av. W1—5E 37
Oxford Ct. EC4—1F 53
(off Cannon St.)
Oxford Dri. SE1—2A 54
Oxford Gdns. W10—5E 33
Oxford Ga. W6—5F 47
Oxford Pl. NW10—5A 4
(off Press Rd.)
Oxford Rd. E15—3F 29
(in two parts)
Oxford Rd. N4—3C 10
Oxford Rd. NW6—1C 34
Oxford Rd. SE19—5F 95
Oxford Rd. SW15—2A 76
Oxford Sq. W2—5A 36
Oxford St. W1—5C 36
Oxgate Cen. NW2—4D 5
Oxgate Ct. NW2—4C 4
Oxgate Gdns. NW2—5D 5
Oxgate La. NW2—4D 5
Oxgate Pde. NW2—4C 4
Oxley Clo. SE1—1B 68
Oxleys Rd. NW2—5D 5
Oxonian St. SE22—2B 82
Oxo Tower Wharf. —1C 52
Oxo Tower Wharf. SE1—1C 52
Oystercatcher Clo. E16—5D 45
Oystergate Wlk. EC4—1F 53
(off Swan La.)
Oyster Row. E1—5E 41
Ozolins Way. E16—5C 44

Pablo Neruda Clo. SE24—2D 81
Pace Pl. E1—5D 41
Pacific Rd. E16—5C 44
Packenham Ho. E2—2B 40
(off Wellington Row)
Packington Sq. N1—5E 25
(in three parts)
Packington St. N1—5D 25
Padbury. SE17—1A 68
(off Bagshot St.)
Padbury Ct. E2—2B 40

Padbury Ho. NW8 —3A 36 (off Tresham Cres.)
Paddenswick Rd. W6 —4C 46
Paddington. —5F 35
Paddington Grn. W2 —4F 35
Paddington St. W1 —4C 36
Paddock Clo. SE3 —5C 72
Paddock Clo. SE26 —4F 97
Paddock Rd. NW2 —5C 4
Padfield Rd. SE5 —1E 81
Padstow Ho. E14 —1B 56
Pagden St. SW8 —4D 65
Pageant Cres. SE16 —2A 56
Pageantmaster Ct. EC4 (off Ludgate Hill) —5D 39
Page Grn. Rd. N15 —1C 12
Page Grn. Ter. N15 —1B 12
Page Ho. SE10 —2E 71 (off Welland St.)
Page St. SW1 —5F 51
Page's Wlk. SE1 —5A 54
Pages Yd. W4 —2B 60
Paget Rd. N16 —3F 11
Paget St. EC1 —2D 39
Pagham Ho. W10 —3E 33 (off Sutton Way)
Pagin Ho. N15 —1A 12 (off Braemar Rd.)
Pagnell St. SE14 —3B 70
Pagoda Gdns. SE3 —5F 71
Paignton Rd. N15 —1A 12
Painsthorpe Rd. N16 —5A 12
Painswick Ct. SE15 —3B 68 (off Daniel Gdns.)
Pakeman Ho. SE1 —3D 53 (off Surrey Row)
Pakeman St. N7 —5B 10
Pakenham Clo. SW12 —1C 92
Pakenham St. WC1 —2B 38
Pakington Ho. SW9 —5A 66 (off Stockwell Gdns. Est.)
Palace Av. W8 —3D 49
Palace Ct. NW3 —2D 21
Palace Ct. W2 —1D 49 (off Moscow Rd.)
Palace Gdns. M. W8 —2D 49
Palace Gdns. Ter. W8 —2C 48
Palace Ga. W8 —3E 49
Palace Grn. W8 —2D 49
Palace Mans. W14 —5A 48 (off Hammersmith Rd.)
Palace M. SW1 —5C 50 (off Eaton Ter.)
Palace M. SW6 —3C 62
Palace Pl. SW1 —4E 51
Palace Pl. Mans. W8 —3D 49 (off Kensington Ct.)
Palace Rd. N8 —1F 9 (in two parts)
Palace Rd. SW2 —1B 94
Palace St. SW1 —4E 51
Palace Vw. SE12 —2C 100
Palamon Ct. SE1 —1B 68 (off Cooper's Rd.)
Palamos Rd. E10 —3C 14
Palatine Av. N16 —1A 26
Palatine Rd. N16 —1A 26
Palermo Rd. NW10 —1C 32
Palewell Comn. Dri. SW14 —3A 74
Palfrey Pl. SW8 —3B 66
Palgrave Gdns. NW1 —3A 36
Palgrave Ho. SE5 —3E 67 (off Wyndham Est.)
Palgrave Rd. W12 —4B 46
Palissy St. E2 —2B 40 (in two parts)
Pallant Ho. SE1 —4F 53 (off Tabard St.)
Pallett Way. SE18 —4F 73
Palliser Ct. W14 —1A 62
Palliser Ho. SE10 —2F 71 (off Trafalgar Rd.)
Palliser Rd. W14 —1A 62
Pall Mall. SW1 —2E 51
Pall Mall E. SW1 —2F 51
Pall Mall Pl. SW1 —2E 51 (off Pall Mall)
Palm Clo. E10 —5D 15
Palm Ct. SE15 —3B 68 (off Garnies Clo.)
Palmer Ct. NW10 —5A 18 (in two parts)
Palmer Pl. N7 —2C 24
Palmer Rd. E13 —3D 45
Palmer's Rd. E2 —1F 41
Palmerston Ho. SE1 —3C 52 (off Westminster Bri. Rd.)
Palmerston Ho. W8 —2C 48 (off Kensington Pl.)
Palmerston Mans. W14 —2A 62 (off Queen's Club Gdns.)
Palmerston Rd. E7 —3D 31
Palmerston Rd. NW6 —4B 20 (in two parts)
Palmerston Way. SW8 —3D 65
Palmer St. SW1 —4F 51
Palm Tree Ho. SE14 —3F 69 (off Barlborough St.)
Pamela Ho. E8 —5B 26
Pamela Wlk. E8 —5C 26 (off Marlborough Av.)
Pancras La. EC4 —5E 39
Pancras Rd. NW1 —1F 37
Pandora Rd. NW6 —3C 20
Pangbourne. NW1 —2E 37 (off Stanhope St.)
Pangbourne Av. W10 —4E 33
Pankhurst Av. E16 —2D 59
Pankhurst Clo. SE14 —3F 69
Panmure Clo. N5 —1D 25
Panmure Rd. SE26 —3D 97
Panorama Ct. N6 —1E 9
Pansy Gdns. W12 —1C 46
Panther Dri. NW10 —2A 18
Panton St. SW1 —1F 51
Panyer All. EC4 —5E 39 (off Newgate St.)
Paper Bldgs. EC4 —1C 52 (off Crown Office Row)
Paper Mill Wharf. E14 —1A 56
Papillons Wlk. SE3 —5C 72
Papworth Gdns. N7 —2B 24
Papworth Way. SW2 —5C 80
Parade Mans. NW4 —1D 5
Parade M. SE27 —2D 95
Parade, The. N4 —3C 10
Parade, The. SE4 —5B 70 (off Up. Brockley Rd.)
Parade, The. SE26 —3D 97 (off Wells Pk. Rd.)
Parade, The. SW11 —3B 64
Paradise Pas. N7 —2C 24
Paradise Rd. SW4 —5A 66
Paradise Row. E2 —2D 41
Paradise St. SE16 —3D 55
Paradise Wlk. SW3 —2B 64
Paragon Clo. E16 —5C 44
Paragon M. SE1 —5F 53
Paragon Pl. SE3 —5B 72
Paragon Rd. E9 —3E 27
Paragon, The. SE3 —5B 72
Paramount Building. EC1 (off St John St.) —3D 39
Paramount Ct. WC1 —3E 37
Parbury Rd. SE23 —4A 84
Pardoner Ho. SE1 —4F 53 (off Pardoner St.)
Pardoner St. SE1 —4F 53 (in two parts)
Pardon St. EC1 —3D 39
Parfett St. E1 —4C 40 (in two parts)
Parfitt Clo. NW3 —3E 7
Parfrey St. W6 —2E 61
Paris Garden. SE1 —2D 53
Paris Ho. E2 —1D 41 (off Old Bethnal Grn. Rd.)
Park App. SE16 —4D 55
Park Av. E15 —3A 30
Park Av. NW2 —3E 19
Park Av. NW11 —3D 7
Park Av. SW14 —2A 74
Park Av. N. NW10 —2D 19
Park Bus. Cen. NW6 —2C 34
Park Clo. E9 —5E 27
Park Clo. NW2 —5D 5
Park Clo. SW1 —3B 50
Park Clo. W4 —2A 60
Park Clo. W14 —4B 48
Park Ct. E17 —1D 15
Park Ct. SE26 —5D 97
Park Ct. SW11 —4D 65
Park Cres. NW1 —3D 37
Park Cres. M. E. W1 —3D 37
Park Cres. M. W. W1 —3D 37
Parkcroft Rd. SE12 —5B 86
Park Dri. NW11 —3D 7
Park Dri. SE7 —2F 73
Park Dri. SW14 —3A 74
Park Dwellings. NW3 —2B 22
Park End. NW3 —1A 22
Parker Clo. E16 —2F 59
Parker Ho. E14 —3C 56 (off Admirals Way)
Parker M. WC2 —5A 38

Parke Rd. *SW13* —4C **60**
Parkers Row. *SE1* —3C **54**
Parker St. *E16* —2F **59**
Parker St. *WC2* —5A **38**
Parkfield Av. *SW14* —2A **74**
Parkfield Ct. *SE14* —4B **70**
(off Parkfield Rd.)
—5C **64**
Parkfield Ind. Est. *SW11*
Parkfield Rd. *NW10* —4D **19**
Parkfield Rd. *SE14* —4B **70**
Parkfields. *SW15* —2E **75**
Parkfields Av. *NW9* —3A **4**
Parkfield St. *N1* —1C **38**
Park Gdns. *E10* —3C **14**
Park Ga. *SE3* —1B **86**
Parkgate M. *N6* —2E **9**
Parkgate Rd. *SW11* —3A **64**
Park Gro. *E15* —5C **30**
Park Gro. Rd. *E11* —4A **16**
Pk. Hall Rd. *SE21* —3E **95**
Pk. Hall Trad. Est. *SE21*
—3E **95**
Parkham St. *SW11* —4A **64**
Park Hill. *SE23* —2D **97**
Park Hill. *SW4* —3F **79**
Pk. Hill Ct. *SW17* —3B **92**
Parkhill Rd. *NW3* —2B **22**
Parkhill Wlk. *NW3* —2B **22**
Parkholme Rd. *E8* —3C **26**
Park Ho. Pas. *N6* —2C **8**
Parkhouse St. *SE5* —3F **67**
Parkhurst Ct. *N7* —1A **24**
Parkhurst Rd. *N7* —1A **24**
Parkinson Ho. *SW1* —5E **51**
(off Tachbrook St.)
Parkland Ct. *E15* —2A **30**
(off Maryland Rd.)
Parkland Gdns. *SW19* —1F **89**
Parklands. *N6* —3D **9**
Parklands Rd. *SW16* —5D **93**
Park La. *E15* —5F **29**
Park La. *W1* —1B **50**
Pk. Lee Ct. *N16* —2A **12**
Park Lodge. *NW8* —4F **21**
Park Lorne. *NW8* —2A **36**
(off Park Rd.)
Park Mans. *NW4* —1D **5**
Park Mans. *NW8* —1A **36**
(off Allitsen Rd.)
Park Mans. *SW1* —3B **50**
(off Brompton Rd.)
Park Mans. *SW8* —2A **66**
Park Mans. *SW11* —4B **64**
(off Prince of Wales Dri.)
Parkmead. *SW15* —4D **75**
Park M. *SE24* —5E **81**
Park Pde. *NW10* —1B **32**
Park Pl. *E14* —2C **56**
Park Pl. *SW1* —2E **51**
Park Pl. Vs. *W2* —4E **35**
Park Ri. *SE23* —1A **98**
Park Ri. Rd. *SE23* —1A **98**
Park Rd. *E6* —5E **31**
Park Rd. *E10* —3C **14**

Park Rd. *E12* —3D **17**
Park Rd. *E15* —5C **30**
Park Rd. *E17* —1B **14**
Park Rd. *N8* —1F **9**
Park Rd. *NW4* —2C **4**
Park Rd. *NW8 & NW1* —2A **36**
Park Rd. *NW9* —2A **4**
Park Rd. *NW10* —5A **18**
Park Rd. *SW19* —5A **92**
Park Rd. *W4* —2A **60**
Park Rd. N. *W4* —1A **60**
Park Row. *SE10* —1F **71**
Parkside. *NW2* —5C **4**
Parkside. *SE3* —3B **72**
Parkside. *SW1* —3B **50**
(off Knightsbridge)
Parkside. *SW19* —3F **89**
Parkside. *W3* —2A **46**
Parkside Av. *SW19* —5F **89**
Parkside Bus. Est. *SE8*
—2A **70**
Parkside Ct. *E11* —1C **16**
(off Wanstead Pl.)
Parkside Cres. *N7* —5C **10**
Parkside Est. *E9* —5E **27**
Parkside Gdns. *SW19* —4F **89**
Parkside Rd. *SW11* —4C **64**
Park Sq. E. *NW1* —3D **37**
Park Sq. M. *NW1* —3C **36**
(off Up. Harley St.)
Park Sq. W. *NW1* —3D **37**
Parkstead Rd. *SW15* —3C **74**
Park Steps. *W2* —1A **50**
(off St George's Fields)
Parkstone Rd. *SE15* —5C **68**
Park St. *SE1* —2E **53**
Park St. *W1* —1C **50**
Park, The. *NW6* —1C **8**
Park, The. *NW11* —3D **7**
Park, The. *SE23* —1E **97**
Parkthorne Rd. *SW12* —5F **79**
Park Towers. *W1* —2D **51**
(off Brick St.)
Park Vw. *N5* —1E **25**
Parkview Ct. *SW6* —5A **62**
Parkview Ct. *SW18* —3C **76**
Pk. View Est. *E2* —1F **41**
Pk. View Gdns. *NW4* —1E **5**
Pk. View Ho. *SE24* —4D **81**
(off Hurst St.)
Pk. View Mans. *N4* —2D **11**
Pk. View Rd. *NW10* —1B **18**
Pk. Village E. *NW1* —1D **37**
Pk. Village W. *NW1* —1D **37**
Parkville Rd. *SW6* —3B **62**
Park Vista. *SE10* —2F **71**
Park Wlk. *N6* —2C **8**
Park Wlk. *SE10* —3F **71**
Park Wlk. *SW10* —2E **63**
Parkway. *NW1* —5D **23**
Park Way. *NW11* —1A **6**
Park West. *W2* —5A **36**
(off Edgware Rd.)
Park W. Pl. *W2* —5A **36**
Park Wharf. *SE8* —1A **70**
(off Evelyn St.)

Parkwood. *NW8* —5B **22**
(off St Edmund's Ter.)
Parkwood M. *N6* —1D **9**
Parkwood Rd. *SW19* —5B **90**
Parliament Ct. *E1* —4A **40**
(off Artillery La.)
Parliament Hill. —5B **8**
Parliament Hill. *NW3* —1A **22**
Parliament Hill Mans. *NW5*
—1C **22**
Parliament Sq. *SW1* —3A **52**
Parliament St. *SW1* —3A **52**
Parliament Vw. *SE1* —5B **52**
Parma Cres. *SW11* —2B **78**
Parmiter Ind. Cen. *E2* —1D **41**
(off Parmiter St.)
Parmiter St. *E2* —1D **41**
Parmoor Ct. *EC1* —3E **39**
(off Gee St.)
Parnell Clo. *W12* —4D **47**
Parnell Ho. *WC1* —4F **37**
Parnell Rd. *E3* —5B **28**
(in two parts)
Parnham St. *E14* —5A **42**
(in two parts)
Parolles Rd. *N19* —3E **9**
Parr Ct. *N1* —1F **39**
(off New North Rd.)
Parrington Ho. *SW4* —4F **79**
Parr Rd. *E6* —5F **31**
Parr St. *N1* —1F **39**
Parry Ho. *E1* —2D **55**
(off Green Bank)
Parry Rd. *W10* —2A **34**
(in two parts)
Parry St. *SW8* —2A **66**
Parsifal Rd. *NW6* —2C **20**
Parsonage St. *E14* —5E **57**
Parsons Green. —4C **62**
Parson's Grn. *SW6* —4C **62**
Parson's Grn. La. *SW6*
—4C **62**
Parsons Ho. *W2* —3F **35**
(off Hall Pl.)
Parsons Lodge. *NW6* —4D **21**
(off Priory Rd.)
Parson's Rd. *E13* —1E **45**
Parthenia Rd. *SW6* —4C **62**
Partington Clo. *N19* —3F **9**
Partridge Clo. *E16* —4F **45**
Partridge Ct. *EC1* —3D **39**
(off Cyprus St.)
Pascall Ho. *SE17* —2E **67**
(off Draco St.)
Pascal St. *SW8* —3F **65**
Pascoe Rd. *SE13* —3F **85**
Pasley Clo. *SE17* —1D **67**
Passage, The. *W6* —4E **47**
Passfield Dri. *E14* —4D **43**
Passfields. *SE6* —3D **99**
Passfields. *W14* —1B **62**
(off Star St.)
Passing All. *EC1* —4D **39**
(off St John St.)
Passmore St. *SW1* —1C **64**
Paston Clo. *E5* —5F **13**

Paston Cres. *SE12* —5D **87**
Pastor Ct. *N6* —1E **9**
Pastor St. *SE11* —5D **53**
(in two parts)
Pasture Rd. *SE6* —1B **100**
Patcham Ter. *SW8* —4D **65**
*Patchway Ct. SE15 —2A **68***
(off Newent Clo.)
Patent Ho. *E14* —4D **43**
Paternoster Row. *EC4* —5D **39**
Paternoster Sq. *EC4* —5D **39**
*Paterson Ct. EC1 —2F **39***
(off St Lukes Est.)
Pater St. *W8* —4C **48**
Pathfield Rd. *SW16* —5F **93**
Patience Rd. *SW11* —5A **64**
*Patina Wlk. SE16 —2A **56***
(off Capstan Way)
Patio Clo. *SW4* —4F **79**
Patmore Est. *SW8* —4E **65**
Patmore Ho. *N16* —2A **26**
Patmore St. *SW8* —4E **65**
*Patmos Lodge. SW9 —4D **67***
(off Elliott Rd.)
Patmos Rd. *SW9* —3D **67**
Paton Clo. *E3* —2C **42**
*Paton Ho. SW9 —5B **66***
(off Stockwell Rd.)
Paton St. *EC1* —2E **39**
Patrick Coman Ho. EC1
*(off Finsbury Est.) —2D **39***
Patrick Connolly Gdns. *E3*
—2D **43**
Patrick Pas. *SW11* —5A **64**
Patrick Rd. *E13* —2E **45**
Patriot Sq. *E2* —1D **41**
Patrol Pl. *SE6* —4D **85**
Patshull Pl. *NW5* —3E **23**
Patshull Rd. *NW5* —3E **23**
Pattenden Rd. *SE6* —1B **98**
Patten Ho. *N16* —3E **11**
Patten Rd. *SW18* —5A **78**
*Patterdale. NW1 —2D **37***
(off Osnaburgh St.)
Patterdale Clo. *Brom* —5B **100**
Patterdale Rd. *SE15* —3E **69**
Pattern Ho. *EC1* —3D **39**
*Pattinson Point. E16 —4C **44***
(off Fife Rd.)
*Pattison Ho. SE1 —3E **53***
(off Redcross Way)
Pattison Rd. *NW2* —5C **6**
Paul Clo. *E15* —4A **30**
Paulet Rd. *SE5* —5D **67**
*Pauline Ho. E1 —4C **40***
(off Old Montague St.)
Paul Julius Clo. *E14* —1F **57**
Pauls Ho. *E3* —4B **42**
Paul St. *E15* —5A **30**
Paul St. *EC2* —3F **39**
Paul's Wlk. *EC4* —1E **53**
Paultons Sq. *SW3* —2F **63**
Paultons St. *SW3* —2F **63**
Pauntley St. *N19* —3E **9**
*Pavan Ct. E2 —2E **41***
(off Sceptre Rd.)
Paveley Dri. *SW11* —3A **64**
*Paveley Ho. N1 —1B **38***
(off Priory Grn. Est.)
Paveley St. *NW8* —2A **36**
*Pavement, The. E11 —3E **15***
(off Hainault Rd.)
Pavement, The. *SW4* —2E **79**
Pavilion Rd. *SW1* —4B **50**
Pavilion St. *SW1* —4B **50**
Pavilion, The. *SW8* —3F **65**
*Pavillion Ter. W12 —5E **33***
(off Wood La.)
Pawsey Clo. *E13* —5D **31**
Paxton Ct. *SE12* —3E **101**
*Paxton Ct. SE26 —4A **98***
(off Adamsrill Rd.)
Paxton Pl. *SE27* —4A **96**
Paxton Rd. *SE23* —3A **98**
Paxton Rd. *W4* —2A **60**
Paxton Ter. *SW1* —2D **65**
*Payne Ho. N1 —5B **24***
(off Barnsbury Est.)
Paynell Ct. *SE3* —1A **86**
Payne Rd. *E3* —1D **43**
Paynesfield Av. *SW14* —1A **74**
Payne St. *SE8* —3B **70**
Paynes Wlk. *W6* —2A **62**
Peabody Av. *SW1* —1D **65**
*Peabody Bldgs. E1 —1C **54***
(off John Fisher St.)
*Peabody Bldgs. E2 —1D **41***
(off Cambridge Cres.)
*Peabody Bldgs. EC1 —3E **39***
(off Roscoe St.)
*Peabody Bldgs. SW3 —2A **64***
(off Lawrence St.)
Peabody Clo. *SE10* —4D **71**
*Peabody Clo. SW1 —1D **65***
(off Lupus St.)
*Peabody Ct. EC1 —3E **39***
(off Roscoe St.)
*Peabody Ct. SE5 —4F **67***
(off Kimpton Rd.)
*Peabody Est. E1 —1F **55***
(off Glasmis Pl.)
*Peabody Est. EC1 —3C **38***
(off Farringdon La.)
*Peabody Est. EC1 —3E **39***
(off Whitecross St.,
in two parts)
Peabody Est. *N1* —5E **25**
*Peabody Est. SE1 —3E **53***
(off Mint St.)
Peabody Est. *SE1* —2C **52**
(Hatfield St.)
Peabody Est. *SE1* —2E **53**
(Southwark St.)
Peabody Est. *SE24* —5D **81**
*Peabody Est. SW1 —5E **51***
(off Vauxhall Bri. Rd.)
Peabody Est. *SW3* —2A **64**
*Peabody Est. SW6 —2B **62***
(off Lillie Rd.)
Peabody Est. *SW11* —2A **78**
Peabody Est. *W6* —1E **61**
Peabody Est. *W10* —4E **33**
Peabody Hill. *SE21* —1D **95**
Peabody Sq. *SE1* —3D **53**
(in two parts)
*Peabody Tower. EC1 —3E **39***
(off Golden La.)
*Peabody Trust. SE17 —5F **53***
(off Rodney Rd.)
Peabody Yd. *N1* —5E **25**
Peachey Edwards Ho. E2
*(off Teesdale St.) —2D **41***
Peach Rd. *W10* —2F **33**
Peachum Rd. *SE3* —2B **72**
(in two parts)
Peachwalk M. *E3* —1F **41**
Peacock St. *SE17* —5D **53**
*Peacock Wlk. E16 —5D **45***
(off Mortlake Rd.)
Peacock Wlk. *N6* —2D **9**
*Peacock Yd. SE17 —1D **67***
(off Iliffe St.)
Peak Hill. *SE26* —4E **97**
Peak Hill Av. *SE26* —4E **97**
Peak Hill Gdns. *SE26* —4E **97**
*Peak Ho. N4 —3E **11***
(off Woodberry Down Est.)
Peak, The. *SE26* —3E **97**
Pearcefield Av. *SE23* —1E **97**
Pear Clo. *SE14* —3A **70**
*Pear Ct. SE15 —3B **68***
(off Thruxton Way)
Pearcroft Rd. *E11* —4F **15**
Peardon St. *SW8* —5D **65**
Pearfield Rd. *SE23* —3A **98**
Pearl Clo. *NW2* —2F **5**
Pearl St. *E1* —2D **55**
Pearman St. *SE1* —4C **52**
Pear Pl. *SE1* —3C **52**
Pear Rd. *E11* —5F **15**
Pearscroft Ct. *SW6* —4D **63**
Pearscroft Rd. *SW6* —4D **63**
Pearse St. *SE15* —2A **68**
Pearson's Av. *SE14* —4C **70**
Pearson St. *E2* —1B **40**
Peartree. *SE26* —5A **98**
Peartree Av. *SW17* —3E **91**
Pear Tree Clo. *E2* —5B **26**
Pear Tree Ct. *EC1* —3C **38**
Pear Tree Ho. *SE4* —1B **84**
Peartree La. *E1* —1E **55**
Pear Tree St. *EC1* —3E **39**
Pear Tree Way. *SE10* —5C **58**
Peary Ho. *NW10* —4A **18**
Peary Pl. *E2* —2E **41**
Peckarmans Wood. *SE26*
—3C **96**
Peckett Sq. *N5* —1E **25**
Peckford Clo. *SW9* —5C **66**
Peckford Pl. *SW9* —5C **66**
Peckham. —4C 68
Peckham Gro. *SE15* —3A **68**
Peckham High St. *SE15*
—4C **68**
Peckham Hill St. *SE15*
—3C **68**
Peckham Pk. Rd. *SE15*
—3C **68**

Peckham Rd. *SE5 & SE15* —4A **68**
Peckham Rye. *SE15 & SE22* —1C **82**
Peckham Sq. *SE15* —4C **68**
*Pecks Yd. E1 —4B **40***
(off Hanbury St.)
Peckwater St. *NW5* —2E **23**
Pedlar's Wlk. *N7* —2B **24**
Pedley St. *E1* —3B **40**
Pedro St. *E5* —5F **13**
Pedworth Gdns. *SE16* —5E **55**
Peek Cres. *SW19* —5F **89**
Peel Gro. *E2* —1E **41**
(in two parts)
*Peel Pas. W8 —2C **48***
(off Peel St.)
Peel Precinct. *NW6* —1C **34**
Peel St. *W8* —2C **48**
Peerless St. *EC1* —2F **39**
Pegasus Clo. *N5* —1F **25**
Pegasus Pl. *SE11* —2C **66**
Pegasus Pl. *SW6* —4C **62**
*Pegasus Tower. SE14 —3A **70***
(off Woodpecker Rd.)
Pegley Gdns. *SE12* —2C **100**
Pekin Clo. *E14* —5C **42**
*Pekin Ho. E14 —5C **42***
(off Pekin St.)
Pekin St. *E14* —5C **42**
*Peldon Wlk. N1 —5D **25***
(off Popham St.)
Pelham Clo. *SE5* —1A **82**
*Pelham Ct. SW3 —5A **50***
(off Fulham Rd.)
Pelham Cres. *SW7* —5A **50**
*Pelham Ho. W14 —5B **48***
(off Mornington Av.)
Pelham Pl. *SW7* —5A **50**
Pelham St. *SW7* —5F **49**
Pelican Est. *SE15* —4B **68**
Pelican Ho. *SE8* —5B **56**
Pelican Pas. *E1* —3E **41**
Pelican Stairs. *E1* —2E **55**
Pelican Wlk. *SW9* —2D **81**
Pelier St. *SE17* —2E **67**
Pelinore Rd. *SE6* —2A **100**
Pella Ho. *SE11* —1B **66**
Pellant Rd. *SW6* —3A **62**
Pellatt Rd. *SE22* —3B **82**
Pellerin Rd. *N16* —2A **26**
*Pellew Ho. E1 —3D **41***
(off Somerford St.)
Pelling St. *E14* —5C **42**
Pelly Rd. *E13* —5C **30**
(in two parts)
Pelter St. *E2* —2B **40**
(in two parts)
Pelton Rd. *SE10* —1A **72**
Pember Rd. *NW10* —2F **33**
Pemberton Gdns. *N19* —5E **9**
*Pemberton Ho. SE26 —4C **96***
(off High Level Dri.)
Pemberton Pl. *E8* —4D **27**
Pemberton Rd. *N4* —1C **10**
Pemberton Row. *EC4* —5C **38**
Pemberton Ter. *N19* —5E **9**
Pembridge Cres. *W11* —1C **48**
Pembridge Gdns. *W2* —1C **48**
Pembridge M. *W11* —1C **48**
Pembridge Pl. *SW15* —3C **76**
Pembridge Pl. *W2* —1C **48**
Pembridge Rd. *W11* —1C **48**
Pembridge Sq. *W2* —1C **48**
Pembridge Vs. *W11 & W2* —1C **48**
Pembroke Bldgs. *NW10* —2C **32**
Pembroke Clo. *SW1* —3C **50**
*Pembroke Cotts. W8 —4C **48***
(off Pembroke Sq.)
Pembroke Gdns. *W14* —5B **48**
Pembroke Gdns. Clo. *W8* —4C **48**
*Pembroke Ho. W2 —5D **35***
(off Hallfield Est.)
*Pembroke M. E1 —3E **41***
(off Wessex St.)
Pembroke M. *E3* —2A **42**
Pembroke M. *W8* —4C **48**
Pembroke Pl. *W8* —4C **48**
Pembroke Rd. *E17* —1D **15**
Pembroke Rd. *N15* —1B **12**
Pembroke Rd. *W8* —5B **48**
Pembroke Sq. *W8* —4C **48**
Pembroke St. *N1* —4A **24**
(in two parts)
Pembroke Vs. *W8* —5C **48**
Pembroke Wlk. *W8* —5C **48**
Pembrook M. *SW11* —2F **77**
Pembry Clo. *SW9* —4C **66**
Pembury Clo. *E5* —2D **27**
Pembury Pl. *E5* —2D **27**
Pembury Rd. *E5* —2D **27**
Pemell Clo. *E1* —3E **41**
*Pemell Ho. E1 —3E **41***
(off Pemell Clo.)
Penally Pl. *N1* —5F **25**
*Penang Ho. E1 —2D **55***
(off Prusom St.)
Penang St. *E1* —2D **55**
Penarth Cen. *SE15* —2E **69**
Penarth St. *SE15* —2E **69**
Penberth Rd. *SE6* —2E **99**
Pencombe M. *W11* —1B **48**
Pencraig Way. *SE15* —2D **69**
Penda's Mead. *E9* —1A **28**
Pendennis Ho. *SE8* —5A **56**
Pendennis Rd. *SW16* —4A **94**
Penderry Ri. *SE6* —2F **99**
Penderyn Way. *N7* —1F **23**
Pendle Ho. *SE26* —3C **96**
Pendle Rd. *SW16* —5D **93**
Pendlestone Rd. *E17* —1D **15**
Pendragon Rd. *Brom* —3B **100**
Pendragon Wlk. *NW9* —1A **4**
*Pendrell Ho. WC2 —5F **37***
(off New Compton St.)
Pendrell Rd. *SE4* —5A **70**
Pendulum M. *E8* —2B **26**
Penerley Rd. *SE6* —1D **99**
*Penfield Lodge. W9 —4C **34***
(off Admiral Wlk.)
Penfields Ho. *N7* —3A **24**
Penfold Pl. *NW1* —4A **36**
Penfold St. *NW8 & NW1* —3F **35**
Penford Gdns. *SE9* —1F **87**
Penford St. *SE5* —5D **67**
Penge Ho. *SW11* —1F **77**
Penge Rd. *E13* —5E **31**
Penhall Rd. *SE7* —5F **59**
*Penhurst Pl. SE1 —4B **52***
(off Carlisle La.)
Peninsula Ct. *E14* —4D **57**
Peninsula Heights. *SE1* —1A **66**
*Peninsula Pk. SE7 —5C **58***
(off Peninsula Pk. Rd.)
Peninsular Pk. Rd. *SE7* —5C **58**
Penley Ct. *WC2* —1B **52**
*Penmayne Ho. SE11 —1C **66***
(off Kennings Way)
Pennack Rd. *SE15* —2B **68**
*Penn Almshouses. SE10 —4E **71***
(off Greenwich S. St.)
Pennant M. *W8* —5D **49**
Pennard Rd. *W12* —3E **47**
Penner Clo. *SW19* —2A **90**
Pennethorne Clo. *E9* —5E **27**
Pennethorne Ho. *SW11* —1F **77**
Pennethorne Rd. *SE15* —3D **69**
*Penn Ho. NW8 —3A **36***
(off Mallory St.)
Pennine Dri. *NW2* —4F **5**
Pennine La. *NW2* —4A **6**
Pennine Pde. *NW2* —4A **6**
Pennington Clo. *SE27* —4F **95**
Pennington Ct. *SE16* —2A **56**
Pennington St. *E1* —1D **55**
Pennington Way. *SE12* —2D **101**
Penn Rd. *N7* —2A **24**
Penn St. *N1* —5F **25**
Pennyfields. *E14* —1C **56**
(in two parts)
*Pennyford Ct. NW8 —3F **35***
(off St John's Wood Rd.)
Penny M. *SW12* —5D **79**
*Pennymoor Wlk. W9 —3B **34***
(off Ashmore Rd.)
Penpoll Rd. *E8* —3D **27**
Penrith Clo. *SW15* —3A **76**
Penrith Pl. *SE27* —2D **95**
Penrith Rd. *N15* —1F **11**
Penrith St. *SW16* —5E **93**
Penrose Gro. *SE17* —1E **67**
Penrose Ho. *SE17* —1E **67**
(in two parts)
Penrose St. *SE17* —1E **67**
*Penryn Ho. SE11 —1C **66***
(off Seaton Clo.)

Penryn St. *NW1* —1F **37**
Penry St. *SE1* —5A **54**
Pensbury Pl. *SW8* —5E **65**
Pensbury St. *SW8* —5E **65**
Penshurst. *NW5* —3C **22**
Penshurst Ho. SE15 —2E **69**
  (off Lovelinch Clo.)
Penshurst Rd. *E9* —4F **27**
Pentland Clo. *NW11* —4A **6**
Pentland Gdns. *SW18* —4E **77**
Pentland St. *SW18* —4E **77**
Pentlow St. *SW15* —1E **75**
Pentney Rd. *SW12* —1E **93**
Penton Gro. *N1* —1C **38**
Penton Ho. N1 —1C **38**
  (off Donegal St.)
Penton Pl. *SE17* —1D **67**
Penton Ri. *WC1* —2B **38**
Penton St. *N1* —1C **38**
Pentonville. —1B **38**
Pentonville Rd. *N1* —1B **38**
Pentridge St. *SE15* —3B **68**
Penwith Rd. *SW18* —2C **90**
Penwood Ho. *SW15* —4B **74**
Penwortham Rd. *SW16*
  —5D **93**
Penywern Rd. *SW5* —1C **62**
Penzance Ho. SE11 —1C **66**
  (off Seaton Clo.)
Penzance Pl. *W11* —2A **48**
Penzance St. *W11* —2A **48**
Peony Gdns. *W12* —1C **46**
Peperfield. WC1 —2B **38**
  (off Cromer St.)
Pepler Ho. W10 —3A **34**
  (off Wornington Rd.)
Pepler M. *SE5* —1B **68**
Peploe Rd. *NW6* —1F **33**
  (in two parts)
Peppermead Sq. *SE4* —3C **84**
Peppermint Pl. *E11* —5A **16**
Pepper St. *E14* —4D **57**
Pepper St. *SE1* —3E **53**
Peppie Clo. *N16* —4A **12**
  (in two parts)
Pepys Clo. *SW4* —1D **79**
Pepys Cres. *E16* —2C **58**
Pepys Ho. E2 —2E **41**
  (off Kirkwall Pl.)
Pepys Rd. *SE14* —4F **69**
Pepys St. *EC3* —1A **54**
Perceval Av. *NW3* —2A **22**
Perch St. *E8* —1B **26**
*Percival David Foundation of
  Chinese Art. —3F **37**
  (off Gordon Sq.)
Percival St. *EC1* —3D **39**
Percy Cir. *WC1* —2B **38**
Percy M. W1 —4F **37**
  (off Rathbone Pl.)
Percy Pas. W1 —4E **37**
  (off Rathbone St.)
Percy Rd. *E11* —2A **16**
Percy Rd. *E16* —4A **44**
Percy Rd. *W12* —3C **46**
Percy St. *W1* —4F **37**

Percy Yd. *WC1* —2B **38**
Peregrine Clo. *NW10* —2A **18**
Peregrine Ct. SE8 —2C **70**
  (off Edward St.)
Peregrine Ct. *SW16* —4B **94**
Peregrine Ho. EC1 —2D **39**
  (off Hall St.)
Perham Rd. *W14* —1A **62**
Perifield. *SE21* —1E **95**
Periton Rd. *SE9* —2F **87**
Perkins Ho. *E14* —4B **42**
Perkin's Rents. *SW1* —4F **51**
Perkins Sq. SE1 —2E **53**
  (off Porter St.)
Perks Clo. *SE3* —1A **86**
Perley Ho. *E3* —4B **42**
Perran Rd. *SW2* —1D **95**
Perren St. *NW5* —3D **23**
Perrers Rd. *W6* —5D **47**
Perrin Ho. *NW6* —2C **34**
Perrin's Ct. *NW3* —1E **21**
Perrin's La. *NW3* —1E **21**
Perrin's Wlk. *NW3* —1E **21**
Perronet Ho. SE1 —4D **53**
  (off Princess St.)
Perry Av. *W3* —5A **32**
Perry Ct. *E14* —1C **70**
Perry Ct. *N15* —1A **12**
Perryfield Way. *NW9* —1B **4**
Perry Hill. *SE6* —3B **98**
Perrymead St. *SW6* —4C **62**
Perryn Ho. *W3* —1A **46**
Perryn Rd. *SE16* —4D **55**
Perryn Rd. *W3* —2A **46**
Perry Ri. *SE23* —3A **98**
Perry's Pl. *W1* —5F **37**
Perry Va. *SE23* —2E **97**
Persant Rd. *SE6* —2A **100**
Perseverance Pl. *SW9* —3C **66**
Perseverance Works. E2
  (off Kingsland Rd.) —2A **40**
Perth Av. *NW9* —2A **4**
Perth Clo. *SE5* —2F **81**
Perth Ho. *N1* —4B **24**
Perth Rd. *E10* —3A **14**
Perth Rd. *E13* —1D **45**
Perth Rd. *N4* —3C **10**
Perystreete. *SE23* —2E **97**
Peter Av. *NW10* —4D **19**
Peter Best Ho. E1 —5D **41**
  (off Nelson St.)
Peterboat Clo. SE10 —5A **58**
Peterborough Ct. *EC4* —5C **38**
Peterborough Gdns. *Ilf*
  —2F **17**
Peterborough M. *SW6*
  —5C **62**
Peterborough Rd. *E10*
  —1E **15**
Peterborough Rd. *SW6*
  —5C **62**
Peterborough Vs. *SW6*
  —4D **63**
Peter Butler Ho. SE1 —3C **54**
  (off Wolseley St.)

Peterchurch Ho. SE15 —2D **69**
  (off Commercial Way)
Petergate. *SW11* —2E **77**
Peter Ho. SW8 —3A **66**
  (off Luscombe Way)
Peterley Bus. Cen. *E2* —1D **41**
Peter Scott Vis. Cen., The.
  —4D **61**
Peters Ct. W2 —5D **35**
  (off Porchester Rd.)
Petersfield Ri. *SW15* —1D **89**
Petersham Ho. SW7 —5F **49**
  (off Kendrick M.)
Petersham La. *SW7* —4E **49**
Petersham M. *SW7* —4E **49**
Petersham Pl. *SW7* —4E **49**
Peter's Hill. *EC4* —1E **53**
Peter's La. *EC1* —4D **39**
Peter's Path. *SE26* —4D **97**
Peterstow Clo. *SW19* —2A **90**
Peter St. *W1* —1F **51**
Petherton Ho. N4 —3E **11**
  (off Woodberry Down Est.)
Petherton Rd. *N5* —2E **25**
Petiver Clo. *E9* —4E **27**
Petley Rd. *W6* —2F **61**
Peto Pl. *NW1* —3D **37**
Peto St. N. *E16* —5B **44**
Peto St. S. *E16* —1B **58**
Petrie Clo. *NW2* —3A **20**
Petros Gdns. *NW3* —3E **21**
Petticoat La. *E1* —4A **40**
Petticoat Sq. *E1* —5B **40**
Petticoat Tower. E1 —5B **40**
  (off Petticoat Sq.)
Pettiward Clo. *SW15* —2E **75**
Pett St. *SE18* —5F **59**
Petty France. *SW1* —4E **51**
Petworth St. *SW11* —4A **64**
Petyt Pl. *SW3* —2A **64**
Petyward. *SW3* —5A **50**
Pevensey Rd. *E7* —1B **30**
Pevensey Rd. *SW17* —4F **91**
Peveril Ho. SE1 —4F **53**
  (off Rephidim St.)
Peyton Pl. *SE10* —3E **71**
Pharamond. *NW2* —3F **19**
Pheasant Clo. *E16* —5D **45**
Phelp St. *SE17* —2F **67**
Phene St. *SW3* —2A **64**
Philadelphia Ct. SW10
  (off Uverdale Rd.) —3E **63**
Philbeach Gdns. *SW5* —1B **62**
Phil Brown Pl. SW8 —1D **79**
  (off Wandsworth Rd.)
Philchurch Pl. *E1* —5C **40**
Philip Ct. W2 —4F **35**
  (off Hall Pl.)
Philip Ho. NW6 —5D **21**
  (off Mortimer Pl.)
Philippa Gdns. *SE9* —3F **87**
Philip St. *E13* —3C **44**
Philip Wlk. *SE15* —1C **82**
  (in three parts)
Phillimore Gdns. *NW10*
  —5E **19**

Phillimore Gdns. *W8* —3C **48**
Phillimore Gdns. Clo. *W8*
　　　　　　—4C **48**
Phillimore Pl. *W8* —3C **48**
Phillimore Ter. *W8* —4C **48**
　(off Allen St.)
Phillimore Wlk. *W8* —4C **48**
Phillipp St. *N1* —5A **26**
　(in two parts)
Philpot La. *EC3* —1A **54**
Philpot Sq. *SW6* —1D **77**
Philpot St. *E1* —5D **41**
Phineas Pett Rd. *SE9* —1F **87**
Phipps Ho. *SE7* —1D **73**
　(off Woolwich Rd.)
Phipps Ho. *W12* —1D **47**
　(off White City Est.)
Phipp St. *EC2* —3A **40**
Phoebeth Rd. *SE13* —3C **84**
Phoenix Bus. Cen. *E3* —4C **42**
Phoenix Clo. *E8* —5B **26**
Phoenix Clo. *E14* —5C **56**
Phoenix Ct. *NW1* —1F **37**
　(off Purchese St.)
Phoenix Ct. *SE14* —2A **70**
　(off Chipley St.)
Phoenix Pl. *WC1* —3B **38**
Phoenix Rd. *NW1* —2F **37**
Phoenix Rd. *SE20* —5E **97**
Phoenix Rd. *WC2* —5F **37**
Phoenix Wharf Rd. *SE1*
　(off Tanner St.) —3B **54**
Phoenix Yd. *WC1* —2B **38**
　(off Kings Cross Rd.)
Physic Pl. *SW3* —2B **64**
Piazza, The. *WC2* —1A **52**
　(off Covent Garden)
Piccadilly. *W1* —2D **51**
Piccadilly Arc. *SW1* —2E **51**
　(off Piccadilly)
Piccadilly Circus. —1F 51
Piccadilly Cir. *W1* —1E **51**
Piccadilly Pl. *W1* —1E **51**
　(off Piccadilly)
Pickard St. *EC1* —2D **39**
Pickering Clo. *E9* —4F **27**
Pickering Ho. *W2* —5E **35**
　(off Hallfield Est.)
Pickering M. *W2* —5D **35**
Pickering Pl. *SW1* —2E **51**
　(off St James's St.)
Pickering St. *N1* —5D **25**
Pickets St. *SW12* —5D **79**
Pickfords Wharf. *N1* —1E **39**
Pickfords Wharf. *SE1* —2F **53**
Pickwick Ho. *SE16* —3C **54**
　(off George Row)
Pickwick Ho. *W11* —2F **47**
　(off St Ann's Rd.)
Pickwick Rd. *SE21* —5F **81**
Pickwick St. *SE1* —3E **53**
Pickworth Clo. *SW8* —3A **66**
Picton Pl. *W1* —5C **36**
Picton St. *SE5* —3F **67**
Pied Bull Yd. *WC1* —4A **38**
　(off Bury Pl.)

Pier Head. *E1* —2D **55**
　(off Wapping High St.)
Pierhead Wharf. *E1* —2D **55**
　(off Wapping High St.)
Pier Ho. *SW3* —2A **64**
Piermont Rd. *SE22* —3D **83**
Pierpoint Building. *E14*
　　　　　　—3B **56**
Pierrepont Arc. *N1* —1D **39**
　(off Pierrepont Row)
Pierrepont Row. *N1* —1D **39**
　(off Camden Pas.)
Pier St. *E14* —5E **57**
　(in two parts)
Pier Ter. *SW18* —2D **77**
Piggott St. *E14* —5C **42**
Pigott St. *E14* —5C **42**
Pike Clo. *Brom* —5D **101**
Pikemans Ct. *SW5* —5C **48**
　(off W. Cromwell Rd.)
Pikethorne. *SE23* —2F **97**
Pilgrimage St. *SE1* —3F **53**
Pilgrim Hill. *SE27* —4E **95**
Pilgrim Ho. *SE1* —4F **53**
　(off Lansdowne Pl.)
Pilgrims Cloisters. *SE5*
　(off Sedgmoor Pl.) —3A **68**
Pilgrim's La. *NW3* —1F **21**
Pilgrims M. *E14* —1A **58**
Pilgrim's Pl. *NW3* —1F **21**
Pilgrim St. *EC4* —5D **39**
Pilgrims Way. *N19* —3F **9**
Pilkington Rd. *SE15* —5D **69**
Pilot Clo. *SE8* —2B **70**
Pilot Ind. Cen. *NW10* —3A **32**
Pilsden Clo. *SW19* —1F **89**
Pilton Pl. *SE17* —1E **67**
　(off Pingle St.)
Pilton Pl. Est. *SE17* —1E **67**
Pimlico. —1E 65
Pimlico Ho. *SW1* —1D **65**
　(off Ebury Bri. Rd.)
Pimlico Rd. *SW1* —1C **64**
Pimlico Wlk. *N1* —2A **40**
　(off Aske St.)
Pinchin St. *E1* —1C **54**
Pincombe Ho. *SE17* —1F **67**
Pincott Pl. *SE4* —1F **83**
Pindar St. *EC2* —4A **40**
Pindock M. *W9* —3D **35**
Pineapple Ct. *SW1* —4E **51**
　(off Wilfred St.)
Pine Av. *E15* —2F **29**
Pine Clo. *E10* —4D **15**
Pine Clo. *N19* —4E **9**
Pinedene. *SE15* —4D **69**
Pinefield Clo. *E14* —1C **56**
Pine Gro. *N4* —4A **10**
Pine Gro. *SW19* —5B **90**
Pine Ho. *SE16* —3E **55**
　(off Ainsty Est.)
Pine Ho. *W10* —3A **34**
　(off Droop St.)
Pinehurst Ct. *W11* —5B **34**
　(off Colville Gdns.)
Pinemartin Clo. *NW2* —5E **5**

Pine M. *NW10* —1F **33**
Pine Rd. *NW2* —1E **19**
Pine St. *EC1* —3C **38**
Pine Tree Ho. *SE14* —3F **69**
　(off Reaston St.)
Pinewood Clo. *SW4* —4F **79**
Pinfold Rd. *SW16* —4A **94**
Pinkerton Pl. *SW16* —4F **93**
Pinnace Ho. *E14* —4E **57**
Pinnell Rd. *SE9* —2F **87**
Pinner Ct. *NW8* —3F **35**
　(off St John's Wood Rd.)
Pintail Clo. *E6* —4F **45**
Pintail Ct. *SE8* —2B **70**
　(off Pilot Clo.)
Pinter Ho. *SW9* —5A **66**
　(off Grantham Rd.)
Pinto Way. *SE3* —2D **87**
Pioneer St. *SE15* —4C **68**
Pioneer Way. *W12* —5D **33**
Piper Clo. *N7* —2B **24**
Pippin Clo. *NW2* —5C **4**
Pirbright Rd. *SW18* —1B **90**
Pirie Clo. *SE5* —1F **81**
Pirie St. *E16* —2D **59**
Pitcairn Ho. *E8* —4E **27**
Pitchford St. *E15* —4F **29**
Pitfield Est. *N1* —2A **40**
Pitfield St. *N1* —2A **40**
Pitfold Clo. *SE12* —4C **86**
Pitfold Rd. *SE12* —4C **86**
Pitman Ho. *SE8* —4C **70**
Pitman St. *SE5* —3E **67**
　(in two parts)
Pitmaston Ho. *SE13* —5E **71**
　(off Lewisham Rd.)
Pitsea Pl. *E1* —5F **41**
Pitsea St. *E1* —5F **41**
Pitt Cres. *SW19* —4D **91**
Pitt's Head M. *W1* —2C **50**
Pitt St. *W8* —3C **48**
Pixley St. *E14* —5B **42**
Plaisterers Highwalk. *EC2*
　(off Noble St.) —4E **39**
Plaistow. —2D 45
Plaistow Gro. *E15* —5B **30**
Plaistow Pk. Rd. *E13* —1D **45**
Plaistow Rd. *E15 & E13*
　　　　　　—5B **30**
Plaistow Wharf. *E16* —2C **58**
Plane St. *SE26* —3D **97**
Planetree Ct. *W6* —5F **47**
　(off Brook Grn.)
Plane Tree Ho. *SE8* —2A **70**
　(off Etta St.)
Plane Tree Wlk. *SE19* —5A **96**
Plantain Gdns. *E11* —5F **15**
　(off Hollydown Way,
　　　　　　in two parts)
Plantain Pl. *SE1* —3F **53**
Plantation, The. *SE3* —5C **72**
Plantation Wharf. *SW11*
　　　　　　—1E **77**
Plasel Ct. *E13* —5D **31**
　(off Pawsey Clo.)
Plashet. —3F 31

Plashet Gro. *E6* —5E **31**
Plashet Rd. *E13* —5C **30**
Plassy Rd. *SE6* —5D **85**
Plate Ho. *E14* —1D **71**
*Platina St. EC2 —3F **39***
(off Tabernacle St.)
Plato Rd. *SW2* —2A **80**
Platt's La. *NW3* —1C **20**
Platt St. *NW1* —1F **37**
Platt, The. *SW15* —1F **75**
Plaxton Ct. *E11* —5B **16**
Playfair Ho. *E14* —5C **42**
*Playfair Mans. W14 —2A **62***
(off Queen's Club Gdns.)
Playfair St. *W6* —1E **61**
Playfield Cres. *SE22* —3B **82**
Playford Rd. *N4* —4B **10**
(in two parts)
Playgreen Way. *SE6* —3C **98**
Playhouse Yd. *EC4* —5D **39**
Plaza Pde. *NW6* —1D **35**
Plaza, The. *W1* —5E **37**
Pleasance Rd. *SW15* —3D **75**
Pleasance, The. *SW15* —2D **75**
Pleasant Pl. *N1* —4D **25**
Pleasant Row. *NW1* —5D **23**
*Plender Pl. NW1 —5E **23***
(off Plender St.)
Plender St. *NW1* —5E **23**
Pleshey Rd. *N7* —1F **23**
Plevna Cres. *N15* —1A **12**
Plevna St. *E14* —4E **57**
Pleydell Av. *W6* —5B **46**
*Pleydell Ct. EC4 —5C **38***
(off Lombard La.)
*Pleydell Est. EC1 —2E **39***
(off Lever St.)
*Pleydell St. EC4 —5C **38***
(off Bouverie St.)
Plimsoll Clo. *E14* —5D **43**
Plimsoll Rd. *N4* —5C **10**
Plough Ct. *EC3* —1F **53**
Plough La. *SE22* —4B **82**
Plough La. *SW19 & SW17* —5D **91**
Ploughmans Clo. *NW1* —5F **23**
Plough Pl. *EC4* —5C **38**
Plough Rd. *SW11* —1F **77**
Plough St. *E1* —5B **40**
Plough Ter. *SW11* —2F **77**
Plough Way. *SE16* —5F **55**
Plough Yd. *EC2* —3A **40**
*Plover Ho. SW9 —3C **66***
(off Brixton Rd.)
Plover Way. *SE16* —4A **56**
*Plowden Bldgs. EC4 —1C **52***
(off Middle Temple La.)
Plumber's Row. *E1* —4C **40**
Plumbridge St. *SE10* —4D **71**
*Plume Ho. SE10 —2D **71***
(off Creek Rd.)
Plummer Rd. *SW4* —5F **79**
Plumtree Ct. *EC4* —5D **39**
*Plymouth Ho. SE10 —3D **71***
(off Devonshire Dri.)
Plymouth Rd. *E16* —4C **44**
Plymouth Wharf. *E14* —5F **57**
Plympton Av. *NW6* —4B **20**
Plympton Pl. *NW8* —3A **36**
Plympton Rd. *NW6* —4B **20**
Plympton St. *NW8* —3A **36**
Pocklington Clo. W12
*(off Goldhawk Rd.) —4C **46***
Pocklington Lodge. *W12* —4C **46**
Pocock St. *SE1* —3D **53**
Podmore Rd. *SW18* —2E **77**
Poet's Rd. *N5* —2F **25**
Point Clo. *SE10* —4E **71**
Pointers Clo. *E14* —1D **71**
Point Hill. *SE10* —3E **71**
Point Pleasant. *SW18* —2C **76**
*Point Ter. E7 —2D **31***
(off Claremont Rd.)
Point West. *W8* —5D **49**
Poland St. *W1* —5E **37**
Polebrook Rd. *SE3* —1E **87**
Polecroft La. *SE6* —2B **98**
*Polesworth Ho. W2 —4C **34***
(off Alfred Rd.)
Pollard Clo. *E16* —1C **58**
Pollard Clo. *N7* —1B **24**
Pollard Ho. *N1* —1B **38**
Pollard Row. *E2* —2C **40**
Pollard St. *E2* —2C **40**
Pollen St. *W1* —5E **37**
Pollitt Dri. *NW8* —3F **35**
*Pollock Ho. W10 —3A **34***
(off Kensal Rd.)
Pollock's Toy Mus. —4E 37
Polsted Rd. *SE6* —5B **84**
Polworth Rd. *SW16* —5A **94**
Polygon Rd. *NW1* —1F **37**
*Polygon, The. NW8 —5F **21***
(off Avenue Rd.)
Polygon, The. *SW4* —2E **79**
Pomell Way. *E1* —5B **40**
*Pomeroy Ho. W11 —5A **34***
(off Lancaster Rd.)
Pomeroy St. *SE14* —3E **69**
Pomfret Rd. *SE5* —1D **81**
Pomoja La. *N19* —4A **10**
Pond Clo. *SE3* —5B **72**
Pond Cotts. *SE21* —1A **96**
Ponder St. *N7* —4B **24**
(in two parts)
Pond Farm Est. *E5* —5E **13**
Pondfield Ho. *SE27* —5E **95**
Pond Ho. *SW3* —5A **50**
Pond Mead. *SE21* —4F **81**
Pond Pl. *SW3* —5A **50**
Pond Rd. *E15* —1A **44**
Pond Rd. *SE3* —5B **72**
Pond Sq. *N6* —3C **8**
Pond St. *NW3* —2A **22**
Ponler St. *E1* —5D **41**
Ponsard Rd. *NW10* —2D **33**
Ponsford St. *E9* —3E **27**
Ponsonby Pl. *SW1* —1F **65**
Ponsonby Rd. *SW15* —5D **75**
Ponsonby Ter. *SW1* —1F **65**
Pontefract Rd. *Brom* —5B **100**
Ponton Rd. *SW8* —3F **65**
Pont St. *SW1* —4B **50**
Pont St. M. *SW1* —4B **50**
Pontypool Pl. *SE1* —3D **53**
Pool Clo. *Beck* —5C **98**
Pool Ct. *SE6* —2C **98**
*Poole Ho. SE11 —4C **52***
(off Lambeth Wlk.)
Poole Rd. *E9* —3F **27**
*Pooles Bldgs. WC1 —3C **38***
(off Mount Pleasant)
Pooles La. *SW10* —3E **63**
Pooles Pk. *N4* —4C **10**
Poole St. *N1* —5F **25**
*Pool Ho. NW8 —4F **35***
(off Penfold St.)
Poolmans St. *SE16* —3F **55**
Poonah St. *E1* —5E **41**
Pope Clo. *SW19* —5F **91**
*Pope Ho. SE5 —3F **67***
(off Elmington Est.)
Pope's Head All. *EC3* —5F **39**
Pope's Rd. *SW9* —1C **80**
Pope St. *SE1* —3A **54**
Popham Rd. *N1* —5E **25**
Popham St. *N1* —5D **25**
(in two parts)
Poplar. —1D 57
Poplar Bath St. *E14* —1D **57**
Poplar Bus. Pk. *E14* —1E **57**
Poplar Clo. *E9* —2B **28**
Poplar Ct. *SW19* —5C **90**
Poplar Gro. *W6* —3E **47**
Poplar High St. *E14* —1D **57**
*Poplar Ho. SE4 —2B **84***
(off Wickham Rd.)
*Poplar Ho. SE16 —3F **55***
(off Woodland Cres.)
*Poplar M. W12 —2E **47***
(off Uxbridge Rd.)
Poplar Pl. *W2* —1D **49**
Poplar Rd. *SE24* —2E **81**
Poplars Av. *NW2* —3E **19**
Poplars Rd. *E17* —1D **15**
Poplar Wlk. *SE24* —1E **81**
(in two parts)
Poppins Ct. *EC4* —5D **39**
Poppleton Rd. *E11* —1A **16**
Porchester Clo. *SE5* —2E **81**
Porchester Ct. *W2* —1D **49**
Porchester Gdns. *W2* —1D **49**
Porchester Gdns. M. *W2* —5D **35**
*Porchester Ga. W2 —1D **49***
(off Bayswater Rd., in two parts)
*Porchester Ho. E1 —5D **41***
(off Philpot St.)
Porchester Mead. *Beck* —5C **98**
Porchester M. *W2* —5D **35**
Porchester Pl. *W2* —5A **36**

Porchester Rd. W2—5D 35
Porchester Sq. W2—5D 35
Porchester Ter. W2—1E 49
Porchester Ter. N. W2—5D 35
Porden Rd. SW2—2B 80
Porlock Ho. SE26—3C 96
Porlock Rd. W10—3F 33
Porlock St. SE1—3F 53
Porson Ct. SE13—1D 85
Portal Clo. SE27—3C 94
Porta Way. E3—3B 42
Portbury Clo. SE15—4C 68
Port Cres. E13—3D 45
Portcullis Ho. SW1—3A 52 (off Bridge St.)
Portelet Ct. N1—5A 26 (off De Beauvoir Est.)
Portelet Rd. E1—2F 41
Porten Houses. W14—4A 48 (off Porten Rd.)
Porten Rd. W14—4A 48
Porter Sq. N19—3A 10
Porter St. SE1—2E 53
Porter St. W1—4B 36
Porters Wlk. E1—1D 55 (off Pennington St.)
Porteus Rd. W2—4E 35
Portgate Clo. W9—3B 34
Porthcawe Rd. SE26—4A 98
Portia Ct. SE11—1D 67 (off Opal St.)
Portia Way. E3—3B 42
Porticos, The. SW3—2F 63 (off Kings Rd.)
Portinscale Rd. SW15—3A 76
Portland Av. N16—2B 12
Portland Ct. SE1—4F 53 (off Gt. Dover St.)
Portland Ct. SE14—2A 70 (off Whitcher Clo.)
Portland Cres. SE9—2F 101
Portland Gdns. N4—1D 11
Portland Gro. SW8—4B 66
Portland Ho. SW1—4E 51 (off Stag Pl.)
Portland M. W1—5E 37
Portland Pl. W1—3D 37
Portland Ri. N4—3D 11
Portland Ri. Est. N4—3E 11
Portland Rd. SE9—2F 101
Portland Rd. W11—1A 48
Portland Rd. Brom—4E 101
Portland Sq. E1—2D 55
Portland St. SE17—1F 67
Portland Wlk. SE17—2F 67
Portman Av. SW14—1A 74
Portman Clo. W1—5B 36
Portman Ga. NW1—3A 36 (off Broadley Ter.)
Portman Mans. W1—4B 36 (off Chiltern St.)
Portman M. S. W1—5C 36
Portman Pl. E2—2E 41
Portman Sq. W1—5C 36
Portman St. W1—5C 36
Portman Towers. W1—5B 36
Portmeers Clo. E17—1B 14
Portnall Rd. W9—1B 34
Portobello Ct. Est. W11—5B 34
Portobello M. W11—1C 48
Portobello Rd. W10—4A 34
Portobello Rd. W11—5B 34
Portobello Road Market.—4A 34
Portpool La. WC1—4C 38
Portree St. E14—5F 43
Portsdown Av. NW11—1B 6
Portsdown M. NW11—1B 6
Portsea Hall. W2—5B 36 (off Portsea Pl.)
Portsea M. W2—5A 36 (off Portsea Pl.)
Portsea Pl. W2—5A 36
Portslade Rd. SW8—5E 65
Portsmouth M. E16—2D 59
Portsmouth Rd. SW15—5D 75
Portsmouth St. WC2—5B 38
Portsoken St. EC3—1B 54
Portswood Pl. SW15—4B 74
Portugal St. WC2—5B 38
Portway. E15—5B 30
Portway Gdns. SE18—3F 73
Pory Ho. SE11—5B 52
Poseidon Ct. E14—5C 56
Postern, The. EC2—4E 39 (off Wood St.)
Post Office App. E7—2D 31
Post Office Ct. EC4—5F 39 (off Barbican)
Post Office Way. SW8—3F 65
Potier St. SE1—4F 53
Potterne Clo. SW19—5F 75
Potters Fields. SE1—2A 54
Potter's La. SW16—5F 93
Potters Lodge. E14—1E 71
Potters Rd. SW6—5E 63
Pottery La. W11—2A 48
Pottery St. SE16—3D 55
Pott St. E2—2D 41
Poulner Way. SE15—3B 68 (in two parts)
Poulton Clo. E8—3D 27
Poultry. EC2—5F 39
Pound La. NW10—3C 18
Pound Pk. Rd. SE7—5F 59
Pountney Rd. SW11—1C 78
Povey Ho. SE17—5A 54 (off Tatum St.)
Powell Rd. E5—5D 13
Powell's Wlk. W4—2A 60
Powergate Bus. Pk. NW10—2A 32
Powerscroft Rd. E5—1E 27
Powis Ct. W11—5B 34 (off Powis Gdns.)
Powis Gdns. NW11—2B 6
Powis Gdns. W11—5B 34
Powis M. W11—5B 34
Powis Pl. WC1—3A 38
Powis Rd. E3—2D 43
Powis Sq. W11—5B 34 (in two parts)
Powis Ter. W11—5B 34
Powlett Pl. NW1—4C 22
Pownall Rd. E8—5C 26
Powster Rd. Brom—5C 100
Poynders Ct. SW4—4E 79
Poynders Gdns. SW4—5E 79
Poynders Rd. SW4—4E 79
Poynings Rd. N19—5E 9
Poynter Ho. NW8—3F 35 (off Fisherton St.)
Poynter Ho. W11—2F 47 (off Queensdale Cres.)
Poyntz Rd. SW11—5B 64
Poyser St. E2—1D 41
Praed M. W2—5F 35
Praed St. W2—5F 35
Pragel St. E13—1E 45
Pragnell Rd. SE12—2D 101
Prague Pl. SW2—3A 80
Prah Rd. N4—4C 10
Prairie St. SW8—5C 64
Pratt M. NW1—5E 23
Pratt St. NW1—5E 23
Pratt Wlk. SE11—5B 52
Prayle Gro. NW2—3F 5
Preachers Ct. EC1—3D 39 (off Charterhouse Sq.)
Prebend Gdns. W6 & W4 (in two parts)—5B 46
Prebend Mans. W4—5B 46 (off Chiswick High Rd.)
Prebend St. N1—5E 25
Precinct, The. N1—5E 25 (in two parts)
Premier Corner. W9—1B 34
Premiere Pl. E14—1C 56
Premier Ho. N1—4D 25
Premier Pl. SW15—2A 76
Prendergast Rd. SE3—1A 86
Prentice Ct. SW19—5B 90
Prentis Rd. SW16—4F 93
Prentiss Ct. SE7—5F 59
Presburg St. E5—5F 13
Prescot St. E1—1B 54
Prescott Ho. SE5—2D 67 (off Hillingdon St.)
Prescott Pl. SW4—1F 79
Presentation M. SW2—2B 94
President Dri. E1—2D 55
President Ho. EC1—2D 39
President Quay. E1—2B 54 (off St Katherine's Way)
President St. EC1—2E 39 (off Central St.)
Press Ho. NW10—5A 4
Press Rd. NW10—5A 4
Prestage Way. E14—1E 57
Prestbury Rd. E7—4E 31
Prested Rd. SW11—2A 78
Prestige Way. NW4—1E 5
Preston Clo. SE1—5A 54

Preston Dri.—Priory Ho.

Preston Dri. *E11* —1E **17**
Preston Gdns. *NW10* —3B **18**
Preston Ho. *SE1* —4B **54**
  (off Stanworth St.)
Preston Ho. *SE17* —5A **54**
  (off Preston Clo.)
Preston Pl. *NW2* —3C **18**
Preston Rd. *E11* —1A **16**
Preston Rd. *SE19* —5D **95**
Preston's Rd. *E14* —1E **57**
Prestwich Ter. *SW4* —3E **79**
Prestwood Ho. *SE16* —4D **55**
  (off Drummond Rd.)
Prestwood St. *N1* —1E **39**
Pretoria Rd. *E11* —3F **15**
Pretoria Rd. *E16* —3B **44**
Pretoria Rd. *SW16* —5D **93**
Priam Ho. *E2* —1D **41**
  (off Old Bethnal Grn. Rd.)
Price Clo. *SW17* —3B **92**
Price' St. *SW11* —1F **77**
Price Ho. *N1* —5E **25**
  (off Britannia Row)
Price's St. *SE1* —2D **53**
Price's Yd. *N1* —5B **24**
Prichard Ct. *N7* —3B **24**
Prideaux Pl. *W3* —1A **46**
Prideaux Pl. *WC1* —2B **38**
Prideaux Rd. *SW9* —1A **80**
Priestfield Rd. *SE23* —3A **98**
Priestley Clo. *N16* —2B **12**
Priestley Ho. *EC1* —3E **39**
  (off Old St.)
Priestley Way. *NW2* —3C **4**
Priest's Bri. *SW14 & SW15*
  —1A **74**
Priest's Ct. *EC2* —5E **39**
  (off Foster La.)
Prima Rd. *SW9* —3C **66**
Prime Meridian Line, The.
  —3F **71**
Primrose Clo. *SE6* —5E **99**
Primrose Clo. *SW12* —5F **79**
Primrose Gdns. *NW3* —3A **22**
Primrose Hill. —5C 22
Primrose Hill. *EC4* —5C **38**
Primrose Hill Ct. *NW3* —4B **22**
Primrose Hill Rd. *NW3*
  —4B **22**
Primrose Hill Studios. *NW1*
  —5C **22**
Primrose Mans. *SW11*
  —4C **64**
Primrose M. *NW1* —4B **22**
  (off Sharpleshall St.)
Primrose M. *SE3* —3C **72**
Primrose Rd. *E10* —3D **15**
Primrose Sq. *E9* —4E **27**
Primrose St. *EC2* —4A **40**
Primrose Wlk. *SE14* —3A **70**
Primula St. *W12* —5C **32**
Prince Albert Ct. *NW8* —5B **22**
  (off Prince Albert Rd.)
Prince Albert Rd. *NW1 &*
  NW8 —2A **36**
Prince Arthur M. *NW3* —1E **21**

Prince Arthur Rd. *NW3*
  —2E **21**
Prince Charles Dri. *NW4*
  —2E **5**
Prince Charles Rd. *SE3*
  —5B **72**
Prince Consort Rd. *SW7*
  —4E **49**
Princedale Rd. *W11* —2A **48**
Prince Edward Mans. *W2*
  (off Hereford Rd.) —1C **48**
Prince Edward Rd. *E9* —3B **28**
Prince George Rd. *N16*
  —1A **26**
Prince Henry Rd. *SE7* —3F **73**
Prince John Rd. *SE9* —3F **87**
Princelet St. *E1* —4B **40**
Prince of Wales Dri. *SW11 &*
  SW8 —4A **64**
Prince of Wales Mans. *SW11*
  —4C **64**
Prince of Wales Pas. *NW1*
  (off Hampstead Rd.) —2E **37**
Prince of Wales Rd. *E16*
  —5E **45**
Prince of Wales Rd. *NW5*
  —3C **22**
Prince of Wales Rd. *SE3*
  —5B **72**
Prince of Wales Ter. *W4*
  —1A **60**
Prince of Wales Ter. *W8*
  —3D **49**
Prince Regent Ct. *NW8*
  (off Avenue Rd.) —1A **36**
Prince Regent Ct. *SE16*
  (off Edward Sq.) —1A **56**
Prince Regent La. *E13 & E16*
  —2D **45**
Prince Regent M. *NW1*
  (off Hampstead Rd.) —2E **37**
Prince Regent's Ga. *NW8*
  —3A **36**
Princes Arc. *W1* —2E **51**
  (off Piccadilly)
Princes Cir. *WC2* —5A **38**
Princes Clo. *N4* —3D **11**
Princes Clo. *SW4* —1E **79**
Princes Ct. *SE16* —4B **56**
Prince's Ct. *SW3* —4B **50**
  (off Brompton Rd.)
Prince Ct. Bus. Cen. *E1*
  —1D **55**
Prince's Gdns. *SW7* —4F **49**
Prince's Ga. *SW7* —3F **49**
  (in six parts)
Prince's Ga. Ct. *SW7* —3F **49**
Prince's Ga. M. *SW7* —4F **49**
Prince's M. *W2* —1D **49**
Princes Pde. *NW11* —1A **6**
  (off Golders Grn. Rd.)
Princes Pk. Av. *NW11* —1A **6**
Princes Pl. *SW1* —2E **51**
  (off Duke St.)
Princes Pl. *W11* —2A **48**
Prince's Ri. *SE13* —5E **71**

Princes Riverside Rd. *SE16*
  —2F **55**
Princes Rd. *SW14* —1A **74**
Prince's Rd. *SW19* —5C **90**
Princess Alice Ho. *W10*
  —3E **33**
Princess Ct. *N6* —2E **9**
Princess Ct. *W1* —4B **36**
  (off Bryanston Pl.)
Princess Ct. *W2* —1D **49**
  (off Queensway)
Princess Cres. *N4* —4D **11**
Princess Louise Clo. *W2*
  —4F **35**
Princess Mary Ho. *SW1*
  (off Vincent St.) —5F **51**
Princess May Rd. *N16*
  —1A **26**
Princess M. *NW3* —2F **21**
Prince's Sq. *W2* —1D **49**
Princess Rd. *NW1* —5C **22**
Princess Rd. *NW6* —1C **34**
Princess St. *SE1* —4D **53**
Princess St. *EC2* —5F **39**
Princes St. *W1* —5D **37**
Princes Ter. *E13* —5D **31**
Prince St. *SE8* —2B **70**
Princes Way. *SW19* —5F **75**
Prince's Yd. *W11* —2A **48**
  (off Princedale Rd.)
Princethorpe Ho. *W2* —4D **35**
  (off Woodchester Sq.)
Princethorpe Rd. *SE2* —4F **97**
Princeton Ct. *SW15* —1F **75**
Princeton St. *WC1* —4B **38**
Principal Sq. *E9* —2F **27**
Pringle Gdns. *SW16* —4E **93**
  (in two parts)
Pring St. *W10* —1F **47**
Printers Inn Ct. *EC4* —5C **38**
Printers M. *E3* —5A **28**
Printer St. *EC4* —5C **38**
Printing Ho. Yd. *E2* —2A **40**
Printon Ho. *E3* —4B **42**
Print Village. *SE15* —5B **68**
Priolo Rd. *SE7* —1E **73**
Prior Bolton St. *N1* —3D **25**
Prioress Rd. *SE27* —3D **95**
Prioress St. *SE1* —4A **54**
Prior St. *SE10* —3E **71**
Priory Av. *E17* —1C **14**
Priory Av. *W4* —5A **46**
Priory Ct. *E6* —5E **31**
Priory Ct. *E9* —2F **27**
Priory Ct. *EC4* —5D **39**
  (off Pilgrim St.)
Priory Ct. *SW8* —4F **65**
Priory Gdns. *N6* —1D **9**
Priory Gdns. *SW13* —1B **74**
Priory Gdns. *W4* —5A **46**
Priory Grn. Est. *N1* —1B **38**
Priory Gro. *SW8* —4A **66**
Priory Ho. *E1* —4B **40**
  (off Folgate St.)
Priory Ho. *EC1* —3D **39**
  (off Sans Wlk.)

236 Mini London

Priory Ho. *SW1* —1F **65**
(off Rampayne St.)
Priory La. *SW15* —4A **74**
Priory M. *SW8* —4A **66**
Priory Pk. *SE3* —1B **86**
Priory Pk. Rd. *NW6* —5B **20**
(in two parts)
Priory Rd. *E6* —5F **31**
Priory Rd. *NW6* —5D **21**
Priory St. *E3* —2D **43**
Priory Ter. *NW6* —5D **21**
Priory, The. *SE3* —2B **86**
(in two parts)
Priory Wlk. *SW10* —1E **63**
Pritchard Ho. *E2* —1D **41**
(off Ada Pl.)
Pritchard's Rd. *E2* —5C **26**
Priter Rd. *SE16* —4C **54**
Priter Way. *SE16* —4C **54**
Probert Rd. *SW2* —3C **80**
Probyn Ho. *SW1* —5F **51**
(off Page St.)
Probyn Rd. *SW2* —2D **95**
Procter Ho. *SE1* —1C **68**
(off Avondale Sq.)
Procter Ho. *SE5* —3F **67**
(off Picton St.)
Procter St. *WC1* —4B **38**
Project Pk. *E3* —3F **43**
Promenade App. Rd. *W4*
—3A **60**
Promenade, The. *W4* —5A **60**
Prospect Clo. *SE26* —4D **97**
Prospect Cotts. *SW18*
—2C **76**
Prospect Ho. *N1* —1C **38**
(off Donegal St.)
Prospect Ho. *SE1* —4D **53**
(off Gaywood St.)
Prospect Ho. *SE8* —2B **70**
(off Evelyn St.)
Prospect Pl. *E1* —2E **55**
Prospect Pl. *N7* —1A **24**
Prospect Pl. *NW2* —5B **6**
Prospect Pl. *NW3* —1E **21**
Prospect Pl. *W4* —1A **60**
Prospect Quay. *SW18* —2C **76**
(off Lightermans Wlk.)
Prospect Rd. *NW2* —5B **6**
Prospect St. *SE16* —4D **55**
Prospect Va. *SE18* —5F **59**
Prospect Wharf. *E1* —1E **55**
Prospero Rd. *N19* —3F **9**
Protea Clo. *E16* —3B **44**
Prothero Rd. *SW6* —3A **62**
Prout Gro. *NW10* —1A **18**
Prout Rd. *E5* —5D **13**
Provence St. *N1* —1E **39**
Providence Clo. *E9* —5F **27**
Providence Ct. *W1* —1C **50**
Providence Pl. *N1* —5D **25**
Providence Row. *N1* —1B **38**
(off Pentonville Rd.)
Providence Row Clo. *E2*
—2D **41**
Providence Sq. *SE1* —3C **54**

Providence Tower. *SE16*
—3C **54**
(off Bermondsey Wall W.)
Providence Yd. *E2* —2C **40**
(off Ezra St.)
Provost Est. *N1* —1F **39**
(off Provost St.)
Provost Rd. *NW3* —4B **22**
Provost St. *N1* —1F **39**
Prowse Pl. *NW1* —4E **23**
Prudent Pas. *EC2* —5E **39**
(off King St.)
Prusom St. *E1* —2D **55**
Pryors, The. *NW3* —5F **7**
Pudding La. *EC3* —1F **53**
Pudding Mill La. *E15* —5D **29**
Puddle Dock. *EC4* —1D **53**
(in two parts)
Pugin Ct. *N1* —4C **24**
(off Liverpool Rd.)
Pulborough Rd. *SW18*
—5B **76**
Pulford Rd. *N15* —1F **11**
Pulham Ho. *SW8* —3B **66**
(off Dorset Rd.)
Pullen's Bldgs. *SE17* —1D **67**
(off Iliffe St.)
Pullman Ct. *SW2* —1A **94**
Pullman Gdns. *SW15* —4E **75**
Pullman M. *SE12* —3D **101**
Pulross Rd. *SW9* —1B **80**
Pulteney Clo. *E3* —5B **28**
Pulteney Ter. *N1* —5B **24**
(in two parts)
Pulton Ho. *SE4* —2A **84**
(off Turnham Rd.)
Pulton Pl. *SW6* —3C **62**
Puma Ct. *E1* —4B **40**
Pump Ct. *EC4* —5C **38**
Pumping Sta. Rd. *W4* —3A **60**
Pump La. *SE14* —3E **69**
Punderson's Gdns. *E2*
—2D **41**
Purbeck Dri. *NW2* —4F **5**
Purbeck Ho. *SW8* —3B **66**
(off Bolney St.)
Purbrook Est. *SE1* —3A **54**
Purbrook St. *SE1* —4A **54**
Purcell Cres. *SW6* —3F **61**
Purcell Ho. *SW10* —2F **63**
(off Milman's St.)
Purcell Mans. *W14* —2A **62**
(off Queen's Club Gdns.)
Purcell M. *NW10* —4A **18**
Purcell St. *N1* —1A **40**
Purchese St. *NW1* —1F **37**
Purdon Ho. *SE15* —4C **68**
(off Peckham High St.)
Purdy St. *E3* —3D **43**
Purelake M. *SE13* —1F **85**
(off Marischal Rd.)
Purley Av. *NW2* —4A **6**
Purley Pl. *N1* —4D **25**
Purneys Rd. *SE9* —2F **87**
Purser Ho. *SW2* —4C **80**
(off Tulse Hill)

Pursers Cross Rd. *SW6*
(in two parts) —4B **62**
Purves Rd. *NW10* —2D **33**
Pusey Ho. *E14* —5C **42**
Putney. —2A 76
Putney Bri. *SW15 & SW6*
—1A **76**
Putney Bri. App. *SW6* —1A **76**
Putney Bri. Rd. *SW15 &*
SW18 —2A **76**
Putney Comn. *SW15* —1E **75**
Putney Exchange Shop. Cen.
SW15 —2F **75**
Putney Heath. —4E 75
Putney Heath. *SW15* —5D **75**
Putney Heath La. *SW15*
—4F **75**
Putney High St. *SW15*
—2F **75**
Putney Hill. *SW15* —5F **75**
(in two parts)
Putney Pk. Av. *SW15* —2C **74**
Putney Pk. La. *SW15* —2D **75**
Putney Vale. —3C 88
Putney Vale Crematorium.
SW15 —2C **88**
Pylon Trad. Est. *E16* —3A **44**
Pymers Mead. *SE21* —1E **95**
Pym Ho. *SW9* —5C **66**
Pynfolds. *SE16* —3D **55**
Pynnersmead. *SE24* —3E **81**
Pyrford Ho. *SW9* —2D **81**
Pyrland Rd. *N5* —2F **25**
Pyrmont Gro. *SE27* —3D **95**
Pytchley Cres. *SE19* —5E **95**
Pytchley Rd. *SE22* —1A **82**

Quadrangle Clo. *SE1* —5A **54**
Quadrangle, The. *SE24*
—3E **81**
Quadrangle, The. *SW10*
—4E **63**
Quadrangle, The. *W2* —5A **36**
Quadrant Arc. *W1* —1E **51**
(off Regent St.)
Quadrant Gro. *NW5* —2B **22**
Quadrant Ho. *SE1* —2D **53**
(off Burrell St.)
Quadrant, The. *W10* —2F **33**
Quaggy Wlk. *SE3* —2C **86**
Quain Mans. *W14* —2A **62**
(off Queen's Club Gdns.)
Quaker Ct. *E1* —3B **40**
(off Quaker St.)
Quaker Ct. *EC1* —3E **39**
(off Banner St.)
Quakers Pl. *E7* —2F **31**
Quaker St. *E1* —3B **40**
Quality Ct. *WC2* —5C **38**
(off Chancery La.)
Quantock Gdns. *NW2* —4F **5**
Quantock Ho. *N16* —3B **12**
Quarley Way. *SE15* —3B **68**
Quarrendon St. *SW6* —5C **62**
Quarry Rd. *SW18* —4E **77**

Quarterdeck, The. *E14* —3C **56**
Quarter Mile La. *E10* —1D **29**
Quay Ho. *E14* —3C **56**
Quayside Cotts. E1 —2C **54**
(off Mew St.)
Quayside Ct. SE16 —2F **55**
(off Abbotshade Rd.)
Quayside Ho. *E14* —2C **56**
Quebec M. *W1* —5B **36**
Quebec Way. SE16 —3F **55**
Quebec Way Ind. Est. *SE16*
—3A **56**
Quedgeley Ct. SE15 —2B **68**
(off Ebley Clo.)
Queen Alexandra Mans. WC1
(off Bidborough St.) —2A **38**
Queen Alexandra's Ct. SW19
—5B **90**
Queen Anne M. *W1* —4D **37**
Queen Anne Rd. *E9* —3F **27**
Queen Anne's Ct. SE10
(off Park Row) —1F **71**
Queen Anne's Gdns. *W4*
—4A **46**
Queen Annes Ga. *SW1*
—3F **51**
Queen Anne's Gro. *W4*
—4A **46**
Queen Anne St. *W1* —4D **37**
Queen Anne's Wlk. WC1
(off Queen Sq.) —3A **38**
Queen Anne Ter. *E1* —1D **55**
(off Sovereign Clo.)
Queen Caroline St. *W6*
—5E **47**
Queen Catherine Ho. SW6
(off Wandon Rd.) —3D **63**
Queen Elizabeth Bldgs. EC4
—1C **52**
(off Middle Temple La.)
Queen Elizabeth Hall.
(off Waterloo Rd.) —2B **52**
Queen Elizabeth Ho. *SW12*
—5C **78**
Queen Elizabeth II Conference
Cen. —3F **51**
(off Broad Sanctuary)
Queen Elizabeth's Clo. N16
—4F **11**
Queen Elizabeth's College.
SE10 —3E **71**
Queen Elizabeth St. *SE1*
—3A **54**
Queen Elizabeth's Wlk. N16
—3F **11**
Queen Elizabeth Wlk. *SW13*
—4C **60**
Queenhithe. *EC4* —1E **53**
Queen Margaret Flats. E2
(off St Jude's Rd.) —2D **41**
Queen Margaret's Gro. *N1*
—2A **26**
Queen Mary Rd. *SE19*
—5D **95**
Queen Marys Bldgs. SW1
(off Stillington St.) —5E **51**

Queen Mary's Ct. *SE10*
(off Park Row) —2F **71**
Queen of Denmark Ct. *SE16*
—4B **56**
Queensberry M. W. *SW7*
—5F **49**
Queensberry Pl. *SW7* —5F **49**
Queensberry Way. *SW7*
—5F **49**
Queensborough M. *W2*
—1E **49**
Queensborough Pas. W2
—1E **49**
(off Queensborough M.)
Queensborough Studios. W2
—1E **49**
(off Queensborough M.)
Queensborough Ter. *W2*
—1D **49**
Queensbridge Ct. E2 —5B **26**
(off Queensbridge Rd.)
Queensbridge Rd. *E8 & E2*
—3B **26**
Queensbury St. *N1* —4E **25**
Queen's Cir. *SW8* —3D **65**
Queen's Club. —1A **62**
(Tennis)
Queen's Club Gdns. *W14*
—2A **62**
Queens Ct. *NW6* —2D **21**
Queen's Ct. NW8 —1F **35**
(off Queen's Ter.)
Queens Ct. *SE23* —2D **97**
Queens Ct. W2 —1D **49**
(off Queensway)
Queen's Cres. *NW5* —3C **22**
Queenscroft Rd. *SE9* —3F **87**
Queensdale Cres. *W11*
—2F **47**
Queensdale Pl. *W11* —2A **48**
Queensdale Rd. *W11* —2F **47**
Queensdale Wlk. *W11* —2A **48**
Queensdown Rd. *E5* —1D **27**
Queens Dri. *E10* —2C **14**
Queens Dri. *N4* —4D **11**
Queen's Elm Pde. SW3
(off Old Church St.) —1F **63**
Queen's Elm Sq. *SW3* —1F **63**
Queen's Gdns. *NW4* —1E **5**
Queen's Gdns. *W2* —1E **49**
Queen's Ga. *SW7* —3E **49**
Queen's Ga. Gdns. *SW7*
—4E **49**
Queens Ga. Gdns. *SW15*
—2D **75**
Queensgate Pl. *NW6* —4C **20**
Queen's Ga. Pl. *SW7* —4E **49**
Queen's Ga. Pl. M. *SW7*
—4E **49**
Queen's Ga. Ter. *SW7* —4E **49**
Queen's Gro. *NW8* —5F **21**
Queen's Gro. Studios. *NW8*
—5F **21**
Queen's Head St. *N1* —5D **25**

Queen's Head Yd. *SE1* —2F **53**
(off Borough High St.)
Queens Ho. *SW8* —3A **66**
(off S. Lambeth Rd.)
Queen's House, The. —2F **71**
(off Romney Rd.)
Queen's Ice Rink. —1D **49**
Queensland Pl. *N7* —1C **24**
Queensland Rd. *N7* —1C **24**
Queen's Mkt. *E13* —5E **31**
Queensmead. *NW8* —5F **21**
Queensmere Clo. *SW19*
—2F **89**
Queensmere Ct. *SW13*
—3B **60**
Queensmere Rd. *SW19*
—2F **89**
Queen's M. *W2* —1D **49**
(in two parts)
Queensmill Rd. *SW6* —3F **61**
Queen's Pde. NW2 —3E **19**
(off Walm La.)
Queens Pde. NW4 —1E **5**
(off Queens Rd.)
Queens Pk. Ct. *W10* —2F **33**
Queen's Park Rangers F.C.
—2D **47**
Queen Sq. *WC1* —3A **38**
Queen Sq. Pl. WC1 —3A **38**
(off Queen Sq.)
Queen's Quay. EC4 —1E **53**
(off Up. Thames St.)
Queens Ride. *SW13 & SW15*
—1C **74**
Queens Rd. *E11* —2F **15**
Queens Rd. *E13* —5D **31**
Queens Rd. *E17* —1B **14**
Queens Rd. *NW4* —1E **5**
Queen's Rd. *SE15 & SE14*
—4D **69**
Queen's Rd. *SW14* —1A **74**
Queens Rd. *SW19* —5C **90**
Queens Rd. W. *E13* —1C **44**
Queen's Row. *SE17* —2F **67**
Queen's Ter. *E1* —3E **41**
Queen's Ter. *E13* —5D **31**
Queen's Ter. *NW8* —5F **21**
Queensthorpe Rd. *SE26*
—4F **97**
Queenstown M. *SW11*
—5D **65**
Queenstown Rd. *SW8*
—2D **65**
Queen St. *EC4* —1E **53**
(in two parts)
Queen St. *W1* —2D **51**
Queen St. Pl. *EC4* —1E **53**
Queensville Rd. *SW12* —5F **79**
Queens Wlk. *SW1* —2E **51**
Queen's Wlk., The. SE1
(off Waterloo Rd.) —2B **52**
Queen's Wlk., The. SE1
(Barge Ho.) —1C **52**
Queen's Wlk., The. SE1
(Morgan's La.) —2A **54**
Queen's Way. *NW4* —1E **5**

Queensway. W2 —5D 35
Queens Wharf. W6 —1E 61
Queenswood Ct. SE27 —4F 95
Queenswood Ct. SW4 —3A 80
Queenswood Gdns. E11 —3D 17
Queens Wood Rd. N10 —1D 9
Queenswood Rd. SE23 —3F 97
Queen's Yd. W1 —4E 37
Queen Victoria Memorial. —3E 51
Queen Victoria Seaman's Rest. E14 —5D 43
Queen Victoria St. EC4 —1D 53
Queen Victoria Ter. E1 —1D 55 (off Sovereign Clo.)
Quemerford Rd. N7 —2B 24
Quendon Ho. W10 —3E 33 (off Sutton Way)
Quenington Ct. SE15 —2B 68
Quentin Ho. SE1 —3C 52 (off Gray St., in two parts)
Quentin Pl. SE13 —1A 86
Quentin Rd. SE3 —1A 86
Quernmore Clo. Brom —5C 100
Quernmore Rd. N4 —1C 10
Quernmore Rd. Brom —5C 100
Querrin St. SW6 —5E 63
Quested Ct. E8 —2D 27 (off Brett Rd.)
Quex M. NW6 —5C 20
Quex Rd. NW6 —5C 20
Quick Rd. W4 —1A 60
Quick St. N1 —1D 39
Quick St. M. N1 —1D 39
Quickswood. NW3 —4A 22
Quill La. SW15 —2F 75
Quill St. N4 —5C 10
Quilp St. SE1 —3E 53 (in two parts)
Quilter Ho. W10 —2B 34
Quilter St. E2 —2C 40
Quinton Ho. SW8 —3A 66 (off Wyvil Rd.)
Quinton St. SW18 —2E 91
Quixley St. E14 —1F 57
Quorn Rd. SE22 —2A 82

Rabbit Row. W8 —2C 48
Raby St. E14 —5A 42
Rachel Point. E5 —1C 26
Racine. SE5 —4A 68 (off Peckham Rd.)
Rackham M. SW16 —5E 93
Rackstraw Ho. NW3 —4B 22
Racton Rd. SW6 —2C 62
Radbourne Clo. E5 —1F 27
Radbourne Rd. SW12 —5E 79
Radcliffe Av. NW10 —1C 32
Radcliffe Ho. SE16 —5D 55 (off Anchor St.)
Radcliffe Path. SW8 —5D 65
Radcliffe Rd. SE1 —4A 54
Radcliffe Sq. SW15 —4F 75
Radcot Point. SE23 —3F 97
Radcot St. SE11 —1C 66
Raddington Rd. W10 —4A 34
Radford Ho. E14 —4D 43
Radford Ho. N7 —2B 24
Radford Rd. SE13 —4E 85
Radipole Rd. SW6 —4B 62
Radland Rd. E16 —5B 44
Radlet Av. SE26 —3D 97
Radlett Clo. E7 —3B 30
Radlett Pl. NW8 —5A 22
Radley Ct. SE16 —3F 55
Radley Ho. NW1 —3B 36 (off Gloucester Pl.)
Radley M. W8 —4C 48
Radley Sq. E5 —4E 13
Radley Ter. E16 —4B 44 (off Hermit Rd.)
Radlix Rd. E10 —3C 14
Radnor M. W2 —5F 35
Radnor Pl. W2 —5A 36
Radnor Rd. NW6 —5A 20
Radnor Rd. SE15 —3C 68
Radnor St. EC1 —2E 39
Radnor Ter. W14 —5B 48
Radnor Wlk. E14 —5C 56 (off Barnsdale Av.)
Radnor Wlk. SW3 —1A 64
Radstock St. SW11 —3A 64 (in two parts)
Raeburn Clo. NW11 —1E 7
Raeburn St. SW2 —2A 80
Raffles Sq. E15 —4F 29
Raglan Ct. SE12 —3C 86
Raglan Rd. E17 —1E 15
Raglan St. NW5 —3D 23
Railey M. NW5 —2E 23
Railton Rd. SE24 —2C 80
Railway App. N4 —1C 10
Railway App. SE1 —2F 53
Railway Arches. E10 —2D 15 (off Capworth St.)
Railway Arches. E11 —4A 16 (off Leytonstone High Rd.)
Railway Arches. E11 —3F 15 (off Sidings, The)
Railway Arches. E17 —1C 14 (off Yunus Khan Clo.)
Railway Av. SE16 —3E 55 (in two parts)
Railway Children Wlk. Brom —2C 100
Railway Cotts. SW19 —4D 91
Railway Gro. SE14 —3B 70
Railway M. E3 —2C 42 (off Wellington Way)
Railway M. W11 —5A 34
Railway Ri. SE22 —2A 82
Railway Side. SW13 —1A 74 (in two parts)
Railway St. N1 —1A 38
Railway Ter. SE13 —3D 85
Rainbow Av. E14 —1D 71
Rainbow Ct. SE14 —2A 70 (off Chipley St.)
Rainbow Quay. SE16 —4A 56
Rainbow St. SE5 —3A 68
Raine St. E1 —2D 55
Rainham Clo. SW11 —4A 78
Rainham Ho. NW1 —5E 23 (off Bayham Pl.)
Rainham Rd. NW10 —2E 33
Rainhill Way. E3 —2C 42 (in two parts)
Rainsborough Av. SE8 —5A 56
Rainsford St. W2 —5A 36
Rainton Rd. SE7 —1C 72
Rainville Rd. W6 —2E 61
Raleana Rd. E14 —2E 57
Raleigh Clo. NW4 —1E 5
Raleigh Ct. SE16 —2F 55 (off Clarence M.)
Raleigh Gdns. SW2 —4B 80
Raleigh Ho. E14 —3D 57 (off Admirals Way)
Raleigh Ho. SW1 —2F 65 (off Dolphin Sq.)
Raleigh M. N1 —5D 25 (off Packington St.)
Raleigh St. N1 —5D 25
Ralph Brook Ct. N1 —2F 39 (off Chart St.)
Ralph Ct. W2 —5D 35 (off Queensway)
Ralston St. SW3 —1B 64
Ramac Ind. Est. SE7 —5D 59
Ramac Way. SE7 —5D 59
Ramar Ho. E1 —4C 40 (off Hanbury St.)
Rambler Clo. SW16 —4E 93
Rame Clo. SW17 —5C 92
Ramilles Clo. SW2 —4A 80
Ramillies Pl. W1 —5E 37
Ramillies Rd. W4 —5A 46
Ramillies St. W1 —5E 37
Rampart St. E1 —5D 41
Rampayne St. SW1 —1F 65
Ram Pl. E9 —3E 27
Ramsay Ho. NW8 —1A 36 (off Townshend Est.)
Ramsay M. SW3 —2A 64
Ramsay Rd. E7 —1A 30
Ramsdale Rd. SW17 —5C 92
Ramsden Rd. SW12 —4C 78
Ramsey Clo. NW9 —1B 4
Ramsey Ho. SW9 —3C 66 (off Vassall Rd.)
Ramsey St. E2 —3C 40
Ramsey Wlk. N1 —3F 25 (off Handa Wlk.)
Ramsfort Ho. SE16 —5D 55 (off Camilla Rd.)
Ramsgate Clo. E16 —2D 59
Ramsgate St. E8 —3B 26
Ram St. SW18 —3D 77
Rancliffe Gdns. SE9 —2F 87
Randall Av. NW2 —4A 4

Randall Clo. *SW11* —4A **64**
Randall Pl. *SE10* —3E **71**
Randall Rd. *SE11* —1B **66**
Randall Row. *SE11* —5B **52**
Randalls Rents. SE16 —4B **56**
(off Gulliver St.)
Randell's Rd. *N1* —5A **24**
(in two parts)
Randisbourne Gdns. *SE6*
—3D **99**
Randlesdown Rd. *SE6*
(in two parts) —4C **98**
Randolph App. *E16* —5E **45**
Randolph Av. *W9* —1D **35**
Randolph Cres. *W9* —3E **35**
Randolph Gdns. *NW6* —1D **35**
Randolph M. *W9* —3E **35**
Randolph Rd. *E17* —1D **15**
Randolph Rd. *W9* —3E **35**
Randolph St. *NW1* —4E **23**
Ranelagh Av. *SW6* —1B **76**
Ranelagh Av. *SW13* —5C **60**
Ranelagh Bri. *W2* —4D **35**
Ranelagh Gdns. *SW6* —1A **76**
Ranelagh Gdns. *W6* —5B **46**
Ranelagh Gdns. Mans. SW6
(off Ranelagh Gdns.) —1A **76**
Ranelagh Gro. *SW1* —1C **64**
Ranelagh Ho. SW3 —1B **64**
(off Elystan Pl.)
Ranelagh Rd. *E11* —1A **30**
Ranelagh Rd. *E15* —1A **44**
Ranelagh Rd. *NW10* —1B **32**
Ranelagh Rd. *SW1* —1E **65**
Rangbourne Ho. *N7* —2A **24**
Rangefield Rd. *Brom*
—5A **100**
Rangemoor Rd. *N15* —1B **12**
Ranger's House. —4F **71**
Rangers Sq. *SE10* —4F **71**
Rangoon St. EC3 —5B **40**
(off Crutched Friars)
Rankine Ho. SE1 —4E **53**
(off Bath Ter.)
Ranmere St. *SW12* —1D **93**
Rannoch Rd. *W6* —2E **61**
Rannock Av. *NW9* —2A **4**
Ransome's Dock Bus. Cen.
SW11 —3A **64**
Ransom Rd. *SE7* —5E **59**
Ranston St. *NW1* —4A **36**
Ranulf Rd. *NW2* —1B **20**
Ranwell Clo. *E3* —5B **28**
Rapesco Ho. SE14 —3A **70**
(off Goodwood Rd.)
Raphael Ct. SE16 —1D **69**
(off Stubbs Dri.)
Raphael St. *SW7* —3B **50**
Rapley Ho. E2 —2C **40**
(off Turin St.)
Rashleigh Ct. *SW8* —5D **65**
Rashleigh Ho. WC1 —2A **38**
(off Thanet St.)
Rastell Av. *SW2* —2F **93**
Ratcliff. —5A **42**
Ratcliffe Clo. *SE12* —5C **86**

Ratcliffe Cross St. *E1* —5F **41**
Ratcliffe Ho. *E14* —5A **42**
Ratcliffe La. *E1* —5A **42**
Ratcliffe La. *E14* —5A **42**
Ratcliff Orchard. *E1* —1F **55**
Ratcliff Rd. *E7* —2E **31**
Rathbone Ho. *NW6* —5C **20**
Rathbone Mkt. *E16* —4B **44**
Rathbone Pl. *W1* —4F **37**
Rathbone Point. *E5* —1C **26**
Rathbone St. *E16* —4B **44**
Rathbone St. *W1* —4E **37**
Rathcoole Gdns. *N8* —1B **10**
Rathfern Rd. *SE6* —1B **98**
Rathgar Rd. *SW9* —1D **81**
Rathlin Wlk. *N1* —3F **25**
Rathmell Dri. *SW4* —4F **79**
Rathmore Rd. *SE7* —1D **73**
Rattray Ct. *SE6* —2B **100**
Rattray Rd. *SW2* —2C **80**
Raul Rd. *SE15* —5C **68**
Raveley St. *NW5* —1E **23**
(in two parts)
Ravenet St. *SW11* —4D **65**
Ravenfield Rd. *SW17* —3B **92**
Ravenhill Rd. *E13* —1E **45**
Raven Ho. SE16 —5F **55**
(off Tawny Way)
Ravenna Rd. *SW15* —3F **75**
Raven Row. *E1* —4D **41**
Ravensbourne Ct. *SE6*
—5C **84**
Ravensbourne Ho. NW8
(off Broadley St.) —4A **36**
Ravensbourne Ho. *Brom*
—5F **99**
Ravensbourne Mans. SE8
(off Berthon St.) —2C **70**
Ravensbourne Pk. *SE6*
—5C **84**
Ravensbourne Pk. Cres. *SE6*
—5B **84**
Ravensbourne Pl. *SE13*
—5D **71**
Ravensbourne Rd. *SE6*
—5B **84**
Ravensbury Rd. *SW18*
—2C **90**
Ravensbury Ter. *SW18*
—2D **91**
Ravenscar. NW1 —5E **23**
(off Bayham St.)
Ravenscar Rd. *Brom* —4A **100**
Ravenscourt Av. *W6* —5C **46**
Ravenscourt Gdns. *W6*
—5C **46**
Ravenscourt Pk. *W6* —4C **46**
Ravenscourt Pk. Mans. W6
—4D **47**
(off Paddenswick Rd.)
Ravenscourt Pl. *W6* —5D **47**
Ravenscourt Rd. *W6* —5D **47**
(in two parts)
Ravenscourt Sq. *W6* —4C **46**
Ravenscroft Av. *NW11* —2B **6**
Ravenscroft Clo. *E16* —4C **44**

Ravenscroft Rd. *E16* —4C **44**
Ravenscroft St. *E2* —1B **40**
Ravensdale Rd. *N16* —2B **12**
Ravensdon St. *SE11* —1C **66**
Ravenshaw St. *NW6* —2B **20**
Ravenslea Rd. *SW12* —5B **78**
Ravensleigh Gdns. Brom
—5D **101**
Ravensmede Way. *W4*
—5B **46**
Ravenstone. *SE17* —1A **68**
Ravenstone Rd. *NW9* —1B **4**
Ravenstone St. *SW12* —1C **92**
Ravens Way. *SE12* —3C **86**
Ravenswood Rd. *SW12*
—5D **79**
Ravensworth Rd. *NW10*
—2D **33**
Ravent Rd. *SE11* —5B **52**
Ravey St. *EC2* —3A **40**
Rav Pinter Clo. N16 —2A **12**
Rawalpindi Ho. *E16* —3B **44**
Rawchester Clo. *SW18*
—1B **90**
Rawlings St. *SW3* —5B **50**
Rawlinson Ct. *NW2* —2E **5**
Rawlinson Ho. SE13 —2F **85**
(off Mercator Rd.)
Rawlinson Point. E16 —4B **44**
(off Fox Rd.)
Rawreth Wlk. N1 —5E **25**
(off Basire St.)
Rawson St. *SW11* —4C **64**
(in two parts)
Rawstone Wlk. *E13* —1C **44**
Rawstorne Pl. *EC1* —2D **39**
Rawstorne St. *EC1* —2D **39**
Rayburne Ct. *W14* —4A **48**
Raydon St. *N19* —4D **9**
Rayford Av. *SE12* —5B **86**
Ray Gunter Ho. SE17 —1D **67**
(off Marsland Clo.)
Ray Ho. N1 —5F **25**
(off Colville Est.)
Rayleigh Rd. *E16* —2D **59**
Raymede Towers. W10
(off Treverton St.) —4F **33**
Raymond Bldgs. *WC1* —4B **38**
Raymond Clo. *SE26* —5E **97**
Raymond Rd. *E13* —5E **31**
Raymond Rd. *SW19* —5A **90**
Raymouth Ho. SE16 —5B **55**
(off Rotherhithe New Rd.)
Raymouth Rd. *SE16* —5D **55**
Raynald Ho. *SW16* —3A **94**
Rayne Ho. *W9* —3D **35**
(off Delaware Rd.)
Rayners Rd. *SW15* —3A **76**
Rayner Towers. E10 —2C **14**
(off Albany Rd.)
Raynes Av. *E11* —2E **17**
Raynham. W2 —5A **36**
(off Norfolk Cres.)
Raynham Rd. *W6* —5D **47**
Raynor Pl. *N1* —4E **25**

Ray St. *EC1* —3C **38**
*Ray St. Bri. EC1 —3C **38***
(off Farringdon Rd.)
Ray Wlk. *N7* —4B **10**
Reachview Clo. *NW1* —4E **23**
Read Ct. *E17* —1C **14**
*Reade Ho. SE10 —2F **71***
(off Trafalgar Gro.)
Reade Wlk. *NW10* —4A **18**
*Read Ho. SE11 —2C **66***
(off Clayton St.)
*Reading Ho. SE15 —2C **68***
(off Friary Est.)
*Reading Ho. W2 —5E **35***
(off Hallfield Est.)
Reading La. *E8* —3D **27**
Reapers Clo. *NW1* —5F **23**
*Reardon Ho. E1 —2D **55***
(off Reardon St.)
Reardon Path. *E1* —2D **55**
(in two parts)
Reardon St. *E1* —2D **55**
Reaston St. *SE14* —3F **69**
Reckitt Rd. *W4* —1A **60**
Record St. *SE15* —2E **69**
Recovery St. *SW17* —5A **92**
Recreation Rd. *SE26* —4F **97**
Rector St. *N1* —5E **25**
Rectory Cres. *E11* —1E **17**
(in two parts)
Rectory Fld. Cres. *SE7* —3E **73**
Rectory Gdns. *SW4* —1E **79**
Rectory Gro. *SW4* —1E **79**
Rectory La. *SW17* —5C **92**
Rectory Orchard. *SW19* —4A **90**
Rectory Rd. *N16* —4B **12**
Rectory Rd. *SW13* —5C **60**
Rectory Sq. *E1* —4F **41**
*Reculver Ho. SE15 —2E **69***
(off Lovelinch Clo.)
Reculver Rd. *SE16* —1F **69**
Red Anchor Clo. *SW3* —2F **63**
Redan Pl. *W2* —5D **35**
Redan St. *W14* —4F **47**
Redan Ter. *SE5* —5D **67**
Redberry Gro. *SE26* —3E **97**
Redbourne Ho. *E14* —5B **42**
*Redbourn Ho. W10 —3E **33***
(off Sutton Way)
Redbridge. —1F 17
Redbridge Gdns. *SE5* —3A **68**
Redbridge La. E. *Ilf* —1F **17**
Redbridge La. W. *E11* —1D **17**
Redbridge Roundabout. (Junct.) —1F **17**
Redburn St. *SW3* —2B **64**
Redcar St. *SE5* —3E **67**
Redcastle Clo. *E1* —1E **55**
Redchurch St. *E1* —3B **40**
*Redcliffe Clo. SW5 —1D **63***
(off Old Brompton Rd.)
Redcliffe Gdns. *SW5 & SW10* —1D **63**
Redcliffe M. *SW10* —1D **63**
Redcliffe Pl. *SW10* —2E **63**
Redcliffe Rd. *SW10* —1E **63**
Redcliffe Sq. *SW10* —1D **63**
Redcliffe St. *SW10* —2D **63**
Redclyffe Rd. *E6* —5E **31**
*Redclyf Ho. E1 —3E **41***
(off Cephas St.)
Redcross Way. *SE1* —3E **53**
Redding Ho. *SE18* —4F **59**
Reddins Rd. *SE15* —2C **68**
Redenham Ho. SW15
*(off Ellisfield Dri.) —5C **74***
Rede Pl. *W2* —5C **34**
Redesdale St. *SW3* —2A **64**
*Redfern Ho. E15 —5B **30***
(off Redriffe Rd.)
Redfern Rd. *NW10* —4A **18**
Redfern Rd. *SE6* —5E **85**
Redfield La. *SW5* —5C **48**
Redfield M. *SW5* —5D **49**
*Redford Wlk. N1 —5E **25***
(off Popham St.)
Redgate Ter. *SW15* —4F **75**
Redgrave Rd. *SW15* —1F **75**
*Redgrave Ter. E2 —2C **40***
(off Derbyshire St.)
Redhill Ct. *SW2* —2C **94**
Redhill St. *NW1* —1D **37**
*Red Ho. Sq. N1 —4E **25***
(off Ashby Gro.)
Redington Gdns. *NW3* —1D **21**
*Redington Ho. N1 —1B **38***
(off Priory Grn. Est.)
Redington Rd. *NW3* —5D **7**
Redlands Way. *SW2* —5B **80**
*Red Lion Clo. SE17 —2F **67***
(off Red Lion Row)
Red Lion Ct. *EC4* —5C **38**
Red Lion Ct. *SE1* —2E **53**
Red Lion Row. *SE17* —2E **67**
Red Lion Sq. *SW18* —3C **76**
Red Lion Sq. *WC1* —4B **38**
Red Lion St. *WC1* —4B **38**
*Red Lion Yd. W1 —2D **51***
(off Waverton St.)
*Redman Ho. EC1 —4C **38***
(off Bourne Est.)
*Redman Ho. SE1 —3E **53***
(off Borough High St.)
Redman's Rd. *E1* —4E **41**
Redmead La. *E1* —2C **54**
*Redmill Ho. E1 —3D **41***
(off Headlam St.)
*Redmond Ho. N1 —5B **24***
(off Barnsbury Est.)
Redmore Rd. *W6* —5D **47**
Red Path. *E9* —3A **28**
Red Pl. *W1* —1C **50**
Red Post Hill. *SE24 & SE21* —2F **81**
Red Post Ho. *E6* —4F **31**
Redriffe Rd. *E13* —5B **30**
Redriff Est. *SE16* —4B **56**
Redriff Rd. *SE16* —5F **55**
Red Rover. (Junct.) —2C **74**
*Redrup Ho. SE14 —2F **69***
(off John Williams Clo.)
Redruth Rd. *E9* —5E **27**
Redstart Clo. *E6* —4F **45**
Redstart Clo. *SE14* —3A **70**
Redvers St. *N1* —2A **40**
Redwald Rd. *E5* —1F **27**
Redwood Clo. *SE16* —2A **56**
Redwood Ct. *N19* —2F **9**
Redwood Ct. *NW6* —4A **20**
*Redwood Mans. W8 —4D **49***
(off Chantry Sq.)
Redwood M. *SW4* —1D **79**
Redwoods. *SW15* —1C **88**
Reece M. *SW7* —5F **49**
Reed Clo. *E16* —4C **44**
Reed Clo. *SE12* —3C **86**
Reedham St. *SE15* —5C **68**
Reedholm Vs. *N16* —1F **25**
Reed's Pl. *NW1* —4E **23**
Reedworth St. *SE11* —5C **52**
Reef Ho. *E14* —4E **57**
Rees St. *N1* —5E **25**
Reets Farm Clo. *NW9* —1A **4**
Reeves Av. *NW9* —2A **4**
*Reeves Ho. SE1 —3C **52***
(off Baylis Rd.)
Reeves M. *W1* —1C **50**
Reeves Rd. *E3* —3D **43**
Reform St. *SW11* —5B **64**
Regal Clo. *E1* —4C **40**
Regal La. *NW1* —5C **22**
Regal Pl. *E3* —2B **42**
*Regal Pl. SW6 —3D **63***
(off Maxwell Rd.)
Regal Row. *SE15* —4E **69**
Regan Way. *N1* —1A **40**
*Regency Ho. NW1 —3D **37***
(off Osnaburgh St.)
Regency Lawn. *NW5* —5D **9**
Regency Lodge. NW3
*(off Adelaide Rd.) —4F **21***
Regency M. *NW10* —3C **18**
Regency Pl. *SW1* —5F **51**
Regency St. *SW1* —5F **51**
*Regency Ter. SW7 —1F **63***
(off Fulham Rd.)
*Regent Ct. NW8 —2A **36***
(off North Bank)
*Regent Ho. W14 —5A **48***
(off Windsor Way)
Regent Pl. *SW19* —5E **91**
Regent Pl. *W1* —1E **51**
Regent Rd. *SE24* —4D **81**
Regent's Bri. Gdns. *SW8* —3A **66**
Regents Canal Ho. *E14* —5A **42**
*Regents Ct. E8 —5B **26***
(off Pownall Rd.)
Regents Ho. Ga. *E14* —1A **56**
Regents M. *NW8* —1E **35**

Regent's Park. —1D 37
Regent's Pk. —2C 36
*Regents Pk. Est. NW1 (off Robert St.) —2E **37***
Regent's Pk. Gdns. M. *NW1* —5B **22**
*Regent's Pk. Ho. NW1 (off Park Rd.) —2A **36***
Regent's Pk. Open Air Theatre. —2C 36
Regent's Pk. Rd. *NW1* (in two parts) —4B **22**
Regent's Pk. Ter. *NW1* —5D **23**
Regent's Pl. *SE3* —5C **72**
*Regents Plaza. NW6 —1D **35** (off Kilburn High Rd.)*
Regent Sq. *E3* —2D **43**
Regent Sq. *WC1* —2A **38**
Regent's Row. *E8* —5C **26**
Regent St. *NW10* —2F **33**
Regent St. *SW1* —1F **51**
Regent St. *W1* —5D **37**
*Regents Wharf. E8 —5D **27** (off Wharf Pl.)*
Regents Wharf. *N1* —1B **38**
Regina Ct. *SE16* —3E **55**
*Reginald Pl. SE8 —3C **70** (off Deptford High St.)*
Reginald Rd. *E7* —4C **30**
Reginald Rd. *SE8* —3C **70**
Reginald Sq. *SE8* —3C **70**
Regina Rd. *N4* —3B **10**
*Regis Ct. NW1 —4B **36** (off Melcombe Pl.)*
*Regis Ho. W1 —4C **36** (off Beaumont St.)*
Regis Pl. *SW2* —2B **80**
Regis Rd. *NW5* —2D **23**
*Regnart Bldgs. NW1 —2E **37** (off Euston St.)*
Reigate Rd. *Brom* —3B **100**
Reighton Rd. *E5* —5C **12**
Relay Rd. *W12* —2E **47**
Relf Rd. *SE15* —1C **82**
Reliance Arc. *SW9* —2C **80**
*Reliance Sq. EC2 —3A **40** (off Anning St.)*
Relton M. *SW7* —4A **50**
*Rembold Ho. SE10 —4E **71** (off Blissett St.)*
Rembrandt Clo. *E14* —4F **57**
*Rembrandt Clo. SW1 —1C **64** (off Graham Ter.)*
*Rembrandt Ct. SE16 —1D **69** (off Stubbs Dri.)*
Rembrandt Rd. *SE13* —2A **86**
Remembrance Rd. *E7* —1F **31**
Remington Rd. *E6* —5F **45**
Remington Rd. *N15* —1F **11**
Remington St. *EC1* —1D **39**
Remnant St. *WC2* —5B **38**
*Remsted Ho. NW6 —5D **21** (off Mortimer Cres.)*
*Remus Building, The. EC1 (off Hardwick St.) —2C **38***
Remus Rd. *E3* —4C **28**
Rendlesham Rd. *E5* —1C **26**
Renforth St. *SE16* —4E **55**
Renfrew Rd. *SE11* —5D **53**
Renmuir St. *SW17* —5B **92**
Rennell St. *SE13* —1E **85**
*Rennie Cotts. E1 —3E **41** (off Pemell Clo.)*
*Rennie Ct. SE1 —2D **53** (off Stamford St.)*
Rennie Est. *SE16* —5D **55**
*Rennie Ho. SE1 —4E **53** (off Bath Ter.)*
Rennie St. *SE1* —2D **53** (in two parts)
*Renoir Ct. SE16 —1D **69** (off Stubbs Dri.)*
Rensburg Rd. *E17* —1F **13**
Renters Av. *NW4* —1E **5**
Renton Clo. *SW2* —4B **80**
Rephidim St. *SE1* —4A **54**
Replingham Rd. *SW18* —1B **90**
Reporton Rd. *SW6* —3A **62**
Repton Ho. *E14* —5A **42**
*Repton Ho. SW1 —5E **51** (off Charlwood St.)*
Repton St. *E14* —5A **42**
Reservoir Rd. *SE4* —5A **70**
Restell Clo. *SE3* —2A **72**
Reston Pl. *SW7* —3E **49**
Restoration Sq. *SW11* —4F **63**
*Restormel Ho. SE11 —5C **52** (off Chester Way)*
Retcar Clo. *N19* —4D **9**
*Retcar Pl. N19 —4D **9** (off Retcar Clo.)*
Retford St. *N1* —1A **40**
Retreat Ho. *E9* —3E **27**
Retreat Pl. *E9* —3E **27**
Retreat, The. *SW14* —1A **74**
Reunion Row. *E1* —1D **55**
Reveley Sq. *SE16* —3A **56**
Revelon Rd. *SE4* —2A **84**
Revelstoke Rd. *SW18* —2B **90**
Reverdy Rd. *SE1* —5C **54**
Review Rd. *NW2* —4B **4**
Rewell St. *SW6* —3E **63**
Rex Pl. *W1* —1C **50**
Reydon Av. *E11* —1E **17**
Reynard Clo. *SE4* —1A **84**
Reynard Pl. *SE14* —2A **70**
Reynolds Clo. *NW11* —2D **7**
*Reynolds Ho. NW8 —1F **35** (off Wellington Rd.)*
*Reynolds Ho. SW1 —5F **51** (off Erasmus St.)*
Reynolds Pl. *SE3* —3D **73**
Reynolds Rd. *SE15* —2E **83**
Rheidol M. *N1* —1E **39**
Rheidol Ter. *N1* —5E **25**
Rhoda St. *E2* —3B **40**
*Rhodes Ho. N1 —2F **39** (off Provost Est.)*
*Rhodes Ho. W12 —2D **47** (off White City Est.)*
Rhodesia Rd. *E11* —4F **15**
Rhodesia Rd. *SW9* —5A **66**
Rhodes St. *N7* —2B **24**
Rhodeswell Rd. *E14* —4A **42**
Rhondda Gro. *E3* —2A **42**
Rhyl St. *NW5* —3C **22**
*Ribblesdale Ho. NW6 —5C **20** (off Kilburn Va.)*
Ribblesdale Rd. *SW16* —5D **93**
Ribbon Dance M. *SE5* —4F **67**
Ricardo St. *E14* —5D **43**
Ricards Rd. *SW19* —5B **90**
*Riceyman Ho. WC1 —2C **38** (off Lloyd Baker St.)*
*Richard Anderson Ct. SE14 (off Monson Rd.) —3F **69***
*Richard Burbidge Mans. SW13 —2E **61** (off Brasenose Dri.)*
*Richard Ho. SE16 —5E **55** (off Silwood St.)*
Richard Ho. Dri. *E16* —5F **45**
*Richard Neale Ho. E1 —1D **55** (off Cornwall St.)*
Richardson Clo. *E8* —5B **26**
*Richardson Ct. SW4 —5A **66** (off Studley Rd.)*
Richardson Rd. *E15* —1A **44**
*Richardson's M. W1 —3E **37** (off Warren St.)*
Richard's Pl. *SW3* —5A **50**
Richard St. *E1* —5D **41**
Richbell Pl. *WC1* —4B **38**
Richborne Ter. *SW8* —3B **66**
*Richborough Ho. SE15 (off Sharratt St.) —2E **69***
Richborough Rd. *NW2* —1A **20**
Richford Ga. *W6* —4E **47**
Richford Rd. *E15* —5B **30**
Richford St. *W6* —3E **47**
Rich Ind. Est. *SE15* —2D **69**
Rich La. *SW5* —1D **63**
*Richman Ho. SE8 —1B **70** (off Grove St.)*
Richmond Av. *N1* —5B **24**
Richmond Av. *NW10* —3E **19**
Richmond Bldgs. *W1* —5F **37**
Richmond Clo. *E17* —1B **14**
*Richmond Cotts. W14 —5A **48** (off Hammersmith Rd.)*
*Richmond Ct. SW1 —3B **50** (off Sloane St.)*
Richmond Cres. *N1* —5B **24**
Richmond Gro. *N1* —4D **25** (in two parts)
*Richmond Ho. NW1 —1D **37** (off Park Village E.)*
*Richmond Ho. SE17 —1F **67** (off Portland St.)*
Richmond M. *W1* —5F **37**
Richmond Rd. *E7* —2D **31**
Richmond Rd. *E8* —4B **26**
Richmond Rd. *E11* —4F **15**
Richmond Rd. *N15* —1A **12**

Richmond St. *E13* —1C **44**
Richmond Ter. *SW1* —3A **52**
Richmond Way. *E11* —4C **16**
Richmond Way. *W12 & W14*
    —3F **47**
Richmount Gdns. *SE3* —1C **86**
Rich St. *E14* —1B **56**
Rickard Clo. *SW2* —1C **94**
Rickett St. *SW6* —2C **62**
Rickman Ho. E1 —2E **41**
 (off Rickman St.)
Rickman St. *E1* —3E **41**
Rick Roberts Way. *E15*
    —5E **29**
Rickthorne Rd. *N19* —4A **10**
Rickyard Path. *SE9* —2F **87**
Riddell Ct. *SE5* —1B **68**
Riddons Rd. *SE12* —3E **101**
Ridgdale St. *E3* —1D **43**
Ridgebrook Rd. *SE3* —1F **87**
Ridge Ct. *SE22* —5C **82**
Ridge Hill. *NW11* —3A **6**
Ridge Rd. *N8* —1B **10**
Ridge Rd. *NW2* —5B **6**
Ridge Way. *SE19* —5A **96**
Ridgeway Dri. *Brom* —4D **101**
Ridgeway Gdns. *N6* —2F **9**
Ridgeway, The. *NW11* —3B **6**
Ridgewell Clo. *N1* —5E **25**
Ridgewell Clo. *SE26* —4B **98**
Ridgmount Gdns. *WC1*
    —4F **37**
Ridgmount Pl. *WC1* —4F **37**
Ridgmount Rd. *SW18* —3D **77**
Ridgmount St. *WC1* —4F **37**
Ridgway. *SW19* —5F **89**
Ridgway Pl. *SW19* —5A **90**
Ridgway Rd. *SW9* —1D **81**
Ridgwell Rd. *E16* —4E **45**
Riding Ho. St. *W1* —4D **37**
Ridings Clo. *N6* —2E **9**
Riding, The. *NW11* —2B **6**
Ridley Ct. *SW16* —5A **94**
Ridley Rd. *E7* —1E **31**
Ridley Rd. *E8* —2B **26**
Ridley Rd. *NW10* —1C **32**
Riffel Rd. *NW2* —2E **19**
Rifle Ct. *SE11* —2C **66**
Rifle Pl. *W11* —2F **47**
Rifle St. *E14* —4D **43**
Rigault Rd. *SW6* —5A **62**
Rigden St. *E14* —5D **43**
Rigeley Rd. *NW10* —2C **32**
Rigg App. *E10* —3F **13**
Rigge Pl. *SW4* —2F **79**
Riggindale Rd. *SW16* —5F **93**
Riley Ho. SW10 —3F **63**
 (off Riley St.)
Riley Rd. *SE1* —4B **54**
Riley St. *SW10* —2F **63**
Rill Ho. SE5 —3F **67**
 (off Harris St.)
Rinaldo Rd. *SW12* —5D **79**
Ringcroft St. *N7* —2C **24**
Ringford Rd. *SW18* —3B **76**
Ringlet Clo. *E16* —4D **45**

Ringmer Av. *SW6* —4A **62**
Ringmer Gdns. *N19* —4A **10**
Ringmore Ri. *SE23* —5D **83**
Ring Rd. *W12* —2E **47**
Ringsfield Ho. *SE17* —1E **67**
 (off Bronti Clo.)
Ringstead Rd. *SE6* —5D **85**
Ring, The. *W2* —1F **49**
Ringwood Gdns. *E14* —5C **56**
Ringwood Gdns. *SW15*
    —1C **88**
Ringwood Rd. *E17* —1B **14**
Ripley Gdns. *SW14* —1A **74**
Ripley Ho. SW1 —2E **65**
 (off Churchill Gdns.)
Ripley M. *E11* —1A **16**
Ripley Rd. *E16* —5E **45**
Ripon Gdns. *Ilf* —1F **17**
Ripplevale Gro. *N1* —4B **24**
Risborough. SE17 —5E **53**
Risborough Ho. NW1
 (off Mallory St.) —3A **36**
Risborough St. *SE1* —3D **53**
Risdon St. *SE16* —4E **55**
Riseholme Ct. *E9* —3B **28**
Riseldine Rd. *SE23* —4A **84**
Rise, The. *E11* —1C **16**
Rise, The. *NW10* —1A **18**
Risinghill St. *N1* —1B **38**
Rising Sun Ct. EC1 —1D **39**
 (off Cloth Fair)
Rita Rd. *SW8* —2A **66**
Ritches Rd. *N15* —1E **11**
Ritchie Ho. *E14* —5F **43**
Ritchie Ho. *N19* —3F **9**
Ritchie Ho. SE16 —4E **55**
 (off Howland Est.)
Ritchie St. *N1* —1C **38**
Ritherdon Rd. *SW17* —2C **92**
Ritson Ho. N1 —5B **24**
 (off Barnsbury Est.)
Ritson Rd. *E8* —3C **26**
Rivaz Pl. *E9* —3E **27**
Riven Ct. W2 —5D **35**
 (off Inverness Ter.)
Riverbank Rd. *Brom*
    —3C **100**
River Barge Clo. *E14* —3E **57**
River Clo. *E11* —1E **17**
River Ct. *SE1* —1D **53**
Rivercourt Rd. *W6* —5D **47**
Riverdale. *SE13* —2E **85**
Riverdale Dri. *SW18* —1D **91**
Riverdale Shop. Cen. *SE13*
    —1E **85**
Riverfleet. WC1 —2A **38**
 (off Birkenhead St.)
River Ho. *SE26* —3D **97**
Rivermead Ct. *SW6* —1B **76**
Rivermead Ho. *E9* —2A **28**
River Pk. Trad. Est. *E14*
    —4B **56**
River Pl. *N1* —4E **25**
Riversdale Rd. *N5* —5D **11**
Riverside. *NW4* —2D **5**
Riverside. *SE7* —4D **59**

Riverside. *WC1* —2A **38**
 (off Birkenhead St.)
Riverside Bus. Cen. *SW18*
    —1D **91**
Riverside Clo. *E5* —3E **13**
Riverside Ct. *SE3* —2B **86**
Riverside Ct. *SE16* —2F **55**
Riverside Ct. *SW8* —2F **65**
Riverside Dri. *NW11* —1A **6**
Riverside Dri. *W4* —3A **60**
Riverside Gdns. *W6* —1D **61**
Riverside Rd. *E15* —1E **43**
Riverside Rd. *N15* —1C **12**
Riverside Rd. *SW17* —4D **91**
Riverside Wlk. *SE10* —4A **58**
 (Morden Wharf Rd.)
Riverside Wlk. *SE10* —3F **57**
 (Tunnel Av.)
Riverside Wlk. *SW6* —1A **76**
Riverside Wlk. W4 —2B **60**
 (off Chiswick Wharf)
Riverside Workshops. *SE1*
    —2E **53**
River St. *EC1* —2C **38**
River Ter. *W6* —1E **61**
River Ter. WC2 —1B **52**
 (off Lancaster Pl.)
Riverton Clo. *W9* —2B **34**
Riverview Gdns. *SW13*
    —2D **61**
Riverview Heights. SE16
    —3C **54**
 (off Bermondsey Wall W.)
Riverview Pk. *SE6* —2C **98**
River Wlk. *W6* —3E **61**
River Way. *SE10* —4B **58**
 (in two parts)
Rivet Ho. SE1 —1B **68**
 (off Coopers Rd.)
Rivington Bldgs. *EC2* —2A **40**
Rivington Ct. *NW10* —5C **18**
Rivington Pl. *EC2* —2A **40**
Rivington St. *EC2* —2A **40**
Rivington Wlk. *E8* —5C **26**
Rixon St. *N7* —5C **10**
Rixsen Rd. *E12* —2F **31**
Roach Rd. *E3* —4C **28**
Roads Pl. *N19* —4A **10**
Roan St. *SE10* —2E **71**
Robert Adam St. *W1* —5C **36**
Roberta St. *E2* —2C **40**
Robert Bell Ho. SE16 —5C **54**
 (off Rouel Rd.)
Robert Clo. *W9* —3E **35**
Robert Dashwood Way. *SE17*
    —5E **53**
Robert Gentry Ho. *W14*
    —1A **62**
Robert Jones Ho. SE16
 (off Rouel Rd.) —5C **54**
Robert Keen Clo. *SE15*
    —4C **68**
Robert Lowe Clo. *SE14*
    —3F **69**
Robert Owen Ho. *SW6*
    —4F **61**

Robert Runcie Ct. *SW9*
—2B **80**
Roberts Clo. *SE16* —3F **55**
Roberts Ct. N1 —*5D 25*
(off Essex Rd.)
Roberts M. *SW1* —4C **50**
Robertson Rd. *E15* —5E **29**
Robertson St. *SW8* —1D **79**
Roberts Pl. *EC1* —3C **38**
Robert St. *NW1* —2D **37**
Robert St. *WC2* —1A **52**
Robeson St. *E3* —4B **42**
Robin Ct. *E14* —4E **57**
Robin Ct. *SE16* —5C **54**
Robin Cres. *E6* —4F **45**
Robin Gro. *N6* —4C **8**
Robin Hood. (Junct.) —3A **88**
Robin Hood Gdns. (Junct.)
—1E **57**
(off Robin Hood La.,
in two parts)
Robin Hood La. *E14* —1E **57**
Robin Hood La. *SW15*
—3A **88**
Robin Hood Rd. *SW19 &*
SW15 —5C **88**
Robin Hood Way. *SW15 &*
SW20 —3A **88**
Robin Ho. NW8 —1A **36**
(off Barrow Hill Est.)
Robinia Cres. *E10* —4D **15**
Robins Ct. *SE12* —3E **101**
Robinscroft M. *SE10* —4E **71**
Robinson Clo. *E11* —5A **16**
Robinson Ct. N1 —*5D 25*
(off St Mary's Path)
Robinson Ho. *E14* —4C **42**
Robinson Ho. W10 —*5F 33*
(off Bramley Rd.)
Robinson Rd. *E2* —1E **41**
Robinson Rd. *SW17 &*
SW19 —5A **92**
Robinson St. *SW3* —2B **64**
Robinwood Pl. *SW15* —4A **88**
Robsart St. *SW9* —5B **66**
Robson Av. *NW10* —4C **18**
Robson Clo. *E6* —5F **45**
Robson Rd. *SE27* —3D **95**
Roby Ho. EC1 —*3E 39*
(off Mitchell St.)
Rochdale Rd. *E17* —2C **14**
Rochdale Way. *SE8* —3C **70**
Roche Ho. *E14* —1B **56**
Rochelle Clo. *SW11* —2F **77**
Rochelle St. *E2* —2B **40**
(in two parts)
Rochemont Wlk. E8 —*5C 26*
(off Pownell Rd.)
Rochester Av. *E13* —5E **31**
Rochester Ct. E2 —*3D 41*
(off Wilmot St.)
Rochester Ho. *SE1* —3F **53**
Rochester Ho. SE15 —*2E 69*
(off Sharratt St.)

Rochester M. *NW1* —4E **23**
Rochester Pl. *NW1* —3E **23**
Rochester Rd. *NW1* —3E **23**
Rochester Row. *SW1* —5E **51**
Rochester Sq. *NW1* —4E **23**
Rochester St. *SW1* —4F **51**
Rochester Ter. *NW1* —3E **23**
Rochester Wlk. SE1 —*2F 53*
(off Stoney St.)
Rochester Way. *SE3 & SE9*
—4D **73**
Rochester Way Relief Rd.
SE3 & SE9 —4D **73**
Rochford Clo. *E6* —1F **45**
Rochford Wlk. *E8* —4C **26**
Rochfort Ho. *SE8* —1B **70**
Rock Av. *SW14* —1A **74**
Rockbourne M. *SE23* —1F **97**
Rockbourne Rd. *SE23*
—1F **97**
Rockell's Pl. *SE22* —4D **83**
Rockfield Ho. SE10 —*2E 71*
(off Welland St.)
Rock Gro. Way. *SE16* —5C **54**
(in two parts)
Rockhall Rd. *NW2* —1F **19**
Rockhampton Clo. *SE27*
—4C **94**
Rockhampton Rd. *SE27*
—4C **94**
Rock Hill. *SE26* —4B **96**
Rockingham Clo. *SW15*
—2B **74**
Rockingham St. *SE1* —4E **53**
Rockland Rd. *SW15* —2A **76**
Rockley Ct. W14 —*3F 47*
(off Rockley Rd.)
Rockley Rd. *W14* —3F **47**
Rockmount Rd. *SE19* —5F **95**
Rocks La. *SW13* —4C **60**
Rock St. *N4* —4C **10**
Rockwell Gdns. *SE19* —5A **96**
Rockwood Pl. *W12* —3E **47**
Rocliffe St. *N1* —1D **39**
Rocombe Cres. *SE23* —5E **83**
Rocque Ho. SW6 —*3B 62*
(off Estcourt Rd.)
Rocque La. *SE3* —1B **86**
Rodale Mans. *SW18* —4D **77**
Rodborough Ct. W9 —*3C 34*
(off Hermes Clo.)
Rodborough Rd. *NW11*
—3C **6**
Rodenhurst Rd. *SW4* —4E **79**
Roden St. *N7* —5B **10**
Roderick Rd. *SE16* —5E **55**
(off Raymouth Rd.)
Roderick Rd. *NW3* —1B **22**
Rodgers Ho. SW4 —*5F 79*
(off Clapham Pk. Est.)
Rodin Ct. N1 —*5D 25*
(off Essex Rd.)
Roding Ho. N1 —*5C 24*
(off Barnsbury St.)
Roding La. S. *Ilf & Wfd G*
—1F **17**

Roding M. *E1* —2C **54**
Roding Rd. *E5* —1F **27**
Rodmarton St. *W1* —4B **36**
Rodmell. *WC1* —2A **38**
(off Regent Sq.)
Rodmere St. *SE10* —1A **72**
Rodmill La. *SW2* —5A **80**
Rodney Ct. *NW8* —3E **35**
Rodney Ho. *E14* —5D **57**
Rodney Ho. N1 —*1B 38*
(off Donegal St.)
Rodney Ho. SW1 —*1E 65*
(off Dolphin Sq.)
Rodney Ho. W11 —*1C 48*
(off Pembridge Cres.)
Rodney Pl. *SE17* —5E **53**
Rodney Rd. *SE17* —5E **53**
Rodney St. *N1* —1B **38**
Rodway Rd. *SW15* —5C **74**
Rodwell Rd. *SE22* —4B **82**
Roebuck Ho. SW1 —*4E 51*
(off Palace Ho.)
Roedean Cres. *SW15* —4A **74**
Roehampton. —5C **74**
Roehampton Clo. *SW15*
—2C **74**
Roehampton Ga. *SW15*
—4A **74**
Roehampton High St. *SW15*
—5C **74**
Roehampton Lane. (Junct.)
—1D **89**
Roehampton La. *SW15*
—2C **74**
Roehampton Va. *SW15*
—3B **88**
Roffey St. *E14* —3E **57**
Rogate Ho. *E5* —5C **12**
Roger Dowley Ct. *E2* —1E **41**
Roger Harriss Almshouses.
(off Gift La.) *E15* —*5B 30*
Rogers Est. *E2* —2E **41**
Rogers Ho. SW1 —*5F 51*
(off Page St.)
Rogers Rd. *E16* —5B **44**
Rogers Rd. *SW17* —4F **91**
Roger St. *WC1* —3B **38**
Rohere Ho. *EC1* —2E **39**
Rojack Rd. *SE23* —1F **97**
Rokeby Rd. *SE4* —5B **70**
Rokeby St. *E15* —5F **29**
Rokell Ho. Beck —*5D 99*
(off Beckenham Hill Rd.)
Roland Gdns. *SW7* —1E **63**
Roland Ho. SW7 —*1E 63*
(off Cranley M.)
Roland M. *E1* —4F **41**
Roland Way. *SE17* —1F **67**
Roland Way. *SW7* —1E **63**
Rollins St. *SE15* —2E **69**
Rollit St. *N7* —2C **24**
Rolls Bldgs. *EC4* —5C **38**
Rollscourt Av. *SE24* —3E **81**
Rolls Pas. WC2 —*5C 38*
(off Chancery La.)
Rolls Rd. *SE1* —1B **68**

Rolt St. *SE8* —2A **70**
(in two parts)
Romanfield Rd. *SW2* —5B **80**
Roman Ho. *EC2* —4E **39**
(off Wood St.)
Roman Ri. *SE19* —5F **95**
Roman Rd. *E2 & E3* —2E **41**
Roman Rd. *E3* —5B **28**
Roman Rd. *E6* —3F **45**
Roman Rd. *NW2* —5E **5**
Roman Rd. *N7* —3B **24**
Roman Way. *SE15* —3E **69**
Roma Read Clo. *SW15*
—5D **75**
Romayne Ho. *SW4* —1F **79**
Romberg Rd. *SW17* —3C **92**
Romborough Gdns. *SE13*
—3E **85**
Romborough Way. *SE13*
—3E **85**
Romero Clo. *SW9* —1B **80**
Romero Sq. *SE3* —2E **87**
Romeyn Rd. *SW16* —3B **94**
Romford Rd. *E15 & E7*
—3A **30**
Romford St. *E1* —4C **40**
Romilly Rd. *N4* —4D **11**
Romilly St. *W1* —1F **51**
Romily Ct. *SW6* —5A **62**
Rommany Rd. *SE27* —4F **95**
(in two parts)
Romney Clo. *NW11* —3E **7**
Romney Clo. *SE14* —3E **69**
Romney Ct. *NW3* —3A **22**
Romney Ct. W12 —3F **47**
(off Shepherd's Bush Grn.)
Romney M. *W1* —4C **38**
Romney Rd. *SE10* —2F **71**
Romney Row. NW2 —4F **5**
(off Brent Ter.)
Romney St. *SW1* —4A **52**
Romola Rd. *SE24* —1D **95**
Ronald Av. *E15* —2A **44**
Ronald Buckingham Ct. SE16
(off Kenning St.) —3E **55**
Ronald Ho. *SE3* —2E **87**
Ronaldshay. *N4* —3C **10**
Ronalds Rd. *N7* —2C **24**
(in three parts)
Ronald St. *E1* —5E **41**
Rona Rd. *NW3* —1C **22**
Rona Wlk. N1 —3F **25**
(off Ramsey Wlk.)
Rondu Rd. *NW2* —2A **20**
Ronver Rd. *SE12* —1B **100**
Rood La. *EC3* —1A **54**
Rookery Clo. *NW9* —1B **4**
Rookery Rd. *SW4* —2E **79**
Rookery Way. *NW9* —1B **4**
Rooke Way. *SE10* —1B **72**
Rookstone Rd. *SW17*
—5B **92**
Rook Wlk. *E6* —5F **45**
Rookwood Rd. *N16* —2B **12**
Rootes Dri. *W10* —4F **33**

Ropemaker Rd. *SE16*
—3A **56**
Ropemakers Fields. *E14*
—1B **56**
Ropemaker St. *EC2* —4F **39**
Roper La. *SE1* —3A **54**
Ropers Orchard. SW3
(off Danvers St.) —2A **64**
Ropers Wlk. *SW2* —5C **80**
Ropery Bus. Pk. *SE7* —5E **59**
Ropery St. *E3* —3B **42**
Rope St. *SE16* —5A **56**
Rope Wlk. Gdns. *E1* —5C **40**
Ropley St. *E2* —1C **40**
Rosa Alba M. *N5* —1E **25**
Rosalind Ho. N1 —1A **40**
(off Arden Ho.)
Rosaline Rd. *SW6* —3A **62**
Rosaline Ter. SW6 —3A **62**
(off Rosaline Rd.)
Rosamond St. *SE26* —3D **97**
Rosary Gdns. *SW7* —5E **49**
Rosaville Rd. *SW6* —3B **62**
Roscoe St. *EC1* —3E **39**
(in two parts)
Roscoe St. Est. *EC1* —3E **39**
Rose All. EC2 —4A **40**
(off Bishopsgate)
Rose All. *SE1* —2E **53**
Rose & Crown Ct. EC2
(off Foster La.) —5E **39**
Rose & Crown Yd. *SW1*
—2E **51**
Rosebank. *SW6* —3E **61**
Rosebank Gdns. *E3* —1B **42**
Rosebank Rd. *E17* —1D **15**
Rosebank Wlk. *NW1* —4F **23**
Roseberry Gdns. *N4* —1D **11**
Roseberry Pl. *E8* —3B **26**
Roseberry St. *SE1* —5D **55**
Rosebery Av. *E12* —3F **31**
Rosebery Av. *EC1* —3C **38**
Rosebery Ct. EC1 —3C **38**
(off Rosebery Av.)
Rosebery Gdns. *N8* —1A **10**
Rosebery Rd. *SW2* —4A **80**
Rosebery Sq. EC1 —3C **38**
(off Rosebery Av.)
Rosebury Rd. *SW6* —5D **63**
Rose Bush Ct. *NW3* —2B **22**
Rose Ct. E1 —4B **40**
(off Wentworth St.)
Rosecroft Av. *NW3* —5C **6**
Rosecroft Gdns. *NW2* —5C **4**
Rosedale Ct. *N5* —1D **25**
Rosedale Ho. *N16* —3F **11**
Rosedale Rd. *E7* —2E **31**
Rosedale Ter. W6 —4D **47**
(off Dalling Rd.)
Rosedene. *NW6* —5F **19**
Rosedene Av. *SW16* —3B **94**
Rosedene Ter. *E10* —4D **15**
Rosedew Rd. *W6* —2F **61**
Rosefield Gdns. *E14* —1C **56**
Roseford Ct. W12 —3F **47**
(off Shepherd's Bush Grn.)

Rosehart M. *W11* —5C **34**
Rosehill Rd. *SW18* —4E **77**
Roseleigh Av. *N5* —1D **25**
Rosemary Ct. SE8 —2B **70**
(off Dorking Clo.)
Rosemary Dri. *E14* —5F **43**
Rosemary Dri. *Ilf* —1F **17**
Rosemary Ho. *N1* —5F **25**
(off Colville Est.)
Rosemary Rd. *SE15* —3B **68**
Rosemary Rd. *SW17* —3E **91**
Rosemary St. *N1* —5F **25**
Rosemead. *NW9* —2B **4**
Rosemont Rd. *NW3* —3E **21**
Rosemoor St. *SW3* —5B **50**
Rosemount Point. *SE23*
—3F **97**
Rosenau Cres. *SW11* —4B **64**
Rosenau Rd. *SW11* —4A **64**
Rosendale Rd. *SE21* —3F **95**
Rosendale Rd. *SE24 & SE21*
—5E **81**
Roseneath Rd. *SW11* —4C **78**
Rosenthal Rd. *SE6* —4D **85**
Rosenthorpe Rd. *SE15*
—3F **83**
Roserton St. *E14* —3E **57**
Rose Sq. *SW7* —1F **63**
Rose St. *WC2* —1A **52**
(in two parts)
Rosethorn Clo. *SW12* —5F **79**
Rosetta Clo. *SW8* —3A **66**
Roseveare Rd. *SE12* —4E **101**
Rose Way. *SE12* —3C **86**
Roseway. *SE21* —4F **81**
Rosewood Ct. *E11* —1F **29**
Rosewood Gdns. *SE13*
—5E **71**
Rosewood Ho. *SW8* —2B **66**
Rosewood Sq. *W12* —5C **32**
Rosher Clo. *E15* —4F **29**
Roshni Ho. *SW17* —5A **92**
Ros Ho. E1 —2D **55**
(off Prusom St.)
Rosina St. *E9* —3F **27**
Roskell Rd. *SW15* —1F **75**
Roslin Way. *Brom* —5C **100**
Rosmead Rd. *W11* —1A **48**
Rosoman Pl. *EC1* —3C **38**
Rosoman St. *EC1* —2C **38**
Rosscourt Mans. SW1
—4D **51**
(off Buckingham Pal. Rd.)
Rossdale Rd. *SW15* —2E **75**
Rosse M. *SE3* —4D **73**
Rossendale St. *E5* —4D **13**
Rossendale Way. *NW1*
—5E **23**
Rosseth M. *NW8* —5F **21**
Rossetti Ct. WC1 —4F **37**
(off Ridgmount Pl.)
Rossetti Ho. *SW1* —5F **51**
(off Erasmus St.)
Rossetti M. *NW8* —5F **21**
Rossetti Rd. *SE16* —1D **69**
Rossington St. *E5* —4C **12**

Rossiter Rd. *SW12* —1D **93**
Rosslyn Av. *SW13* —1A **74**
Rosslyn Hill. *NW3* —1F **21**
Rosslyn M. *NW3* —1F **21**
Rosslyn Pk. M. *NW3* —2F **21**
Rosslyn Park R.U.F.C.
—2B **74**
Rossmore Clo. *NW1* —3A **36**
(off Rossmore Rd.)
Rossmore Ct. *NW1* —3B **36**
Rossmore Rd. *NW1* —3A **36**
Ross Way. *SE9* —1F **87**
Rostella Rd. *SW17* —4F **91**
Rostrevor Av. *N15* —1B **12**
Rostrevor M. *SW6* —4B **62**
Rostrevor Rd. *SW6* —4B **62**
Rostrevor Rd. *SW19* —5C **90**
Rotary St. *SE1* —4D **53**
Rothay. *NW1* —2D **37**
(off Albany St.)
Rothbury Hall. *SE10* —5A **58**
(off Azof St.)
Rothbury Rd. *E9* —4B **28**
Rotherfield Ct. *N1* —4F **25**
(off Rotherfield St.,
in two parts)
Rotherfield St. *N1* —4E **25**
Rotherham Wlk. *SE1* —2D **53**
(off Nicholson St.)
Rotherhithe. —3E 55
Rotherhithe New Rd. *SE16*
—1D **69**
Rotherhithe Old Rd. *SE16*
—5F **55**
Rotherhithe St. *SE16* —3E **55**
Rother Ho. *SE15* —2D **83**
Rotherwick Ho. *E1* —1C **54**
(off Thomas More St.)
Rotherwick Rd. *NW11* —2C **6**
Rotherwood Rd. *SW15*
—1F **75**
Rothery St. *N1* —5D **25**
(off St Marys Path)
Rothesay Ct. *SE6* —2B **100**
(off Cumberland Pl.)
Rothesay Ct. *SE11* —2C **66**
(off Harleyford St.)
Rothesay Ct. *SE12* —3D **101**
Rothley Ct. *NW8* —3F **35**
(off St John's Wood Rd.)
Rothsay Rd. *E7* —4E **31**
Rothsay St. *SE1* —4A **54**
Rothsay Wlk. *E14* —5C **56**
(off Charnwood Gdns.)
Rothschild St. *SE27* —4D **95**
Roth Wlk. *N7* —4B **10**
Rothwell St. *NW1* —5B **22**
Rotten Row. *NW3* —3E **7**
Rotten Row. *SW7 & SW1*
—3A **50**
Rotterdam Dri. *E14* —4E **57**
Rouel Rd. *SE16* —4C **54**
(Old Jamaica Rd.)
Rouel Rd. *SE16* —5C **54**
(Yalding Rd.)
Roundacre. *SW19* —2F **89**

Roundel Clo. *SE4* —2B **84**
Roundhay Clo. *SE23* —2F **97**
Round Hill. *SE26* —2E **97**
Roundhouse Theatre, The.
—4C **22**
Roundtable Rd. *Brom*
—3B **100**
Roundwood Rd. *NW10*
—3B **18**
Rounton Rd. *E3* —3C **42**
Roupell Rd. *SW2* —1B **94**
Roupell St. *SE1* —2C **52**
Rousden St. *NW1* —4E **23**
Rouse Gdns. *SE21* —4A **96**
Routemaster Clo. *E13* —2D **45**
Routh Rd. *SW18* —5A **78**
Rover Ho. *N1* —5A **26**
(off Whitmore Est.)
Rowallan Rd. *SW6* —3A **62**
Rowan Rd. *E13* —1D **45**
(off High St.)
Rowan Ct. *SE15* —3B **68**
(off Garnies Clo.)
Rowan Ct. *SW11* —4B **78**
Rowan Lodge. *W8* —4D **49**
(off St Mary's Pl.)
Rowan Rd. *W6* —5F **47**
Rowans Bowl. *N4* —4C **10**
Rowan Ter. *W6* —5F **47**
(off Rowan Rd.)
Rowan Wlk. *N2* —1E **7**
Rowan Wlk. *N19* —4E **9**
Rowan Wlk. *W10* —3A **34**
Rowberry Clo. *SW6* —3E **61**
Rowcross St. *SE1* —1B **68**
Rowditch La. *SW11* —5C **64**
Rowdon Av. *NW10* —4D **19**
Rowe La. *E9* —2E **27**
Rowena Cres. *SW11* —5A **64**
Rowfant Rd. *SW17* —1C **92**
Rowhill Rd. *E5* —1D **27**
Rowington Clo. *W2* —4D **35**
Rowland Ct. *E16* —3B **44**
Rowland Gro. *SE26* —3D **97**
Rowland Hill Ho. *SE1* —3D **53**
Rowland Hill St. *NW3* —2A **22**
Rowlands Clo. *N6* —1C **8**
Rowley Gdns. *N4* —2E **11**
Rowley Ho. *SE8* —1C **70**
(off Watergate St.)
Rowley Rd. *N15* —1E **11**
Rowley Way. *NW8* —5D **21**
Rowntree Clifford Clo. *E13*
—3D **45**
Rowntree Rd. *NW6* —3C **20**
Rowse Clo. *E15* —5E **29**
Rowstock Gdns. *N7* —2F **23**
Roxburgh Rd. *SE27* —5D **95**
Roxby Pl. *SW6* —2C **62**
Roxley Rd. *SE13* —4D **85**
Roxwell Rd. *W12* —3C **46**
Roxwell Trad. Pk. *E17* —2A **14**
Royal Academy of Arts.
—1E **51**
Royal Albert Hall. —3F **49**
Royal Albert Way. *E16* —1F **59**

Royal Arc. *W1* —1E **51**
(off Old Bond St.)
Royal Av. *SW3* —1B **64**
Royal Av. Ho. *SW3* —1B **64**
(off Royal Av.)
Royal Belgrave Ho. *SW1*
(off Hugh St.) —5D **51**
Royal Ceremonial Dress
Collection, The. —2D **49**
Royal Cir. *SE27* —3C **94**
Royal Clo. *N16* —3A **12**
Royal Clo. *SE8* —2B **70**
Royal Clo. *SW19* —2F **89**
Royal College St. *NW1*
—4E **23**
Royal Ct. *EC3* —5F **39**
(off Finch La.)
Royal Ct. *SE16* —4B **56**
Royal Courts of Justice.
—5C **38**
Royal Cres. *W11* —2F **47**
Royal Cres. M. *W11* —2F **47**
Royal Duchess M. *SW12*
—5D **79**
Royal Exchange. —5F **39**
Royal Exchange Av. *EC3*
(off Finch La.) —5F **39**
Royal Exchange Bldgs. *EC2*
—5F **39**
(off Threadneedle St.)
Royal Festival Hall. —2B **52**
Royal Hill. *SE10* —3E **71**
Royal Hill Ct. *SE10* —3E **71**
(off Greenwich High St.)
Royal Hospital Chelsea Mus.
—1C **64**
Royal Hospital Rd. *SW3*
—2B **64**
Royal London Ind. Est. *NW10*
—1A **32**
Royal M. *SW1* —4D **51**
Royal Mews, The. —4D **51**
Royal Mint Ct. *EC3* —1B **54**
Royal Mint Pl. *E1* —1C **54**
(off Cartwright St.)
Royal Mint St. *E1* —1B **54**
Royal National Theatre.
—2B **52**
Royal Naval Pl. *SE14* —3B **70**
Royal Oak Ct. *N1* —2A **40**
(off Pitfield St.)
Royal Oak Pl. *SE22* —4D **83**
Royal Oak Rd. *E8* —3D **27**
Royal Oak Yd. *SE1* —3A **54**
Royal Observatory
Greenwich. —3F **71**
Royal Opera Arc. *SW1* —2F **51**
Royal Opera House. —5A **38**
Royal Orchard Clo. *SW18*
—5A **76**
Royal Pde. *SE3* —5B **72**
Royal Pde. *SW6* —3A **62**
(off Dawes Rd.)
Royal Pde. M. *SE3* —5B **72**
(off Royal Pde.)
Royal Pl. *SE10* —3E **71**

Royal Rd. *E16* —5E **45**
Royal Rd. *SE17* —2D **67**
Royal St. *SE1* —4B **52**
Royal Tower Lodge. E1
 (off Cartwright St.) —1C **54**
Royalty M. W1 —5F **37**
 (off Dean St.)
Royalty Studios. W10 —3F **33**
 (off Lancaster Rd.)
Royal Victoia Pl. *E16* —2D **59**
Royal Victoria Patriotic
 Building. SW18 —4F **77**
Royal Victor Pl. *E3* —1F **41**
Royal Westminster Lodge.
 SW1 —5F **51**
 (off Elverton St.)
Roycroft Clo. *SW2* —1C **94**
Roydon Clo. SW11 —5B **64**
 (off Battersea Pk. Rd.)
Roy Sq. *E14* —1A **56**
Royston Ct. E13 —5C **30**
 (off Stopford Rd.)
Royston Ct. *SE24* —4E **81**
Royston Gdns. *Ilf* —1F **17**
Royston Ho. SE15 —2D **69**
 (off Friary Est.)
Royston Pde. *Ilf* —1F **17**
Royston St. *E2* —1E **41**
Rozel Ct. *N1* —5A **26**
Rozel Rd. *SW4* —1E **79**
Rubens Pl. *SW4* —2A **80**
Rubens St. *SE6* —2B **98**
Ruby St. *SE15* —2D **69**
Ruby Triangle. *SE15* —2D **69**
Ruckholt Clo. *E10* —5D **15**
Ruckholt Rd. *E10* —1D **29**
Rucklidge Av. *NW10* —1B **32**
Rucklidge Pas. *NW6* —1B **34**
Rucklidge Pas. NW10
 (off Rucklidge Av.) —1B **32**
Rudall Cres. *NW3* —1F **21**
Rudbeck Ho. SE15 —3C **68**
 (off Peckham Pk. Rd.)
Ruddington Clo. *E5* —1A **28**
Rudge Ho. SE16 —4C **54**
 (off Jamaica Rd.)
Rudgwick Ter. *NW8* —5A **22**
Rudloe Rd. *SW12* —5E **79**
Rudolf Pl. *SW8* —2A **66**
Rudolph Rd. *E13* —1B **44**
Rudolph Rd. *NW6* —1C **34**
Rufford St. *N1* —5A **24**
Rufus Ho. SE1 —4B **54**
 (off Abbey St.)
Rufus St. *EC1* —2A **40**
Rugby Mans. W14 —5A **48**
 (off Bishop King's Rd)
Rugby Rd. *W4* —3A **46**
Rugby St. *WC1* —3B **38**
Rugg St. *E14* —1C **56**
Rugless Ho. *E14* —3E **57**
Ruislip St. *SW17* —4B **92**
Rumball Ho. SE5 —3A **68**
 (off Harris St.)
Rumbold Rd. *SW6* —3D **63**
Rum Clo. *E1* —1E **55**

Rumford Ho. *SE1* —4E **53**
 (off Tiverton St.)
Rumsey M. *N4* —5D **11**
Rumsey Rd. *SW9* —1B **80**
Runacres Ct. *SE17* —1E **67**
Runbury Circ. *NW9* —4A **4**
Runcorn Pl. *W11* —1A **48**
Rundell Cres. *NW4* —1D **5**
Rundell Tower. *SW8* —4B **66**
Runnymede Ct. *SW15*
 —1C **88**
Runnymede Ho. *E9* —1A **28**
Rupack St. *SE16* —3E **55**
Rupert Ct. *W1* —1F **51**
Rupert Gdns. *SW9* —5D **67**
Rupert Ho. *SE11* —5C **52**
Rupert Rd. *N19* —5F **11**
 (in two parts)
Rupert Rd. *NW6* —1B **34**
Rupert Rd. *W4* —4A **46**
Rupert St. *W1* —1F **51**
Ruscoe Rd. *E16* —5B **44**
Rusham Rd. *SW12* —4B **78**
Rushcroft Rd. *SW2* —2C **80**
Rushey Grn. *SE6* —5D **85**
Rushey Mead. *SE4* —3C **84**
Rushford Rd. *SE4* —4B **84**
Rushgrove Av. *NW9* —1A **4**
Rushgrove Pde. *NW9* —1A **4**
Rush Hill M. SW11 —1C **78**
 (off Rush Hill Rd.)
Rush Hill Rd. *SW11* —1C **78**
Rushmead. *E2* —2D **41**
Rushmere Pl. *SW19* —5F **89**
Rushmore Cres. *E5* —1F **27**
Rushmore Ho. W14 —4A **48**
 (off Russell Rd.)
Rushmore Rd. E5 —1E **27**
 (in three parts)
Rusholme Gro. *SE19* —5A **96**
Rusholme Rd. *SW15* —4F **75**
Rushton Ho. *SW8* —5F **65**
Rushton St. *N1* —1F **39**
Rushworth St. *SE1* —3D **53**
Ruskin Av. *E12* —3F **31**
Ruskin Clo. *NW11* —1D **7**
Ruskin Ct. SE5 —1F **81**
 (off Champion Hill)
Ruskin Ho. SW1 —5F **51**
 (off Herrick St.)
Ruskin Mans. W14 —2A **62**
 (off Queen's Club Gdns.)
Ruskin Pk. Ho. *SE5* —1F **81**
Ruskin Wlk. *SE24* —3E **81**
Rusper Ho. *NW2* —5E **5**
Rusper Ct. SW9 —5A **66**
 (off Clapham Rd.)
Russell Clo. *SE7* —3E **73**
Russell Clo. *W4* —2B **60**
Russell Ct. *E10* —2D **15**
Russell Ct. SE15 —5D **69**
 (off Heaton Rd.)
Russell Ct. SW1 —2E **51**
 (off Cleveland Row)
Russell Ct. *SW16* —5B **94**
Russell Ct. *WC1* —3A **38**

Russell Gdns. *NW11* —1A **6**
Russell Gdns. *W14* —4A **48**
Russell Gdns. M. W14
 —3A **48**
Russell Gro. *SW9* —3C **66**
Russell Ho. *E14* —5C **42**
Russell Ho. SW1 —1E **65**
 (off Cambridge St.)
Russell Lodge. SE1 —4F **53**
 (off Spurgeon St.)
Russell Pde. NW11 —1A **6**
 (off Golders Grn. Rd.)
Russell Pl. *NW3* —2A **22**
Russell Rd. *E10* —1D **15**
Russell Rd. *E16* —5C **44**
Russell Rd. *N8* —1F **9**
Russell Rd. *N15* —1A **12**
Russell Rd. *NW9* —1B **4**
Russell Rd. *W14* —4A **48**
Russell's Footpath. SW16
 —5A **94**
Russell Sq. *WC1* —4A **38**
Russell St. *WC2* —1A **52**
Russell Yd. *SW15* —2A **76**
Russet Cres. *N7* —2B **24**
Russett Way. *SE13* —5D **71**
Russia Ct. EC2 —2E **39**
 (off Russia Row)
Russia Dock Rd. *SE16*
 —2A **56**
Russia Row. *EC2* —2E **39**
Russia Wlk. *SE16* —3A **56**
Rusthall Av. *W4* —5A **46**
Rustic Wlk. E16 —5D **45**
 (off Lambert Rd.)
Ruston M. *W11* —5A **34**
Ruston Rd. *SE18* —4F **59**
Ruston St. *E3* —5B **28**
Rust Sq. *SE5* —3F **67**
Rutford Rd. *SW16* —5A **94**
Ruth Ct. *E3* —1A **42**
Rutherford Ho. E1 —3D **41**
 (off Brady St.)
Rutherford St. *SW1* —5F **51**
Ruth Ho. W10 —3A **34**
 (off Kensal Rd.)
Ruthin Clo. *NW9* —1A **4**
Ruthin Rd. *SE3* —2C **72**
Ruthven St. *E9* —5F **27**
Rutland Ct. *SE5* —2F **81**
Rutland Ct. SW7 —3A **50**
 (off Rutland Gdns.)
Rutland Gdns. *N4* —1D **11**
Rutland Gdns. *SW7* —3A **50**
Rutland Gdns. M. SW7
 —3A **50**
Rutland Ga. *SW7* —3A **50**
Rutland Ga. M. SW7 —3A **50**
 (off Rutland Ga.)
Rutland Gro. *W6* —1D **61**
Rutland Ho. W8 —4D **49**
 (off Marloes Rd.)
Rutland M. *NW8* —5D **21**
Rutland M. E. SW7 —4A **50**
 (off Ennismore St.)

Rutland M. S. SW7 —4A 50 (off Ennismore St.)
Rutland M. W. SW7 —4A 50 (off Rutland Ga.)
Rutland Pk. NW2 —3E 19
Rutland Pk. SE6 —2B 98
Rutland Pk. Gdns. NW2 (off Rutland Pk.) —3E 19
Rutland Pk. Mans. NW2 —3E 19
Rutland Pl. EC1 —3D 39
Rutland Rd. E7 —4F 31
Rutland Rd. E9 —5F 27
Rutland Rd. E17 —1C 14
Rutland St. SW7 —4A 50
Rutland Wlk. SE6 —2B 98
Rutley Clo. SE17 —2D 67
Rutt's Ter. SE14 —4F 69
Ruvigny Gdns. SW15 —1F 75
Ryan Clo. SE3 —2D 87
Rycott Path. SE22 —5C 82
Ryculff Sq. SE3 —5B 72
Rydal Gdns. SW15 —5A 88
Rydal Rd. SW16 —4F 93
Rydal Water. NW1 —2E 37
Rydens Ho. SE9 —3E 101
Ryder Clo. Brom —5D 101
Ryder Ct. E10 —4D 15
Ryder Ct. SW1 —2E 51 (off Ryder St.)
Ryder Dri. SE16 —1D 69
Ryder Ho. E1 —3E 41 (off Colebert Av.)
Ryder M. E9 —2E 27
Ryder's Ter. NW8 —1E 35
Ryder St. SW1 —2E 51
Ryder Yd. SW1 —2E 51
Ryde Va. Rd. SW12 —2E 93
Rydons Clo. SE9 —1F 87
Rydon St. N1 —5E 25
Rydston Clo. N7 —4A 24
Ryecotes Mead. SE21 —1A 96
Ryecroft Lodge. SW16 —5D 95
Ryecroft Rd. SE13 —3E 85
Ryecroft Rd. SW16 —5C 94
Ryecroft St. SW6 —4D 63
Ryedale. SE22 —4D 83
Ryefield Path. SW15 —1C 88
Ryefield Rd. SE19 —5E 95
Rye Hill Pk. SE15 —2E 83
Rye Ho. SE16 —3E 55 (off Swan Rd.)
Rye Ho. SW1 —1D 65 (off Ebury Bri. Rd.)
Ryelands Cres. SE12 —4E 87
Rye La. SE15 —4C 68
Rye Pas. SE15 —1C 82
Rye Rd. SE15 —2F 83
Rye Wlk. SW15 —3F 75
Ryfold Rd. SW19 —3C 90
Rylandes Rd. NW2 —5C 4
Ryland Rd. NW5 —3D 23
Rylett Cres. W12 —3B 46
Rylett Rd. W12 —3B 46
Rylston Rd. SW6 —2B 62
Rymer St. SE24 —4D 81
Rysbrack St. SW3 —4B 50

Saatchi Gallery. —5D 21
Sabbarton St. E16 —5B 44
Sabella Ct. E3 —1B 42
Sabine Rd. SW11 —1B 78
Sable St. N1 —4D 25
Sach Rd. E5 —4D 13
Sackville Ho. SW16 —3A 94
Sackville St. W1 —1E 51
Sackville Way. SE22 —1C 96
Saddlers M. SW8 —4A 66
Saddle Yd. W1 —2D 51
Sadler Ho. EC1 —2D 39 (off Spa Grn. Est.)
Sadler's Wells Theatre. —2C 38
Saffron Av. E14 —1F 57
Saffron Clo. NW11 —1B 6
Saffron Ct. E15 —2A 30 (off Maryland Pk.)
Saffron Hill. EC1 —4C 38
Saffron St. EC1 —4C 38
Saffron Wharf. SE1 —3B 54
Sage St. E1 —1E 55
Sage Way. WC1 —2B 38 (off Cubitt St.)
Saigasso Clo. E16 —5F 45
Sailmakers Ct. SW6 —5E 63
Sail St. SE11 —5B 52
Sainfoin Rd. SW17 —2C 92
Sainsbury Rd. SE19 —5A 96
St Agnes Clo. E9 —5E 27
St Agnes Pl. SE11 —2C 66
St Aidan's Rd. SE22 —4D 83
St Alban's Av. W4 —4A 46
St Alban's Clo. NW11 —3C 6
St Albans Ct. EC2 —5E 39 (off Wood St.)
St Albans Gro. W8 —4D 49
St Alban's La. NW11 —3C 6
St Albans Mans. W8 —4D 49 (off Kensington Ct. Pl.)
St Alban's Pl. N1 —5D 25
St Albans Rd. NW5 —5C 8
St Alban's Rd. NW10 —5A 18
St Alban's St. SW1 —1F 51 (in two parts)
St Albans Ter. W6 —2A 62
St Albans Vs. NW5 —5C 8
St Alfege Pas. SE10 —2E 71
St Alfege Rd. SE7 —2F 73
St Alphage Garden. EC2 (in two parts) —4E 39
St Alphage Highwalk. EC2 (off London Wall) —4E 39
St Alphage Ho. EC2 —4F 39 (off Fore St.)
St Alphonsus Rd. SW4 —2E 79
St Amunds Clo. SE6 —4C 98
St Andrews Chambers. W1 (off Wells St.) —4E 37
St Andrew's Clo. NW2 —5D 5
St Andrews Clo. SE16 (off Ryder Dri.) —1D 69
St Andrew's Ct. SW18 —2E 91
St Andrew's Gro. N16 —3F 11
St Andrew's Hill. EC4 —1D 53 (in two parts)
St Andrews Mans. W1 (off Dorset St.) —4C 36
St Andrews Mans. W14 (off St Andrews Rd.) —2A 62
St Andrew's M. N16 —3A 12
St Andrew's M. SE3 —3C 72
St Andrews M. SW12 —1F 93
St Andrew's Pl. NW1 —3D 37
St Andrew's Rd. E11 —1A 16
St Andrew's Rd. E13 —2D 45
St Andrew's Rd. NW10 —3D 19
St Andrew's Rd. NW11 —1B 6
St Andrew's Rd. W3 —1A 46
St Andrew's Rd. W14 —2A 62
St Andrews Sq. W11 —5A 34
St Andrew St. EC1 —4C 38
St Andrews Way. E3 —3D 43
St Andrew's Wharf. SE1 —3B 54
St Anne's Clo. N6 —5C 8
St Anne's Ct. NW6 —5A 20
St Anne's Ct. W1 —5F 37
St Anne's Flats. NW1 —2F 37 (off Doric Way)
St Anne's Pas. E14 —5B 42
St Anne's Rd. E11 —4F 15
St Anne's Row. E14 —5B 42
St Anne's St. E14 —5B 42
St Anne's Trad. Est. E14 —5B 42
St Ann's Cres. SW18 —4D 77
St Ann's Gdns. NW5 —3C 22
St Ann's Hill. SW18 —3D 77
St Ann's Ho. WC1 —2C 38 (off Margery St.)
St Ann's La. SW1 —4F 51
St Ann's Pk. Rd. SW18 —4E 77
St Ann's Pas. E14 —5B 42
St Ann's Pas. SW13 —1A 74
St Ann's Rd. N15 —1D 11
St Ann's Rd. SW13 —5B 60
St Ann's Rd. W11 —1F 47
St Ann's St. SW1 —4F 51
St Ann's Ter. NW8 —1F 35
St Ann's Vs. W11 —2F 47
St Anselm's Pl. W1 —1D 51
St Anthony's Clo. E1 —2C 54
St Anthony's Clo. SW17 —2A 92
St Anthony's Flats. NW1 (off Aldenham St.) —1F 37
St Antony's Rd. E7 —4D 31
St Asaph Rd. SE4 —1F 83
St Aubins Ct. N1 —5F 25
St Aubyn's Av. SW19 —5B 90

St Augustine's Ho. NW1
 (off Werrington St.) —2F 37
St Augustine's Mans. SW1
 (off Bloomburg St.) —5E 51
St Augustine's Path. N5
—1E 25
St Augustine's Rd. NW1
—4F 23
St Austell Rd. SE13 —5E 71
St Barnabas Clo. SE22
—3A 82
St Barnabas Rd. E17 —1C 14
St Barnabas St. SW1 —1C 64
St Barnabas Ter. E9 —2F 27
St Barnabas Vs. SW8 —4A 66
St Bartholomew's Clo. SE26
—4D 97
St Benedict's Clo. SW17
—5C 92
St Benet's Clo. SW17 —2A 92
St Benet's Pl. EC3 —1F 53
St Bernard's Clo. SE27
—4F 95
St Bernard's Rd. E6 —5F 31
St Botolph Row. EC3 —5B 40
St Botolph St. EC3 —5B 40
St Brelades Ct. N1 —5A 26
St Briavel's Ct. SE15 —3A 68
 (off Lynbrook Clo.)
St Bride's Av. EC4 —5D 39
 (off Bride La.)
St Bride's Church. —5D 39
 (off Bride La.)
St Bride's Pas. EC4 —5D 39
 (off Dorset Ri.)
St Bride St. EC4 —5D 39
St Catherine's Clo. SW17
—2A 92
St Catherine's Ct. W4 —4A 46
St Catherine's Dri. SE14
—5F 69
St Catherines M. SW3 —5B 50
St Catherines Tower. E10
—2D 15
St Chad's Pl. WC1 —2A 38
St Chad's St. WC1 —2A 38
 (in two parts)
St Charles Pl. W10 —4A 34
St Charles Sq. W10 —4F 33
St Chrishoper's Ho. NW1
 (off Bridgeway St.) —1E 37
St Christopher's Pl. W1
—5C 36
St Clair Rd. E13 —1D 45
St Clare St. EC3 —5B 40
St Clement's Ct. EC4 —1F 53
 (off Clements La.)
St Clement's Ct. N7 —3B 24
St Clements Ct. SE14 —2F 69
 (off Myers La.)
St Clement's Heights. SE26
—3C 96
St Clement's La. WC2 —5B 38
St Clements Mans. SW6
 (off Lillie Rd.) —2F 61
St Clement St. N7 —4C 24

St Clements Yd. SE22 —2B 82
St Cloud Rd. SE27 —4E 95
St Crispin's Clo. NW3 —1A 22
St Cross St. EC1 —4C 38
St Cuthbert's Rd. NW2
—3B 20
St Cyprian's St. SW17 —4B 92
St Davids Clo. SE16 —1D 69
 (off Masters Dri.)
St David's Pl. NW4 —2D 5
St Davids Sq. E14 —1D 71
St Denis Rd. SE27 —4F 95
St Dionis Rd. SW6 —5B 62
St Donatt's Rd. SE14 —4B 70
St Dunstan's All. EC3 —1A 54
 (off St Dunstans Hill)
St Dunstan's Av. W3 —1A 46
St Dunstan's Ct. EC4 —5C 38
St Dunstan's Gdns. W3
—1A 46
St Dunstans Hill. EC3 —1A 54
St Dunstan's La. EC3 —1A 54
St Dunstan's Rd. E7 —3D 31
St Dunstan's Rd. W6 —1F 61
St Edmund's Clo. NW8
—5B 22
St Edmund's Clo. SW17
—2A 92
St Edmund's Ct. NW8 —5B 22
 (off St Edmund's Ter.)
St Edmunds Sq. SW13
—2E 61
St Edmund's Ter. NW8
—5A 22
St Edward's Clo. NW11 —1C 6
St Edwards Ct. E10 —2D 15
St Edwards Ct. NW11 —1C 6
St Elizabeth Ct. E10 —2D 15
St Elmo Rd. W12 —2B 46
 (in two parts)
St Elmos Rd. SE16 —3A 56
St Ermin's Hill. SW1 —4F 51
 (off Broadway)
St Ervan's Rd. W10 —4B 34
St Eugene Ct. NW6 —5A 20
 (off Salusbury Rd.)
St Faith's Rd. SE21 —1D 95
St Fillans Rd. SE6 —1E 99
St Francis' Ho. NW1 —1F 37
 (off Bridgeway St.)
St Francis Rd. SE22 —2A 82
St Frideswides M. E14
 (off Lodore St.) —5E 43
St Gabriel's Clo. E11 —3D 17
St Gabriels Mnr. SE5 —4D 67
 (off Cormont Rd.)
St Gabriels Rd. NW2 —2F 19
St George's Av. E7 —4D 31
St George's Av. N7 —1B 23
St George's Bldgs. SE1
—4D 53
 (off St George's Rd.)
St George's Cir. SE1 —4D 53
St George's Clo. NW11 —1B 6
St George's Clo. SW8 —4E 65
St Georges Ct. EC4 —5D 39

St George's Ct. SW15 —2B 76
St George's Dri. SW1 —5D 51
St George's Fields. W2
—5A 36
St George's Gro. SW17
—3F 91
St George's Ho. NW1 —1F 37
 (off Bridgeway St.)
St George's La. EC3 —1F 53
 (off Pudding La.)
St George's Mans. SW1
 (off Causton St.) —1F 65
St George's M. NW1 —4B 22
St Georges M. SE1 —4C 52
 (off Westminster Bri. Rd.)
St Georges Pde. SE6 —2B 98
St George's Path. SE4
 (off Adelaide Av.) —2C 84
St George's Rd. E7 —4D 31
St George's Rd. E10 —5E 15
St George's Rd. NW11 —1B 6
St George's Rd. SE1 —4C 52
St George's Rd. W4 —3A 46
St George's Rd. E7 —4D 31
St George's Sq. E14 —1A 56
St George's Sq. SE8 —5B 56
St George's Sq. SW1 —1F 65
St George's Sq. M. SW1
—1F 65
St George's Ter. NW1 —4B 22
St George St. W1 —1D 51
St George's Way. SE15
—2A 68
St George's Wharf. SE1
 (off Shad Thames) —3B 54
St Gerards Clo. SW4 —3E 79
St German's Pl. SE3 —4C 72
St German's Rd. SE23 —1A 98
St Giles Cir. W1 —5F 37
St Giles Ct. WC2 —5A 38
 (off St Giles High St.)
St Giles High St. WC1 —5F 37
St Giles Pas. WC2 —5F 37
 (off New Compton St.)
St Giles Rd. SE5 —3A 68
St Giles Ter. EC2 —4E 39
 (off Beech St.)
St Giles Tower. SE5 —4A 68
 (off Gables Clo.)
St Gothard Rd. SE27 —4F 95
 (in two parts)
St Helena Ho. WC1 —2C 38
 (off Margery St.)
St Helena Rd. SE16 —5F 55
St Helena St. WC1 —2C 38
St Helen's Gdns. W10 —4F 33
St Helen's Pl. EC2 —5A 40
St Helier Ct. N1 —5A 26
 (off De Beauvoir Est.)
St Helier's Rd. E10 —1E 15
St Hilda's Clo. NW6 —5F 19
St Hilda's Clo. SW17 —2A 92
St Hilda's Rd. SW13 —2D 61
St Hubert's Ho. E14 —4C 56
St Hughes Clo. SW17 —2A 92
St James SE14 —4A 70

St James Apartments. *E17*
  (off High St.) —1A **14**
St James Ct. *E2* —2C **40**
  (off Bethnal Grn. Rd.)
St James Ct. *E12* —4E **17**
St James Ct. *SE3* —4D **73**
St James Ct. *SW1* —4E **51**
St James Gro. *SW11* —5B **64**
St James M. *E14* —4E **57**
St James M. *E17* —1A **14**
  (off St James's St.)
St James Residences. *W1*
  (off Brewer St.) —1F **51**
St James' Rd. *E15* —2B **30**
St James's. —2F 51
St James's. *SW1* —2E **51**
St James's App. *E2* —3A **40**
St James's Chamber. *SW1*
  (off Jermyn St.) —2E **51**
St James's Clo. *NW8* —5B **22**
  (off St James's Ter M.)
St James's Clo. *SW17* —2B **92**
St James's Cres. *SW9* —1C **80**
St James's Dri. *SW17 &*
  SW12 —1B **92**
  —2A **48**
St James's Gdns. *W11*
St James's Mkt. *SW1* —1F **51**
St James's Palace. —3E **51**
St James's Pk. —3F **51**
St James's Pas. *EC3* —5A **40**
  (off Duke's Pl.)
St James's Pl. *SW1* —2E **51**
St James's Rd. *SE1* —2C **68**
St James's Rd. *SE16* —4C **54**
St James's Sq. *SW1* —2E **51**
St James's St. *E17* —1A **14**
St James's St. *SW1* —2E **51**
St James's Ter. *NW8* —5B **22**
  (off Prince Albert Rd.)
St James's Ter. M. *NW8*
  —5B **22**
St James St. *W6* —1E **61**
St James's Wlk. *EC1* —3D **39**
St James Ter. *SW12* —1C **92**
St John's. —5C 70
St John's Av. *NW10* —5B **18**
St John's Av. *SW15* —3F **75**
St Johns Chu. Rd. *E9* —2E **27**
St John's Clo. *SW6* —3C **62**
St John's Ct. *N4* —4D **11**
St John's Ct. *N5* —1D **25**
St John's Ct. *SE13* —5E **71**
St John's Ct. *W6* —5D **47**
  (off Glenthorne Rd.)
St John's Cres. *SW9* —1C **80**
St Johns Dri. *SW18* —1D **91**
St John's Est. *N1* —1F **39**
St John's Est. *SE1* —3D **41**
  (off Fair St.)
St John's Gdns. *W11* —1A **48**
St John's Gate. —3D **39**
  (off St John's La.)
St John's Gro. *N19* —4E **9**
St John's Gro. *SW13* —5B **60**
St John's Hill. *SW11* —3F **77**

St John's Hill Gro. *SW11*
  —2F **77**
St John's Ho. *E14* —5E **57**
St Johns Ho. *SE17* —2F **67**
  (off Lytham St.)
St John's La. *EC1* —3D **39**
St John's M. *W11* —5C **34**
St John's Pk. *SE3* —3B **72**
St John's Pk. Mans. *N19*
  —5E **9**
St John's Path. *EC1* —3D **39**
  (off Britton St.)
St Johns Pathway. *SE23*
  —1E **97**
St John's Pl. *EC1* —3D **39**
St John's Rd. *E16* —5C **44**
St John's Rd. *N15* —1A **12**
St John's Rd. *NW11* —1B **6**
St John's Rd. *SW11* —2A **78**
St John's Sq. *EC1* —3D **39**
St John's Ter. *E7* —3D **31**
St John's Ter. *SW15* —3A **88**
  (off Kingston Va.)
St John's Ter. *W10* —3F **33**
St John St. *EC1* —1C **38**
St John's Va. *SE8* —5C **70**
St John's Vs. *N19* —4F **9**
St John's Vs. *W8* —4D **49**
St John's Way. *N19* —4E **9**
St John's Wood. —1F 35
St John's Wood Ct. *NW8*
  —2F **35**
  (off St John's Wood Rd.)
St John's Wood High St. *NW8*
  —1F **35**
St John's Wood Pk. *NW8*
  —5F **21**
St John's Wood Rd. *NW8*
  —3F **35**
St John's Wood Ter. *NW8*
  —1F **35**
St Joseph's Clo. *W10* —4A **34**
St Josephs Ct. *SE7* —2D **73**
St Joseph's Flats. *NW1*
  —2F **37**
  (off Drummond Cres.)
St Joseph's St. *SW8* —4D **65**
St Joseph's Va. *SE3* —1F **85**
St Jude's Rd. *E2* —1D **41**
St Jude St. *N1* —2A **26**
St Julian's Clo. *SW16* —4C **94**
St Julian's Farm Rd. *SE27*
  —4C **94**
St Julian's Rd. *NW6* —5C **20**
St Katharine Docks. —2C **54**
St Katharine's Precinct. *NW1*
  —1D **37**
St Katharine's Way. *E1*
  (in two parts) —2B **54**
St Katherine's Row. *EC3*
  (off Fenchurch St.) —1A **54**
St Katherines Wlk. *W11*
  (off St Ann's Rd.) —2F **47**
St Kilda's Rd. *N16* —3F **11**
St Kitts Ter. *SE19* —5A **96**
St Laurence Clo. *NW6* —5F **19**

St Lawrence Cotts. *E14*
  —2E **57**
St Lawrence Ct. *N1* —4F **25**
  (off De Beauvoir Est.)
St Lawrence Ho. *SE1* —4A **54**
  (off Purbrook St.)
St Lawrence St. *E14* —2E **57**
St Lawrence Ter. *W10* —4A **34**
St Lawrence Way. *SW9*
  —5C **66**
St Leonard M. *N1* —1A **40**
St Leonard's Ct. *N1* —2F **39**
  (off New N. Rd.)
St Leonard's Rd. *E14* —4D **43**
  (in two parts)
St Leonard's Rd. *NW10*
  —3A **32**
St Leonards Sq. *NW5* —3C **22**
St Leonard's St. *E3* —2D **43**
St Leonard's Ter. *SW3* —1B **64**
St Loo Av. *SW3* —2A **64**
St Louis Rd. *SE27* —4F **95**
St Lucia Dri. *E15* —5B **30**
St Luke's. —3E 39
St Luke's Av. *SW4* —2F **79**
St Luke's Clo. *EC1* —3E **39**
St Lukes Clo. *E10* —2D **15**
  (off Capworth St.)
St Luke's Est. *EC1* —2F **39**
St Lukes M. *W11* —5B **34**
St Luke's Rd. *W11* —4B **34**
St Luke's Sq. *E16* —5B **44**
St Luke's St. *SW3* —1A **64**
St Luke's Yd. *W9* —1B **34**
  (in two parts)
St Margaret's Clo. *EC2*
  (off Lothbury) —5F **39**
St Margarets Ct. *SE1* —2E **53**
St Margarets Ct. *SW15*
  —2D **75**
St Margaret's Cres. *SW15*
  —3D **75**
St Margaret's Gro. *E11*
  —5B **16**
St Margaret's La. *W8* —4D **49**
St Margaret's Pas. *SE13*
  —1A **86**
St Margaret's Rd. *E12* —4E **17**
St Margaret's Rd. *NW10*
  —2E **33**
St Margarets Rd. *SE4*
  (in two parts) —2B **84**
St Margaret St. *SW1* —3A **52**
St Mark's Clo. *SE10* —3E **71**
St Marks Clo. *SW6* —4C **62**
St Marks Ct. *E10* —2D **15**
  (off Capworth St.)
St Marks Ct. *NW8* —1E **35**
  (off Abercorn Pl.)
St Mark's Cres. *NW1* —5C **22**
St Mark's Ga. *E9* —4B **28**
St Mark's Gro. *SW10* —3D **63**
St Marks Ho. *SE17* —2F **67**
  (off Lytham St.)
St Marks Ind. Est. *E16*
  —2F **59**

St Mark's Pl. SW19 —5B 90
St Mark's Pl. W11 —5A 34
St Mark's Ri. E8 —2B 26
St Mark's Rd. W10 & W11 —4F 33
St Mark's Sq. NW1 —5C 22
St Mark St. E1 —5B 40
St Martin's Almshouses. NW1 —5E 23
St Martin's Av. E6 —1F 45
St Martin's Clo. NW1 —5E 23
St Martins Ct. N1 —5A 26 (off De Beauvoir Est.)
St Martin's Ct. WC2 —1A 52
St Martins Est. SW2 —1C 94
St Martin's La. WC2 —1A 52
St Martin's-le-Grand. EC1 —5E 39
St Martin's Pl. WC2 —1A 52
St Martin's Rd. SW9 —5B 66
St Martin's St. WC2 —1F 51 (in two parts)
St Martins Way. SW17 —3E 91
St Mary Abbot's Ct. W14 (off Warwick Gdns.) —4B 48
St Mary Abbot's Pl. W8 —4B 48
St Mary Abbot's Ter. W14 —4B 48
St Mary at Hill. EC3 —1A 54
St Mary Axe. EC3 —5A 40
St Marychurch St. SE16 —3E 55
St Mary Graces Ct. E1 —1B 54
St Mary le-Park Ct. SW11 (off Parkgate Rd.) —3A 64
St Mary Newington Clo. SE17 (off Surrey Sq.) —1A 68
St Mary's Av. E11 —2D 17
St Mary's Ct. SE7 —3F 73
St Mary's Ct. W12 —4B 46
St Mary's Est. SE16 —3E 55 (off St Marychurch St.)
St Mary's Flats. NW1 —2F 37
St Mary's Gdns. SE11 —5C 52
St Mary's Ga. W8 —4D 49
St Mary's Gro. N1 —3D 25
St Mary's Gro. SW13 —1D 75
St Mary's Ho. N1 —5D 25 (off St Mary's Path)
St Mary's Mans. W2 —4F 35
St Mary's M. NW6 —4D 21 (in two parts)
St Mary's Path. N1 —5D 25
St Mary's Pl. W8 —4D 49
St Mary's Rd. E10 —5E 15
St Mary's Rd. E13 —1D 45
St Mary's Rd. NW10 —5A 18
St Mary's Rd. NW11 —2A 6
St Mary's Rd. SE15 —4E 69
St Mary's Rd. SW19 —5A 90
St Mary's Sq. W2 —4F 35
St Mary's Ter. W2 —4F 35
St Mary's Tower. EC1 —3E 39 (off Fortune St.)
St Mary's Wlk. SE11 —5C 52
St Matthews Ct. E10 —2D 15 (off Capworth St.)
St Matthews Ct. SE1 —4E 53 (off Meadow Row)
St Matthews Ho. SE17 (off Phelp St.) —2F 67
St Matthew's Lodge. NW1 (off Oakley Sq.) —1E 37
St Matthew's Rd. SW2 —2B 80
St Matthew's Row. E2 —2C 40
St Matthew St. SW1 —4F 51
St Maur Rd. SW6 —4B 62
St Michael's All. EC3 —5F 39
St Michaels Clo. E16 —4F 45
St Michaels Ct. E14 —4E 43 (off St Leonards Rd.)
St Michael's Ct. SE1 —3E 53 (off Trinity St.)
St Michael's Flats. NW1 (off Aldenham St.) —1F 37
St Michael's Gdns. W10 —4A 34
St Michael's Rd. NW2 —1E 19
St Michael's Rd. SW9 —5B 66
St Michael's St. W2 —5F 35
St Michaels Ter. N6 —3C 8 (off South Gro.)
St Mildred's Ct. EC2 —5F 39
St Mildreds Rd. SE6 —5A 86
St Nicholas' Flats. NW1 (off Werrington St.) —1F 37
St Nicholas Glebe. SW17 —5C 92
St Nicholas Ho. SE8 —2C 70 (off Deptford Grn.)
St Nicholas St. SE8 —4B 70
St Norbert Grn. SE4 —2A 84
St Norbert Rd. SE4 —3F 83
St Olaf Ho. SE1 —2F 53 (off Tooley St.)
St Olaf's Rd. SW6 —3A 62
St Olaf Stairs. SE1 —2F 53 (off Tooley St.)
St Olave's Ct. EC2 —5F 39
St Olave's Est. SE1 —3A 54
St Olave's Gdns. SE11 —5C 52
St Olave's Mans. SE11 —5C 52 (off Walnut Tree Wlk.)
St Olave's Ter. SE1 —3A 54 (off Fair St.)
St Oswald's Pl. SE11 —1B 66
St Oswulf St. SW1 —5F 51 (off Erasmus St.)
St Owen Ho. SE1 —4A 54 (off Fendall St.)
St Pancras. —2A 38
St Pancras Commercial Cen. (off Pratt St.) NW1 —5E 23
St Pancras Way. NW1 —4E 23
St Paul's All. EC4 —5D 39 (off St Paul's Chyd.)
St Paul's Av. NW2 —3D 19
St Paul's Av. SE16 —2F 55
St Paul's Cathedral. —5E 39
St Paul's Chyd. EC4 —5D 39 (in two parts)
St Pauls Clo. SE7 —1F 73
St Pauls Ct. SW4 —3F 79
St Pauls Courtyard. SE8 —3C 70
St Paul's Cres. NW1 —4F 23 (in two parts)
St Paul's Dri. E15 —2F 29
St Paul's M. NW1 —4F 23
St Paul's Pl. N1 —3F 25
St Paul's Rd. N1 —3D 25
St Paul's Shrubbery. N1 —3F 25
St Paul's Studios. W6 (off Talgarth Rd.) —1A 62
St Pauls Ter. SE17 —2D 67
St Pauls Tower. E10 —2D 15 (off Beaumont Rd.)
St Paul St. N1 —5E 25 (in two parts)
St Pauls Vw. Apartments. WC1 —2C 38 (off Amwell St.)
St Pauls Way. E3 —4B 42
St Peter's All. EC3 —5F 39 (off Cornhill)
St Peter's Av. E2 —1C 40
St Petersburgh M. W2 —1D 49
St Petersburgh Pl. W2 —1D 49
St Peter's Cen. E1 —2D 55 (off Watts St.)
St Peters Chu. Clo. N1 (off Devonia Rd.) —5D 25
St Peter's Clo. E2 —1C 40
St Peter's Clo. SW17 —2A 92
St Peter's Ct. NW4 —1E 5
St Peter's Gdns. SE27 —3C 94
St Peter's Gro. W6 —5C 46
St Peters Ho. SE17 —2F 67
St Peter's Ho. WC1 —2A 38 (off Regent Sq.)
St Peters Pl. W9 —3D 35
St Peter's Rd. W6 —1C 60
St Peter's Sq. E2 —1C 40
St Peter's Sq. W6 —5B 46
St Peter's St. N1 —5D 25
St Peter's St. M. N1 —1D 39 (off St Peters St.)
St Peter's Ter. SW6 —3B 62
St Peter's Vs. W6 —5C 46
St Peter's Way. N1 —4A 26
St Peter's Wharf. W4 —1C 60
St Philip Ho. WC1 —2C 38 (off Lloyd Baker St.)
St Philip Sq. SW8 —5D 65
St Philip's Rd. E8 —3C 26
St Philip St. SW8 —5D 65
St Philip's Way. N1 —5E 25
St Quintin Av. W10 —4E 33
St Quintin Gdns. W10 —4E 33
St Quintin Rd. E13 —2D 45

St Regis Heights. NW3 —5D 7
St Richard's Ho. NW1 —2F 37
(off Eversholt St.)
St Rule St. SW8 —5E 65
St Saviour's College. SE27
—4F 95
St Saviour's Est. SE1 —3B 54
St Saviour's Rd. SW2 —3B 80
St Saviour's Wharf. SE1
(off Shad Thames) —3B 54
St Saviour's Wharf. SE1
(off Mill St.) —3B 54
Saints Clo. N8 —4D 95
Saints Dri. E7 —2F 31
St Silas Pl. NW5 —3C 22
St Simon's Av. SW15 —3E 75
St Stephen's Av. E17 —1E 15
St Stephen's Av. W12 —3D 47
(in two parts)
St Stephen's Clo. E17 —1D 15
St Stephen's Clo. NW8
—5A 22
St Stephens Ct. N8 —1B 10
St Stephen's Cres. W2
—5C 34
St Stephen's Gdns. SW15
—3B 76
St Stephen's Gdns. W2
(in two parts) —5C 34
St Stephens Gro. SE13
—1E 85
St Stephens Ho. SE17
(off Lytham St.) —2F 67
St Stephens M. W2 —4C 34
St Stephens Pde. E7 —4E 31
St Stephen's Rd. E3 —5A 28
St Stephen's Rd. E6 —4E 31
St Stephen's Rd. E17 —1D 15
St Stephen's Row. EC4
(off Walbrook) —5F 39
St Stephen's Ter. SW8
—3B 66
St Stephen's Wlk. SW7
—5E 49
(off Southwell Gdns.)
St Swithins La. EC4 —1F 53
St Swithun's Rd. SE13
—4F 85
St Thomas Ct. E10 —2D 15
(off Beaumont Rd.)
St Thomas Rd. E16 —5C 44
St Thomas's Gdns. NW5
—3C 22
St Thomas's Pl. E9 —4E 27
St Thomas's Rd. N4 —4C 10
St Thomas's Rd. NW10
—5A 18
St Thomas's Sq. E9 —4E 27
St Thomas St. SE1 —2F 53
St Thomas's Way. SW6
—3B 62
St Vincent Clo. SE27 —5D 95
St Vincent De Paul Ho. E1
(off Jubilee St.) —4E 41
St Vincent Ho. SE1 —4B 54
(off Fendall St.)

St Vincent St. W1 —4C 36
Sala Ho. SE3 —2D 87
Salamanca Pl. SE1 —5B 52
Salamanca St. SE1 & SE11
—5B 52
Salcombe Rd. E17 —2B 14
Salcombe Rd. N16 —2A 26
Salcott Rd. SW11 —3A 78
Salehurst Rd. SE4 —4B 84
Salem Rd. W2 —1D 49
Sale Pl. W2 —4A 36
Sale St. E2 —3C 40
Salford Ho. E14 —5E 57
Salford Rd. SW2 —1F 93
Salisbury Clo. SE17 —5F 53
Salisbury Ct. EC4 —5D 39
Salisbury Ho. E14 —5D 43
Salisbury Ho. EC2 —4F 39
(off London Wall)
Salisbury Ho. N1 —5D 25
(off St Mary's Path)
Salisbury Ho. SW1 —1F 65
(off Drummond Ga.)
Salisbury Ho. SW9 —3C 66
(off Cranmer Rd.)
Salisbury Mans. N4 —1D 11
Salisbury M. SW6 —3B 62
Salisbury Pas. SW6 —3B 62
(off Dawes Rd.)
Salisbury Pavement. SW6
(off Dawes Rd.) —3B 62
Salisbury Pl. SW9 —3D 67
Salisbury Pl. W1 —4B 36
Salisbury Rd. E7 —3C 30
Salisbury Rd. E10 —4E 15
Salisbury Rd. E12 —2F 31
Salisbury Rd. E17 —1E 15
Salisbury Rd. N4 —1D 11
Salisbury Sq. EC4 —5C 38
Salisbury St. NW8 —3A 36
Salisbury Ter. SE15 —1E 83
Salisbury Wlk. N19 —4E 9
Salmen Rd. E13 —1B 44
Salmon La. E1 —5A 42
Salmon La. E14 —5A 42
Salmon M. NW6 —2C 20
Salmon St. E14 —5B 42
Salomons Rd. E13 —4E 45
Salop Rd. E17 —1F 13
Saltcoats Rd. W4 —3A 46
Saltdene. N4 —3B 10
Salterford Rd. SW17 —5C 92
Salter Rd. SE16 —2F 55
Salters Ct. EC4 —5E 39
(off Bow La.)
Salters Hall Ct. EC4 —1F 53
(off Cannon St.)
Salter's Hill. SE19 —5F 95
Salters Rd. W10 —3F 33
Salter St. E14 —1B 56
Salter St. NW10 —2C 32
Saltley Clo. E6 —5F 45
Salterton Rd. N7 —5B 10
Saltoun Rd. SW2 —2C 80
Saltram Cres. W9 —2B 34
Saltwell St. E14 —1C 56

Saltwood Gro. SE17 —1F 67
Saltwood Ho. SE15 —2E 69
(off Lovelinch Clo.)
Salusbury Rd. NW6 —5A 20
Salutation Rd. SE10 —5A 58
Salvador. SW17 —5B 92
Salvin Rd. SW15 —1F 75
Salway Pl. E15 —3F 29
Salway Rd. E15 —3F 29
Samantha Clo. E17 —2B 14
Sam Bartram Clo. SE7 —1E 73
Sambrook Ho. E1 —4E 41
(off Jubilee St.)
Sambrook Ho. SE11 —5C 52
(off Hotspur St.)
Sambruck M. SE6 —1D 99
Samels Ct. W6 —1C 60
Samford Ho. N1 —5C 24
(off Barnsbury Est.)
Samford St. NW8 —3F 35
Samira Clo. E17 —1C 14
Sam Manners Ho. SE10
(off Tuskar St.) —1A 72
Sam March Ho. E14 —5F 43
Sampson Ho. SE1 —2D 53
Sampson St. E1 —2C 54
Samson St. E13 —1E 45
Samuda Est. E14 —4E 57
Samuel Clo. E8 —5B 26
Samuel Clo. SE14 —2F 69
Samuel Ho. E8 —5B 26
Samuel Johnson Clo. SW16
—4B 94
Samuel Jones Ind. Est. SE5
(off Peckham Gro.) —3A 68
Samuel Lewis Bldgs. N1
—3C 24
Samuel Lewis Trust Dwellings.
E8 —2C 26
Samuel Lewis Trust Dwellings.
N15 —1A 12
Samuel Lewis Trust Dwellings.
SE5 —4E 67
(off Warner Rd.)
Samuel Lewis Trust Dwellings.
SW3 —5A 50
(off Ixworth Pl., in two parts)
Samuel Lewis Trust Dwellings.
SW6 —3C 62
(off Vanston Pl.)
Samuel Lewis Trust Dwellings.
(off Lisgar Ter.) W14 —5B 48
Samuel Richardson Ho. W14
(off N. End Cres.) —5B 48
Samuel's Clo. W6 —5E 47
Samuel St. SE15 —3B 68
Sancroft Clo. NW2 —5D 3
Sancroft Ho. SE11 —1B 66
(off Sancroft St.)
Sancroft St. SE11 —1B 66
Sanctuary St. SE1 —3E 53
Sanctuary, The. SW1 —4F 51
(off Broadway Sanctuary)
Sandale Clo. N16 —5F 11
Sandall Ho. E3 —1A 42
Sandall Rd. NW5 —3E 23

Sandal St. *E15* —5A **30**
Sandalwood Clo. *E1* —3A **42**
Sandalwood Mans. *W8*
　　　　　　—4D **49**
Sandbourne. *NW8* —5D **21**
　(off Abbey Rd.)
Sandbourne. *W11* —5C **34**
　(off Dartmouth Clo.)
Sandbourne Rd. *SE4* —5A **70**
Sandbrook Rd. *N16* —5A **12**
Sandby Grn. *SE9* —1F **87**
Sandby Ho. *NW6* —5C **20**
Sandell St. *SE1* —3C **52**
Sanderling Ct. *SE8* —2B **70**
　(off Abinger Gro.)
Sanders Ho. *WC1* —2C **38**
　(off Gt. Percy St.)
Sanderson Clo. *NW5* —1D **23**
Sanderson Ho. *SE18* —1B **70**
　(off Grove St.)
Sanderstead Av. *NW2* —4A **6**
Sanderstead Clo. *SW12*
　　　　　　—5E **79**
Sanderstead Rd. *E10* —3A **14**
Sanders Way. *N19* —3F **9**
Sandfield. *WC1* —2A **38**
　(off Cromer St.)
Sandford Ct. *N16* —3A **12**
Sandford Row. *SE17* —1F **67**
Sandford Rd. *SW6* —3D **63**
Sandgate Ho. *E5* —2D **27**
Sandgate La. *SW18* —1A **92**
Sandgate St. *SE15* —2D **69**
Sandgate Trad. Est. *SE15*
　(off Sandgate St.) —2D **69**
Sandham Ct. *SW4* —4A **66**
Sandhills, The. *SW10* —2E **63**
　(off Limerston St.)
Sandhurst Ct. *SW2* —2A **80**
Sandhurst Ho. *E1* —4E **41**
　(off Wolsey St.)
Sandhurst Mkt. *SE6* —1E **99**
　(off Sangley Rd.)
Sandhurst Rd. *SE6* —1F **99**
Sandifer Dri. *NW2* —5F **5**
Sandilands Rd. *SW6* —4D **63**
Sandison St. *SE15* —1C **82**
Sandland St. *WC1* —4B **38**
Sandlings Clo. *SE15* —5D **69**
Sandmere Rd. *SW4* —2A **80**
Sandown Rd. *SE26* —3D **97**
Sandpiper Clo. *SE16* —3B **56**
Sandpiper Ct. *E14* —4E **57**
Sandpiper Ct. *SE8* —2C **70**
　(off Edward7 St.)
Sandpit Pl. *SE7* —1F **73**
Sandpit Rd. *Brom* —5A **100**
Sandridge Ct. *N4* —4E **11**
Sandridge St. *N19* —4E **9**
Sandringham Clo. *SW19*
　　　　　　—1F **89**
Sandringham Ct. *SE16*
　　　　　　—2F **55**
　(off King & Queen Wharf)
Sandringham Ct. *W1* —5E **37**
　(off Dufour's Pl.)

Sandringham Ct. *W9*
　(off Maida Va.) —2E **35**
Sandringham Flats. *WC2*
　　　　　　—1F **51**
　(off Charing Cross Rd.)
Sandringham Gdns. *N8*
　　　　　　—1A **10**
Sandringham Ho. *W14*
　(off Windsor Way) —5A **48**
Sandringham Rd. *E7*
　　　　　　—2E **31**
Sandringham Rd. *E8*
　　　　　　—2B **26**
Sandringham Rd. *E10*
　　　　　　—1F **15**
Sandringham Rd. *NW2*
　　　　　　—3D **19**
Sandringham Rd. *NW11*
　　　　　　—2A **6**
Sandringham Rd. *Brom*
　　　　　　—5C **100**
Sandrock Rd. *SE13* —1C **84**
Sand's End La. *SW6* —4D **63**
Sandstone Pl. *N19* —4D **9**
Sandstone Rd. *SE12*
　　　　　　—2D **101**
Sandtoft Rd. *SE7* —2D **73**
Sandwell Cres. *NW6* —3C **20**
Sandwich Ho. *SE16* —3E **55**
　(off Swan Rd.)
Sandwich Ho. *WC1* —2A **38**
　(off Sandwich St.)
Sandwich St. *WC1* —2A **38**
Sandy Ho. *NW3* —4D **7**
Sandys Row. *E1* —4A **40**
Sanford La. *N16* —5B **12**
　(in two parts)
Sanford St. *SE14* —2A **70**
Sanford Ter. *N16* —5B **12**
Sanford Wlk. *N16* —4B **12**
Sanford Wlk. *SE14* —2A **70**
Sangley Rd. *SE6* —5D **85**
Sangora Rd. *SW11* —2F **77**
Sankey Ho. *E2* —1E **41**
　(off St James's Av.)
Sansom Rd. *E11* —4B **16**
Sansom St. *SE5* —4F **67**
Sans Wlk. *EC1* —3C **38**
Santley Ho. *SE1* —3C **52**
Santley St. *SW4* —2B **80**
Santos Rd. *SW18* —3C **76**
Sapcote Trad. Est. *NW10*
　　　　　　—3B **18**
Saperton Wlk. *SE11* —5B **52**
　(off Juxon St.)
Sapperton Ct. *EC1* —3E **39**
　(off Gee St.)
Sapphire Ct. *E1* —1C **54**
　(off Cable St.)
Sapphire Rd. *SE8* —5A **56**
Saracens Head Yd. *EC3*
　(off Jewry St.) —5B **40**
Saracen St. *E14* —5C **42**
Sarah Ho. *E1* —5D **41**
　(off Commercial Rd.)

Sarah St. *N1* —2A **40**
Sarah Swift Ho. *SE1* —3F **53**
　(off Kipling St.)
Sara La. Ct. *N1* —1A **40**
　(off Stanway St.)
Saratoga Rd. *E5* —1E **27**
Sardinia St. *WC2* —5B **38**
Sarjant Path. *SW19* —2F **89**
　(off Blincoe Clo.)
Sark Wlk. *E16* —5D **45**
Sarnesfield Ho. *SE15* —2D **69**
　(off Pencraig Way)
Sarratt Ho. *W10* —4E **33**
　(off Sutton Way)
Sarre Rd. *NW2* —2B **20**
Sarsfeld Rd. *SW12* —2B **92**
Sartor Rd. *SE15* —2F **83**
Sarum Ter. *E3* —3B **42**
Satanita Clo. *E16* —5F **45**
Satchwell Rd. *E2* —2C **40**
Satchwell St. *E2* —2C **40**
Sattar M. *N16* —5F **11**
　(off Clissold Rd.)
Saul Ct. *SE15* —2B **68**
Sauls Grn. *E11* —5A **16**
Saunders Clo. *E14* —1B **56**
Saunders Ho. *W11* —2F **47**
Saunders Ness Rd. *E14*
　　　　　　—1E **71**
Saunders St. *SE11* —5C **52**
Savage Gdns. *EC3* —1A **54**
　(in two parts)
Savernake Ho. *N4* —2E **11**
Savernake Rd. *NW3* —1B **22**
Savile Row. *W1* —1E **51**
Saville Rd. *E16* —2F **59**
Savill Ho. *SW4* —4F **79**
Savona Ho. *SW8* —3E **65**
Savona St. *SW8* —3E **65**
Savoy Bldgs. *WC2* —1B **52**
　(off Strand)
Savoy Clo. *E15* —5A **30**
Savoy Ct. *NW3* —5E **7**
Savoy Ct. *WC2* —1B **52**
Savoy Hill. *WC2* —1B **52**
Savoy Pl. *WC2* —1A **52**
Savoy Row. *WC2* —1B **52**
　(off Savoy St.)
Savoy Steps. *WC2* —1B **52**
　(off Savoy Row)
Savoy St. *WC2* —1B **52**
Savoy Way. *WC2* —1B **52**
　(off Savoy Hill)
Sawkins Clo. *SW19* —2A **90**
Sawley Rd. *W12* —2B **46**
Sawmill Yd. *E3* —5A **28**
Sawyer Ct. *NW10* —4A **18**
Sawyer St. *SE1* —3E **53**
Saxby Rd. *SW2* —5A **80**
Saxonbury Ct. *N7* —2A **24**
Saxon Clo. *E17* —2C **14**
Saxonfield Clo. *SW2* —1B **94**
Saxon Rd. *E3* —1B **42**
Saxton Clo. *SE13* —1F **85**
Sayes Ct. *SE8* —2B **70**
Sayes Ct. St. *SE8* —2B **70**

Scafell. NW1 —2E **37**
(off Stanhope St.)
Scala St. W1 —4E **37**
Scampston M. *W10* —5F **33**
Scandrett St. *E1* —2D **55**
Scarba Wlk. N1 —3F **25**
(off Marquess Rd.)
Scarborough Rd. *E11* —3F **15**
Scarborough Rd. *N4* —3C **10**
Scarborough St. *E1* —5B **40**
Scarlet Rd. *SE6* —3A **100**
Scarlette Mnr. Way. *SW2*
—5C **80**
Scarsbrook Rd. *SE3* —1F **87**
Scarsdale Pl. *W8* —4D **49**
Scarsdale Vs. *W8* —4C **48**
Scarth Rd. *SW13* —1B **74**
Scawen Rd. *SE8* —1A **70**
Scawfell St. *E2* —1B **40**
Sceaux Gdns. *SE5* —4A **68**
Sceptre Ct. *E1* —1B **54**
(off Tower Hill)
Sceptre Ho. *E1* —3E **41**
(off Malcolm Rd.)
Schafer Ho. *NW1* —2E **37**
Schofield Wlk. *SE3* —3C **72**
Scholars Rd. *SW12* —1E **93**
Scholefield Rd. *N19* —3F **9**
Scholey Ho. *SW11* —1A **78**
Schomberg Ho. *SW1* —5F **51**
(off Page St.)
Schonfeld Sq. *N16* —4F **11**
School App. *E2* —2A **40**
Schoolbank Rd. *SE10*
—4B **58**
Schoolbell M. *E3* —1A **42**
School Ho. SE1 —5A **54**
(off Quadrangle Clo.)
School Ho. La. *E1* —1F **55**
School Rd. *NW10* —3A **32**
Schooner Clo. *E14* —4F **57**
Schooner Clo. *SE16* —3F **55**
Schubert Rd. *SW15* —3B **76**
Science Mus. —4F **49**
Sclater St. *E1* —3B **40**
Scoble Pl. *N16* —1B **26**
Scoles Cres. *SW2* —1C **94**
Scoresby St. *SE1* —2D **53**
Scorton Ho. N1 —1A **40**
(off Whitmore Est.)
Scotch House. (Junct.)
—3B **50**
Scoter Ct. SE8 —2B **70**
(off Abinger Gro.)
Scotia Building. E1 —1F **55**
(off Jardine Rd.)
Scotia Ct. SE16 —4F **55**
(off Canada Est.)
Scotia Rd. *SW2* —5C **80**
Scotland Pl. *SW1* —2A **52**
Scotney Ho. *E9* —3E **27**
Scotsdale Rd. *SE12* —3D **87**
Scotson Ho. SE11 —5C **52**
(off Marylee Way)
Scotswood St. *EC1* —3C **38**
Scott Ellis Gdns. *NW8* —2F **35**

Scott Ho. *E13* —1C **44**
(off Queens Rd. W.)
Scott Ho. E14 —3C **56**
(off Admirals Way)
Scott Ho. N1 —5F **25**
(off Sherborne St.)
Scott Ho. N7 —3B **24**
(off Caledonian Rd.)
Scott Ho. NW1 —3A **36**
(off Ashmill St.)
Scott Ho. NW10 —4A **18**
(off Stonebridge Pk.)
Scott Lidgett Cres. *SE16*
—3C **54**
Scott Russell Pl. *E14* —1D **71**
Scott's Rd. *E10* —3E **15**
Scott's Rd. *W12* —3D **47**
Scott's Sufferance Wharf. SE1
(off Mill St.) —3B **54**
Scott St. *E1* —3D **41**
Scott's Yd. EC4 —1F **53**
(off Gophir La.)
Scoulding Ho. *E14* —4C **56**
Scoulding Rd. *E16* —5C **44**
Scouler St. *E14* —1E **57**
Scout App. *NW10* —1A **18**
Scout La. *SW4* —1E **79**
Scovell Cres. *SE1* —3E **53**
(off McCoid Way)
Scovell Rd. *SE1* —3E **53**
Scriven St. *E8* —5B **26**
Scriven St. *E8* —5B **26**
Scrooby St. *SE6* —4D **85**
Scrope Ho. EC1 —4C **38**
(off Bourne Est.)
Scrubs La. *NW10* —2C **32**
Scrutton Clo. *SW12* —5F **79**
Scrutton St. *EC2* —3A **40**
Scutari Rd. *SE22* —3E **83**
Scylla Rd. *SE15* —1C **82**
(in two parts)
Seabright St. *E2* —2D **41**
Seacole Clo. *W3* —5A **32**
Seaford Ho. SE16 —3E **55**
(off Swan Rd.)
Seaford St. *WC1* —2B **38**
Seaforth Cres. *N5* —2E **25**
Seaforth Pl. SW1 —4E **51**
(off Buckingham Ga.)
Seagar Bldgs. *SE8* —4C **70**
Seagar Pl. *E3* —4B **42**
Seagrave Clo. *E1* —4F **41**
Seagrave Lodge. SW6
(off Seagrave Rd.) —2C **62**
Seagrave Rd. *SW6* —2C **62**
Seagry Rd. *E11* —2C **16**
Seal Ho. SE1 —4F **53**
(off Pardoner St.)
Seal St. *E8* —1B **26**
Searle Pl. *N4* —3B **10**
Searles Clo. *SW11* —3A **64**
Searles Rd. *SE1* —5F **53**
Searson Ho. SE17 —5D **53**
(off Canterbury Pl.)
Sears St. *SE5* —3F **67**
Seaton Clo. *E13* —3C **44**

Seaton Clo. *SE11* —1C **66**
Seaton Clo. *SW15* —1D **89**
Seaton Point. *E5* —1C **26**
Sebastian Ho. N1 —1A **40**
(off Hoxton St.)
Sebastian St. EC1 —2D **39**
Sebbon St. *N1* —4D **25**
Sebright Ho. E2 —1C **40**
(off Coate St.)
Sebright Pas. *E2* —1C **40**
Secker Ho. SW9 —5D **67**
(off Loughborough Est.)
Secker St. *SE1* —2C **52**
Second Av. *E13* —2C **44**
Second Av. *E17* —1C **14**
Second Av. *SW14* —1A **74**
Second Av. *W3* —2B **46**
Second Av. *W10* —3A **34**
Sedan Way. *SE17* —1A **68**
Sedding St. *SW1* —5C **50**
Sedding Studios. SW1
(off Sedding St.) —5C **50**
Seddon Highwalk. *EC2*
(off Barbican) —4E **39**
Seddon Ho. EC2 —4E **39**
(off Beech St.)
Seddon St. *WC1* —2B **38**
Sedgebrook Rd. *SE3* —5F **73**
Sedgeford Rd. *W12* —2D **46**
Sedgehill Rd. *SE6* —4C **98**
Sedgeway. *SE6* —1B **100**
Sedgmoor Pl. *SE5* —3A **68**
Sedgwick Ho. *E3* —4C **42**
Sedgwick Rd. *E10* —4E **15**
Sedgwick St. *E9* —2F **27**
Sedleigh Rd. *SW18* —4B **76**
Sedlescombe Rd. *SW6*
—2C **62**
Sedley Ct. *SE26* —2D **97**
Sedley Ho. SE11 —1B **66**
(off Newburn St.)
Sedley Pl. *W1* —5D **37**
Seeley Dri. *SE21* —4A **96**
Seelig Av. *NW9* —2C **4**
Seely Rd. *SW17* —5C **92**
Seething La. *EC3* —1A **54**
Sefton St. *SW15* —1E **75**
Segal Clo. *SE23* —5A **84**
Sekforde St. *EC1* —3D **39**
Selbie Av. *NW10* —2B **18**
Selborne Rd. *SE5* —5F **67**
Selbourne Ho. SE1 —3F **53**
(off Gt. Dover St.)
Selby Clo. *E6* —4F **45**
Selby Ho. W10 —2A **34**
(off Beethoven St.)
Selby Rd. *E11* —5A **16**
Selby Rd. *E13* —4D **45**
Selby St. *E1* —3C **40**
Selcroft Ho. SE10 —1B **72**
(off Glenister Rd.)
Selden Ho. *SE15* —5F **69**
(off Selden Rd.)
Selden Rd. *SE15* —5E **69**
Selden Wlk. *N7* —4B **10**

*Seldon Ho. SW1 —1E **65***
(off Churchill Gdns.)
*Seldon Ho. SW8 —3E **65***
(off Stewart's Rd.)
Selhurst Clo. *SW19* —1F **89**
*Selina Ho. NW8 —3F **35***
(off Frampton St.)
Selkirk Rd. *SW17* —4A **92**
Sellincourt Rd. *SW17* —5A **92**
Sellons Av. *NW10* —5B **18**
Selsdon Rd. *E11* —2C **16**
Selsdon Rd. *E13* —5E **31**
Selsdon Rd. *NW2* —4B **4**
Selsdon Rd. *SE27* —3C **94**
Selsdon Way. *E14* —4D **57**
Selsea Pl. *N16* —2A **26**
Selsey St. *E3* —4C **42**
Selsey St. *E14* —4C **42**
*Selway Ho. SW8 —4A **66***
(off S. Lambeth Rd.)
Selwood Pl. *SW7* —1F **63**
Selwood Ter. *SW7* —1F **63**
Selworthy Clo. *E11* —1C **16**
Selworthy Rd. *SE6* —3B **98**
*Selwyn Ct. E17 —1C **14***
(off Yunus Khan Clo.)
Selwyn Ct. *SE3* —1B **86**
Selwyn Rd. *E3* —1B **42**
Selwyn Rd. *E13* —5D **31**
Selwyn Rd. *NW10* —4A **18**
Semley Ga. *E9* —3B **28**
*Semley Ho. SW1 —5D **51***
(off Semley Pl.)
Semley Pl. *SW1* —5C **50**
Senate St. *SE15* —5E **69**
Senior St. *W2* —4D **35**
Senlac Rd. *SE12* —1D **101**
Sennen Wlk. *SE9* —3F **101**
Senrab St. *E1* —5F **41**
*Seraph Ct. EC1 —2E **39***
(off Moreland St.)
Serbin Clo. *E10* —2E **15**
Sergeant Ind. Est. *SW18* —4D **77**
Serica Ct. *SE10* —3E **71**
Serjeant's Inn. *EC4* —5C **38**
Serle St. *WC2* —5B **38**
*Sermon La. EC4 —5E **39***
(off Carter La.)
Serpentine Gallery. —3F 49
Serpentine Rd. *W2* —2A **50**
Setchell Rd. *SE1* —5B **54**
Setchell Way. *SE1* —5B **54**
Seth St. *SE16* —3E **55**
Settle Rd. *E13* —1C **44**
Settles St. *E1* —4C **40**
Settrington Rd. *SW6* —5D **63**
Seven Dials. *WC2* —5A **38**
*Seven Dials Ct. WC2 —5A **38***
(off Short Gdns.)
Sevenoaks Rd. *SE4* —4A **84**
Seven Sisters Rd. *N7 & N4* —5B **10**
Seven Sisters Rd. *N15* —1F **11**
Seven Stars Corner. *W6* —4C **46**
Severnake Clo. *E14* —5C **56**
Severn Way. *NW10* —2B **18**
Severus Rd. *SW11* —2A **78**
Seville M. *N1* —4A **26**
Seville St. *SW1* —3B **50**
Sevington Rd. *NW4* —1D **5**
Sevington St. *W9* —3D **35**
Sewardstone Rd. *E2* —1E **41**
Seward St. *EC1* —2D **39**
Sewdley St. *E5* —5F **13**
Sewell St. *E13* —2C **44**
Sextant Av. *E14* —5F **57**
*Sextons Ho. SE10 —2E **71***
(off Bardsley La.)
Seymour Ct. *NW2* —4D **5**
Seymour Gdns. *SE4* —1A **84**
*Seymour Ho. NW1 —2F **37***
(off Churchway)
*Seymour Ho. WC1 —3A **38***
(off Tavistock Pl.)
Seymour M. *W1* —5C **36**
Seymour Pl. *W1* —4B **36**
Seymour Rd. *E6* —1F **45**
Seymour Rd. *E10* —3B **14**
Seymour Rd. *N8* —1C **10**
Seymour Rd. *SW18* —5B **76**
Seymour Rd. *SW19* —3F **89**
Seymour Rd. Ind. Est. *E10* —3B **14**
Seymour St. *W2 & W1* —5B **36**
Seymour Wlk. *SW10* —2E **63**
Seyssel St. *E14* —5E **57**
Shaa Rd. *W3* —1A **46**
Shackleton Clo. *SE23* —2D **97**
Shackleton Ct. *E14* —1C **70**
Shackleton Ct. *W12* —3D **47**
*Shackleton Ho. E1 —2E **55***
(off Prusom St.)
Shackleton Ho. *NW10* —4A **18**
Shacklewell. —1B 26
Shacklewell Grn. *E8* —1B **26**
Shacklewell Ho. *E8* —1B **26**
Shacklewell La. *N16* —2B **26**
Shacklewell Rd. *N16* —1B **26**
Shacklewell Row. *E8* —1B **26**
Shacklewell St. *E2* —2B **40**
Shad Thames. *SE1* —2B **54**
Shadwell. —1D 55
*Shadwell Gdns. E1 —1E **55***
(off Sutton St.)
Shadwell Pier Head. *E1* —1E **55**
*Shadwell Pl. E1 —1E **55***
(off Shadwell Gdns.)
Shaftesbury Av. *WC1 & WC2* —5A **38**
Shaftesbury Cen. W10
*(off Barlby Rd.) —3F **33***
*Shaftesbury Ct. N1 —1F **39***
(off Shaftesbury St)
*Shaftesbury Ct. SW6 —4D **63***
(off Maltings Pl.)
Shaftesbury Ct. *SW16* —3F **93**
Shaftesbury Gdns. *NW10* —3A **32**
Shaftesbury Lodge. E14
*(off Upper N. St.) —5D **43***
*Shaftesbury M. SE1 —4F **53***
(off Falmouth Rd.)
Shaftesbury M. *SW4* —3E **79**
*Shaftesbury M. W8 —4C **48***
(off Stratford Rd.)
*Shaftesbury Pl. EC2 —4E **39***
(off London Wall)
*Shaftesbury Pl. W14 —5B **48***
(off Warwick Rd.)
Shaftesbury Point. E13
*(off High St.) —1C **44***
Shaftesbury Rd. *E7* —4E **31**
Shaftesbury Rd. *E10* —3C **14**
Shaftesbury Rd. *E17* —1D **15**
Shaftesbury Rd. *N19* —3A **10**
Shaftesbury St. *N1* —1E **39**
(in two parts)
Shafto M. *SW1* —4B **50**
Shafton M. *E9* —5F **27**
Shafton Rd. *E9* —5F **27**
Shaftsbury Ct. *SE5* —2F **81**
Shafts Ct. *EC3* —5A **40**
*Shahjalal Ho. E2 —1C **40***
(off Pritchards Rd.)
Shakespeare Rd. *SE24* —3D **81**
Shakespeare's Globe Exhibition. —2E 53
(off Shakespeare's Globe Theatre)
Shakespeare's Globe Theatre. —2E 53
Shakespeare Tower. EC2
*(off Beech St.) —4E **39***
Shakspeare M. *N16* —1A **26**
Shakspeare Wlk. *N16* —1A **26**
Shalcomb St. *SW10* —2E **63**
Shalden Ho. *SW15* —4B **74**
Shalfleet Dri. *W10* —1F **47**
*Shalford Ct. N1 —1D **39***
(off Charlton Pl.)
Shalford Ho. *SE1* —4F **53**
Shamrock St. *SW4* —1F **79**
Shandon Rd. *SW4* —4E **79**
Shand St. *SE1* —3A **54**
Shandy St. *E1* —4F **41**
Shanklin Rd. *N8* —1F **9**
Shanklin Way. *SE15* —3B **68**
Shannon Clo. *NW2* —5F **5**
Shannon Ct. *N16* —5A **12**
Shannon Gro. *SW9* —2B **80**
Shannon Pl. *NW8* —1A **36**
Shanti Ct. *SW18* —1C **90**
Shap St. *E2* —1B **40**
Shardcroft Av. *SE24* —3D **81**
Shardeloes Rd. *SE14* —5B **70**
Shard's Sq. *SE15* —2C **68**
Sharnbrook Ho. *W14* —2C **62**
Sharon Gdns. *E9* —5E **27**
Sharp Ho. *SW8* —1D **79**
Sharpleshall St. *NW1* —4B **22**

Sharpness Ct. SE15 —3B **68**
(off Daniel Gdns.)
Sharratt St. SE15 —2E **69**
Sharsted St. SE17 —1D **67**
Sharwood. WC1 —1B **38**
(off Penton Ri.)
Shaver's Pl. SW1 —1F **51**
(off Coventry St.)
Shawbrooke Rd. SE9 —3E **87**
Shawbury Rd. SE22 —3B **82**
Shawfield St. SW3 —1A **64**
Shawford Ct. SW15 —5C **74**
Shaw Path. Brom —3B **100**
Shaw Rd. SE22 —2A **82**
Shaw Rd. Brom —3B **100**
Shaws Cotts. SE23 —3A **98**
Shearling Way. N7 —3A **24**
Shearman Rd. SE3 —2B **86**
Shearwater Ct. SE8 —2B **70**
(off Abinger Gro.)
Sheenewood. SE26 —4D **97**
Sheengate Mans. SW14
—2A **74**
Sheen Gro. N1 —5C **24**
Sheepcote La. SW11 —5B **64**
Sheep La. E8 —5D **27**
Sheep Wlk. M. SW19 —5F **89**
Sheerwater Rd. E16 —4F **45**
Sheffield Sq. E3 —2B **42**
Sheffield St. WC2 —5B **38**
Sheffield Ter. W8 —2C **48**
Shelburne Rd. N7 —1B **24**
Shelbury Rd. SE22 —3D **83**
Sheldon Av. N6 —2A **8**
Sheldon Clo. SE12 —3D **87**
Sheldon Ct. SW8 —4A **66**
(off Lansdowne Grn.)
Sheldon Rd. NW2 —1F **19**
Sheldrake Ho. SE16 —5F **55**
(off Tawny Way)
Sheldrake Pl. W8 —3C **48**
Shelduck Clo. E15 —2B **30**
Shelduck Ct. SE8 —2B **70**
(off Pilot Clo.)
Shelford Pl. N16 —5F **11**
Shelgate Rd. SW11 —3A **78**
Shelley Av. E12 —3F **31**
Shelley Clo. SE15 —5D **69**
Shelley Ct. E10 —2D **15**
(off Skelton's La.)
Shelley Ct. N19 —3B **10**
Shelley Ct. SW3 —2B **64**
(off Tite St.)
Shelley Ho. E2 —2E **41**
(off Cornwall Av.)
Shelley Ho. SE17 —1E **67**
(off Browning St.)
Shelley Ho. SW1 —2E **65**
(off Churchill Gdns.)
Shelley Rd. NW10 —5A **18**
Shelley Way. SW19 —5F **91**
Shellness Rd. E5 —2D **27**
Shell Rd. SE13 —1D **85**
Shellwood Rd. SW11
—5B **64**
Shelmerdine Clo. E3 —4C **42**

Shelton St. WC2 —5A **38**
(in two parts)
Shene Ho. EC1 —4C **38**
(off Bourne Est.)
Shenfield Ho. SE18 —4F **73**
(off Portway Gdns.)
Shenfield St. N1 —1A **40**
(in two parts)
Shenley Rd. SE5 —4A **68**
Shepherd Clo. W1 —1C **50**
(off Lees Pl.)
Shepherdess Pl. N1 —2E **39**
Shepherdess Wlk. N1 —1E **39**
Shepherd Ho. E14 —5D **43**
(off Dorman Way)
Shepherd Mkt. W1 —2D **51**
Shepherd's Bush. —3E 47
Shepherd's Bush Grn. W12
—3E **47**
Shepherd's Bush Mkt. W12
—3E **47**
Shepherd's Bush Pl. W12
—3F **47**
Shepherd's Bush Rd. W6
—5E **47**
Shepherd's Clo. N6 —1D **9**
Shepherds Ct. W12 —3F **47**
(off Shepherd's Bush Grn.)
Shepherd's Hill. N6 —1D **9**
Shepherds La. E9 —3F **27**
Shepherd's Path. NW3
(off Lyndhurst Rd.) —2F **21**
Shepherds Pl. W1 —1C **50**
Shepherds Wlk. NW2 —4C **4**
Shepherds Wlk. NW3 —2F **21**
Sheppard Dri. SE16 —1D **69**
Sheppard Ho. E2 —1C **40**
(off Warner Pl.)
Sheppard Ho. SW2 —1C **94**
Sheppard St. E16 —3B **44**
Shepperton Rd. N1 —5E **25**
Sheppey Wlk. N1 —3E **25**
*Shepton Houses. E2 —2E **41***
(off Welwyn St.)
Sherard Ct. N7 —5A **10**
Sheraton Ho. SW1 —2D **65**
(off Churchill Gdns.)
Sheraton St. W1 —5F **37**
Sherborne Ho. SW1 —1D **65**
Sherborne Ho. SW8 —3B **66**
(off Bolney St.)
Sherborne La. EC4 —1F **53**
Sherborne St. N1 —5F **25**
Sherboro Rd. N15 —1B **12**
Sherbrooke Ho. E2 —1E **41**
(off Bonner Rd.)
Sherbrooke Rd. SW6 —3A **62**
Shere Ho. SE1 —4F **53**
(off Gt. Dover St.)
Sherfield Gdns. SW15 —4B **74**
Sheridan Bldgs. WC2
(off Martlett Ct.) —5A **38**
Sheridan Ct. NW6 —4E **21**
(off Belsize Rd.)
Sheridan Ho. E1 —5E **41**
(off Tarling St.)

Sheridan Ho. SE11 —5C **52**
(off Wincott St.)
Sheridan M. E11 —1D **17**
(off High St.)
Sheridan Pl. SW13 —1B **74**
Sheridan Rd. E7 —5B **16**
Sheridan St. E1 —5D **41**
Sheridan Wlk. NW11 —1C **6**
Sheringham. NW8 —5F **21**
Sheringham Ho. NW1
(off Lisson St.) —4A **36**
Sheringham Rd. N7 —3B **24**
Sherington Rd. SE7 —2D **73**
Sherlock Ct. NW8 —5F **21**
(off Dorman Way)
Sherlock Holmes Mus.
(off Baker St.) —3B **36**
Sherlock M. W1 —4C **36**
Sherrard Rd. E7 & E12
—3E **31**
Sherrick Grn. Rd. NW10
—2D **19**
Sherriff Rd. NW6 —3C **20**
Sherrin Rd. E10 —1D **29**
Sherston Ct. SE17 —5D **53**
(off Newington Butts)
Sherston Ct. WC1 —2C **38**
(off Attneave St.)
Sherwin Ho. SE11 —2C **66**
(off Kennington Rd.)
Sherwin Rd. SE14 —4F **69**
Sherwood. NW6 —4A **20**
Sherwood Clo. SW13 —1D **75**
Sherwood Ct. SW11 —1E **77**
Sherwood Ct. W1 —4B **36**
Sherwood Gdns. E14 —5C **56**
Sherwood Gdns. SE16
—1C **68**
Shetland Rd. E3 —1B **42**
Shifford Path. SE23 —3F **97**
Shillaker Ct. W3 —2B **46**
Shillibeer Pl. W1 —4A **36**
(off York St.)
Shillingford St. N1 —4D **25**
Shillingstone Ho. W14
(off Russell Rd.) —4A **48**
Shinfield St. W12 —5E **33**
Ship & Mermaid Row. SE1
—3F **53**
Shipka Rd. SW12 —1D **93**
*Shiplake Ho. E2 —2B **40***
(off Arnold Cir.)
Shipman Rd. E16 —5D **45**
Shipman Rd. SE23 —2F **97**
Ship St. SE8 —4C **70**
Ship Tavern Pas. EC3 —1A **54**
*Shipton Ho. E2 —1B **40***
(off Shipton St.)
Shipton St. E2 —1B **40**
Shipway Ter. N16 —5B **12**
Shipwright Rd. SE16 —3A **56**
Shipwright Yd. SE1 —2A **54**
Ship Yd. E14 —1D **71**
Shirburn Clo. SE23 —5E **83**
Shirbutt St. E14 —1D **57**

Shirebrook Rd. *SE3* —1F **87**
Shirehall Clo. *NW4* —1F **5**
Shirehall Gdns. *NW4* —1F **5**
Shirehall La. *NW4* —1F **5**
Shirehall Pk. *NW4* —1F **5**
Shire Pl. *SW18* —5E **77**
Shirland M. *W9* —2B **34**
Shirland Rd. *W9* —2B **34**
Shirlbutt St. *E14* —1D **57**
Shirley Gro. *SW11* —1C **88**
Shirley Ho. *SE5* —3F **67**
(off Picton St.)
Shirley Ho. Dri. *SE7* —3E **73**
Shirley Rd. *E15* —4A **30**
Shirley Rd. *W4* —3A **46**
Shirley St. *E16* —5B **44**
Shirlock Rd. *NW3* —1B **22**
Shobroke Clo. *NW2* —5E **5**
Shoe La. *EC4* —5C **38**
Shooters Hill Rd. *SE3 &*
 SE18 —3E **73**
Shooters Hill Rd. *SE10 &*
 SE3 —4E **71**
Shoot Up Hill. *NW2* —2A **20**
Shore Bus. Cen. *E9* —4E **27**
Shoreditch. —2A 40
Shoreditch Ct. *E8* —4B **26**
(off Queensbridge Rd.)
Shoreditch High St. *E1*
 —3A **40**
Shoreham Clo. *SW18* —3D **77**
Shore Ho. *SW8* —1D **79**
Shore M. *E9* —4E **27**
(off Shore Rd.)
Shore Pl. *E9* —4E **27**
Shore Rd. *E9* —4E **27**
Shorncliffe Rd. *SE1* —1B **68**
Shorndean St. *SE6* —1E **99**
Shorrold's Rd. *SW6* —3B **62**
Shortcroft Mead Ct. *NW10*
(off Cooper Rd.) —2C **18**
Shorter St. *EC3* —1B **54**
Shortlands. *W6* —5F **47**
Shortlands Ho. *E17* —1B **14**
Shortlands Rd. *E10* —2D **15**
Short Rd. *E11* —4A **16**
Short Rd. *W4* —2A **60**
Shorts Gdns. *WC2* —5A **38**
Short St. *SE1* —3C **52**
Short Wall. *E15* —2E **43**
Short Way. *SE9* —1F **87**
Shottendane Rd. *SW6*
 —4C **62**
Shottery Clo. *SE9* —3F **101**
Shottfield Av. *SW14* —2A **74**
Shottsford. *W11* —5C **34**
(off Ledbury Rd.)
Shoulder of Mutton All. *E14*
 —1A **56**
Shouldham St. *W1* —4A **36**
Shrewsbury Ct. *EC1* —3E **39**
(off Whitecross St.)
Shrewsbury Cres. *NW10*
 —5A **18**
Shrewsbury Ho. *SW8* —2B **66**
(off Meadow Rd.)

Shrewsbury M. *W2* —4C **34**
(off Chepstow Rd.)
Shrewsbury Rd. *E7* —2F **31**
Shrewsbury Rd. *W2* —5C **34**
Shrewsbury St. *W10* —3E **33**
Shroffold Rd. *Brom* —4A **100**
Shropshire Pl. *WC1* —3E **37**
Shroton St. *NW1* —4A **36**
Shrubbery Clo. *N1* —5E **25**
Shrubbery Rd. *SW16* —4A **94**
Shrubbery, The. *E11* —1D **17**
Shrubland Rd. *E8* —5C **26**
Shrubland Rd. *E10* —2C **14**
Shrubland Rd. *E17* —1C **14**
Shrublands Clo. *SE26* —3E **97**
Shrubsall Clo. *SE9* —1F **101**
Shuna Wlk. *N1* —3F **25**
Shurland Gdns. *SE15* —3B **68**
Shuters Sq. *W14* —1B **62**
Shuttle St. *E1* —3C **40**
Shuttleworth Rd. *SW11*
 —5A **64**
Sibella Rd. *SW4* —5F **65**
Sibthorpe Rd. *SE12* —4D **87**
Sicilian Av. *WC1* —4A **38**
(off Vernon Pl.)
Sidbury St. *SW6* —4A **62**
Sidcup Rd. *SE12 & SE9*
 —3E **87**
Siddons Ho. *W2* —4F **35**
(off Harbet Rd.)
Siddons La. *NW1* —3B **36**
Siddons Rd. *SE23* —2A **98**
Side Rd. *E17* —1B **14**
Sidford Ho. *SE1* —4C **52**
(off Cosser St.)
Sidford Pl. *SE1* —4C **52**
Sidgwick Ho. *SW9* —5B **66**
(off Lingham St.)
Sidings M. *N7* —5C **10**
Sidings, The. *E11* —3E **15**
Sidlaw Ho. *N16* —3B **12**
Sidmouth Ho. *SE15* —3C **68**
(off Lympstone Gdns.)
Sidmouth Ho. *W1* —5A **36**
(off Cato St.)
Sidmouth Pde. *NW10* —4E **19**
Sidmouth Rd. *E10* —5E **15**
Sidmouth Rd. *NW2* —4E **19**
Sidmouth St. *WC1* —2B **38**
Sidney Boyd Ct. *NW6* —4C **20**
Sidney Est. *E1* —5E **41**
(Bromhead St.)
Sidney Est. *E1* —4E **41**
(Wolsey St.)
Sidney Godley (VC) Ho. *E2*
(off Digby St.) —2E **41**
Sidney Gro. *EC1* —1D **39**
Sidney Rd. *E7* —5C **16**
Sidney Rd. *SW9* —5B **66**
Sidney Sq. *E1* —4E **41**
Sidney St. *E1* —4D **41**
Sidworth St. *E8* —4D **27**
Siebert Rd. *SE3* —2C **72**
Siege Ho. *E1* —5D **41**
(off Sidney St.)

Siemens Rd. *SE18* —4F **59**
Sienna Ter. *NW2* —4C **4**
Sigdon Pas. *E8* —2C **26**
Sigdon Rd. *E8* —2C **26**
Sigmund Freud Statue.
(off Adelaide Rd.) —3F **21**
Signmakers Yd. *NW1* —5D **23**
(off Delancey St.)
Silbury Ho. *SE26* —3C **96**
Silbury St. *N1* —2F **39**
Silchester Rd. *W10* —5F **33**
Silesia Bldgs. *E8* —4D **27**
Silex St. *SE1* —3D **53**
Silk Clo. *SE12* —3C **86**
Silk Ct. *E2* —2C **40**
(off Squirries St.)
Silk Mills Pas. *SE13* —5D **71**
Silk Mills Path. *SE13* —5D **71**
Silk Mills Sq. *E9* —3B **28**
Silks Ct. *E11* —3B **16**
Silk St. *EC2* —4E **39**
Sillitoe Ho. *N1* —5F **25**
(off Colville Est.)
Silsoe Ho. *NW1* —1D **37**
Silverbirch Wlk. *NW5* —3C **22**
Silverburn Ho. *SW9* —4D **67**
(off Lothian Rd.)
Silver Clo. *SE14* —3A **70**
Silverdale. *NW1* —2E **37**
(off Hampstead Rd.)
Silverdale. *SE26* —4E **97**
Silverdale Dri. *SE9* —2F **101**
Silverdale Ho. *EC1* —3D **39**
(off Goswell Rd.)
Silvermere Rd. *SE6* —5D **85**
Silver Pl. *W1* —5E **37**
Silver Rd. *SE13* —1D **85**
(in two parts)
Silver Rd. *W12* —1F **47**
Silverthorn. *NW8* —5D **21**
(off Abbey Rd.)
Silverthorne Rd. *SW8*
 —5D **65**
Silverton Rd. *W6* —2F **61**
Silvertown. —2F 59
Silvertown Way. *E16* —5A **44**
Silver Wlk. *SE16* —2A **56**
Silvester Ho. *E1* —5D **41**
(off Varden St.)
Silvester Ho. *E2* —2E **41**
(off Sceptre Rd.)
Silvester Ho. *W11* —5B **34**
(off Basing St.)
Silvester Rd. *SE22* —3B **82**
Silvester St. *SE1* —3F **53**
Silvocea Way. *E14* —5F **43**
Silwood Est. *SE16* —5E **55**
Silwood St. *SE16* —5E **55**
Simla Ho. *SE1* —3F **53**
(off Kipling Est.)
Simms Rd. *SE1* —5C **54**
Simnel Rd. *SE12* —5D **87**
Simon Clo. *W11* —1B **48**
Simon Ct. *W9* —2C **34**
(off Saltram Cres.)
Simonds Rd. *E10* —4C **14**

Simone Ct.—Solon New Rd. Est.

Simone Ct. *SE26* —3E **97**
Simons Ct. *N16* —4B **12**
Simons Wlk. *E15* —2F **29**
Simpson Dri. *W3* —5A **32**
Simpson Ho. *NW8* —2A **36**
Simpson Ho. *SE11* —1B **66**
Simpson's Rd. *E14* —1D **57**
Simpson St. *SW11* —5A **64**
Simrose Ct. *SW18* —3C **76**
Sims Wlk. *SE3* —2B **86**
Sinclair Clo. *W14* —3F **47**
Sinclair Gdns. *NW11* —1F **5**
Sinclair Ho. *WC1* —2A **38**
(off Sandwich St.)
Sinclair Mans. *W14* —3F **47**
(off Richmond Way)
Sinclair Pl. *SE4* —4C **84**
Sinclair Rd. *W14* —3F **47**
Singer St. *EC1* —2F **39**
Sir Abraham Dawes Cotts.
SW15 —2A **76**
Sir Alexander Clo. *W3* —2B **46**
Sir Alexander Rd. *W3* —2B **46**
Sirdar Rd. *W11* —1F **47**
Sirinham Point. *SW8* —2B **66**
(off Meadow Rd.)
Sirius Building. *E1* —1F **55**
(off Jardine Rd.)
Sir John Soane's Mus.
—5B **38**
Sir Nicholas Garrow Ho. *W10*
(off Kensal Rd.) —3A **34**
Sir Oswald Stoll Foundation,
The. *SW6* —3D **63**
(off Fulham Rd.)
Sir Oswald Stoll Mans. *SW6*
(off Fulham Rd.) —3D **63**
Sir William Powell's
Almshouses. *SW6* —5A **62**
Sise La. *EC4* —5F **39**
(off Queen Victoria St.)
Siskin Clo. *SE16* —5F **55**
(off Tawny Way)
Sispara Gdns. *SW18* —4B **76**
Sissinghurst Clo. *Brom*
—5A **100**
Sissinghurst Ho. *SE15*
(off Sharratt St.) —2E **69**
Sister Mabel's Way. *SE15*
—3C **68**
Sisters Av. *SW11* —1B **78**
Sistova Rd. *SW12* —1D **93**
Sisulu Pl. *SW9* —1C **80**
Sivill Ho. *E2* —2B **40**
(off Columbia St.)
Siward Rd. *SW17* —3E **91**
Six Acres Est. *N4* —4C **10**
Six Bridges Ind. Est. *SE1*
—1C **68**
Sixth Av. *W10* —2A **34**
Skardu Rd. *NW2* —2A **20**
Skeena Hill. *SW18* —5A **76**
Skeggs Ho. *E14* —4E **57**
Skelbrook St. *SW18* —2E **91**
Skelgill Rd. *SW15* —2B **76**
Skelley Rd. *E15* —4B **30**

Skelton Clo. *E8* —3B **26**
Skelton Rd. *E7* —3C **30**
Skelton's La. *E10* —2D **15**
Skelwith Rd. *W6* —2E **61**
Skenfrith Ho. *SE15* —2D **69**
(off Commercial Way)
Sketchley Gdns. *SE16*
—1F **69**
Skiers St. *E15* —5A **30**
Skiffington Clo. *SW2* —1C **94**
Skinner Ct. *E2* —1D **41**
Skinner Pl. *SW1* —5C **50**
(off Bourne St.)
Skinners La. *EC4* —1E **53**
Skinner's Row. *SE10* —4D **71**
Skinner St. *EC1* —2C **38**
Skipton Ho. *SE1* —4B **84**
Skipwith Ho. *EC1* —4C **38**
(off Bourne Est.)
Skipworth Rd. *E9* —5E **27**
Skomer Wlk. *N1* —3E **25**
Skua Ct. *SE8* —2B **70**
(off Dorking Clo.)
Skyline Plaza Building. *E1*
—5C **40**
(off Commercial Rd.)
Skylines. *E14* —3E **57**
Sladebrook Rd. *SE3* —1F **87**
Sladen Pl. *E5* —1D **27**
Slade Tower. *E10* —4C **14**
(off Leyton Grange Est.)
Slade Wlk. *SE17* —2D **67**
Slagrove Pl. *SE4* —3C **84**
Slaidburn St. *SW10* —2E **63**
Slaithwaite Rd. *SE13* —2E **85**
Slaney Clo. *NW10* —4E **19**
Slaney Pl. *N7* —2C **24**
Sleaford Ind. Est. *SW8*
—3E **65**
Sleaford St. *SW8* —3E **65**
Sleigh Ho. *E2* —2E **41**
(off Bacton St.)
Slievemore Clo. *SW4* —1F **79**
Slindon Ct. *N16* —5B **12**
Slingsby Pl. *WC2* —1A **52**
Slippers Pl. *SE16* —4D **55**
Sloane Av. *SW3* —5A **50**
Sloane Ct. E. *SW3* —1C **64**
Sloane Ct. W. *SW3* —1C **64**
Sloane Gdns. *SW1* —5C **50**
Sloane Sq. *SW1* —5B **50**
Sloane St. *SW1* —3B **50**
Sloane Ter. *SW1* —5C **50**
Sloane Ter. Mans. *SW1*
—5C **50**
Sloman Ho. *W10* —2A **34**
(off Beethoven St.)
Sly St. *E1* —5D **41**
Smallbrook M. *W2* —5F **35**
Smalley Clo. *N16* —5B **12**
Smalley Rd. Est. *N16*
(off Smalley Clo.) —5B **12**
Smallwood Rd. *SW17*
—4F **91**
Smart's Pl. *WC1* —5A **38**
Smart St. *E2* —2F **41**

Smeaton Ct. *SE1* —4E **53**
Smeaton Rd. *SW18* —5C **76**
Smeaton St. *E1* —2D **55**
Smedley St. *SW8 & SW4*
—5F **65**
Smeed Rd. *E3* —4C **28**
Smiles Pl. *SE13* —5E **71**
Smith Clo. *SE16* —2F **55**
Smithfield St. *EC1* —4D **39**
Smithies Ct. *E15* —2E **29**
Smith's Ct. *W1* —1F **51**
(off Gt. Windmill St.)
Smiths Point. *E13* —5C **30**
(off Brooks Rd.)
Smith Sq. *SW1* —4A **52**
Smith St. *SW3* —1B **64**
Smith's Yd. *SW18* —2E **91**
Smith Ter. *SW3* —1B **64**
Smithwood Clo. *SW19*
—1A **90**
Smithy St. *E1* —4E **41**
Smokehouse Yd. *EC1* —4D **39**
(off St John St.)
Smugglers Way. *SW18*
—2D **77**
Smyrk's Rd. *SE17* —1A **68**
Smyrna Rd. *NW6* —4C **20**
Smythe St. *E14* —1D **57**
Snaresbrook. —1C 16
Snarsgate St. *W10* —4E **33**
Sneath Av. *NW11* —2B **6**
Sneyd Rd. *NW2* —2E **19**
Snipe Ct. *SE8* —2A **70**
(off Rolt St.)
Snowberry Clo. *E11* —1F **29**
Snowbury Rd. *SW6* —5D **63**
Snowden Dri. *NW9* —1A **4**
Snowden St. *EC2* —3A **40**
Snow Hill. *EC1* —4D **39**
Snow Hill Ct. *EC1* —5D **39**
(in two parts)
Snowman Ho. *NW6* —5D **21**
Snowsfields. *SE1* —3F **53**
Snowshill Rd. *E12* —2F **31**
Soames St. *SE15* —1B **82**
Soane Ct. NW1 —4E **23**
(off St Pancras Way)
Soho. —5E 37
Soho Sq. *W1* —5F **37**
Soho St. *W1* —5F **37**
Sojourner Truth Clo. *E8*
—3D **27**
Solander Gdns. *E1* —1E **55**
Solarium Ct. *SE1* —5B **54**
(off Alscot Rd.)
Soldene Ct. *N7* —2B **24**
(off George's Rd.)
Solebay St. *E1* —3A **42**
Solent Ri. *E13* —2D **44**
Solent Rd. *NW6* —2C **20**
Soley M. *WC1* —2C **38**
Solna Av. *SW15* —3E **75**
Solomon's Pas. *SE15* —2D **83**
Solon New Rd. *SW4* —2A **80**
Solon New Rd. Est. *SW4*
—2A **80**

258 Mini London

Solon Rd. SW2—2A 80
Solway Clo. E8—3B 26 (off Queensbridge Rd.)
Solway Rd. SE22—2C 82
Somali Rd. NW2—2B 20
Somer Ct. SW6—2C 62 (off Anselm Rd.)
Somerfield Ho. SE16—1F 69
Somerfield Rd. N4—4D 11
Somerford Gro. N16—1B 26
Somerford Gro. Est. N16 —1B 26
Somerford St. E1—3D 41
Somerford Way. SE16 —3A 56
Somerleyton Pas. SW9 —2D 81
Somerleyton Rd. SW9 —2C 80
Somers Clo. NW1—1F 37
Somers Cres. W2—5A 36
Somerset Est. SW11—4F 63
Somerset Gdns. N6—2C 8
Somerset Gdns. SE13 —5D 71
Somerset House. —1B 52
Somerset Rd. E17—1C 14
Somerset Rd. SW19—3F 89
Somerset Sq. W14—3A 48
Somers Pl. SW2—5B 80
Somers Rd. SW2—4B 80
Somers Town. —2F 37
Somerton Rd. NW2—5A 6
Somerton Rd. SE15—2D 83
Somertrees Av. SE12 —2D 101
Somerville Av. SW13—2D 61
Somerville Point. SE16 —3B 56
Sonderburg Rd. N7—4B 10
Sondes St. SE17—2F 67
Sonia Gdns. NW10—1B 18
Sonning Ho. E2—2B 40 (off Swanfield St.)
Soper Clo. SE23—1F 97
Sophia Clo. N7—3B 24
Sophia Rd. E10—3D 15
Sophia Rd. E16—5D 45
Sophia Sq. SE16—1A 56 (off Sovereign Cres.)
Sopwith Way. SW8—3D 65
Sorensen Ct. E10—4D 15 (off Leyton Grange Est.)
Sorrel Gdns. E6—4F 45
Sorrel La. E14—5F 43
Sorrell Clo. SE14—3A 70
Sorrell Clo. SW9—5C 66
Sotheby Rd. N5—5D 11
Sotheran Clo. E8—5C 26
Sotheron Rd. SW6—3D 63
Soudan Rd. SW11—4B 64
Souldern Rd. W14—4F 47
S. Access Rd. E17—2A 14
Southacre. W2—5A 36 (off Hyde Pk. Cres.)
S. Africa Rd. W12—2D 47
Southall Pl. SE1—3F 53
Southampton Bldgs. WC2 —4C 38
Southampton Pl. WC1 —4A 38
Southampton Rd. NW5 —2B 22
Southampton Row. WC1 —4A 38
Southampton St. WC2 —1A 52
Southampton Way. SE5 —3F 67
Southam St. W10—3A 34
S. Audley St. W1—1C 50
South Av. NW10—3E 33
Southbank Bus. Cen. SW8 —2F 65
Southbank Bus. Cen. SW11 —4B 64
South Bank Cen. —2B 52
South Bank Cen. SE1—2B 52 (off Belvedere Rd.)
S. Birkbeck Rd. E11—5F 15
S. Black Lion La. W6—1C 60
South Block. SE1—3B 52 (off Westminster Bri. Rd.)
S. Bolton Gdns. SW5—1E 63
Southborough Ho. SE17 (off Surrey Gro.) —1A 68
Southborough Rd. E9—5F 27
Southbourne Gdns. SE12 —3D 87
S. Branch Av. NW10—3E 33
South Bromley. —5F 43
Southbrook M. SE12—4B 86
Southbrook Rd. SE12 —4B 86
Southbury. NW8—5E 21 (off Loudoun Rd.)
S. Carriage Dri. SW7 & SW1 —3F 49
S. Circular Rd. SW15—2C 74
South Clo. N6—1D 9
S. Colonnade, The. E14 —2C 56
Southcombe St. W14—5A 48
Southcote Rd. N19—1E 23
South Cres. E16—3F 43
South Cres. WC1—4F 37
Southcroft Rd. SW17 & SW16—5C 92
S. Croxted Rd. SE21—3F 95
Southdean Gdns. SW19 —2B 90
Southdown. N7—3A 24
South Dri. E12—5F 17
S. Eaton Pl. SW1—5C 50
S. Edwardes Sq. W8—4B 48
Southend. —4F 99
South End. W8—4D 49
S. End Clo. NW3—1A 22
S. End Grn. NW3—1A 22
Southend La. SE26 & SE6 —4B 98
S. End Rd. NW3—1A 22
Southend Rd. Beck—5D 99
S. End Row. W8—4D 49
Southerngate Way. SE14 —3A 70
Southern Gro. E3—2B 42
Southern Rd. E13—1D 45
Southern Row. W10—3A 34
Southern St. N1—1B 38
Southernwood Retail Pk. SE1 —1B 68
Southerton Rd. W6—5E 47
S. Esk Rd. E7—3E 31
Southey Ho. SE17—1E 67 (off Browning St.)
Southey M. E16—2C 58
Southey Rd. N15—1A 12
Southey Rd. SW9—4C 66
Southfield Ct. E11—5B 16
Southfields. —1C 90
Southfields M. SW18—4C 76
Southfields Pas. SW18 —4C 76
Southfields Rd. SW18—4C 76
Southgate Gro. N1—4F 25
Southgate Rd. N1—5F 25
South Gro. E17—1B 14
South Gro. N6—3C 8
South Gro. N15—1F 11
South Gro. Ho. N6—3C 8
South Hackney. —4F 27
South Hampstead. —4E 21
S. Hill Pk. NW3—1A 22
S. Hill Pk. Gdns. NW3—5A 8
Southill St. E14—5D 43
S. Island Pl. SW9—3B 66
South Kensington. —5F 49
S. Kensington Sta. Arc. SW7 (off Pelham St.) —5F 49
South Lambeth. —3A 66
S. Lambeth Pl. SW8—1A 66
S. Lambeth Rd. SW8—2A 66
Southlands Dri. SW19—2F 89
South Lodge. NW8—1F 35
South Lodge. SW7—3A 50 (off Knightsbridge)
South London Gallery. (off Peckham Rd.) —4A 68
Southmead Rd. SW19 —1A 90
S. Molton La. W1—5D 37
S. Molton Rd. E16—5C 44
S. Molton St. W1—5D 37
Southmoor Way. E9—3B 28
S. Oak Rd. SW16—4B 94
Southolm St. SW11—4D 65
Southover. Brom—5C 100
South Pde. SW3—1F 63
South Pde. W4—5A 46
S. Park Cres. SE6—1A 100
S. Park M. SW6—1D 77
S. Park Rd. SW19—5E 91
South Pl. EC2—4F 39
South Pl. M. EC2—4F 39
S. Quay Plaza. E14—3D 57
South Ri. W2—1A 50 (off St George's Fields)

South Rd. *SE23* —2F **97**
South Row. *SE3* —5B **72**
S. Sea St. *SE16* —4B **56**
South Side. *W6* —4B **46**
Southside Comn. *SW19*
　　　　　　　　—5E **89**
Southside Ind. Est. SW8
　(off Havelock Ter.) —4E **65**
South Sq. *NW11* —1D **7**
South Sq. *WC1* —4C **38**
South St. *W1* —2C **50**
S. Tenter St. *E1* —1B **54**
South Ter. *SW7* —5A **50**
South Tottenham. —1B 12
Southvale Rd. *SE3* —5A **72**
Southview Av. *NW10* —2B **18**
Southview Clo. *SW17* —5C **92**
Southview Rd. *Brom* —4F **99**
South Vs. *NW1* —3F **23**
Southville. *SW8* —4F **65**
Southwark. —2E 53
Southwark Bri. *SE1 & EC4*
　　　　　　　　—1E **53**
Southwark Bri. Bus. Cen. SE1
　(off Tower Bri. Rd.) —2E **53**
Southwark Bri. Office Village.
　　　　　　　SE1 —2E **53**
　(off Southwark Bri. Rd.)
Southwark Bri. Rd. *SE1*
　　　　　　　　—4D **53**
Southwark Cathedral.
　(off Montague Clo.) —2F **53**
Southwark Pk. Est. *SE16*
　　　　　　　　—4D **55**
Southwark Pk. Rd. *SE16*
　　　　　　　　—5B **54**
Southwark St. *SE1* —2D **53**
Southwater Clo. *E14* —5B **42**
Southway. *NW11* —1D **7**
Southwell Gdns. *SW7* —5E **49**
Southwell Gro. Rd. *E11*
　　　　　　　　—4A **16**
Southwell Ho. SE16 —5D **55**
　(off Anchor St.)
Southwell Rd. *SE5* —1E **81**
S. W. India Dock Entrance.
　　　　　　E14 —3E **57**
S. W. India Dock Rd. *E14*
　　　　　　　　—3E **57**
Southwest Rd. *E11* —3F **15**
S. Wharf Rd. *W2* —5F **35**
Southwick M. *W2* —5F **35**
Southwick Pl. *W2* —5A **36**
Southwick St. *W2* —5A **36**
Southwick Yd. W2 —5A **36**
　(off Titchborne Row)
Southwold Mans. W9 —2C **34**
　(off Widley Rd.)
Southwold Rd. *E5* —4D **13**
Southwold Av. *N6* —2D **9**
Southwood Ct. EC1 —2D **39**
　(off Wynyatt St.)
Southwood Ct. *NW11* —1D **7**
S. Woodford to Barking
　Relief Rd. *E11 & Bark*
　　　　　　　　—1F **17**

Southwood Hall. *N6* —1D **9**
Southwood Heights. *N6*
　　　　　　　　—2D **9**
Southwood Ho. W11 —1A **48**
　(off Avondale Pk. Rd.)
Southwood La. *N6* —3C **8**
Southwood Lawn Rd. *N6*
　　　　　　　　—2C **8**
Southwood Mans. N6 —1C **8**
　(off Southwood La.)
Southwood Pk. *N6* —2C **8**
Southwood Smith Ho. E2
　(off Florida St.) —2D **41**
Southwood Smith St. N1
　　　　　　　　—5D **25**
　(off Old Royal Free Sq.)
S. Worple Av. *SW14* —1A **74**
Southwyck Ho. *SW9* —2D **81**
Sovereign Clo. *E1* —1D **55**
Sovereign Cres. *SE16* —1A **56**
Sovereign Ho. E1 —3D **41**
　(off Cambridge Heath Rd.)
Sovereign M. *E2* —1B **40**
Spa Ct. *SW16* —4B **94**
Spafield St. *EC1* —3C **38**
Spa Grn. Est. *EC1* —2D **39**
Spalding Ho. *SE4* —2A **84**
Spalding Rd. *NW4* —2E **5**
Spalding Rd. *SW17* —5D **93**
Spanby Rd. *E3* —3C **42**
Spaniards Clo. *NW11* —3F **7**
Spaniards End. *NW11* —3E **7**
Spaniards Rd. *NW3* —4E **7**
Spanish Pl. *W1* —5C **36**
Spanish Rd. *SW18* —3E **77**
Sparke Ter. E16 —5B **44**
　(off Clarkson Rd.)
Spa Rd. *SE16* —4B **54**
Sparrick's Row. *SE1* —3F **53**
Sparrow Ho. E1 —3E **41**
　(off Cephas Av.)
Sparsholt Rd. *N19* —3B **10**
Sparta St. *SE10* —4E **71**
Speakman Ho. SE4 —1A **84**
　(off Arica Rd.)
Spearman Ho. *E14* —5C **42**
Spear M. *SW5* —5C **48**
Spears Rd. *N19* —3A **10**
Spectacle Works. *E13* —2E **45**
Spedan Clo. *NW3* —5C **7**
Speed Highwalk. *EC2* —4E **39**
　(off Silk St.)
Speed Ho. EC2 —4F **39**
　(off Silk St.)
Speedwell St. *SE8* —3C **70**
Speedy Pl. WC1 —2A **38**
　(off Cromer St.)
Speke's Monument. —1E 49
Speldhurst Rd. *E9* —4F **27**
Speldhurst Rd. *W4* —4A **46**
Spellbrook Wlk. *N1* —5E **25**
Spelman Ho. *E1* —4C **40**
　(off Spelman St.)
Spelman St. *E1* —4C **40**
　(in two parts)
Spence Clo. *SE16* —3B **56**

Spencer Dri. *N2* —1E **7**
Spencer House. —2E 51
　(off St James's Pl.)
Spencer Ho. *NW4* —1D **5**
Spencer Mans. W14 —2A **62**
　(off Queen's Club Gdns.)
Spencer M. SW8 —4B **66**
　(off S. Lambeth Rd.)
Spencer M. W6 —2A **62**
　(off Queen's Club Gdns.)
Spencer Park. —3F 77
Spencer Pk. *SW18* —3F **77**
Spencer Pl. *N1* —4D **25**
Spencer Ri. *NW5* —1D **23**
Spencer Rd. *E6* —5F **31**
Spencer Rd. *N8* —1B **10**
　(in two parts)
Spencer Rd. *SW11* —2F **77**
Spencer St. *EC1* —2D **39**
Spencer Wlk. *NW3* —1F **21**
Spencer Wlk. *SW15* —2F **75**
Spenlow Ho. SE16 —4C **54**
　(off Jamaica Rd.)
Spenser Gro. *N16* —2A **26**
　(in two parts)
Spenser M. *SE21* —2F **95**
Spenser Rd. *SE24* —3D **81**
Spenser St. *SW1* —4E **51**
Spensley Wlk. *N16* —5F **11**
Spert St. *E14* —1A **56**
Spey St. *E14* —4E **43**
Spezia Rd. *NW10* —1C **32**
Spice Ct. E1 —1C **54**
　(off Asher Way)
Spice Quay Heights. *SE1*
　　　　　　　　—2B **54**
Spicer Clo. *SW9* —5D **67**
Spindrift Av. *E14* —5C **56**
Spinnaker Ho. *E14* —3C **56**
Spinney Gdns. *SE19* —5B **96**
Spinney, The. *SW13* —3D **61**
Spinney, The. *SW16* —3E **93**
Spire Ho. W2 —1E **49**
　(off Lancaster Ga.)
Spirit Quay. *E1* —2C **54**
Spitalfields. —4B 40
Spital Sq. *E1* —4B **40**
Spital Sq. *E1* —4A **40**
Spital St. *E1* —4C **40**
Spital Yd. *EC2* —4A **40**
Splendour Wlk. SE16 —1E **69**
　(off Verney Rd.)
Spode Ho. SE11 —4C **52**
　(off Lambeth Wlk.)
Spode Wlk. *NW6* —2D **21**
Sportsbank St. *SE6* —5E **85**
Spratt Hall Rd. *E11* —1C **16**
Spriggs Ho. *N1* —4D **25**
　(off Canonbury Rd.)
Sprimont Pl. *SW3* —1B **64**
Springall St. *SE15* —3D **69**
Springalls Wharf. SE16
　　　　　　　　—3C **54**
　(off Bermondsey Wall W.)
Springbank Rd. *SE13* —4F **85**
Springbank Wlk. *NW1* —4F **23**

Spring Ct. *NW6* —3B **20**
Springdale M. *N16* —1F **25**
Springdale Rd. *N16* —1F **25**
Springfield. *E5* —3D **13**
Springfield Gdns. *E5* —3D **13**
Springfield Gdns. *NW9* —1A **4**
Springfield Gro. *SE7* —2E **73**
Springfield La. *NW6* —5D **21**
Springfield Mt. *NW9* —1A **4**
Springfield Ri. *SE26* —3D **97**
(in two parts)
Springfield Rd. *E15* —2A **44**
Springfield Rd. *E17* —1B **14**
Springfield Rd. *NW8* —5E **21**
Springfield Rd. *SE26* —5D **97**
Springfield Rd. *SW19* —5B **90**
Springfield Wlk. *NW6* —5D **21**
Spring Gdns. *N5* —2E **25**
Spring Gdns. *SW1* —2F **51**
Spring Hill. *E5* —2C **12**
Spring Hill. *SE26* —4E **97**
Springhill Clo. *SE5* —1F **81**
Spring Ho. WC1 —2C **38**
  (off Margery St.)
Spring La. *E5* —2D **13**
Spring M. *W1* —4B **36**
Spring Pk. Dri. *N4* —3E **11**
Spring Pas. *SW15* —1F **75**
Spring Path. *NW3* —2F **21**
Spring Pl. *NW5* —2D **23**
Springrice Rd. *SE13* —4F **85**
Spring St. *W2* —5F **35**
Spring Tide Clo. *SE15* —4C **68**
Spring Va. Ter. *W14* —4F **47**
Spring Wlk. *E1* —4C **40**
Springwater. WC1 —4B **38**
  (off New North St.)
Springwell Av. *NW10* —5B **18**
Springwell Clo. *SW16* —4B **94**
Springwell Rd. *SW16* —4C **94**
Sprowston M. *E7* —3C **30**
Sprowston Rd. *E7* —2C **30**
Spruce Ho. SE16 —3F **55**
  (off Woodland Cres.)
Sprules Rd. *SE4* —5A **70**
Spurgeon St. *SE1* —4F **53**
Spurling Rd. *SE22* —2B **82**
Spur Rd. SE1 —3C **52**
  (off Station App. Rd.)
Spur Rd. *SW1* —3E **51**
Spurstowe Rd. *E8* —3D **27**
Spurstowe Ter. *E8* —3D **27**
Square Rigger Row. *SW11*
  —1E **77**
Square, The. *W6* —1E **61**
Squarey St. *SW17* —3E **91**
Squire Gdns. NW8 —2F **35**
  (off Grove End Rd.)
Squires Ct. *SW4* —4A **66**
Squires Ct. *SW19* —4C **90**
Squires M. *NW3* —5F **7**
Squirrels, The. *SE13* —1F **85**
Squirries St. *E2* —2C **40**
Stables Mkt., The. *NW1*
  —4D **23**
Stables M. *SE27* —5E **95**

Stables, The. *W10* —5F **33**
  (off Bassett Rd.)
Stables Way. *SE11* —1C **66**
Stable Way. *W10* —5E **33**
Stable Yd. SW1 —3E **51**
  (off St James' Pal.)
Stable Yd. *SW15* —1E **75**
Stable Yd. Rd. *SW1* —3E **51**
Stableyard, The. *SW9* —5B **66**
Stacey Clo. *E10* —1F **15**
Stacey St. *N7* —5C **10**
Stacey St. *WC2* —5F **37**
Stack Ho. *SW1* —5C **50**
  (off Cundy St.)
Stackhouse St. *SW3* —4B **50**
  (off Pavilion Rd.)
Stacy Path. *SE5* —3A **68**
Stadium Rd. E. *NW4* —2D **5**
Stadium St. *SW10* —3E **63**
Staffa Rd. *E10* —3A **14**
Stafford Clo. *E17* —1B **14**
  (in two parts)
Stafford Clo. *NW6* —3B **34**
  (in two parts)
Stafford Ct. *SW8* —3A **66**
Stafford Cripps Ho. E2
  —2E **41**
  (off Globe Rd.)
Stafford Cripps Ho. SW6
  (off Clem Attlee Ct.) —2B **62**
Stafford Mans. SW1 —4E **51**
  (off Stafford Pl.)
Stafford Mans. *SW4* —2A **80**
Stafford Mans. SW11 —3B **64**
  (off Albert Bri. Rd.)
Stafford Pl. *SW1* —4E **51**
Stafford Rd. *E3* —1B **42**
Stafford Rd. *E7* —4E **31**
Stafford Rd. *NW6* —2C **34**
Staffordshire St. *SE15* —4C **68**
Stafford St. *W1* —2E **51**
Stafford Ter. *W8* —4C **48**
Staff St. *EC1* —2F **39**
Stag Lane. (Junct.) —2B **88**
Stag La. *SW15* —3B **88**
Stag Pl. *SW1* —4E **51**
Stainer Ho. *SE3* —2E **87**
Stainer St. *SE1* —2F **53**
Staining La. *EC2* —5E **39**
Stainsbury St. *E2* —1E **41**
Stainsby Pl. *E14* —5C **42**
Stainsby Rd. *E14* —5C **42**
Stainton Rd. *SE6* —4F **85**
Stalbridge Flats. W1 —5C **36**
  (off Lumley St.)
Stalbridge St. *NW1* —4A **36**
Stalham St. *SE16* —4D **55**
Stamford Brook Arches. *W6*
  —5C **46**
Stamford Brook Av. *W6*
  —4B **46**
Stamford Brook Gdns. *W6*
  —4B **46**
Stamford Brook Mans. W6
  (off Goldhawk Rd.) —5B **46**
Stamford Brook Rd. *W6*
  —4B **46**

Stamford Clo. *NW3* —5E **7**
  (off Heath St.)
Stamford Ct. *W6* —5C **46**
Stamford Ga. *SW6* —3D **63**
Stamford Gro. E. *N16* —3C **12**
Stamford Gro. W. *N16*
  —3C **12**
Stamford Hill. —3B **12**
Stamford Hill. *N16* —4B **12**
Stamford Lodge. *N16* —2B **12**
Stamford Rd. *E6* —5F **31**
Stamford Rd. *N1* —4A **26**
Stamford Rd. *N15* —1C **12**
Stamford Rd. *SE1* —2C **52**
Stamford Wharf. *SE1* —1C **52**
Stamp Pl. *E2* —1B **40**
Stanard Clo. *N16* —2A **12**
Stanboard Way. *E14* —4C **56**
Stanborough Pas. *E8* —3B **26**
Stanbridge Rd. *SW15* —1E **75**
Stanbury Ct. *NW3* —3B **22**
Stanbury Rd. *SE15* —5D **69**
  (in two parts)
Standard Pl. EC2 —2A **40**
  (off Rivington St.)
Standen Rd. *SW18* —5B **76**
Standish Ho. SE3 —2D **87**
  (off Elford Clo.)
Standish Ho. *W6* —5C **46**
  (off St Peter's Gro.)
Standlake Point. *SE23*
  —3F **97**
Stane Pas. *SW16* —5A **94**
Stanesgate Ho. SE15 —3C **68**
  (off Friary Est.)
Stane Way. *SE18* —3F **73**
Stanfield Ho. NW8 —3F **35**
  (off Frampton St.)
Stanfield Rd. *E3* —1A **42**
Stanford Ct. *SW6* —4D **63**
Stanford Pl. *SE17* —5A **54**
Stanford Rd. *W8* —4D **49**
Stanford St. *SW1* —5F **51**
Stangate. *SE1* —4B **52**
  (off Royal St.)
Stanhope Clo. *SE16* —3F **55**
Stanhope Gdns. *N4* —1D **11**
Stanhope Gdns. *N6* —1D **9**
Stanhope Gdns. *SW7* —5E **49**
Stanhope Ga. *W1* —2C **50**
Stanhope Ho. SE8 —3B **70**
  (off Adolphus St.)
Stanhope M. E. *SW7* —5E **49**
Stanhope M. S. *SW7* —5E **49**
Stanhope M. W. *SW7* —5E **49**
Stanhope Pde. *NW1* —2E **37**
Stanhope Pl. *W2* —5B **36**
Stanhope Rd. *E17* —1D **15**
Stanhope Rd. *N6* —1E **9**
Stanhope Row. *W1* —2D **51**
Stanhope Ter. *W2* —1F **49**
Stanier Clo. *W14* —1B **62**
Stanlake M. *W12* —2E **47**
Stanlake Rd. *W12* —2E **47**
Stanlake Vs. *W12* —2E **47**

Stanley Clo. SW8 —2B 66
Stanley Cohen Ho. EC1
—3E 39
(off Golden La. Est.)
Stanley Cres. W11 —1B 48
Stanley Gdns. NW2 —2E 19
Stanley Gdns. W3 —3A 46
Stanley Gdns. W11 —1B 48
Stanley Gdns. M. W11
—1B 48
(off Kensington Pk. Rd.)
Stanley Gro. SW8 —5C 64
Stanley Ho. E14 —5C 42
Stanley Pas. NW1 —1A 38
Stanley Rd. E10 —1D 15
Stanley Rd. E12 —2F 31
Stanley Rd. E15 —5F 29
Stanley Rd. NW9 —2C 4
Stanley St. SE8 —3B 70
Stanley Ter. N19 —4A 10
Stanmer St. SW11 —4A 64
Stanmore Pl. NW1 —5D 23
Stanmore Rd. E11 —3B 16
Stanmore St. N1 —5B 24
Stannard Cotts. E1 —3E 41
(off Fox Clo.)
Stannard Rd. E8 —3C 26
Stannary Pl. SE11 —1C 66
(off Stannary St.)
Stannary St. SE11 —1C 66
Stansbury Ho. W10 —2A 34
(off Beethoven St.)
Stansfeld Rd. E6 —4F 45
Stansfield Ho. SE1 —5B 54
(off Balaclava Rd.)
Stansfield Rd. SW9 —1B 80
Stanstead Gro. SE6 —1B 98
Stanstead Rd. E11 —1D 17
Stanstead Rd. SE23 & SE6
—1F 97
Stanswood Gdns. SE5
—3A 68
Stanthorpe Clo. SW16
—5A 94
Stanthorpe Rd. SW16
—5A 94
Stanton Ho. SE10 —2E 71
(off Thames St.)
Stanton Rd. SE26 —4B 98
Stanton Rd. SW13 —5B 60
Stanton Sq. SE26 —4B 98
Stanton Way. SE26 —4B 98
Stanway St. N1 —1A 40
(in three parts)
Stanway St. N1 —1A 40
Stanwick Rd. W14 —5B 48
Stanworth St. SE1 —4B 54
Stanyhurst. SE23 —1A 98
Staplefield Clo. SW2 —1A 94
Stapleford Clo. SW19
—5A 76
Staplehurst Rd. SE13 —3F 85
Staple Inn. WC1 —4C 38
(off Staple Inn Bldgs.)
Staple Inn Bldgs. WC1
—4C 38

Staples Clo. SE16 —2A 56
Staples Corner. (Junct.)
—3D 5
Staples Corner Bus. Pk.
NW2 —3D 5
Staple St. SE1 —3F 53
Stapleton Hall Rd. N4 —3B 10
Stapleton Ho. E2 —2D 41
(off Ellsworth St.)
Stapleton Rd. SW17 —3C 92
Star All. EC3 —1A 54
(off Fenchurch St.)
Starboard Way. E14 —4C 56
Starcross St. NW1 —2E 37
Starfield Rd. W12 —3C 46
Star La. E16 —3A 44
Starling Ho. NW8 —1A 36
(off Barrow Hill Est.)
Star Pl. E1 —1C 54
Star Rd. W14 —2B 62
Star St. W2 —5A 36
Star Yd. WC2 —5C 38
Statham Gro. N16 —1F 25
Statham Ho. SW8 —4E 65
(off Wadhurst Rd.)
Station App. E7 —1D 31
Station App. E11 —1C 16
Station App. NW10 —2B 32
Station App. SE3 —1D 87
Station App. SE12 —4C 86
(off Burnt Ash Hill)
Station App. SE26 —4E 97
(Sydenham Rd.)
Station App. SE26 —5B 98
(Worsley Bri. Rd.)
Station App. SW6 —1A 76
Station App. SW16 —5F 93
Station App. Rd. SE1 —3C 52
Station Av. SW9 —1D 81
Station Ct. E10 —2D 15
(off Kings Clo.)
Station Cres. SE3 —1C 72
Stationer's Hall Ct. EC4
—5D 39
Station Pde. NW2 —3E 19
Station Pde. SW12 —1C 92
Station Pas. SE15 —4E 69
Station Path. E8 —3D 27
(off Graham Rd.)
Station Path. SW6 —1B 76
Station Pl. N4 —4C 10
Station Ri. SE27 —2D 95
Station Rd. E7 —1C 30
Station Rd. E10 —5E 15
Station Rd. E12 —1F 31
Station Rd. E17 —1A 14
Station Rd. N19 —5E 9
Station Rd. NW4 —1C 4
Station Rd. NW10 —1B 32
Station Rd. SE13 —1E 85
Station Rd. SE20 —5E 97
Station Rd. SW13 —5B 60
Station Sta. E15 —4F 29
Station Ter. NW10 —1F 33
Station Ter. SE5 —4E 67
Station Ter. M. SE3 —1C 72

Station Way. SE15 —5C 68
Staunton Ho. SE17 —5A 54
(off Tatum St.)
Staunton St. SE8 —2B 70
Staveley. NW1 —2E 37
(off Varndell St.)
Staveley Clo. E9 —2E 27
Staveley Clo. N7 —1A 24
Staveley Clo. SE15 —4D 69
Staveley Gdns. W4 —4A 60
Staveley Rd. W4 —3A 60
Staverton Rd. NW2 —4E 19
Stave Yd. Rd. SE16 —2A 56
Stavordale Rd. N5 —1D 25
Stayner's Rd. E1 —3F 41
Steadman Ct. EC1 —3E 39
(off Old St.)
Stead St. SE17 —5F 53
Stean St. E8 —5B 26
Stebbing Ho. W11 —2F 47
(off Queensdale Cres.)
Stebondale St. E14 —5E 57
Stedham Pl. WC1 —5A 38
(off New Oxford St.)
Steedman St. SE17 —5E 53
Steele Ho. E15 —1A 44
(off Eve Rd.)
Steele Rd. E11 —1A 30
Steele's M. N. NW3 —3B 22
Steele's M. S. NW3 —3B 22
Steele's Rd. NW3 —3B 22
Steele's Studios. NW3
—3B 22
Steel's La. E1 —5E 41
Steelyard Pas. EC4 —1F 53
(off Allhallows La.)
Steen Way. SW22 —3A 82
Steep Hill. SW16 —3F 93
Steeple Clo. SW6 —5A 62
Steeple Clo. SW19 —5A 90
Steeple Ct. E1 —3D 41
Steeple Wlk. N1 —5E 25
(off Basire St.)
Steerforth St. SW18 —2E 91
Steers Way. SE16 —3A 56
Stelfox Ho. WC1 —2B 38
(off Penton Ri.)
Stella Rd. SW17 —5B 92
Stellman Clo. E5 —5C 12
Stephan Clo. E8 —5C 26
Stephendale Rd. SW6 —1D 77
Stephen Fox Ho. W4 —1A 60
(off Chiswick La.)
Stephen M. W1 —4F 37
Stephen Pl. SW4 —1E 79
Stephens Ct. E16 —3B 44
Stephens Ct. SE4 —1A 84
Stephenson Ho. SE1 —4E 53
Stephenson Rd. E17 —1A 14
Stephenson St. E16 —3A 44
Stephenson St. NW10
—2A 32
Stephenson Way. NW1
—3E 37
Stephen's Rd. E15 —5A 30
Stephen St. W1 —4F 37

Stepney. —4F 41
Stepney Causeway. *E1* —5F **41**
Stepney Grn. *E1* —4E **41**
Stepney High St. *E1* —4F **41**
Stepney Way. *E1* —4D **41**
Sterling Clo. *NW10* —4C **18**
Sterling Gdns. *SE14* —2A **70**
Sterling Ho. *SE3* —2D **87**
Sterling St. *SW7* —4A **50**
Sterndale Rd. *W6* —4F **47**
Sterne St. *W12* —3F **47**
Sternhall La. *SE15* —1C **82**
Sternhold Av. *SW2* —2F **93**
Sterry St. *SE1* —3F **53**
Steucers La. *SE23* —1A **98**
Steve Biko La. *SE6* —4C **98**
Steve Biko Rd. *N7* —5C **10**
Stevedore St. *E1* —2D **55**
Stevenage Rd. *SW6* —3F **61**
Stevens Av. *E9* —3E **27**
Stevens Clo. *Beck* —5C **98**
Stevenson Clo. *SE16* —1C **68**
*Stevenson Ho. NW8 —5E **21***
(off Boundary Rd.)
Stevens St. *SE1* —4A **54**
Steventon Rd. *W12* —1B **46**
Steward St. *E1* —4A **40**
(in two parts)
Stewart Rd. *E15* —1F **29**
Stewart's Gro. *SW3* —1F **63**
Stewart's Rd. *SW8* —3E **65**
Stewart St. *E14* —3E **57**
Stew La. *EC4* —1E **53**
Stileman Ho. *E3* —4B **42**
Stillingfleet Rd. *SW13* —2C **60**
Stillington St. *SW1* —5E **51**
Stillness Rd. *SE23* —4A **84**
Stirling Rd. *E13* —1D **45**
Stirling Rd. *SW9* —5A **66**
*Stockbeck. NW1 —1E **37***
(off Ampthill Est.)
Stock Exchange. —5F 39
Stockfield Rd. *SW16* —3B **94**
*Stockholm Ho. E1 —1C **54***
(off Swedenborg Gdns.)
Stockholm Rd. *SE16* —1E **69**
Stockholm Way. *E1* —2C **54**
Stockhurst Clo. *SW15* —5E **61**
*Stockleigh Hall. NW8 —1A **36***
(off Prince Albert Rd.)
Stock Orchard Cres. *N7* —2B **24**
Stock Orchard St. *N7* —2B **24**
Stocks Pl. *E14* —1B **56**
Stock St. *E13* —1C **44**
*Stockton Ho. E2 —2D **41***
(off Ellsworth St.)
Stockwell. —5B 66
Stockwell Av. *SW9* —1B **80**
Stockwell Gdns. *SW9* —4B **66**
Stockwell Gdns. Est. *SW9* —5A **66**
Stockwell Grn. *SW9* —5B **66**
Stockwell Grn. Ct. *SW9* —5B **66**
Stockwell La. *SW9* —5B **66**
Stockwell M. *SW9* —5B **66**
Stockwell Pk. Cres. *SW9* —5B **66**
Stockwell Pk. Est. *SW9* —5B **66**
Stockwell Pk. Rd. *SW9* —4B **66**
Stockwell Pk. Wlk. *SW9* —1C **80**
Stockwell Rd. *SW9* —5B **66**
Stockwell St. *SE10* —2E **71**
Stockwell Ter. *SW9* —4B **66**
Stoddart Ho. *SW8* —2B **66**
Stofield Gdns. *SE9* —3F **101**
Stoford Clo. *SW19* —5A **76**
Stokenchurch St. *SW6* —4D **63**
Stoke Newington. —5B 12
Stoke Newington Chu. St. *N16* —5F **11**
Stoke Newington Comn. *N16* —4B **12**
Stoke Newington High St. *N16* —5B **12**
Stoke Newington Rd. *N16* —2B **26**
Stoke Pl. *NW10* —2B **32**
Stokesley St. *W12* —5B **32**
Stokes Rd. *E6* —3F **45**
Stoll Clo. *NW2* —5E **5**
Stoms Path. *SE6* —5C **98**
*Stondon Ho. E15 —5B **30***
(off John St.)
Stondon Pk. *SE23* —4A **84**
Stondon Wlk. *E6* —1F **45**
Stonebridge. —5A 18
Stonebridge Pk. *NW10* —4A **18**
Stonebridge Rd. *N15* —1B **12**
*Stone Bldgs. WC2 —4B **38***
(off Chancery La.)
Stone Clo. *SW4* —5E **65**
Stonecutter St. *EC4* —5D **39**
Stonefield. *N7* —4B **10**
Stonefield St. *N1* —5C **24**
Stonefield Way. *SE7* —3F **73**
*Stone Hall. W8 —4D **49***
(off St Margarets's La.)
Stonehall Av. *Ilf* —1F **17**
Stone Hall Gdns. *W8* —4D **49**
Stone Hall Pl. *W8* —4D **49**
Stonehills Ct. *SE21* —3A **96**
*Stonehouse. NW1 —5E **23***
(off Plender St.)
*Stone Ho. Ct. EC3 —5A **40***
(off Houndsditch)
Stone Lake Ind. Pk. *SE7* —5E **59**
Stone Lake Retail Pk. *SE7* —5E **59**
Stoneleigh M. *E3* —1A **42**
Stoneleigh Pl. *W11* —1F **47**
Stoneleigh St. *W11* —1F **47**
Stoneleigh Ter. *N19* —4D **9**
Stonell's Rd. *SW11* —4B **78**
Stonenest St. *N4* —3B **10**
Stones End St. *SE1* —3E **53**
Stoneyard La. *E14* —1D **57**
Stoneycroft Clo. *SE12* —5B **86**
Stoney La. *E1* —5B **40**
Stoney St. *SE1* —2F **53**
Stonhouse St. *SW4* —2F **79**
Stonor Rd. *W14* —5B **48**
Stopes St. *SE15* —3B **68**
Stopford Rd. *E13* —5C **30**
Stopford Rd. *SE17* —1D **67**
*Stopher Ho. SE1 —3D **53***
(off Webber St.)
Storers Quay. *E14* —5F **57**
Store St. *E15* —2F **29**
Store St. *WC1* —4F **37**
*Storey Ct. NW8 —2F **35***
(off St John's Wood Rd.)
Storey Ho. *E14* —1D **57**
Storey Rd. *N6* —1B **8**
Storey's Ga. *SW1* —3F **51**
Stories M. *SE5* —5A **68**
Stories Rd. *SE5* —1A **82**
Stork Rd. *E7* —3B **30**
Stork's Rd. *SE16* —4C **54**
Stormont Rd. *N6* —2B **8**
Stormont Rd. *SW11* —1C **78**
*Storrington. WC1 —2A **38***
(off Regent Sq.)
Story St. *N1* —4B **24**
*Stothard Ho. E1 —3E **41***
(off Amiel St.)
Stothard St. *E1* —3E **41**
Stott Clo. *SW18* —4F **77**
Stoughton Clo. *SE11* —5B **52**
Stoughton Clo. *SW15* —1C **88**
Stourcliffe Clo. *W1* —5B **36**
Stourcliffe St. *W2* —5B **36**
Stourhead Clo. *SW19* —5F **75**
*Stourhead Ho. SW1 —1F **65***
(off Tachbrook St.)
Stour Rd. *E3* —4C **28**
Stowage. *SE8* —2C **70**
Stowe Ho. *NW11* —1E **7**
Stowe Rd. *W12* —3D **47**
Stracey Rd. *E7* —1C **30**
Stracey Rd. *NW10* —5A **18**
Stradbroke Rd. *N5* —1E **25**
Stradella Rd. *SE24* —4E **81**
*Strafford Ho. SE8 —1B **70***
(off Grove St.)
Strafford St. *E14* —3C **56**
Strahan Rd. *E3* —2A **42**
Straightsmouth. *SE10* —3E **71**
Strait Rd. *E6* —1F **59**
Strakers Rd. *SE15* —2D **83**
*Strale Ho. N1 —5A **26***
(off Whitmore Est.)
Strand. *WC2* —1A **52**
Strand La. *WC2* —1B **52**
Strang Ho. *N1* —5E **25**
Strangways Ter. *W14* —4B **48**
Stranraer Way. *N1* —4A **24**
Strasburg Rd. *SW11* —4C **64**
Stratford. —4F 29
Stratford Cen., The. *E15* —4F **29**

Stratford Circus Arts Cen.
　　　　—3F 29
Stratford Gro. *SW15* —2F 75
Stratford Marsh. —4D 29
Stratford New Town. —2E 29
Stratford Office Village, The.
　　　　E15 —4A 30
(off Romford Rd.)
Stratford Pl. *W1* —5D 37
Stratford Rd. *E13* —5B 30
(in two parts)
Stratford Rd. *W8* —4C 48
Stratford Shop. Cen. *E15*
　　　　—4F 29
(off Stratford Cen., The)
Stratford Studios. *W8* —4C 48
Stratford Vs. *NW1* —4E 23
Stratham Ct. *N19* —5A 10
(off Alexander Rd.)
Strathan Clo. *SW18* —4A 76
Strathaven Rd. *SE12* —4D 87
Strathblaine Rd. *SW11*
　　　　—3F 77
Strathdale. *SW16* —5B 94
Strathdon Dri. *SW17* —3F 91
Strathearn Pl. *W2* —5A 36
Strathearn Rd. *SW19* —5C 90
Stratheden Pde. *SE3* —3C 72
Stratheden Rd. *SE3* —4C 72
Strathleven Rd. *SW2* —3A 80
Strathmore Ct. *NW8* —2A 36
(off Park Rd.)
Strathmore Gdns. *W8* —2C 48
Strathmore Rd. *SW19* —3C 90
Strathnairn St. *SE1* —5C 54
Strathray Gdns. *NW3* —3A 22
Strath Ter. *SW11* —2A 78
Strathville Rd. *SW18* —2C 90
Strattondale St. *E14* —4E 57
Stratton St. *W1* —2D 51
Strauss Rd. *W4* —3A 46
Streakes Fld. Rd. *NW2* —4C 4
Streatham. —4A 94
Streatham Clo. *SW16* —2A 94
Streatham Common. —5A 94
Streatham Comn. N. *SW16*
　　　　—5A 94
Streatham Comn. S. *SW16*
　　　　—5A 94
Streatham Ct. *SW16* —3A 94
Streatham High Rd. *SW16*
　　　　—4A 94
Streatham Hill. —1A 94
Streatham Hill. *SW2* —2A 94
Streatham Ice Rink. —5A 94
Streatham Park. —4E 93
Streatham Pl. *SW2* —5A 80
Streatham St. *WC1* —5A 38
Streathbourne Rd. *SW17*
　　　　—2C 92
Streatley Pl. *NW3* —1E 21
Streatley Rd. *NW6* —4B 20
Streetfield M. *SE3* —1C 86
Streimer Rd. *E15* —1E 43
Strelley Way. *W3* —1A 46
Stretton Mans. *SE8* —1C 70

Strickland Ct. *SE15* —1C 82
Strickland Ho. *E2* —2B 40
(off Chambord St.)
Strickland Row. *SW18*
　　　　—5F 77
Strickland St. *SE8* —5C 70
Stride Rd. *E13* —1B 44
Stringer Ho. *N1* —5A 26
(off Whitmore Est.)
Strode Rd. *E7* —1C 30
Strode Rd. *NW10* —3C 18
Strode Rd. *SW6* —3A 62
Strome Ho. *NW6* —1D 35
(off Carlton Va.)
Strone Rd. *E7 & E12* —3E 31
Stronsa Rd. *W12* —3B 46
Strood Ho. *SE1* —4C 26
(off Staple St.)
Stroud Cres. *SW15* —3C 88
Stroud Green. —2B 10
Stroud Grn. Rd. *N4* —3B 10
Stroudley Ho. *SW8* —4E 65
Stroudley Wlk. *E3* —2D 43
Stroud Rd. *SW19* —3C 90
Strouts Pl. *E2* —2B 40
Strudwick Ct. *SW4* —4A 66
(off Binfield Rd.)
Strutton Ground. *SW1* —4F 51
Strype St. *E1* —4B 40
Stuart Av. *NW9* —2C 4
Stuart Ho. *W14* —5A 48
(off Windsor Way)
Stuart Mill Ho. *N1* —1B 38
Stuart Rd. *NW6* —2C 34
(in two parts)
Stuart Rd. *SE15* —2E 83
Stuart Rd. *SW19* —3C 90
Stuart Tower. *W9* —2E 35
(off Maida Va.)
Stubbs Dri. *SE16* —1D 69
Stubbs Ho. *SW1* —5F 51
(off Erasmus St.)
Stubbs Point. *E16* —3C 44
Stucley Ho. *NW1* —4D 23
Studdridge St. *SW6* —5C 62
(in two parts)
Studd St. *N1* —5D 25
Studholme Ct. *NW3* —1C 20
Studholme St. *SE15* —3D 69
Studio Pl. *SW1* —3B 50
(off Kinnerton St.)
Studland. *SE17* —1F 67
(off Portland St.)
Studland Rd. *SE26* —5F 97
Studland St. *W6* —5D 47
Studley Clo. *E5* —2A 28
Studley Ct. *E14* —1F 57
Studley Dri. *Ilf* —1F 17
Studley Est. *SW4* —4A 66
Studley Rd. *E7* —3D 31
Studley Rd. *SW4* —4A 66
Stukeley Rd. *E7* —4D 31
Stukeley St. *WC2* —5A 38
Stumps Hill La. *Beck* —5C 98
Stunell Ho. *SE14* —2F 69
(off John Williams Clo.)

Sturdee Ho. *E2* —1C 40
(off Horatio St.)
Sturdy Rd. *SE15* —5D 69
Sturgeon Rd. *SE17* —1E 67
Sturgess Av. *NW4* —2D 5
Sturge St. *SE1* —3E 53
Sturmer Way. *N7* —2B 24
Sturminster Ho. *SW8* —3B 66
(off Dorset Rd.)
Sturry St. *E14* —5D 43
Sturt St. *N1* —1E 39
(off Wenlock Rd.)
Stutfield St. *E1* —5C 40
Styles Gdns. *SW9* —1D 81
Styles Ho. *SE1* —2D 53
(off Hatfields)
Sudbourne Rd. *SW2* —3A 80
Sudbrooke Rd. *SW12* —4B 78
Sudbury Ct. *E5* —1A 28
Sudbury Cres. *SW8* —4F 65
Sudbury Cres. *Brom* —5C 100
Sudbury Ho. *SW18* —3D 77
Sudeley St. *N1* —1D 39
Sudlow Rd. *SW18* —3C 76
Sudrey St. *SE1* —3E 53
Suffield Ho. *SE17* —1D 67
(off Berryfield Rd.)
Suffolk Ct. *E10* —2C 14
Suffolk La. *EC4* —1F 53
Suffolk Pl. *SW1* —2F 51
Suffolk Rd. *E13* —2C 44
Suffolk Rd. *N15* —1F 11
Suffolk Rd. *NW10* —4A 18
Suffolk Rd. *SW13* —3B 60
Suffolk St. *E7* —1C 30
Suffolk St. *SW1* —1F 51
Sugar Bakers Ct. *EC3* —5A 40
(off Creechurch La.)
Sugar Ho. La. *E15* —1E 43
Sugar Loaf Wlk. *E2* —2E 41
Sugar Quay. *EC3* —1A 54
(off Lwr. Thames St.)
Sugar Quay Wlk. *EC3* —1A 54
Sugden Rd. *SW11* —1C 78
Sugden Rd. *SW19* —5E 91
Sugden St. *SE5* —2F 67
(off Depot St.)
Sulby Ho. *SE4* —2A 84
(off Turnham Rd.)
Sulgrave Gdns. *W6* —3E 47
Sulgrave Rd. *W6* —4E 47
Sulina Rd. *SW2* —5A 80
Sulivan Ct. *SW6* —5C 62
Sulivan Enterprise Cen. *SW6*
　　　　—1D 77
Sulivan Rd. *SW6* —1C 76
Sullivan Av. *E16* —4F 45
Sullivan Clo. *SW11* —1A 78
Sullivan Ct. *N16* —2B 12
Sullivan Ho. *SE11* —5B 52
(off Vauxhall St.)
Sullivan Ho. *SW1* —2D 65
(off Churchill Gdns.)
Sullivan Rd. *SE11* —5D 53
Sultan St. *SE5* —3E 67
Sumatra Rd. *NW6* —2C 20
Sumburgh Rd. *SW12* —4C 78

Summercourt Rd. *E1* —5E **41**
Summerfield Av. *NW6* —1A **34**
Summerfield St. *SE12* —5B **86**
Summerhouse Rd. *N16*
     —4A **12**
Summerley St. *SW18* —2D **91**
Summersby Rd. *N6* —1D **9**
Summers Rd. *EC1* —3C **38**
Summerstown. —3E 91
Summerstown. *SW17* —3E **91**
Summit Clo. *NW2* —2A **20**
Summit Est. *N16* —2C **12**
Sumner Av. *SE15* —4B **68**
Sumner Bldgs. SE1 —2E **53**
    (off Sumner St.)
Sumner Ct. *SW8* —3A **66**
Sumner Est. *SE15* —3B **68**
Sumner Ho. *E3* —4D **43**
Sumner Pl. *SW7* —5F **49**
Sumner Pl. M. *SW7* —5F **49**
Sumner Rd. *SE15* —2B **68**
    (in two parts)
Sumner St. *SE1* —2D **53**
Sumpter Clo. *NW3* —3E **21**
Sunbeam Cres. *W10* —3E **33**
Sunbeam Rd. *NW10* —3A **32**
Sunbury Av. *SW14* —2A **74**
Sunbury Av. Pas. *SW14*
    —2A **74**
Sunbury Ho. E2 —2B **40**
    (off Swanfield St.)
Sunbury Ho. SE14 —2F **69**
    (off Myers La.)
Sunbury La. *SW11* —4F **63**
    (in two parts)
Sunbury Workshops. E2
    (off Swanfield St.) —2B **40**
Sun Ct. EC3 —5F **39**
    (off Cornhill)
Suncroft Pl. *SE26* —3E **97**
Sunderland Ct. *SE22* —5C **82**
Sunderland Mt. *SE23* —2F **97**
Sunderland Rd. *SE23* —1F **97**
Sunderland Ter. *W2* —5D **35**
Sunderland Way. *E12* —4F **17**
Sundew Av. *W12* —1C **46**
Sundew Clo. *W12* —1C **46**
Sundorne Rd. *SE7* —1E **73**
Sundra Wlk. *E1* —3F **41**
Sundridge. —5E 101
Sunfields Pl. *SE3* —3D **73**
Sunflower Dri. *E8* —4B **26**
Sun-in-the-Sands. (Junct.)
    —3D **73**
Sun-in-the-Sands. *SE3*
    —3C **72**
Sun La. *SE3* —3D **73**
Sunlight Clo. *SW19* —5E **91**
Sunlight Sq. *E2* —2D **41**
Sunningdale Av. *W3* —1A **46**
Sunningdale Clo. SE16
    (off Ryder Dri.) —1D **69**
Sunningdale Gdns. W8
    (off Stratford Rd.) —4C **48**
Sunninghill Rd. *SE13* —5D **71**
Sunnydale Rd. *SE12* —3D **87**

Sunnydene St. *SE26* —4A **98**
Sunnyhill Clo. *E5* —1A **28**
Sunnyhill Rd. *SW16* —4A **94**
Sunnymead Rd. *NW9* —2A **4**
Sunnymead Rd. *SW15*
    —3D **75**
Sunnyside. *NW2* —5B **6**
Sunnyside. *SW19* —5A **90**
Sunnyside Houses. NW2
    (off Sunnyside) —5B **6**
Sunnyside Pas. *SW19*
    —5A **90**
Sunnyside Rd. *E10* —3C **14**
Sunnyside Rd. *N19* —2F **9**
Sun Pas. SE16 —4C **54**
    (off Old Jamaica Rd.)
Sunray Av. *SE24* —2F **81**
Sun Rd. *W14* —1B **62**
Sunset Rd. *SE5* —2E **81**
Sun St. *EC2* —4F **39**
    (in two parts)
Sun St. Pas. *EC2* —4A **40**
Sunwell St. *SE15* —4D **69**
Sun Wharf. SE8 —3D **71**
    (off Creekside)
Surma Clo. *E1* —3C **40**
Surrendale Pl. *W9* —3C **34**
Surrey Canal Rd. *SE15 &
    SE14* —2E **69**
Surrey County Cricket Club.
    —2B **66**
Surrey Gdns. *N4* —1E **11**
Surrey Gro. *SE17* —1A **68**
Surrey Ho. SE16 —2F **55**
    (off Rotherhithe St.)
Surrey La. *SW11* —4A **64**
Surrey La. Est. *SW11* —4A **64**
Surrey M. *SE27* —4A **96**
Surrey Mt. *SE23* —1D **97**
Surrey Quays Rd. *SE16*
    —4E **55**
Surrey Quays Shop. Cen.
    SE16 —4F **55**
Surrey Rd. *SE15* —3F **83**
Surrey Row. *SE1* —3D **53**
Surrey Sq. *SE17* —1A **68**
Surrey Steps. WC2 —1B **52**
    (off Surrey St.)
Surrey St. *E13* —2D **45**
Surrey St. *WC2* —1B **52**
Surrey Ter. *SE17* —1A **68**
Surrey Water Rd. *SE16*
    —2F **55**
Surridge Ct. SW9 —5A **66**
    (off Clapham Rd.)
Surr St. *N7* —2A **24**
Susan Constant Ct. *E14*
    —1F **57**
Susannah St. *E14* —5D **43**
Susan Rd. *SE3* —5D **73**
Sussex Clo. *N19* —4A **10**
Sussex Ct. SE10 —2E **71**
    (off Roan St.)
Sussex Gdns. *N4* —1E **11**
Sussex Gdns. *N6* —1B **8**

Sussex Gdns. *W2* —1F **49**
Sussex Ga. *N6* —1B **8**
Sussex Lodge. W2 —5F **35**
    (off Sussex Pl.)
Sussex Mans. SW7 —5F **49**
    (off Old Brompton Rd.)
Sussex Mans. WC2 —1A **52**
    (off Maiden La.)
Sussex M. E. W2 —5F **35**
    (off Clifton Pl.)
Sussex M. W. *W2* —1F **49**
Sussex Pl. *NW1* —3B **36**
Sussex Pl. *W2* —5F **35**
Sussex Pl. *W6* —1E **61**
Sussex Sq. *W2* —1F **49**
Sussex St. *E13* —2D **45**
Sussex St. *SW1* —1D **65**
Sussex Wlk. *SW9* —2D **81**
    (in two parts)
Sussex Way. *N19 & N7*
    (in four parts) —3F **9**
Sutcliffe Clo. *NW11* —1D **7**
Sutherland Av. *W9* —3C **34**
Sutherland Ct. *N16* —5F **11**
Sutherland Ct. W9 —3C **34**
    (off Surrendale Pl.)
Sutherland Gdns. *SW14*
    —1A **74**
Sutherland Gro. *SW18*
    —4A **76**
Sutherland Ho. *W8* —4D **49**
Sutherland Pl. *W2* —5C **34**
Sutherland Point. E5 —1D **27**
    (off Brackenfield Clo.)
Sutherland Rd. *E3* —1B **42**
Sutherland Rd. *W4* —2A **60**
Sutherland Row. *SW1*
    —1D **65**
Sutherland Sq. *SE17* —1E **67**
Sutherland St. *SW1* —1D **65**
Sutherland Wlk. *SE17* —1E **67**
Sutlej Rd. *SE7* —3E **73**
Sutterton St. *N7* —3B **24**
Sutton Ct. Rd. *E13* —2E **45**
Sutton Est. EC1 —2F **39**
    (off City Rd.)
Sutton Est. *W10* —4E **33**
Sutton Est., The. N1 —4D **25**
Sutton Est., The. SW3
    (off Cale St.) —1A **64**
Sutton Pl. *E9* —2E **27**
Sutton Rd. *E13* —3B **44**
Sutton Row. *W1* —5F **37**
Sutton Sq. *E9* —2E **27**
Sutton St. *E1* —1E **55**
Sutton's Way. *EC1* —3E **39**
Sutton Wlk. *SE1* —2B **52**
Sutton Way. *W10* —3E **33**
Swaby Rd. *SW18* —1E **91**
Swaffield Rd. *SW18* —5D **77**
Swains La. *N6* —3C **8**
Swainson Rd. *W3* —3B **46**
Swallands Rd. *SE6* —3C **98**
    (in two parts)
Swallow Clo. *SE14* —4F **69**
Swallow Ct. *SE12* —5C **86**

Swallow Ct. W9 —4C **34**
(off Admiral Wlk.)
Swallow Dri. NW10 —3A **18**
Swallowfield Rd. SE7 —1D **73**
Swallow Gdns. SW16 —5F **93**
Swallow Ho. NW8 —1A **36**
(off Barrow Hill Est.)
Swallow Pas. W1 —5D **37**
(off Swallow Pl.)
Swallow Pl. W1 —5D **37**
Swallow St. W1 —1E **51**
Swanage Ho. SW8 —3B **66**
(off Dorset Rd.)
Swanage Rd. SW18 —4E **77**
Swan App. E6 —4F **45**
Swanbourne. SE17 —5E **53**
(off Wansey St.)
Swanbourne Ho. NW8
(off Capland St.) —3A **36**
Swan Cen., The. SW17
—3D **91**
Swan Ct. E14 —5B **42**
Swan Ct. SW3 —1A **64**
Swandon Way. SW18 —3D **77**
Swanfield St. E2 —2B **40**
Swan La. EC4 —1F **53**
Swanley Ho. SE17 —1A **68**
(off Kinglake Est.)
Swan Mead. SE1 —4A **54**
Swan M. SW6 —4B **62**
Swan M. SW9 —5B **66**
Swanne Ho. SE10 —3E **71**
(off Gloucester Cir.)
Swan Pas. E1 —1B **54**
(off Royal Mint Pl.)
Swan Pl. SW13 —5B **60**
Swan Rd. SE16 —3E **55**
Swanscombe Ho. W11
(off St Ann's Rd.) —2F **47**
Swanscombe Point. E16
(off Clarkson Rd.) —4B **44**
Swanscombe Rd. W4 —1A **60**
Swanscombe Rd. W11
—2F **47**
Swan St. SE1 —4E **53**
Swan St. SE18 —4F **59**
(in two parts)
Swanton Gdns. SW19 —1F **89**
Swan Wlk. SW3 —2B **64**
Swanwick Clo. SW15 —5B **74**
Swan Yd. N1 —3D **25**
Swathling Ho. SW15 —4B **74**
(off Tunworth Cres.)
Swaton Rd. E3 —3C **42**
Swedeland Ct. E1 —4A **40**
(off Bishopsgate)
Swedenborg Gdns. E1
—1D **55**
Sweden Ga. SE16 —4A **56**
Swedish Quays. SE16
—4A **56**
Sweeney Cres. SE1 —3B **54**
Swell Ct. E17 —1C **14**
Swete St. E13 —1C **44**
Sweyn Pl. SE3 —5C **72**
Swift Lodge. W9 —3C **34**

(off Admiral Wlk.)
Swiftsden Way. Brom
—5A **100**
Swift St. SW6 —4B **62**
Swinbrook Rd. W10 —4A **34**
Swinburne Ct. SE5 —2F **81**
(off Basingdon Way)
Swinburne Ho. E2 —2E **41**
(off Roman Rd.)
Swinburne Rd. SW15 —2C **74**
Swindon St. W12 —2D **47**
Swinford Gdns. SW9 —1D **81**
Swinley Ho. NW1 —2D **37**
(off Redhill St.)
Swinnerton St. E9 —2A **28**
Swinton Pl. WC1 —2B **38**
Swinton St. WC1 —2B **38**
Swiss Cen. WC2 —1F **51**
(off Wardour St.)
Swiss Cottage. (Junct.)
—4F **21**
Swiss Cottage. NW3 —4F **21**
Swiss Ct. WC2 —1F **51**
(off Panton St.)
Swiss Ter. Rd. NW6 —4F **21**
Sybil M. N4 —1D **11**
Sybil Phoenix Clo. SE8
—1F **69**
Sybil Thorndike Casson Ho.
SW5 —1C **62**
(off Old Brompton Rd.)
Sybourn St. E17 —2B **14**
Sycamore Av. E3 —5B **28**
Sycamore Clo. E16 —3A **44**
Sycamore Clo. SE9 —2F **101**
Sycamore Clo. W3 —2A **46**
Sycamore Ct. E7 —3C **30**
Sycamore Ct. NW6 —5C **20**
(off Bransdale Clo.)
Sycamore Gdns. W12 —3D **47**
Sycamore Gro. SE6 —4E **85**
Sycamore Ho. SE16 —3F **55**
(off Woodland Cres.)
Sycamore Ho. W6 —3D **47**
Sycamore Lodge. W8
(off St Mary's Pl.) —4D **49**
Sycamore M. SW4 —1E **79**
Sycamore St. EC1 —3B **89**
Sycamore St. EC1 —3E **39**
Sycamore Wlk. W10 —3A **34**
Sydcote. SE21 —1E **95**
Sydenham. —4E **97**
Sydenham Av. SE26 —5D **97**
Sydenham Cotts. SE12
—2E **97**
Sydenham Hill. SE23 &
SE26 —1D **97**
Sydenham Hill. SE26 —3E **97**
Sydenham Pk. Mans. SE26
(off Sydenham Pk.) —3E **97**
Sydenham Pk. Rd. SE26
—3E **97**
Sydenham Pl. SE27 —3D **95**
Sydenham Ri. SE23 —2D **97**
Sydenham Rd. SE26 —4E **97**
Sydmons Ct. SE23 —5E **83**

Sydner M. N16 —1B **26**
Sydner Rd. N16 —1B **26**
Sydney Clo. SW3 —5F **49**
Sydney Gro. NW4 —1E **5**
Sydney M. SW3 —5F **49**
Sydney Pl. SW7 —5F **49**
Sydney Rd. E11 —1D **17**
Sydney St. SW3 —1A **64**
Sylvan Gro. NW2 —1F **19**
Sylvan Gro. SE15 —2D **69**
Sylvan Rd. E7 —3C **30**
Sylvan Rd. E11 —1C **16**
Sylvan Rd. E17 —1C **14**
Sylvester Path. E8 —3D **27**
Sylvester Rd. E8 —3D **27**
Sylvester Rd. E17 —2B **14**
Sylvia Ct. N1 —1F **39**
Symes M. NW1 —1E **37**
Symington Ho. SE1 —4F **53**
(off Deverell St.)
Symington M. E9 —2F **27**
Symister M. N1 —2A **40**
(off Coronet St.)
Symons St. SW3 —5B **50**
Syon Lodge. SE12 —5C **86**
Syringa Ho. SE4 —1B **84**

Tabard Ct. E14 —5E **43**
(off Lodore St.)
Tabard Garden Est. SE1
—4F **53**
Tabard Ho. SE1 —4F **53**
(off Manciple St.)
Tabard St. SE1 —3F **53**
Tabernacle Av. E13 —3C **44**
Tabernacle St. EC2 —3F **39**
Tableer Av. SW4 —3E **79**
Tabley Rd. N7 —1A **24**
Tabor Rd. W6 —4D **47**
Tachbrook Est. SW1 —1F **65**
Tachbrook M. SW1 —5E **51**
Tachbrook St. SW1 —5E **51**
(in two parts)
Tack M. SE4 —1C **84**
Tadema Ho. NW8 —3F **35**
(off Penfold St.)
Tadema Rd. SW10 —3E **63**
Tadmor St. W12 —2F **47**
Tadworth Ho. SE1 —3D **53**
(off Webber St.)
Tadworth Rd. NW2 —4C **4**
Taeping St. E14 —5D **57**
Taffrail Ho. E14 —1D **71**
Taft Way. E3 —2D **43**
Tailworth St. E1 —4C **40**
(off Chicksand St.)
Tait Ct. SW8 —4A **66**
(off Lansdowne Grn.)
Tait Ho. SE1 —2C **52**
(off Greet St.)
Takhar M. SW11 —5A **64**
Talacre Rd. NW5 —3C **22**
Talbot Ct. EC3 —1F **53**
(off Gracechurch St.)
Talbot Cres. NW4 —1C **4**

Talbot Gro. Ho. W11 —5A **34**
(off Lancaster Rd.)
Talbot Ho. E14 —5D **43**
Talbot Pl. SE3 —5A **72**
Talbot Rd. E7 —1C **30**
Talbot Rd. N6 —1C **8**
Talbot Rd. SE22 —2A **82**
Talbot Rd. W11 & W2
(in two parts) —5B **34**
Talbot Sq. W2 —5F **35**
Talbot Wlk. NW10 —3A **18**
Talbot Wlk. W11 —5A **34**
Talbot Yd. SE1 —2F **53**
Talcott Path. SW2 —1C **94**
Talfourd Pl. SE15 —4B **68**
Talfourd Rd. SE5 —4B **68**
Talgarth Mans. W14 —1A **62**
(off Talgarth Rd.)
Talgarth Rd. W6 & W14
—1F **61**
Talgarth Wlk. NW9 —1A **4**
Talia Ho. E14 —4E **57**
Talina Cen. SW6 —4E **63**
Talisman Sq. SE26 —4C **96**
Tallack Rd. E10 —3B **14**
Talleyrand Ho. SE5 —5E **67**
(off Lilford Rd.)
Tallis Clo. E16 —5D **45**
Tallis Gro. SE7 —2D **73**
Tallis St. EC4 —1C **52**
Tallis Vw. NW10 —3A **18**
Talmage Clo. SE23 —5E **83**
Talma Rd. SW2 —2C **80**
Talwin St. E3 —2D **43**
Tamar Clo. E3 —5B **28**
Tamar Ho. SE11 —1C **66**
(off Kennington La.)
Tamarind Ct. W8 —4D **49**
(off St Margaret's La.)
Tamarind Yd. E1 —2C **54**
(off Kennet St.)
Tamarisk Sq. W12 —1B **46**
Tamar St. SE7 —4F **59**
Tamworth. N7 —3A **24**
Tamworth St. SW6 —2C **62**
Tancred Rd. N4 —2D **11**
Tanfield Av. NW2 —1B **18**
Tangley Gro. SW15 —4B **74**
Tangmere. WC1 —2B **38**
(off Sidmouth St.)
Tanhurst Ho. SW2 —5B **80**
(off Redlands Way)
Tankerton Houses. WC1
(off Tankerton St.) —2A **38**
Tankerton St. WC1 —2A **38**
Tankridge Rd. NW2 —4D **5**
Tanner Ho. SE1 —3A **54**
(off Tanner St.)
Tanneries, The. E1 —3E **41**
(off Cephas Av.)
Tanner Point. E13 —5C **30**
(off Pelly Rd.)
Tanner's Hill. SE8 —4B **70**
Tanner St. SE1 —3A **54**
(in two parts)
Tannington Ter. N5 —5D **11**

Tannsfeld Rd. SE26 —5F **97**
Tansley Clo. N7 —2F **23**
Tanswell St. SE1 —3C **52**
Tantallon Rd. SW12 —1C **92**
Tant Av. E16 —5B **44**
Tanza Rd. NW3 —1B **22**
Tapley Ho. SE1 —3C **54**
(off Wolseley St.)
Taplow. SE17 —1F **67**
(off Thurlow St.)
Taplow Ho. E2 —2B **40**
(off Palissy St.)
Taplow St. N1 —1E **39**
Tappesfield Rd. SE15 —1E **83**
Tapp St. E1 —3D **41**
Tarbert Rd. SE22 —3A **82**
Tarbert Wlk. E1 —1E **55**
Tariff Cres. SE8 —5B **56**
Tarleton Gdns. SE23 —2D **97**
Tarling Ho. E1 —5D **41**
(off Tarling St.)
Tarling Rd. E16 —5B **44**
Tarling St. E1 —5E **41**
Tarling St. Est. E1 —5E **41**
Tarns, The. NW1 —2E **37**
(off Varndell St.)
Tarn St. SE1 —4E **53**
Tarplett Ho. SE14 —2E **69**
(off John Williams Clo.)
Tarquin Ho. SE26 —4C **96**
(off High Level Dri.)
Tarragon Clo. SE14 —3A **70**
Tarragon Gro. SE26 —5F **97**
Tarranbrae. NW6 —4A **20**
Tarrant Ho. E2 —2E **41**
(off Roman Rd.)
Tarrant Pl. W1 —4B **36**
Tarrington Clo. SW16 —3F **93**
Tartan Ho. E14 —5E **43**
Tarver Rd. SE17 —1D **67**
Tarves Way. SE10 —3D **71**
Tasker Ho. E14 —4B **42**
Tasker Rd. NW3 —2B **22**
Tasman Ct. E14 —5D **57**
Tasman Ho. E1 —2D **55**
(off Clegg St.)
Tasman Rd. SW9 —1A **80**
Tasman Wlk. E16 —5F **45**
Tasso Rd. W6 —2A **62**
Tasso Yd. W6 —2A **62**
(off Tasso Rd.)
Tatchbury Ho. SW15 —4B **74**
(off Tunworth Cres.)
Tate Britain. —5A **52**
Tate Modern. —2D **53**
Tatnell Rd. SE23 —4A **84**
Tatsfield Ho. SE1 —4F **53**
(off Pardoner St.)
Tatton Cres. N16 —2B **12**
Tatum St. SE17 —5F **53**
Tauheed Clo. N4 —4E **11**
Taunton Ho. W2 —5E **35**
(off Hallfield Est.)
Taunton M. NW1 —3B **36**
Taunton Pl. NW1 —3B **36**
Taunton Rd. SE12 —3A **86**

Taverners Clo. W11 —2A **48**
Taverner Sq. N5 —1E **25**
Tavern La. SW9 —5C **66**
Tavern Quay. SE16 —5A **56**
Tavistock Clo. N16 —2A **26**
Tavistock Ct. WC1 —3F **37**
(off Tavistock Sq.)
Tavistock Cres. W11 —4B **34**
(in three parts)
Tavistock Ho. WC1 —3F **37**
Tavistock M. W11 —5B **34**
Tavistock Pl. WC1 —3A **38**
Tavistock Rd. E7 —1B **30**
Tavistock Rd. E15 —3B **30**
Tavistock Rd. N4 —1F **11**
Tavistock Rd. NW10 —1B **32**
Tavistock Rd. W11 —5B **34**
(in two parts)
Tavistock Sq. WC1 —3F **37**
Tavistock St. WC2 —1A **52**
(in two parts)
Tavistock Ter. N19 —5F **9**
Tavistock Tower. SE16
—4A **56**
Taviton St. WC1 —3F **37**
Tavy Clo. SE11 —1C **66**
(off White Hart St.,
in two parts)
Tawny Way. SE16 —5F **55**
Taybridge Rd. SW11 —1C **78**
Tay Bldgs. SE1 —4A **54**
(off Decima St.)
Tayburn Clo. E14 —5E **43**
Tayler Ct. NW8 —5F **21**
(off Dorman Way)
Taylor Clo. SE8 —2B **70**
Taylor Ct. E15 —2E **29**
Taylors Grn. W3 —5A **32**
Taylors La. NW10 —4A **18**
Taylor's La. SE26 —4D **97**
Taymount Grange. SE23
—2E **97**
Taymount Ri. SE23 —2E **97**
Tayport Clo. N1 —4A **24**
Tayside Ct. SE5 —2F **81**
Teak Clo. SE16 —2A **56**
Tealby Ct. N7 —2B **24**
(off George's Rd.)
Teal Clo. E16 —4F **45**
Teal Ct. NW10 —3A **18**
Teal Ct. SE8 —2B **70**
(off Abinger Gro.)
Teale St. E2 —1C **40**
Teasel Way. E15 —2A **44**
Ted Roberts Ho. E2 —1D **41**
(off Parmiter St.)
Tedworth Gdns. SW3 —1B **64**
Tedworth Sq. SW3 —1B **64**
Teesdale Clo. E2 —1C **40**
Teesdale Rd. E11 —1B **16**
Teesdale St. E2 —1D **41**
Teesdale Yd. E2 —1D **41**
Tee, The. W3 —5A **32**
Teignmouth Clo. SW4 —2F **79**
Teignmouth Rd. NW2 —2F **19**
Telecom Tower, The. —4E **37**

Telegraph Hill. *NW3* —5D **7**
Telegraph Pas. *SW2* —5A **80**
Telegraph Pl. *E14* —5D **57**
Telegraph Quarters. SE10
  (off Park Row) —1F **71**
Telegraph Rd. *SW15* —5D **75**
Telegraph St. *EC2* —5F **39**
Teleman Sq. *SE3* —2D **87**
Telephone Pl. *SW6* —2B **62**
Telfer Ho. *EC1* —2E **39**
  (off Lever St.)
Telferscot Rd. *SW12* —1F **93**
Telford Av. *SW2* —1F **93**
Telford Clo. *E17* —2A **14**
Telford Ho. SE1 —4E **53**
  (off Tiverton St.)
Telford Rd. *NW9* —1C **4**
Telford Rd. *W10* —4A **34**
Telfords Yd. E1 —1C **54**
  (off Pennington St.)
Telford Ter. SW1 —2E **65**
  (off Churchill Gdns.)
Telford Way. *W3* —4A **32**
Tell Gro. *SE22* —2B **82**
Tellson Av. *SE18* —4F **73**
Temair Ho. SE10 —3D **71**
  (off Tarves Way)
Temeraire St. *SE16* —3E **55**
Tempelhof Av. *NW4* —2E **5**
Temperley Rd. *SW12* —5C **78**
Templar Ct. NW8 —2F **35**
  (off St John's Wood Rd.)
Templar Ho. *NW2* —3B **20**
Templars Av. *NW11* —1B **6**
Templars Ho. *E15* —2D **29**
Templar St. *SE5* —5D **67**
Temple Av. EC4 —1C **52**
Temple Bar. —5C 38
  (off Strand)
Temple Chambers. EC4
  (off Temple Av.) —1C **52**
Temple Clo. *E11* —2A **16**
Templecombe Rd. *E9* —5E **27**
Temple Ct. SW8 —3A **66**
  (off Thorncroft St.)
Temple Dwellings. E2 —1D **41**
  (off Temple St.)
Temple Fortune. —1B 6
Temple Fortune Hill. *NW11*
  —1C **6**
Temple Fortune La. *NW11*
  —1B **6**
Temple Fortune Pde. *NW11*
  —1B **6**
Temple Gdns. EC4 —1C **52**
  (off Middle Temple La.)
Temple Gdns. *NW11* —1B **6**
Temple Gro. *NW11* —1C **6**
Temple La. *EC4* —5C **38**
Templemead Clo. *W3* —5A **32**
Templemead Ho. *E9* —1A **28**
Temple Mill La. *E10 & E15*
  (in two parts) —1D **29**
Temple Mills. —1D 29
Temple Pl. *WC2* —1B **52**
Temple Rd. *E6* —5F **31**

Temple Rd. *NW2* —1E **19**
Temple St. *E2* —1D **41**
Templeton Clo. *N15* —1F **11**
Templeton Clo. *N16* —2A **26**
Templeton Pl. *SW5* —5C **48**
Templeton Rd. *N15* —1F **11**
Temple W. M. SE11 —4D **53**
  (off West Sq.)
Templewood Av. *NW3* —5D **7**
Templewood Gdns. *NW3*
  —5D **7**
Templewood Point. NW2
  (off Granville Rd.) —4B **6**
Tenbury Clo. *E7* —2F **31**
Tenbury Ct. *SW12* —1F **93**
Tenby Ho. W2 —5E **35**
  (off Hallfield Est.)
Tenby Mans. *W1* —4C **36**
  (off Nottingham St.)
Tench St. *E1* —2D **55**
Tenda Rd. *SE16* —5D **55**
Tenham Av. *SW2* —1F **93**
Tenison Ct. *W1* —1E **51**
Tenison Way. *SE1* —2B **52**
Tenniel Clo. *W2* —1E **49**
Tennis St. *SE1* —3F **53**
Tennyson Av. *E11* —2C **16**
Tennyson Av. *E12* —4F **31**
Tennyson Ct. SW6 —4D **63**
  (off Maltings Pl.)
Tennyson Ho. *SE17* —1E **67**
  (off Browning St.)
Tennyson Mans. *W14* —2B **62**
  (off Queen's Club Gdns.)
Tennyson Rd. *E10* —3D **15**
Tennyson Rd. *E15* —4A **30**
Tennyson Rd. *E17* —1B **14**
Tennyson Rd. *NW6* —5B **20**
  (in two parts)
Tennyson Rd. *SW19* —5E **91**
Tennyson St. *SW8* —5D **65**
Tenterden Ho. *SE17* —1A **68**
  (off Surrey Gro.)
Tenterden St. *W1* —5D **37**
Tenter Ground. *E1* —4B **40**
Tenter Pas. E1 —5B **40**
  (off N. Tenter St.)
Tent St. *E1* —3D **41**
Terborch Way. *SE22* —3A **82**
Teredo St. *SE16* —4F **55**
  (in two parts)
Terling Clo. *E11* —5B **16**
Terling Ho. W10 —4E **33**
  (off Sutton Way)
Terling Wlk. *N1* —5E **25**
  (off Popham St.)
Terminus Pl. *SW1* —4D **51**
Terrace Av. *NW10* —3E **33**
Terrace Gdns. *SW13* —5B **60**
Terrace Rd. *E9* —4E **27**
Terrace Rd. *E13* —1C **44**
Terraces, The. NW8 —1F **35**
  (off Queen's Ter.)
Terrace, The. EC4 —5C **38**
  (off Crown Office Row)
Terrace, The. *NW6* —5C **20**

Terrace, The. *SE8* —5B **56**
  (off Longshore)
Terrace, The. *SE23* —5A **84**
Terrace, The. *SW13* —5A **60**
Terrace Wlk. SW11 —3B **64**
  (off Albert Bri. Rd.)
Terrapin Rd. *SW17* —3D **93**
Terretts Pl. *N1* —4D **25**
  (off Upper St.)
Terrick Ho. SE11 —5C **52**
  (off Reedworth St.)
Territorial Ho. *SE11* —5C **52**
  (off Reedworth St.)
Tessa Sanderson Pl. SW8
  —1D **79**
  (off Daley Thompson Way)
Testerton Wlk. *W11* —1F **47**
Tetbury Pl. *N1* —5D **25**
Tetcott Rd. *SW10* —3E **63**
  (in two parts)
Teversham La. *SW8* —4A **66**
Teviot Est. *E14* —4D **43**
Teviot St. *E14* —3E **43**
Tewkesbury Av. *SE23* —1D **97**
Tewkesbury Clo. *N15* —1F **11**
Tewkesbury Rd. *N15* —1F **11**
Thackeray Clo. *SW3* —1B **64**
Thackeray Ct. W14 —4A **48**
  (off Blythe Rd.)
Thackeray Ho. WC1 —3A **38**
  (off Herbrand St.)
Thackeray M. *E8* —3C **26**
Thackeray Rd. *E6* —1F **45**
Thackeray Rd. *SW8* —5D **65**
Thackeray St. *W8* —4D **49**
Thakeham Clo. *SE26* —4D **97**
Thalia Clo. *SE10* —2F **71**
Thame Rd. *SE16* —3F **55**
Thames Av. *SW10* —4E **63**
Thames Barrier Ind. Area.
  SE18 —4F **59**
  (off Faraday Way)
Thames Barrier Vis. Cen.
  —4F **59**
Thamesbrook. SW3 —1A **64**
  (off Dovehouse St.)
Thames Circ. *E14* —5C **56**
Thames Ct. *SE15* —3B **68**
  (off Daniel Gdns.)
Thames Cres. *W4* —3A **60**
Thames Exchange Building.
  EC4 —1E **53**
  (off Up. Thames St.)
Thames Flood Barrier, The.
  —4E **59**
Thames Ho. *EC4* —1E **53**
  (off Up. Thames St.)
Thames Ho. SW1 —5A **52**
  (off Millbank)
Thameside Ind. Est. *E16*
  —3F **59**
Thames Pl. *SW15* —1F **75**
  (in two parts)
Thames Quay. *E14* —3D **57**
Thames Quay. *SW10* —4E **63**
  (off Chelsea Harbour)
Thames Rd. *E16* —2F **59**

Thames Rd. Ind. Est. E16 —3F 59
Thames St. SE10 —2D 71
Thames Wlk. SW11 —3A 64
Thanet Ho. WC1 —2A 38
Thanet Lodge. NW2 —3A 20 (off Mapesbury Rd.)
Thanet St. WC1 —2A 38
Thanet Wharf. SE8 —2D 71 (off Copperas St.)
Thane Vs. N7 —5B 10
Thane Works. N7 —5B 10
Thant Clo. E10 —5D 15
Thavie's Inn. EC1 —5C 38
Thaxted Ct. N1 —1F 39 (off Fairbank Est.)
Thaxted Ho. SE16 —5E 55 (off Abbeyfield Est.)
Thaxton Rd. W14 —2B 62
Thayer St. W1 —5C 36
Theatre Mus. —1A 52 (off Russell St.)
Theatre Royal. —3F 29
Theatre Sq. E15 —3F 29
Theatre St. SW11 —1B 78
Theberton St. N1 —5C 24
Theed St. SE1 —2C 52
Thelma Gdns. SE3 —4F 73
Theobald Rd. E17 —2B 14
Theobalds Ct. N4 —5E 11
Theobald's Rd. WC1 —4B 38
Theobald St. SE1 —4F 53
Theodore Ct. SE13 —4F 85
Theodore Rd. SE13 —4F 85
Therapia Rd. SE22 —4E 83
Theresa Rd. W6 —5C 46
Therfield Ct. N4 —4E 11
Thermopylae Ga. E14 —5D 57
Theseus Wlk. N1 —1D 39 (off City Garden Row)
Thessaly Ho. SW8 —3E 65 (off Thessaly Rd.)
Thessaly Rd. SW8 —3E 65
Thesus Ho. E14 —5E 43
Thetford Ho. SE1 —4B 54 (off Maltby St.)
Theydon Rd. E5 —4E 13
Theydon St. E17 —2B 14
Third Av. E13 —2C 44
Third Av. E17 —1C 14
Third Av. W3 —2B 46
Third Av. W10 —2A 34
Thirleby Rd. SW1 —4E 51
Thirlmere. NW1 —2D 37 (off Cumberland Mkt.)
Thirlmere Rd. SW16 —4F 93
Thirsk Rd. SW11 —1C 78
Thistle Gro. SW10 —1E 63
Thistle Ho. E14 —5E 43
Thistlewaite Rd. E5 —5D 13
Thistlewood Clo. N7 —4B 10
Thistley Ct. SE8 —2D 71
Thomas Baines Rd. SW11 —1F 77
Thomas Burt Ho. E2 —2D 41 (off Canrobert St.)
Thomas Darby Ct. W11 (off Lancaster Rd.) —5A 34
Thomas Dean Rd. SE26 —4B 98
Thomas Dinwiddy Rd. SE12 —2D 101
Thomas Doyle St. SE1 —4D 53
Thomas Hollywood Ho. E2 (off Approach Rd.) —1E 41
Thomas La. SE6 —5C 84
Thomas More Highwalk. EC2 (off Beech St.) —4E 39
Thomas More Ho. EC2 (off Beech St.) —4E 39
Thomas More Sq. E1 —1C 54 (off Thomas More St.)
Thomas More St. E1 —1C 54
Thomas Neals Shop. Mall. WC2 —5A 38 (off Earlham St.)
Thomas N. Ter. E16 —4B 44 (off Barking Rd.)
Thomas Pl. W8 —4D 49
Thomas Rd. E14 —5B 42
Thomas Rd. Ind. Est. E14 (in two parts) —4C 42
Thompson Ho. SE14 —2E 69 (off John Williams Clo.)
Thompson Rd. SE22 —4B 82
Thompson's Av. SE5 —3E 67
Thomson Ho. E14 —5C 42
Thomson Ho. SE17 —5A 54 (off Tatum St.)
Thomson Ho. SW1 —1F 65 (off Bessborough Pl.)
Thorburn Sq. SE1 —5C 54
Thoresby St. N1 —2E 39
Thornaby Ho. E2 —2D 41 (off Canrobert St.)
Thornbury Clo. N16 —2A 26
Thornbury Ct. W11 —1C 48 (off Chepstow Vs.)
Thornbury Rd. SW2 —4A 80
Thornbury Sq. N6 —3E 9
Thornby Rd. E5 —5E 13
Thorncliffe Rd. SW4 —4A 80
Thorncombe Rd. SE22 —3A 82
Thorncroft St. SW8 —3A 66
Thorndean St. SW18 —2E 91
Thorndike Clo. SW10 —3E 63
Thorndike Ho. SW1 —1F 65 (off Vauxhall Bri. Rd.)
Thorndike St. SW1 —5F 51
Thorne Clo. E11 —1A 30
Thorne Clo. E16 —5C 44
Thorne Ho. E2 —2E 41 (off Roman Rd.)
Thorne Ho. E14 —4E 57
Thorne Pas. SW13 —5A 60
Thorne Rd. SW8 —3A 66
Thorne St. SW13 —1A 74
Thorney Ct. SW7 —3E 49 (off Palace Ga.)
Thorney Cres. SW11 —3F 63
Thorney St. SW1 —5A 52
Thornfield Ho. E14 —1C 56
Thornfield Rd. W12 —3D 47
Thornford Rd. SE13 —3E 85
Thorngate Rd. W9 —3C 34
Thorngrove Rd. E13 —5D 31
Thornham Gro. E15 —2F 29
Thornham St. SE10 —2D 71
Thornhaugh M. WC1 —3F 37
Thornhaugh St. WC1 —3F 37
Thornhill Bri. Wharf. N1 —5B 24
Thornhill Cres. N1 —4B 24
Thornhill Gdns. E10 —4D 15
Thornhill Gro. N1 —4B 24
Thornhill Ho. W4 —1A 60 (off Wood St.)
Thornhill Houses. N1 —4C 24
Thornhill Rd. E10 —4D 15
Thornhill Rd. N1 —4C 24
Thornhill Sq. N1 —4B 24
Thornicroft Ho. SW9 —5B 66 (off Stockwell Rd.)
Thornlaw Rd. SE27 —4C 94
Thornsbeach Rd. SE6 —1E 99
Thornsett Rd. SW18 —1D 91
Thorn Ter. SE15 —1E 83
Thornton Av. SW2 —1F 93
Thornton Av. W4 —5A 46
Thornton Gdns. SW12 —1F 93
Thornton Ho. SE17 —5A 54 (off Townsend St.)
Thornton Pl. W1 —4B 36
Thornton Rd. E11 —4F 15
Thornton Rd. SW12 —5F 79
Thornton Rd. SW14 —2A 74
Thornton Rd. Brom —5C 100
Thornton St. SW9 —5C 66
Thornton Way. NW11 —1D 7
Thorntree Rd. SE7 —1F 73
Thornville St. SE8 —4C 70
Thornwood Rd. SE13 —3A 86
Thornycroft Ho. W4 —1A 60 (off Fraser St.)
Thorogood Gdns. E15 —2A 30
Thorold Ho. SE1 —3E 53 (off Pepper St.)
Thorparch Rd. SW8 —4F 65
Thorpebank Rd. W12 —2C 46
Thorpe Clo. SE26 —4F 97
Thorpe Clo. W10 —5A 34
Thorpedale Rd. N4 —4A 10
Thorpe Ho. N1 —5B 24 (off Barnsbury Est.)
Thorpe Rd. E7 —1B 30
Thorpe Rd. N15 —1A 12
Thorpewood Av. SE26 —2D 97
Thorsden Way. SE19 —5A 96
Thorverton Rd. NW2 —5A 6
Thoydon Rd. E3 —1A 42
Thrale Rd. SW16 —4E 93
Thrale St. SE1 —2E 53
Thrasher Clo. E8 —5B 26
Thrawl St. E1 —4B 40
Thrayle Ho. SW9 —1B 80 (off Benedict Rd.)

Threadgold Ho. N1 —3F ***25***
(off Dovercourt Est.)
Threadneedle St. *EC2* —5F **39**
Three Barrels Wlk. EC4
(off Queen St. Pl.) —1E ***53***
Three Colt Corner. E2 & E1
(off Cheshire St.) —3C ***40***
Three Colts La. *E2* —3D **41**
Three Colt St. *E14* —5B **42**
Three Cups Yd. WC1 —4B ***38***
(off Sandland St.)
Three Kings Yd. *W1* —1D **51**
Three Mill La. *E3* —2E **43**
Three Oak La. *SE1* —3B **54**
Three Quays. EC3 —1A ***54***
(off Tower Hill)
Three Quays Wlk. *EC3* —1A **54**
Threshers Pl. *W11* —1A **48**
Thriffwood. *SE26* —3E **97**
Thring Ho. SW9 —5B ***66***
(off Stockwell Rd.)
Throckmorten Rd. *E16* —5D **45**
Throgmorton Av. *EC2* —5F **39**
(in two parts)
Throgmorton St. *EC2* —5F **39**
Thrush St. *SE17* —1E **67**
Thruxton Way. *SE15* —3B **68**
Thurbarn Rd. *SE6* —5D **99**
Thurland Ho. SE16 —5D ***55***
(off Camilla Rd.)
Thurland Rd. *SE16* —4C **54**
Thurlby Rd. *SE27* —4C **94**
Thurleigh Av. *SW12* —4C **78**
Thurleigh Rd. *SW12* —5B **78**
Thurlestone Rd. *SE27* —3C **94**
Thurloe Clo. *SW7* —5A **50**
Thurloe Ct. SW3 —5A ***50***
(off Fulham Ct.)
Thurloe Pl. *SW7* —5F **49**
Thurloe Pl. M. SW7 —5F ***49***
(off Thurloe Pl.)
Thurloe Sq. *SW7* —5A **50**
Thurloe St. *SW7* —5F **49**
Thurlow Hill. *SE21* —1E **95**
Thurlow Ho. *SW16* —3A **94**
Thurlow Pk. Rd. *SE21* —2D **95**
Thurlow Rd. *NW3* —2F **21**
Thurlow St. *SE17* —1F **67**
(in two parts)
Thurlow Ter. *NW5* —2C **22**
Thurlow Wlk. *SE17* —1A **68**
(in two parts)
Thurnscoe. NW1 —5E ***23***
(off Pratt St.)
Thursley Gdns. *SW19* —2F **89**
Thursley Ho. SW2 —5B ***80***
(off Holmewood Gdns.)
Thurso Ho. *NW6* —1D **35**
Thurso St. *SW17* —4F **91**
Thurstan Dwellings. WC2
(off Newton St.) —5A ***38***
Thurston Ind. Est. *SE13* —1D **85**
Thurston Rd. *SE13* —5D **71**
Thurtle Rd. *E2* —1B **40**
Tibbatts Rd. *E3* —3D **43**
Tibbenham Pl. *SE6* —2C **98**
Tibbenham Wlk. *E13* —1B **44**
Tibberton Sq. *N1* —5E **25**
Tibbet's Clo. *SW19* —1F **89**
Tibbet's Corner. (Junct.) —5F **75**
Tibbet's Ride. *SW15* —5F **75**
Tiber Gdns. *N1* —5A **24**
Ticehurst Rd. *SE23* —2A **98**
Tickford Ho. *NW8* —2A **36**
Tidal Basin Rd. *E16* —1B **58**
Tidbury Ct. SW8 —3E ***65***
(off Stewart's Rd.)
Tideswell Rd. *SW15* —2E **75**
Tideway Ct. *SE16* —2F **55**
Tideway Ho. *E14* —3C **56**
Tideway Ind. Est. SW8
(off Kirtling St.) —2E ***65***
Tideway Wlk. *SW8* —2E **65**
Tidey St. *E3* —4C **42**
Tidworth Rd. *E3* —3C **42**
Tierney Rd. *SW2* —1A **94**
Tiffany Heights. *SW18* —5C **76**
Tiger Way. *E5* —1D **27**
Tilbrook Rd. *SE3* —1E **87**
Tilbury Clo. *SE15* —3B **68**
Tilbury Ho. SE14 —2F ***69***
(off Myers La.)
Tilbury Rd. *E10* —2E **15**
Tildesley Rd. *SW15* —4E **75**
Tilehurst Rd. *SW18* —1F **91**
Tile Kiln La. *N6* —3D **9**
Tile Kiln Studios. *N6* —3E **9**
Tile Yd. *E14* —5B **42**
Tileyard Rd. *N7* —4A **24**
Tilford Gdns. *SW19* —1F **89**
Tilford Ho. SW2 —5B ***80***
(off Holmewood Gdns.)
Tilia Rd. *E5* —1D **27**
Tilia Wlk. *SW9* —2D **81**
Tilleard Ho. W10 —2A ***34***
(off Herries St.)
Tiller Rd. *E14* —4C **56**
Tillett Sq. *SE16* —3A **56**
Tillet Way. *E2* —2C **40**
Tilling Rd. *NW2* —3E **5**
Tillman St. *E1* —5D **41**
Tilloch St. *N1* —4B **24**
Tillotson Ct. SW8 —3F ***65***
(off Wandsworth Rd.)
Tilney Ct. *EC1* —3E **39**
Tilney Gdns. *N1* —3F **25**
Tilney St. *W1* —2C **50**
Tilson Gdns. *SW12* —5A **80**
Tilson Ho. *SW2* —5A **80**
Tilston Clo. *E11* —5B **16**
Tilton St. *SW6* —2A **62**
Timberland Clo. *SE15* —3C **68**
Timberland Rd. *E1* —5D **41**
Timber Mill Way. *SW4* —1F **79**
Timber Pond Rd. *SE16* —2F **55**
Timber St. *EC1* —3E **39**
Timberwharf Rd. *N16* —1C **12**
Timber Wharves Est. *E14* —5C **56**
Timbrell Pl. *SE16* —2B **56**
Time Sq. *E8* —2B **26**
Timothy Clo. *SW4* —3E **79**
Timothy Rd. *E3* —4B **42**
Timsbury Wlk. *SW15* —1C **88**
Tindal St. *SW9* —4D **67**
Tinderbox All. *SW14* —1A **74**
Tinniswood Clo. *N5* —2C **24**
Tinsley Rd. *E1* —4E **41**
Tintagel Cres. *SE22* —2B **82**
Tintagel Gdns. *SE22* —2B **82**
Tintern Clo. *SW15* —3A **76**
Tintern Ho. NW1 —1D ***37***
(off Augustus St.)
Tintern Ho. SW1 —5D ***51***
(off Abbots Mnr.)
Tintern Path. NW9 —1A ***4***
(off Fryent Gro.)
Tintern St. *SW4* —2A **80**
Tinto Rd. *E16* —3C **44**
Tinworth St. *SE1* —1A **66**
Tipthorpe Rd. *SW11* —1C **78**
Tisbury Ct. W1 —1F ***51***
(off Wardour St.)
Tisdall Pl. *SE17* —5F **53**
Tissington Ct. *SE16* —5E **55**
Titan Bus. Est. SE8 —3C ***70***
(off Ffinch St.)
Titchborne Row. *W2* —5A **36**
Titchfield Rd. *NW8* —5A **22**
Titchwell Rd. *SW18* —1F **91**
Tite St. *SW3* —1B **64**
Titmuss St. *W12* —3E **47**
Tiverton Rd. *N15* —1F **11**
Tiverton Rd. *NW10* —5F **19**
Tiverton St. *SE1* —4E **53**
Tivoli Ct. *SE16* —2B **56**
Tivoli Gdns. *SE18* —5F **59**
(in two parts)
Tivoli Rd. *N8* —1F **9**
Tivoli Rd. *SE27* —5E **95**
Tobacco Dock. *E1* —1D **55**
Tobacco Quay. *E1* —1D **55**
Tobago St. *E14* —3C **56**
Tobin Clo. *NW3* —4A **22**
Toby La. *E1* —3A **42**
Todds Wlk. *N7* —4B **10**
Tokenhouse Yd. *EC2* —5F **39**
Token Yd. *SW15* —2A **76**
Toland Sq. *SW15* —3C **74**
Tolchurch. W11 —5B ***34***
(off Dartmouth Clo.)
Tollbridge Clo. *W10* —3A **34**
Tollet St. *E1* —3F **41**
Tollgate Dri. *SE21* —2A **96**
Tollgate Gdns. *NW6* —1D **35**
Tollgate Ho. NW6 —1D ***35***
(off Tollgate Gdns.)
Tollgate Rd. *E16 & E6* —4E **45**
Tollhouse Way. *N19* —4E **9**
Tollington Pk. *N4* —4B **10**
Tollington Pl. *N4* —4B **10**

Tollington Rd. N7—1B 24
Tollington Way. N7—5A 10
Tolmers Sq. NW1—3E 37
(in two parts)
Tolpaide Ho. SE11—5C 52
(off Hotspur St.)
Tolpuddle Av. E13—5E 31
(off Queens Rd.)
Tolpuddle St. N1—1C 38
Tolsford Rd. E5—2D 27
Tom Groves Clo. E15—2F 29
Tom Hood Clo. E15—2F 29
Tom Jenkinson Rd. E16
—2C 58
Tomkyns Ho. SE11—5C 52
(off Distin St.)
Tomlin's Gro. E3—2C 42
Tomlinson Clo. E2—2B 40
Tomlins Ter. E14—5A 42
Tomlins Wlk. N7—4B 10
Tom Nolan Clo. E15—1A 44
Tompion Ho. EC1—3D 39
(off Percival St.)
Tompion St. EC1—2D 39
(in two parts)
Tom Smith Clo. SE10—2A 72
Tomson Ho. SE1—4B 54
(off Riley Rd.)
Tom Williams Ho. SW6
(off Clem Attlee Ct.)—2B 62
Tonbridge Houses. WC1
(off Tonbridge St.)—2A 38
Tonbridge St. WC1—2A 38
Tonbridge Wlk. WC1—2A 38
(off Tonbridge St.)
Toneborough. NW8—5D 21
(off Abbey Rd.)
Tonsley Hill. SW18—3D 77
Tonsley Pl. SW18—3D 77
Tonsley Rd. SW18—3D 77
Tonsley St. SW18—3D 77
Tony Cannell M. E3—2B 42
Took's Ct. WC2—5C 38
Tooley St. SE1—2F 53
Tooting.—5A 92
Tooting Bec.—3C 92
Tooting Bec Gdns. SW16
(in two parts) —4F 93
Tooting Bec Rd. SW17 &
SW16—3C 92
Tooting B'way. SW17—5A 92
Tooting Graveney.—5B 92
Tooting Gro. SW17—5A 92
Tooting High St. SW17
—5A 92
Tooting Mkt. SW17—4B 92
Topaz Wlk. NW2—2F 5
Topham Ho. SE10—3E 71
(off Prior St.)
Topham St. EC1—3C 38
Topley St. SE9—2E 87
Topmast Point. E14—3C 56
Topp Wlk. NW2—4E 5
Topsfield Clo. N8—1F 9
Topsfield Pde. N8—1A 10
Topsfield Rd. N8—1A 10
Topsham Rd. SW17—3B 92
Torbay Ct. NW1—4D 23
Torbay Mans. NW6—5B 20
(off Willesden La.)
Torbay Rd. NW6—4B 20
Torbay St. NW1—4D 23
Tor Ct. W8—3C 48
Torcross Dri. SE23—2E 97
Tor Gdns. W8—3C 48
Tor Ho. N6—1D 9
Tornay Ho. N1—1B 38
(off Priory Grn. Est.)
Torney Ho. E9—4E 27
Toronto Rd. E11—1F 29
Torquay St. W2—4D 35
Torrance Clo. SE7—2F 73
Torrens Ct. SE5—1F 81
Torrens Rd. E15—3B 30
Torrens Rd. SW2—3B 80
Torrens Sq. E15—3B 30
Torrens St. EC1—1C 38
Torres Sq. E14—1C 70
Torriano Av. NW5—2F 23
Torriano Cotts. NW5—2E 23
Torriano M. NW5—2E 23
Torridge Gdns. SE15—2E 83
Torridon Ho. NW6—1D 35
(off Randolph Gdns.)
Torridon Rd. SE6 & SE13
—5F 85
Torrington Ct. SE26—5C 96
(off Crystal Pal. Pk. Rd.)
Torrington Pl. E1—2C 54
Torrington Pl. WC1—4F 37
Torrington Sq. WC1—3F 37
Tortington Ho. SE15—3C 68
(off Friary Est.)
Torwood Rd. SW15—3C 74
Tothill Ho. SW1—5F 51
(off Page St.)
Tothill St. SW1—3F 51
Tottan Ter. E1—5F 41
Tottenhall. NW1—4C 22
(off Ferdinand St.)
Tottenham Ct. Rd. W1
—3E 37
Tottenham La. N8—1A 10
Tottenham M. W1—4E 37
Tottenham Rd. N1—3A 26
Tottenham St. W1—4E 37
Totterdown St. SW17—4B 92
Toulmin St. SE1—3E 53
Toulon St. SE5—3E 67
Toulouse Ct. SE16—1D 69
(off Rossetti Rd.)
Tourist Info. Cen.—5E 39
(City of London)
Tourist Info. Cen.—2E 71
(Greenwich)
Tourist Info. Cen.—2E 85
(Lewisham)
Tourist Info. Cen.—4A 40
(Liverpool Street Station)
Tourist Info. Cen.—4B 40
(off Commerical St.,
Tower Hamlets)
Tourist Info. Cen.—2F 53
(off Tooley St., Southwark)
Tourist Info. Cen.—4D 51
(Victoria Station)
Tourist Info. Cen.—3B 52
(Waterloo International
Terminal)
Tournay Rd. SW6—3B 62
Tours Pas. SW11—2E 77
Toussaint Wlk. SE16—4C 54
Tovy Ho. SE1—1C 68
(off Avondale Sq.)
Towcester Rd. E3—3D 43
Tower Bri. SE1 & E1—2B 54
Tower Bri. App. E1—2B 54
Tower Bri. Bus. Complex.
SE16—4C 54
Tower Bridge Experience.
(off Tower Bri.)—2B 54
Tower Bri. Plaza. SE1—2B 54
Tower Bri. Rd. SE1—4A 54
Tower Bri. Sq. SE1—3B 54
(off Queen Elizabeth St.)
Tower Bri. Wharf. E1—2C 54
Tower Bldgs. E1—2D 55
(off Brewhouse La.)
Tower Clo. NW3—2F 21
Tower Ct. E5—2B 12
Tower Ct. N1—4E 25
(off Canonbury St.)
Tower Ct. NW8—1A 36
(off Mackennal St.)
Tower Ct. WC2—5A 38
(off Tower St.)
Tower 42.—5A 40
Tower Hamlets Rd. E7
—1B 30
Tower Hill. (Junct.)—1B 54
Tower Hill. EC3—1A 54
Tower Hill Ter. EC3—1A 54
(off Byward St.)
Tower Ho. E1—4C 40
(off Fieldgate St.)
Tower Mill Rd. SE15—3B 68
Tower of London, The.
—1B 54
Tower Pl. EC3—1A 54
(off Lwr. Thames St.)
Tower Rd. NW10—4C 18
Tower Royal. EC4—1F 53
Tower St. WC2—5A 38
Towncourt Path. N4—3E 11
Town Hall Rd. SW11—1B 78
Town Hall Wlk. N16—1F 25
(off Church Wlk.)
Townley Ct. E15—3B 30
Townley Rd. SE22—3A 82
Townley St. SE17—1F 67
(in two parts)
Townmead Bus. Cen. SW6
—1E 77
Townmead Rd. SW6—1D 77
Townsend Ho. EC1—3D 39
(off Finsbury Est.)
Townsend Ho. SE1—5C 54
(off Strathnairn St.)

Townsend La. *NW9* —2A **4**
Townsend Rd. *N15* —1B **12**
Townsend St. *SE17* —5A **54**
Townsend Yd. *N6* —3D **9**
Townshend Ct. NW8 —1A **36**
(off Townshend Rd.)
Townshend Est. *NW8* —1A **36**
Townshend Rd. *NW8* —5A **22**
(in two parts)
Towns Ho. *SW4* —1F **79**
Towpath, The. *SW10* —4F **63**
Towpath Wlk. *E9* —2B **28**
Towton Rd. *SE27* —2E **95**
Toynbee St. *E1* —4B **40**
Toyne Way. *N6* —1B **8**
Tracey Av. *NW2* —2E **19**
Tradescant Rd. *SW8* —3A **66**
Tradewinds Ct. E1 —1C **54**
(off Asher Way)
Trafalgar Av. *SE15* —1B **68**
Trafalgar Clo. *SE16* —4A **56**
Trafalgar Gdns. *E1* —4F **41**
Trafalgar Gdns. W8 —4D **49**
(off South End)
Trafalgar Gro. *SE10* —2F **71**
Trafalgar Ho. SE17 —1E **67**
(off Bronti Clo.)
Trafalgar Rd. *SE10* —2F **71**
Trafalgar Square. —2A **52**
Trafalgar Sq. *WC2* —2F **51**
Trafalgar St. *SE17* —1F **67**
Trafalgar Way. *E14* —2E **57**
Trafford Clo. *E15* —2D **29**
Trafford Ho. N1 —1F **39**
(off Cranston Est.)
Traitors' Gate. —2B **54**
(off Tower of London, The)
Tralee Ct. SE16 —1D **69**
(off Masters Dri.)
Tramway Av. *E15* —4A **30**
Tranley M. *NW3* —1A **22**
Tranmere Rd. *SW18* —2E **91**
Tranquil Pas. *SE3* —5B **72**
Tranquil Va. *SE3* —5A **72**
Transay Wlk. *N1* —3F **25**
Transept St. *NW1* —4A **36**
Transom Clo. *SE16* —5A **56**
Transom Sq. *E14* —1D **71**
Tranton Rd. *SE16* —4C **54**
Trappes Ho. SE16 —5D **55**
(off Camilla Rd.)
Travers Ho. *SE10* —2F **71**
(off Trafalgar Gro.)
Travers Rd. *N7* —5C **10**
Travis Ho. *SE10* —4E **71**
Treadgold St. *W11* —1F **47**
Treadway St. *E2* —1D **41**
Treasury Pas. SW1 —3A **52**
(off Downing St.)
Treaty St. *N1* —5B **24**
Trebeck St. *W1* —2D **51**
Trebovir Rd. *SW5* —1C **62**
Treby St. *E3* —3B **42**
Trecastle Way. *N7* —1F **23**
Tredegar M. *E3* —2B **42**
Tredegar Rd. *E3* —1B **42**

Tredegar Sq. *E3* —2B **42**
Tredegar Ter. *E3* —2B **42**
Trederwen Rd. *E8* —5C **26**
Tredown Rd. *SE26* —5E **97**
Tredwell Clo. *SW2* —2B **94**
Tredwell Rd. *SE27* —4D **95**
Treen Av. *SW13* —1B **74**
Tree Rd. *E16* —5E **45**
Treewall Gdns. *Brom* —4D **101**
Trefil Wlk. *N7* —1A **24**
Trefoil Rd. *SW18* —3E **77**
Tregaron Av. *N8* —1A **10**
Tregarvon Rd. *SW11* —2C **78**
Tregothnan Rd. *SW9* —1A **80**
Tregunter Rd. *SW10* —2D **63**
Treherne Ct. *SW9* —4D **67**
Treherne Ct. *SW17* —4C **92**
Trehern Rd. *SW14* —1A **74**
Trehurst St. *E5* —2A **28**
Trelawney Est. *E9* —3E **27**
Trelawney Ho. SE1 —3E **53**
(off Pepper St.)
Trelawn Rd. *E10* —5E **15**
Trelawn Rd. *SW2* —3C **80**
Trellick Tower. W10 —3B **34**
(off Golborne Rd.)
Trellis Sq. *E3* —2B **42**
Treloar Gdns. *SE19* —5F **95**
Tremadoc Rd. *SW4* —2F **79**
Tremaine Clo. *SE4* —5C **70**
Trematon Ho. SE11 —1C **66**
(off Kennings Way)
Tremlett Gro. *N19* —5E **9**
Tremlett M. *N19* —5E **9**
Trenchard Ct. *NW4* —1C **4**
Trenchard St. *SE10* —1F **71**
Trenchold St. *SW8* —2A **66**
Trendell Ho. *E14* —5C **42**
Trenmar Gdns. *NW10* —2D **33**
Trentham St. *SW18* —1C **90**
Trent Ho. *SE15* —2E **83**
Trent Rd. *SW2* —3B **80**
Treport St. *SW18* —5D **77**
Tresco Ho. SE11 —1C **66**
(off Sancroft St.)
Tresco Rd. *SE15* —2D **83**
Tresham Cres. *NW8* —3A **36**
Tresham Wlk. *E9* —2E **27**
Tresidder Ho. *SW4* —5F **79**
Tressell Clo. *N1* —4D **25**
Tressillian Cres. *SE4* —1C **84**
Tressillian Rd. *SE4* —2B **84**
Tress Pl. SE1 —2D **53**
(off Blackfriars Rd.)
Trevanion Rd. *W14* —5A **48**
Trevelyan Gdns. *NW10*
—5E **19**
Trevelyan Ho. SE5 —3D **67**
(off John Ruskin St.)
Trevelyan Rd. *E15* —1B **30**
Trevelyan Rd. *SW17* —5A **92**
Trevenna Ho. *SE23* —3F **97**
(off Dacres Rd.)
Treveris St. *SE1* —2D **53**
Treverton St. *W10* —3A **34**

Treverton Towers. *W10*
(off Treverton St.) —4F **33**
Treves Ho. E1 —3C **40**
(off Vallance Rd.)
Treville St. *SW15* —5D **75**
Treviso Rd. *SE23* —2F **97**
Trevithick Ho. SE16 —5D **55**
(off Rennie Est.)
Trevithick St. *SE8* —2C **70**
Trevone Ct. *SW2* —5A **80**
(off Doverfield Rd.)
Trevor Pl. *SW7* —3A **50**
Trevor Sq. *SW7* —3B **50**
Trevor St. *SW7* —3A **50**
Trevor Wlk. SW7 —3A **50**
(off Trevor Pl.)
Trevose Ho. *SE11* —1B **66**
(off Orsett St.)
Trewint St. *SW18* —2E **91**
Trewsbury Rd. *SE26* —5F **97**
Triangle Bus. Cen., The.
NW10 —2B **32**
Triangle Ct. *E16* —4F **45**
Triangle Pl. *SW4* —2F **79**
Triangle Rd. *E8* —5D **27**
Triangle, The. *E8* —5D **27**
Triangle, The. EC1 —3D **39**
(off Cyrus St.)
Tricycle Theatre. —4B **20**
Trident Bus. Cen. *SW17*
—5B **92**
Trident Ho. *E14* —5E **43**
Trident St. *SE16* —5F **55**
Trig La. *EC4* —1E **53**
Trigon Rd. *SW8* —3B **66**
Trilby Rd. *SE23* —2F **97**
Trimdon. *NW1* —5E **23**
Trim St. *SE14* —2B **70**
Trinder Gdns. *N19* —3A **10**
Trinder Rd. *N19* —3A **10**
Trinidad Ho. *E14* —1B **56**
Trinidad St. *E14* —1B **56**
Trinity Buoy Wharf. *E14*
—1A **58**
Trinity Chu. Pas. *SW13*
—2D **61**
Trinity Chu. Rd. *SW13*
—2D **61**
Trinity Chu. Sq. *SE1* —4E **53**
Trinity Clo. *E8* —3B **26**
Trinity Clo. *E11* —4A **16**
Trinity Clo. *NW3* —1F **21**
Trinity Clo. *SE13* —2F **85**
Trinity Clo. *SW4* —2E **79**
Trinity Ct. SE1 —4E **53**
(off Brockham St.)
Trinity Ct. *SE7* —5F **59**
Trinity Ct. *SE26* —3E **97**
Trinity Ct. W2 —5E **35**
(off Gloucester Ter.)
Trinity Ct. WC1 —3B **38**
(off Gray's Inn Rd.)
Trinity Cres. *SW17* —2B **92**
Trinity Gdns. *E16* —4B **44**
Trinity Gdns. *SW9* —2B **80**
Trinity Grn. *E1* —3E **41**

Trinity Gro. *SE10* —4E **71**
Trinity Hospital Almshouses.
  (off High Bri.) SE10 —1F **71**
Trinity Ho. SE1 —4E **53**
  (off Bath Ter.)
Trinity M. *W10* —5F **33**
Trinity Path. *SE23* —3E **97**
Trinity Pier. *E14* —1A **58**
Trinity Pl. *EC3* —1B **54**
Trinity Ri. *SW2* —1C **94**
Trinity Rd. *SW18 & SW17*
                    —2E **77**
Trinity Rd. *SW19* —5C **90**
Trinity Sq. *EC3* —1A **54**
Trinity St. *E16* —4B **44**
Trinity St. *SE1* —3E **53**
  (in two parts)
Trinity Tower. E1 —1C **54**
  (off Vaughan Way)
Trinity Wlk. *NW3* —3E **21**
Trinity Way. *W3* —1A **46**
Trio Pl. *SE1* —3E **53**
Tristan Ct. SE8 —2B **70**
  (off Dorking Clo)
Tristan Sq. *SE3* —1A **86**
Tristram Rd. *Brom* —4B **100**
Triton Ho. *E14* —5D **57**
Triton Sq. *NW1* —3E **37**
Tritton Rd. *SE21* —3F **95**
**Trocadero Entertainment
           Cen.** —1F **51**
Trocette Mans. SE1 —4A **54**
  (off Bermondsey St.)
Trojan Ct. *NW6* —4A **20**
Trojan Ind. Est. *NW10* —3B **18**
Troon Clo. *SE16* —1D **69**
Troon St. *E1* —5A **42**
Trossachs Rd. *SE22* —3A **82**
Trothy Rd. *SE1* —5C **54**
Trotman Ho. SE14 —4E **69**
  (off Pomeroy St.)
Trott St. *SW11* —4A **64**
Troughton Rd. SE7 —1D **73**
Troutbeck. *NW1* —2D **37**
  (off Albany St.)
Troutbeck Rd. *SE14* —4A **70**
Trouville Rd. *SW4* —4E **79**
Trowbridge Rd. *E9* —3B **28**
Troy Ct. W8 —4C **48**
  (off Kensington High St.)
Troy Rd. *SE19* —5F **95**
Troy Town. *SE15* —1C **82**
Trumans Rd. *N16* —2B **26**
Trumpington Rd. *E7* —1B **30**
Trump St. *EC2* —5E **39**
Trundle St. SE1 —3E **53**
  (off Weller St.)
Trundley's M. *SE8* —1F **69**
Trundley's Rd. *SE8* —1F **69**
Trundley's Ter. *SE8* —5F **55**
Truro Gdns. *Ilf* —2F **17**
Truro St. *NW5* —3C **22**
Truslove Rd. *SE27* —5C **94**
Trussley Rd. *W6* —4E **47**
Trust Wlk. *SE21* —1D **95**
Tryfan Clo. *Ilf* —1F **17**

Tryon Cres. *E9* —5E **27**
Tryon St. *SW3* —1B **64**
Tubbs Rd. *NW10* —1B **32**
Tucklow Wlk. *SW15* —5B **74**
Tudor Av. *E17* —2B **14**
Tudor Clo. *N6* —2E **9**
Tudor Clo. *NW3* —2A **22**
Tudor Clo. *SW2* —4B **80**
Tudor Ct. *N1* —3A **26**
Tudor Ct. SE16 —2F **55**
  (off Princes Riverside Rd.)
Tudor Gdns. *SW13* —1A **74**
Tudor Gro. *E9* —4E **27**
Tudor Rd. *E9* —4E **27**
Tudor Ho. W14 —5F **47**
  (off Windsor Way)
Tudor Rd. *E6* —5B **44**
Tudor Rd. *E9* —5D **27**
Tudor Stacks. *SE24* —2E **81**
Tudor St. *EC4* —1C **52**
Tudway Rd. *SE3* —1D **87**
Tufnell Park. —1E **23**
Tufnell Pk. Rd. *N19 & N7*
                    —1E **23**
Tufton Ct. SW1 —4A **52**
  (off Tufton St.)
Tufton St. *SW1* —4A **52**
Tugela St. *SE6* —2B **98**
Tulse Hill. —1D **95**
Tulse Hill. *SW2* —4C **80**
Tulse Hill Est. *SW2* —4C **80**
Tulse Ho. *SW2* —4C **80**
Tulsemere Rd. *SE27* —2E **95**
Tunbridge Ho. EC1 —2D **39**
  (off Spa Grn. Est.)
Tunis Rd. *W12* —2E **47**
Tunley Grn. *E14* —4B **42**
Tunley Rd. *NW10* —5A **18**
Tunley Rd. *SW17* —1C **92**
Tunmarsh La. *E13* —2D **45**
Tunnel App. *E14* —1A **56**
Tunnel App. *SE10* —3A **58**
Tunnel App. *SE16* —3E **55**
Tunnel Av. *SE10* —3F **57**
  (in two parts)
Tunnel Av. Trad. Est. *SE10*
                    —3F **57**
Tunnel Rd. *SE16* —3E **55**
Tunstall Rd. *SW9* —2B **80**
Tunworth Cres. *SW15* —4B **74**
Tun Yd. SW8 —5D **65**
  (off Silverthorne Rd.)
Tupelo Rd. *E10* —4D **15**
Tupman Ho. SE16 —3C **54**
  (off Scott Lidgett Cres.)
Turenne Clo. *SW18* —2E **77**
Turin St. *E2* —2C **40**
Turk's Head Yd. *EC1* —4D **39**
Turk's Row. *SW3* —1B **64**
Turle Rd. *N4* —4B **10**
Turlewray Clo. *N4* —3B **10**
Turley Clo. *E15* —5A **30**
Turnagain La. EC4 —5D **39**
  (off Farringdon St.)
Turnberry Clo. SE16 —1D **69**
  (off Ryder Dri.)

Turnberry Quay. *E14* —4D **57**
Turnbull Ho. *N1* —5D **25**
Turnchapel M. *SW4* —1D **79**
Turner Clo. *NW11* —1D **7**
Turner Clo. *SE5* —3D **67**
Turner Ct. SE —3E **55**
  (off Albion St.)
Turner Dri. *NW11* —1D **7**
Turner Ho. NW8 —1A **36**
  (off Townshend Est.)
Turner Ho. SW1 —5F **51**
  (off Herrick St.)
Turner Pl. *SW11* —3A **78**
Turner's All. *EC3* —1A **54**
Turners Rd. *E14 & E3* —4B **42**
Turner St. *E1* —4D **41**
Turner St. *E16* —5B **44**
Turners Wood. *NW11* —2E **7**
Turneville Rd. *W14* —2B **62**
Turney Rd. *SE21* —5E **81**
Turnham Green. —1A **60**
Turnham Grn. Ter. *W4*
                    —5A **46**
Turnham Grn. Ter. M. *W4*
                    —5A **46**
Turnham Rd. *SE4* —3A **84**
Turnmill St. *EC1* —3D **39**
Turnour Ho. E1 —5D **41**
  (off Walburgh St.)
Turnpike Clo. *SE8* —3B **70**
Turnpike Ho. *EC1* —2D **39**
Turnpin La. *SE10* —2E **71**
Turnstone Clo. *E13* —2C **44**
Turpentine La. *SW1* —1D **65**
Turpin Ho. *SW11* —4D **65**
Turpin Way. *N19* —4F **9**
  (in two parts)
Turquand St. *SE17* —5E **53**
Turret Gro. *SW4* —1E **79**
Turville Ho. NW8 —3A **36**
  (off Grendon St.)
Turville St. *E2* —3B **40**
Tuscan Ho. E2 —2E **41**
  (off Knottisford St.)
Tuskar St. *SE10* —2A **72**
Tustin Est. *SE15* —2E **69**
Tutshill Ct. SE15 —3A **68**
  (off Newent Clo.)
Tuttle Ho. SW1 —1F **65**
  (off Aylesford St.)
Tweedale St. *E15* —2E **29**
Tweed Ho. *E14* —3E **43**
Tweedmouth Rd. *E13* —1D **45**
Tweezer's All. WC2 —1C **52**
  (off Milford La.)
Twelvetrees Cres. *E3 & E16*
  (in two parts) —3E **43**
Twickenham Rd. *E11* —4E **15**
Twig Folly Clo. *E2* —1F **41**
Twilley St. *SW18* —5D **77**
Twine Ct. *E1* —1E **55**
Twine Ter. E3 —3B **42**
  (off Ropery St.)
Twisden Rd. *NW5* —1D **23**
Twycross M. *SE10* —1A **72**
Twyford Ho. *N5* —5D **11**

Twyford Ho. N15 —1A ***12*** *(off Chisley Rd.)*
Twyford Pl. *WC2* —5B **38**
Twyford St. *N1* —5B **24**
Tyas Rd. *E16* —3B **44**
Tyburn Way. *W1* —1B **50**
Tyers Est. SE1 —3A ***54*** *(off Bermondsey St.)*
Tyers Ga. *SE1* —3A **54**
Tyers St. *SE11* —1B **66**
Tyers Ter. *SE11* —1B **66**
Tyler Clo. *E2* —1B **40**
Tyler's Ct. W1 —5F ***37*** *(off Wardour St.)*
Tyler St. *SE10* —1A **72** (in two parts)
Tylney Av. *SE19* —5B **96**
Tylney Ho. E1 —5D ***41*** *(off Nelson St.)*
Tylney Rd. *E7* —1E **31**
Tyndale Ct. *E14* —1D **71**
Tyndale La. *N1* —4D **25**
Tyndale Mans. N1 —4D ***25*** *(off Upper St.)*
Tyndale Ter. *N1* —4D **25**
Tyndall Gdns. *E10* —4E **15**
Tyndall Rd. *E10* —4E **15**
Tyneham Clo. *SW11* —1C **78**
Tyneham Rd. *SW11* —5C **64**
Tynemouth St. *SW6* —5E **63**
Tyne St. *E1* —5B **40**
Tynley Av. *SE19* —5B **96**
Tynwald Ho. *SE26* —3C **96**
Type St. *E2* —1F **41**
Tyrawley Rd. *SW6* —4D **63**
Tyrell Ho. Beck —5D ***99*** *(off Beckenham Hill Rd.)*
Tyrols Rd. *SE23* —1F **97**
Tyrrell Ho. SW1 —2E ***65*** *(off Churchill Gdns.)*
Tyrrell Rd. *SE22* —2C **82**
Tyrrel Way. *NW9* —2B **4**
Tyrwhitt Rd. *SE4* —1C **84**
Tysoe St. *EC1* —2C **38**
Tyson Gdns. *SE23* —5E **83**
Tyson Rd. *SE23* —5E **83**
Tyssen Pas. *E8* —3B **26**
Tyssen Rd. *N16* —5B **12**
Tyssen St. *E8* —3B **26**
Tytherton. E2 —1E ***41*** *(off Cyprus St.)*
Tytherton Rd. *N19* —5F **9**

Uamvar St. *E14* —4D **43**
Udall St. *SW1* —5E **51**
Udimore Ho. W10 —4E ***33*** *(off Sutton Way)*
Uffington Rd. *NW10* —5C **18**
Uffington Rd. *SE27* —4C **94**
Ufford St. *SE1* —3C **52**
Ufton Gro. *N1* —4F **25**
Ufton Rd. *N1* —4F **25** (in two parts)
Uhura Sq. *N16* —5A **12**
Ujima Ct. *SW16* —4A **94**
Ullathorne Rd. *SW16* —4E **93**
Ullin St. *E14* —4E **43**
Ullswater Clo. *SW15* —4A **88**
Ullswater Cres. *SW15* —4A **88**
Ullswater Ho. SE15 —2E ***69*** *(off Hillbeck Clo.)*
Ullswater Rd. *SE27* —2D **95**
Ullswater Rd. *SW13* —3C **60**
Ulster Pl. *NW1* —3D **37**
Ulster Ter. NW1 —3C ***36*** *(off Outer Circ.)*
Ulundi Rd. *SE3* —2A **72**
Ulva Rd. *SW15* —3F **75**
Ulverscroft Rd. *SE22* —3B **82**
Ulverstone Rd. *SE27* —2D **95**
Ulysses Rd. *NW6* —2B **20**
Umberston St. *E1* —5C **40**
Umbria St. *SW15* —4C **74**
Umfreville Rd. *N4* —1D **11**
Undercliff Rd. *SE13* —1C **84**
Underhill Ho. *E14* —4C **42**
Underhill Pas. NW1 —5D ***23*** *(off Camden High St.)*
Underhill Rd. *SE22* —3C **82**
Underhill St. *NW1* —5D **23**
Undershaft. *EC3* —5A **40**
Undershaw Rd. *Brom* —3B **100**
Underwood Ct. E10 —3D ***15*** *(off Leyton Grange Est.)*
Underwood Rd. *E1* —3C **40**
Underwood Row. *N1* —2E **39**
Underwood St. *N1* —2E **39**
Undine Rd. *E14* —5D **57**
Undine St. *SW17* —5B **92**
Unicorn Building. E1 —1F ***55*** *(off Jardine Rd.)*
Union Clo. *E11* —1F **29**
Union Cotts. *E15* —4A **30**
Union Ct. EC2 —5A ***40*** *(off Old Broad St.)*
Union Ct. *SW4* —5A **66**
Union Dri. *E1* —3A **42**
Union Gro. *SW8* —5F **65**
Union M. *SW4* —5A **66**
Union Rd. *SW8 & SW4* —5F **65**
Union Sq. *N1* —5E **25**
Union St. *E15* —5F **29**
Union St. *SE1* —2D **53**
Union Theatre. —2D 53 *(off Union St.)*
Union Wlk. *E2* —2A **40**
Union Yd. *W1* —5D **37**
Unit Workshops. E1 —5C ***40*** *(off Adler St.)*
Unity Clo. *NW10* —3C **18**
Unity Clo. *SE19* —5E **95**
Unity M. *NW1* —1F **37**
Unity Way. *SE7* —4F **59**
Unity Wharf. SE1 —3B ***54*** *(off Mill St.)*
University Rd. *SW19* —5F **91**
University St. *WC1* —3E **37**
Unwin Clo. *SE15* —2C **68**
Unwin Mans. W14 —2B ***62*** *(off Queen's Club Gdns.)*
Unwin Rd. *SW7* —4F **49**
Upbrook M. *W2* —5E **35**
Upcerne Rd. *SW10* —3E **63**
Upgrove Mnr. Way. *SE24* —5C **80**
Upham Pk. Rd. *W4* —5A **46**
Upland M. *SE22* —3C **82**
Upland Rd. *E13* —3C **44**
Upland Rd. *SE22* —3C **82**
Uplands Rd. *N8* —1B **10**
Upnall Ho. *SE15* —2E **69**
Upnor Way. *SE17* —1A **68**
Up. Addison Gdns. *W14* —3A **48**
Up. Bardsey Wlk. N1 —3E ***25*** *(off Douglas Rd. N.)*
Up. Belgrave St. *SW1* —4C **50**
Up. Berenger Wlk. SW10 (off Berenger Wlk.) —3F ***63***
Up. Berkeley St. *W2* —5B **36**
Up. Blantyre Wlk. SW10 (off Blantyre Wlk.) —3F ***63***
Up. Brockley Rd. *SE4* —1B **84**
Up. Brook St. *W1* —1C **50**
Up. Caldy Wlk. N1 —4E ***25*** *(off Caldy Wlk.)*
Up. Camelford Wlk. W11 (off St Mark's Rd.) —5A ***34***
Up. Cheyne Row. *SW3* —2A **64**
Upper Clapton. —4D 13
Up. Clapton Rd. *E5* —4D **13**
Up. Clarendon Wlk. W11 (off Clarendon Rd.) —5A ***34***
Up. Dartrey Wlk. SW10 (off Whistler Wlk.) —3E ***63***
Up. Dengie Wlk. N1 —5E ***25*** *(off Baddow Wlk.)*
Upper Feilde. W1 —1C ***50*** *(off Park St.)*
Up. Grosvenor St. *W1* —1C **50**
Upper Ground. *SE1* —2C **52**
Up. Gulland Wlk. N1 —3E ***25*** *(off Oronsay Wlk.)*
Up. Hampstead Wlk. *NW3* —1E **21**
Up. Handa Wlk. N1 —3F ***25*** *(off Handa Wlk.)*
Up. Hawkwell Wlk. N1 —5E ***25*** *(off Maldon Rd.)*
Up. Hilldrop Est. *N7* —2F **23**
Upper Holloway. —4E 9
Up. James St. *W1* —1E **51**
Up. John St. *W1* —1E **51**
Up. Lismore Wlk. N1 —3F ***25*** *(off Clephane St.)*
Upper Mall. *W6* —1C **60** (in two parts)
Upper Marsh. *SE1* —4B **52**
Up. Montagu St. *W1* —4B **36**
Up. North St. *E14* —4C **42**
Up. Park Rd. *NW3* —2B **22**

Up. Phillimore Gdns. *W8*
—3C **48**
Up. Ramsey Wlk. *N1* —3F **25**
(off Ramsey Wlk.)
Up. Rawreth Wlk. *N1* —5E **25**
(off Basire St.)
Up. Richmond Rd. *SW15*
—2B **74**
Upper Rd. *E13* —2C **44**
Up. St Martin's La. *WC2*
—1A **52**
Up. Sheppey Wlk. *N1* —3E **25**
(off Skomer Wlk.)
Upper St. *N1* —1C **38**
Upper Sydenham. —3D 97
Up. Tachbrook St. *SW1*
—5E **51**
Up. Talbot Wlk. *W11* —5A **34**
(off Talbot Wlk.)
Upper Ter. *NW3* —5E **7**
Up. Thames St. *EC4* —1D **53**
Up. Tollington Pk. *N4* —3C **10**
(in two parts)
Upperton Rd. E. *E13* —2E **45**
Upperton Rd. W. *E13* —2E **45**
Upper Tooting. —3B 92
Up. Tooting Pk. *SW17* —2B **92**
Up. Tooting Rd. *SW17*
—4B **92**
Up. Tulse Hill. *SW2* —5B **80**
Up. Whistler Wlk. *SW10*
—3E **63**
(off Worlds End Est.)
Up. Wimpole St. *W1* —4C **36**
Up. Woburn Pl. *WC1* —2F **37**
Upstall St. *SE5* —4D **67**
Upton. —4C 30
Upton Av. *E7* —4C **30**
Upton La. *E7* —4C **30**
Upton Lodge. *E7* —3C **30**
Upton Park. —1F 45
Upton Pk. Rd. *E7* —4D **31**
Upwey Ho. *N1* —5A **26**
Upwood Rd. *SE12* —4C **86**
Urlwin St. *SE5* —2E **67**
Urlwin Wlk. *SW9* —4C **66**
Urmston Dri. *SW19* —1A **90**
Urmston Ho. *E14* —5E **57**
Ursula M. *N4* —3E **11**
Ursula St. *SW11* —4A **64**
Urswick Rd. *E9* —2E **27**
Usborne M. *SW8* —3B **66**
Usher Rd. *E3* —5B **28**
Usher-Walker Ho. *E16* —3F **43**
(off South Cres.)
Usk Rd. *SW11* —2E **77**
Usk St. *E2* —2F **41**
Utopia Village. *NW1* —4C **22**
Uverdale Rd. *SW10* —3E **63**
Uxbridge Rd. *W12* —2B **46**
Uxbridge St. *W8* —2C **48**

Vale Clo. *W9* —2E **35**
Vale Cotts. *SW15* —3A **88**
Vale Ct. *W3* —2B **46**

Vale Ct. *W9* —2E **35**
Vale Cres. *SW15* —4A **88**
Vale End. *SE22* —2B **82**
Vale Est., The. *W3* —2A **46**
Vale Gro. *N4* —2E **11**
Vale Gro. *Slou* —3A **46**
Vale Lodge. *SE23* —2E **97**
Valentia Pl. *SW9* —2C **80**
Valentine Ct. *SE23* —2F **97**
(in two parts)
Valentine Pl. *SE1* —3D **53**
Valentine Rd. *E9* —3F **27**
Valentine Row. *SE1* —3D **53**
Vale Of Health. —5E 7
Vale of Health. *NW3* —5F **7**
Vale Pde. *SW15* —3A **88**
Valerian Way. *E15* —2A **44**
Vale Ri. *NW11* —3B **6**
Vale Rd. *E7* —3D **31**
Vale Rd. *N4* —2E **11**
Vale Row. *N5* —5D **11**
Vale Royal. *N7* —4A **24**
Vale Royal Ho. *WC2* —1F **51**
(off Charing Cross Rd.)
Vale St. *SE27* —3F **95**
Valeswood Rd. *Brom*
—5B **100**
Vale Ter. *N4* —1E **11**
Vale, The. *NW11* —5F **5**
Vale, The. *SW3* —2F **63**
Vale, The. *W3* —2A **46**
Valetta Gro. *E13* —1C **44**
Valetta Rd. *W3* —3A **46**
Valette Ho. *E9* —3E **27**
Valette St. *E9* —3E **27**
Valiant Ho. *E7* —1E **73**
Vallance Rd. *E2 & E1* —3C **40**
Valleyfield Rd. *SW16* —5B **94**
Valley Gro. *SE7* —1E **73**
Valley Rd. *SW16* —5B **94**
Valley Side. *SE7* —1F **73**
Valliere Rd. *NW10* —2C **46**
Valmar Rd. *SE5* —4E **67**
Valmar Trad. Est. *SE5* —4E **67**
Val McKenzie Av. *N7* —5C **10**
Valnay St. *SW17* —5B **92**
Valois Ho. *SE1* —4B **54**
(off Grange, The)
Valonia Gdns. *SW18* —4B **76**
Vanbrugh Clo. *E16* —4F **45**
Vanbrugh Ct. *SE11* —5C **52**
(off Wincott St.)
Vanbrugh Fields. *SE3* —2B **72**
Vanbrugh Hill. *SE10 & SE3*
—1B **72**
Vanbrugh Pk. *SE3* —3B **72**
Vanbrugh Pk. Rd. *SE3*
—3B **72**
Vanbrugh Pk. Rd. W. *SE3*
—3B **72**
Vanbrugh Rd. *W4* —4A **46**
Vanbrugh Ter. *SE3* —4B **72**
Vanburgh Ho. *E1* —4B **40**
(off Folgate St.)
Vancouver Rd. *SE23* —2A **98**
Vanderbilt Rd. *SW18* —1D **91**

Vandome Clo. *E16* —5D **45**
Vandon Pas. *SW1* —4E **51**
Vandon St. *SW1* —4E **51**
Vandyke Clo. *SW15* —5F **75**
Vandyke Cross. *SE9* —3F **87**
Vandy St. *EC2* —3A **40**
Vane Clo. *NW3* —2F **21**
Vane St. *SW1* —5E **51**
Vange Ho. W10 —4E **33**
(off Sutton Way)
Van Gogh Ct. *E14* —4F **57**
Vanguard Building. *E14*
—3B **56**
Vanguard Clo. *E16* —4C **44**
Vanguard St. *SE8* —4C **70**
Vanguard Trad. Est. *E15*
—5E **29**
Vanneck Sq. *SW15* —3C **74**
Vanoc Gdns. *Brom* —4C **100**
Vansittart Rd. *E7* —1B **30**
Vansittart St. *SE14* —3A **70**
Vanston Pl. *SW6* —3C **62**
Vantage M. E14 —2E **57**
(off Preston's Rd.)
Vantrey Ho. *SE11* —5C **52**
(off Marylee Way)
Vant Rd. *SW17* —5B **92**
Varcoe Rd. *SE16* —1D **69**
Vardens Rd. *SW11* —2F **77**
Varden St. *E1* —5D **41**
Vardon Clo. *W3* —5A **32**
Vardon Ho. *SE10* —4E **71**
Varley Ho. NW6 —5C **20**
(off Brondesbury Rd.)
Varley Rd. *E16* —5D **45**
Varna Rd. *SW6* —3A **62**
Varndell St. *NW1* —2E **37**
Vartry Rd. *N15* —1F **11**
Vassall Rd. *SW9* —3C **66**
Vat Ho. SW8 —3A **66**
(off Rita Rd.)
Vauban Est. *SE1* —4B **54**
Vauban St. *SE16* —4B **54**
Vaudeville Ct. *N4* —4C **10**
Vaughan Av. *NW4* —1C **4**
Vaughan Av. *W6* —5B **46**
Vaughan Est. *E2* —2B **40**
(off Diss St.)
Vaughan Ho. SE1 —3D **53**
(off Blackfriars Rd.)
Vaughan Rd. *SW4* —5E **79**
Vaughan Rd. *E15* —3B **30**
Vaughan Rd. *SE5* —5E **67**
Vaughan St. *SE16* —3B **56**
Vaughan Way. *E1* —1C **54**
Vaughan Williams Clo. *SE8*
—3C **70**
Vauxhall. —1A 66
Vauxhall Bri. *SW1 & SE1*
—1A **66**
Vauxhall Bri. Rd. *SW1* —4E **51**
Vauxhall Cross. (Junct.)
—1A **66**
Vauxhall Distribution Pk. SW8
—2F **65**
(off Post Office Way)

Vauxhall Gro. SW8 —2B 66
Vauxhall St. SE11 —1B 66
Vauxhall Wlk. SE11 —1B 66
Veda Rd. SE13 —2C 84
Velde Way. SE22 —3A 82
Venables St. NW8 —3F 35
Vencourt Pl. W6 —5C 46
Venetian Rd. SE5 —5E 67
Venetia Rd. N4 —1D 11
Venice Ct. SE5 —3E 67
(off Bowyer St.)
Venner Rd. SE26 —5E 97
Venn Ho. N1 —5B 24
(off Barnsbury Est.)
Venn St. SW4 —2E 79
Ventnor Rd. SE14 —3F 69
Venture Ct. SE12 —5C 86
Venue St. E14 —4E 43
Vera Lynn Clo. E7 —1C 30
Vera Rd. SW6 —4A 62
Verbena Clo. E16 —3B 44
Verbena Gdns. W6 —1C 60
Verdant Ct. SE6 —5A 86
(off Verdant La.)
Verdant La. SE6 —5A 86
Verdi Ho. W10 —1A 34
(off Herries St.)
Verdun Rd. SW13 —2C 60
Vereker Rd. W14 —1A 62
Vere St. W1 —5D 37
Verity Clo. W11 —1A 48
Ver Meer Ct. E14 —4F 57
Vermeer Gdns. SE15 —2E 83
Vermont Rd. SW18 —4D 77
Verney Ho. NW8 —3A 36
(off Jerome Cres.)
Verney Rd. SE16 —2C 68
Verney St. NW10 —5A 4
Verney Way. SE16 —1D 69
Vernon Ct. NW2 —5B 6
Vernon Ho. SE11 —1B 66
(off Vauxhall St.)
Vernon Ho. WC1 —4A 38
(off Vernon Pl.)
Vernon M. W14 —5A 48
(off Vernon St.)
Vernon Pl. WC1 —4A 38
Vernon Ri. WC1 —2B 38
Vernon Rd. E3 —1B 42
Vernon Rd. E11 —3A 16
Vernon Rd. E15 —4A 30
Vernon Rd. SW14 —1A 74
Vernon Sq. WC1 —2B 38
Vernon St. W14 —5A 48
Vernon Yd. W11 —1B 48
Verona Ct. SE14 —2F 69
(off Myers La.)
Verona Rd. E7 —4C 30
Veronica Ho. SE4 —1B 84
Veronica Rd. SW17 —2D 93
Verran Rd. SW12 —5D 79
Verulam Av. E17 —1B 14
Verulam Bldgs. WC1 —4B 38
(off Grays Inn)
Verulam Ct. NW9 —2C 4
Verulam St. WC1 —4C 38
Verwood Ho. SW8 —3B 66
(off Cobbett St.)
Verwood Lodge. E14 —4F 57
Veryan Ct. N8 —1F 9
Vesage Ct. EC1 —4C 38
(off Leather La.)
Vesey Path. E14 —5D 43
Vespan Rd. W12 —3C 46
Vessey Path. E14 —5D 43
Vesta Rd. SE4 —5A 70
Vestris Rd. SE23 —2F 97
Vestry Ct. SW1 —4F 51
(off Monck St.)
Vestry M. SE5 —4A 68
Vestry Rd. SE5 —4A 68
Vestry St. N1 —2F 39
Vevey St. SE6 —2B 98
Viaduct Bldgs. EC1 —4C 38
Viaduct Pl. E2 —2D 41
Viaduct St. E2 —2D 41
Vian St. SE13 —1D 85
Viant Ho. NW10 —4A 18
Vibart Gdns. SW2 —5B 80
Vibart Wlk. N1 —5A 24
(off Outram Pl.)
Vicarage Ct. W8 —3D 49
Vicarage Cres. SW11 —4F 63
Vicarage Gdns. W8 —2C 48
Vicarage Ga. W8 —2D 49
Vicarage Gro. SE5 —4F 67
Vicarage La. E15 —4A 30
Vicarage Path. N8 —2A 10
Vicarage Rd. E10 —2C 14
Vicarage Rd. E15 —4B 30
Vicarage Rd. NW4 —1C 4
Vicarage Rd. SW14 —3A 74
Vicarage Wlk. SW11 —4F 63
Vicarage Way. NW10 —5A 4
Vicar's Clo. E9 —5E 27
Vicars Clo. E15 —5C 30
Vicar's Hill. SE13 —2D 85
Vicars Oak Rd. SE19 —5A 96
Vicar's Rd. NW5 —2C 22
Viceroy Ct. NW8 —1A 36
(off Prince Albert Rd.)
Viceroy Rd. SW8 —4A 66
Vickery Ct. EC1 —3E 39
(off Bartholomew Sq.)
Victor Cazalet Ho. N1 —5D 25
(off Gaskin St.)
Victoria & Albert Mus. —4F 49
Victoria Arc. SW1 —4D 51
(off Victoria St.)
Victoria Av. E6 —5F 31
Victoria Av. EC2 —4A 40
Victoria Bldgs. E8 —5D 27
(off Mare St.)
Victoria Colonnade. WC1 —4A 38
(off Southampton Row)
Victoria Cotts. E1 —4C 40
(off Deal St.)
Victoria Ct. SE26 —5E 97
Victoria Cres. N15 —1A 12
Victoria Cres. SE19 —5A 96
Victoria Dock Rd. E16 —5B 44
Victoria Dri. SW19 —5F 75
Victoria Embkmt. SW1 & WC2 —3A 52
Victoria Gdns. W11 —2C 48
Victoria Gro. W8 —4E 49
Victoria Gro. M. W2 —1C 48
Victoria Hall. E16 —2C 58
(off Wesley Av., in two parts)
Victoria Ho. SW1 —5E 51
(off Francis St.)
Victoria Ho. SW1 —1D 65
(off Ebury Bri. Rd.)
Victoria Ho. SW8 —3A 66
(off S. Lambeth Rd.)
Victoria Ind. Est. W3 —4A 32
Victoria Mans. NW2 —4D 19
Victoria Mans. SW8 —3A 66
(off S. Lambeth Rd.)
Victoria M. NW6 —5C 20
Victoria M. SW4 —2D 79
Victoria M. SW18 —1E 91
Victorian Gro. N16 —1A 26
Victorian Rd. N16 —5A 12
Victoria Pk. —5A 28
Victoria Pk. Ind. Cen. E9
(off Rothbury Rd.) —4C 28
Victoria Pk. Rd. E9 —5E 27
Victoria Pk. Sq. E2 —2E 41
Victoria Pas. NW8 —3F 35
(off Fisherton St.)
Victoria Pl. Shop. Cen. SW1 —5D 51
Victoria Point. E13 —1C 44
(off Victoria Rd.)
Victoria Ri. SW4 —1D 79
Victoria Rd. E11 —1A 30
Victoria Rd. E13 —1C 44
Victoria Rd. N4 —2B 10
Victoria Rd. NW6 —1B 34
Victoria Rd. NW10 —4A 32
Victoria Rd. SW14 —1A 74
Victoria Rd. W3 —4A 32
Victoria Rd. W8 —4E 49
Victoria Sq. SW1 —4D 51
Victoria St. E15 —4A 30
Victoria St. SW1 —4E 51
Victoria Ter. N4 —3C 10
Victoria Ter. NW10 —3B 32
Victoria Ter. SW8 —5D 65
Victoria Way. SE7 —1D 73
Victoria Wharf. E14 —1A 56
Victoria Wharf. SE8 —1B 70
(off Dragoon Rd.)
Victoria Works. NW2 —4D 5
Victoria Yd. E1 —5C 40
Victor Rd. NW10 —2D 33
Victory Ct. W9 —3C 34
(off Hermes Clo.)
Victory Pl. E14 —1A 56
Victory Pl. SE17 —5F 53
Victory Wlk. SE8 —4C 70
Victory Way. SE16 —3A 56
View Clo. N6 —2B 8
View Ct. SE12 —3E 101

View Cres. *N8* —1F **9**
Viewfield Rd. *SW18* —4B **76**
View Rd. *N6* —2B **8**
Vigilant Clo. *SE26* —4C **96**
Vigo St. *W1* —1E **51**
Viking Clo. *E3* —1A **42**
*Viking Ct. SW6 —2C **62***
(off Halford Rd.)
Viking Gdns. *E6* —3F **45**
*Viking Ho. SE5 —5E **67***
(off Denmark Rd.)
Viking Pl. *E10* —3B **14**
*Village Clo. NW3 —2F **21***
(off Belsize La.)
*Village Ct. SE3 —1A **86***
(off Hurren Clo.)
Village, The. *NW3* —4E **7**
Village, The. *SE7* —2E **73**
Village Way. *NW10* —1A **18**
Village Way. *SE24* —4F **81**
Villa Rd. *SW9* —1C **80**
Villas on the Heath. *NW3* —5E **7**
Villa St. *SE17* —1F **67**
*Villa Wlk. SE17 —1F **67***
(off Inville Rd.)
Villiers Clo. *E10* —4C **14**
Villiers Rd. *NW2* —3C **18**
Villiers St. *WC2* —2A **52**
Vincennes Est. *SE27* —4F **95**
Vincent Clo. *SE16* —3A **56**
Vincent Ct. *N4* —3A **10**
Vincent Ct. *SW9* —4B **66**
*Vincent Ct. W1 —5B **36***
(off Seymour Pl.)
Vincent Gdns. *NW2* —5B **4**
*Vincent Ho. SW1 —5F **51***
(off Vincent Sq.)
Vincent M. *E3* —1C **42**
Vincent Sq. *SW1* —5F **51**
Vincent Sq. Mans. SW1
*(off Walcott St.) —5E **51***
Vincent St. *E16* —4B **44**
Vincent St. *SW1* —5F **51**
Vincent Ter. *N1* —1D **39**
Vince St. *EC1* —2F **39**
Vine Ct. *E1* —4C **40**
Vinegar St. *E1* —2D **55**
*Vinegar Yd. SE1 —3A **54***
(off St Thomas St.)
Vine Hill. *EC1* —3C **38**
Vine La. *SE1* —2A **54**
Vineries, The. *SE6* —1C **98**
Vine Rd. *E15* —4B **30**
Vine Rd. *SW13* —1B **74**
Vinery Way. *W6* —4D **47**
*Vine Sq. W14 —1B **62***
(off Star Rd.)
Vine St. *EC3* —5B **40**
Vine St. *W1* —1E **51**
Vine St. Bri. *EC1* —3C **38**
*Vine Yd. SE1 —3E **53***
(off Sanctuary St.)
Vineyard Clo. *SE6* —1C **98**
Vineyard Hill Rd. *SW19* —4B **90**
*Vineyard M. EC1 —3C **38***
(off Vineyard Wlk.)
Vineyard Wlk. *EC1* —3C **38**
Viney Rd. *SE13* —1D **85**
Vining St. *SW9* —2C **80**
Vinopolis, City of Wine.
*(off Bank End) —2F **53***
Vintners Ct. *EC4* —1E **53**
*Vintners Hall. EC4 —1E **53***
(off Up. Thames St.)
Vintners Pl. *EC4* —1E **53**
Viola Sq. *W12* —1B **46**
Violet Clo. *E16* —3A **44**
Violet Clo. *SE8* —2B **70**
Violet Hill. *NW8* —1E **35**
*Violet Hill Ho. NW8 —1E **35***
(off Violet Hill)
Violet Rd. *E3* —3D **43**
Violet Rd. *E17* —1C **14**
Violet St. *E2* —3D **41**
V.I.P. Trading Est. *SE7* —5E **59**
Virgil Pl. *W1* —4B **36**
Virgil St. *SE1* —4B **52**
*Virginia Ct. SE16 —3F **55***
(off Eleanor Clo.)
*Virginia Ct. WC1 —3F **37***
(off Burton St.)
Virginia Ho. *E14* —1E **57**
Virginia Rd. *E2* —2B **40**
Virginia St. *E1* —1C **54**
Virginia Wlk. *SW2* —4B **80**
*Viscount Ct. W2 —5C **34***
(off Pembridge Vs.)
Viscount St. *EC1* —3E **39**
Vista Dri. *Ilf* —1F **17**
Vista, The. *SE9* —4F **87**
*Vittoria Ho. N1 —5B **24***
(off High Rd.)
Vivian Av. *NW4* —1D **5**
Vivian Comma Clo. *N4* —5D **11**
*Vivian Mans. NW4 —1D **5***
(off Vivian Av.)
Vivian Rd. *E3* —1A **42**
Vivian Sq. *SE15* —1D **83**
Vogans Mill. *SE1* —3B **54**
*Vollasky Ho. E1 —4C **40***
(off Daplyn St.)
Voltaire Rd. *SW4* —1F **79**
Volt Av. *NW10* —2A **32**
Voluntary Pl. *E11* —1C **16**
Vorley Rd. *N19* —4E **9**
Voss St. *E2* —2C **40**
Voyager Bus. Est. SE16
*(off Spa Rd.) —4C **54***
Vulcan Rd. *SE4* —5B **70**
Vulcan Sq. *E14* —5D **57**
Vulcan Ter. *SE4* —5B **70**
Vulcan Way. *N7* —3B **24**
Vyner Rd. *W3* —1A **46**
Vyner St. *E9* —5D **27**

Wadding St. *SE17* —5F **53**
Waddington Rd. *E15* —2F **29**
Waddington St. *E15* —3F **29**
*Wade Ho. SE1 —3C **54***
(off Parkers Row)
Wadeson St. *E2* —1D **41**
Wade's Pl. *E14* —1D **57**
Wadham Gdns. *NW3* —5A **22**
Wadham Rd. *SW15* —2A **76**
Wadhurst Rd. *SW8* —4E **65**
Wadhurst Rd. *W4* —4A **46**
Wadley Rd. *E11* —2A **16**
Wager St. *E3* —3B **42**
Waghorn Rd. *E13* —5E **31**
Waghorn St. *SE15* —1C **82**
Wagner St. *SE15* —3E **69**
Wainford Clo. *SW19* —5F **75**
Waite Davies Rd. *SE12* —5B **86**
Waite St. *SE15* —2B **68**
*Waithman St. EC4 —5D **39***
(off Apothecary St.)
Wakefield Ct. *SE26* —5E **97**
Wakefield Gdns. *Ilf* —1F **17**
Wakefield Ho. *SE15* —4C **68**
Wakefield M. *WC1* —2A **38**
Wakefield Rd. *N15* —1B **12**
Wakefield St. *E6* —5F **31**
Wakefield St. *WC1* —3A **38**
Wakeford Clo. *SW4* —3E **79**
Wakeham St. *N1* —3F **25**
Wakehurst Rd. *SW11* —3A **78**
Wakeling St. *E1* —5A **42**
Wakeling St. *E14* —5A **42**
*Wakelin Ho. N1 —4D **25***
(off Sebbon St.)
Wakelin Ho. *SE23* —5A **84**
Wakelin Rd. *E15* —1A **44**
Wakeman Rd. *NW10* —2E **33**
Wakley St. *EC1* —2D **39**
Walberswick St. *SW8* —3A **66**
Walbrook. *EC4* —1F **53**
(in three parts)
Walbrook Wharf. EC4
*(off Bell Wharf La.) —1E **53***
Walburgh St. *E1* —5D **41**
Walcorde Av. *SE17* —5E **53**
*Walcot Gdns. SE11 —5C **52***
(off Kennington Rd.)
Walcot Sq. *SE11* —5C **52**
Walcott St. *SW1* —5E **51**
Waldeck Gro. *SE27* —3D **95**
Waldemar Av. *SW6* —4A **62**
Waldemar Rd. *SW19* —5C **90**
Walden Ct. *SW8* —4F **65**
*Walden Ho. SW1 —5C **50***
(off Pimlico Rd.)
Waldenshaw Rd. *SE23* —1E **97**
Walden St. *E1* —5D **41**
Waldo Clo. *SW4* —3E **79**
Waldo Rd. *NW10* —2C **32**
(in two parts)
Waldram Cres. *SE23* —1E **97**
Waldram Pk. Rd. *SE23* —1F **97**
Waldram Pl. *SE23* —1E **97**
Waldron M. *SW3* —2F **63**
Waldron Rd. *SW18* —3E **91**

Walerand Rd. *SE13* —5E **71**
Waleran Flats. *SE1* —5A **54**
Wales Clo. *SE15* —3D **69**
Wales Farm Rd. *W3* —4A **32**
Waley St. *E1* —4A **42**
Walford Ho. *E1* —5D **41**
Walford Rd. *N16* —1A **26**
Walham Green. —4D 63
Walham Grn. Ct. SW6
  (off Waterford Rd.) —3D *63*
Walham Gro. *SW6* —3C **62**
Walham Ri. *SW19* —5A **90**
Walham Yd. *SW6* —3C **62**
Walker Ho. *NW1* —1F **37**
Walker's Ct. W1 —1F *51*
  (off Brewer St.)
Walkerscroft Mead. *SE21*
  —1E **95**
Walkers Pl. *SW15* —2A **76**
Walkford Way. *SE15* —3B **68**
Walkinshaw Ct. N1 —4E *25*
  (off Rotherfield St.)
Wallace Collection. —5C 36
Wallace Ct. *NW1* —4A *36*
  (off Old Marylebone Rd.)
Wallace Ho. *N7* —3B *24*
  (off Caledonian Rd.)
Wallace Rd. *N1* —3E **25**
Wallace Way. N19 —4F *9*
  (off St John's Way)
Wallbutton Rd. *SE4* —5A **70**
Wallcote Av. *NW2* —3F **5**
Wall Ct. N4 —3B *10*
  (off Stroud Grn. Rd.)
Waller Rd. *SE14* —4F **69**
Waller Way. *SE10* —3D **71**
Wallflower St. *W12* —1B **46**
Wallgrave Rd. *SW5* —5D **49**
Wallingford Av. *W10* —4F **33**
Wallis All. SE1 —3E *53*
  (off Marshalsea Rd.)
Wallis Clo. *SW11* —1F **77**
Wallis Ho. *SE14* —4A **70**
Wallis Rd. *E9* —3B **28**
Wallis's Cotts. SW2 —5A *80*
Wallorton Gdns. *SW14*
  —2A **74**
Wallside. EC2 —4E *39*
  (off Beech St.)
Wall St. *N1* —3F **25**
Wallwood Rd. *E11* —2F **15**
Wallwood St. *E3* —4B **42**
Wallwood St. *E14* —4B **42**
Walmer Ho. W10 —5F *33*
  (off Bramley Rd.)
Walmer Pl. W1 —4B *36*
  (off Walmer St.)
Walmer Rd. *W10* —5E **33**
Walmer Rd. *W11* —1A **48**
Walmer St. *W1* —4B **36**
Walm La. *NW2* —3E **19**
Walney Wlk. *N1* —3E **25**
Walnut Clo. *SE8* —2B **70**
Walnut Ct. W8 —4D *49*
  (off St Mary's Pl.)
Walnut Gdns. *E15* —2A **30**

Walnut Rd. *E10* —4C **14**
Walnut Tree Clo. *SW13*
  —4B **60**
Walnut Tree Cotts. *SW19*
  —5A **90**
Walnut Tree Ho. SW10
  (off Tregunter Rd.) —2D *63*
Walnut Tree Rd. *SE10*
  (in two parts) —1A **72**
Walnut Tree Wlk. *SE11*
  —5C **52**
Walpole Ct. *W14* —4F **47**
  (off Blythe Rd.)
Walpole Ho. SE1 —3C *52*
  (off Westminster Bri. Rd.)
Walpole M. *NW8* —5F **21**
Walpole M. *SW19* —5F **91**
Walpole Rd. *E6* —4E **31**
Walpole Rd. *SW19* —5F **91**
Walpole St. *SW3* —1B **64**
Walsham Clo. *N16* —3C **12**
Walsham Ho. *SE14* —5F **69**
Walsham Ho. SE17 —1F *67*
  (off Blackwood St.)
Walsham Rd. *SE14* —5F **69**
Walsingham. *NW8* —5F **21**
Walsingham Lodge. *SW13*
  —4C **60**
Walsingham Mans. SW6
  (off Fulham Rd.) —3D *63*
Walsingham Dri. *SW11*
  —4C **78**
Walsingham Rd. *E5* —5C **12**
Walston Ho. SW1 —1F *65*
  (off Aylesford St.)
Walter Grn. Ho. SE15 —4E *69*
  (off Lausanne Rd.)
Walters Clo. SE17 —5F *53*
  (off Brandon St.)
Walters Ho. SE11 —2D *67*
  (off Brandon Est.)
Walter St. *E2* —2F **41**
Walters Way. *SE23* —4F **83**
Walter Ter. *E1* —5F **41**
Walterton Rd. *W9* —3B **34**
Waltham Ho. *NW8* —5E **21**
Walton Clo. *E5* —5F **13**
Walton Clo. *NW2* —4D **5**
Walton Clo. *SW8* —3A **66**
Walton Dri. *NW10* —3A **18**
Walton Ho. *E2* —3B **40**
Walton Pl. *SW3* —4B **50**
Walton Rd. *E13* —1E **45**
Walton St. *SW3* —5A **50**
Walt Whitman Clo. *SE24*
  —2D **81**
Walworth. —1E 67
Walworth Pl. *SE17* —1E **67**
Walworth Rd. *SE1 & SE17*
  —5E **53**
Wanborough Dri. *SW15*
  —1D **89**
Wandle Ho. NW8 —4A *36*
  (off Penfold St.)
Wandle Ho. *Brom* —5F **99**
Wandle Rd. *SW17* —2A **92**

Wandle Way. *SW18* —1D **91**
Wandon Rd. *SW6* —3D **63**
  (in two parts)
Wandsworth. —3D 77
Wandsworth Bri. *SW6 &*
  SW18 —1D **77**
Wandsworth Bri. Rd. *SW6*
  —4D **63**
Wandsworth Common.
  —1B **92**
Wandsworth Comn. W. Side.
  SW18 —3E **77**
Wandsworth Gyratory.
  (Junct.) —3D **77**
Wandsworth High St. *SW18*
  —3C **76**
Wandsworth Plain. *SW18*
  —3D **77**
Wandsworth Rd. *SW8*
  —1D **79**
Wandsworth Shop. Cen.
  SW18 —4D **77**
Wangford Ho. SW9 —2D *81*
  (off Loughborough Pk.)
Wanless Rd. *SE24* —1E **81**
Wanley Rd. *SE5* —2F **81**
Wanlip Rd. *E13* —3D **45**
Wansbeck Rd. *E9 & E3*
  —4B **28**
Wansdown Pl. *SW6* —3D **63**
Wansey St. *SE17* —5E **53**
Wanstead. —1D 17
Wanstead Gdns. *Ilf* —1F **17**
Wanstead La. *Ilf* —1F **17**
Wanstead Pk. Av. *E12* —3F **17**
Wanstead Pk. Rd. *Ilf* —1F **17**
Wanstead Pl. *E11* —1C **16**
Wantage Rd. *SE12* —3B **86**
Wapping. —2D 55
Wapping Dock St. *E1* —2D **55**
Wapping High St. *E1* —2C **54**
Wapping La. *E1* —1D **55**
Wapping Wall. *E1* —2E **55**
Warbeck Rd. *W12* —3D **47**
Warburton Clo. N1 —3A *26*
  (off Culford Rd.)
Warburton Ho. E8 —5D *27*
  (off Warburton St.)
Warburton Rd. *E8* —5D **27**
Warburton St. *E8* —5D **27**
Wardalls Gro. *SE14* —3E **69**
Wardalls Ho. SE8 —2B *70*
  (off Staunton St.)
Wardell Ho. SE10 —2E *71*
  (off Welland St.)
Warden Rd. *NW5* —3C **22**
Wardens Gro. *SE1* —2E **53**
Wardle St. *E9* —2F **27**
Wardley St. *SW18* —5D **77**
Wardo Av. *SW6* —4A **62**
Wardour M. W1 —5E *37*
  (off D'Arblay St.)
Wardour St. *W1* —5E **37**
Ward Point. *SE11* —5C **52**
Ward Rd. *E15* —5F **29**
Ward Rd. *N19* —5E **9**

Wardrobe Pl. EC4 —5D 39
(off Carter La.)
Wardrobe Ter. EC4 —1D 53
(off Addle Hill)
Wareham Ho. SW8 —3B 66
Warfield Rd. NW10 —2F 33
Warfield Yd. NW10 —2F 33
(off Warfield Rd.)
Wargrave Av. N15 —1B 12
Wargrave Ho. E2 —2B 40
(off Navarre St.)
Warham Rd. N4 —1C 10
Warham St. SE5 —3D 67
Waring St. SE27 —4E 95
Warley Clo. E10 —3B 14
Warley St. E2 —2F 41
Warlock Rd. W9 —3B 34
Warlters Clo. N7 —1A 24
Warlters Rd. N7 —1A 24
Warltersville Mans. N19
—2A 10
Warltersville Rd. N19 —2A 10
Warmington Clo. E5 —5F 13
Warmington Rd. SE24
—4E 81
Warmington St. E13 —3C 44
Warmington Tower. SE14
—4A 70
Warmley Ct. SE15 —2A 68
(off Newent Ct.)
Warmsworth. NW1 —5E 23
(off Pratt St.)
Warndon St. SE16 —5F 55
Warneford St. E9 —5D 27
Warner Clo. E15 —2A 30
Warner Clo. NW9 —2B 4
Warner Ho. NW8 —2E 35
Warner Ho. SE13 —5D 71
(off Russett Way)
Warner Pl. E2 —1C 40
Warner Rd. SE5 —4E 67
Warner St. EC1 —3C 38
Warner Ter. E14 —4C 42
(off Broomfield)
Warner Yd. EC1 —3C 38
(off Warner St.)
Warnford Ho. SW15 —4A 74
(off Tunworth Cres.)
Warnham. WC1 —2B 38
(off Sidmouth St.)
Warnham Ho. SW2 —5B 80
(off Up. Tulse Hill)
Warple M. W3 —3A 46
Warple Way. W3 —2A 46
(in two parts)
Warren Av. E10 —5E 15
Warren Clo. SE21 —5E 81
Warrender Rd. N19 —5E 9
Warren Dri., The. E11 —2E 17
Warren Gdns. E15 —2F 29
Warren M. W1 —3E 37
Warren Pl. E1 —5F 41
(off Caroline St.)
Warren Rd. E10 —5E 15
Warren Rd. E11 —1E 17
(in two parts)

Warren Rd. NW2 —4B 4
Warren St. W1 —3D 37
Warren Wlk. SE7 —2E 73
Warriner Gdns. SW11 —4B 64
Warringtons Cres. W9 —3E 35
Warrington Gdns. W9 —3E 35
Warrington Pl. E14 —2E 57
(off Yabsley S)
Warspite Ho. E14 —5D 57
Warspite Rd. SE18 —4F 59
Warton Rd. E15 —4E 29
Warwick. W14 —5B 48
(off Kensington Village)
Warwick Av. W9 & W2
—3D 35
Warwick Chambers. W8
—4C 48
(off Pater St.)
Warwick Ct. WC1 —4B 38
Warwick Cres. W2 —4E 35
Warwick Dri. SW15 —1D 75
Warwick Est. W2 —4D 35
Warwick Gdns. N4 —1E 11
Warwick Gdns. W14 —4B 48
Warwick Gro. E5 —4D 13
Warwick Ho. SW1 —5C 66
Warwick Ho. St. SW1 —2F 51
Warwick La. EC4 —5D 39
Warwick Pas. EC4 —5D 39
(off Old Bailey)
Warwick Pl. W9 —4E 35
Warwick Pl. N. SW1 —5E 51
Warwick Rd. E11 —1D 17
Warwick Rd. E12 —2F 31
Warwick Rd. E15 —3B 30
Warwick Rd. W14 & SW5
—5B 48
Warwick Row. SW1 —4E 51
Warwickshire Path. SE8
—3B 70
Warwickshire Rd. N16
—1A 26
Warwick Sq. EC4 —5D 39
Warwick Sq. SW1 —1E 65
Warwick Sq. M. SW1 —5E 51
Warwick St. W1 —1E 51
Warwick Ter. E10 —1F 15
(off Lea Bri. Rd.)
Warwick Way. SW1 —1D 65
Warwick Yd. EC1 —3E 39
Washington Clo. E3 —2D 43
Washington Rd. E6 —4E 31
Washington Rd. SW13
—3C 60
Wasps R.U.F.C. —2D 47
(Queens Park Rangers
Football Ground)
Wastdale Rd. SE23 —1F 97
Waterbank Rd. SE6 —3D 99
Water Brook La. NW4 —1E 5
Watercress Pl. N1 —4A 26
Waterden Cres. E15 —2C 28
Waterden Rd. E15 —2C 28
Waterer Ho. SE6 —4E 99
Waterfall Cotts. SW19 —5F 91
Waterfall Rd. SW19 —5F 91
Waterfall Ter. SW17 —5A 92

Waterford Ho. W11 —1B 48
(off Kensington Pk. Rd.)
Waterford Rd. SW6 —3D 63
(in two parts)
Water Gdns., The. W2 —5A 36
Watergate. EC4 —1D 53
Watergate St. SE8 —2C 70
Watergate Wlk. WC2 —2A 52
Waterhead. NW1 —2E 37
(off Varndell St.)
Waterhouse Clo. E16 —4F 45
Waterhouse Clo. NW3 —2F 21
Waterhouse Clo. W6 —5F 47
Waterhouse Sq. EC1 —4C 38
Wateridge Clo. E14 —4C 56
Water La. E15 —3A 30
Water La. EC3 —1A 54
Water La. NW1 —4D 23
Water La. SE14 —3E 69
Waterloo Bri. WC2 & SE1
—1B 52
Waterloo Clo. E9 —2E 27
Waterloo Gdns. E2 —1E 41
Waterloo Pas. NW6 —4B 20
Waterloo Pl. SW1 —2F 51
Waterloo Rd. E6 —4E 31
Waterloo Rd. E7 —2B 30
Waterloo Rd. E10 —2C 14
Waterloo Rd. NW2 —3C 4
Waterloo Rd. SE1 —2B 52
Waterloo Ter. N1 —4D 25
Waterlow Ct. NW11 —2D 7
Waterlow Rd. N19 —3E 9
Waterman Building. E14
—3B 56
Waterman St. SW15 —1F 75
Waterman's Wlk. EC4 —1F 53
(off Allhallows La.)
Watermans Wlk. SE16
—3A 56
Waterman Way. E1 —2D 55
Watermead Ho. E9 —2A 28
Watermeadow La. SW6
—5E 63
Watermead Rd. SE6 —4E 99
Watermint Quay. N16 —2C 12
Waters Edge. SW6 —4E 61
Waterside. E17 —1E 13
Waterside Clo. E3 —5B 28
Waterside Clo. SE16 —3C 56
Waterside Ho. E14 —3D 57
Waterside Pl. NW1 —5C 22
Waterside Point. SW11
—3A 64
Waterside Way. SW17 —4E 91
Waterson St. E2 —2A 40
Waters Pl. SW15 —5E 61
Waters Rd. SE6 —3A 100
Water St. WC2 —1C 52
(off Maltravers St.)
Water Tower Pl. N1 —5C 24
Waterworks La. E5 —4F 13
Waterworks Rd. SW2 —4B 80
Watford Clo. SW11 —4A 64
Watford Rd. E16 —4C 44

Watford Way. NW4 —1D 5
Watkinson Rd. N7 —3B 24
Watling Ct. EC4 —5E 39
(off Watling St.)
Watling Gdns. NW2 —3A 20
Watling St. EC4 —5E 39
Watling St. SE15 —2A 68
Watlington Gro. SE26 —5A 98
Watney Mkt. E1 —5D 41
Watney St. E1 —5D 41
Watson Clo. N16 —2F 25
Watson's M. W1 —4A 36
Watson's St. SE8 —3C 90
Watson St. E13 —1D 45
Watsons Yd. NW2 —4C 4
Wattisfield Rd. E5 —5E 13
Watts Gro. E3 —4C 42
Watts Point. E13 —5C 30
(off Brooks Rd.)
Watts St. E1 —2D 55
Watts St. SE15 —4B 68
Wat Tyler Rd. SE10 & SE3
—5E 71
Wavel M. NW6 —4D 21
Wavel Pl. SE26 —4B 96
Wavendon Av. W4 —1A 60
Waveney Av. SE15 —2D 83
Waveney Clo. E1 —2C 54
Waveney St. SE15 —2D 83
Waverley Ct. NW6 —4A 20
Waverley Ct. SE26 —5E 97
Waverley Pl. N4 —4D 11
Waverley Pl. NW8 —1F 35
Waverley Rd. N8 —1A 10
Waverton Ho. E3 —5B 28
Waverton Rd. SW18 —5E 77
Waverton St. W1 —2C 50
Wavertree Ct. SW2 —1A 94
Wavertree Rd. SW2 —1B 94
Waxlow Rd. NW10 —1A 32
Wayford St. SW11 —5A 64
Wayland Av. E8 —2C 26
Wayland Ho. SW9 —5C 66
(off Robsart St.)
Waylett Ho. SE11 —1B 66
(off Loughborough St.)
Waylett Pl. SE27 —3D 95
Wayman Ct. E8 —3D 27
Wayne Kirkum Way. NW6
—2B 20
Waynflete Sq. W10 —1F 47
Waynflete St. SW18 —2E 91
Wayside. NW11 —3A 6
Weald Clo. SE16 —1D 69
Weald Sq. E5 —4C 12
Weardale Rd. SE13 —2F 85
Wearmouth Ho. E3 —4B 42
Wear Pl. E2 —2D 41
(in two parts)
Wearside Rd. SE13 —2D 85
Weatherbury. W2 —5C 34
(off Talbot Rd.)
Weatherbury Ho. N19 —5F 9
(off Wedmore St.)
Weatherley Clo. E3 —4B 42

Weavers Ho. E11 —1C 16
(off New Wanstead)
Weavers La. SE1 —2A 54
Weavers Ter. SW6 —2C 62
(off Micklethwaite Rd.)
Weaver St. E1 —3C 40
Weavers Way. NW1 —5F 23
Weaver Wlk. SE27 —4E 95
Webb Clo. W10 —3E 33
Webber Row. SE1 —3D 53
(in two parts)
Webber St. SE1 —3C 52
Webb Est. E5 —2C 12
Webb Gdns. E13 —3D 44
Webb Ho. SW8 —3F 65
Webb Pl. NW10 —2B 32
Webb Rd. SE3 —2B 72
Webb's Rd. SW11 —2B 78
Webb St. SE1 —4A 54
Webheath. NW6 —4B 20
(off Netherwood St.)
Webster Rd. E11 —5E 15
Webster Rd. SE16 —4C 54
Wedderburn Rd. NW3 —2F 21
Wedgewood Ho. SW1 —1D 65
(off Churchill Gdns.)
Wedgwood Ho. SE11 —4C 52
(off Lambeth Wlk.)
Wedgwood M. W1 —5F 37
Wedgwood Wlk. NW6 —2D 21
(off Dresden Clo.)
Wedlake St. W10 —3A 34
Wedmore Ct. N19 —4F 9
Wedmore Gdns. N19 —4F 9
Wedmore M. N19 —5F 9
Wedmore St. N19 —5F 9
Weech Rd. NW6 —1C 20
Weedington Rd. NW5 —2C 22
Weedon Ho. W12 —5C 32
Weekley Sq. SW11 —1F 77
Weigall Rd. SE12 —3C 86
Weighhouse St. W1 —5C 36
Weir Rd. SW12 —5E 79
Weir Rd. SW19 —3D 91
Weir's Pas. NW1 —2F 37
Weiss Rd. SW15 —1F 75
Welbeck Av. Brom —4C 100
Welbeck Ct. W14 —5B 48
(off Addison Bri. Pl.)
Welbeck Ho. W1 —5D 37
(off Welbeck St.)
Welbeck Rd. E6 —2F 45
Welbeck St. W1 —4C 36
Welbeck Way. W1 —5D 37
Welby Ho. N19 —2F 9
Welby St. SE5 —4D 67
Welcome Ct. E17 —2C 14
(off Boundary Rd.)
Welfare Rd. E15 —4A 30
Welford Clo. E5 —5F 13
Welford Ct. NW1 —4D 23
(off Castlehaven Rd.)
Welford St. SW8 —5E 65
Welford Pl. SW19 —4A 90
Welham Rd. SW17 & SW16
—5C 92

Welland Ct. SE6 —2B 98
(off Oakham Clo.)
Welland Ho. SE15 —2E 83
Welland M. E1 —2C 54
Welland St. SE10 —2E 71
Wellby Ct. E13 —5E 31
Well Clo. SW16 —4B 94
Wellclose Sq. E1 —1C 54
(in two parts)
Wellclose St. E1 —1C 54
Wellcome Cen. for Medical
Science. —3F 37
(off Euston Rd.)
Well Cottage Clo. E11 —1E 17
Well Ct. EC4 —5E 39
(in two parts)
Weller Ho. SE16 —3C 54
(off George Row)
Wellers Ct. NW1 —1A 38
Weller St. SE1 —3E 53
Wellesley Av. W6 —4D 47
Wellesley Clo. SE7 —1E 73
Wellesley Ct. NW2 —4C 4
Wellesley Ct. NW8 —2E 35
(off Maida Va.)
Wellesley Ho. SW1 —1D 65
(off Ebury Bri. Rd.)
Wellesley Mans. W14
(off Edith Vs.) —1B 62
Wellesley Pl. NW1 —2F 37
Wellesley Pl. NW5 —2C 22
Wellesley Rd. E11 —1C 16
Wellesley Rd. E17 —1C 14
Wellesley Rd. NW5 —2C 22
Wellesley St. E1 —4F 41
Wellesley Ter. N1 —2E 39
Wellfield Rd. SW16 —4A 94
Wellfield Wlk. SW16 —5B 94
(in two parts)
Wellfit St. SE24 —1D 81
Wellgarth Rd. NW11 —3D 7
Wellington Av. N15 —1B 12
Wellington Bldgs. SW1
—1C 64
Wellington Clo. SE14 —4E 69
Wellington Clo. W11 —5C 34
Wellington Ct. NW8 —1F 35
(off Wellington Rd.)
Wellington Ct. SW1 —3B 50
(off Knightsbridge)
Wellington Ct. SW6 —4D 63
(off Maltings Pl.)
Wellington Est. E2 —1E 41
Wellington Gdns. SE7 —2E 73
Wellington Gro. SE10 —3F 71
Wellington Mans. E10 —3C 14
Wellington M. N7 —3B 24
(off Roman Rd.)
Wellington M. SE7 —2E 73
Wellington M. SE22 —2C 82
Wellington M. SW16 —3F 93
Wellington Mus. —3C 50
Wellington Pk. Est. NW2
—3C 4
Wellington Pas. E11 —1C 16
(off Wellington Rd.)

Wellington Pl. *E11* —1C **16**
Wellington Pl. *NW8* —2F **35**
Wellington Rd. *E7* —1B **30**
Wellington Rd. *E10* —3A **14**
Wellington Rd. *E11* —1C **16**
Wellington Rd. *NW8* —1F **35**
Wellington Rd. *NW10*
—2F **33**
Wellington Rd. *SW19*
—2C **90**
Wellington Row. *E2* —2B **40**
Wellington Sq. *SW3* —1B **64**
Wellington St. *WC2* —1B **52**
Wellington Ter. *E1* —2D **55**
Wellington Ter. *W11* —1C **48**
Wellington Way. *E3* —2C **42**
Wellmeadow Rd. *SE13* &
(in two parts) *SE6* —4A **68**
Well Pl. *NW3* —5F **7**
Well Rd. *NW3* —5F **7**
Wells Ct. *NW6* —1C **34**
(off Cambridge Av.)
Wells Gdns. *Ilf* —2F **17**
Wells Ho. *EC1* —2C **38**
(off Spa Grn. Est.)
Wells Ho. *SE16* —4E **55**
(off Howland Est.)
Wells Ho. Brom —5D **101**
(off Pike Clo.)
Wells Ho. Rd. *NW10* —4A **32**
Wells M. *W1* —4E **37**
Wells Pk. Rd. *SE26* —3C **96**
Wells Ri. *NW8* —5B **22**
Wells Rd. *W12* —3E **47**
Wells Sq. *WC1* —2B **38**
Wells St. *W1* —4E **37**
Wells Ter. *N4* —4C **10**
Well St. *E9* —4E **27**
Well St. *E15* —3A **30**
Wells Way. *SE5* —2F **67**
Wells Way. *SW7* —4F **49**
Wells Yd. *N7* —2C **24**
Well Wlk. *NW3* —1F **21**
Welsford St. *SE1* —5C **54**
(in two parts)
Welsh Clo. *E13* —2C **44**
Welsh Ho. *E1* —2D **55**
(off Wapping La.)
Welshpool Ho. *E8* —5C **26**
Welshpool St. *E8* —5C **26**
(in two parts)
Welshside Wlk. *NW9* —1A **4**
Welstead Ho. *E1* —5D **41**
(off Cannon St. Rd.)
Welstead Way. *W4* —5B **46**
Weltje Rd. *W6* —5C **46**
Welton Ct. *SE5* —4A **68**
Welwyn St. *E2* —2E **41**
Wembury M. *N6* —2E **9**
Wembury Rd. *N6* —2D **9**
Wemyss Rd. *SE3* —5B **72**
Wendell Rd. *W12* —4B **46**
Wendle Ct. *SW8* —2A **66**
Wendon St. *E3* —5B **28**
Wendover. *SE17* —1A **68**
(in two parts)

Wendover Ct. *NW2* —5C **6**
Wendover Ct. *W1* —4C **36**
(off Chiltern St.)
Wendover Ho. *W1* —4C **36**
(off Chiltern St.)
Wendover Rd. *NW10* —1B **32**
Wendover Rd. *SE9* —1F **87**
Wenham Ho. *SW8* —3E **65**
(off Ascalon St.)
Wenlake Ho. *EC1* —3E **39**
(off Old St.)
Wenlock Barn Est. *N1* —1F **39**
(off Wenlock St.)
Wenlock Ct. *N1* —1F **39**
Wenlock Rd. *N1* —1E **39**
Wenlock St. *N1* —1E **39**
Wennington Rd. *E3* —1F **41**
Wensdale Ho. *E5* —4C **12**
Wentland Clo. *SE6* —2F **99**
Wentland Rd. *SE6* —2F **99**
Wentworth Ct. *W6* —2A **62**
(off Laundry Rd.)
Wentworth Cres. *SE15*
—3C **68**
Wentworth Dwellings. *E1*
(off Wentworth St.) —5B **40**
Wentworth M. *E3* —3A **42**
Wentworth Rd. *E12* —1F **31**
Wentworth Rd. *NW11* —1B **6**
Wentworth St. *E1* —5B **40**
Werrington St. *NW1* —1E **37**
Werter Rd. *SW15* —2A **76**
Wesleyan Pl. *NW5* —1D **23**
Wesley Av. *E16* —2C **58**
Wesley Av. *NW10* —2A **32**
Wesley Clo. *N7* —4B **10**
Wesley Clo. *SE17* —5D **53**
Wesley Rd. *E10* —2E **15**
Wesley Sq. *W11* —5A **34**
Wesley St. *W1* —4C **36**
Wessex Gdns. *NW11* —3A **6**
Wessex Ho. *SE1* —1B **68**
Wessex St. *E2* —2E **41**
Wessex Way. *NW11* —3A **6**
Westacott Clo. *N19* —3F **9**
W. Arbour St. *E1* —5F **41**
West Av. *NW4* —1F **5**
West Bank. *N16* —2A **12**
West Beckton. —5F 45
Westbere Rd. *NW2* —1A **20**
West Block. *SE1* —3B **52**
(off Addington St.)
Westbourne Bri. *W2* —4E **35**
Westbourne Cres. *W2* —1F **49**
Westbourne Cres. M. *W2*
—1F **49**
(off Westbourne Cres.)
Westbourne Dri. *SE23* —2F **97**
Westbourne Gdns. *W2*
—5D **35**
Westbourne Green. —5B 34
Westbourne Gro. *W11 & W2*
—1B **48**
Westbourne Gro. M. *W11*
—5C **34**

Westbourne Gro. Ter. *W2*
—5D **35**
Westbourne Ho. *SW1* —1D **65**
Westbourne Pk. Pas. *W2*
—4C **34**
(off Alfred Rd., in two parts)
Westbourne Pk. Rd. *W11 &
W2* —5A **34**
Westbourne Pk. Vs. *W2*
—4C **34**
Westbourne Rd. *N7* —3B **24**
Westbourne Rd. *SE26* —5F **97**
Westbourne St. *W2* —1F **49**
Westbourne Ter. *SE23* —2F **97**
(off Waldram Pk. Rd.)
Westbourne Ter. *W2* —5E **35**
Westbourne Ter. M. *W2*
—5E **35**
Westbourne Ter. Rd. *W2*
—4D **35**
Westbourne Ter. Rd. Bri. *W2*
—4E **35**
(off Westbourne Ter. Rd.)
Westbridge Clo. *W12* —3C **46**
Westbridge Rd. *SW11* —4F **63**
West Brompton. —2D 63
Westbrook Ho. *E2* —2E **41**
(off Victoria Pk. Sq.)
Westbrook Rd. *SE3* —4D **73**
Westbury Rd. *E7* —3D **31**
Westbury St. *SW8* —5E **65**
(off Portslade Rd.)
Westbury Ter. *E7* —3D **31**
W. Carriage Dri. *W2* —1A **50**
W. Central St. *WC1* —5A **38**
W. Centre Av. *NW10* —3D **33**
Westcombe Ct. *SE3* —3B **72**
Westcombe Hill. *SE3* —3C **72**
Westcombe Pk. Rd. *SE3*
—2A **72**
Westcote Rd. *SW16* —5E **93**
West Cotts. *NW6* —2C **20**
Westcott Clo. *N15* —1B **12**
Westcott Ho. *E14* —1C **56**
Westcott Rd. *SE17* —2D **67**
Westcroft Clo. *NW2* —1A **20**
Westcroft Sq. *W6* —5C **46**
Westcroft Way. *NW2* —1A **20**
W. Cromwell Rd. *W14* &
SW5 —1B **62**
W. Cross Route. *W10* —1F **47**
Westdean Av. *SE12* —1D **101**
W. Dean Clo. *SW18* —4D **77**
Westdown Rd. *E15* —1E **29**
Westdown Rd. *SE6* —5C **84**
West Dri. *SW16* —4E **93**
West Dulwich. —2F 95
W. Eaton Pl. *SW1* —5C **50**
W. Eaton Pl. M. *SW1* —5C **50**
(off W. Eaton Pl.)
W. Ella Rd. *NW10* —4A **18**
W. End Av. *E10* —1F **15**
W. End Ct. *NW6* —4D **21**
W. End La. *NW6* —2C **20**
Westerdale Rd. *SE10* —1C **72**
Westerfield Rd. *N15* —1B **12**

Westerham. NW1 —5E **23**
  (off Bayham St.)
Westerham Ho. SE1 —4F **53**
  (off Law St.)
Westerham Rd. *E10* —2D **15**
Westerley Cres. *SE26*
  —5B **98**
Western Av. *NW11* —1F **5**
Western Beach Apartments.
  E16 —1C **58**
Western Circus. (Junct.)
  —1B **46**
Western Ct. W9 —1B **34**
  (off Carlton Va.)
Western La. *SW12* —5C **78**
Western M. *W9* —3B **34**
Western Pl. *SE16* —3E **55**
Western Rd. *E13* —1E **45**
Western Rd. *E17* —1E **15**
Western Rd. *SW9* —1C **80**
Western Ter. W6 —1C **60**
  (off Chiswick Mall)
Westferry Cir. *E14* —2C **56**
Westferry Rd. *E14* —1B **56**
Westfield Clo. *SW10* —3E **63**
Westfield Ho. SE16 —5F **55**
  (off Rotherhithe New Rd.)
Westfield Ho. *SW18* —1D **91**
Westfields. *SW13* —1B **74**
Westfields Av. *SW13* —1A **74**
Westfield St. *SE18* —4F **59**
Westfield Way. *E1* —2A **42**
W. Garden Pl. *W2* —5A **36**
West Gdns. *E1* —1D **55**
West Gdns. *SW17* —5A **92**
Westgate Ct. SE12 —1C **100**
  (off Burnt Ash Hill)
Westgate Ct. SW9 —1C **80**
  (off Canterbury Cres.)
Westgate M. W10 —3A **34**
  (off West Row)
Westgate St. *E8* —5D **27**
Westgate Ter. *SW10* —1D **63**
West Gro. *SE10* —4E **71**
Westgrove La. *SE10* —4E **71**
W. Halkin St. *SW1* —4C **50**
W. Hallowes. *SE9* —1F **101**
West Ham. —5C 30
W. Ham La. *E15* —4F **29**
West Hampstead. —3D 21
W. Hampstead M. *NW6*
  —3D **21**
West Ham United F.C.
  —1F **45**
W. Harding St. *EC4* —5C **38**
W. Heath Av. *NW11* —3C **6**
W. Heath Clo. *NW3* —5C **6**
W. Heath Ct. *NW11* —3C **6**
W. Heath Dri. *NW11* —3C **6**
W. Heath Gdns. *NW3* —5C **6**
W. Heath Rd. *NW3* —4C **6**
West Hendon. —2C 4
West Hill. —4B 76
West Hill. *SW15 & SW18*
  —5F **75**
W. Hill Ct. *N6* —5C **8**

Westhill Pk. *N6* —4B **8**
  (in two parts)
W. Hill Rd. *SW18* —4B **76**
Westhope Ho. E2 —3C **40**
  (off Derbyshire St.)
Westhorne Av. *SE12 & SE9*
  —5C **86**
Westhorpe Rd. *SW15* —1E **75**
West Ho. Clo. *SW19* —1A **90**
W. India Av. *E14* —2C **56**
W. India Dock Rd. *E14*
  (in two parts) —1B **56**
W. India Ho. *E14* —1C **56**
West Kensington. —5B 48
W. Kensington Ct. W14
  (off Edith Vs.) —1B **62**
W. Kensington Mans. W14
  —1B **62**
  (off Beaumont Cres.)
West Kilburn. —2B 34
Westlake. SE16 —5E **55**
  (off Rotherhithe New Rd.)
Westland Pl. *EC1* —2F **39**
Westlands Ter. *SW12* —4E **79**
West La. *SE16* —3D **55**
Westleigh Av. *SW15* —3D **75**
Westleigh Ct. *E11* —1C **16**
West London Crematorium.
  NW10 —3D **33**
Westmacott Ho. NW8
  (off Hatton St.) —3F **35**
West Mall. W8 —2C **48**
  (off Palace Gdns. Ter.)
Westmead. *SW15* —4D **75**
W. Mersea Clo. *E16* —2D **59**
West M. SW1 —5D **51**
  (off W. Warwick Pl.)
Westmill Ct. N4 —4E **11**
  (off Brownswood Rd.)
Westminster. —3A 52
Westminster Abbey. —4A 52
*Westminster Abbey Chapter
  House.* —4A 52
  (off Westminster Abbey)
Westminster Bri. *SW1 & SE1*
  —3A 52
Westminster Bri. Rd. *SE1*
  —3B 52
Westminster Bus. Sq. *SE1*
  —1B 66
Westminster Ct. E11 —1C **16**
  (off Cambridge Pk.)
Westminster Ct. SE16 —2F **55**
  (off King & Queen Wharf)
Westminster Gdns. SW1
  (off Marsham St.) —5A 52
Westminster Hall. —3A 52
  (off St Margaret St.)
Westminster Ind. Est. *SE18*
  —4F **59**
Westminster Mans. SW1
  —4F 51
Westminster Pal. Gdns. SW1
  (off Artillery Row) —4F 51
Westminster R.C. Cathedral.
  —4E 51

Westmoor St. *SE7* —4E **59**
Westmoreland Pl. *SW1*
  —1D **65**
Westmoreland Rd. *SE17*
  (in two parts) —2F **67**
Westmoreland Rd. *SW13*
  —4B **60**
Westmoreland St. *W1*
  —4C **36**
Westmoreland Ter. *SW1*
  —1D **65**
Westmoreland Wlk. *SE17*
  (in three parts) —2F **67**
Westmoreland Clo. E12
  —4F **17**
Westmorland Rd. *E17*
  —1C **14**
West Norwood. —3D 95
West Norwood Crematorium.
  SE27 —3E 95
Westonbirt Ct. SE15 —2B **68**
  (off Ebley Clo.)
Weston Ct. *N4* —5E **11**
West One Ho. W1 —4E **37**
  (off Wells St.)
Weston Ho. *E9* —5E **27**
  (off King Edward's Rd.)
Weston Ho. *NW6* —4A **20**
Weston Pk. *N8* —1A **10**
Weston Ri. *WC1* —2B **38**
Weston St. *SE1* —3A **54**
  (in three parts)
Weston Wlk. *E8* —4D **27**
Westover Hill. *NW3* —4C **6**
Westover Rd. *SW18* —5E **77**
Westow Hill. *SE19* —5A **96**
Westow St. *SE19* —5A **96**
West Pk. *SE9* —2F **101**
West Parkside. *SE10* —3A **58**
West Pier. *E1* —2D **55**
West Pl. *SW19* —5E **89**
West Point. *E14* —1B **56**
West Point. *SE1* —1C **68**
Westport Rd. *E13* —3D **45**
Westport St. *E1* —5F **41**
W. Poultry Av. *EC1* —4D **39**
West Quarters. *W12* —5C **32**
West Quay. *SW10* —4E **63**
West Ri. W2 —1A **50**
  (off St George's Fields)
West Rd. *E15* —5B **30**
West Rd. *SE1* —3B **52**
West Rd. *SW3* —1B **64**
West Rd. *SW4* —3F **79**
Westrow. *SW15* —4E **75**
West Row. *W10* —3A **34**
W. Side Comn. *SW19* —5E **89**
Westside Ct. W9 —3C **34**
  (off Elgin Av.)
West Smithfield. *EC1* —4D **39**
West Sq. *SE11* —4D **53**
West St. *E2* —1D **41**
West St. *E11* —5A **16**
West St. *WC2* —5F **37**
W. Tenter St. *E1* —5B **40**
Westvale M. W3 —3A **46**
W. View Clo. *NW10* —2B **18**

Westview Clo. *W10* —5E **33**
Westville Rd. *W12* —3C **46**
W. Warwick Pl. *SW1* —5E **51**
West Way. *NW10* —5A **4**
Westway. *W2* —4C **34**
Westway. *W10 & W9* —4B **34**
Westway. *W12 & W10*
    —1B **46**
Westwell M. *SW16* —5A **94**
Westwell Rd. *SW16* —5A **94**
Westwell Rd. App. *SW16*
    —5A **94**
Westwick Gdns. *W14* —3F **47**
Westwood Gdns. *SW13*
    —1B **74**
Westwood Hill. *SE26* —5C **96**
Westwood Pk. *SE23* —5D **83**
Westwood Pl. *SE26* —4C **96**
Westwood Rd. *E16* —2D **59**
Westwood Rd. *SW13* —1B **74**
Wetherby Gdns. *SW5* —5E **49**
Wetherby Mans. SW5 —1D 63
    (off Earl's Ct. Sq.)
Wetherby M. *SW5* —1D **63**
Wetherby Pl. *SW7* —5E **49**
Wetherden St. *E17* —2B **14**
Wetherell Rd. *E9* —5F **27**
Wetland Cen., The. —4D 61
Wevco Wharf. *SE16* —2D **69**
Wevell Ho. N6 —2C 8
    (off Hillcrest)
Wexford Ho. E1 —4E 41
    (off Sidney St.)
Wexford Rd. *SW12* —5B **78**
Weybourne St. *SW18* —2E **91**
Weybridge Ct. SE16 —1D 69
    (off Argyle Way)
Weybridge Point. *SW11*
    —5B **64**
Weydown Clo. *SW19* —1A **90**
Weyhill Rd. *E1* —5C **40**
Weyman Rd. *SE3* —4E **73**
Weymouth Ct. E2 —1B 40
    (off Weymouth Ter.)
Weymouth Ho. SW8 —3B 66
    (off Bolney St.)
Weymouth M. *W1* —4D **37**
Weymouth St. *W1* —4C **36**
Weymouth Ter. *E2* —1B **40**
Whadcoat St. *N4* —4C **10**
Whalebone Ct. EC2 —5F 39
    (off Telegraph St.)
Whalebone La. *E15* —4A **30**
Whales Yd. E15 —4A 30
    (off West Ham La.)
Wharfdale Rd. *N1* —1A **38**
Wharfedale Ct. *E5* —1F **27**
Wharfedale Ho. NW6 —5D 21
    (off Kilburn Va.)
Wharfedale St. *SW10*
    —1D **63**
Wharf Pl. *E2* —5D **27**
Wharf Rd. *E15* —5B **29**
Wharf Rd. *N1* —1E **39**
Wharf Rd. *NW1* —5F **23**
Wharfside Rd. *E16* —4A **44**

Wharf St. *E16* —4A **44**
Wharf, The. *EC3* —2B **54**
Wharton Clo. *NW10* —3A **18**
Wharton Cotts. *WC1* —2C **38**
Wharton Ho. SE1 —4B 54
    (off Maltby St.)
Wharton St. *WC1* —2B **38**
Whateley Rd. *SE22* —3B **82**
Whatman Ho. *E14* —5B **42**
Whatman Rd. *SE23* —5F **83**
Wheatland Ho. *SE22* —1A **82**
Wheatlands Rd. *SW17*
    —3C **92**
Wheatley Ho. SW15 —5C 74
    (off Ellisfield Dri.)
Wheatley St. *W1* —4C **36**
Wheat Sheaf Clo. *E14* —5D **57**
Wheatsheaf La. *SW6* —3E **61**
Wheatsheaf La. *SW8* —3A **66**
    (in two parts)
Wheatsheaf Ter. *SW6* —3B **62**
Wheatstone Rd. *W10* —4A **34**
Wheeler Gdns. N1 —5A 24
    (off Outram Pl.)
Wheel Ho. *E14* —1D **71**
Wheelwright St. *N7* —4B **24**
Wheler Ho. E1 —3B 40
    (off Quaker St.)
Wheler St. *E1* —3B **40**
Whellock Rd. *W4* —4A **46**
Whetstone Pk. *WC2* —5B **38**
Whetstone Rd. *SE3* —5E **73**
Whewell Rd. *N19* —4A **10**
Whidborne Clo. *SE8* —5C **70**
Whidborne St. *WC1* —2A **38**
Whinfell Clo. *SW16* —5F **93**
Whinyates Rd. *SE9* —1F **87**
Whipps Cross. *E11* —1B **16**
Whipps Cross. *E17* —1F **15**
Whipps Cross Rd. *E11*
    —1F **15**
    (in two parts)
Whiskin St. *EC1* —2D **39**
Whistler M. *SE15* —3B **68**
Whistlers Av. *SW11* —3F **63**
Whistler St. *N5* —2D **25**
Whistler Tower. SW10 —3E 63
    (off Worlds End Est.)
Whistler Wlk. *SW10* —3F **63**
Whiston Ho. N1 —4D 25
    (off Richmond Gro.)
Whiston Rd. *E2* —1B **40**
    (in two parts)
Whitbread Rd. *SE4* —2A **84**
Whitburn Rd. *SE13* —2D **85**
Whitby Clo. *N7* —1A **24**
Whitby Ho. NW8 —5E 21
    (off Boundary Rd.)
Whitby St. *E1* —3B **40**
    (in two parts)
Whitcher Clo. *SE14* —2A **70**
Whitcher Pl. *NW1* —3E **23**
Whitchurch Ho. *W10* —5F **33**
    (off Kingsdown Clo.)
Whitchurch Rd. *W11* —1F **47**
Whitcomb Ct. *SW1* —1F **51**
    (off Whitcomb St.)

Whitcomb St. *WC2* —1F **51**
Whiteadder Way. *E14* —5D **57**
Whitear Wlk. *E15* —3F **29**
Whitebeam Clo. *SW9* —3B **66**
White Bear Pl. NW3 —1F 21
White Bear Yd. EC1 —3C 38
    (off Clerkenwell Rd.)
Whitechapel. —4C 40
Whitechapel High St. *E1*
    —5B **40**
Whitechapel Rd. *E1* —4C **40**
White Chu. La. E1 —5C 40
White Chu. Pas. E1 —5C 40
    (off White Chu. La.)
White City. —1D 47
White City. (Junct.) —5E **33**
White City Clo. *W12* —1E **47**
White City Est. *W12* —1D **47**
White City Rd. *W12* —1E **47**
White Conduit St. *N1* —1C **38**
Whitecross Pl. *EC2* —4F **39**
Whitecross St. *EC1* —3E **39**
Whitefield Av. *NW2* —3E **5**
Whitefield Clo. *SW18* —4A **76**
Whitefoot La. *Brom* —6E **99**
Whitefoot Ter. *Brom* —3A **100**
Whitefriars St. *EC4* —5C **38**
Whitehall. *SW1* —2A **52**
Whitehall Ct. *SW1* —2A **52**
    (in two parts)
Whitehall Gdns. SW1 —2A 52
    (off Horseguards Av.)
Whitehall Pk. *N19* —3E **9**
Whitehall Pl. *E7* —2C **30**
Whitehall Pl. *SW1* —2A **52**
White Hart Ct. EC2 —4A 40
    (off Bishopsgate)
White Hart La. *NW10* —3B **18**
White Hart La. *SW13* —1A **74**
White Hart St. *SE11* —1C **66**
White Hart Yd. *SE1* —2F **53**
Whitehaven St. *NW8* —3A **36**
Whitehead Clo. *SW18* —5E **77**
Whiteheads Gro. *SW3* —5A **50**
White Heather Ho. WC1
    (off Cromer St.) —2A **38**
White Horse All. EC1 —4D 39
    (off Cowcross St.)
White Horse La. *E1* —3F **41**
Whitehorse M. *SE1* —4C **52**
White Horse Rd. *E1* —4A **42**
    (in two parts)
White Horse St. *W1* —2D **51**
White Horse Yd. *EC2* —5F **39**
White Ho. SW4 —5F 79
    (off Clapham Pk. Est.)
White Ho. *SW11* —4F **63**
Whitehouse Est. *E10* —1E **15**
White Ho., The. NW1 —3D 37
    (off Albany St.)
White Kennett St. *E1* —5A **40**
Whitelands Ho. *SW3* —1B **64**
    (off Cheltenham Ter.)
Whitelegg Rd. *E13* —1B **44**
Whiteley Rd. *SE19* —5F **95**
Whiteleys Cen. *W2* —5D **35**

Whiteley's Cotts. W14 —5B 48
White Lion Ct. EC3 —5A 40 (off Cornhill)
White Lion Ct. SE15 —2E 69
White Lion Hill. EC4 —1D 53
White Lion St. N1 —1C 38
White Lodge Clo. N2 —1F 7
White Lyon Ct. EC2 —3E 39 (off Fann St.)
White Post La. E9 —4B 28
White Post St. SE15 —3E 69
White Rd. E15 —4A 30
White's Grounds. SE1 —3A 54
White's Grounds Est. SE1 —3A 54 (off White's Grounds)
White's Row. E1 —4B 40
Whites Sq. SW4 —2F 79
Whitestone La. NW3 —5E 7
Whitestone Wlk. NW3 —5E 7
Whiteswan M. W4 —1A 60
Whitethorn Ho. E1 —2E 55 (off Prusom St.)
Whitethorn Pas. E3 —3C 42
Whitethorn St. E3 —4C 42
Whitfield Ho. NW1 —3A 36 (off Salisbury St.)
Whitfield Pl. W1 —3E 37 (off Whitfield St.)
Whitfield Rd. E6 —4E 31
Whitfield Rd. SE3 —4F 71
Whitfield St. W1 —3E 37
Whitgift Ho. SE11 —5B 52
Whitgift St. SE11 —5B 52
Whitley Ho. SW1 —2E 65 (off Churchill Gdns.)
Whitlock Dri. SW19 —5A 76
Whitman Ho. E2 —2E 41 (off Cornwall Av.)
Whitman Rd. E3 —3A 42
Whitmore Est. N1 —5A 26
Whitmore Gdns. NW10 —1E 33
Whitmore Ho. E2 —5A 26 (off Whitmore Est.)
Whitmore Rd. N1 —5A 26
Whitnell Way. SW15 —3E 75
Whitney Rd. E10 —2D 15
Whitstable Ho. W10 —5F 33 (off Silchester Rd.)
Whittaker Rd. E6 —4E 31
Whittaker St. SW1 —5C 50
Whittaker Way. SE1 —5C 54
Whitta Rd. E12 —1F 31
Whittell Gdns. SE26 —3E 97
Whittingham Ct. W4 —3A 60
Whittingstall Rd. SW6 —4B 62
Whittington Av. EC3 —5A 40
Whittington Ct. N2 —1B 8
Whittle Clo. E17 —1A 14
Whittlesey St. SE1 —2C 52
Whitton Wlk. E3 —2C 42
Whitwell Rd. E13 —2C 44
Whitworth Ho. SE1 —4E 53
Whitworth St. SE10 —1A 72
Whorlton Rd. SE15 —1D 83
Whyteville Rd. E7 —3D 31
Whytlaw Ho. E3 —4B 42
Wickersley Rd. SW11 —5C 64
Wickers Oake. SE19 —4B 96
Wicker St. E1 —5D 41
Wickfield Ho. SE16 —3D 55 (off Wilson Gro.)
Wickford Ho. E1 —3E 41 (off Wickford St.)
Wickford St. E1 —3E 41
Wickham Clo. E1 —4E 41
Wickham Gdns. SE4 —1B 84
Wickham Ho. E1 —4F 41 (off Jamaica St.)
Wickham M. SE4 —5B 70
Wickham Rd. SE4 —2B 84
Wickham St. SE11 —1B 66
Wick La. E3 —5C 28 (in two parts)
Wicklow Ho. N16 —3B 12
Wicklow St. WC1 —2B 38
Wick M. E9 —3A 28
Wick Rd. E9 —3F 27
Wicks Clo. SE9 —4F 101
Wick Sq. E9 —3B 28
Wicksteed Ho. SE1 —4E 53
Wickway Ct. SE15 —2B 68 (off Cator St.)
Wickwood St. SE5 —5D 67
Widdenham Rd. N7 —1B 24
Widdin St. E15 —4A 30
Widegate St. E1 —4A 40
Widford Ho. N1 —1D 39 (off Colebrooke Rd.)
Widgeon Clo. E16 —5D 45
Widley Rd. W9 —2C 34
Wigan Ho. E5 —3D 13
Wightman Rd. N8 & N4 —1C 10
Wigmore Hall. —5D 37 (off Wigmore St.)
Wigmore Pl. W1 —5D 37
Wigmore St. W1 —5C 36
Wigram Ho. E14 —1D 57
Wigram Rd. E11 —1E 17
Wigston Rd. E13 —3D 45
Wigton Pl. SE11 —1C 66
Wilberforce Rd. N4 —4D 11
Wilberforce Rd. NW9 —1C 4
Wilberforce Way. SW19 —5F 89
Wilbraham Ho. SW8 —3A 66 (off Wandsworth Rd.)
Wilbraham Pl. SW1 —5B 50
Wilby M. W11 —2B 48
Wilcox Clo. SW8 —3A 66 (in two parts)
Wilcox Ho. E3 —4B 42
Wilcox Pl. SW1 —4E 51
Wilcox Rd. SW8 —3A 66
Wild Ct. WC2 —5B 38 (in two parts)
Wildcroft Mnr. SW15 —5E 75
Wildcroft Rd. SW15 —5E 75
Wilde Clo. E8 —5C 26
Wilde Pl. SW18 —5F 77
Wilderness M. SW4 —2D 79
Wilderton Rd. N16 —2A 12
Wildfell Rd. SE6 —5D 85
Wild Goose Dri. SE14 —4E 69
Wild Hatch. NW11 —1C 6
Wild's Rents. SE1 —4A 54
Wild St. WC2 —5A 38
Wildwood Clo. SE12 —5B 86
Wildwood Gro. NW3 —3E 7
Wildwood Ri. NW11 —3E 7
Wildwood Rd. NW11 —1D 7
Wildwood Ter. NW11 —3E 7
Wilfred Ct. N15 —1F 11 (off South Gro.)
Wilfred Owen Clo. SW19 —5E 91
Wilfred St. SW1 —4E 51
Wilkie Ho. SW1 —1F 65 (off Cureton St.)
Wilkie Way. SE22 —1C 96
Wilkins Ho. SW1 —2D 65 (off Churchill Gdns.)
Wilkinson Ct. SW17 —4F 91
Wilkinson Ho. N1 —1F 39 (off Cranston Est.)
Wilkinson Rd. E16 —5E 45
Wilkinson St. SW8 —3B 66
Wilkin St. NW5 —3C 22
Wilkin St. M. NW5 —3D 23
Wilks Pl. N1 —1A 40
Willan Wall. E16 —1B 58
Willard St. SW8 —1D 79
Will Crooks Gdns. SE9 —2E 87
Willesden. —3C 18
Willesden Green. —3D 19
Willesden La. NW2 & NW6 —3E 19
Willes Rd. NW5 —3D 23
Willett Ho. E13 —1D 45 (off Queens Rd. W.)
William Banfield Ho. SW6 (off Munster Rd.) —5B 62
William Blake Ho. SW11 —4A 64
William Bonney Est. SW4 —2F 79
William Caslon Ho. E2 (off Patriot Sq.) —1D 41
William Channing Ho. E2 (off Canrobert St.) —2D 41
William Clo. SE13 —1E 85
William Cobbett Ho. W8 (off Scarsdale Pl.) —4D 49
William Dromey Ct. NW6 —4B 20
William Dunbar Ho. NW6 (off Albert Rd.) —1B 34
William Dyce M. SW16 —4F 93
William Ellis Way. SE16 (off St James's Rd.) —4C 54
William Evans Ho. SE8 (off Bush Rd.) —5F 55
William Fenn Ho. E2 —2C 40 (off Shipton Rd.)

William IV St. WC2 —1A 52
William Gdns. SW15 —3D 75
William Gibbs Ct. SW1
  (off Old Pye St.) —4F 51
William Gunn Ho. NW3
  —2A 22
William Guy Gdns. E3
  —2D 43
William Henry Wlk. SW8
  —2F 65
William Hunt Mans. SW13
  —2E 61
William Margrie Clo. SE15
  —5C 68
William M. SW1 —3B 50
William Morley Clo. E6
  —5F 31
William Morris Ho. W6
  —2F 61
William Morris Way. SW6
  —1E 77
William Paton Ho. E16
  —5D 45
William Pl. E3 —1B 42
William Rathbone Ho. E2
  (off Florida St.) —2D 41
William Rd. NW1 —2D 37
William Rushbrooke Ho.
  SE16 —5C 54
  (off Rouel Rd.)
William Saville Ho. NW6
  (off Denmark Rd.) —1B 34
Williams Clo. N8 —1F 9
Williams Clo. SW6 —3A 62
Williams Ho. NW2 —5E 5
  (off Stoll Clo.)
Williamson Clo. SE10 —1B 72
Williamson Ct. SE17 —1E 67
Williamson Rd. N4 —1D 11
Williamson St. N7 —1A 24
William Sq. SE16 —1A 56
  (off Sovereign Cres.)
William St. E10 —1D 15
William St. SW1 —3B 50
William White Ct. E13 —5E 31
  (off Green St.)
William Wood Ho. SE26
  (off Shrublands Clo.) —3E 97
Willifield Way. NW11 —1C 6
Willingham Clo. NW5 —2E 23
Willingham Ter. NW5 —2E 23
Willington Rd. SW9 —1A 80
Willington Rd. SW9 —1A 80
Willis Ho. E14 —1D 57
Willis Rd. E15 —1B 44
Willis St. E14 —5D 43
Willoughby Highwalk. EC2
  (off Moor La.) —4F 39
Willoughby Ho. E1 —2D 55
  (off Reardon Path)
Willoughby Ho. EC2 —4F 39
  (off Moor La.)
Willoughby Pas. E14 —2C 56
Willoughby Rd. NW3 —1F 21
Willoughbys, The. SW15
  —1A 74

Willoughby St. WC1 —4A 38
  (off Gt. Russell St.)
Willoughby Way. SE7 —5D 59
Willow Av. SW13 —5B 60
Willow Bank. SW6 —1A 76
Willow Bri. Rd. N1 —3E 25
Willowbrook Est. SE15
  —3C 68
Willow Bus. Pk. SE26 —3E 97
Willow Clo. SE6 —1B 100
Willow Ct. E11 —4A 13
  (off Trinity Clo.)
Willow Ct. EC2 —3A 40
  (off Willow St.)
Willow Ct. NW6 —4A 20
Willow Ct. W4 —3A 60
  (off Corney Reach Way)
Willowdene. N6 —2B 8
Willowdene. SE15 —3D 69
Willow Farm La. SW15
  —1D 75
Willow Gro. E13 —1C 44
Willow Ho. W10 —3F 33
  (off Maple Wlk.)
Willow Lodge. SW6 —4F 61
Willow Pl. SW1 —5E 51
Willow Rd. NW3 —1F 21
Willows Ter. NW10 —1B 32
  (off Rucklidge Av.)
Willow St. EC2 —3A 40
Willow Tree Clo. E3 —5A 28
Willow Tree Clo. SW18
  —1D 91
Willow Va. W12 —2C 46
Willow Wlk. SE1 —4A 54
Willow Way. SE26 —3E 97
Willow Way. W11 —1F 47
Willsbridge Ct. SE15 —2B 68
Wilman Gro. E8 —4C 26
Wilmcote Ho. W2 —4D 35
  (off Woodchester Sq.)
Wilment Ct. NW2 —5E 5
Wilmer Lea Clo. E15 —4F 29
Wilmer Pl. N16 —4B 12
Wilmington Sq. WC1 —2C 38
  (in two parts)
Wilmington St. WC1 —2C 38
Wilmot Clo. SE15 —3C 68
Wilmot Rd. E10 —4D 15
Wilmot St. E2 —3D 41
Wilmot St. NW1 —4E 23
Wilna Rd. SW18 —5E 77
Wilsham St. W11 —2F 47
Wilshaw Ho. SE8 —3C 70
Wilshaw St. SE14 —4C 70
Wilson Gro. SE16 —3D 55
Wilson Rd. E6 —2F 45
Wilson Rd. SE5 —4A 68
Wilson's Pl. E14 —5B 42
Wilson's Rd. W6 —1F 61
Wilson St. EC2 —4F 39
Wilson Wlk. W6 —5B 46
  (off Prebend Gdns.)
Wiltern Ct. NW2 —3A 20

Wilton Av. W4 —1A 60
Wilton Ct. E1 —5D 41
  (off Cavell St.)
Wilton Cres. SW1 —3C 50
Wilton Est. E8 —3C 26
Wilton M. SW1 —4C 50
Wilton Pl. SW1 —3C 50
Wilton Rd. SW1 —4D 51
Wilton Row. SW1 —3C 50
Wilton Sq. N1 —5F 25
Wilton St. SW1 —4D 51
Wilton Ter. SW1 —4C 50
Wilton Vs. N1 —5F 25
  (off Wilton Sq.)
Wilton Way. E8 —3C 26
Wiltshire Clo. SW3 —5B 50
Wiltshire Ct. N4 —3B 10
  (off Marquis Rd.)
Wiltshire Gdns. N4 —1E 11
Wiltshire Rd. SW9 —1C 80
Wiltshire Row. N1 —5F 25
  (off Bridport Pl.)
Wimbart Rd. SW2 —5B 80
Wimbledon. —5B 90
Wimbledon. —3A 90
  (All England Tennis Club)
Wimbledon Bri. SW19 —5B 90
Wimbledon Common.
  —5C 88
Wimbledon Common
  Postmill. —3E 89
Wimbledon Common
  Windmill Mus. —3E 89
Wimbledon Greyhound
  Stadium. —4E 91
Wimbledon Hill Rd. SW19
  —5A 90
Wimbledon Lawn Tennis
  Mus. —3A 90
(Wimbledon All England
  Lawn Tennis &
  Croquet Club)
Wimbledon Mus. of
  Local History. —5A 90
Wimbledon Park. —3C 90
Wimbledon Pk. Rd. SW19 &
  SW18 —2A 90
Wimbledon Pk. Side. SW19
  —3F 89
Wimbledon Rd. SW17 —4E 91
Wimbledon Stadium Bus.
  Cen. SW17 —3D 91
Wimbolt St. E2 —2C 40
Wimborne Clo. SE12 —3B 86
Wimborne Ct. SW12 —3E 93
Wimborne Ho. E16 —1B 58
  (off Victoria Dock Rd.)
Wimborne Ho. NW1 —3A 36
  (off Harewood Av.)
Wimborne Ho. SW8 —3B 66
  (off Dorset Rd.)
Wimbourne Ct. N1 —1F 39
  (off Wimbourne St.)
Wimbourne St. N1 —1F 39
Wimpole M. W1 —4D 37
Wimpole St. W1 —4D 37

Winans Wlk. SW9 —5C 66
Wincanton Rd. SW18 —5B 76
Winchcombe Bus. Cen. SE15
—2A 68
Winchcombe Ct. SE15
(off Longhope Clo.) —2A 68
Winchcomb Gdns. SE9
—1F 87
Winchelsea Clo. SW15
—3F 75
Winchelsea Ho. SE16 —3E 55
(off Swan Rd.)
Winchelsea Rd. E7 —5C 16
Winchelsea Rd. NW10
—5A 18
Winchendon Rd. SW6 —4B 62
Winchester Av. NW6 —5A 20
Winchester Clo. SE17 —5D 53
Winchester Ct. W8 —3C 48
Winchester Ho. SE18 —3F 73
(off Portway Gdns.)
Winchester Ho. SW3 —2F 63
(off Beaufort St.)
Winchester Ho. SW9 —3C 66
Winchester Ho. W2 —5E 35
(off Hallfield Est.)
Winchester Pl. E8 —2B 26
Winchester Pl. N6 —3D 9
Winchester Rd. N6 —2D 9
Winchester Rd. NW3 —4F 21
Winchester Sq. SE1 —2F 53
(off Winchester Wlk.)
Winchester St. SW1 —1D 65
Winchester Wlk. SE1 —2F 53
Winchfield Ho. SW15
—4B 74
Winchfield Rd. SE26 —5A 98
Winch Ho. E14 —4D 57
Winch Ho. SW10 —3E 63
(off King's Rd.)
Winchilsea Ho. NW8 —2F 35
(off St John's Wood Rd.)
Wincott St. SE11 —5C 52
Windermere. NW1 —2D 37
(off Albany St.)
Windermere Av. NW6 —5A 20
Windermere Ct. SW13
—2B 60
Windermere Ho. E3 —3B 42
Windermere Point. SE15
(off Old Kent Rd.) —3E 69
Windermere Rd. N19 —4E 9
Windermere Rd. SW15
—4A 88
Winders Rd. SW11 —5A 64
(in two parts)
Windfield Clo. SE26 —4F 97
Windlass Pl. SE8 —5A 56
Windlesham Gro. SW19
—1F 89
Windley Clo. SE23 —2E 97
Windmill. WC1 —4B 38
(New N. St.)
Windmill Clo. SE1 —5C 54
(off Beatrice Rd.)
Windmill Clo. SE13 —5E 71

Windmill Ct. NW2 —3A 20
Windmill Dri. SW4 —3D 79
Windmill Hill. NW3 —5E 7
Windmill La. E15 —3F 29
Windmill M. W4 —5A 46
Windmill Pas. W4 —5A 46
Windmill Rd. SW18 —4F 77
Windmill Rd. SW19 —4D 89
Windmill Rd. W4 —5A 46
Windmill Row. SE11 —1C 66
Windmill St. W1 —4F 37
(in two parts)
Windmill Wlk. SE1 —2C 52
Windrose Clo. SE16 —3F 55
Windrush Clo. SW11 —2F 77
Windrush La. SE23 —3F 97
Windsock Clo. SE16 —5B 56
Windsor Cen., The. N1
(off Windsor St.) —5D 25
Windsor Clo. SE27 —4E 95
Windsor Cotts. SE14 —3B 70
(off Amersham Gro.)
Windsor Ct. NW3 —1C 20
Windsor Ct. NW11 —1A 6
(off Golders Grn. Rd.)
Windsor Ct. SE16 —1F 55
(off King & Queen Wharf)
Windsor Ct. SW3 —1A 64
(off Jubilee Pl.)
Windsor Ct. SW11 —5F 63
Windsor Ct. W2 —1D 49
(off Moscow Rd.)
Windsor Ct. W10 —5F 33
(off Darfield Way)
Windsor Gdns. W9 —4C 34
Windsor Gro. SE27 —4E 95
Windsor Hall. E16 —2D 59
(off Wesley Av.,
in two parts)
Windsor Ho. N1 —1E 39
Windsor Ho. NW1 —2D 37
(off Cumberland Mkt.)
Windsor M. SE6 —1E 99
Windsor M. SE23 —1A 98
Windsor M. SW18 —5E 77
(off Wilna Rd.)
Windsor Pl. SW1 —4E 51
Windsor Rd. E7 —2D 31
Windsor Rd. E10 —4D 15
Windsor Rd. E11 —3C 16
Windsor Rd. N7 —5A 10
Windsor Rd. NW2 —3D 19
Windsor St. N1 —5D 25
Windsor Ter. N1 —2E 39
Windsor Wlk. SE5 —5F 67
Windsor Way. W6 —5F 47
Windsor Wharf. E9 —3C 28
Windspoint Dri. SE15
—2D 69
Windus Rd. N16 —3B 12
Windus Wlk. N16 —3B 12
Windy Ridge Clo. SW19
—5F 89
Wine Clo. E1 —1E 55
Wine Office Ct. EC4 —5C 38
Winford Ct. SE15 —4D 69

Winford Ho. E3 —4B 28
Winforton St. SE10 —4E 71
Winfrith Rd. SW18 —5E 77
Wingate Rd. W6 —4D 47
Wingfield Ho. E2 —2B 40
(off Virginia Rd.)
Wingfield Ho. NW6 —1D 35
(off Tollgate Gdns.)
Wingfield M. SE15 —1C 82
Wingfield Rd. E15 —1A 30
Wingfield Rd. E17 —1D 15
Wingfield St. SE15 —1C 82
Wingford Rd. SW2 —4A 80
Wingmore Rd. SE24 —1E 81
Wingrad Ho. E1 —4E 41
(off Jubilee St.)
Wingrave. SE17 —5F 53
(in three parts)
Wingrave Rd. W6 —2E 61
Wingreen. NW8 —5D 21
(off Abbey Rd.)
Wingrove Rd. SE6 —2A 100
Winicotte Ho. W2 —4F 35
(off Princess Louise Clo.)
Winifred Ter. E13 —1C 44
(off Victoria Rd.)
Winkfield Rd. E13 —1D 45
Winkley St. E2 —1D 41
Winkworth Cotts. E1 —3E 41
(off Cephas St.)
Winlaton Rd. Brom —4F 99
Winnett St. W1 —1F 51
Winnington Clo. N2 —1F 7
Winnington Ho. SE5 —3E 67
(off Wyndham Est.)
Winnington Rd. N2 —1F 7
Winn Rd. SE12 —1C 100
Winscombe St. NW5 —5D 9
Winsford Rd. SE6 —3B 98
Winsham Gro. SW11 —3C 78
Winsham Ho. NW1 —2F 37
(off Churchway)
Winslade Rd. SW2 —3A 80
Winslade Way. SE6 —5D 85
Winsland M. W2 —5F 35
Winsland St. W2 —5F 35
Winsley St. W1 —5E 37
Winslow. SE17 —1A 68
Winslow Clo. NW10 —5A 4
Winslow Rd. W6 —2E 61
Winstanley Est. SW11 —1F 77
Winstanley Rd. SW11 —1F 77
Winston Av. NW9 —2A 4
Winston Churchill's Britain
at War Experience. —2A 54
(off Tooley St.)
Winston Ho. N1 —1F 39
(off Cherbury St.)
Winston Ho. WC1 —3F 37
(off Endsleigh St.)
Winston Rd. N16 —1F 25
Winterbourne Ho. W11
(off Portland Rd.) —1A 48
Winterbourne Rd. SE6
—1B 98
Winterbrook Rd. SE24 —4E 81

Winterfold Clo. *SW19* —2A **90**
Wintergreen Clo. *E6* —4F **45**
*Winterleys. NW6 —1B **34***
(off Albert Rd.)
*Winter Lodge. SE16 —1C **68***
(off Fern Wlk.)
*Winterslow Ho. SE5 —5E **67***
(off Flaxman Rd.)
Winterstoke Rd. *SE6* —1B **98**
*Winterton Ho. E1 —5E **41***
(off Deancross St.)
Winterton Pl. *SW10* —2E **63**
Winterwell Rd. *SW2* —3A **80**
Winthorpe Rd. *SW15* —2A **76**
Winthrop St. *E1* —4D **41**
Winton Way. *SW16* —5C **94**
Wirrall Ho. *SE26* —3C **96**
*Wisbech. N4 —3B **10***
(off Lorne Rd.)
Wisden Ho. *SW8* —2B **66**
Wiseman Rd. *E10* —4C **14**
Wise Rd. *E15* —5F **29**
Wiseton Rd. *SW17* —1A **92**
Wishart Rd. *SE3* —5F **73**
*Wisley Ho. SW1 —1F **65***
(off Rampayne St.)
Wisley Rd. *SW11* —3C **78**
Wisteria Rd. *SE13* —2F **85**
Witanhurst La. *N6* —3C **8**
Witan St. *E2* —2D **41**
Witham Ct. *E10* —5D **15**
Witherington Rd. *N5* —2C **24**
Withers Pl. *EC1* —3E **39**
Withycombe Rd. *SW19* —5F **75**
*Witley Ct. WC1 —3A **38***
(off Coram St.)
Witley Ho. *SW2* —5A **80**
Witley Rd. *N19* —4E **9**
Witney Path. *SE23* —3F **97**
Wittersham Rd. *Brom* —5B **100**
Wivenhoe Clo. *SE15* —1D **83**
Wiverton Rd. *SE26* —5E **97**
Wixom Ho. *SE3* —2E **87**
Wix's La. *SW4* —1D **79**
*Woburn Ct. SE16 —1D **69***
(off Masters Dri.)
Woburn M. *WC1* —3F **37**
Woburn Pl. *WC1* —3A **38**
Woburn Sq. *WC1* —3F **37**
Woburn Wlk. *WC1* —2F **37**
Wodehouse Av. *SE5* —4B **68**
Woking Clo. *SW15* —2B **74**
*Wolcot Ho. NW1 —1E **37***
(off Aldenham St.)
Wolfe Cres. *SE7* —1F **73**
Wolfe Cres. *SE16* —3F **55**
*Wolfe Ho. W12 —1D **47***
(off White City Est.)
Wolffe Gdns. *E15* —3B **30**
Wolfington Rd. *SE27* —4D **95**
Wolfram Clo. *SE13* —3A **86**
Wolftencroft Clo. *SW11* —1A **78**
Wollaston Clo. *SE1* —5E **53**
*Wollett Ct. NW1 —4E **23***
(off St Pancras Way)
Wolseley Av. *SW19* —2C **90**
Wolseley Rd. *E7* —4D **31**
Wolseley Rd. *N8* —1F **9**
Wolseley St. *SE1* —3C **54**
*Wolsey Ct. SW11 —4A **64***
(off Westbridge Rd.)
Wolsey M. *NW5* —3E **23**
Wolsey Rd. *N1* —2F **25**
Wolsey St. *E1* —4E **41**
Wolverley St. *E2* —2D **41**
Wolverton. *SE17* —1A **68**
(in two parts)
Wolverton Gdns. *W6* —5F **47**
Womersley Rd. *N8* —1B **10**
Wontner Clo. *N1* —4E **25**
Wontner Rd. *SW17* —2B **92**
Woodall Clo. *E14* —1D **57**
Woodbank Rd. *Brom* —3B **100**
Woodbastwick Rd. *SE26* —5F **97**
Woodberry Down. *N4* —2E **11**
Woodberry Down Est. *N4*
(in two parts) —2E **11**
Woodberry Gro. *N4* —2E **11**
Woodbine Pl. *E11* —1C **16**
Woodbine Ter. *E9* —3E **27**
Woodborough Rd. *SW15* —2D **75**
Woodbourne Av. *SW16* —3F **93**
Woodbourne Clo. *SW16* —3A **94**
Woodbridge Clo. *N7* —4B **10**
Woodbridge Ho. *E11* —3B **16**
Woodbridge St. *EC1* —3D **39**
(in two parts)
Woodburn Clo. *NW4* —1F **5**
Woodbury Ho. *SE26* —3C **96**
Woodbury St. *SW17* —5A **92**
Woodchester Sq. *W2* —4D **35**
Woodchurch Rd. *NW6* —4C **20**
Wood Clo. *E2* —3C **40**
Wood Clo. *NW9* —2A **4**
Woodcock Ho. *E14* —4C **42**
Woodcocks. *E16* —4E **45**
Woodcombe Cres. *SE23* —1E **97**
*Woodcote Ho. SE8 —2B **70***
(off Prince St.)
Woodcote Pl. *SE27* —5D **95**
Woodcote Rd. *E11* —2C **16**
Woodcroft M. *SE8* —5A **56**
*Wood Dene. SE15 —4D **69***
(off Queen's Rd.)
Wood Dri. *Chst* —5F **101**
Woodend. *SE19* —5E **95**
Wooder Gdns. *E7* —1C **30**
Woodfall Rd. *N4* —4C **10**
Woodfall St. *SW3* —1B **64**
Woodfarrs. *SE5* —2F **81**
Wood Fld. *NW3* —2B **22**
Woodfield Av. *SW16* —3F **93**
Woodfield Gro. *SW16* —3F **93**
*Woodfield Ho. SE23 —3F **97***
(off Dacres Rd.)
Woodfield La. *SW16* —3F **93**
Woodfield Pl. *W9* —3B **34**
Woodfield Rd. *W9* —4B **34**
*Woodford Ct. W14 —3F **47***
(off Shepherd's Bush Grn.)
Woodford Rd. *E7* —5D **17**
Woodger Rd. *W12* —3E **47**
Woodget Clo. *E6* —5F **45**
Woodgrange Rd. *E7* —2D **31**
*Woodhall. NW1 —2E **37***
(off Robert St.)
Woodhall Av. *SE21* —3B **96**
Woodhall Dri. *SE21* —3B **96**
Woodham Rd. *SE6* —3E **99**
Woodhatch Clo. *E6* —4F **45**
Woodhayes Rd. *SW19* —5E **89**
Woodheyes Rd. *NW10* —2A **18**
Woodhill. *SE18* —5F **59**
Woodhouse Gro. *E12* —3F **31**
Woodhouse Rd. *E11* —5B **16**
Woodin St. *E14* —4D **43**
Woodison St. *E3* —3A **42**
Woodland Clo. *SE19* —5A **96**
*Woodland Ct. E11 —1C **16***
(off New Wanstead)
Woodland Cres. *SE10* —2A **72**
Woodland Cres. *SE16* —3F **55**
Woodland Gro. *SE10* —1A **72**
Woodland Hill. *SE19* —5A **96**
Woodland Rd. *SE19* —5A **96**
Woodlands. *NW11* —1A **6**
Woodlands Art Gallery. —2C 72
Woodlands Av. *E11* —3D **17**
Woodlands Clo. *NW11* —1A **6**
Woodlands Ct. *SE23* —5D **83**
Woodlands Ga. *SW15* —3B **76**
Woodlands Ho. *NW6* —4A **20**
Woodlands Pk. Rd. *N15* —1D **11**
Woodlands Pk. Rd. *SE10* —2A **72**
Woodlands Rd. *E11* —4A **16**
Woodlands Rd. *SW13* —1B **74**
Woodlands St. *SE13* —5F **85**
Woodlands, The. *N5* —1E **25**
Woodlands, The. *SE13* —5F **85**
Woodland St. *E8* —3B **26**
Woodlands Way. *SW15* —3B **76**
Woodland Ter. *SE7* —5F **59**
Woodland Wlk. *NW3* —2A **22**
Woodland Wlk. *SE10* —1A **72**
Woodland Wlk. *Brom*
(in two parts) —4A **100**
Wood La. *N6* —1D **9**
Wood La. *NW9* —2A **4**
Wood La. *W12* —5E **33**
Woodlawn Clo. *SW15* —3B **76**
Woodlawn Rd. *SW6* —3F **61**
Woodlea Rd. *N16* —5A **12**

Woodleigh Gdns. SW16 —3A 94
Woodmans Gro. NW10 —2B 18
Woodman's M. W12 —4D 33
Woodmere Clo. SW11 —1C 78
Woodnook Rd. SW16 —5D 93
Woodpecker Rd. SE14 —2A 70
Wood Point. E16 —4C 44 (off Fife Rd.)
Woodquest Av. SE24 —3E 81
Woodridge Clo. NW2 —5D 5
Woodriffe Rd. E11 —2F 15
Woodrush Clo. SE14 —3A 70
Wood's Bldgs. E1 —4D 41 (off Winthrop St.)
Woodseer St. E1 —4B 40
Woodsford. SE17 —1F 67 (off Portland St.)
Woodsford Sq. W14 —3A 48
Woodside. SW19 —5B 90
Woodside Av. N6 & N10 —1B 8
Woodside Ct. E12 —3E 17
Woodside M. SE22 —3B 82
Woodside Rd. E13 —3E 45
Woods M. W1 —1B 50
Woodsome Rd. NW5 —5C 8
Woods Pl. SE1 —4A 54
Woodspring Rd. SW19 —2A 90
Woods Rd. SE15 —4D 69
Woodstock Av. NW11 —2A 6
Woodstock Ct. SE11 —1B 66
Woodstock Ct. SE12 —4C 86
Woodstock Gro. W12 —3F 47
Woodstock M. W1 —4C 36 (off Westmoreland St.)
Woodstock Rd. E7 —4E 31
Woodstock Rd. N4 —3C 10
Woodstock Rd. NW11 —2B 6
Woodstock Rd. W4 —5A 46
Woodstock St. W1 —5D 37
Woodstock Ter. E14 —1D 57
Wood St. E16 —1D 59
Wood St. EC2 —5E 39
Wood St. W4 —1A 60
Woodsyre. SE26 —4B 96
Woodthorpe Rd. SW15 —2D 75
Wood Va. N10 —1E 9
Wood Va. SE23 —1D 97
Wood Va. Est. SE23 —5E 83
Woodvale Wlk. SE27 —5E 95
Woodvale Way. NW11 —5F 5
Woodview Clo. N4 —2D 11
Woodview Clo. SW15 —4A 88
Woodville. SE3 —4D 73
Woodville Clo. SE12 —3C 86
Woodville Gdns. NW2 —2F 5
Woodville Ho. SE1 —4B 54 (off Grange Wlk.)
Woodville Rd. E11 —3B 16
Woodville Rd. N1 —2A 26
Woodville Rd. NW6 —1B 34
Woodville Rd. NW11 —2F 5
Woodward Av. NW4 —1C 4
Woodwarde Rd. SE22 —4A 82
Woodwell St. SW18 —3E 77
Wood Wharf. SE10 —2E 71
Wood Wharf Bus. Pk. E14 (in two parts) —2D 57
Woodyard Clo. NW5 —2C 22
Woodyard La. SE21 —5A 82
Woodyates Rd. SE12 —4C 86
Woolacombe Rd. SE3 —4E 73
Woolcombes Ct. SE16 —2F 55 (off Princes Riverside Rd.)
Wooler St. SE17 —1F 67
Woolf M. WC1 —3F 37 (off Burton Pl.)
Woolgar M. N16 —2A 26 (off Gillett St.)
Woollaston Rd. N4 —1D 11
Woolley Ho. SW9 —1D 81 (off Loughborough Rd.)
Woolmead Av. NW9 —2C 4
Woolmore St. E14 —1E 57
Woolneigh St. SW6 —1D 77
Woolridge Way. E9 —4E 27
Wool Rd. SW20 —5D 89
Woolstaplers Way. SE16 —4C 54
Woolstone Rd. SE23 —2A 98
Woolwich Chu. St. SE18 —4F 59
Woolwich Dockyard Ind. Est. SE18 —4F 59
Woolwich Rd. SE10 & SE7 —1B 72
Wooster Gdns. E14 —5F 43
Wooster Pl. SE1 —5F 53 (off Searles Rd.)
Wootton St. SE1 —2C 52
Worcester Clo. NW2 —5D 5
Worcester Dri. W4 —3A 46
Worcester Ho. SE11 —4C 52 (off Kennington Rd.)
Worcester Ho. SW9 —3C 66 (off Cranmer Rd.)
Worcester Ho. W2 —5E 35 (off Hallfield Est.)
Worcester M. NW6 —3D 21
Worcester Rd. SW19 —5B 90
Wordsworth Av. E12 —4F 31
Wordsworth Ho. NW6 (off Stafford Rd.) —2C 34
Wordsworth Pl. NW3 —2B 22
Wordsworth Rd. N16 —1A 26
Wordsworth Rd. SE1 —5B 54
Worfield St. SW11 —3A 64
Worgan St. SE11 —1B 66
Worgan St. SE16 —5F 55
Worland Rd. E15 —4A 30
Worlds End Est. SW10 —3F 63
World's End Pas. SW10 —3F 63 (off Worlds End Est.)
World's End Pl. SW10 —3F 63 (off Worlds End Est.)
Worlidge St. W6 —1E 61
Worlingham Rd. SE22 —2B 82
Wormholt Rd. W12 —1C 46
Wormwood St. EC2 —5A 40 (in two parts)
Wornington Rd. W10 —3A 34 (in two parts)
Wornum Ho. W10 —1A 34 (off Kilburn La.)
Woronzow Rd. NW8 —5F 21
Worple Rd. M. SW19 —5B 90
Worple St. SW14 —1A 74
Worship St. EC2 —3F 39
Worslade Rd. SW17 —4F 91
Worsley Bri. Rd. SE26 & Beck —4B 98
Worsley Ho. SE23 —2D 97
Worsley Rd. E11 —1A 30
Worsopp Dri. SW4 —3E 79
Worth Gro. SE17 —1F 67
Worthing Clo. E15 —5A 30
Worthington Ho. EC1 —2C 38 (off Myddelton Pas.)
Wortley Rd. E6 —4F 31
Wotton Ct. E14 —1F 57
Wotton Rd. NW2 —5E 5
Wotton Rd. SE8 —2B 70
Wouldham Rd. E16 —5B 44
Wragby Rd. E11 —5A 16
Wrayburn Ho. SE16 —3C 54 (off Llewellyn St.)
Wray Cres. N4 —4A 10
Wren Av. NW2 —2E 19
Wren Clo. E16 —5B 44
Wren Ho. SW1 —1F 65 (off Aylesford St.)
Wren Landing. E14 —2C 56
Wrenn Ho. SW13 —2E 61
Wren Rd. SE5 —4F 67
Wren's Pk. Ho. E5 —4D 13
Wren St. WC1 —3B 38
Wrentham Av. NW10 —1F 33
Wrenthorpe Rd. Brom —4A 100
Wrestlers Ct. EC3 —5A 40 (off Clark's Pl.)
Wrexham Rd. E3 —1C 42
Wricklemarsh Rd. SE3 (in two parts) —5D 73
Wrigglesworth St. SE14 —3F 69
Wright Clo. SE13 —2F 85
Wright Rd. N1 —3A 26
Wrights Grn. SW4 —2F 79
Wright's La. W8 —4D 49
Wright's Rd. E3 —1B 42 (in two parts)
Wrotham Ho. SE1 —4F 53 (off Law St.)
Wrotham Rd. NW1 —4E 23
Wrottesley Rd. NW10 —1C 32
Wroughton Rd. SW11 —3B 78
Wroxton Rd. SE15 —5E 69
Wulfstan St. W12 —4B 32
Wyatt Clo. SE16 —3B 56
Wyatt Dri. SW13 —2D 61

Wyatt Ho. NW8 —3F ***35***
(off Frampton St.)
Wyatt Ho. *SE3* —5B **72**
Wyatt Pk. Rd. *SW2* —2A **94**
Wyatt Rd. *E7* —3C **30**
Wyatt Rd. *N5* —5E **11**
Wybert St. *NW1* —3E **37**
Wycherley Clo. *SE3* —3B **72**
Wychombe Studios. *NW3* —3B **22**
Wychwood End. *N6* —2E **9**
Wychwood Way. *SE19* —5F **95**
Wyclif Ct. EC1 —2D ***39***
(off Wyclif St.)
Wycliffe Rd. *SW11* —5C **64**
Wyclif St. *EC1* —2D **39**
Wycombe Gdns. *NW11* —4C **6**
Wycombe Ho. NW8 —3A ***36***
(off Grendon St.)
Wycombe Pl. *SW18* —4E **77**
Wydeville Mnr. Rd. *SE12* —4D **101**
Wye St. *SW11* —5F **63**
Wyfold Rd. *SW6* —3A **62**
Wykeham Ct. NW4 —1E ***5***
(off Wykeham Rd.)
Wyke Rd. *E3* —4C **28**
Wyldes Clo. *NW11* —3E **7**
Wyleu St. *SE23* —5A **84**
Wyllen Clo. *E1* —3E **41**
Wymans Way. *E7* —1E **31**
Wymering Mans. W9 —2C ***34***
(off Wymering Rd., in two parts)
Wymering Rd. *W9* —2C **34**
Wymond St. *SW15* —1E **75**
Wynan Rd. *E14* —1D **71**
Wyndcliff Rd. *SE7* —2D **73**
Wyndham Cres. *N19* —5E **9**
Wyndham Deedes Ho. E2
(off Hackney Rd.) —1C ***40***
Wyndham Est. *SE5* —3E **67**
Wyndham Ho. *E14* —3D **57**
Wyndham M. *W1* —4B **36**
Wyndham Pl. *W1* —4B **36**
Wyndham Rd. *E6* —4F **31**
Wyndham Rd. *SE5* —3E **67**
Wyndham St. *W1* —4B **36**
Wyndham Yd. *W1* —4B **36**
Wyneham Rd. *SE24* —3F **81**
Wynell Rd. *SE23* —3F **97**
Wynford Ho. N1 —1B ***38***
(off Priory Grn. Est.)
Wynford Rd. *N1* —1B **38**
Wynne Ho. *SE14* —4F **69**
Wynne Rd. *SW9* —5C **66**
Wynnstay Gdns. *W8* —4C **48**
Wynter St. *SW11* —2E **77**
Wynyard Ho. SE11 —1B ***66***
(off Newburn St.)
Wynyard Ter. *SE11* —1B **66**
Wynyatt St. *EC1* —2D **39**
Wythburn Ct. W1 —5B ***36***
(off Wythburn Pl.)
Wythburn Pl. *W1* —5B **36**
Wythes Rd. *E16* —2F **59**
Wyvil Rd. *SW8* —3A **66**
Wyvis St. *E14* —4D **43**

Yabsley St. *E14* —2E **57**
Yalding Rd. *SE16* —4C **54**
Yale Ct. *NW6* —2D **21**
Yardley St. *WC1* —2C **38**
(in two parts)
Yarmouth Cres. *N17* —1D **13**
Yarmouth Pl. *W1* —2D **51**
Yarnfield Sq. *SE15* —4C **68**
Yarrow Cres. *E6* —4F **45**
Yarrow Ho. *E14* —4E **57**
Yateley St. *SE18* —4F **59**
Yates Ho. E2 —2C ***40***
(off Roberta St.)
Yeate St. *N1* —4F **25**
Yeatman Rd. *N6* —1B **8**
Yeats Clo. *NW10* —2A **18**
Yeats Clo. *SE13* —5F **71**
Yeldham Rd. *W6* —1F **61**
Yelverton Rd. *SW11* —5F **63**
Yeoman Clo. *SE27* —3D **95**
Yeoman Ct. SE1 —1B ***68***
(off Cooper's Rd.)
Yeoman's Row. *SW3* —4A **50**
Yeoman St. *SE8* —5A **56**
Yeoman's Yd. E1 —1B ***54***
(off Chamber St.)
Yeo St. *E3* —4D **43**
Yerbury Rd. *N19* —5F **9**
(in two parts)
Yewfield Rd. *NW10* —3B **18**
Yew Gro. *NW2* —1F **19**
Yew Tree Ct. NW11 —1B ***6***
(off Bridge La.)
Yew Tree Lodge. *SW16* —4E **93**
Yew Tree Rd. *W12* —1B **46**
Yoakley Rd. *N16* —4A **12**
Yoke Clo. *N7* —3A **24**
Yolande Gdns. *SE9* —3F **87**
Yonge Pk. *N4* —5C **10**
York Av. *SE17* —1E **67**
York Bri. *NW1* —3C **36**
York Bldgs. *WC2* —1A **52**
York Clo. SE5 —5E ***67***
(off Lilford Rd.)
York Ga. *NW1* —3C **36**
York Gro. *SE15* —4E **69**
York Hill. *SE27* —3D **95**
York Ho. *SE1* —4B **52**
York Ho. W1 —4B ***36***
(off York St.)
York Ho. Pl. *W8* —3D **49**
York Mans. SW5 —1D ***63***
(off Earl's Ct. Rd.)
York Mans. SW11 —4C ***64***
(off Prince of Wales Dri.)
York Mans. W1 —4C ***36***
(off Chiltern St.)
York M. *NW5* —2D **23**
York Pl. *SW11* —1F **77**
York Pl. WC2 —1A ***52***
(off Villiers St.)
York Pl. Mans. NW1 —4B ***36***
(off Baker St.)
York Ri. *NW5* —5D **9**
York Rd. *E7* —3C **30**
York Rd. *E10* —5E **15**
York Rd. *E17* —1F **13**
York Rd. *SE1* —3B **52**
York Rd. *SW18 & SW11* —2E **77**
York Rd. *SW19* —5E **91**
Yorkshire Clo. *N16* —5A **12**
Yorkshire Grey. (Junct.) —3F **87**
Yorkshire Grey Pl. *NW3* —1E **21**
Yorkshire Grey Yd. WC1
(off Eagle St.) —4B ***38***
Yorkshire Pl. *E14* —5A **42**
Yorkshire Rd. *E14* —5A **42**
Yorkshire St. *E14* —5A **42**
York Sq. *E14* —5A **42**
York St. *W1* —4B **36**
York St. Chambers. W1
(off York St.) —4B ***36***
York Ter. E. *NW1* —3C **36**
York Ter. W. *NW1* —3C **36**
Yorkton St. *E2* —1C **40**
York Way. *N7 & N1* —3F **23**
York Way Ct. N1 —5A ***24***
(off Tiber Gdns.)
York Way Est. *N7* —3A **24**
Young Ct. *NW6* —4A **20**
Young Rd. *E16* —5E **45**
Youngs Bldgs. EC1 —3E ***39***
(off Old St.)
Youngs Ct. *SW11* —4C **64**
Young St. *W8* —3D **49**
Young Vic Theatre, The.
(off Cut, The) —3C ***52***
Yukon Rd. *SW12* —5D **79**
Yuletide Clo. *NW10* —4A **18**
Yunus Khan Clo. *E17* —1C **14**

Zampa Rd. *SE16* —1E **69**
Zander Ct. *E2* —2C **40**
Zangwill Rd. *SE3* —4F **73**
Zealand Ho. SE5 —5E ***67***
(off Denmark Rd.)
Zealand Rd. *E3* —1A **42**
Zennor Rd. *SW12* —1E **93**
Zennor Rd. Ind. Est. *SW12* —1E **93**
Zenoria St. *SE22* —2B **82**
Zetland Ho. W8 —4D ***49***
(off Marloes Rd.)
Zetland St. *E14* —4D **43**
Zoar St. *SE1* —2E **53**
Zoffany St. *N19* —4F **9**

HOSPITALS and HOSPICES
covered by this atlas
with their map square reference

N.B. Where Hospitals and Hospices are not named on the map, the reference given is for the road in which they are situated.

ATHLONE HOUSE —3B **8**
Hampstead La.
LONDON
N6 4RX
Tel: 020 83485231

BARNES HOSPITAL —1A **74**
S. Worple Way
LONDON
SW14 8SU
Tel: 020 88784981

BELVEDERE DAY HOSPITAL —5C **18**
341 Harlesden Rd., LONDON
NW10 3RX
Tel: 020 84593562

BLACKHEATH BMI HOSPITAL, THE
—1B **86**
40-42 Lee Ter., LONDON
SE3 9UD
Tel: 020 83187722

BOLINGBROKE HOSPITAL —3A **78**
Bolingbroke Gro., LONDON
SW11 6HN
Tel: 020 72237411

BRITISH HOME & HOSPITAL FOR
INCURABLES —5D **95**
Crown La., LONDON
SW16 3JB
Tel: 020 86708261

CAMDEN MEWS DAY HOSPITAL —3E **23**
1-5 Camden M., LONDON
NW1 9DB
Tel: 020 75304780

CHARING CROSS HOSPITAL —2F **61**
Fulham Pal. Rd., LONDON
W6 8RF
Tel: 020 88461234

CHELSEA & WESTMINSTER HOSPITAL
—2E **63**
369 Fulham Rd., LONDON
SW10 9NH
Tel: 020 87468000

COTTAGE DAY HOSPITAL —3A **92**
Springfield University Hospital
61 Glenburnie Rd., LONDON
SW17 7DJ
Tel: 020 86826514

CROMWELL HOSPITAL, THE —5D **49**
162-174 Cromwell Rd.
LONDON
SW5 0TU
Tel: 020 74602000

DEVONSHIRE HOSPITAL, THE —4C **36**
29-31 Devonshire St.
LONDON
W1N 1RF
Tel: 020 74867131

EAST HAM MEMORIAL HOSPITAL —4F **31**
Shrewsbury Rd.
LONDON
E7 8QR
Tel: 0208 5865000

EASTMAN DENTAL HOSPITAL & DENTAL
INSTITUTE, THE —3B **38**
256 Gray's Inn Rd.
LONDON
WC1X 8LD
Tel: 020 79151000

EDENHALL MARIE CURIE CENTRE —2F **21**
11 Lyndhurst Gdns.
LONDON
NW3 5NS
Tel: 020 77940066

FLORENCE NIGHTINGALE DAY HOSPITAL
—4A **36**
1B Harewood Row
LONDON
NW1 6SE
Tel: 020 7259940

FLORENCE NIGHTINGALE HOSPITAL —4A **36**
11-19 Lisson Gro.
LONDON
NW1 6SH
Tel: 020 72583828

GAINSBOROUGH CLINIC, THE —4C **52**
22 Barkham Ter.
LONDON
SE1 7PW
Tel: 020 79285633

GORDON HOSPITAL —5F **51**
Bloomburg St.
LONDON
SW1V 2RH
Tel: 020 87468733

GREAT ORMOND STREET HOSPITAL
FOR CHILDREN —3A **38**
Great Ormond St., LONDON
WC1N 3JH
Tel: 020 74059200

GREENWICH DISTRICT HOSPITAL —1B **72**
Vanbrugh Hill, LONDON
SE10 9HE
Tel: 020 88588141

GUY'S HOSPITAL —2F **53**
St Thomas St., LONDON
SE1 9RT
Tel: 020 79555000

GUY'S NUFFIELD HOUSE —3F **53**
Newcomen St., LONDON
SE1 1YR
Tel: 020 79554257

HAMMERSMITH & NEW QUEEN
CHARLOTTE'S HOSPITAL —5D **33**
Du Cane Rd., LONDON
W12 0HS
Tel: 020 83831000

HARLEY STREET CLINIC, THE —4D **37**
35 Weymouth St., LONDON
W1N 4BJ
Tel: 020 79357700

HEART HOSPITAL, THE —4C **36**
16-18 Westmoreland St., LONDON
W1G 8PH
Tel: 020 75738888

HIGHGATE PRIVATE HOSPITAL —1B **8**
17 View Rd., LONDON
N6 4DJ
Tel: 020 83414182

HOMERTON HOSPITAL —2F **27**
Homerton Row, LONDON
E9 6SR
Tel: 020 85105555

HOSPITAL FOR TROPICAL DISEASES —3E **37**
Mortimer Mkt., Capper St., LONDON
WC1E 6AU
Tel: 020 73879300

HOSPITAL OF ST JOHN & ST ELIZABETH
—1F **35**
60 Grove End Rd., LONDON
NW8 9NH
Tel: 020 72865126

KING EDWARD VII'S HOSPITAL FOR
OFFICERS —4C **36**
5-10 Beaumont St., LONDON
W1N 2AA
Tel: 020 74864411

KING'S COLLEGE HOSPITAL —5F **67**
Denmark Hill, LONDON
SE5 9RS
Tel: 020 77374000

KING'S COLLEGE HOSPITAL, DULWICH
—2A **82**
East Dulwich Gro., LONDON
SE22 8PT
Tel: 020 77374000

LATIMER DAY HOSPITAL —4E **37**
40 Hanson St., LONDON
W1W 6UL
Tel: 020 73809187

LEWISHAM UNIVERSITY HOSPITAL —3D **85**
Lewisham High St., LONDON
SE13 6LH
Tel: 020 83333000

LISTER HOSPITAL, THE —1D **65**
Chelsea Bri. Rd., LONDON
SW1W 8RH
Tel: 020 77303417

LONDON BRIDGE HOSPITAL —2F **53**
27 Tooley St., LONDON
SE1 2PR
Tel: 020 74073100

LONDON CHEST HOSPITAL —1E **41**
Bonner Rd., LONDON
E2 9JX
Tel: 020 73777000

LONDON CLINIC, THE —3C **36**
20 Devonshire Pl., LONDON
W1N 2DH
Tel: 020 79354444

LONDON FOOT HOSPITAL —3E **37**
33 & 40 Fitzroy Sq., LONDON
W1P 6AY
Tel: 020 75304500

LONDON INDEPENDENT HOSPITAL —4F **41**
1 Beaumont Sq., LONDON
E1 4NL
Tel: 020 77900990

LONDON LIGHTHOUSE —5A **34**
111-117 Lancaster Rd.
LONDON
W11 1QT
Tel: 020 77921200

LONDON WELBECK HOSPITAL —4C **36**
27 Welbeck St., LONDON
W1G 8EN
Tel: 020 72242242

MAITLAND DAY HOSPITAL —1E **27**
143-153 Lwr. Clapton Rd.
LONDON
E5 8EQ
Tel: 020 89195600

MAUDSLEY HOSPITAL, THE —5F **67**
Denmark Hill,
LONDON
SE5 8AZ
Tel: 020 77036333

Hospitals & Hospices

MIDDLESEX HOSPITAL, THE —4E **37**
Mortimer St., LONDON
W1N 8AA
Tel: 020 76368333

MILDMAY MISSION HOSPITAL —2B **40**
Hackney Rd., LONDON
E2 7NA
Tel: 020 76136300

MOORFIELDS EYE HOSPITAL —2F **39**
162 City Rd., LONDON
EC1V 2PD
Tel: 020 72533411

NATIONAL HOSPITAL FOR NEUROLOGY &
NEUROSURGERY, THE —3A **38**
Queen Sq., LONDON
WC1N 3BG
Tel: 020 78373611

NEWHAM GENERAL HOSPITAL —3E **45**
Glen Rd., LONDON
E13 8SL
Tel: 020 74764000

OBSTETRIC HOSPITAL, THE —3E **37**
Huntley St., LONDON
WC1E 6DH
Tel: 020 73879300

PARKSIDE HOSPITAL —3F **89**
53 Parkside, LONDON
SW19 5NX
Tel: 020 89718000

PLAISTOW HOSPITAL —1E **45**
Samson St., LONDON
E13 9EH
Tel: 020 85866200

PORTLAND HOSPITAL FOR WOMEN &
CHILDREN, THE —3D **37**
209 Gt. Portland St., LONDON
W1N 6AH
Tel: 020 75804400

PRINCESS GRACE HOSPITAL —3C **36**
42-52 Nottingham Pl., LONDON
W1M 3FD
Tel: 020 74861234

PRINCESS LOUISE HOSPITAL —4F **33**
St Quintin Av.,
LONDON
W10 6DL
Tel: 020 89690133

QUEEN MARY'S HOSPITAL —5E **7**
23 E. Heath Rd., LONDON
NW3 1DU
Tel: 020 74314111

QUEEN MARY'S UNIVERSITY HOSPITAL
—4C **74**
Roehampton La., LONDON
SW15 5PN
Tel: 020 87896611

RICHARD HOUSE CHILDREN'S HOSPICE
—1F **59**
Richard Ho. Dri.
LONDON
E16 3RG
Tel: 020 75110222

ROEHAMPTON PRIORY HOSPITAL —2B **74**
Priory La.
LONDON
SW15 5JJ
Tel: 020 88768261

ROYAL BROMPTON HOSPITAL —1A **64**
Sydney St.
LONDON
SW3 6NP
Tel: 020 73528121

ROYAL BROMPTON HOSPITAL (ANNEXE)
—1F **63**
Fulham Rd.
LONDON
SW3 6HP
Tel: 020 73528121

ROYAL FREE HOSPITAL, THE —2A **22**
Pond St.,
LONDON
NW3 2QG
Tel: 020 77940500

ROYAL HOSPITAL FOR NEURO-DISABILITY
—4A **76**
West Hill, LONDON
SW15 3SW
Tel: 020 87804500

ROYAL LONDON HOMOEOPATHIC
HOSPITAL, THE —4A **38**
Gt. Ormond St., LONDON
WC1N 3HR
Tel: 020 78378833

ROYAL LONDON HOSPITAL (MILE END)
—3F **41**
Bancroft Rd., LONDON
E1 4DG
Tel: 020 7377 7920

ROYAL LONDON HOSPITAL (WHITECHAPEL)
—4D **41**
Whitechapel Rd., LONDON
E1 1BB
Tel: 020 7377 7000

ROYAL MARSDEN HOSPITAL (FULHAM),
THE —1F **63**
Fulham Rd., LONDON
SW3 6JJ
Tel: 020 73528171

ROYAL NATIONAL ORTHOPAEDIC
HOSPITAL (OUTPATIENTS) —3D **37**
45-51 Bolsover St.,
LONDON
W1P 8AQ
Tel: 020 89542300

ROYAL NATIONAL THROAT, NOSE & EAR
HOSPITAL —2B **38**
330 Gray's Inn Rd., LONDON
WC1X 8DA
Tel: 020 79151300

ST ANDREW'S HOSPITAL —3D **43**
Devas St., LONDON
E3 3NT
Tel: 020 74764000

ST ANN'S HOSPITAL —1E **11**
St Ann's Rd., LONDON
N15 3TH
Tel: 020 84426000

ST BARTHOLOMEW'S HOSPITAL —4D **39**
W. Smithfield, LONDON
EC1A 7BE
Tel: 020 73777000

ST CHARLES HOSPITAL —4F **33**
Exmoor St., LONDON
W10 6DZ
Tel: 020 89692488

ST CHRISTOPHER'S HOSPICE —5E **97**
51-59 Lawrie Pk. Rd., LONDON
SE26 6DZ
Tel: 020 87789252

ST CLEMENT'S HOSPITAL —2B **42**
2A Bow Rd., LONDON
E3 4LL
Tel: 020 7377 7000

ST GEORGE'S HOSPITAL (TOOTING) —5F **91**
Blackshaw Rd., LONDON
SW17 0QT
Tel: 020 86721255

ST JOHN'S HOSPICE —1F **35**
Hospital of St John & St Elizabeth,
60 Grove End Rd., LONDON
NW8 9NH
Tel: 020 72865126

ST JOSEPH'S HOSPICE —5D **27**
Mare St., LONDON
E8 4SA
Tel: 020 85256000

ST LUKE'S HOSPITAL FOR THE CLERGY
—3E **37**
14 Fitzroy Sq., LONDON
W1T 6AH
Tel: 020 73884954

ST MARY'S HOSPITAL —5F **35**
Praed St., LONDON
W2 1NY
Tel: 020 77256666

ST PANCRAS HOSPITAL —5F **23**
4 St Pancras Way
LONDON
NW1 0PE
Tel: 020 75303500

ST THOMAS' HOSPITAL —4B **52**
Lambeth Pal. Rd., LONDON
SE1 7EH
Tel: 020 79289292

SOUTH LONDON AND MAUDSLEY TRUST
—1A **80**
108 Landor Rd., LONDON
SW9 9NT
Tel: 020 74116100

SOUTHWOOD HOSPITAL —2C **8**
70 Southwood La., LONDON
N6 5SP
Tel: 020 83408778

SPRINGFIELD UNIVERSITY HOSPITAL
—3A **92**
61 Glenburnie Rd., LONDON
SW17 7DJ
Tel: 020 86826000

TRINITY HOSPICE —2D **79**
30 Clapham Comn. N. Side
LONDON
SW4 0RN
Tel: 020 77871000

UNITED ELIZABETH GARRETT ANDERSON &
SOHO HOSPITALS FOR WOMEN —2F **37**
144 Euston Rd.
LONDON
NW1 2AP
Tel: 020 73872501

UNIVERSITY COLLEGE HOSPITAL —3E **37**
Gower St., LONDON
WC1E 6AU
Tel: 020 73879300

THE WELLINGTON HOSPITAL, THE —2F **35**
8a Wellington Pl., LONDON
NW8 9LE
Tel: 020 75865959

WESTERN OPHTHALMIC HOSPITAL —4B **36**
153 Marylebone Rd.
LONDON
NW1 5QH
Tel: 020 78866666

WHIPPS CROSS HOSPITAL —1F **15**
Whipps Cross Rd.,
LONDON
E11 1NR
Tel: 020 85395522

WHITTINGTON NHS TRUST —4E **9**
Highgate Hill
LONDON
N19 5NF
Tel: 020 72723070

WILLESDEN COMMUNITY HOSPITAL —4C **18**
Harlesden Rd.
LONDON
NW10 3RY
Tel: 020 84591292

RAIL, CROYDON TRAMLINK, DOCKLANDS LIGHT RAILWAY AND LONDON UNDERGROUND STATIONS

with their map square reference

Acton Central Station. Rail —2A **46**
Aldgate East Station. Tube —5B **40**
Aldgate Station. Tube —5B **40**
All Saints Station. DLR —1D **57**
Angel Station. Tube —1C **38**
Archway Station. Tube —4E **9**
Arsenal Station. Tube —5C **10**

Baker Street Station. Tube —3B **36**
Balham Station. Rail & Tube —1D **93**
Bank Station. Tube & DLR —5F **39**
Barbican Station. Rail & Tube —4E **39**
Barnes Bridge Station. Rail —5B **60**
Barnes Station. Rail —1C **74**
Barons Court Station. Tube —1A **62**
Battersea Park Station. Rail —3D **65**
Bayswater Station. Tube —1D **49**
Beckenham Hill Station. Rail —5E **99**
Bellingham Station. Rail —3D **99**
Belsize Park Station. Tube —2A **22**
Bermondsey Station. Tube —4C **54**
Bethnal Green Station. Rail —3D **41**
Bethnal Green Station. Tube —2E **41**
Blackfriars Station. Rail & Tube —1D **53**
Blackheath Station. Rail —1B **86**
Blackwall Station. DLR —1E **57**
Bond Street Station. Tube —5D **37**
Borough Station. Tube —3E **53**
Bow Church Station. DLR —2C **42**
Bow Road Station. Tube —2C **42**
Brent Cross Station. Tube —2F **5**
Brixton Station. Rail & Tube —2C **80**
Brockley Station. Rail —1A **84**
Bromley-by-Bow Station. Tube —2E **43**
Brondesbury Park Station. Rail —5A **20**
Brondesbury Station. Rail —4B **20**

Caledonian Road & Barnsbury Station. Rail —4B **24**
Caledonian Road Station. Tube —3B **24**
Cambridge Heath Station. Rail —1D **41**
Camden Road Station. Rail —4E **23**
Camden Town Station. Tube —5D **23**
Canada Water Station. Tube —3E **55**
Canary Wharf Station. DLR —2C **56**
Canning Town Station. Rail, DLR & Tube —5A **44**
Cannon Street Station. Rail & Tube —1F **53**
Canonbury Station. Rail —2E **25**
Catford Bridge Station. Rail —5C **84**
Catford Station. Rail —5C **84**
Chalk Farm Station. Tube —4C **22**
Chancery Lane Station. Tube —4C **38**
Charing Cross Station. Rail & Tube —2A **52**

Charlton Station. Rail —1E **73**
City Thameslink Station. Rail —5D **39**
Clapham Common Station. Tube —2E **79**
Clapham High Street Station. Rail —1F **79**
Clapham Junction Station. Rail —1A **78**
Clapham North Station. Tube —1A **80**
Clapham South Station. Rail —4D **79**
Clapton Station. Rail —4D **13**
Covent Garden Station. Rail —1A **52**
Cricklewood Station. Rail —1F **19**
Crofton Park Station. Rail —3B **84**
Crossharbour Station. DLR —4D **57**
Crouch Hill Station. Rail —2B **10**
Custom House Station. Rail & DLR —1D **59**
Cutty Sark Station. DLR —2E **71**

Dalston Kingsland Station. Rail —2A **26**
Denmark Hill Station. Rail —5F **67**
Deptford Bridge Station. DLR —4C **70**
Deptford Station. Rail —3C **70**
Devons Road Station. DLR —3D **43**
Dollis Hill Station. Tube —2C **18**
Drayton Park Station. Rail —1C **24**

Earl's Court Station. Tube —5D **49**
Earlsfield Station. Rail —1E **91**
East Acton Station. Tube —5B **32**
East Dulwich Station. Rail —2A **82**
East India Station. DLR —1F **57**
East Putney Station. Tube —3A **76**
Edgware Road Station. Tube —4A **36**
Edgware Road Station. Tube —4A **36**
Elephant & Castle Station. Rail & Tube —5E **53**
Elverson Road Station. DLR —5D **71**
Embankment Station. Tube —2A **52**
Essex Road Station. Rail —4E **25**
Euston Square Station. Tube —3E **37**
Euston Station. Rail & Tube —2F **37**

Farringdon Station. Rail & Tube —4D **39**
Fenchurch Street Station. Rail —1A **54**
Finchley Road & Frognal Station. Rail —2E **21**
Finchley Road Station. Tube —3E **21**
Finsbury Park Station. Rail & Tube —4C **10**
Forest Gate Station. Rail —2C **30**
Forest Hill Station. Rail —2E **97**
Fulham Broadway Station. Tube —3C **62**

Gipsy Hill Station. Rail —5A **96**
Gloucester Road Station. Tube —5E **49**
Golders Green Station. Tube —3C **6**
Goldhawk Road Station. Tube —3E **47**

Index to Stations

Goodge Street Station. Tube —4F **37**
Gospel Oak Station. Rail —1C **22**
Great Portland Street Station. Tube —3D **37**
Green Park Station. Tube —2E **51**
Greenwich Station. Rail & DLR —3D **71**
Grove Park Station. Rail —3D **101**

Hackney Central Station. Rail —3D **27**
Hackney Downs Station. Rail —2D **27**
Hackney Wick Station. Rail —3C **28**
Hammersmith Station. Tube —5E **47**
Hampstead Heath Station. Rail —1A **22**
Hampstead Station. Tube —1E **21**
Harlesden Station. Rail & Tube —1A **32**
Harringay Green Lanes Station. Rail —1D **11**
Harringay Station. Rail —1C **10**
Haydons Road Station. Rail —5E **91**
Hendon Central Station. Tube —1D **5**
Hendon Station. Rail —1C **4**
Herne Hill Station. Rail —4D **81**
Heron Quays Station. DLR —2C **56**
High Street, Kensington Station. Tube —3D **49**
Highbury & Islington Station. Rail & Tube —3D **25**
Highgate Station. Tube —1D **9**
Hither Green Station. Rail —4A **86**
Holborn Station. Tube —5B **38**
Holland Park Station. Tube —2B **48**
Holloway Road Station. Tube —2B **24**
Homerton Station. Rail —3F **27**
Honor Oak Park Station. Rail —4F **83**
Hyde Park Corner Station. Tube —3C **50**

Island Gardens Station. DLR —1E **71**

Kennington Station. Tube —1D **67**
Kensal Green Station. Rail & Tube —2E **33**
Kensal Rise Station. Rail —1F **33**
Kensington Olympia Station. Rail & Tube —4A **48**
Kentish Town Station. Rail & Tube —2E **23**
Kentish Town West Station. Rail —3D **23**
Kidbrooke Station. Rail —1D **87**
Kilburn High Road Station. Rail —5D **21**
Kilburn Park Station. Tube —1C **34**
Kilburn Station. Tube —3B **20**
King's Cross St Pancras Station. Tube —2A **38**
King's Cross Station. Rail —1A **38**
King's Cross Thameslink Station. Rail —2A **38**
Knightsbridge Station. Tube —3B **50**

Ladbroke Grove Station. Tube —5A **34**
Ladywell Station. Rail —3D **85**
Lambeth North Station. Tube —4C **52**
Lancaster Gate Station. Tube —1F **49**
Latimer Road Station. Tube —1F **47**
Lee Station. Rail —4C **86**
Leicester Square Station. Tube —1A **52**
Lewisham Station. Rail & DLR —1E **85**
Leyton Midland Road Station. Rail —3E **15**
Leyton Station. Tube —5E **15**
Leytonstone High Road Station. Rail —4A **16**

Leytonstone Station. Tube —3A **16**
Limehouse Station. Rail & DLR —5A **42**
Liverpool Street Station. Rail & Tube —4A **40**
London Bridge Station. Rail & Tube —2F **53**
London Fields Station. Rail —4D **27**
Loughborough Junction Station. Rail —1D **81**
Lower Sydenham Station. Rail —5B **98**

Maida Vale Station. Tube —2D **35**
Manor House Station. Tube —2E **11**
Manor Park Station. Rail —1F **31**
Mansion House Station. Tube —1E **53**
Marble Arch Station. Tube —5B **36**
Maryland Station. Rail —3A **30**
Marylebone Station. Rail & Tube —3B **36**
Maze Hill Station. Rail —2A **72**
Mile End Station. Tube —3B **42**
Monument Station. Tube —1F **53**
Moorgate Station. Rail & Tube —4F **39**
Mornington Crescent Station. Tube —1E **37**
Mudchute Station. DLR —5D **57**

Neasden Station. Tube —2A **18**
New Cross Gate Station. Rail & Tube —4A **70**
New Cross Station. Rail & Tube —3B **70**
North Acton Station. Tube —4A **32**
North Dulwich Station. Rail —3F **81**
North Greenwich Station. Tube —3A **58**
Notting Hill Gate Station. Tube —2C **48**
Nunhead Station. Rail —5E **69**

Old Street Station. Rail & Tube —3F **39**
Oval Station. Tube —2C **66**
Oxford Circus Station. Tube —5E **37**

Paddington Station. Rail & Tube —5F **35**
Parsons Green Station. Tube —4C **62**
Peckham Rye Station. Rail —5C **68**
Penge East Station. Rail —5E **97**
Piccadilly Circus Station. Tube —1F **51**
Pimlico Station. Tube —1F **65**
Plaistow Station. Tube —1B **44**
Poplar Station. DLR —1D **57**
Prince Regent Station. DLR —1E **59**
Pudding Mill Lane Station. DLR —5D **29**
Putney Bridge Station. Tube —1B **76**
Putney Station. Rail —2A **76**

Queen's Road (Peckham) Station. Rail —4E **69**
Queens Park Station. Rail & Tube —1B **34**
Queenstown Road (Battersea) Station. Rail —4D **65**
Queensway Station. Tube —1D **49**

Ravenscourt Park Station. Tube —5D **47**
Rectory Road Station. Rail —5B **12**
Redbridge Station. Tube —1F **17**
Regent's Park Station. Tube —3D **37**
Rotherhithe Station. Tube —3E **55**
Royal Albert Station. DLR —1F **59**

Index to Stations

Royal Oak Station. Tube —4D **35**
Royal Victoria Station. DLR —1C **58**
Russell Square Station. Tube —3A **38**

St James Street, Walthamstow Station. Rail —1A **14**
St James's Park Station. Tube —3F **51**
St John's Wood Station. Tube —1F **35**
St Johns Station. Rail —5C **70**
St Pancras Station. Rail —2A **38**
St Paul's Station. Tube —5E **39**
Shadwell Station. DLR —1D **55**
Shepherd's Bush Station. Tube —3F **47**
Shepherd's Bush Station. Tube —2E **47**
Shoreditch Station. Tube —3B **40**
Silvertown & City Airport Station. Rail —2F **59**
Sloane Square Station. Tube —5C **50**
Snaresbrook Station. Tube —1C **16**
South Bermondsey Station. Rail —1E **69**
South Hampstead Station. Rail —4E **21**
South Kensington Station. Tube —5F **49**
South Quay Station. DLR —3D **57**
South Tottenham Station. Rail —1B **12**
Southfields Station. Tube —1B **90**
Southwark Station. Tube —2D **53**
Stamford Brook Station. Tube —5B **46**
Stamford Hill Station. Rail —2A **12**
Stepney Green Station. Tube —3F **41**
Stockwell Station. Tube —5A **66**
Stoke Newington Station. Rail —4B **12**
Stratford (Low Level) Station. Rail —4F **29**
Stratford Station. Rail, Tube & DLR —4F **29**
Streatham Hill Station. Rail —2A **94**
Streatham Station. Rail —5F **93**
Surrey Quays Station. Tube —5F **55**
Swiss Cottage Station. Tube —4F **21**
Sydenham Hill Station. Rail —3B **96**
Sydenham Station. Rail —4E **97**

Temple Station. Tube —1B **52**
Tooting Bec Station. Tube —3C **92**
Tooting Broadway Station. Tube —5A **92**
Tottenham Court Road Station. Tube —5F **37**
Tower Gateway Station. DLR —1B **54**
Tower Hill Station. Tube —1B **54**
Tufnell Park Station. Tube —1E **23**
Tulse Hill Station. Rail —2D **95**
Turnham Green Station. Tube —5A **46**

Upper Holloway Station. Rail —4F **9**
Upton Park Station. Tube —5E **31**

Vauxhall Station. Rail & Tube —1A **66**
Victoria Coach Station Station. Bus —5D **51**
Victoria Station. Rail & Tube —4D **51**

Walthamstow Queens Road Station. Rail —1C **14**
Wandsworth Common Station. Rail —1B **92**
Wandsworth Road Station. Rail —5E **65**
Wandsworth Town Station. Rail —2D **77**
Wanstead Park Station. Rail —1D **31**
Wanstead Station. Tube —1D **17**
Wapping Station. Tube —2E **55**
Warren Street Station. Tube —3E **37**
Warwick Avenue Station. Tube —3E **35**
Waterloo East Station. Rail —2C **52**
Waterloo International Station. Rail —3B **52**
Waterloo Station. Rail & Tube —3C **52**
West Brompton Station. Rail & Tube —2C **62**
West Dulwich Station. Rail —2F **95**
West Ham Station. Tube —2A **44**
West Ham Station. Rail —2A **44**
West Hampstead Station. Rail —3C **20**
West Hampstead Station. Tube —3D **21**
West Hampstead Thameslink Station. Rail —3C **20**
West India Quay Station. DLR —1C **56**
West Kensington Station. Tube —1B **62**
West Norwood Station. Rail —4D **95**
Westbourne Park Station. Tube —4B **34**
Westcombe Park Station. Rail —1C **72**
Westferry Station. DLR —1C **56**
Westminster Station. Tube —3A **52**
White City Station. Tube —1E **47**
Whitechapel Station. Tube —4D **41**
Willesden Green Station. Tube —3E **19**
Willesden Junction Station. Rail & Tube —2B **32**
Wimbledon Park Station. Tube —3C **90**
Wimbledon Station. Rail, CT & Tube —5B **90**
Woodgrange Park Station. Rail —2F **31**